ENJOY A FULL YEAR

FREE

Thanks for adding **The Taste of Home Cookbook** to your kitchen library! Soon you'll discover the very best recipes from the pages of the world's #1 cooking magazine, *Taste of Home.* And now you can keep the scrumptious recipes coming throughout the year— **FREE**! Here's how

$23.94 VALUE

Perfect Party Foods | Cinco de Mayo Specialties

COOKING · CARING · SHARING
tasteof**home**
simply
mouth~watering!
* Lemon prize-winners
* 23 luscious desserts
* Light & tasty chicken

30 never-fail main dishes

#1 Cooking Magazine in the World!

*taste*of*home*

FREE SUBSCRIPTION CARD

Return this card today to claim your Free Subscription (a $23.94 value) to *Taste of Home* magazine. You'll enjoy a full year of new recipes and fresh cooking ideas delivered to your home, along with premium access to more than 33,000 recipes at www.TasteofHome.com.

YES! PLEASE START MY FREE 1-YEAR SUBSCRIPTION TO *TASTE OF HOME* MAGAZINE!

NAME _____
(please print)

ADDRESS _____

CITY _____

STATE_____ ZIP _____

E-MAIL _____

Free subscription to *Taste of Home* magazine valid with purchase of The Taste of Home Cookbook from select retailers and available only by returning this card. *Taste of Home* is published 6 times per year at the annual cover price of $23.94. Please allow 4-6 weeks for delivery of your first FREE issue.

DETACH HERE & MAIL TODAY!

QJ0TTP4T

MAIL THIS CARD TODAY!

Now Give Your Family the Fresh Flavors They Crave!

As a *Taste of Home* subscriber, you'll look forward to:

- **Hundreds of mouth-watering recipes** from home cooks, all tested and approved by the Taste of Home Test Kitchen.

- More delicious dishes made with everyday, **easy-to-find ingredients**.

- Top winners from **national recipe contests**.

- Dozens of **Clip & Keep Recipe Cards** to add to your cookbook.

- **Color photos** for picture-perfect results.

- **Instant on-line access** to premium subscriber-only content and over *33,000* recipes at www.TasteofHome.com!

FROM: _____

_____

_____

MAIL THIS CARD TODAY!

PLACE
STAMP
HERE

taste of home

**SUBSCRIPTION FULFILLMENT CENTER
PO BOX 5509
HARLAN IA 51593-1009**

COOKING | CARING | SHARING

THE taste of home COOKBOOK

About our special Cooks Who Care edition

Welcome to our greatest cookbook ever. The **Cooks Who Care** edition of *The Taste of Home Cookbook* celebrates good food **and** good people.

We've included **21** stories about people who make a difference. They donate their time to put their culinary skills to good use by helping the less fortunate.

Some of them prepare meals for the homeless, sick or elderly in their communities, some bake to raise money for charities near to their hearts, and some have found their own special ways to help others. These good-for-the-soul stories are about cooking, caring and sharing.

We at *Taste of Home* are proud to sponsor the **Cooks Who Care** program. We hope reading these stories will inspire you to to give back to your community.

You'll find a heartwarming story on each of the 21 chapter tabs in this book. For recipes from these cooks, for more information about starting your own local effort, and for **301** bonus recipes from *Taste of Home*, please go to **tasteofhome.com/CookbookBonus** and type in the access code **ICare**.

Catherine

Catherine Cassidy
Editor in Chief

taste of home BOOKS

REIMAN MEDIA GROUP, INC.
GREENDALE, WISCONSIN

taste of home | Reader's Digest

A TASTE OF HOME/READER'S DIGEST BOOK

© 2009 REIMAN MEDIA GROUP, INC.
  5400 SOUTH 60TH STREET
  GREENDALE WI 53129
  All rights reserved.

TASTE OF HOME AND READER'S DIGEST ARE
REGISTERED TRADEMARKS OF THE READER'S DIGEST
ASSOCIATION, INC.

EDITOR IN CHIEF: **CATHERINE CASSIDY**
VICE PRESIDENT, EXECUTIVE EDITOR/BOOKS: **HEIDI REUTER LLOYD**
CREATIVE DIRECTOR: **ARDYTH COPE**
FOOD DIRECTOR: **DIANE WERNER RD**
SENIOR EDITOR/BOOKS: **MARK HAGEN**
EDITOR: **JANET BRIGGS**
PROJECT EDITORS: **JULIE KASTELLO, KRIS KRUEGER,**
JULIE SCHNITTKA, BETH KONG
ART DIRECTOR: **EDWIN ROBLES, JR.**
DIETITIAN: **PEGGY WOODWARD RD**
CONTENT PRODUCTION SUPERVISOR: **JULIE WAGNER**
DESIGN LAYOUT ARTISTS: **CATHERINE FLETCHER, KATHY CRAWFORD,**
KATHLEEN BUMP, EMMA ACEVEDO
PROOFREADERS: **LINNE BRUSKEWITZ, JEAN DUERST, VICKI JENSEN**
RECIPE ASSET SYSTEM: **COLEEN MARTIN, SUE A. JURACK,**
SUSAN GUENTHER
PREMEDIA SUPERVISOR: **SCOTT BERGER**
RECIPE TESTING & EDITING: **TASTE OF HOME TEST KITCHEN**
FOOD PHOTOGRAPHY: **TASTE OF HOME PHOTO STUDIO**
EDITORIAL ASSISTANTS: **BARB CZYSZ, MARIE BRANNON**

CHIEF MARKETING OFFICER: **LISA KARPINSKI**
VICE PRESIDENT, BOOK MARKETING: **DAN FINK**

THE READER'S DIGEST ASSOCIATION, INC.
PRESIDENT AND CHIEF EXECUTIVE OFFICER: **MARY G. BERNER**
PRESIDENT, RDA FOOD & ENTERTAINING: **SUZANNE M. GRIMES**
PRESIDENT, CONSUMER MARKETING: **DAWN ZIER**

READER'S DIGEST TRADE PUBLISHING
PRESIDENT/PUBLISHER, TRADE PUBLISHING: **HAROLD CLARKE**
ASSOCIATE PUBLISHER: **ROSANNE MCMANUS**
VICE PRESIDENT, SALES & MARKETING: **STACEY ASHTON**

COVER PHOTOGRAPHY
PHOTOGRAPHERS: **DAN ROBERTS, ROB HAGEN,**
GRACE NATOLI SHELDON
FOOD STYLISTS: **JIM RUDE, JENNIFER JANZ, DIANE ARMSTRONG**
SET STYLISTS: **STEPHANIE MARCHESE, DEE DEE JACQ**

TASTE OF HOME GUIDELINES

- The Nutrition Facts provided in *The Taste of Home Cookbook* are calculated using products that include the normal amount of fat, sugars and sodium (for example whole milk or chicken broth rather than fat-free milk or reduced-sodium chicken broth) unless otherwise noted. Nutrition Facts reflect only the amount of marinade absorbed during preparation.

- Nutrition Facts are calculated with the first measurement of an ingredient in a range (2 to 3 tablespoons), the first ingredient listed (1/4 cup half-and-half cream or heavy whipping cream) and the second serving size (12 to 14 servings).

- Optional ingredients or garnishes without a specific amount are not included in the Nutrition Facts. Other ingredients will be noted if they are not included, such as assorted crackers.

- Recipes have been tested in a 1,100-watt microwave.

- Temperatures provided are in degrees Fahrenheit (°F).

International Standard Book Number (10): **0-89821-729-6**
International Standard Book Number (13): **978-0-89821-729-2**
Library of Congress Control Number: **2008943196**

"Timeless Recipes from Trusted Home Cooks" is a registered trademark of Reiman Media Group, Inc.

"Cooking Caring Sharing" and "Cooks Who Care" are registered trademarks of Reiman Media Group, Inc.

FOR OTHER TASTE OF HOME BOOKS AND PRODUCTS,
VISIT **www.tasteofhome.com.**
FOR MORE READER'S DIGEST PRODUCTS
AND INFORMATION,
VISIT **www.rd.com** (IN THE UNITED STATES)
www.rd.ca (IN CANADA)

PRINTED IN CHINA (LPP)
1 3 5 7 9 10 8 6 4 2

CONTENTS

One Recipe...Four Ways!
Cook the way that fits your lifestyle

Welcome to the newly revised *Taste of Home Cookbook* from the staff and readers of *Taste of Home* magazine, the No. 1 cooking publication in the world. This exciting new edition has 64 more pages, 429 more recipes **and** a new feature—One Recipe...Four Ways!

We took 80 all-time-favorite foods and prepared them four different ways—classic, time-saver, light and serves 2. Each of these 80 fabulous foods is featured on a lifestyle spread that lets **you** choose the recipe that best fits the way you want to cook that day. Here are the choices:

Classic Recipes are how Mom cooked—from-scratch using a combination of fresh and convenience ingredients. These recipes show you how to make a wide variety of foods, using traditional preparation techniques and cooking methods for wonderful home-cooked results.

Time-Saver Recipes require less effort to make, less time to cook or both, yet they taste like you spent hours preparing them. The recipes use more convenience products, are easier to prepare, have shorter ingredient lists and may have quicker cooking methods, such as using the stovetop or microwave instead of the oven. These recipes also feature the simplicity of the bread machine and slow cooker. You just prep it and forget it—the appliances do the rest.

Light Recipes are designed for those who are watching their calories. These recipes start with ingredients that are lower in fat, cholesterol, carbohydrates and sodium—then they're cooked using methods with minimal salt and fat. They'll show you that lower-calorie foods can look and taste great!

Serves 2 Recipes have been scaled down to make the perfect amount for two. Most entrees and sides don't have leftovers. The baked goods and desserts generally make more than two servings, but their yield is smaller than a comparable full-size recipe.

> **Share your recipes on-line for a chance to have your recipe published in a *Taste of Home* cookbook! Visit us at www.tasteofhome.com/cookbookrecipes**

Besides the One Recipe...Four Ways feature, *The Taste of Home Cookbook* is packed with tips, techniques and other recipes to make your cooking experience a pleasure. *The Taste of Home Cookbook* has more than 1,375 family favorites to choose from...plus plenty of useful information! Inside you'll find:

- **1,375+ fabulous recipes and variations,** all made from easy-to-find, everyday ingredients, all shared by trusted home cooks just like you.

- **Nutrition Facts for every recipe,** so you can quickly identify the recipes that meet your family's dietary needs.

- **Prep and cook times on each recipe** that allow you to judge at a glance if the recipe will fit into your cooking schedule.

- **More than 1,375 full-color photos,** many paired with recipes to showcase the finished dish, so you'll know exactly how it will look on your table.

- **Hundreds of tips, techniques and how-to's** from the experts on our Test Kitchen staff. This will answer your questions and help you enjoy family-pleasing results from any recipe. Plus, *Taste of Home* readers share their tried-and-true tips and practical kitchen wisdom.

- **Easy-to-follow references and indexes.** In addition to the alphabetical listing on the back of each chapter divider tab, there is a master alphabetical index at the end of the book. Plus, there is a comprehensive index organized by major ingredients, cooking techniques and food categories.

- **Other special features,** including the handy five-ring binder, which lays flat on your counter, splash guards to keep your book's pages clean and safe from splatters, and tabbed dividers for quick reference.

- **Our guarantee that absolutely every recipe will work!** Taste of Home Test Kitchen home economists have tested each recipe so that it will turn out perfectly in your own kitchen—every single time you make it!

Best of all, with this book you can enjoy the home-style goodness for which *Taste of Home* is trusted and loved. Whether you're a new friend or a longtime fan, you're sure to find a delicious dish for every occasion in *The Taste of Home Cookbook*.

angels with spatulas

Bakers create birthday cakes & memories

Tina Ellis and Amanda Bowyer

> *Growing up, I always had a special cake on my birthday, so it's hard for me to imagine a child not having one.*
> ~Amanda Bowyer

Angels aren't always outfitted with halos and wings. Some are equipped with aprons, hand mixers and lots and lots of cake pans.

Well, at least that's true of the angels who bake for Angel Cakes Charity, a nonprofit organization in the Boise, Idaho, area that creates special-occasion cakes for hospice patients, underprivileged kids, vets and other deserving people.

"Angel Cakes Charity was born out of my love for baking and the realization that there are children in Idaho not receiving a cake to celebrate their birthday," explains Tina Ellis, executive director.

To remedy that, the organization honors the birthdays with the gift of a homemade cake. "The children might be in foster care where both money and time are limited, or they might be homeless and in a shelter," Tina says.

"We also make very special birthday cakes for hospice patients. We ask about a person's life and bake a cake to capture an aspect of that life and the taste of a cake they have always loved."

Launched in January 2008, Angel Cakes Charity now averages 50 homemade cakes each month and regularly bakes for nursing homes, families staying at the Ronald McDonald house and a few other organizations.

About 60 volunteers, known as Angel Bakers, donate all of the ingredients, decorations and wrappings for the cakes. They range from beginning bakers to experts and can choose to bake from once a month to twice a week.

One such Angel Baker is Amanda Bowyer of Caldwell, Idaho, who discovered the joy of baking in childhood when she received an Easy-Bake Oven.

"I just do this because I love to do it," she says. "I especially love decorating the kids' cakes. I love the bright, vibrant colors. Growing up, I always had a special cake on my birthday, so it's hard for me to imagine a child not having one."

A Wilton-trained cake decorator, Amanda has taught workshops to other Angel Bakers.

She also has 200 cake pans that she lends out to make special shaped cakes for recipients.

"The recipients are so thankful. It means a lot to them that someone cared enough to spend the time to do that for them," she says.

taste of home

cooks who care

DO YOU KNOW A COOK WHO CARES?
If you or someone you know cooks for a charitable, spiritual or other cause, tell us about it at **tasteofhome.com/CookbookBonus**

Kitchen Basics

Measuring Tools And Techniques

To ensure delicious and consistent cooking results, it's important to know how to accurately and correctly measure ingredients. Not all measuring cups are the same, and not all ingredients are measured in the same manner. There are specific measuring cups designed for measuring liquid and dry ingredients, and they are not interchangeable.

A liquid measuring cup is either clear glass or transparent plastic with a handle and a pour spout. Liquid measures are available in 1-cup, 2-cup, 4-cup and 8-cup sizes. They are used for milk, honey, molasses, corn syrup, water and oil.

A dry measuring cup is made from metal or plastic and has a handle. The food to be measured should be even with the rim of the cup. Dry measuring cups usually come in a set with 1/4-cup, 1/3-cup, 1/2-cup and 1-cup sizes. Some sets may have additional sizes such as 1/8 cup or 2/3 cup.

Dry measures are used for flour and sugar. They also are used to measure shortening, sour cream, yogurt and applesauce. While these ingredients are not "dry," they can mound when measured. The dry measure allows you to level the ingredient with the top of the cup for an accurate measurement.

Standard measuring spoons are used to measure both liquid and dry ingredients. Sets often include a 1/4 teaspoon, 1/2 teaspoon, 1 teaspoon and 1 tablespoon. Some sets are available with a 1/8 teaspoon.

Weight and Measure Equivalents

TEASPOON AND TABLESPOON MEASURES		
Dash or pinch	=	less than 1/8 teaspoon
1-1/2 teaspoons	=	1/2 tablespoon
3 teaspoons	=	1 tablespoon; 1/2 fluid ounce
4-1/2 teaspoons	=	1-1/2 tablespoons
2 tablespoons	=	1/8 cup; 1 fluid ounce
4 tablespoons	=	1/4 cup; 2 fluid ounces
8 tablespoons	=	1/2 cup; 4 fluid ounces
12 tablespoons	=	3/4 cup; 6 fluid ounces
16 tablespoons	=	1 cup; 8 fluid ounces; 1/2 pint

CUP MEASURES		
1/8 cup	=	2 tablespoons; 1 fluid ounce
1/4 cup	=	4 tablespoons; 2 fluid ounces
1/3 cup	=	5-1/3 tablespoons
1/2 cup	=	8 tablespoons; 4 fluid ounces
2/3 cup	=	10-2/3 tablespoons
3/4 cup	=	12 tablespoons; 6 fluid ounces
7/8 cup	=	3/4 cup plus 2 tablespoons
1 cup	=	16 tablespoons; 8 fluid ounces; 1/2 pint
2 cups	=	1 pint; 16 fluid ounces
4 cups	=	2 pints; 1 quart; 32 fluid ounces

PINTS, QUARTS, GALLONS AND POUNDS		
1/2 pint	=	1 cup; 8 fluid ounces
1 pint	=	2 cups; 16 fluid ounces
1 quart	=	4 cups; 32 fluid ounces
1 gallon	=	4 quarts; 16 cups
1/4 pound	=	4 ounces
1/2 pound	=	8 ounces
3/4 pound	=	12 ounces
1 pound	=	16 ounces

Proper Measuring Techniques

Measuring Liquid

Place a liquid measuring cup on a level surface. For a traditional liquid measuring cup, view the amount at eye level to be sure of an accurate measure. Do not lift cup to check the level. Some newer liquid measuring cups are designed so that they can be accurately read from above.

For sticky liquids such as molasses, corn syrup or honey, spray the measuring cup with cooking spray before adding the liquid. This will make it easier to pour out the liquid and clean the cup.

Measuring Sour Cream and Yogurt

Spoon sour cream and yogurt into a dry measuring cup, then level top by sweeping a metal spatula or flat side of a knife across the top of the cup.

Measuring Brown Sugar

Since brown sugar has a unique moist texture, it needs to be packed into a dry measuring cup. Firmly press or "pack" brown sugar into the cup with your fingers or the back of a spoon. Level with the rim of the cup. Brown sugar should hold the shape of the cup when it is turned out.

Using Measuring Spoons

For dry ingredients such as flour, sugar or spices, heap the ingredient into the spoon over a canister or waxed paper. With a metal spatula or flat side of a knife, level with the rim of the spoon.

For shortening or butter, spread into spoon and level off. For liquids, pour into measuring spoon over a bowl or custard cup.

Measuring Dry Ingredients

For dry ingredients such as flour, sugar or cornmeal, spoon ingredients into a dry measuring cup over a canister or waxed paper. Fill cup to overflowing, then level by sweeping a metal spatula or flat side of a knife across the top.

Measuring Bulk Dry Ingredients

Spoon bulk dry ingredients such as cranberries, raisins or chocolate chips into the measuring cup. If necessary, level the top with a spatula or flat side of a knife.

Measuring Shortening

Press shortening into a dry measuring cup with a spatula to make sure it is solidly packed without air pockets. With a metal spatula or flat side of a knife, level with the rim. Some shortenings come in sticks and may be measured like butter.

Measuring Butter

The wrappers for sticks of butter come with markings for tablespoons, 1/4 cup, 1/3 cup and 1/2 cup. Use a knife to cut off the desired amount.

Measuring Tip

Never measure over the batter because some may spill, adding too much to the batter.

Kitchen Cutlery

A basic set of knives is essential to any well-equipped kitchen. There are a variety of knives made from many materials. The best knives, made from high-carbon steel, are resistant to corrosion (unlike carbon steel) and remain sharper longer than stainless steel.

A. Steel

This long, thin rod with a handle is used to smooth out small rough spots on the edge of a knife blade and to reset the edge of the blade. You can also use a whetstone or electric knife sharpener to sharpen knives.

B. Chef's Knife

This 8-in. to 10-in. multipurpose knife is used for mincing, chopping and dicing.

C. Santoku

This is a Japanese variation of a chef's knife. The 6-1/2-in. to 7-in. multipurpose knife is used for mincing, chopping, dicing and slicing. The blade's dimple design helps reduce drag during slicing.

D. Carving Knife

This 8-in. to 10-in. knife is perfect for slicing roasts and turkey.

E. Serrated or Bread Knife

This knife's serrated blade is used for slicing breads, cakes and delicate foods. An 8-in. knife is most versatile, but a range of lengths is available.

F. Utility Knife

This 6-in. knife is the right size to slice small foods.

G. Boning Knife

This knife's 5-in. or 6-in. tapered blade is designed to remove the meat from poultry, beef, pork or fish bones.

H. Paring Knife

This 3-in. to 4-in. knife is used for peeling, mincing and slicing small foods.

I. Kitchen Shears

This versatile tool is used to snip fresh herbs, disjoint chicken, trim pastry, etc.

Caring for Knives

To keep knives sharp, cut foods on a soft plastic or wooden cutting board. Ceramic, granite, metal and other hard surfaces will dull the blades.

Always wash and dry knives by hand immediately after use. Never let them soak in water or wash in the dishwasher. Store knives in a slotted wooden block or hang them on a magnetic rack especially designed for knives. Proper storage will protect knife edges, keep blades sharper longer and guard against injury.

Using a Steel

Rest the tip of the steel on the work surface. Hold your knife at a 20° angle to the steel. Start with the heel of the blade against the steel and draw the blade up across the steel until you reach the tip of the knife. Repeat five times on both sides of knife blade. Repeat as needed.

Common Cutting and Chopping Techniques

Mincing and Chopping
Holding the handle of a chef's knife with one hand, rest the fingers of your other hand on the top of the blade near the tip. Using the handle to guide and apply pressure, move knife in an arc across the food with a rocking motion until pieces of food are the desired size. Mincing results in pieces no larger than 1/8 in., and chopping produces 1/4-in. to 1/2-in. pieces.

Dicing and Cubing Vegetables
1) Using a utility knife, trim each side of the vegetable, squaring it off. Cut lengthwise into evenly spaced strips. The narrower the strips, the smaller the pieces will be. Dicing results in 1/8-in. to 1/4-in. uniform pieces, and cubing yields 1/2-in. to 1-in. uniform pieces.

2) Stack the strips and cut lengthwise into uniform-sized strips.

3) Arrange the square-shaped strips into a pile and cut widthwise into cubes.

Making Bias/Diagonal Cuts
Holding a chef's knife at an angle to the length of the food, slice as thick or thin as desired. This technique is often used in stir-fry recipes.

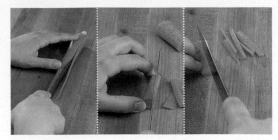

Making Julienne Strips
1) Using a utility knife, cut a thin strip from one side of vegetable. Turn so flat side is down.

2) Cut widthwise into 2-in. lengths, then cut each piece lengthwise into thin strips.

3) Stack the strips and cut lengthwise into thinner strips.

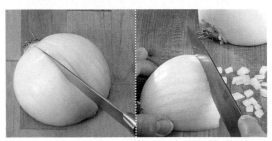

Chopping an Onion
1) To quickly chop an onion, peel and cut in half from the root to the top. Leaving root attached, place flat side down on work surface. Cut vertically through the onion, leaving the root end uncut.

2) Cut across the onion, discarding root end. The closer the cuts, the finer the onion will be chopped. This method can also be used for shallots.

Peeling and Mincing Fresh Garlic
Using the blade of a chef's knife, crush garlic clove. Peel away skin. Mince as directed at top left.

Slicing or Chopping a Sweet Pepper

1) Cut top and bottom off pepper and discard. Cut each side from pepper by slicing close to the center and then down. Scrape out seeds and discard.

2) Cut away any ribs.

3) Place cut side down on work surface and flatten slightly with your hand. Cut lengthwise into strips, then widthwise into pieces if desired.

Peeling
Placing your thumbs on the fruit or vegetable, move the blade of a paring or utility knife toward you.

Snipping Fresh Herbs
Hold herbs over a small bowl and make 1/8-in. to 1/4-in. cuts with a kitchen shears.

Freezing Herbs
You can freeze chopped herbs in freezer containers or bags and just use the amount you need directly from the freezer.

Common Cooking Techniques

To Fry
Place food, such as chicken, in 1/2 to 1 in. of hot oil in a skillet. Fry, uncovered, until food is browned and cooked through.

To Saute
Place food, such as fresh vegetables, in a small amount of hot oil in a skillet or saute pan. Cook quickly and stir frequently.

To Steam
Place food, such as beans, in a perforated basket (steamer insert) set just above, but not touching, the boiling water in a saucepan. Cover pan and allow food to cook in the steam given off by the boiling water.

To Braise
In a Dutch oven, brown meat, such as pork ribs, in a little oil, then add a small amount of liquid. Cover and simmer until cooked.

Cookware

Using the right cookware can help simplify meal preparation. It's best to start with a basic selection for everyday cooking, then add to it as needed.

Most kitchens should have a large (5-qt. or larger) Dutch oven, two saucepans with lids (a 1-qt. and a 2- or 3-qt.), a 10-in. to 12-in. skillet with lid, an 8-in. or 9-in. saute/omelet pan and a shallow roaster. A stockpot, double boiler, steamer insert basket, griddle and additional saucepans and skillets are also useful.

Selecting Cookware

Good cookware should do two things: conduct heat quickly and then evenly distribute that heat over the pan's surface to cook food evenly. These qualities are determined by the type of material the pan is made from and its thickness. There are pros and cons to the different materials used in cookware.

Of all the metals used, **copper** conducts heat the best but is expensive, requires polishing and reacts with acidic ingredients. That is why copper pans are lined with tin or stainless steel. **Aluminum** is less expensive and is also a good heat conductor, but aluminum also reacts with acidic ingredients. **Anodized aluminum** cookware has a surface that is electrochemically treated. This treatment produces a cookware that does not react to acidic foods. It is also easier to clean and is resistant to food sticking and scratches. **Cast iron** also conducts heat well but is heavy and must be seasoned periodically. **Stainless steel** is a poor heat conductor but is durable and remains looking like new for years. Manufacturers combine stainless steel with an aluminum or copper core or bottom for durable, even-cooking pans.

Thicker-gauge cookware offers more even heating so it is less likely to burn foods or have hot spots. Generally, the heavier a pan feels when picked up, the thicker the gauge is.

Pans with nonstick surfaces make cleanup a breeze. This feature is handy for skillets and saute pans but usually not necessary for saucepans, Dutch ovens and large pots.

The handles should feel comfortable in your hand, stay cool while cooking and be oven-safe. Pots with two handles are easier to pick up when full. Lids should fit tightly.

Seasoning Cast Iron

Cast-iron pans should be seasoned before using to protect the surface and prevent food from sticking. One way to season a cast-iron skillet is to brush the inside with vegetable oil or coat with shortening. Bake at 300° for 1 hour. When cool, wipe it dry with paper towels. Repeat one or two times.

8-IN. SAUTE/OMELET PAN

12-IN. SKILLET WITH LID

10-IN. SKILLET

3-QT. SAUCEPAN

1-QT. SAUCEPAN

ROASTER

Choosing Bakeware

The recipes in this book call for standard-size baking pans and baking dishes. For best results, use the pan size called for in the recipe. However, there are some substitutions (see Bakeware Substitution on page 14).

Baking pans are made of metal. Aluminum pans with dull finishes give the best overall baking results. Pans with dark finishes often cook and brown foods more quickly. If you use pans with dark finishes, you may need to adjust the baking time and cover tops of baked goods with foil to prevent overbrowning. Insulated pans generally take longer to bake and brown foods.

Baking dishes are made of ovenproof glass or ceramic. They are often used for casseroles, egg dishes and saucy meat dishes. Always use glass or ceramic baking dishes when marinating foods or making dishes with tomato sauce. If you substitute a glass baking dish in a recipe calling for a metal baking pan, reduce the oven temperature by 25° to avoid overbaking and overbrowning.

Measuring Bakeware

To measure your bakeware's diameter, length or width, use a ruler and measure from one inside top edge to the opposite inside top edge. To measure the height, place a ruler on the outside of the dish and measure from the bottom to a top edge. For volume, fill the pan or dish to the rim with water, using a large liquid measuring cup. Keep track of how much water it took to fill the pan.

Basic Bakeware

A well-stocked kitchen should have the following items:

1) 9-in. x 1-1/2-in. round baking pan (two to three)
2) 13-in. x 9-in. x 2-in. baking pan and/or dish (3 qt.)
3) 10-in. fluted tube pan
4) 15-in. x 10-in. x 1-in. baking pan (jelly-roll pan)
5) Baking sheets (without sides) in assorted sizes
6) 9-in. springform pan
7) 9-in. pie plate
8) 12-cup muffin pan (standard size)
9) 6-oz. custard cups (set of six)
10) 9-in. x 5-in. x 3-in. loaf pan (two) and 8-in. x 4-in. x 2-in. loaf pan (two)
11) 9-in. x 9-in. x 2-in. and 8-in. x 8-in. x 2-in. square baking dishes and/or pans
12) 10-in. tube pan

These other items are also nice to have on hand:

- 11-in. x 7-in. x 2-in. baking pan and/or dish (2 qt.)
- 9-in. deep-dish pie plate
- 9-in. fluted tart pan with removable bottom
- 10-in. springform pan
- 5-3/4-in. x 3-in. x 2-in. loaf pan (three to four)
- Miniature muffin pans
- 10-oz. custard cups (set of six)
- 8-in. fluted tube pan

Bakeware Substitution

If you don't have the right pan for a recipe, here are a few substitutions.
(Remember that using smaller pans will require less baking time.)

IF YOU DON'T HAVE THIS PAN(S):	USE THIS PAN(S) INSTEAD:
One 9-in. x 5-in. x 3-in. loaf pan	Three 5-3/4-in. x 3-in. x 2-in. loaf pans
One 8-in. x 4-in. x 2-in. loaf pan	Two 5-3/4-in. x 3-in. x 2-in. loaf pans
One 9-in. round baking pan	One 8-in. square baking dish
Two 9-in. round baking pans	One 13-in. x 9-in. x 2-in. baking pan
One 10-in. fluted tube pan	One 10-in. tube pan or two 9-in. x 5-in. x 3-in. loaf pans
One 13-in. x 9-in. x 2-in. baking pan	Two 9-in. round baking pans or two 8-in. square baking dishes

Kitchen Tools and Gadgets

When equipping a new kitchen, there are so many tools and gadgets to consider.
Start with the basics listed below before expanding to specialty items.

Apple corer

Blender *and/or* food processor

Can and bottle opener

Canisters

Citrus juicer

Colander

Cookie cutters

Corkscrew

Cutting boards, wood and plastic

Dough cutter/scraper

Egg separator

Egg slicer

Garlic press

Hand grater/shredder

Ladles, large and small

Measuring cups, dry and liquid

Measuring spoons

Meat fork

Meat mallet/tenderizer

Metal skewers

Metal strainer *or* sieve

Mixers, stand *and/or* hand

Mixing bowls

Pancake turners

Pastry bag and tips

Pastry blender

Pastry brush

Pastry wheel

Pepper mill *or* shaker

Pie server

Pizza cutter

Plastic spoons

Plastic storage and freezer containers

Potato masher

Rolling pin

Salad spinner

Salt shaker

Slotted spoons, large and small

Spatulas, rubber and metal

Thermometers, instant-read, candy/deep-fat, meat, oven, refrigerator/freezer

Timer

Tongs

Vegetable peeler

Wire whisks in assorted sizes

Wire racks

Wooden spoons

Kitchen Textiles:

Dishcloths

Dish towels

Hand towels

Hot pads/mitts

Kitchen string

Pastry cloth

Rolling pin cover

Food Safety

To ensure the foods you serve are safe to eat, follow these basic, but important, food safety rules.

Keep it clean. Before handling any food, thoroughly wash your hands in hot, soapy water. Make sure all work surfaces, cutting boards, knives and any other utensils have been cleaned in hot, soapy water. And, after handling raw food, clean hands and utensils in hot, soapy water.

Cutting boards can be sanitized with a mixture of 1 teaspoon chlorine bleach in 1 quart of water. Allow the bleach-water to stand on the cutting board for several minutes before rinsing. Let the board air dry or dry with clean paper towels.

Keep it separate. Don't cross-contaminate foods, which means allowing the juices of raw meats, poultry and fish to come in contact with other foods. Reusing a cutting board, countertop, sink, plate, knife or other utensil that came in contact with raw meat without first thoroughly washing it in hot, soapy water can cause cross-contamination. Never reuse the package material, such as foam meat trays or plastic wrap, from meat, poultry or fish.

It is not recommended that you wash raw poultry, beef, veal, pork, lamb or seafood before cooking. Any bacteria that may be present on the surface of these foods will be destroyed by properly cooking the food. Washing these items will contaminate the sink, which can cause cross-contamination if not cleaned right away.

Keep it at the right temperature. Keep hot foods hot and cold foods cold. Cooked foods and uncooked foods that require refrigeration should be left at room temperature for only up to 2 hours and only 1 hour if it is a hot day. Use warming trays, slow cookers and chafing dishes to keep hot foods to at least 140°. Use ice bowls (see page 45) or ice to keep foods cold.

Always cook foods to the proper temperatures.

140° for fully cooked ham.

145° for medium-rare beef, lamb and veal.

160° for medium beef, lamb and veal; pork, fresh ham or partially cooked ham and egg dishes.

165° for ground chicken and turkey, stuffing, casseroles and leftovers.

170° for well-done beef, well-done lamb, chicken and turkey breasts.

180° for whole chicken and turkey, thighs and wings, duck, goose and pheasant.

Food Safety Tip

Purchase several different colored plastic cutting boards. Use a different color for different items, such as green for fruits and vegetables, yellow for poultry and red for meat.

Basic Table Setting

Setting the table is often a hurried task that leaves family members wondering about the correct placement of the flatware, plates, napkins and glassware. You don't have to add stress to your dinner plans, just start with a basic table setting to dress up your dinner table and set the mood for your dinner party or gathering.

A basic setting is appropriate for most occasions, and for a more formal setting, you just add to the basic pieces as needed.

1) The dinner plate is positioned in the center of the place setting and everything else is placed around it.

2) Flatware is arranged around the plate in the order in which it will be used:

   • To the left of the plate is the dinner fork. If a salad is to be served, the salad fork is placed to the left of the dinner fork.

   • To the right of the plate is the knife and spoon. The knife is placed to the right of the plate with the sharp edge toward the plate. To the right of the knife is the spoon.

3) A water glass goes above the knife.

4) Napkins can be placed under the forks or on the plate for an informal setting.

Lightening Up Recipes

Food plays a key role in many social occasions, from family celebrations to office potlucks to neighborhood block parties. And many cooks want to prepare recipes that not only taste great, but are a bit healthier.

This cookbook contains hundreds of recipes that our Taste of Home Test Kitchen dietitians have approved as lighter recipes. Look for ▨ to identify these lighter recipes at a glance.

If a recipe is not designated as light, you still can see how it fits into your family's diet, because every recipe in this cookbook includes Nutrition Facts.

But you may have some of your own "special" recipes handed down that you feel are no longer appropriate because they are higher in fat, cholesterol, sugar or sodium. You can still serve them if you take the time to make them healthier.

Success in lighter cooking comes from trial and error, so don't be afraid to experiment. Consider making gradual changes in recipes. Rather than replace all of an ingredient with its lighter version, consider replacing only a portion with the lower-fat product. This way you'll see how your changes affect the flavor and texture of the recipe, as well as how your family responds to eating lighter.

Cutting Fat

For entrees and side dishes, use cooking methods that add little or no fat. Roasting, broiling, grilling, sauteing, stir-frying, poaching and steaming are great ways to cook meats and vegetables using a small amount of fat—or none at all.

Choose leaner cuts of meat and trim any visible fat from the meat. Roast, broil or grill meat on a rack to allow fat to drip off during cooking. Remove and discard skin from chicken or turkey after cooking.

Instead of topping meats or veggies with heavy gravies or cheesy sauces, season them with flavorful herbs, spices or condiments. Try dry herb rubs and tangy fruit salsas on grilled meats and lemon juice and fresh herbs on steamed vegetables.

When preparing cheesy casseroles, creamy soups or rich sauces, consider using the lighter versions of the ingredients called for in the recipe. Try using reduced-fat sour cream, shredded cheese and cream soups instead of their full-fat counterparts. Fat-free half-and-half cream or fat-free evaporated milk can be used in place of half-and-half cream in many recipes.

For creamy dips, spreads and salad dressings, use the fat-free or reduced-fat varieties of sour cream, cream cheese, mayonnaise and cottage cheese. Plain yogurt can often be used in place of sour cream.

In baked goods, you can use applesauce as a fat substitute as well as pureed canned pears, peaches, apricots and plums, baby food fruit purees or mashed bananas. Try replacing half of the butter, margarine, shortening or oil with the fat substitute. For instance, if a recipe calls for 1/2 cup butter, use 1/4 cup butter and 1/4 cup puree.

To cut fat in desserts, use reduced-fat whipped topping, reduced-fat graham cracker crusts, fat-free frozen yogurt and fat-free ice cream toppings.

Lowering Cholesterol

To cut cholesterol, limit foods that are higher in saturated fats, such as butter and shortening, in your diet. Use monounsaturated fats such as safflower oil, olive oil and canola oil or polyunsaturated fats such as sunflower oil, soybean oil and corn oil. Or use butter-flavored cooking spray when practical.

You can also reduce cholesterol by limiting the number of egg yolks in recipes. In breakfast recipes and baked goods, you can replace at least a portion of the whole eggs with egg whites or egg substitute. When reducing eggs in a from-scratch recipe, substitute two egg whites or 1/4 cup egg substitute for one whole egg. It's usually best to leave at least one whole egg in the recipe.

Trimming Sodium

Rely on fresh or frozen vegetables rather than canned ones which have high sodium levels. Use reduced-sodium broths, soups and soy sauce instead of their higher-sodium counterparts. Instead of seasoning with salt, use flavored vinegars, citrus juices, salt-free seasoning blends and fresh or dried herbs and spices.

Reducing Sugar

When preparing baked goods, start by simply reducing the amount of sugar 25%. Or try reducing it 50% and add a sugar replacement to make up for the other half. The Taste of Home Test Kitchen home economists have had the best luck with the sugar substitute Splenda Sugar Blend for Baking. They also use Splenda Granules for puddings, sweet sauces and other desserts that are not baked.

To reduce the amount of sugar in other dessert recipes, consider using the sugar-free versions of products like gelatin and instant pudding and replace jams with reduced-sugar jam and fruit spreads. Instead of topping cakes or brownies with canned frosting, sprinkle with a little confectioners' sugar. To enhance taste when using less sugar, use spices like cinnamon, cardamom, allspice, nutmeg and mace. Also consider extracts, such as vanilla and almond, to add more flavor.

Menu-Planning Pointers

Meals should be planned using recipes that contain a variety of foods, flavors, colors and textures. Begin your menu planning with the main dish. Next choose the side dishes and desserts that complement the main dish. For example, if you are planning to serve a beef roast, consider serving a colorful vegetable to add eye appeal to the plate. Serve only one strong-flavored food per meal.

Select recipes that can be prepared and served together in the allotted time frame. Two dishes that are baked at the same temperature can be cooked in the same oven without any adjustments to the baking time. Make a cooking schedule listing the recipes that can be prepared in advance, recipes that need to be started first because they require more cooking or chilling time and recipes that need to be prepared at the last minute. Once your planning is complete, make a shopping list according to the layout of your grocery store to reduce shopping time.

Serve hot foods hot and cold foods cold. Don't let any food remain at room temperature for more than 2 hours (1 hour in hot weather).

Menu Ideas for Special Occasions

Stocking Up and Storage Guidelines

Stocking your pantry, refrigerator and freezer with the ingredients and foods you use most often can simplify menu planning and dinner preparation. Having a variety of meat, poultry and seafood in the freezer makes it easy to select a main dish. And keeping your refrigerator and pantry stocked with the fresh foods and packaged products called for in your favorite recipes means there's no need to make a last-minute shopping trip. Plus, it's helpful to know you have these items stocked in your kitchen should you want to serve an impromptu meal to unexpected guests.

Stocking up can trim your grocery bill in the long run, too, because you can take advantage of weekly sales and more economical bulk pricing. But you won't save money if the items you buy spoil or lose their flavor before you use them up. So carefully choose the size of packages to be sure you'll finish them before the use-by dates listed. If you know you won't be using an item within a day or two and it's suitable for freezer storage, freeze it immediately using the guidelines that follow.

Pantry Storage

Check the sell-by or use-by dates on pantry items. Discard items that are past those dates. In the pantry, store opened items tightly closed and place in a cool, dry place. Times given in the charts on pages 19-20 are for pantry storage of opened items.

Refrigerated Foods

The use-by date on refrigerated items is only for the unopened item. Use the times given in the chart for opened foods. Keep the refrigerator temperature between 34°-40°. In the refrigerator, store leftovers in covered refrigerator containers or wrap them in plastic wrap or foil. Resealable plastic bags also are great for storage.

Frozen Foods

For the best quality, foods should be frozen in a freezer that maintains 0° and is at least two-thirds full. Cool cooked food quickly before freezing. Store food in containers that are moisture-proof and vapor-proof, such as foil, freezer bags, freezer wrap and plastic freezer containers. Remove as much air as possible when packaging the food. Label and date packages before freezing. Spread out the packages for quicker freezing, and then stack them after they are solidly frozen.

Defrost foods in the refrigerator, microwave oven or cold water. Generally, small items will defrost overnight in the refrigerator. Most items take 1 or 2 days. Bulky, large items will take even longer to thaw. To defrost in a microwave oven, follow the manufacturer's directions. To defrost in cold water, place food in a watertight plastic storage bag. Place the bag in cold water. Change the water every 30 minutes until the food is thawed.

OPENED FOOD ITEM	REFRIGERATOR TEMP. 34° TO 40°	FREEZER TEMP. 0°
DAIRY		
Butter	1 to 3 months	6 to 9 months
Cheese		
Brie	1 week	6 months
Cottage/Ricotta	1 week	not suitable
Cream Cheese	2 weeks	not suitable
Cheddar, Brick, Swiss, Monterey Jack	3 to 4 weeks	6 months
Mozzarella	1 week	6 months
Parmesan/Romano, Grated	2 months	6 months
Cream		
Ultrapasteurized	1 month	not suitable
Heavy Whipping or Half-and-Half	3 days	2 to 4 months
Eggs		
Whole, In the shell	4 to 5 weeks	not suitable
Whites or Yolks, Uncooked	2 to 4 days	12 months
Milk		
Milk	7 days	3 months
Buttermilk	7 to 14 days	3 months
Evaporated or Sweetened Condensed	4 to 5 days	
Margarine	4 to 5 months	12 months
Sour Cream	7 to 21 days	not suitable
Yogurt	7 to 14 days	1 to 2 months
MEATS—BEEF, PORK, LAMB		
Fresh		
Chops	3 to 5 days	4 to 6 months
Ground or Stew Meat	1 to 2 days	3 to 4 months
Roasts	3 to 5 days	4 to 12 months
Sausage, Fresh	1 to 2 days	1 to 2 months
Steaks	3 to 5 days	6 to 12 months
Leftover Cooked Meats/Casseroles	1 to 4 days	2 to 3 months
Processed Meats		
Bacon	7 days	1 month
Ham	3 to 5 days	1 to 2 months
Luncheon Meats	3 to 5 days	1 to 2 months
POULTRY		
Chicken/Turkey		
Whole	1 to 2 days	1 year
Parts	1 to 2 days	9 months
Leftover, Cooked	1 to 4 days	1 to 4 months
FISH AND SEAFOOD		
Lean Fish (Fillets/Steaks)		
Cod, Sole, Halibut, Orange Roughy, Flounder	1 to 2 days	6 months
Fatty Fish (Fillets/Steaks)		
Catfish, Perch, Salmon, Whitefish	1 to 2 days	2 to 3 months
Crab, Cooked	1 to 2 days	3 months
Scallops/Shrimp		
Uncooked	1 to 2 days	3 to 6 months
Cooked	3 to 4 days	3 months
Leftover, Cooked Seafood	3 to 4 days	3 to 6 months

OPENED FOOD ITEM	PANTRY STORAGE TEMP. 70°	REFRIGERATOR TEMP. 34° TO 40°	FREEZER TEMP. 0°
STAPLES			
Baking Powder	18 months		
Baking Soda	18 months		
Bouillon Cubes	1 year		
Bread	2 to 7 days	4 to 7 days	3 months
Canned Goods			
Fish and Seafood		2 days	
Fruit		1 week	
Pasta Sauces		5 days	
Vegetables		2 to 3 days	
Cereal			
Cook before eating	6 months		
Ready to eat	2 to 3 months		
Cornmeal	12 months		
Cornstarch	18 months		
Flour			
All-Purpose	15 months		
Whole Wheat	6 months		
Fruit, Dried	6 months		
Honey	12 months		
Jam and Jelly		12 months	
Ketchup or Chili Sauce		4 to 6 months	
Mayonnaise		2 months	
Mustard		6 to 12 months	
Nuts	3 to 6 months	3 to 6 months	6 to 12 months
Oils			
Canola or Corn Oil	6 months		
Olive Oil	4 months		
Peanut Butter	2 to 3 months		
Pickles		1 to 2 months	
Pies			
Custard		2 to 3 days	not suitable
Fruit, Unbaked			8 months
Fruit, Baked		4 to 5 days	1 to 2 months
Pumpkin		4 to 5 days	2 months
Rice			
Brown	1 month	6 months	
White	2 years		
Salad Dressings		3 months	
Salsa		1 month	
Shortening	8 months		
Soy Sauce		12 months	
Sugar			
Brown	4 months		
Granulated	2 years		
Worcestershire Sauce	12 months		

Herbs and Spices

Seasoned cooks know that a pinch of this herb and a dash of that spice can really perk up a dish. A well-stocked spice rack can be one of the quickest and least expensive ways to add flair to ordinary meals. Store dried herbs and spices in tightly closed glass or heavy-duty plastic containers. It's best to keep them in a cool, dry place; avoid storing them in direct sunlight, over the stove or near other heat sources.

For best flavor, keep dried herbs and ground spices for up to 6 months. They can be used if they are older, but the flavors might not be as intense. Whole spices can be stored for 1 to 2 years.

Select fresh herbs that are fragrant with bright, fresh-looking leaves. Avoid those with wilted, yellowing or browning leaves. Wrap fresh herbs in a slightly damp paper towel and place in a resealable plastic bag. Press as much air as possible out of the bag and seal. Store in the refrigerator for 5 to 7 days.

To substitute dried herbs for fresh, use one-third less. For example if a recipe calls for 1 tablespoon fresh, use 1 teaspoon dried.

Allspice
Available as whole, dried berries or ground. Tastes like, cinnamon, cloves and nutmeg. Use for baked goods, jerked meats, sauces, sausage, preserves, roasts, root vegetables.

Aniseed
Available as oval, greenish-brown seeds. Licorice-like flavor similar to fennel. Use for cookies, cakes, breads, pickles, stews, seafood, beets, cauliflower, pasta sauces.

Basil
Available as fresh green or purple leaves or dried and crushed. Sweet flavor with hints of mint, pepper and cloves. Use for tomato sauce, pestos, chicken, meat, zucchini, summer squashes.

Bay Leaf
Available as whole, fresh or dried, dull green leaves. Savory, spicy and aromatic. Use for soups, stews, casseroles, pickles, meat.

Black/White Pepper
Available whole, cracked, coarse or ground (black); whole or ground (white). Black has a sharp, hot piney flavor; white is milder. Use for all types of cooking; white adds pepper flavor without flecks.

Caraway Seeds
Available as light to dark brown seeds. Sweet blend of dill and anise flavors. Use for breads, cakes, biscuits, pork, cheese, potatoes, sauerkraut.

Cardamom
Available as pods, brownish-black seeds or ground. Sweet, spicy flavor and slightly pungent. Use for baked goods, chicken, curries, meat.

Cayenne Pepper
Available ground, also known as ground red pepper. Pungent, hot flavor. Use for chili, soups, sauces, beans, poultry, meat, seafood.

Celery Seed
Available as light-brown or tan seeds. Strong and bitter flavor. Use for fish, eggs, cheese, salad dressings.

Chervil
Available as fresh leaves or dried and crushed. Fresh has a hint of anise and dry has a hint of parsley flavor. Use for fish, eggs, poultry, salads.

Chives
Available as fresh or freeze-dried hollow stems. Delicate and peppery, mild onion flavor. Use for potatoes, eggs, sauces, seafood, salads.

Cilantro

Available as fresh leaves. When dried, it's known as coriander. Pungent, strong flavor. Use for ethnic dishes (such as Mexican or Asian), salsa, tomatoes, chicken, pork, seafood.

Cinnamon

Available as sticks or ground. Sweet and pungent flavor. Use for baked goods, fruit desserts, warm beverages.

Cloves

Available whole or ground. Pungent, medicinal, sweet flavor. Use for baked goods, fruit desserts, ham, lamb, warm beverages.

Coriander

Available as dried and crushed leaves, seeds or ground seeds. Mildly sweet, spicy flavor. Use for ethnic dishes (North African, Mediterranean, Asian), stews, curries, pork, lentils.

Cumin

Available as seeds and ground. Pungent, earthy, slightly bitter flavor. Use for beans, chili, pork, chicken, stews.

Dill

Available as fresh leaves, dried and crushed or seeds. Fresh, sweet, grassy flavor. Use for pickles, fish, cucumbers, breads, tomatoes.

Fennel

Available as seeds. Sweet and mildly licorice-like flavor. Use for baked goods, seafood, sausage, pork.

Ginger

Available as fresh root, crystallized or ground. Pungent, sweet, spicy, hot flavor. Use for baked goods, pumpkin, pork, chicken.

Mace

Available ground. Nutmeg-like flavor. Use for baked goods, poultry, fish.

Marjoram

Available as fresh leaves, dried and crushed. Oregano-like flavor. Use for tomato dishes, meat, poultry, seafood, vegetables.

Mint

Available as fresh leaves or dried and crushed. Fresh, strong, cool flavor. Use for lamb, salsas, vegetables, meats.

Mustard

Available ground or as seeds. Pungent, sharp, hot flavor. Use for meats, vinaigrettes, seafood, sauces.

Nutmeg

Available whole or ground. Sweet, spicy flavor. Use for baked goods, custards, vegetables, poultry, meat.

Oregano

Available as fresh leaves, dried and crushed or ground. Pungent, slightly bitter flavor. Use for tomato dishes, chicken, pork, lamb, vegetables.

Paprika

Available ground. Mild to hot, sweet flavor. Use for poultry, shellfish, meat, vegetables.

Parsley

Available as fresh leaves, curly or Italian (flat-leaf), or dried and flaked. Fresh, slightly peppery flavor. Use for poultry, seafood, tomatoes, pasta, vegetables.

Poppy Seeds

Available as seeds. Nut-like flavor. Use for baked goods, fruits, pasta.

Rosemary

Available as fresh leaves on stems or dried. Pungent flavor with a hint of pine. Use for lamb, poultry, pork, vegetables.

Saffron

Available as threads (whole stigmas) or powder. Pungent, bitter flavor. Use for bouillabaisse, curries, fish, poultry, rice.

Sage

Available as fresh leaves, dried and crushed or rubbed. Pungent, slightly bitter, musty mint flavor. Use for pork, poultry, stuffing.

Salt, Kosher

Available only as noniodized. Coarser, larger grains with fluffier look. Less sodium per teaspoon than table salt. Use for brines, salt crusts on meats and fish, marinades, savory dishes, coating rims of glasses.

Salt, Sea

Available in many varieties and in large or fine grains. Color ranges from white to clay to pinkish-brown to gray. Less salty than table salt but may impart other subtle flavors. Use at the end of cooking to season food.

Salt, Table

Available as iodized (to help prevent goiter) and non-iodized. Has anticaking agent added to keep it flowing. Boosts food's flavor and acts as a preservative. Use for savory foods, baked goods.

Savory

Available as fresh leaves, dried and crushed or ground. Piquant blend of mint and thyme. Use for beans, lentils, lamb, poultry.

Sesame Seeds

Available as seeds. Nut-like flavor. Use for breads, chicken, seafood, noodles, chickpeas.

Tarragon

Available as fresh leaves or dried and crushed. Strong, spicy, anise-like flavors. Use for poultry, seafood, meats, vegetables.

Thyme

Available as fresh leaves or dried and crushed. Pungent, earthy, spicy flavor. Use for meat, poultry, lentils, soups, stews.

Turmeric

Available ground. Pungent, bitter, earthy flavor. Use for curries, lamb, chicken, meat, beans, lentils.

Glossary

While you use this book, there will be common cooking terms in each chapter that are defined here. Within some chapters, you may find that the more specific terms for that chapter will be defined within it.

A

Al Dente: An Italian term meaning "to the tooth" used to describe pasta that is cooked but still firm.

Au Jus: Natural, unthickened juices that collect while roasting meats.

B

Bake: To cook in an oven surrounded by dry heat. When baking, preheat the oven before placing the food in it.

Baste: To moisten foods while cooking by brushing with pan juices, butter, margarine, oil or a reserved marinade.

Batter: A mixture made of flour and a liquid such as milk. It may also include other ingredients such as sugar, butter, shortening or oil, eggs, leaveners and flavorings. The consistency of batters ranges from thin to thick. Thin batters are pourable, such as pancakes or cakes. Thick batters can be dropped from a spoon, such as quick breads.

Beat: To rapidly mix with a spoon, fork, wire whisk or electric mixer.

Betty: A baked fruit dessert that alternates layers of sweetened fruit with cake, cookies or bread crumbs.

Bias Cut: To cut foods diagonally into slices. Most often used in stir-fries.

Blanch: To cook for a few minutes in boiling water. This technique is used to help remove peels, to partially cook foods as a preparation step in a recipe or to prepare foods for freezing.

Blend: To combine several ingredients with a spoon, electric mixer, blender or food processor.

Boil: To heat liquids until bubbles form that cannot be stirred down. In the case of water, the temperature will reach 212° at sea level.

Bone: To remove raw or cooked meat from bones. (See Boning Chicken Breasts on page 219.)

Braise: To cook slowly in a small amount of liquid in a covered pan on the stovetop or in the oven. Generally used for less tender cuts of meat.

Breading: A coating of fine bread crumbs or crackers used on meat, fish or vegetables.

Broil: To cook foods about 4 to 6 inches from a heat source.

Brown: To cook foods in a small amount of fat over medium to high heat until the food becomes brown, sealing in the juices and developing rich pan drippings.

Browned Bits: Little flecks of browned food that are left in the bottom of a pan after browning or cooking meat or poultry.

Buckle: A baked, cake-like fruit dessert made with berries. Named because the cake sometimes buckles under the weight of the topping.

Butterfly: To split foods, such as chicken breast, boneless meat or shrimp, lengthwise in half, leaving the meat attached along one side.

C

Caramelize: To heat sugar in a skillet or saucepan over low heat until melted and golden brown. Also refers to cooking onions in butter until soft, caramel-colored and rich in flavor.

Chill: To cool foods to below room temperature (40° or less) by placing in the refrigerator, freezer or an ice bath.

Chop: To cut foods into 1/4-inch to 1/2-inch pieces.

Clarify: To remove sediment and suspended particles from a liquid. Clarified butter has the milk solids removed, which allows the clarified butter to be heated to a higher temperature without smoking.

Coat: To dip or roll foods in flour, bread crumbs, sugar or a sauce until covered.

"Coats Spoon": To leave a thin, even, smooth film on the back of a metal spoon. This is a doneness test for stirred custards.

Cobbler: A fruit dessert with a biscuit topping. The topping can be either in a single layer or dropped over the fruit to give a cobblestone effect.

Combine: To place several ingredients in a single bowl or container and mix thoroughly.

Cooking in Liquid: To simmer meat covered with liquid for a long time. Generally used for less tender cuts of meat to tenderize the meat.

Cool: To bring foods to room temperature (about 70°).

Core: To remove the seed area of an apple or pear using a coring tool or a small knife.

Cream: To beat softened butter, margarine or shortening alone or with sugar using a spoon or mixer until light and fluffy.

Crimp: To seal the edge of a double-crusted pie by pinching or pressing the crusts together with your fingers, fork or other utensil.

Crisp: A baked fruit dessert that has a crumb topping over fruit. The topping generally has flour, sugar and butter and may or may not have oats, nuts and spices. The topping gets crisp while baking.

Crisp-Tender: A stage of vegetable cooking where the vegetables are cooked until they are crunchy yet tender enough to be pierced with a fork.

Crush: To reduce foods to crumbs, paste or powder. Herbs can be crushed with a mortar and pestle. Garlic cloves and fresh gingerroot can be crushed with the side of a knife.

Cube: To cut foods into 1/2-inch to 1-inch square pieces.

Cut in: To break down and distribute cold butter, margarine or shortening into a flour mixture using a pastry blender or two knives.

D

Dash: A measurement less than 1/8 teaspoon that is used for herbs, spices or hot pepper sauce. This is not an accurate measurement.

Deep-Fat Fry: To cook foods in enough hot oil so that the food floats in the oil.

Deglaze: To add water, broth or wine to a pan in which food, usually meat, has been cooked to remove the browned bits to make a rich gravy.

Dice: To cut foods into small cubes (1/8-inch to 1/4-inch cubes).

Direct Heat: To cook foods on an outdoor grill directly over coals or heat source.

Dissolve: To stir a solid food with a liquid until none of the solid remains, such as yeast with warm water or gelatin in boiling water.

Dollop: A small mound of soft food such as whipped cream or whipped topping.

Dot: To break up butter into small pieces and distribute over the top of a pie or dough.

Dough: A thick mixture made of flour and a liquid that is not pourable. It may include ingredients such as sugar, butter, shortening or oil, eggs, leaveners and flavorings. It may be stiff enough to be worked with by hand (kneading bread dough, for example).

Dredge: To lightly coat foods with flour or bread crumbs.

Dress: To toss salads with salad dressing. Also, to remove the internal organs of fish, poultry or game.

Drippings: The juices and melted fat that collect in the bottom of the pan as meat is cooked. The juices and some of the fat from the drippings can be used in gravies and sauces.

Drizzle: To slowly spoon or pour a thin stream of an icing, melted butter or other liquid over food.

Dust: To lightly sprinkle with confectioners' sugar, baking cocoa or flour.

Dutch Oven: A multipurpose cooking pot that can range in size from 5 to 8 quarts and is used to roast meats, cook soups and stews, boil pasta or steam vegetables.

E

Egg Wash: A mixture of beaten egg, egg yolk or egg white and water that is brushed over breads, rolls, pastries or pie crusts before baking. Egg washes give the final baked product a shiny brown finish.

Emulsify: To combine through a whisking action two liquids that traditionally separate, such as oil and vinegar, into a uniform mixture.

Extracts: The distilled essential oils from plant materials, which are then dissolved in alcohol. Common examples are vanilla and almond.

F

Filet: A boneless cut of meat.

Fillet: A boneless piece of fish.

Flake: To separate foods into small pieces. The term is frequently used when describing the doneness of fish.

Flavorings: Chemical compounds that replicate the flavor of a particular food or plant and do not originate from the plant material. Common examples are maple, banana and coconut.

Flute: To make a V-shape or scalloped edge on pie crust with thumb and fingers.

Fold: A method of mixing to combine light or delicate ingredients such as whipped cream or egg whites with other ingredients without beating. A rubber spatula is used to gently cut down through the ingredients, move across the bottom of the bowl and bring up part of the mixture.

Food Coloring: Used to tint foods and is available in liquids, gels or pastes.

Full Rolling Boil: A vigorous boil in which the bubbles cannot be stirred down and continuously break the surface.

Freeze: To store foods in the freezer.

Frost: To cover a cake, cupcake or cookie with a spreadable frosting.

Fry: To cook foods in a small amount of fat over medium to high heat.

G

Garnish: A decorative and edible accompaniment to give a dish more eye appeal and sometimes a flavor boost.

Glaze: To coat the exterior of sweet or savory foods with a thin, glossy mixture.

Grate: To rub ingredients such as citrus peel, spices and chocolate over a grater to produce very fine particles.

Grease: To rub the inside of a baking dish or pan with shortening, butter or oil, or to coat with cooking spray to keep the contents from sticking.

Grease and Flour: To rub the inside of a baking dish or pan with a thin layer of shortening, butter or oil, or coat with cooking spray and then dust with flour. The excess flour is shaken out of the pan. Cakes baked in round baking pans or fluted tube pans generally require the pan to be greased and floured.

Grill: To cook foods outside on a grid over hot charcoals or a gas flame. Also refers to an indoor countertop electrical appliance.

Grind: To transform a solid piece of food into smaller pieces using a food processor, blender or mortar and pestle.

H

Headspace: An area left unfilled between the top of the food in a home canning jar or freezer container and the bottom of the lid. (See Boiling-Water-Bath Basics on page 496.)

Hull: To remove the green stem and leaves of strawberries.

Husk: To remove the outer leaves from an ear of corn.

I

Ice: To spread a thin frosting over cakes or cookies.

Indirect Heat: To cook foods on an outdoor grill over a drip pan with the coals (or other heat source) placed on one or both sides of the drip pan. Indirect heat is used for cooking larger cuts of meat or less tender cuts of meat.

J

Jelly Roll: A dessert made by spreading a filling, jelly or whipped cream over a sponge cake baked in a 15-inch x 10-inch x 1-inch pan and rolling into a log. Jelly-roll style is used when any food is filled and rolled into a log shape.

Julienne: To cut foods into long, thin matchstick shapes about 2 inches long and 1/8 inch thick. (See Making Julienne Strips on page 10.)

K

Knead: To work dough by using a pressing and folding action to make it smooth and elastic.

L

Line: To cover a baking sheet with a piece of parchment paper, waxed paper or foil to prevent sticking.

M

Marble: To swirl light and dark batters in a cake, bar cookie, pie or cheesecake. The batters should not be combined into one color; there should still be two distinct batters after marbling.

Marinate: To tenderize and/or flavor foods, usually meat or raw vegetables, by placing in a liquid mixture of oil, vinegar, wine, lime or lemon juice, herbs and spices.

Mince: To cut foods into very fine pieces no larger than 1/8 inch.

Mix: To stir or beat two or more ingredients together with a spoon or a fork until well combined.

Moisten: To add enough liquid to dry ingredients while stirring gently to make a wet, but not runny, mixture. Often used in the preparation of muffins.

P
....

Pan-Broil: To cook tender cuts of meat, uncovered, in a skillet on the stovetop without the addition of any fat or liquid.

Pan-Dressed: Fish or small game with the internal organs and head removed, making it ready for cooking.

Pan-Fry: To cook tender cuts of meat, uncovered, in a skillet on the stovetop with the addition of fat but no liquid.

Parboil: To boil foods, usually vegetables, until partially cooked. Most often used when vegetables are finished using another cooking method or chilled for marinated salads or appetizer dips.

Partially Set: The consistency of chilled gelatin (resembles unbeaten egg whites) before fruits, vegetables and nuts can be added without floating.

Peel: To remove the skin from fruits and vegetables. To remove the peel, use a small sharp knife, a grater, a vegetable peeler or zester. Also, the outer portion of a citrus fruit is known as the peel.

Pinch: A measurement less than 1/8 teaspoon of a seasoning or spice that is easily held between the thumb and index finger. This is not an accurate measurement.

Pipe: To force a soft mixture such as whipped cream, frosting or meringue through a pastry bag for a fancy shape.

Pit: To remove the seed from fruit. Also refers to the seed in cherries, peaches, nectarines and avocados.

Plump: To soak dried fruit such as raisins and cherries in liquid until softened.

Poach: To cook meat, fish, eggs or fruits in hot (160° to 180°) liquid, which is just below a simmer. For meats and fish, the liquid can be flavored with salt, bay leaves, onion, celery and white wine if desired. Fruits are often poached in a sugar syrup.

Preheat: To bring an oven up to the baking temperature before baking.

Press: Often called a cookie press. Used to extrude cookie dough in decorative shapes.

Prick: To pierce food or pastry with the tines of a fork to prevent them from bursting or rising during baking. Also used when roasting ducks and geese to remove excess fat under the skin.

Process: To combine, blend, chop or puree foods in a food processor or blender.

Proof: To check the quality of yeast before using. To proof yeast, dissolve yeast and a little sugar in warm water (110° to 115°) and let stand for 5 minutes. If the yeast is alive, there will be a thick foam on the surface. To proof also refers to letting yeast dough rise after it has been shaped and before baking.

Pulse: To process foods in a food processor or in a blender using short bursts of power. This is accomplished by quickly turning the machine on and off.

Punch Down: To use a fist to deflate risen yeast dough after the first rising.

Puree: To mash solid foods into a smooth mixture using a food processor, food mill, blender or sieve.

R
....

Reduce: To thicken sauces and gravy by boiling down and evaporating a portion of the liquid in an uncovered pan.

Refrigerate: To place in the refrigerator to chill.

Roast: To cook meat or vegetables with a dry heat as in cooking in an oven without the addition of liquid. Also refers to large cuts of meat that are intended to be roasted.

Rounded Teaspoon or Tablespoon: To mound dough slightly in measuring spoon.

Roux: A French term for a mixture of flour and fat that is cooked together until golden brown and used to thicken gumbos, soups and sauces.

S
....

Saute: To cook or lightly brown foods in butter, margarine or oil until tender.

Scald: To heat milk or cream over low heat until just before it boils. Look for small bubbles around the edge of the liquid.

Score: To make thin slashes on the surface of breads to decorate and allow steam to escape during baking.

Seed: To remove seeds from fruits and vegetables.

Seize: To become thick and lumpy. Seizing happens when a small amount of liquid comes in contact with melted chocolate.

Separate: To remove the egg white from the egg yolk.

Shred: To cut or tear foods into long, thin strips, such as cooked chicken. In the case of soft cheese, carrots or potatoes, a metal shredder is used.

Shuck: To remove the meat of oysters, clams, etc. from their shells. Also refers to removing the husk from an ear of corn.

Sift: To pass dry ingredients such as flour or confectioners' sugar through a fine-mesh strainer or sifter to remove lumps, add air and combine several dry ingredients.

Simmer: To cook liquids alone or a combination of ingredients with liquid just under the boiling point (180° to 200°). The surface of the liquid will have some movement and there may be small bubbles around the side of pan.

Skim: To remove with a spoon a layer of fat or foam that rises from the top of cooking liquids. (See Making Pan Gravy on page 488.)

Snip: To cut herbs into small pieces using a kitchen shears.

Soft Peaks: The stage of beating egg whites or heavy whipping cream when the beater is lifted from the mixture and the points of the peaks curl over.

Soften: To bring butter, margarine or cream cheese to a soft consistency by holding at room temperature for a short time.

Spice Bag: A container made out of cheesecloth to hold whole spices and/or herbs. The bag makes it easy to remove and discard the spices or herbs before serving. (See Making a Spice Bag on page 65.)

Steam: To cook foods covered on a rack or in a steamer basket over a small amount of boiling water. Most often used for vegetables.

Steep: To place dry foods, such as tea leaves, in hot water to extract flavor and/or color.

Stew: To cover food with liquid and slowly cook over low heat in a tightly covered pot. This cooking method tenderizes tough cuts of meat and allows flavors to blend.

Stiff Peaks: The stage of beating egg whites or heavy whipping cream when the beater is lifted from the mixture and the points of peaks stand straight up.

Stir: To blend a combination of ingredients by hand using a spoon in a circular motion.

Stir-Fry: To quickly saute meats and vegetables while stirring constantly in a wok or skillet.

Stock: A long-simmered broth made from meat, poultry, fish and/or vegetables with herbs and spices.

Strain: To separate solids from liquid by pouring through a sieve or colander.

Stud: To insert seasonings like whole cloves into the surface of food, such as a ham.

Stuff: To fill a cavity in fish, poultry or pork chops with a bread or rice, vegetable, fruit or nut mixture. (See Stuffing, Roasting and Carving a Whole Turkey on page 240.)

T

Tear: To use your hands to pull food apart into unevenly sized pieces, such as when tearing salad greens.

Thread: To place pieces of meat and vegetables onto skewers as when making kabobs.

Toss: To quickly and gently mix ingredients with a spoon or fork. Often done with flour and candied fruit in baked goods.

Truss: To tie the legs and wings of poultry close to the body before roasting. If poultry is stuffed, the openings are closed with skewers that are tied or closed with string.

W

Warm: To hold foods at a low temperature, usually around 200°, without further cooking.

Water Bath: To place a baking dish containing food, such as a custard or souffle, in a large dish. The larger dish is filled with hot or boiling water. The food is then baked in the water bath to promote even cooking.

Weave: To thread food on a skewer using a back and forth motion. The term is also used to describe the action when making a lattice top for a pie.

Whip: To beat rapidly by hand or with an electric mixer to add air and increase volume.

Whisk: A multi-looped, wire mixing utensil with a handle used to whip sauces, eggs, cream, etc. to a smooth, airy consistency. Also means to whip ingredients together.

Z

Zest: *See Peel.*

little bites reap big rewards

70 micro-businesses start up around the world

Virginia Galloway

> *I knew this program could make a significant difference in the lives of people who live in dire poverty.*
>
> ~Virginia Galloway

Although she graduated some time ago, Virginia Galloway keeps finding good reasons to stay at the University of St. Thomas in Houston, Texas.

"I believe it's my obligation to help and encourage our students in any way that I can," she acknowledges with a smile. For years, Virginia has been working along with university students and cooking for the Basilian Fathers at the school.

"I assist the students in setting the tables, making meals and serving dinner to the Fathers," she says. "I've given many impromptu cooking lessons along the way...frequently referring to recipes and tips from *Taste of Home*."

When Ida Orbe, a student whose family is from Tunisia, asked Virginia to make hors d'oeuvres for a fund-raiser, she couldn't say no. Ida wanted to raise money for the Center for International Studies' Micro-Credit Program, which offers micro-loans (an average of just $50) to small entrepreneurs in developing countries.

"I knew this program could make a significant difference in the lives of people who live in dire poverty," says Virginia. "I was delighted to donate my time and cooking skills to help our students help others."

Together, Virginia, Ida and nine other students took over the Fathers' kitchen, working until 1 a.m. the night before the event. They washed and chopped vegetables, created little pastries, prepared hummus and made mini cheesecakes—along with many other treats.

And they cooked up quite a success!

"We raised over $10,000, which aided the Micro-Credit Program in dispatching loans to over 70 beneficiaries all over the world," says Virginia. Seventy percent of those went to female entrepreneurs.

The loans helped people do everything from opening a retail store in the Ukraine to starting honey farming in Mexico.

"The evening was such a success," says Virginia, "that we're making it an annual event!"

Recipes

Tips

Appetizers & Beverages

Appetizers not only stimulate the appetite before the main course but also can be served in place of a meal. But don't overdo it. Instead, prepare a few good choices or make one spectacular item and fill in with other easy but delicious foods.

You can choose from hot, cold and room temperature foods. When selecting your appetizers, choose recipes that will give a variety of colors, textures (soft and crunchy) and flavors (sour, salty, savory, sweet, spicy or subtle). Look for appetizers that make a nice presentation and require no last-minute fussing.

How Much to Serve

The amount per person varies on the length of the party and the focus of the appetizers.

- For a social hour before dinner, plan on serving 3 or 4 different appetizers and allow 4 to 5 bites per person.

- For an open-house affair, plan on serving 4 to 5 different appetizers and allow 4 to 6 bites per person per hour.

- For an appetizer buffet that is served in place of a meal, plan on serving 6 to 8 different appetizers and allow 10 to 14 bites per person.

Tips for Tasty Appetizers

Allow cheese balls, dips and spreads that contain cream cheese to stand at room temperature for 15 minutes before serving for easier spreading and more flavor.

Place dips in colorful, edible bowls such as red or green cabbage shells or cored sweet red, yellow or green peppers. Fruit dips can be spooned into melon, orange or grapefruit shells.

Tenderize firm vegetable dippers such as broccoli, green beans and cauliflower by blanching (see page 358) them in boiling water for a minute or two to cook partially. They should still remain crisp. After blanching, immediately plunge the vegetables in ice water to stop the cooking. Drain well before serving.

Add splashes of color by garnishing appetizer platters with sprigs of freshly picked herbs, lemon wedges, grape clusters, fresh berries or small hot peppers. For a lighter feel, decorate with citrus peel curls, fresh chives or edible flowers.

For plates, puddle the dipping sauce for a savory item or ice cream topping for a sweet food on the plate and top with the food. Or dust the plate with cocoa powder or confectioners' sugar.

Try radishes, sweet red pepper strips, sugar snap peas and cherry tomatoes in addition to your usual vegetable dippers.

Prepare appetizers ahead of serving time but store in the refrigerator; wrap tightly with foil or plastic wrap.

Keep cold appetizers on ice when your gathering takes you out-of-doors in the warm months (see How to Make an Ice Bowl on page 45). And keep hot appetizers hot to keep them safe from spoilage.

Cheese Tip

Select sharp cheddar when using packaged shredded cheese for recipes that you'd like to have a bolder flavor. If you will be shredding cheese at home from bulk cheddar, you can choose from mild, medium, sharp and extra sharp.

Savory Swiss Cheesecake

PREP: 15 min. **BAKE:** 40 min. + chilling

Marjorie Turner, Pearisburg, Virginia

Big on Swiss cheese flavor, this creamy spread is irresistible at a festive buffet table. It's terrific when entertaining because it is made ahead.

> 1 cup finely crushed thin wheat crackers
> 3 tablespoons butter, melted
> 12 ounces reduced-fat cream cheese
> 2 cartons (8 ounces *each*) reduced-fat plain yogurt
> 1 egg
> 1 egg yolk
> 1/4 teaspoon dried basil
> 1/8 teaspoon dried rosemary, crushed
> 2 cups (8 ounces) shredded reduced-fat Swiss cheese

Assorted crackers

1) In a small bowl, combine cracker crumbs and butter. Press onto the bottom of a 9-in. springform pan; set aside.

2) In a large mixing bowl, beat cream cheese until smooth. Add the yogurt, egg, egg yolk, basil and rosemary; beat on low speed just until blended. Stir in Swiss cheese.

3) Pour into prepared crust. Place pan on a baking sheet. Bake at 350° for 40-50 minutes or until center is almost set. Cool on a wire rack for 10 minutes. Carefully run a knife around edge of pan to loosen; cool 1 hour longer.

4) Refrigerate overnight. Remove sides of pan. Cut into wedges; serve with crackers. Refrigerate leftovers.

Yield: 16 servings.

NUTRITION FACTS: 1 piece (calculated without crackers) equals 169 calories, 11 g fat (7 g saturated fat), 57 mg cholesterol, 170 mg sodium, 7 g carbohydrate, trace fiber, 9 g protein.

FIESTA CHEESE BALL

Fiesta Cheese Ball

PREP: 15 min. + chilling

Virginia Horst, Mesa, Washington

For a change of pace, shape individual servings of this cheese spread into smaller balls, then roll in paprika or chopped nuts.

> 1 package (8 ounces) cream cheese, softened
> 1/4 cup shredded Colby-Monterey Jack cheese
> 3 to 4 tablespoons minced fresh cilantro
> 2 to 3 tablespoons grated onion
> 1 tablespoon chili powder
> 1 teaspoon dried minced garlic
> 1/2 teaspoon garlic salt
> 1/4 teaspoon dried oregano
> 1/4 teaspoon crushed red pepper flakes
> 1/8 teaspoon ground cumin
> 1/8 to 1/4 teaspoon hot pepper sauce
> 1/4 cup minced fresh parsley

Assorted crackers

1) In a small mixing bowl, beat cream cheese. Add the cheese, cilantro, onion, chili powder, garlic, garlic salt, oregano, red pepper flakes, cumin and hot pepper sauce.

2) Cover and refrigerate for at least 1 hour. Shape into a ball. Roll in parsley. Cover and refrigerate for 8 hours or overnight. Serve with crackers.

Yield: 1 cheese ball.

NUTRITION FACTS: 2 tablespoons cheese ball (calculated without crackers) equals 79 calories, 7 g fat (5 g saturated fat), 23 mg cholesterol, 153 mg sodium, 1 g carbohydrate, trace fiber, 2 g protein.

Shaping a Cheese Ball

Keep hands and countertop clean by spooning the cheese mixture onto a piece of plastic wrap. Working from the underside of the wrap, pat the mixture into a ball. Complete recipe as directed.

1 package (10 ounces) frozen chopped spinach, thawed and squeezed dry
1 cup (4 ounces) shredded cheddar cheese
1 can (8 ounces) water chestnuts, drained and chopped
5 bacon strips, cooked and crumbled
1 green onion, chopped
2 teaspoons dill weed
1 garlic clove, minced
1/2 teaspoon seasoned salt
1/8 teaspoon pepper
1 unsliced round loaf (1 pound) sourdough bread

Raw vegetables

1) In a large mixing bowl, beat cream cheese and mayonnaise. Stir in the spinach, cheese, water chestnuts, bacon, onion and seasonings.

2) Cut a 1-1/2-in. slice off top of the bread; set aside. Carefully hollow out bottom, leaving a 1/2-in. shell. Cube removed bread and set aside. Fill the shell with spinach dip; replace top. Wrap in heavy-duty foil; place on a baking sheet.

3) Bake at 375° for 1-1/4 to 1-1/2 hours or until dip is heated through. Open foil carefully. Serve warm with bread cubes and vegetables.

Yield: 4-1/2 cups.

NUTRITION FACTS: 1/4 cup dip (calculated without bread cubes or vegetables) equals 105 calories, 7 g fat (4 g saturated fat), 20 mg cholesterol, 303 mg sodium, 6 g carbohydrate, 1 g fiber, 6 g protein.

Fruit and Caramel Brie

PREP/TOTAL TIME: 15 min.

Tracy Schuhmacher, Penfield, New York

I'm a stay-at-home mother with two boys and I enjoy cooking—especially appetizers. Brie is one of my favorite cheeses and this sweet-savory recipe is party-special but quite easy to throw together.

1 round (8 ounces) Brie cheese, rind removed
1/3 cup caramel ice cream topping
1/4 cup dried cranberries
1/4 cup chopped dried apples
1/4 cup chopped walnuts
1 loaf (1 pound) French bread baguette, sliced and toasted

1) Place Brie in a microwave-safe bowl. In a small bowl, combine the caramel topping, cranberries, apples and walnuts. Spread over Brie. Microwave, uncovered, on high for 60-90 seconds or until cheese is heated through and slightly melted. Serve with toasted baguette slices.

Yield: 8 servings.

NUTRITION FACTS: 1 serving equals 412 calories, 16 g fat (6 g saturated fat), 28 mg cholesterol, 568 mg sodium, 57 g carbohydrate, 4 g fiber, 12 g protein.

Baked Spinach Dip Loaf

PREP: 15 min. **BAKE:** 1-1/4 hours

Frieda Meding, Trochu, Alberta

This baked version of spinach dip is a twist on the traditional cold variety. To save time, make and chill the dip overnight. Spoon the dip into the bread bowl and bake before guests arrive.

2 packages (8 ounces *each*) cream cheese, softened
1 cup mayonnaise

Hot Bean Dip

PREP/TOTAL TIME: 15 min.

Michelle Sawatzky, Isle, Minnesota

This thick and tasty party-starter takes advantage of prepared taco sauce and canned refried beans.

1 pound ground beef
1/4 cup chopped onion
1 can (16 ounces) refried beans
1-1/4 cups shredded Monterey Jack cheese
1/2 cup taco sauce

Tortilla chips

1) In a large skillet, cook beef and onion over medium heat until meat is no longer pink; drain. Reduce heat. Stir in the refried beans, Monterey Jack cheese and taco sauce; cook and stir until cheese is melted. Serve warm with tortilla chips.

Yield: 3-1/2 cups.

NUTRITION FACTS: 1/4 cup (calculated without tortilla chips) equals 124 calories, 6 g fat (3 g saturated fat), 27 mg cholesterol, 225 mg sodium, 6 g carbohydrate, 2 g fiber, 10 g protein.

BEER DIP

1 tablespoon Worcestershire sauce
1 cup (4 ounces) shredded cheddar cheese
Seafood seasoning *or* paprika, optional
Crackers *and/or* raw vegetables

1) In a large microwave-safe bowl, combine the cornstarch and the wine or broth until smooth. Add cream cheese.

2) Cover and microwave on high for 45 seconds; stir. Microwave 45-75 seconds longer or until smooth and slightly thickened.

3) Stir in the crab, cream, parsley and Worcestershire sauce. Cover and microwave on high for 45 seconds; stir. Add cheddar cheese; heat 45-60 seconds longer. Stir until the cheese is melted. Sprinkle with seafood seasoning if desired. Serve with crackers and vegetables.

Yield: about 3 cups.

NUTRITION FACTS: 2 tablespoons dip (calculated without crackers or vegetables) equals 71 calories, 5 g fat (3 g saturated fat), 29 mg cholesterol, 114 mg sodium, 1 g carbohydrate, trace fiber, 5 g protein.

Beer Dip
PREP/TOTAL TIME: 5 min.

Michelle Long, New Castle, Colorado

Ranch dressing mix flavors this fast-to-fix mixture that's loaded with shredded cheese. This thick dip is made to go with pretzels. It's one of those snacks that when you start eating it, you can't stop! This dip can be prepared with any type of beer, including nonalcoholic beer.

2 packages (8 ounces *each*) cream cheese, softened
1/3 cup beer *or* nonalcoholic beer
1 envelope ranch salad dressing mix
2 cups (8 ounces) shredded cheddar cheese
Pretzels

1) In a large mixing bowl, beat the cream cheese, beer and dressing mix until smooth. Stir in cheese. Serve with pretzels. Refrigerate leftovers.

Yield: 3-1/2 cups.

NUTRITION FACTS: 2 tablespoons (calculated without pretzels) equals 89 calories, 8 g fat (5 g saturated fat), 26 mg cholesterol, 177 mg sodium, 1 g carbohydrate, 0 fiber, 3 g protein.

Party Crab Dip
PREP/TOTAL TIME: 15 min.

Kimberly McGuire, Dunlap, Illinois

Nothing shaves time from party preparations like a no-fuss appetizer, and this flavorful seafood spread is a perfect example. Serve it with crackers or toasted bread rounds.

1 teaspoon cornstarch
1/2 cup white wine *or* chicken broth
1 package (8 ounces) cream cheese, cubed
2 cans (6 ounces *each*) crabmeat, drained, flaked and cartilage removed
2 tablespoons half-and-half cream
2 tablespoons minced fresh parsley

Artichoke Dip
PREP/TOTAL TIME: 30 min.

Mrs. William Garner, Austin, Texas

Give this golden dip some color after baking by sprinkling the top with sliced fresh tomatoes and chives.

1 can (14 ounces) water-packed artichoke hearts, rinsed and drained
1 cup mayonnaise
1/3 to 1/2 cup grated Parmesan cheese
1 garlic clove, minced
Dash hot pepper sauce
Paprika, optional
Assorted crackers

1) In a large bowl, combine the artichoke hearts, mayonnaise, Parmesan cheese, garlic and hot pepper sauce. Transfer to a greased 1-qt. baking dish. Sprinkle with paprika if desired.

2) Bake, uncovered, at 350° for 20-25 minutes or until top is lightly browned. Serve warm with crackers.

Yield: 2 cups.

NUTRITION FACTS: 2 tablespoons dip (calculated without crackers) equals 117 calories, 12 g fat (2 g saturated fat), 6 mg cholesterol, 168 mg sodium, 2 g carbohydrate, 0 fiber, 1 g protein.

■ **Zippy Artichoke Dip:** Add 1 can (4 ounces) drained chopped green chilies to the mayonnaise mixture. Bake as directed.

■ **Cheesy Artichoke Dip:** Add 1 cup (4 ounces) shredded mozzarella cheese, 1 tablespoon chopped onion, 1 tablespoon minced fresh parsley and 1/4 teaspoon garlic salt to the mayonnaise mixture. Bake as directed.

ARTICHOKE DIP

Garlic Feta Spread
PREP/TOTAL TIME: 10 min.

Theresa Conroy, Santa Rosa, California

With lots of garlic and feta cheese, this creamy spread is packed with flavor. It's a big hit at parties.

     4 ounces reduced-fat cream cheese
    1/3 cup fat-free mayonnaise
     1 to 2 garlic cloves, minced
    1/4 teaspoon dried basil, crushed
    1/4 teaspoon dried oregano, crushed
    1/8 teaspoon dill weed
    1/8 teaspoon dried thyme, crushed
     4 ounces crumbled feta cheese
Fresh vegetables *and/or* crackers

1) In a food processor, combine the first seven ingredients; cover and process until smooth. Transfer to a small bowl; stir in feta cheese. Serve with vegetables and/or crackers.

Yield: 1-1/4 cups.

NUTRITION FACTS: 2 tablespoons (calculated without fresh vegetables or crackers) equals 63 calories, 5 g fat (3 g saturated fat), 17 mg cholesterol, 224 mg sodium, 2 g carbohydrate, trace fiber, 3 g protein.

Warm Broccoli Cheese Spread
PREP: 15 min. **BAKE:** 25 min.

Patricia Moore, Toledo, Ohio

I cut this recipe out of a newspaper and decided to trim it down by substituting fat-free and reduced-fat ingredients.

     1 package (8 ounces) fat-free cream cheese, cubed
     1 cup (8 ounces) reduced-fat sour cream
     1 envelope Italian salad dressing mix
     1 package (10 ounces) frozen chopped broccoli, thawed, drained and patted dry
     2 cups (8 ounces) shredded reduced-fat cheddar cheese, *divided*
Reduced-fat wheat snack crackers

1) In a large mixing bowl, beat the cream cheese, sour cream and salad dressing mix until blended. Fold in the broccoli and 1-1/2 cups cheese.

2) Spoon into a shallow 1-qt. baking dish coated with cooking spray. Bake, uncovered, at 350° for 20 minutes. Sprinkle with remaining cheese. Bake 5 minutes longer or until cheese is melted. Serve warm with crackers.

Yield: 3-1/2 cups.

NUTRITION FACTS: 1/4 cup equals 96 calories, 5 g fat (4 g saturated fat), 19 mg cholesterol, 287 mg sodium, 4 g carbohydrate, 1 g fiber, 8 g protein.

Pretzel Mustard Dip
PREP: 10 min. + chilling

Bonnie Capper-Eckstein, Maple Grove, Minnesota

Perfect for just a little snack, this recipe makes about 1/2 cup. It's also a tasty sandwich spread.

    1/4 cup mayonnaise
    1/4 cup prepared yellow *or* Dijon mustard
     2 tablespoons finely chopped onion
     1 tablespoon ranch salad dressing mix
  2-1/4 teaspoons prepared horseradish
Pretzels

1) In a small bowl, combine the mayonnaise, mustard, chopped onion, salad dressing mix and horseradish.

2) Cover and refrigerate for at least 30 minutes. Serve with pretzels.

Yield: about 1/2 cup.

NUTRITION FACTS: 2 tablespoons dip (calculated without pretzels) equals 125 calories, 11 g fat (2 g saturated fat), 5 mg cholesterol, 547 mg sodium, 4 g carbohydrate, 1 g fiber, 1 g protein.

WARM BROCCOLI CHEESE SPREAD

Keeping Dips Warm

Warm dips can be prepared ahead and then heated in a slow cooker instead of the oven. A slow cooker will also keep your dip warm during a party.

Eggplant Dip

PREP: 20 min. **COOK:** 20 min.

Linda Roberson, Cordova, Tennessee

Pleasantly surprise guests by offering this unique dip. For a little Mediterranean flair, serve it with pita wedges.

- 3 cups cubed eggplant
- 1 medium onion, chopped
- 1/3 cup finely chopped sweet red pepper
- 1 jar (4-1/2 ounces) sliced mushrooms, drained
- 4 garlic cloves, minced
- 1/3 cup olive oil
- 1 jar (6 ounces) stuffed olives, drained and chopped
- 1 can (6 ounces) tomato paste
- 2 tablespoons red wine vinegar
- 1-1/2 teaspoons sugar
- 1 teaspoon salt
- 1/2 teaspoon dried oregano

Hot pepper sauce to taste

Pita bread wedges *or* tortilla *or* corn chips

1) In a skillet, combine the first six ingredients. Cover and cook over medium heat for 10 minutes or until tender. Stir in olives, tomato paste, vinegar, sugar, salt, oregano and hot pepper sauce; bring to a boil. Reduce the heat; cover and simmer for 20-30 minutes or until flavors are blended.

2) Serve warm or at room temperature with pita wedges or chips.

Yield: 3 cups.

NUTRITION FACTS: 2 tablespoons dip (calculated without pita bread or chips) equals 53 calories, 4 g fat (trace saturated fat), 0 cholesterol, 247 mg sodium, 4 g carbohydrate, 1 g fiber, 1 g protein.

Simple Guacamole

PREP/TOTAL TIME: 10 min.

Heidi Main, Anchorage, Alaska

Because avocados can brown quickly, it's best to make this guacamole just before serving.

- 2 medium ripe avocados
- 1 tablespoon lemon juice
- 1/4 cup chunky salsa
- 1/8 to 1/4 teaspoon salt

1) Peel and chop avocados; place in a small bowl. Sprinkle with lemon juice. Add salsa and salt; mash coarsely with a fork. Chill until serving.

Yield: 1-1/2 cups.

NUTRITION FACTS: 2 tablespoons guacamole equals 53 calories, 5 g fat (1 g saturated fat), 0 cholesterol, 51 mg sodium, 3 g carbohydrate, 2 g fiber, 1 g protein.

Chopping Avocados

Place halved and peeled avocados in a bowl and use a potato masher or pastry blender to quickly break up the avocados.

Orange-Ginger Fruit Dip

PREP/TOTAL TIME: 5 min.

Trisha Faulk, Athens, Michigan

With just four ingredients, this dip is great for last-minute entertaining. It can also be served with gingersnaps.

- 1 package (8 ounces) cream cheese, softened
- 1 jar (7 ounces) marshmallow creme
- 1 tablespoon grated orange peel
- 1/8 teaspoon ground ginger

Assorted fresh fruit

1) In a small mixing bowl, beat cream cheese until smooth. Beat in the marshmallow creme, orange peel and ginger. Chill until serving. Serve with fruit.

Yield: 2-1/2 cups.

NUTRITION FACTS: 2 tablespoons dip (calculated without fruit) equals 73 calories, 4 g fat (2 g saturated fat), 12 mg cholesterol, 42 mg sodium, 9 g carbohydrate, trace fiber, 1 g protein.

Horseradish Mustard Dip

PREP/TOTAL TIME: 10 min.

Shirley Glaab, Hattiesburg, Mississippi

This versatile vegetable dip is also great on ham, turkey or roast beef sandwiches. To suit more timid tastes, cut the horseradish back to 2 teaspoons.

- 3/4 cup fat-free plain yogurt
- 3 tablespoons minced chives
- 2 tablespoons reduced-fat mayonnaise
- 1 tablespoon snipped fresh dill *or* 1 teaspoon dill weed
- 1 tablespoon prepared horseradish
- 1 tablespoon Dijon mustard
- 1/4 teaspoon salt
- 1/8 teaspoon white pepper

Assorted fresh vegetables

1) In a small bowl, combine the yogurt, chives, mayonnaise, dill, horseradish, mustard, salt and pepper. Chill until serving. Serve with vegetables.

Yield: 1 cup.

NUTRITION FACTS: 1/4 cup (calculated without vegetables) equals 51 calories, 3 g fat (1 g saturated fat), 4 mg cholesterol, 338 mg sodium, 5 g carbohydrate, 1 g fiber, 2 g protein.

Six-Layer Dip

PREP: 20 min. + chilling

Etta Gillespie, Elmendorf, Texas

Tortilla chips make great scoopers for this dip. Serve in a glass bowl to show off the pretty layers.

- 2 medium ripe avocados, peeled and sliced
- 2 tablespoons lemon juice
- 1/2 tablespoon garlic salt
- 1/8 teaspoon hot pepper sauce
- 1 cup (8 ounces) sour cream

SIX-LAYER DIP

1 can (2-1/4 ounces) chopped ripe olives, drained
1 jar (16 ounces) thick and chunky salsa, drained
2 medium tomatoes, seeded and chopped
1 cup (8 ounces) shredded cheddar cheese
Tortilla chips

1) In a large bowl, mash the avocados with lemon juice, garlic salt and hot pepper sauce. Spoon into a 10-in. deep-dish pie plate or serving bowl.

2) Layer with the sour cream, olives, salsa, tomatoes and cheese. Cover and refrigerate for at least 1 hour. Serve with chips.

Yield: 2-1/2 cups.

NUTRITION FACTS: 2 tablespoons dip (calculated without chips) equals 88 calories, 7 g fat (3 g saturated fat), 14 mg cholesterol, 313 mg sodium, 5 g carbohydrate, 3 g fiber, 4 g protein.

Five-Fruit Salsa

PREP: 20 min. + chilling **BAKE:** 10 min.

Catherine Dawe, Kent, Ohio

You'll find it hard to stop eating this fresh, fruity salsa and homemade cinnamon tortilla chips! For extra zest, toss in some of the jalapeno seeds.

2 cups chopped fresh cantaloupe
6 green onions, chopped
3 kiwifruit, peeled and finely chopped
1 medium navel orange, peeled and finely chopped
1 medium sweet yellow pepper, chopped
1 medium sweet red pepper, chopped
2 jalapeno peppers, seeded and chopped
1 can (8 ounces) crushed unsweetened pineapple, drained

CINNAMON TORTILLA CHIPS:
10 flour tortillas (8 inches)
1/4 cup butter, melted

1/3 cup sugar
2 teaspoons ground cinnamon
1 cup finely chopped fresh strawberries

1) In a large bowl, combine the cantaloupe, onions, kiwi, orange, peppers and pineapple. Cover and refrigerate for 8 hours or overnight.

2) For chips, brush tortillas with butter; cut into eight wedges. Combine sugar and cinnamon; sprinkle over the tortillas. Place on ungreased baking sheets. Bake at 350° for 10-14 minutes or just until crisp.

3) Just before serving, drain salsa if desired. Stir in strawberries. Serve the fruit salsa with cinnamon tortilla chips.

Yield: 8 cups.

Editor's Note: When cutting or seeding hot peppers, use rubber or plastic gloves to protect your hands. Avoid touching your face.

NUTRITION FACTS: 1/2 cup salsa with 5 chips equals 150 calories, 5 g fat (2 g saturated fat), 8 mg cholesterol, 189 mg sodium, 29 g carbohydrate, 2 g fiber, 4 g protein.

Texas Caviar

PREP: 10 min. + chilling

Kathy Faris, Lytle, Texas

Be prepared to hand out this tangy salsa recipe when you take it to get-togethers. Black-eyed peas are a delicious ingredient.

1 can (15-1/2 ounces) black-eyed peas, rinsed and drained
3/4 cup chopped sweet red pepper
3/4 cup chopped green pepper
1 medium onion, chopped
3 green onions, chopped
1/4 cup minced fresh parsley
1 jar (2 ounces) diced pimientos, drained
1 garlic clove, minced
1 bottle (8 ounces) fat-free Italian salad dressing
Baked tortilla chips

1) In a large bowl, combine the peas, peppers, onions, parsley, pimientos and garlic. Pour salad dressing over pea mixture; stir gently to coat.

2) Cover and refrigerate for 24 hours. Serve with tortilla chips.

Yield: 4 cups.

NUTRITION FACTS: 1/2 cup (calculated without chips) equals 148 calories, 1 g fat (trace saturated fat), 1 mg cholesterol, 661 mg sodium, 30 g carbohydrate, 5 g fiber, 5 g protein.

No-Fuss Ice Bowl

Fill a large glass or plastic serving bowl with ice cubes or crushed ice. Fill a smaller bowl with dip and set on top of the ice. Replace the ice as it melts.

APPETIZING MEATBALLS

 CLASSIC: Seven dozen tender meatballs are shaped from 2 pounds ground beef to make this crowd-pleasing snack. Cranberry Appetizer Meatballs are coated with a sweet and tangy sauce suitable for large holiday gatherings.

 TIME-SAVER: The name Easy Meatballs says it all. This recipe uses three prepared products to create a saucy, savory appetizer in just 15 minutes.

 LIGHT: Lean ground turkey replaces the ground beef in Saucy Asian Meatballs, which helps reduce the cholesterol. Using reduced-sodium soy sauce keeps the sodium at an acceptable level.

 SERVES 2: A ketchup-based barbecue sauce coats the eight meatballs in Tangy Turkey Meatballs. To make just the right number of meatballs for a pair, the recipe calls for a third pound ground turkey.

Cranberry Appetizer Meatballs

PREP: 25 min. **BAKE:** 15 min.

Jim Ulberg, Elk Rapids, Michigan

- 2 eggs, beaten
- 1 cup dry bread crumbs
- 1/3 cup minced fresh parsley
- 1/3 cup ketchup
- 2 tablespoons finely chopped onion
- 2 tablespoons soy sauce
- 2 garlic cloves, minced
- 1/2 teaspoon salt
- 1/4 teaspoon pepper
- 2 pounds ground beef

CRANBERRY SAUCE:

- 1 can (16 ounces) whole-berry cranberry sauce
- 1 bottle (12 ounces) chili sauce
- 1 tablespoon brown sugar
- 1 tablespoon prepared mustard
- 1 tablespoon lemon juice
- 2 garlic cloves, minced

1) In a large bowl, combine the eggs, bread crumbs, parsley, ketchup, onion, soy sauce, garlic, salt and pepper. Crumble beef over mixture and mix well. Shape into 1-in. balls.

2) Place meatballs on a rack in a shallow baking pan. Bake, uncovered, at 400° for 15 minutes or until no longer pink. Transfer with a slotted spoon to a slow cooker or chafing dish.

3) Combine sauce ingredients in a saucepan; simmer for 10 minutes, stirring occasionally. Pour over meatballs. Serve warm.

Yield: about 7 dozen.

NUTRITION FACTS: 1 meatball equals 42 calories, 2 g fat (1 g saturated fat), 12 mg cholesterol, 122 mg sodium, 4 g carbohydrate, trace fiber, 3 g protein.

■ **Sweet and Soy Appetizer Meatballs:** Omit the Cranberry Sauce from recipe above. In a small saucepan, combine 3 tablespoons plus 2 tea- spoons cornstarch with 1/3 cup reduced-sodium soy sauce and 3 tablespoons lemon juice until smooth. Stir in 1-1/2 cups orange marmalade and 3 minced garlic cloves. Bring to a boil; cook and stir for 2 minutes or until thickened. Pour over meatballs and serve warm.

■ **Barbecue Appetizer Meatballs:** Omit the Cranberry Sauce from recipe above. In a large saucepan, combine 1/2 cup *each* packed brown sugar, water, cider vinegar and ketchup, 1/4 cup Dijon-mayonnaise blend and 2 cans (8 ounces *each*) drained pineapple. Bring to a boil over medium heat. Reduce the heat; simmer, uncovered, for 5 minutes. Pour over meatballs and serve warm.

EASY MEATBALLS

Easy Meatballs

PREP/TOTAL TIME: 15 min.

Christine Smoot, Childress, Texas

- 24 frozen cooked Italian meatballs (1/2 ounce *each*), thawed
- 1 cup barbecue sauce
- 1/2 cup sweet-and-sour sauce

1) Place the meatballs in a 3-qt. microwave-safe dish; cover and microwave on high for 3-4 minutes or until heated through.

2) In a small microwave-safe bowl, combine the sauces; cover and heat on high for 2-3 minutes or until heated through. Pour over meatballs; cover and microwave on high for 1-2 minutes, stirring occasionally.

Yield: 2 dozen.

NUTRITION FACTS: 1 meatball equals 60 calories, 4 g fat (2 g saturated fat), 11 mg cholesterol, 233 mg sodium, 4 g carbohydrate, trace fiber, 2 g protein.

SAUCY ASIAN MEATBALLS

Saucy Asian Meatballs

PREP: 20 min. **BAKE:** 20 min.

Lisa Varner, Greenville, South Carolina

    2 garlic cloves, minced
  1/2 teaspoon ground ginger
    1 teaspoon plus 1/4 cup reduced-sodium soy sauce, *divided*
    1 pound lean ground turkey
  1/4 cup rice wine vinegar
  1/4 cup tomato paste
    2 tablespoons molasses
    1 teaspoon hot pepper sauce

1) In a large bowl, combine the garlic, ginger and 1 teaspoon soy sauce. Crumble turkey over mixture and mix well. Shape into 1-in. balls.

2) Place in a 13-in. x 9-in x 2-in. baking dish coated with cooking spray. Bake, uncovered, at 350° for 20-25 minutes or until meat is no longer pink.

3) In a large saucepan, combine the vinegar, tomato paste, molasses, pepper sauce and remaining soy sauce. Cook and stir over medium heat for 3-5 minutes. Add the meatballs; heat through.

Yield: 3 dozen.

NUTRITION FACTS: 1 meatball equals 26 calories, 1 g fat (trace saturated fat), 10 mg cholesterol, 87 mg sodium, 2 g carbohydrate, trace fiber, 2 g protein.

CUTTING THE FAT FROM MEATBALLS ▪▪▪

To reduce the amount of fat in meatballs and cut cleanup time, I bake them in a 400° oven for 20 minutes instead of frying them on the stovetop. Baking them on a rack in a broiler pan allows the grease to drip away.

—Rita L., Dracut, Massachusetts

Tangy Turkey Meatballs

PREP: 15 min. **COOK:** 20 min.

Taste of Home Test Kitchen

    2 tablespoons dry bread crumbs
    2 tablespoons chopped green pepper
    1 egg white
    1 garlic clove, minced
    2 drops Louisiana-style hot sauce
  1/3 pound lean ground turkey
    1 teaspoon canola oil

SAUCE:

  1/4 cup ketchup
    2 tablespoons water
    4 teaspoons lemon juice
    4 teaspoons red wine vinegar
    2 teaspoons brown sugar
    2 teaspoons molasses
  1/2 teaspoon ground mustard
  1/4 to 1/2 teaspoon chili powder
  1/8 to 1/4 teaspoon cayenne pepper
  1/8 teaspoon pepper

1) In a large bowl, combine the bread crumbs, green pepper, egg white, garlic and hot sauce. Crumble turkey over mixture and mix well. Shape into 1-in. balls. In a small nonstick skillet, brown meatballs in oil over medium heat; drain.

2) Combine the sauce ingredients; pour over meatballs. Bring to a boil. Reduce heat; cover and simmer for 10 minutes or until heated through.

Yield: 8 meatballs.

NUTRITION FACTS: 1 meatball equals 63 calories, 2 g fat (trace saturated fat), 15 mg cholesterol, 134 mg sodium, 6 g carbohydrate, trace fiber, 4 g protein.

TANGY TURKEY MEATBALLS

Double Sausage Stromboli

PREP: 20 min. + rising **BAKE:** 20 min.

Connie Atchley, Westport, Indiana

Every bite of this wonderful stromboli is packed with pepperoni, sausage and cheese. For a hearty lunch, cut it into 6 or 8 slices.

- 1 pound bulk pork sausage
- 28 pepperoni slices, chopped
- 3/4 cup shredded part-skim mozzarella *or* cheddar cheese
- 1 package (16 ounces) hot roll mix
- 1 cup warm water (120° to 130°)
- 2 tablespoons butter, softened
- 1 egg, beaten
- 1 tablespoon dried oregano
- 1-1/2 teaspoons vegetable oil

1) In a large skillet, cook sausage over medium heat until no longer pink; add pepperoni. Drain well and pat dry with paper towels; stir in cheese and set aside.

2) In a large bowl, combine contents of hot roll mix, water, butter and egg until dough pulls away from side of bowl and holds together. Turn onto a lightly floured surface; knead until smooth and elastic, about 5 minutes. Cover and let rest for 5 minutes.

3) Pat dough into a greased 15-in. x 10-in. x 1-in. baking pan. Spread sausage mixture lengthwise down the center third of dough; sprinkle with oregano. Fold sides over filling; press edges lightly to seal. Cover and let rise until doubled, about 30 minutes.

4) Brush with oil. Bake at 375° for 20-25 minutes or until golden brown. Let stand for 5 minutes before cutting.

Yield: 12-14 servings.

NUTRITION FACTS: 1 piece equals 245 calories, 13 g fat (5 g saturated fat), 39 mg cholesterol, 466 mg sodium, 24 g carbohydrate, 1 g fiber, 8 g protein.

SPICY PORK BAGUETTE BITES

Spicy Pork Baguette Bites

PREP: 20 min. + marinating **BAKE:** 30 min.

Virginia Anthony, Jacksonville, Florida

Here's an interesting twist on mini cocktail sandwiches. Lime mayonnaise provides a cool counterpoint to the nicely spiced pork, and toasted baguette slices contribute to the crunch.

- 1 teaspoon paprika
- 1/2 teaspoon salt
- 1/2 teaspoon dried oregano
- 1/2 teaspoon ground cumin
- 1/4 teaspoon garlic powder
- 1/4 teaspoon cayenne pepper
- 1/4 teaspoon pepper
- 1 pork tenderloin (1 pound)

LIME MAYONNAISE:

- 1/2 cup mayonnaise
- 1 tablespoon lime juice
- 1/2 teaspoon grated lime peel
- 1 French bread baguette (1 pound), sliced and toasted

Additional grated lime peel, optional

1) In a bowl, combine the first seven ingredients; rub over tenderloin. Place in a large resealable plastic bag; seal and refrigerate overnight.

2) Place tenderloin on a rack in a foil-lined shallow roasting pan. Bake, uncovered, at 425° for 30-35 minutes or until a meat thermometer reads 160°. Let stand for 5 minutes.

3) Meanwhile, in a small bowl, combine the mayonnaise, lime juice and peel. Thinly slice the pork; serve on toasted bread with a dollop of lime mayonnaise. Sprinkle with additional lime peel if desired.

Yield: 20-24 appetizers.

NUTRITION FACTS: 1 baguette bite equals 137 calories, 6 g fat (1 g saturated fat), 12 mg cholesterol, 195 mg sodium, 14 g carbohydrate, 1 g fiber, 5 g protein.

Sausage Cheese Bites

PREP/TOTAL TIME: 30 min.

Nancy Reichert, Thomasville, Georgia

These baked snacks can be frozen, then reheated in a 375° oven for 6 to 8 minutes. If your family prefers foods with more spice, substitute hot pork sausage and pepper Jack cheese.

- 1 pound mild pork sausage
- 4 cups buttermilk biscuit mix
- 2 cups (8 ounces) shredded cheddar cheese
- 1 cup water

1) Crumble sausage into a skillet; cook over medium heat until no longer pink. Drain.

2) In a large bowl, combine biscuit mix and cheese. Add sausage and stir until well blended. Stir in water just until mixed. Shape into 1-1/2-in. balls.

3) Place on greased baking sheets. Bake at 375° for about 15 minutes or until golden.

Yield: 16 servings.

NUTRITION FACTS: 3 pieces equals 230 calories, 14 g fat (6 g saturated fat), 25 mg cholesterol, 579 mg sodium, 19 g carbohydrate, 1 g fiber, 7 g protein.

Smoky Cheese-Stuffed Jalapenos
PREP: 40 min. **GRILL:** 10 min.

Lin Sines, Oak Point, Texas

These spicy jalapenos are sure to start your meal off with a bang. This is the perfect appetizer for any gathering. Whenever my company has an outdoor event, I'm not allowed to come without them.

- 15 large jalapeno peppers
- 2 cups (8 ounces) shredded cheddar-Monterey Jack cheese
- 4 ounces cream cheese, softened
- 1/2 cup minced fresh cilantro
- 1/4 teaspoon garlic powder
- 1/4 teaspoon paprika
- 15 bacon strips

1) Cut stems off jalapenos; remove seeds and membranes. In a small mixing bowl, beat the cheeses, cilantro, garlic powder and paprika until blended. Stuff 1 tablespoon into each jalapeno; wrap a strip of bacon around each.

2) Grill peppers, covered, over medium-hot heat for 4-5 minutes on each side or until bacon is crisp and filling is heated through. Serve warm.

Yield: 15 appetizers.

Editor's Note: This may also be broiled. Broil 4-6 in. from heat for time given in recipe. When cutting or seeding hot peppers, use rubber or plastic gloves to protect your hands. Avoid touching your face.

NUTRITION FACTS: 2 stuffed jalapenos equals 259 calories, 22 g fat (13 g saturated fat), 58 mg cholesterol, 460 mg sodium, 4 g carbohydrate, 1 g fiber, 13 g protein.

Coconut Chicken Bites
PREP: 10 min. + chilling **COOK:** 5 min./batch

Linda Schwarz, Bertrand, Nebraska

These tender nuggets are great for nibbling thanks to the coconut, cumin, celery salt and garlic powder that season them. Serve them alone or with sweet-sour sauce.

- 2 cups flaked coconut
- 1 egg
- 2 tablespoons milk
- 3/4 pound boneless skinless chicken breasts, cut into 3/4-inch pieces
- 1/2 cup all-purpose flour
- Oil for deep-fat frying
- 1 teaspoon celery salt
- 1/2 teaspoon garlic powder
- 1/2 teaspoon ground cumin

1) In a blender or food processor, process coconut until finely chopped. Transfer to a bowl and set aside. In another bowl, combine egg and milk.

2) Toss chicken with flour; dip in egg mixture, then in coconut. Place in a single layer on a baking sheet. Refrigerate for 30 minutes.

3) In an electric skillet or deep-fat fryer, heat 2 in. of oil to 375°. Fry chicken, a few pieces at time, for 1-1/2 minutes on each side or until golden brown.

4) Drain on paper towels; place in a bowl. Sprinkle with celery salt, garlic powder and cumin; toss to coat. Serve warm.

Yield: 3 dozen.

NUTRITION FACTS: 3 pieces equals 166 calories, 10 g fat (6 g saturated fat), 34 mg cholesterol, 185 mg sodium, 12 g carbohydrate, 1 g fiber, 7 g protein.

BACON SWISS BREAD

Bacon Swiss Bread
PREP: 15 min. **BAKE:** 20 min.

Shirley Mills, Tulsa, Oklahoma

I'm a busy mom, so I'm always looking for fast and easy recipes. These savory slices of jazzed-up French bread are great with soup and salad.

- 1 loaf (1 pound) French bread (20 inches)
- 2/3 cup butter, softened
- 1/3 cup chopped green onions
- 4 teaspoons prepared mustard
- 5 slices process Swiss cheese
- 5 bacon strips

1) Cut bread into 1-in.-thick slices, leaving slices attached at bottom. In a bowl, combine the butter, onions and mustard; spread on both sides of each slice of bread.

2) Cut each cheese slice diagonally into four triangles; place between the slices of bread. Cut bacon in half widthwise and then lengthwise; drape a piece over each slice.

3) Place the loaf on a double thickness of heavy-duty foil. Bake at 400° for 20-25 minutes or until bacon is crisp.

Yield: 10 servings.

NUTRITION FACTS: 1 piece equals 332 calories, 23 g fat (12 g saturated fat), 49 mg cholesterol, 651 mg sodium, 24 g carbohydrate, 2 g fiber, 8 g protein.

WINGING IT

 CLASSIC: Some like it hot! These Spicy Hot Wings are baked for 50 minutes, then served with a homemade blue cheese dipping sauce to cool the burn.

 TIME-SAVER: A package of chicken wingettes eliminates the need to cut the wings into pieces in Barbecue Wings. To shorten the cooking time, these wings are deep-fat fried rather than baked in the oven.

 LIGHT: Chicken wings are higher in fat and calories than chicken breast meat. For a tasty substitute with less fat and fewer calories, try Mini Chicken Kabobs. Marinated chicken breast cubes are glazed with a honey-soy sauce.

 SERVES 2: Peachy Chicken Wings use packaged wingettes. This convenient product allows you to easily take out just the right number of wing pieces. You can keep the rest in the freezer for the next time you crave these tasty wings.

SPICY HOT WINGS

Spicy Hot Wings

PREP: 25 min. **BAKE:** 50 min.

Anna Free, Plymouth, Ohio

- 10 chicken wings (about 2 pounds)
- 1/2 cup butter, melted
- 2 to 5 teaspoons hot pepper sauce
- 3/4 teaspoon garlic salt
- 1/4 teaspoon paprika

DIPPING SAUCE:

- 3/4 cup sour cream
- 1 tablespoon dried minced onion
- 1 tablespoon milk
- 1/2 cup crumbled blue cheese
- 1/4 teaspoon garlic salt
- 1/8 teaspoon ground mustard

Paprika, optional

Celery sticks, optional

1) Cut chicken wings into three sections; discard wing tips. Place wings in a greased 15-in. x 10-in. x 1-in. baking pan. Combine the butter, hot pepper sauce, garlic salt and paprika; pour over wings.

2) Bake at 375° for 30 minutes. Turn; bake 20-25 minutes longer or until chicken juices run clear.

3) Meanwhile, for sauce, combine the sour cream, onion, milk, cheese, garlic salt and mustard in a blender. Cover and process until smooth. Pour into a bowl; sprinkle with paprika if desired. Cover and refrigerate until serving.

4) Drain wings. Serve with sauce and celery if desired.

Yield: 8 servings.

NUTRITION FACTS: 1 piece equals 122 calories, 10 g fat (6 g saturated fat), 35 mg cholesterol, 191 mg sodium, 1 g carbohydrate, trace fiber, 6 g protein.

Barbecue Wings

PREP/TOTAL TIME: 30 min.

Sara Yarrington, Salem, New Hampshire

Oil for deep-fat frying

- 1 package (40 ounces) fresh *or* frozen chicken wingettes, thawed
- 1/2 cup barbecue sauce
- 1 tablespoon butter
- 1 teaspoon celery seed
- 1 teaspoon hot pepper sauce

1) In an electric skillet or deep-fat fryer, heat oil to 375°. Fry chicken wings, a few at a time, for

BARBECUE WINGS

8 minutes or until golden brown and juices run clear, turning occasionally. Drain on paper towels.

2) In a small microwave-safe bowl, combine the barbecue sauce, butter, celery seed and hot pepper sauce. Cover and microwave on high for 1 minute or until heated through. Place the chicken wings in a large bowl; add sauce and toss to coat.

Yield: 6 servings.

NUTRITION FACTS: 1 piece equals 156 calories, 13 g fat (3 g saturated fat), 37 mg cholesterol, 88 mg sodium, 1 g carbohydrate, trace fiber, 9 g protein.

WINGS AT THE READY ■■■

Chicken wings are always a hit when we entertain, but planning ahead makes it easier to prepare them. I buy whole chicken wings in bulk, cut them into three pieces, discard the wing tips and store the pieces in freezer bags. Then, on the day of the party, preparing the appetizers is a snap!

—Lorraine Caland, Thunder Bay, Ontario

Mini Chicken Kabobs

PREP: 20 min. + marinating **COOK:** 5 min.

Norma Wells, Cookson, Oklahoma

- 1/4 cup reduced-sodium soy sauce
- 2 teaspoons sugar
- 1/2 teaspoon salt

Dash *each* pepper, garlic powder and ground ginger

- 1/2 pound boneless skinless chicken breasts, cut into 1-inch cubes
- 1 small green pepper, cut into 1/2-inch pieces
- 2 cans (8 ounces *each*) pineapple chunks, drained
- 1 teaspoon honey

1) In a small bowl, combine the soy sauce, sugar, salt, pepper, garlic powder and ginger. Pour half of the marinade into a resealable plastic bag; add the chicken. Seal bag and turn to coat; refrigerate for 30 minutes. Cover and refrigerate remaining marinade for basting.

2) Drain and discard marinade. For each kabob, thread a piece of chicken, green pepper and pineapple onto a wooden toothpick. Place kabobs on a microwave-safe plate. Add honey to the reserved marinate.

3) Microwave kabobs on high for 3-4 minutes or until chicken juices run clear, turning occasionally. Baste with reserved marinade during the last minute of cooking.

Yield: 3 dozen.

NUTRITION FACTS: 1 kabob equals 14 calories, trace fat (trace saturated fat), 31 mg cholesterol, 95 mg sodium, 2 g carbohydrate, trace fiber, 1 g protein.

PEACHY CHICKEN WINGS

Peachy Chicken Wings

PREP: 15 min. + marinating **BAKE:** 50 min.

Linda Walker, Dumfries, Virginia

- 2 tablespoons reduced-sodium soy sauce
- 2 tablespoons peach preserves
- 1-1/2 teaspoons lemon juice
- 1/4 teaspoon ground ginger
- 1/4 teaspoon minced garlic
- 8 chicken wingettes

1) In a large resealable plastic bag, combine the first five ingredients; add chicken wings. Seal bag and turn to coat; refrigerate for 8 hours or overnight.

2) Transfer wings to a 13-in. x 9-in. x 2-in. baking dish coated with cooking spray. Bake, uncovered, at 350° for 50-60 minutes or until chicken juices run clear, turning every 10 minutes.

Yield: 2 servings.

Editor's Note: This recipe was prepared with the first and second sections of the chicken wings.

NUTRITION FACTS: 1 piece equals 114 calories, 71 g fat (2 g saturated fat), 29 mg cholesterol, 179 mg sodium, 4 g carbohydrate, trace fiber, 9 g protein.

Disjointing Chicken Wings

1) Place chicken wing on a cutting board. With a sharp knife, cut between the joint at the top of the tip end. Discard tips or use for preparing chicken broth.

2) Take remaining wing and cut between the joints. Proceed with recipe as directed.

CHICKEN-PESTO PAN PIZZA

⏱Chicken-Pesto Pan Pizza

PREP/TOTAL TIME: 30 min.

Juanita Fleck, Bullhead City, Arizona

A packaged pesto mix is the tasty replacement for traditional tomato sauce in this tempting pizza.

- 1 tube (13.8 ounces) refrigerated pizza crust
- 1/2 cup water
- 3 tablespoons olive oil
- 1 envelope pesto sauce mix
- 1 package (10 ounces) frozen chopped spinach, thawed and squeezed dry
- 1/2 cup ricotta cheese
- 1/4 cup chopped onion
- 2 cups shredded cooked chicken
- 1 jar (4-1/2 ounces) sliced mushrooms, drained
- 4 plum tomatoes, sliced
- 1 cup (4 ounces) shredded Swiss cheese
- 1/4 cup grated Romano cheese

1) Unroll pizza crust into an ungreased 15-in. x 10-in. x 1-in. baking pan; flatten dough and build up edges slightly. Prick dough several items with a fork. Bake at 425° for 7 minutes or until lightly browned.

2) Meanwhile, combine the water, oil and pesto sauce mix in a saucepan. Cook until heated through (do not boil). Add the spinach, ricotta and onion; mix well. Spread over crust.

3) Top with the chicken, mushrooms, tomatoes and Swiss and Romano cheeses. Bake at 425° for 7 minutes or until crust is golden and cheese is melted.

Yield: 8 servings.

NUTRITION FACTS: 1 slice equals 368 calories, 16 g fat (6 g saturated fat), 54 mg cholesterol, 866 mg sodium, 32 g carbohydrate, 3 g fiber, 24 g protein.

Marinated Shrimp

PREP: 10 min. + marinating

Margaret DeLong, Lake Butler, Florida

To keep the shrimp cold on a buffet table, serve them in a pretty ice bowl. See page 45 for directions.

- 2 pounds cooked medium shrimp, peeled and deveined
- 1 medium red onion, cut into rings and separated
- 2 medium lemons, cut into slices
- 1 cup pitted ripe olives, drained
- 1/2 cup olive oil
- 1/3 cup minced fresh parsley
- 3 tablespoons lemon juice
- 3 tablespoons red wine vinegar
- 1 garlic clove, minced
- 1 bay leaf
- 1 tablespoon minced fresh basil *or* 1 teaspoon dried basil
- 1 teaspoon salt
- 1 teaspoon ground mustard
- 1/4 teaspoon pepper

1) In a 3-qt. glass serving bowl, combine the shrimp, onion, lemons and olives.

2) In a jar with a tight-fitting lid, combine the remaining ingredients; shake well. Pour over shrimp mixture and stir gently to coat.

3) Cover and refrigerate for 24 hours, stirring occasionally. Discard bay leaf before serving.

Yield: 14 servings.

NUTRITION FACTS: 3 shrimp with 1 olive equals 157 calories, 10 g fat (1 g saturated fat), 99 mg cholesterol, 350 mg sodium, 3 g carbohydrate, 1 g fiber, 13 g protein.

MARINATED SHRIMP

Empanaditas

PREP: 20 min. **BAKE:** 20 min.

Mary Ann Kosmas, Minneapolis, Minnesota

Empanaditas can be frozen after sealing. When ready to use, place frozen empanaditas on a greased baking sheet, brush with milk and bake at 375° for 30-35 minutes.

- 1/2 pound boneless skinless chicken breast halves, thinly sliced
- 1 tablespoon vegetable oil
- 1/8 teaspoon ground cumin
- 1 can (4 ounces) chopped green chilies, drained
- 1/2 cup shredded pepper Jack cheese *or* Monterey Jack cheese
- 2 tablespoons all-purpose flour

Pastry for 2 double-crust pies
- 1/4 cup milk

1) In a large skillet, saute chicken in oil for 7-8 minutes or until juices run clear. Sprinkle with cumin. Chop into very small pieces and place in a bowl. Add chilies and cheese. Sprinkle with flour; toss to coat.

2) Turn pastry dough onto a floured surface; roll to 1/8-in. thickness. Cut with a 2-in. round cutter. Fill each circle with about 1 tablespoon of filling. Wet edges of circle with water.

3) Fold half of pastry over filling; seal with fingers, then press with the tines of a fork. Repeat until all filling is used.

4) Place on a greased baking sheet. Brush lightly with milk. Bake at 375° for 20-25 minutes or until golden brown. Serve warm.

Yield: 3 dozen.

NUTRITION FACTS: 1 empanadita equals 126 calories, 7 g fat (3 g saturated fat), 10 mg cholesterol, 115 mg sodium, 12 g carbohydrate, trace fiber, 3 g protein.

Savory Rye Snacks

PREP/TOTAL TIME: 20 min.

Connie Simon, Durand, Michigan

I make the flavorful spread in advance and refrigerate it. Then all I need to do to have a quick snack is put it on the rye bread and bake.

- 1 cup sliced green onions
- 1 cup (4 ounces) shredded Monterey Jack cheese
- 1 cup (4 ounces) shredded cheddar cheese
- 1 cup mayonnaise
- 1 can (4 ounces) mushroom stems and pieces, drained
- 1/2 cup chopped ripe olives
- 1/2 cup chopped stuffed olives
- 1 loaf (1 pound) snack rye bread

1) In a bowl, combine onions, cheeses, mayonnaise, mushrooms and olives.

2) Spread on bread; place on ungreased baking sheets. Bake at 350° for 8-10 minutes or until bubbly.

Yield: 4 dozen.

NUTRITION FACTS: 3 pieces equals 242 calories, 17 g fat (5 g saturated fat), 19 mg cholesterol, 496 mg sodium, 15 g carbohydrate, 2 g fiber, 6 g protein.

How to Make an Ice Bowl

1) Place ice cubes over the bottom of a 2-1/2- or 3-qt. bowl. Center a 1-1/2- or 1-qt. bowl on top of the ice cubes. Weigh the smaller bowl down with ice cubes or a can of frozen juice. Place freezer tape across both bowls to hold them in place.

2) Use a wooden skewer to tuck fresh herbs, citrus slices or edible flowers between the ice cubes.

3) Pour cold water between the bowls until the water is about 2 in. from the bottom. Freeze. Add another inch of water and freeze. If desired, add or reposition herbs, citrus slices or flowers. Repeat until water is about 1/2 in. below bowl rim.

4) Remove tape from sides of bowls and ice cubes or juice can from smaller bowl. Fill smaller bowl with warm, not hot, water and let stand for 1-2 minutes. Carefully lift out of large bowl. Dip large bowl in warm, not hot, water. Remove from ice bowl. Use bowl immediately for shrimp, dips or fresh fruits.

Mini Shrimp Rolls

PREP: 45 min. **BAKE:** 15 min.

Jennifer Jones, Pine City, New York

These tasty tidbits are better for you than traditional egg rolls because they're baked.

- 1 pound cooked medium shrimp, peeled and deveined
- 6 ounces reduced-fat cream cheese
- 1 cup (4 ounces) shredded part-skim mozzarella cheese
- 1-1/2 cups finely chopped cabbage
- 3 green onions, finely chopped
- 1/2 cup shredded carrot
- 1 tablespoon reduced-sodium soy sauce
- 2 garlic cloves, minced
- 48 wonton wrappers
- 2 tablespoons all-purpose flour
- 3 tablespoons water

1) Chop shrimp; set aside. In a mixing bowl, beat cream cheese until smooth. Add mozzarella cheese; mix well. Stir in the cabbage, onions, carrot, soy sauce, garlic and shrimp.

2) For each shrimp roll, place 1 tablespoon of shrimp mixture across the bottom third of a wonton wrapper to within 1/4 in. of bottom and side edges. Combine flour and water until smooth; brush a 1/4-in.-wide strip on side edges and fold side edges over 1/4 in.

3) Brush sides and top edges with water mixture. Fold bottom third of wonton wrapper over filling, then bring top over and pinch edges to seal.

4) Lightly spray rolls with cooking spray. Place on a baking sheet coated with cooking spray. Bake at 400° for 15-18 minutes or until golden brown, turning once. Serve warm.

Yield: 4 dozen.

NUTRITION FACTS: 3 shrimp rolls equals 153 calories, 4 g fat (2 g saturated fat), 70 mg cholesterol, 317 mg sodium, 16 g carbohydrate, 1 g fiber, 11 g protein.

SEAFOOD TRIANGLES

Seafood Triangles

PREP: 30 min. **BAKE:** 10 min./batch

Tarsia Nichols, Prineville, Oregon

One chilly Easter, my creative clan was looking for an appetizer that would break family traditions and warm hearts...and we came up with these spicy bites filled with shrimp and crabmeat.

- 3 tablespoons chopped green onions
- 3 tablespoons butter, *divided*
- 1/2 pound uncooked shrimp, peeled, deveined and quartered
- 1/4 cup white wine *or* chicken broth
- 4 teaspoons cornstarch
- 1/3 cup 2% milk
- 1/2 cup grated Parmesan cheese
- 1 can (6 ounces) crabmeat, drained, flaked and cartilage removed
- 1 teaspoon sugar
- 1 teaspoon lemon juice
- 1/4 teaspoon cayenne pepper
- 1/8 teaspoon white pepper, optional
- 22 sheets phyllo dough (14 inch x 9 inch sheet size)
- 1 egg white, beaten

1) In a large nonstick skillet, saute onions in 1 tablespoon butter until tender. Add shrimp and wine or broth; cook and stir over medium-high heat for 2 minutes or until shrimp turn pink. Using a slotted spoon, remove shrimp.

2) Combine cornstarch and milk until smooth; stir into the cooking juices. Bring to a boil; cook and stir for 2 minutes or until thickened. Reduce heat to low. Stir in the Parmesan cheese, crab, sugar, lemon juice, cayenne, white pepper if desired and shrimp. Remove from the heat; cool.

3) On a dry surface, carefully remove two sheets of phyllo dough and place on top of each other (keep remaining dough covered with plastic wrap to prevent drying). Melt remaining butter. Cut sheets widthwise into six strips about 2 in. wide. Lightly brush the tops with butter.

4) Place a rounded teaspoonful of shrimp mixture near lower right corner of each strip. Fold left corner of dough over filling, forming a triangle. Fold triangle up, then fold over, forming another triangle. Continue folding like a flag for the length of the strip.

5) Place triangles on ungreased baking sheets. Brush tops with egg white. Bake at 400° for 7-10 minutes or until golden brown. Serve warm.

Yield: 5-1/2 dozen.

NUTRITION FACTS: 4 triangles equals 110 calories, 4 g fat (2 g saturated fat), 37 mg cholesterol, 218 mg sodium, 10 g carbohydrate, 1 g fiber, 7 g protein.

Cheesy Sausage Nachos

PREP: 30 min. **BAKE:** 10 min.

Jane Sodergren, Red Wing, Minnesota

Set a platter of these nachos on the table and stand back as guests dive in! This dish can be used as an appetizer as well as an entree.

- 3/4 pound bulk pork sausage
- 1/4 cup chopped onion
- 3 cups diced fresh tomatoes, *divided*
- 3/4 cup picante sauce
- 4 cups tortilla chips
- 3 cups (12 ounces) shredded Monterey Jack cheese, *divided*
- 1 medium ripe avocado, diced

1) Crumble sausage into a large skillet; add onion. Cook over medium heat until meat is no longer pink; drain well.

2) Add 2 cups tomatoes and picante sauce. Bring to a boil. Reduce heat; simmer, uncovered, for 20 minutes or until most of the liquid has evaporated.

3) Sprinkle tortilla chips over a 12-in. pizza pan. Top with 2 cups cheese and the sausage mixture; sprinkle with remaining cheese.

4) Bake at 350° for 8-10 minutes or until cheese is melted. Sprinkle with avocado and remaining tomatoes.

Yield: 8-10 servings.

NUTRITION FACTS: 1/2 cup nachos equals 290 calories, 22 g fat (10 g saturated fat), 42 mg cholesterol, 442 mg sodium, 12 g carbohydrate, 2 g fiber, 12 g protein.

■ **Cheesy Turkey Nachos:** Substitute 3/4 pound ground turkey for the bulk pork sausage.

Feta Bruschetta

PREP/TOTAL TIME: 30 min.

Stacey Rinehart, Eugene, Oregon

You won't believe the compliments you'll receive when you greet guests with these wonderful appetizers. Each crispy bite offers the savory tastes of feta cheese, tomatoes, basil and garlic.

- 1/4 cup butter, melted
- 1/4 cup olive oil
- 10 slices French bread (1 inch thick)
- 1 package (4 ounces) crumbled feta cheese
- 2 to 3 garlic cloves, minced
- 1 tablespoon minced fresh basil *or* 1 teaspoon dried basil
- 1 large tomato, seeded and chopped

1) In a small bowl, combine butter and oil; brush onto both sides of bread. Place on a baking sheet. Bake at 350° for 8-10 minutes or until lightly browned on top.

FETA BRUSCHETTA

2) Combine the feta cheese, garlic and basil; sprinkle over toast. Top with tomato. Bake 8-10 minutes longer or until heated through. Serve warm.

Yield: 10 appetizers.

NUTRITION FACTS: 1 piece equals 296 calories, 14 g fat (5 g saturated fat), 18 mg cholesterol, 547 mg sodium, 35 g carbohydrate, 3 g fiber, 8 g protein.

Ham 'n' Cheese Quiches

PREP: 15 min. + chilling **BAKE:** 30 min.

Virginia Abraham, Oxford, Mississippi

When I need festive finger food, I reach for the recipe for these quiches featuring cheese in both the crust and the filling.

- 1/2 cup cold butter
- 1 jar (5 ounces) process sharp cheese spread
- 1 cup all-purpose flour
- 2 tablespoons water

FILLING:

- 1 egg
- 1/2 cup milk
- 1/4 teaspoon salt
- 1/2 cup finely chopped fully cooked ham
- 1/2 cup shredded Monterey Jack cheese

1) In a small bowl, cut butter and cheese spread into flour until well blended. Add water and toss with a fork until a ball forms. Refrigerate for 1 hour.

2) Press tablespoonfuls onto the bottom and up the sides of greased miniature muffin cups. In a bowl, beat egg, milk and salt. Stir in ham and cheese. Spoon a rounded teaspoonful into each shell.

3) Bake at 350° for 30 minutes or until golden brown. Let stand for 5 minutes before serving.

Yield: 2 dozen.

NUTRITION FACTS: 3 quiches equals 265 calories, 19 g fat (12 g saturated fat), 81 mg cholesterol, 645 mg sodium, 15 g carbohydrate, trace fiber, 8 g protein.

HOT-FROM-THE-OVEN PIZZA

 CLASSIC: A from-scratch crust sets Homemade Pizza Supreme apart from all others. Covered with a homemade sauce and then sprinkled with pepperoni, Canadian bacon, peppers and olives, this eye-appealing appetizer really satisfies.

 TIME-SAVER: Sliced tomato and mozzarella cheese are the simple toppings for Tomato Pizza Bread. A refrigerated pizza crust cuts prep time, so you can be serving these savory squares in half an hour.

 LIGHT: After one bite of Blue Cheese Appetizer Pizza, you won't even miss the meat. A bold combo of ingredients, including basil, garlic, red onion, tomato and blue cheese, provides plenty of flavor but less fat and calories than Homemade Pizza Supreme.

 SERVES 2: Starting with a single sandwich roll is a quick and easy way to make two servings of yummy Pepperoni Bread. The tasty snack gets its zip from spicy pepperoni.

HOMEMADE PIZZA SUPREME

Homemade Pizza Supreme

PREP: 45 min. + rising **BAKE:** 30 min.

Gaylene Anderson, Sandy, Utah

- 1 package (1/4 ounce) active dry yeast
- 2 cups warm water (110° to 115°)
- 3 tablespoons vegetable oil
- 1-1/2 teaspoons salt
- 4 to 6 cups all-purpose flour

SAUCE:
- 2 cans (8 ounces *each*) tomato sauce
- 1-1/2 teaspoons grated onion
- 1 teaspoon dried oregano
- 1/4 teaspoon salt
- 1/8 teaspoon pepper

TOPPINGS:
- 4 cups (16 ounces) shredded part-skim mozzarella cheese
- 4 ounces Canadian bacon, diced
- 1 package (3-1/2 ounces) sliced pepperoni

- 1 medium sweet red pepper, sliced
- 1 medium green pepper, sliced
- 1 can (2-1/4 ounces) sliced ripe olives, drained
- 1 cup chopped onion
- 1 cup grated Parmesan cheese
- 1/2 cup minced fresh basil

1) In a large mixing bowl, dissolve yeast in warm water. Add the oil, salt and 2 cups flour. Beat on medium speed for 3 minutes. Stir in enough remaining flour to form a soft dough.

2) Turn onto a floured surface; knead until smooth and elastic, about 6-8 minutes. Place in a greased bowl, turning once to grease top. Cover and let rest in a warm place for 10 minutes.

3) Combine sauce ingredients; set aside. Divide dough in half. On a floured surface, roll each portion into a 13-in. circle. Transfer to two greased 12-in. pizza pans; build up edges slightly.

TOMATO PIZZA BREAD

4) Bake at 375° for 15 minutes or until lightly browned. Spread with sauce; sprinkle with toppings. Bake for 15-20 minutes or until cheese is melted.

Yield: 2 pizzas (10 slices each).

NUTRITION FACTS: 1 slice equals 231 calories, 10 g fat (4 g saturated fat), 23 mg cholesterol, 653 mg sodium, 23 g carbohydrate, 1 g fiber, 12 g protein.

Tomato Pizza Bread

PREP/TOTAL TIME: 30 min.

Kimberly Mason, Broken Arrow, Oklahoma

- 1 tube (10 ounces) refrigerated pizza crust
- 2 garlic cloves, minced
- 1/2 teaspoon dried oregano
- 1 cup (4 ounces) shredded part-skim mozzarella cheese, *divided*
- 1 plum tomato, halved lengthwise and thinly sliced
- 1/2 teaspoon Italian seasoning, optional

1) On a greased baking sheet, roll pizza crust into a 12-in. x 8-in. rectangle. Bake at 425° for 6-8 minutes or until the edges are lightly browned. Sprinkle with garlic, oregano and half of the cheese.

2) Arrange tomato slices in a single layer over cheese. Top with remaining cheese and Italian seasoning if desired. Bake 6-8 minutes longer or until cheese is melted and crust is lightly browned.

Yield: 8 servings.

NUTRITION FACTS: 1 piece equals 132 calories, 4 g fat (1 g saturated fat), 8 mg cholesterol, 303 mg sodium, 18 g carbohydrate, 1 g fiber, 7 g protein.

Blue Cheese Appetizer Pizza

PREP: 15 min. + rising **BAKE:** 20 min.

Kathy Stanaway, DeWitt, Michigan

- 1 loaf (1 pound) frozen bread dough, thawed
- 3 tablespoons olive oil
- 2 teaspoons dried basil
- 2 teaspoons dried oregano
- 1 teaspoon garlic powder
- 1 small red onion, thinly sliced and separated into rings
- 2 plum tomatoes, chopped
- 1 cup (4 ounces) shredded part-skim mozzarella cheese, *divided*
- 3 ounces crumbled blue cheese
- 2 tablespoons grated Parmesan cheese

BLUE CHEESE APPETIZER PIZZA

1) Divide bread dough in half. Press each portion onto the bottom of a 12-in. pizza pan coated with cooking spray; build up edges slightly. Prick dough several times with a fork. Cover and let rise in a warm place for 30 minutes.

2) Brush dough with oil. Combine the basil, oregano and garlic powder; sprinkle over dough.

3) Bake at 425° for 10 minutes. Arrange onion and tomatoes over crust; sprinkle with cheeses. Bake 8-10 minutes longer or until golden brown.

Yield: 2 pizzas (10 slices each).

NUTRITION FACTS: 1 slice equals 118 calories, 5 g fat (2 g saturated fat), 7 mg cholesterol, 228 mg sodium, 13 g carbohydrate, 1 g fiber, 5 g protein.

Pepperoni Bread

PREP/TOTAL TIME: 20 min.

Sherry Adams, Mount Ayr, Iowa

- 1 French *or* Italian sandwich roll (about 4 to 5 inches long)
- 2 to 3 tablespoons pizza sauce
- 8 slices slices turkey pepperoni
- 1/4 cup shredded part-skim mozzarella cheese

1) Slice roll in half lengthwise. Place on baking sheet. Spread pizza sauce over each half. Top with pepperoni. Sprinkle with mozzarella cheese.

2) Bake at 350° for 10 minutes or until heated through. Broil 4 in. from the heat for 2 minutes or until cheese is bubbly and golden brown.

Yield: 2 servings.

NUTRITION FACTS: 1 serving equals 427 calories, 18 g fat (5 g saturated fat), 147 mg cholesterol, 2,410 mg sodium, 23 g carbohydrate, 1 g fiber, 43 g protein.

CARAMELIZED ONION TARTLETS

Caramelized Onion Tartlets

PREP: 40 min. **BAKE:** 15 min.

Jerri Hansen, Council Bluffs, Iowa

Cooking onions in sugar mellows their strong flavor, so even folks who don't care for onions will find these elegant tartlets irresistible.

> 2 tablespoons plus 1/2 cup butter, *divided*
> 2 large sweet onions, chopped
> 1/4 cup sugar
> 3/4 cup hot water
> 1 tablespoon beef bouillon granules
> 1 cup (4 ounces) shredded Swiss cheese
> 8 sheets phyllo dough (14 inches x 9 inches)

1) In a large skillet, melt 2 tablespoons butter over medium heat. Add onions and sugar. Cook for 15-20 minutes or until the onions are golden brown, stirring frequently.

2) Stir in water and bouillon. Bring to a boil. Reduce heat; simmer, uncovered, for 5-7 minutes or until liquid has evaporated. Remove from the heat; stir in cheese.

3) Melt remaining butter. Place one sheet of phyllo dough on a work surface; brush with butter (brush to distribute evenly). Repeat with a second sheet; brush with butter. Cut into 12 squares. (Keep remaining phyllo covered with plastic wrap and a damp towel to prevent drying.) Repeat three times, making 48 squares.

4) Press one square into a greased miniature muffin cup. Top with another square of phyllo, placing corners off center. Spoon about 1 tablespoon onion mixture into cup. Repeat with remaining

phyllo squares and onion mixture. Bake at 375° for 10-15 minutes or until golden brown. Serve warm.

Yield: 2 dozen.

NUTRITION FACTS: 3 pieces equals 247 calories, 18 g fat (11 g saturated fat), 51 mg cholesterol, 521 mg sodium, 17 g carbohydrate, 1 g fiber, 6 g protein.

Holiday Appetizer Puffs

PREP: 20 min. **BAKE:** 25 min.

Kathy Fielder, Dallas, Texas

These are so versatile. Instead of crab, you can also use your favorite chicken or tuna salad.

> 1 cup water
> 1/2 cup butter
> 1/2 teaspoon salt
> 1 cup all-purpose flour
> 4 eggs

FILLING:

> 1 package (8 ounces) cream cheese, softened
> 1/4 cup mayonnaise
> 1 can (6 ounces) crabmeat, drained and cartilage removed
> 1/2 cup shredded Swiss cheese
> 1 tablespoon snipped chives
> 1 teaspoon garlic salt
> 1 teaspoon Worcestershire sauce
> 1/4 teaspoon pepper

1) In a small saucepan, bring water, butter and salt to a boil. Add flour all at once and stir until a smooth ball forms. Remove from the heat; let stand for 5 minutes.

2) Add eggs, one at a time, beating well after each addition. Continue beating until the mixture is smooth and shiny.

3) Drop by rounded teaspoonfuls 2 in. apart onto greased baking sheets. Bake at 400° for 25-30 minutes or until golden. Remove to wire racks. Immediately slit puffs to allow steam to escape.

4) When cool, split puffs open; remove tops and set aside. Discard soft dough from inside.

5) In a small mixing bowl, beat cream cheese and mayonnaise until smooth. Stir in remaining filling ingredients. Just before serving, spoon filling into puffs; replace tops.

Yield: 4 dozen.

NUTRITION FACTS: 3 puffs equals 195 calories, 16 g fat (8 g saturated fat), 98 mg cholesterol, 369 mg sodium, 7 g carbohydrate, trace fiber, 7 g protein.

◖Black Bean Quesadillas

PREP/TOTAL TIME: 30 min.

Jane Epping, Iowa City, Iowa

Topped with salsa and sour cream, these crisp wedges are always a hit. You can also add chopped onion, black olives and green chilies.

2 cans (15 ounces *each*) black beans, rinsed and drained

1-2/3 cups salsa, *divided*

10 flour tortillas (8 inches)

2 cups (8 ounces) shredded Colby-Monterey Jack cheese

1/3 cup sour cream

1) In a bowl, mash the beans; add 1 cup salsa. Place five tortillas on ungreased baking sheets; spread with bean mixture. Sprinkle with cheese; top with the remaining tortillas.

2) Bake at 350° for 15-18 minutes or until crisp and heated through. Cut into wedges. Serve with sour cream and remaining salsa.

Yield: 30 wedges.

NUTRITION FACTS: 1 wedge with about 1 teaspoon salsa and 1 teaspoon sour cream equals 113 calories, 4 g fat (2 g saturated fat), 10 mg cholesterol, 237 mg sodium, 14 g carbohydrate, 1 g fiber, 5 g protein.

Corn Salsa Tostadas

PREP/TOTAL TIME: 20 min.

Laurie Todd, Columbus, Mississippi

These south-of-the-border treats are sure to satisfy cravings for something a little spicy.

3 flour tortillas (8 inches)

3/4 cup fat-free sour cream

3 teaspoons minced fresh cilantro, *divided*

2 green onions, finely chopped

1/4 teaspoon garlic powder

3/4 cup fresh *or* frozen corn, thawed

1 plum tomato, diced

1 tablespoon chopped jalapeno pepper

2 tablespoons orange juice

1 teaspoon canola oil

1/2 teaspoon salt

1) With a 2-in. round cutter, cut 12 circles from each tortilla. Coat both sides of circles with cooking spray. Place in a single layer on a baking sheet. Bake at 400° for 4-5 minutes or until crisp. Cool.

2) In a small bowl, combine the sour cream, 1 teaspoon cilantro, onions and garlic powder; cover and refrigerate. In another bowl, combine the corn, tomato, jalapeno, orange juice, oil, salt and remaining cilantro; cover and refrigerate.

3) Just before serving, spread 1 teaspoon sour cream mixture over each tostada. Using a slotted spoon, top each with a teaspoonful of corn salsa.

Yield: 3 dozen.

Editor's Note: When cutting or seeding hot peppers, use rubber or plastic gloves to protect your hands. Avoid touching your face.

NUTRITION FACTS: 6 tostadas equals 141 calories, 3 g fat (trace saturated fat), 3 mg cholesterol, 347 mg sodium, 25 g carbohydrate, 1 g fiber, 5 g protein.

Canadian Bacon Potato Skins

PREP: 30 min. **BAKE:** 15 min.

Mary Plummer, De Soto, Kansas

Need a fun appetizer or a tasty side dish? These potato skins are sure to fill the bill! Potato shells are topped with Canadian bacon, chopped tomato and reduced-fat cheese.

6 large baking potatoes (12 ounces *each*)

2 teaspoons canola oil

1/8 teaspoon hot pepper sauce

1 teaspoon chili powder

1 medium tomato, seeded and finely chopped

2/3 cup chopped Canadian bacon

2 tablespoons finely chopped green onion

1 cup (4 ounces) shredded reduced-fat cheddar cheese

1/2 cup reduced-fat sour cream

1) Place potatoes on a microwave-safe plate; prick with a fork. Microwave, uncovered, on high for 14-17 minutes or until tender but firm, turning once. Let stand for 5 minutes. Cut each potato in half lengthwise. Scoop out pulp, leaving a 1/4-in. shell (discard pulp or save for another use).

2) Combine oil and hot pepper sauce; brush over potato shells. Sprinkle with chili powder. Cut each potato shell in half lengthwise. Place on baking sheets coated with cooking spray. Sprinkle with the tomato, bacon, onion and cheese.

3) Bake at 450° for 12-14 minutes or until heated through and cheese is melted. Serve with sour cream.

Yield: 8 servings.

NUTRITION FACTS: 3 potato skins equals 211 calories, 7 g fat (4 g saturated fat), 21 mg cholesterol, 309 mg sodium, 29 g carbohydrate, 5 g fiber, 11 g protein.

CANADIAN BACON POTATO SKINS

IRRESISTIBLE STUFFED MUSHROOMS

 CLASSIC: Ham, bacon and two kinds of cheese combine to make the flavorful filling for Italian Stuffed Mushrooms. They're baked in the oven until tender and taste fabulous when served warm.

 TIME-SAVER: In less than 20 minutes, you can be tempting guests with impressive Bacon-Stuffed Mushrooms. They're filled with four simple ingredients and broiled for just a few minutes.

 LIGHT: A meatless filling made with fresh spinach, reduced-fat ricotta, and water chestnuts and pecans for crunch gives the lighter spin to Spinach Cheese Mushrooms. Although you'd never guess by its flavor, one mushroom is lower in calories, fat and sodium than one classic Italian Stuffed Mushroom.

 SERVES 2: For a special appetizer that serves two, try Savory Stuffed Mushrooms. The filling gets spark from green pepper, onion and cayenne. And because the recipe makes six, each of you can enjoy three delicious mushrooms.

ITALIAN STUFFED MUSHROOMS

Italian Stuffed Mushrooms

PREP/TOTAL TIME: 30 min.

Virginia Slater, West Sunbury, Pennsylvania

- 4 bacon strips, diced
- 30 large fresh mushrooms
- 1 cup onion and garlic salad croutons, crushed
- 1 cup (4 ounces) shredded part-skim mozzarella cheese
- 1 medium tomato, finely chopped
- 1/4 pound ground fully cooked ham
- 1/4 cup grated Parmesan cheese
- 2 tablespoons minced fresh parsley
- 1-1/2 teaspoons minced fresh oregano *or* 1/2 teaspoon dried oregano

1) In a large skillet, cook bacon over medium heat until crisp. Using a slotted spoon, remove to paper towels; drain, reserving 1 tablespoon drippings.

2) Remove stems from mushrooms; set caps aside. Finely chop half of the stems (save the remaining for another use). Add chopped stems to drippings with bacon; saute for 2-3 minutes. Remove from the heat. Stir in the remaining ingredients.

3) Firmly stuff crouton mixture into mushroom caps. Place in a greased 15-in. x 10-in. x 1-in. baking pan. Bake at 425° for 12-15 minutes or until mushrooms are tender.

Yield: 15 servings.

NUTRITION FACTS: 1 stuffed mushroom equals 43 calories, 3 g fat (1 g saturated fat), 6 mg cholesterol, 114 mg sodium, 2 g carbohydrate, trace fiber, 3 g protein.

Bacon-Stuffed Mushrooms

PREP/TOTAL TIME: 20 min.

Angela Coffman, Stewartsville, Missouri

- 1 package (8 ounces) cream cheese, softened
- 1/2 cup real bacon bits
- 1 tablespoon chopped green onion
- 1/4 teaspoon garlic powder
- 1 pound whole fresh mushrooms, stems removed

1) In a small mixing bowl, beat cream cheese until smooth. Stir in the bacon, onion and garlic powder. Spoon into mushroom caps. Broil 4-6 in. from the heat for 4-6 minutes or until heated through. Serve warm.

Yield: about 2 dozen.

NUTRITION FACTS: 1 mushroom equals 46 calories, 4 g fat (2 g saturated fat), 12 mg cholesterol, 103 mg sodium, 1 g carbohydrate, trace fiber, 2 g protein.

SAVORY STUFFED MUSHROOMS

Spinach Cheese Mushrooms

PREP/TOTAL TIME: 25 min.

Debbie Hert, Columbus, Indiana

- 1/2 pound fresh torn spinach
- 2 tablespoons water
- 3/4 cup reduced-fat ricotta cheese
- 3 tablespoons butter, softened
- 1 egg
- 2/3 cup grated Parmesan cheese
- 1/2 cup water chestnuts, chopped
- 1/3 cup finely chopped pecans, *divided*
- 56 large fresh mushrooms (about 3-1/2 pounds)

Refrigerated butter-flavored spray

1) In a large saucepan, bring spinach and water to a boil. Reduce heat; cover and cook for 3 minutes. Drain; squeeze dry and finely chop. In a large mixing bowl, beat ricotta and butter until smooth. Beat in egg. Stir in Parmesan cheese, water chestnuts, 3 tablespoons pecans and chopped spinach.

2) Remove stems from mushrooms (discard or save for another use). Spray inside of mushroom caps with butter-flavored spray. Place caps on a baking sheet coated with cooking spray. Stuff with spinach mixture; sprinkle with remaining pecans.

3) Bake, uncovered, at 400° for 15-20 minutes or until lightly browned.

Yield: 28 servings.

Editor's Note: This recipe was tested with I Can't Believe It's Not Butter Spray.

NUTRITION FACTS: 1 mushroom equals 26 calories, 2 g fat (1 g saturated fat), 7 mg cholesterol, 27 mg sodium, 2 g carbohydrate, trace fiber, 2 g protein.

Savory Stuffed Mushrooms

PREP/TOTAL TIME: 30 min.

Pam Miller, Kokomo, Indiana

- 6 large fresh mushrooms
- 4-1/2 teaspoons finely chopped green pepper
- 4-1/2 teaspoons finely chopped onion
- 1 tablespoon butter
- 3/4 cup cubed day-old bread
- 1/8 teaspoon salt
- 1/8 teaspoon pepper

Dash cayenne pepper

1) Remove stems from mushrooms and finely chop; set caps aside. In a skillet, saute the stems, green pepper and onion in butter until tender. Remove from the heat. Stir in the bread cubes, salt, pepper and cayenne.

2) Stuff into mushroom caps. Place in a baking dish coated with cooking spray. Bake, uncovered, at 350° for 15 minutes or until stuffing is lightly browned.

Yield: 2 servings.

NUTRITION FACTS: 1 stuffed mushroom equals 36 calories, 2 g fat (1 g saturated fat), 5 mg cholesterol, 94 mg sodium, 4 g carbohydrate, trace fiber, 1 g protein.

Preparing Mushrooms For Stuffing

Hold the mushroom cap in one hand and grab the stem with the other hand. Twist to snap off the stem; place caps on a greased baking sheet. Mince or finely chop stems.

Turkey Tortilla Roll-Ups

PREP/TOTAL TIME: 10 min.

Darlene Brenden, Salem, Oregon

You won't have to take a long time to make these tasty, hearty snacks. Cooked chicken or cold cuts also work well.

- 3/4 cup sour cream
- 6 flour tortillas (8 inches)
- 1-1/2 cups diced cooked turkey
- 1 cup (4 ounces) finely shredded cheddar cheese
- 1 cup shredded lettuce
- 1/2 cup chopped ripe olives
- 1/2 cup chunky salsa

1) Spread 2 tablespoons sour cream over each tortilla. Top with the turkey, cheese, lettuce, olives and salsa.

2) Roll up each tortilla tightly; wrap in plastic wrap. Refrigerate until serving. Unwrap and cut each roll-up into 6 pieces.

Yield: 12 servings.

NUTRITION FACTS: 3 pieces equals 177 calories, 8 g fat (4 g saturated fat), 33 mg cholesterol, 297 mg sodium, 15 g carbohydrate, 1 g fiber, 11 g protein.

Marinated Olives

PREP: 10 min. + marinating

Marguerite Shaeffer, Sewell, New Jersey

These olives are nice to have for get-togethers because they're simple to make and add a little zest to the buffet table offerings.

- 2 cups large stuffed olives, drained
- 1 cup pitted kalamata olives, drained
- 1 cup pitted medium ripe olives, drained
- 1/4 cup olive oil
- 2 tablespoons lemon juice
- 1 tablespoon minced fresh thyme *or* 1 teaspoon dried thyme
- 2 teaspoons minced fresh rosemary *or* 1/2 teaspoon dried rosemary, crushed
- 2 teaspoons grated lemon peel
- 4 garlic cloves, slivered

Pepper to taste

1) Place olives in a bowl. Combine the remaining ingredients; pour over olives and stir.

2) Cover and refrigerate for 1-2 days before serving, stirring several times each day. Olives may be refrigerated for 2 weeks. Serve with a slotted spoon.

Yield: 4 cups.

NUTRITION FACTS: 1/4 cup equals 98 calories, 10 g fat (1 g saturated fat), 0 cholesterol, 572 mg sodium, 3 g carbohydrate, trace fiber, trace protein.

Marinated Mozzarella Cubes

PREP: 10 min. + marinating

Arline Roggenbuck, Shawano, Wisconsin

Jars of these marinated cheese cubes make wonderful gifts any time of the year...if you can bear to part with them!

- 1 pound part-skim mozzarella cheese, cut into 1-inch cubes
- 1 jar (7 ounces) roasted red peppers, drained and cut into bite-size pieces
- 6 fresh thyme sprigs
- 2 garlic cloves, minced
- 1-1/4 cups olive oil
- 2 tablespoons minced fresh rosemary
- 2 teaspoons Italian seasoning
- 1/4 teaspoon crushed red pepper flakes

Bread *or* crackers

1) In a quart jar with a tight-fitting lid, layer a third of the cheese, peppers, thyme and garlic. Repeat layers twice.

2) In a small bowl, combine the oil, rosemary, Italian seasoning and pepper flakes; mix well. Pour into jar; seal and turn upside down.

3) Refrigerate overnight, turning several times. Serve with bread or crackers.

Yield: 12-16 servings.

NUTRITION FACTS: 1 serving (calculated without bread or crackers) equals 121 calories, 10 g fat (4 g saturated fat), 22 mg cholesterol, 224 mg sodium, 1 g carbohydrate, trace fiber, 6 g protein.

MARINATED MOZZARELLA CUBES

Cayenne Pretzels

PREP: 10 min. **BAKE:** 1-1/4 hours

Gayle Zebo, Warren, Pennsylvania

These easy-to-coat, well-seasoned pretzels were a huge hit at my daughter's graduation party. The longer they sit, the spicier they get!

> 1 cup vegetable oil
> 1 envelope ranch salad dressing mix
> 1 teaspoon garlic salt
> 1 teaspoon cayenne pepper
> 1 pound (12 cups) pretzel sticks

1) In a small bowl, combine the oil, dressing mix, garlic salt and cayenne. Divide pretzels between two ungreased 15-in. x 10-in. x 1-in. baking pans. Pour oil mixture over pretzels; stir to coat.

2) Bake at 200° for 1-1/4 to 1-1/2 hours or until golden brown, stirring occasionally. Cool completely. Store in an airtight container.

Yield: 3 quarts.

NUTRITION FACTS: 3/4 cup equals 236 calories, 15 g fat (2 g saturated fat), 0 cholesterol, 690 mg sodium, 24 g carbohydrate, 1 g fiber, 3 g protein.

Spiced Pecans

PREP: 10 min. **BAKE:** 1 hour

Miriam Herschberger, Holmesville, Ohio

Toasting nuts intensifies their flavor, and the sweet, sugar-cinnamon coating on these pecans is irresistible.

> 1 egg white
> 1 teaspoon cold water
> 4 cups (about 1 pound) pecan halves
> 1/2 cup sugar
> 1/2 teaspoon ground cinnamon
> 1/4 teaspoon salt

1) In a small mixing bowl, beat egg white lightly. Add water; beat until frothy but not stiff. Add pecans; stir until well coated.

2) Combine the sugar, cinnamon and salt. Sprinkle over pecans; toss to mix. Spread in a greased 15-in. x 10-in. x 1-in. baking pan. Bake at 250° for 1 hour, stirring occasionally.

Yield: 12 servings.

NUTRITION FACTS: 1/3 cup equals 283 calories, 26 g fat (2 g saturated fat), 0 cholesterol, 54 mg sodium, 13 g carbohydrate, 4 g fiber, 4 g protein.

Super Trail Mix

Need a quick snack without any fuss—then try this kid pleaser. In a large bowl, combine 5 cups *each* miniature pretzel twists, Honey-Nut Cheerios and Corn Chex with 2 cups *each* salted mix nuts and dried banana or apple chips or M&M's or Reese's pieces.

SMACKIN' GOOD SNACK MIX

Smackin' Good Snack Mix

PREP: 15 min. **BAKE:** 40 min. + cooling

Lucile Cline, Wichita, Kansas

Tailgaters love to munch, so this crunchy snack mix is perfect for a pregame spread. Everyone who has tried it likes it. I'm a retired Extension home economist, and have won a ribbon at the state fair with this recipe.

> 6 cups original Bugles
> 5 cups nacho cheese-flavored Bugles
> 4 cups miniature cheese crackers
> 1 package (6 ounces) miniature colored fish-shaped crackers
> 3 cups miniature pretzels
> 2 cups Crispix
> 2 cups lightly salted cashews
> 3/4 cup butter-flavored popcorn oil
> 2 envelopes (1 ounce *each*) ranch salad dressing mix

1) In a large bowl, combine the first seven ingredients. Combine oil and dressing mix; pour over cracker mixture and toss to coat.

2) Transfer to three greased 15-in. x 10-in. x 1-in. baking pans. Bake at 250° for 40-45 minutes or until crisp, stirring occasionally. Cool on wire racks. Store in an airtight container.

Yield: 6 quarts.

NUTRITION FACTS: 3/4 cup equals 217 calories, 13 g fat (3 g saturated fat), 1 mg cholesterol, 437 mg sodium, 22 g carbohydrate, 1 g fiber, 4 g protein.

Garnishes for Beverages

Part of the enjoyment of drinking a cool, refreshing beverage is its presentation. Add a simple garnish, and a delicious drink becomes a festive drink. Here are no-fuss suggestions to give beverages a little pizzazz.

Place fresh berries, such as raspberries or strawberries, and a fresh mint leaf in ice cube trays and fill partway with water. Freeze and use as ice cubes.

For a more delicate look, use flowers, such as pansies, rose petals or dianthus, for ice cubes. If using flowers, make sure to properly identify flowers before picking. Double-check that they're edible and have not been treated with chemicals.

Skewer various fruits with bamboo or reusable picks. Some suggestions are:

- Place a slice of star fruit on the end of a skewer and place in the drink.

- Cut 3/4-inch-thick slices of seedless watermelon, cantaloupe and honeydew, then cut out the melon with a small, heart-shaped cookie or appetizer cutter. Thread several pieces of melon or one of each melon on a skewer.

- Take a slice of orange, lemon or lime and make a cut from the center to one end. Twist the slice and thread onto a skewer. If desired, thread strawberries or small pieces of fruit between each turn of the citrus fruit slice.

- Using a vegetable peeler, peel wide strips of citrus fruit peel. With a sharp knife, trim the long edges so they are smooth. Weave peel accordion-style onto skewers. If desired, add a piece of fruit or mint to one end.

Other Simple Garnishes

To Decorate a Rim of a Glass
Use a wedge of pineapple or citrus fruit slice, a slice of strawberry or a whole strawberry, a curl of citrus peel.

To Make a Citrus Curl
Use a citrus stripper to remove a long continuous strip of peel. Tightly wind the strip around a straw and secure ends with waterproof tape; let stand for 20 minutes. The longer it stands, the longer the strip will hold its shape. To use, remove tape and slip off straw or unwind from the straw.

For a Sugar- or Salt-Coated Rim
Dip rim of glass in water, then dip in coarse sugar or salt. Or use colored sugar to match your party theme.

For a Cold Shake or Iced Coffee
Melt semisweet chocolate chips and place in a small resealable plastic bag. Cut off a small piece of the corner of the bag and pipe a design on waxed paper (the design should not be too thin). Let stand until set and gently peel off the paper. Top your shake or coffee with whipped cream and insert the chocolate garnish. Or hang the garnish off the side of the glass.

For a Frosted Glass
Place in the freezer 15-30 minutes before using. Fill with ice and a cold beverage.

Citrus Punch
PREP: 5 min. + chilling

Dianne Conway, London, Ontario

Zesty, fruity flavors combine in this refreshing punch that's easy to double for larger groups.

>   2 cups pineapple juice
>   2 cups orange juice
>   1 cup grapefruit juice
>   1 cup lemonade
>   2 cups ginger ale, chilled

1) In a large pitcher, combine the fruit juices and lemonade. Refrigerate until chilled.

2) Just before serving, pour into a punch bowl. Slowly add ginger ale.

Yield: 8 servings (2 quarts).

NUTRITION FACTS: 1 cup equals 109 calories, trace fat (trace saturated fat), 0 cholesterol, 7 mg sodium, 27 g carbohydrate, trace fiber, 1 g protein.

Cold Punches
Chill all punch ingredients before mixing so that you don't have to dilute the punch with ice to get it cold. Or consider garnishing a cold punch with an ice ring (which lasts longer than ice cubes) made from punch ingredients instead of water.

Sangria

PREP: 15 min. + chilling

Taste of Home Test Kitchen

This is a great make-ahead beverage because it allows time for the flavors to blend together.

  1 bottle (750 ml) Zinfandel *or* other fruity red wine
3/4 cup orange juice
1/3 cup unsweetened pineapple juice
1/4 cup superfine sugar
  1 medium orange, sliced
  1 medium lemon, sliced
  1 medium lime, cut into wedges

1) In a pitcher, combine the wine, orange juice, pineapple juice and sugar; stir until sugar is dissolved.

2) Add fruit; press lightly with a wooden spoon.

3) Refrigerate for 2-4 hours. Serve over ice.

Yield: 5 servings.

NUTRITION FACTS: 3/4 cup equals 186 calories, trace fat (trace saturated fat), 0 cholesterol, 8 mg sodium, 23 g carbohydrate, 1 g fiber, 1 g protein.

Fresh Lime Margaritas

PREP/TOTAL TIME: 15 min.

Taste of Home Test Kitchen

This basic margarita recipe is easy to modify to your tastes. Try it frozen or with strawberries!

  4 lime wedges
  1 tablespoon kosher salt
1/2 cup gold tequila
1/4 cup Triple Sec
1/4 cup lime juice
1/4 cup lemon juice
  2 tablespoons superfine sugar
1-1/3 cups crushed ice

1) Using lime wedges, moisten rim of four glasses. Holding each glass upside down, dip rim into salt; set aside.

2) In a pitcher, combine the tequila, Triple Sec, lime juice, lemon juice and sugar; stir until sugar is dissolved. Serve in prepared glasses over ice.

Yield: 4 servings.

NUTRITION FACTS: 1/3 cup equals 149 calories, trace fat (trace saturated fat), 0 cholesterol, 1,413 mg sodium, 16 g carbohydrate, trace fiber, trace protein.

■ **Frozen Lime Margaritas:** Reduce lemon and lime juices to 2 tablespoons *each*. Increase the superfine sugar to 1/4 cup and the crushed ice to 4 cups. Add 3/4 cup limeade concentrate. Prepare glasses as directed. In a blender, combine the tequila, Triple Sec, lime juice, lemon juice, limeade concentrate, superfine sugar and ice; cover and process until smooth.

■ **Frozen Strawberry Margaritas:** Follow directions for Frozen Lime Margaritas, except reduce ice to 2 cups and add 2 cups frozen unsweetened strawberries.

Champagne Party Punch

PREP: 15 min. + chilling

Taste of Home Test Kitchen

To make this punch even more festive, float an ice ring in the punch.

  1 cup sugar
  1 cup water
  2 cups unsweetened apple juice
  2 cups unsweetened pineapple juice
1/2 cup lemon juice
1/3 cup frozen orange juice concentrate, thawed
1/4 cup lime juice
  2 cups ice cubes
  1 quart ginger ale, chilled
  1 bottle (750 ml) champagne, chilled

1) In a large pitcher, combine the sugar and water; stir until sugar is dissolved. Add the apple juice, pineapple juice, lemon juice, orange juice concentrate and lime juice. Refrigerate until serving.

2) Just before serving, pour into a punch bowl and add ice cubes. Slowly add the ginger ale and champagne.

Yield: 16-18 servings (3-1/2 quarts).

NUTRITION FACTS: 3/4 cup equals 129 calories, trace fat (trace saturated fat), 0 cholesterol, 8 mg sodium, 26 g carbohydrate, trace fiber, trace protein.

Making an Ice Ring

1) Fill a ring mold halfway with water. Freeze until solid. Top with your choice of fruit. Add lemon leaves if desired. Add enough water to almost cover fruit. Freeze until solid.

2) Unmold by wrapping the bottom of the mold with a hot, damp dishcloth. Turn out onto a baking sheet; place in punch bowl fruit side up.

COSMOPOLITAN

Cosmopolitan
PREP/TOTAL TIME: 5 min.

Taste of Home Test Kitchen

Lively color graces this signature drink. Its refreshing and slightly tart taste is perfect for a ladies' night out or at a party. During the holidays, use fresh cranberries for a festive garnish.

Ice cubes
- 2 ounces vodka
- 2 ounces cranberry juice
- 1/2 ounce lime juice
- 1/2 ounce triple sec

Fresh cranberries and lime wedge

1) Fill a shaker three-fourths full with ice. Add the vodka, juices and triple sec. Cover and shake for 10-15 seconds or until condensation forms on outside of shaker. Strain into a chilled cocktail glass. Garnish with cranberries and lime as desired.

Yield: 1 serving.

NUTRITION FACTS: 1 serving equals 215 calories, trace fat (trace saturated fat), 0 cholesterol, 5 mg sodium, 16 g carbohydrate, trace fiber, trace protein.

Martini
PREP/TOTAL TIME: 5 min.

Taste of Home Test Kitchen

Martinis can be made with either vodka or gin. Our taste panel's preference was for the gin, but try them both and decide for yourself. Be warned, this is a strong and serious drink.

Ice cubes
- 3 ounces gin *or* vodka
- 1/2 ounce dry vermouth

Pimiento-stuffed olives

1) Fill a mixing glass or tumbler three-fourths full with ice. Add gin or vodka and vermouth; stir until condensation forms on outside of glass. Strain into a chilled cocktail glass. Garnish with olives as desired.

Yield: 1 serving.

Editor's Note: This recipe makes a dry martini. Use less vermouth for an extra-dry martini; use more for a "wet" martini. You may also serve the martini over ice in a rocks glass.

NUTRITION FACTS: 2/3 cup equals 209 calories, 0 fat (0 saturated fat), 0 cholesterol, 5 mg sodium, trace carbohydrate, 0 fiber, 0 protein.

Daiquiris
PREP/TOTAL TIME: 10 min.

Taste of Home Test Kitchen

This daiquiri blends sweet and tart to perfection. For a party, make it in chilled pitchers, then pour over ice before serving.

- 5 to 5-1/2 cups ice cubes, *divided*
- 3/4 cup light rum
- 2-1/2 ounces lime juice
- 2 ounces simple syrup *or* bar syrup

Lime slices

1) Fill a shaker three-fourths full with ice. Divide remaining ice among four hurricane or cocktail glasses; set aside.

2) Add the rum, lime juice and simple syrup to shaker; cover and shake for 10-15 seconds or until condensation forms on outside of shaker. Strain into prepared glasses. Garnish with lime slices as desired.

Yield: 4 servings.

NUTRITION FACTS: 2/3 cup equals 161 calories, trace fat (trace saturated fat), 0 cholesterol, 2 mg sodium, 17 g carbohydrate, trace fiber, trace protein.

Mojito
PREP/TOTAL TIME: 5 min.

Taste of Home Test Kitchen

The traditional Mojito is made with rum, which is both pleasant and mildly sweet. The version made with tequila is more tart and has a more distinctive alcohol taste, but is still refreshing.

- 1 to 2 lime wedges
- 2 mint sprigs
- 2 teaspoons confectioners' sugar
- 3/4 to 1 cup ice cubes
- 2 ounces light rum
- 1/2 cup club soda, chilled

Mint sprig and lime slice

1) Squeeze lime wedge into a highball glass; drop lime into the glass. Add mint and confectioners' sugar; muddle. Add ice. Pour rum and club soda into glass; stir. Garnish with mint and lime as desired.

Yield: 1 serving.

NUTRITION FACTS: 1 cup equals 149 calories, trace fat (trace saturated fat), 0 cholesterol, 2 mg sodium, 5 g carbohydrate, trace fiber, trace protein.

■ **Tequila Mojito:** Substitute silver tequila (such as Jose Cuervo Clasico) for the rum.

Brandy Slush

PREP: 15 min. + freezing

Taste of Home Test Kitchen

This slush with a hint of citrus keeps you cool on hot summer days. You'll like the mix even if you're not a tea lover.

> 4 individual green *or* black tea bags
> 9 cups water, *divided*
> 2 cups brandy
> 1 can (12 ounces) frozen lemonade concentrate, thawed
> 1 can (12 ounces) frozen orange juice concentrate, thawed

EACH SERVING:

> 1/4 cup lemon-lime soda, chilled

Orange *or* lemon slice

1) Place tea bags in a bowl. Bring 2 cups water to a boil; pour over tea bags. Cover and steep for 5 minutes. Discard tea bags. Transfer tea to a large pitcher; stir in the brandy, lemonade concentrate, juice concentrate and remaining water. Pour into a 4-qt. freezer container. Freeze overnight or until set.

2) For each serving, scoop 3/4 cup slush into a rocks glass. Pour lemon-lime soda into the glass; garnish with orange or lemon slices as desired.

Yield: 21 servings (about 4 quarts slush mix).

NUTRITION FACTS: 1 serving equals 129 calories, trace fat (trace saturated fat), 0 cholesterol, 8 mg sodium, 20 g carbohydrate, trace fiber, trace protein.

Holiday Eggnog

PREP: 15 min. **COOK:** 25 min. + chilling

Taste of Home Test Kitchen

For a nice, rich and creamy treat, try this eggnog recipe. You can serve it plain or add rum for adult holiday guests.

> 6 eggs
> 3/4 cup sugar

> 1/4 teaspoon salt
> 4 cups milk, *divided*
> 1 tablespoon vanilla extract
> 1/2 teaspoon ground nutmeg
> 1 cup heavy whipping cream

Additional whipped cream and ground nutmeg, optional

1) In a large heavy saucepan, whisk together the eggs, sugar and salt. Gradually add 2 cups milk. Cook over low heat, stirring constantly, until a thermometer reads 160°, about 25 minutes.

2) Pour into a large bowl; stir in the vanilla, nutmeg and remaining milk. Place the bowl in an ice-water bath; stir frequently until mixture is cool. If mixture separates, process in a blender until smooth. Cover and refrigerate for at least 3 hours.

3) When ready to serve, in a small mixing bowl, beat cream on high speed until soft peaks form; whisk gently into cooled mixture. Pour into a chilled punch bowl. If desired, top with dollops of whipped cream and sprinkle with nutmeg.

Yield: 6 servings (about 4 cups).

NUTRITION FACTS: 3/4 cup equals 413 calories, 25 g fat (14 g saturated fat), 289 mg cholesterol, 256 mg sodium, 34 g carbohydrate, 0 fiber, 12 g protein.

■ **Spiked Holiday Eggnog:** Reduce milk to 3-1/4 cups. Heat 2 cups milk with eggs, sugar and salt. Add 1-1/4 cups milk with vanilla and nutmeg. After mixture has cooled in ice bath, stir in 3/4 cup rum, brandy or bourbon. Proceed as recipe directs.

Old-Fashioned Chocolate Malted Milk

PREP/TOTAL TIME: 10 min.

Taste of Home Test Kitchen

With a few ingredients, you can make this old-fashioned favorite just like the old malt shops used to serve!

> 2 cups vanilla ice cream
> 2/3 cup cold milk
> 2 tablespoons malted milk powder
> 2 tablespoons chocolate syrup
> 2 to 4 tablespoons whipped cream

1) In a blender, combine the ice cream, milk, malted milk powder and chocolate syrup; cover and process until smooth.

2) Pour into chilled glasses. Top with a dollop of whipped cream; serve immediately.

Yield: 2 servings.

NUTRITION FACTS: 1-1/3 cup equals 430 calories, 19 g fat (12 g saturated fat), 75 mg cholesterol, 217 mg sodium, 59 g carbohydrate, 1 g fiber, 9 g protein.

APRICOT PEACH SMOOTHIES

frozen raspberries and 1 teaspoon vanilla extract. Cover and process until smooth.

■ **Strawberry Smoothies:** In a blender or food processor, combine 1 cup milk, 1 cup strawberry yogurt, 1 pint vanilla ice cream, 1 quartered medium banana, 1/2 cup frozen unsweetened strawberries and 1 tablespoon honey. Cover and process until smooth.

Strawberry Cooler

PREP/TOTAL TIME: 10 min.

Judy Robertson, Russell Springs, Kentucky

This refreshing beverage is easy to double. Just make two batches ahead of time and add ginger ale and ice when you're ready for more!

    3 cups water
    5 cups sliced fresh strawberries
3/4 to 1 cup sugar
 1/4 cup lemon juice
    2 teaspoons grated lemon peel
    1 cup ginger ale
Crushed ice
Whole strawberries, optional

1) In a blender, process the water, strawberries, sugar, lemon juice and peel in batches until smooth. Strain the berry seeds if desired.

2) Pour into a pitcher; stir in the ginger ale. Serve over ice. Garnish with whole berries if desired.

Yield: 8 servings.

NUTRITION FACTS: 1 cup equals 116 calories, trace fat (trace saturated fat), 0 cholesterol, 3 mg sodium, 29 g carbohydrate, 2 g fiber, 1 g protein.

Apricot Peach Smoothies

PREP/TOTAL TIME: 10 min.

DeAnn Alleva, Hudson, Wisconsin

The mellow mingling of peach, banana and apricot flavors makes this refreshing smoothie so soothing. A spark of lemon adds a little tang but honey keeps it on the lightly sweet side.

    1 can (5-1/2 ounces) apricot nectar
    1 medium ripe banana, frozen and cut into chunks
    1 cup (8 ounces) fat-free vanilla yogurt
    2 cups sliced fresh *or* frozen unsweetened peaches
    1 tablespoon lemon juice
    1 tablespoon honey
    1 teaspoon grated lemon peel
    6 ice cubes

1) In a blender or food processor, combine all of the ingredients. Cover and process until smooth. Pour into glasses; serve immediately.

Yield: 4 servings.

NUTRITION FACTS: 1 cup equals 160 calories, trace fat (0 saturated fat), 2 mg cholesterol, 35 mg sodium, 37 g carbohydrate, 3 g fiber, 4 g protein.

■ **Raspberry Cream Smoothies:** In a blender or food processor, combine 1 cup orange juice, 1 cup raspberry yogurt, 1 cup frozen vanilla yogurt, 1/2 cup frozen banana chunks, 1-1/2 cups

Spicy Tomato Juice

PREP/TOTAL TIME: 10 min.

Susan Zambito, New Orleans, Louisiana

A few ingredients make this spicy beverage ideal for a brunch.

    1 can (11-1/2 ounces) V8 *or* tomato juice, chilled
 1/4 cup beef broth
 1/4 teaspoon pepper
 1/8 teaspoon celery salt
 1/8 teaspoon Worcestershire sauce
Dash hot pepper sauce, optional
Celery sticks, optional

1) In a small pitcher, combine first six ingredients. Serve over ice with celery sticks if desired.

Yield: 2 servings.

NUTRITION FACTS: 1 cup equals 40 calories, trace fat (trace saturated fat), 0 cholesterol, 644 mg sodium, 8 g carbohydrate, 1 g fiber, 1 g protein.

■ **Spiked Spicy Tomato Juice:** Add 1/4 cup vodka to the juice mixture.

Raspberry Refresher

PREP: 10 min. **COOK:** 20 min. + chilling

Doreen Patterson, Qualicum Beach, British Columbia

This recipe explodes with raspberry flavor! It's a wonderful summertime treat.

>   8 cups fresh *or* frozen raspberries, thawed
> 1-1/2 cups sugar
>   2/3 cup cider vinegar
> 2-1/2 cups cold water, *divided*
>   2 liters ginger ale, chilled

1) In a large saucepan, crush the berries. Stir in sugar, vinegar and 1/2 cup water. Bring to a boil; reduce heat. Simmer, uncovered, for 20 minutes. Strain to remove seeds; refrigerate.

2) Just before serving, stir in the ginger ale and remaining water. Serve over ice.

Yield: 14 servings (about 3-1/2 quarts).

NUTRITION FACTS: 1 cup equals 169 calories, trace fat (trace saturated fat), 0 cholesterol, 11 mg sodium, 43 g carbohydrate, 5 g fiber, 1 g protein.

Springtime Lime Slushy

PREP: 10 min. + freezing

Joyce Minge-Johns, Jacksonville, Florida

For more fun variations, try using your favorite gelatin and sherbet flavors.

> 2 packages (3 ounces *each*) lime gelatin
> 2 cups boiling water
> 2 cups cold water
> 2 quarts lime sherbet
> 3 cups ginger ale, chilled

1) In a freezer container, dissolve gelatin in boiling water. Stir in the cold water and sherbet until combined. Freeze for 4 hours or until set.

2) Remove from the freezer 45 minutes before serving. For each serving, place 1 cup of slush mixture in a glass; add about 1/3 cup ginger ale.

Yield: 8 servings.

NUTRITION FACTS: 1 cup equals 313 calories, 3 g fat (2 g saturated fat), 9 mg cholesterol, 123 mg sodium, 71 g carbohydrate, 0 fiber, 4 g protein.

Old-Fashioned Strawberry Soda

PREP/TOTAL TIME: 10 min.

Ginger Hubbard, Anderson, Missouri

Strawberries and ice cream blend together in this creamy favorite. Adding ginger ale gives it a fun, bubbly twist.

>   1 cup milk
> 1/2 cup fresh *or* frozen strawberries
> 1/2 cup vanilla ice cream, softened
>   2 tablespoons sugar

> 2 to 3 drops red food coloring, optional
> 1 cup ginger ale, chilled

1) In a blender container, combine the milk, strawberries, ice cream, sugar and food coloring if desired; cover and process until smooth.

2) Pour into two tall glasses. Add ginger ale and serve immediately.

Yield: 2 servings.

NUTRITION FACTS: 1 cup equals 242 calories, 8 g fat (5 g saturated fat), 31 mg cholesterol, 95 mg sodium, 39 g carbohydrate, 1 g fiber, 5 g protein.

Homemade Lemonade

PREP: 5 min. **COOK:** 10 min. + chilling

Rebecca Baird, Salt Lake City, Utah

This old-fashioned thirst quencher gets a little fizz from club soda, creating a refreshing, sweet-tart beverage.

> 3 cups sugar
> 2 cups water
> 1 cup lemon peel strips (about 6 lemons)
> 3 cups lemon juice (about 14 lemons)
> 1 bottle (1 liter) club soda, chilled

1) In a large saucepan, heat sugar and water over medium heat until sugar is dissolved, stirring frequently. Stir in lemon strips. Bring to a boil. Reduce heat; simmer, uncovered, for 5 minutes.

2) Remove from the heat. Cool slightly. Stir in lemon juice; cover and refrigerate until chilled. Discard lemon strips. Pour mixture into a pitcher and gradually stir in club soda.

Yield: 10 cups.

NUTRITION FACTS: 1 cup equals 251 calories, 0 fat (0 saturated fat), 0 cholesterol, 22 mg sodium, 66 g carbohydrate, trace fiber, trace protein.

■ **Orange Lemonade:** Heat 1-3/4 cups sugar with 2-1/2 cups water as directed. Cool sugar syrup. Add 1-1/2 cups *each* lemon and orange juices, and 2 tablespoons *each* grated lemon and orange peels. Refrigerate until chilled. Strain lemonade before serving. For each serving, fill a glass with 1/2 cup of lemonade mixture and 1/2 cup of chilled water or club soda. Add ice and serve.

■ **Spiked Lemonade:** Omit club soda. Prepare and chill as directed. Stir in 1 cup light rum or vodka. For each serving, place 3/4 to 1 cup ice in a tall glass. Pour lemonade mixture into glass.

Liquifying Ice in a Blender

Chill and thicken beverages with ice by placing all ingredients except ice in blender. Cover and process on high until blended. With the motor running, remove feeder cap in the center of cover and drop in one ice cube at a time. Continue until all the ice is liquified or until the beverage is as thick as desired.

Coffee

A good cup of coffee starts with a clean pot, fresh cold water and fresh coffee. Coffee manufacturers will generally recommend between 1 to 2 tablespoons ground coffee per 3/4 cup (6 ounces) of water; check the package for the recommendation of the brand you are using. If you are grinding the beans, grind only enough for what you are planning to use.

When serving coffee at a party, use insulated carafes to keep the coffee warm for up to 2 hours. Offer guests both decaf and regular. Choose a quality basic coffee and allow your guests the option to flavor their own mugs with orange twists, flavored liqueurs or syrups such as hazelnut.

Store unopened containers of ground, instant and freeze-dried coffee at room temperature for up to a year. Once the package is open, it loses its flavor quickly. Store opened packages in the refrigerator for up to 3 weeks. If there is more ground coffee than you would use in 3 weeks, divide the remaining ground coffee into weekly portions and store in the freezer in airtight, freezerproof containers.

Coffee beans should be used within 3 weeks. Store beans in the freezer in airtight, freezerproof containers for up to 1 year. Thaw beans before grinding.

TOFFEE-FLAVORED COFFEE

Toffee-Flavored Coffee
PREP/TOTAL TIME: 15 min.

Taste of Home Test Kitchen

With its chocolate toffee flavor, this soothing java drink makes mornings pleasantly perk along. Treat yourself to a cup in the afternoon as a special pick-me-up.

1/2 cup heavy whipping cream
 1 tablespoon confectioners' sugar
1/2 cup milk chocolate toffee bits
 5 cups hot brewed coffee
 2 tablespoons butterscotch ice cream topping

1) In a small mixing bowl, beat cream until it begins to thicken. Add confectioners' sugar; beat until stiff peaks form. Stir toffee bits into coffee; let stand for 30 seconds. Strain and discard any undissolved toffee bits.

2) Pour coffee into mugs; top with whipped cream and drizzle with butterscotch topping.

Yield: 5 servings.

NUTRITION FACTS: 1 cup equals 242 calories, 17 g fat (10 g saturated fat), 52 mg cholesterol, 150 mg sodium, 22 g carbohydrate, trace fiber, 1 g protein.

Iced Coffee
PREP/TOTAL TIME: 5 min.

Jenny Reece, Lowry, Minnesota

When I first tried iced coffee, I didn't think I'd like it. But I created this fast-to-fix version, and it's a refreshing alternative to hot coffee.

 4 teaspoons instant coffee granules
 1 cup boiling water
Artificial sweetener equivalent to 4 teaspoons sugar, optional
 1 cup fat-free milk
 4 teaspoons chocolate syrup
1/8 teaspoon vanilla extract
Ice cubes

1) In a small bowl, dissolve coffee in water. Add sweetener if desired. Stir in the milk, chocolate syrup and vanilla; mix well. Serve over ice.

Yield: 2 servings.

NUTRITION FACTS: 1 cup equals 79 calories, 1 g fat (0 saturated fat), 2 mg cholesterol, 76 mg sodium, 15 g carbohydrate, 0 fiber, 5 g protein.

Hot Ginger Coffee
PREP/TOTAL TIME: 25 min.

Audrey Thibodeau, Mesa, Arizona

This is wonderful after skiing or sledding. Try the crystallized ginger in baked goods or over ice cream.

 6 tablespoons ground coffee (not instant)
 1 tablespoon grated orange peel
 1 tablespoon chopped crystallized *or* candied ginger
1/2 teaspoon ground cinnamon
 6 cups cold water
Whipped cream, cinnamon sticks *and/or* additional orange peel, optional

1) Combine the coffee, orange peel, ginger and cinnamon; pour mixture into a coffee filter. Brew according to manufacturer's directions using the 6 cups cold water.

2) Pour into mugs; garnish with whipped cream, cinnamon sticks and orange peel if desired.

Yield: 6 servings.

Editor's Note: Look for crystallized or candied ginger in the spice or baking section of your grocery store.

NUTRITION FACTS: 1 cup equals 22 calories, trace fat (trace saturated fat), 0 cholesterol, 3 mg sodium, 5 g carbohydrate, trace fiber, 1 g protein.

Cinnamon Mocha Coffee
PREP/TOTAL TIME: 20 min.

Bernice Morris, Marshfield, Missouri

One snowy day, my neighbor called and invited me over to try a new drink she'd made. It was delicious! This spiced coffee is a lovely treat any time of year.

- 1/2 cup ground dark roast coffee
- 1 tablespoon ground cinnamon
- 1/4 teaspoon ground nutmeg
- 5 cups water
- 1 cup milk
- 1/3 cup chocolate syrup
- 1/4 cup packed brown sugar
- 1 teaspoon vanilla extract

Whipped cream, optional

1) In a small bowl, combine the coffee grounds, cinnamon and nutmeg; pour into a coffee filter of a drip coffeemaker. Add water; brew according to manufacturer's directions.

2) In a large saucepan, combine the milk, chocolate syrup and brown sugar. Cook over low heat until sugar is dissolved, stirring occasionally. Stir in the vanilla and brewed coffee. Ladle into mugs; garnish with whipped cream if desired.

Yield: 6 servings.

NUTRITION FACTS: 1 cup equals 126 calories, 2 g fat (1 g saturated fat), 6 mg cholesterol, 34 mg sodium, 25 g carbohydrate, 1 g fiber, 3 g protein.

Easy Cappuccino
PREP/TOTAL TIME: 10 min.

Taste of Home Test Kitchen

Traditionally, a cappuccino is one part espresso mixed with one part steamed milk, then topped with one part foamed milk. This recipe lets you duplicate your favorite coffeehouse beverage, minus the specialized equipment.

- 1/2 cup milk
- 1/3 cup hot brewed Easy Espresso (recipe follows)

1) Place milk in a 1-cup microwave-safe measuring cup. Microwave, uncovered, on high for 1 minute or until milk is hot and small bubbles form around edge of cup.

2) Place a metal whisk in cup; whisk vigorously by holding whisk handle loosely between palms and quickly rubbing hands back and forth. Remove

CINNAMON MOCHA COFFEE

foam to a small measuring cup as it forms. Continue whisking until foam measures 1/3 cup; set aside.

3) Pour Easy Espresso into a mug; pour in remaining hot milk. Spoon foam over top and serve immediately.

Yield: 1 serving.

Editor's Note: You may also use a portable mixer with whisk attachment to froth the milk.

NUTRITION FACTS: 1 cup equals 76 calories, 4 g fat (3 g saturated fat), 17 mg cholesterol, 61 mg sodium, 6 g carbohydrate, 0 fiber, 4 g protein.

Easy Espresso
PREP/TOTAL TIME: 10 min.

Taste of Home Test Kitchen

Capture the classic taste of espresso without the hassle of expensive brewing equipment! For best flavor, serve espresso immediately. Pour leftover espresso in ice cube trays and freeze to use later in cold drinks.

- 1/2 cup ground coffee (French *or* other dark roast)
- 1-1/2 cups cold water

Lemon twists, optional

1) Place ground coffee in the filter of a drip coffeemaker. Add water; brew according to manufacturer's instructions. Serve immediately in espresso cups with lemon twists if desired.

Yield: 4 servings.

Editor's Note: This recipe was tested with Starbucks French Roast ground coffee.

NUTRITION FACTS: 1/3 cup equals 7 calories, trace fat (0 saturated fat), 0 cholesterol, 7 mg sodium, 1 g carbohydrate, 0 fiber, trace protein.

IRISH COFFEE

1-1/3 cups fat-free milk
Sugar substitute equivalent
  to 2 teaspoons sugar
  2/3 cup hot strong brewed coffee
Ground cinnamon *or* baking cocoa,
  optional

1) In a small saucepan, combine milk and sugar substitute. Whisk over medium heat until foamy and steaming (do not boil).

2) Slowly pour into mugs. Pour coffee through the foam. Sprinkle with cinnamon or cocoa if desired.

Yield: 2 servings.

Editor's Note: This recipe was tested with Splenda No Calorie Sweetener.

NUTRITION FACTS: 1 cup equals 61 calories, 1 g fat (1 g saturated fat), 3 mg cholesterol, 86 mg sodium, 9 g carbohydrate, 0 fiber, 6 g protein.

Tea

Tea is available in loose leaves or tea bags and in a variety of types—black, green and oolong—and blends. A good cup of tea starts with fresh cold water and your favorite tea blend.

For tea bags, bring water to a rolling boil and pour over the tea bag in a cup or small pot and let steep (stand) for 3 to 5 minutes depending on the blend of tea. Remove and discard the tea bag after steeping so the tea does not become bitter.

For loose leaf tea, warm the tea pot with warm water; add 1 round teaspoon of tea leaves for each 6-ounce cup. Pour boiling water over tea leaves and steep. Again, it is best if leaves are removed and discarded or the tea is strained and poured into another pot.

If stored properly, tea will stay fresh from 1-1/2 to 2 years. Moisture, temperature, light and odors will affect the quality of the tea. So it is best to store tea in an airtight container that keeps light out. Keep the container in a cool dry place. And store different types of teas separately to prevent flavors from mingling.

Sweet Spiced Tea
PREP: 15 min. **COOK:** 20 min.

Taste of Home Test Kitchen

Welcome guests in from the cold with this honey-laden hot tea. Regular tea can be used with equally good results.

  3 cinnamon sticks (3 inches)
  2 orange peel strips (1 to 3 inches)
 12 whole cloves
 12 whole allspice
  3 quarts water
 12 orange-flavored black tea bags
2/3 cup honey

Irish Coffee
PREP/TOTAL TIME: 10 min.

Taste of Home Test Kitchen

Creme de menthe adds a colorful touch to the cream. But made without, the coffee still lives up to its reputation as a relaxing after-dinner drink.

  2 teaspoons sugar
  2 ounces Irish whiskey
  2 cups hot strong-brewed coffee
    (French *or* other dark roast)
1/4 cup heavy whipping cream
  1 teaspoon green creme de menthe

1) Divide sugar and whiskey between two mugs; stir in coffee. In a small chilled mixing bowl, beat cream and creme de menthe until thickened. Gently spoon onto tops of drinks, allowing cream to float. Serve immediately.

Yield: 2 servings.

Editor's Note: You may also use a portable mixer with whisk attachment to thicken the cream mixture in a 1-cup measuring cup.

NUTRITION FACTS: 1 cup equals 203 calories, 11 g fat (7 g saturated fat), 41 mg cholesterol, 21 mg sodium, 8 g carbohydrate, 0 fiber, 1 g protein.

Stovetop Latte
PREP/TOTAL TIME: 10 min.

Delores Ward, Decatur, Indiana

Skip the trip to the trendy coffee shop and brew this good-for-you version of latte in the comfort of your own home. It's a great winter warm-up!

1 tablespoon lemon juice
Orange slices, optional

1) Place the cinnamon sticks, orange peel, cloves and allspice on a double thickness of cheesecloth. Bring up corners of cloth; tie with string to form a bag. Place water and spice bag in a large kettle or Dutch oven; bring to a boil. Remove from the heat. Add tea bags; cover and steep for 5 minutes. Discard tea bags.

2) Add honey and lemon juice to tea; bring to a boil. Discard spice bag. Serve tea in mugs. Garnish with orange slices if desired.

Yield: 3 quarts.

NUTRITION FACTS: 1 cup equals 61 calories, 0 fat (0 saturated fat), 0 cholesterol, 1 mg sodium, 16 g carbohydrate, trace fiber, trace protein.

BREWED ICED TEA IN MINUTES ∎∎∎

To make iced tea in a hurry, I put two family-size tea bags in the basket of my automatic drip coffee maker. I prepare the tea like I was making coffee. When it's done, I add sugar, cold water and ice to suit our tastes. It's terrific on sticky summer days.

—Mary P., Bedford, Pennsylvania

Raspberry Iced Tea
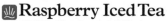

PREP: 10 min. + chilling

Lois McGrady, Hillsville, Virginia

I like to serve this beverage on hot summer days over raspberry ice cubes.

    4 quarts water
1-1/2 cups sugar
    1 package (12 ounces) frozen unsweetened raspberries
   10 individual tea bags
  1/4 cup lemon juice

1) In a Dutch oven, bring water and sugar to a boil. Remove from the heat; stir until sugar is dissolved. Add the raspberries, tea bags and lemon juice. Cover and steep for 3 minutes.

2) Strain; discard berries and tea bags. Refrigerate until chilled. Serve over ice.

Yield: 16 servings (4 quarts).

Editor's Note: To make fruited ice cubes, see Garnishes for Beverages on page 56.

NUTRITION FACTS: 1 cup equals 83 calories, trace fat (0 saturated fat), 0 cholesterol, 1 mg sodium, 21 g carbohydrate, 1 g fiber, trace protein.

∎ **Touch-of-Mint Iced Tea:** Bring 2 quarts of water to a boil. Steep 5 individual tea bags for 5 minutes and discard; cool for 15 minutes. Add 1-1/3 cups packed fresh mint and steep for 5 minutes. Strain tea and stir in 1 cup lemonade concentrate. Refrigerate until chilled. Serve over ice. Makes about 2 quarts.

RASPBERRY ICED TEA

Summertime Fruit Tea

PREP/TOTAL TIME: 15 min.

Rosalee Dixon, Sardis, Mississippi

Pineapple-orange juice gives ordinary iced tea a refreshing citrus flavor.

  12 cups water, *divided*
1-1/2 cups sugar
   9 individual tea bags
   1 can (12 ounces) frozen lemonade concentrate, thawed
   1 can (12 ounces) frozen pineapple-orange juice concentrate, thawed

1) In a Dutch oven, bring 4 cups water to a boil. Stir in sugar until dissolved. Remove from the heat; add tea bags.

2) Steep for 5-8 minutes. Discard tea bags. Stir in juice concentrates and remaining water. Serve over ice.

Yield: 3-1/2 quarts.

NUTRITION FACTS: 1 cup equals 173 calories, trace fat (trace saturated fat), 0 cholesterol, 15 mg sodium, 44 g carbohydrate, trace fiber, trace protein.

Making a Spice Bag

Keep spices together so they can be removed from a saucepan or Dutch oven by placing them on several layers of cotton cheesecloth that have been cut into 3-in. squares. Bring up corners of cloth and tie with kitchen string to form a bag.

CHAI

1/2 teaspoon vanilla extract
1/4 cup whipped cream
Ground cinnamon, optional

1) In a small saucepan, mix the cocoa and sugar; add water and stir until smooth. Bring to a boil, stirring constantly. Boil for 1 minute. Reduce heat; stir in milk and heat through.

2) Remove from the heat and stir in vanilla. Pour into 2 cups; top with whipped cream and sprinkle with cinnamon if desired.

Yield: 2 servings.

NUTRITION FACTS: 1 cup equals 235 calories, 10 g fat (6 g saturated fat), 39 mg cholesterol, 129 mg sodium, 28 g carbohydrate, 1 g fiber, 9 g protein.

■ **Maple Hot Chocolate:** Omit whipped cream and cinnamon. Add 1 tablespoon butter to cocoa mixture before bringing it to a boil. Add 3 large marshmallows with the milk and heat until marshmallows are melted. Add 1/2 teaspoon maple flavoring with the vanilla. Pour into mugs and top with additional marshmallows.

■ **Cozy Hot Mocha:** Reduce milk to 1 cup. Add 1 cup strong-brewed coffee. Proceed as directed.

Mulled Cider

PREP: 5 min. **COOK:** 30 min.

Taste of Home Test Kitchen

This is a classic warmer-upper that you can serve on chilly winter days. You can pass the brandy separately for those adults who want it.

   3 cinnamon sticks (3 inches)
   3 whole cloves
   2 whole allspice
   1 bay leaf
   3 quarts apple cider *or* apple juice
1/4 cup orange juice
1/4 cup lemon juice
   1 tablespoon grated orange peel
   2 tablespoons brown sugar
Dash salt
   1 to 1-1/2 cups brandy, optional

1) Place the cinnamon stick, cloves, allspice and bay leaf on a double thickness of cheesecloth; bring up corners of cloth and tie with kitchen string to form a bag.

2) In a large saucepan, combine the apple cider, juices, orange peel, brown sugar, salt and spice bag. Bring to a boil. Reduce heat to medium-low; simmer, uncovered, for 30 minutes to blend flavors.

3) Discard spice bag. Strain cider mixture and stir in brandy if desired. Serve immediately.

Yield: 13 servings (about 3 quarts).

NUTRITION FACTS: 1 cup (calculated without brandy) equals 122 calories, 0 fat (0 saturated fat), 0 cholesterol, 35 mg sodium, 31 g carbohydrate, trace fiber, trace protein.

Chai

PREP/TOTAL TIME: 25 min.

Terese Block, Waukesha, Wisconsin

Chai (rhymes with "pie") is a spiced milk tea that's becoming more popular. This recipe is just as tasty as any coffeehouse chai I've tried.

   2 cups water
   2 individual tea bags
   1 cinnamon stick
   6 cardamom seeds, crushed
   1 whole clove
1/4 teaspoon ground ginger
2-1/2 cups milk
1/3 cup sugar
Sweetened whipped cream, ground cinnamon and cinnamon sticks, optional

1) In a small saucepan, combine the first six ingredients. Bring to a boil. Reduce heat; cover and simmer for 5 minutes.

2) Stir in milk. Return to a boil; boil for 1 minute, then strain. Stir in sugar until dissolved. Top with whipped cream, sprinkle with cinnamon and garnish with a cinnamon stick if desired.

Yield: 4 servings.

NUTRITION FACTS: 1 cup equals 159 calories, 5 g fat (3 g saturated fat), 21 mg cholesterol, 75 mg sodium, 24 g carbohydrate, trace fiber, 5 g protein.

Cozy Hot Chocolate

PREP/TOTAL TIME: 10 min.

Marie Hattrup, Moro, Oregon

This mixes up a perfect mugful for two. If maple is your favorite flavor, try that as well.

   2 tablespoons baking cocoa
   2 tablespoons sugar
1/4 cup water
   2 cups milk

feeding las vegas

Church packs free lunch & breakfast for homeless

The Brown Baggers

> *It's in our hearts, and we just show up. We feel touched that we can do something to help.*
>
> ~Kay Fine

Even in Las Vegas, someone is watching out for those whose luck has gone bad.

Volunteers arrive at the First Presbyterian Church hall at 8 a.m. on the last Saturday of every month to make 450 brown bag breakfasts and lunches to hand out to the area's homeless.

Each of the Brown Baggers, as they're called, brings one or two dozen hard-boiled eggs and two or three dozen cookies, preferably homemade. Then they get to work assembling sandwiches and stuffing paper bags.

"This terrific group of dedicated people has such a good time as they busily perform their tasks," says Kay Fine, a deacon at the church. "We feel blessed by the camaraderie. And those of us who do it feel dedicated to it. At least 20 to 25 of the 30 volunteers have come every month for 5 years now."

The 200 breakfast bags usually include a hard-cooked egg, breakfast bar, applesauce and juice. The 250 brown bag lunches are typically filled with a peanut butter and jelly sandwich, fresh carrots, applesauce, chips and a few homemade cookies. All 450 bags have an illustrated Bible verse in English and Spanish enclosed. Each bag is accompanied by a bottle of water.

Beth More, also a deacon, often uses *Taste of Home* recipes to make the cookies she brings, Kay notes. Her favorite recipe is Almond Chocolate Cookies from *Taste of Home*, but her Chocolate Drop Cookies are also quite popular.

When all the sandwiches are made and all the bags are packed, group members head to an area in Las Vegas known as "the zone" near the Salvation Army, where a large population of homeless is found. The lunches are handed out to those who line up for them, while the breakfast bags are delivered to Amazing Grace ministry, which distributes them the next morning during its Sunday sermon.

The meals are well received by those in line. "They're always very polite, very thankful," says Kay.

"We love to do this. There's not a one of us who ever misses it if we have any choice. It's in our hearts, and we just show up. We feel touched that we can do something to help—even if it's not much. It is truly a wonderful way to be Christ's hands here in our own little corner of the globe."

You can find some of Beth's recipes in the Web exclusive online at tasteofhome.com/CookbookBonus **Type in access code ICare**

taste of home
cooks who care

DO YOU KNOW A COOK WHO CARES?
If you or someone you know cooks for a charitable, spiritual or other cause, tell us about it at **tasteofhome.com/CookbookBonus**

Recipes

Tips

SOUPS & SANDWICHES

Soups & Sandwiches

Soups are versatile and can satisfy many menu-planning needs. Use a light broth or a cream-based soup as a first course. A full-bodied bean or a loaded chicken vegetable soup just needs a crisp salad or a hearty bread to complete the meal. Or just a cupful is a perfect accompaniment to a sandwich or salad.

Useful Definitions

The following terms are specific to this chapter. You can also refer to the Glossary (pages 24-28).

Bisque: A thick, rich pureed soup often made with seafood but may be made with poultry or vegetables.

Broth: Made from simmering meats, poultry, fish or vegetables, broths have less body than stocks. Broths and stocks may be used interchangeably for the recipes in this book.

Chili: A hearty dish usually made with tomatoes and chili powder, but some chili dishes are white. The variations on chili seem endless. A chili can be mild or hot, have ground beef, stew meat, sausage, poultry or be meatless. It may have macaroni or spaghetti or no pasta at all.

Chowder: A chunky, thick, rich soup frequently made with seafood or vegetables, such as corn, but it can be made with other meat. Chowders have a milk or cream base and may be thickened with flour.

Consommé: A completely degreased, clarified stock. It has a rich flavor, and due to its high gelatin content, will set up when chilled.

Creamed Soups: Pureed soups with a smooth, silky texture. The main flavor is frequently a single vegetable, such as asparagus or carrot. They may be thickened with flour or potatoes and can be made without cream.

Gazpacho: An uncooked cold soup. The most common version uses tomatoes, cucumbers, sweet peppers, onion and garlic.

Gumbo: A hearty stew-like soup usually served with white rice that starts with a dark roux (see page 84) of flour and oil or butter. It may contain shellfish, chicken, sausage, ham, tomatoes, onions, garlic, sweet peppers and celery. In addition to the roux, okra is used as a thickening agent.

Stocks: Usually made with meaty bones (possibly roasted), meat and vegetables. Stock should be clear, be free of grease and have a subtle flavor.

Making Stocks, Broths & Soups

Start making a stock with cold water. Just cover the bones, meat and/or vegetables with water. Add seasonings but do not salt (add salt, if necessary, after cooking). Bring slowly to a boil over low heat. Using a ladle, skim foam from the top of liquid. If water evaporates, add enough additional water to cover the bones, meat and/or vegetables. Skim fat or remove solidified fat after chilling. Strain stock; divide among several containers. Place containers in an ice bath to cool quickly. When chilled, refrigerate or freeze.

Add little or no salt, as well as other flavors, when making stock since it concentrates as it simmers and the liquid evaporates. Taste the soup when it is just about ready to be served and add enough salt to suit your family's preferences.

Add a pinch of turmeric or simmer an unpeeled whole yellow onion in the cooking liquid for golden homemade chicken and turkey broths.

Store soups in the refrigerator for up to 3 days. If there is rice or pasta in the soup, you may want to cook and store them separately, since they may continue to absorb the liquid.

Many broth-based soups freeze well for up to 3 months. Thaw in the refrigerator before reheating. It's best not to freeze soups prepared with potatoes, fruit, cheese, sour cream, yogurt, eggs, milk or cream.

Making Chicken Stock and Soup

1) Remove the excess fat from the cut-up chicken. In a kettle or Dutch oven, combine chicken, vegetables, cold water and seasonings.

2) Bring to a boil over low heat. Skim foam as it rises to the top of the water. Reduce heat; cover and simmer until the chicken is tender, about 1 hour.

3) Remove chicken; let stand until cool enough to handle. Remove chicken from bones; discard skin and bones. Dice chicken; use immediately or cover and refrigerate. Chill broth several hours or overnight; lift fat from surface of broth and discard.

4) Bring soup to a boil; add noodles. Cook until tender. Stir in reserved chicken; heat through.

Straining Stock or Broth

Remove meat and bones from stock. Line a colander with a double thickness of cheesecloth; place in a large heat-resistant bowl. Pour stock into colander. Discard vegetables, seasonings and cheesecloth. For a clear stock or broth, do not press liquid from vegetables and seasonings in the colander.

Chicken Broth

PREP: 25 min. **COOK:** 1-1/2 hours

Nila Grahl, Gurnee, Illinois

Whether you're making a chicken soup or just a broth to use in other dishes, this recipe makes a tasty base for most anything.

 1 broiler/fryer chicken (3 to 4 pounds), cut up
10 cups water
 1 large carrot, sliced
 1 large onion, sliced
 1 celery rib, sliced
 1 garlic clove, minced
 1 bay leaf
 1 teaspoon dried thyme
 1 teaspoon salt
1/4 teaspoon pepper

1) In a large soup kettle or Dutch oven, combine all the ingredients. Slowly bring to a boil over low heat. Cover and simmer for 45-60 minutes or until the meat is tender, skimming the surface as foam rises.

2) Remove chicken and set aside until cool enough to handle. Remove and discard skin and bones. Chop chicken; set aside for soup or save for another use.

3) Strain broth through a cheesecloth-lined colander, discarding vegetables and bay leaf. If using immediately, skim fat or refrigerate for 8 hours or overnight, then remove fat from surface. Broth can be covered and refrigerated for up to 3 days or frozen for 4 to 6 months.

Yield: about 2 quarts.

NUTRITION FACTS: 1 cup equals 105 calories, 5 g fat (1 g saturated fat), 33 mg cholesterol, 331 mg sodium, 3 g carbohydrate, 1 g fiber, 11 g protein.

■ **Chicken Noodle Soup:** Place broth in a large saucepan or Dutch oven. Add 2 sliced large carrots, 2 sliced celery ribs and 1 chopped onion. Bring to a boil. Reduce heat; cover and simmer for 10 minutes or until the vegetables are tender. Add 2 cups uncooked fine egg noodles and reserved chicken. Bring to a boil. Reduce heat; cover and simmer for 6 minutes. Stir in 1 cup frozen peas and 1/2 cup frozen cut beans; cook for 2-4 minutes or until beans and noodles are tender.

■ **Chicken Soup with Spaetzle:** Prepare Chicken Noodle Soup as directed, omitting the noodles, peas and beans. With the carrots, add 1 minced garlic clove. With the chicken, add 2 cups sliced fresh mushrooms. For spaetzle, combine 1-1/4 cups all-purpose flour, and 1/8 teaspoon *each* baking powder and salt. Stir in 1 beaten egg and 1/4 cup *each* water and milk until blended. Drop batter by 1/2 teaspoonfuls onto boiling soup. Cook, uncovered, 10 minutes or until spaetzle float.

BETTER CHICKEN NOODLE SOUP ■■■

When I make my favorite chicken noodle soup, I find it tastes better if I refrigerate the soup without the noodles. When it's time to serve, I add the noodles to the amount of soup I'm going to use and cook them until tender.

—Martha D., Nineveh, Indiana

Vegetable Broth

PREP: 45 min. **COOK:** 1-3/4 hours

Taste of Home Test Kitchen

The flavors of celery and mushrooms came through in this vegetable broth. Use it in place of chicken or beef broth.

- 2 tablespoons olive oil
- 2 medium onions, cut into wedges
- 2 celery ribs, cut into 1-inch pieces
- 1 whole garlic bulb, separated into cloves and peeled
- 3 medium leeks, white and light green parts only, cleaned and cut into 1-inch pieces
- 3 medium carrots, cut into 1-inch pieces
- 8 cups water
- 1/2 pound fresh mushrooms, quartered
- 1 cup packed fresh parsley sprigs
- 4 sprigs fresh thyme
- 1 teaspoon salt
- 1/2 teaspoon whole peppercorns
- 1 bay leaf

1) Heat oil in a stockpot over medium heat until hot. Add the onions, celery and garlic. Cook and stir for 5 minutes or until tender. Add leeks and carrots; cook and stir 5 minutes longer. Add the water, mushrooms, parsley, thyme, salt, peppercorns and bay leaf; bring to a boil. Reduce heat; simmer, uncovered, for 1 hour.

2) Remove from the heat. Strain through a cheesecloth-lined colander; discard vegetables. If using immediately, skim fat or refrigerate for 8 hours or overnight, then remove fat from surface. Broth can be covered and refrigerated for up to 3 days or frozen for up to 4 to 6 months.

Yield: 5-1/2 cups.

NUTRITION FACTS: 1 cup equals 148 calories, 6 g fat (1 g saturated fat), 0 cholesterol, 521 mg sodium, 22 g carbohydrate, 5 g fiber, 4 g protein.

Homemade Beef Broth

PREP: 25 min. **COOK:** 5-1/2 hours

Taste of Home Test Kitchen

Roasting the soup bones gives this soup base a delicious beefy flavor.

- 4 pounds meaty beef soup bones (beef shanks *or* short ribs)
- 3 medium carrots, cut into chunks
- 3 celery ribs, cut into chunks
- 2 medium onions, quartered
- 1/2 cup warm water
- 3 bay leaves
- 3 garlic cloves
- 8 to 10 whole peppercorns
- 3 to 4 sprigs fresh parsley
- 1 teaspoon *each* dried thyme, marjoram and oregano
- 3 quarts cold water

1) Place soup bones in a large roasting pan. Bake, uncovered, at 450° for 30 minutes. Add the carrots, celery and onions. Bake 30 minutes longer; drain fat.

2) Using a slotted spoon, transfer bones and vegetables to a large Dutch oven. Add warm water to the roasting pan; stir to loosen browned bits from pan. Transfer pan juices to kettle. Add seasonings and enough cold water just to cover.

3) Slowly bring to a boil, about 30 minutes. Reduce heat; simmer, uncovered, for 4-5 hours, skimming the surface as foam rises. If necessary, add hot water during the first 2 hours to keep ingredients covered.

4) Remove beef bones and set aside until cool enough to handle. If desired, remove meat from bones; discard bones and save meat for another use. Strain broth through a cheesecloth-lined colander, discarding vegetables and seasonings.

5) If using immediately, skim fat or refrigerate for 8 hours or overnight, then remove fat from surface. Broth can be covered and refrigerated for up to 3 days or frozen for 4 to 6 months.

Yield: about 2-1/2 quarts.

NUTRITION FACTS: 1 cup equals 209 calories, 10 g fat (4 g saturated fat), 56 mg cholesterol, 61 mg sodium, 6 g carbohydrate, 2 g fiber, 22 g protein.

Lightening Up Soups

It's easy to bring smile-fetching soup to the front burner of a food-smart meal plan. Keep the following secrets in mind when you're lightening up your soup du jour.

Skip the salt—Set down the salt shaker and stir in additional herbs or a salt-free seasoning blend into your soup instead. When recipes call for canned chicken broth, substitute the reduced-sodium variety.

Thin thickeners—Watching your weight doesn't mean writing off creamy soups. Puree a cooked peeled potato and reduced-fat milk or fat-free half-and-half to a creamy consistency. Slowly stir the mixture into the heated soup to thicken it. Then heat through, but do not boil. To thicken southwestern soups and chili, add pureed cooked beans.

Cut back on beef—Try preparing a recipe with additional vegetables or pasta in place of beef. Or, consider replacing beef with cooked poultry now and again.

TIMELESS TURKEY SOUP

 CLASSIC: Danish Turkey Dumpling Soup is truly a from-scratch recipe. It brings water and a turkey carcass to a slow simmer to create a homemade broth, which is then enhanced with fresh veggies. It's topped with egg dumplings, then served. If you like, dice some cooked turkey and add to the soup before you cook the dumplings.

 TIME-SAVER: Cooked turkey is combined with canned chicken broth and pumpkin for an interesting flavor twist in Tuscan Turkey Soup. Though it tastes like it simmered all day, it can be on the table in just 30 minutes.

 LIGHT: Fewer than 100 calories per serving makes Old-Fashioned Turkey Soup the choice for calorie-counters. It starts with a homemade broth and lots of vegetables. Store leftovers in the freezer to enjoy later.

 SERVES 2: Several vegetables and spiral pasta add substance to Chunky Turkey Vegetable Soup. Since it calls for a small amount of fresh vegetables you're likely to have on hand, such as potato, carrot, celery and onion, there's no worry about what to do with leftover canned veggies.

DANISH TURKEY DUMPLING SOUP

Danish Turkey Dumpling Soup

PREP: 35 min. **COOK:** 3 hours

Karen Sue Garback-Pristera, Albany, New York

- 1 leftover turkey carcass (from a 12- to 14-pound turkey)
- 9 cups water
- 3 teaspoons chicken bouillon granules
- 1 bay leaf
- 1 can (14-1/2 ounces) stewed tomatoes, cut up
- 1 medium turnip, peeled and diced
- 2 celery ribs, chopped
- 1 medium onion, chopped
- 1 medium carrot, chopped
- 1/4 cup minced fresh parsley
- 1 teaspoon salt

DUMPLINGS:

- 1/2 cup water
- 1/4 cup butter, cubed
- 1/2 cup all-purpose flour
- 1 teaspoon baking powder
- 1/8 teaspoon salt
- 2 eggs
- 1 tablespoon minced fresh parsley

1) Place the turkey carcass, water, bouillon and bay leaf in a Dutch oven or soup kettle; slowly bring to a boil over low heat. Reduce heat; cover and simmer for 1-1/2 hours.

2) Remove carcass and set aside until cool enough to handle. Remove and discard bones. Chop turkey; set aside for soup.

3) Strain the broth through a cheesecloth-lined colander; disard bay leaf and cheesecloth. If using immediately, skim fat or refrigerate for 8 hours or overnight, then remove fat from surface. Stock may be refrigerated for up to 3 days or frozen for 4 to 6 months.

4) Return strained broth to pan. Add the tomatoes, vegetables, parsley, salt and reserved turkey. Bring to a boil. Reduce heat; cover and simmer for 25-30 minutes or until vegetables are crisp-tender.

5) For dumplings, in a large saucepan, bring water and butter to a boil. Combine the flour, baking powder and salt; add all at once to pan and stir until a smooth ball forms. Remove from heat; let stand for 5 minutes. Add eggs, one at a time, beating well after each addition. Continue beating until mixture is smooth and shiny. Stir in parsley.

6) Drop batter in 12 mounds onto simmering soup. Cover and simmer for 20 minutes or until a toothpick inserted in a dumpling comes out clean (do not lift cover while simmering).

Yield: 6 servings (about 2 quarts).

NUTRITION FACTS: 1-1/2 cups equals 221 calories, 11 g fat (6 g saturated fat), 122 mg cholesterol, 1,197 mg sodium, 19 g carbohydrate, 2 g fiber, 11 g protein.

Tuscan Turkey Soup

PREP/TOTAL TIME: 30 min.

Marie McConnell, Shelbyville, Illinois

- 1 cup chopped onion
- 1 cup chopped celery
- 1 teaspoon minced garlic
- 2 tablespoons olive oil
- 2 cans (14-1/2 ounces *each*) chicken broth
- 2 cups cubed cooked turkey
- 1 can (15 ounces) solid-pack pumpkin
- 1 can (15 ounces) white kidney *or* cannellini beans, rinsed and drained
- 1/2 teaspoon salt
- 1/2 teaspoon dried basil
- 1/4 teaspoon pepper

Grated Parmesan cheese, optional

1) In a large saucepan, saute the onion, celery and garlic in oil until tender.

2) Stir in the broth, turkey, pumpkin, beans, salt, basil and pepper. Bring to a boil. Reduce heat; simmer, uncovered, for 10-15 minutes or until heated through, stirring occasionally. Serve with Parmesan cheese if desired.

Yield: 8 servings (2 quarts).

NUTRITION FACTS: 1 cup (calculated without Parmesan cheese) equals 166 calories, 6 g fat (1 g saturated fat), 29 mg cholesterol, 698 mg sodium, 14 g carbohydrate, 5 g fiber, 14 g protein.

Old-Fashioned Turkey Soup

PREP: 25 min. **COOK:** 2-3/4 hours

Linda Sand, Winsted, Connecticut

- 1 leftover turkey carcass (from a 12-pound turkey)
- 5 quarts water

SOUP:

- 3 cups cubed cooked turkey
- 1 can (28 ounces) stewed tomatoes
- 1 large onion, chopped
- 2 large carrots, shredded
- 1 cup chopped celery
- 1 package (10 ounces) frozen chopped spinach, thawed
- 3/4 cup fresh *or* frozen peas
- 3/4 cup uncooked long grain rice
- 4 chicken bouillon cubes
- 2 teaspoons salt
- 3/4 teaspoon pepper
- 1/2 teaspoon dried marjoram
- 1/2 teaspoon dried thyme

1) Place the turkey carcass and water in a Dutch oven or soup kettle; slowly bring to a boil over low heat. Cover and simmer for 1-1/2 hours.

2) Remove carcass and discard. Strain the broth through a cheesecloth-lined colander. If using immediately, skim fat or refrigerate for 8 hours or overnight, then remove fat from surface. Stock may be refrigerated for up to 3 days or frozen for 4 to 6 months.

3) For soup, return strained broth to pan. Add the turkey, vegetables, rice, bouillon and seasonings; bring to a boil. Reduce heat; cover and simmer for 30 minutes or until rice and vegetables are tender.

Yield: 22 servings (5-1/2 quarts).

NUTRITION FACTS: 1 cup equals 96 calories, 2 g fat (1 g saturated fat), 23 mg cholesterol, 522 mg sodium, 11 g carbohydrate, 2 g fiber, 9 g protein.

■ **Turkey Barley Soup:** Prepare stock as directed in steps 1 and 2 above. For soup, omit stewed tomatoes and rice. Bring stock to a boil; add 1 cup uncooked medium pearl barley. Reduce heat; cover and simmer for 30 minutes. Add remaining ingredients. Cook, uncovered, for 20-25 minutes or until barley and vegetables are tender.

Chunky Turkey Vegetable Soup

PREP/TOTAL TIME: 25 min.

Suzanne Fawkes, Cameron, Missouri

- 3 cups cups turkey *or* chicken broth
- 1/2 cup frozen baby lima beans, thawed
- 1/3 cup cubed peeled potato
- 1/3 cup sliced carrot
- 1/3 cup sliced celery
- 2 tablespoons chopped onion
- 3/4 cup cubed cooked turkey *or* chicken
- 1/2 cup cooked spiral pasta
- 1 tablespoon minced fresh parsley

1) In a large saucepan, combine the broth, lima beans, potato, carrot, celery and onion. Bring to a boil. Reduce heat; cover and cook for 15 minutes or until vegetables are tender.

2) Add turkey and pasta; cook until heated through. Stir in parsley.

Yield: 2 servings.

Editor's Note: If your family does not care for lima beans, use white kidney beans or black beans.

NUTRITION FACTS: 1-1/2 cups equals 242 calories, 3 g fat (1 g saturated fat), 51 mg cholesterol, 284 mg sodium, 27 g carbohydrate, 4 g fiber, 25 g protein.

Italian Wedding Soup

PREP: 20 min. **COOK:** 15 min.

Nancy Ducharme, Deltona, Florida

This soup always satisfies! I add cooked pasta at the end of the cooking time to keep it from getting mushy.

- 1 egg
- 3/4 cup grated Parmesan *or* Romano cheese
- 1/2 cup dry bread crumbs
- 1 small onion, chopped
- 3/4 teaspoon salt, *divided*
- 1-1/4 teaspoons garlic powder, *divided*
- 1-1/4 teaspoons pepper, *divided*
- 2 pounds ground beef
- 2 quarts chicken broth
- 1/3 cup chopped fresh spinach
- 1 teaspoon onion powder
- 1 teaspoon dried parsley flakes
- 1-1/4 cups cooked medium pasta shells

1) In a large bowl, combine the egg, cheese, bread crumbs, onion, 1/4 teaspoon salt, 1/4 teaspoon garlic powder and 1/4 teaspoon pepper. Crumble beef over mixture; mix well. Shape into 1-in. balls.

2) In a Dutch oven, brown meatballs in small batches; drain. Add the broth, spinach, onion powder, parsley and remaining salt, pepper and garlic powder; bring to a boil. Reduce heat; simmer, uncovered, for 5 minutes. Stir in pasta; heat through.

Yield: 12 servings (3 quarts).

NUTRITION FACTS: 1 cup equals 226 calories, 12 g fat (5 g saturated fat), 72 mg cholesterol, 942 mg sodium, 9 g carbohydrate, trace fiber, 20 g protein.

French Onion Soup

PREP: 30 min. **COOK:** 30 min.

Lise Thomson, Magrath, Alberta

My version of onion soup has a slightly sweet flavor that makes it unique.

- 6 cups thinly sliced onions
- 1 tablespoon sugar
- 1/2 teaspoon pepper
- 1/3 cup vegetable oil
- 6 cups beef broth
- 8 slices French bread (3/4 inch thick), toasted
- 1/2 cup shredded Parmesan *or* Swiss cheese

1) In a Dutch oven, cook the onions, sugar and pepper in oil over medium low heat for 20 minutes or until onions are caramelized, stirring frequently. Add the broth; bring to a boil. Reduce heat; cover and simmer for 30 minutes.

2) Ladle soup into ovenproof bowls. Top each with a slice of French bread; sprinkle with cheese. Broil

FRENCH ONION SOUP

4-6 in. from heat until cheese is melted. Serve immediately.

Yield: 8 servings (2 quarts).

NUTRITION FACTS: 1 cup equals 330 calories, 13 g fat (3 g saturated fat), 4 mg cholesterol, 1,092 mg sodium, 43 g carbohydrate, 4 g fiber, 10 g protein.

Beef Barley Soup

PREP: 10 min. **COOK:** 2 hours 20 min.

Ellen McCleary, Scotland, Ontario

I came across this recipe years ago at a recipe exchange through a church group. The contributor didn't sign her name, so I don't know who to thank. But my husband and son thank me for preparing it by helping themselves to seconds and thirds!

- 1-1/2 pounds ground beef
- 1 medium onion, chopped
- 3 celery ribs, sliced
- 3 cans (10-1/2 ounces *each*) condensed beef consomme, undiluted
- 1 can (28 ounces) diced tomatoes, undrained
- 4 medium carrots, sliced
- 2 cups water
- 1 can (10-3/4 ounces) condensed tomato soup, undiluted
- 1/2 cup medium pearl barley
- 1 bay leaf

1) In a Dutch oven or soup kettle, cook the beef, onion and celery over medium heat until the meat is no longer pink; drain.

2) Add the remaining ingredients; bring to a boil. Reduce heat; simmer, uncovered, for 2 hours or until barley is tender. Discard bay leaf.

Yield: 12 servings (3 quarts).

NUTRITION FACTS: 1 serving equals 168 calories, 5 g fat (2 g saturated fat), 29 mg cholesterol, 452 mg sodium, 17 g carbohydrate, 4 g fiber, 13 g protein.

Ravioli Soup

PREP: 20 min. **COOK:** 45 min.

Shelley Way, Cheyenne, Wyoming

So fast and easy to make, this soup always hits the spot.

- 1 pound ground beef
- 2 cups water
- 1 can (28 ounces) crushed tomatoes, undrained
- 1 can (14-1/2 ounces) crushed tomatoes, undrained
- 1 can (6 ounces) tomato paste
- 1-1/2 cups chopped onions
- 1/4 cup minced fresh parsley
- 2 garlic cloves, minced
- 3/4 teaspoon dried basil
- 1/2 teaspoon dried oregano
- 1/2 teaspoon onion salt
- 1/2 teaspoon sugar
- 1/2 teaspoon salt
- 1/4 teaspoon pepper
- 1/4 teaspoon dried thyme
- 1 package (9 ounces) refrigerated cheese ravioli
- 1/4 cup grated Parmesan cheese

1) In a Dutch oven, cook beef over medium heat until no longer pink; drain. Add the next 14 ingredients; bring to a boil. Reduce heat; cover and simmer for 30 minutes.

2) Meanwhile, cook ravioli according to package directions; drain. Add to soup and heat through. Stir in the Parmesan cheese. Serve immediately.

Yield: 10 servings (2-1/2 quarts).

NUTRITION FACTS: 1 cup equals 235 calories, 8 g fat (4 g saturated fat), 42 mg cholesterol, 542 mg sodium, 25 g carbohydrate, 4 g fiber, 17 g protein.

Hearty Split Pea Soup

PREP: 15 min. **COOK:** 1-1/2 hours

Barbara Link, Rancho Cucamonga, California

For a different spin on split pea soup, try this recipe. The flavor is peppery rather than smoky.

HEARTY SPLIT PEA SOUP

- 1 package (16 ounces) dried split peas
- 8 cups water
- 2 medium potatoes, peeled and cubed
- 2 large onions, chopped
- 2 medium carrots, chopped
- 2 cups cubed fully cooked lean ham or cooked corned beef
- 1/2 cup chopped celery
- 5 teaspoons reduced-sodium chicken bouillon granules
- 1 teaspoon dried marjoram
- 1 teaspoon poultry seasoning
- 1 teaspoon rubbed sage
- 1/2 to 1 teaspoon pepper
- 1/2 teaspoon dried basil

1) In a Dutch oven or soup kettle, combine all ingredients; bring to a boil. Reduce heat; cover and simmer for 1-1/4 to 1-1/2 hours or until peas and vegetables are tender.

Yield: 12 servings (3 quarts).

NUTRITION FACTS: 1/2 cup equals 198 calories, 2 g fat (trace saturated fat), 9 mg cholesterol, 440 mg sodium, 32 g carbohydrate, 11 g fiber, 15 g protein.

Lentil Soup

PREP: 10 min. **COOK:** 1-1/4 hours

Joyce Pyra, North Battleford, Saskatchewan

This is a great soup because it can be easily doubled. Try it topped with shredded cheddar cheese.

- 1 cup dried lentils, rinsed
- 6 cups chicken broth
- 2 cups chopped onions
- 1 garlic clove, minced
- 1 tablespoon vegetable oil
- 2-1/2 cups chopped fresh tomatoes
- 1 cup sliced carrots
- 1/2 teaspoon dried thyme
- 1/4 teaspoon dried marjoram

1) In a large saucepan, bring lentils and chicken broth to a boil. Reduce heat; cover and simmer for 30 minutes.

2) Meanwhile, in a large skillet, saute onions and garlic in oil; add to saucepan. Add the tomatoes, carrots, thyme and marjoram. Cook 30 minutes longer or until lentils and vegetables are tender.

Yield: about 8 servings (2 quarts).

NUTRITION FACTS: 1 cup equals 142 calories, 3 g fat (trace saturated fat), 0 cholesterol, 712 mg sodium, 22 g carbohydrate, 9 g fiber, 9 g protein.

SPICE UP YOUR LENTIL SOUP ■■■

I spice up my lentil soup by substituting salsa for half of the tomatoes.

—Myriam P., Sandwich, New Hampshire

STICK-TO-YOUR-RIBS BEAN SOUP

 CLASSIC: Ham and Bean Soup uses dried beans and ham to make a delicious and economical soup. It's a classic combination your family will love!

 TIME-SAVER: Three types of canned beans as well as seasoned canned broth hurry along Southwestern Bean Soup. Its quick prep makes it ideal for weeknight dining.

 LIGHT: Herbed Black Bean Soup brings the sodium down by cooking the dried beans in reduced-sodium chicken broth and using salt-free seasoning blend and no-salt-added tomato paste. It's a good choice for those watching their sodium intake.

 SERVES 2: A rich and satisfying soup, White Bean Bisque gets its zip from cayenne pepper, garlic and Italian sausage. One individual Italian sausage link with the casing removed will do for the amount of sausage listed in the recipe.

HAM AND BEAN SOUP

Ham and Bean Soup

PREP: 30 min. + soaking **COOK:** 1-1/2 hours

Amanda Reed, Milford, Delaware

I learned to make this soup when we lived in Pennsylvania near several Amish families. It's a great way to use up ham and mashed potatoes. It freezes well, too.

- 1 pound dried navy beans
- 2 medium onions, chopped
- 2 teaspoons vegetable oil
- 2 celery ribs, chopped
- 10 cups water
- 4 cups cubed fully cooked ham
- 1 cup mashed potatoes (without added milk and butter)
- 1/2 cup shredded carrot
- 2 tablespoons Worcestershire sauce
- 1 teaspoon salt
- 1/2 teaspoon dried thyme
- 1/2 teaspoon pepper
- 2 bay leaves
- 1 meaty ham bone *or* 2 smoked ham hocks
- 1/4 cup minced fresh parsley

1) Place beans in a Dutch oven or soup kettle; add water to cover by 2 in. Bring to a boil; boil for 2 minutes. Remove from the heat; cover and let stand for 1 to 4 hours or until beans are softened. Drain and rinse beans, discarding liquid.

2) In the same pan, saute onions in oil for 2 minutes. Add celery; cook until tender. Stir in the beans, water, ham, potatoes, carrot, Worcestershire sauce, salt, thyme, pepper and bay leaves. Add ham bone. Bring to a boil. Reduce heat; cover and simmer for 1-1/4 to 1-1/2 hours or until beans are tender. Discard bay leaves.

3) Remove ham bone; and set aside until cool enough to handle. Remove ham from bone and cut into cubes. Discard bone. Return ham to soup. Garnish soup with parsley.

Yield: 15 servings (3-3/4 quarts).

NUTRITION FACTS: 1 cup equals 213 calories, 6 g fat (2 g saturated fat), 27 mg cholesterol, 675 mg sodium, 25 g carbohydrate, 6 g fiber, 15 g protein.

Southwestern Bean Soup

PREP/TOTAL TIME: 25 min.

Jackie Hacker, Seville, Ohio

- 1 large onion, chopped
- 1 teaspoon vegetable oil
- 2 cans (15 ounces *each*) black beans, rinsed and drained
- 2 cans (14-1/2 ounces *each*) diced tomatoes with garlic and onion
- 2 cans (14-1/2 ounces *each*) chicken *or* vegetable broth
- 1 can (16 ounces) kidney beans, rinsed and drained
- 1 can (15 ounces) cannellini *or* white kidney beans, rinsed and drained
- 1-1/2 cups fresh *or* frozen corn
- 4 garlic cloves, minced
- 1-1/2 teaspoons ground cumin
- 1-1/2 teaspoons chili powder
- 1/8 to 1/4 teaspoon hot pepper sauce

1) In a Dutch oven or soup kettle, saute the onion in oil until tender. Stir in the remaining ingredients;

bring to a boil. Reduce heat; simmer, uncovered, for 5 minutes or until heated through.

Yield: 12 servings (3 quarts).

NUTRITION FACTS: 1 cup equals 129 calories, 1 g fat (trace saturated fat), 0 cholesterol, 481 mg sodium, 24 g carbohydrate, 6 g fiber, 7 g protein.

Herbed Black Bean Soup

PREP: 30 min. + soaking **COOK:** 2 hours

Audrey Thibodeau, Gilbert, Arizona

- 1 pound dried black beans
- 6 cups reduced-sodium chicken broth
- 4 cups water
- 1-1/2 cups chopped onions
- 1 cup thinly sliced celery
- 1 large carrot, chopped
- 1/2 cup *each* chopped green, sweet red and yellow peppers
- 2 garlic cloves, minced
- 3 tablespoons olive oil
- 1/4 cup no-salt-added tomato paste
- 3 tablespoons minced fresh parsley
- 1 tablespoon chopped fresh oregano *or* 1 teaspoon dried oregano
- 1 tablespoon minced fresh thyme *or* 1 teaspoon dried thyme
- 1-1/2 teaspoons ground cumin
- 1 teaspoon pepper
- 3/4 teaspoon salt-free seasoning blend
- 3 bay leaves

1) Place beans in a Dutch oven or soup kettle; add water to cover by 2 in. Bring to a boil; boil for 2 minutes. Remove from the heat; cover and let stand for 1 to 4 hours or until beans are softened. Drain and rinse beans, discarding liquid.

2) Return beans to pan; add broth and water. Bring to a boil. Reduce heat; cover and simmer for 1 hour or until the beans are almost tender. Meanwhile, in a large skillet, saute the onions, celery, carrot, peppers and garlic in oil until tender.

3) Add the tomato paste, herbs and seasonings to the bean mixture. Add the sauteed vegetables; bring to a boil. Reduce heat; cover and simmer for 1 hour or until beans are tender. Discard bay leaves.

Yield: 12 servings (3 quarts).

NUTRITION FACTS: 1 cup equals 203 calories, 4 g fat (0 saturated fat), 2 mg cholesterol, 77 mg sodium, 31 g carbohydrate, 5 g fiber, 10 g protein.

White Bean Bisque

PREP: 15 min. **COOK:** 20 min.

Linda Miranda, Wakefield, Rhode Island

- 1/4 cup shredded Parmesan cheese

Cayenne pepper

- 1/4 pound Italian turkey sausage links
- 2 tablespoons chopped onion
- 1 teaspoon olive oil
- 1 garlic clove, minced
- 1 can (15 ounces) white kidney *or* cannellini beans, rinsed and drained
- 1 cup reduced-sodium chicken broth
- 1/4 cup heavy whipping cream
- 2 teaspoons sherry, optional
- 1 teaspoon minced fresh parsley
- 1/8 teaspoon salt
- 1/8 teaspoon dried thyme

1) Spoon Parmesan cheese into six mounds 3 in. apart on a parchment paper-lined baking sheet. Spread into 1-1/2-in. circles. Sprinkle with a dash of cayenne. Bake at 400° for 5-6 minutes or until light golden brown. Cool.

2) In a saucepan, cook sausage and onion in oil over medium heat until meat is no longer pink; drain. Remove and keep warm.

3) In the same pan, saute garlic for 1-2 minutes or until tender. Stir in the beans, broth, cream, sherry if desired, parsley, salt, thyme and a dash of cayenne. Bring to a boil. Reduce heat; simmer, uncovered, for 12-15 minutes or until heated through. Cool slightly.

4) Transfer to a blender; cover and process on high until almost blended. Pour into soup bowls; sprinkle with sausage mixture and Parmesan crisps.

Yield: 2 servings.

NUTRITION FACTS: 1 cup equals 425 calories, 22 g fat (10 g saturated fat), 82 mg cholesterol, 1,218 mg sodium, 33 g carbohydrate, 8 g fiber, 23 g protein.

Preparing Dried Beans for Cooking

Soak dried beans such as navy, great northern, pinto and kidney beans before cooking. There are two methods for soaking beans—the quick soaking method, which takes a little over an hour, and the overnight method. See instructions for both methods in the Beans & Grains chapter on page 345.

WHITE BEAN BISQUE

Southern Garden Soup

PREP/TOTAL TIME: 30 min.

Leslie Owens, Poplar Bluff, Missouri

Filled with garden-fresh flavors of cauliflower, asparagus and spinach, this soup is my favorite way to use up summer's produce.

12-1/4	cups water, *divided*
1/2	cup pearl onions
5	chicken bouillon cubes
2	cups cauliflowerets
2	pounds fresh asparagus, cut into 1/2-inch pieces
1	can (8 ounces) sliced water chestnuts, drained
1	cup chopped fresh spinach
1/2	cup chopped chives
1/2	teaspoon dried marjoram
1/2	teaspoon salt
1/8 to 1/4	teaspoon pepper
1/8	teaspoon ground nutmeg
3	tablespoons cornstarch

1) In a Dutch oven, bring 6 cups water to a boil. Add pearl onions; boil for 3 minutes. Drain and rinse in cold water; peel and set aside.

2) In a 3-qt. saucepan, bring 6 cups water and bouillon to a boil. Add cauliflower and onions; cover and cook for 5 minutes. Add the asparagus, water chestnuts, spinach and seasonings; cover and cook for 5 minutes or until asparagus is tender.

3) Combine cornstarch and remaining water until smooth; stir into soup. Bring to a boil; cook and stir for 2 minutes or until thickened. Serve immediately.

Yield: 9 servings (2-1/4 quarts).

NUTRITION FACTS: 1 cup equals 58 calories, 1 g fat (trace saturated fat), trace cholesterol, 770 mg sodium, 11 g carbohydrate, 2 g fiber, 3 g protein.

Gazpacho

PREP: 15 min. + chilling

Robynn Shannon, Alexandria, Virginia

Nothing equals the taste of an ice-cold bowl of gazpacho on a hot summer day. This soup is a wonderful way to use up homegrown tomatoes.

3	cups chopped seeded peeled fresh tomatoes
2	celery ribs, finely chopped
1	medium green pepper, finely chopped
1	medium cucumber, peeled, seeded and finely chopped
1/4	cup minced fresh parsley
1	tablespoon minced chives
1	green onion, thinly sliced
1	garlic clove, minced

GAZPACHO

1	can (46 ounces) tomato juice
1/3	cup red wine vinegar
1/4	cup olive oil
1	teaspoon salt
1/2	teaspoon Worcestershire sauce
1/2	teaspoon pepper

Seasoned croutons

1) In a large bowl, combine the tomatoes, celery, green pepper, cucumber, parsley, chives, onion, garlic, tomato juice, vinegar, oil, salt, Worcestershire sauce and pepper.

2) Cover and refrigerate for several hours or overnight. Garnish each serving with croutons.

Yield: 10 servings (2-1/2 quarts).

NUTRITION FACTS: 1 cup (calculated without croutons) equals 94 calories, 6 g fat (1 g saturated fat), 0 cholesterol, 757 mg sodium, 11 g carbohydrate, 2 g fiber, 2 g protein.

Roasted Tomato Soup

PREP: 70 min. **COOK:** 15 min.

Kriss Erickson, Kalauea, Hawaii

The big fresh tomato taste of this savory soup makes it a great first course. You can enjoy it hot or chilled.

3	pounds tomatoes
1/3	cup olive oil, *divided*
6	garlic cloves, minced
2	tablespoons chopped fresh thyme *or* 2 teaspoons dried thyme
2	cups chopped onion
1/4	cup minced fresh basil *or* 1 tablespoon dried basil
1	can (14-1/2 ounces) chicken broth
1/2	cup half-and-half cream

Salt and pepper to taste

1) Core tomatoes; place in a roasting pan. Drizzle with 1/4 cup oil; sprinkle with garlic and thyme. Bake, uncovered, at 350° for 1 hour, turning occasionally.

2) In a large saucepan, saute onion in remaining oil until softened. Add roasted tomatoes and basil;

cook for 5 minutes. Add broth; bring to a boil. Cook and stir for 5 minutes.

3) Put through a sieve or food mill; return puree to pan. In a small saucepan over medium-low heat, warm half-and-half (do not boil). Stir the half-and-half, salt and pepper into soup.

Yield: 4-6 servings.

NUTRITION FACTS: 1 cup equals 211 calories, 15 g fat (3 g saturated fat), 10 mg cholesterol, 304 mg sodium, 17 g carbohydrate, 4 g fiber, 4 g protein.

BEEFY TOMATO SOUP ■■■

After browning 1/2 pound of ground beef in a Dutch oven, I turn it into a speedy soup. I add two cans of tomato soup diluted with milk and 1 cup of cooked macaroni. I also like to sprinkle in some parsley flakes for additional color.

—Wilma Wood, Milton, Wisconsin

Cream of Butternut Soup

PREP: 35 min. **COOK:** 30 min.

Shelly Snyder, Lafayette, Colorado

Ginger, turmeric, cinnamon and a little sherry do an incredible job of seasoning this slightly sweet soup. After I lightened up this recipe I received from a friend in South Africa, it quickly became a family favorite.

- 1 cup chopped onion
- 2 celery ribs, chopped
- 2 tablespoons butter
- 2 cans (14-1/2 ounces *each*) reduced-sodium chicken broth
- 1 teaspoon sugar
- 1 bay leaf
- 1/2 teaspoon salt
- 1/2 teaspoon ground ginger
- 1/2 teaspoon ground turmeric
- 1/4 teaspoon ground cinnamon
- 1 butternut squash (2-1/2 pounds), peeled and cubed
- 3 medium potatoes, peeled and cubed

CREAM OF BUTTERNUT SOUP

- 1-1/2 cups 1% milk
- 2 tablespoons sherry *or* additional reduced-sodium chicken broth

1) In a large saucepan coated with cooking spray, cook onion and celery in butter until tender. Stir in the broth, sugar, bay leaf, salt, ginger, turmeric and cinnamon.

2) Add the squash and potatoes. Bring to a boil. Reduce the heat; cover and simmer for 15-20 minutes or until vegetables are tender.

3) Remove from the heat; cool slightly. Discard bay leaf. In a blender, puree vegetable mixture in batches. Return to the pan. Stir in milk and sherry or broth; heat through (do not boil).

Yield: 8 servings.

NUTRITION FACTS: 1-1/4 cups equals 159 calories, 4 g fat (2 g saturated fat), 9 mg cholesterol, 487 mg sodium, 29 g carbohydrate, 6 g fiber, 5 g protein.

Cream of Carrot Soup

PREP: 15 min. **COOK:** 20 min. + cooling

Ruth Andrewson, Leavenworth, Washington

This rich, yummy soup is versatile, too. You can substitute most any vegetable with excellent results. For a quick garnish, top with some shredded fresh carrot.

- 4 cups chicken broth
- 4 large carrots, cut into chunks
- 1/2 cup heavy whipping cream
- 1 teaspoon sugar

1) In a large saucepan, bring broth and carrots to a boil. Reduce heat; simmer, uncovered, for 15 minutes or until carrots are tender. Cool for 10 minutes.

2) In a blender, cover and process soup in small batches until smooth; return to the pan. Stir in cream and sugar; heat through.

Yield: 5 servings.

NUTRITION FACTS: 1 cup equals 122 calories, 9 g fat (5 g saturated fat), 33 mg cholesterol, 773 mg sodium, 8 g carbohydrate, 2 g fiber, 3 g protein.

■ **Cream of Asparagus Soup:** Substitute 1-1/2 pounds fresh asparagus for the carrots. Cut asparagus into 1-in. pieces. Simmer for 5-7 minutes or until tender.

■ **Cream of Broccoli Soup:** Substitute 3 cups chopped fresh broccoli for the carrots. Simmer 7-10 minutes or until tender.

■ **Cream of Cauliflower Soup:** Substitute 3 cups cauliflower florets for the carrots. Simmer for 7-10 minutes or until tender.

Garnishes for Soups

Dress up a soup with a sprinkle of nuts, chopped fresh herbs, sliced green onions, slivers of fresh vegetables, croutons, shredded cheese or crumbled bacon.

TRIED-AND-TRUE MINESTRONE

 CLASSIC: Tomatoes, carrots and cabbage simmered slowly in beef broth give this Italian-favorite Minestrone a fabulous blend of flavors. Beans, pasta and ground beef are added to make it both family-pleasing and filling.

 TIME-SAVER: Pesto Minestrone makes quick use of canned vegetable broth, refrigerated tortellini and prepared pesto. This uniquely flavored minestrone is ready in 30 minutes.

 LIGHT: Calories and fat are cut in Turkey Minestrone by using lean ground turkey instead of ground beef. Italian turkey sausage spices it up a bit.

 SERVES 2: For smaller households, Simple Minestrone simmers to a perfect 3-cup yield. Pantry staples, including canned broth, canned tomatoes and dried herbs, make it easy to prepare.

MINESTRONE

Minestrone
PREP: 20 min. **COOK:** 1-1/2 hours
Virginia Bauer, Wapakoneta, Ohio
- 2 cups coarsely chopped onions
- 1 cup sliced celery
- 1/4 cup minced fresh parsley
- 2 garlic cloves, minced
- 1/4 cup vegetable oil
- 5 cups beef broth
- 2 cups chopped tomatoes *or* 1 can (14-1/2 ounces) diced tomatoes, drained
- 1 can (15 ounces) tomato sauce
- 2 cups coarsely chopped cabbage
- 1 cup sliced fresh carrots
- 2 teaspoons dried basil *or* Italian seasoning
- 1/2 teaspoon salt
- 1/4 teaspoon pepper
- 1-1/2 pounds ground beef
- 1-1/2 cups sliced zucchini

- 1 cup cut fresh green beans
- 1 can (16 ounces) kidney beans, rinsed and drained
- 1 can (15 ounces) garbanzo beans *or* chickpeas, rinsed and drained
- 1 cup uncooked ditalini *or* 4 ounces spaghetti, broken into 3-inch pieces
- 1 cup grated Parmesan cheese

1) In an 8-qt. soup kettle, saute the onions, celery, parsley and garlic in oil until tender. Stir in the broth, tomatoes, tomato sauce, cabbage, carrots, basil, salt and pepper. Bring to a boil. Reduce heat; cover and simmer for 1 hour.

2) In a large skillet, cook beef over medium heat until no longer pink; drain and set aside. Stir into soup along with the zucchini, beans and pasta. Cover and simmer for 15 to 20 minutes or until the vegetables and pasta are tender. Top each serving with Parmesan cheese.

Yield: 20 servings (5 quarts).

NUTRITION FACTS: 1 cup equals 209 calories, 9 g fat (3 g saturated fat), 26 mg cholesterol, 538 mg sodium, 19 g carbohydrate, 4 g fiber, 14 g protein.

Pesto Minestrone
PREP/TOTAL TIME: 30 min.
Natalie Cataldo, Des Moines, Iowa
- 1/2 cup chopped onion
- 1 teaspoon minced garlic
- 2 teaspoons olive oil
- 2-1/4 cups water
- 2 cups frozen mixed vegetables
- 1 can (14-1/2 ounces) vegetable broth
- 3/4 teaspoon dried oregano
- 1/2 teaspoon salt
- 1/2 teaspoon pepper
- 1 package (9 ounces) refrigerated cheese tortellini
- 2 cups diced zucchini
- 2 tablespoons prepared pesto

1) In a large saucepan, saute onion and garlic in oil until tender. Stir in the water, mixed vegetables, broth, oregano, salt and pepper. Bring to a boil. Reduce heat; cover and simmer for 3 minutes.

2) Add the tortellini, zucchini and pesto. Simmer, uncovered, 6-8 minutes longer or until pasta and vegetables are tender.

Yield: 4 servings.

NUTRITION FACTS: 1 cup equals 337 calories, 12 g fat (4 g saturated fat), 30 mg cholesterol, 1,063 mg sodium, 47 g carbohydrate, 7 g fiber, 15 g protein.

Turkey Minestrone
PREP/TOTAL TIME: 30 min.

Betty Christensen, Victoria, British Columbia

- 2/3 cup chopped onion
- 2 tablespoons canola oil
- 1/2 pound lean ground turkey
- 1/2 pound hot Italian turkey sausage links, casings removed
- 1/2 cup minced fresh parsley
- 2 garlic cloves, minced
- 1 teaspoon dried oregano
- 1 teaspoon dried basil
- 2 cans (14-1/2 ounces *each*) Italian stewed tomatoes
- 6 cups chicken broth
- 1 medium zucchini, sliced
- 1 package (10 ounces) frozen mixed vegetables
- 1 can (16 ounces) kidney beans, rinsed and drained
- 1-1/2 cups cooked elbow macaroni
- 2 tablespoons cider vinegar
- 1/2 teaspoon salt, optional

Pinch pepper

1) In a large kettle over medium heat, saute onion in oil until tender, about 4 minutes. Add the next six ingredients; cook over medium heat until meat is no longer pink.

2) Add the tomatoes, broth, zucchini and mixed vegetables; cover and cook over on low heat for 5 minutes. Add the beans, macaroni, vinegar, salt if desired and pepper; simmer for 3-4 minutes or until heated through.

Yield: 16 servings (4 quarts).

NUTRITION FACTS: 1 cup equals 132 calories, 4 g fat (1 g saturated fat), 20 mg cholesterol, 538 mg sodium, 15 g carbohydrate, 3 g fiber, 9 g protein.

Simple Minestrone
PREP: 15 min. COOK: 35 min.

Regina Cook, Fort Worth, Texas

- 1 bacon strip, diced
- 1/3 cup smoked turkey kielbasa, quartered

SIMPLE MINESTRONE

- 1 small onion, chopped
- 1 garlic clove, minced
- 1/4 cup chopped carrot
- 2 tablespoons chopped celery
- 1 cup reduced-sodium chicken broth
- 1 cup canned diced tomatoes, undrained
- 1 can (5-1/2 ounces) reduced-sodium tomato juice
- 1/4 cup chopped zucchini
- 1/2 teaspoon dried basil
- 1/4 teaspoon dried oregano
- 1/8 teaspoon pepper
- 1/3 cup canned pinto beans, rinsed and drained
- 1/4 cup cooked elbow macaroni
- 1 tablespoon grated Parmesan cheese

1) In a large saucepan, cook bacon over medium heat until crisp. Using a slotted spoon, remove to paper towel. In the drippings, saute the sausage, onion and garlic for 3 minutes. Stir in the carrot and celery. Cook and stir 2 minutes longer or until sausage is lightly browned; drain.

2) Stir in the broth, tomatoes, tomato juice, zucchini and seasonings. Bring to a boil. Reduce heat; cover and simmer for 10 minutes or until vegetables are tender. Stir in the beans and macaroni; heat through. Sprinkle with Parmesan cheese and bacon.

Yield: 2 servings.

NUTRITION FACTS: 1-1/2 cups equals 267 calories, 9 g fat (3 g saturated fat), 45 mg cholesterol, 1,256 mg sodium, 28 g carbohydrate, 6 g fiber, 18 g protein.

MONTEREY JACK CHEESE SOUP

Monterey Jack Cheese Soup

PREP/TOTAL TIME: 30 min.

Susan Salenski, Copemish, Michigan

Main-meal soups are something I'm always on the lookout for. I love cheese, and our kids like anything with Mexican flavor. Serve it with tacos, nachos or a loaf of bread.

> 1   cup chicken broth
> 1   large tomato, peeled, seeded and diced
> 1/2 cup finely chopped onion
> 2   tablespoons chopped green chilies
> 1   garlic clove, minced
> 2   tablespoons butter
> 2   tablespoons all-purpose flour
> Salt and pepper to taste
> 3   cups milk, *divided*
> 1-1/2 cups (6 ounces) shredded Monterey Jack cheese

1) In a 3-qt. saucepan, combine the broth, tomato, onion, chilies and garlic; bring to a boil. Reduce heat; cover and simmer for 10 minutes or until vegetables are tender. Remove from the heat and set aside.

2) In another saucepan, melt butter. Stir in the flour, salt and pepper until smooth; gradually stir in 1-1/2 cups milk. Bring to a boil; cook and stir for 1 minute or until thickened.

3) Slowly stir into vegetable mixture. Reduce heat; add cheese and remaining milk. Cook and stir over low heat until cheese is melted. Serve immediately.

Yield: 5 servings.

NUTRITION FACTS: 1 cup (calculated without salt and pepper) equals 286 calories, 20 g fat (12 g saturated fat), 62 mg cholesterol, 503 mg sodium, 13 g carbohydrate, 1 g fiber, 14 g protein.

Southwestern Corn Chowder

PREP: 20 min. **COOK:** 25 min.

Nancy Winters, Moorpark, California

This chowder gets a little spice from picante sauce.

> 4   boneless skinless chicken breast halves, cut into 3/4-inch cubes
> 1   medium onion, cut into thin wedges
> 1   tablespoon vegetable oil
> 2   teaspoons ground cumin
> 2   cans (14-1/2 ounces *each*) chicken broth
> 1   package (10 ounces) frozen corn
> 3/4 cup picante sauce
> 1/2 cup chopped sweet red pepper
> 1/2 cup chopped green pepper
> 2   tablespoons minced fresh cilantro
> 2   tablespoons cornstarch
> 2   tablespoons water
> Shredded Monterey Jack cheese, optional

1) In a 3-qt. saucepan, cook chicken and onion in oil until chicken juices run clear. Stir in cumin. Add broth, corn and picante sauce; bring to a boil. Reduce heat; cover and simmer for 15 minutes. Stir in peppers and cilantro.

2) Combine cornstarch and water until smooth; stir into soup. Bring to a boil; cook and stir for 2 minutes or until slightly thickened. Spoon into bowls; top with cheese if desired.

Yield: 7 servings (about 2 quarts).

NUTRITION FACTS: 1 cup (calculated without cheese) equals 164 calories, 4 g fat (1 g saturated fat), 36 mg cholesterol, 611 mg sodium, 16 g carbohydrate, 2 g fiber, 16 g protein.

Manhattan Clam Chowder

PREP: 10 min. **COOK:** 45 min.

Joan Hopewell, Columbus, New Jersey

This chowder also cooks up wonderfully in a slow cooker. Just add all the ingredients and let it cook all day.

> 1   cup chopped onion
> 2/3 cup chopped celery
> 2   teaspoons minced green pepper
> 1   garlic clove, minced
> 2   tablespoons butter
> 2   cups hot water
> 1   cup cubed peeled potatoes
> 1   can (28 ounces) diced tomatoes, undrained
> 2   cans (6-1/2 ounces *each*) minced clams, undrained
> 1   teaspoon salt
> 1/2 teaspoon dried thyme
> 1/4 teaspoon pepper
> Dash cayenne pepper
> 2   teaspoons minced fresh parsley

1) In a 3-qt. saucepan, cook the onion, celery, green pepper and garlic in butter over low heat for 20 minutes, stirring frequently.

2) Add water and potatoes; bring to a boil. Reduce heat; cover and simmer for 15 minutes or until potatoes are tender.

3) Add the tomatoes, clams, salt, thyme, pepper and cayenne; heat through. Stir in parsley. Serve immediately.

Yield: 6-8 servings (about 2 quarts).

NUTRITION FACTS: 1 cup equals 91 calories, 3 g fat (2 g saturated fat), 15 mg cholesterol, 652 mg sodium, 13 g carbohydrate, 3 g fiber, 5 g protein.

New England Fish Chowder
PREP: 25 min. **COOK:** 40 min.

Dorothy Noonan, Quincy, Massachusetts

Adjust the flavor of this soup by adding a bay leaf or dried thyme to the water when cooking the potatoes (then discard the bay leaf). Servings can also be garnished with chopped fresh parsley or crumbled cooked bacon.

1-1/2 cups sliced onions
   4 tablespoons butter, *divided*
1-1/2 cups water
   3 medium potatoes, peeled and diced
1-1/4 teaspoons salt
1/2 teaspoon pepper
   2 tablespoons all-purpose flour
1-1/4 cups milk
   1 can (12 ounces) evaporated milk
   1 pound fresh *or* frozen haddock fillets, cut into large chunks

1) In a large saucepan, saute onions in 2 tablespoons butter. Add the water, potatoes, salt and pepper. Bring to a boil. Reduce heat; cover and simmer for 25 minutes or until potatoes are tender.

2) Combine the flour and milk until smooth. Stir into potato mixture along with evaporated milk. Add fish and the remaining butter; bring to a boil. Reduce heat; cook 5-10 minutes longer or until fish is opaque.

Yield: 8 servings (2 quarts).

NUTRITION FACTS: 1 cup equals 262 calories, 11 g fat (7 g saturated fat), 68 mg cholesterol, 534 mg sodium, 24 g carbohydrate, 2 g fiber, 17 g protein.

■ **New England Salmon Chowder:** Omit haddock and add 1 pound fresh *or* frozen salmon cut into chunks. To use 1 pound canned salmon, remove the skin and bones; add to the soup along with milk.

■ **New England Clam Chowder:** Omit the haddock and add two cans (6-1/2 ounces each) drained chopped clams along with the milk. For a stronger clam flavor, substitute 1 bottle (8 ounces) clam juice for 1 cup of the water.

MEXICAN SHRIMP BISQUE

Mexican Shrimp Bisque
PREP/TOTAL TIME: 30 min.

Karen Harris, Castle Rock, Colorado

I enjoy both Cajun and Mexican cuisine, and this rich, elegant soup combines the best of both. I serve it with a crispy green salad and glass of white wine for a simple but very special meal.

1/2 cup chopped onion
   2 garlic cloves, minced
   1 tablespoon olive oil
   1 tablespoon all-purpose flour
   1 cup water
1/2 cup heavy whipping cream
   1 tablespoon chili powder
   2 teaspoons sodium-free chicken bouillon granules
1/2 teaspoon ground cumin
1/2 teaspoon ground coriander
1/2 pound uncooked medium shrimp, peeled and deveined
1/2 cup sour cream
Fresh cilantro and cubed avocado, optional

1) In a large saucepan, saute onion and garlic in oil until tender. Stir in flour until blended. Stir in the water, cream, chili powder, bouillon, cumin and coriander; bring to a boil. Reduce heat; cover and simmer for 5 minutes.

2) Cut shrimp into bite-size pieces; add to soup. Simmer 5 minutes longer or until shrimp turn pink. Gradually stir 1/2 cup hot soup into sour cream; return all to the pan, stirring constantly. Heat through (do not boil). Garnish with cilantro and avocado if desired.

Yield: 3 cups.

NUTRITION FACTS: 1 cup equals 327 calories, 24 g fat (12 g saturated fat), 180 mg cholesterol, 199 mg sodium, 12 g carbohydrate, 2 g fiber, 17 g protein.

FLAVORFUL, FILLING GUMBOS

 CLASSIC: The base of Louisiana Gumbo is homemade chicken broth. It gets added flavor with a traditional brown roux. Loaded with fresh vegetables, meat, shrimp and seasonings, it is a hearty soup. The broth can be made one day and the gumbo can be finished the next day.

 TIME-SAVER: In contrast to the Louisiana Gumbo recipe, the short ingredient list and easy prep of Gumbo in a Jiffy assures this dish is on the table in 20 minutes. This recipe makes good use of canned broth, canned tomatoes with green peppers and onion, and instant rice.

 LIGHT: Sausage, ham and chicken not only lend great flavor to Louisiana Gumbo, unfortunately they add calories, cholesterol and sodium, too. Southern Seafood Gumbo lowers these levels, making a more heart-smart version, by substituting catfish for the sausage, ham and chicken.

 SERVES 2: Ham and Chicken Gumbo makes about 2 cups, so it is perfectly portioned for two people. It uses cooked chicken and ham—a great use of leftovers. This recipe omits the sausage and shrimp to keep the yield small.

LOUISIANA GUMBO

Louisiana Gumbo

PREP: 20 min. **COOK:** 2-1/4 hours

Gloria Mason, Springhill, Louisiana

- 1 broiler/fryer chicken (3 to 3-1/2 pounds), cut up
- 2 quarts water
- 3/4 cup all-purpose flour
- 1/2 cup vegetable oil
- 1/2 cup sliced green onions
- 1/2 cup chopped onion
- 1/2 cup chopped green pepper
- 1/2 cup chopped sweet red pepper
- 1/2 cup chopped celery
- 2 garlic cloves, minced
- 1/2 pound fully cooked smoked sausage, cut into 1-inch cubes
- 1/2 pound fully cooked ham, cut into 3/4-inch cubes
- 1/2 pound uncooked medium fresh *or* frozen shrimp, thawed, peeled and deveined
- 1 cup cut fresh *or* frozen okra (3/4-inch pieces)

- 1 can (16 ounces) kidney beans, rinsed and drained
- 1/2 teaspoon salt
- 1/4 teaspoon pepper
- 1/4 teaspoon hot pepper sauce
- 6 cups hot cooked rice

1) Place the chicken and water in a Dutch oven. Slowly bring to a boil. Reduce heat; cover and simmer 45-60 minutes or until chicken is tender, skimming the surface as foam rises.

2) Remove chicken and set aside until cool enough to handle. Remove and discard skin and bones. Cut chicken into bite-size pieces.

3) Strain the broth through a cheesecloth-lined colander; skim fat. Reserve 6 cups broth. Any remaining broth can be covered and refrigerated for up to 3 days or frozen for 4 to 6 months.

4) In a Dutch oven, combine flour and oil until smooth; cook and stir over medium-low heat for 2-3 minutes or until browned. Stir in the onions, peppers, celery and garlic; cook for 5 minutes or until vegetables are tender.

5) Stir in the sausage, ham and reserved broth and chicken. Bring to a boil. Reduce heat; cover and simmer for 45 minutes.

Browning a Roux

Thicken gravy and soup using a roux, which is a mixture of fat and flour. In a traditional gumbo, flour is added to the fat and heated until it reaches a reddish-brown color. It is important to stir while the mixture is browning.

6) Add the shrimp, okra, beans, salt, pepper and hot pepper sauce; cover and simmer 10 minutes longer or until shrimp is cooked. Spoon 1 cup gumbo into bowl and top with 1/2 cup rice.

Yield: 12 servings.

NUTRITION FACTS: 1 cup equals 473 calories, 22 g fat (6 g saturated fat), 94 mg cholesterol, 646 mg sodium, 38 g carbohydrate, 3 g fiber, 29 g protein.

Gumbo in a Jiffy
PREP/TOTAL TIME: 20 min.

Amy Flack, Homer City, Pennsylvania

- 3 Italian turkey sausage links, sliced
- 1 can (14-1/2 ounces) diced tomatoes with green peppers and onions, undrained
- 1 can (14-1/2 ounces) reduced-sodium chicken broth
- 1/2 cup water
- 1 cup uncooked instant rice
- 1 can (7 ounces) whole kernel corn, drained

1) In a large saucepan, cook sausage over medium heat until no longer pink; drain.

2) Stir in the tomatoes, broth and water; bring to a boil. Stir in rice and corn; cover and remove from the heat. Let stand for 5 minutes.

Yield: 6 servings.

NUTRITION FACTS: 1 cup equals 194 calories, 6 g fat (1 g saturated fat), 34 mg cholesterol, 888 mg sodium, 22 g carbohydrate, 2 g fiber, 12 g protein.

Southern Seafood Gumbo
PREP: 25 min. **COOK:** 35 min.

Susan Wright, Champaign, Illinois

- 1 medium onion, chopped
- 2 celery ribs with leaves, chopped
- 1 medium green pepper, chopped
- 3 garlic cloves, minced
- 1 tablespoon olive oil
- 1 bottle (46 ounces) spicy hot V8 juice
- 1 can (14-1/2 ounces) diced tomatoes, undrained
- 1/4 teaspoon cayenne pepper
- 1 package (16 ounces) frozen sliced okra, thawed
- 1 pound catfish fillets, cut into 3/4-inch cubes
- 3/4 pound uncooked medium shrimp, peeled and deveined
- 3 cups cooked long grain rice

1) In a large saucepan, saute the onion, celery, green pepper and garlic in oil until tender. Stir in the V8 juice, tomatoes and cayenne; bring to a boil. Reduce heat; cover and simmer for 10 minutes.

GUMBO IN A JIFFY

2) Stir in okra and catfish; cook 8 minutes longer. Add the shrimp; cook about 7 minutes longer or until shrimp turn pink. Place rice in individual serving bowls; top with gumbo.

Yield: 12 servings.

NUTRITION FACTS: 1 cup gumbo with 1/4 cup rice equals 180 calories, 5 g fat (1 g saturated fat), 60 mg cholesterol, 512 mg sodium, 22 g carbohydrate, 3 g fiber, 14 g protein.

Ham and Chicken Gumbo
PREP: 10 min. **COOK:** 45 min.

Jean Leonard, Houston, Texas

- 3 bacon strips, cut into 1/2-inch pieces
- 1/3 cup chopped onion
- 1 garlic clove, minced
- 1/2 cup cubed fully cooked ham
- 1/4 cup cubed cooked chicken
- 1 cup frozen sliced okra
- 1 can (8 ounces) diced tomatoes, undrained
- 1 cup chicken broth
- 1/2 teaspoon Worcestershire sauce
- 1/8 teaspoon salt
- 4 drops hot pepper sauce

Hot cooked rice

1) In a large skillet, cook bacon over medium heat just until crisp. Add onion and cook until bacon is crisp and onion is soft, stirring constantly. Add the garlic, ham and chicken; cook for 2 minutes, stirring constantly.

2) Stir in the okra, tomatoes and broth; bring to a boil. Reduce heat; cover and simmer for 30 minutes. Add the Worcestershire sauce, salt and hot pepper sauce. Serve over rice.

Yield: 2 servings.

NUTRITION FACTS: 1 cup (calculated without rice) equals 307 calories, 20 g fat (6 g saturated fat), 60 mg cholesterol, 1,548 mg sodium, 14 g carbohydrate, 4 g fiber, 19 g protein.

TUSCAN SOUP

◐Tuscan Soup

PREP/TOTAL TIME: 30 min.

Rosemary Goetz, Hudson, New York

This meatless soup can be prepared in a flash. It's perfect after working full-time outside the home.

- 1 small onion, chopped
- 1 small carrot, sliced
- 1 tablespoon olive oil
- 2 cans (14-1/2 ounces *each*) chicken broth
- 1 cup water
- 3/4 teaspoon salt
- 1/4 teaspoon pepper
- 1 can (15 to 16 ounces) white kidney *or* great northern beans, rinsed and drained
- 2/3 cup uncooked small spiral pasta
- 3 cups thinly sliced fresh escarole *or* spinach

1) In a 2-qt. saucepan, saute onion and carrot in oil until onion is tender. Add the broth, water, salt and pepper; bring to a boil. Stir in beans and pasta; return to a boil.

2) Reduce heat; cover and simmer for 15 minutes or until pasta and vegetables are tender, stirring occasionally. Add escarole; heat through.

Yield: 4 servings.

NUTRITION FACTS: 1 cup equals 196 calories, 5 g fat (1 g saturated fat), 0 cholesterol, 1,432 mg sodium, 30 g carbohydrate, 6 g fiber, 9 g protein.

Wild Rice Soup

PREP: 30 min. **COOK:** 1 hour

Elienore Myhre, Balaton, Minnesota

Wild rice has an intense, nutty flavor. It's delicious in this soup, and a small amount goes a long way in satisfying a hungry diner.

- 1/3 cup uncooked wild rice
- 1 tablespoon vegetable oil
- 1 quart water
- 1 medium onion, chopped
- 1 celery rib, finely chopped
- 1 medium carrot, finely chopped
- 1/2 cup butter
- 1/2 cup all-purpose flour
- 3 cups chicken broth
- 2 cups half-and-half cream
- 1/2 teaspoon dried rosemary, crushed
- 1 teaspoon salt

1) In a medium saucepan, combine the rice, oil and water; bring to a boil. Reduce heat; cover and simmer for 30 minutes.

2) Meanwhile, in a Dutch oven, cook the onion, celery and carrot in butter until vegetables are almost tender. Stir in flour until blended; cook and stir for 2 minutes. Slowly stir in broth and undrained rice. Bring to a boil; cook and stir for 2 minutes or until slightly thickened.

3) Reduce heat; stir in the cream, rosemary and salt. Simmer, uncovered, for about 20 minutes or until rice is tender.

Yield: 8 servings (about 2 quarts).

NUTRITION FACTS: 1 cup equals 270 calories, 19 g fat (11 g saturated fat), 61 mg cholesterol, 797 mg sodium, 17 g carbohydrate, 1 g fiber, 5 g protein.

Creamy White Chili

PREP: 10 min. **COOK:** 40 min.

Laura Brewer, Lafayette, Indiana

I got this wonderful recipe from my sister-in-law, who made a big batch and served a crowd one night. It was a hit. Plus, it's easy and quick.

- 1 pound boneless skinless chicken breasts, cut into 1/2-inch cubes
- 1 medium onion, chopped
- 1-1/2 teaspoons garlic powder
- 1 tablespoon vegetable oil
- 2 cans (15-1/2 ounces *each*) great northern beans, rinsed and drained
- 1 can (14-1/2 ounces) chicken broth
- 2 cans (4 ounces *each*) chopped green chilies
- 1 teaspoon salt
- 1 teaspoon ground cumin
- 1 teaspoon dried oregano

CREAMY WHITE CHILI

1/2 teaspoon pepper
1/4 teaspoon cayenne pepper
1 cup (8 ounces) sour cream
1/2 cup heavy whipping cream

1) In a large saucepan, saute chicken, onion and garlic powder in oil until chicken is no longer pink. Add the beans, broth, chilies and seasonings. Bring to a boil.

2) Reduce heat; simmer, uncovered, for 30 minutes. Remove from the heat; stir in sour cream and cream. Serve immediately.

Yield: 7 servings.

NUTRITION FACTS: 1 cup equals 334 calories, 16 g fat (8 g saturated fat), 81 mg cholesterol, 1,045 mg sodium, 24 g carbohydrate, 7 g fiber, 22 g protein.

Cincinnati Chili
PREP: 20 min. **COOK:** 1-3/4 hours
Edith Koritansky, Thompson, Ohio

Cinnamon and cocoa give a rich brown color to this hearty chili. One heaping dish will warm you up on a cold day.

1 pound ground beef
1 pound ground pork
4 medium onions, chopped
6 garlic cloves, minced
2 cans (16 ounces *each*) kidney beans, rinsed and drained
1 can (28 ounces) crushed tomatoes
1/4 cup white vinegar
1/4 cup baking cocoa
2 tablespoons chili powder
2 tablespoons Worcestershire sauce
4 teaspoons ground cinnamon
3 teaspoons dried oregano
2 teaspoons ground cumin
2 teaspoons ground allspice
2 teaspoons hot pepper sauce
3 bay leaves
1 teaspoon sugar
Salt and pepper to taste
Hot cooked spaghetti
Shredded cheddar cheese, sour cream, chopped tomatoes and green onions

1) In a Dutch oven or soup kettle, cook beef, pork, onions and garlic over medium heat until meat is no longer pink; drain.

2) Add the beans, tomatoes, vinegar, cocoa and seasonings; bring to a boil. Reduce heat; cover and simmer for 1-1/2 hours or until heated through.

3) Discard bay leaves. Serve over spaghetti. Garnish with cheese, sour cream, tomatoes and onions.

Yield: 8 servings.

NUTRITION FACTS: 1 cup (calculated without spaghetti, cheese, sour cream, tomatoes and green onions) equals 421 calories, 16 g fat (6 g saturated fat), 75 mg cholesterol, 443 mg sodium, 38 g carbohydrate, 11 g fiber, 32 g protein.

CINCINNATI CHILI

CHILL-CHASING CHILI

 CLASSIC: A combination of nine herbs and spices was the inspiration for its name, Spiced Chili. This recipe is versatile enough to be cooked in a slow cooker or simmered on the stovetop.

 TIME-SAVER: Jalapeno Pepper Chili gets its heat from two main seasonings—chili powder and jalapeno pepper. Extra flavor comes from canned tomatoes with garlic and onion. A minimum of chopping and measuring, plus a fast heating on the stovetop, makes this great for a busy day.

 LIGHT: Bulgur Chili creates the texture of ground beef with a good-for-you grain, bulgur. Your family won't even miss the meat. As an added benefit, this recipe uses reduced-sodium tomato juice.

 SERVES 2: Just 1/2 pound of ground beef is used to create two hearty servings of Chili con Carne. It also features the classic chili spice combination of chili powder, oregano and cumin.

SPICED CHILI

Spiced Chili

PREP: 20 min. **COOK:** 4 hours

Julie Brendt, Gold River, California

- 1-1/2 pounds ground beef
- 1/2 cup chopped onion
- 4 garlic cloves, minced
- 2 cans (16 ounces *each*) kidney beans, rinsed and drained
- 2 cans (15 ounces *each*) tomato sauce
- 2 cans (14-1/2 ounces *each*) stewed tomatoes, cut up
- 1 cup water
- 2 bay leaves
- 1/4 cup chili powder
- 1 tablespoon salt
- 1 tablespoon brown sugar
- 1 tablespoon dried basil
- 1 tablespoon Italian seasoning
- 1 tablespoon dried thyme
- 1 tablespoon pepper
- 1 teaspoon dried oregano
- 1 teaspoon dried marjoram

Shredded cheddar cheese, optional

1) In a large skillet, cook the beef, onion and garlic over medium heat until meat is no longer pink; drain.

2) Transfer to a 5-qt. slow cooker. Stir in the beans, tomato sauce, tomatoes, water and seasonings.

3) Cover and cook on low for 4-5 hours. Discard bay leaves. Garnish with cheese if desired.

Yield: 12 servings (about 3 quarts).

NUTRITION FACTS: 1 cup equals 236 calories, 7 g fat (3 g saturated fat), 38 mg cholesterol, 1,240 mg sodium, 25 g carbohydrate, 6 g fiber, 18 g protein.

■ **Stovetop Spiced Chili:** If you like to make the chili on the stovetop, use a Dutch oven instead of a skillet to cook the beef, onion and garlic. Add the beans, tomato sauce, tomatoes, water and seasonings to the Dutch oven. Bring to boil. Reduce heat; cover and simmer for 45 minutes. Discard bay leaves.

Jalapeno Pepper Chili

PREP/TOTAL TIME: 30 min.

Tonya Michelle Burkhard, Englewood, Florida

- 1/2 pound ground beef
- 1/2 pound ground pork
- 2 cans (16 ounces *each*) kidney beans, rinsed and drained
- 2 cans (14-1/2 ounces *each*) diced tomatoes with garlic and onion, undrained

JALAPENO PEPPER CHILI

1 can (14-1/2 ounces) beef broth
1 can (8 ounces) tomato sauce
2 tablespoons chili powder
1 jalapeno pepper, seeded and chopped
12 hard rolls (about 4-1/2 inches), optional
Shredded cheddar cheese, sliced green onions and sour cream, optional

1) In a large saucepan, cook beef and pork over medium heat until no longer pink; drain. Stir in the beans, tomatoes, broth, tomato sauce, chili powder and jalapeno. Bring to a boil. Reduce heat; cover and simmer for 20 minutes.

2) Serve in soup bowls or if desired, cut the top fourth off of each roll; carefully hollow out bottom, leaving a 1/2-in. shell. Cube removed bread. Spoon chili into bread bowls. Serve with cubed bread, shredded cheddar cheese, sliced green onions and sour cream if desired.

Yield: 12 servings.

Editor's Note: When cutting or seeding hot peppers, use rubber or plastic gloves to protect your hands. Avoid touching your face.

NUTRITION FACTS: 3/4 cup equals 292 calories, 8 g fat (2 g saturated fat), 22 mg cholesterol, 778 mg sodium, 40 g carbohydrate, 4 g fiber, 16 g protein.

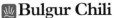

Bulgur Chili
PREP: 10 min. + standing **COOK:** 30 min.
Jeraldine Hall, Ravenden Springs, Arkansas

3/4 cup bulgur
2 cups boiling water
1-1/2 cups finely chopped green peppers
1 large onion, chopped
2 teaspoons vegetable oil
2 cups reduced-sodium tomato juice
1 can (16 ounces) kidney beans, rinsed and drained
1 can (15 ounces) ranch-style beans, undrained
1 can (14-1/2 ounces) diced tomatoes, undrained
1 can (8 ounces) tomato sauce
1 cup water
2 to 3 tablespoons chili powder
2 garlic cloves, minced
1/2 teaspoon ground cumin
1/8 to 1/4 teaspoon cayenne pepper
3/4 cup shredded reduced-fat cheddar cheese

1) Place bulgur in a large bowl; stir in boiling water. Cover and let stand for 30 minutes or until most of the liquid is absorbed. Drain and squeeze dry.

BULGUR CHILI

2) In a large saucepan, saute green peppers and onion in oil until tender. Stir in the bulgur, tomato juice, beans, tomatoes, tomato sauce, water, chili powder, garlic, cumin and cayenne. Bring to a boil. Reduce heat; cover and simmer for 20-25 minutes or until heated through. Garnish with cheese.

Yield: 9 servings.

Editor's Note: Look for bulgur in the cereal, rice or organic food aisle of your grocery store.

NUTRITION FACTS: 1 cup equals 195 calories, 3 g fat (1 g saturated fat), 5 mg cholesterol, 657 mg sodium, 33 g carbohydrate, 7 g fiber, 11 g protein.

Chili con Carne
PREP: 10 min. **COOK:** 1-1/2 hours
Karleen Warkentin, McAllen, Texas

1/2 pound ground beef
1/2 cup chopped onion
1 garlic clove, minced
1 can (10 ounces) diced tomatoes and green chilies
1 can (8 ounces) tomato sauce
3/4 cup canned pinto beans, rinsed and drained
2-1/2 teaspoons chili powder
1/2 teaspoon dried oregano
1/4 teaspoon salt, optional
1/4 teaspoon ground cumin
1/4 teaspoon pepper

1) In a large saucepan, cook the beef, onion and garlic over medium heat until meat is no longer pink; drain.

2) Stir in the tomatoes, tomato sauce, beans, chili powder, oregano, salt if desired, cumin and pepper. Bring to a boil. Reduce heat; cover and simmer for 1 hour.

Yield: 2 servings.

NUTRITION FACTS: 1-1/3 cups equals 357 calories, 12 g fat (4 g saturated fat), 41 mg cholesterol, 1,247 mg sodium, 34 g carbohydrate, 10 g fiber, 31 g protein.

Sandwiches

Sandwiches are often defined as a portable meal between two pieces of bread or on a roll, perfect for taking to picnics, school or work.

Sandwiches come in a variety of sizes and shapes. Many are handheld, while some need to be eaten with a knife and fork. Sandwiches can be served hot or cold, presented open-faced, stacked high or enclosed in a tortilla.

Sandwich Pizzazz

Take the humdrum out of a deli sandwich by replacing butter or mayonnaise with one of these quick-to-make spreads. Just slather or drizzle over bread or rolls.

- **Horseradish Mayonnaise:** Mix 1/4 cup mayonnaise with 1-1/2 teaspoons *each* chopped green onions and prepared horseradish.

- **Italian-Style Mayonnaise:** Mix 1/4 cup mayonnaise with 3/4 teaspoon tomato paste and 1/8 teaspoon dried basil.

- **Tapenade Mayonnaise:** Mix 2 tablespoons *each* mayonnaise and finely chopped ripe or Greek olives, 1/8 teaspoon minced garlic and a dash *each* dried thyme and pepper.

- **Avocado Sandwich Spread:** Mash 1/2 of a large avocado and mix in 1 tablespoon minced green onion, 1 teaspoon white balsamic vinegar and 1/8 teaspoon *each* salt and pepper.

- **Chimichurri Sandwich Spread:** Whisk together 2 tablespoons olive oil, 1 tablespoon *each* red wine vinegar, minced onion and minced fresh cilantro, 1 minced garlic clove, 1/4 teaspoon dried oregano and 1/8 teaspoon *each* salt and cayenne pepper.

- **Oil and Vinegar Drizzle:** Whisk together 2 tablespoons *each* olive oil and white wine vinegar, 1 tablespoon grated Parmesan cheese, 1 teaspoon sugar, 1/4 teaspoon *each* dried oregano and paprika and 1/8 teaspoon *each* garlic powder and ground mustard.

- **Sun-Dried Tomato Spread:** Mix 2 tablespoons *each* mayonnaise and finely chopped oil-packed sun-dried tomatoes and 2 teaspoons minced red onion.

- **Artichoke Pepperoncini Sandwich Spread:** Process 1/3 cup rinsed and drained water-packed artichoke hearts with 2 whole pepperoncini peppers in a food processor until spreadable but not smooth.

Tasty Sandwich Topper

Out of mayo? Try spreading your bread or roll with ranch or a creamy Caesar salad dressing.

Shredded French Dip

PREP: 5 min. **COOK:** 6 hours

Carla Kimball, Callaway, Nebraska

A chuck roast slow-simmered in a beefy broth is delicious when shredded and spooned onto rolls. I like to serve the cooking juices in individual cups for dipping.

- 1 **boneless beef chuck roast (3 pounds), trimmed**
- 1 **can (10-1/2 ounces) condensed French onion soup, undiluted**
- 1 **can (10-1/2 ounces) condensed beef consomme, undiluted**
- 1 **can (10-1/2 ounces) condensed beef broth, undiluted**
- 1 **teaspoon beef bouillon granules**
- 8 **to 10 French *or* Italian rolls, split**

1) Halve roast and place in a 3-qt. slow cooker. Combine the soup, consomme, broth and bouillon; pour over roast. Cover and cook on low for 6-8 hours or until meat is tender.

2) Remove meat and shred with two forks. Serve on rolls. Skim fat from cooking juices and serve as a dipping sauce.

Yield: 10 servings.

NUTRITION FACTS: 1 serving equals 399 calories, 15 g fat (5 g saturated fat), 91 mg cholesterol, 1,104 mg sodium, 30 g carbohydrate, 2 g fiber, 33 g protein.

SHREDDED FRENCH DIP

Shredding Meat for Sandwiches

Remove meat from broth and place in a shallow pan. With two forks, pull meat into thin shreds.

Pork BBQ Sandwiches

PREP: 35 min. **COOK:** 4-1/2 hours

Julie Fella, Skaneateles, New York

When having a crowd over, you can serve this barbecue on mini rolls for a great-tasting appetizer.

- 1 bone-in pork shoulder roast (about 4 pounds)
- 1 cup water
- 1 teaspoon salt
- 2 cups finely chopped celery
- 1/3 cup steak sauce
- 1/4 cup packed brown sugar
- 1/4 cup cider vinegar
- 2 teaspoons lemon juice
- 2 teaspoons chili sauce
- 1 teaspoon ketchup
- 2 medium onions, sliced
- 2 teaspoons sugar
- 1 tablespoon olive oil
- 1 tablespoon butter
- 16 hoagie buns, split

1) In a Dutch oven, bring the pork roast, water and salt to a boil. Reduce heat; cover and simmer for 3-1/2 to 4 hours or until the meat is very tender.

2) Remove meat and let stand until cool enough to handle. Discard bone; shred meat with two forks. Skim fat from pan juices.

3) Stir in the celery, steak sauce, brown sugar, vinegar, lemon juice, chili sauce, ketchup and shredded pork. Bring to a boil. Reduce heat; cover and simmer for 1 hour.

4) In a large skillet, cook onions and sugar in oil and butter over low heat for 20-30 minutes or until golden brown and tender, stirring occasionally. Serve pork and onions on buns.

Yield: 16 servings.

NUTRITION FACTS: 1 sandwich equals 422 calories, 16 g fat (6 g saturated fat), 59 mg cholesterol, 660 mg sodium, 43 g carbohydrate, 2 g fiber, 26 g protein.

Italian Beef Sandwiches

PREP: 20 min. **COOK:** 8 hours

Kristin Swihart, Perrysburg, Ohio

You can enjoy this beef mixture right away, but it also freezes well. Store individual portions in the freezer and take them out for a quick lunch or dinner.

- 1 jar (11-1/2 ounces) pepperoncinis
- 1 boneless beef chuck roast (3-1/2 to 4 pounds)
- 1/4 cup water
- 1-3/4 teaspoons dried basil
- 1-1/2 teaspoons garlic powder
- 1-1/2 teaspoons dried oregano
- 1-1/4 teaspoons salt

ITALIAN BEEF SANDWICHES

- 1/4 teaspoon pepper
- 1 large onion, sliced and quartered
- 10 to 12 hard rolls, split

1) Drain pepperoncinis, reserving liquid. Remove and discard stems of peppers; set peppers aside. Cut roast into large chunks; place a third of the meat in a 5-qt. slow cooker. Add water.

2) In a small bowl, combine the seasonings; sprinkle half over beef. Layer with half of the remaining meat, then onion, reserved peppers and liquid. Top with remaining meat and herb mixture.

3) Cover and cook on low for 8-9 hours or until meat is tender. Shred beef with two forks. Using a slotted spoon, serve beef and peppers on rolls.

Yield: 10-12 servings.

Editor's Note: Look for pepperoncinis (pickled peppers) in the pickle and olive section of your grocery store.

NUTRITION FACTS: 1 sandwich equals 376 calories, 15 g fat (5 g saturated fat), 86 mg cholesterol, 1,132 mg sodium, 27 g carbohydrate, 2 g fiber, 31 g protein.

Tasty Sandwiches

If you enjoy grilled sandwiches, you may want to invest in an electric or stovetop griddle, which will allow you to grill four to six sandwiches at a time.

When assembling sandwiches ahead, spread them with butter or margarine to seal the bread and keep the meat's moisture from being absorbed into the bread.

Enhance a sandwich with toppings such as guacamole, salsa, cheese spreads, mayonnaise, Swiss cheese, blue cheese, sauteed mushrooms or strips of crisp bacon.

CHEESE STEAK SUBS

Cheese Steak Subs

PREP/TOTAL TIME: 30 min.

Taste of Home Test Kitchen

Thin slices of roast beef are topped with peppers, onions and cheese to create this satisfying stacked sandwich. Accompany it with deli potato salad and peanut butter brownies, or serve French fries and store-bought sugar cookies.

- 1/2 cup julienned sweet red pepper
- 1/2 cup julienned green pepper
- 1/2 cup sliced onion
- 1/2 teaspoon vegetable oil
- 2 slices part-skim mozzarella cheese
- 4 ounces thinly sliced deli roast beef
- 2 submarine sandwich buns, split

1) In a small skillet, saute the peppers and onion in oil until tender. Cut cheese slices in half. Place beef and cheese on the bottom of each bun.

2) Broil 4 in. from the heat for 1-2 minutes or until cheese is melted. Top with pepper mixture and bun tops.

Yield: 2 servings.

NUTRITION FACTS: 1 sandwich equals 599 calories, 16 g fat (6 g saturated fat), 45 mg cholesterol, 1,679 mg sodium, 77 g carbohydrate, 5 g fiber, 34 g protein.

Champion Beef Sandwiches

PREP/TOTAL TIME: 15 min.

Ann Eastman, Santa Monica, California

When I have time, I like to prepare a roast with this much-requested recipe in mind. But when I need a quick meal in a hurry, I use deli roast beef with delicious results.

- 1/2 cup sour cream
- 1 tablespoon dry onion soup mix
- 1 tablespoon prepared horseradish, drained
- 1/8 teaspoon pepper

- 8 slices rye *or* pumpernickel bread
- 1/2 pound sliced roast beef

Lettuce leaves

1) In a small bowl, combine the first four ingredients. Spread 1 tablespoon on each slice of bread. Top four slices of bread with roast beef and lettuce; cover with remaining bread.

Yield: 4 servings.

NUTRITION FACTS: 1 sandwich equals 318 calories, 11 g fat (6 g saturated fat), 60 mg cholesterol, 1,401 mg sodium, 34 g carbohydrate, 4 g fiber, 18 g protein.

Greek Pitas

PREP: 20 min. + chilling COOK: 5 min.

Lisa Hockersmith, Bakersfield, California

These taste like gyros but can be made right at home! Plus, you can prepare the meat and sauce ahead of time for added convenience.

- 1 cup (8 ounces) plain yogurt
- 1 cup diced peeled cucumber
- 1 teaspoon dill weed
- 1/4 teaspoon seasoned salt
- 1/4 cup olive oil
- 1/4 cup lemon juice
- 2 tablespoons Dijon mustard
- 2 garlic cloves, minced
- 1-1/2 teaspoons dried oregano
- 1 teaspoon dried thyme
- 1-1/4 pounds lean boneless pork, thinly sliced
- 6 pita breads (6 inches), halved and warmed
- 1 medium tomato, chopped
- 2 tablespoons chopped onion

1) In a small bowl, combine the yogurt, cucumber, dill and seasoned salt; cover and refrigerate for 6 hours or overnight.

2) In a large resealable plastic bag, combine the oil, lemon juice, mustard, garlic, oregano and thyme; add pork. Seal bag and turn to coat; refrigerate for 6 hours or overnight, turning occasionally.

CHAMPION BEEF SANDWICH

3) Drain and discard marinade. In a skillet, stir-fry pork for about 4 minutes or until no longer pink. Stuff into pita halves; top with cucumber sauce, tomato and onion.

Yield: 6 servings.

NUTRITION FACTS: 2 filled pita halves equals 375 calories, 12 g fat (4 g saturated fat), 60 mg cholesterol, 509 mg sodium, 38 g carbohydrate, 2 g fiber, 27 g protein.

Quesadilla
PREP/TOTAL TIME: 10 min.

Amber Waddell, Grand Rapids, Michigan

This single-serving quesadilla is a snap to make. It is equally as delicious made with cooked chicken, turkey, pork or beef.

- 1 to 2 teaspoons vegetable oil
- 2 flour tortillas (6 inches)
- 1/2 cup shredded cheddar cheese, *divided*
- 1/2 cup cubed cooked chicken, turkey, pork *or* beef
- 1/4 cup sliced fresh mushrooms
- 1/2 cup shredded Monterey Jack cheese, *divided*

Sour cream and salsa, optional

1) Heat oil in a nonstick skillet, add one tortilla. Layer with half the cheddar cheese, all of the chicken and mushrooms and half the Monterey Jack cheese. Top with the second tortilla.

2) Cover and heat until cheese melts and bottom tortilla is crisp and golden brown. Turn over; sprinkle remaining cheese on top.

3) Cook until bottom tortilla is crisp and golden brown and cheese is melted. Cut into wedges; serve with sour cream and salsa if desired.

Yield: 1 serving.

NUTRITION FACTS: 1 quesadilla equals 768 calories, 49 g fat (25 g saturated fat), 173 mg cholesterol, 1,152 mg sodium, 29 g carbohydrate, trace fiber, 53 g protein.

California Clubs
PREP/TOTAL TIME: 10 min.

Diane Cigel, Stevens Point, Wisconsin

Ranch dressing and Dijon mustard create a tasty sauce to top this sandwich. Pairing tomato and avocado with the chicken and bacon is just the right combination on sourdough bread.

- 1/2 cup ranch salad dressing
- 1/4 cup Dijon mustard
- 8 slices sourdough bread, toasted
- 4 boneless skinless chicken breast halves, cooked and sliced
- 1 large tomato, sliced
- 1 medium ripe avocado, peeled and sliced
- 12 bacon strips, cooked and drained

CALIFORNIA CLUBS

1) In a small bowl, combine salad dressing and mustard; spread on each slice of bread.

2) On four slices of bread, layer the chicken, tomato, avocado and bacon. Top with remaining bread.

Yield: 4 servings.

NUTRITION FACTS: 1 sandwich equals 837 calories, 41 g fat (9 g saturated fat), 84 mg cholesterol, 1,765 mg sodium, 74 g carbohydrate, 7 g fiber, 42 g protein.

Santa Fe Chicken Heroes
PREP/TOTAL TIME: 20 min.

Bonnie Link, Goose Creek, South Carolina

The Southwestern seasonings make these sandwiches spicy and flavorful. You can adjust the crushed red pepper and chili powder to your tastes.

- 6 boneless skinless chicken breast halves
- 1 tablespoon vegetables oil
- 1/4 to 1/2 teaspoon pepper
- 1/4 to 1/2 teaspoons crushed red pepper flakes
- 1/4 to 1/2 teaspoon chili powder
- 6 slices Monterey Jack cheese
- 6 French *or* Italian rolls, split
- 2 tablespoons butter, melted

Lettuce leaves and tomato slices

Salsa *or* picante sauce, optional

1) Coat grill rack with cooking spray before starting the grill. Pound chicken breasts slightly to flatten evenly. Brush both sides with oil. Combine seasonings; sprinkle on both sides of chicken.

2) Grill, uncovered, over medium-hot heat for 6-8 minutes; turn and grill 4-6 minutes longer or until chicken is tender and no longer pink. Top with cheese; allow to melt, about 2 minutes.

3) Brush rolls with butter; grill just until toasted. Place lettuce, tomato and chicken on rolls; top with salsa or picante sauce if desired.

Yield: 6 servings.

NUTRITION FACTS: 1 sandwich (calculated without lettuce and tomato) equals 322 calories, 15 g fat (7 g saturated fat), 41 mg cholesterol, 494 mg sodium, 30 g carbohydrate, 1 g fiber, 15 g protein.

CHICKEN SALAD CROISSANTS

Chicken Salad Croissants

PREP/TOTAL TIME: 15 min.

Laura Koziarski, Battle Creek, Michigan

This tempting chicken salad gets its special taste from Swiss cheese and pickle relish. It's a favorite of my brother, who insists I make it when he visits.

       2   cups cubed cooked chicken
       1   cup cubed Swiss cheese
     1/2   cup dill pickle relish
     2/3   cup mayonnaise
       1   tablespoon minced fresh parsley
       1   teaspoon lemon juice
     1/2   teaspoon seasoned salt
     1/8   teaspoon pepper
   Lettuce leaves
       6   croissants, split

1) In a large bowl, combine the chicken, cheese and pickle relish. Combine the mayonnaise, parsley, lemon juice, seasoned salt and pepper; add to chicken mixture and mix well.

2) Place a lettuce leaf on each croissant; top with about 1/2 cup of the chicken mixture.

Yield: 6 servings.

NUTRITION FACTS: 1 serving (calculated without lettuce) equals 607 calories, 41 g fat (14 g saturated fat), 109 mg cholesterol, 1,001 mg sodium, 34 g carbohydrate, 2 g fiber, 25 g protein.

Open-Faced Crab Salad Sandwiches

PREP/TOTAL TIME: 25 min.

Lanie Kappe, Santa Ana, California

Everyone loved the crab salad my mother-in-law contributed to a family gathering, so I reduced the fat in her recipe for this version. Serve it hot or cold or as a spread for crackers.

     1/2   cup reduced-fat mayonnaise
     1/8   teaspoon salt

     1/8   teaspoon pepper
       2   packages (8 ounces *each*) imitation crabmeat, chopped
       1   cup (4 ounces) shredded part-skim mozzarella cheese
     1/4   cup chopped sweet red pepper
     1/4   cup chopped green onions
     1/4   cup chopped celery
       1   loaf (8 ounces) unsliced French bread, halved lengthwise

1) In a large bowl, combine the mayonnaise, salt and pepper. Stir in the crab, cheese, red pepper, onions and celery. Spoon over bread halves.

2) Place on a baking sheet. Broil 5 in. from the heat for 7-8 minutes or until lightly browned. Cut into 3-in. pieces.

Yield: 8 servings.

NUTRITION FACTS: 1 piece equals 236 calories, 9 g fat (3 g saturated fat), 44 mg cholesterol, 420 mg sodium, 24 g carbohydrate, 1 g fiber, 13 g protein.

Turkey Tenderloin Sandwiches

PREP: 10 min. + marinating **GRILL:** 10 min.

Kathy Thompson, Clifton, Colorado

We loved these absolutely delicious tenderloins when we visited the Iowa State Fair. We had to wait in line for more than an hour to order them, but with this recipe, we can enjoy them regularly.

       4   turkey breast tenderloins (4 ounces *each*)
     1/4   cup canola oil
     1/4   cup sherry *or* chicken broth
     1/4   cup reduced-sodium soy sauce
       2   tablespoons lemon juice
       2   tablespoons dried minced onion
     1/4   teaspoon ground ginger
     1/8   teaspoon pepper
       4   whole wheat hamburger buns, split
       1   slice red onion, separated into rings
       4   slices tomato
       4   lettuce leaves

1) Flatten tenderloins to 3/4-in. thickness. In a large resealable plastic bag, combine the oil, sherry or broth, soy sauce, lemon juice, onion, ginger and pepper; add turkey. Seal bag and turn to coat; refrigerate at least 3 hours, turning occasionally.

2) If grilling the turkey, coat grill rack with cooking spray before starting the grill. Drain and discard marinade. Grill turkey, uncovered, over medium heat or broil 4 in. from the heat for 4-5 minutes on each side or until juices run clear. Serve on buns with onion, tomato and lettuce.

Yield: 4 servings.

NUTRITION FACTS: 1 sandwich equals 281 calories, 7 g fat (1 g saturated fat), 56 mg cholesterol, 421 mg sodium, 25 g carbohydrate, 4 g fiber, 31 g protein.

Three-Meat Stromboli

PREP: 20 min. **BAKE:** 35 min.

Lorelei Hull, Luling, Louisiana

This hearty sandwich features three different meats. But you can easily vary the stromboli filling to your liking and have delicious results.

- 2 loaves (1 pound *each*) frozen bread dough, thawed
- 2 tablespoons Dijon mustard
- 1/2 cup grated Parmesan cheese, *divided*
- 1/4 pound pastrami, finely chopped
- 1/4 pound pepperoni, finely chopped
- 1/4 pound hard salami, finely chopped
- 1 cup (4 ounces) shredded Swiss cheese
- 1 egg, beaten

1) Roll each loaf of bread into a 12-in. x 7-in. rectangle. Spread mustard to within 1 in. of edges. Sprinkle each with 2 tablespoons of Parmesan cheese.

2) Combine the pastrami, pepperoni, salami and Swiss cheese; sprinkle over dough. Top with the remaining Parmesan. Brush edges of dough with egg. Roll up jelly-roll style, beginning with a long side. Seal edge and ends.

3) Place seam side down on a greased baking sheet; cut three slits in the top of each loaf. Bake at 350° for 35-40 minutes. Slice; serve warm.

Yield: 2 loaves (12-16 servings each).

NUTRITION FACTS: 1 slice equals 135 calories, 6 g fat (2 g saturated fat), 18 mg cholesterol, 377 mg sodium, 15 g carbohydrate, 1 g fiber, 7 g protein.

■ **Three-Cheese Meat Stromboli:** Substitute a 1/4 pound chopped fully cooked ham for the pastrami and omit the pepperoni. Use 3/4 cup *each* shredded mozzarella and cheddar cheeses for the Swiss cheese. Add 1/4 cup chopped roasted red pepper to the meat-cheese mixture. Proceed as recipe directs.

Ham and Swiss Stromboli

PREP: 15 min. **BAKE:** 30 min.

Pat Raport, Gainesville, Florida

This pretty swirled sandwich loaf is fast, easy and versatile. Fill it with anything your family likes. Try it with sliced pepperoni and provolone cheese, or anchovies and ripe olives.

- 1 tube (11 ounces) refrigerated crusty French loaf
- 6 ounces thinly sliced deli ham
- 6 green onions, sliced
- 8 bacon strips, cooked and crumbled
- 1-1/2 cups (6 ounces) shredded Swiss cheese

1) Unroll dough on a greased baking sheet. Place ham over dough to within 1/2 in. of edges; sprinkle evenly with onions, bacon and cheese.

2) Roll up jelly-roll style, starting with a long side. Pinch seams to seal and tuck ends under. Place seam side down on baking sheet. With a sharp knife, cut several 1/4-in.-deep slits on top of loaf.

3) Bake at 350° for 26-30 minutes or until golden brown. Cool slightly before slicing. Serve warm.

Yield: 8 servings.

NUTRITION FACTS: 1 piece equals 289 calories, 15 g fat (8 g saturated fat), 46 mg cholesterol, 725 mg sodium, 19 g carbohydrate, 1 g fiber, 18 g protein.

Double-Cheese Beef Panini

PREP/TOTAL TIME: 30 min.

Lisa Huff, Clive, Iowa

Nothing beats a piping hot panini when it comes to a speedy, satisfying lunch or supper. Blue cheese and horseradish give my family-approved sandwich zip.

- 1/3 cup mayonnaise
- 1/4 cup crumbled blue cheese
- 2 teaspoons prepared horseradish
- 1/8 teaspoon pepper
- 1 large sweet onion, thinly sliced
- 1 tablespoon olive oil
- 8 slices white bread
- 8 slices provolone cheese
- 8 slices deli roast beef
- 2 tablespoons butter, softened

1) In a small bowl, combine the mayonnaise, blue cheese, horseradish and pepper; set aside. In a large skillet, saute onion in oil until tender.

2) Spread mayonnaise mixture over one side of each slice of bread. On four slices, layer one piece of cheese, two slices of roast beef, sauteed onion and another piece of cheese; top with remaining bread.

3) Spread butter over both sides of sandwiches. Cook on a panini maker or indoor grill for 2-3 minutes or until bread is browned and cheese is melted.

Yield: 4 servings.

NUTRITION FACTS: 1 piece equals 639 calories, 44 g fat (18 g saturated fat), 91 mg cholesterol, 1,340 mg sodium, 31 g carbohydrate, 2 g fiber, 29 g protein.

DOUBLE-CHEESE BEEF PANINI

Boston Subs

PREP/TOTAL TIME: 20 min.

Sue Erdos, Meriden, Connecticut

My mother has made these sandwiches ever since she left her hometown of Boston many years ago. They're quick to prepare and travel well. The recipe is great for parties if you use a loaf of French or Italian bread instead of the individual rolls.

1/2 cup mayonnaise

12 submarine sandwich buns, split

1/2 cup Italian salad dressing, *divided*

1/4 pound *each* thinly sliced bologna, deli ham, hard salami, pepperoni and olive loaf

1/4 pound thinly sliced provolone cheese

1 medium onion, diced

1 medium tomato, diced

1/2 cup diced dill pickles

1 cup shredded lettuce

1 teaspoon dried oregano

1) Spread mayonnaise on inside of buns. Brush with half of the salad dressing. Layer deli meats and cheese on bun bottoms.

2) Top with onion, tomato, pickles and lettuce. Sprinkle with oregano and drizzle with remaining dressing. Replace bun tops.

Yield: 12 servings.

NUTRITION FACTS: 1 sandwich equals 682 calories, 33 g fat (9 g saturated fat), 45 mg cholesterol, 1,863 mg sodium, 72 g carbohydrate, 4 g fiber, 22 g protein.

Italian Submarine Sandwich

PREP: 15 min. + chilling

Susan Brown, Richland, Washington

I first sampled this at a dinner where it was served as an appetizer, and I almost didn't have room for the main course! Since then, it's become our family's standard sandwich.

1 can (4-1/4 ounces) chopped ripe olives

2 jars (2 ounces *each*) diced pimientos, drained

2/3 cup chopped pimiento-stuffed olives

1/2 cup minced fresh parsley

1/2 cup olive oil

3 garlic cloves, minced

1 teaspoon dried oregano

1/4 teaspoon pepper

1 loaf (1 pound) unsliced Italian bread

1/3 pound thinly sliced fully cooked ham

1/3 pound thinly sliced Genoa salami

1/3 pound thinly sliced provolone cheese

1) In a jar with tight-fitting lid, combine the first eight ingredients; cover and shake well. Cover and refrigerate for at least 12 hours.

2) Cut bread in half lengthwise; hollow out top and bottom, leaving a 1-in. shell. (Discard removed bread or save for another use.) Drain 2 tablespoons liquid from olive mixture; spread on the inside of bread top. Spoon 1 cup olive mixture evenly into bottom of bread shell.

3) Layer with the ham, salami and cheese; spread with remaining olive mixture. Replace bread top. Slice into serving-size pieces.

Yield: 4-6 servings.

NUTRITION FACTS: 1 slice equals 631 calories, 41 g fat (11 g saturated fat), 51 mg cholesterol, 1,875 mg sodium, 44 g carbohydrate, 3 g fiber, 25 g protein.

Buffalo Chicken Lettuce Wraps

PREP/TOTAL TIME: 25 min.

Priscilla Gilbert, Indian Harbour Beach, Florida

These homemade buffalo chicken wraps are excellent. Honey and lime juice help tone down the hot wing sauce for a refreshing zip. They're perfect for lunch or a light summer meal with a tall glass of ice-cold lemonade.

1/3 cup crumbled blue cheese

1/4 cup mayonnaise

2 tablespoons milk

4-1/2 teaspoons lemon juice

1 tablespoon minced fresh parsley

1 teaspoon Worcestershire sauce

1 pound boneless skinless chicken breasts, cubed

1 teaspoon salt

1 tablespoon vegetable oil

1/4 cup lime juice

1/4 cup Louisiana-style hot sauce

1/4 cup honey

1 small cucumber, halved lengthwise, seeded and thinly sliced

BUFFALO CHICKEN LETTUCE WRAPS

1 celery rib, thinly sliced
3/4 cup julienned carrots
8 Bibb *or* Boston lettuce leaves

1) For dressing, in a small bowl, combine the first six ingredients. Cover and refrigerate until serving.

2) Sprinkle chicken with salt. In a large skillet, cook chicken in oil until no longer pink. Combine the lime juice, hot sauce and honey; pour over chicken. Bring to a boil. Reduce heat; simmer, uncovered, for 2-3 minutes or until heated through. Remove from the heat; stir in the cucumber, celery and carrots.

3) Spoon 1/2 cup chicken mixture onto each lettuce leaf; fold sides over filling and secure with a toothpick. Serve with blue cheese dressing.

Yield: 8 servings.

NUTRITION FACTS: 1 wrap equals 194 calories, 10 g fat (2 g saturated fat), 39 mg cholesterol, 459 mg sodium, 12 g carbohydrate, 1 g fiber, 13 g protein.

Turkey Muffuletta

PREP: 30 min. + chilling

Gilda Lester, Wilmington, North Carolina

You have to resist the temptation to eat this impressive, multi-layered sandwich immediately! It needs to "rest" at least 30 minutes in the refrigerator to allow the flavors to meld. But it's worth the wait.

1 loaf (1 pound) unsliced Italian bread
1/3 cup olive oil
3 tablespoons balsamic vinegar
1 tablespoon minced fresh basil *or* 1 teaspoon dried basil
1 garlic clove, minced
1/2 teaspoon salt
1/4 teaspoon crushed red pepper flakes
3/4 pound sliced deli turkey
6 ounces provolone cheese, thinly sliced
1 jar (7 ounces) roasted sweet red peppers, drained and sliced
1/2 cup sliced pimiento-stuffed olives
1 large tomato, sliced
3 tablespoons shredded Romano cheese
1 tablespoon minced fresh oregano *or* 1 teaspoon dried oregano
1/4 teaspoon pepper

1) Cut bread in half lengthwise; carefully hollow out top and bottom, leaving a 1-in. shell (discard removed bread or save for another use).

2) In a bowl, combine the oil, vinegar and seasonings; brush over cut sides of bread. In bottom bread shell, layer turkey, provolone cheese, red peppers, olives and tomato. Sprinkle with Romano cheese, oregano and pepper. Replace bread top.

3) Wrap in plastic wrap; refrigerate for 30 minutes. Cut into slices.

Yield: 6 servings.

NUTRITION FACTS: 1 slice equals 517 calories, 25 g fat (7 g saturated fat), 46 mg cholesterol, 1,861 mg sodium, 46 g carbohydrate, 2 g fiber, 26 g protein.

Grilled Veggie Wraps

PREP: 15 min. + marinating GRILL: 15 min.

Britani Sepanski, Indianapolis, Indiana

I love this vegetable marinade, but the key to this recipe's success is the three-cheese spread.

2 tablespoons balsamic vinegar
1-1/2 teaspoons minced fresh basil
1-1/2 teaspoons olive oil
1-1/2 teaspoons molasses
3/4 teaspoon minced fresh thyme
1/8 teaspoon salt
1/8 teaspoon pepper
1 medium zucchini, cut lengthwise into 1/4-inch slices
1 medium sweet red pepper, cut into 1-inch pieces
1 medium red onion, cut into 1/2-inch slices
4 ounces whole fresh mushrooms, cut into 1/2-inch pieces
4 ounces fresh sugar snap peas
1/2 cup crumbled feta cheese
3 tablespoons reduced-fat cream cheese
2 tablespoons grated Parmesan cheese
1 tablespoon reduced-fat mayonnaise
4 flour tortillas (8 inches)
4 romaine leaves

1) In a large resealable plastic bag, combine the first seven ingredients; add vegetables. Seal bag and turn to coat; refrigerate for 2 hours, turning once.

2) Drain and reserve marinade. Combine cheeses and mayonnaise; set aside. Place vegetables in a grill basket. Grill, uncovered, over medium-high heat for 5 minutes.

3) Set aside 1 teaspoon marinade. Turn vegetables; baste with remaining marinade. Grill 5-8 minutes longer or until tender. Brush one side of each tortilla with reserved marinade. Place tortillas, marinade side down, on grill for 1-3 minutes or until lightly toasted.

4) Spread 3 tablespoons of cheese mixture over ungrilled side of each tortilla. Top with romaine and 1 cup grilled vegetables; roll up.

Yield: 4 servings.

NUTRITION FACTS: 1 wrap equals 332 calories, 14 g fat (6 g saturated fat), 26 mg cholesterol, 632 mg sodium, 39 g carbohydrate, 4 g fiber, 13 g protein.

Taco Avocado Wraps

PREP/TOTAL TIME: 30 min.

Renee Rutherford, Andover, Minnesota

I came up with this one summer when we wanted a light supper and didn't want to turn on the oven. We also serve it for lunch or a snack.

- 1 package (8 ounces) cream cheese, softened
- 1/2 cup sour cream
- 1 can (4 ounces) chopped green chilies, drained
- 1 tablespoon taco seasoning
- 4 flour tortillas (10 inches), warmed
- 2 medium ripe avocados, peeled and sliced
- 2 plum tomatoes, thinly sliced
- 5 green onions, sliced
- 1 can (4 ounces) sliced ripe olives, drained

1) In a small bowl, combine the cream cheese, sour cream, chilies and taco seasoning.

2) Spread about 1/2 cup over each tortilla. Top with the avocados, tomatoes, onions and olives; roll up.

Yield: 4 servings.

NUTRITION FACTS: 1 serving equals 683 calories, 47 g fat (20 g saturated fat), 82 mg cholesterol, 1,158 mg sodium, 47 g carbohydrate, 12 g fiber, 14 g protein.

TACO AVOCADO WRAPS

Mozzarella Tuna Melts

PREP/TOTAL TIME: 30 min.

Jo Maasberg, Farson, Wyoming

While soup simmers for my lunch, I assemble these tasty melts. Using a mini food processor to chop the celery and onion for the filling helps shave prep time.

- 1 can (6 ounces) water-packed tuna, drained and flaked
- 1/4 cup finely chopped celery
- 1/4 cup finely chopped onion
- 1/4 cup mayonnaise
- 4 hamburger buns, split
- 4 part-skim mozzarella cheese slices
- 4 tomato slices
- 4 lettuce leaves

1) In a small bowl, combine the tuna, celery, onion and mayonnaise. Spread on bottom of buns; set bun tops aside. Top tuna mixture with a slice of cheese and tomato.

2) Place on an ungreased baking sheet. Bake, uncovered, at 350° for 12-15 minutes or until heated through and cheese is melted. Top each with a lettuce leaf; replace bun tops.

Yield: 4 servings.

NUTRITION FACTS: 1 sandwich equals 363 calories, 20 g fat (6 g saturated fat), 40 mg cholesterol, 575 mg sodium, 25 g carbohydrate, 2 g fiber, 20 g protein.

Toasted Reubens

PREP/TOTAL TIME: 15 min.

Patty Kile, Plymouth Meeting, Pennsylvania

When New Yorkers taste my Reuben, they say it's like those served by delis in "The Big Apple." For a little less kick, omit the horseradish from the mayonnaise mixture.

- 1/2 cup mayonnaise
- 3 tablespoons ketchup
- 2 tablespoons sweet pickle relish
- 1 tablespoon prepared horseradish
- 4 teaspoons prepared mustard
- 8 slices rye bread
- 1 pound thinly sliced deli corned beef
- 4 slices Swiss cheese
- 1 can (8 ounces) sauerkraut, rinsed and well drained
- 2 tablespoons butter

1) In a small bowl, combine the mayonnaise, ketchup, pickle relish and horseradish; set aside. Spread mustard on one side of four slices of bread, then layer with the corned beef, cheese, sauerkraut and mayonnaise mixture; top with remaining bread.

2) In a large skillet, melt butter over medium heat. Add sandwiches; cover and cook on both sides until bread is lightly toasted and cheese is melted.

Yield: 4 servings.

NUTRITION FACTS: 1 sandwich equals 705 calories, 45 g fat (15 g saturated fat), 124 mg cholesterol, 2,830 mg sodium, 41 g carbohydrate, 6 g fiber, 34 g protein.

lending a helping hand

Deacons make home-cooked meals for less fortunate

Cooking and caring go hand in hand at the First United Presbyterian Church of West Pittston, Pennsylvania.

For the past 15 years, the nine members of the church's Board of Deacons have prepared a hot, nutritious meal for area homeless men at least once or twice each year.

The meal, one of the church's many outreach efforts, is performed with other area churches, civic organizations and VISION Inc., a nonprofit organization that provides services for homeless men in the Wyoming Valley.

"Two of our neighboring churches are among the 20 congregations that provide space for the shelter on a rotating basis, usually one week at a time," explains Rev. Jim Thyren, the church's pastor.

The men are transported from VISION's drop-in center to the host church around dinnertime. The deacons rotate with other service organizations to provide the meal for shelter residents on each of the seven nights. The men stay overnight at the host church and then are returned to the drop-in center the next morning.

"The men enjoy hearty meals such as one-dish casseroles, stews,

chili, baked ham and chicken," says Carol Ferguson, a deacon for four years. One entree that was a big hit was Meat Loaf for a Mob found on the *Taste of Home* Web site. "We received rave reviews," Carol says. "Some of the men said, 'This is the best meat loaf I've ever tasted.'"

Other main dishes that were well received were Slumgullion, a Spanish rice casserole, and Swedish Meatballs, using a recipe from Rev. Thyren. "My grandparents were Swedish," he says. "While my grandmother's recipe is long gone, our family has been using this recipe for more than 40 years."

Each meal is accompanied by side dishes, bread or rolls and dessert.

The deacons handle all aspects of the meal from start to finish. They develop a menu, do the shopping, recruit additional help if needed, prepare the food, transport it to the host church, serve the meal and help clean up. The number of men served ranges from 30 to just over 50.

"They've been very appreciative when they get a home-cooked meal," Thyren says. "And they especially like the variety."

Church deacons

> "
> *Some of the men said, 'This is the best meat loaf I've ever tasted.'*
> ~Carol Ferguson
> "

You can find some of Rev. Thyren's recipes in the Web exclusive online at tasteofhome.com/ CookbookBonus **Type in access code ICare**

taste of home
cooks who care

DO YOU KNOW A COOK WHO CARES?

If you or someone you know cooks for a charitable, spiritual or other cause, tell us about it at **tasteofhome.com/CookbookBonus**

Recipes

Tips

Beef & Veal

Beef and ground beef are staples in many kitchens and lend themselves to many cooking methods. When purchasing beef and ground beef, you'll want to select beef with a bright, cherry-red color and without any gray or brown patches. Select veal that has a fine-grained texture and is creamy pink in color.

Make sure the package is cold and free of holes or tears. Also make sure the package does not have excessive liquid, as this might indicate that the meat was subjected to improper temperatures.

Purchase before the "sell-by" date on the packaging for best quality.

Determine the amount of beef or veal you need to buy based on the cut and amount of bone:

- 1 pound of bone-in roasts yields 2-1/2 servings.
- 1 pound of bone-in steaks yields 2 servings.
- 1 pound of boneless cuts that will be trimmed of fat yields 2-1/2 to 3-1/2 servings.
- 1 pound of lean boneless cuts without waste —such as eye of round, flank and tenderloin— yields 3 to 4 servings.

Marinate less tender cuts of beef to tenderize and add flavor. A tenderizing marinade contains an acidic ingredient such as lemon juice, vinegar, yogurt or wine. Marinades without an acid can be used to flavor tender cuts.

Marinate meat in the refrigerator, turning or stirring several times to evenly coat. Always marinate meat in the refrigerator unless you are marinating it for 30 minutes or less.

Allow 6 to 24 hours to tenderize less tender cuts of large steaks or roasts. Marinating longer than 24 hours will result in a mushy surface texture. Smaller cuts, such as cubes for kabobs or thin steaks, can be marinated in a few hours.

Set aside a portion of marinade before adding the beef if the marinade is to be used later for basting or as a serving sauce. Allow 1/4 cup of marinade for each pound of beef.

Apply a "rub" or blend of seasonings, such as fresh or dried herbs and spices, to the surface of uncooked cuts, such as roasts or steaks. Rubs add a burst of flavor to the meat but do not tenderize.

Choose an appropriate cooking method for the cut you select. Tender cuts can be cooked quickly using dry-heat methods (broiling, grilling, pan-broiling, pan-frying, roasting and stir-frying); less tender cuts need to be cooked slowly using moist-heat methods (braising and cooking in liquid.)

Lightening Up Beef

Whether you want to serve your family more meatless meals or simply reduce some of the meat in family favorites, consider the following ideas for savvy standbys:

Cut back with casseroles—Replace some of the meat called for in your best hot dish with a combination of finely chopped carrots, celery and nuts. Or substitute a portion of the meat with grains such as cooked rice, couscous, barley or bulgur.

Believe in beans—Legumes are protein-rich substitutes for the meat and poultry found in many dishes, particularly soups and stews. Feel free to experiment and get creative with beans that are new to you.

Make pasta a preference—Skip the ground beef usually added to spaghetti sauce, and stir in sliced mushrooms or chopped peppers instead. And you won't miss the meat in your lasagna if you replace it with sauteed vegetables such as sliced zucchini or eggplant.

Cooking Methods for Beef and Veal

CUT/TYPE	BRAISE	BROIL	GRILL	ROAST	PAN-BROIL	PAN-FRY	COOKING IN LIQUID
BEEF ROASTS							
BOTTOM ROUND ROAST	•		•				
BRISKET	•						•
CHUCK ROAST	•						
RIB EYE ROAST			•	•			
RIB ROAST			•	•			
SIRLOIN TIP ROAST				•			
TENDERLOIN			•	•			
TRI-TIP ROAST			•	•			
BEEF STEAKS							
BOTTOM ROUND STEAK	•	•	•				
CUBE STEAK					•	•	
FLANK STEAK	•	•	•				
PORTERHOUSE STEAK		•	•			•	
RIB EYE STEAK		•	•		•	•	
RIB STEAK		•	•				
SIRLOIN STEAK		•	•		•	•	
SKIRT STEAK	•	•	•				
T-BONE STEAK		•			•	•	
TENDERLOIN STEAK		•	•		•	•	
TOP LOIN STEAK		•	•		•	•	
TOP ROUND STEAK	•	•	•				
BEEF RIBS							
BACK RIBS	•			•			
SHORT RIBS	•						•
BEEF—OTHERS							
BEEF SHANKS	•						•
BEEF STEW MEAT	•						•
GROUND BEEF PATTIES		•	•		•	•	
LIVER						•	
VEAL ROASTS							
BONELESS BREAST	•			•			
BONELESS LEG ROAST				•			
BONELESS RUMP ROAST	•			•			
BONELESS SHOULDER ROAST	•						
LOIN ROASTS				•			
RIB ROAST				•			
SHOULDER ARM ROAST	•			•			
VEAL CHOPS							
LOIN CHOPS	•	•	•			•	
RIB CHOPS	•	•	•			•	
VEAL STEAKS							
SHOULDER ARM STEAK	•					•	
SHOULDER BLADE STEAK	•					•	

Roasting Beef and Veal

Place meat on a rack in a shallow roasting pan with the fat side up. Insert an oven-safe meat thermometer in the thickest portion of the muscle without touching bone or fat. Or use an instant-read thermometer toward the end of the roasting time. If the roast needs to cook longer, remove the instant-read thermometer before you return the roast to the oven.

Roast without liquid, uncovered, according to the temperature and time given in the chart below or provided in the recipe. Because roasts will continue to cook after being removed from the oven, remove the meat when the meat thermometer reads 5-10° below desired doneness. Cover with foil and let stand for 10-15 minutes before carving.

CUT	WEIGHT	COOKING TIME (MINUTES PER POUND)			OVEN TEMP.
		MEDIUM-RARE 145°	MEDIUM 160°	WELL-DONE 170°	
BEEF RIB EYE ROAST (small end)	3 to 4 lbs. 4 to 6 lbs.	25 to 30 20 to 25	30 to 35 25 to 30	35 to 38 30 to 35	350° 350°
BEEF RIB ROAST	4 to 6 lbs. (2 ribs)	22 to 25	25 to 30	30 to 35	350°
	6 to 8 lbs. (2 to 4 ribs)	19 to 22	22 to 28	28 to 33	350°
BEEF ROUND TIP ROAST	3 to 4 lbs. 4 to 6 lbs.	30 to 35 25 to 30	33 to 38 30 to 35	38 to 42 35 to 40	325° 325°
BEEF TRI-TIP ROAST	1-1/2 to 2 lbs.	30 to 60 (minutes total)	40 to 45 (minutes total)		425°
BEEF BONELESS ROLLED RUMP ROAST	4 to 6 lbs.		22 to 27	30	325°
BEEF EYE OF ROUND ROAST	2 to 3 lbs.	35 to 45			325°
BEEF TENDERLOIN	4 to 5 lbs.	50 to 60 (minutes total)	60 to 70 (minutes total)	70 to 80 (minutes total)	425°
VEAL LOIN ROAST	3 to 4 lbs.		34 to 36	38 to 40	325°
VEAL BONELESS LEG ROAST	2 to 3 lbs.		18 to 20	22 to 24	325°
VEAL RIB ROAST	4 to 5 lbs.		25 to 27	29 to 31	325°
VEAL BONELESS SHOULDER ROAST	2-1/2 to 3 lbs.		31 to 34	34 to 37	325°

Defrosting Guidelines

The thicker the package, the longer it will take to defrost. Here are some guidelines for defrosting beef or veal in the refrigerator:

- For 1/2- to 3/4-in.-thick ground beef or veal patties, allow at least 12 hours.
- For 1- to 1-1/2-in.-thick meat pieces or packages of ground beef or veal, allow at least 24 hours.
- For steaks, allow 12 to 24 hours.
- For a large roast or a thick pot roast, allow about 6 hours per pound.

Cuts of Beef

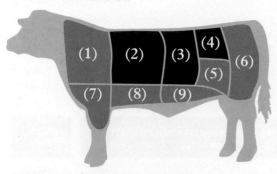

■ TENDER   ■ LESS TENDER

Chuck (1)

Chuck Arm Pot Roast

Chuck Shoulder
Pot Roast, Boneless

Chuck Shoulder
Steak, Boneless

Chuck Mock
Tender Steak

Chuck Pot Roast,
Boneless

Chuck 7-Bone
Pot Roast

Chuck Short Ribs

Rib (2)

Rib Roast, Large End

Rib Steak, Small End,
Boneless

Rib Eye Roast

Rib Eye Steak

Short Loin (3)

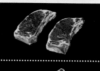
Top Loin (Strip) Steaks

T-Bone Steak

Porterhouse Steak

Beef Tenderloin Roast

Top Sirloin (4)

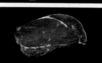
Top Sirloin Steak, Boneless

Bottom Sirloin (5)

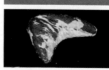
Tri-Tip Roast

Round (6)

Top Round Steak

Round Steak, Boneless

Bottom Round
Rump Roast

Eye Round Roast

Round Tip Roast,
Cap Off

Shank & Brisket (7)

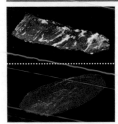

Brisket, Whole, Boneless

Plate & Flank (8 & 9)

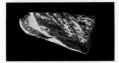

Skirt Steak, Boneless

Flank Steak

Other Cuts

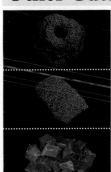

Ground Beef

Cube Steak

Beef Stew Meat

Photos Courtesy of The Beef Checkoff.

Veal

Leg

Leg Rump Roast, Boneless

Loin

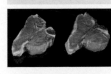

Loin Chops

Rib

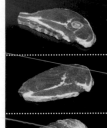

Rib Chops

Shoulder

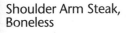

Shoulder Arm Steak

Shoulder Arm Steak,
Boneless

Shoulder Arm Roast,
Boneless

Shoulder Blade Steak

Breast

Breast, Boneless

Beef and Veal Grilling Chart

The cooking times shown below are for medium-rare to medium doneness. For beef, a meat thermometer should read 145° for medium-rare, 160° for medium and 170° for well-done.

Veal is done when a meat thermometer reads 160° for medium and 170° for well-done. Ground beef and veal should be 160°. For direct grilling, turn meat halfway through grilling time.

CUT	WEIGHT OR THICKNESS	HEAT	COOKING TIME
BEEF ROASTS			
RIB EYE STEAK	1 in.	Medium/Direct	11 to 14
	1-1/2 in.	Medium/Direct	17 to 22
T-BONE, PORTERHOUSE OR TOP LOIN STEAK (BONELESS STRIP)	3/4 in.	Medium/Direct	10 to 12
	1 in.	Medium/Direct	15 to 18
	1-1/2 in.	Medium/Direct	19 to 23
TENDERLOIN STEAK	1 in.	Medium/Direct	13 to 15
	1-1/2 in.	Medium/Direct	14 to 16
TOP SIRLOIN STEAK (BONELESS)	1 in.	Medium/Direct	17 to 21
	1-1/2 in.	Medium/Direct	22 to 26
	2 in.	Medium/Direct	28 to 33
FLANK STEAK*	1-1/2 to 2 lbs.	Medium/Direct	12 to 15
SKIRT STEAK	1/4 to 1/2 in.	High/Direct	6 to 8
TOP ROUND STEAK*	1 in.	Medium/Direct	16 to 18
CHUCK SHOULDER STEAK*	1 in.	Medium/Direct	16 to 20
TENDERLOIN ROAST	2 to 3 lbs.	Medium-Hot/Indirect	45 to 60
	4 to 5 lbs.	Medium-Hot/Indirect	1 to 1-1/4 hours
TRI-TIP	1-3/4 to 2 lbs.	Medium/Indirect	35 to 45
GROUND BEEF OR VEAL PATTY	4 oz. and 1/2 in.	Medium/Direct	11 to 14
VEAL			
LOIN OR RIB CHOP	1 in.	Medium/Direct	12 to 14
ARM OR BLADE STEAK*	3/4 in.	Medium/Direct	16 to 18

★ These cuts of meat are best when marinated before grilling.

Doneness Test for Steak

To test for doneness, insert an instant-read thermometer horizontally from the side, making sure to get the reading in the center of the steak.

SEASONED RIB ROAST

Seasoned Rib Roast

PREP: 10 min. **BAKE:** 1-3/4 hours + standing

Evelyn Gebhardt, Kasilof, Alaska

Gravy made from the drippings of this boneless beef rib roast is exceptional. You can also use a rib eye roast.

- 1-1/2 teaspoons lemon-pepper seasoning
- 1-1/2 teaspoons paprika
- 3/4 teaspoon garlic salt
- 1/2 teaspoon dried rosemary, crushed
- 1/4 teaspoon cayenne pepper
- 1 boneless beef rib roast (3 to 4 pounds)

1) In a small bowl, combine the seasonings; rub over roast. Place roast fat side up on a rack in a shallow roasting pan.

2) Bake, uncovered, at 350° for 1-3/4 to 2-1/2 hours or until meat reaches desired doneness (for medium-rare, a meat thermometer should read 145°; medium, 160°; well-done, 170°).

3) Remove to a warm serving platter. Let stand for 10-15 minutes before carving.

Yield: 6-8 servings.

NUTRITION FACTS: 5 ounces cooked beef equals 434 calories, 34 g fat (14 g saturated fat), 110 mg cholesterol, 342 mg sodium, trace carbohydrate, trace fiber, 30 g protein.

Herbed Roast Beef

PREP: 10 min. **BAKE:** 2-1/2 hours + standing

Kerry Sullivan, Longwood, Florida

This is a great recipe to serve guests, and it can be easily doubled for a larger group.

- 1 bone-in beef rib roast (4 to 6 pounds)
- 1 teaspoon fennel seed, crushed
- 1 teaspoon dried rosemary, crushed
- 1 teaspoon *each* dried basil, marjoram, savory and thyme
- 1 teaspoon rubbed sage
- 1 medium onion, sliced
- 3 fresh rosemary sprigs

HORSERADISH SAUCE:
- 3/4 cup sour cream
- 2 tablespoons prepared horseradish
- 1 tablespoon snipped chives
- 4-1/2 teaspoons lemon juice

1) Trim and tie roast if desired. In a small bowl, combine the fennel seed, crushed rosemary, basil, marjoram, savory, thyme and sage; rub over roast.

2) Place fat side up in a roasting pan. Top with onion and rosemary sprigs. Bake, uncovered, at 350° for 2 to 3 hours or until meat reaches desired doneness (for medium-rare, a meat thermometer should read 145°; medium, 160°; well-done, 170°).

3) Discard onion and rosemary. Let roast stand for 10-15 minutes before slicing. Meanwhile, in a small bowl, combine the sauce ingredients. Serve with beef.

Yield: 8 servings.

NUTRITION FACTS: 5 ounces cooked beef equals 544 calories, 42 g fat (18 g saturated fat), 138 mg cholesterol, 120 mg sodium, 4 g carbohydrate, 1 g fiber, 35 g protein.

Carving Standing Rib Roasts

1) To carve a standing rib roast, place meat on a cutting board with large side down and rib bones to one side. Make a 1- to 2-in. cut along the curve of the bone to separate meat from bone.

2) Slice meat horizontally into 1/4-in. to 1/2-in. slices from the top edge to the bones. Repeat slicing, loosening meat from bone as necessary.

Peppery Roast Beef

PREP: 5 min. **BAKE:** 2-1/2 hours + standing

Maureen Brand, Somers, Iowa

With its spicy coating and creamy horseradish sauce, this tender roast is sure to be the star of any meal, whether it's a sit-down dinner or serve-yourself potluck.

- 1 tablespoon olive oil
- 1 tablespoon seasoned pepper
- 2 garlic cloves, minced
- 1/2 teaspoon dried thyme
- 1/4 teaspoon salt
- 1 boneless beef eye round roast (4 to 5 pounds)

HORSERADISH SAUCE:

- 1 cup (8 ounces) sour cream
- 2 tablespoons lemon juice
- 2 tablespoons milk
- 2 tablespoons prepared horseradish
- 1 tablespoon Dijon mustard
- 1/4 teaspoon salt
- 1/8 teaspoon pepper

1) In a small bowl, combine the oil, seasoned pepper, garlic, thyme and salt; rub over roast. Place fat side up on a rack in a shallow roasting pan.

2) Bake, uncovered, at 325° for 2-1/2 to 3 hours or until meat reaches desired doneness (for medium-rare, a meat thermometer should read 145°; medium, 160°; well-done, 170°). Let stand for 10 minutes before slicing.

3) In a small bowl, combine the sauce ingredients. Serve with roast.

Yield: 10-12 servings.

NUTRITION FACTS: 4 ounces cooked beef with 4-1/2 teaspoons sauce equals 228 calories, 10 g fat (4 g saturated fat), 83 mg cholesterol, 211 mg sodium, 3 g carbohydrate, trace fiber, 30 g protein.

PEPPERY ROAST BEEF

TENDERLOIN WITH CREAMY GARLIC SAUCE

Tenderloin with Creamy Garlic Sauce

PREP: 25 min. **BAKE:** 25 min. + standing

Beth Taylor, Chapin, South Carolina

I like to serve this main course with green beans, garlic mashed potatoes and seven-layer salad for a special holiday dinner. The garlic sauce is also good with pork or poultry.

- 1 jar (8 ounces) Dijon mustard, *divided*
- 10 garlic cloves, peeled, *divided*
- 2 tablespoons whole black peppercorns, coarsely crushed, *divided*
- 3 tablespoons vegetable oil, *divided*
- 1 beef tenderloin (4 to 5 pounds), halved
- 2 cups heavy whipping cream
- 1 cup (8 ounces) sour cream

1) In a blender, combine half of the mustard, eight garlic cloves and 1 tablespoon peppercorns; cover and process for 1 minute, scraping the sides occasionally. Add 1 tablespoon oil; process until a paste forms. Spread over beef.

2) In a large skillet, heat the remaining oil over medium-high heat. Brown beef, one piece at a time, on all sides. Place in a shallow roasting pan coated with cooking spray.

3) Bake, uncovered, at 400° for 25-45 minutes or until meat reaches desired doneness (for medium-rare, a meat thermometer should read 145°; medium, 160°; well-done, 170°). Remove to a warm serving platter. Let stand for 10-15 minutes.

4) Meanwhile, mince the remaining garlic. In a saucepan, combine garlic, whipping cream, sour cream and remaining mustard and peppercorns. Cook and stir over low heat until heated through. Slice beef; serve with the sauce.

Yield: 12 servings.

NUTRITION FACTS: 4 ounces cooked beef with 1/4 cup sauce equals 499 calories, 38 g fat (18 g saturated fat), 163 mg cholesterol, 553 mg sodium, 5 g carbohydrate, trace fiber, 33 g protein.

Spinach-Stuffed Beef Tenderloin

PREP: 30 min. **BAKE:** 40 min. + standing

Taste of Home Test Kitchen

Make this entree the centerpiece of Christmas dinner, and you're sure to be serving up seconds.

- 1/2 pound fresh mushrooms, chopped
- 4 green onions, sliced
- 2 tablespoons olive oil, *divided*
- 2 garlic cloves, minced, *divided*
- 2 packages (10 ounces *each*) fresh spinach leaves
- 1 teaspoon salt, *divided*
- 1/8 to 1/4 teaspoon cayenne pepper
- 1 whole beef tenderloin (about 3-1/2 pounds), trimmed
- 1/4 teaspoon onion powder
- 1/4 teaspoon coarsely ground pepper

1) In a large nonstick skillet, saute mushrooms and onions in 1 tablespoon oil for 2 minutes. Add half of the garlic; cook until mushrooms are tender. Add spinach, 1/2 teaspoon salt and cayenne. Cook until the spinach is wilted. Remove from the heat; set aside.

2) Cut a lengthwise slit down the center of tenderloin to within 3/4 in. of bottom. Open so meat lies flat. Spread with spinach stuffing. Fold one side of meat over stuffing; tie several times with kitchen string. Rub remaining oil over beef.

3) Combine the onion powder, pepper and remaining garlic and salt; rub over beef. Place on a rack in a shallow roasting pan.

4) Bake, uncovered, at 425° for 40-55 minutes or until meat reaches desired doneness (for medium-rare, a meat thermometer should read 145°; medium, 160°; well-done, 170°). Let stand for 10-15 minutes. Remove string before slicing.

Yield: 12 servings.

NUTRITION FACTS: 1 serving equals 241 calories, 12 g fat (4 g saturated fat), 83 mg cholesterol, 298 mg sodium, 3 g carbohydrate, 2 g fiber, 3 g protein.

Herbed Beef Tenderloin

PREP: 5 min. + marinating
GRILL: 30 min. + standing

Paul Verner, Wooster, Ohio

Grilling is a hobby of mine. This nicely seasoned dish is one of my family's favorites. Try it with baked potatoes and garden-fresh veggies.

- 1 beef tenderloin (4 to 5 pounds)
- 1/2 cup olive oil
- 2 green onions, finely chopped
- 2 garlic cloves, minced
- 1 tablespoon *each* dried basil, thyme and rosemary, crushed
- 1 tablespoon balsamic vinegar

Slicing Boneless Roasts

To slice boneless roasts, slice the meat vertically across the grain into 1/4-in. to 1/2-in. slices. If the roast is tied, remove the string as you carve to help hold the roast together.

- 1 tablespoon Dijon mustard
- 1 teaspoon salt
- 1 teaspoon pepper

1) Place tenderloin in a large resealable heavy-duty plastic bag. In a bowl, combine the remaining ingredients; pour over meat. Seal bag and turn to coat; refrigerate overnight.

2) Prepare grill for indirect medium-hot heat, using a drip pan. Drain and discard marinade from beef. Place beef over direct heat.

3) Grill, covered, over medium-hot heat for 10-15 minutes or until beef is browned, turning frequently. Move beef to indirect side of the grill.

4) Cover and grill for 20-25 minutes longer or until meat reaches desired doneness (for medium-rare, a meat thermometer should read 145°; medium, 160°; well-done, 170°). Let stand for 10 minutes before slicing.

Yield: 12 servings.

NUTRITION FACTS: 4 ounces cooked beef equals 256 calories, 13 g fat (4 g saturated fat), 95 mg cholesterol, 129 mg sodium, 1 g carbohydrate, 1 g fiber, 32 g protein.

FROM ROAST TO SALAD ▪▪▪

When I have leftover roast beef, I slice the beef in narrow strips and add onions, sweet peppers and Italian salad dressing. I toss it all together and refrigerate this salad to allow the flavors to blend. You don't even need to heat up the oven to enjoy this dish, which makes the most of leftovers.

—Elizabeth Blondefield, San Jose, California

COMPANY-PLEASING ROASTS

 CLASSIC: A beef rib roast is one of the premier roasts for tenderness and juiciness. The Roast Prime Rib recipe accentuates the beef with garlic, onion and a savory spice rub for an entree that's perfect when entertaining.

 TIME-SAVER: Sirloin Roast with Gravy requires only a few minutes of prep before the slow cooker takes over. You can start this roast and have time to run errands before you make the tasty soy-based gravy.

 LIGHT: A tender and leaner beef sirloin tip roast makes a special-occasion dinner that's also calorie- and cholesterol-friendly. Pepper-Crusted Sirloin Roast calls for a fresh blend of rosemary, mint and mustard to enhance the beef flavor.

 SERVES 2: This meat-and-potatoes recipe, Prime Rib and Potatoes, makes a hearty holiday meal. Just add a salad or vegetable, and dinner is served.

Roast Prime Rib

PREP: 10 min. **BAKE:** 1-3/4 hours + standing

Wendell Obermeier, Charles City, Iowa

- 1 tablespoon ground mustard
- 1-1/2 teaspoons salt
- 1/2 teaspoon paprika
- 1/4 teaspoon ground allspice
- 1/4 teaspoon pepper
- 1 boneless beef rib roast
  (4 to 5 pounds), rolled and tied
- 1 small onion, cut into thin slivers
- 2 garlic cloves, cut into slivers

Fresh parsley sprigs

1) In a small bowl, combine the mustard, salt, paprika, allspice and pepper. Using a sharp knife, cut long deep slits in the top of the roast, approximately 1 in. apart.

2) Stuff each slit with onion, garlic, parsley and a small amount of spice mixture. Rub remaining spice mixture on the outside of the roast.

3) Place on a rack in a shallow roasting pan. Bake, uncovered, at 350° for 1-3/4 to 1-1/2 hours or until meat reaches desired doneness (for medium-rare, a meat thermometer should read 145°; medium, 160°; well-done, 170°). Let stand for 10-15 minutes before carving.

Yield: 10 servings.

NUTRITION FACTS: 8 ounces cooked beef equals 470 calories, 36 g fat (14 g saturated fat), 117 mg cholesterol, 445 mg sodium, 1 g carbohydrate, trace fiber, 33 g protein.

Reducing Pan Juices for Gravy

To thicken pan juices without flour, remove the meat to a warm serving platter. Transfer pan juices along with browned bits to a saucepan. Bring to a boil; cook, uncovered, until the liquid evaporates enough that it thickens to a gravy consistency.

SIRLOIN ROAST WITH GRAVY

Sirloin Roast with Gravy

PREP: 15 min. **COOK:** 5-1/2 hours

Rita Clark, Monument, Colorado

- 1 boneless beef sirloin tip roast
  (about 3 pounds)
- 1 to 2 tablespoons coarsely ground pepper
- 1-1/2 teaspoons minced garlic
- 1/4 cup reduced-sodium soy sauce
- 3 tablespoons balsamic vinegar
- 1 tablespoon Worcestershire sauce
- 2 teaspoons ground mustard
- 2 tablespoons cornstarch
- 1/4 cup cold water

1) Rub roast with pepper and garlic; cut in half and place in a 3-qt. slow cooker. Combine the soy sauce, vinegar, Worcestershire sauce and mustard; pour over beef. Cover and cook on low for 5-1/2 to 6 hours or until the meat is tender.

2) Remove roast and keep warm. Strain cooking juices into a small saucepan; skim fat. Combine cornstarch and water until smooth; gradually stir

into cooking juices. Bring to a boil; cook and stir for 2 minutes or until thickened. Cut roast into slices. Serve with gravy.

Yield: 10 servings.

NUTRITION FACTS: 4 ounces cooked beef with 3 tablespoons gravy equals 185 calories, 6 g fat (2 g saturated fat), 72 mg cholesterol, 318 mg sodium, 4 g carbohydrate, trace fiber, 26 g protein.

Pepper-Crusted Sirloin Roast

PREP: 15 min. **BAKE:** 2-1/4 hours + standing

Mary Ann Griffin, Saginaw, Michigan

> 1 boneless beef sirloin tip roast (4 pounds)
> 2 tablespoons Dijon mustard
> 1 tablespoon coarsely ground pepper
> 1 tablespoon minced fresh rosemary *or* 1 teaspoon dried rosemary, crushed
> 1 tablespoon minced fresh mint *or* 1 teaspoon dried mint

1) Place roast fat side up on a rack in a shallow roasting pan; spread with mustard. Combine the pepper, rosemary and mint; press into mustard.

2) Bake, uncovered, at 350° for 2-1/4 to 3 hours or until meat reaches desired doneness (for medium-rare, a meat thermometer should read 145°; medium, 160°; well-done, 170°). Let stand for 10-15 minutes before slicing.

Yield: 12-16 servings.

NUTRITION FACTS: 1 serving equals 141 calories, 5 g fat (2 g saturated fat), 60 mg cholesterol, 96 mg sodium, 1 g carbohydrate, trace fiber, 21 g protein.

Give Your Roast a Rest

When preparing a special roast for company, remember that many recipes instruct you to let the roast stand or rest before carving. This is important because it allows the meat to reabsorb and distribute its juices more evenly. A roast may need to rest anywhere from 10 to 20 minutes, depending on its size. So plan ahead to use this time to tend to the last-minute touches needed to complete the rest of your menu.

Prime Rib and Potatoes

PREP: 10 min. **BAKE:** 1-3/4 hours + standing

Richard Fairchild, Orange, California

> 1 tablespoon olive oil
> 1 small garlic clove, minced
> 1 standing beef rib roast (about 3 pounds and 2 ribs)
> 2 large baking potatoes

1) Combine the oil and garlic; rub evenly over roast. Place roast fat side up in a small roasting pan. Place a potato on each side of roast.

2) Bake, uncovered, at 350° for 1-3/4 to 2-1/2 hours or until meat reaches desired doneness (for medium-rare, a meat thermometer should read 145°; medium, 160°; well-done, 170°). Let stand for 10 minutes before carving.

Yield: 2 servings.

NUTRITION FACTS: 1 serving equals 1,807 calories, 120 g fat (46 g saturated fat), 370 mg cholesterol, 309 mg sodium, 67 g carbohydrate, 6 g fiber, 109 g protein.

PRIME RIB AND POTATOES

Beef Wellington

PREP: 45 min. + chilling **BAKE:** 40 min. + standing

Janaan Cunningham, Greendale, Wisconsin

This very impressive-looking yet easy-to-make dish can be prepared ahead. Just finish when your guests arrive.

1 beef tenderloin (4 to 5 pounds)

MADEIRA SAUCE:

2 cans (10-1/2 ounces *each*) condensed beef consomme, undiluted

2 tablespoons tomato paste

1/2 teaspoon beef bouillon granules

2 tablespoons butter, softened

2 tablespoons all-purpose flour

1/2 cup Madeira wine

FILLING:

2 cups chopped fresh mushrooms

4 shallots, chopped

1/4 pound sliced deli ham, chopped

1/4 cup minced fresh parsley

1 package (17.3 ounces) frozen puff pastry sheets, thawed

2 tablespoons milk

1) Place the tenderloin in a greased 15-in. x 10-in. x 1-in. baking pan; fold ends under tenderloin. Bake, uncovered, at 475° for 20-25 minutes or until browned. Cover and refrigerate for at least 2 hours or until chilled.

2) For sauce, in a large saucepan, combine the consomme, tomato paste and bouillon granules. Bring to a boil. Reduce heat; simmer, uncovered, for 20 minutes or until reduced to 2 cups.

3) Combine butter and flour until smooth. Stir into sauce, a teaspoon at a time. Bring to a boil; cook and stir for 2 minutes or until thickened. Remove from the heat; stir in wine and set aside.

4) For the filling, in a large skillet, combine the mushrooms, shallots, ham and 2 tablespoons Madeira sauce. Cook over low heat for 10 minutes or until liquid has evaporated, stirring occasionally. Set aside.

5) On a lightly floured surface, unfold one puff pastry sheet; cut lengthwise along one fold line, forming two rectangles. Cut smaller rectangle into a 6-in. x 3-in. rectangle; use remaining piece for decorations if desired. Moisten a 6-in. edge of large rectangle with water. Attach the smaller rectangle along that edge, pressing lightly to seal. Transfer to an ungreased baking sheet.

6) Spread half of the filling down the center of pastry. Place the tenderloin on the filling. Spread the remaining filling over the top of meat. Roll out remaining puff pastry into a rectangle 8 in. wide and 5 in. longer than the tenderloin; place over the meat. Brush pastry edges with milk; fold edges under meat.

7) Bake, uncovered, at 425° for 40 minutes (meat will be medium); cover lightly with foil if needed. Transfer to a serving platter. Let stand for 15 minutes before slicing. Rewarm Madeira sauce if necessary. Serve with tenderloin.

Yield: 12-16 servings.

NUTRITION FACTS: 1 serving equals 394 calories, 21 g fat (7 g saturated fat), 79 mg cholesterol, 380 mg sodium, 21 g carbohydrate, 3 g fiber, 28 g protein.

ROAST BEEF REVIVAL ■■■

I heat hickory-smoked barbecue sauce with a little water and brown sugar, then add thin slices of leftover roast beef. Once it's heated, I serve it on buns.

—Florence Beaudoin, Windsor, Ontario

Yankee-Doodle Sirloin Roast

PREP: 10 min. + marinating
BAKE: 2 hours + standing

Laurie Neverman, Denmark, Wisconsin

Marinating the meat overnight really boosts the flavor of this family-pleasing roast.

1/2 cup beef broth

1/2 cup teriyaki *or* soy sauce

1/4 cup vegetable oil

2 tablespoons brown sugar

2 tablespoons finely chopped onion

3 garlic cloves, minced

1 teaspoon Worcestershire sauce

1/2 teaspoon hot pepper sauce

1 boneless beef sirloin tip roast (about 4 pounds)

1) In a large resealable plastic bag, combine the first eight ingredients; add roast. Seal bag and turn to coat; refrigerate overnight.

2) Drain and discard marinade. Place roast on a rack in a shallow roasting pan.

BEEF WELLINGTON

3) Bake, uncovered, at 350° for 1-1/2 to 2-1/4 hours or until meat reaches desired doneness (for medium-rare, a meat thermometer should read 145°; medium, 160°; well-done, 170°). Let stand for 10-15 minutes before slicing.

Yield: 12-14 servings.

Editor's Note: To grill the roast, grill, covered, over indirect medium heat for 1-1/2 to 2-1/4 hours or until meat reaches desired doneness.

NUTRITION FACTS: 3 ounces cooked beef equals 183 calories, 8 g fat (2 g saturated fat), 69 mg cholesterol, 247 mg sodium, 2 g carbohydrate, trace fiber, 25 g protein.

Slicing Corned Beef

For melt-in-your-mouth corned beef, thinly slice the meat across the grain.

Corned Beef Dinner

PREP: 10 min. **COOK:** 9 hours

Michelle Rhodes, Fort Bliss, Texas

This traditional meal is a must for St. Patrick's Day but great any time of the year. A slow cooker makes it easy.

      4 to 5 medium red potatoes, quartered
      2 cups fresh baby carrots, halved lengthwise
      3 cups chopped cabbage
      1 corned beef brisket (3-1/2 pounds) with spice packet
      3 cups water
      1 tablespoon caraway seeds

1) Place the potatoes, carrots and cabbage in a 5-qt. slow cooker. Cut brisket in half; place over vegetables. Add the water, caraway seeds and contents of spice packet.

2) Cover and cook on low for 9-10 hours or until the meat and vegetables are tender.

Yield: 8 servings.

NUTRITION FACTS: 1 serving equals 457 calories, 30 g fat (9 g saturated fat), 107 mg cholesterol, 2,452 mg sodium, 14 g carbohydrate, 3 g fiber, 31 g protein.

Slow Cooker Tips

Choose the correct size slow cooker for your recipe. A slow cooker should be from half to three-quarters full.

Cut roasts over 3 pounds in half to ensure proper and even cooking. Trim as much fat from meat to avoid greasy gravy.

Do not remove the lid during cooking unless the recipe specifically says to stir or add an ingredient. Removing the lid allows a significant amount of heat to be lost and will increase the cooking time.

SLOW-COOKED COFFEE BEEF ROAST

Slow-Cooked Coffee Beef Roast

PREP: 15 min. **COOK:** 8 hours

Charles Trahan, San Dimas, California

Day-old coffee is the key to this flavorful beef roast that simmers in the slow cooker until it's fall-apart tender. Try it once, and I'm sure you'll cook it again.

      1 boneless beef sirloin tip roast (2-1/2 pounds), cut in half
      2 teaspoons canola oil
  1-1/2 cups sliced fresh mushrooms
    1/3 cup sliced green onions
      2 garlic cloves, minced
  1-1/2 cups brewed coffee
      1 teaspoon Liquid Smoke, optional
    1/2 teaspoon salt
    1/2 teaspoon chili powder
    1/4 teaspoon pepper
    1/4 cup cornstarch
    1/3 cup cold water

1) In a large nonstick skillet, brown roast on all sides in oil over medium-high heat. Place in a 5-qt. slow cooker.

2) In the same skillet, saute mushrooms, onions and garlic until tender; stir in the coffee, Liquid Smoke if desired, salt, chili powder and pepper. Pour over roast.

3) Cover and cook on low for 8-10 hours or until meat is tender. Remove roast and keep warm. Pour cooking juices into a 2-cup measuring cup; skim fat.

4) In a saucepan, combine cornstarch and water until smooth. Gradually stir in 2 cups cooking juices. Bring to a boil; cook and stir for 2 minutes or until thickened. Serve with sliced beef.

Yield: 6 servings.

NUTRITION FACTS: 3 ounces cooked beef with 1/3 cup gravy equals 209 calories, 7 g fat (2 g saturated fat), 82 mg cholesterol, 244 mg sodium, 6 g carbohydrate, trace fiber, 28 g protein.

BIG ON BRISKETS

 CLASSIC: A brisket is a good cut to use when entertaining. It's usually large, and there is little waste. As demonstrated in Cranberry-Mushroom Beef Brisket, this less-tender cut of beef is frequently cooked one day and reheated the next, which cuts down on last-minute preparation.

 TIME-SAVER: The slow cooker, with its low temperature and slow cooking, is a great appliance to make Brisket for a Bunch. This recipe takes just 20 minutes to assemble, then pop it in the slow cooker and leave it until mealtime.

 LIGHT: Brisket with Gravy limits the serving size to 3 ounces of cooked brisket. By being mindful of the serving size, you can better control your calorie intake.

 SERVES 2: A smoky homemade barbecue sauce coats the small brisket in Rocky Mountain Brisket. If you like, purchase a large brisket and cut it into 1-pound pieces. Use one piece for this recipe. Wrap the other pieces individually and freeze until ready to use.

CRANBERRY-MUSHROOM BEEF BRISKET

Cranberry-Mushroom Beef Brisket

PREP: 30 min. **BAKE:** 4 hours + chilling

Margaret Welder, Madrid, Iowa

- 2 cups beef broth
- 1/2 cup cranberry juice concentrate
- 1/4 cup red wine vinegar
- 4-1/2 teaspoons chopped fresh rosemary *or* 1-1/2 teaspoons dried rosemary, crushed
- 4 garlic cloves, minced
- 1 large onion, thinly sliced
- 1 fresh beef brisket (4 pounds)
- 1/2 teaspoon salt
- 1/4 teaspoon pepper
- 1/4 cup all-purpose flour
- 1/4 cup cold water
- 1/4 to 1/2 teaspoon browning sauce, optional
- 1 pound fresh mushrooms, sliced
- 1-1/2 cups dried cranberries

1) In a large bowl, combine the broth, cranberry juice concentrate, vinegar, rosemary and garlic; pour into a large roasting pan. Top with onion slices.

2) Season beef with salt and pepper; place fat side up in pan. Cover; bake at 325° for 3 to 3-1/2 hours or until tender. Remove meat and thinly slice meat across the grain. Cover and refrigerate overnight.

3) For gravy, skim fat from cooking juices; pour into a saucepan. Combine flour, water and browning sauce if desired until smooth; stir into cooking juices. Bring to a boil; cook and stir for 2 minutes or until thickened. Cover and refrigerate.

4) Place beef slices in a shallow baking dish; top with mushrooms, cranberries and gravy. Cover and bake at 325° for 60-65 minutes or until heated through and mushrooms are tender.

Yield: 10-12 servings.

Editor's Note: This is a fresh beef brisket, not corned beef.

NUTRITION FACTS: 1 serving equals 383 calories, 19 g fat (7 g saturated fat), 90 mg cholesterol, 313 mg sodium, 24 g carbohydrate, 2 g fiber, 28 g protein.

Brisket for a Bunch

PREP: 20 min. **COOK:** 7 hours

Dawn Fagerstrom, Warren, Minnesota

- 1 fresh beef brisket (2-1/2 pounds), cut in half
- 1 tablespoon vegetable oil
- 1/2 cup chopped celery
- 1/2 cup chopped onion
- 3/4 cup beef broth
- 1/2 cup tomato sauce
- 1/4 cup water
- 1/4 cup sugar
- 2 tablespoons onion soup mix
- 1 tablespoon cider vinegar
- 12 hamburger buns, split

1) In a large skillet, brown the brisket in oil on each side; transfer to a slow cooker. In the same skillet, saute celery and onion for 1 minute. Gradually add the broth, tomato sauce and water; stir to loosen the browned bits from pan. Add the sugar, soup mix and vinegar; bring to a boil. Pour over brisket.

2) Cover and cook on low for 7-8 hours or until meat is tender. Let stand for 5 minutes before slicing. Skim fat from cooking juices. Serve meat in buns with cooking juices.

Yield: 10 servings.

Editor's Note: This is a fresh beef brisket, not corned beef.

NUTRITION FACTS: 3 ounces cooked beef equals 404 calories, 18 g fat (6 g saturated fat), 68 mg cholesterol, 583 mg sodium, 33 g carbohydrate, 2 g fiber, 25 g protein.

Brisket with Gravy

PREP: 10 min. **BAKE:** 3 hours 50 min.

Margaret Haugh Heilman, Houston, Texas

- 1 fresh beef brisket (about 4 pounds)
- 1/2 teaspoon pepper
- 1 large onion, thinly sliced and separated into rings
- 1 can (12 ounces) beer *or* nonalcoholic beer
- 1/2 cup chili sauce
- 3 tablespoons brown sugar
- 2 garlic cloves, minced
- 2 tablespoons cornstarch
- 1/4 cup cold water

1) Place beef in a roasting pan. Sprinkle with pepper and top with onion. Combine the beer, chili sauce, brown sugar and garlic; stir until sugar is dissolved. Pour over meat.

BRISKET FOR A BUNCH

2) Cover and bake at 325° for 3-1/2 hours. Uncover; bake 15-30 minutes longer or until onions are lightly browned and meat is tender. Remove meat and onions to a serving platter and keep warm.

3) Pour drippings and loosened browned bits into a saucepan. Skim fat. Combine cornstarch and water until smooth. Gradually stir into pan drippings. Bring to a boil; cook and stir for 2 minutes or until thickened. Slice meat thinly across the grain. Serve with gravy.

Yield: 12 servings.

Editor's Note: This is a fresh beef brisket, not corned beef.

NUTRITION FACTS: 3 ounces cooked beef equals 270 calories, 12 g fat (4 g saturated fat), 88 mg cholesterol, 389 mg sodium, 9 g carbohydrate, 1 g fiber, 28 g protein.

Rocky Mountain Brisket

PREP: 20 min. **BAKE:** 3 hours

Judy Ehrhart, Gonzales, Louisiana

- 1 fresh beef brisket (1 pound)
- 1-1/2 teaspoons chili powder
- 1/2 teaspoon pepper
- 1/4 teaspoon salt
- 1-1/2 teaspoons Liquid Smoke, optional
- 1 bay leaf

BARBECUE SAUCE:

- 2/3 cup ketchup
- 2 tablespoons water
- 4 teaspoons Worcestershire sauce
- 1 tablespoon butter
- 1 tablespoon brown sugar
- 1 teaspoon ground mustard
- 1/2 teaspoon celery seed
- 1/2 teaspoon Liquid Smoke, optional

Dash cayenne pepper

Dash pepper

1) Place brisket fat side up in an 11-in. x 7-in. x 2-in. baking dish coated with cooking spray. Combine the chili powder, pepper and salt; rub over brisket. Sprinkle with Liquid Smoke if desired. Add bay leaf. Cover and bake at 325° for 2-1/2 hours or until meat is almost tender. Drain; discard juices and bay leaf.

2) In a small saucepan, combine all the sauce ingredients. Bring to a boil over medium heat. Pour over brisket. Cover and bake 30 minutes longer or until meat is tender and sauce is heated through. Thinly slice brisket across the grain.

Yield: 3 servings.

Editor's Note: This is a fresh beef brisket, not corned beef.

NUTRITION FACTS: 5 ounces cooked beef equals 406 calories, 24 g fat (10 g saturated fat), 101 mg cholesterol, 1,021 mg sodium, 22 g carbohydrate, 1 g fiber, 27 g protein.

BRAISED BEEF WITH BARLEY

Braised Beef with Barley

PREP: 30 min. **COOK:** 2 hours 20 min.

June Formanek, Belle Plaine, Iowa

Braising works well for less tender cuts of meat and brings out the flavor of the chuck roast in this recipe. Barley, mushrooms and peas are a wonderful addition to the meal.

> 1 boneless chuck roast (2 to 2-1/2 pounds)
> 1 tablespoon vegetable oil
> 1 medium onion, chopped
> 1/2 pound fresh mushrooms, sliced
> 3 garlic cloves, minced
> 1 can (14-1/2 ounces) beef broth
> 1 bay leaf
> 1-1/2 teaspoons salt
> 1/4 teaspoon pepper
> 1/2 cup medium pearl barley
> 1 cup frozen peas
> 1/3 cup sour cream, optional

1) In a Dutch oven, brown meat in oil on all sides over medium-high heat. Remove roast and set aside. Drain, reserving 1 tablespoon of drippings. Saute the onion, mushrooms and garlic in drippings until tender.

2) Return roast to the pan. Add the broth, bay leaf, salt and pepper; bring to a boil. Reduce heat; cover and simmer for 1-1/2 hours. Add barley. Cover and simmer for 45 minutes or until meat and barley are tender. Add peas; cover and simmer for 5 minutes or until peas are tender. Discard bay leaf.

3) Set the roast and barley aside; keep warm. Skim fat from pan juices. If desired, add sour cream to the pan juices; stir until heated through over low heat (do not boil). Slice roast; serve with barley and gravy.

Yield: 6 servings.

NUTRITION FACTS: 1 serving equals 380 calories, 17 g fat (6 g saturated fat), 98 mg cholesterol, 922 mg sodium, 21 g carbohydrate, 5 g fiber, 35 g protein.

Braising Beef

1) Heat oil in a Dutch oven over medium-high. Brown roast on all sides, turning with a sturdy meat fork.

2) Combine liquid ingredients and seasonings; pour over roast. Cover and simmer for 1 to 2 hours or bake at 325° for 2 to 3 hours or until tender. Proceed with recipe.

Thickening Pan Juices from Braised Beef

Remove meat to a warm serving platter; skim fat from pan juices. (See Step 1 of Making Pan Gravy on page 488.) Measure juices and transfer to a saucepan. For each cup of juices, combine 3 tablespoons all-purpose flour and 1/3 cup cold water until smooth. Stir flour mixture into pan; bring to a boil, stirring constantly. Cook and stir for 2 minutes or until thickened, adding additional water if necessary. Season to taste with salt and pepper.

GERMAN SAUERBRATEN

German Sauerbraten

PREP: 10 min. + marinating
COOK: 3 hours 10 min.

Cathy Eland, Highstown, New Jersey

Our family loves it when Mom prepares this wonderful old-world dish. The tender beef has a bold blend of mouthwatering seasonings.

- 2 teaspoons salt
- 1 teaspoon ground ginger
- 1 beef top round roast (about 4 pounds)
- 2-1/2 cups water
- 2 cups cider vinegar
- 2 medium onions, sliced
- 1/3 cup sugar
- 2 tablespoons mixed pickling spices
- 1 teaspoon whole peppercorns
- 8 whole cloves
- 2 bay leaves
- 2 tablespoons vegetable oil
- 14 to 16 gingersnaps, crushed

1) Combine salt and ginger; rub over roast. Place in a deep glass bowl. In a saucepan, combine water, vinegar, onions, sugar and seasonings; bring to a boil. Pour over roast; turn to coat. Cover and refrigerate for 2 days, turning twice a day.

2) Remove roast, reserving marinade; pat roast dry. In a large kettle or Dutch oven, brown roast on all sides in oil over medium-high heat.

3) Strain marinade, reserving half of the onions and seasonings. Pour 1 cup of marinade and reserved onions and seasonings over roast (cover and refrigerate remaining marinade). Bring to a boil. Reduce heat; cover and simmer for 3 hours or until meat is tender.

4) Strain cooking liquid, discarding the onions and seasonings. Measure liquid; if necessary, add enough reserved marinade to equal 3 cups. Pour

into a saucepan and bring to a full rolling boil; boil for 1 minute. Add gingersnaps. Reduce heat; simmer, uncovered, until gravy is thickened. Slice roast and serve with gravy.

Yield: 14 servings.

NUTRITION FACTS: 3-1/2 ounces cooked beef with about 3 tablespoons gravy equals 241 calories, 7 g fat (2 g saturated fat), 73 mg cholesterol, 420 mg sodium, 15 g carbohydrate, 1 g fiber, 30 g protein.

Hungarian Goulash

PREP: 20 min. **COOK:** 1-1/2 hours

Joan Rose, Langley, British Columbia

With tender beef and a rich flavorful sauce, this entree is an all-time favorite with my family.

- 1 pound beef stew meat, cut into 1-inch cubes
- 1 pound lean boneless pork, cut into 1-inch cubes
- 2 large onions, thinly sliced
- 2 tablespoons vegetable oil
- 2 cups water
- 2 tablespoons paprika
- 1/2 teaspoon salt
- 1/2 teaspoon dried marjoram
- 1 tablespoon all-purpose flour
- 1 cup (8 ounces) sour cream

Hot cooked noodles

1) In a large skillet, brown beef, pork and onions in oil over medium heat; drain. Add the water, paprika, salt and marjoram; bring to a boil. Reduce heat; cover and simmer for 1-1/2 hours or until meat is tender.

2) Combine flour and sour cream until smooth; stir into meat mixture. Bring to a boil over medium heat; cook and stir for 1-2 minutes or until thickened and bubbly. Serve over noodles.

Yield: 6-8 servings.

NUTRITION FACTS: 1 cup goulash (calculated without noodles) equals 273 calories, 16 g fat (7 g saturated fat), 89 mg cholesterol, 212 mg sodium, 6 g carbohydrate, 1 g fiber, 24 g protein.

Carving Chuck Roasts

1) To carve arm or blade chuck roasts, first separate the individual muscles by cutting around each muscle and bone.

2) Carve each muscle across the grain of the meat to desired thickness.

HOME-STYLE POT ROASTS

 CLASSIC: Down-Home Pot Roast is just like Mom would make with potatoes, onions and carrots. Sweet red pepper and cabbage are easy additions for extra flavor and color.

 TIME-SAVER: Chuck roast is cooked to delectable tenderness in a slow cooker in Cajun-Style Pot Roast. Tapioca is added to thicken the gravy while it cooks, eliminating the need to make gravy before serving.

 LIGHT: Marinated Pot Roast uses a beef top round roast, which is a lean cut of beef. The recipe calls for marinating the meat in a wine-soy sauce mixture overnight to help tenderize the roast and give it extra flavor.

 SERVES 2: A small beef chuck steak takes the place of chuck roast in Maple Pot Roast. This smaller cut gives two generous servings. If you can only find a chuck roast in your grocery store, cut the roast into smaller portions and freeze the unused part.

Down-Home Pot Roast

PREP: 15 min. **COOK:** 2 hours 35 min.

Lenore Rein, Kelliher, Saskatchewan

- 1 boneless beef sirloin tip roast (3 pounds)
- 1 tablespoon canola oil
- 1 can (14-1/2 ounces) reduced-sodium beef broth
- 3 tablespoons cider vinegar
- 2 garlic cloves, minced
- 1/2 teaspoon dried basil
- 1/4 teaspoon dried thyme
- 1 small head cabbage, cut into wedges
- 4 medium potatoes, quartered
- 2 medium onions, cut into chunks
- 3 medium carrots, cut into chunks
- 1 medium sweet red pepper, cut into 1-inch pieces
- 1/2 teaspoon salt
- 1/2 teaspoon pepper
- 1/4 cup all-purpose flour
- 1/4 cup cold water

1) In a Dutch oven, brown roast on all sides in oil over medium-high heat; drain. Add broth. Pour vinegar over roast. Sprinkle with garlic, basil and thyme. Bring to a boil. Reduce heat; cover and simmer for 2 hours, turning roast occasionally. Add water if needed. Skim off fat.

2) Add vegetables to pan. Sprinkle with salt and pepper. Cover and simmer for 35-45 minutes or until vegetables and meat are tender. Remove meat and vegetables to a serving platter and keep warm.

3) For gravy, pour drippings and loosened browned bits into a measuring cup. Skim fat, reserving 2 cups drippings. Return drippings to pan.

4) Combine flour and cold water until smooth; gradually stir into drippings. Bring to a boil; cook

and stir for 2 minutes or until thickened. Serve with meat and vegetables.

Yield: 12 servings.

NUTRITION FACTS: 3 ounces cooked beef with 2 tablespoons sauce equals 258 calories, 7 g fat (2 g saturated fat), 61 mg cholesterol, 235 mg sodium, 25 g carbohydrate, 4 g fiber, 25 g protein.

CAJUN-STYLE POT ROAST

Cajun-Style Pot Roast

PREP: 15 min. **COOK:** 6 hours

Ginger Menzies, Oak Creek, Colorado

- 1 boneless beef chuck roast (2 to 3 pounds)
- 2 tablespoons Cajun seasoning
- 1 tablespoon olive oil
- 2 cans (10 ounces *each*) diced tomatoes and green chilies
- 1 medium sweet red pepper, chopped
- 1-1/2 cups chopped celery
- 3/4 cup chopped onion

1/4 cup quick-cooking tapioca
1-1/2 teaspoons minced garlic
1 teaspoon salt
Hot cooked rice

1) Cut roast in half; sprinkle with Cajun seasoning. In a large skillet, brown roast in oil on all sides; drain. Transfer to a 5-qt. slow cooker.

2) Combine the tomatoes, red pepper, celery, onion, tapioca, garlic and salt; pour over roast. Cover and cook on low for 6-8 hours or until meat is tender. Slice and serve with rice.

Yield: 6 servings.

NUTRITION FACTS: 1 serving (calculated without rice) equals 328 calories, 17 g fat (6 g saturated fat), 98 mg cholesterol, 1,336 mg sodium, 13 g carbohydrate, 2 g fiber, 31 g protein.

MAPLE POT ROAST

Marinated Pot Roast

PREP: 10 min. + marinating **COOK:** 8 hours

Marijane Rea, Portland, Oregon

1 cup dry white wine *or* beef broth
1/3 cup reduced-sodium soy sauce
1 tablespoon olive oil
4 garlic cloves, minced
2 green onions, thinly sliced
1-1/2 teaspoons ground ginger
1/4 teaspoon pepper
4 whole cloves
1 boneless beef top round roast (4 pounds)
5 teaspoons cornstarch
5 teaspoons cold water

1) In a gallon-size resealable plastic bag, combine the first eight ingredients. Cut roast in half; add to marinade. Seal bag and turn to coat; refrigerate overnight.

2) Place roast and marinade in a 5-qt. slow cooker. Cover and cook on low for 8-10 hours or until meat is tender. Remove roast to a serving platter and keep warm. Pour cooking juices into a 2-cup measuring cup; discard whole cloves

3) In a saucepan, combine cornstarch and cold water until smooth; stir in 1-1/2 cups cooking juices. Bring to a boil; cook and stir for 2 minutes or until thickened. Serve with the roast.

Yield: 12 servings.

NUTRITION FACTS: 3 ounces cooked beef with 2 tablespoons gravy equals 174 calories, 6 g fat (2 g saturated fat), 59 mg cholesterol, 255 mg sodium, 3 g carbohydrate, trace fiber, 25 g protein.

Maple Pot Roast

PREP: 15 min. **COOK:** 2 hours

Amy Miazga, Cohoes, New York

3/4 pound boneless beef chuck steak (3/4 to 1 inch thick)
1/4 cup orange juice

1/4 cup maple syrup
4-1/2 teaspoons red wine vinegar
1-1/2 teaspoons Worcestershire sauce
1 teaspoon grated orange peel
1/8 teaspoon salt
1/8 teaspoon pepper
1 medium carrot, cut into 2-inch pieces
1 celery rib, cut into 2-inch pieces
8 fresh pearl onions, peeled
1 large potato, peeled and cut into 2-inch pieces

1) In a Dutch oven coated with cooking spray, brown meat on both sides. Combine the orange juice, syrup, vinegar, Worcestershire sauce, orange peel, salt and pepper; pour over roast. Bring to a boil. Reduce heat; cover and simmer for 1 hour.

2) Add the carrot, celery and onions; cover and simmer for 20 minutes. Add potato; cover and simmer for 20 minutes or until tender. Serve roast and vegetables with pan juices.

Yield: 2 servings.

Editor's Note: For information on how to peel pearl onions, see page 391.

NUTRITION FACTS: 6 ounces cooked beef with 3/4 cup cooked vegetables equals 619 calories, 17 g fat (6 g saturated fat), 111 mg cholesterol, 304 mg sodium, 80 g carbohydrate, 6 g fiber, 38 g protein.

Pot Roast Doneness Test

Pot roasts are done when a long handled fork can be inserted into the thickest part of the roast easily. If the pot roast is cooked until it falls apart, the meat is actually overcooked and will be stringy, tough and dry.

MONGOLIAN FONDUE

Mongolian Fondue

PREP: 15 min. + chilling **COOK:** 20 min.

Marion Lowery, Medford, Oregon

Mealtime is so much fun when fondue is on the menu. I made this recipe after tasting something similar in a restaurant.

- 1/2 cup soy sauce
- 1/4 cup water
- 1 teaspoon white wine vinegar
- 1-1/2 teaspoons minced garlic, *divided*
- 1 cup sliced carrots (1/4 inch thick)
- 2 cans (14-1/2 ounces *each*) beef broth
- 1 teaspoon minced fresh gingerroot
- 2 pounds boneless beef sirloin steak, cut into 2-1/2-inch x 1/4-inch strips
- 1 pound turkey breast, cut into 2-1/2-inch x 1/4-inch strips
- 1 pound uncooked large shrimp, peeled and deveined
- 3 small zucchini, cut into 1/2-inch slices
- 1 *each* medium sweet red, yellow and green pepper, cut into 1-inch chunks
- 1 to 2 cups whole fresh mushrooms
- 1 cup cubed red onion (1-inch pieces)
- 1 jar (7 ounces) hoisin sauce
- 1 jar (4 ounces) Chinese hot mustard

1) In a saucepan, combine the soy sauce, water, vinegar and 1/2 teaspoon garlic; bring to a boil. Remove from the heat. Cover and refrigerate for at least 1 hour.

2) In a small saucepan, cook carrots in a small amount of water for 3 minutes or until crisp-tender; drain and pat dry.

3) In a large saucepan, bring broth, ginger and remaining garlic to a boil. Transfer to a fondue pot and keep warm.

4) Pat meat and shrimp dry with paper towels. Use fondue forks to cook beef to desired doneness. Cook turkey until juices run clear. Cook shrimp until pink. Cook vegetables until they reach desired doneness. Serve with hoisin sauce, mustard sauce and reserved garlic-soy sauce.

Yield: 8 servings.

NUTRITION FACTS: 1 serving equals 364 calories, 8 g fat (2 g saturated fat), 184 mg cholesterol, 1,826 mg sodium, 21 g carbohydrate, 3 g fiber, 50 g protein.

Marinated Beef Fondue

PREP: 15 min. + marinating **COOK:** 5 min./batch

DeEtta Rasmussen, Fort Madison, Iowa

Guests will enjoy cooking this boldly seasoned meat, then dipping it in either zippy horseradish or barbecue sauce.

- 3/4 cup soy sauce
- 1/4 cup Worcestershire sauce
- 2 garlic cloves, minced
- 2-1/2 pounds beef tenderloin, cut into 1-inch cubes
- 2-1/2 pounds pork tenderloin, cut into 1-inch cubes

HORSERADISH SAUCE:

- 1 cup (8 ounces) sour cream
- 3 tablespoons prepared horseradish
- 1 tablespoon chopped onion
- 1 teaspoon white vinegar
- 1/2 teaspoon salt
- 1/4 teaspoon pepper

BARBECUE SAUCE:

- 1 can (8 ounces) tomato sauce
- 1/3 cup steak sauce
- 2 tablespoons brown sugar
- 6 to 9 cups peanut *or* vegetable oil

1) In a resealable plastic bag, combine the first three ingredients; add meat. Seal bag and turn to coat; refrigerate for 4 hours, turning occasionally.

2) Meanwhile, in a small bowl, combine horseradish sauce ingredients; cover and refrigerate.

3) In another bowl, combine the tomato sauce, steak sauce and brown sugar; cover and refrigerate. Drain and discard marinade. Pat meat dry.

4) Using one fondue pot for every six people, heat 2-3 cups oil in each pot to 375°. Use fondue forks to cook meat in oil until it reaches desired doneness. Serve with the horseradish and barbecue sauces.

Yield: 12-16 servings.

NUTRITION FACTS: 1 serving equals 272 calories, 13 g fat (5 g saturated fat), 94 mg cholesterol, 680 mg sodium, 5 g carbohydrate, trace fiber, 30 g protein.

Beef Tenderloin Stroganoff

PREP/TOTAL TIME: 30 min.

Elizabeth Deguit, Richmond Hill, Georgia

This entree is easy to prepare, and it's a great dish to serve company. Using tenderloin makes it special.

- 2 tablespoons all-purpose flour
- 1-1/2 pounds beef tenderloin, cut into thin strips
- 2 tablespoons olive oil
- 2 tablespoons butter
- 1-1/2 cups beef broth
- 1/4 cup sour cream
- 2 tablespoons tomato paste
- 1/2 teaspoon paprika

Salt to taste

Hot cooked noodles

1) Place flour in a resealable plastic bag; add beef, a few pieces at a time, and shake to coat. In a large skillet, brown beef in oil and butter over medium heat.

2) Gradually stir in broth; bring to a boil. Reduce heat to low. In a bowl, combine sour cream, tomato paste, paprika and salt; slowly stir in sour cream mixture (do not boil).

3) Cook, uncovered, over low heat for 15-20 minutes, stirring frequently. Serve over noodles.

Yield: 4-6 servings.

NUTRITION FACTS: 1 serving (calculated without salt and noodles) equals 312 calories, 21 g fat (9 g saturated fat), 89 mg cholesterol, 305 mg sodium, 4 g carbohydrate, trace fiber, 24 g protein.

Freezing Leftover Tomato Paste

A tablespoon or two of tomato paste adds richness and color to many savory dishes. Here's a tip for storing leftover tomato paste. Line a baking sheet with waxed paper. Mound the tomato paste in 1-tablespoon portions on the waxed paper. Freeze until firm, then transfer to a resealable freezer bag.

BEEF STEW WITH POTATO DUMPLINGS

Beef Stew with Potato Dumplings

PREP: 10 min. **COOK:** 1 hour 50 min.

Shawn Asiala, Del Ray Beach, Florida

You could call me a "recipe tinkerer." It's fun for me to take a recipe, substitute ingredients, add seasonings to spice it up and make the final result my own!

- 1/4 cup all-purpose flour
- 3/4 teaspoon salt
- 1/2 teaspoon pepper
- 2 pounds beef stew meat
- 2 medium onions, chopped
- 2 tablespoons vegetable oil
- 2 cans (10-1/2 ounces *each*) condensed beef broth, undiluted
- 3/4 cup water
- 1 tablespoon red wine vinegar
- 6 medium carrots, cut into 2-inch chunks
- 2 bay leaves
- 1 teaspoon dried thyme
- 1/4 teaspoon garlic powder

DUMPLINGS:

- 1 egg
- 3/4 cup seasoned dry bread crumbs
- 1 tablespoon all-purpose flour
- 1 tablespoon minced fresh parsley
- 1 tablespoon minced onion
- 1/2 teaspoon dried thyme
- 1/2 teaspoon salt
- 1/2 teaspoon pepper
- 2-1/2 cups finely shredded raw potatoes

Additional all-purpose flour

1) In a plastic bag, combine the flour, salt and pepper. Add meat; toss to coat. In a Dutch oven, cook meat along with onions in oil until the meat is browned on all sides and onions are tender.

2) Stir in the broth, water, vinegar, carrots and seasonings; bring to a boil. Reduce heat; cover and simmer for 1-1/2 hours or until meat is almost tender. Discard bay leaves.

3) In a large bowl, beat egg; add the crumbs, flour, parsley, onion and seasonings. Stir in potatoes; mix well. With floured hands, shape into 1-1/2-in. balls. Dust with flour.

4) Bring stew to a boil; drop dumplings onto stew. Cover and simmer for 30 minutes (do not lift cover while simmering). Serve immediately.

Yield: 6 servings.

NUTRITION FACTS: 1 serving (calculated without additional all-purpose flour) equals 487 calories, 18 g fat (5 g saturated fat), 130 mg cholesterol, 1,486 mg sodium, 42 g carbohydrate, 5 g fiber, 38 g protein.

SAVORY STEWS

 CLASSIC: This sure-to-satisfy beef stew is loaded with beef stew meat, potatoes and carrots. Cider Beef Stew is simmered in apple cider or juice for a delicious taste twist.

 TIME-SAVER: The ground beef and frozen veggies in Beefy Vegetable Stew not only make for easy prep, but require a shorter cooking time. Your family can enjoy this hearty meal even on busy weeknights.

 LIGHT: Calories are trimmed in Southwestern Beef Stew by using beef round steak, which is one of the leanest cuts of beef available, yet there's no reduction in flavor.

SERVES 2: Beef Burgundy is an elegant stew that has a subtle blend of flavors from the tomato paste, currant jelly and Burgundy wine.

CIDER BEEF STEW

Cider Beef Stew
PREP: 30 min. **COOK:** 1-3/4 hours

Joyce Glaesemann, Lincoln, Nebraska

- 2 pounds beef stew meat, cut into 1-inch cubes
- 2 tablespoons vegetable oil
- 3 cups apple cider *or* juice
- 2 tablespoons cider vinegar
- 2 teaspoons salt, optional
- 1/4 to 1/2 teaspoon dried thyme
- 1/4 teaspoon pepper
- 3 medium potatoes, peeled and cubed
- 4 medium carrots, cut into 3/4-inch pieces
- 3 celery ribs, cut into 3/4-inch pieces
- 2 medium onions, cut into wedges
- 1/4 cup all-purpose flour
- 1/4 cup water

1) In a Dutch oven, brown beef on all sides in oil over medium-high heat; drain. Add the cider, vinegar, salt if desired, thyme and pepper; bring to a boil. Reduce heat; cover and simmer for 1-1/4 hours.

2) Add the potatoes, carrots, celery and onions; return to a boil. Reduce heat; cover and simmer for 30-35 minutes or until beef and vegetables are tender.

3) Combine flour and water until smooth; stir into stew. Bring to a boil; cook and stir for 2 minutes or until slightly thickened.

Yield: 8 servings.

NUTRITION FACTS: 1 cup equals 315 calories, 12 g fat (0 saturated fat), 70 mg cholesterol, 238 mg sodium, 29 g carbohydrate, 0 fiber, 24 g protein.

Beefy Vegetable Stew
PREP: 5 min. **COOK:** 45 min.

Theresa Lynne and Don Stone
Bakersfield, California

- 1 pound ground beef
- 1 can (28 ounces) stewed tomatoes, cut up
- 1 can (15 ounces) tomato sauce
- 1 package (16 ounces) frozen California-blend vegetables
- 1 cup frozen corn
- 1 cup frozen broccoli cuts
- 2 cups water
- 1 tablespoon beef bouillon granules
- 1/2 teaspoon salt
- 1/4 teaspoon pepper
- 1/4 teaspoon garlic powder

1) In a Dutch oven, cook beef over medium heat until no longer pink; drain. Add the remaining ingredients. Bring to a boil. Reduce heat; cover and simmer for 40-45 minutes, stirring occasionally.

Yield: 10-12 servings.

NUTRITION FACTS: 1 cup equals 137 calories, 5 g fat (2 g saturated fat), 25 mg cholesterol, 614 mg sodium, 14 g carbohydrate, 3 g fiber, 11 g protein.

BEEF BURGUNDY

Southwestern Beef Stew

PREP: 10 min. **COOK:** 1-3/4 hours

Betty Jean Howard, Prineville, Oregon

- 1-1/2 pounds boneless beef round steak, cut into 1/2-inch cubes
- 1 can (14-1/2 ounces) beef broth
- 1 cup cubed peeled potatoes
- 1 cup sliced carrots
- 1 cup chopped onion
- 1/4 cup chopped sweet red pepper
- 1 jalapeno pepper, seeded and chopped
- 1 garlic clove, minced
- 1-1/2 teaspoons chili powder
- 1/2 teaspoon salt
- 1 can (14-1/2 ounces) diced tomatoes, undrained
- 2 tablespoons all-purpose flour
- 2 tablespoons water
- 2 tablespoons minced fresh cilantro

1) In a Dutch oven coated with cooking spray, brown meat on all sides over medium-high heat. Add the broth, potatoes, carrots, onion, red pepper, jalapeno, garlic, chili powder and salt. Bring to a boil. Reduce heat; cover and simmer for 30 minutes or until potatoes and carrots are tender. Add tomatoes; cover and cook 1 hour longer or until meat is tender.

2) Combine flour and water until smooth; stir into pot. Stir in cilantro. Bring to a boil; cook and stir for 2 minutes or until thickened.

Yield: 6 servings.

Editor's Note: When cutting or seeding hot peppers, use rubber or plastic gloves to protect your hands. Avoid touching your face.

NUTRITION FACTS: 1 cup equals 222 calories, 6 g fat (2 g saturated fat), 72 mg cholesterol, 600 mg sodium, 16 g carbohydrate, 3 g fiber, 26 g protein.

Beef Burgundy

PREP: 30 min. **COOK:** 1-1/4 hours

Diana Bachelder, Winter Haven, Florida

- 3/4 pound boneless beef chuck roast, cut into 1-inch cubes
- 2 tablespoons olive oil, *divided*
- 1 tablespoon butter
- 4 teaspoons all-purpose flour
- 1 teaspoon red currant jelly *or* seedless raspberry jam
- 1 teaspoon tomato paste
- 1-1/4 cups chicken broth
- 1/4 cup Burgundy wine *or* additional chicken broth
- 2 bacon strips, cooked and crumbled
- 1-1/2 cups sliced fresh mushrooms
- 1 cup pearl onions, peeled
- 1 cup fresh baby carrots

Dash pepper

Hot cooked egg noodles, optional

1) In a saucepan, brown beef cubes on all sides in 1 tablespoon oil. Remove and set aside. In the same pan, melt butter. Stir in the flour, jelly and tomato paste until smooth; gradually add broth and wine or additional broth. Bring to a boil; cook and stir for 1 minute or until thickened.

2) Add beef and bacon. Return to a boil. Reduce heat; cover and simmer for 45-50 minutes or until meat is tender.

3) In a small skillet, saute mushrooms in remaining oil until tender. Add the mushrooms, onions, carrots and pepper to beef mixture. Cover and cook 20-25 minutes longer or until vegetables are tender. Serve over noodles if desired.

Yield: 2 servings.

Editor's Note: For information on how to peel pearl onions, see page 391.

NUTRITION FACTS: 1 cup (calculated without noodles) equals 651 calories, 39 g fat (13 g saturated fat), 131 mg cholesterol, 890 mg sodium, 30 g carbohydrate, 2 g fiber, 40 g protein.

Serve It in Bread Bowls

For an attractive presentation that's delicious, too, serve stew in individual bread bowls. Many bakeries carry small round loaves specifically for this purpose. If you cannot find any, look for extra-large crusty buns or firm sourdough rolls instead.

Cut the top off of each loaf or bun and scoop out the interior to create a bowl. Place each bread bowl on a plate and ladle the stew into the bowl right before serving. Serve tops alongside.

Beef Fillets with Portobello Sauce

PREP/TOTAL TIME: 30 min.

Christel Stein, Tampa, Florida

These tasty steaks seem special, but they are fast enough for everyday dinners. We serve them with crusty French bread, mixed salad and a light lemon dessert.

> 2 beef tenderloin steaks
> (4 ounces *each*)
> 1/2 cup dry red wine *or*
> reduced-sodium beef broth
> 1 teaspoon all-purpose flour
> 1/2 cup reduced-sodium beef broth
> 1 teaspoon *each* steak sauce,
> Worcestershire sauce and
> ketchup
> 1/2 teaspoon ground mustard
> 4 ounces fresh baby portobello
> mushrooms, sliced
> 1/4 teaspoon pepper
> 1/8 teaspoon salt
> 1 tablespoon minced chives,
> optional

1) In a large nonstick skillet coated with cooking spray, brown steaks on both sides over medium-high heat. Remove and keep warm.

2) Reduce heat to medium. Add wine or broth to pan, stirring to loosen browned bits; cook for 2-3 minutes or until the liquid is reduced by half. Combine flour and broth until smooth; whisk into the pan juices. Add steak sauce, Worcestershire sauce, ketchup and mustard. Bring to a boil.

3) Return steaks to the skillet; add mushrooms. Cook for 4-5 minutes on each side or until meat reaches desired doneness (for medium-rare, a meat thermometer should read 145°; medium, 160°; well-done, 170°). Sprinkle with pepper, salt and chives if desired.

Yield: 2 servings.

NUTRITION FACTS: 1 steak with 1/3 cup sauce equals 255 calories, 8 g fat (3 g saturated fat), 72 mg cholesterol, 422 mg sodium, 7 g carbohydrate, 1 g fiber, 26 g protein.

Surf 'n' Turf Tenderloin

PREP/TOTAL TIME: 30 min.

Colleen Gonring, Brookfield, Wisconsin

The twist on this recipe is that the steaks are stuffed with shrimp. It looks tricky but is really a cinch.

> 1 tablespoon finely chopped onion
> 1 garlic clove, minced
> 2 tablespoons olive oil, *divided*
> 2 tablespoons butter, *divided*
> 1/4 cup beef broth
> 16 uncooked medium shrimp
> (about 1/2 pound), peeled and
> deveined

SURF 'N' TURF TENDERLOIN

> 1 tablespoon minced fresh parsley
> 4 beef tenderloin steaks (1-1/2 to 2
> inches thick and 6 ounces *each*)

1) In a small skillet, saute onion and garlic in 1 tablespoon oil and 1 tablespoon butter until tender. Add broth; cook and stir for 1 minute. Add the shrimp; cook and stir until shrimp turn pink, about 3-5 minutes. Add parsley.

2) Meanwhile, make a horizontal cut three-fourths of the way through each steak. Place three shrimp in each pocket. Set aside remaining shrimp and sauce for garnish; keep warm.

3) In a large skillet, heat remaining oil and butter over medium-high heat. Add steaks; cook until meat reaches desired doneness (about 10-13 minutes for medium, 160°), turning once. Top with remaining shrimp and sauce.

Yield: 4 servings.

NUTRITION FACTS: 1 serving equals 453 calories, 30 g fat (11 g saturated fat), 205 mg cholesterol, 282 mg sodium, 1 g carbohydrate, trace fiber, 43 g protein.

Balsamic-Seasoned Steak

PREP/TOTAL TIME: 25 min.

Taste of Home Test Kitchen

A two-ingredient sauce makes this sirloin so delicious. You'll love its simple preparation and scrumptious Swiss cheese topping.

> 2 tablespoons balsamic vinegar
> 2 teaspoons steak sauce
> 1 boneless beef sirloin steak
> (1 pound)
> 1/4 teaspoon coarsely ground pepper
> 2 ounces reduced-fat Swiss cheese,
> cut into thin strips

1) In a small bowl, combine vinegar and steak sauce; set aside. Rub steak with pepper. Place on a broiler pan. Broil 4 in. from heat for 7 minutes.

2) Turn; spoon half of the steak sauce mixture over steak. Broil 5-7 minutes longer or until meat reaches desired doneness (for medium-rare, a meat thermometer should read 145°; medium, 160°; well-done, 170°).

3) Remove steak to a cutting board; cut across the grain into 1/4-in. slices. Place on a foil-lined baking sheet; drizzle with juices from cutting board and remaining steak sauce mixture. Top with cheese. Broil for 1 minute or until cheese is melted.

Yield: 4 servings.

NUTRITION FACTS: 3 ounces cooked beef with 1/2 ounce of cheese equals 188 calories, 8 g fat (3 g saturated fat), 70 mg cholesterol, 116 mg sodium, 2 g carbohydrate, trace fiber, 26 g protein.

T-Bones with Onions
PREP/TOTAL TIME: 30 min.

Sheree Quate, Cave Junction, Oregon

Steak gets a dressy treatment when topped with onion slices flavored with honey and mustard. I found this recipe on a bag of charcoal more than 10 years ago.

> 3 large onions, cut into 1/4-inch-thick slices
> 2 tablespoons honey
> 1/2 teaspoon salt
> 1/2 teaspoon ground mustard
> 1/2 teaspoon paprika
> 1/2 teaspoon pepper
> 4 beef T-bone steaks (1 inch thick and 12 ounces *each*)

Additional salt and pepper

1) Place onions in the center of a piece of heavy-duty foil (about 20 in. x 18 in.). Drizzle with honey; sprinkle with the salt, mustard, paprika and pepper.

2) Fold foil over onions and seal tightly. Season steaks with additional salt and pepper. Grill onions and steaks, covered, over medium heat. Grill onions for 10-12 minutes on each side or until tender.

3) Grill steak for 7-10 minutes on each side or until meat reaches desired doneness (for medium-rare, a meat thermometer should read 145°; medium 160°; well-done, 170°). Let steak stand for 3-5 minutes. Serve with onions.

Yield: 4 servings.

NUTRITION FACTS: 1 serving (calculated without additional salt and pepper) equals 695 calories, 46 g fat (18 g saturated fat), 131 mg cholesterol, 434 mg sodium, 19 g carbohydrate, 2 g fiber, 49 g protein.

T-BONES WITH ONIONS

Tips for Grilling Steaks

Trim steaks to avoid flare-ups, leaving a thin layer of fat if desired to help maintain juiciness. Pat dry with paper towels before grilling—a dry steak will brown better than a moist one.

Santa Fe Strip Steaks
PREP/TOTAL TIME: 25 min.

Joan Hallford, North Richland Hills, Texas

If you love Southwestern flavor, this recipe certainly provides it!

> 1/2 cup chopped onion
> 1 tablespoon olive oil
> 2 cans (4 ounces *each*) chopped green chilies
> 1/2 cup fresh cilantro leaves
> 1 jalapeno pepper, seeded
> 2 teaspoons red currant jelly
> 1 teaspoon chicken bouillon granules
> 1 teaspoon Worcestershire sauce
> 1 garlic clove, peeled
> 1/2 teaspoon seasoned salt
> 1/4 teaspoon dried oregano

Salt and pepper to taste

> 1/2 cup shredded Monterey Jack cheese, optional
> 4 New York strip steaks (about 1 inch and 7 ounces *each*)

1) In a small saucepan, saute onion in oil until tender. Transfer to a blender or food processor. Add the green chilies, cilantro, jalapeno, jelly, bouillon, Worcestershire sauce, garlic, seasoned salt and oregano; cover and process until smooth.

2) Return mixture to saucepan. Bring to a boil. Reduce heat; simmer, uncovered, for 10 minutes. Set aside and keep warm.

3) Sprinkle steaks with salt and pepper. Broil 4-6 in. from heat for 4-8 minutes on each side or until meat reaches desired doneness (for medium-rare, a meat thermometer should read 145°; medium, 160°; well-done, 170°).

4) Serve steaks with green chili sauce and sprinkle with cheese if desired.

Yield: 4 servings.

Editor's Note: Steak may be known as strip steak, Kansas City steak, New York Strip steak, Ambassador Steak or boneless Club Steak in your region. Steaks may also be grilled, uncovered, over medium heat. When cutting or seeding hot peppers, use rubber or plastic gloves to protect your hands. Avoid touching your face.

NUTRITION FACTS: 1 serving (calculated without salt and pepper) equals 457 calories, 31 g fat (11 g saturated fat), 109 mg cholesterol, 727 mg sodium, 8 g carbohydrate, 2 g fiber, 36 g protein.

Peppercorn Steaks

PREP/TOTAL TIME: 30 min.

Taste of Home Test Kitchen

These tender peppered steaks get plenty of zip from a quick-to-fix sauce seasoned with mustard and Worcestershire.

    1 tablespoon whole black
       peppercorns, crushed
    2 New York strip steaks
       (8 ounces *each*)
    2 to 3 tablespoons butter, melted
    1 to 2 garlic cloves, minced
    1 tablespoon Worcestershire sauce
  1/2 cup red wine *or* beef broth
    1 teaspoon ground mustard
  1/2 teaspoon sugar
    2 teaspoons cornstarch
    1 tablespoon water

1) Rub pepper over both sides of steaks. Refrigerate for 15 minutes. In an ungreased skillet, brown steaks on both sides over medium-high heat.

2) Reduce heat to medium; add butter and garlic; cook for 4-6 minutes, turning steaks once. Add Worcestershire sauce; cook 4-6 minutes longer, turning once, or until meat reaches desired doneness (for medium-rare, a meat thermometer should read 145°; medium, 160°; well-done, 170°). Remove steaks and keep warm.

3) Combine wine or broth, mustard and sugar; add to the pan. Stir to loosen browned bits. Combine cornstarch and water until smooth; add to pan. Bring to a boil; cook and stir for 2 minutes or until thickened. Serve with the steaks.

Yield: 2 servings.

Editor's Note: Steak may be known as strip steak, Kansas City steak, New York Strip steak, Ambassador Steak or boneless Club Steak in your region.

NUTRITION FACTS: 1 serving equals 626 calories, 43 g fat (19 g saturated fat), 155 mg cholesterol, 301 mg sodium, 8 g carbohydrate, trace fiber, 41 g protein.

Garlic Grilled Steaks

PREP/TOTAL TIME: 20 min.

Taste of Home Test Kitchen

For a mouthwatering change of taste at your next barbecue, take steak to new flavor heights by basting your choice of cuts with a great garlic blend.

   10 garlic cloves
  1-1/2 teaspoons salt
  1/2 teaspoon pepper
    2 tablespoons olive oil
    1 tablespoon lemon juice
    2 teaspoons Worcestershire sauce
    4 New York strip steak *or* 4 boneless
       beef rib eye steaks (1-1/4 inches
       thick and 8 ounces *each*)

1) With a mortar and pestle, combine the garlic, salt and pepper. Add the oil, lemon juice and Worcestershire sauce and mix to form a paste.

2) Grill steaks, covered, over medium heat for 6-8 minutes on each side or until meat reaches desired doneness (for medium-rare, a meat thermometer should read 145°; medium, 160°; well-done, 170°).

3) Brush with garlic mixture during the last few minutes of grilling. Let stand for 3-5 minutes before serving.

Yield: 4 servings.

NUTRITION FACTS: 1 serving equals 525 calories, 38 g fat (13 g saturated fat), 124 mg cholesterol, 1,013 mg sodium, 3 g carbohydrate, trace fiber, 41 g protein.

PINWHEEL FLANK STEAKS

Pinwheel Flank Steaks

PREP: 20 min. + marinating **GRILL:** 20 min.

Nancy Tafoya, Fort Collins, Colorado

This yummy, elegant-looking main dish is easy to make. Plus, so much prep can be done in advance.

  1-1/2 pounds beef flank steak
  1/4 cup olive oil
    2 tablespoons red wine vinegar
    2 teaspoons Worcestershire sauce
    2 teaspoons Italian seasoning
  1-1/2 teaspoons garlic powder
  1-1/2 teaspoons pepper, *divided*
    1 teaspoon seasoned salt
    8 bacon strips, cooked and crumbled
    2 garlic cloves, minced
  1/4 cup minced fresh parsley
  1/4 cup finely chopped onion
  1/2 teaspoon salt

1) Flatten steak to 1/4-in. thickness. In a large resealable plastic bag, combine the oil, vinegar, Worcestershire sauce, Italian seasoning, garlic powder, 1 teaspoon pepper and seasoned salt; add the steak.

2) Seal bag and turn to coat; refrigerate for 8 hours or overnight. Drain and discard marinade.

3) Combine the bacon, garlic, parsley, onion, salt and remaining pepper; sprinkle over steak to within 1 in. of edges. Roll up jelly-roll style, starting with a long side; tie with kitchen string at about 1-in. intervals. Cut into 1-1/4-in. rolls.

4) Coat grill rack with cooking spray before starting the grill. Grill steak rolls, uncovered, over medium heat for 10-12 minutes on each side or until meat reaches desired doneness (for medium-rare, a meat thermometer should read 145°; medium, 160°; well-done, 170°). Cut and remove string before serving.

Yield: 6 servings.

NUTRITION FACTS: 1 serving equals 265 calories, 17 g fat (6 g saturated fat), 61 mg cholesterol, 663 mg sodium, 2 g carbohydrate, trace fiber, 25 g protein.

Sirloin Veggie Kabobs

PREP: 30 min. + marinating **GRILL:** 10 min.

Trisha Ward, Atlanta, Georgia

Planning your Labor Day cookout menu will be no work at all when you have my classic kabob recipe to call on. Feel free to use cauliflower or other favorite vegetables.

2/3 cup chili sauce
1/2 cup dry red wine *or* beef broth
1/2 cup balsamic vinegar
2 tablespoons canola oil
4-1/2 teaspoons Worcestershire sauce
4-1/2 teaspoons dried minced onion
1 garlic clove, minced
1/2 teaspoon ground mustard
1/4 teaspoon salt
1 pound boneless beef sirloin steak, cut into 3/4-inch cubes
16 fresh baby portobello *or* large white mushrooms, halved
2 medium red onions, cut into wedges
1 medium sweet red pepper, cut into 3/4-inch pieces
1 medium sweet yellow pepper, cut into 3/4-inch pieces

SIRLOIN VEGGIE KABOBS

1) In a small bowl, combine the first nine ingredients; mix well. Pour half into a large resealable plastic bag; add beef cubes. Seal bag and turn to coat. Pour the remaining marinade into another large resealable plastic bag; add mushrooms, onions and peppers. Seal the bag and turn to coat. Refrigerate beef and vegetables for up to 4 hours.

2) If grilling kabobs, coat grill rack with cooking spray before starting grill. Drain and discard marinade from beef. Drain vegetables, reserving marinade for basting. On eight metal or soaked wooden skewers, alternately thread beef and vegetables.

3) Grill, covered, over medium heat or broil 4-6 in. from the heat for 3-4 minutes on each side or until meat reaches desired doneness, turning three times and basting frequently with reserved marinade.

Yield: 4 servings.

NUTRITION FACTS: 2 kabobs equals 268 calories, 10 g fat (2 g saturated fat), 63 mg cholesterol, 480 mg sodium, 20 g carbohydrate, 2 g fiber, 24 g protein.

Grilled Asian Flank Steak

PREP: 15 min. + marinating **GRILL:** 15 min.

Shawn Solley, Morgantown, West Virginia

The Chinese five-spice powder and hoisin sauce add a distinctive Asian flair to this grilled flank steak.

1/4 cup Worcestershire sauce
1/4 cup reduced-sodium soy sauce
3 tablespoons honey
1 tablespoon sesame oil
1 teaspoon Chinese five-spice powder
1 teaspoon minced garlic
1/2 teaspoon minced fresh gingerroot
1 beef flank steak (1-1/2 pounds)
2 tablespoons hoisin sauce
3 green onions, thinly sliced
1 tablespoon sesame seeds, toasted, optional

1) In a large resealable plastic bag, combine the first seven ingredients; add the steak. Seal bag and turn to coat; refrigerate overnight.

2) Drain and discard marinade. Grill steak, covered, over medium heat for 6-7 minutes on each side or until meat reaches desired doneness (for medium-rare, a meat thermometer should read 145°; medium, 160°; well-done, 170°). Let stand for 5 minutes.

3) Meanwhile, place the hoisin sauce in a small microwave-safe dish. Microwave on high for 10-20 seconds or until heated through. Thinly slice steak across the grain. Drizzle with hoisin sauce. Garnish with green onions. Sprinkle with sesame seeds if desired.

Yield: 6 servings.

NUTRITION FACTS: 3 ounces cooked beef equals 193 calories, 9 g fat (4 g saturated fat), 54 mg cholesterol, 241 mg sodium, 5 g carbohydrate, trace fiber, 22 g protein.

Steak Fajitas

PREP/TOTAL TIME: 30 min.

Shirley Hilger, Lincoln, Nebraska

Strips of sirloin pick up plenty of spicy flavor from a marinade seasoned with cayenne pepper and cumin. These colorful fajitas are speedy and satisfying.

- 1/4 cup orange juice
- 1/4 cup white vinegar
- 4 garlic cloves, minced
- 1 teaspoon seasoned salt
- 1 teaspoon dried oregano
- 1 teaspoon ground cumin
- 1/4 teaspoon cayenne pepper
- 1 pound boneless beef sirloin steak, cut into 1/4-inch strips
- 1 medium onion, thinly sliced
- 1 medium green pepper, thinly sliced
- 1 medium sweet red pepper, thinly sliced
- 2 tablespoons vegetable oil, *divided*
- 4 to 6 flour tortillas (10 inches), warmed

Shredded cheddar cheese, picante sauce and sour cream, optional

1) In a large resealable plastic bag, combine the orange juice, vinegar, garlic and seasonings; add the beef. Seal bag and turn to coat; set aside. In a skillet, saute onion and peppers in 1 tablespoon oil until crisp-tender; remove and set aside.

2) Drain and discard marinade. In the same skillet, cook beef in remaining oil for 2-4 minutes or until it reaches desired doneness. Return vegetables to pan; heat through.

3) Spoon meat and vegetables onto tortillas. If desired, top with cheese and serve with picante sauce and sour cream.

Yield: 4-6 servings.

NUTRITION FACTS: 1 fajita equals 305 calories, 11 g fat (3 g saturated fat), 42 mg cholesterol, 422 mg sodium, 27 g carbohydrate, 5 g fiber, 19 g protein.

STEAK FAJITAS

Asparagus Beef Stir-Fry

PREP: 15 min. + marinating **COOK:** 15 min.

Debby Peterson, Niagara, Wisconsin

This stir-fry is popular, especially when I put a little extra bite in it with the red pepper flakes. To make sure the steak is tender, cut it into thin strips across the grain.

- 2 tablespoons reduced-sodium soy sauce, *divided*
- 2 tablespoons dry red wine *or* beef broth, *divided*
- 1/2 pound boneless beef sirloin steak, cut into thin strips
- 1 tablespoon cornstarch
- 1/2 cup water
- 4 teaspoons canola oil, *divided*
- 1 small onion, thinly sliced
- 1 pound fresh asparagus, trimmed and cut into 1-inch pieces
- 2 celery ribs, thinly sliced
- 1 garlic clove, minced
- 1/8 to 1/4 teaspoon crushed red pepper flakes

Hot cooked rice, optional

1) In a large resealable plastic bag, combine 1 tablespoon of soy sauce and 1 tablespoon wine or broth; add beef. Seal bag and turn to coat; refrigerate for 30 minutes.

2) In a small bowl, combine the cornstarch, water and remaining soy sauce and wine or broth until smooth; set aside.

3) In a large nonstick skillet or wok, stir-fry beef in 2 teaspoons oil for 3-4 minutes or until no longer pink. Remove with a slotted spoon and keep warm.

4) Stir-fry onion in remaining oil for 1 minute. Add asparagus; stir-fry for 2 minutes. Add celery, garlic and red pepper flakes; stir-fry 4-6 minutes longer or until vegetables are crisp-tender.

5) Stir cornstarch mixture and add to the pan. Bring to a boil; cook and stir for 2 minutes or until thickened. Add beef; heat through. Serve with rice if desired.

Yield: 3 servings.

NUTRITION FACTS: 1-1/3 cups equals 211 calories, 10 g fat (2 g saturated fat), 42 mg cholesterol, 461 mg sodium, 11 g carbohydrate, 3 g fiber, 18 g protein.

Spinach Beef Stir-Fry

PREP: 10 min. + marinating **COOK:** 20 min.

LaVerne Heath, Fountain, North Carolina

With soy-marinated strips of steak and fresh colorful vegetables, this mouthwatering stir-fry sizzles with flavor! This versatile entree can also be made with chicken breasts instead of beef. If you like zucchini or squash, toss some in.

- 1/4 cup reduced-sodium soy sauce
- 1 boneless beef sirloin steak (1 pound), cut into thin strips
- 2 teaspoons cornstarch

1/2 teaspoon beef bouillon granules

1/2 teaspoon Chinese five-spice powder

1/2 cup water

2 tablespoons canola oil, *divided*

1 cup sliced fresh carrots

1 medium green pepper, julienned

1 cup sliced celery

1 cup sliced fresh mushrooms

1 can (8 ounces) sliced water chestnuts, drained

1/2 cup sliced green onions

6 cups torn fresh spinach

Hot cooked rice, optional

1) Place soy sauce in a large resealable plastic bag; add steak. Seal bag and turn to coat; refrigerate for up to 2 hours. Drain and discard soy sauce.

2) In a bowl, combine the cornstarch, bouillon, five-spice powder and water until smooth; set aside. In a large nonstick skillet or wok, stir-fry beef in batches in 1 tablespoon hot oil until beef is no longer pink. Remove from skillet and set aside.

3) Stir-fry carrots in remaining oil for 2 minutes. Add the green pepper, celery and mushrooms; stir-fry for 3 minutes. Add the water chestnuts and onions; stir-fry for 2 minutes or until the vegetables are crisp-tender.

4) Stir cornstarch mixture and add to the pan. Bring to a boil; cook and stir for 2 minutes. Add spinach and beef; cook and stir until spinach is wilted and beef is heated through. Serve over rice if desired.

Yield: 4 servings.

NUTRITION FACTS: 1-1/4 cups equals 280 calories, 13 g fat (3 g saturated fat), 63 mg cholesterol, 597 mg sodium, 16 g carbohydrate, 6 g fiber, 25 g protein.

Tips for Stir-Frying

To make it easier to slice the meat into thin strips, partially freeze it before slicing. It takes about 30 minutes in the freezer to partially freeze thin cuts of meat.

Cut and prepare all the ingredients before you begin to stir-fry, including any sauces that are added at the end of cooking.

Select a wok or skillet large enough to accommodate the volume of food you'll be stir-frying. If the food is crowded in the pan, it will steam. If necessary, stir-fry the food in batches.

Don't place the stir-fried food on the same plate that held the uncooked meat when cooking in batches. Use a clean plate or bowl.

Add oil, when called for, to the pan and heat until hot before adding the food.

Stir any sauce that has a thickener, such as cornstarch, before adding to the pan.

GINGERED PEPPER STEAK

Gingered Pepper Steak

PREP/TOTAL TIME: 15 min.

Susan Adair, Somerset, Kentucky

This wonderfully tender steak is a treat even for folks not watching their diet. When my mother-in-law shared the recipe, she said it cooks up in no time...and she was right.

2 teaspoons sugar

2 teaspoons cornstarch

1/4 teaspoon ground ginger

1/4 cup reduced-sodium soy sauce

1 tablespoon white wine vinegar

1 pound beef flank steak, thinly sliced

2 medium green peppers, julienned

1 teaspoon vegetable oil

Hot cooked rice, optional

1) In a large bowl, combine the sugar, cornstarch, ginger, soy sauce and vinegar until smooth. Add beef and toss to coat; set aside.

2) In a large skillet or wok, stir-fry green peppers in oil until crisp-tender, about 3 minutes. Remove with a slotted spoon and keep warm.

3) Add beef with marinade to pan; stir-fry for 3 minutes or until meat reaches desired doneness. Return peppers to pan; heat through. Serve over rice if desired.

Yield: 4 servings.

NUTRITION FACTS: 1 cup equals 218 calories, 9 g fat (4 g saturated fat), 54 mg cholesterol, 674 mg sodium, 8 g carbohydrate, 1 g fiber, 23 g protein.

✿ Seasoned Swiss Steak

PREP: 35 min. **COOK:** 1-1/2 hours

Edna Hoffman, Hebron, Indiana

Tender beef and vegetables are combined in this recipe with a gravy that melds tomato, brown sugar and mustard.

1/4 cup all-purpose flour
1 tablespoon ground mustard
1 teaspoon salt, *divided*
1/4 teaspoon pepper, *divided*
1-1/2 pounds boneless beef top round steak (about 1 inch thick), cut into serving-size pieces
2 tablespoons vegetable oil
1 cup diced carrots
1/2 cup chopped onion
1/2 cup chopped green pepper
1 tablespoon brown sugar
1 tablespoon Worcestershire sauce
1 can (14-1/2 ounces) diced tomatoes, undrained
1/4 cup cold water

1) Combine the flour, mustard, 1/2 teaspoon salt and 1/8 teaspoon pepper; set aside 2 tablespoons for gravy. Rub remaining flour mixture over steak. Pound with a meat mallet to tenderize.

2) In a large skillet, brown steak in oil over medium-high heat. Transfer to a greased 2-1/2-qt. baking dish. Top with carrots, onion, green pepper, brown sugar and Worcestershire sauce. Pour tomatoes over all.

3) Cover and bake at 350° for 1-1/2 to 2 hours or until meat and vegetables are tender. Transfer meat and vegetables to a serving dish; keep warm. Strain pan juices into a measuring cup; add water to measure 1 cup.

4) In a saucepan, combine reserved flour mixture with cold water until smooth. Whisk in pan juices. Bring to a boil; cook and stir for 2 minutes or until thickened. Add remaining salt and pepper. Serve over steak.

Yield: 6 servings.

NUTRITION FACTS: 1 serving equals 249 calories, 9 g fat (2 g saturated fat), 64 mg cholesterol, 549 mg sodium, 14 g carbohydrate, 3 g fiber, 28 g protein.

Beef Potpie

PREP: 30 min. **BAKE:** 45 min. + standing

Lucile Cline, Wichita, Kansas

Filling and comforting, this meat pie is a delicious way to put leftover roast beef to use. Grated onion adds a nice flavor to the pie crust.

1/4 cup *each* chopped onion, green pepper and sweet red pepper
2 garlic cloves, minced
1 tablespoon vegetable oil
3 cups cubed cooked roast beef

2 cups frozen cubed hash brown potatoes
1 can (10-3/4 ounces) condensed cream of mushroom soup, undiluted
1 package (10 ounces) frozen corn
1 jar (4-1/2 ounces) sliced mushrooms, drained
1 teaspoon Worcestershire sauce
1/8 teaspoon salt
Dash pepper

ONION PASTRY:
2-1/2 cups all-purpose flour
1-1/4 teaspoons salt
1 cup butter-flavored shortening
4 teaspoons grated onion
4 to 5 tablespoons cold water

1) In a large skillet, saute the onion, peppers and garlic in oil for 3 minutes. Stir in the beef, potatoes, soup, corn, mushrooms, Worcestershire sauce, salt and pepper. Bring to a boil. Reduce heat; cover and simmer for 10 minutes.

2) For pastry, combine flour and salt in a large bowl. Cut in shortening until crumbly; sprinkle with onion. Gradually add water, tossing with a fork until dough forms a ball.

3) Divide dough in half so that one ball is slightly larger than the other. On a lightly floured surface, roll out larger ball to fit a 9-in. deep-dish pie plate.

4) Transfer pastry to plate; trim even with edge. Add filling. Roll out remaining pastry to fit top of pie; place over filling. Trim, seal and flute edges. Cut slits in top.

5) Bake at 375° for 45-50 minutes or until filling is bubbly and crust is golden brown. Let stand for 15 minutes before cutting.

Yield: 8 servings.

NUTRITION FACTS: 1 serving equals 625 calories, 39 g fat (11 g saturated fat), 54 mg cholesterol, 785 mg sodium, 46 g carbohydrate, 3 g fiber, 21 g protein.

✿ Slow-Cooked Short Ribs

PREP: 25 min. **COOK:** 9 hours

Pam Halfhill, Wapakoneta, Ohio

Smothered in a mouthwatering barbecue sauce, these meaty ribs are a popular entree wherever I serve them. The recipe is great for a busy cook—after everything is combined, the slow cooker does all the work!

2/3 cup all-purpose flour
2 teaspoons salt
1/2 teaspoon pepper
4 to 4-1/2 pounds boneless beef short ribs
1/4 to 1/3 cup butter
1 large onion, chopped
1-1/2 cups beef broth

3/4 cup red wine vinegar
3/4 cup packed brown sugar
1/2 cup chili sauce
1/3 cup ketchup
1/3 cup Worcestershire sauce
5 garlic cloves, minced
1-1/2 teaspoons chili powder

1) In a large resealable plastic bag, combine the flour, salt and pepper. Add ribs in batches and shake to coat. In a large skillet, brown ribs in butter.

2) Transfer to a 6-qt. slow cooker. In the same skillet, combine the remaining ingredients. Cook and stir until mixture comes to a boil; pour over ribs. Cover and cook on low for 9-10 hours or until meat is tender.

Yield: 12 servings.

NUTRITION FACTS: 4 ounces equals 631 calories, 47 g fat (21 g saturated fat), 107 mg cholesterol, 901 mg sodium, 27 g carbohydrate, 1 g fiber, 24 g protein.

SLOW-COOKED SHORT RIBS

Sticky Bones
PREP: 30 min. + marinating **BAKE:** 1 hour
Berta Joy, Gering, Nebraska
I never had a recipe for short ribs that impressed me...until this one!

1 cup white vinegar
1/2 cup ketchup
1/2 cup honey
2 tablespoons Worcestershire sauce
1 teaspoon salt
1 teaspoon ground mustard
1 teaspoon paprika
1 garlic clove, minced

1/4 teaspoon pepper
4 pounds bone-in beef short ribs

1) In a small saucepan, combine the vinegar, ketchup, honey, Worcestershire sauce, salt, mustard, paprika, garlic and pepper. Bring to a boil. Reduce heat; cover and simmer for 15 minutes. Set aside 1 cup for basting.

2) Cool remaining marinade. Pour the remaining marinade in a large resealable plastic bag; add ribs. Seal bag and turn to coat; refrigerate for at least 2 hours.

3) Drain and discard marinade. Bake ribs, uncovered, at 325° for 1 hour or until meat is tender, basting frequently with reserved marinade.

Yield: 4 servings.

NUTRITION FACTS: 1 serving equals 449 calories, 21 g fat (9 g saturated fat), 109 mg cholesterol, 685 mg sodium, 27 g carbohydrate, trace fiber, 37 g protein.

Liver with Peppers and Onions
PREP/TOTAL TIME: 25 min.
Naomi Giddis, Grawn, Michigan
A simple breading of flour, salt and pepper keeps the liver tender. The sauce adds wonderful flavor.

1/2 cup all-purpose flour
1 teaspoon salt
1/4 teaspoon pepper
1 pound liver, cut into bite-size pieces
1 large onion, thinly sliced and separated into rings
1 medium green pepper, cut into 1-inch pieces
1 sweet red pepper, cut into 1-inch pieces
4 tablespoons vegetable oil, *divided*
1 tablespoon cornstarch
1 cup beef broth
2 tablespoons soy sauce

Hot cooked rice *or* noodles

1) In a large bowl or resealable plastic bag, combine the flour, salt and pepper. Add liver; toss to coat.

2) In a large skillet, cook onion and peppers in 2 tablespoons oil until crisp-tender. Remove from pan; set aside. In same skillet, cook and stir liver in remaining oil for 5-7 minutes or until meat is no longer pink.

3) In a small bowl, combine cornstarch, broth and soy sauce until smooth; stir into liver. Bring to a boil; cook and stir for 2 minutes or until thickened. Return vegetables to the skillet; heat through. Serve over rice or noodles.

Yield: 4-6 servings.

NUTRITION FACTS: 1 serving (calculated without rice or noodles) equals 245 calories, 12 g fat (2 g saturated fat), 332 mg cholesterol, 898 mg sodium, 17 g carbohydrate, 2 g fiber, 16 g protein.

SNOW PEAS AND BEEF SALAD

Snow Peas and Beef Salad

PREP: 35 min. + chilling

Janeen Kilpatrick, Fairbury, Illinois

In this delicious main-dish salad, savory strips of broiled steak are lightly dressed along with water chestnuts, mushrooms and onions, then tossed with crisp snow peas. Ketchup and ginger add a bit of zip to the sweet dressing.

- 1 beef flank steak (1 pound)
- 1/4 cup ketchup
- 2 tablespoons canola oil
- 2 tablespoons lemon juice
- 1 tablespoon brown sugar
- 1/4 teaspoon *each* garlic powder, garlic salt, ground ginger and pepper
- 1/2 pound fresh mushrooms, sliced
- 1 can (8 ounces) sliced water chestnuts, drained
- 1 medium onion, sliced and separated into rings
- 1 cup fresh *or* frozen snow peas, thawed
- 12 lettuce leaves
- 2 medium tomatoes, cut into wedges

1) Broil steak 4-6 in. from the heat for 8-10 minutes on each side or until a meat thermometer reads 170°. Cool completely. Thinly slice meat across the grain; place in a large resealable plastic bag.

2) In a jar with tight-fitting lid, combine the ketchup, oil, lemon juice, brown sugar and seasonings; shake well. Pour over meat; seal bag and turn to coat. Add the mushrooms, water chestnuts and onion.

3) Refrigerate for 8 hours or overnight, turning occasionally. Just before serving, add snow peas. Serve on lettuce; garnish with tomatoes.

Yield: 6 servings.

NUTRITION FACTS: About 1 cup salad with 2 lettuce leaves and 1/3 of a tomato equals 304 calories, 15 g fat (5 g saturated fat), 54 mg cholesterol, 263 mg sodium, 19 g carbohydrate, 4 g fiber, 25 g protein.

Roast Beef Pasta Salad

PREP/TOTAL TIME: 20 min.

Sandy Shields, Mead, Washington

I made this salad one hot summer day. The cool dish was a refreshing selection that was very well received. It's great to serve all year long.

- 1 package (16 ounces) spiral pasta
- 2 cups julienned cooked roast beef
- 1 cup chopped green pepper
- 1 cup sliced celery
- 3/4 cup chopped red onion
- 1/2 cup chopped sweet red pepper
- 1/3 cup chopped dill pickle
- 2 to 3 green onions, sliced

DRESSING:

- 2 tablespoons beef bouillon granules
- 1/4 cup boiling water
- 1/2 cup milk
- 2 cups mayonnaise
- 1 cup (8 ounces) sour cream
- 1 teaspoon dill weed

Dash pepper

1) Cook the pasta according to package directions; drain and rinse in cold water. Place in a large bowl; add the beef, green pepper, celery, onion, red pepper, pickle and green onions.

2) For dressing, dissolve bouillon in water. Add the milk, mayonnaise, sour cream, dill and pepper; mix well. Toss with pasta mixture. Cover and refrigerate until serving.

Yield: 12 servings.

NUTRITION FACTS: 1 cup equals 539 calories, 39 g fat (9 g saturated fat), 51 mg cholesterol, 682 mg sodium, 32 g carbohydrate, 2 g fiber, 13 g protein.

ROAST BEEF PASTA SALAD

Sirloin Caesar Salad

PREP: 5 min. + marinating **GRILL:** 15 min.

Carol Sinclair, St. Elmo, Illinois

A tangy sauce that combines bottled salad dressing, lemon juice and Dijon mustard flavors this filling main-dish salad. You save on cleanup time because both the steak and bread are cooked on the grill.

- 1 cup Caesar salad dressing
- 1/4 cup Dijon mustard
- 1/4 cup lemon juice
- 1 boneless top sirloin steak (3/4 inch thick and 1 pound)
- 6 slices French bread (1 inch thick)
- 12 cups torn romaine
- 1 medium tomato, chopped

1) In a bowl, combine the salad dressing, mustard and lemon juice; set aside 3/4 cup. Pour 3/4 cup dressing mixture in a large resealable plastic bag; add steak.

2) Seal bag and turn to coat; refrigerate for 1 hour, turning occasionally. Cover and refrigerate remaining dressing mixture.

3) Coat grill rack with cooking spray before starting the grill. Brush both sides of bread with 1/4 cup of the reserved dressing mixture.

4) Grill bread, uncovered, over medium heat for 1-2 minutes on each side or until lightly toasted. Wrap in foil and set aside.

5) Drain and discard marinade from steak. Grill, covered, over medium heat for 5-8 minutes on each side or until meat reaches desired doneness (for medium-rare, a meat thermometer should read 145°; medium, 160°; well-done, 170°).

6) Place romaine and tomato on serving platter. Slice steak diagonally; arrange over salad. Serve with the bread and remaining dressing.

Yield: 6 servings.

NUTRITION FACTS: 1 serving equals 424 calories, 18 g fat (3 g saturated fat), 57 mg cholesterol, 836 mg sodium, 39 g carbohydrate, 4 g fiber, 25 g protein.

Veal Cutlet with Red Peppers

PREP: 15 min. + standing **COOK:** 45 min.

Karen Johnson, Battle Creek, Michigan

I've made this meal for many guests over the years, and they all tell me how much they enjoy it. It's very pretty with red bell pepper strips served alongside the cutlets.

- 1-1/2 pounds veal cutlets (about 1/4 inch thick)
- 1/4 cup lemon juice
- 2 tablespoons olive oil
- 2 teaspoons grated lemon peel
- 2 garlic cloves, minced
- 1 teaspoon sugar
- 1 teaspoon salt
- 1 teaspoon paprika

VEAL CUTLET WITH RED PEPPERS

- 1/2 teaspoon ground mustard
- 1/2 teaspoon ground nutmeg
- 1/2 cup all-purpose flour
- 6 tablespoons butter, *divided*
- 2 medium onions, sliced
- 2 medium sweet red peppers, julienned
- 1/2 pound fresh mushrooms, sliced
- 1 can (14-1/2 ounces) chicken broth
- 2 teaspoons cornstarch
- 2 teaspoons water

1) Place veal in a 13-in. x 9-in. x 2-in. dish; set aside. In a medium bowl, combine the lemon juice, oil, lemon peel, garlic, sugar, salt, paprika, mustard and nutmeg; reserve 2 tablespoons. Pour the remaining marinade over veal. Let stand for 30 minutes at room temperature.

2) Discard marinade from veal. Place flour in a shallow dish; coat veal with flour, shaking off excess. In a large skillet, brown veal slices, two at a time, in 4 tablespoons butter; set aside.

3) In the same skillet, saute the onions, red peppers and mushrooms in remaining butter until tender, stirring to loosen browned bits. Stir in broth and reserved marinade; cover and simmer 10 minutes.

4) Combine cornstarch and water until smooth. Stir into vegetable mixture. Bring to a boil; cook and stir for 2-3 minutes or until thickened. Add the veal; heat through.

Yield: 6 servings.

Editor's Note: This recipe was tested with a veal cutlet or veal for scallopini, not processed veal cube steaks.

NUTRITION FACTS: 1 serving equals 413 calories, 27 g fat (12 g saturated fat), 105 mg cholesterol, 826 mg sodium, 20 g carbohydrate, 3 g fiber, 23 g protein.

Asparagus Veal Cordon Bleu

PREP/TOTAL TIME: 30 min.

Jeanne Molloy, Feeding Hills, Massachusetts

I try to make varied meals for two that are both appetizing and interesting. I sometimes double this recipe so we can have the leftovers for lunch the next day.

- 8 fresh asparagus spears, trimmed
- 2 tablespoons water
- 2 veal cutlets (6 ounces *each*)
- 1/4 teaspoon salt
- 1/8 teaspoon pepper
- 2 garlic cloves, minced
- 1 tablespoon olive oil
- 4 large fresh mushrooms, sliced
- 2 thin slices prosciutto *or* deli ham
- 1/2 cup shredded Italian cheese blend

1) Place asparagus and water in an 11-in. x 7-in. x 2-in. microwave-safe dish. Cover and microwave on high for 2-3 minutes or until crisp-tender; drain and set aside.

2) If necessary, flatten veal to 1/4-in. thickness; sprinkle with salt and pepper. In a small skillet, saute garlic in oil. Add veal; brown for 2-3 minutes on each side.

3) Transfer to an ungreased 11-in. x 7-in. x 2-in. baking dish. In the pan drippings, saute the mushrooms until tender; spoon over veal. Top each with four asparagus spears and a slice of prosciutto. Sprinkle with cheese.

4) Bake, uncovered, at 350° for 5-10 minutes or until cheese is melted.

Yield: 2 servings.

NUTRITION FACTS: 1 serving equals 492 calories, 33 g fat (12 g saturated fat), 155 mg cholesterol, 1,106 mg sodium, 6 g carbohydrate, 2 g fiber, 44 g protein.

ASPARAGUS VEAL CORDON BLEU

Veal Chops with Mustard-Sage Crust

PREP: 15 min. **BAKE:** 25 min.

Taste of Home Test Kitchen

We used stone-ground mustard to flavor these moist veal chops that bake in the oven.

- 4 veal chops (8 ounces *each*)
- 1/2 teaspoon pepper
- 1/4 teaspoon salt
- 1 cup soft bread crumbs
- 3 tablespoons stone-ground mustard
- 2 tablespoons minced fresh sage
- 2 garlic cloves, minced

1) Sprinkle veal chops on both sides with pepper and salt. Place bread crumbs in a shallow bowl. Combine mustard, sage and garlic; spread over one side of each chop, then coat with crumbs.

2) Place chops coated side up on a rack in a shallow roasting pan. Bake at 450° for 25-30 minutes or until a meat thermometer reads 160°.

Yield: 4 servings.

NUTRITION FACTS: 1 veal chop equals 98 calories, 4 g fat (1 g saturated fat), 27 mg cholesterol, 457 mg sodium, 8 g carbohydrate, 1 g fiber, 8 g protein.

French Veal Chops

PREP: 15 min. **BAKE:** 30 min.

Betty Biehl, Mertztown, Pennsylvania

Perfectly portioned for two, this effortless entree can easily be doubled to serve four.

- 2 veal chops (1 inch thick)
- 1/2 teaspoon salt

Dash pepper

- 1 tablespoon vegetable oil
- 1/2 cup chopped onion
- 2 tablespoons butter, *divided*
- 1/4 cup chicken broth
- 1/3 cup dry bread crumbs
- 2 tablespoons grated Parmesan cheese

1) Sprinkle veal chops with salt and pepper. In a skillet, brown chops on both sides in oil. Sprinkle onion into a greased shallow baking dish; dot with 1 tablespoon butter. Top with chops; drizzle with broth.

2) Melt remaining butter; toss with bread crumbs and Parmesan cheese. Sprinkle over top.

3) Bake, uncovered, at 350° for 30-35 minutes or until the meat is no longer pink and a meat thermometer reads 160°.

Yield: 2 servings.

NUTRITION FACTS: 1 serving equals 469 calories, 31 g fat (13 g saturated fat), 144 mg cholesterol, 1,146 mg sodium, 17 g carbohydrate, 1 g fiber, 31 g protein.

VEAL SCALLOPINI

Veal Scallopini

PREP/TOTAL TIME: 25 min.

Karen Bridges, Downers Grove, Illinois

My husband and I prepare this veal dish for birthdays and other special occasions.

- 2 tablespoons all-purpose flour
- 1/8 teaspoon salt
- 1/8 teaspoon pepper
- 1 egg
- 1/2 to 3/4 pound veal cutlets
- 2 tablespoons olive oil
- 4 ounces fresh mushrooms, halved
- 1 cup chicken broth
- 2 tablespoons Marsala wine

Hot cooked spaghetti

1) In a shallow bowl, combine the flour, salt and pepper. In another shallow bowl, lightly beat the egg.

2) Pound veal to 1/4-in. thickness. Dip in egg, then coat with flour mixture. In a large skillet, brown veal in oil on both sides.

3) Stir in the mushrooms, broth and wine. Bring to a boil. Reduce heat; simmer, uncovered, for 5-10 minutes or until mushrooms are tender. Serve over spaghetti.

Yield: 2 servings.

NUTRITION FACTS: 1 serving (calculated without spaghetti) equals 395 calories, 27 g fat (7 g saturated fat), 180 mg cholesterol, 697 mg sodium, 10 g carbohydrate, 1 g fiber, 25 g protein.

Complementing Veal's Flavor

Veal has a delicate taste, which allows the more flavorful ingredients in a recipe to shine. Herbs and spices that complement veal include marjoram, rosemary, sage, oregano, black pepper, cinnamon, garlic, mustard, nutmeg, bay leaf and thyme.

Buying and Cooking Ground Beef

Ground beef is often labeled using the cut of meat that it is ground from, such as ground chuck or ground round. (Ground beef comes from a combination of beef cuts.) Ground beef can also be labeled according to the fat content of the ground mixture or the percentage of lean meat to fat, such as 85% or 90% lean. The higher the percentage, the leaner the meat.

Select ground beef that is bright red in color and is in a tightly sealed package. Purchase all ground beef before the "sell-by" date.

Purchase the amount you need: 1 pound of ground beef serves 3 to 4.

Handle the mixture as little as possible when shaping hamburgers, meat loaves or meatballs to keep the final product light in texture.

Cook ground beef until it is well-done and no longer pink. For patties and loaves, where it is difficult to judge color, make sure a meat thermometer reads 160° before serving.

Sloppy Joe Sandwiches

PREP: 5 min. **COOK:** 35 min.

Laurie Hauser, Rochester, New York

This is one of those recipes that cooks love because it's quick, easy and inexpensive. Brown sugar adds a touch of sweetness. In addition to rolls, the beef mixture is tasty over rice, biscuits or baked potatoes as well.

- 1 pound ground beef
- 1 cup ketchup
- 1/4 cup water
- 2 tablespoons brown sugar
- 2 teaspoons Worcestershire sauce
- 2 teaspoons prepared mustard
- 1/2 teaspoon garlic powder
- 1/2 teaspoon onion powder
- 1/2 teaspoon salt
- 4 hamburger buns, split

1) In a large saucepan, cook beef over medium heat until no longer pink; drain. Stir in the ketchup, water, brown sugar, Worcestershire sauce, mustard, garlic powder, onion powder and salt.

2) Bring to a boil. Reduce heat; cover and simmer for 30-40 minutes. Serve on buns.

Yield: 4 servings.

NUTRITION FACTS: 1 sandwich equals 439 calories, 16 g fat (6 g saturated fat), 75 mg cholesterol, 1,360 mg sodium, 46 g carbohydrate, 2 g fiber, 27 g protein.

FAMILY-FAVORITE MEAT LOAVES

 CLASSIC: This traditional oven-baked meat loaf takes about 1-1/2 hours to bake. The savory combination of sage and Worcestershire sauce in South Dakota Meat Loaf nicely complements the ground beef.

 TIME-SAVER: Nothing can beat the microwave for a speedy meat loaf—this one cooks in only 10 minutes! Sweet-and-Sour Meat Loaf gets a fast flavor boost from onion soup mix.

 LIGHT: Lean ground beef, egg whites, 1% milk and whole wheat flour transform a typical meat loaf into a lighter counterpart. Flavorful Meat Loaf contains a blend of seasonings that will please most any palate.

 SERVES 2: Mom's Meat Loaf makes two individual loaves from 1/2 pound of ground beef. As an added bonus, the small loaves bake faster; they're done in 40 minutes.

SOUTH DAKOTA MEAT LOAF

South Dakota Meat Loaf
PREP: 10 min. **BAKE:** 1 hour 25 min. + standing

Lauree Buus, Rapid City, South Dakota

- 1 egg, lightly beaten
- 1/3 cup evaporated milk
- 3/4 cup quick-cooking oats
- 1/4 cup chopped onion
- 2 tablespoons Worcestershire sauce
- 1 teaspoon salt
- 1/2 teaspoon rubbed sage
- 1/8 teaspoon pepper
- 1-1/2 pounds ground beef
- 1/4 cup ketchup

1) In a large bowl, combine the egg, milk, oats, onion, Worcestershire sauce and seasonings. Crumble beef over mixture and mix well.

2) Press into an ungreased 8-in. x 4-in. x 2-in. loaf pan. Bake, uncovered, at 350° for 1-1/4 hours; drain.

3) Drizzle with ketchup; bake 10 minutes longer or until meat is no longer pink and a meat thermom-

eter reads 160°. Let stand for 5-10 minutes before slicing.

Yield: 6 servings.

NUTRITION FACTS: 1 piece equals 308 calories, 16 g fat (7 g saturated fat), 115 mg cholesterol, 646 mg sodium, 12 g carbohydrate, 1 g fiber, 26 g protein.

Sweet-and-Sour Meat Loaf
PREP/TOTAL TIME: 25 min.

Deb Thompson, Lincoln, Nebraska

- 1 egg, lightly beaten
- 5 tablespoons ketchup, *divided*
- 2 tablespoons prepared mustard
- 1/2 cup dry bread crumbs
- 2 tablespoons onion soup mix
- 1/4 teaspoon salt
- 1/4 teaspoon pepper
- 1 pound lean ground beef
- 1/4 cup sugar
- 2 tablespoons brown sugar
- 2 tablespoons cider vinegar

SWEET-AND-SOUR MEAT LOAF

FLAVORFUL MEAT LOAF

1) In a large bowl, combine the egg, 2 tablespoons ketchup, mustard, bread crumbs, dry soup mix, salt and pepper. Crumble beef over mixture and mix well. Shape into an oval loaf.

2) Place in a shallow 1-qt. microwave-safe dish. Cover and microwave on high for 10-12 minutes or until the meat is no longer pink and a meat thermometer reads 160°; drain.

3) Meanwhile in a small bowl, combine the sugars, vinegar and remaining ketchup; drizzle over meat loaf. Cover and microwave on high for 2-3 minutes longer or until heated through. Let stand for 10 minutes before slicing.

Yield: 4 servings.

NUTRITION FACTS: 4 ounces equals 353 calories, 11 g fat (4 g saturated fat), 122 mg cholesterol, 944 mg sodium, 37 g carbohydrate, 1 g fiber, 25 g protein.

Flavorful Meat Loaf

PREP: 15 min. **BAKE:** 45 min. + standing

Lillian Wittler, Wayne, Nebraska

- 2 egg whites
- 1/2 cup 1% milk
- 3 slices whole wheat bread, torn into pieces
- 1/4 cup finely chopped onion
- 1 teaspoon Worcestershire sauce
- 1/4 teaspoon onion powder
- 1/4 teaspoon garlic powder
- 1/4 teaspoon ground mustard
- 1/4 teaspoon rubbed sage
- 1/4 teaspoon pepper
- 1 pound lean ground beef
- 3 tablespoons ketchup

1) In a large bowl, beat egg whites. Add milk and bread; let stand for 5 minutes. Stir in the onion, Worcestershire sauce and seasonings. Crumble beef over mixture and mix well.

2) Shape into a loaf in an 11-in. x 7-in. x 2-in. baking pan coated with cooking spray. Bake, uncovered, at 350° for 35 minutes; drain.

3) Spoon ketchup over loaf. Bake 10-20 minutes longer or until a meat thermometer reads 160°. Let stand for 10 minutes before slicing.

Yield: 5 servings.

NUTRITION FACTS: 1 piece equals 228 calories, 9 g fat (4 g saturated fat), 35 mg cholesterol, 307 mg sodium, 13 g carbohydrate, 1 g fiber, 23 g protein.

Mom's Meat Loaf

PREP: 15 min. **BAKE:** 40 min.

Michelle Beran, Caflin, Kansas

- 1 egg
- 1/4 cup 2% milk
- 1/3 cup crushed saltines
- 3 tablespoons chopped onion
- 1/4 teaspoon salt
- 1/8 teaspoon rubbed sage

Dash pepper

- 1/2 pound lean ground beef
- 1/4 cup ketchup
- 2 tablespoons brown sugar
- 1/4 teaspoon Worcestershire sauce

1) In a large bowl, beat egg. Add the milk, cracker crumbs, onion, salt, sage and pepper. Crumble beef over mixture and mix well. Shape into two loaves; place in a shallow baking dish coated with cooking spray.

2) Combine the ketchup, brown sugar and Worcestershire sauce; spoon over meat loaves. Bake at 350° for 40-45 minutes or until meat is no longer pink and a meat thermometer reads 160°; drain.

Yield: 2 mini meat loaves.

NUTRITION FACTS: 1 mini meat loaf equals 337 calories, 12 g fat (4 g saturated fat), 162 mg cholesterol, 898 mg sodium, 31 g carbohydrate, 1 g fiber, 27 g protein.

MOM'S MEAT LOAF

EASY-ON-THE-BUDGET SALISBURY STEAKS

 CLASSIC: Salisbury Steak with Onion Gravy will appeal to your budget as well as your taste buds. The savory gravy will be a hit on mashed potatoes, rice or pasta.

 TIME-SAVER: Rely on your microwave to get dinner on the table in record time when fixing Speedy Salisbury Steak. No flavor is sacrificed in this tasty entree.

 LIGHT: Lower-calorie ingredients, such as lean ground beef, reduced-fat reduced-sodium cream soup and fat-free milk, are used in Simple Salisbury Steak. These ingredient choices help cut the calories by more than 50% from Salisbury Steak with Onion Gravy.

 SERVES 2: Baby portobello mushrooms and balsamic vinegar jazz up the ground beef in Salisbury Steak with Portobello Sauce, a meaty main dish portioned for a pair.

Salisbury Steak with Onion Gravy

PREP: 10 min. **COOK:** 25 min.

Kim Kidd, Freedom, Pennsylvania

    1 egg
    1 can (10-1/2 ounces) condensed
       French onion soup, undiluted,
       divided
 1/2 cup dry bread crumbs
 1/4 teaspoon salt
Dash pepper
1-1/2 pounds ground beef
 1/4 cup water
 1/4 cup ketchup
    1 teaspoon Worcestershire sauce
 1/2 teaspoon prepared mustard
    1 tablespoon all-purpose flour
    2 tablespoons cold water
    6 cups hot cooked egg noodles
Chopped fresh parsley, optional

1) In a large bowl, beat egg. Stir in 1/3 cup of soup, bread crumbs, salt and pepper. Crumble beef over mixture; mix gently. Shape into six oval patties.

2) In a skillet, brown patties over medium heat for 3-4 minutes on each side. Remove and set aside; drain. Add the water, ketchup, Worcestershire sauce, mustard and remaining soup to skillet. Bring to a boil.

3) Return patties to skillet. Reduce heat; cover and simmer for 15 minutes or until meat is no longer pink. Remove patties.

4) Combine flour and cold water until smooth. Stir into pan. Bring to a boil; cook and stir for 2 minutes or until thickened. Serve patties and gravy over noodles. Garnish with parsley if desired.

Yield: 6 servings.

NUTRITION FACTS: 1 serving equals 458 calories, 18 g fat (6 g saturated fat), 149 mg cholesterol, 767 mg sodium, 42 g carbohydrate, 2 g fiber, 31 g protein.

SPEEDY SALISBURY STEAK

Speedy Salisbury Steak

PREP/TOTAL TIME: 20 min.

Cindy Stephenson, Bullard, Texas

    1 egg, lightly beaten
 1/2 cup soft bread crumbs
 1/4 cup chopped onion
    2 teaspoons Worcestershire sauce
 1/2 teaspoon garlic powder
    1 pound ground beef

GRAVY:

    2 tablespoons all-purpose flour
    1 can (14-1/2 ounces) beef broth
 1/4 cup ketchup
    1 tablespoon Worcestershire sauce
 1/4 teaspoon dried basil
    1 jar (4-1/2 ounces) sliced
       mushrooms, drained
Mashed potatoes

1) In a large bowl, combine the first five ingredients. Crumble beef over mixture and mix well. Shape into four patties; place in a shallow 2-qt. microwave-safe dish.

2) Cover and microwave at 70% power for 5-6 minutes. Meanwhile, in a small bowl, combine flour and broth until smooth. Stir in the ketchup, Worcestershire sauce, basil and mushrooms.

3) Turn patties; drain. Pour gravy over patties. Cover and microwave at 70% power for 5-6 minutes. Gently stir gravy; cover and let stand for 5 minutes. Serve over mashed potatoes.

Yield: 4 servings.

NUTRITION FACTS: 1 serving (calculated without mashed potatoes) equals 312 calories, 16 g fat (6 g saturated fat), 128 mg cholesterol, 842 mg sodium, 14 g carbohydrate, 1 g fiber, 27 g protein.

Quick Substitute

If you don't have time to make mashed potatoes, serve the patties and gravy on toast. Simply toast the bread while the meat is cooking in the microwave.

Simple Salisbury Steak

PREP/TOTAL TIME: 30 min.

Elouise Bonar, Hanover, Illinois

- 1 egg
- 1/3 cup dry bread crumbs
- 1 can (10-3/4 ounces) reduced-fat reduced-sodium condensed cream of mushroom soup, undiluted, *divided*
- 1/4 cup finely chopped onion
- 1 pound lean ground beef
- 1/2 cup fat-free milk
- 1/4 teaspoon browning sauce, optional
- 1/4 teaspoon salt
- 1-1/2 cups sliced fresh mushrooms

1) In a bowl, combine the egg, bread crumbs, 1/4 cup soup and onion. Crumble the beef over mixture and mix well. Shape into six patties. In a large nonstick skillet, brown the patties on both sides; drain.

2) In a bowl, combine the milk, browning sauce if desired, salt and remaining soup; stir in mushrooms. Pour over patties. Reduce heat; cover and simmer for 15-20 minutes or until meat is no longer pink.

Yield: 6 servings.

NUTRITION FACTS: 1 serving equals 212 calories, 9 g fat (3 g saturated fat), 67 mg cholesterol, 599 mg sodium, 11 g carbohydrate, trace fiber, 20 g protein.

Salisbury Steak with Portobello Sauce

PREP/TOTAL TIME: 25 min.

Taste of Home Test Kitchen

- 3/4 pound lean ground beef
- 1/4 teaspoon salt
- 1/8 teaspoon pepper
- 3 tablespoons port wine *or* beef broth
- 2 tablespoons chopped shallots
- 1-1/2 teaspoons balsamic vinegar
- 1/2 cup sliced baby portobello mushrooms
- 1-1/2 teaspoons all-purpose flour
- 1/2 cup beef broth
- 1 teaspoon Worcestershire sauce
- 1 teaspoon ketchup
- 1/8 teaspoon dried rosemary, crushed

1) In a bowl, combine the beef, salt and pepper; shape into two oval patties. In a skillet, cook patties over medium heat until no longer pink.

2) Meanwhile, in a saucepan, combine the wine or broth, shallots and vinegar. Bring to a boil; cook for 5 minutes or until thickened. Toss the mushrooms with flour; add to saucepan. Stir in the broth, Worcestershire sauce, ketchup and rosemary. Bring to a boil; cook and stir for 3-5 minutes or until mushrooms are tender. Drain patties; serve with sauce.

Yield: 2 servings.

NUTRITION FACTS: 1 patty with 1/3 cup sauce equals 313 calories, 13 g fat (5 g saturated fat), 83 mg cholesterol, 673 mg sodium, 8 g carbohydrate, trace fiber, 34 g protein.

SALISBURY STEAK WITH PORTOBELLO SAUCE

MEATBALLS WITH CREAM SAUCE

Meatballs with Cream Sauce

PREP: 15 min. **BAKE:** 20 min.

Michelle Thompson, Smithfield, Utah

I get raves from my husband and our three fussy children when I serve these satisfying meatballs with mashed potatoes. The savory cream sauce gives a new twist to meatballs.

      1   egg, lightly beaten
    1/4   cup milk
      2   tablespoons ketchup
      1   teaspoon Worcestershire sauce
    3/4   cup quick-cooking oats
    1/4   cup finely chopped onion
    1/4   cup minced fresh parsley
      1   teaspoon salt
    1/4   teaspoon pepper
  1-1/2   pounds lean ground beef
      3   tablespoons all-purpose flour

CREAM SAUCE:
      2   tablespoons butter
      2   tablespoons all-purpose flour
    1/4   teaspoon dried thyme
Salt and pepper to taste
      1   can (14 ounces) chicken broth
    2/3   cup heavy whipping cream
      2   tablespoons minced fresh parsley

1) In a large bowl, combine the first nine ingredients. Crumble beef over mixture and mix well. Shape into 1-1/2-in. balls. Roll in flour, shaking off excess. Place 1 in. apart on greased 15-in. x 10-in. x 1-in. baking pans.

2) Bake, uncovered, at 400° for 10 minutes. Turn meatballs; bake 12-15 minutes longer or until meat is no longer pink.

3) Meanwhile, for sauce, melt butter in a saucepan over medium heat. Stir in the flour, thyme, salt and pepper until smooth. Gradually add broth and cream. Bring to a boil; cook and stir for 2 minutes or until thickened.

4) Drain meatballs on paper towels; transfer to a serving dish. Top with sauce; sprinkle with parsley.

Yield: 6 servings.

NUTRITION FACTS: 1 serving (calculated without the salt and pepper in cream sauce) equals 389 calories, 24 g fat (12 g saturated fat), 139 mg cholesterol, 874 mg sodium, 16 g carbohydrate, 1 g fiber, 27 g protein.

Making Meatballs of Equal Size

1) Lightly pat meat mixture into a 1-in.-thick rectangle. Cut the rectangle into the same number of squares as meatballs in the recipe.

2) Gently roll each square into a ball.

Teriyaki Meatballs

PREP: 20 min. **BAKE:** 20 min.

Evette Nowicki, Oak Harbor, Washington

The Asian-inspired sauce gets its sweetness from pineapple as well as yellow and red peppers. This one-time appetizer was changed so many times because of my family's suggestions that it eventually became a main course.

      2   cans (8 ounces *each*) pineapple chunks
      1   medium onion, finely chopped
    1/4   cup finely chopped sweet yellow pepper
    1/4   cup finely chopped sweet red pepper
    1/2   cup dry bread crumbs
    1/2   teaspoon ground ginger
    1/4   teaspoon salt
      1   pound lean ground beef

SAUCE:
    1/4   cup vegetable oil
    1/4   cup soy sauce
      3   tablespoons honey

2 tablespoons white vinegar
3/4 teaspoon garlic powder
1/2 teaspoon ground ginger

1) Drain pineapple, reserving 1/4 cup juice; set pineapple aside. In a bowl, combine the onion, peppers, bread crumbs, ginger, salt and reserved pineapple juice. Crumble beef over mixture and mix well. Shape into 1-in. balls.

2) Place the sauce ingredients in a blender; cover and process for 1 minute. Place 2 tablespoons of sauce in a greased 13-in. x 9-in. x 2-in. baking dish. Add meatballs. Pour remaining sauce over meatballs.

3) Bake, uncovered, at 400° for 20 minutes or until meat is no longer pink. Gently stir pineapple into sauce or place one pineapple chunk on each meatball; secure with a toothpick.

Yield: 42 meatballs.

Editor's Note: To serve these meatballs as an appetizer, place the cooked meatballs in a chafing dish.

NUTRITION FACTS: 8 meatballs equals 394 calories, 18 g fat (4 g saturated fat), 44 mg cholesterol, 1,009 mg sodium, 37 g carbohydrate, 2 g fiber, 21 g protein.

Baking Meatballs & Meat Loaves

Place shaped meatballs on a rack in a shallow baking pan. Bake at 400° until no longer pink, about 20 minutes for 1-1/2-in. meatballs.

For meat loaf, insert an instant-read thermometer in the center of the loaf near the end of the baking time. When it reads 160°, the meat loaf is done. After baking, drain any fat. Let the meat loaf stand for 5-10 minutes before slicing.

VEGETABLE BEEF STIR-FRY

Vegetable Beef Stir-Fry
PREP/TOTAL TIME: 25 min.

Taste of Home Test Kitchen

You can now find sliced fresh shiitake mushrooms in the produce section of your local grocery store.

1 pound lean ground beef
2 cups cut fresh asparagus (1-inch pieces)
1 can (8 ounces) sliced water chestnuts, drained
1 package (5 ounces) sliced fresh shiitake mushrooms
1 teaspoon minced garlic
2 teaspoons sesame oil
2 tablespoons cornstarch
1-1/2 cups beef broth
1/3 cup hoisin sauce
2 tablespoons reduced-sodium soy sauce
1 teaspoon minced fresh gingerroot
1 large tomato, chopped
Hot cooked rice, optional

1) In a large skillet or wok, cook beef over medium heat until no longer pink; drain and set aside. In the same pan, stir-fry the asparagus, water chestnuts, mushrooms and garlic in oil for 5 minutes or until crisp-tender.

2) In a small bowl, combine the cornstarch, broth, hoisin sauce, soy sauce and ginger until blended; pour over vegetables. Return beef to the pan. Bring to a boil; cook and stir for 2 minutes or until thickened. Remove from the heat; stir in the tomato. Serve with rice if desired.

Yield: 4 servings.

NUTRITION FACTS: 1 cup equals 338 calories, 12 g fat (4 g saturated fat), 56 mg cholesterol, 1,040 mg sodium, 31 g carbohydrate, 5 g fiber, 27 g protein.

TRADITIONAL CABBAGE ROLLS

 CLASSIC: A meaty beef-pork mixture is rolled in large cabbage leaves in Old-Fashioned Cabbage Rolls. These are slowly baked in the oven in tomato sauce for tasty, tender results.

 TIME-SAVER: All the classic flavors of a cabbage roll are in this easy, slow-cooked casserole. Stuffed Cabbage Casserole doesn't require filling and forming the rolls, which saves you time in the kitchen.

 LIGHT: Your family won't miss the meat in Vegetarian Cabbage Rolls. It's replaced with bulgur, zucchini and red and green peppers for great flavor and extra nutrition.

 SERVES 2: Just 1/4 pound of ground beef and pork sausage are used to make these four savory Cabbage Rolls. If you buy 1-pound packages of ground beef and pork sausage, divide the meat into 1/4-pound patties, wrap individually and freeze. That way, you can remove just the amount needed to make this recipe or another one.

Old-Fashioned Cabbage Rolls

PREP: 25 min. **BAKE:** 1-1/2 hours

Florence Krantz, Bismarck, North Dakota

- 1 medium head cabbage (3 pounds)
- 1/2 pound ground beef
- 1/2 pound ground pork
- 1 can (15 ounces) tomato sauce, *divided*
- 1 small onion, chopped
- 1/2 cup uncooked long grain rice
- 1 tablespoon dried parsley flakes
- 1/2 teaspoon salt
- 1/2 teaspoon dill weed
- 1/8 teaspoon cayenne pepper
- 1 can (14-1/2 ounces) diced tomatoes, undrained
- 1/2 teaspoon sugar

1) In a Dutch oven, cook cabbage in boiling water for 2-3 minutes just until leaves fall off head. Set aside 12 large leaves for rolls. Cut out the thick vein from the bottom of each reserved leaf, making a V-shaped cut. Set aside remaining cabbage.

OLD-FASHIONED CABBAGE ROLLS

2) In a bowl, combine beef, pork, 1/2 cup tomato sauce, onion, rice, parsley and seasonings. Place about 1/4 cup meat mixture on each cabbage leaf; overlap cut ends of leaf. Fold in sides. Beginning from cut end, roll up completely to enclose filling.

3) Slice the remaining cabbage; place in Dutch oven. Arrange the cabbage rolls seam side down over sliced cabbage. Combine the tomatoes, sugar and remaining tomato sauce; pour over the rolls. Cover and bake at 350° for 1-1/2 hours or until tender and a meat thermometer reads 160°.

Yield: 6 servings.

NUTRITION FACTS: 2 cabbage rolls equals 260 calories, 10 g fat (4 g saturated fat), 50 mg cholesterol, 694 mg sodium, 23 g carbohydrate, 3 g fiber, 18 g protein.

Stuffed Cabbage Casserole

PREP: 20 min. **COOK:** 4 hours

Joann Alexander, Center, Texas

- 1 pound ground beef
- 1/3 cup chopped onion
- 4 cups chopped cabbage
- 1 medium green pepper, chopped
- 1 cup uncooked instant rice
- 1 cup water
- 1 can (6 ounces) tomato paste
- 1 can (14-1/2 ounces) diced tomatoes, undrained
- 1/2 cup ketchup
- 2 tablespoons cider vinegar
- 1 to 2 tablespoons sugar, optional
- 1 tablespoon Worcestershire sauce
- 1 teaspoon salt
- 1/2 teaspoon pepper
- 1/4 teaspoon garlic powder

1) In a large skillet, cook beef and onion over medium heat until meat is no longer pink; drain. Transfer to a 5-qt. slow cooker; add cabbage, green pepper and rice.

2) In a large bowl, combine the water and tomato paste. Stir in the remaining ingredients. Pour over beef mixture; mix well. Cover and cook on low for 4-5 hours or until rice and vegetables are tender.

Yield: 6 servings.

NUTRITION FACTS: 1 cup equals 295 calories, 10 g fat (4 g saturated fat), 50 mg cholesterol, 815 mg sodium, 34 g carbohydrate, 5 g fiber, 19 g protein.

Vegetarian Cabbage Rolls

PREP: 30 min. **BAKE:** 15 min.

Michelle Dougherty, Lewiston, Idaho

1-1/2	cups chopped fresh mushrooms
1	cup diced zucchini
3/4	cup chopped green pepper
3/4	cup chopped sweet red pepper
3/4	cup vegetable broth
1/2	cup bulgur
1	teaspoon dried basil
1/2	teaspoon dried marjoram
1/2	teaspoon dried thyme
1/4	teaspoon pepper
6	tablespoons shredded Parmesan cheese, *divided*
2	teaspoons lemon juice
1	large head cabbage
1	can (8 ounces) tomato sauce
1/8	teaspoon hot pepper sauce

1) In a large saucepan, combine the first 10 ingredients. Bring to a boil over medium heat. Reduce heat; cover and simmer for 5 minutes. Remove from the heat; let stand for 5 minutes. Stir 4 tablespoons Parmesan cheese and lemon juice into vegetable mixture.

2) Cook cabbage in boiling water just until leaves fall off head. Set aside eight large leaves for rolls (refrigerate remaining cabbage for another use). Cut out the thick vein from each leaf, making a V-shaped cut.

3) Place a heaping 1/3 cupful beef mixture onto each cabbage leaf; overlap cut ends of leaf. Fold in sides. Beginning from cut end, roll up completely to enclose filling.

4) Combine tomato sauce and hot pepper sauce; pour 1/3 cup into a 2-qt. baking dish. Place cabbage rolls in dish; spoon remaining sauce over top. Cover and bake at 400° for 15 minutes or until heated through. Sprinkle with remaining Parmesan cheese.

Yield: 4 servings.

Editor's Note: Look for bulgur in the cereal, rice or organic food aisle of your grocery store.

NUTRITION FACTS: 2 cabbage rolls equals 142 calories, 3 g fat (1 g saturated fat), 5 mg cholesterol, 675 mg sodium, 25 g carbohydrate, 6 g fiber, 8 g protein.

Shaping Cabbage Rolls

1) Place head of cabbage in boiling water just until outer leaves begin to loosen. Remove cabbage from water and remove leaves that come off easily. Place cabbage back in water if more leaves are needed. For easier rolling, cut out thick vein from each leaf, making a V-shaped cut.

2) Place 2-3 tablespoons of ground beef mixture on each cabbage leaf; fold up sides, beginning from cut end. Roll up to completely enclose meat mixture in leaf. Fasten with a toothpick.

Cabbage Rolls

PREP: 20 min. **BAKE:** 1 hour

Lucille Proctor, Panguitch, Utah

4	large cabbage leaves
1/4	pound ground beef
1/4	pound bulk pork sausage
1/4	cup chopped onion
1/2	cup cooked rice
1	teaspoon Worcestershire sauce
1/2	teaspoon Dijon mustard
1	egg
1	cup tomato juice
2	tablespoons brown sugar, optional

1) In a large saucepan, cook the cabbage leaves in boiling water for 5 minutes; drain and set aside. Meanwhile, in a skillet, cook the beef, sausage and onion over medium heat until meat is no longer pink; drain. Stir in the rice, Worcestershire sauce, mustard and egg; mix well.

2) Cut out the thick vein from the bottom of each reserved leaf, making a V-shaped cut. Place about 1/3 cup beef mixture onto each cabbage leaf; overlap cut ends of leaf. Fold in sides. Beginning from the cut end, roll up completely to enclose filling. Place with seam side down in a greased 11-in. x 7-in. x 2-in. baking dish.

3) Pour juice over rolls; sprinkle with brown sugar if desired. Cover and bake at 350° for 50 minutes. Uncover and bake 10 minutes longer.

Yield: 2 servings.

NUTRITION FACTS: 2 cabbage rolls equals 357 calories, 20 g fat (7 g saturated fat), 164 mg cholesterol, 798 mg sodium, 22 g carbohydrate, 2 g fiber, 21 g protein.

THE PERFECT HAMBURGER

The Perfect Hamburger

PREP/TOTAL TIME: 20 min.

Shirley Kidd, New London, Minnesota

My family calls this the "perfect" burger because we think the chili sauce and horseradish add just the right amount of zip. But you can add or change the seasonings to your liking.

   1 egg, lightly beaten

SEASONINGS:

   2 tablespoons chili sauce

   1 teaspoon dried minced onion

   1 teaspoon prepared horseradish

   1 teaspoon Worcestershire sauce

1/2 teaspoon salt

Dash pepper

BURGER:

   1 pound lean ground beef

   4 hamburger buns, split

Optional toppings: sliced tomato, onion, pickles and condiments

1) Coat grill rack with cooking spray before starting the grill. In a large bowl, combine the egg and seasonings. Crumble beef over mixture and mix well. Shape into four 3/4-in.-thick patties.

2) Grill, covered, over medium heat for 5-7 minutes on each side or until a meat thermometer reads 160° and juices run clear. Serve on buns with desired toppings.

Yield: 4 servings.

Editor's Note: To broil burgers, broil 4 in. from heat for 5-7 minutes on each side or until a meat thermometer reads 160° and juices run clear.

NUTRITION FACTS: 1 burger equals 321 calories, 12 g fat (4 g saturated fat), 109 mg cholesterol, 758 mg sodium, 24 g carbohydrate, 1 g fiber, 27 g protein.

■ **Bacon Burgers:** Replace the seasonings with 1/2 cup shredded cheddar cheese, 1 small onion, chopped, 2 tablespoons ketchup, 1 tablespoon each Parmesan cheese and Worcestershire sauce, 1/2 teaspoon salt and pepper.

Shape into six patties. Wrap 1 bacon strip around each patty; secure with a toothpick. Grill as directed.

■ **Herbed Burgers:** Omit egg. Replace seasoning mix with 5 teaspoons sour cream, 3/4 teaspoon dried parsley flakes, 1/2 teaspoon salt and 1/8 teaspoon pepper. Shape into four patties. Grill as directed.

■ **Taco Burgers:** Replace seasoning mix with 3 tablespoons taco seasoning mix, 2 teaspoons instant minced onion and 3/4 cup finely crushed corn chips. Shape into six patties. Grill as directed.

Testing Burgers For Doneness

Cook beef, pork and lamb burgers to 160°; cook chicken or turkey burgers to 165°. To test for doneness, use tongs to hold burger while inserting instant-read thermometer horizontally from a side. Make sure thermometer is far enough in to read the temperature in the center.

Greek Pasta and Beef

PREP: 30 min. **BAKE:** 45 min.

Dorothy Bateman, Carver, Massachusetts

This casserole gives everyday macaroni and cheese an international flavor. A co-worker who's a pro at Greek cooking shared the recipe.

   1 package (16 ounces) elbow macaroni

   1 pound ground beef

   1 large onion, chopped

   1 garlic clove, minced

   1 can (8 ounces) tomato sauce

1/2 cup water

   1 teaspoon salt

1/2 teaspoon ground cinnamon

1/4 teaspoon ground nutmeg

1/4 teaspoon pepper

   1 egg, lightly beaten

1/2 cup grated Parmesan cheese

SAUCE:

   1 cup butter

1/4 cup all-purpose flour

1/4 teaspoon ground cinnamon
3 cups milk
2 eggs, lightly beaten
1/3 cup grated Parmesan cheese

1) Cook macaroni according to package directions. In a large skillet, cook beef, onion and garlic over medium heat until meat is no longer pink; drain. Stir in the tomato sauce, water and seasonings. Cover and simmer for 10 minutes, stirring occasionally. Drain macaroni.

2) In a large bowl, combine the macaroni, egg and Parmesan cheese; set aside. In a large saucepan, melt butter; stir in flour and cinnamon until smooth. Gradually add milk. Bring to a boil over medium heat; cook and stir for 2 minutes or until slightly thickened.

3) Remove from the heat. Stir a small amount of hot mixture into eggs; return all to pan, stirring constantly. Stir in cheese.

4) In a greased 3-qt. baking dish, spread half of the macaroni mixture. Top with beef mixture and remaining macaroni mixture. Pour sauce over the top. Bake, uncovered, at 350° for 45-50 minutes or until bubbly and heated through. Let stand for 5 minutes before serving.

Yield: 12 servings.

NUTRITION FACTS: 1 serving equals 445 calories, 26 g fat (14 g saturated fat), 132 mg cholesterol, 607 mg sodium, 35 g carbohydrate, 2 g fiber, 19 g protein.

ITALIAN STEW

Italian Stew
PREP: 10 min. **COOK:** 30 min.

Taste of Home Test Kitchen

Escarole, a salad green of the chicory family, has broad wavy jagged-edged green outer leaves that whiten near the core. Wash each leaf well, pat dry and trim off white core.

1 pound ground beef
1/2 pound bulk mild Italian sausage
1 cup chopped onion

1 can (15 ounces) cannellini or white kidney beans, rinsed and drained
2 cups cut fresh green beans
1 can (14-1/2 ounces) Italian stewed tomatoes
1 cup vegetable broth
1 can (6 ounces) tomato paste
2 teaspoons dried oregano
1 teaspoon salt
1/2 teaspoon pepper
1 bunch escarole, trimmed and torn
1/2 cup shredded Parmesan cheese

1) In a large skillet or Dutch oven, cook the beef, sausage and onion over medium heat until meat is no longer pink; drain.

2) Add cannellini, green beans, tomatoes, broth, tomato paste, oregano, salt and pepper. Bring to a boil. Reduce heat; cover and simmer for 15 minutes.

3) Add escarole; cover and simmer 5 minutes longer or until escarole is wilted. Sprinkle with Parmesan cheese.

Yield: 6 servings.

NUTRITION FACTS: 1-1/2 cups equals 339 calories, 14 g fat (6 g saturated fat), 57 mg cholesterol, 1,252 mg sodium, 28 g carbohydrate, 9 g fiber, 26 g protein.

Brief Burritos
PREP/TOTAL TIME: 15 min.

Ginger Burow, Fredericksburg, Texas

With three children in school, evenings are often hectic and short on time—especially during the holiday season. I can put this dish together after school and still have time to run back to town for evening activities. Best of all, the kids love it.

1 pound ground beef
1 can (16 ounces) refried beans
1 can (10 ounces) diced tomatoes and green chilies, drained
1/2 cup chili sauce
8 flour tortillas (10 inches), warmed
1/2 cup shredded cheddar cheese
1/2 cup sour cream

1) In a large skillet, cook beef over medium heat until no longer pink; drain. Stir in the refried beans, tomatoes and chili sauce; heat through.

2) Spoon about 1/2 cup down the center of each tortilla; top with cheese and sour cream. Fold ends and sides over filling. Serve immediately.

Yield: 8 burritos.

NUTRITION FACTS: 1 burrito equals 430 calories, 14 g fat (7 g saturated fat), 50 mg cholesterol, 1,022 mg sodium, 46 g carbohydrate, 9 g fiber, 21 g protein.

SATISFYING GROUND BEEF CASSEROLES

 CLASSIC: Sour cream and cream cheese give this comforting casserole a rich, creamy texture. Beef Noodle Bake pleases all ages.

 TIME-SAVER: Convenience products, like cream of mushroom soup, instant rice and stuffing mix, trim the prep when assembling Microwave Beef Casserole. And the microwave assures it's on the table in less than half an hour.

 LIGHT: The wise use of lower-fat ingredients, such as lean ground turkey, dry milk powder and reduced-fat cream cheese, really cuts the calories in Ground Turkey Noodle Bake. But what isn't cut is all the homey taste.

 SERVES 2: A cheesy corn bread tops a chili-seasoned ground beef mixture with south-of-the-border flair in Mexican Spoon Bread Casserole. It's just the right size for two people.

BEEF NOODLE BAKE

Beef Noodle Bake

PREP: 15 min. **BAKE:** 35 min.

Evelyne Olechnowicz, Valencia, Pennsylvania

- 1-1/2 pounds ground beef
- 1 small onion, chopped
- 2 cans (8 ounces *each*) tomato sauce
- 1 cup (8 ounces) sour cream
- 1 package (3 ounces) cream cheese, cubed and softened
- 1 teaspoon sugar
- 1/2 to 1 teaspoon garlic salt
- 7 cups uncooked wide egg noodles, cooked and drained
- 1 cup (4 ounces) shredded cheddar cheese

1) In a large skillet, cook beef and onion until meat is no longer pink; drain. Remove from the heat; stir in the tomato sauce, sour cream, cream cheese, sugar and garlic salt.

2) Place half of the noodles in a greased 13-in. x 9-in. x 2-in. baking dish; top with half of the beef mixture. Repeat layers. Cover and bake at 350° for 30-35 minutes or until heated through. Sprinkle with cheese; bake 3-5 minutes longer or until cheese is melted.

Yield: 6 servings.

NUTRITION FACTS: 1 serving equals 559 calories, 29 g fat (17 g saturated fat), 160 mg cholesterol, 584 mg sodium, 38 g carbohydrate, 2 g fiber, 33 g protein.

Microwave Beef Casserole

PREP/TOTAL TIME: 30 min.

Joan Hallford, North Richland Hills, Texas

- 1 pound ground beef
- 1 small onion, chopped
- 1/2 cup uncooked instant rice
- 1-1/2 cups water, *divided*
- 1 can (10-3/4 ounces) condensed cream of mushroom soup, undiluted
- 1 cup slivered almonds
- 5 large fresh mushrooms, chopped
- 1 package (6 ounces) seasoned stuffing mix
- 1/4 cup butter, melted

1) Crumble beef into a microwave-safe 3-qt. dish; add onion. Loosely cover and microwave on high for 3-5 minutes or until meat is no longer pink, stirring twice; drain. Stir in rice and 1/2 cup water. Cover and cook for 2 minutes. Stir in the soup, almonds and mushrooms.

2) In a large bowl, combine the stuffing mix, butter and remaining water; spoon over beef mixture. Microwave, uncovered, for 1-3 minutes or until heated through.

Yield: 4-6 servings.

NUTRITION FACTS: 1-1/2 cups equals 510 calories, 30 g fat (10 g saturated fat), 73 mg cholesterol, 988 mg sodium, 36 g carbohydrate, 4 g fiber, 25 g protein.

Ground Turkey Noodle Bake

PREP: 35 min. **BAKE:** 15 min.

Ruby Williams, Bogalusa, Louisiana

- 3 cups uncooked wide egg noodles
- 1/2 pound lean ground turkey
- 1 medium onion, chopped
- 1 can (15 ounces) tomato sauce
- 1 teaspoon Italian seasoning
- 2/3 cup nonfat dry milk powder
- 1/2 cup water
- 4 ounces reduced-fat cream cheese, cubed
- 1 tablespoon minced fresh parsley
- 1 garlic clove, minced
- 1-1/4 cups shredded part-skim mozzarella cheese

1) Cook noodles according to package directions. Meanwhile, in a large skillet, cook turkey and onion over medium heat until turkey is no longer pink; drain. Stir in tomato sauce and Italian seasoning. Bring to a boil. Reduce heat; cover and simmer for 10 minutes.

2) In a saucepan, combine milk powder, water, cream cheese, parsley and garlic. Cook and stir over medium heat until cream cheese is melted.

3) Drain noodles; add to cream cheese mixture. Transfer to an 8-in. square baking dish coated with cooking spray. Top with turkey mixture. Sprinkle with mozzarella cheese.

4) Bake, uncovered, at 375° for 15-20 minutes or until cheese is melted.

Yield: 6 servings.

NUTRITION FACTS: 1 serving equals 281 calories, 11 g fat (6 g saturated fat), 71 mg cholesterol, 676 mg sodium, 25 g carbohydrate, 2 g fiber, 21 g protein.

Mexican Spoon Bread Casserole

PREP: 25 min. **BAKE:** 25 min.

Paula Lock, Glenwood, Arkansas

- 1/2 pound ground beef
- 1 small onion, chopped
- 2 tablespoons chopped green pepper
- 1 garlic clove, minced
- 2/3 cup tomato sauce
- 1/2 cup frozen corn, thawed
- 2 tablespoons sliced ripe olives
- 3/4 teaspoon chili powder
- 1/2 teaspoon salt

Dash pepper

TOPPING:

- 3 tablespoons cornmeal
- 1/2 cup milk

- 1/8 teaspoon salt
- 1/4 cup shredded cheddar cheese
- 1 egg, lightly beaten

1) In a large skillet, cook the beef, onion, green pepper and garlic over medium heat until meat is no longer pink; drain. Add the tomato sauce, corn, olives, chili powder, salt and pepper; bring to a boil. Reduce heat; simmer, uncovered, for 10 minutes.

2) Meanwhile, in a large saucepan, combine the cornmeal, milk and salt; bring to a boil, stirring frequently. Remove from the heat. Stir in cheese and egg.

3) Spoon meat mixture into an ungreased 1-qt. baking dish. Pour topping over meat mixture. Bake, uncovered, at 375° for 22-26 minutes or until a knife inserted near the center comes out clean.

Yield: 2 servings.

NUTRITION FACTS: 1 cup equals 436 calories, 20 g fat (10 g saturated fat), 185 mg cholesterol, 1,418 mg sodium, 31 g carbohydrate, 4 g fiber, 33 g protein.

Cut Calories in Ground Beef Casseroles

Ground beef casseroles can be easily lightened up by using a leaner ground meat. See chart below for calorie, fat and cholesterol content of 4 ounces cooked ground meat.

TYPE OF BEEF	CALORIES	FAT	SAT. FAT	CHOL.
GROUND BEEF 70% lean/30% fat	232	16g	6g	71mg
GROUND CHUCK 80% lean/20% fat	204	13g	5g	71mg
GROUND ROUND 85% lean/15% fat	193	12g	4g	71mg
GROUND SIRLOIN 90% lean/10% fat	175	9g	4g	71mg
GROUND TURKEY 85% lean/15% fat	220	17g	4g	85mg
LEAN GROUND TURKEY 93% lean/7% fat	170	8g	2g	80mg
EXTRA LEAN GROUND TURKEY 99% lean/1% fat	120	1g	0g	55mg

GARLIC BEEF ENCHILADAS

Garlic Beef Enchiladas

PREP: 30 min. **BAKE:** 40 min.

Jennifer Standridge, Kennesaw, Georgia

Enchiladas are typically prepared with corn tortillas, but my husband and I prefer flour tortillas. I use them in this saucy casserole that has home-cooked flavor and a subtle kick.

> 1 pound ground beef
> 1 medium onion, chopped
> 2 tablespoons all-purpose flour
> 1 tablespoon chili powder
> 1 teaspoon salt
> 1 teaspoon garlic powder
> 1/2 teaspoon ground cumin
> 1/4 teaspoon rubbed sage
> 1 can (14-1/2 ounces) stewed tomatoes

SAUCE:

> 4 to 6 garlic cloves, minced
> 1/3 cup butter
> 1/2 cup all-purpose flour
> 1 can (14-1/2 ounces) beef broth
> 1 can (15 ounces) tomato sauce
> 1 to 2 tablespoons chili powder
> 1 to 2 teaspoons ground cumin
> 1 to 2 teaspoons rubbed sage
> 1/2 teaspoon salt
> 10 flour tortillas (7 inches)
> 2 cups (8 ounces) shredded Colby-Monterey Jack cheese

1) In a saucepan, cook beef and onion over medium heat until meat is no longer pink; drain. Stir in the flour and seasonings until blended. Stir in tomatoes; bring to a boil. Reduce heat; cover and simmer for 15 minutes.

2) Meanwhile, in another saucepan, saute garlic in butter until tender. Stir in flour until blended. Gradually stir in broth; bring to a boil. Cook and stir for 2 minutes or until thickened. Stir in tomato sauce and seasonings; heat through.

3) Pour 1-1/2 cups sauce into an ungreased 13-in. x 9-in. x 2-in. baking dish. Spread 1/4 cup beef mixture down center of each tortilla; top with 1-2 tablespoons cheese. Roll up tightly; place seam side down over sauce. Top with remaining sauce.

4) Cover and bake at 350° for 30-35 minutes. Sprinkle with remaining cheese. Bake, uncovered, 10-15 minutes longer or until the cheese is melted.

Yield: 4-6 servings.

NUTRITION FACTS: 1-1/2 enchiladas equals 637 calories, 36 g fat (18 g saturated fat), 111 mg cholesterol, 2,070 mg sodium, 47 g carbohydrate, 3 g fiber, 33 g protein.

Stuffed Green Peppers

PREP: 20 min. **BAKE:** 1 hour

Marlene Karnemaat, Fremont, Michigan

This classic recipe is a great way to enjoy fresh green peppers.

> 6 medium green peppers
> 1-1/2 pounds uncooked lean ground beef
> 1 cup cooked long grain rice
> 1/2 cup chopped onion
> 1/2 cup chopped celery
> 1 small tomato, seeded and chopped
> 1 garlic clove, minced
> 1 teaspoon salt
> 1/4 teaspoon pepper
> 1 can (10-3/4 ounces) condensed tomato soup, undiluted
> 1/2 teaspoon dried basil
> 1/2 cup shredded sharp cheddar cheese

1) Cut tops off peppers and remove seeds. In a large kettle, cook peppers in boiling water for 3 minutes. Drain and immediately place in ice water; invert onto paper towels.

2) In a bowl, combine beef, rice, onion, celery, tomato, garlic, salt and pepper. Spoon into peppers. Place in a greased 13-in. x 9-in. x 2-in. baking dish. Combine soup and basil; spoon over. Cover and bake at 350° for 55-60 minutes or until the beef is no longer pink. Sprinkle with cheese; bake 5 minutes longer or until the cheese is melted.

Yield: 6 servings.

NUTRITION FACTS: 1 stuffed pepper equals 312 calories, 11 g fat (5 g saturated fat), 66 mg cholesterol, 836 mg sodium, 25 g carbohydrate, 4 g fiber, 27 g protein.

Parboiling Peppers

Bring water to a boil in a Dutch oven or soup kettle. Cook seeded whole peppers until crisp-tender, about 2-3 minutes depending on the size of the pepper. Remove from the water with tongs and invert onto paper towels to drain before stuffing.

chef for a night

Dream job wows the crowd at cafe fund-raiser

While dining with her husband at a cafe in their home state of Connecticut, Ruth Hartunion Alumbaugh saw a poster that whet her appetite.

"Want to be the guest chef of the month?" the sign asked. A lifelong cooking enthusiast and a *Taste of Home* field editor, Ruth answered "Yes!" with excitement.

The Willimantic Brewing Co. cafe's promotion offered locals the chance to plan and prepare a menu for an evening with a portion of the proceeds going to charity.

Clad in a white chef's coat on the big night, Ruth created an appetizer and three entrees with help from the restaurant's staff. Ruth had spread the word around town about her celebrity gig, so the restaurant was packed. In fact, people were turned away. The menu sold out.

Her Lamb Kabobs with Bulgur Pilaf, which reflect her Armenian heritage, were the biggest hit. They were completely gone in the first two hours.

Ruth also treated diners to 100 "thank-you" cupcakes.

The restaurant was so impressed with the turnout that Ruth received 10 percent of the night's profits—$1,300. The staff of her designated charity, the Willimantic Public Library children's department, was astounded with her gift, Ruth says. "We spend a lot of time there, so it's nice that they now know how much we appreciate them."

And for Ruth the cook, working in a restaurant kitchen was a dream come true.

"So much counter space, and I didn't have to wash a single dish," she says. "The dishwashers were my heroes!"

Ruth Hartunion Alumbaugh

> " *It's nice that they now know how much we appreciate them.*
>
> ~Ruth Hartunion Alumbaugh

Recipes

Tips

PORK & LAMB

Pork & Lamb

PORK

Today's pork is easier than ever to cook because it's lean and tender. Follow the techniques and guidelines below for cooking your favorite cuts of pork, and you'll have perfect results every time!

Purchase before the "sell-by" date on the packaging for best quality. Make sure the package is cold and has no holes or tears.

Due to breeding and feeding changes over the last 20 years, the fat content of pork has been reduced to make it a leaner product.

Some of the leanest cuts of pork are boneless loin roasts or chops, boneless sirloin roasts or chops and bone-in pork loin chops. Ounce for ounce, pork tenderloin is almost as lean as boneless skinless chicken breast.

Determine the amount of pork you need to buy based on the cut and amount of bone. Follow these guidelines:

- 1 pound of bone-in roasts, chops or ham yields 2-1/2 to 3 servings.
- 1 pound of boneless roasts, chops or ham yields 3 to 4 servings.
- 1 pound of spareribs yields 1-1/4 servings.

Defrosting Guidelines

Plan more time for thicker packages because they take longer to defrost. Here are some guidelines for thawing pork in the refrigerator:

- For a 1- to 1-1/2-in.-thick package of ground pork, allow at least 24 hours.
- For 1-in.-thick chops, allow 12 to 14 hours.
- For a small roast, allow 3 to 5 hours per pound.
- For a large roast, allow 4 to 7 hours per pound.

Reading the Label

Meat labels give you a variety of information. The label states the type of meat (beef, pork, veal or lamb), the wholesale cut (loin, rib, shoulder, leg, etc.) and the retail cut (steak, chops, roast, etc.). The label also states the "sell-by" date, weight of the meat, cost per pound and total price.

The wholesale cut is an indication of tenderness; for example, a loin or rib chop will be more tender than a shoulder or leg chop. Tenderness helps determine an appropriate cooking method. Tender cuts are best cooked with dry-heat methods (grilling, broiling, roasting, pan-frying, pan-broiling and stir-frying). Less-tender cuts are better cooked by moist-heat methods (braising or cooking in liquid).

Cooking Pork

Don't overcook lean, fresh pork. It cooks quickly and will become dry and tough if cooked too long. Use a meat thermometer to check doneness. Pork is done at 160°. Cook large roasts to 155°, then tent with foil and allow to stand for 10-15 minutes. The internal temperature will rise to 160°. At 160°, the internal color of boneless roasts may be faint pink, and bone-in roasts may be slightly pink near the bone. The juices may have a hint of pink or be clear.

Use dry-heat cooking methods (broiling, grilling, pan-broiling, roasting and stir-frying) when a firm texture is desired for cuts of pork because, unlike beef, pork cuts vary little in tenderness. The moist-heat method of braising is used for a fork-tender texture.

CUT/TYPE	BRAISE	BROIL	GRILL	ROAST	PAN-BROIL	PAN-FRY	COOK IN LIQUID
ROASTS							
BOSTON BUTT ROAST	•			•			
CROWN ROAST				•			
LOIN ROAST				•			
PICNIC SHOULDER	•			•			
PORK LEG				•			
RIB ROAST				•			
TENDERLOIN	•	•	•	•			
WHOLE OR HALF HAM				•			
CHOPS							
BLADE CHOPS	•	•	•		•	•	
LOIN CHOPS	•	•	•		•		
RIB CHOPS	•	•	•		•		
STEAKS							
ARM STEAKS	•				•	•	
BLADE STEAKS	•	•	•		•	•	
RIBS							
BACK RIBS	•	•	•	•			•
COUNTRY-STYLE RIBS	•	•	•	•			•
SPARERIBS	•	•	•	•			•
OTHER							
GROUND PORK PATTIES		•	•		•	•	
HAM SLICES		•	•	•	•	•	
PORK CUBES	•	•	•				
TENDERLOIN SLICES						•	

Roasting Fresh Pork and Ham

Place meat on a rack in a shallow roasting pan with the fat side up. Insert an oven-safe meat thermometer in the thickest portion of the muscle without touching bone or fat. Or use an instant-read thermometer toward the end of the roasting time. If the roast needs to cook longer, make sure to remove the instant-read thermometer before you return the roast to the oven.

Roast without liquid, uncovered, according to the temperature and time given in the chart below or in the recipe. Roasts continue to cook after being removed from the oven, so remove the meat when the meat thermometer reads 5-10° below desired doneness. Cover with foil and let stand for 10-15 minutes before carving.

CUT	WEIGHT	COOKING TIME (MINUTES PER POUND)	OVEN TEMP.	DONENESS
PORK LOIN ROAST, BONE-IN	3 to 5 lbs.	20 to 30	350°	160°
PORK LOIN ROAST, BONELESS	2 to 4 lbs.	20 to 30	350°	160°
PORK CROWN ROAST	6 to 8 lbs.	20 to 25	350°	160°
SHOULDER ROAST OR BOSTON BUTT	3 to 6 lbs.	30 to 40	350°	160°
LEG-HALF (FRESH HAM OR PICNIC)	3-1/2 lbs.	35 to 40	350°	160°
PORK TENDERLOIN	1/2 to 1 lb.	20 to 30 (minutes total)	425° or 450°	160°
SPARERIBS	1 to 1-1/2 lbs.	1-1/2 to 2 (hours total)	350°	tender
WHOLE HAM, FULLY COOKED, BONE-IN	10 to 14 lbs.	15 to 18	325°	140°
HALF HAM, FULLY COOKED, BONE-IN	5 to 7 lbs.	18 to 25	325°	140°
HAM, FULLY COOKED, BONELESS	4 to 6 lbs.	18 to 20	325°	140°

Carving a Rib Roast

1) To serve the roast as boneless slices, hold the roast upright by using paper towels to hold the rib bones with one hand. With a carving knife, cut between the meat and the rib bones. If the chine bone (backbone) is attached, cut between the meat and chine bone to remove.

2) Place the meat cut side down on a cutting board. Cut into slices.

3) To serve the roast with rib bones attached, place roast with rib bones to one side of a cutting board. Hold the meat steady with a meat fork. Using a carving knife, cut between the bones, following along the curve of the bone.

Cuts of Pork

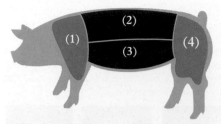

■ **TENDER** ■ **LESS TENDER**

Shoulder (1)

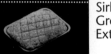
Blade Steak

Picnic Shoulder

Shoulder Cut
Boneless Pork Butt

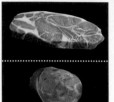
Sirloin Cuts
Ground Pork,
Extra Lean

Arm Picnic Roast

Loin (2)

Boneless Loin Roast

Center Rib Roast

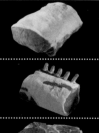
Loin Chop

Center Cut Roast

Pork Rib Chop

Pork Tenderloin

Pork Top Loin Chop

Sirloin Chop

Back Ribs

Sirloin Steaks

Side (3)

Country-Style
Spareribs

Spareribs

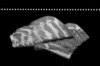
St. Louis-Style Ribs

Leg (4)

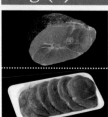
Smoked Ham

Sandwich Steaks

Photos courtesy of the National Pork Board.

Pork Grilling Chart

Pork, fresh pork sausages and ground pork are done when the temperature reaches 160°. Cooked sausages are done when they are heated through.

CUT	WEIGHT OR THICKNESS	HEAT	COOKING TIME
LOIN OR RIB CHOP (BONE-IN)	3/4 to 1 in. 1-1/4 to 1-1/2 in.	Medium/Direct Medium/Direct	8 to 10 min. 12 to 18 min.
LOIN CHOP (BONELESS)	3/4 to 1 in. 1-1/4 to 1-1/2 in.	Medium/Direct Medium/Direct	8 to 10 min. 12 to 18 min.
BACK RIBS OR SPARERIBS	3 to 4 lbs.	Medium/Indirect	1-1/2 to 2 hours
TENDERLOIN	3/4 to 1 lb.	Medium-Hot/Indirect	25 to 40 min.
LOIN ROAST (BONE-IN OR BONELESS)	3 to 5 lbs.	Medium/Indirect	1-1/4 to 1-3/4 hours
KABOBS	1-in. cubes	Medium/Direct	10 to 15 min.
SAUSAGE, COOKED		Medium/Direct	3 to 7 min. or until heated through
SAUSAGE, FRESH	4 oz.	Medium/Indirect	20 to 30 min.
PORK PATTIES	4 oz. and 1/2 in.	Medium/Direct	8 to 10 min.

Grilled Rosemary Pork Roast

PREP: 15 min. + marinating **GRILL:** 1-1/4 hours

Christine Wilson, Sellersville, Pennsylvania

When we're expecting guests for dinner, I often serve this flavorful grilled pork roast.

   3 medium tart apples, peeled and chopped
   1 cup unsweetened apple cider *or* juice
   3 green onions, chopped
   3 tablespoons honey
   1 to 2 teaspoons dried rosemary, crushed
   2 garlic cloves, minced
   1 boneless pork loin roast (3 pounds)

1) In a small saucepan, combine the apples, cider, onions, honey, rosemary and garlic; bring to a boil. Reduce heat; simmer, uncovered, for 5 minutes. Cool to room temperature.

2) Place pork roast in a large resealable plastic bag; add half of marinade. Seal bag and turn to coat; chill overnight, turning occasionally. Transfer the remaining marinade to a bowl; cover and chill.

3) Coat grill rack with cooking spray before starting the grill. Prepare grill for indirect heat, using a drip pan. Drain and discard marinade from pork.

GRILLED ROSEMARY PORK ROAST

4) Grill roast, covered, over indirect medium heat for 1-1/4 to 1-3/4 hours or until a meat thermometer reads 160°, turning occasionally. Let stand for 10 minutes before slicing. Heat reserved marinade; serve with pork.

Yield: 8 servings.

NUTRITION FACTS: 4-1/2 ounces cooked pork with 1 tablespoon sauce equals 260 calories, 8 g fat (3 g saturated fat), 85 mg cholesterol, 52 mg sodium, 13 g carbohydrate, 1 g fiber, 33 g protein.

PESTO PORK ROAST

Pesto Pork Roast

PREP: 30 min. **BAKE:** 1-1/2 hours + standing

Jennifer Magrey, Sterling, Connecticut

I came up with this recipe when I was left with a bit of pesto from another recipe and also had an abundance of tomatoes from the garden. I serve a green salad with fresh mozzarella and balsamic vinaigrette on the side.

- 1/4 cup plus 2 tablespoons olive oil, *divided*
- 2 cups loosely packed basil leaves
- 1/2 cup grated Parmesan cheese
- 4 garlic cloves, peeled
- 12 plum tomatoes
- 1-1/2 teaspoons pepper, *divided*
- 1 teaspoon kosher salt, *divided*
- 1 bone-in pork loin roast (4 to 5 pounds)
- 1 package (16 ounces) egg noodles

1) For pesto, in a blender, combine 1/4 cup oil, basil, Parmesan cheese and garlic. Cover and process until blended. Remove 2 tablespoons pesto to a small bowl; stir in remaining oil and set aside.

2) Cut each tomato into four slices; place in a greased shallow roasting pan. Sprinkle with 1 teaspoon pepper and 1/2 teaspoon salt. Sprinkle remaining pepper and salt over roast; place over tomato slices. Spread remaining pesto over roast.

3) Bake, uncovered, at 350° for 1-1/2 to 2 hours or until a meat thermometer reads 160°. Remove roast and keep warm. Let stand for 10 minutes before slicing.

4) Cook noodles according to package directions; drain and place in a large bowl. Using a slotted spoon, remove tomatoes from roasting pan and add to noodles. Add reserved pesto and toss to coat. Serve with pork.

Yield: 6-8 servings.

NUTRITION FACTS: 1 serving equals 584 calories, 25 g fat (7 g saturated fat), 149 mg cholesterol, 426 mg sodium, 46 g carbohydrate, 3 g fiber, 43 g protein.

Herb-Stuffed Pork Loin

PREP: 20 min. **BAKE:** 1 hour 20 min. + standing

Michele Montgomery, Lethbridge, Alberta

I prepare this pork roast often when I'm entertaining guests. It's especially good with garden-fresh herbs, but dried work nicely as well.

- 1 boneless pork loin roast (3 pounds)
- 1/4 cup Dijon mustard
- 4 garlic cloves, minced
- 1/3 cup minced chives
- 1/4 cup minced fresh sage *or* 4 teaspoons rubbed sage
- 2 tablespoons minced fresh thyme *or* 2 teaspoons dried thyme
- 1 tablespoon minced fresh rosemary *or* 1 teaspoon dried rosemary, crushed
- 2-3/4 teaspoons pepper, *divided*
- 1 teaspoon salt, *divided*
- 1 tablespoon olive oil

1) Starting about a third in from one side, make a lengthwise slit down the roast to within 1/2 in. of the bottom. Turn roast over and make another lengthwise slit, starting about a third in from the opposite side. Open roast so it lies flat; cover with plastic wrap. Flatten to 3/4-in. thickness; remove plastic wrap.

2) Combine mustard and garlic; rub two-thirds of the mixture over roast. Combine the chives, sage, thyme, rosemary, 3/4 teaspoon pepper and 1/2 teaspoon salt. Sprinkle two-thirds of the herb mixture over roast.

3) Roll up jelly-roll style, starting with a long side; tie several times with kitchen string. Rub oil over roast; sprinkle with remaining salt and pepper.

4) If grilling the roast, coat grill rack with cooking spray before starting the grill. Grill roast, covered, over indirect medium heat or bake, uncovered, at 350° for 1 hour.

HERB-STUFFED PORK LOIN

5) Brush remaining mustard mixture over roast; sprinkle with remaining herb mixture. Grill or bake 20-25 minutes longer or until a meat thermometer reads 160°. Let stand 10 minutes before slicing.

Yield: 12 servings.

NUTRITION FACTS: 1 serving equals 199 calories, 10 g fat (3 g saturated fat), 69 mg cholesterol, 372 mg sodium, 2 g carbohydrate, 1 g fiber, 25 g protein.

SEASONED PORK RIB ROAST

Seasoned Pork Rib Roast

PREP: 10 min. + chilling
BAKE: 1-1/2 hours + standing

Joyce Kramer, Donalsonville, Georgia

My husband created this, and it's a specialty of the house. The simple seasoning also works well on pork chops, beef roast and chicken.

> 1 tablespoon garlic powder
> 1 tablespoon onion powder
> 1 tablespoon dried marjoram
> 1 tablespoon dried parsley flakes
> 1 to 2 teaspoons cayenne pepper
> 1 bone-in pork rib roast (about 4 pounds)

1) In a small bowl, combine the garlic powder, onion powder, marjoram, parsley and cayenne. Rub over roast. Cover and refrigerate overnight.

2) Place roast bone side down in a shallow roasting pan. Bake, uncovered, at 350° 1-1/2 to 1-3/4 hours or until a meat thermometer reads 160°. Let stand for 10-15 minutes before carving.

Yield: 8 servings.

NUTRITION FACTS: 4-1/2 ounces equals 356 calories, 24 g fat (9 g saturated fat), 111 mg cholesterol, 88 mg sodium, 2 g carbohydrate, trace fiber, 30 g protein.

Corn-Stuffed Crown Roast

PREP: 20 min. **BAKE:** 2-1/2 hours + standing

Dorothy Swanson, St. Louis, Missouri

My mother always made this elegant entree for company dinners and special family celebrations. There's a "wow!" effect when it's set on the table.

> 1 pork crown roast (about 7 pounds and 12 ribs)
> 1/2 teaspoon pepper, *divided*
> 1 cup chopped celery
> 1 cup chopped onion
> 1 cup butter
> 6 cups corn bread stuffing
> 2 cups frozen corn, thawed
> 2 jars (4-1/2 ounces *each*) sliced mushrooms, undrained
> 1 teaspoon salt
> 1 teaspoon poultry seasoning

1) Place roast on a rack in a large roasting pan. Sprinkle with 1/4 teaspoon pepper. Cover rib ends with small pieces of foil. Bake, uncovered, at 350° for 2 hours.

2) In a Dutch oven, saute celery and onion in butter until tender. Stir in stuffing, corn, mushrooms, salt, poultry seasoning and remaining pepper. Loosely spoon 1-3 cups into center of roast. Place remaining stuffing in a greased 2-qt. baking dish.

3) Bake the roast for 30-60 minutes or until a meat thermometer reads 160° and juices run clear. Cover and bake extra stuffing for 30-40 minutes. Transfer roast to serving platter. Let stand for 10 minutes. Remove foil; cut between ribs to serve.

Yield: 12 servings.

NUTRITION FACTS: 1 serving equals 545 calories, 30 g fat (15 g saturated fat), 124 mg cholesterol, 826 mg sodium, 30 g carbohydrate, 3 g fiber, 38 g protein.

CORN-STUFFED CROWN ROAST

SUCCULENT PORK ROAST

 CLASSIC: Perfect for entertaining, Roast Pork with Raspberry Sauce looks impressive, tastes fabulous and serves a crowd. A large rolled pork loin roast is rubbed with seasonings, roasted in the oven and served with a warm fruit sauce.

 TIME-SAVER: You'll need just 10 minutes and a handful of ingredients to start Teriyaki Pork Roast, then let your slow cooker handle the rest. While you do other things, it simmers the meat to an amazing tenderness.

 LIGHT: Tuscan Pork Roast allows you to enjoy the same generous 4-ounce portion of pork roast, but with fewer calories. Dried herbs and a small amount of heart-healthy olive oil provide extra flavor without a lot of extra calories.

 SERVES 2: Don't cross roasts off your menu because you have a smaller household. The recipe for Petite Pork Roast calls for a one-pound pork sirloin roast, so it's just the right size for two—with no leftovers to be forgotten in the back of the fridge.

Roast Pork with Raspberry Sauce

PREP: 15 min. **BAKE:** 1 hour 10 min. + standing

Carolyn Zimmerman, Fairbury, Illinois

- 1 teaspoon salt
- 1 teaspoon rubbed sage
- 1 teaspoon pepper
- 1 boneless rolled pork loin roast (3-1/2 to 4 pounds)

SAUCE:

- 1 package (10 ounces) frozen sweetened raspberries, thawed
- 1-1/2 cups sugar
- 1/4 cup white vinegar
- 1/4 teaspoon *each* ground ginger, nutmeg and cloves
- 1/4 cup cornstarch
- 1 tablespoon butter, melted
- 1 tablespoon lemon juice
- 3 to 4 drops red food coloring, optional

1) Combine the salt, sage and pepper; rub over entire roast. Place roast fat side up on a rack in a shallow roasting pan. Bake, uncovered, at 350° for 70-80 minutes or until a meat thermometer reads 160°.

2) For the sauce, drain raspberries, reserving liquid. Set berries aside. Add enough water to juice to measure 3/4 cup. In a saucepan, combine the sugar, vinegar, spices and 1/2 cup raspberry juice. Bring to a boil. Reduce heat; simmer, uncovered, for 10 minutes.

3) Combine cornstarch and remaining raspberry juice until smooth; stir into the saucepan. Bring to a boil; cook and stir for 2 minutes or until thickened. Remove from the heat. Stir in the butter, lemon juice, food coloring if desired and reserved raspberries.

4) Let roast stand for 10-15 minutes before slicing. Serve with raspberry sauce.

Yield: 10 servings.

NUTRITION FACTS: 4 ounces pork equals 366 calories, 9 g fat (3 g saturated fat), 82 mg cholesterol, 294 mg sodium, 41 g carbohydrate, 1 g fiber, 31 g protein.

Teriyaki Pork Roast

PREP: 10 min. **COOK:** 6 hours + standing

Debbie Dunaway, Kettering, Ohio

- 1 boneless pork shoulder roast (3 to 4 pounds), trimmed
- 1 cup packed brown sugar
- 1/3 cup unsweetened apple juice
- 1/3 cup soy sauce

TERIYAKI PORK ROAST

1/2 teaspoon salt
1/4 teaspoon pepper
2 tablespoons cornstarch
3 tablespoons cold water

1) Cut roast in half; rub with brown sugar. Place in a 5-qt. slow cooker. Pour apple juice and soy sauce over roast. Sprinkle with salt and pepper. Cover and cook on low for 6 to 6-1/2 hours or until meat is tender.

2) Remove roast; cover and let stand for 15 minutes. Meanwhile, strain cooking juices and return to slow cooker. Combine cornstarch and cold water until smooth; gradually stir into juices. Cover and cook on high for 15 minutes or until thickened. Slice pork; serve with gravy.

Yield: 6-8 servings.

NUTRITION FACTS: 4 ounces equals 545 calories, 21 g fat (7 g saturated fat), 194 mg cholesterol, 945 mg sodium, 30 g carbohydrate, trace fiber, 56 g protein.

PETITE PORK ROAST

Tuscan Pork Roast

PREP: 10 min. + marinating
BAKE: 1-1/2 hours + standing

Diane Toomey, Methuen, Massachusetts

3 garlic cloves, minced
2 tablespoons olive oil
1 tablespoon fennel seed, crushed
1 tablespoon dried rosemary, crushed
1 teaspoon salt
1/4 teaspoon pepper
1 boneless pork loin roast (3 pounds)

1) In a small bowl, combine the garlic, oil and seasonings; rub over pork roast. Cover and refrigerate overnight.

2) Place roast on a rack in a shallow roasting pan. Bake, uncovered, at 350° for 1-1/2 hours or until a meat thermometer reads 160°, basting occasionally with pan juices. Let stand for 10 minutes before slicing.

Yield: 10 servings.

NUTRITION FACTS: 4 ounces cooked pork equals 229 calories, 10 g fat (3 g saturated fat), 80 mg cholesterol, 282 mg sodium, 1 g carbohydrate, 1 g fiber, 31 g protein.

Using an Herb Rub

Crush any large herbs; combine all herbs. Sprinkle mixture over entire roast and rub into the surface of the meat. Roast as directed.

Petite Pork Roast

PREP: 10 min. + marinating
BAKE: 1 hour + standing

Rita Applegate, La Mesa, California

1 teaspoon fennel seed
1 teaspoon caraway seeds
1 tablespoon reduced-sodium soy sauce
1/8 teaspoon ground mustard
1 boneless pork sirloin roast (1 pound)

SAVORY MUSTARD SAUCE:

1 tablespoon ground mustard
1/2 teaspoon cornstarch
2 tablespoons water
4-1/2 teaspoons light corn syrup
1-1/2 teaspoons cider vinegar

1) Combine fennel and caraway seeds. In a small bowl, combine soy sauce and mustard; rub over roast. Roll roast in seeds. Cover and refrigerate for at least 2 hours.

2) Place roast fat side up on a rack in a shallow roasting pan. Bake, uncovered, at 325° for 60-80 minutes or until a meat thermometer reads 160°. Cover and let stand for 10 minutes.

3) For sauce, in a small saucepan, combine the mustard, cornstarch and water until smooth. Stir in corn syrup and vinegar. Bring to a boil; cook and stir for 1-2 minutes or until thickened. Serve with roast.

Yield: 2 servings.

NUTRITION FACTS: 1 serving with 2 tablespoons sauce equals 395 calories, 15 g fat (5 g saturated fat), 136 mg cholesterol, 411 mg sodium, 15 g carbohydrate, 1 g fiber, 48 g protein.

GRILLED PORK WITH HOT MUSTARD

Grilled Pork with Hot Mustard

PREP: 5 min. + marinating **GRILL:** 25 min.

Kyle Spencer, Havre, Montana

I love Chinese food, and this soy sauce-marinated tenderloin is one of my favorites. It's terrific served warm or cold, especially when dipped in the zippy sauce.

- 1/4 cup reduced-sodium soy sauce
- 2 tablespoons dry red wine *or* chicken broth
- 1 tablespoon brown sugar
- 1 tablespoon honey
- 1/2 teaspoon ground cinnamon
- 2 pork tenderloins (3/4 pound *each*)

HOT MUSTARD:

- 1/4 cup Dijon mustard
- 1 tablespoon honey
- 1 teaspoon prepared horseradish
- 2 teaspoons sesame seeds, toasted

1) In a large resealable plastic bag, combine the soy sauce, wine or broth, sugar, honey and cinnamon; add pork. Seal bag and turn to coat; refrigerate for 8 hours or overnight.

2) Drain and discard marinade. Grill pork, covered, over indirect medium-hot heat for 25-40 minutes or until a meat thermometer reads 160°. Let stand for 5 minutes before slicing.

3) In a small bowl, combine the mustard, honey and horseradish. Slice pork, sprinkle with sesame seeds. Serve with hot mustard.

Yield: 6 servings.

NUTRITION FACTS: One serving equals 197 calories, 7 g fat (2 g saturated fat), 62 mg cholesterol, 408 mg sodium, 6 g carbohydrate, 1 g fiber, 26 g protein.

Pepper-Crusted Pork Tenderloin

PREP: 5 min. **BAKE:** 50 min. + standing

Taste of Home Test Kitchen

Guests will be impressed by this elegant entree and its golden crumb coating with peppery pizzazz. The meat slices up so moist and tender, you can serve it without sauce and still have a taste-tempting main dish.

- 2 pork tenderloins (3/4 pound *each*)
- 3 tablespoons Dijon mustard
- 1 tablespoon 1% buttermilk
- 2 teaspoons minced fresh thyme
- 1 to 2 teaspoons coarsely ground pepper
- 1/4 teaspoon salt
- 2/3 cup soft bread crumbs

1) Place tenderloins side by side and tie together with kitchen string. In a small bowl, combine the mustard, buttermilk, thyme, pepper and salt; spread over surface of meat. Press crumbs onto meat.

2) Place on a rack in a shallow roasting pan. Cover and bake at 425° for 15 minutes. Uncover; bake 35-40 minutes longer or until a meat thermometer reads 160°. Let stand for 10 minutes. Remove string before slicing.

Yield: 6 servings.

NUTRITION FACTS: 3 ounces cooked pork equals 178 calories, 5 g fat (1 g saturated fat), 67 mg cholesterol, 383 mg sodium, 6 g carbohydrate, trace fiber, 25 g protein.

PEPPER-CRUSTED PORK TENDERLOIN

SPINACH-STUFFED PORK TENDERLOIN

Spinach-Stuffed Pork Tenderloin

PREP: 15 min. **BAKE:** 25 min. + standing

Taste of Home Test Kitchen

This roast recipe comes complete with an easy lesson on how to butterfly and stuff the meat with a mouthwatering filling. Just follow the directions (plus we added helpful how-to photos).

- 1 pork tenderloin (about 1 pound)
- 1/2 teaspoon celery salt, *divided*
- 1/2 teaspoon garlic powder, *divided*
- 1/2 teaspoon pepper, *divided*
- 4 slices provolone cheese
- 2 cups fresh spinach
- 2 thin slices deli ham (1/2 ounce *each*)

1) Cut a lengthwise slit down the center of the tenderloin to within 1/2 in. of bottom. Open tenderloin so it lies flat. On each half, make another lengthwise slit down the center to within 1/2 in. of bottom; cover with plastic wrap.

2) Flatten to 1/4-in. thickness. Remove plastic wrap; sprinkle pork with 1/4 teaspoon celery salt, 1/4 teaspoon garlic powder and 1/4 teaspoon pepper. Layer with the cheese, spinach and ham. Press down gently.

3) Roll up jelly-roll style, starting with a long side. Tie the roast at 1-1/2-in. to 2-in. intervals with kitchen string. Sprinkle with remaining celery salt, garlic powder and pepper. Place on a rack in a shallow baking pan.

4) Bake, uncovered, at 425° for 25-30 minutes or until a meat thermometer reads 160°. Transfer to a serving platter. Let stand for 10 minutes before slicing.

Yield: 4 servings.

NUTRITION FACTS: 1 serving equals 248 calories, 12 g fat (6 g saturated fat), 87 mg cholesterol, 588 mg sodium, 2 g carbohydrate, 1 g fiber, 32 g protein.

Stuffing a Tenderloin

1) Cut a lengthwise slit down the center of the tenderloin to within 1/2 in. of bottom.

2) Open tenderloin so it lies flat. On each half, make another lengthwise slit down the center to within 1/2 in. of bottom.

3) Cover with plastic wrap. Flatten to 1/4-in. thickness.

4) Remove plastic wrap. Layer or stuff as recipe directs

5) Roll up jelly-roll style, starting with a long side. Tie roast at 1-1/2-in. to 2-in. intervals with kitchen string.

New England Boiled Dinner

PREP: 10 min. **COOK:** 2 hours

Natalie Cook, Scarborough, Maine

This has been a popular dinner among our family for a long time. When we moved to California in 1960, I'd make it often to remind us of New England. We're back home now and continue to enjoy this scrumptious dish.

- 1 smoked boneless pork shoulder butt roast (2 to 2-1/2 pounds)
- 1 pound fresh carrots, sliced lengthwise and halved
- 8 medium red potatoes, peeled and halved
- 2 medium onions, cut into quarters
- 1 large head cabbage, cut into quarters
- 1 large turnip, peeled and cut into quarters
- 1 large rutabaga, peeled, halved and sliced

1) Place pork roast in a large Dutch oven; cover with water. Bring to a boil. Reduce heat; cover and simmer for 1 hour.

2) Add the remaining ingredients; return to a boil. Reduce heat. Cover and simmer for 1 hour or until the vegetables are tender; drain.

Yield: 8-10 servings.

NUTRITION FACTS: 1 serving equals 350 calories, 17 g fat (6 g saturated fat), 52 mg cholesterol, 1,120 mg sodium, 36 g carbohydrate, 9 g fiber, 17 g protein.

Pennsylvania Pot Roast

PREP: 10 min. **COOK:** 8 hours 10 min.

Donna Wilkinson, Monrovia, Maryland

This heartwarming one-dish meal is adapted from a Pennsylvania Dutch recipe. I start the pot roast cooking before I leave for church, add vegetables when I get home and then just sit back and relax until it's done.

- 1 boneless pork shoulder roast (2-1/2 to 3 pounds), halved
- 1-1/2 cups beef broth
- 1/2 cup sliced green onions
- 1 teaspoon dried basil
- 1 teaspoon dried marjoram
- 1/2 teaspoon salt
- 1/2 teaspoon pepper
- 1 bay leaf
- 6 medium red potatoes, cut into 2-inch chunks
- 4 medium carrots, cut into 2-inch chunks
- 7 to 8 fresh mushrooms, quartered
- 1/4 cup all-purpose flour
- 1/2 cup cold water

Browning sauce, optional

1) Place roast in a 5-qt. slow cooker; add the broth, onions and seasonings. Cover and cook on high for 2 hours. Add the vegetables.

2) Cover and cook on low for 6 hours or until vegetables are tender. Remove the meat and vegetables; keep warm. Discard bay leaf.

3) In a saucepan, combine flour and cold water until smooth; stir in 1-1/2 cups cooking juices. Bring to a boil; cook and stir for 2 minutes or until thickened. Add browning sauce if desired. Serve with roast and vegetables.

Yield: 6 servings.

NUTRITION FACTS: 1 serving equals 331 calories, 12 g fat (4 g saturated fat), 78 mg cholesterol, 490 mg sodium, 28 g carbohydrate, 4 g fiber, 26 g protein.

Pork 'n' Pepper Tortillas

PREP: 15 min. **COOK:** 8-1/2 hours

Rita Hahnbaum, Muscatine, Iowa

I season a pork roast with onions, garlic and spices, and then cook it slowly until tender. I shred the flavorful meat and wrap it in tortillas for a wonderful main dish.

- 1 boneless pork shoulder roast (2-1/2 to 3 pounds), halved
- 1 cup boiling water
- 2 teaspoons beef bouillon granules
- 3 garlic cloves, minced
- 1 tablespoon dried basil
- 1 tablespoon dried oregano
- 1 teaspoon ground cumin
- 1 teaspoon pepper

1 teaspoon dried tarragon
1 teaspoon white pepper
2 medium onions, sliced
1 *each* large green, sweet red and yellow pepper, sliced
1 tablespoon butter
12 flour tortillas (8 inches), warmed
Shredded lettuce, chopped ripe olives, sliced jalapeno peppers and sour cream, optional

1) Place roast in a 5-qt. slow cooker. Combine the water, bouillon, garlic and seasonings; pour over roast. Top with onions. Cover and cook on high for 1 hour. Reduce heat to low. Cook for 7-8 hours or until pork is very tender.

2) When cool enough to handle, remove meat from bone. Shred meat and return to slow cooker; heat through. Meanwhile, in a skillet, saute peppers in butter until tender.

3) Using a slotted spoon, place about 1/2 cup pork and onion mixture down the center of each tortilla; top with peppers.

4) Add the lettuce, olives, jalapenos and sour cream if desired. Fold sides of tortilla over filling.

Yield: 12 servings.

NUTRITION FACTS: 1 tortilla equals 417 calories, 16 g fat (5 g saturated fat), 110 mg cholesterol, 489 mg sodium, 31 g carbohydrate, 2 g fiber, 36 g protein.

Useful Definitions

For additional terms, refer to the Glossary on pages 24-28.

Baby Back Ribs: Ribs that come from the blade and center section of the pork loin. They are called baby back ribs because they are smaller than spareribs.

Country-Style Ribs: Meaty ribs from the rib end of the pork loin. They are sold both in slabs and individually with and without bones.

Spareribs: Curved ribs from the pork belly. While they are the least meaty of the ribs, they have a meaty pork flavor.

St. Louis-Style Ribs: Spareribs with the breastbone removed.

Hot 'n' Spicy Spareribs

PREP: 10 min. + marinating
GRILL: 1 hour 40 min.

Myra Innes, Auburn, Kansas
I keep this dry rub in a shaker on my shelf so I have it ready in an instant.

2 tablespoons brown sugar
2 tablespoons paprika
2 tablespoons pepper
1 tablespoon chili powder

HOT 'N' SPICY SPARERIBS

1-1/2 teaspoons salt
1-1/2 teaspoons crushed red pepper flakes
1 teaspoon garlic powder
6 pounds pork spareribs
6 sheets (40 inches x 18 inches) heavy-duty foil

1) In a small bowl, combine sugar and seasonings. Rub all of it onto both sides of ribs. Make two stacks of three sheets of foil. Place half of the ribs in the center of each stack.

2) Bring opposite long edges of foil together; fold down several times. Fold the short edges toward the food and crimp tightly to prevent leaks. Refrigerate overnight. Remove from refrigerator 30 minutes before grilling.

3) Place foil packets over indirect medium heat. Grill, covered, for 1-1/2 hours or until tender, turning foil packets over after 45 minutes. Remove ribs from foil; place over direct heat. Grill, uncovered, for 10-15 minutes or until crisp, turning once.

Yield: 8 servings.

NUTRITION FACTS: 1 serving equals 1,310 calories, 97 g fat (35 g saturated fat), 383 mg cholesterol, 1,204 mg sodium, 12 g carbohydrate, 2 g fiber, 93 g protein.

Tips for Great Ribs

Start ribs ahead if time does not permit tenderizing and cooking ribs on the same day. Cook the ribs until they are tender, about 1 hour, then refrigerate. The next day, brush the ribs with sauce and bake until heated through, basting with sauce as desired.

Hold ribs until serving time or transport hot cooked ribs to a party by placing them in heavy-duty foil and then in a brown paper bag. The ribs can stand this way for up to 1 hour.

FINGER-LICKIN' RIBS

 CLASSIC: Basted with a sweet homemade sauce, mouth-watering Maple Barbecued Ribs are so tasty they're sure to become a family tradition at your house.

 TIME-SAVER: After only 20 minutes of prep, Lazy Man's Ribs are ready for the slow cooker. Then forget about them until they're cooked oh-so-tender and delicious.

 LIGHT: A serving of Chinese Pork Ribs has fewer than half the calories and fat of Maple Barbecued Ribs. Yet they're just as taste-tempting. Plus, they're a snap to prepare in the slow cooker.

 SERVES 2: The recipe for Thick 'n' Zesty Ribs starts with two pounds of baby back ribs, so it serves two people quite nicely. The full-flavored sauce is simple to make with ketchup, a little vinegar and pantry seasonings.

Maple Barbecued Ribs

PREP: 10 min. **BAKE:** 1-1/2 hours

Linda Russell, Exeter, Ontario

- 3 pounds pork spareribs
- 1 cup maple syrup
- 1 small onion, chopped
- 1 tablespoon sesame seeds
- 1 tablespoon white vinegar
- 1 tablespoon Worcestershire sauce
- 1 tablespoon chili sauce
- 2 garlic cloves, minced
- 1/2 teaspoon salt
- 1/2 teaspoon ground ginger
- 1/4 teaspoon ground mustard
- 1/8 teaspoon pepper

1) Cut ribs into serving-size pieces. Place ribs bone side down on a rack in a shallow roasting pan. Bake at 350° for 1 hour; drain.

2) Meanwhile, in a small saucepan, combine the remaining ingredients; cook and stir over medium heat until mixture comes to a boil.

3) Pour sauce over ribs. Bake, uncovered, at 350° for 30-45 minutes longer or until tender, basting occasionally.

Yield: 6 servings.

NUTRITION FACTS: 1 serving equals 576 calories, 33 g fat (12 g saturated fat), 128 mg cholesterol, 367 mg sodium, 39 g carbohydrate, trace fiber, 31 g protein.

■ **Honey Barbecued Ribs:** Bake ribs for 1 hour as directed above. In a bowl, combine 3 tablespoons lemon juice, 2 tablespoons *each* vegetable oil and honey, 1 tablespoon *each* dried minced onion and soy sauce, 1 teaspoon *each* salt and paprika, 1/2 teaspoon dried oregano and 1/8 teaspoon garlic powder. Brush some of glaze on ribs. Bake 30-45 minutes longer, brushing occasionally with remaining glaze.

■ **Plum Glazed Ribs:** Bake ribs for 1 hour as directed in recipe. In a small bowl, combine 6 tablespoons *each* soy sauce, plum jam and honey, and

2 minced garlic cloves. Brush some of glaze on ribs. Bake 30-45 minutes longer, brushing occasionally with remaining glaze.

Tenderizing Ribs

Tenderize ribs so the meat pulls easily from the bones. First, place serving-size portions on a rack in a shallow baking pan. Cover tightly with foil and bake at 350° for 1 hour; drain. Then finish cooking as the recipe directs.

Lazy Man's Ribs

PREP: 20 min. **COOK:** 5-1/2 hours

Allan Stackhouse Jr., Jennings, Louisiana

- 2-1/2 pounds pork baby back ribs, cut into eight pieces
- 2 teaspoons Cajun seasoning
- 1 medium onion, sliced
- 1 cup ketchup
- 1/2 cup packed brown sugar
- 1/3 cup orange juice
- 1/3 cup cider vinegar
- 1/4 cup molasses
- 2 tablespoons Worcestershire sauce
- 1 tablespoon barbecue sauce
- 1 teaspoon stone-ground mustard
- 1 teaspoon paprika
- 1/2 teaspoon garlic powder
- 1/2 teaspoon Liquid Smoke, optional

Dash salt

- 5 teaspoons cornstarch
- 1 tablespoon water

1) Rub ribs with Cajun seasoning. Layer ribs and onion in a 5-qt. slow cooker.

2) In a small bowl, combine the ketchup, brown sugar, orange juice, vinegar, molasses, Worcestershire sauce, mustard, paprika, garlic powder, Liquid Smoke if desired and salt. Pour over ribs. Cover and cook on low for 5-1/2 to 6-1/2 hours or until meat is tender.

3) Remove ribs and keep warm. Strain cooking juices and skim fat; transfer to a saucepan. Combine cornstarch and water until smooth; stir into juices. Bring to a boil; cook and stir for 2 minutes or until thickened. Serve with ribs.

Yield: 4 servings.

NUTRITION FACTS: 1 serving equals 753 calories, 39 g fat (14 g saturated fat), 153 mg cholesterol, 1,335 mg sodium, 70 g carbohydrate, 2 g fiber, 33 g protein.

SWEET SPARERIBS ■■■

When I bake spareribs, I add apricot preserves and a little honey to my favorite barbecue sauce and brush over the meal. It's tangy and delicious!

—*Geri Lesch, New Port Richey, Florida*

Chinese Pork Ribs

PREP: 10 min. **COOK:** 6 hours

June Ross, Belmont, North Carolina

1/4 cup reduced-sodium soy sauce

1/3 cup reduced-sugar orange marmalade

3 tablespoons ketchup

2 garlic cloves, minced

3 to 4 pounds bone-in country-style pork ribs

LAZY MAN'S RIBS

THICK 'N' ZESTY RIBS

1) In a bowl, combine the soy sauce, marmalade, ketchup and garlic. Pour half into a 5-qt. slow cooker. Top with ribs; drizzle with remaining sauce. Cover and cook on low for 6 hours or until tender. Thicken cooking juices if desired.

Yield: 6-8 servings.

NUTRITION FACTS: 1 serving equals 273 calories, 14 g fat (5 g saturated fat), 86 mg cholesterol, 562 mg sodium, 8 g carbohydrate, trace fiber, 27 g protein.

Thick 'n' Zesty Ribs

PREP: 10 min. **BAKE:** 1 hour 25 min.

Helen Tucker, Wooster, Ohio

2 pounds pork baby back ribs, cut into serving-size pieces

1/2 teaspoon garlic powder

1/2 cup ketchup

1/4 cup white vinegar

2 tablespoons sugar

3/4 teaspoon chili powder

1/2 teaspoon salt

1/2 teaspoon paprika

1/2 teaspoon ground mustard

1/4 teaspoon pepper

1) Place the ribs in a 13-in. x 9-in. x 2-in. baking dish coated with cooking spray. Rub with garlic powder. Bake, uncovered, at 350° for 45 minutes.

2) In a small bowl, combine the remaining ingredients. Drain ribs; pour half of the sauce over ribs. Bake, uncovered, 40-50 minutes longer or until meat is tender, basting several times with remaining sauce.

Yield: 2 servings.

NUTRITION FACTS: 1 serving equals 890 calories, 62 g fat (23 g saturated fat), 245 mg cholesterol, 1,975 mg sodium, 30 g carbohydrate, 1 g fiber, 52 g protein.

Corn-Stuffed Pork Chops

PREP: 15 min. **BAKE:** 35 min.

Kimberly Andresen, Chiefland, Florida

Here's a main course that's impressive enough for guests but simple enough for weeknights. The moist stuffing takes only a few moments to prepare.

1/4 cup chopped onion
1/4 cup chopped green pepper
 1 tablespoon butter
3/4 cup corn bread stuffing mix
1/2 cup frozen corn, thawed
 2 tablespoons diced pimientos
1/4 teaspoon salt
1/8 teaspoon ground cumin
1/8 teaspoon pepper
 4 bone-in pork rib chops
   (7 ounces *each*)

1) In a large skillet, saute onion and green pepper in butter for 3-4 minutes or until tender. Stir in the stuffing mix, corn, pimientos, salt, cumin and pepper.

2) Cut a pocket in each pork chop by making a horizontal slice almost to the bone; fill with stuffing. Secure with toothpicks if necessary.

3) Place in an 11-in. x 7-in. x 2-in. baking dish coated with cooking spray. Bake, uncovered, at 375° for 35-40 minutes or until meat juices run clear. Discard toothpicks before serving.

Yield: 4 servings.

NUTRITION FACTS: 1 stuffed pork chop equals 297 calories, 12 g fat (5 g saturated fat), 94 mg cholesterol, 433 mg sodium, 14 g carbohydrate, 1 g fiber, 32 g protein.

PORK CHOPS WITH HERBED CREAM SAUCE

Pork Chops with Herbed Cream Sauce

PREP/TOTAL TIME: 30 min.

Edith Ruth Muldoon, Baldwin, New York

This recipe is perfect for a spur-of-the-moment lunch or no-fuss dinner. The meat cooks up moist and tender, and the bouillon lends instant flavor to the gravy.

 4 pork rib chops (7 ounces *each*), 1/2 inch thick
 2 tablespoons vegetable oil
 1 tablespoon all-purpose flour
1/2 teaspoon beef bouillon granules
 1 tablespoon minced fresh parsley
1/2 teaspoon dried basil, thyme *or* tarragon
2/3 cup milk *or* half-and-half cream
 2 tablespoons water
1/8 to 1/4 teaspoon pepper

1) In a large skillet, cook pork chops in oil until the juices run clear. Remove and keep warm; drain.

2) Stir the flour, bouillon, parsley and basil into the skillet. Gradually stir in the milk, water and pepper until smooth. Bring to a boil; cook and stir for 2 minutes or until thickened. Spoon over chops.

Yield: 4 servings.

NUTRITION FACTS: 1 pork chop with 2 tablespoons sauce equals 278 calories, 17 g fat (5 g saturated fat), 69 mg cholesterol, 156 mg sodium, 4 g carbohydrate, trace fiber, 27 g protein.

CORN-STUFFED PORK CHOPS

Making a Pocket in a Pork Chop

Use a sharp knife to cut a pocket in a pork chop. Make a horizontal slit in the middle of the chop by slicing from the edge almost to the bone.

Braised Pork Chops

PREP/TOTAL TIME: 30 min.

Marilyn Larsen, Port Orange, Florida

An easy herb rub gives sensational taste to these boneless pork loin chops that can be cooked on the stovetop in minutes.

- 1 teaspoon rubbed sage
- 1 teaspoon dried rosemary, crushed
- 1 garlic clove, minced
- 1/2 teaspoon salt
- 1/8 teaspoon pepper
- 4 boneless pork loin chops (1/2 inch thick and 4 ounces *each*)
- 1 tablespoon butter
- 1 tablespoon olive oil
- 3/4 cup dry white wine *or* apple juice, *divided*
- 1 tablespoon minced fresh parsley

1) Combine the sage, rosemary, garlic, salt and pepper; rub over both sides of pork chops. In a large nonstick skillet, brown chops on both sides in butter and oil. Remove.

2) Add 1/2 cup wine or juice to the skillet; bring to a boil. Return chops to pan. Reduce heat; cover and simmer for 8-10 minutes or until meat juices run clear, basting occasionally. Remove chops to a serving platter and keep warm.

3) Add remaining wine or juice to the skillet. Bring to a boil, loosening any browned bits from pan. Cook, uncovered, until liquid is reduced to 1/2 cup. Pour over pork chops; sprinkle with parsley.

Yield: 4 servings.

NUTRITION FACTS: 1 pork chop equals 232 calories, 11 g fat (4 g saturated fat), 79 mg cholesterol, 383 mg sodium, 1 g carbohydrate, trace fiber, 24 g protein.

Lime-Glazed Pork Chops

PREP/TOTAL TIME: 25 min.

Jacqui Correa, Landing, New Jersey

A wonderful, sweet-sour citrus glaze makes my recipe for tender chops tangy and tasty. The grilled chops are great for picnics and barbecues.

- 1/3 cup orange marmalade
- 1 jalapeno pepper, seeded and finely chopped
- 2 tablespoons lime juice
- 1 teaspoon grated fresh gingerroot
- 4 bone-in pork loin chops (8 ounces *each*)
- 4 teaspoons minced fresh cilantro

Lime wedges

1) For glaze, in a small saucepan, combine the marmalade, jalapeno, lime juice and ginger. Cook and stir over medium heat for 5 minutes or until marmalade melts. Remove from heat; set aside.

LIME-GLAZED PORK CHOPS

2) Coat grill rack with cooking spray before starting the grill. Grill pork chops, covered, over medium heat for 6-7 minutes on each side or until juices run clear, brushing with glaze during the last 5 minutes of grilling. Sprinkle with cilantro and serve with lime wedges.

Yield: 4 servings.

Editor's Note: When cutting or seeding hot peppers, use rubber or plastic gloves to protect your hands. Avoid touching your face.

NUTRITION FACTS: 1 pork chop equals 286 calories, 8 g fat (3 g saturated fat), 86 mg cholesterol, 85 mg sodium, 18 g carbohydrate, 1 g fiber, 34 g protein.

Honey Citrus Chops

PREP: 5 min. + marinating **GRILL:** 10 min.

Cheryl Stawicki, Yorkville, Illinois

Three handy ingredients make a fantastic marinade for boneless pork chops. It's a grilled favorite we enjoy all summer.

- 2/3 cup lemon-lime soda
- 1/2 cup soy sauce
- 1/4 cup honey
- 6 boneless pork loin chops (3/4 inch thick and 6 ounces *each*)

1) In a large resealable plastic bag, combine the soda, soy sauce and honey; add the pork. Seal bag and turn to coat; refrigerate overnight, turning occasionally.

2) Coat grill rack with cooking spray before starting the grill. Drain and discard marinade. Grill, covered, over medium heat for 4-5 minutes on each side or until juices run clear.

Yield: 6 servings.

NUTRITION FACTS: 1 serving equals 260 calories, 10 g fat (4 g saturated fat), 82 mg cholesterol, 662 mg sodium, 7 g carbohydrate, trace fiber, 34 g protein.

MOIST, TENDER PORK CHOPS

 CLASSIC: The inviting aroma of Baked Pork Chops and Apples will bring your family to the dinner table the first time you call. The skillet-browned chops are baked with sliced apples, raisins, cinnamon, cloves and brown sugar, then draped with a fruity sauce.

 TIME-SAVER: Enjoy a hearty entree without turning on the oven when you prepare Sweet 'n' Tangy Pork Chops. An easy sauce made with everyday ingredients coats the tender pork chops as they cook on the stovetop.

 LIGHT: For satisfying fare that's on the lighter side, try Breaded Pork Chops. Egg whites rather than whole eggs are used to help the breading cling, which reduces cholesterol. The chops are baked, not browned in oil, to reduce the fat.

 SERVES 2: Two butterflied pork chops are marinated, then broiled in this impressive meal for two. Smothered Pork Chops get a special treatment when topped with sauteed mushrooms and pepper Jack cheese.

Baked Pork Chops and Apples

PREP: 15 min. **BAKE:** 40 min.

Naomi Giddis, Two Buttes, Colorado

- 6 bone-in pork loin chops (3/4 inch thick and 7 ounces *each*)
- 1/2 teaspoon salt
- 1 tablespoon vegetable oil
- 2 medium baking apples, peeled and sliced
- 1/4 cup raisins
- 4 tablespoons brown sugar, *divided*
- 1/4 to 1/2 teaspoon ground cinnamon
- 1/8 teaspoon ground cloves
- 1 tablespoon lemon juice
- 1/4 cup apple juice
- 1/4 cup orange juice

1) Sprinkle pork chops with salt. In a large skillet, brown chops in oil; set aside. Place apples and raisins in a greased 13-in. x 9-in. x 2-in. baking dish. Combine 2 tablespoons brown sugar, cinnamon and cloves; sprinkle over apples. Drizzle with lemon juice. Put pork chops on top.

2) Bake, uncovered, at 325° for 40-45 minutes or until chops are tender and juices run clear.

3) In a saucepan, combine apple juice, orange juice and remaining brown sugar; bring to a boil. Reduce heat and simmer 10 minutes. Serve with chops.

Yield: 6 servings.

NUTRITION FACTS: 1 serving equals 287 calories, 11 g fat (3 g saturated fat), 86 mg cholesterol, 264 mg sodium, 16 g carbohydrate, trace fiber, 30 g protein.

SWEET 'N' TANGY PORK CHOPS

Sweet 'n' Tangy Pork Chops

PREP/TOTAL TIME: 25 min.

Dennis Wolcott, Blossburg, Pennsylvania

- 4 bone-in pork loin chops (1 inch and 7 ounces *each*)
- 2 tablespoons vegetable oil
- 1 cup (8 ounces) tomato sauce
- 1/2 cup packed brown sugar
- 2 tablespoons cider vinegar
- 1-1/2 teaspoons Worcestershire sauce
- 1 teaspoon celery salt
- 1/2 teaspoon ground nutmeg
- 1/2 teaspoon pepper

1) In a large skillet, brown pork chops in oil. Combine the remaining ingredients; add to skillet. Bring to a boil. Reduce heat; simmer, uncovered, for 8-10 minutes or until pork juices run clear. Spoon sauce over pork chops.

Yield: 4 servings.

NUTRITION FACTS: 1 pork chop equals 388 calories, 15 g fat (4 g saturated fat), 86 mg cholesterol, 726 mg sodium, 31 g carbohydrate, 1 g fiber, 31 g protein.

BREADED PORK CHOPS

Breaded Pork Chops

PREP: 10 min. + chilling **BAKE:** 25 min.

Taste of Home Test Kitchen

- 2 tablespoons all-purpose flour
- 4 egg whites
- 1/2 teaspoon Worcestershire sauce
- 1/2 teaspoon balsamic vinegar
- 1/8 teaspoon hot pepper sauce
- 3/4 cup dry bread crumbs
- 3 tablespoons grated Parmesan cheese
- 1/2 teaspoon dried thyme
- 1/4 teaspoon salt
- 1/4 teaspoon paprika
- 6 boneless pork loin chops (1/2 inch thick and 4 ounces *each*)

Refrigerated butter-flavored spray

1) Place flour in a shallow dish. In another shallow dish, beat the egg whites, Worcestershire sauce, vinegar and hot pepper sauce. In a third dish, combine the bread crumbs, Parmesan cheese, thyme, salt and paprika. Coat pork chops with flour. Dip into egg mixture, then coat with crumb mixture. Place on a plate; cover and chill for 1 hour.

2) Place chops in a 13-in. x 9-in. x 2-in. baking dish coated with cooking spray; spritz chops with butter-flavored spray. Bake, uncovered, at 350° for 25-28 minutes or until juices run clear.

Yield: 6 servings.

Editor's Note: This recipe was tested with I Can't Believe It's Not Butter Spray.

NUTRITION FACTS: 1 pork chop equals 250 calories, 8 g fat (3 g saturated fat), 74 mg cholesterol, 372 mg sodium, 12 g carbohydrate, trace fiber, 29 g protein.

Thickness Matters

If the pork chops you're cooking aren't as thick as what is called for in the recipe, go ahead and use them anyway. Just remember to adjust the cooking time. Thinner chops will cook more quickly and thicker chops will take longer.

Smothered Pork Chops

PREP: 15 min. + marinating **BROIL:** 10 min.

Danielle Binkley, New Carlisle, Ohio

- 1/2 cup olive oil
- 1 tablespoon lemon juice
- 3 garlic cloves, minced
- 2 teaspoons grated lemon peel
- 1/2 teaspoon salt
- 1/2 teaspoon pepper
- 1/2 teaspoon *each* dried basil, parsley flakes and rosemary, crushed
- 2 boneless butterflied pork chops (1/2 inch thick and 8 ounces *each*)

TOPPING:
- 1 cup sliced fresh mushrooms
- 2 tablespoons butter
- 1/4 teaspoon salt
- 1/8 teaspoon pepper
- 2 slices pepper Jack cheese

1) In a large resealable plastic bag, combine the oil, lemon juice, garlic, lemon peel, salt, pepper, basil, parsley and rosemary; add the pork. Seal bag and turn to coat; refrigerate for 2 hours or overnight.

2) Drain and discard marinade. Broil pork chops 3-4 in. from the heat for 5-6 minutes on each side or until no pink remains and a meat thermometer reads 160°.

3) Meanwhile, in a small skillet, saute mushrooms in butter until tender; sprinkle with salt and pepper. Using a slotted spoon, place mushrooms on pork chops. Cover each with a cheese slice. Broil for 1-2 minutes longer or until cheese is melted.

Yield: 2 servings.

NUTRITION FACTS: 1 pork chop equals 1,012 calories, 87 g fat (24 g saturated fat), 169 mg cholesterol, 1,203 mg sodium, 6 g carbohydrate, 1 g fiber, 52 g protein.

SMOTHERED PORK CHOPS

Country-Style Pork Medallions

PREP: 20 min. **COOK:** 20 min.

Pamela Jessen, Calgary, Alberta

Be prepared to hand out recipes after you pass around this impressive pork entree. Dinner guests can't believe how easy it is. I think leftovers would be great in sandwiches...but I've never had any to sample!

- 2 pork tenderloins (1 pound *each*)
- 6 tablespoons butter, *divided*
- 2 small onions, sliced and separated into rings
- 3/4 pound small fresh mushrooms
- 2 small apples, cored and cut into rings

APPLE CREAM SAUCE:

- 1 cup apple cider *or* juice
- 1 package (8 ounces) cream cheese, cubed
- 1/4 cup apple brandy *or* additional apple cider
- 1 teaspoon dried basil

1) Cut pork into 1/2-in. slices; flatten to 1/4-in. thickness. In a large skillet, cook pork in batches in 3 tablespoons butter over medium-high heat until juices run clear. Remove to a serving platter and keep warm.

2) In the same skillet, saute onions and mushrooms in remaining butter for 4 minutes or until crisp-tender. Add apples; saute for 3-4 minutes or until vegetables and apples are tender. Arrange over pork.

3) Add cider and cream cheese to the skillet; cook and stir over medium heat for 3 minutes or until cheese is melted and sauce is smooth. Stir in brandy or additional cider and basil; heat through. Serve with pork and vegetables.

Yield: 6 servings.

NUTRITION FACTS: 1 serving equals 304 calories, 21 g fat (12 g saturated fat), 86 mg cholesterol, 199 mg sodium, 12 g carbohydrate, 2 g fiber, 15 g protein.

COUNTRY-STYLE PORK MEDALLIONS

Pork Medallions with Sauteed Apples

PREP/TOTAL TIME: 30 min.

Clara M. Coulston, Washington Court House, Ohio

When it comes to healthy, easy and flavorful entrees, this dish is tops. The pork doesn't have much fat, and it's wonderful with the apple slices.

- 1 pork tenderloin (1 pound), cut into 1-inch slices
- 3/4 teaspoon dried thyme
- 1/2 teaspoon paprika
- 1/4 teaspoon salt
- 1/4 teaspoon pepper
- 1/4 cup sliced green onions
- 1 garlic clove, minced
- 1 tablespoon butter
- 2 medium apples, cut into wedges
- 2 teaspoons cornstarch
- 2/3 cup reduced-sodium chicken broth
- 1/4 cup unsweetened apple juice

1) Flatten pork to 1/2-in. thickness. Combine the thyme, paprika, salt and pepper; sprinkle over both sides of pork. Broil pork 3-4 in. from the heat for 3-4 minutes on each side or until juices run clear; keep warm.

2) In a nonstick skillet, saute onions and garlic in butter until tender. Add the apples; cook and stir for 2 minutes or until crisp-tender. Combine the cornstarch, broth and apple juice until smooth; stir into apple mixture. Bring to a boil; cook and stir for 1-2 minutes or until thickened. Serve with pork.

Yield: 4 servings.

NUTRITION FACTS: 3 ounces cooked pork with 1/2 cup apples equals 251 calories, 10 g fat (4 g saturated fat), 85 mg cholesterol, 335 mg sodium, 15 g carbohydrate, 3 g fiber, 25 g protein.

Caramelized Pork Slices

PREP/TOTAL TIME: 15 min.

Elisa Lochridge, Tigard, Oregon

This easy treatment for pork caught my eye when I saw the word "caramelized." I like to serve this over noodles or rice...or with mashed potatoes.

- 1 pork tenderloin (1 pound), cut into 1-inch slices
- 2 teaspoons canola oil
- 2 garlic cloves, minced
- 2 tablespoons brown sugar
- 1 tablespoon orange juice
- 1 tablespoon molasses
- 1/2 teaspoon salt
- 1/4 teaspoon pepper

1) Flatten pork slices to 1/2-in. thickness. In a nonstick skillet, brown pork in oil over medium-high heat. Remove and keep warm.

2) In the same skillet, saute garlic for 1 minute; stir in the brown sugar, orange juice, molasses, salt and pepper. Return pork to pan; cook, uncovered, for 3-4 minutes or until pork is no longer pink.

Yield: 4 servings.

NUTRITION FACTS: 3 ounces cooked pork equals 200 calories, 6 g fat (2 g saturated fat), 74 mg cholesterol, 355 mg sodium, 11 g carbohydrate, 1 g fiber, 24 g protein.

Warm Fajita Salad

PREP: 10 min. + marinating **COOK:** 10 min.

Bobbie Jo Yokley, Franklin, Kentucky

When I didn't have tortillas in the house to wrap up the meat in this recipe, I made it into a hearty salad instead. It was delicious!

   1 cup lime juice
1/4 cup chicken broth
1/4 cup soy sauce
   2 garlic cloves, minced
   1 tablespoon vegetable oil
   1 teaspoon sugar
   1 teaspoon Liquid Smoke, optional
3/4 teaspoon ground cumin
1/2 teaspoon dried oregano
1/4 teaspoon ground ginger
1/4 teaspoon hot pepper sauce
   1 pound boneless pork loin, trimmed and cut into thin strips
   1 large onion, sliced
   1 medium green pepper, cut into strips
   1 medium sweet yellow pepper, cut into strips
   1 tablespoon lemon juice
   6 cups torn romaine
 12 cherry tomatoes, quartered

1) In a large resealable plastic bag, combine the lime juice, broth, soy sauce, garlic, oil, sugar and seasonings. Reserve 2 tablespoons; cover and refrigerate.

2) Add pork to remaining marinade. Seal bag and turn to coat; refrigerate for 30 minutes to 3 hours, turning occasionally.

3) Drain pork, discarding marinade. Heat reserved marinade in a large skillet over medium-high heat. Add the pork, onion and peppers; stir-fry for 3-4 minutes or until pork is no longer pink. Drizzle with lemon juice. Remove from the heat.

4) Arrange lettuce on four individual plates; top with meat mixture and tomatoes.

Yield: 4 servings.

NUTRITION FACTS: 1 cup equals 278 calories, 11 g fat (3 g saturated fat), 67 mg cholesterol, 1,044 mg sodium, 19 g carbohydrate, 4 g fiber, 29 g protein.

WARM FAJITA SALAD

Pork Schnitzel

PREP/TOTAL TIME: 20 min.

Joyce Folker, Paraowan, Utah

I often like to serve this German dish with mashed potatoes and cinnamon applesauce. It's one of my husband's favorite meals.

   6 boneless pork cutlets (1/2 inch thick)
1/2 cup all-purpose flour
   2 teaspoons seasoned salt
1/2 teaspoon pepper
   2 eggs
1/4 cup milk
1-1/2 cups dry bread crumbs
   2 teaspoons paprika
   6 tablespoons vegetable oil

DILL SAUCE:
1-1/2 cups chicken broth, *divided*
   2 tablespoons all-purpose flour
1/2 teaspoon dill weed
   1 cup (8 ounces) sour cream

1) Flatten pork cutlets to 1/4-in. thickness. In a shallow bowl, combine the flour, seasoned salt and pepper. In another bowl, beat eggs and milk. In a third bowl, combine bread crumbs and paprika. Dip cutlets into flour mixture, then into egg mixture and coat with crumb mixture.

2) In a large skillet, cook pork in oil, a few pieces at a time, for 3-4 minutes per side or until meat is no longer pink. Remove to a platter; keep warm.

3) For sauce, pour 1 cup broth into skillet, scraping bottom of pan to loosen browned bits. Combine flour and remaining broth until smooth; stir into skillet. Bring to a boil. Cook; stir for 2 minutes or until thickened. Reduce heat. Stir in dill and sour cream; heat through (do not boil). Pour over pork.

Yield: 6 servings.

NUTRITION FACTS: 1 serving equals 412 calories, 25 g fat (8 g saturated fat), 107 mg cholesterol, 1,025 mg sodium, 32 g carbohydrate, 1 g fiber, 11 g protein.

MARINATED PORK KABOBS

🐚 Marinated Pork Kabobs

PREP: 15 min. + marinating **GRILL:** 30 min.

Bobbie Jo Miller, Fallon, Nevada

This recipe was originally for lamb, but I adapted it to pork and adjusted the spices. It's always requested when the grill comes out for the season.

- 2 cups plain yogurt
- 2 tablespoons lemon juice
- 4 garlic cloves, minced
- 1/2 teaspoon ground cumin
- 1/4 teaspoon ground coriander
- 2 pounds pork tenderloin, cut into 1-1/2-inch cubes
- 8 small white onions, halved
- 8 cherry tomatoes
- 1 medium sweet red pepper, cut into 1-1/2-inch pieces
- 1 medium green pepper, cut into 1-1/2-inch pieces

1) In a large resealable plastic bag, combine the yogurt, lemon juice, garlic, cumin and coriander; add pork. Seal bag and turn to coat; refrigerate for 6 hours or overnight.

2) Drain and discard marinade. Alternately thread the pork, onions, tomatoes and peppers on eight metal or soaked bamboo skewers. Grill, covered, over medium heat for about 15-20 minutes or until meat juices run clear.

Yield: 8 servings.

NUTRITION FACTS: 1 serving equals 190 calories, 5 g fat (2 g saturated fat), 67 mg cholesterol, 63 mg sodium, 11 g carbohydrate, 2 g fiber, 25 g protein.

Pork Noodle Casserole

PREP: 25 min. **BAKE:** 45 min.

Bernice Morris, Marshfield, Missouri

Less expensive cuts of pork become tender and tasty in this creamy meal-in-one casserole.

- 2 cups uncooked egg noodles
- 2 pounds boneless pork, cut into 3/4-inch cubes
- 2 medium onions, chopped
- 2 cans (15-1/4 ounces *each*) whole kernel corn, drained
- 2 cans (10-3/4 ounces *each*) condensed cream of mushroom soup, undiluted
- 1/2 teaspoon salt
- 1/2 teaspoon pepper

1) Cook noodles according to package directions. In a large skillet, cook pork and onions over medium heat until meat is no longer pink. Drain noodles. Stir the noodles, corn, soup, salt and pepper into pork mixture.

2) Transfer to a greased 3-qt. baking dish. Cover and bake at 350° for 30 minutes. Uncover; bake 15 minutes longer.

Yield: 8 servings.

NUTRITION FACTS: 1 serving equals 355 calories, 12 g fat (4 g saturated fat), 79 mg cholesterol, 1,078 mg sodium, 29 g carbohydrate, 3 g fiber, 28 g protein.

Peanut Butter Pork with Spicy Dipping Sauce

PREP: 20 min. + marinating **GRILL:** 15 min.

Dennis Gilroy, Stover, Missouri

These skewers are one of my favorite things to prepare. They have a wonderfully different flavor and are great with hot cooked rice.

- 1/4 cup creamy peanut butter
- 2 tablespoons soy sauce
- 2 tablespoons ground coriander
- 1 tablespoon lemon juice
- 1 tablespoon vegetable oil
- 2 teaspoons ground cumin
- 1/2 teaspoon chili powder
- 1 garlic clove, minced
- 1 pork tenderloin (1 pound), cut into 1-inch cubes

SPICY DIPPING SAUCE:

- 1/4 cup soy sauce
- 1/4 cup white vinegar
- 2 tablespoons water
- 1 garlic clove, minced
- 1 tablespoon molasses
- 1/2 teaspoon crushed red pepper flakes

1) In a large resealable plastic bag, combine the peanut butter, soy sauce, coriander, lemon juice, oil, cumin, chili powder and garlic; add pork. Seal bag and turn to coat; refrigerate several hours or overnight.

2) Meanwhile, combine all of the sauce ingredients; cover and chill at least 1 hour. Coat grill rack with cooking spray before starting the grill. Drain and discard marinade from pork.

3) Thread meat on metal or soaked wooden skewers, leaving a small space between pieces. Grill, covered, over medium heat for 10-15 minutes or until meat is no longer pink, turning several times. Serve with sauce.

Yield: 4 servings.

NUTRITION FACTS: 1 serving equals 232 calories, 10 g fat (2 g saturated fat), 63 mg cholesterol, 1,237 mg sodium, 7 g carbohydrate, 2 g fiber, 27 g protein.

PORK CHOW MEIN

Pork Chow Mein

PREP: 15 min. + marinating **COOK:** 15 min.

Helen Carpenter, Albuquerque, New Mexico

I give all the credit for my love of cooking and baking to my mother, grandmother and mother-in-law. That trio inspired delicious dishes like this hearty skillet dinner.

- 1 pound boneless pork loin
- 2 garlic cloves, minced
- 4 tablespoons soy sauce, *divided*
- 2 tablespoons cornstarch
- 1/2 to 1 teaspoon ground ginger
- 1 cup chicken broth
- 1 tablespoon vegetable oil
- 1 cup thinly sliced carrots
- 1 cup thinly sliced celery
- 1 cup chopped onion
- 1 cup coarsely chopped cabbage
- 1 cup coarsely chopped fresh spinach

Hot cooked rice

1) Cut pork into 4-in. x 1/4-in. strips; place in a bowl. Add garlic and 2 tablespoons soy sauce. Cover and refrigerate for 2-4 hours.

2) Meanwhile, combine the cornstarch, ginger, broth and remaining soy sauce until smooth; set aside. Heat oil in a large skillet or wok on high; stir-fry pork until no longer pink. Remove; keep warm.

3) Add carrots and celery; stir-fry for 3-4 minutes. Add the onion, cabbage and spinach; stir-fry for 2-3 minutes. Stir broth mixture; stir into skillet along with pork. Bring to a boil; cook and stir for 3-4 minutes or until thickened. Serve immediately over rice.

Yield: 6 servings.

NUTRITION FACTS: 1 cup (calculated without rice) equals 162 calories, 6 g fat (2 g saturated fat), 38 mg cholesterol, 561 mg sodium, 10 g carbohydrate, 2 g fiber, 17 g protein.

Sweet-and-Sour Pork

PREP/TOTAL TIME: 20 min.

Gloria Kobiak, Loveland, Colorado

You couldn't ask for a better blend of sweet-and-sour flavors! This recipe has it.

- 1/4 cup cornstarch
- 1 egg, beaten
- 1-1/2 pounds boneless pork, cut into 1/2-inch cubes
- 3 tablespoons vegetable oil, *divided*
- 2 medium carrots, sliced
- 1 medium onion, chopped
- 1 garlic clove, minced
- 1 medium green pepper, cut into 1-inch pieces
- 2 tablespoons water
- 1 can (8 ounces) unsweetened pineapple chunks

SAUCE:

- 1 tablespoon cornstarch
- 1/3 cup packed brown sugar
- 1/4 cup chicken broth
- 1/4 cup white wine vinegar
- 1 tablespoon soy sauce
- 1/2 teaspoon minced fresh gingerroot

Hot cooked rice

1) In a large bowl, combine cornstarch and egg until smooth. Add pork; toss to coat. In a skillet or wok, stir-fry half of the pork in 1 tablespoon oil until no longer pink; remove. Repeat with remaining pork and 1 tablespoon oil. Set pork aside; keep warm.

2) Stir-fry the carrots, onion and garlic in the remaining oil for 3 minutes. Add green pepper and water; stir-fry for 2 minutes. Drain pineapple, reserving 1/4 cup juice. Add pineapple and pork to pan.

3) Combine cornstarch and brown sugar. Stir in chicken broth, vinegar and soy sauce until smooth. Add ginger and reserved pineapple juice; add to pan. Bring to a boil; cook and stir for 2 minutes or until thickened. Serve over rice.

Yield: 6 servings.

NUTRITION FACTS: 1 serving (calculated without rice) equals 351 calories, 14 g fat (4 g saturated fat), 102 mg cholesterol, 268 mg sodium, 29 g carbohydrate, 2 g fiber, 26 g protein.

Spiedis

PREP: 10 min. + marinating GRILL: 10 min.

Gertrude Skinner, Binghamton, New York

Spiedis is a traditional Italian dish featuring skewered meat grilled like kabobs, then wrapped in Italian bread and eaten like a sandwich. The seasonings in this recipe work well with pork, beef, lamb, poultry and other meats.

    1   cup vegetable oil
  2/3 cup cider vinegar
    2   tablespoons Worcestershire sauce
  1/2 medium onion, finely chopped
  1/2 teaspoon salt
  1/2 teaspoon sugar
  1/2 teaspoon dried basil
  1/2 teaspoon dried marjoram
  1/2 teaspoon dried rosemary, crushed
2-1/2 pounds boneless lean pork, beef, lamb, venison, chicken *or* turkey, cut into 1-1/2- to 2-inch cubes

Italian rolls *or* hot dog buns

1) In a large resealable plastic bag, combine the oil, vinegar, Worcestershire sauce, onion and seasonings; add meat. Seal bag and turn to coat; refrigerate for 24 hours, turning occasionally.

2) Coat grill rack with cooking spray before starting the grill. Drain and discard marinade. Thread meat on metal or soaked wooden skewers.

3) Grill, covered, over medium heat for 10-15 minutes or until meat reaches desired doneness. Remove meat from skewers and serve on Italian rolls or hot dog buns.

Yield: 8 servings.

NUTRITION FACTS: 1 serving (calculated without Italian rolls) equals 323 calories, 22 g fat (5 g saturated fat), 83 mg cholesterol, 156 mg sodium, 2 g carbohydrate, trace fiber, 29 g protein.

Country Skillet Supper

PREP/TOTAL TIME: 15 min.

Arlene Snyder, Millerstown, Pennsylvania

This is a super-quick way to use leftover pork. With hearty potatoes and bright green peas, it's creamy, comforting and so tasty.

  1 small onion, chopped
  1 tablespoon vegetable oil
  1 can (10-3/4 ounces) condensed cream of celery soup, undiluted
1/2 cup milk
  1 teaspoon Worcestershire sauce
1/4 teaspoon salt
1/8 teaspoon pepper
  1 cup cubed cooked pork
  1 cup cubed cooked potatoes
  1 cup frozen peas, thawed

Biscuits, optional

1) In a large skillet, saute onion in oil until tender. Stir in the soup, milk, Worcestershire, salt and pepper; mix well.

2) Add the pork, potatoes and peas; heat through. Serve with biscuits if desired.

Yield: 2-3 servings.

NUTRITION FACTS: 1 serving equals 326 calories, 15 g fat (5 g saturated fat), 52 mg cholesterol, 1,058 mg sodium, 30 g carbohydrate, 4 g fiber, 20 g protein.

Pork Fried Rice for Two

PREP/TOTAL TIME: 25 min.

Laura Kittleson, Casselberry, Florida

My husband and I often make this appealing stir-fry.

1/8 teaspoon Chinese five-spice powder
  6 ounces boneless pork loin, cut into 1/4-inch cubes
1/2 teaspoon fennel seed, crushed
1-1/2 teaspoons canola oil, *divided*
  2 cups broccoli florets
  1 celery rib with leaves, sliced
1/2 cup shredded carrot
1/4 cup chopped green onions
1-1/2 cups cold cooked brown rice
  1 tablespoon reduced-sodium soy sauce
1/8 teaspoon pepper

1) Sprinkle five-spice powder over pork and toss to coat. In a large nonstick skillet or wok coated with cooking spray, stir-fry pork for 3 minutes or until brown. Remove and keep warm.

2) Stir-fry fennel seed in 3/4 teaspoon oil for 30 seconds. Add the broccoli, celery, carrot and onions; stir-fry for 3 minutes or until crisp-tender. Remove and keep warm.

3) Stir-fry rice in remaining oil for 2 minutes. Stir in soy sauce and pepper. Return pork and vegetables to pan; cook and stir until heated through.

Yield: 2 servings.

NUTRITION FACTS: 1-3/4 cups equals 367 calories, 10 g fat (2 g saturated fat), 50 mg cholesterol, 417 mg sodium, 44 g carbohydrate, 5 g fiber, 26 g protein.

Pueblo Green Chili Stew

PREP: 15 min. COOK: 1 hour

Helen LaBrake, Rindge, New Hampshire

Green chilies add a little spice to this flavorful pork stew featuring corn, potatoes and tomatoes.

  2 pounds lean boneless pork, cut into 1-1/2-inch cubes
  1 tablespoon vegetable oil
  3 cans (11 ounces *each*) whole kernel corn, drained
  2 celery ribs, chopped
  2 medium potatoes, peeled and cubed
  2 medium tomatoes, coarsely chopped

3 cans (4 ounces *each*) chopped
  green chilies
4 cups chicken broth
2 teaspoons ground cumin
1 teaspoon dried oregano
1 teaspoon salt, optional

1) In a large Dutch oven, brown pork in oil in batches over medium-high heat. Add remaining ingredients. Bring to a boil. Reduce heat; cover and simmer for 1 hour or until pork is tender.

Yield: 8 servings (about 2-1/2 quarts).

NUTRITION FACTS: 1-1/4 cups equals 333 calories, 10 g fat (3 g saturated fat), 67 mg cholesterol, 1,017 mg sodium, 29 g carbohydrate, 4 g fiber, 28 g protein.

Spiced Pork Potpie

PREP: 30 min. **BAKE:** 30 min.

Kay Krause, Sioux Falls, South Dakota

This scrumptious meat pie smells just like autumn as it bakes! I changed the original pastry crust to this fuss-free batter crust.

1-1/2 pounds cubed pork shoulder roast
1/2 cup butter, *divided*
2 cups apple cider *or* juice
1 cup water
1 cup chopped peeled tart apple
1/2 cup dried cranberries
1/2 cup dried pitted prunes, chopped
2 teaspoons ground cinnamon

1-1/2 teaspoons ground ginger
2 whole cloves
6 tablespoons all-purpose flour
1 can (15 ounces) sweet potatoes, drained and cubed

CRUST:
1 cup all-purpose flour
1-1/2 teaspoons baking powder
1/2 teaspoon salt
3/4 cup milk
1/2 cup butter, melted

1) In a Dutch oven, cook pork in 2 tablespoons butter until no longer pink. Add the cider and water; bring to a boil. Reduce heat; simmer, uncovered, for 10 minutes. Stir in the fruit and spices; simmer 10 minutes longer.

2) Melt remaining butter; stir in flour until smooth. Slowly add to meat mixture. Bring to a boil; cook for 1-2 minutes or until thickened. Discard cloves. Stir in sweet potatoes. Pour into a greased 3-qt. baking dish.

3) For crust, combine the flour, baking powder and salt in a bowl. Combine the milk and butter; stir into dry ingredients until smooth. Spread over filling. Bake at 400° for 28-32 minutes or until crust is browned.

Yield: 6 servings.

NUTRITION FACTS: 1 cup equals 857 calories, 46 g fat (24 g saturated fat), 215 mg cholesterol, 777 mg sodium, 70 g carbohydrate, 5 g fiber, 42 g protein.

WARMING PORK STEW

 CLASSIC: A Dutch oven helps simmer up a filling meal of Lumberjack Stew. The chunky mixture is loaded with tender pork, colorful carrots, green beans and pearl onions.

 TIME-SAVER: Cut your time at the stove in half with Harvest Stew, which gets its flavor from squash and apples. It's simple to assemble and cooks while you slice some bread and set the table.

 LIGHT: Creamy bowls of Pork Tenderloin Stew are brimming with pork and a bounty of fresh vegetables. Yet each serving has fewer calories and less fat and sodium than Lumberjack Stew, thanks in part to fat-free milk, reduced-fat sour cream and reduced-sodium broth.

 SERVES 2: Two hearty appetites are sure to be satisfied with the generous 1-1/2-cup servings of Sweet Potato Pork Stew. Starting with three-quarters of a pound of chop suey meat and just one sweet potato and onion gives just the right yield.

LUMBERJACK STEW

Lumberjack Stew

PREP: 15 min. **COOK:** 2 hours

Bonnie Tetzlaff, Iola, Wisconsin

- 2 pounds boneless pork, trimmed and cut into 1-inch cubes
- 1 teaspoon salt
- 1 teaspoon sugar
- 1/2 teaspoon pepper
- 1/2 teaspoon paprika
- 2 tablespoons vegetable oil
- 1 cup sliced onion
- 1 garlic clove, minced
- 3 cups water
- 1 tablespoon lemon juice
- 1 teaspoon Worcestershire sauce
- 2 chicken bouillon cubes
- 2 bay leaves
- 6 medium carrots, cut into 1-inch pieces
- 1 package (10 ounces) pearl onions, peeled

- 3 cups frozen cut green beans
- 3 tablespoons cornstarch
- 1/2 cup cold water

1) Toss pork with the salt, sugar, pepper and paprika. In a Dutch oven, brown in oil on all sides. Add sliced onion and garlic; cook over medium heat for 5 minutes.

2) Add the water, lemon juice, Worcestershire sauce, bouillon and bay leaves; cover and simmer for 1 hour.

3) Add the carrots and pearl onions; cover and simmer for 40 minutes. Add beans; cover and simmer for 10 minutes.

4) Combine cornstarch and cold water until smooth; stir into stew. Bring to a boil; cook and stir for 2 minutes or until thickened. Discard bay leaves.

Yield: 6 servings.

NUTRITION FACTS: 1 cup equals 350 calories, 14 g fat (4 g saturated fat), 89 mg cholesterol, 935 mg sodium, 22 g carbohydrate, 4 g fiber, 34 g protein.

Harvest Stew

PREP: 20 min. **COOK:** 40 min.

Taste of Home Test Kitchen

- 1-1/2 pounds boneless pork loin roast, cut into 1-inch cubes
- 1 medium onion, chopped
- 2 garlic cloves, minced
- 2 tablespoons butter
- 3 cups chicken broth
- 3/4 teaspoon salt
- 1/4 teaspoon dried rosemary, crushed
- 1/4 teaspoon rubbed sage
- 1 bay leaf
- 1 medium butternut squash, peeled and cubed (3 cups)
- 2 medium apples, peeled and cubed

1) In a large saucepan, cook the pork, onion and garlic in butter over medium heat until meat is no longer pink; drain. Add the broth, salt, rosemary, sage and bay leaf. Bring to a boil. Reduce heat; cover and simmer for 10 minutes.

2) Add the squash and apples; simmer, uncovered, for 20 minutes or until squash and apples are tender. Discard bay leaf.

Yield: 6 servings.

NUTRITION FACTS: 1 cup equals 289 calories, 11 g fat (5 g saturated fat), 79 mg cholesterol, 867 mg sodium, 23 g carbohydrate, 6 g fiber, 26 g protein.

PORK TENDERLOIN STEW

Pork Tenderloin Stew

PREP: 20 min. **COOK:** 40 min.

Janet Allen, Belleville, Illinois

 2 pork tenderloins (1 pound *each*), cut into 1-inch cubes
 1 tablespoon olive oil
 1 medium onion, chopped
 1 garlic clove, minced
 1 can (14-1/2 ounces) reduced-sodium chicken broth
 2 pounds red potatoes, peeled and cubed
 1 cup sliced fresh carrots
 1 cup sliced celery
 1/2 pound sliced fresh mushrooms
 2 tablespoons cider vinegar
 2 teaspoons sugar
 1-1/2 teaspoons dried tarragon
 1 teaspoon salt
 2 tablespoons all-purpose flour
 1/2 cup fat-free milk
 1/2 cup reduced-fat sour cream

1) In a large nonstick skillet, cook pork in batches in oil over medium heat until no longer pink; remove and keep warm.

2) In the same pan, saute onion and garlic until crisp-tender. Add the broth, vegetables, vinegar, sugar, tarragon and salt; bring to a boil. Reduce heat; cover and simmer for 25-30 minutes or until vegetables are tender.

3) Combine flour and milk until smooth; gradually stir into vegetable mixture. Bring to a boil; cook and stir for 2 minutes or until thickened. Add pork and heat through. Reduce heat; stir in sour cream just before serving (do not boil).

Yield: 8 servings.

NUTRITION FACTS: 1-1/4 cups equals 293 calories, 7 g fat (3 g saturated fat), 68 mg cholesterol, 521 mg sodium, 28 g carbohydrate, 3 g fiber, 28 g protein.

Sweet Potato Pork Stew

PREP: 10 min. **COOK:** 35 min.

Susan Schlenvogt, Waukesha, Wisconsin

 3/4 pound pork chop suey meat
 1 tablespoon Dijon mustard
 3 tablespoons all-purpose flour
 1 tablespoon brown sugar
 1 small garlic clove, minced
 1 tablespoon vegetable oil
 1 cup reduced-sodium chicken broth
 1 small onion, quartered
 1 medium sweet potato, peeled and cubed
 1/4 teaspoon salt
 1/8 teaspoon pepper
 1 tablespoon minced fresh parsley

1) In a small bowl, toss pork with mustard. In a large resealable plastic bag, combine flour and brown sugar; add pork and shake to coat.

2) In a large saucepan coated with cooking spray, cook pork and garlic in oil until pork is browned on all sides. Stir in broth. Bring to a boil. Reduce heat; cover and simmer for 15 minutes.

3) Stir in the onion, sweet potato, salt and pepper. Return to a boil. Reduce heat; cover and simmer 15-20 minutes longer or until meat is no longer pink and vegetables are tender. Stir in parsley.

Yield: 2 servings.

NUTRITION FACTS: 1-1/2 cups equals 492 calories, 17 g fat (5 g saturated fat), 100 mg cholesterol, 848 mg sodium, 44 g carbohydrate, 4 g fiber, 40 g protein.

Canadian Bacon with Apples

PREP/TOTAL TIME: 20 min.

Paula Marchesi, Lenhartsville, Pennsylvania

No one can resist Canadian bacon and apples coated with a delicious brown sugar glaze.

1/2 cup packed brown sugar
1 tablespoon lemon juice
1/8 teaspoon pepper
1 large unpeeled red apple
1 large unpeeled green apple
1 pound sliced Canadian bacon

1) In a large skillet, combine the brown sugar, lemon juice and pepper. Cook and stir over medium heat until sugar is dissolved.

2) Cut each apple into 16 wedges; add to brown sugar mixture. Cook over medium heat for 5-7 minutes until tender, stirring occasionally. Remove apples to a serving platter with a slotted spoon; keep warm.

3) Add Canadian bacon to the skillet; cook over medium heat for 3 minutes or until heated through, turning once. Transfer to platter. Pour remaining brown sugar mixture over apples and bacon. Serve immediately.

Yield: 6 servings.

NUTRITION FACTS: 1 serving equals 199 calories, 4 g fat (1 g saturated fat), 28 mg cholesterol, 744 mg sodium, 30 g carbohydrate, 2 g fiber, 12 g protein.

Zippy Praline Bacon

PREP/TOTAL TIME: 20 min.

Myrt Pflannkuche, Pell City, Alabama

Three simple ingredients give bacon an entirely new taste. It's a real treat at any breakfast table.

1 pound sliced bacon
3 tablespoons brown sugar
1-1/2 teaspoons chili powder
1/4 cup finely chopped pecans

1) Line two 15-in. x 10-in. x 1-in. baking pans with foil. Arrange bacon in a single layer in pans. Bake at 425° for 10 minutes; drain.

2) Combine the brown sugar and chili powder; sprinkle over bacon. Sprinkle with pecans. Bake 5-10 minutes longer or until bacon is crisp. Drain on paper towels.

Yield: 10 servings.

NUTRITION FACTS: 2 slices equals 124 calories, 10 g fat (3 g saturated fat), 13 mg cholesterol, 244 mg sodium, 5 g carbohydrate, trace fiber, 5 g protein.

Breakfast Patties

PREP/TOTAL TIME: 30 min.

Jeannine Stallings, East Helena, Montana

This homemade sausage is terrific because it's lean, holds together well and shrinks very little when cooked. It's incredibly easy to mix up a batch and make any breakfast special.

1/4 cup water
2 teaspoons salt
2 teaspoons rubbed sage
1 teaspoon pepper
1/2 teaspoon ground nutmeg
1/4 teaspoon crushed red pepper flakes
1/8 teaspoon ground ginger
2 pounds ground pork

1) In a large bowl, combine water and seasonings. Add pork and mix well. Shape into eight 4-in. patties.

2) In a large skillet, cook patties over medium heat for 5-6 minutes on each side or until no longer pink in the center and a meat thermometer reads 160°.

Yield: 8 patties.

NUTRITION FACTS: 1 patty equals 241 calories, 17 g fat (6 g saturated fat), 76 mg cholesterol, 649 mg sodium, trace carbohydrate, trace fiber, 21 g protein.

Biscuits and Sausage Gravy

PREP/TOTAL TIME: 15 min.

Sue Baker, Jonesboro, Arkansas

I adapted an old Southern recipe to make it more my own, and now my family prefers it.

- 1/4 pound bulk pork sausage
- 2 tablespoons butter
- 2 to 3 tablespoons all-purpose flour
- 1/4 teaspoon salt
- 1/8 teaspoon pepper
- 1-1/4 to 1-1/3 cups milk

Warm biscuits

1) In a skillet, cook sausage over medium heat until no longer pink; drain. Add butter and heat until melted. Add the flour, salt and pepper; cook and stir until blended.

2) Gradually add the milk, stirring constantly. Bring to a boil; cook and stir for 2 minutes or until thickened. Serve over biscuits.

Yield: 2 servings.

NUTRITION FACTS: 3/4 cup (calculated without biscuits) equals 337 calories, 27 g fat (14 g saturated fat), 72 mg cholesterol, 718 mg sodium, 14 g carbohydrate, trace fiber, 10 g protein.

BISCUITS AND SAUSAGE GRAVY

Brats with Onions

PREP: 20 min. **COOK:** 20 min.

Gunnard Stark, Rotunda West, Florida

After years of eating plain old brats, I came up with this great-tasting version slathered in zippy onions. Enjoy juicy bratwurst for dinner with plenty left over for meals later in the week.

- 3 cans (12 ounces *each*) beer or 4-1/2 cups chicken broth
- 3 large onions, thinly sliced and separated into rings
- 6 garlic cloves, minced
- 1 tablespoon hot pepper sauce
- 2 to 3 teaspoons celery salt
- 2 to 3 teaspoons pepper
- 1 teaspoon chili powder
- 15 fresh bratwurst links (3-1/2 to 4 pounds)
- 15 hot dog buns *or* brat buns, split

1) In a Dutch oven, combine the beer or broth, onion, garlic, pepper sauce, celery salt, pepper and chili powder.

2) Bring to a boil. Add bratwurst. Reduce heat; simmer, uncovered, for 20-25 minutes or until bratwurst is firm and cooked. Drain, reserving onions.

3) Broil brats 4 in. from heat or grill over medium heat for 4-5 minutes or until browned, turning once. Serve on buns with reserved onions.

Yield: 15 brats.

NUTRITION FACTS: 1 brat equals 512 calories, 25 g fat (9 g saturated fat), 51 mg cholesterol, 1,341 mg sodium, 40 g carbohydrate, 3 g fiber, 18 g protein.

TASTY PIZZA TOPPER ■■■

When I have extra bratwurst after a barbecue, I slice it up and sprinkle the pieces on top of a frozen pizza before baking. It tastes great, and kids like it, too.

—Larry Von Gunten, Jefferson City, Missouri

Bratwurst Stew

PREP: 20 min. **COOK:** 25 min.

Deborah Elliott, Ridge Spring, South Carolina

Using leftover brats hurries along the preparation of this satisfying stew. When time is short, this flavorful combination is so good and easy. I usually have all the ingredients handy.

- 2 cans (14-1/2 ounces *each*) chicken broth
- 4 medium carrots, cut into 3/4-inch chunks
- 2 celery ribs, cut into 3/4-inch chunks
- 1 medium onion, chopped
- 1/2 to 1 teaspoon dried thyme
- 1/2 teaspoon dried basil
- 1/2 teaspoon salt
- 1/4 to 1/2 teaspoon garlic powder
- 3 cups chopped cabbage
- 2 cans (15-1/2 ounces *each*) great northern beans, rinsed and drained
- 5 fully cooked bratwurst links, cut into 3/4-inch slices

1) In a large saucepan, combine the broth, carrots, celery, onion and seasonings. Bring to a boil.

2) Reduce heat; cover and simmer for 15 minutes. Add the cabbage; cover and cook for 10 minutes. Stir in beans and bratwurst; heat through.

Yield: 10 servings.

NUTRITION FACTS: 1 serving equals 229 calories, 12 g fat (4 g saturated fat), 26 mg cholesterol, 917 mg sodium, 20 g carbohydrate, 6 g fiber, 12 g protein.

POLISH KRAUT AND APPLES

⏲ Polish Kraut and Apples

PREP: 10 min. **COOK:** 4 hours

Caren Markee, Crystal Lake, Illinois

My family loves this hearty, heartwarming meal on cold winter nights. The tender apples and brown sugar add a bit of sweetness to the smoked sausage. I like making it because the prep time is very short.

- 1 can (14 ounces) sauerkraut, rinsed and well drained
- 1 package (16 ounces) smoked Polish sausage, cut into chunks
- 3 medium tart apples, peeled and cut into eighths
- 1/2 cup packed brown sugar
- 1/2 teaspoon caraway seeds, optional
- 1/8 teaspoon pepper
- 3/4 cup apple juice

1) Place half of the sauerkraut in an ungreased 3-qt. slow cooker. Top with sausage, apples, brown sugar, caraway seeds if desired and pepper. Top with remaining sauerkraut.

2) Pour apple juice over all. Cover and cook on low for 4-5 hours or until apples are tender.

Yield: 4 servings.

NUTRITION FACTS: 1 cup equals 546 calories, 31 g fat (12 g saturated fat), 81 mg cholesterol, 1,630 mg sodium, 52 g carbohydrate, 4 g fiber, 15 g protein.

HEARTY KIELBASA MEALS ■■■

I stock my freezer with two easy main dishes. I buy two links of kielbasa or smoked sausage, cut them into 1/4-inch slices and fry them in a skillet. I pour a large jar of sauerkraut into one large mircrowave-safe freezer container and a large can of baked beans into another. I divide the sausage slices between the two containers, put the lids on and place them in the freezer. Each can be thawed in the fridge for a day before warming in the microwave.

—Katie Weed, Topeka, Kansas

Smoked Sausage Stew

PREP: 15 min. **COOK:** 1 hour

Ella Jay Tubbs, Fort Worth, Texas

Condensed bean and bacon soup adds fast flavor to this stew. It simmers together in about an hour, which is perfect after a long day.

- 2 cans (11-1/2 ounces *each*) condensed bean and bacon soup
- 1 can (14-1/2 ounces) diced tomatoes, undrained
- 2 cups water
- 2 medium potatoes, diced
- 1 cup sliced carrots
- 1 cup sliced celery
- 1 teaspoon chili powder
- 12 ounces fully cooked smoked sausage, thinly sliced

1) In a saucepan, combine the soup, tomatoes and water. Add the potatoes, carrots, celery and chili powder. Bring to a boil.

2) Reduce heat; cover and simmer for 20 minutes. Add sausage; cover and simmer 40 minutes longer.

Yield: 8 servings (2 quarts).

NUTRITION FACTS: 1 cup equals 310 calories, 15 g fat (6 g saturated fat), 32 mg cholesterol, 1,138 mg sodium, 31 g carbohydrate, 7 g fiber, 13 g protein.

⏲ Spicy Cajun Stew

PREP/TOTAL TIME: 20 min.

Elizabeth Freise, Bryn Mawr, Pennsylvania

Packed with sausage, rice and vegetables, this dish is surprisingly quick and easy since it has just five ingredients.

- 1 package (16 ounces) smoked Polish sausage, cut into 1/4-inch slices
- 2 cans (10 ounces *each*) diced tomatoes and green chilies, undrained
- 1 can (14-1/2 ounces) chicken broth
- 1 package (10 ounces) frozen chopped spinach, thawed and squeezed dry
- 1/2 to 3/4 cup uncooked instant rice

1) In a large skillet, saute sausage until lightly browned; drain. Add tomatoes and broth. Bring to a boil. Stir in spinach.

2) Return to a boil; cook for 2 minutes. Stir in the rice. Cover and remove from the heat. Let stand for 5 minutes. Stir with a fork.

Yield: 5 servings.

NUTRITION FACTS: 1 serving equals 356 calories, 25 g fat (10 g saturated fat), 64 mg cholesterol, 1,604 mg sodium, 17 g carbohydrate, 3 g fiber, 15 g protein.

SAUSAGE CALZONES

Sausage Calzones

PREP: 35 min. + rising **BAKE:** 20 min.

Janine Colasurdo, Chesapeake, Virginia

My husband and I both enjoy cooking Italian food. We took the filling we usually use for ravioli and wrapped it in a dough to make these excellent calzones. The Italian sausage blends so beautifully with the cheeses and spinach.

- 1 package (1/4 ounce) active dry yeast
- 1/2 cup warm water (110° to 115°)
- 3/4 cup warm milk (110° to 115°)
- 2 tablespoons plus 2 teaspoons olive oil, *divided*
- 1-1/2 teaspoons salt
- 1 teaspoon sugar
- 3 to 3-1/4 cups all-purpose flour
- 1 pound bulk Italian sausage
- 1 package (10 ounces) frozen chopped spinach, thawed and squeezed dry
- 1 carton (15 ounces) ricotta cheese
- 1/2 cup grated Parmesan cheese
- 1 tablespoon minced fresh parsley
- 1/8 teaspoon pepper
- 2 tablespoons cornmeal
- 1/2 teaspoon garlic salt
- 1-1/2 cups pizza sauce, warmed

1) In a large mixing bowl, dissolve yeast in warm water. Add the milk, 2 tablespoons oil, salt, sugar and 2 cups flour; beat until smooth. Stir in enough remaining flour to form a soft dough.

2) Turn onto a floured surface; knead until smooth and elastic, 6-8 minutes. Place in a greased bowl, turning once to grease top. Cover and let rise in a warm place until doubled, about 1 hour.

3) Meanwhile, in a large skillet, cook sausage over medium heat until no longer pink; drain. Add the spinach, cheeses, parsley and pepper; mix well.

4) Punch dough down; divide into six pieces. On a floured surface, roll each piece into an 8-in. circle.

Top each with 2/3 cup filling. Fold dough over filling; pinch to seal.

5) Place on greased baking sheets sprinkled with cornmeal. Brush tops lightly with remaining oil; sprinkle with garlic salt.

6) Bake at 400° for 20-25 minutes or until golden brown. Serve with pizza sauce.

Yield: 6 servings.

NUTRITION FACTS: 1 calzone equals 616 calories, 28 g fat (11 g saturated fat), 68 mg cholesterol, 1,619 mg sodium, 63 g carbohydrate, 5 g fiber, 29 g protein.

Italian Sloppy Joes
PREP: 20 min. **COOK:** 30 min.

Kimberly Speakman, McKinney, Texas

My mother used to make these for us when we were kids. When I left home, I was sure to take the recipe with me.

- 1 pound bulk Italian sausage
- 1 pound bulk hot Italian sausage
- 4 garlic cloves, minced
- 1 cup chopped green pepper
- 1/2 cup chopped onion
- 1 can (15 ounces) tomato sauce
- 2 tablespoons minced fresh parsley
- 1 teaspoon dried oregano
- 1/2 teaspoon chili powder
- 1/4 teaspoon fennel seed
- 8 to 10 French *or* submarine rolls, split
- 3/4 cup shredded part-skim mozzarella cheese

1) In a large saucepan or Dutch oven, cook sausage, garlic, green pepper and onion over medium heat until the sausage is no longer pink; drain.

2) Add the tomato sauce and seasonings; bring to a boil. Reduce heat; cover and simmer for 30 minutes. Spoon about 1/2 cup onto each roll; sprinkle with cheese.

Yield: 8-10 servings.

NUTRITION FACTS: 1 serving equals 344 calories, 18 g fat (6 g saturated fat), 41 mg cholesterol, 877 mg sodium, 30 g carbohydrate, 2 g fiber, 15 g protein.

ITALIAN SLOPPY JOES

POLENTA WITH ITALIAN SAUSAGE

Polenta with Italian Sausage

PREP: 25 min. **COOK:** 15 min.

Peggy Ratliff, North Tazewell, Virginia

My mom brought this recipe over from Europe. Polenta is a coarse-textured cornmeal that makes the hearty base to this main dish.

> 4 cups water, *divided*
> 1 cup cornmeal
> 1 teaspoon salt
> 1 pound Italian sausage links
> 2 garlic cloves, minced
> 1 can (14-1/2 ounces) Italian stewed tomatoes
> 1 can (6 ounces) tomato paste
> 2 tablespoons minced fresh parsley
> 1/4 cup shredded Parmesan cheese

1) In a bowl, combine 1 cup water and cornmeal. In a saucepan, bring salt and remaining water to a boil. Slowly stir in cornmeal mixture. Reduce heat; cook for 15 minutes, stirring frequently.

2) Meanwhile, in a large skillet, cook the sausage and garlic over medium heat until sausage is no longer pink; drain. Cool slightly. Cut sausage into 1-in. pieces; return to skillet. Add the tomatoes, tomato paste and parsley; bring to a boil. Remove from the heat.

3) Spread half of the cornmeal mixture in a serving dish; top with half of the sausage mixture. Repeat layers. Sprinkle with Parmesan cheese. Serve immediately.

Yield: 6 servings.

NUTRITION FACTS: 1 piece equals 267 calories, 11 g fat (4 g saturated fat), 32 mg cholesterol, 1,057 mg sodium, 29 g carbohydrate, 5 g fiber, 12 g protein.

Chicago-Style Pan Pizza

PREP: 20 min. **BAKE:** 25 min.

Nikki MacDonald, Sheboygan, Wisconsin

I developed a love for Chicago's deep-dish pizzas while attending college in the Windy City. This simple recipe relies on frozen bread dough, so I can indulge in the mouthwatering sensation without leaving home.

> 1 loaf (1 pound) frozen bread dough, thawed
> 1 pound bulk Italian sausage
> 2 cups (8 ounces) shredded part-skim mozzarella cheese
> 1/2 pound sliced fresh mushrooms
> 1 small onion, chopped
> 2 teaspoons olive oil
> 1 can (28 ounces) diced tomatoes, drained
> 3/4 teaspoon dried oregano
> 1/2 teaspoon salt
> 1/2 teaspoon fennel seed, crushed
> 1/4 teaspoon garlic powder
> 1/2 cup grated Parmesan cheese

1) Press dough onto the bottom and up the sides of a greased 13-in. x 9-in. x 2-in. baking dish. In a large skillet, cook sausage over medium heat until no longer pink; drain. Sprinkle over dough. Top with mozzarella cheese.

2) In a skillet, saute mushrooms and onion in oil until onion is tender. Stir in the tomatoes, oregano, salt, fennel seed and garlic powder. Spoon over mozzarella cheese.

3) Sprinkle with Parmesan cheese. Bake at 350° for 25-35 minutes or until crust is golden brown.

Yield: 8 slices.

NUTRITION FACTS: 2 pieces equals 786 calories, 38 g fat (15 g saturated fat), 97 mg cholesterol, 2,110 mg sodium, 75 g carbohydrate, 8 g fiber, 42 g protein.

CHICAGO-STYLE PAN PIZZA

About Ham

You can choose from several kinds of fully cooked hams. A bone-in ham can be purchased whole or cut in half. Rump (butt) portions are more expensive because they have more meat and less bone than the shank cuts. Boneless hams are also available.

Buy ham with a rosy pink color. The meat should be firm to the touch when pressed. Calorie-conscious cooks should look for extra-lean ham. Note that most hams in grocery stores have been cured, smoked and fully cooked. So they can be served warm (internal temperature 140°) or cold. On the other hand, country hams have been salt-cured, smoked and aged. They're usually labeled "cook before eating," so you'll want to follow the cooking directions on the package.

Useful Definitions

Refer to the Glossary on pages 24-28 for more terms.

Butt End: The round end of a ham.

Country-Style Ham: Also known as old-fashioned or Southern-style ham. This type of ham has been dry-cured with salt, sugar and spices and may be smoked. No water has been added to the ham. These hams can be salty and should be prepared according to package directions.

Cured Ham: Infused with a solution of sugar, salt and nitrite to enhance flavor and shelf life. A cured ham can also be smoked.

Fresh Ham: From the hind leg and has not been smoked or cured.

Fully Cooked Ham: Cooked and smoked and/or cured. It can be eaten without heating but is generally heated to 140° for optimal flavor.

Picnic Ham: Not considered a true ham because it is from the foreleg not the hind leg. It also has a portion of the shoulder.

Prosciutto: Thinly sliced Italian-style ham that is salt-cured and air-dried for 10 months to 2 years. It is not smoked.

Shank End: The narrow end of a ham.

Smithfield Ham: Processed in the Smithfield area of Virginia. This seasoned hickory-smoked ham is usually aged for 6 to 12 months. The ham is dark in color, lean and salty. Prepare according to package directions.

Smoked Ham: Processed by being exposed to smoke or by having Liquid Smoke applied to the surface. A smoked ham can also be cured.

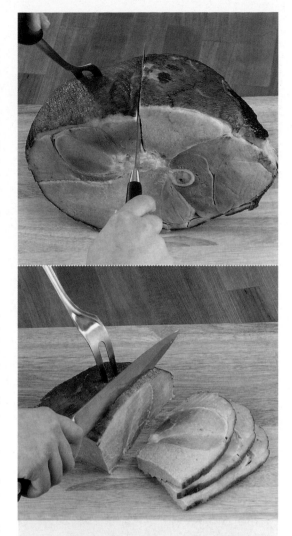

Carving a Half Ham with Bone

1) Place ham fat side up on a carving board. Using a meat fork to anchor the ham, make a horizontal cut with a carving knife from the one side of the ham to the bone. Position the cut in about middle of the ham along the natural break between the muscles. Make a second cut from the top of the ham to the first cut. Remove the large meaty area of the ham from the bone. Remove the two remaining large meaty sections in the same manner. The meat left on the ham bone may be used for soup or picked off and used in salads or casseroles.

2) Place the meaty piece of ham cut side down on a cutting board. Cut into slices.

HAM WITH CHERRY SAUCE

⏱Ham with Cherry Sauce

PREP: 15 min. **COOK:** 4 hours

Carol Lee Jones, Taylors, South Carolina

I often fix this tasty ham topped with a thick cherry sauce. It's such a favorite that I've served it at Easter dinners, church breakfasts and a friend's wedding brunch.

- 1   boneless fully cooked ham (3 to 4 pounds)
- 1/2 cup apple jelly
- 2   teaspoons prepared mustard
- 2/3 cup ginger ale, *divided*
- 1   can (21 ounces) cherry pie filling
- 2   tablespoons cornstarch

1) Score surface of ham, making diamond shapes 1/2 in. deep. In a small bowl, combine the jelly, mustard and 1 tablespoon ginger ale; rub over scored surface of ham.

2) Cut ham in half; place in a 5-qt. slow cooker. Cover and cook on low for 4-5 hours or until a meat thermometer reads 140° and ham is heated through. Baste with cooking juices toward end of cooking time.

3) For the sauce, place pie filling in a saucepan. Combine cornstarch and remaining ginger ale; stir into pie filling until blended. Bring to a boil; cook and stir for 2 minutes or until thickened. Serve over ham.

Yield: 10-12 servings.

NUTRITION FACTS: 4 ounces equals 284 calories, 10 g fat (3 g saturated fat), 60 mg cholesterol, 1,469 mg sodium, 28 g carbohydrate, trace fiber, 21 g protein.

SWEET, SLOW-COOKED HAM ■■■

When entertaining, I like to prepare a boneless ham in my slow cooker. I drizzle honey and pineapple juice over the ham before piercing it with some whole cloves. I then cook it on low for 6-8 hours or until it's done. The results are always juicy and delicious, and I have plenty of time to tend to other things.

—Vicki Whitworth, Camden, Tennessee

Raspberry-Chipotle Glazed Ham

PREP: 10 min. **BAKE:** 2 hours 20 min.

Mary Lou Wayman, Salt Lake City, Utah

Looking to liven up your same-old holiday ham? Try this recipe, which features a sweet and spicy sauce.

- 1   bone-in fully cooked spiral-sliced ham (9 to 10 pounds)
- 2-1/4 cups seedless raspberry jam
- 3   tablespoons white vinegar
- 3   chipotle peppers in adobo sauce, drained, seeded and minced
- 3 to 4 garlic cloves, minced
- 1   tablespoon coarsely ground pepper

1) Place ham on a rack in a shallow roasting pan. Bake, uncovered, at 325° for 2 to 2-1/2 hours or until a meat thermometer reads 130°.

2) In a small saucepan, combine the jam, vinegar, peppers and garlic. Bring to a boil. Reduce heat; simmer, uncovered, for 5 minutes. Brush some of the sauce over ham. Bake 20 minutes longer or until meat thermometer reads 140°, brushing twice with sauce. Sprinkle pepper over ham. Serve with remaining sauce.

Yield: 16-20 servings.

NUTRITION FACTS: 4 ounces equals 342 calories, 5 g fat (1 g saturated fat), 45 mg cholesterol, 1,852 mg sodium, 39 g carbohydrate, trace fiber, 37 g protein.

Scoring and Studding Ham

With a sharp knife, make diagonal cuts in a diamond pattern about 1/2 in. deep in the surface of the ham. Push whole cloves in a decorative pattern in the diamonds.

Ham with Maple Gravy

PREP: 35 min. **BAKE:** 1 hour 30 min.

Sue Ward, Thunder Bay, Ontario

When you make this hearty dish, the wonderful aroma coming from the kitchen is sure to create some big appetites!

- 1   fully cooked boneless ham (6 pounds)
- 30 whole cloves
- 3/4 cup maple syrup, *divided*
- 4   teaspoons ground mustard
- 2   cups apple juice
- 3   tablespoons cornstarch
- 3   tablespoons water
- 2   tablespoons butter
- 6   medium tart apples, cored and cut into 1/2-inch slices

HAM WITH MAPLE GRAVY

1) Place ham on a rack in a shallow roasting pan. Score the surface of the ham, making diamond shapes 1/2 in. deep; insert a clove in each diamond.

2) Combine 1/2 cup maple syrup and mustard; pour over ham. Pour apple juice into the roasting pan. Bake at 325° for 1-1/2 to 2 hours or until a meat thermometer reads 140°, basting frequently.

3) Remove ham and keep warm. Transfer the pan juices to a saucepan. Combine cornstarch and water until smooth; add to saucepan. Bring to a boil; cook and stir for 1 minute or until thickened.

4) Meanwhile, in a skillet, melt butter over medium heat. Add apples and remaining maple syrup. Cover and cook for 10-15 minutes, stirring occasionally. Slice ham; serve with the apples and gravy.

Yield: 14 servings.

NUTRITION FACTS: 4 ounces ham equals 328 calories, 9 g fat (3 g saturated fat), 103 mg cholesterol, 2,036 mg sodium, 27 g carbohydrate, 2 g fiber, 36 g protein.

Apple Ham Steak
PREP/TOTAL TIME: 30 min.

Mildred Sherrer, Fort Worth, Texas

For an easy one-dish meal, you can't beat this ham steak.

1-1/2 cups instant rice
1 medium onion, chopped
2 celery ribs, chopped
6 tablespoons butter, *divided*
2-1/2 cups apple juice, *divided*
1 teaspoon salt
1 pound boneless fully cooked ham steak, cut into fourths
2 medium tart apples, peeled and sliced
2 tablespoons brown sugar
1/4 teaspoon ground cinnamon
2 tablespoons raisins
1 tablespoon cornstarch
Hot cooked rice

1) In a saucepan, saute rice, onion and celery in 2 tablespoons butter until tender. Add 1-1/2 cups apple juice and salt. Bring to a boil. Cover and remove from the heat; let stand for 5 minutes.

2) Meanwhile, in a skillet, cook ham in remaining butter until lightly browned. Remove and keep warm. In the same skillet, cook and stir apples, brown sugar and cinnamon over medium heat until apples are almost tender, about 5 minutes. Stir in raisins.

3) In a bowl, combine cornstarch and remaining apple juice just until smooth; add to the skillet. Bring to a boil; cook and stir for 2 minutes or until thickened. Return ham to skillet and heat through. Serve over rice.

Yield: 4 servings.

NUTRITION FACTS: 1 serving equals 649 calories, 27 g fat (14 g saturated fat), 106 mg cholesterol, 2,242 mg sodium, 77 g carbohydrate, 4 g fiber, 25 g protein.

Sweet-Sour Ham Balls
PREP: 20 min. **BAKE:** 45 min.

Dorothy Pritchett, Wills Point, Texas

Pineapple, brown sugar and mustard combine to create a tangy sauce for these savory ham and pork balls. I like to keep a batch on hand for card parties and other occasions.

4 eggs, lightly beaten
1/4 cup chopped onion
1-1/2 cups soft bread crumbs
2 pounds ground ham
1 pound ground pork
2 cans (8 ounces *each*) crushed pineapple, undrained
1 cup packed brown sugar
1/4 cup prepared mustard
2 tablespoons cider vinegar

1) In a bowl, combine the eggs, onion and bread crumbs. Crumble meat over mixture and mix well. Shape into 1-1/2-in. balls. Place in two greased 13-in. x 9-in. x 2-in. baking dishes.

2) In a blender, combine the pineapple, brown sugar, mustard and vinegar; cover and process until smooth. Pour over ham balls.

3) Bake, uncovered, at 350° for 45-50 minutes or until a meat thermometer reads 160°, basting occasionally with sauce.

Yield: 5 dozen.

Editor's Note: Ham balls may be frozen. Prepare as directed and pour sauce over ham balls. Do not bake at this point. Freeze in dinner sized portions. Thaw completely in the refrigerator. Bake as directed in recipe.

NUTRITION FACTS: 3 ham balls equals 482 calories, 26 g fat (9 g saturated fat), 166 mg cholesterol, 1,326 mg sodium, 33 g carbohydrate, 1 g fiber, 29 g protein.

MOTHER'S HAM CASSEROLE

Mother's Ham Casserole

PREP: 35 min. **BAKE:** 25 min.

Linda Childers, Murfreesboro, Tennessee

One of my mother's favorite dishes, this recipe always brings back fond memories of her when I prepare it. It's a terrific use of leftover ham from a holiday dinner.

- 2 cups cubed peeled potatoes
- 1 large carrot, sliced
- 2 celery ribs, chopped
- 3 cups water
- 2 cups cubed fully cooked ham
- 2 tablespoons chopped green pepper
- 2 teaspoons finely chopped onion
- 7 tablespoons butter, *divided*
- 3 tablespoons all-purpose flour
- 1-1/2 cups milk
- 3/4 teaspoon salt
- 1/8 teaspoon pepper
- 1 cup (4 ounces) shredded cheddar cheese
- 1/2 cup soft bread crumbs

1) In a saucepan, bring the potatoes, carrot, celery and water to a boil. Reduce heat; cover and cook about 15 minutes or until tender. Drain.

2) In a large skillet, saute the ham, green pepper and onion in 3 tablespoons butter until tender. Add to the potato mixture. Transfer to a greased 1-1/2-qt. baking dish.

3) In a saucepan, melt the remaining butter; stir in flour until smooth. Gradually add milk, salt and pepper. Bring to a boil; cook and stir for 2 minutes or until thickened. Reduce heat; add cheese and stir until melted.

4) Pour over the ham mixture. Sprinkle with bread crumbs. Bake, uncovered, at 375° for 25-30 minutes or until heated through.

Yield: 4-6 servings.

NUTRITION FACTS: 1 cup equals 374 calories, 25 g fat (15 g saturated fat), 89 mg cholesterol, 1,208 mg sodium, 22 g carbohydrate, 2 g fiber, 17 g protein.

Quick Golden Stew

PREP/TOTAL TIME: 30 min.

Merry McNally, Ionia, Michigan

This complete meal can be prepared in a hurry. Yet it has a rich goodness that tastes like you fussed.

- 4 carrots, cut into 1-inch pieces
- 1-1/2 cups peeled and diced potatoes
- 2 medium onions, cut into chunks

Water

- 1 package (10 ounces) frozen peas, defrosted
- 2 cups cubed fully cooked ham
- 1 can (10-3/4 ounces) cream of celery soup, undiluted
- 1 jar (8 ounces) process cheese spread

1) In a large saucepan or Dutch oven, combine the carrots, potatoes, onions and just enough water to cover. Bring to a boil. Reduce heat; cover and cook for 10 minutes or until vegetables are tender.

2) Add peas and ham; cover and cook 5 minutes longer. Drain water. Stir in soup and cheese; heat through.

Yield: 4 servings.

NUTRITION FACTS: 1 cup equals 323 calories, 14 g fat (8 g saturated fat), 50 mg cholesterol, 1,654 mg sodium, 32 g carbohydrate, 6 g fiber, 18 g protein.

Pretty Penne Ham Skillet

PREP/TOTAL TIME: 30 min.

Kathy Stephan, West Seneca, New York

I enjoy experimenting with herbs and spices to cut down on salt and sugar. Parsley, basil and oregano season this tasty main dish.

- 1 package (16 ounces) penne pasta
- 3 cups cubed fully cooked ham
- 1 large sweet red pepper, diced
- 1 medium onion, chopped
- 1/4 cup minced fresh parsley
- 2 garlic cloves, minced
- 1-1/2 teaspoons minced fresh basil *or* 1/2 teaspoon dried basil
- 1-1/2 teaspoons minced fresh oregano *or* 1/2 teaspoon dried oregano
- 1/4 cup olive oil
- 3 tablespoons butter
- 1 can (14-1/2 ounces) chicken broth
- 1 tablespoon lemon juice
- 1/2 cup shredded Parmesan cheese

1) Cook pasta according to package directions. Meanwhile, in a large skillet, saute the ham, red pepper, onion, parsley, garlic, basil and oregano in oil and butter for 4-6 minutes or until ham is browned and vegetables are tender.

2) Stir in broth and lemon juice. Bring to a boil. Reduce heat; simmer, uncovered, for 10-15 minutes or until liquid is reduced by half. Drain pasta; stir into ham mixture. Sprinkle with Parmesan cheese.

Yield: 6 servings.

NUTRITION FACTS: 1-1/2 cups equals 567 calories, 24 g fat (8 g saturated fat), 57 mg cholesterol, 1,344 mg sodium, 62 g carbohydrate, 4 g fiber, 27 g protein.

BAKED HAM SANDWICHES ■■■

When I have leftover baked ham, I grind it and combine it with chopped olives and green pepper, shredded cheddar cheese, Dijon mustard and mayonnaise. Then I stuff this mixture into hard rolls. Wrapped in foil and baked at 375° for 30 minutes, these make tasty hot sandwiches.

—*Marion S., Joseph, Oregon*

Kentucky Stuffed Peppers

PREP: 30 min. **BAKE:** 40 min.

Lucille Terry, Frankfort, Kentucky

This colorful and delicious dish is my own variation on stuffed peppers, which usually feature ground beef. The ham and mushrooms are a nice change from the ordinary.

  4 large sweet *and/or* yellow peppers
  1 can (14-1/2 ounces) diced tomatoes
  1 large onion, chopped
  2 tablespoons butter
  2 cups cooked rice
  1 jar (4-1/2 ounces) sliced mushrooms, drained
  1 cup diced fully cooked ham
  1 teaspoon sugar
Dash hot pepper sauce
  3/4 cup shredded cheddar cheese

1) Cut tops off peppers and remove seeds. In a Dutch oven, cook peppers in boiling water for 3-5 minutes. Drain and rinse in cold water. Place peppers upside down on paper towels; set aside.

2) Drain tomatoes, reserving the juice; set tomatoes and juice aside. In a large skillet, saute onion in butter until tender. Add the rice, mushrooms, ham, sugar, hot pepper sauce and reserved tomatoes; mix well. Loosely spoon into peppers.

3) Place in an ungreased 2-qt. baking dish. Pour reserved tomato juice over peppers.

4) Cover and bake at 350° for 35-40 minutes; sprinkle with cheese. Bake 5 minutes longer or until the cheese is melted.

Yield: 4 servings.

NUTRITION FACTS: 1 stuffed pepper equals 375 calories, 15 g fat (9 g saturated fat), 56 mg cholesterol, 904 mg sodium, 45 g carbohydrate, 7 g fiber, 16 g protein.

Ham a la King

PREP/TOTAL TIME: 20 min.

Jean Grubb, Bastrop, Texas

My mom and I used to have a catering business, and this recipe was a popular choice from our menu. It looks elegant on the plate and always gets rave reviews. Being able to make the sauce a day ahead is a big plus.

  1 package (10 ounces) frozen puff pastry shells
1/4 cup butter, cubed
1/4 cup all-purpose flour
  1 teaspoon chicken bouillon granules
1/2 cup hot water
1-1/2 cups milk
  3 slices process American cheese
  1 teaspoon Worcestershire sauce
  1 teaspoon prepared mustard
  2 cups cubed fully cooked ham
1/2 cup frozen peas, thawed, optional
  1 can (2-1/4 ounces) sliced ripe olives, drained
  2 tablespoons diced pimientos
  2 tablespoons minced fresh parsley

1) Bake the pastry shells according to package directions. Meanwhile, in a saucepan, melt butter; stir in flour until smooth.

2) Dissolve bouillon in water. Gradually add milk and bouillon to the saucepan. Bring to a boil; cook and stir for 2 minutes or until thickened.

3) Reduce heat; add the cheese, Worcestershire sauce and mustard; stir until the cheese is melted. Add the ham, peas if desired, olives, pimientos and parsley; heat through. Serve in pastry shells.

Yield: 6 servings.

NUTRITION FACTS: 1 filled pastry shell equals 487 calories, 31 g fat (12 g saturated fat), 60 mg cholesterol, 1,232 mg sodium, 35 g carbohydrate, 3 g fiber, 17 g protein.

HAM A LA KING

LAMB

Lamb is a wonderfully tender and moist meat that lends itself to a variety of cooking styles and an assortment of flavor possibilities.

Purchase before the "sell-by" date on the packaging for best quality. Look for lamb that is pinkish red. Be sure the package is cold and has no holes or tears.

Determine the amount of lamb you need to buy based on the cut and amount of bone:

- 1 pound of bone-in roasts yields 2-1/2 servings.
- 1 pound of bone-in steaks yields 2 servings.
- 1 pound of bone-in rib or loin chops yields 2 servings.
- 1 pound of rack of lamb yields 2 servings.

Don't be afraid to use generous amounts of fresh garlic and herbs when cooking lamb. These bold flavors will enhance any cut.

Use a meat thermometer when roasting lamb to ensure the meat is cooked just the way you like it. For best flavor and tenderness, serve roasted lamb medium-rare to medium-well (see page 189).

Serve lamb piping hot for best flavor. Warm oven-safe platters and dinner plates in the oven before serving to keep your entree hot. Use hot pads when handling warm plates.

Useful Definitions

For additional terms, refer to the Glossary on pages 24-28.

Fell: A thin membrane that covers the fat. To remove, use a sharp knife to loosen the fell and peel off.

Frenching: Refers to when about 1-1/2 in. of the meat is removed from the bones. This treatment is frequently done with rack of lamb.

Lamb: Meat from a sheep that is less than 1 year old.

Mutton: Meat from a sheep that is over 1 year old.

Defrosting Guidelines

The thicker the package, the longer it will take to thaw. Here are some guidelines for defrosting lamb in the refrigerator.

- For 1- to 1-1/2-in.-thick packages of ground lamb or meat pieces, allow at least 24 hours.
- For 1-in.-thick chops, allow 12 to 14 hours.
- For a small roast, allow 3 to 5 hours per pound.
- For a large roast, allow 4 to 7 hours per pound.

Cooking Methods for Lamb

CUT/TYPE	BRAISE	BROIL	GRILL	ROAST	PAN-BROIL	PAN-FRY	COOK IN LIQUID
ROASTS							
BREAST	•			•			
CENTER LEG ROAST				•			
LEG OF LAMB				•			
LOIN ROAST				•			
RACK OF LAMB		•	•	•			
CHOPS							
ARM CHOPS	•	•	•		•	•	
BLADE CHOPS	•	•	•		•	•	
LOIN CHOPS	•	•	•		•	•	
RIB CHOPS	•	•	•		•	•	
SHOULDER ROAST	•			•			
OTHER							
GROUND LAMB PATTIES		•	•		•		
LEG STEAK		•	•		•	•	
SHANKS	•						•
STEW CUBES	•						•

Roasting Lamb

Place meat fat side up on a rack in a shallow roasting pan. Insert an oven-safe meat thermometer in the thickest portion of the muscle without touching bone or fat. Or use an instant-read thermometer toward the end of the roasting time. If the meat needs to cook longer, remove the instant-read thermometer before you return the meat to the oven.

Roast without liquid, uncovered, according to the temperature and time given in the chart below or in your recipe. Because roasts will continue to cook after being removed from the oven, remove it when the meat thermometer reads 5-10° below desired doneness. Cover with foil and let stand for 10-15 minutes before carving.

CUT	WEIGHT	COOKING TIME (MINUTES PER POUND)			OVEN TEMP.
		MEDIUM-RARE 145°	MEDIUM 160°	WELL-DONE 170°	
LEG-WHOLE, BONE-IN	5 to 7 lbs.	20 to 25	25 to 30	30 to 35	325°
LEG-SHANK HALF OR SHOULDER, BONE-IN	3 to 4 lbs.	30 to 35	40 to 45	45 to 50	325°
LEG, BONELESS	4 to 7 lbs.	25 to 30	30 to 35	35 to 40	325°
RACK OF LAMB	1-1/2 to 2-1/2 lbs.	25 to 30	30 to 35	35 to 40	375°

Lamb Grilling Chart

Lamb chops and steaks are done when a meat thermometer reads 145° for medium-rare, 160° for medium and 170° for well-done. Ground lamb is done when the temperature reaches 160°. For direct grilling, turn meat halfway through grilling time.

CUT	WEIGHT OR THICKNESS	HEAT	COOKING TIME
RIB OR LOIN CHOPS	1 in.	Medium/Direct	10 to 18 min.
LEG OF LAMB (BONE-IN)	5 to 7 lbs.	Medium-Low/Indirect	1-3/4 to 2-3/4 hours
LEG OF LAMB (BONELESS)	3 to 4 lbs.	Medium-Low/Indirect	1-1/2 to 2-1/2 hours
RACK OF LAMB	1 to 1-1/2 lbs.	Medium/Direct	25 to 35 min.
KABOBS	1-in. cubes	Medium/Direct	8 to 12 min.
LAMB PATTIES	4 oz. and 1/2 in. thick	Medium/Direct	8 to 10 min.

Lamb Nutritional Facts

The numbers given below are for the calorie, fat and cholesterol content in 4 ounces of cooked lamb.

CUT OF LAMB	CALORIES	FAT	SATURATED FAT	CHOLESTEROL
ARM CHOP	250	11 g	4 g	118 mg
LEG OF LAMB	215	9 g	4 g	101 mg
LOIN CHOP	245	11 g	4 g	108 mg
RACK OF LAMB	238	13 g	6 g	91 mg
RIB CHOP	238	13 g	6 g	91 mg
SHANK	187	6 g	2 g	104 mg

Cuts of Lamb

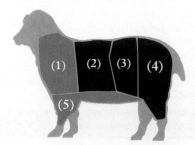

■ **TENDER** ■ **LESS TENDER**

Shoulder (1)

Arm Chop

Blade Chop

Square Cut
Shoulder Whole

Rib (2)

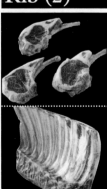

Rib Lamb Chop

Rack of Lamb

Photos courtesy of the National Pork Board.

Loin (3)

Loin Lamb Roast

Loin Lamb Chops

Leg (4)

Whole Leg

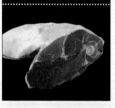

Boneless Leg of Lamb

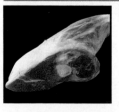

Half Leg of Lamb
Shank Portion

Center Leg Roast

Foreshank & Breast (5)

Lamb Shank

ITALIAN LEG OF LAMB

Italian Leg of Lamb

PREP: 10 min. + marinating
BAKE: 2-1/4 hours + standing

Mary Ann Marino, West Pittsburg, Pennsylvania

When this pleasantly seasoned roast appears on my table, no one walks away hungry. Garlic, lemon juice and seasonings make each bite of this succulent lamb irresistible.

  1/2 to 2/3 cup lemon juice
  1/2 cup olive oil
   2   tablespoons dried oregano
   2   teaspoons ground mustard
   1   teaspoon garlic powder
   4   garlic cloves, minced
   1   boneless leg of lamb
       (4 to 5 pounds)

1) In a small bowl, combine the lemon juice, oil and seasonings. Pour half of the marinade into a large resealable plastic bag; add lamb. Seal bag and turn to coat; refrigerate for at least 2 hours or overnight. Cover and refrigerate the remaining marinade.

2) Drain and discard marinade from lamb. Place lamb fat side up on a rack in a shallow roasting pan. Bake, uncovered, at 325° for 2-1/4 to 3 hours or until meat reaches desired doneness (for medium-rare, a meat thermometer should read 145°; medium, 160°; well-done, 170°), basting occasionally with reserved marinade. Let stand for 10-15 minutes before slicing.

Yield: 11 servings.

NUTRITION FACTS: 4 ounces cooked lamb equals 254 calories, 15 g fat (4 g saturated fat), 84 mg cholesterol, 66 mg sodium, 1 g carbohydrate, trace fiber, 26 g protein.

SIMPLE LEG OF LAMB ■■■

When preparing roast leg of lamb, I rub the meat with ground ginger and some lemon juice. This treatment takes away the strong lamb aroma and makes the meat taste excellent.

—Georgia M., Hudson, Florida

Roast Lamb with Plum Sauce

PREP: 30 min. **BAKE:** 2-1/2 hours + standing

Dorothy Pritchett, Wills Point, Texas

The sweet-and-spicy plum sauce makes a delightful glaze. Then serve the extra alongside the lamb.

   1   bone-in leg of lamb (5 to 6 pounds)
   3   garlic cloves, slivered
  1/2 cup thinly sliced green onions
  1/4 cup butter
   1   jar (12 ounces) plum jam
  1/2 cup chili sauce
  1/4 cup white grape juice
   1   tablespoon lemon juice
  1/2 teaspoon ground allspice
   1   tablespoon dried parsley flakes

1) Remove thin fat covering from the roast. Make slits in meat; insert a garlic sliver in each. Place on a rack in a large roasting pan. Bake, uncovered, at 325° for 1-1/2 hours.

2) For plum sauce, in a saucepan, saute onions in butter until tender. Add jam, chili sauce, grape juice, lemon juice and allspice. Bring to a boil; stir occasionally. Simmer, uncovered, for 10 minutes.

3) Baste roast with sauce. Bake 1 hour longer, or until meat reaches desired doneness (for medium-rare, a meat thermometer should read 145°; medium, 160°; and well-done, 170°), basting occasionally with plum sauce.

4) Bring the remaining sauce to a boil; stir in parsley. Let roast stand for 10-15 minutes before carving. Serve remaining sauce with roast.

Yield: 11 servings.

NUTRITION FACTS: 4 ounces cooked lamb with 1 tablespoon sauce equals 300 calories, 11 g fat (5 g saturated fat), 104 mg cholesterol, 253 mg sodium, 25 g carbohydrate, trace fiber, 26 g protein.

Carving a Leg of Lamb

1) Cut a few 1/4-in. slices on the thin side of the leg and remove to a platter. Turn roast over so it rests on the cut surface.

2) Hold roast steady by using paper towels around bone with one hand. With a carving knife, make a series of 1/4-in. slices along leg down to bone. Then cut along the bone to free slices.

CRUSTY ROAST LEG OF LAMB

Crusty Roast Leg of Lamb

PREP: 20 min. **BAKE:** 2 hours + standing

Millie Vickery, Lena, Illinois

For Easter dinner, St. Patrick's Day or another spring occasion, this tender and flavorful lamb roast is a perfect choice. Potatoes and apples cooked with the meat add to its home-style appeal.

> 1 boneless leg of lamb (4 to 5 pounds)
> 1 cup soft bread crumbs (about 2 slices)
> 2 tablespoons butter, melted
> 1/2 teaspoon herbes de Provence

Dash salt and pepper

> 1 large onion, finely chopped
> 1 can (14-1/2 ounces) chicken broth
> 2-1/2 pounds medium potatoes, peeled and cut into wedges
> 1 large tart apple, sliced

1) Place leg of lamb on a rack in a roasting pan. In a small bowl, combine the bread crumbs, butter and seasonings; spread over meat. Place onion in pan; pour broth over onion. Bake, uncovered, at 325° for 1 hour.

2) Add potatoes; bake 30 minutes longer. Add apple; bake 30 minutes longer or until potatoes are tender and meat reaches desired doneness (for medium-rare, a meat thermometer should read 145°; medium, 160°; well-done, 170°).

3) Remove vegetables and apple and keep warm. Let roast stand for 10-15 minutes before slicing.

Yield: 10 servings.

Editor's Note: Look for herbes de Provence in the spice aisle of your grocery store.

NUTRITION FACTS: 1 serving equals 349 calories, 13 g fat (6 g saturated fat), 116 mg cholesterol, 316 mg sodium, 21 g carbohydrate, 2 g fiber, 36 g protein.

Dijon Leg of Lamb

PREP: 10 min. + marinating
GRILL: 1-1/2 hours + standing

Christy Porter, Englewood, Colorado

This special entree is always on our Easter table, and I serve it for other events all year.

> 1 boneless leg of lamb (4 to 5 pounds)
> 1 cup Dijon mustard
> 1/2 cup soy sauce
> 2 tablespoons olive oil
> 1 tablespoon chopped fresh rosemary *or* 1 teaspoon dried rosemary, crushed
> 1 teaspoon ground ginger
> 1 garlic cloves, minced

1) Cut leg of lamb horizontally from one long side to within 1 in. of opposite side. Open meat so it lies flat; trim and discard fat. Place lamb in a large resealable plastic bag.

2) In a small bowl, whisk the remaining ingredients. Pour 1 cup of marinade over lamb. Seal bag and turn to coat; refrigerate overnight. Cover and refrigerate remaining marinade.

3) Coat grill rack with cooking spray before starting the grill. Prepare grill for indirect heat, using a drip pan. Drain and discard marinade. Place lamb over drip pan.

4) Grill, covered, over medium-low heat for 1-1/2 to 2-1/2 hours or until meat reaches desired doneness (for medium-rare, a meat thermometer should read 145°; medium, 160°; well-done, 170°). Let stand for 10 minutes before slicing. Warm reserved mustard sauce; serve with lamb.

Yield: 9 servings.

NUTRITION FACTS: 4 ounces cooked lamb with 1 tablespoon mustard sauce equals 320 calories, 17 g fat (5 g saturated fat), 113 mg cholesterol, 1,578 mg sodium, 3 g carbohydrate, trace fiber, 38 g protein.

Rack of Lamb

PREP: 10 min. **BAKE:** 30 min.

Bob Paffenroth, Brookfield, Wisconsin

I often bake this rack of lamb and always have great results.

> 4 racks of lamb (1 to 1-1/2 pounds *each*), trimmed
> 2 tablespoons Dijon mustard
> 1 cup soft bread crumbs
> 1/4 cup minced fresh parsley
> 1/4 teaspoon salt
> 1/4 teaspoon pepper
> 1/4 cup butter, melted
> 1 garlic clove, minced

1) Place lamb on a rack in a greased large roasting pan; brush with mustard. In a small bowl, combine the bread crumbs, parsley, salt and pepper. Press onto the meat. Combine butter and garlic; drizzle over the meat.

2) Bake, uncovered, at 375° for 30-35 minutes or until meat reaches desired doneness (for medium-rare, a meat thermometer should read 145°; medium, 160°; well-done, 170°). Remove from the oven and cover loosely with foil. Let stand for 5-10 minutes before slicing.

Yield: 8 servings.

NUTRITION FACTS: 4-1/2 ounces cooked lamb equals 247 calories, 16 g fat (7 g saturated fat), 82 mg cholesterol, 319 mg sodium, 3 g carbohydrate, trace fiber, 21 g protein.

Lamb with Mint Salsa

PREP: 15 min. + marinating **BAKE:** 20 min.

Taste of Home Test Kitchen

Tender slices of meat are served with a refreshing salsa that will have guests licking their lips.

- 5 teaspoons olive oil
- 2 garlic cloves, minced
- 1 teaspoon *each* dried basil, thyme and rosemary, crushed
- 1/2 teaspoon salt
- 1/4 teaspoon pepper
- 2 racks of lamb (8 ribs *each*)

MINT SALSA:

- 1 cup minced fresh mint
- 1 small cucumber, peeled, seeded and chopped
- 1/2 cup seeded chopped tomato
- 1/3 cup finely chopped onion
- 1/3 cup chopped sweet yellow pepper
- 1 jalapeno pepper, seeded and chopped
- 3 tablespoons lemon juice
- 2 tablespoons sugar
- 2 garlic cloves, minced
- 3/4 teaspoon ground ginger
- 1/4 teaspoon salt

1) In a small bowl, combine the oil, garlic and seasonings. Rub over lamb. Place in a roasting pan; cover and refrigerate for 1 hour. In a bowl, combine the salsa ingredients; cover and refrigerate until serving.

2) Bake lamb, uncovered, at 425° for 20-30 minutes or until meat reaches desired doneness (for medium-rare, a meat thermometer should read 145°; medium, 160°; well-done, 170°). Cover loosely with foil and let stand for 5-10 minutes before slicing. Serve with mint salsa.

Yield: 8 servings (2 cups salsa).

Editor's Note: When cutting or seeding hot peppers, use rubber or plastic gloves to protect your hands. Avoid touching your face.

NUTRITION FACTS: 2 ribs with 1/4 cup salsa equals 191 calories, 9 g fat (3 g saturated fat), 60 mg cholesterol, 278 mg sodium, 7 g carbohydrate, 1 g fiber, 20 g protein.

Lamb with Raspberry Sauce

PREP/TOTAL TIME: 30 min.

Scott Beatrice, Lakeland, Florida

I like to surprise my wife with creative dishes like these lamb chops dressed up with a wonderful fruity sauce.

- 2 cups fresh *or* frozen unsweetened raspberries
- 3/4 cup finely chopped seeded peeled cucumber
- 1/2 cup finely chopped peeled tart apple
- 2 tablespoons white grape juice
- 1 to 2 tablespoons sugar
- 4 garlic cloves, minced
- 3 tablespoons olive oil
- 8 lamb loin chops (6 to 7 ounces *each* and 1 to 1-1/2 inches thick)

1) Place raspberries in a blender or food processor; cover and process until pureed. Strain and discard seeds; transfer puree to a small saucepan.

2) Stir in cucumber, apple, grape juice and sugar. Bring to a boil. Reduce heat; simmer, uncovered, for 5-7 minutes or until apple is tender.

3) Meanwhile, in a large skillet, saute garlic in oil until tender. Add lamb chops. Cook, uncovered, for 7-10 minutes on each side or until meat reaches desired doneness (for medium-rare, a meat thermometer should read 145°; medium, 160°; well-done, 170°). Serve with raspberry sauce.

Yield: 4 servings.

NUTRITION FACTS: 1 serving equals 460 calories, 24 g fat (6 g saturated fat), 136 mg cholesterol, 122 mg sodium, 15 g carbohydrate, 5 g fiber, 44 g protein.

LAMB WITH RASPBERRY SAUCE

SPECIAL-OCCASION LAMB CHOPS

 CLASSIC: A homemade mushroom mixture that's sauteed on the stove is tucked into Stuffed Lamb Chops before baking. Mint jelly is a traditional accompaniment.

 TIME-SAVER: Broiling rather than baking trims cooking time from Glazed Lamb Chops, so you can have them table-ready in less than half an hour. They're dressed up with a simple sauce for fast flavor.

 LIGHT: Southwestern Lamb Chops have fewer calories and fat and a mere fraction of the sodium of classic Stuffed Lamb Chops. A lighter sauce made with orange sections, sweet onion and jalapenos adds the finishing touch to the grilled lamb.

 SERVES 2: An elegant dinner for two is a breeze when you start ahead of time by marinating Lemon Herb Lamb Chops. The two chops are broiled for only a few minutes to keep them tender and juicy.

Stuffed Lamb Chops

PREP: 20 min. **BAKE:** 45 min.

Sarah Thompson, Milwaukee, Wisconsin

- 1/2 cup chopped fresh mushrooms
- 1/2 cup finely chopped celery
- 1 tablespoon finely chopped onion
- 2 tablespoons butter
- 1-1/4 cups dry bread crumbs, *divided*
- 1 tablespoon minced fresh parsley
- 3/4 teaspoon salt, *divided*
- 2 eggs, lightly beaten
- 2 tablespoons milk

Dash paprika

- 6 boneless lamb loin chops (1-1/2 inches thick and 5 ounces *each*)

Mint jelly

1) In a large skillet, saute the mushrooms, celery and onion in butter until tender. Stir in 1/2 cup bread crumbs, parsley and 1/4 teaspoon salt; set aside.

2) In a shallow bowl, combine the eggs and milk. In another shallow bowl, combine the paprika and remaining bread crumbs and salt.

3) Cut a pocket in each chop by horizontally cutting almost to the bone; stuff with mushroom mixture. Dip chops in egg mixture, then coat with crumb mixture. Let stand for 5 minutes.

4) Place in an ungreased 9-in. square baking pan. Bake, uncovered, at 400° for 30 minutes. Turn chops over; bake 15 minutes longer or until meat reaches desired doneness (for medium-rare, a meat thermometer should read 145°; medium, 160°; well-done, 170°). Serve with mint jelly.

Yield: 6 servings.

NUTRITION FACTS: 1 stuffed lamb chop (calculated without mint jelly) equals 331 calories, 14 g fat (6 g saturated fat), 161 mg cholesterol, 583 mg sodium, 17 g carbohydrate, 1 g fiber, 32 g protein.

GLAZED LAMB CHOPS

Glazed Lamb Chops

PREP/TOTAL TIME: 25 min.

Mitzi Sentiff, Annapolis, Maryland

- 1/3 cup orange juice concentrate
- 1/3 cup barbecue sauce
- 4 lamb loin chops (1 inch thick and about 6 ounces *each*)

1) In a small saucepan, combine the orange juice concentrate and barbecue sauce. Cook and stir over medium heat for 3-4 minutes or until heated through; set aside 1/3 cup for serving. Spread remaining sauce over both sides of lamb chops. Place on a broiler pan.

2) Broil 4-6 in. from the heat for 4-9 minutes on each side or until meat reaches desired doneness (for medium-rare, a meat thermometer should read 145°; medium, 160°; well-done, 170°). Serve with reserved sauce.

Yield: 4 servings.

NUTRITION FACTS: 1 lamb chop equals 209 calories, 7 g fat (3 g saturated fat), 68 mg cholesterol, 251 mg sodium, 12 g carbohydrate, trace fiber, 22 g protein.

Southwestern Lamb Chops

PREP/TOTAL TIME: 30 min.

Margaret Pache, Mesa, Arizona

- 1 cup orange juice
- 2 jalapeno peppers, seeded and finely chopped
- 1 teaspoon ground cumin
- 1/2 teaspoon salt, optional

Dash pepper

- 3/4 cup halved sliced sweet onion
- 4 teaspoons cornstarch
- 1/4 cup cold water
- 1 cup fresh orange sections
- 2 tablespoons minced fresh cilantro
- 8 lamb loin chops (1 inch thick and 4 ounces *each*)

1) In a small saucepan, combine the orange juice, jalapeno, cumin, salt if desired and pepper. Cook over medium-high heat until mixture begins to simmer. Stir in onion.

2) Combine cornstarch and water until smooth; gradually add to the sauce. Bring to a boil over medium heat; cook and stir for 2 minutes or until thickened and bubbly. Remove from the heat. Stir in oranges and cilantro; keep warm.

3) Grill the lamb chops, covered, over medium heat for 4-9 minutes on each side or until a meat reaches desired doneness (for medium-rare, a meat thermometer should read 145°; medium, 160°; well-done, 170°). Serve with orange sauce.

Yield: 4 servings.

Editor's Note: When cutting or seeding hot peppers, use plastic gloves to protect your hands. Avoid touching your face. Mandarin oranges can be used for orange segments to hurry along this entree. Gently fold into the sauce so they don't break apart.

NUTRITION FACTS: 2 lamb chops equals 281 calories, 10 g fat (3 g saturated fat), 90 mg cholesterol, 83 mg sodium, 18 g carbohydrate, 2 g fiber, 30 g protein.

Lemon Herb Lamb Chops

PREP: 5 min. + marinating **BROIL:** 10 min.

Mildred Sherrer, Fort Worth, Texas

- 1/4 cup olive oil
- 1 tablespoon lemon juice
- 1 garlic clove, minced
- 1 teaspoon grated lemon peel
- 1/4 teaspoon salt
- 1/4 teaspoon dried basil
- 1/4 teaspoon dried rosemary, crushed
- 1/4 teaspoon pepper
- 2 lamb loin chops (1 inch thick and 6 ounces *each*)

1) In a large resealable plastic bag, combine the oil, lemon juice, garlic, lemon peel and seasonings; add the chops. Seal bag and turn to coat; refrigerate for at least 2 hours or overnight.

2) Drain and discard marinade. Broil lamb 3-4 in. from the heat for 4-9 minutes on each side or until meat reaches desired doneness (for medium-rare, a meat thermometer should read 145°; medium, 160°; well-done, 170°).

Yield: 2 servings.

NUTRITION FACTS: 1 lamb chop equals 303 calories, 23 g fat (5 g saturated fat), 68 mg cholesterol, 238 mg sodium, 1 g carbohydrate, trace fiber, 22 g protein.

SOUTHWESTERN LAMB CHOPS

ROCKY MOUNTAIN GRILL

🔥 Rocky Mountain Grill

PREP: 10 min. + marinating **GRILL:** 10 min.

Rick Wertheimer, Englewood, Colorado

Rubbed sage adds wonderful seasoning to the lamb loin chops that also get a little kick from cayenne pepper.

- 2 tablespoons water
- 2 tablespoons red wine vinegar
- 2 tablespoons vegetable oil
- 1-1/2 teaspoons rubbed sage
- 1 teaspoon grated onion
- 1/2 teaspoon lemon-pepper seasoning
- 1/2 teaspoon Dijon mustard
- 1/8 to 1/4 teaspoon cayenne pepper
- 4 bone-in lamb loin chops
  (1 inch thick and 4 ounces *each*)

1) In a small bowl, combine the water, vinegar, oil and seasonings. Pour 1/4 cup into a large resealable plastic bag; add lamb. Seal bag and turn to coat; refrigerate overnight. Cover and refrigerate remaining marinade for basting.

2) Coat grill rack with cooking spray before starting the grill. Drain and discard marinade; grill chops, covered, over medium heat for 4 minutes.

3) Turn; baste with reserved marinade. Grill for 4 minutes. Turn and grill 1-2 minutes longer or until meat reaches desired doneness (for medium-rare, a meat thermometer should read 145°; medium, 160°; well-done, 170°).

Yield: 4 servings.

NUTRITION FACTS: 1 serving equals 151 calories, 10 g fat (2 g saturated fat), 45 mg cholesterol, 95 mg sodium, 1 g carbohydrate, trace fiber, 14 g protein.

Thicker Stews

If your stew needs just a little extra thickening, stir in a few tablespoons of fresh white, whole wheat or rye bread crumbs.

Wyoming Lamb Stew

PREP: 30 min. **BAKE:** 2 hours

Sandra Ramsey, Elk Mountain, Wyoming

I'll often double this recipe and make a big batch because leftovers come in handy around my busy house.

- 5 bacon strips, diced
- 1/4 cup all-purpose flour
- 1 teaspoon salt
- 1/2 teaspoon pepper
- 6 lamb shanks (about 6 pounds)
- 1 can (28 ounces) diced tomatoes, undrained
- 1 can (14-1/2 ounces) beef broth
- 1 can (8 ounces) tomato sauce
- 2 cans (4 ounces *each*) mushroom stems and pieces, drained
- 2 medium onions, chopped
- 1 cup chopped celery
- 1/2 cup minced fresh parsley
- 2 tablespoons prepared horseradish
- 1 tablespoon cider vinegar
- 2 teaspoons Worcestershire sauce
- 1 garlic clove, minced

1) In a Dutch oven, cook bacon over medium heat until crisp. Using a slotted spoon, remove to paper towels to drain, reserving drippings. Set bacon aside.

WYOMING LAMB STEW

2) In a large resealable plastic bag, combine the flour, salt and pepper; add lamb shanks, one at a time, and shake to coat. In bacon drippings, brown shanks on all sides; drain. Add remaining ingredients.

3) Bring to a boil. Cover and bake at 325° for 2 to 2-1/2 hours or until the meat is very tender; skim fat. Garnish with bacon.

Yield: 6 servings.

Editor's Note: If you like, make the stew a day ahead. Cool, then refrigerate. Before reheating, lift off fat from top of stew. Bring to a boil over medium-high heat. Reduce heat; cover and simmer until heated through.

NUTRITION FACTS: 1 serving equals 569 calories, 31 g fat (13 g saturated fat), 171 mg cholesterol, 1,423 mg sodium, 21 g carbohydrate, 5 g fiber, 49 g protein.

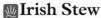Irish Stew

PREP: 5 min. **COOK:** 1-3/4 hours

Lois Gelzer, Cape Elizabeth, Maine

This satisfying stew is chock-full of potatoes, turnips, carrots and lamb. Served with Irish soda bread, it makes a hearty St. Patrick's Day meal.

>   1-1/2 pounds lamb stew meat
>   2 teaspoons olive oil
>   4 cups water
>   2 cups sliced peeled potatoes
>   1 medium onion, sliced
>   1/2 cup sliced carrot
>   1/2 cup cubed turnip
>   1 teaspoon salt
>   1/2 teaspoon *each* dried marjoram, thyme and rosemary, crushed
>   1/8 teaspoon pepper
>   2 tablespoons all-purpose flour
>   2 tablespoons fat-free milk
>   1/2 teaspoon browning sauce, optional
>   3 tablespoons minced fresh parsley

1) In a Dutch oven, brown lamb in oil over medium high heat. Add water; bring to a boil. Reduce heat; cover and simmer for 1 hour.

2) Add the potatoes, onion, carrot, turnip and seasonings. Bring to a boil. Reduce heat; cover and simmer for 30 minutes or until the vegetables are tender.

3) In a small bowl, combine the flour, milk and browning sauce if desired until smooth; stir into stew. Add parsley. Bring to a boil; cook and stir for 2 minutes or until thickened.

Yield: 6 servings.

NUTRITION FACTS: 1-1/2 cups equals 279 calories, 9 g fat (3 g saturated fat), 92 mg cholesterol, 469 mg sodium, 17 g carbohydrate, 2 g fiber, 31 g protein.

HUNGARIAN LAMB STEW

Hungarian Lamb Stew

PREP: 30 min. **COOK:** 2 hours

Joyce Snedden, Casper, Wyoming

Full-flavored Hungarian paprika comes in mild and hot forms, and hot Hungarian paprika packs a punch similar to cayenne pepper. The milder variety works well unless you like a little more kick!

>   3 slices bacon, cut into 1-inch pieces
>   2 medium onions, thinly sliced
>   2 pounds lamb stew meat, cut into 1-inch cubes
>   2 tablespoons Hungarian paprika
>   1 teaspoon salt
>   1 teaspoon caraway seeds
>   1 garlic clove, minced
>   1 medium green pepper, sliced, *divided*
>   1 medium sweet red pepper, sliced, *divided*
>   1 cup water
>   3 medium potatoes, peeled and cut into 3/4-inch pieces
>   1 large tomato, sliced

1) In a Dutch oven, cook bacon over medium heat until crisp. Using a slotted spoon, remove to paper towel. Reserve drippings. Cook onions in drippings until tender. Remove onions. Brown meat in drippings on all sides over medium-high heat.

2) Return bacon and onions to pan along with the paprika, salt, caraway, garlic and half the peppers. Add water. Bring to a boil. Reduce heat; cover and simmer for 1-1/2 hours. Add additional water if necessary.

3) Stir in potatoes and remaining peppers. Bring to a boil. Reduce heat; simmer for 20 minutes. Add tomato; simmer 10 minutes longer or until meat and vegetables are tender.

Yield: 9 servings.

NUTRITION FACTS: 1 cup equals 241 calories, 10 g fat (4 g saturated fat), 71 mg cholesterol, 388 mg sodium, 15 g carbohydrate, 2 g fiber, 23 g protein.

LAMB FAJITAS

Lamb Fajitas

PREP: 15 min. + marinating **COOK:** 15 min.

Bonnie Hiller, Powell, Wyoming

My family enjoys these fajitas, which are a popular change of pace from grilled or roasted lamb.

- 1 boneless leg of lamb *or* lamb shoulder (3 to 4 pounds)
- 1/2 cup vegetable oil
- 1/2 cup lemon juice
- 1/3 cup soy sauce
- 1/3 cup packed brown sugar
- 1/4 cup cider vinegar
- 3 tablespoons Worcestershire sauce
- 1 tablespoon ground mustard
- 1/2 teaspoon pepper
- 1 large green pepper, sliced
- 1 large sweet red pepper, sliced
- 1 large onion, sliced
- 16 flour tortillas (8 inches), warmed

Chopped tomato and cucumber, optional

1) Cut lamb into thin bite-size strips. In a large resealable plastic bag, combine oil, lemon juice, soy sauce, sugar, vinegar, Worcestershire, mustard and pepper; add lamb. Seal bag and turn to coat; refrigerate for 3 hours, turning occasionally.

2) Place the lamb and marinade in a Dutch oven or large saucepan; bring to a boil. Reduce heat; cover and simmer for 8-10 minutes or until meat is tender. Add peppers and onion; cook until vegetables are crisp-tender, about 4 minutes.

3) Using a slotted spoon, place meat and vegetables on tortillas; top with tomato and cucumber if desired. Fold in sides of tortilla and serve.

Yield: 8 servings.

NUTRITION FACTS: 1 serving equals 697 calories, 30 g fat (6 g saturated fat), 95 mg cholesterol, 1,251 mg sodium, 67 g carbohydrate, 1 g fiber, 40 g protein.

Lamb with Apricots

PREP: 15 min. **BAKE:** 1-1/2 hours

Rachel Delano, Tappahannock, Virginia

This was a favorite of mine growing up. Dried apricots add a touch of sweetness to the lamb.

- 1 large onion, chopped
- 2 tablespoons olive oil
- 1 boneless lamb shoulder roast (2-1/2 to 3 pounds), cubed
- 1 teaspoon *each* ground cumin, cinnamon and coriander

Salt and pepper to taste

- 1/2 cup dried apricots, halved
- 1/4 cup orange juice
- 1 tablespoon ground almonds
- 1/2 teaspoon grated orange peel
- 1-1/4 cups chicken broth
- 1 tablespoon sesame seeds, toasted

1) In a large skillet, saute onion in oil until tender. Add the lamb and seasonings. Cook and stir for 5 minutes or until meat is browned. Add apricots, orange juice, almonds and orange peel.

2) Transfer to a 2-1/2-qt. baking dish. Stir in broth. Cover and bake at 350° for 1-1/2 hours or until meat is tender. Sprinkle with sesame seeds.

Yield: 8 servings.

NUTRITION FACTS: 1 cup (calculated without salt and pepper) equals 280 calories, 19 g fat (7 g saturated fat), 70 mg cholesterol, 199 mg sodium, 9 g carbohydrate, 2 g fiber, 19 g protein.

Curried Lamb Stir-Fry

PREP/TOTAL TIME: 15 min.

Priscilla Root, Englewood, Colorado

Apple is a deliciously different addition to this mildly seasoned stir-fry. Tender strips of lamb contrast nicely with the crunchy snow peas and water chestnuts.

- 1 teaspoon cornstarch
- 1/4 teaspoon curry powder
- 1/4 cup chicken broth
- 1 tablespoon soy sauce
- 3/4 pound boneless lamb, cut into 1/8-inch strips
- 1 small onion, chopped
- 2 garlic cloves, minced
- 2 tablespoons vegetable oil, *divided*
- 1 small red apple, chopped
- 1/2 cup chopped green pepper
- 1/2 cup sliced celery
- 1 can (8 ounces) sliced water chestnuts, drained
- 6 ounces fresh *or* frozen snow peas
- 1/4 teaspoon ground ginger

Hot cooked rice

1) In a small bowl, combine cornstarch and curry powder. Stir in broth and soy sauce until smooth; set aside. In a large skillet or wok, saute lamb, onion and garlic in 1 tablespoon oil until meat is browned. Remove and keep warm.

2) In the same skillet, stir-fry apple, green pepper, celery, water chestnuts, peas and ginger in remaining oil until crisp-tender. Add lamb mixture.

3) Stir broth mixture and add to skillet. Bring to a boil; cook and stir for 2 minutes or until thickened. Serve over rice.

Yield: 4 servings.

NUTRITION FACTS: 1 serving (calculated without rice) equals 250 calories, 12 g fat (3 g saturated fat), 47 mg cholesterol, 345 mg sodium, 19 g carbohydrate, 4 g fiber, 18 g protein.

Greek Lamb Kabobs

PREP: 10 min. + marinating **GRILL:** 15 min.

Kathy Herrola, Martinez, California

We have a gas grill and use it year-round, especially to make these tender, juicy kabobs. The lamb marinates overnight, and the attractive skewers can be quickly assembled the next day.

1/2 cup lemon juice
4 teaspoons olive oil
2 tablespoons dried oregano
6 garlic cloves, minced
1 pound boneless lean lamb, cut into 1-inch cubes
16 cherry tomatoes
1 large green pepper, cut into 1-inch pieces
1 large onion, cut into 1-inch wedges

1) In a small bowl, combine the lemon juice, oil, oregano and garlic. Remove 1/4 cup for basting; cover and refrigerate. Pour the remaining marinade into a large resealable plastic bag; add the lamb. Seal bag and turn to coat; refrigerate for at least 8 hours or overnight, turning occasionally.

2) Coat grill rack with cooking spray before starting the grill. Drain and discard marinade from lamb. On eight metal or soaked wooden skewers, alternately thread lamb, tomatoes, green pepper and onion.

3) Grill kabobs, uncovered, over medium heat for 3 minutes on each side. Baste with reserved marinade. Grill 8-10 minutes longer or until meat reaches desired doneness (for medium-rare, a meat thermometer should read 145°; medium, 160°; well-done, 170°), turning and basting frequently.

Yield: 4 servings.

NUTRITION FACTS: 2 kabobs equals 226 calories, 9 g fat (3 g saturated fat), 74 mg cholesterol, 83 mg sodium, 13 g carbohydrate, 2 g fiber, 25 g protein.

Mediterranean Lamb and Bean Salad

PREP: 30 min. + chilling

Lora Winckler, Benton City, Washington

This savory salad combines lamb, artichokes, beans and feta cheese with a tangy dressing. It's also good with chicken or beef in place of the lamb.

1 pound boneless leg of lamb
2 jars (6-1/2 ounces *each*) marinated artichoke hearts, drained
1 can (16 ounces) kidney beans, rinsed and drained
2 cups frozen cut green beans, thawed
1/2 cup julienned sweet red pepper
1/4 cup chopped red onion
1/2 cup fat-free Italian salad dressing
1/4 cup red wine vinegar
1/4 teaspoon pepper
Crumbled reduced-fat feta cheese, optional

1) Grill lamb, covered, over medium heat for 10-20 minutes or until meat reaches desired doneness (for medium-rare, a meat thermometer should read 145°; medium, 160°; well-done, 170°). Cut into cubes.

2) In a large bowl, combine the lamb, artichokes, kidney beans, green beans, red pepper and onion. In a small bowl, combine the salad dressing, vinegar and pepper; drizzle over salad and toss to coat. Cover and refrigerate for at least 4 hours. Serve with feta cheese if desired.

Yield: 6 servings.

Editor's Note: Boneless leg of lamb roasts usually weigh more than one pound. For this recipe cut off the amount needed. Then cut up the rest of the roast for stew or kabobs. Freeze the extra lamb for up to 12 months.

NUTRITION FACTS: 1 cup equals 289 calories, 14 g fat (4 g saturated fat), 43 mg cholesterol, 700 mg sodium, 22 g carbohydrate, 5 g fiber, 19 g protein.

MEDITERRANEAN LAMB AND BEAN SALAD

GREEK PASTA BAKE

Greek Pasta Bake

PREP: 40 min. **BAKE:** 60 min.

Carol Stevens, Basye, Virginia

Lemon and herbs are complemented by the subtle taste of cinnamon in this pasta bake.

- 1/2 pound ground beef
- 1/2 pound ground lamb
- 1 large onion, chopped
- 4 garlic cloves, minced
- 3 teaspoons dried oregano
- 1 teaspoon dried basil
- 1/2 teaspoon salt
- 1/4 teaspoon pepper
- 1/4 teaspoon dried thyme
- 1 can (15 ounces) tomato sauce
- 1 can (14-1/2 ounces) diced tomatoes, undrained
- 1 tablespoon lemon juice
- 1 teaspoon sugar
- 1/4 teaspoon ground cinnamon
- 2 cups uncooked rigatoni *or* large tube pasta
- 4 ounces feta cheese, crumbled

1) In a large skillet, cook beef and lamb over medium heat until no longer pink; drain. Stir in onion, garlic, oregano, basil, salt, pepper and thyme; mix well. Add the tomato sauce, tomatoes and lemon juice.

2) Bring to a boil. Reduce heat; simmer, uncovered, for 20 minutes, stirring occasionally. Stir in the sugar and cinnamon. Simmer, uncovered, 15 minutes longer.

3) Meanwhile, cook the pasta according to package directions; drain. Stir into meat mixture. Transfer to a greased 2-qt. baking dish. Sprinkle with cheese.

4) Cover and bake at 325° for 45 minutes. Uncover; bake 15 minutes longer or until heated through.

Yield: 6 servings.

NUTRITION FACTS: 1 serving equals 316 calories, 12 g fat (6 g saturated fat), 54 mg cholesterol, 840 mg sodium, 29 g carbohydrate, 4 g fiber, 22 g protein.

Herbed Lamb Kabobs

PREP: 15 min. + marinating **GRILL:** 20 min.

Janet Dingler, Cedartown, Georgia

This colorful kabob wouldn't be the same without its delicious herb marinade and tender-crisp vegetables. Together, they add delicious flavor and texture to the lamb pieces.

- 1 cup vegetable oil
- 1 medium onion, chopped
- 1/2 cup lemon juice
- 1/2 cup minced fresh parsley
- 3 to 4 garlic cloves, minced
- 2 teaspoons salt
- 2 teaspoons dried marjoram
- 2 teaspoons dried thyme
- 1/2 teaspoon pepper
- 2 pounds boneless lamb, cut into 1-inch cubes
- 1 medium red onion, cut into wedges
- 1 large green pepper, cut into 1-inch pieces
- 1 large sweet red pepper, cut into 1-inch pieces

1) In a small bowl, combine the oil, onion, lemon juice, parsley, garlic and seasonings. Pour 1 cup into a large resealable plastic bag; add lamb. Seal bag and turn to coat; refrigerate for 6-8 hours. Cover and refrigerate remaining marinade for basting.

2) Drain and discard marinade. On eight metal or soaked wooden skewers, alternately thread the lamb, onion and peppers. Grill, uncovered, over medium heat for 10-13 minutes on each side or until meat reaches desired doneness (for medium-rare, a meat thermometer should read 145°; medium, 160°; well-done, 170°), basting frequently with reserved marinade.

Yield: 8 servings.

NUTRITION FACTS: 1 kabob equals 366 calories, 28 g fat (5 g saturated fat), 69 mg cholesterol, 591 mg sodium, 6 g carbohydrate, 2 g fiber, 22 g protein.

HERBED LAMB KABOBS

lots cookin' at this mission

Family-run business gives away its profits

Molly's work crew

> *Since opening in 2004, we've served more than 20,000 people.*
>
> ~Molly Lloyd

With the help of hard-working family members and hundreds of volunteers, Molly Lloyd of Bainbridge, Ohio, has shown how a catering business can touch hearts, not just stomachs.

She and her siblings have converted an abandoned church in nearby Bourneville into Belltower Mission, a banquet facility for weddings, business meetings and other gatherings. Every dollar minus costs goes to mission work and the community.

"There's nothing fancy; it's all home-style food," says Molly. "My sister-in-law, Denise Litter, and I do most of the cooking, using our own tried-and-true recipes."

Twice-baked potatoes, baked steak, pecan-crusted chicken, homemade rolls and fruit pies are just a few of the popular items on the menu. Says Molly, "Since opening in 2004, we've served more than 20,000 people."

Belltower Mission supports Campus Crusade for Christ and a "church planter" in Africa, several children's charities and other special needs.

Molly traces the start of her charitable venture to 2001, when she prepared meals as a fundraiser for a youth group mission trip. Soon, others began asking her to cater.

She recalls, "One day I was driving through Bourneville, the town where I grew up, and saw a 'for sale' sign outside an old, vacant Presbyterian church I'd always loved. I heard God say, 'I'll give you this building for your mission.'"

Molly, her sister and three brothers (who own a construction company) purchased the church in 2003 and began extensive renovations.

Nine months later, Belltower Mission opened. Family members Mark, Denise, Joe, Kim, Art, Ann and Laura Litter, along with Molly's husband, Byron, help cook, shop, decorate, serve and clean up for events. All leftovers are boxed up as meals for the elderly.

Says Molly, "The community's reaction has been wonderful. Many who have received help have since come to volunteer at Belltower Mission."

DO YOU KNOW A COOK WHO CARES?
If you or someone you know cooks for a charitable, spiritual or other cause, tell us about it at **tasteofhome.com/CookbookBonus**

You can find one of Molly's recipes in the Web exclusive online at tasteofhome.com/CookbookBonus **Type in access code ICare**

Recipes

Tips

Poultry

Beyond chicken, poultry also includes turkey, duck, pheasant, geese and Cornish game hens. This chapter is filled with ways to roast, bake, cook and enjoy poultry in all its forms. Here are some poultry basics to help you get started.

The skin color of chicken ranges from white to deep yellow. The skin color is due to the chicken's diet and is not an indication of freshness or quality.

While duck and geese breasts are darker in color than chicken and turkey breasts, they are still considered white meat. Duck and geese breasts are darker because these birds fly and use their breast muscles more than chickens and turkeys.

Duck and geese are generally found in the freezer case of supermarkets. During the holiday season, it is easier to find them fresh.

Make sure the package of poultry is cold and has no holes or tears. Place package in a plastic bag to prevent it from leaking onto any other groceries.

Purchase before the "sell-by" date on the packaging for best quality. Refrigerate or freeze poultry immediately when you return home from the grocery store. Use uncooked poultry within 1 to 2 days of purchase.

Never defrost frozen poultry at room temperature. Thaw in the refrigerator (see Defrosting Guidelines on page 207), in cold water (see Defrosting in Cold Water on page 207) or in the microwave oven (refer to manufacturer's directions).

Always wash your hands and anything that has come in contact with the uncooked poultry (knives, cutting boards, countertops) with hot, soapy water to avoid contamination with other foods.

Cook poultry breasts to an internal temperature of 170°. Cook whole poultry and dark meat to 180°. Cook ground chicken and turkey to 165°. Stuffing in whole poultry should be cooked to 165°.

Pierce poultry with a fork in several places. The juices of thoroughly cooked poultry should run clear. Cubes and strips of chicken and turkey are cooked when they are no longer pink and juices run clear.

Purchasing Poultry

The amount of poultry you need to buy depends on the variety, portion and amount of bone.

TYPE OF POULTRY	SERVINGS PER POUND
CHICKEN, WHOLE	1 to 2
CHICKEN PARTS (BONE-IN, SKIN ON)	2 to 3
CHICKEN BREASTS (BONELESS, SKINLESS)	3 to 4
TURKEY, WHOLE (12 POUNDS OR LESS)	1
TURKEY, WHOLE (12 POUNDS OR MORE)	2
TURKEY PARTS (THIGHS, BONE-IN BREASTS)	2 to 3
TURKEY BREAST (BONELESS)	3 to 4
DUCK, WHOLE	1
GOOSE, WHOLE	1
CORNISH GAME HENS	1 to 2

Cooking Methods for Poultry

CUT/TYPE	BROIL	FRY	GRILL	ROAST	SAUTE
CHICKEN					
BREAST, CUBES FOR KABOBS	•		•		
BREAST, BONE-IN	•		•	•	
BREAST, BONELESS	•	•	•		
BROILER/FRYER HALVES	•		•	•	
DRUMSTICKS	•	•	•		
PARTS	•	•	•		
THIGHS	•	•			
WHOLE			•	•	
CORNISH GAME HENS					
HALVES	•		•	•	
WHOLE			•	•	
TURKEY					
BREAST (WHOLE & HALF)			•	•	
BREAST TENDERLOIN, CUBES OR STRIPS					•
BREAST TENDERLOINS, WHOLE	•	•	•		
CUTLETS	•	•	•		
GROUND TURKEY PATTIES	•	•	•		
WHOLE			•	•	

Useful Definitions

Refer to the Glossary on pages 24-28 for more terms.

Basted or Self-Basted: The chicken or turkey has been injected or marinated with a solution of water, broth or stock that contains a fat, such as butter, spices and flavor enhancers.

Broiler/Fryer: A chicken about 7 weeks old that weighs 2-1/2 to 4-1/2 pounds.

Capon: A castrated male chicken between 4 and 8 months old that weighs 4 to 7 pounds.

Chicken Leg: The attached drumstick and thigh.

Chicken Quarter: A quarter of the chicken, which may be the leg or breast quarter. The leg quarter contains the drumstick, thigh and portion of the back. The breast quarter contains the breast, wing and portion of the back.

Cornish Game Hen: A small broiler/fryer that is less than 30 days old and weighs 1-1/2 to 2 pounds.

Cut-Up Chicken: A broiler/fryer that has been cut into two breast halves, two thighs, two drumsticks and two wings. It may or may not have the back.

Drummette: The first section of a chicken wing.

Drumstick: The lower portion of the leg.

Free Range or Free Roaming: The poultry was not confined to a chicken house but was allowed outside to forage for food.

Fresh Poultry: Uncooked poultry that has never been commercially stored below 26°.

Giblets: The heart, liver, neck and gizzard.

Hen or Tom Turkey: Indicates whether the turkey was female (hen) or male (tom). Tom turkeys are usually larger than hen turkeys. Hen or tom turkeys should be equally tender.

Roaster: A chicken between 3 and 5 months old that weighs 5 to 7 pounds.

Split Chicken: A broiler/fryer that was cut lengthwise in half.

Roasting Poultry

Remove giblets that are usually stored in a packet in the neck area of the bird. Use for preparing broth if desired. Remove and discard any large pockets of fat that may be present in the neck area.

For whole poultry, drain juices and blot cavity dry with paper towels. Currently, the USDA does not advise washing poultry before cooking. If you do, wash the sink with hot, soapy water or sanitize with a mild bleach solution of 1 teaspoon chlorine bleach to 1 quart of water. This will help prevent cross-contamination to other foods that are washed in the sink.

Rub the inside cavity and neck area with salt. Place breast side up on a rack in a shallow roasting pan.

For chicken, turkey or Cornish game hens, brush the skin with oil or melted butter. For ducklings and geese, prick the skin all over with a fork. This allows the fat from the fat layer under the skin to drip out of the bird while it roasts. With a baster, remove and discard fat from the bottom of the roaster as it accumulates. Because duck and goose drippings are very rich with fat, gravy is not usually prepared from it.

Insert an oven-safe meat thermometer into the thigh area of large birds, not touching bone. Or for large or small birds, use an instant-read thermometer toward the end of roasting time. If the bird needs to cook longer, make sure to remove the instant-read thermometer before you return it to the oven.

Roast, uncovered, without liquid according to the temperature and time given in the chart below or recipe. The roasting times provided in the chart below are for defrosted poultry that is refrigerator cold.

If poultry browns too quickly, tent with foil. Because roasts will continue to cook after being removed from the oven, remove them when the internal temperature is 5-10° below desired doneness. Cover with foil and let stand for 10-20 minutes before removing any stuffing and carving. (See Stuffing, Roasting and Carving a Whole Turkey on page 240.)

TYPE OF POULTRY (*UNSTUFFED)	WEIGHT	COOKING TIME (MINUTES PER POUND)	OVEN TEMP.	DONENESS
BROILER/FRYER CHICKEN	3 to 4 lbs.	23 to 25	350°	180°
ROASTING CHICKEN, WHOLE	5 to 7 lbs.	23 to 25	350°	180°
CAPON, WHOLE	4 to 8 lbs	22 to 30	350°	180°
CORNISH GAME HENS	1-1/4 to 1-1/2 lbs.	50 to 60 (minutes total)	350°	180°
DUCKLING, WHOLE (DOMESTIC)	4 to 6 lbs.	30 to 35	350°	180°
GOOSE, WHOLE (DOMESTIC)	8 to 12 lbs.	15 to 21	350°	180°
TURKEY, WHOLE	8 to 12 lbs. 12 to 14 lbs. 14 to 18 lbs. 18 to 20 lbs. 20 to 24 lbs.	15 to 20 15 to 17 14 to 16 13 to 14 12 to 13-1/2	325°	180°
TURKEY BREAST, WHOLE	4 to 6 lbs.	22 to 30	325°	170°
TURKEY BREAST, HALF	1-3/4 to 3-1/2 lbs.	35 to 40	325°	170°
TURKEY BREAST, ROAST	1-1/4 to 1-3/4 lbs.	45 to 60	325°	170°

* For stuffed birds, add 15 to 45 minutes to the roasting time.

Poultry Grilling Chart

Chicken and turkey breasts and turkey tenderloins are done when they reach a temperature of 170°; whole chickens and turkeys at 180° as measured in the thigh.

Kabobs and strips are done when juices run clear. Ground chicken or turkey patties are done at 165°. For direct grilling, turn meat halfway through grilling time.

CUT	WEIGHT OR THICKNESS	HEAT	COOKING TIME
CHICKEN			
BROILER/FRYER, WHOLE	3 to 4 lbs.	Medium/Indirect	1-1/4 to 1-3/4 hours
ROASTER, WHOLE	5 to 6 lbs.	Medium/Indirect	1-3/4 to 2-1/4 hours
MEATY BONE-IN PIECES, BREAST HALVES, LEGS, QUARTERS	1-1/4 to 1-1/2 lbs.	Medium/Indirect or Medium/Direct	40 to 50 min. 35 to 45 min.
BONE-IN THIGHS, DRUMSTICKS, WINGS	3 to 7 oz. *each*	Medium-Low/Direct or Medium/Indirect	15 to 30 min. 20 to 30 min.
BREAST HALVES, BONELESS	6 oz. *each*	Medium/Direct	10 to 15 min.
KABOBS	1-in. cubes	Medium/Direct	10 to 15 min.
CORNISH GAME HENS	1-1/2 to 2 lbs.	Medium/Indirect	45 to 60 min.
TURKEY			
WHOLE, UNSTUFFED	8 to 11 lbs.	Medium/Indirect	2 to 3 hours
	12 to 16 lbs.	Medium/Indirect	3 to 4 hours
BREAST (BONE-IN)	4 to 5 lbs.	Medium/Indirect	1-1/2 to 2 hours
BREAST (BONELESS)	1-1/4 to 1-3/4 lbs.	Medium/Indirect	1 to 1-1/4 hours
TENDERLOINS	8 oz.	Medium/Direct	15 to 20 min.
DRUMSTICKS OR THIGHS	1/2 to 1-1/2 lbs.	Medium/Indirect	45 to 75 min.
PATTY	4 oz. and 1/2 in.	Medium/Direct	10 to 12 min.

Baking Chicken Pieces

Here are general guidelines for baking chicken pieces. Sauces and additional ingredients may affect cooking time and/or temperature. Place chicken pieces in a single layer in a baking pan. Bake, uncovered, for the time listed in the chart below.

TYPE OF POULTRY	WEIGHT	COOKING TIME at 350° to 375° (in minutes)	DONENESS
CHICKEN BREAST, BONE-IN	6-8 oz. *each*	30 to 40	170°
CHICKEN BREAST, BONELESS	4 oz. *each*	20 to 30	170°
CHICKEN LEGS	8 oz. *each*	40 to 50	180°
CHICKEN THIGHS	4 oz. *each*	40 to 50	180°
CHICKEN DRUMSTICKS	4 oz. *each*	35 to 45	180°
CHICKEN WINGS	2 to 3 oz. *each*	30 to 40	Juices run clear

Defrosting Guidelines

Defrosting times for poultry depend on the weight and thickness of the package. When defrosting poultry in the refrigerator, place a tray under the package to catch any liquid or juices and to keep the refrigerator clean. Here are some timelines for defrosting poultry in the refrigerator:

- For bone-in parts or a small whole chicken, allow at least 1 to 2 days.
- For duck or goose parts, allow at least 1 day.
- For a whole duck or goose, allow at least 2 days.
- For a whole turkey or large whole chicken, allow 24 hours for every 4 pounds.

Defrosting in Cold Water

Cold-water thawing is an option that takes less time than thawing in the refrigerator but requires more attention.

The poultry must be in a leakproof bag such as its original, tightly sealed wrapper. If its package is not leakproof, place it in a heavy-duty resealable plastic bag.

Submerge the wrapped poultry in cold tap water. Change the water every 30 minutes until the bird is thawed. For this method, allow 30 minutes for every pound.

Storing Leftovers

Any perishable food should not stand at room temperature for longer than 2 hours. So within 2 hours of roasting, the poultry meat should be removed from the carcass and put away in the refrigerator or freezer. If desired, slice, cube or cut the meat into strips. Leftover poultry parts or pieces can be packaged without being cut up.

Meat and leftover poultry casseroles can be refrigerated for 3 to 4 days, stuffing for up to 3 days and gravy for 2 days. Stuffing can be frozen for 1 to 2 months, and meat and casseroles for up to 6 months. Homemade gravy does not freeze well.

Cutting Up a Whole Chicken

1) Pull the leg and thigh away from the body. With a small sharp knife, cut through the skin to expose the joint.

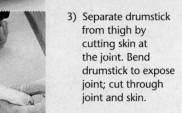

2) Cut through joint, then cut skin around thigh to free leg. Repeat with other leg.

3) Separate drumstick from thigh by cutting skin at the joint. Bend drumstick to expose joint; cut through joint and skin.

4) Pull wing away from the body. Cut through skin to expose joint. Cut through joint and skin to separate wing from body. Repeat.

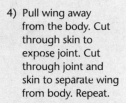

5) Snip along each side of the backbone between rib joints with kitchen or poultry shears.

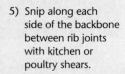

6) Hold chicken breast in both hands (skin side down) and bend it back to snap breastbone. Turn over. With a knife, cut in half along breastbone. Breastbone will remain attached to one of the halves.

SUNDAY STUFFED CHICKEN

 CLASSIC: Apple-Stuffed Chicken combines apples and nuts in a stuffing mix for a whole broiler/fryer. It roasts in the oven for over an hour until it's crispy and golden.

 TIME-SAVER: You'll get the dining experience of a stuffed chicken in half the time with Corny Chicken Bake. This all-in-one casserole takes advantage of a corn bread stuffing mix and boneless chicken breasts, and bakes in just 25 minutes.

 LIGHT: The package directions for the stuffing mix in Apple-Stuffed Chicken call for 1/4 cup butter. By switching to a rice-based stuffing, Roasted Chicken with Basil-Rice Stuffing eliminates the fat and calories from the butter. Removing the skin before serving also cuts the calories.

SERVES 2: Glazed Cornish Hen with Rice Pilaf gives you the look of a stuffed chicken but in a size perfectly suited for two.

APPLE-STUFFED CHICKEN

Apple-Stuffed Chicken
PREP: 20 min. **BAKE:** 1 hour 20 min. + standing
Joan Wrigley, Lynden, Washington

- 1 package (6 ounces) chicken-flavored stuffing mix
- 1 broiler/fryer chicken (3-1/2 to 4 pounds)
- 1/2 teaspoon salt
- 1/4 teaspoon pepper
- 1 tablespoon vegetable oil
- 1 cup chopped peeled apple
- 1/4 cup chopped celery
- 1/4 cup chopped walnuts
- 1/4 cup raisins
- 1/2 teaspoon grated lemon peel

GLAZE:
- 1/2 cup apple jelly
- 1 tablespoon lemon juice
- 1/2 teaspoon ground cinnamon

1) Prepare stuffing according to package directions. Meanwhile, sprinkle inside of chicken with salt and pepper; rub outside with oil.

2) In a large bowl, mix stuffing with the apple, celery, nuts, raisins and lemon peel. Lightly stuff chicken. Place breast side up on a rack in a shallow roasting pan. Bake, uncovered, at 350° for 1 hour.

3) In a saucepan, combine the glaze ingredients. Bring to a simmer; heat, uncovered, for 3 minutes. Brush over chicken.

4) Bake 20-30 minutes longer or until a meat thermometer reads 180°, brushing occasionally with glaze. Cover with foil and let stand for 10-15 minutes. Remove stuffing, then carve chicken.

Yield: 6 servings.

NUTRITION FACTS: 1 serving equals 547 calories, 23 g fat (5 g saturated fat), 102 mg cholesterol, 806 mg sodium, 46 g carbohydrate, 2 g fiber, 38 g protein.

Corny Chicken Bake
PREP: 15 min. **BAKE:** 25 min.
Barbara Ramstack, Fond du Lac, Wisconsin

- 3 cups corn bread stuffing mix
- 1 can (14-3/4 ounces) cream-style corn
- 1/3 cup finely chopped onion
- 1 celery rib, chopped
- 4 boneless skinless chicken breast halves (4 ounces *each*)
- 1/4 cup packed brown sugar
- 1/4 cup butter, melted
- 3 tablespoons spicy brown mustard

1) In a large bowl, combine the stuffing mix, corn, onion and celery. Spoon into a greased 11-in. x 7-in. x 2-in. baking dish. Top with chicken.

2) In a small bowl, combine the brown sugar, butter and mustard; drizzle over the chicken. Bake, uncovered, at 400° for 25-30 minutes or until chicken juices run clear.

Yield: 4 servings.

NUTRITION FACTS: 1 serving equals 438 calories, 14 g fat (7 g saturated fat), 46 mg cholesterol, 1,353 mg sodium, 65 g carbohydrate, 3 g fiber, 12 g protein.

ROASTED CHICKEN WITH BASIL-RICE STUFFING

Roasted Chicken with Basil-Rice Stuffing

PREP: 25 min. **BAKE:** 1 hour + standing

Edna Hoffman, Hebron, Indiana

- 1/4 cup chopped celery
- 1-1/2 teaspoons butter
- 1 cup cooked long grain rice
- 2 tablespoons minced fresh parsley
- 1 tablespoon sliced green onion
- 1 tablespoon minced fresh basil *or* 1 teaspoon dried basil
- 2-1/4 teaspoons sunflower kernels *or* chopped almonds
- 1/8 teaspoon salt

Dash pepper

- 1 broiler/fryer chicken (3 pounds)

1) In a small skillet, saute celery in butter until crisp-tender. In a large bowl, combine the celery, rice, parsley, onion, basil, sunflower kernels, salt and pepper. Stuff chicken. Tie drumsticks together with kitchen string if desired. Place breast side up on a rack in a roasting pan.

2) Bake, uncovered, at 350° for 1 to 1-1/4 hours or until juices run clear and a meat thermometer reads 180° for chicken and 165° for stuffing. Cover and let stand for 10 minutes. Remove and discard skin. Remove stuffing, then carve chicken.

Yield: 3-4 servings.

NUTRITION FACTS: 1 serving equals 311 calories, 11 g fat (3 g saturated fat), 114 mg cholesterol, 191 mg sodium, 12 g carbohydrate, 1 g fiber, 38 g protein.

Glazed Cornish Hen With Rice Pilaf

PREP: 70 min. **BAKE:** 45 min. + standing

Taste of Home Test Kitchen

- 1 cup cooked long grain rice
- 1/2 cup cooked wild rice
- 1/2 cup chopped peeled tart apple
- 1/4 cup white wine *or* apple juice
- 2 tablespoons slivered almonds
- 1/4 teaspoon salt
- 1/4 teaspoon poultry seasoning

Dash curry powder

- 1/4 cup peach preserves
- 1 tablespoon Dijon mustard
- 1 teaspoon prepared horseradish
- 1/4 teaspoon dried tarragon
- 1 Cornish game hen (20 ounces), split lengthwise

1) In a bowl, combine the first eight ingredients; set aside. In a small saucepan, combine the preserves, mustard, horseradish and tarragon. Cook and stir over medium heat until preserves are melted.

2) Carefully loosen skin around hen breast, thighs and drumsticks. Set aside 1/4 cup glaze; spoon remaining glaze under skin.

3) Place the rice mixture in two mounds in an 11-in. x 7-in. x 2-in. baking dish coated with cooking spray; arrange hen halves skin side up over rice.

4) Bake, uncovered, at 400° for 45-55 minutes or until meat juices run clear. Let stand for 10 minutes. Warm reserved glaze. Remove and discard skin from hen halves; brush with glaze.

Yield: 2 servings.

NUTRITION FACTS: 1 Cornish hen half (skin removed), with 1 cup rice mixture equals 516 calories, 89 g fat (1 g saturated fat), 1,117 mg cholesterol, 890 mg sodium, 71 g carbohydrate, 23 g fiber, 331 g protein.

EASY WAY TO REMOVE STUFFING ■■■

When baking a stuffed turkey or chicken, I put the stuffing on a square of cheesecloth and tie it in a loose knot. I then stuff the knotted cheesecloth into the bird and roast as usual. To serve, I simply remove the cheesecloth. This eliminates scooping.

—Beth W., Bremerton, Washington

Harvest Stuffed Chicken

PREP: 20 min. **BAKE:** 2-1/4 hours + standing

Jodi Cigel, Stevens Point, Wisconsin

This roasted chicken is easy enough to prepare every day, yet special enough for company. The corn bread and fresh savory enhance the flavor of the homemade stuffing.

- 1 package (7-1/2 ounces) corn bread/muffin mix, prepared as directed and crumbled *or* 3 cups corn bread crumbs
- 3 cups unseasoned stuffing croutons
- 1/2 cup *each* chopped celery, fresh mushrooms and fully cooked ham
- 1/4 cup chopped sweet red pepper
- 1/4 cup chopped green onions
- 4 teaspoons chopped fresh savory *or* 1 teaspoon dried savory
- 3/4 teaspoon salt
- 1/2 teaspoon pepper
- 3 tablespoons vegetable oil
- 1 to 1-1/2 cups chicken broth
- 1 roasting chicken (6 to 7 pounds)

1) In a large bowl, combine corn bread crumbs and croutons. In a large skillet, saute the celery, mushrooms, ham, red pepper, onions, savory, salt and pepper in oil until vegetables are tender. Add to crumb mixture. Stir in enough broth to moisten.

2) Stuff chicken. Place breast side up on a rack in a large roasting pan.

3) Bake, uncovered, at 350° for 2-1/4 to 3 hours or until a meat thermometer reads 180° for chicken and 165° for stuffing. Let stand for 10-15 minutes before removing stuffing and carving.

Yield: 6 servings.

Editor's Note: Stuffing may be baked separately in a 2-qt. covered baking dish at 350° for 45 minutes.

NUTRITION FACTS: 1 serving equals 817 calories, 44 g fat (11 g saturated fat), 193 mg cholesterol, 1,179 mg sodium, 39 g carbohydrate, 2 g fiber, 63 g protein.

■ **Herb-Rubbed Stuffed Chicken:** In a small bowl, combine 1 teaspoon *each* onion salt and vegetable oil, 1/2 teaspoon *each* dried thyme and dried rosemary, crushed, and 1/4 teaspoon *each* grated orange peel and pepper. Rub over chicken before baking.

Poultry Tips

A 3-1/2-pound whole chicken will yield about 3 cups of diced cooked chicken.

If you don't plan to stuff a whole chicken or turkey, place 1 to 2 cups total of chopped celery, carrot and onion into the cavity. These veggies will add some flavor to the pan juices. Discard vegetables before carving.

HARVEST STUFFED CHICKEN

Golden Glazed Fryer

PREP: 10 min. **GRILL:** 40 min.

Peggy West, Georgetown, Delaware

This moist, grilled chicken has a pleasant coating that's a nice change of pace from tomato-based sauces. This recipe has been passed down in my family for generations.

- 1 broiler/fryer chicken (3 to 4 pounds), cut up
- 1/2 cup vegetable oil
- 1/2 cup cider vinegar
- 1 egg, lightly beaten
- 4 teaspoons salt
- 1-1/2 teaspoons poultry seasoning
- 1/4 teaspoon pepper

1) Coat grill rack with cooking spray before starting the grill. Grill chicken, covered, skin side down over medium heat for 15 minutes. Turn; cover and grill 15 minutes longer.

2) Meanwhile, combine the remaining ingredients; brush over chicken. Grill for 5 minutes. Turn and brush with glaze; grill 5 minutes longer or until a meat thermometer reads 180° in the thigh and 170° in the breast. Discard any unused glaze.

Yield: 6 servings.

NUTRITION FACTS: 1 serving equals 334 calories, 24 g fat (5 g saturated fat), 105 mg cholesterol, 867 mg sodium, 1 g carbohydrate, trace fiber, 28 g protein.

Apricot-Glazed Cornish Hens

PREP: 20 min. **BAKE:** 1-1/4 hours

Ruth Andrewson, Leavenworth, Washington

These flavorful hens are a tasty sized-right twist on the conventional bird. Filled with a well-seasoned stuffing, they make perfect individual servings.

- 3 tablespoons chopped celery
- 3 tablespoons chopped onion
- 1/4 cup butter, cubed

3 cups dry bread cubes

1 can (4 ounces) mushroom stems and pieces, drained

1-1/2 teaspoons poultry seasoning

1/2 teaspoon rubbed sage

1/4 teaspoon salt

1/4 teaspoon pepper

3 to 4 tablespoons chicken broth

4 Cornish game hens (20 ounces *each*)

1 jar (12 ounces) apricot preserves, warmed

4 green onions (green part only), optional

Fresh rosemary sprigs, optional

1) In a large skillet, saute celery and onion in butter until tender; remove from the heat. Add the bread cubes, mushrooms and seasonings. Stir in enough broth just to moisten.

2) Stuff hens. Tie drumsticks together. Place breast side up on a rack in a large shallow baking pan. Cover and bake at 350° for 45 minutes.

3) Brush with preserves. Bake, uncovered, 30-45 minutes longer or until meat juices run clear, basting every 10-15 minutes.

4) If using green onions, first soften them in boiling water or the microwave for a few seconds, then tie over the string used to tie the drumsticks together. Garnish platter with rosemary if desired.

Yield: 4 servings.

NUTRITION FACTS: 1 Cornish hen with 1/4 of the stuffing equals 1,009 calories, 42 g fat (15 g saturated fat), 216 mg cholesterol, 1,239 mg sodium, 116 g carbohydrate, 4 g fiber, 43 g protein.

Chicken and Rice Dinner

PREP: 15 min. **BAKE:** 55 min.

Denise Baumert, Dalhart, Texas

In this easy and tasty recipe, the chicken bakes up to a beautiful golden brown while the moist rice is packed with flavor. The taste is unbeatable.

1 broiler/fryer chicken (3-1/2 to 4 pounds), cut up

1/4 to 1/3 cup all-purpose flour

2 tablespoons vegetable oil

2-1/3 cups water

1-1/2 cups uncooked long grain rice

1 cup milk

1 teaspoon salt

1 teaspoon poultry seasoning

1/2 teaspoon pepper

Minced fresh parsley

1) Dredge chicken pieces in flour. In a large skillet, brown chicken on all sides in oil over medium heat.

2) In a large bowl, combine the next six ingredients. Pour into a greased 13-in. x 9-in. x 2-in. baking dish. Top with chicken.

3) Cover lightly with foil. Bake at 350° for 55 minutes or until rice and chicken are tender and a meat thermometer inserted in chicken reads 180°. Sprinkle with parsley before serving.

Yield: 6 servings.

NUTRITION FACTS: 3 ounces cooked chicken (skin removed) with 3/4 cup rice mixture equals 541 calories, 23 g fat (6 g saturated fat), 108 mg cholesterol, 504 mg sodium, 43 g carbohydrate, 1 g fiber, 38 g protein.

NO-FUSS GLAZE ■■■

To make an excellent glaze for chicken, turkey or pork, I combine a half cup of whatever jelly or jam I have on hand with a tablespoon of Dijon mustard. Apricot jam and red currant jelly work well. If the spread is on the tart side (like orange marmalade), I add brown sugar.

—Isabel K., Longville, Minnesota

Brunswick Stew

PREP: 1 hour + cooling **COOK:** 45 min.

Mildred Sherrer, Fort Worth, Texas

This stew is a traditional dish from the Southeast. My version, containing beans, vegetables and chicken, turns out great every time.

1 broiler/fryer chicken (3-1/2 to 4 pounds), cut up

1 cup water

4 medium potatoes, peeled and cubed

2 medium onions, sliced

1 can (15-1/4 ounces) lima beans, rinsed and drained

1 teaspoon salt

1/2 teaspoon pepper

Dash cayenne pepper

1 can (15-1/4 ounces) whole kernel corn, drained

1 can (14-1/2 ounces) diced tomatoes, undrained

1/4 cup butter, cubed

1/2 cup dry bread crumbs

1) In a Dutch oven, slowly bring the chicken and water to a boil. Cover and simmer for 45-60 minutes or until chicken is tender, skimming the surface as foam rises.

2) Remove chicken and set aside until cool enough to handle. Remove and discard skin and bones. Cube chicken and return to broth.

3) Add the potatoes, onions, beans and seasonings. Bring to a boil. Reduce heat; simmer, uncovered, for 30 minutes or until potatoes are tender. Stir in remaining ingredients. Simmer, uncovered, for 10 minutes or until slightly thickened.

Yield: 6 servings.

NUTRITION FACTS: 1 serving equals 589 calories, 25 g fat (9 g saturated fat), 123 mg cholesterol, 1,147 mg sodium, 47 g carbohydrate, 7 g fiber, 40 g protein.

DOWN-HOME FRIED CHICKEN

 CLASSIC: Fried chicken is comfort food at its best. In Buttermilk Fried Chicken with Gravy, the chicken is first soaked in buttermilk to help tenderize it before frying. The chicken is served with a milk-based gravy for a Southern flair.

 TIME-SAVER: Jump on the fast track with Fried Chicken Nuggets. Cubes of chicken breast are dipped in a pancake batter, then deep-fat fried. Frying small pieces of boneless chicken cuts the actual cooking time to 5 minutes per batch.

 LIGHT: The cooking method makes all the difference in Oven-Fried Chicken. It bakes in the oven, eliminating the oil absorbed during frying. So there's much less fat per serving.

 SERVES 2: Who needs a whole chicken when Country Fried Chicken calls for just chicken thighs and drumsticks? They're breaded and fried to yield two generous servings of juicy fried chicken.

Buttermilk Fried Chicken With Gravy
PREP: 15 min. + chilling **COOK:** 1 hour

Vera Reid, Laramie, Wyoming

- 1 broiler/fryer chicken (3-1/2 to 4 pounds), cut up
- 1 cup buttermilk
- 1 cup all-purpose flour
- 1-1/2 teaspoons salt
- 1/2 teaspoon pepper

Oil for frying

GRAVY:

- 3 tablespoons all-purpose flour
- 1 cup milk
- 1-1/2 to 2 cups water

Salt and pepper, optional

1) Place the chicken in a large shallow dish. Pour buttermilk over; cover and refrigerate for 1 hour. Combine the flour, salt and pepper in a large resealable plastic bag. Drain chicken; add to flour mixture, one piece at a time, and shake to coat. Shake off excess; let stand on waxed paper for 15 minutes before frying.

2) Heat 1/8 to 1/4 in. of oil in a large skillet; fry chicken until browned on all sides. Cover and simmer, turning occasionally, for 40-45 minutes or until juices run clear and chicken is tender. Uncover and cook 5 minutes longer. Remove chicken; drain on paper towels and keep warm.

3) Drain all but 1/4 cup drippings from skillet; stir in flour until blended. Gradually add milk, then 1-1/2 cups water. Bring to a boil over medium heat; cook and stir for 2 minutes or until thickened. Add remaining water if needed. Season with salt and pepper if desired. Serve with chicken.

Yield: 6 servings.

NUTRITION FACTS: 1 serving equals 532 calories, 34 g fat (7 g saturated fat), 108 mg cholesterol, 611 mg sodium, 17 g carbohydrate, 1 g fiber, 36 g protein.

■ **Tasty Fried Chicken:** To the flour mixture, add 1 tablespoon paprika, 1/2 teaspoon *each* garlic powder and onion powder, 1/4 teaspoon *each* rubbed sage and dried thyme and 1/8 teaspoon baking powder. Prepare as directed.

■ **Home-Style Fried Chicken:** To the flour mixture, add 1/4 teaspoon *each* ground cumin, dried oregano and paprika. Prepare as directed.

Fried Chicken Nuggets
PREP/TOTAL TIME: 25 min.

Dorothy Smith, El Dorado, Arkansas

- 2-1/2 pounds boneless skinless chicken breasts, cut into 1-inch cubes
- 2-2/3 cups pancake mix
- 1-1/2 cups lemon-lime soda
- 1/4 cup butter, melted

Oil for deep-fat frying

1) Place chicken in a 2-qt. microwave-safe bowl. Cover and microwave on high for 6-8 minutes or

BUTTERMILK FRIED CHICKEN WITH GRAVY

until juices run clear, stirring every 2 minutes; drain. In a shallow bowl, combine the pancake mix, soda and butter.

2) Heat oil in an electric skillet or deep-fat fryer to 375°. Dip chicken cubes into batter; fry in oil, in batches, for about 2 minutes on each side or until golden brown. Drain on paper towels.

Yield: 8-10 servings.

NUTRITION FACTS: 3 ounces cooked chicken equals 382 calories, 19 g fat (4 g saturated fat), 75 mg cholesterol, 482 mg sodium, 26 g carbohydrate, 2 g fiber, 26 g protein.

OVEN-FRIED CHICKEN

Oven-Fried Chicken

PREP: 10 min. **BAKE:** 50 min.

Daucia Brooks, Westmoreland, Tennessee

- 1/2 cup cornmeal
- 1/2 cup dry bread crumbs
- 1 teaspoon dried tarragon
- 1 teaspoon ground ginger
- 1/2 teaspoon salt
- 1/4 teaspoon cayenne pepper
- 1/4 teaspoon pepper
- 3 egg whites
- 2 tablespoons fat-free milk
- 1/2 cup all-purpose flour
- 6 bone-in chicken breast halves
  (6 ounces *each*)

Refrigerated butter-flavored spray

1) In a shallow bowl, combine the first seven ingredients. In another shallow bowl, whisk egg whites and milk. Place flour in a third shallow bowl. Coat chicken with flour; dip in the egg white mixture, then roll in cornmeal mixture.

2) Place in a 15-in. x 10-in. x 1-in. baking pan coated with cooking spray. Bake, uncovered, at 350° for 40 minutes. Spritz with butter-flavored spray. Bake 10-15 minutes longer or until juices run clear and a meat thermometer reads 170°.

Yield: 6 servings.

Editor's Note: This recipe was tested with I Can't Believe It's Not Butter Spray.

NUTRITION FACTS: 1 chicken breast half equals 248 calories, 2 g fat (1 g saturated fat), 63 mg cholesterol, 375 mg sodium, 24 g carbohydrate, 1 g fiber, 30 g protein.

Country Fried Chicken

PREP: 10 min. **COOK:** 25 min.

Rebekah Miller, Rocky Mountain, Virginia

- 1/3 cup all-purpose flour
- 1 teaspoon garlic salt
- 1 teaspoon pepper
- 1/2 teaspoon paprika
- 1/4 teaspoon poultry seasoning
- 1 egg
- 1/4 cup 2% milk
- 2 bone-in chicken thighs
  (6 ounces *each*)
- 2 chicken drumsticks
  (4 ounces *each*)
- 1/3 cup canola oil

1) In a large resealable plastic bag, combine the first five ingredients. In a shallow bowl, beat the egg and milk. Add chicken to bag, a few pieces at a time, and shake to coat. Dip into egg mixture, then return to flour mixture and shake again. Remove from bag and let stand for 5 minutes.

2) Fry chicken in oil until golden brown on all sides. Reduce heat to medium; cook until a meat thermometer reads 180°, about 15 minutes.

Yield: 2 servings.

NUTRITION FACTS: 1 serving equals 732 calories, 56 g fat (8 g saturated fat), 213 mg cholesterol, 1,053 mg sodium, 19 g carbohydrate, 1 g fiber, 37 g protein.

COUNTRY FRIED CHICKEN

NO-MESS BREADED CHICKEN ■■■

When breading chicken, I coat the pieces with mayonnaise instead of egg. The mayonnaise clings to the chicken and doesn't drip like the egg does. Plus, it adds nice flavor.

—*Vita G., Central Islip, New York*

Chicken and Dumplings

PREP: 15 min. **COOK:** 1 hour 50 min.

Edna Hoffman, Hebron, Indiana

Made with homemade broth and dumplings, this dish is an old-fashioned treat. It's worth the effort to enjoy its wonderful flavors.

- 1 broiler/fryer chicken (3-1/2 to 4 pounds), cut up
- 2 to 2-1/4 quarts water
- 1/2 cup sliced celery
- 1/2 cup sliced carrots
- 2 fresh parsley sprigs
- 1 bay leaf
- 1 teaspoon salt
- 1/4 teaspoon pepper

DUMPLINGS:

- 3/4 cup all-purpose flour
- 1 tablespoon minced fresh parsley
- 1 teaspoon baking powder
- 1/4 teaspoon salt
- Dash ground nutmeg
- 1/3 cup milk
- 1 egg, lightly beaten
- 1 tablespoon vegetable oil

GRAVY:

- 1/4 cup all-purpose flour
- 1/2 cup water
- 1/4 teaspoon salt
- 1/8 teaspoon pepper

1) In a large Dutch oven, combine the first eight ingredients. Slowly bring to a boil over low heat. Cover and simmer for 45-60 minutes or until meat is tender, skimming surface as foam rises.

2) In a bowl, combine the flour, parsley, baking powder, salt and nutmeg; stir in milk, egg and oil just until moistened. Drop batter by tablespoonfuls onto simmering broth.

3) Cover and simmer for 12-15 minutes or until a toothpick inserted in a dumpling comes out clean (do not lift the cover while simmering). Remove the dumplings and chicken with a slotted spoon to a serving dish; keep warm.

4) Strain broth, discarding vegetables and bay leaf and reserving 2 cups for gravy. (Remaining broth can be covered and refrigerated for up to 3 days or frozen for 4-6 months.)

5) Place reserved broth in a saucepan; bring to a boil. Combine flour, water, salt and pepper until smooth; gradually stir into broth. Cook and stir over medium heat for 2 minutes or until thickened. Pour over chicken and dumplings.

Yield: 4 servings.

NUTRITION FACTS: 1 serving equals 606 calories, 30 g fat (8 g saturated fat), 209 mg cholesterol, 1,144 mg sodium, 25 g carbohydrate, 1 g fiber, 54 g protein.

Stuffing Bone-In Chicken Breasts

1) Work fingers under the skin to loosen and form a pocket.

2) Lightly fill each pocket with the stuffing mixture. Proceed with recipe.

Spinach-Stuffed Chicken

PREP: 15 min. **BAKE:** 1 hour

Barbara Eitemiller, Churchville, Maryland

A mixture of spinach, spices and three kinds of cheese is tucked into these chicken breasts. They bake to a beautiful golden brown, so they look lovely on the plate, too.

- 2 packages (10 ounces *each*) frozen chopped spinach, thawed and squeezed dry
- 1 cup (4 ounces) shredded Swiss cheese
- 3/4 cup ricotta cheese
- 1/3 cup grated Parmesan cheese
- 3 tablespoons finely chopped onion
- 1 garlic clove, minced
- 1/4 teaspoon salt
- 1/4 teaspoon ground nutmeg
- 1/4 teaspoon pepper

SPINACH-STUFFED CHICKEN

6 bone-in chicken breast halves
(8 ounces *each*)
2 tablespoons olive oil
1 teaspoon paprika
1/2 teaspoon dried oregano
1/2 teaspoon dried thyme
Additional paprika, optional

1) In a large bowl, combine the spinach, cheeses, onion, garlic, salt, nutmeg and pepper. Carefully loosen the skin on one side of each chicken breast half to form a pocket.

2) Stuff 1/2 cup spinach mixture into each pocket. Place chicken skin side up in a greased 15-in. x 10-in. x 1-in. baking pan. Combine the oil, paprika, oregano and thyme; brush over chicken. Sprinkle with additional paprika if desired.

3) Bake, uncovered, at 350° for 1 to 1-1/4 hours or until a meat thermometer inserted into the breast meat reads 170° and juices run clear.

Yield: 6 servings.

NUTRITION FACTS: 1 stuffed chicken breast half equals 461 calories, 24 g fat (10 g saturated fat), 144 mg cholesterol, 430 mg sodium, 7 g carbohydrate, 3 g fiber, 53 g protein.

Garlic Lime Chicken

PREP: 15 min. + marinating **BAKE:** 30 min.

Dorothy Smith, El Dorado, Arkansas

I love garlic, and this golden-brown chicken with its fragrant spices and citrus tang is an excellent way to showcase its flavor.

1/2 cup lime juice
1/4 cup cider vinegar
6 garlic cloves, minced
2 tablespoons minced fresh oregano *or* 2 teaspoons dried oregano
1 tablespoon dried coriander
2 teaspoons pepper
1 teaspoon salt
1 teaspoon paprika
8 bone-in chicken breast halves
(8 ounces *each*)
1/4 cup vegetable oil

1) In a large resealable plastic bag, combine the lime juice, vinegar, garlic and seasonings; add chicken. Seal bag and turn to coat; refrigerate for 8 hours or overnight.

2) Discard marinade. In a skillet, brown chicken on all sides in oil. Transfer to a greased 15-in. x 10-in. x 1-in. baking pan.

3) Bake, uncovered, at 375° for 30-35 minutes or until a meat thermometer reads 170° and juices run clear.

Yield: 8 servings.

NUTRITION FACTS: 1 chicken breast half equals 209 calories, 7 g fat (2 g saturated fat), 90 mg cholesterol, 153 mg sodium, 1 g carbohydrate, trace fiber, 33 g protein.

Yogurt-Marinated Chicken

PREP: 5 min. + marinating **GRILL:** 45 min.

Naheed Saleem, Stamford, Connecticut

This tender marinated chicken gets its zing from the chili powder and cumin. For variety, add a tablespoon of tomato paste to the marinade or replace the chili powder with chopped green chilies.

1/2 cup fat-free yogurt
3 garlic cloves, minced
2 tablespoons lemon juice
1 tablespoon canola oil
1 teaspoon sugar
1 teaspoon chili powder
1 tablespoon minced fresh gingerroot
1/2 teaspoon salt
1/2 teaspoon ground cumin
6 bone-in chicken breast halves
(6 ounces *each*)

1) In a large resealable plastic bag, combine the yogurt, garlic, lemon juice, oil, sugar and seasonings; add chicken. Seal bag and turn to coat; refrigerate for 8 hours or overnight.

2) Coat grill rack with cooking spray before starting the grill. Prepare the grill for indirect heat. Drain and discard marinade.

3) Grill chicken, covered, bone side down over indirect medium heat for 20 minutes. Turn; grill 25-35 minutes longer or until juices run clear and a meat thermometer reads 170°.

Yield: 6 servings.

NUTRITION FACTS: 1 chicken breast half equals 149 calories, 4 g fat (1 g saturated fat), 68 mg cholesterol, 163 mg sodium, 2 g carbohydrate, trace fiber, 25 g protein.

YOGURT-MARINATED CHICKEN

ZESTY BARBECUED CHICKEN

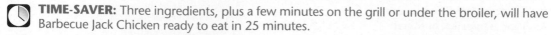

CLASSIC: A homemade barbecue sauce adds a tangy coating to a cut-up chicken in George's Barbecued Chicken. The oven bakes the chicken to a juicy tenderness.

TIME-SAVER: Three ingredients, plus a few minutes on the grill or under the broiler, will have Barbecue Jack Chicken ready to eat in 25 minutes.

LIGHT: Switching to just breast meat helps reduce the calories and fat in Oven-Barbecued Chicken.

SERVES 2: Two chicken leg quarters offer two hearty portions in Barbecued Chicken Legs. If you prefer white meat, use chicken breast quarters and cook until a meat thermometer reads 170°.

BARBECUE JACK CHICKEN

George's Barbecued Chicken

PREP: 15 min. **BAKE:** 45 min.

George Summer, Denver, Colorado

- 2 tablespoons chopped onion
- 1/3 cup vegetable oil, *divided*
- 2 cups ketchup
- 1/2 cup cider vinegar
- 2 tablespoons lemon juice
- 1 tablespoon hot pepper sauce
- 2/3 cup Worcestershire sauce
- 1 broiler/fryer chicken
  (3-1/2 to 4 pounds), cut up

1) In a large saucepan, saute onion in 1 tablespoon oil until tender. Add the ketchup, vinegar, lemon juice, hot pepper sauce and Worcestershire sauce. Bring to a boil. Reduce heat; simmer, uncovered, for 10 minutes, stirring occasionally.

2) In a large skillet, brown chicken on all sides in remaining oil over medium-high heat; drain. Transfer to a 13-in. x 9-in. x 2-in. baking pan.

3) Pour sauce over chicken. Bake, uncovered, at 350° for 45-60 minutes or until juices run clear and a meat thermometer reads 180°.

Yield: 6 servings.

NUTRITION FACTS: 4-1/2 ounces cooked chicken equals 503 calories, 29 g fat (6 g saturated fat), 102 mg cholesterol, 1,348 mg sodium, 29 g carbohydrate, 1 g fiber, 34 g protein.

Barbecue Jack Chicken

PREP/TOTAL TIME: 25 min.

Taste of Home Test Kitchen

- 4 boneless skinless chicken breast halves (6 ounces *each*)
- 4 slices pepper Jack cheese
- 1 cup barbecue sauce

1) Carefully cut a pocket in each chicken breast half. Fill with cheese; secure with metal or soaked wooden skewers.

2) Grill chicken, covered, over medium heat or broil 4 in. from the heat for 6-8 minutes on each side or until juices run clear, basting frequently with barbecue sauce.

Yield: 4 servings.

NUTRITION FACTS: 1 chicken breast half equals 120 calories, 4 g fat (2 g saturated fat), 31 mg cholesterol, 572 mg sodium, 8 g carbohydrate, 1 g fiber, 11 g protein.

Oven-Barbecued Chicken
PREP: 20 min. BAKE: 45 min.

Marge Wagner, Roselle, Illinois

- 6 bone-in chicken breast halves (8 ounces *each*)
- 1/3 cup chopped onion
- 3/4 cup ketchup
- 1/2 cup water
- 1/3 cup white vinegar
- 3 tablespoons brown sugar
- 1 tablespoon Worcestershire sauce
- 1 teaspoon ground mustard
- 1/4 teaspoon salt
- 1/8 teaspoon pepper

1) In a nonstick skillet coated with cooking spray, brown chicken over medium heat. Transfer to a 13-in. x 9-in. x 2-in. baking dish coated with cooking spray.

2) Remove skillet from stovetop and recoat with cooking spray; cook onion over medium heat until tender. Stir in the remaining ingredients. Bring

BARBECUED CHICKEN LEGS

to a boil. Reduce heat; simmer, uncovered, for 15 minutes. Pour over chicken. Bake, uncovered, at 350° for 45-55 minutes or until chicken juices run clear and a meat thermometer reads 170°.

Yield: 6 servings.

NUTRITION FACTS: 1 chicken breast half equals 241 calories, 4 g fat (1 g saturated fat), 90 mg cholesterol, 563 mg sodium, 17 g carbohydrate, 1 g fiber, 34 g protein.

Barbecued Chicken Legs
PREP: 10 min. BAKE: 50 min.

Agnes Golian, Garfield Heights, Ohio

- 2 chicken leg quarters
- 1 tablespoon canola oil
- 1/4 cup ketchup
- 2 tablespoons Worcestershire sauce
- 1 tablespoon sugar
- 1 tablespoon cider vinegar
- 1 tablespoon steak sauce

Dash hot pepper sauce

1) In a large nonstick skillet, brown chicken in oil. Transfer to an 8-in. square baking dish coated with cooking spray. In a bowl, combine the ketchup, Worcestershire sauce, sugar, vinegar, steak sauce and hot pepper sauce; pour over chicken.

2) Bake, uncovered, at 350° for 50-60 minutes or until a meat thermometer reads 180°, basting with sauce every 15 minutes.

Yield: 2 servings.

NUTRITION FACTS: 1 serving equals 412 calories, 23 g fat (5 g saturated fat), 105 mg cholesterol, 755 mg sodium, 19 g carbohydrate, trace fiber, 31 g protein.

OVEN-BARBECUED CHICKEN

Crab-Stuffed Chicken Breasts

PREP: 25 min. **BAKE:** 35 min.

Therese Bechtel, Montgomery Village, Maryland

*This elegant dish is often on the menu when I cook for guests.
The versatile sauce is also delicious on pork chops.*

- 4 tablespoons butter, *divided*
- 1/4 cup all-purpose flour
- 1 cup chicken broth
- 3/4 cup milk
- 1/4 cup chopped onion
- 1 can (6 ounces) crabmeat, drained, flaked and cartilage removed
- 1 can (4 ounces) mushroom stems and pieces, drained
- 1/3 cup crushed saltines (about 10 crackers)
- 2 tablespoons minced fresh parsley
- 1/2 teaspoon salt

Dash pepper

- 4 boneless skinless chicken breast halves (6 ounces *each*)
- 1 cup (4 ounces) shredded Swiss cheese
- 1/2 teaspoon paprika

Additional minced fresh parsley, optional

Hot cooked rice, optional

1) In a small saucepan, melt 3 tablespoons butter. Stir in flour until smooth. Gradually stir in broth and milk. Bring to a boil; cook and stir for 2 minutes. Remove from the heat; set aside.

2) In a small skillet, saute onion in remaining butter until tender. Add the crab, mushrooms, cracker crumbs, parsley, salt, pepper and 2 tablespoons of the white sauce; heat through.

3) For each chicken breast half, make a horizontal cut along one long side almost to the other side; leave chicken breasts attached at opposite side. Open breast so it lies flat; cover with plastic wrap and flatten chicken to 1/4-in. thickness. Remove plastic wrap.

4) Spoon about 1/2 cup of the crab mixture on each chicken breast half. Fold in sides and roll up. Secure with toothpicks. Place in a greased 1-1/2-qt. baking dish. Top with remaining white sauce. Cover and bake at 350° for 30 minutes or until chicken juices run clear.

5) Sprinkle with the cheese and paprika. Bake, uncovered, 5 minutes longer or until cheese is melted. Remove toothpicks before serving. Sprinkle with additional parsley and serve with rice if desired.

Yield: 4 servings.

NUTRITION FACTS: 1 stuffed chicken breast half equals 520 calories, 26 g fat (14 g saturated fat), 193 mg cholesterol, 1,129 mg sodium, 15 g carbohydrate, 1 g fiber, 55 g protein.

CHICKEN KIEV

Chicken Kiev

PREP: 15 min. + freezing **BAKE:** 35 min.

Karin Erickson, Burney, California

From holiday suppers to potlucks, this is one of my most-requested meals. Folks love the mildly seasoned chicken roll-ups.

- 1/4 cup butter, softened
- 1 tablespoon minced chives
- 1 garlic clove, minced
- 6 boneless skinless chicken breast halves (8 ounces *each*)
- 3/4 cup crushed cornflakes
- 2 tablespoons minced fresh parsley
- 1/2 teaspoon paprika
- 1/3 cup buttermilk

Hot cooked rice, optional

1) In a small bowl, combine the butter, chives and garlic. Shape into a 3-in. x 2-in. rectangle. Cover and freeze until firm, about 30 minutes.

2) Flatten chicken to 1/4-in. thickness. Cut the butter mixture lengthwise into six pieces; place one piece in center of each chicken breast half. Fold short sides over butter; fold long sides over and secure with toothpicks.

3) In a shallow dish, combine the cornflakes, parsley and paprika. Place buttermilk in another shallow dish. Dip the chicken into buttermilk, then coat evenly with cornflake mixture.

4) Place chicken seam side down in a greased 13-in. x 9-in. x 2-in. baking dish. Bake, uncovered, at 425° for 35-40 minutes or until no longer pink. Remove toothpicks before serving. Serve over rice if desired.

Yield: 6 servings.

NUTRITION FACTS: 1 stuffed chicken breast equals 357 calories, 13 g fat (6 g saturated fat), 146 mg cholesterol, 281 mg sodium, 10 g carbohydrate, trace fiber, 47 g protein.

Chicken Supreme

PREP: 20 min. + chilling **BAKE:** 50 min.

Marlene Nutter, Thedford, Nebraska

Monterey Jack cheese tucked inside and crushed croutons in the coating make this entree extra special.

        4 ounces Monterey Jack cheese
      1/2 cup butter, softened
        1 teaspoon minced fresh parsley
        1 teaspoon dried oregano
      1/2 to 1 teaspoon dried marjoram
        8 boneless skinless chicken breast halves (6 ounces *each*)
      1/2 teaspoon seasoned salt
      1/2 cup all-purpose flour
        2 eggs, beaten
    1-3/4 cups crushed Caesar salad croutons
      1/2 cup white wine *or* chicken broth

1) Cut cheese into eight 2-1/2-in. x 1-in. x 3/8-in. strips. In a bowl, combine the butter, parsley, oregano and marjoram; spread 1-1/2 teaspoons over each cheese strip. Cover and refrigerate cheese and remaining butter mixture at least 2 hours.

2) Flatten chicken to 1/8-in. thickness; sprinkle with seasoned salt. Place a cheese strip on each piece of chicken. Roll up and tuck in ends; secure with toothpicks. Coat chicken on all sides with flour. Dip in eggs, then coat with croutons. Place seam side down in a greased 13-in. x 9-in. x 2-in. baking dish. Bake, uncovered, at 350° for 30 minutes.

3) In a saucepan, combine wine or broth and reserved butter mixture; heat until butter is melted. Pour over chicken. Bake 20-25 minutes longer or until chicken juices run clear. Remove toothpicks before serving.

Yield: 8 servings.

NUTRITION FACTS: 1 stuffed chicken breast half equals 436 calories, 23 g fat (12 g saturated fat), 193 mg cholesterol, 498 mg sodium, 12 g carbohydrate, 1 g fiber, 41 g protein.

Crispy Chicken Cutlets

PREP/TOTAL TIME: 20 min.

Debra Smith, Brookfield, Missouri

These moist and tender cutlets feature a nutty coating and go well with buttered egg noodles.

        4 boneless skinless chicken breast halves (6 ounces *each*)
        1 egg white

CRISPY CHICKEN CUTLETS

      3/4 cup finely chopped pecans
        3 tablespoons all-purpose flour
      1/4 teaspoon salt
      1/4 teaspoon pepper
        1 tablespoon butter
        1 tablespoon vegetable oil

1) Flatten chicken to 1/4-in. thickness. In a shallow bowl, lightly beat egg white. In another shallow bowl, combine the pecans, flour, salt and pepper. Dip chicken in egg white, then coat with pecan mixture. Let stand for 5 minutes.

2) In a large skillet, brown chicken in butter and oil over medium heat for 4-6 minutes on each side or until juices run clear.

Yield: 4 servings.

NUTRITION FACTS: 1 chicken breast half equals 418 calories, 26 g fat (5 g saturated fat), 102 mg cholesterol, 272 mg sodium, 8 g carbohydrate, 2 g fiber, 38 g protein.

■ **Pecan Parmesan Chicken:** Combine 1/3 cup soft bread crumbs, 3 tablespoons ground pecans, 3 tablespoons grated Parmesan cheese, 3/4 teaspoon dried oregano, 1/4 teaspoon *each* seasoned salt and dried basil and a dash pepper. Dip chicken in egg white beaten with 1 teaspoon cornstarch, then in pecan mixture. Cook as directed above.

IMPRESSIVE CHICKEN ROLLS

 CLASSIC: In this Chicken Cordon Bleu recipe, chicken breasts are pounded thin so they will be larger and thinner. This makes it easier to enclose the ham and Swiss cheese in the chicken roll, resulting in an elegant presentation.

 TIME-SAVER: Chicken breasts are pounded thin, then wrapped around cheese and broccoli before being popped into the microwave. The easier prep and speedy cooking make Broccoli Chicken Roll-Ups a great pick for a weeknight dinner.

 LIGHT: In Apple-Stuffed Chicken Breasts, the traditional ham-and-cheese filling of Cordon Bleu is replaced with sauteed apple and onion, bread crumbs and herbs. This switch creates a delectable chicken roll and reduces the calories, fat and sodium.

 SERVES 2: The simpler technique of wrapping the chicken breast around the filling is also used in Asparagus-Stuffed Chicken Breasts. A microwaved Hollandaise Sauce adds a flavorful final touch to the chicken rolls.

Chicken Cordon Bleu

PREP: 15 min. **BAKE:** 40 min.

Jim Wick, Orlando, Florida

- 4 boneless skinless chicken breast halves (8 ounces *each*)
- 2 tablespoons butter, softened
- 1 teaspoon dried thyme
- 4 thin slices fully cooked ham
- 4 thin slices Swiss cheese
- 8 bacon strips
- 2 eggs
- 1/2 cup milk
- 1/2 cup all-purpose flour
- 3/4 cup dry bread crumbs
- 1/2 teaspoon garlic powder
- 1 teaspoon dried oregano
- 1/4 cup shredded Parmesan cheese

1) Flatten chicken to 1/8-in. thickness; spread butter on the insides. Sprinkle with thyme. Top with a slice of ham and Swiss cheese; roll up tightly. Wrap each with two strips of bacon and secure with toothpicks.

Making a Stuffed Chicken Roll

1) Spread stuffing in center of flatten chicken breast.

2) Roll up jelly roll-style, tucking in sides. Secure with toothpicks.

2) In a shallow bowl, beat eggs and milk. Place flour in another bowl. Combine the bread crumbs, garlic powder, oregano and Parmesan cheese. Dip each chicken roll-up in egg mixture; coat with flour. Dip each again in egg mixture, then coat with crumbs.

3) Place on a greased baking sheet. Bake, uncovered, at 350° for 40-45 minutes or until chicken juices run clear. Remove toothpicks before serving.

Yield: 4 servings.

NUTRITION FACTS: 1 stuffed chicken breast half equals 883 calories, 51 g fat (23 g saturated fat), 320 mg cholesterol, 1,084 mg sodium, 30 g carbohydrate, 1 g fiber, 71 g protein.

Broccoli Chicken Roll-Ups

PREP/TOTAL TIME: 20 min.

Joyce Hooker, Knightstown, Indiana

- 4 boneless skinless chicken breast halves (6 ounces *each*)
- 2 slices process American cheese, *divided*
- 1 cup chopped fresh *or* frozen broccoli, thawed
- 1 tablespoon all-purpose flour
- 1/2 cup milk
- 1 tablespoon white wine *or* chicken broth
- 1 teaspoon minced fresh parsley
- 1/4 teaspoon salt
- 1/8 teaspoon pepper

1) Flatten chicken to 1/4-in. thickness. Cut one cheese slice into four strips; place one strip in the center of each piece of chicken. Top with broccoli. Fold chicken in half and secure with toothpicks.

2) Place seam side down around the outside of a greased 8-in. square microwave-safe dish. Cover and microwave on high for 3-1/2 to 6 minutes or until chicken juices run clear; keep warm.

3) In a microwave-safe bowl, combine the flour, milk, wine or broth, parsley, salt and pepper until blended. Microwave, uncovered, on high for 1 to 1-1/2 minutes or until thickened. Dice remaining cheese slice; add to the sauce and stir until melted. Pour over chicken. Cook, uncovered, on high for 20 seconds or until heated through.

Yield: 4 servings.

NUTRITION FACTS: 1 chicken roll-up equals 187 calories, 6 g fat (3 g saturated fat), 72 mg cholesterol, 346 mg sodium, 5 g carbohydrate, 1 g fiber, 26 g protein.

Apple-Stuffed Chicken Breasts
PREP: 35 min. COOK: 30 min.

Lois Gallup Edwards, Citrus Heights, California

- 6 boneless skinless chicken breast halves (6 ounces *each*)
- 1 teaspoon salt, *divided*
- 1/4 teaspoon pepper
- 1/2 cup finely chopped onion
- 2 garlic cloves, minced
- 3 tablespoons butter, *divided*
- 1 medium apple, peeled and grated
- 3/4 cup soft bread crumbs
- 1/4 teaspoon dried basil
- 1/4 teaspoon dried rosemary, crushed
- 1/4 cup all-purpose flour
- 1/2 cup unsweetened apple juice
- 1 tablespoon sherry *or* additional unsweetened apple juice

1) Flatten chicken to 1/4-in. thickness. Combine 1/2 teaspoon salt and pepper; sprinkle over both sides of chicken. Set aside.

2) In a small nonstick skillet, saute onion and garlic in 1 tablespoon butter until tender. Add apple; saute 1 minute longer. Stir in the bread crumbs, basil, rosemary and remaining salt; heat through.

3) Place 3 tablespoons of apple mixture on each piece of chicken. Roll up and secure with toothpicks; coat with flour. In a large nonstick skillet, cook chicken in 1 tablespoon butter until browned on all sides. Remove and keep warm.

4) Stir apple juice and sherry or additional juice into pan, stirring to loosen any browned bits. Return chicken to pan. Bring to a boil. Reduce heat; cover and simmer for 15-20 minutes or until chicken juices run clear.

5) Remove chicken to a serving platter; discard toothpicks. Add remaining butter to pan juices; whisk until blended. Serve with chicken.

Yield: 6 servings.

NUTRITION FACTS: 1 serving equals 143 calories, 7 g fat (4 g saturated fat), 31 mg cholesterol, 497 mg sodium, 14 g carbohydrate, 1 g fiber, 7 g protein.

ASPARAGUS-STUFFED CHICKEN BREASTS

Asparagus-Stuffed Chicken Breasts
PREP/TOTAL TIME: 25 min.

Renee Smith, Clinton Township, Michigan

- 2 boneless skinless chicken breast halves (6 ounces *each*)
- 1 tablespoon Dijon mustard
- 1 green onion, finely chopped
- 10 asparagus spears, trimmed
- 3 tablespoons crushed butter-flavored crackers

HOLLANDAISE SAUCE:

- 1/4 cup butter, cubed
- 2 egg yolks
- 2 teaspoons lemon juice
- 1 teaspoon water
- 1/8 teaspoon salt
- 1/4 cup sliced almonds, toasted

1) Flatten chicken to 1/4-in. thickness. Spread with mustard; sprinkle with onion. Place asparagus spears down the center of chicken; fold over and secure with toothpicks if necessary.

2) Place seam side down in an ungreased 8-in. square microwave-safe dish. Sprinkle with cracker crumbs. Microwave, uncovered, on high for 6-8 minutes or until chicken juices run clear. Keep warm.

3) For sauce, in a small microwave-safe bowl, melt butter. Gradually whisk in egg yolks, lemon juice, water and salt. Microwave, uncovered, at 30% power for 30 seconds or until mixture reaches 160° and is thickened, stirring once. Discard toothpicks. Top with sauce; sprinkle with almonds.

Yield: 2 servings.

NUTRITION FACTS: 1 serving equals 495 calories, 39 g fat (17 g saturated fat), 321 mg cholesterol, 696 mg sodium, 13 g carbohydrate, 3 g fiber, 26 g protein.

Chicken with Sun-Dried Tomatoes

PREP: 15 min. **COOK:** 30 min.

Heather Nandell, Johnston, Iowa

Sun-dried tomatoes provide intense flavor in this delightful chicken entree. If you have all the ingredients for this dish ready before you start to cook, the recipe comes together quickly.

- 1/2 cup plus 3 tablespoons reduced-sodium chicken broth, *divided*
- 1/4 cup chopped dry-packed sun-dried tomatoes
- 1/2 cup sliced fresh mushrooms
- 1 green onion, thinly sliced
- 2 teaspoons minced garlic, *divided*
- 4 boneless skinless chicken breast halves (4 ounces *each*)
- 1 teaspoon olive oil
- 2 teaspoons cornstarch
- 1/2 teaspoon dried basil
- 1/4 teaspoon salt
- 1/4 teaspoon pepper
- 1/2 cup fat-free milk

Hot cooked pasta, optional

1) In a small saucepan, bring 1/2 cup broth to a boil; remove from the heat. Stir in sun-dried tomatoes; let stand for 10 minutes.

2) Meanwhile, in a large nonstick skillet coated with cooking spray, saute the mushrooms, onion and 1 teaspoon garlic for 1 minute. Stir in the remaining broth; cook 2 minutes longer or until mushrooms are tender. Remove mushroom mixture and set aside.

CHICKEN WITH SUN-DRIED TOMATOES

3) Rub chicken with remaining garlic. In the same skillet, brown chicken in oil for 3 minutes on each side. Stir in tomato mixture; bring to a boil. Reduce heat; cover and simmer for 10-12 minutes or until chicken juices run clear. Remove chicken and keep warm.

4) In a small bowl, combine the cornstarch, basil, salt and pepper. Stir in milk until smooth; add to tomato mixture. Bring to a boil; cook and stir for 1-2 minutes or until thickened. Stir in mushroom mixture. Slice chicken; top with sauce. Serve with pasta if desired.

Yield: 4 servings.

NUTRITION FACTS: 1 chicken breast half with 1/4 cup sauce equals 190 calories, 5 g fat (1 g saturated fat), 66 mg cholesterol, 416 mg sodium, 7 g carbohydrate, 1 g fiber, 29 g protein.

Baked Lemon Chicken

PREP: 10 min. **BAKE:** 25 min.

Marion Lowery, Medford, Oregon

Right out of the oven or cold the next day, this chicken is delicious. It's moist, tender and lemony with a nice crunch.

- 3 tablespoons butter, melted
- 2 tablespoons lemon juice
- 1 garlic clove, minced
- 1/2 teaspoon salt
- 1/4 teaspoon pepper
- 1/2 cup seasoned bread crumbs
- 4 boneless skinless chicken breast halves (4 ounces *each*)

1) In a shallow bowl, combine the butter, lemon juice, garlic, salt and pepper. Place bread crumbs in another bowl.

BAKED LEMON CHICKEN

Flattening Chicken Breasts (Option 2)

1) Hold sharp knife parallel to cutting board and along one long side of breast; cut almost in half, leaving breast attached at one side.

2) Open breast so it lies flat; cover with plastic wrap. Using flat side of a meat mallet, lightly pound to 1/8-in. thickness.

2) Dip chicken in butter mixture, then coat with crumbs. Place in a greased 13-in. x 9-in. x 2-in. baking dish. Drizzle with the remaining butter mixture.

3) Bake, uncovered, at 350° for 25-30 minutes or until juices run clear.

Yield: 4 servings.

NUTRITION FACTS: 1 chicken breast half equals 255 calories, 12 g fat (6 g saturated fat), 86 mg cholesterol, 652 mg sodium, 11 g carbohydrate, 1 g fiber, 25 g protein.

Chicken Nuggets
PREP/TOTAL TIME: 30 min.

Cathryn White, Newark, Delaware

With a crisp golden coating, these moist and tender bite-size pieces of chicken are greeted with enthusiasm whenever I serve them.

> 1 cup dry bread crumbs
> 1/2 cup grated Parmesan cheese
> 2 teaspoons dried basil
> 2 teaspoons dried thyme
> 2 teaspoons paprika
> 1 teaspoon salt
> 1 teaspoon pepper
> 3/4 cup butter, melted
> 2-1/2 pounds boneless skinless chicken breasts, cut into 1-inch cubes

1) In a shallow bowl, combine the bread crumbs, Parmesan cheese and seasonings. Place butter in another shallow bowl. Dip chicken in butter, then roll in bread crumb mixture.

2) Place in a greased 15-in. x 10-in. x 1-in. baking pan. Bake, uncovered, at 400° for 15-20 minutes or until juices run clear.

Yield: 8 servings.

NUTRITION FACTS: 1 serving equals 383 calories, 23 g fat (13 g saturated fat), 128 mg cholesterol, 747 mg sodium, 11 g carbohydrate, 1 g fiber, 33 g protein.

Chicken Parmigiana
PREP: 10 min. **BAKE:** 35 min.

Rhonda Schiel, Magnolia, Texas

A nicely seasoned breading coats the tender chicken breasts in this attractive entree. When I have extra time, I make my own herbed tomato sauce instead of using prepared spaghetti sauce.

> 1/2 cup dry bread crumbs
> 3 tablespoons grated Parmesan cheese
> 3/4 teaspoon Italian seasoning
> 1/2 teaspoon garlic powder
> 1/2 teaspoon salt
> 1/4 cup egg substitute
> 4 boneless skinless chicken breast halves (4 ounces *each*)
> 1 jar (26 ounces) meatless spaghetti sauce
> 3/4 cup shredded part-skim mozzarella cheese
> 1/4 cup shredded Parmesan cheese

1) In a shallow bowl, combine the bread crumbs, grated Parmesan cheese, Italian seasoning, garlic powder and salt. In another bowl, beat egg substitute. Dip chicken in egg substitute, then roll in crumb mixture.

2) Place in a 13-in. x 9-in. x 2-in. baking dish coated with cooking spray. Bake, uncovered, at 375° for 10 minutes on each side.

3) Pour spaghetti sauce over chicken; bake for 5 minutes. Sprinkle with shredded cheeses; bake 10 minutes longer or until chicken juices run clear.

Yield: 4 servings.

Editor's Note: If you prefer, use 1 lightly beaten egg may be used in place of the egg substitute.

NUTRITION FACTS: 1 serving equals 412 calories, 15 g fat (5 g saturated fat), 88 mg cholesterol, 1,420 mg sodium, 32 g carbohydrate, 5 g fiber, 37 g protein.

CHICKEN PARMIGIANA

SAVORY CHICKEN CACCIATORE

 CLASSIC: Cut-up chicken is simmered in a homemade herbed tomato mixture, making Chicken Cacciatore big on flavor. Serve with your favorite pasta to make the most of the delicious sauce.

 TIME-SAVER: Cubes of boneless chicken are sauteed in Chicken Cacciatore Skillet, then simmered in jarred spaghetti sauce, dressed up with herbs and mushrooms.

 LIGHT: Mushroom Chicken Cacciatore uses chicken breasts and half the fat of Chicken Cacciatore, which saves calories. It also conveniently simmers in a slow cooker.

 SERVES 2: Mom's Chicken Cacciatore is down-sized for two by creating just the right amount of homemade sauce for a pair of bone-in chicken breasts.

CHICKEN CACCIATORE

Chicken Cacciatore
PREP: 15 min. **COOK:** 1-1/4 hours

Barbara Roberts, Courtenay, British Columbia

- 1 broiler/fryer chicken (3-1/2 to 4 pounds), cut up
- 1/4 cup all-purpose flour

Salt and pepper to taste

- 2 tablespoons olive oil
- 2 tablespoons butter
- 1 large onion, chopped
- 2 celery ribs, sliced diagonally
- 1 large green pepper, cut into strips
- 1/2 pound fresh mushrooms, sliced
- 1 can (28 ounces) diced tomatoes, undrained
- 1 can (8 ounces) tomato sauce
- 1 can (6 ounces) tomato paste
- 1 cup dry red wine *or* water
- 1 teaspoon dried thyme
- 1 teaspoon dried rosemary, crushed
- 1 teaspoon dried oregano
- 1 teaspoon dried basil
- 3 garlic cloves, minced
- 1 tablespoon sugar

Hot cooked pasta
Shredded Parmesan cheese

1) Dust chicken with flour. Season with salt and pepper. In a large skillet, brown chicken on all sides in oil and butter over medium-high heat. Remove chicken and keep warm.

2) In same skillet, saute the onion, celery, green pepper and mushrooms for 5 minutes. Stir in the tomatoes, tomato sauce, tomato paste, wine or water, herbs, garlic and sugar. Bring to a boil. Reduce heat; cover and simmer for 30 minutes.

3) Return chicken to the pan. Cover and simmer for 45-60 minutes or until tender. Serve over pasta; sprinkle with Parmesan cheese.

Yield: 6 servings.

NUTRITION FACTS: 4-1/2 ounces cooked chicken (calculated without salt, pepper, pasta and Parmesan cheese) equals 517 calories, 25 g fat (8 g saturated fat), 112 mg cholesterol, 790 mg sodium, 28 g carbohydrate, 6 g fiber, 39 g protein.

Chicken Cacciatore Skillet
PREP: 5 min. **COOK:** 30 min.

Norma Lavanchy, Douglas, Arizona

- 1/2 pound boneless skinless chicken breasts, cut into 1-inch cubes
- 1/4 cup chopped onion
- 2 garlic cloves, minced
- 1-1/2 cups reduced-sodium chicken broth, *divided*
- 3/4 cup chopped green pepper
- 1 can (4 ounces) mushroom stems and pieces, drained
- 1 bay leaf
- 1/4 teaspoon dried oregano
- 1/4 teaspoon dried basil
- 1/4 teaspoon pepper
- 3/4 cup uncooked long grain rice
- 1 cup meatless spaghetti sauce

1) In a large skillet, cook the chicken, onion and garlic in 3 tablespoons broth until chicken juices run clear. Stir in the green pepper, mushrooms, bay leaf, oregano, basil, pepper and remaining broth.

2) Bring to a boil. Add the rice. Reduce heat; cover and simmer for 20-25 minutes or until the rice is tender. Add the spaghetti sauce; heat through. Discard bay leaf.

Yield: 4 servings.

NUTRITION FACTS: 1 cup equals 250 calories, 1 g fat (trace saturated fat), 33 mg cholesterol, 641 mg sodium, 40 g carbohydrate, 3 g fiber, 19 g protein.

MUSHROOM CHICKEN CACCIATORE

Mushroom Chicken Cacciatore

PREP: 20 min. **COOK:** 4 hours

Jane Bone, Cape Coral, Florida

   4 boneless skinless chicken breast halves (6 ounces *each*)
   2 tablespoons vegetable oil
   1 can (15 ounces) tomato sauce
   2 cans (4 ounces *each*) sliced mushrooms, drained
   1 medium onion, chopped
  1/4 cup red wine *or* chicken broth
   2 garlic cloves, minced
  1-1/4 teaspoons dried oregano
  1/2 teaspoon dried thyme
  1/8 to 1/4 teaspoon salt
  1/8 teaspoon pepper
Hot cooked spaghetti

1) In a large skillet, brown chicken in oil on both sides. Transfer to a 3-qt. slow cooker. In a bowl, combine the tomato sauce, mushrooms, onion, wine or broth, garlic, oregano, thyme, salt and pepper; pour over chicken.

2) Cover and cook on low for 4-5 hours or until a meat thermometer reads 170°. Serve over spaghetti.

Yield: 4 servings.

NUTRITION FACTS: 1 serving (calculated without spaghetti) equals 255 calories, 10 g fat (2 g saturated fat), 68 mg cholesterol, 744 mg sodium, 11 g carbohydrate, 3 g fiber, 28 g protein.

Mom's Chicken Cacciatore

PREP: 25 min. **COOK:** 50 min.

Cheri Sassman, Utica, New York

  1/4 cup all-purpose flour
  3/4 teaspoon salt, *divided*
  1/4 teaspoon pepper
   2 bone-in chicken breast halves (8 ounces *each*)
   2 tablespoons olive oil, *divided*
  1-3/4 cups sliced fresh mushrooms
  1/2 cup chopped onion
   1 garlic clove, minced
  1/3 cup tomato paste
   1 cup water
   2 tablespoons white wine *or* chicken broth
  1/4 teaspoon *each* dried thyme, parsley flakes and oregano
  1/4 teaspoon ground allspice
Hot cooked spaghetti

1) In a large resealable plastic bag, combine the flour, 1/2 teaspoon salt and pepper. Add chicken and shake to coat.

2) In a large skillet, brown chicken in 1 tablespoon oil. Remove and keep warm. In the same skillet, saute the mushrooms, onion and garlic in remaining oil. Stir in tomato paste until combined. Gradually add water and wine or broth. Stir in the thyme, parsley, oregano, allspice and remaining salt. Return chicken to the pan.

3) Bring to a boil. Reduce heat; cover and simmer for 40-45 minutes or until a meat thermometer reads 170°. Serve with spaghetti.

Yield: 2 servings.

NUTRITION FACTS: 1 chicken breast half with about 1 cup sauce (calculated without spaghetti) equals 494 calories, 24 g fat (5 g saturated fat), 111 mg cholesterol, 1,018 mg sodium, 22 g carbohydrate, 5 g fiber, 44 g protein.

MOM'S CHICKEN CACCIATORE

CREOLE SKILLET DINNER

Creole Skillet Dinner
PREP: 15 min. **COOK:** 30 min.

Bonnie Brann, Pasco, Washington
This colorful dish replaced my traditional turkey at one holiday dinner. It's a recipe from my former neighbor.

    4 cups chicken broth
2-1/2 cups uncooked long grain rice
    1 cup chopped red onion
1-1/2 teaspoons minced garlic, *divided*
1-1/4 teaspoons chili powder
    1 teaspoon salt
  1/2 teaspoon ground turmeric
  1/4 teaspoon pepper
    1 bay leaf
    1 medium sweet red pepper, julienned
    1 medium green pepper, julienned
    2 green onions, sliced
    1 teaspoon minced fresh parsley
  1/2 teaspoon dried basil
  1/2 teaspoon dried thyme
  1/4 teaspoon hot pepper sauce
    2 tablespoons butter
    1 cup sliced fresh mushrooms
    1 medium tomato, chopped
    1 cup frozen peas
    1 pound boneless skinless chicken breasts, thinly sliced
    2 tablespoons lemon juice
  1/3 cup sliced almonds, toasted

1) In a large saucepan, bring the broth, rice, red onion, 1 teaspoon garlic, chili powder, salt, turmeric, pepper and bay leaf to a boil. Reduce heat; cover and simmer for 20 minutes or until rice is tender.

2) Meanwhile, in a large skillet, cook and stir the peppers, green onions, parsley, basil, thyme, hot pepper sauce and remaining garlic in butter over medium-high heat for 2 minutes. Add the mushrooms; cook until peppers are crisp-tender. Add tomato and peas; heat through. Remove from the heat. Discard bay leaf from rice. Add rice to vegetable mixture. Keep warm.

3) In another skillet, cook and stir chicken in lemon juice over medium-high heat until juices run clear. Add to rice mixture; toss. Sprinkle with almonds.

Yield: 6 servings.

NUTRITION FACTS: 1-1/4 cups equals 491 calories, 10 g fat (3 g saturated fat), 52 mg cholesterol, 1,131 mg sodium, 75 g carbohydrate, 5 g fiber, 26 g protein.

Thai-Style Chicken
PREP: 10 min. + marinating **BAKE:** 20 min.

Vicki Floden, Story City, Iowa
When you add the chicken to the peppery marinade the night before, there isn't much dinner preparation the following day.

1/4 cup reduced-sodium soy sauce
  3 tablespoons lemon juice
  3 tablespoons minced fresh basil
    or 1 tablespoon dried basil
  2 tablespoons fat-free plain yogurt
  2 teaspoons grated lemon peel
  3 garlic cloves, minced
  1 teaspoon ground ginger
1/2 to 1 teaspoon crushed red pepper flakes
  4 boneless skinless chicken breast halves (4 ounces *each*)

1) In a small bowl, combine the soy sauce, lemon juice, basil, yogurt, lemon peel, garlic, ginger and red pepper flakes. Remove 1/4 cup to another bowl; cover and refrigerate.

2) Pour the remaining marinade into a large resealable plastic bag; add chicken. Seal bag and turn to coat; refrigerate overnight.

3) Drain and discard marinade. Place chicken in a 13-in. x 9-in. x 2-in. baking dish coated with cooking spray. Spoon reserved marinade over chicken. Bake, uncovered, at 375° for 20 minutes or until a meat thermometer reads 170°.

Yield: 4 servings.

NUTRITION FACTS: 1 chicken breast half equals 134 calories, 3 g fat (1 g saturated fat), 63 mg cholesterol, 360 mg sodium, 2 g carbohydrate, trace fiber, 24 g protein.

Bruschetta Chicken
PREP: 10 min. **BAKE:** 30 min.

Carolin Cattoi-Demkiw, Lethbridge, Alberta
My husband and I enjoy serving this tasty chicken to company as well as family. It looks like we fussed, but it's fast and easy to fix.

1/2 cup all-purpose flour
  2 eggs, lightly beaten
  4 boneless skinless chicken breast halves (6 ounces *each*)

BRUSCHETTA CHICKEN

1/4 cup grated Parmesan cheese
1/4 cup dry bread crumbs
1 tablespoon butter, melted
2 large tomatoes, seeded and chopped
3 tablespoons minced fresh basil
2 garlic cloves, minced
1 tablespoon olive oil
1/2 teaspoon salt
1/4 teaspoon pepper

1) Place flour and eggs in separate shallow bowls. Dip chicken in flour, then in eggs. Place in a greased 13-in. x 9-in. x 2-in. baking dish. Combine the Parmesan cheese, bread crumbs and butter; sprinkle over chicken.

2) Loosely cover baking dish with foil. Bake at 375° for 20 minutes. Uncover; bake 5-10 minutes longer or until top is browned.

3) Meanwhile, in a bowl, combine the remaining ingredients. Spoon over the chicken. Return to the oven for 3-5 minutes or until tomato mixture is heated through.

Yield: 4 servings.

NUTRITION FACTS: 1 chicken breast half with tomato topping equals 380 calories, 14 g fat (5 g saturated fat), 185 mg cholesterol, 589 mg sodium, 19 g carbohydrate, 2 g fiber, 42 g protein.

Chicken Fajitas

PREP: 15 min. + marinating **GRILL:** 15 min.

Melinda Ewbank, Fairfield, Ohio

Fresh lime juice helps you bring a taste of Mexico to your dinner table. These colorful fajitas have fresh flavors that appeal to everyone.

2 tablespoons white wine vinegar
2 tablespoons fresh lime juice
2 tablespoons vegetable oil, *divided*
1 tablespoon Worcestershire sauce
1 tablespoon chopped onion
1 garlic clove, minced
1/2 teaspoon salt, optional
1/2 teaspoon dried oregano
1/4 teaspoon ground cumin
1 pound boneless skinless chicken breasts
1 medium green pepper, halved and seeded
1 medium sweet red pepper, halved and seeded
1 medium sweet onion, sliced
6 flour tortillas (8 inches)
Salsa, guacamole, sour cream and shredded cheddar cheese, optional

1) In a large resealable plastic bag, combine the vinegar, lime juice, 1 tablespoon oil, Worcestershire sauce, onion, garlic, salt if desired, oregano and cumin; add chicken. Seal bag and turn to coat; refrigerate at least 4 hours.

2) Coat grill rack with cooking spray before starting the grill. Drain and discard marinade. Lightly brush peppers and onion with remaining oil.

3) Grill vegetables and chicken, covered, over medium heat for 12-15 minutes or until the vegetables begin to soften and chicken juices run clear.

4) Meanwhile, warm tortillas according to package directions. Quickly slice chicken and peppers into strips and separate onion slices into rings.

5) Place chicken and vegetables down the center of tortillas; fold sides over filling. Garnish if desired with salsa, guacamole, sour cream and cheese.

Yield: 6 servings.

NUTRITION FACTS: 1 fajita equals 282 calories, 8 g fat (1 g saturated fat), 42 mg cholesterol, 301 mg sodium, 31 g carbohydrate, 1 g fiber, 20 g protein.

■ **Grilled Beef Fajitas:** Prepare as directed, using 1-1/2 pounds beef flank steak in place of the chicken. Grill over medium heat for 6-8 minutes on each side or until meat reaches desired doneness (for medium-rare, a meat thermometer should read 145°; medium, 160°; well-done, 170°).

CHICKEN FAJITAS

Creamy Braised Chicken

PREP: 10 min. **COOK:** 30 min.

Margaret Haugh Heilman, Houston, Texas

A smooth, delicate cream sauce gives special taste to these tender chicken breasts. This dish is so rich tasting, you'll want to serve it to company.

- 6 cups water
- 1/2 pound pearl onions
- 1 cup thinly sliced onion
- 1/2 cup thinly sliced carrot
- 1/2 cup thinly sliced celery
- 1 tablespoon plus 2 teaspoons butter, *divided*
- 6 boneless skinless chicken breast halves (4 ounces *each*)
- 1 cup dry white wine *or* reduced-sodium chicken broth
- 1-1/3 cups reduced-sodium chicken broth
- 1 tablespoon minced fresh parsley
- 1 teaspoon salt
- 1 teaspoon dried thyme
- 1/8 teaspoon white pepper
- 1 bay leaf
- 3 tablespoons all-purpose flour
- 1/2 cup fat-free evaporated milk
- 1/2 pound fresh mushrooms, quartered

1) In a Dutch oven, bring water to a boil. Add pearl onions; boil for 3 minutes. Drain and rinse in cold water; peel and set aside.

2) In the same pan, saute sliced onion, carrot and celery in 1 tablespoon butter until tender. Remove vegetables; set aside. Add chicken to pan; brown on both sides. Remove and keep warm.

3) Add wine or broth; simmer until reduced to 1/2 cup. Stir in the chicken broth and seasonings. Return chicken to pan; cover and simmer for 5 minutes or until juices run clear. Remove chicken to a serving platter; keep warm.

4) Combine flour and milk until smooth; gradually stir into pan. Bring to a boil; cook and stir for 2 minutes or until thickened. Return vegetables to pan. Remove from the heat; cover and set aside.

5) In a nonstick skillet, saute reserved pearl onions in remaining butter until tender. Remove and set aside. In the same pan, saute mushrooms until tender.

6) Add onions and mushrooms to serving platter. Discard bay leaf from sauce; spoon over chicken and vegetables.

Yield: 6 servings.

NUTRITION FACTS: 1 chicken breast half with 2/3 cup sauce equals 273 calories, 5 g fat (3 g saturated fat), 75 mg cholesterol, 748 mg sodium, 18 g carbohydrate, 2 g fiber, 31 g protein.

Chicken and Shrimp Satay

PREP: 20 min. + marinating **GRILL:** 10 min.

Hannah Barringer, Loudon, Tennessee

I lightened up a recipe that I found in a cookbook, and these grilled kabobs were the tasty result. The scrumptious dipping sauce is always a hit.

- 3/4 pound uncooked medium shrimp, peeled and deveined
- 3/4 pound chicken tenderloin, cut into 1-inch cubes
- 4 green onions, chopped
- 2 garlic cloves, minced
- 1 tablespoon butter
- 1 tablespoon minced fresh parsley
- 1/2 cup white wine *or* chicken broth
- 1 tablespoon lemon juice
- 1 tablespoon lime juice

DIPPING SAUCE:
- 1/4 cup chopped onion
- 1 tablespoon butter
- 2/3 cup reduced-sodium chicken broth
- 1/4 cup reduced-fat chunky peanut butter
- 2-1/4 teaspoons brown sugar
- 3/4 teaspoon lemon juice
- 3/4 teaspoon lime juice
- 1/4 teaspoon salt
- 1/4 teaspoon *each* dried basil, thyme and rosemary, crushed
- 1/8 teaspoon cayenne pepper

1) Thread shrimp and chicken onto 12 metal or soaked wooden skewers. Place in a large shallow dish; set aside.

CREAMY BRAISED CHICKEN

CHICKEN AND SHRIMP SATAY

2) In a small skillet, saute the green onions and garlic in butter. Stir in the parsley, wine or broth, lemon juice and lime juice. Cool slightly. Pour over skewers and turn to coat. Cover and refrigerate for 4 hours, turning every 30 minutes.

3) In a small saucepan, saute onion in butter. Add the remaining sauce ingredients; cook and stir until blended. Remove from the heat; set aside.

4) Coat grill rack with cooking spray before starting the grill; prepare for indirect heat. Drain and discard marinade. Grill skewers, covered, over indirect medium heat for 7-8 minutes, turning often. Brush with 1/4 cup sauce during the last minute of grilling. Serve with remaining sauce.

Yield: 6 servings.

NUTRITION FACTS: 2 kabobs with 2 tablespoons sauce equals 190 calories, 7 g fat (3 g saturated fat), 126 mg cholesterol, 339 mg sodium, 7 g carbohydrate, 1 g fiber, 25 g protein.

Chicken Piccata
PREP/TOTAL TIME: 30 min.

Linda Carver, Cedar Rapids, Iowa

A blend of flour, garlic powder and paprika lightly coats the chicken to give it flavor and keep it moist at the same time.

 1/2 cup all-purpose flour
 1/2 teaspoon garlic powder
 1/2 teaspoon paprika
   2 eggs
   6 tablespoons lemon juice, *divided*
   4 boneless skinless chicken breast halves (6 ounces *each*)
 1/2 cup butter
   2 teaspoons chicken bouillon granules
   1 cup water

1) In a shallow bowl, combine the flour, garlic powder and paprika. In another shallow bowl, beat eggs and 2 tablespoons lemon juice. Dip chicken in egg mixture, then coat with flour mixture.

2) In a large skillet, brown chicken on both sides in butter over medium-high heat. Combine bouillon, water and remaining lemon juice; pour over chicken. Bring to a boil. Reduce heat; cover and simmer for 20 minutes or until juices run clear.

Yield: 4 servings.

NUTRITION FACTS: 1 chicken breast half with 3 tablespoons sauce equals 488 calories, 29 g fat (16 g saturated fat), 262 mg cholesterol, 765 mg sodium, 15 g carbohydrate, 1 g fiber, 40 g protein.

Teriyaki Chicken
PREP: 10 min. + marinating **BAKE:** 35 min.

Jean Clark, Albion, Maine

I developed my own teriyaki sauce that coats the chicken before it bakes up beautifully.

 3/4 cup soy sauce
 1/4 cup vegetable oil
   3 tablespoons brown sugar
   2 tablespoons sherry, optional
 1/2 teaspoon ground ginger
 1/2 teaspoon garlic powder
  12 chicken drumsticks (4 ounces *each*)

1) In a large resealable plastic bag, combine the soy sauce, oil, brown sugar, sherry if desired, ginger and garlic powder; add drumsticks. Seal bag and turn to coat; cover and refrigerate for 1 hour or overnight, turning occasionally.

2) Drain and discard marinade. Place chicken in a single layer on a foil-lined baking sheet. Bake, uncovered, at 350° for 35-45 minutes or until a meat thermometer reads 180° and the juices run clear.

Yield: 6 servings.

NUTRITION FACTS: 2 drumsticks equals 483 calories, 23 g fat (6 g saturated fat), 202 mg cholesterol, 1,098 mg sodium, 3 g carbohydrate, trace fiber, 62 g protein.

TERIYAKI CHICKEN

New Orleans-Style Chicken

PREP: 30 min. **COOK:** 50 min.

Jason Bagley, Pasco, Washington

This hearty one-dish meal is loaded with succulent chunks of chicken, colorful veggies, beans and rice. It's a favorite of mine.

1-1/4	pounds boneless skinless chicken breasts, cut into 1-in. cubes
3	teaspoons canola oil, *divided*
2	medium carrots, chopped
1	large onion, chopped
1	medium green pepper, chopped
1	medium sweet red pepper, chopped
2	portobello mushrooms (3 ounces *each*), chopped
3	garlic cloves, minced
2-3/4	cups hot water
1	can (15 ounces) black beans, rinsed and drained
1	package (8 ounces) red beans and rice mix
1	can (14-1/2 ounces) diced tomatoes, drained
1/3	cup shredded Asiago cheese

1) In a large nonstick skillet, brown chicken in 1 teaspoon oil over medium-high heat; remove and set aside. In the same skillet, saute the carrots, onion and peppers in remaining oil for 10 minutes. Add mushrooms and garlic; saute 1-2 minutes longer or until vegetables are tender.

2) Stir in the water, black beans and red beans and rice mix. Return chicken to the pan; bring to a boil. Reduce heat; cover and simmer for 30-35 minutes or until liquid is absorbed and rice is

tender. Stir in tomatoes; heat through. Just before serving, sprinkle with cheese.

Yield: 6 servings.

Editor's Note: This recipe was prepared with Zatarain's New Orleans-style red beans and rice.

NUTRITION FACTS: 1-1/3 cups equals 381 calories, 7 g fat (2 g saturated fat), 58 mg cholesterol, 891 mg sodium, 50 g carbohydrate, 9 g fiber, 30 g protein.

Garlic Chicken Kabobs

PREP: 10 min. + marinating **GRILL:** 10 min.

Sheri Jean Waked, Loveland, Ohio

Tender and moist, these grilled kabobs are extra special when served with the garlic dipping sauce. This is a lighter version of a dish my Lebanese mother-in-law taught me to make. I reduced the amount of oil and substituted yogurt for mayonnaise.

8	garlic cloves, minced
1/2	teaspoon salt
1/4	cup minced fresh cilantro
1	teaspoon ground coriander
1/2	cup reduced-fat plain yogurt
2	tablespoons lemon juice
1-1/2	teaspoons olive oil
2	pounds boneless skinless chicken breasts, cut into 1-inch cubes

GARLIC DIPPING SAUCE:

4	garlic cloves, minced
1/4	teaspoon salt
2	tablespoons olive oil
1	cup (8 ounces) reduced-fat plain yogurt

1) Place garlic and salt in a small bowl; crush with the back of a sturdy spoon. Add cilantro and coriander; crush together. Add the yogurt, lemon juice and oil; mix well.

2) Pour into a large resealable plastic bag; add the chicken. Seal bag and turn to coat; refrigerate for 2 hours.

3) For dipping sauce, place garlic and salt in a small bowl; crush with the back of a sturdy spoon. Mix in oil. Stir in yogurt. Cover and refrigerate until serving.

4) Coat grill rack with cooking spray before starting the grill. Drain and discard marinade. Thread chicken on eight metal or soaked wooden skewers.

5) Grill kabobs, covered, over medium heat for 3-4 minutes on each side or until juices run clear. Serve with dipping sauce.

Yield: 8 servings.

Editor's Note: To broil, place kabobs on a broiler pan. Broil 4 in. from the heat for 3-4 minutes on each side or until juices run clear.

NUTRITION FACTS: 1 kabob with 2 tablespoons dipping sauce equals 186 calories, 6 g fat (1 g saturated fat), 68 mg cholesterol, 246 mg sodium, 4 g carbohydrate, trace fiber, 28 g protein.

NEW ORLEANS-STYLE CHICKEN

STIR-FRIED CHICKEN AND RICE NOODLES

🌾 Stir-Fried Chicken And Rice Noodles
PREP: 25 min. **COOK:** 20 min.

Kim Pettipas, Oromocto, New Brunswick

This is a great dish to showcase rice noodles. Don't let the ingredients fool you; the stir-fry is very simple.

- 2-1/2 teaspoons cornstarch
- 1/3 cup reduced-sodium soy sauce
- 1/4 cup white wine *or* reduced-sodium chicken broth
- 2 teaspoons sesame oil
- 1-1/2 pounds boneless skinless chicken breasts, cut into 1-inch cubes
- 1/2 cup reduced-sodium chicken broth
- 2 tablespoons sugar
- 1 tablespoon Worcestershire sauce
- 3/4 teaspoon chili powder
- 3 ounces uncooked Asian rice noodles
- 4 teaspoons canola oil, *divided*
- 3 cups fresh broccoli florets
- 2/3 cup chopped green onions
- 3 garlic cloves, minced
- 2 teaspoons minced fresh gingerroot
- 1/4 cup unsalted dry roasted peanuts

1) In a small bowl, combine the cornstarch, soy sauce, wine or broth and sesame oil until smooth. Pour 1/4 cup marinade into a large resealable plastic bag; add the chicken. Seal bag and turn to coat; refrigerate for 20 minutes.

2) Add the broth, sugar, Worcestershire sauce and chili powder to remaining marinade; set aside.

3) Cook the rice noodles according to package directions. Meanwhile, drain and discard the marinade from chicken. In a large nonstick skillet or wok, stir-fry chicken in 2 teaspoons canola oil until juices run clear; remove and keep warm.

4) Stir-fry broccoli in remaining canola oil for 5 minutes. Add the onions, garlic and ginger; stir-fry 3-5 minutes longer or until broccoli is tender. Return chicken to the pan.

5) Stir reserved broth mixture and stir into pan. Bring to a boil; cook and stir for 2 minutes or until thickened. Drain noodles; toss with chicken mixture. Garnish with peanuts.

Yield: 6 servings.

NUTRITION FACTS: 1 cup equals 293 calories, 10 g fat (2 g saturated fat), 63 mg cholesterol, 498 mg sodium, 22 g carbohydrate, 2 g fiber, 27 g protein.

🌾 Curry Chicken
PREP: 20 min. **COOK:** 15 min.

Judie White, Florien, Louisiana

A little curry powder makes this meal-in-one a vibrant change of pace from weeknight staples. I like how the dash of red pepper flakes adds extra spice to the stir-fry.

- 1 tablespoon cornstarch
- 2 teaspoons curry powder
- 1/8 teaspoon crushed red pepper flakes
- 1 cup reduced-sodium chicken broth
- 1 tablespoon reduced-sodium soy sauce
- 1 pound boneless skinless chicken breasts, cut into cubes
- 2 teaspoons canola oil, *divided*
- 1 cup sliced fresh carrots
- 2 garlic cloves, minced
- 3 cups fresh broccoli florets
- 4 green onions, thinly sliced

1) In a small bowl, combine the cornstarch, curry and red pepper flakes. Stir in broth and soy sauce until smooth; set aside.

2) In a large nonstick skillet or wok coated with cooking spray, stir-fry chicken in 1 teaspoon oil for 5-6 minutes or until no longer pink. Remove and keep warm.

3) In the same pan, stir-fry carrots and garlic in remaining oil for 1 minute. Add broccoli; cook for 2 minutes. Add onions; cook 1-2 minutes longer.

4) Stir broth mixture and stir into vegetables. Bring to a boil; cook and stir for 2 minutes or until thickened. Return chicken to the pan; heat through.

Yield: 4 servings.

NUTRITION FACTS: 1 cup equals 194 calories, 5 g fat (1 g saturated fat), 63 mg cholesterol, 389 mg sodium, 10 g carbohydrate, 3 g fiber, 26 g protein.

Hawaiian Baked Chicken

PREP: 5 min. **BAKE:** 35 min.

Leona Callen, Anna Maria, Florida

Here's a sweet and tangy way to dress up chicken. Pineapple and brown mustard pair perfectly for marinating the poultry.

- 12 boneless skinless chicken thighs (4 ounces *each*)
- 2 cans (8 ounces *each*) unsweetened crushed pineapple, undrained
- 1/4 cup sherry *or* chicken broth
- 1/4 cup spicy brown mustard
- 1/4 cup honey
- 2 tablespoons butter, melted
- 1/2 teaspoon paprika

1) Arrange chicken in a shallow baking dish coated with cooking spray. In a small bowl, combine the pineapple, sherry, mustard, honey and butter.

2) Spoon over chicken; sprinkle with paprika. Bake, uncovered, at 400° for 35-45 minutes or until a meat thermometer reads 180°.

Yield: 6 servings.

NUTRITION FACTS: 2 chicken thighs with about 1/4 cup sauce equals 285 calories, 10 g fat (4 g saturated fat), 118 mg cholesterol, 288 mg sodium, 22 g carbohydrate, 1 g fiber, 26 g protein.

Paella

PREP: 20 min. **COOK:** 25 min.

Taste of Home Test Kitchen

Paella is a Spanish dish made with rice, saffron, a variety of meat and shellfish, garlic, onions, tomatoes and other vegetables. It's named for the wide, shallow pan it's cooked in, but you can use a regular skillet.

- 4 cups chicken broth
- 2-1/2 cups uncooked long grain rice
- 1 cup chopped onion
- 2 teaspoons minced garlic, *divided*
- 1 teaspoon salt
- 1/2 teaspoon ground turmeric
- 1/4 teaspoon pepper
- 1 bay leaf
- 1 large green pepper, julienned
- 3 green onions, sliced
- 1 teaspoon minced fresh parsley
- 1 teaspoon dried thyme
- 1/4 teaspoon hot pepper sauce
- 2 tablespoons olive oil
- 1 cup sliced fresh mushrooms
- 2 medium tomatoes, chopped
- 2 cups frozen peas
- 1/2 pound uncooked medium shrimp, peeled and deveined
- 2 tablespoons lemon juice
- 1 pound boneless skinless chicken breasts, thinly sliced

1) In a large saucepan, combine the broth, rice, onion, 1 teaspoon garlic, salt, turmeric, pepper and bay leaf. Bring to a boil. Reduce heat; cover and simmer for 20 minutes or until rice is tender.

2) Meanwhile, in a large skillet, saute the green pepper, green onions, parsley, thyme, hot pepper sauce and remaining garlic in oil for 2 minutes. Add mushrooms. Cook until green pepper is crisp-tender. Add tomatoes and peas; heat through. Discard bay leaf from rice mixture. Stir rice into vegetable mixture and keep warm.

3) In a large nonstick skillet, cook and stir shrimp in lemon juice for 2 minutes. Add chicken; cook until chicken is no longer pink and shrimp has turned pink, about 3-5 minutes. Add to rice mixture; toss.

Yield: 10-12 servings.

NUTRITION FACTS: 1 serving equals 258 calories, 4 g fat (1 g saturated fat), 49 mg cholesterol, 591 mg sodium, 39 g carbohydrate, 3 g fiber, 16 g protein.

Phyllo Chicken

PREP: 15 min. **BAKE:** 35 min.

Joyce Mummau, Mt. Airy, Maryland

Phyllo dough is fun to work with. Its flakiness turns everyday ingredients into a special entree.

- 1/2 cup butter, melted, *divided*
- 12 sheets phyllo dough (14 inches x 9 inches)
- 3 cups diced cooked chicken
- 1/2 pound sliced bacon, cooked and crumbled
- 1 package (9 ounces) frozen chopped broccoli, thawed and drained
- 2 cups (8 ounces) shredded cheddar *or* Swiss cheese
- 6 eggs
- 1 cup half-and-half cream
- 1/2 cup milk
- 1 teaspoon salt
- 1/2 teaspoon pepper

1) Brush sides and bottom of a 13-in. x 9-in. x 2-in. baking dish with some of the melted butter. Place one sheet of phyllo in bottom of dish; lightly brush with butter; repeat with five more sheets of phyllo. Keep remaining phyllo covered with plastic wrap and a damp towel to prevent it from drying out.

2) In a bowl, combine chicken, bacon, broccoli and cheese; spread evenly over phyllo in baking dish. In another bowl, whisk the eggs, cream, milk, salt and pepper; pour over chicken mixture.

3) Cover filling with one sheet of phyllo; brush with butter. Repeat with remaining phyllo dough. Brush top with remaining butter.

PHYLLO CHICKEN

4) Bake, uncovered, at 375° for 35-40 minutes or until a knife inserted near the center comes out clean. Let stand for 5-10 minutes before cutting.

Yield: 12 servings.

NUTRITION FACTS: 1 serving equals 373 calories, 24 g fat (13 g saturated fat), 195 mg cholesterol, 659 mg sodium, 16 g carbohydrate, 1 g fiber, 23 g protein.

Baked Chicken and Acorn Squash

PREP: 20 min. **BAKE:** 1 hour

Connie Svoboda, Elko, Minnesota

With its colorful acorn squash and sweet peaches, this main dish is ideal for harvesttime. The fragrance of rosemary-seasoned chicken baking is heavenly.

     2 small acorn squash (1-1/4 pounds)
     2 to 4 garlic cloves, minced
     2 tablespoons vegetable oil, *divided*
     4 chicken drumsticks (4 ounces *each*)
     4 chicken thighs (4 ounces *each*)
  1/4 cup packed brown sugar
     1 teaspoon salt
     1 tablespoon minced fresh rosemary *or* 1 teaspoon dried rosemary, crushed
     1 can (15-1/4 ounces) sliced peaches, undrained

1) Cut squash in half lengthwise; discard seeds. Cut each half widthwise into 1/2-in. slices; discard ends. Place slices in an ungreased 13-in. x 9-in. x 2-in. baking dish. Sprinkle with garlic and drizzle with 1 tablespoon oil.

2) In a large skillet, brown chicken in remaining oil. Arrange chicken over squash. Combine the

brown sugar, salt and rosemary; sprinkle over chicken. Bake, uncovered, at 350° for 45 minutes, basting with pan juices twice.

3) Pour peaches over chicken and squash. Bake 15 minutes longer or until the chicken juices run clear and the peaches are heated through.

Yield: 4 servings.

NUTRITION FACTS: 1 serving equals 624 calories, 21 g fat (5 g saturated fat), 147 mg cholesterol, 740 mg sodium, 64 g carbohydrate, 5 g fiber, 45 g protein.

Sweet Smoky Chicken Legs

PREP: 10 min. **BAKE:** 1 hour

Jane MacKinnis, Eden, Maryland

This is so easy! Just layer the ingredients in the baking dish, and a wonderful meal is ready in about an hour.

     2 medium onions, sliced
     3 pounds chicken legs
  1/2 cup ketchup
  1/2 cup maple syrup
  1/4 cup white vinegar
     2 tablespoons prepared mustard
     1 teaspoon salt
  1/2 teaspoon Liquid Smoke

1) Place onions in a greased 13-in. x 9-in. x 2-in. baking dish; arrange chicken in a single layer over onions.

2) Combine the ketchup, syrup, vinegar, mustard salt and Liquid Smoke; pour over all, completely coating chicken.

3) Bake, uncovered, at 350° for 1 hour or until juices run clear or a meat thermometer reads 180°, basting several times.

Yield: 6 servings.

NUTRITION FACTS: 1 serving equals 346 calories, 12 g fat (3 g saturated fat), 94 mg cholesterol, 777 mg sodium, 29 g carbohydrate, 1 g fiber, 30 g protein.

BAKED CHICKEN AND ACORN SQUASH

ORIENTAL CHICKEN THIGHS

Oriental Chicken Thighs

PREP: 15 min. **COOK:** 50 min.

Dave Farrington, Midwest City, Oklahoma

A thick, tangy sauce coats the golden chicken pieces in this savory skillet recipe. I like to serve them over long grain rice or with a helping of ramen noodle slaw.

 5 bone-in chicken thighs, skin removed
 5 teaspoons olive oil
 1/3 cup warm water
 1/4 cup packed brown sugar
 2 tablespoons orange juice
 2 tablespoons soy sauce
 2 tablespoons ketchup
 1 tablespoon white vinegar
 4 garlic cloves, minced
 1/2 teaspoon crushed red pepper flakes
 1/4 teaspoon Chinese five-spice powder
 2 teaspoons cornstarch
 2 tablespoons cold water
Hot cooked rice
Sliced green onions

1) In a large skillet, brown chicken in oil over medium heat for 18-20 minutes or until juices run clear. Meanwhile, in a jar with a tight-fitting lid, combine the warm water, brown sugar, orange juice, soy sauce, ketchup, vinegar, garlic, pepper flakes and five-spice powder; shake until sugar is dissolved.

2) Pour over the chicken. Bring to a boil. Reduce heat; simmer, uncovered, for 30-35 minutes or until chicken is tender, turning occasionally.

3) Combine cornstarch and cold water until smooth; gradually stir into skillet. Bring to a boil; cook and stir for 2 minutes or until thickened. Serve with rice. Garnish with green onions.

Yield: 5 servings.

NUTRITION FACTS: 1 serving (calculated without rice and green onions) equals 203 calories, 10 g fat (2 g saturated fat), 46 mg cholesterol, 482 mg sodium, 15 g carbohydrate, trace fiber, 14 g protein.

Chicken Salad with Crispy Wontons

PREP/TOTAL TIME: 30 min.

Kylea Rorabaugh, Kansas City, Missouri

My mom made this when I was growing up, but I added veggies and lightened the sweet-and-sour dressing. I also broil the crispy wontons instead of frying them.

 10 wonton wrappers, cut into 1/4-inch strips
 1/4 cup cider vinegar
 3 tablespoons canola oil
 3/4 teaspoon sesame oil
 2 tablespoons sugar
 3/4 teaspoon salt
 1/4 teaspoon pepper
 5 cups torn romaine
 3 cups cubed cooked chicken breast
 1 medium sweet red pepper, cut into 1/4-inch strips
 1 medium sweet yellow pepper, cut into 1/4-inch strips
 1/2 cup halved grape tomatoes

1) Lightly spritz both sides of wonton strips with cooking spray; place on a baking sheet. Broil 4-6 in. from the heat for 2-3 minutes or until golden brown. Turn strips over; broil 2-3 minutes longer or until golden brown. Remove to wire racks to cool.

2) For dressing, in a small bowl, whisk the vinegar, oils, sugar, salt and pepper; set aside. In a large bowl, combine the romaine, chicken, peppers and tomatoes. Just before serving, drizzle with dressing and toss to coat. Top with wonton strips.

Yield: 10 servings.

NUTRITION FACTS: 1 cup equals 149 calories, 6 g fat (1 g saturated fat), 33 mg cholesterol, 253 mg sodium, 10 g carbohydrate, 1 g fiber, 14 g protein.

Poppy Seed Chicken

PREP: 15 min. **BAKE:** 20 min.

Ernestine Plasek, Houston, Texas

This recipe is the ideal solution when you wonder what to do with leftover cooked chicken.

 1/2 pound fresh mushrooms, sliced
 1 tablespoon butter
 5 cups cubed cooked chicken
 1 can (10-3/4 ounces) condensed cream of chicken soup, undiluted
 1 cup (8 ounces) sour cream
 1 jar (2 ounces) diced pimientos, drained

TOPPING:
 1/2 cup butter, melted
 1-1/3 cups finely crushed butter-flavored crackers
 2 teaspoons poppy seeds

1) In a large skillet, saute mushrooms in butter until tender. Stir in the chicken, soup, sour cream and pimientos. Spoon into a greased 2-qt. baking dish.

2) Combine topping ingredients; sprinkle over chicken mixture. Bake, uncovered, at 350° for 20-25 minutes or until heated through and topping is browned.

Yield: 6 servings.

NUTRITION FACTS: 1 serving equals 619 calories, 41 g fat (19 g saturated fat), 181 mg cholesterol, 848 mg sodium, 21 g carbohydrate, 2 g fiber, 39 g protein.

Baked Chimichangas

PREP/TOTAL TIME: 30 min.

Angela Oelschlaeger, Tonganoxie, Kansas

Usually chimichangas are deep-fried, so my baked version is healthier as well as delicious. You can omit the chilies for less heat.

2-1/2	cups shredded cooked chicken breast
1	cup salsa
1	small onion, chopped
3/4	teaspoon ground cumin
1/2	teaspoon dried oregano
6	flour tortillas (10 inches), warmed
3/4	cup shredded reduced-fat cheddar cheese
1	cup reduced-sodium chicken broth
2	teaspoons chicken bouillon granules
1/8	teaspoon pepper
1/4	cup all-purpose flour
1	cup fat-free half-and-half
1	can (4 ounces) chopped green chilies

BAKED CHIMICHANGAS

1) In a large nonstick skillet, simmer the chicken, salsa, onion, cumin and oregano until heated through and most of liquid is evaporated. Place 1/2 cup down the center of each tortilla; top with 2 tablespoons cheese.

2) Fold sides and ends over filling; roll up. Place seam side down in a 13-in. x 9-in. x 2-in. baking dish coated with cooking spray. Bake, uncovered, at 425° for 15 minutes or until browned.

3) In a saucepan, heat broth, bouillon and pepper until bouillon is dissolved. Combine flour and half-and-half until smooth; stir into broth. Bring to a boil; cook and stir for 2 minutes or until thickened. Stir in chilies; heat through. Cut chimichangas in half; top with sauce.

Yield: 6 servings.

NUTRITION FACTS: 1 chimichanga with 1/3 cup sauce equals 423 calories, 9 g fat (3 g saturated fat), 57 mg cholesterol, 1,326 mg sodium, 47 g carbohydrate, 7 g fiber, 32 g protein.

Pizza on the Grill

PREP: 30 min. **GRILL:** 10 min.

Lisa Boettcher, Columbus, Wisconsin

I make pizza at least once a week. The barbecue flavor mingling with the cheese tastes delicious.

1	package (1/4 ounce) active dry yeast
1	cup warm water (110° to 115°)
2	tablespoons vegetable oil
2	teaspoons sugar
1	teaspoon baking soda
1	teaspoon salt
2-3/4	to 3 cups all-purpose flour

TOPPINGS:

2	cups cubed cooked chicken
1/2	to 3/4 cup barbecue sauce
1/2	cup julienned green pepper
2	cups (8 ounces) shredded Monterey Jack cheese

1) In a large mixing bowl, dissolve yeast in warm water. Add the oil, sugar, baking soda, salt and 2 cups flour. Stir in enough remaining flour to form a soft dough.

2) Turn onto a floured surface; knead until smooth and elastic, about 6-8 minutes. Cover and let rest for 10 minutes. On a floured surface, roll dough into a 13-in. circle. Transfer to a greased 12-in. pizza pan. Build up edges slightly.

3) Grill, covered, over medium heat for 5 minutes. Remove from the grill. Combine chicken and barbecue sauce; spread over crust. Sprinkle with green pepper and cheese. Grill, covered, 5-10 minutes longer or until crust is golden and cheese is melted.

Yield: 4 servings.

NUTRITION FACTS: 1 serving equals 757 calories, 31 g fat (13 g saturated fat), 113 mg cholesterol, 1,525 mg sodium, 73 g carbohydrate, 3 g fiber, 44 g protein.

Stuffing Tips for Poultry

You'll want to prepare about 3/4 cup stuffing for every pound of poultry. Try using sauteed vegetables, cooked meats or egg substitute in place of fresh eggs.

Begin stuffing preparation ahead of time if desired. For example, chop and saute vegetables. Make bread cubes or measure out store-bought stuffing croutons. Combine seasonings. Store wet ingredients separate from dry, and store perishable items in the refrigerator.

Wait until just before you are ready to stuff the bird to heat the broth or water for the stuffing and combine all the ingredients.

Stuff the poultry just before you are ready to bake. Loosely spoon stuffing into the neck and body cavities to allow for expansion as the poultry roasts. See Stuffing, Roasting and Carving a Whole Turkey on page 240.

Stuffed poultry requires longer roasting time—add 15-45 minutes to the time unstuffed poultry takes.

The internal temperature of the stuffing must reach 165° in order to be fully cooked. If the bird is completely cooked and the stuffing has not reached 165°, remove from bird and transfer to a baking dish. Continue baking the stuffing until it reaches 165°.

Bake stuffing in a casserole dish as the poultry bakes. See specific recipes for baking directions.

Cover the whole bird and let it stand for 10-20 minutes before removing the stuffing. Remove all stuffing and store any leftovers in separate containers in the refrigerator.

CIDER-MARINATED TURKEY

Cider-Marinated Turkey

PREP: 20 min. + marinating
GRILL: 2 hours + standing

Wendy Stenman, Germantown, Wisconsin

Make Thanksgiving dinner memorable by serving this golden-brown turkey that's marinated in apple cider, kosher salt and spices.

  8 cups apple cider *or* unsweetened apple juice
1/2 cup kosher salt
  2 bay leaves
  2 sprigs fresh thyme
  8 whole cloves
  5 garlic cloves
  1 teaspoon whole allspice, crushed
  2 medium navel oranges, quartered
  3 quarts cold water
  1 turkey (12 pounds)
  1 medium onion, quartered
  2 medium carrots, halved and quartered
  2 sprigs fresh sage *or* 1 tablespoon rubbed sage
  1 tablespoon canola oil

1) In a large kettle, combine the cider and the seasonings. Bring to a boil. Cook and stir until salt is dissolved. Stir in oranges. Remove from the heat. Add water; cool to room temperature.

2) Remove giblets from turkey; discard. Place a turkey-size oven roasting bag inside a second roasting bag; add turkey. Place in a roasting pan.

3) Carefully pour the cooled marinade into bag. Squeeze out as much air as possible; seal bag and turn to coat. Refrigerate for 12-14 hours; turn several times.

4) Coat grill rack with cooking spray before starting grill. Prepare grill for indirect heat, using a drip pan. Drain and discard marinade. Rinse turkey under cold water; pat dry. Place onion, carrots and sage in cavity. Rub oil over skin. Skewer turkey openings; tie drumsticks together.

5) Place turkey over drip pan. Grill, covered, over indirect medium heat for 2-3 hours or until a meat thermometer reads 180° in the thigh, tenting turkey with foil after about 1 hour. Cover and let stand for 15 minutes.

6) If desired, thicken pan juices for gravy. Remove and discard skin and vegetables in cavity before carving turkey. Serve with gravy.

Yield: 12 servings plus leftovers.

Editor's Note: It is best not to use a prebasted turkey for this recipe. However, if you do, omit the salt in the recipe.

NUTRITION FACTS: 4 ounces light and dark cooked turkey (skin removed, calculated without gravy) equals 198 calories, 6 g fat (2 g saturated fat), 86 mg cholesterol, 244 mg sodium, trace carbohydrate, 0 fiber, 33 g protein.

Stuffed Duckling

PREP: 20 min. **BAKE:** 1-3/4 hours + standing

Joanne Callahan, Far Hills, New Jersey

I started with a basic bread stuffing and added on-hand ingredients until I came up with this pleasing recipe. The stuffing usually disappears long before the bird is gone!

- 1/2 cup chopped onion
- 1 garlic clove, minced
- 1 tablespoon butter
- 2 cups cubed day-old bread
- 1 cup cooked rice
- 1 teaspoon dried basil
- 1 teaspoon dried rosemary, crushed
- 1 teaspoon rubbed sage
- 1 teaspoon dried parsley flakes
- 1 teaspoon salt, *divided*
- 1/8 teaspoon pepper
- 1/2 cup raisins
- 1/2 cup chopped pecans
- 1/4 to 1/3 cup chicken broth
- 1 domestic duckling (4 to 5 pounds)

1) In a large skillet, saute onion and garlic in butter until tender; transfer to a large bowl. Add bread cubes, rice, basil, rosemary, sage, parsley, 1/2 teaspoon salt and pepper. Add raisins, pecans and enough broth to moisten; toss gently.

2) Prick skin of duckling well with a fork. Sprinkle cavity with remaining salt. Lightly stuff bread mixture into duck. Place breast side up on a rack in a shallow roasting pan.

3) Bake, uncovered, at 350° for 1-3/4 to 2 hours or until a meat thermometer reads 180° for duck and 165° for stuffing. Drain fat as it accumulates during roasting. Cover and let stand 20 minutes before removing stuffing and carving.

Yield: 4 servings.

NUTRITION FACTS: 4 ounces cooked meat equals 606 calories, 44 g fat (14 g saturated fat), 108 mg cholesterol, 589 mg sodium, 26 g carbohydrate, 2 g fiber, 26 g protein.

Brown Rice 'n' Apple Stuffed Turkey

PREP: 1 hour **BAKE:** 2-3/4 hours + standing

Taste of Home Test Kitchen

Mouth-watering flavors of autumn permeate this lovely stuffing. Apple bits and plump raisins add fruity flavor to the brown rice.

- 1 can (14-1/2 ounces) reduced-sodium chicken broth
- 1/2 cup unsweetened apple juice, *divided*
- 1/2 teaspoon salt, *divided*
- 1 cup uncooked long grain brown rice

STUFFED DUCKLING

- 1/3 cup raisins
- 1/2 cup *each* chopped celery and onion
- 1 tablespoon butter
- 1 cup chopped tart apple
- 1 teaspoon poultry seasoning
- 1/4 teaspoon pepper
- 1 turkey (10 to 12 pounds)

1) In a saucepan, bring the broth, 1/3 cup juice and 1/4 teaspoon salt to a boil. Stir in rice and raisins. Return to a boil. Reduce heat; cover and simmer for 40-50 minutes or until rice is tender.

2) In a nonstick skillet, cook celery and onion in butter for 2 minutes. Add apple; cook and stir for 3 minutes or until vegetables are tender. Combine the rice mixture, apple mixture, poultry seasoning, pepper and remaining juice and salt.

3) Just before baking, loosely stuff turkey. Skewer turkey openings; tie drumsticks together. Place breast side up on a rack in a roasting pan. Bake, uncovered, at 325° for 2-3/4 to 3 hours or until a meat thermometer reads 180° for the turkey and 165° for the stuffing. (Cover loosely with foil if turkey browns too quickly.)

4) Cover turkey and let stand for 20 minutes. Remove stuffing and carve turkey. If desired, thicken pan drippings for gravy.

Yield: 6 servings plus leftovers.

Editor's Note: Stuffing may be prepared as directed and baked separately in a 1-1/2-qt. baking dish coated with cooking spray. Cover and bake at 325° for 25 minutes. Uncover; bake 10-15 minutes longer or until heated through.

NUTRITION FACTS: 3 ounces cooked turkey with 3/4 cup stuffing (calculated without gravy) equals 286 calories, 8 g fat (3 g saturated fat), 51 mg cholesterol, 443 mg sodium, 37 g carbohydrate, 3 g fiber, 17 g protein.

TEMPTING HOLIDAY TURKEY

 CLASSIC: Classic Stuffed Turkey is perfect for the holidays or any special gathering of family and friends. This has a simple, herb-seasoned mushroom stuffing. If you prefer, omit the mushroom stuffing and use one of the other kinds of stuffings, starting on pages 336 and 337.

 TIME-SAVER: The slow cooker makes short work of your kitchen time in Turkey in a Pot. A boneless turkey breast is cooked in a spiced cranberry-apple juice mixture. The boneless breast is easy to slice, too!

 LIGHT: By roasting an all-white meat turkey breast and discarding the skin before serving, Herbed Turkey Breast reduces both calories and fat.

SERVES 2: When serving two, a whole turkey or even a turkey breast is just too much, leaving a lot of leftovers. A recipe scaled down to just the right size is Citrus Turkey Tenderloin.

CLASSIC STUFFED TURKEY

Classic Stuffed Turkey

PREP: 20 min. **BAKE:** 3-3/4 hours + standing

Kathi Graham, Naperville, Illinois

- 2 large onions, chopped
- 2 celery ribs, chopped
- 1/2 pound fresh mushrooms, sliced
- 1/2 cup butter
- 1 can (14-1/2 ounces) chicken broth
- 1/3 cup minced fresh parsley
- 2 teaspoons rubbed sage
- 1 teaspoon salt
- 1 teaspoon poultry seasoning
- 1/2 teaspoon pepper
- 12 cups unseasoned stuffing cubes

Warm water

- 1 turkey (14 to 16 pounds)

Melted butter

1) In a large skillet, saute the onions, celery and mushrooms in butter until tender. Add broth and seasonings; mix well.

2) Place bread cubes in a large bowl; add mushroom mixture and toss to coat. Stir in enough warm water to reach desired moistness. Just before baking, loosely stuff turkey. Place any remaining stuffing in a greased baking dish; cover and refrigerate. Remove dish from refrigerator 30 minutes before baking.

3) Skewer turkey openings; tie drumsticks together with kitchen string. Place breast side up on a rack in a roasting pan. Brush with melted butter.

4) Bake turkey, uncovered, at 325° for 3-3/4 to 4-1/2 hours or until a meat thermometer reads 180° for the turkey and 165° for the stuffing, basting occasionally with pan drippings. (Cover loosely with foil if turkey browns too quickly.)

5) Bake additional stuffing, covered, for 30 minutes. Uncover; bake 10 minutes longer or until lightly browned.

6) Cover turkey with foil and let stand for 20 minutes before removing stuffing and carving. If desired, thicken pan drippings for gravy.

Yield: 12 servings (10 cups stuffing).

NUTRITION FACTS: 1 serving equals 571 calories, 26 g fat (11 g saturated fat), 153 mg cholesterol, 961 mg sodium, 42 g carbohydrate, 4 g fiber, 44 g protein.

Turkey in a Pot

PREP: 25 min. **COOK:** 5 hours

Lois Woodward, Okeechobee, Florida

- 1 boneless turkey breast (3 to 4 pounds), halved
- 1 can (16 ounces) whole-berry cranberry sauce
- 1/2 cup sugar
- 1/2 cup apple juice
- 1 tablespoon cider vinegar
- 2 garlic cloves, minced
- 1 teaspoon ground mustard

1/2 teaspoon ground cinnamon
1/4 teaspoon ground cloves
1/4 teaspoon ground allspice
2 tablespoons all-purpose flour
1/4 cup cold water
1/4 teaspoon browning sauce,
optional

1) Place the turkey skin side up in a 5-qt. slow cooker. Combine the cranberry sauce, sugar, apple juice, vinegar, garlic, mustard, cinnamon, cloves and allspice; pour over turkey.

2) Cover and cook on low for 5-6 hours or until a meat thermometer reads 170°.

3) Remove turkey to a cutting board; keep warm. Strain cooking juices. In a saucepan, combine flour and water until smooth; gradually stir in strained juices. Bring to a boil; cook and stir for 2 minutes or until thickened. Stir in browning sauce if desired. Serve with sliced turkey.

Yield: 12-16 servings.

NUTRITION FACTS: 4 ounces cooked turkey equals 168 calories, 1 g fat (trace saturated fat), 53 mg cholesterol, 48 mg sodium, 19 g carbohydrate, 1 g fiber, 21 g protein.

Herbed Turkey Breast

PREP: 15 min. **BAKE:** 2-1/2 hours + standing

Alicia Glover, Sterling, Alaska

1 bone-in turkey breast (8-1/2 pounds)
3 tablespoons lemon juice, *divided*
2 tablespoons olive oil, *divided*
2 garlic cloves, minced
1-1/2 teaspoons salt
1 teaspoon grated lemon peel
1 teaspoon dried thyme
3/4 teaspoon pepper
1/2 teaspoon rubbed sage

1) Loosen skin from turkey with fingers, leaving skin attached along bottom edges. Combine 1 tablespoon lemon juice, 1 tablespoon oil, garlic and seasonings; spread under turkey skin. In a small bowl, combine remaining lemon juice and oil; set aside for basting.

2) Place turkey on a rack in a shallow roasting pan. Bake, uncovered, at 350° for 2-1/2 to 3 hours or until a meat thermometer reads 170°, basting every 15-20 minutes with lemon mixture. Let stand for 10 minutes. Remove skin before carving.

Yield: 16 servings.

NUTRITION FACTS: 1 serving equals 158 calories, 3 g fat (1 g saturated fat), 79 mg cholesterol, 246 mg sodium, 1 g carbohydrate, trace fiber, 31 g protein.

Citrus Turkey Tenderloin

PREP: 30 min. **BAKE:** 30 min.

Diane Baker, Bothell, Washington

1 garlic clove, minced
1 turkey tenderloin (about 1/2 pound)
1/3 cup orange juice
1/4 cup plus 1 tablespoon chicken broth, *divided*
1 tablespoon lemon juice
1 teaspoon minced fresh thyme *or* 1/4 teaspoon dried thyme

Salt to taste, optional
Pepper to taste

2 teaspoons cornstarch

1) Rub garlic over all sides of tenderloin. Place in a greased shallow 5-cup baking dish. Pour the orange juice, 1/4 cup broth and lemon juice over turkey. Sprinkle with the thyme, salt if desired and pepper.

2) Cover and bake at 325° for 20 minutes. Uncover; bake 10-20 minutes longer or until meat juices run clear and a meat thermometer reads 170°, basting occasionally. Remove turkey to a serving platter and keep warm.

3) For sauce, pour drippings and loosened browned bits into a measuring cup. Skim the fat; pour the drippings into a small saucepan. Combine cornstarch and remaining broth until smooth; stir into drippings. Bring to a boil; cook and stir for 1-2 minutes or until thickened. Serve with turkey.

Yield: 2 servings.

NUTRITION FACTS: 1 serving equals 155 calories, 2 g fat (trace saturated fat), 56 mg cholesterol, 207 mg sodium, 8 g carbohydrate, trace fiber, 27 g protein.

CITRUS TURKEY TENDERLOIN

Stuffing, Roasting and Carving a Whole Turkey

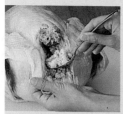

1) Combine the stuffing ingredients as recipe directs. Do not stuff the turkey until you're ready to place it in the oven. Spoon the stuffing loosely into neck cavity.

2) Pull neck skin over stuffing to the back of turkey and secure with a skewer. Tuck wing tips under body to avoid overbrowning while roasting.

3) Loosely spoon stuffing into the body cavity. Tie drumsticks together with kitchen string.

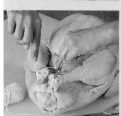

4) Place turkey breast side up on a rack in a shallow roasting pan. Brush with oil or melted butter if desired. Insert an oven-safe meat thermometer into thick portion of inner thigh area, not touching bone. Or use an instant-read thermometer toward end of roasting time.

5) Roast turkey as recipe directs. Baste with pan juices if desired.

6) When breast area has browned, loosely cover with foil to avoid excess browning. Roast until the thermometer reads 180° in the thigh and stuffing is 165°.

7) Place bird on a carving board and remove any stuffing. Holding the end of the drumstick, pull the leg away from the body and cut between the thigh joint and body to remove the entire leg. Repeat with other leg.

8) To separate the drumstick and thigh, cut through the connecting joint.

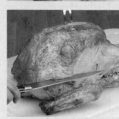

9) Holding drumstick by the end, slice meat into 1/4-in. slices. Cut thigh meat parallel to the bone into 1/4-in. slices.

10) Hold the bird with a meat fork and make a deep cut into the breast meat just above the wing area.

11) Slice down from the top of the breast into the cut made in Step 10. Slice meat 1/4 in. thick. Repeat Steps 10 and 11 on other side of bird.

12) To remove wings, cut through connecting joints by the wing bones and backbone.

LEMON TURKEY WITH COUSCOUS STUFFING

Lemon Turkey with Couscous Stuffing

PREP: 15 min. **BAKE:** 1 hour 25 min. + standing

Kathi Graham, Naperville, Illinois

This moist turkey breast with its unique stuffing is perfect for a special-occasion main dish.

- 1 bone-in turkey breast (4 to 4-1/2 pounds)
- 2 teaspoons olive oil
- 1 teaspoon lemon juice
- 1 garlic clove, minced
- 1/2 teaspoon grated lemon peel
- 1/4 teaspoon salt
- 1/8 teaspoon pepper

STUFFING:
- 1-1/2 cups boiling water
- 1 cup uncooked couscous
- 1 medium carrot, shredded
- 1/2 cup raisins
- 1/3 cup chicken broth
- 1/4 cup slivered almonds, toasted
- 2 tablespoons minced fresh parsley

1) Carefully loosen turkey skin, leaving it attached at the back. Combine the oil, lemon juice, garlic, lemon peel, salt and pepper; spread under turkey skin. Place turkey to one side in a shallow roasting pan coated with cooking spray.

2) For stuffing, in a bowl, pour boiling water over couscous. Cover and let stand for 5 minutes or until water is absorbed. Add remaining ingredients; toss to combine. Spoon stuffing into other side of pan, shaping into an 8-in. x 5-in. x 2-in. mound. Cover pan; bake at 325° for 45 minutes.

3) Uncover turkey; leave stuffing covered. Bake 40-50 minutes longer or until a meat thermometer reads 170°. Cover turkey with foil and let stand for 15 minutes before slicing. Serve with stuffing.

Yield: 8 servings.

NUTRITION FACTS: 4-1/2 ounces cooked turkey (skin removed) with 1/2 cup stuffing equals 303 calories, 4 g fat (1 g saturated fat), 94 mg cholesterol, 181 mg sodium, 26 g carbohydrate, 2 g fiber, 38 g protein.

Roast Christmas Goose

PREP: 10 min. **BAKE:** 2-1/4 hours + standing

Rosemarie Forcum, White Stone, Virginia

I have such fond childhood memories of my mother serving this golden-brown goose for holiday meals.

- 1 goose (10 to 12 pounds)
- Salt and pepper
- 1 medium apple, peeled and quartered
- 1 medium navel orange, peeled and quartered
- 1 medium lemon, peeled and quartered
- 1 cup hot water

1) Sprinkle the goose cavity with salt and pepper. Place apple, orange and lemon in cavity. Place goose breast side up on a rack in a large roasting pan. Prick skin well with a fork. Pour water into pan.

2) Bake, uncovered, at 350° for 2-1/4 to 3 hours or until a meat thermometer reads 185°. If necessary, drain fat from pan as it accumulates. Cover goose with foil and let stand for 20 minutes before carving. Discard fruit.

Yield: 10 servings.

NUTRITION FACTS: 4 ounces cooked meat equals 376 calories, 26 g fat (8 g saturated fat), 108 mg cholesterol, 84 mg sodium, 4 g carbohydrate, 1 g fiber, 30 g protein.

Duck with Cherry Sauce

PREP: 5 min. **BAKE:** 2 hours + standing

Sandy Jenkins, Elkhorn, Wisconsin

This is one of my mom's signature Sunday dishes.

- 1 domestic duckling (4 to 5 pounds)
- 1 jar (12 ounces) cherry preserves
- 1 to 2 tablespoons red wine vinegar

1) Prick skin of duckling well with a fork and place breast side up on a rack in a shallow roasting pan. Tie drumsticks together. Bake, uncovered, at 350° for 2 to 2-1/2 hours or until juices run clear and meat thermometer reads 180°. Drain fat from pan as it accumulates. Cover and let stand 20 minutes before carving.

2) For sauce, combine preserves and vinegar in a small saucepan. Cook and stir over medium heat until heated through. Serve with duck.

Yield: 4-5 servings.

NUTRITION FACTS: 6 ounces cooked duck equals 664 calories, 41 g fat (14 g saturated fat), 123 mg cholesterol, 86 mg sodium, 44 g carbohydrate, 0 fiber, 28 g protein.

TURKEY MARSALA

🌿 Turkey Marsala

PREP: 10 min. **COOK:** 30 min.

Deborah Williams, Peoria, Arizona

This recipe originally called for beef, but I used turkey to make it healthier. It's easy to prepare, but the rich sauce makes it seem like you spent all day in the kitchen. I often serve this with a baked sweet potato and a green vegetable.

- 1 package (20 ounces) turkey breast tenderloins
- 1/4 cup all-purpose flour
- 1/2 teaspoon salt, *divided*
- 1/2 teaspoon pepper, *divided*
- 1 tablespoon olive oil
- 1/2 pound fresh mushrooms, sliced
- 1 tablespoon butter
- 1/2 cup reduced-sodium chicken broth
- 1/2 cup Marsala wine *or* 1/3 cup reduced-sodium chicken broth, 3 tablespoons white grape juice and 2 teaspoons white wine vinegar
- 1 teaspoon lemon juice

1) Cut tenderloins in half and flatten to 3/4-in. thickness. In a large resealable plastic bag, combine the flour, 1/4 teaspoon salt and 1/4 teaspoon pepper. Add turkey and shake to coat.

2) In a large nonstick skillet, cook turkey in oil over medium heat for 7-8 minutes on each side or until juices run clear. Remove and keep warm.

3) In the same skillet, saute mushrooms in butter for 4 minutes or until tender. Stir in the broth and wine or broth mixture. Cook over medium heat for 12-15 minutes or until liquid is reduced by half. Stir in lemon juice and remaining salt and pepper. Serve over turkey.

Yield: 4 servings.

NUTRITION FACTS: 4 ounces cooked turkey with 1/4 cup mushroom mixture equals 295 calories, 8 g fat (3 g saturated fat), 77 mg cholesterol, 482 mg sodium, 12 g carbohydrate, 1 g fiber, 36 g protein.

🌿 Peppery Herbed Turkey Tenderloin

PREP: 10 min. + marinating **COOK:** 15 min.

Virginia Anthony, Jacksonville, Florida

I won the North Carolina Turkey Cook-Off one year with these full-flavored tenderloins in a tasty sauce. Marinating the turkey in wine, garlic, rosemary and thyme gives it a fantastic flavor.

- 3 turkey breast tenderloins (12 ounces *each*)
- 1 cup dry white wine *or* apple juice
- 3 green onions, chopped
- 3 tablespoons minced fresh parsley
- 6 teaspoons olive oil, *divided*
- 1 tablespoon finely chopped garlic
- 3/4 teaspoon dried rosemary, crushed
- 3/4 teaspoon dried thyme
- 1 teaspoon coarsely ground pepper
- 3/4 teaspoon salt, *divided*
- 4 teaspoons cornstarch
- 1 cup reduced-sodium chicken broth

1) Pat tenderloins dry; flatten to 3/4-in. thickness. In a bowl, combine the wine or juice, onions, parsley, 4 teaspoons oil, garlic, rosemary and thyme.

2) Pour 3/4 cup marinade into a large resealable plastic bag; add turkey. Seal bag and turn to coat; refrigerate for at least 4 hours, turning occasionally. Cover and refrigerate remaining marinade.

3) Drain and discard marinade from turkey. Sprinkle turkey with pepper and 1/2 teaspoon salt. In a large nonstick skillet, cook turkey in remaining oil for 5-6 minutes on each side or until no longer pink. Remove and keep warm.

4) In a small bowl, combine the cornstarch, broth, reserved marinade and remaining salt until smooth; pour into skillet. Bring to a boil; cook and stir for 1-2 minutes or until thickened. Slice turkey; serve with sauce.

Yield: 6 servings.

Editor's Note: If using the apple juice instead of wine, add 1 tablespoon white wine vinegar *or* cider vinegar to the marinade.

NUTRITION FACTS: 5 ounces cooked turkey equals 258 calories, 5 g fat (1 g saturated fat), 116 mg cholesterol, 476 mg sodium, 4 g carbohydrate, trace fiber, 41 g protein.

🌀 Turkey Scallopini

PREP/TOTAL TIME: 20 min.

Karen Adams, Seymour, Indiana

Quick-cooking turkey breast slices make it easy to prepare a satisfying meal in minutes. I've also used boneless skinless chicken breast halves.

- 6 turkey breast slices (about 1-1/2 pounds)
- 1/4 cup all-purpose flour

TURKEY SCALLOPINI

1/8 teaspoon salt
1/8 teaspoon pepper
  1 egg
  2 tablespoons water
  1 cup soft bread crumbs
1/2 cup grated Parmesan cheese
1/4 cup butter, cubed
Minced fresh parsley

1) Pound turkey to 1/4-in. thickness. In a shallow bowl, combine the flour, salt and pepper. In another bowl, beat egg and water. On a plate, combine the bread crumbs and Parmesan cheese.

2) Dredge turkey in flour mixture; dip in egg mixture and coat with crumbs. Let stand for 5 minutes.

3) In a large skillet, melt butter over medium-high heat; cook turkey for 2-3 minutes on each side or until juices run clear and coating is golden brown. Sprinkle with parsley.

Yield: 6 servings.

NUTRITION FACTS: 1 serving equals 904 calories, 15 g fat (8 g saturated fat), 483 mg cholesterol, 635 mg sodium, 8 g carbohydrate, trace fiber, 172 g protein.

Citrus Grilled Turkey Breast

PREP: 10 min. **GRILL:** 1-1/2 hours + standing

Taste of Home Test Kitchen

Instead of the usual outdoor barbecue, treat your guests to a sit-down dinner featuring this delicious grilled entree with a luscious herb and citrus gravy.

  1 bone-in turkey breast
    (4 to 5 pounds)
1/4 cup fresh parsley sprigs
1/4 cup fresh basil leaves
  3 tablespoons butter
  4 garlic cloves, halved
1/2 teaspoon salt
  1 medium lemon, thinly sliced
  1 medium orange, thinly sliced

  1 tablespoon cornstarch
  2 tablespoons water
  1 cup orange juice
  1 teaspoon grated orange peel
  1 teaspoon grated lemon peel
1/4 teaspoon pepper

1) Using fingers, carefully loosen the skin from both sides of turkey breast. In a food processor, combine the parsley, basil, butter, garlic and salt; cover and process until smooth.

2) Spread parsley mixture under turkey skin; arrange lemon and orange slices over herb mixture. Secure skin to underside of breast with toothpicks.

3) Coat grill rack with cooking spray before starting the grill. Prepare grill for indirect heat, using a drip pan. Place turkey over drip pan.

4) Grill, covered, over indirect medium heat for 1-1/2 to 2-1/4 hours or until a meat thermometer reads 170° and juices run clear. Cover and let stand for 10 minutes.

5) Meanwhile, pour pan drippings into a measuring cup; skim fat. In a saucepan, combine cornstarch and water until smooth. Add the orange juice, orange peel, lemon peel, pepper and pan drippings. Bring to a boil; cook and stir for 2 minutes or until thickened.

6) Discard the skin, lemon and orange slices from turkey breast. Remove herb mixture from turkey; stir into gravy. Slice turkey and serve with gravy.

Yield: 8 servings plus leftovers.

NUTRITION FACTS: 4 ounces cooked turkey with 3 tablespoons gravy equals 192 calories, 2 g fat (1 g saturated fat), 101 mg cholesterol, 224 mg sodium, 5 g carbohydrate, trace fiber, 35 g protein.

CITRUS GRILLED TURKEY BREAST

◐ Sage Turkey Thighs

PREP: 10 min. **COOK:** 6 hours

Natalie Swanson, Baltimore, Maryland

I created this for my boys, who love dark meat. It's more convenient than cooking a whole turkey.

- 4 medium carrots, halved
- 1 medium onion, chopped
- 1/2 cup water
- 2 garlic cloves, minced
- 1-1/2 teaspoons rubbed sage, *divided*
- 2 turkey thighs *or* drumsticks (2 pounds total)
- 1 teaspoon browning sauce, optional
- 1/4 teaspoon salt
- 1/8 teaspoon pepper
- 1 tablespoon cornstarch
- 1/4 cup cold water

1) In a 3-qt. slow cooker, combine the carrots, onion, water, garlic and 1 teaspoon sage. Top with turkey. Sprinkle with remaining sage. Cover and cook on low for 6-8 hours or until a meat thermometer reads 180°.

2) Remove turkey and keep warm. Strain cooking juices; reserve vegetables and cool slightly. Process vegetables in a food processor until smooth; place in a saucepan. Skim fat from juices; add to pan. Bring to a boil; cook and stir for 2 minutes or until thickened. Serve with turkey.

Yield: 4 servings.

NUTRITION FACTS: 4 ounces cooked turkey with 1/4 cup gravy equals 277 calories, 8 g fat (3 g saturated fat), 96 mg cholesterol, 280 mg sodium, 15 g carbohydrate, 3 g fiber, 34 g protein.

▦ Marinated Turkey Thighs

PREP: 10 min. + marinating
BAKE: 1-1/4 hours + standing

Enid Karp, Encinitas, California

The recipe originally called for lamb shanks, but I tried turkey thighs instead. They're tender and juicy every time.

- 1-1/2 cups buttermilk
- 3 tablespoons dried minced onion
- 1 teaspoon salt
- 1/2 teaspoon pepper
- 1/2 teaspoon celery seed
- 1/2 teaspoon ground coriander
- 1/2 teaspoon ground ginger
- 2 turkey thighs (3/4 pound *each*)

1) In a resealable plastic bag, combine buttermilk, onion, salt, pepper, celery seed, coriander and ginger; add turkey. Seal bag and turn to coat; refrigerate for 8 hours or overnight.

2) Drain and discard marinade. Place turkey in a greased shallow baking dish. Cover and bake at 325° for 45 minutes. Uncover and bake 30-35

TURKEY TETRAZZINI

minutes longer or until juices run clear and a meat thermometer reads 180°. Let stand for 10 minutes before serving.

Yield: 2 servings.

NUTRITION FACTS: 1 serving equals 301 calories, 7 g fat (2 g saturated fat), 204 mg cholesterol, 595 mg sodium, 5 g carbohydrate, trace fiber, 52 g protein.

Turkey Tetrazzini

PREP: 15 min. **BAKE:** 50 min.

Audrey Thibodeau, Gilbert, Arizona

What a great way to use up extra holiday turkey! Plus, it bakes up delicious and bubbly for dinner.

- 1 package (1 pound) linguine
- 6 tablespoons butter
- 6 tablespoons all-purpose flour
- 1/2 teaspoon salt
- 1/4 teaspoon pepper
- 1/8 teaspoon cayenne pepper
- 3 cups chicken broth
- 1 cup heavy whipping cream
- 4 cups cubed cooked turkey
- 1 cup sliced fresh mushrooms
- 1 jar (4 ounces) diced pimientos, drained
- 1/4 cup chopped fresh parsley
- 4 to 5 drops hot pepper sauce
- 1/3 cup grated Parmesan cheese

1) Cook linguine according to package directions. Meanwhile, in a saucepan, melt butter over medium heat. Stir in the flour, salt, pepper and cayenne until smooth. Gradually add broth. Bring to a boil; cook and stir for 2 minutes or until thickened. Remove from the heat; stir in cream.

2) Drain linguine; toss with 2 cups sauce. Transfer to a greased 13-in. x 9-in. x 2-in. baking dish. Make a well in center of noodles, making a space about 6 in. x 4 in.

3) To remaining sauce, add turkey, mushrooms, pimientos, parsley and hot pepper sauce; mix well. Pour into center of dish. Sprinkle with Parmesan cheese.

4) Cover and bake at 350° for 30 minutes. Uncover; bake 20-30 minutes longer or until bubbly.

Yield: 8-10 servings.

NUTRITION FACTS: 1 serving equals 340 calories, 20 g fat (11 g saturated fat), 96 mg cholesterol, 568 mg sodium, 19 g carbohydrate, 1 g fiber, 22 g protein.

Curried Turkey

PREP/TOTAL TIME: 25 min.

Evelyn Gunn, Andrews, Texas

Apple and curry flavors nicely accent the meat. With a salad and rolls, you have an easy meal.

     2 cups milk
     2 chicken bouillon cubes
     2 cups diced peeled apples
     1 cup chopped onion
   1/4 cup vegetable oil
     2 tablespoons all-purpose flour
     2 teaspoons curry powder
   1/2 teaspoon salt
   1/4 teaspoon pepper
     1 tablespoon lemon juice
     4 cups diced cooked turkey
Hot cooked rice

1) In a small saucepan, heat the milk and bouillon, stirring until bouillon is dissolved. Set aside.

2) In a large saucepan, saute apples and onion in oil until tender. Stir in the flour, curry powder, salt and pepper until blended. Gradually add milk mixture and lemon juice. Bring to a boil; cook and stir for 2 minutes or until thickened. Add turkey; heat through. Serve over rice.

Yield: 6 servings.

NUTRITION FACTS: 1 cup (calculated without rice) equals 338 calories, 17 g fat (4 g saturated fat), 82 mg cholesterol, 675 mg sodium, 15 g carbohydrate, 2 g fiber, 31 g protein.

ITALIAN TURKEY SANDWICHES

Italian Turkey Sandwiches

PREP: 10 min. COOK: 5 hours

Carol Riley, Morrison, Illinois

Our family loves these tasty turkey sandwiches.

     1 bone-in turkey breast
       (5-1/2 pounds), skin removed
   1/2 cup chopped green pepper
     1 medium onion, chopped
   1/4 cup chili sauce
     3 tablespoons white vinegar
     2 tablespoons dried oregano
     4 teaspoons beef bouillon granules
    11 kaiser *or* hard rolls, split

1) Cut turkey breast in half along the bone. Place in a 5-qt. slow cooker coated with cooking spray. Add green pepper and onion. Combine the chili sauce, vinegar, oregano and bouillon; pour over turkey and vegetables.

2) Cover and cook on low for 5-6 hours or until meat juices run clear and vegetables are tender. Remove turkey; shred with two forks. Return to cooking juices. Spoon 1/2 cup onto each roll.

Yield: 11 servings.

NUTRITION FACTS: 1 sandwich equals 364 calories, 4 g fat (1 g saturated fat), 102 mg cholesterol, 576 mg sodium, 33 g carbohydrate, 1 g fiber, 46 g protein.

Creamed Turkey over Rice

PREP/TOTAL TIME: 30 min.

Kathi Parker, Craig, Colorado

This is one of our favorite ways to use up leftover turkey.

     1 medium onion, chopped
   1/2 cup chopped celery
   1/4 cup butter
   1/4 cup all-purpose flour
 1-1/2 cups chicken broth
     2 cups cubed cooked turkey
     1 cup milk
   1/2 cup cubed Swiss cheese
     1 tablespoon diced pimientos
   1/2 teaspoon salt
   1/4 teaspoon pepper
   1/4 teaspoon ground nutmeg
Hot cooked long grain and wild rice

1) In a large skillet, saute onion and celery in butter until tender. Stir in flour until blended. Gradually stir in broth. Bring to a boil. Cook; stir 2 minutes.

2) Reduce heat; stir in turkey, milk, cheese, pimientos, salt, pepper and nutmeg. Cook until cheese melts and mixture is heated through. Serve over rice.

Yield: 4 servings.

NUTRITION FACTS: 1 serving (calculated without rice) equals 372 calories, 22 g fat (12 g saturated fat), 107 mg cholesterol, 896 mg sodium, 14 g carbohydrate, 1 g fiber, 30 g protein.

COMFORTING TURKEY POTPIES

 CLASSIC: You can taste the from-scratch goodness in All-American Turkey Potpie. It features a flaky homemade crust and a filling loaded with veggies and cooked turkey.

 TIME-SAVER: Turkey Biscuit Potpie cuts back on prep time by using frozen vegetables, ground turkey and refrigerated biscuits. This easy-to-make casserole takes 30 minutes from start to finish.

 LIGHT: Phyllo Turkey Potpie replaces the pie crust with sheets of phyllo dough coated with butter-flavored spray. This helps reduce the fat grams and calories.

 SERVES 2: If you're not a fan of leftovers, you'll appreciate this casserole just for two. A small tube of refrigerated crescent rolls is used to make the pretty top on Turkey Lattice Pie.

ALL-AMERICAN TURKEY POTPIE

All-American Turkey Potpie
PREP: 30 min. + chilling **BAKE:** 35 min.
Laureen Naylor, Factoryville, Pennsylvania
- 2 cups all-purpose flour
- 1/2 teaspoon salt
- 1/2 cup finely shredded cheddar cheese
- 2/3 cup shortening
- 1 tablespoon cold butter, cubed
- 3 to 4 tablespoons cold water

FILLING:
- 1 cup diced peeled potatoes
- 1/2 cup thinly sliced carrots
- 1/3 cup chopped celery
- 1/4 cup chopped onion
- 1 garlic clove, minced
- 1 tablespoon butter
- 1 cup chicken broth
- 2 tablespoons all-purpose flour
- 1/2 cup milk
- 1-1/2 cups cubed cooked turkey
- 1/2 cup frozen peas, thawed
- 1/2 cup frozen corn, thawed
- 1/2 teaspoon salt
- 1/4 teaspoon dried tarragon
- 1/4 teaspoon pepper

1) In a food processor, combine flour and salt; cover and pulse to blend. Add cheese; pulse until fine crumbs form. Add shortening and butter; pulse until coarse crumbs form. While processing, gradually add water until dough forms a ball.

2) Divide dough in half with one ball slightly larger than the other; wrap in plastic wrap. Refrigerate for 30 minutes.

3) For filling, in a large saucepan, saute the potatoes, carrots, celery, onion and garlic in butter for 5-6 minutes. Add broth; cover and cook for 10 minutes or until vegetables are tender.

4) In a small bowl, combine flour and milk until smooth. Gradually add to vegetable mixture. Bring to a boil; cook and stir for 2 minutes or until thickened. Add the remaining ingredients; simmer 5 minutes longer.

5) Roll out larger pastry ball to fit a 9-in. pie plate; transfer to pie plate. Trim pastry even with edge. Pour hot turkey filling into crust. Roll out remaining pastry to fit top of pie; place over filling. Trim, seal and flute edges. Cut slits in top or make decorative cutouts in pastry.

6) Bake at 350° for 35-45 minutes or until crust is light golden brown. Serve immediately.

Yield: 6 servings.

NUTRITION FACTS: 1 piece equals 551 calories, 31 g fat (11 g saturated fat), 50 mg cholesterol, 704 mg sodium, 47 g carbohydrate, 3 g fiber, 20 g protein.

Turkey Biscuit Potpie
PREP/TOTAL TIME: 30 min.
Vicki Kerr, Portland, Maine
- 1 pound ground turkey
- 3 tablespoons all-purpose flour
- 2 cups milk
- 2-1/2 cups frozen peas and carrots, thawed
- 1/4 to 1/2 teaspoon salt

1/4 teaspoon pepper
1 tube (12 ounces) refrigerated buttermilk biscuits, separated into 10 biscuits

1) In a large skillet coated with cooking spray, cook turkey over medium heat until no longer pink; drain.

2) In a large saucepan, combine flour and milk until smooth. Bring to a boil; cook and stir for 2 minutes or until thickened. Stir in the vegetables, salt, pepper and turkey; keep warm.

3) Place biscuits 2 in. apart on an ungreased baking sheet. Bake at 400° for 5 minutes. Transfer turkey mixture to a greased 8-in. square baking dish. Place nine biscuits over turkey mixture. Bake potpie and remaining biscuit for 5-7 minutes or until biscuits are golden brown.

Yield: 5 servings.

NUTRITION FACTS: 1 serving equals 460 calories, 19 g fat (7 g saturated fat), 75 mg cholesterol, 896 mg sodium, 49 g carbohydrate, 3 g fiber, 26 g protein.

Phyllo Turkey Potpie
PREP: 35 min. **BAKE:** 10 min.
Taste of Home Test Kitchen

6 cups water
2 cups fresh pearl onions
1-1/2 pounds turkey breast tenderloins, cut into cubes
2 tablespoons canola oil, *divided*
2 medium red potatoes, peeled and chopped
1 cup sliced fresh mushrooms
1 can (14-1/2 ounces) reduced-sodium chicken broth
1/2 pound fresh asparagus, trimmed and cut into 1-inch pieces
3 tablespoons sherry *or* additional reduced-sodium chicken broth
3 tablespoons cornstarch
1/2 cup fat-free milk
1-1/2 teaspoons minced fresh thyme
1/2 teaspoon salt
1/4 teaspoon pepper
10 sheets phyllo dough (14 inches x 9 inches)
Refrigerated butter-flavored spray

1) In a Dutch oven, bring water to a boil. Add pearl onions; boil for 3 minutes. Drain and rinse in cold water; peel and set aside.

2) In a large skillet, cook turkey in 1 tablespoon oil over medium heat until juices run clear; remove and keep warm. In the same pan, saute potatoes in remaining oil for 5 minutes. Add onions and mushrooms; saute 3 minutes longer. Add the broth, asparagus and sherry or additional broth.

Bring to a boil. Reduce heat; cover and simmer for 5 minutes or until potatoes are tender.

3) Combine cornstarch and milk until smooth; stir into skillet. Bring to a boil; cook and stir for 2 minutes or until thickened. Drain turkey; add to onion mixture. Stir in the thyme, salt and pepper. Transfer to an 8-in. square baking dish coated with cooking spray.

4) Stack all 10 phyllo sheets. Roll up, starting at a long side; cut into 1/2-in. strips. Place in a large bowl and toss to separate strips. Spritz with butter-flavored spray. Arrange over the turkey mixture; spritz again. Bake, uncovered, at 425° for 10-15 minutes or until golden brown.

Yield: 6 servings.

Editor's Note: This recipe was tested with I Can't Believe It's Not Butter Spray.

NUTRITION FACTS: 1 cup equals 317 calories, 7 g fat (1 g saturated fat), 56 mg cholesterol, 531 mg sodium, 32 g carbohydrate, 2 g fiber, 32 g protein.

Turkey Lattice Pie
PREP: 20 min. **BAKE:** 25 min.
Taste of Home Test Kitchen

1 cup water
1/2 cup frozen mixed vegetables
2 teaspoons chicken bouillon granules
2 tablespoons plus 1/2 teaspoon cornstarch
1 cup milk
1 cup cubed cooked turkey
1/2 cup shredded cheddar cheese
2 teaspoons minced fresh parsley
1/4 teaspoon salt
1/8 teaspoon pepper
1 tube (4 ounces) refrigerated crescent rolls

1) In a saucepan, bring the water, vegetables and bouillon to a boil. Reduce heat; simmer, uncovered, for 3-5 minutes or until vegetables are tender.

2) In a small bowl, combine cornstarch and milk until smooth; add to the vegetable mixture. Bring to a boil; cook and stir for 1-2 minutes or until thickened. Add the turkey, cheese, parsley, salt and pepper. Pour into a greased 8-in. square baking dish.

3) Unroll crescent roll dough; separate into two rectangles. Seal seams and perforations. Place long sides together to form a square; pinch edges together to seal. Cut into eight strips; make a lattice crust over hot turkey mixture. Bake at 375° for 25-30 minutes or until top is golden brown.

Yield: 2 servings.

NUTRITION FACTS: 1 serving equals 583 calories, 28 g fat (13 g saturated fat), 100 mg cholesterol, 1,877 mg sodium, 44 g carbohydrate, 2 g fiber, 36 g protein.

TURKEY MEAT LOAF

🏠 Turkey Meat Loaf

PREP: 10 min. **BAKE:** 1 hour

Judy Prante, Portland, Oregon

A friend once told me this was the best turkey meat loaf she'd ever eaten!

4-1/2 teaspoons water
1-1/2 teaspoons teriyaki sauce
  1 cup bread cubes
  1 egg, beaten
  2 tablespoons chopped onion
  1 tablespoon chopped green pepper
  1 tablespoon *each* shredded part-skim mozzarella and cheddar cheese
Dash *each* garlic powder and celery seed
1/2 pound ground turkey
  1 tablespoon grated Parmesan cheese

1) In a bowl, combine the water, teriyaki sauce and bread cubes; let stand for 5 minutes. Add the egg, onion, green pepper, mozzarella and cheddar cheeses, garlic powder and celery seed. Crumble turkey over mixture and mix well.

2) Pat into an ungreased 5-3/4-in. x 3-in. x 2-in. loaf pan. Sprinkle with Parmesan cheese. Bake, uncovered, at 350° for 1 hour or until a meat thermometer reads 165°; drain.

Yield: 2 servings.

NUTRITION FACTS: 1 serving equals 355 calories, 22 g fat (8 g saturated fat), 192 mg cholesterol, 476 mg sodium, 12 g carbohydrate, 1 g fiber, 25 g protein.

🕐 Tender Turkey Burgers

PREP/TOTAL TIME: 30 min.

Sherry Hulsman, Louisville, Kentucky

These juicy, tender patties on whole wheat buns make a wholesome, satisfying sandwich.

  1 egg, lightly beaten
2/3 cup soft whole wheat bread crumbs
1/2 cup finely chopped celery
1/4 cup finely chopped onion
  1 tablespoon minced fresh parsley
  1 teaspoon Worcestershire sauce
  1 teaspoon dried oregano

1/2 teaspoon salt
1/4 teaspoon pepper
1-1/4 pounds lean ground turkey
  6 whole wheat hamburger buns, split

1) Coat grill rack with cooking spray before starting the grill. In a bowl, combine the first nine ingredients. Crumble turkey over mixture and mix well. Shape into six patties.

2) Grill, covered, over medium heat for 5-6 minutes on each side or until a meat thermometer reads 165° and juices run clear. Serve on buns.

Yield: 6 servings.

Editor's Note: To broil, broil meat 4-6 in. from heat for 5-6 minutes on each side or until a meat thermometer reads 165° and juices run clear.

NUTRITION FACTS: 1 burger equals 293 calories, 11 g fat (3 g saturated fat), 110 mg cholesterol, 561 mg sodium, 27 g carbohydrate, 4 g fiber, 22 g protein.

Almond Turkey Casserole

PREP: 10 min. **BAKE:** 35 min.

Jill Black, Troy, Ontario

A special cousin shared the recipe for this comforting casserole. The almonds and water chestnuts give it a nice crunch.

  2 cans (10-3/4 ounces *each*) condensed cream of mushroom soup, undiluted
1/2 cup mayonnaise
1/2 cup sour cream
  2 tablespoons chopped onion
  2 tablespoons lemon juice
  1 teaspoon salt
1/2 teaspoon white pepper
  5 cups cubed cooked turkey
  3 cups cooked rice
  4 celery ribs, chopped
  1 can (8 ounces) sliced water chestnuts, drained
  1 cup sliced almonds

TOPPING:
1-1/2 cups crushed butter-flavored crackers (about 38 crackers)
1/3 cup butter, melted
1/4 cup sliced almonds

1) In a large bowl, combine soup, mayonnaise, sour cream, onion, lemon juice, salt and pepper. Stir in turkey, rice, celery, water chestnuts and almonds.

2) Transfer to a greased 13-in. x 9-in. x 2-in. baking dish. Combine topping ingredients; sprinkle over turkey mixture. Bake, uncovered, at 350° for 35-40 minutes or until bubbly and golden brown.

Yield: 8 servings.

NUTRITION FACTS: 1 cup equals 678 calories, 41 g fat (12 g saturated fat), 105 mg cholesterol, 1,211 mg sodium, 43 g carbohydrate, 4 g fiber, 34 g protein.

potluck in the park

Dedicated cooks prepare hot meals for hundreds

Potluck in the Park volunteers

> " Our casseroles feed the homeless, veterans in wheelchairs, single parents and college students. "
>
> ~Alison Gilmore

A flurry of serving spoons, dozens of industrial-size casseroles and jumbo coffee urns set the scene every Sunday at O'Bryant Square in downtown Portland, Oregon.

Potluck in the Park, a community-wide program, has been serving hot meals to anyone in need since 1991. An integral part of the effort is Christ Episcopal Church of Lake Oswego. The congregation has faithfully provided the casseroles and beverages for Potluck in the Park for 13 years.

"The heart of the potluck is the casserole because it's warm and offers protein and substance," says Christ Episcopal program coordinator Alison Gilmore.

On average, 250 to 500 people are served each Sunday.

"At our 16th annual BBQ, we fed over 1,000 people in just over two hours," adds Alison's husband and co-coordinator, Larry.

Preparing enough huge casseroles weekly to feed the masses is not an easy task, but with generous donations from the Oregon Culinary Institute and the Western Culinary Institute, the church crew is able to pull it off.

Every Friday, volunteers head to the institutes to pick up "leftovers" from the culinary classes. They collect proteins such as fresh lamb, beef and pork, and starches like potatoes and rice. Back in the church's commercial kitchen, ingredients are sorted and evaluated. Alison and Larry come in on Saturdays to determine which fillers are needed to make tasty hot dishes.

Right after the Sunday service, cooks head to the kitchen to make 12 huge casseroles. They are picked up at 2 p.m. by volunteers for delivery to O'Bryant Square.

Still more church members join dozens of other community volunteers—including Boy Scout troops and service groups—who donate additional foods and help serve the meal.

By 3 p.m., a long line of hungry people wraps around O'Bryant Square.

Says Alison, "Many say, 'bless you,' and 'thank you.' One man lost his job and came for a hot meal in the park. Eventually, he got his job back, and he started serving with us. Once people start helping, they don't stop."

taste of home
cooks who care

DO YOU KNOW A COOK WHO CARES?
If you or someone you know cooks for a charitable, spiritual or other cause, tell us about it at **tasteofhome.com/CookbookBonus**

Recipes

Tips

Seafood

Useful Definitions

Refer to the Glossary on pages 24-28 for more terms.

Dressed Fish: Ready to cook; has been gutted and scaled. It still has its head and tail.

Fillets: From the side of the fish and are boneless. They may or may not be skinless.

Flatfish: Have both eyes on top of a flat body. Flounder, sole, turbot and halibut are flatfish. Generally, flatfish are sold as fillets, but halibut is typically sold as steaks.

Freshwater Fish: From streams, rivers and fresh-water lakes.

Lean Fish: Has a low fat content—it can be as low as 2.5% fat. Lean fish has a delicate texture and mild flavor. Due to the low fat content, it dries out easily during cooking and is best cooked with some liquid or fat. Poaching, steaming and sauteing are recommended cooking methods. And if basted during cooking, it can also be baked, broiled or grilled.

Moderately Fatty Fish: Has a fat content around 6%. It has a firmer texture than lean fish and a neutral flavor. These types of fish can be baked, broiled, grilled, pan-fried or poached.

Fatty Fish: Has a fat content of more than 6% and can be as high as 50%. Due to the high fat content, these fish have a firm, meaty texture and a strong rich flavor. These fish stay moist during cooking and are suitable to be baked, broiled or grilled.

Pan-Dressed Fish: A dressed fish with the head and tail removed.

Roundfish: Have eyes on both sides of its head and a round body. Roundfish are sold dressed or pan-dressed and as steaks or fillets.

Saltwater Fish: Fish from seas or oceans.

Steaks: Cross-sections of large roundfish and contain part of the backbone usually 1/2 to 1 inch thick.

Whole Fish: Needs to be gutted and scaled before cooking.

Whether you like to use fresh or frozen fish, shellfish or canned seafood products, you'll find recipes in this chapter to make a delicious meal. Once you've selected your seafood, remember to closely follow the recipe directions to avoid overcooking.

Buy fresh fish fillets or steaks that have firm, elastic and moist-looking flesh. The skin should be shiny and bright. Whole fish should have eyes that are not sunken or cloudy and a firm body that is springy to the touch. Fresh fish should have a mild smell. Avoid fish with a strong fishy odor, bruised skin and flesh with drying edges.

Buy frozen fish in packages that are solidly frozen, tightly sealed and free of freezer burn and odor.

Follow these guidelines for how much fish to purchase per person.

- 1 pound whole fish yields 1 serving.
- 1 pound pan-dressed fish yields 2 servings.
- 1 pound steaks or fillets yields 3 to 4 servings.

Prepare fresh fish within 1 to 2 days after it is caught or purchased because it is highly perishable. Freshly caught fish should be pan-dressed, washed in cold water, blotted dry with paper towels, placed in an airtight container or heavy-duty plastic bag and refrigerated. Refrigerate freshly caught or purchased fish in the coldest area of your refrigerator.

Wrap fish in freezer paper, heavy-duty foil or heavy-duty plastic bags for long term storage. Freeze fatty fish for up to 3 months and lean fish for up to 6 months.

Not all markets carry all types of fish. The type of fish—lean, moderately fatty and fatty—influences the cooking method. When looking for a fish substitute, it is usually best to substitute within the same fat category.

Fish Traits & Cooking Methods

TYPE	FLAVOR	TEXTURE	FAT LEVEL	BAKE	BROIL	PAN-FRY	GRILL	POACH	SAUTE	STEAM	STEW
BLUEFIN TUNA	Full-Flavored	Firm	Fatty	•	•		•				
BLUEFISH	Full-Flavored	Tender	Fatty	•	•	•	•		•		•
CATFISH	Mild	Medium	Moderately Fatty			•			•		•
COD	Mild	Tender	Lean	•	•		•	•		•	•
FLOUNDER	Mild	Tender	Lean	•	•	•	•	•	•	•	
GROUPER	Mild	Firm	Lean	•	•		•	•		•	•
HADDOCK	Mild	Medium	Lean	•	•	•	•	•			
HALIBUT	Mild	Firm	Lean	•	•	•	•	•		•	
HERRING	Moderate	Tender	Fatty	•	•		•				•
LAKE TROUT	Mild	Medium	Moderately Fatty	•	•	•	•			•	
MACKEREL	Full-Flavored	Medium	Fatty	•	•		•				•
MAHI-MAHI	Sweet, Mild	Firm	Lean	•	•	•	•	•			
OCEAN PERCH	Mild	Soft to Firm	Fatty	•	•	•			•		
ORANGE ROUGHY	Mild	Medium	Lean	•	•		•	•	•	•	
POLLACK	Mild	Medium	Lean	•		•		•		•	
POMPANO	Sweet, Mild	Firm	Moderately Fatty	•	•		•				
RAINBOW TROUT	Mild	Medium	Moderately Fatty						•		
RED SNAPPER	Sweet, Mild	Medium	Lean		•	•	•	•			•
SALMON	Moderate	Medium	Fatty	•	•		•	•		•	
SEA BASS	Moderate	Medium	Moderately Fatty	•	•		•	•	•	•	
SHAD	Full-Flavored	Tender	Fatty	•			•		•		•
SHARK	Mild to Full-Flavored	Firm	Moderately Fatty		•	•	•		•		
SOLE	Mild	Firm	Lean			•	•	•	•	•	•
STRIPED BASS (also called Rockfish)	Sweet, Mild	Firm	Moderately Fatty	•	•		•	•	•		
SWORDFISH	Moderate	Firm	Moderately Fatty	•	•		•		•		
TILAPIA	Sweet, Mild	Firm	Lean	•	•	•	•			•	
WHITEFISH	Moderate	Medium	Moderately Fatty	•	•	•	•				
YELLOW TUNA	Mild	Firm	Moderately Fatty	•	•		•		•		

Defrosting Guidelines

The thicker the package, the longer it will take to defrost. When defrosting fish or shellfish in the refrigerator, place a tray under the package to catch any liquid or juices to keep the refrigerator clean. Allow 12 or more hours to thaw a 1-pound package.

Cold-water thawing is an option that takes less time than refrigeration defrosting, but requires more attention. The fish or shellfish must be in a leakproof bag such as its original tightly sealed wrapper. If its package is not leakproof, place in a heavy-duty plastic bag. Submerge the wrapped seafood in cold tap water. Change the water every 30 minutes until the seafood is thawed. For this method, allow 1 to 2 hours for every pound.

Seafood Grilling Chart

Fish is done when it turns opaque in the thickest portion and flakes into sections. Scallops are done when they turn opaque. Shrimp are done when they turn pink. Watch closely to avoid overcooking. For direct grilling, turn steaks, whole fish, shrimp and scallops halfway through grilling time. Fillets generally do not need to be turned. For ease of turning, use a grill basket.

CUT	WEIGHT OR THICKNESS	HEAT	COOKING TIME (in minutes)
DRESSED FISH	1 lb. 2 to 2-1/2 lbs.	Medium/Direct Medium/Indirect	10 to 15 20 to 30
FILLETS OR STEAKS	1/4 to 1/2 in. 1/2 to 1 in.	High/Direct High/Direct	3 to 5 5 to 10
KABOBS	1-in. cubes	Medium/Direct	8 to 12
SCALLOPS, SEA	1 lb.	Medium/Direct	5 to 8
SHRIMP, MEDIUM	1 lb.	Medium/Direct	5 to 8

FENNEL STUFFED COD

Fennel Stuffed Cod

PREP: 20 min. + chilling **BAKE:** 30 min.

Mary Ellen Wilcox, Schenectady, New York

Moist fish, a super stuffing and a creamy sauce make for a memorable main dish. Fennel has a distinct flavor that works well in this entree.

> 1 cup (8 ounces) plain yogurt
> 2-1/4 cups finely chopped fennel fronds, *divided*
> 1 teaspoon lemon juice
> 1 teaspoon snipped chives
> 1/8 teaspoon salt, optional
> 1/8 teaspoon pepper
> 2 celery ribs, chopped
> 1/4 cup chopped onion
> 2 to 4 tablespoons vegetable oil
> 4 cups stuffing croutons
> 1 cup chicken broth
> 2 eggs, beaten
> 4 cod *or* flounder fillets (1-1/2 pounds)
> 1 medium lemon, sliced

1) For sauce, combine the yogurt, 1/4 cup of fennel, lemon juice, chives, salt if desired and pepper in a bowl. Cover and chill for 2 hours or overnight.

2) In a small skillet, saute celery and onion in oil until tender. Remove from the heat. Stir in the croutons, broth, eggs and remaining fennel. Spoon about 1 cup stuffing mixture onto each fillet; roll fish around stuffing.

3) Transfer to a greased 2-qt. baking dish. Top each with a lemon slice. Bake, uncovered, at 350° for 30-35 minutes or until fish flakes easily with a fork and a thermometer inserted into stuffing reads 160°. Serve with fennel sauce.

Yield: 4 servings.

NUTRITION FACTS: 1 serving equals 476 calories, 15 g fat (3 g saturated fat), 193 mg cholesterol, 869 mg sodium, 47 g carbohydrate, 4 g fiber, 42 g protein.

Golden Catfish Fillets

PREP/TOTAL TIME: 20 min.

Sharon Stevens, Weirton, West Virginia

My grandmother always made these crisp fillets with Granddad's fresh catch from the Ohio River. We'd immediately refrigerate the cleaned, fresh fish and use them within a couple of days.

> 3 eggs
> 3/4 cup all-purpose flour
> 3/4 cup cornmeal
> 1 teaspoon garlic powder
> 1/2 teaspoon salt
> 1/2 teaspoon pepper
> 5 catfish fillets (6 ounces *each*)

Oil for frying

1) In a shallow bowl, beat the eggs until foamy. In another shallow bowl, combine the flour, cornmeal and seasonings. Dip fillets in eggs, then coat with cornmeal mixture.

2) Heat 1/4 in. of oil in a large skillet; fry fish over medium-high heat for 3-4 minutes on each side or until fish flakes easily with a fork.

Yield: 5 servings.

NUTRITION FACTS: 1 fillet equals 377 calories, 16 g fat (4 g saturated fat), 186 mg cholesterol, 359 mg sodium, 24 g carbohydrate, 2 g fiber, 32 g protein.

CATFISH IN GINGER SAUCE

⏱ Catfish in Ginger Sauce

PREP/TOTAL TIME: 15 min.

Mary Dixson, Decatur, Alabama

Whenever I want to serve fish, I turn to this recipe. The fillets always turn out tender and tasty. For even more flavor, spoon extra sauce over the fish before serving.

- 1/2 cup chopped green onions
- 1 tablespoon vegetable oil
- 1/4 teaspoon ground ginger
- 1 teaspoon cornstarch
- 2 tablespoons water
- 1 cup chicken broth
- 1 tablespoon soy sauce
- 1 tablespoon white wine vinegar
- 1/8 teaspoon cayenne pepper
- 4 catfish fillets (6 ounces *each*)

1) In a 2-cup microwave-safe bowl, combine the onions, oil and ginger. Microwave, uncovered, on high for 1-1/2 minutes or until onions are tender.

2) In small bowl, combine the cornstarch and water until smooth. Stir in the broth, soy sauce, vinegar and cayenne. Stir into onion mixture. Microwave, uncovered, at 70% power for 2-3 minutes, stirring after each minute, until sauce comes to a boil.

3) Place catfish in a microwave-safe 3-qt. dish; pour sauce over fish. Cover and microwave on high for 5-6 minutes or until fish flakes easily with a fork.

Yield: 4 servings.

NUTRITION FACTS: 1 serving equals 274 calories, 16 g fat (3 g saturated fat), 80 mg cholesterol, 555 mg sodium, 2 g carbohydrate, trace fiber, 28 g protein.

Breading Fish

Combine dry ingredients in a pie plate or shallow bowl. In another pie plate or bowl, whisk egg, milk and/or other liquid ingredients. Dip fish into egg mixture, then roll gently in dry ingredients. Fry or bake as directed.

🌀 Spinach Catfish Skillet

PREP/TOTAL TIME: 15 min.

Lee Bremson, Kansas City, Missouri

Nestled in a skillet with carrots and spinach, these catfish fillets are nutritious as well as delicious.

- 20 baby carrots
- 4 teaspoons vegetable oil
- 1/2 cup sliced onion
- 2 catfish fillets (6 ounces *each*)
- 2 packages (6 ounces *each*) fresh baby spinach
- 1/4 cup white wine vinegar
- 1/2 teaspoon sugar

1) In a large skillet, stir-fry carrots in oil for 1-2 minutes or until crisp-tender. Add onion; cook and stir for 1 minute. Add catfish; cook for 2-3 minutes on each side. Remove fish and set aside.

2) Add spinach, in batches, stir-frying until slightly wilted. Return fish to skillet. Sprinkle with vinegar and sugar.

3) Cover and cook for 5 minutes or until fish flakes easily with a fork. Remove to a warm serving dish; spoon pan juices over fillets.

Yield: 2 servings.

NUTRITION FACTS: 1 serving equals 397 calories, 23 g fat (4 g saturated fat), 80 mg cholesterol, 280 mg sodium, 17 g carbohydrate, 6 g fiber, 32 g protein.

🌿 Cilantro Lime Cod

PREP: 15 min. **BAKE:** 35 min.

Donna Hackman, Bedford, Virginia

My daughter loves to cook and especially likes dishes with Mexican flair. She bakes these seasoned fish fillets in foil to keep them moist and to cut down on cleanup.

- 4 cod *or* haddock fillets (2 pounds)
- 1/4 teaspoon pepper
- 1 tablespoon dried minced onion
- 1 garlic clove, minced
- 1 tablespoon olive oil
- 1-1/2 teaspoons ground cumin
- 1/4 cup minced fresh cilantro
- 2 limes, thinly sliced
- 2 tablespoons butter, melted

1) Place each fillet on a 15-in. x 12-in. piece of heavy-duty foil. Sprinkle with pepper. In a small saucepan, saute onion and garlic in oil; stir in cumin.

2) Spoon over fillets; sprinkle with cilantro. Place lime slices over each; drizzle with butter.

3) Fold foil around fish and seal tightly. Place on a baking sheet. Bake at 375° for 35-40 minutes or until fish flakes easily with a fork.

Yield: 8 servings.

NUTRITION FACTS: 3 ounces cooked fish equals 131 calories, 5 g fat (2 g saturated fat), 51 mg cholesterol, 91 mg sodium, 2 g carbohydrate, 1 g fiber, 18 g protein.

A NEW TWIST FOR CRUMB COATING ∎∎∎

I coat my baked and deep-fried fish fillets with mashed potato flakes instead of bread crumbs. The key to a thick, crispy coating is to put the flakes in a resealable plastic bag with your seasonings and crush them a bit with a rolling pin. I dip the fillets into a beaten egg, then coat with the potato flake mixture.

—Sandra C., Kenosha, Wisconsin

Oven Fish 'n' Chips

PREP: 20 min. **BAKE:** 25 min.

Janice Mitchell, Aurora, Colorado

Enjoy flavorful fish with a coating that's as crunchy and golden as the deep-fried variety.

> 2 tablespoons olive oil
> 1/4 teaspoon pepper
> 4 medium baking potatoes
>   (1 pound), peeled

FISH:

> 1/3 cup all-purpose flour
> 1/4 teaspoon pepper
> 1 egg, lightly beaten
> 2 tablespoons water
> 2/3 cup crushed cornflakes
> 1 tablespoon grated Parmesan cheese
> 1/8 teaspoon cayenne pepper
> 1 pound haddock fillets

Tartar sauce, optional

1) In a medium bowl, combine oil and pepper. Cut potatoes lengthwise into 1/2-in. strips. Add to oil mixture; toss to coat.

2) Place on a 15-in. x 10-in. x 1-in. baking pan coated with cooking spray. Bake, uncovered, at 425° for 25-30 minutes or until golden brown and crisp.

3) Meanwhile, in a shallow dish, combine flour and pepper. In a second shallow dish, beat egg and water. In a third dish, combine the cornflakes, cheese and cayenne. Dredge fish in flour, then dip in egg mixture and coat with crumb mixture.

4) Place on a baking sheet coated with cooking spray. Bake at 425° for 10-15 minutes or until fish flakes easily with a fork. Serve with chips and tartar sauce if desired.

Yield: 4 servings.

NUTRITION FACTS: 1 serving equals 376 calories, 9 g fat (2 g saturated fat), 120 mg cholesterol, 228 mg sodium, 44 g carbohydrate, 2 g fiber, 28 g protein.

Dill Butter

Make an easy dill butter by combining minced fresh dill with half a cup of softened butter. Chill for at least 2 hours to allow flavors to blend. Use with broiled seafood.

Mediterranean Baked Fish

PREP/TOTAL TIME: 30 min.

Ellen De Munnik, Chesterfield, Michigan

The mouthwatering aroma of this herbed fish dish baking is sure to lure guests to your kitchen. In a pinch, you can use dried herbs and canned diced tomatoes to replace the fresh ingredients.

> 1 cup thinly sliced leeks
>   (white portion only)
> 2 garlic cloves, minced
> 2 teaspoons olive oil
> 12 large fresh basil leaves
> 1-1/2 pounds orange roughy fillets
> 1 teaspoon salt
> 2 plum tomatoes, sliced
> 1 can (2-1/4 ounces) sliced ripe olives, drained
> 1 medium lemon
> 1/8 teaspoon pepper
> 4 fresh rosemary sprigs

1) In a nonstick skillet, saute leeks and garlic in oil until tender; set aside. Coat a 13-in. x 9-in. x 2-in. baking dish with cooking spray.

2) Arrange basil in a single layer in dish; top with fish fillets. Sprinkle with salt. Top with leek mixture. Arrange tomatoes and olives over fish. Thinly slice half of lemon; place over top. Squeeze juice from remaining lemon over all. Sprinkle with pepper.

3) Cover and bake at 425° for 15-20 minutes or until fish flakes easily with a fork. Garnish with rosemary.

Yield: 4 servings.

NUTRITION FACTS: 4-1/2 ounces cooked fish equals 180 calories, 5 g fat (1 g saturated fat), 34 mg cholesterol, 844 mg sodium, 7 g carbohydrate, 1 g fiber, 26 g protein.

MEDITERRANEAN BAKED FISH

Baked Flounder

PREP/TOTAL TIME: 20 min.

Brenda Taylor, Benton, Kentucky

I fix this fish frequently because my whole family enjoys it. The flounder is baked on a bed of mushrooms and green onions and topped with bread crumbs and reduced-fat cheese.

- 2/3   cup sliced green onions
- 1/2   cup sliced fresh mushrooms
- 2   pounds flounder *or* sole fillets
- 1   teaspoon dried marjoram
- 1/2   teaspoon salt
- 1/8   teaspoon pepper
- 2   tablespoons dry white wine *or* chicken broth
- 2   teaspoons lemon juice
- 1/4   cup shredded reduced-fat Mexican cheese blend
- 1/4   cup soft whole wheat bread crumbs
- 2   tablespoons butter, melted

1) Sprinkle the green onions and mushrooms into a 13-in. x 9-in. x 2-in. baking dish coated with cooking spray. Arrange the fish over vegetables, overlapping the thickest end of fillets over the thin end. Sprinkle with marjoram, salt and pepper.

2) Pour wine or broth and lemon juice over fish. Cover with cheese and bread crumbs; drizzle with butter. Bake, uncovered, at 400° for 10-12 minutes or until fish flakes easily with a fork.

Yield: 6 servings.

NUTRITION FACTS: 1 serving equals 212 calories, 7 g fat (4 g saturated fat), 86 mg cholesterol, 438 mg sodium, 5 g carbohydrate, 1 g fiber, 31 g protein.

Baked Orange Roughy With Veggies

PREP/TOTAL TIME: 30 min.

Shannon Messmer, Oklahoma City, Oklahoma

This is a nice meal for two, but the recipe is easily doubled to serve four.

- 3/4   teaspoon lemon-pepper seasoning
- 1/8   teaspoon salt
- 2   orange roughy, red snapper, cod *or* haddock fillets (6 ounces *each*)
- 1/2   cup sliced fresh mushrooms
- 1/4   cup thinly sliced green onions
- 1/4   cup chopped seeded tomato
- 1/4   cup finely chopped green pepper
- 2   tablespoons butter, melted
- 1-1/2   teaspoons orange juice
- 1   cup hot cooked rice
- 4-1/2   teaspoons grated Parmesan cheese, optional

Testing Fish for Doneness

Overcooked fish loses its flavor and becomes tough. As a general guideline, fish is cooked 10 minutes for every inch of thickness.

For fish fillets, check for doneness by inserting a fork at an angle into the thickest portion of the fish and gently parting the meat. When it is opaque and flakes into sections, it is cooked completely. Translucent appearance means it needs to cook a little longer.

Whole fish or steaks are done when the flesh is opaque and is easily removed from the bones. The juices in cooked fish are milky white.

1) Combine lemon-pepper and salt; sprinkle over both sides of fillets. Place in a greased 11-in. x 7-in. x 2-in. baking dish.

2) Combine the mushrooms, onions, tomato and green pepper; spoon over fillets. Combine butter and orange juice; pour over fish and vegetables.

3) Cover and bake at 350° for 20-25 minutes or until fish flakes easily with a fork. Serve over rice. Sprinkle with Parmesan cheese if desired.

Yield: 2 servings.

NUTRITION FACTS: 1 serving equals 490 calories, 14 g fat (7 g saturated fat), 163 mg cholesterol, 665 mg sodium, 27 g carbohydrate, 1 g fiber, 61 g protein.

Curried Red Snapper

PREP: 15 min. **BAKE:** 25 min.

Lynette Kerslake, Corbett, Oregon

My husband and daughter, who don't usually care for fish, love it prepared this way. A tasty curry sauce baked over the fish makes the delicious difference.

- 1-1/2   pounds fresh *or* frozen red snapper, cod, haddock *or* flounder fillets
- 2   medium onions, chopped
- 2   celery ribs, chopped

1 tablespoon butter
1 teaspoon curry powder
3/4 teaspoon salt
1/4 cup milk

1) Place the fish in a greased 13-in. x 9-in. x 2-in. baking dish. In a skillet, saute onions and celery in butter until tender. Add curry powder and salt; mix well. Remove from the heat; stir in milk.

2) Spoon over fish. Bake, uncovered, at 350° for 25 minutes or until fish flakes easily with a fork.

Yield: 6 servings.

NUTRITION FACTS: 1 serving equals 155 calories, 4 g fat (2 g saturated fat), 46 mg cholesterol, 381 mg sodium, 6 g carbohydrate, 1 g fiber, 24 g protein.

Coconut-Crusted Perch
PREP: 20 min. **COOK:** 15 min.

Norma Thurber, Johnston, Rhode Island

A coconut breading lends tropical taste to tender perch served with a sweet-sour sauce for dipping. It's very good with any kind of whitefish.

1/2 cup apricot preserves
1/4 cup ketchup
1/4 cup light corn syrup
2 tablespoons lemon juice
1/4 teaspoon ground ginger
2 cups crushed butter-flavored crackers (about 50 crackers)
1 cup flaked coconut
2 eggs
2 tablespoons evaporated milk
1/2 teaspoon salt
3 pounds perch fillets
1 cup vegetable oil, *divided*

1) For sweet sour sauce, combine the preserves, ketchup, corn syrup, lemon juice and ginger in a

LEMON-SOY SAUCE ROUGHY

small saucepan. Bring to a boil. Reduce heat; simmer, uncovered, for 5 minutes or until slightly thickened. Remove from the heat and keep warm.

2) In a shallow dish, combine the cracker crumbs and coconut. In another shallow dish, whisk the eggs, milk and salt. Dip each fillet in egg mixture, then coat with crumb mixture.

3) In a large skillet, cook fish in 3 tablespoons oil in batches over medium-high heat for 1-2 minutes on each side or until fish flakes easily with a fork, adding oil as needed. Serve with sweet-sour sauce.

Yield: 8 servings.

NUTRITION FACTS: 4-1/2 ounces cooked fish with 4 teaspoons sweet-sour sauce equals 497 calories, 20 g fat (6 g saturated fat), 201 mg cholesterol, 570 mg sodium, 42 g carbohydrate, 1 g fiber, 37 g protein.

Lemon-Soy Sauce Roughy
PREP: 5 min. + marinating **BAKE:** 15 min.

Anne Powers, Munford, Alabama

I enjoy fried fish very much, but my doctor said it's a no-no. So this is a very tasty way to prepare fish without adding lots of extra fat and calories.

1/4 cup lemon juice
1/4 cup reduced-sodium soy sauce
1 tablespoon sugar
1/2 teaspoon ground ginger
4 fresh *or* frozen orange roughy fillets (6 ounces *each*), thawed
1/2 teaspoon salt-free lemon-pepper seasoning

1) In a large resealable plastic bag, combine juice, soy sauce, sugar and ginger; add fish. Seal bag and turn to coat; refrigerate for 30 minutes.

2) Drain and discard marinade. Arrange fillets in a 15-in. x 10-in. x 1-in. baking pan coated with cooking spray; sprinkle with lemon-pepper. Bake, uncovered, at 350° for 12-15 minutes or until fish flakes easily with a fork.

Yield: 4 servings.

NUTRITION FACTS: 1 fillet equals 124 calories, 1 g fat (trace saturated fat), 34 mg cholesterol, 258 mg sodium, 1 g carbohydrate, trace fiber, 25 g protein.

COCONUT-CRUSTED PERCH

LEMON-BATTER FISH

⏱ Lemon-Batter Fish
PREP/TOTAL TIME: 25 min.

Jackie Hannahs, Muskegon, Michigan

The flour-based coating helps keep the fish moist and gives it crispness. The hint of lemon adds tang.

- 1-1/2 cups all-purpose flour, *divided*
- 1 teaspoon baking powder
- 3/4 teaspoon salt
- 1/2 teaspoon sugar
- 1 egg, beaten
- 2/3 cup water
- 2/3 cup lemon juice, *divided*
- 2 pounds perch fillets *or* walleye fillets, cut into pieces

Oil for frying

Lemon wedges, optional

1) In a shallow bowl, combine 1 cup flour, baking powder, salt and sugar; set aside. Combine the egg, water and 1/3 cup lemon juice; stir into dry ingredients until smooth.

2) In separate shallow bowls, place remaining lemon juice and remaining flour. Dip fillets in lemon juice, then flour and coat with the batter.

3) Heat 1 in. of oil in a skillet. Fry pieces, a few at a time, over medium-high heat for 2-3 minutes on each side or until the fish flakes easily with a fork. Drain on paper towels. Garnish with lemon if desired.

Yield: 5 servings.

NUTRITION FACTS: 4-1/2 ounces cooked fish equals 403 calories, 14 g fat (1 g saturated fat), 206 mg cholesterol, 560 mg sodium, 27 g carbohydrate, 1 g fiber, 40 g protein.

About Poaching

Poaching is used for delicate foods, such as fish fillets. The proper temperature for poaching is 160° to 180°, which is lower than simmering.

〰 Poached Orange Roughy With Tarragon Sauce
PREP: 5 min. **BAKE:** 30 min.

Taste of Home Test Kitchen

A flavorful, herb-flecked sauce enhances the mild, poached-to-perfection fish fillets in this recipe.

- 4 cups water
- 1 cup dry white wine *or* vegetable broth
- 1/4 cup chopped celery
- 1/4 cup chopped carrot
- 2 tablespoons chopped onion
- 2 tablespoons lemon juice
- 7 whole peppercorns
- 1 bay leaf
- 2 teaspoons dried tarragon, *divided*
- 4 orange roughy *or* red snapper fillets (4 ounces *each*)
- 1/8 teaspoon *each* salt and white pepper
- 2 tablespoons 2% milk
- 1 egg yolk

1) In a large nonstick skillet, combine water, wine or broth, vegetables, lemon juice, peppercorns, bay leaf and 1-1/2 teaspoons tarragon. Bring to a boil.

2) Reduce heat; add fillets and poach, uncovered, until fish is firm and flakes easily with a fork (about 8-10 minutes per inch of fillet thickness). Remove to a warm serving platter.

3) Strain 1 cup of the cooking liquid; place in a saucepan. Add salt and pepper. Bring to a boil; cook until liquid is reduced to about 1/3 cup. Remove from the heat.

4) In a small bowl, beat milk and egg yolk. Stir 1 tablespoon reduced liquid into egg mixture; return all to the pan, stirring constantly. Stir in remaining tarragon. Bring to a gentle boil over low heat; cook and stir for 1 minute or until thickened. Spoon over fish.

Yield: 4 servings.

NUTRITION FACTS: 1 fillet with 2 tablespoons sauce equals 106 calories, 2 g fat (1 g saturated fat), 76 mg cholesterol, 152 mg sodium, 1 g carbohydrate, 1 g fiber, 18 g protein.

⏱ Salmon with Ginger Pineapple Salsa
PREP/TOTAL TIME: 30 min.

Kathleen Kelley, Roseburg, Oregon

I eat salmon at least twice a week and usually grill it. But it's just as delicious baked with this zesty, ginger pineapple salsa.

- 1 can (20 ounces) unsweetened pineapple tidbits
- 1 cup chopped seeded ripe tomatoes

3 green onions, sliced
1 jalapeno pepper, seeded and chopped
2 tablespoons cider vinegar
2 garlic cloves, minced
1-1/2 teaspoons sesame oil
1 teaspoon honey
1-1/2 teaspoons minced fresh gingerroot
1/4 teaspoon crushed red pepper flakes
3/4 teaspoon salt, *divided*
6 salmon fillets (6 ounces *each*)
3/4 teaspoon ground cumin
1/4 teaspoon pepper

1) Drain pineapple, reserving 1/4 cup juice. In a large bowl, combine the tomatoes, green onions, jalapeno, vinegar, garlic, sesame oil, honey, ginger, red pepper flakes, 1/4 teaspoon salt, pineapple and reserved juice; mix well. Cover and refrigerate until serving.

2) Pat salmon dry with paper towels. Sprinkle with cumin, pepper and remaining salt. Place skin side down in a 13-in. x 9-in. x 2-in. baking dish coated with cooking spray.

3) Bake, uncovered, at 350° for 10-15 minutes or until fish flakes easily with a fork. Serve with salsa.

Yield: 6 servings.

Editor's Note: When cutting or seeding hot peppers, use rubber or plastic gloves to protect your hands. Avoid touching your face.

NUTRITION FACTS: 1 fillet with 1/2 cup salsa equals 374 calories, 20 q fat (4 q saturated fat), 100 mg cholesterol, 405 mg sodium, 14 g carbohydrate, 1 g fiber, 34 g protein.

SALMON WITH GINGER PINEAPPLE SALSA

DOUBLE K GRILLED SALMON

Double K Grilled Salmon

PREP: 10 min. + marinating **GRILL:** 20 min.

Krista Frank, Rhododendron, Oregon

There's a little story behind the name of my favorite salmon recipe. When my husband, Kevin, and I could not find a spicy teriyaki-style marinade to our liking, we created one and named it Double K—for Krista and Kevin. Every time we make this flavorful fish, we get asked how we do it.

1/4 cup packed brown sugar
1/4 cup soy sauce
3 tablespoons unsweetened pineapple juice
3 tablespoons red wine vinegar
3 garlic cloves, minced
1 tablespoon lemon juice
1 teaspoon ground ginger
1/2 teaspoon pepper
1/2 teaspoon hot pepper sauce
1 salmon fillet (2 pounds)

1) In a bowl, combine the first nine ingredients. Pour 3/4 cup into a large resealable plastic bag; add the salmon. Seal bag and turn to coat; refrigerate for 1 hour, turning occasionally. Set aside remaining marinade for basting.

2) Coat grill rack with cooking spray before starting the grill. Drain and discard marinade. Place salmon skin side down on rack. Grill, covered, over medium heat for 5 minutes. Brush with reserved marinade. Grill 15-20 minutes longer or until fish flakes easily with a fork.

Yield: 8 servings.

NUTRITION FACTS: 4 ounces cooked fish equals 246 calories, 12 g fat (2 g saturated fat), 67 mg cholesterol, 532 mg sodium, 9 g carbohydrate, trace fiber, 24 g protein.

CRAB-TOPPED FISH FILLETS

Crab-Topped Fish Fillets
PREP/TOTAL TIME: 30 min.

Mary Tuthill, Ft. Myers Beach, Florida

Elegant but truly no-fuss, this recipe is perfect for company. Toasting the almonds gives them a little more crunch, which is a delightful way to top the fish fillets.

- 4 sole, orange roughy *or* cod fillets (6 ounces *each*)
- 1 can (6 ounces) crabmeat, drained, flaked and cartilage removed *or* 1 cup imitation crabmeat, chopped
- 1/2 cup grated Parmesan cheese
- 1/2 cup mayonnaise
- 1 teaspoon lemon juice

Paprika, optional

- 1/3 cup slivered almonds, toasted

1) Place fillets in a greased 13-in. x 9-in. x 2-in. baking dish. Bake, uncovered, at 350° for 18-22 minutes or until fish flakes easily with a fork.

2) Meanwhile, in a bowl, combine crab, Parmesan cheese, mayonnaise and lemon juice.

3) Drain cooking juices from baking dish; spoon crab mixture over fillets. Broil 5 in. from the heat for 5 minutes or until topping is lightly browned. Sprinkle with paprika if desired and almonds.

Yield: 4 servings.

NUTRITION FACTS: 1 serving equals 457 calories, 31 g fat (5 g saturated fat), 90 mg cholesterol, 585 mg sodium, 2 g carbohydrate, 1 g fiber, 40 g protein.

FRIED FISH ITALIAN-STYLE ■■■

I recently experimented with a lighter and zestier version of fried fish. I lightly brushed tilapia fillets with fat-free Italian salad dressing and then coated them with bread crumbs. I pan-fried the fillets in a small amount of olive oil and I Can't Believe It's Not Butter spray. This eliminated the need for eggs, plus gave the fish zippy flavor without requiring additional seasonings.

—*Marti B., Valley View, Ohio*

Tilapia with Cucumber Relish
PREP/TOTAL TIME: 30 min.

Mary VanHollebeke, Wyandotte, Michigan

My husband isn't big on fish, but he enjoys this mild-tasting tilapia. The relish adds garden-fresh flavor and pretty color.

- 2/3 cup chopped seeded cucumber
- 1/2 cup chopped radishes
- 1 tablespoon tarragon vinegar
- 1 teaspoon olive oil
- 1/2 teaspoon salt, *divided*
- 1/4 teaspoon pepper, *divided*
- 1/8 teaspoon sugar
- 1/8 teaspoon paprika
- 4 tilapia fillets (6 ounces *each*)
- 1 tablespoon butter

1) In a small bowl, combine cucumber and radishes. In another small bowl, whisk the vinegar, oil, 1/4 teaspoon salt, 1/8 teaspoon pepper and sugar. Pour over cucumber mixture; toss to coat evenly. Combine paprika and remaining salt and pepper; sprinkle over fillets.

2) In a large nonstick skillet coated with cooking spray, melt butter. Add fish; cook for 3-4 minutes on each side or until fish flakes easily with a fork. Serve with cucumber relish.

Yield: 4 servings.

NUTRITION FACTS: 1 fillet with 3 tablespoons relish equals 181 calories, 6 g fat (3 g saturated fat), 90 mg cholesterol, 388 mg sodium, 1 g carbohydrate, trace fiber, 32 g protein.

TILAPIA WITH CUCUMBER RELISH

Creole Catfish Fillets
PREP/TOTAL TIME: 15 min.

Dave Bremstone, Plantation, Florida

I rub catfish fillets with a pleasant mixture of seasonings before cooking them quickly on the grill for moist results.

- 3 tablespoons reduced-fat plain yogurt
- 2 tablespoons finely chopped onion

1 tablespoon fat-free mayonnaise
1 tablespoon Dijon mustard
1 tablespoon ketchup
1/2 teaspoon dried thyme
1/4 teaspoon grated lemon peel
1 teaspoon paprika
1/2 teaspoon onion powder
1/4 teaspoon salt
1/8 teaspoon cayenne pepper
4 catfish fillets (4 ounces *each*)
4 lemon wedges

1) In a small bowl, combine the yogurt, onion, mayonnaise, mustard, ketchup, thyme and lemon peel. Cover and refrigerate until serving.

2) In another bowl, combine paprika, onion powder, salt and cayenne; rub over both sides of fillets.

3) Grill, covered, in a grill basket coated with cooking spray over medium-hot heat for 5-6 minutes on each side or until fish flakes easily with a fork. Serve with lemon wedges and yogurt sauce.

Yield: 4 servings.

NUTRITION FACTS: 1 fillet with about 1 tablespoon sauce equals 182 calories, 9 g fat (2 g saturated fat), 54 mg cholesterol, 382 mg sodium, 5 g carbohydrate, 1 g fiber, 19 g protein.

Feta Tomato-Basil Fish

PREP/TOTAL TIME: 20 min.

Alicia Szeszol, Lindenhurst, Illinois

My husband provides the main ingredient in this dish after his summer fishing trips. Feta and Italian tomatoes give it a Mediterranean flavor.

1/3 cup chopped onion
1 garlic clove, minced
2 teaspoons olive oil
1 can (14-1/2 ounces) Italian diced tomatoes, drained
1-1/2 teaspoons minced fresh basil *or* 1/2 teaspoon dried basil

FETA TOMATO-BASIL FISH

SUNSHINE HALIBUT

1 pound walleye, bass *or* other whitefish fillets
4 ounces crumbled feta cheese

1) In a saucepan, saute onion and garlic in oil until tender. Add tomatoes and basil. Bring to a boil. Reduce heat; simmer, uncovered, for 5 minutes.

2) Broil fish 4-6 in. from heat for 5-6 minutes. Top fillets with tomato mixture and cheese. Broil 5-7 minutes longer or until fish flakes easily with a fork.

Yield: 4 servings.

NUTRITION FACTS: 1 serving equals 295 calories, 10 g fat (5 g saturated fat), 172 mg cholesterol, 799 mg sodium, 11 g carbohydrate, 1 g fiber, 38 g protein.

Sunshine Halibut

PREP/TOTAL TIME: 30 min.

Jalayne Luckett, Marion, Illinois

Seasoned with garlic, onion and citrus, these fish fillets are tasty. They look pretty on a bed of shredded carrots.

1/3 cup chopped onion
1 garlic clove, minced
2 tablespoons minced fresh parsley
1/2 teaspoon grated orange peel
4 halibut steaks (6 ounces *each*)
1/4 cup orange juice
1 tablespoon lemon juice
1/4 teaspoon salt
1/4 teaspoon lemon-pepper seasoning

1) In a nonstick skillet coated with cooking spray, saute onion and garlic until tender; remove from the heat. Stir in parsley and orange peel.

2) Place halibut in an 11-in. x 7-in. x 2-in. baking dish coated with cooking spray. Top with onion mixture. Combine orange and lemon juices; pour over fish. Sprinkle with salt and lemon-pepper. Cover and bake at 400° for 15-20 minutes or until fish flakes easily with a fork.

Yield: 4 servings.

NUTRITION FACTS: 4-1/2 ounces cooked fish equals 202 calories, 4 g fat (1 g saturated fat), 54 mg cholesterol, 270 mg sodium, 4 g carbohydrate, trace fiber, 36 g protein.

Salsa Fish Skillet

PREP/TOTAL TIME: 20 min.

Taste of Home Test Kitchen

Zucchini and yellow summer squash add seasonal flair to this colorful fish dish.

> 1 pound halibut steaks *or* other firm whitefish, cut into 1-inch pieces
> 3 teaspoons canola oil, *divided*
> 1 medium yellow summer squash, julienned
> 1 medium zucchini, julienned
> 1 cup sliced fresh mushrooms
> 2 garlic cloves, minced
> 1/4 to 1/2 teaspoon ground cumin
> 1-1/2 cups chunky salsa
> 4 teaspoons minced fresh cilantro

1) In a large nonstick skillet or wok, stir-fry halibut in 2 teaspoons hot oil for 3-4 minutes or until fish flakes easily with a fork; remove and keep warm.

2) Add the yellow squash, zucchini, mushrooms, garlic, cumin and remaining oil to the pan. Stir-fry for 2-3 minutes or until vegetables are crisp-tender. Return fish to the pan. Add salsa; heat through. Sprinkle with cilantro.

Yield: 4 servings.

NUTRITION FACTS: 1 cup equals 207 calories, 6 g fat (1 g saturated fat), 36 mg cholesterol, 486 mg sodium, 11 g carbohydrate, 3 g fiber, 27 g protein.

Removing Skin from a Fillet

1) Use a sharp flexible knife to remove the skin from a fillet. Position the fillet with the tail end closest to you. Starting at the tail end of the fillet, make a small 45° angle cut in the meat to, but not through, the skin. Using that cut as a starting point, insert knife and angle it flat against the skin.

2) Hold the skin taut with one hand and slide the knife along the skin, separating the skin from the fillet. As you push the knife away from you, pull the skin toward you.

Pecan-Crusted Salmon

PREP: 15 min. + standing **BAKE:** 10 min.

Kara Cook, Elk Ridge, Utah

These delicious salmon fillets are wonderful for company since they take only a few minutes to prepare, yet they taste like you fussed. The nutty coating is a nice complement to the fish.

> 4 salmon fillets (about 6 ounces *each*)
> 2 cups milk
> 1 cup finely chopped pecans
> 1/2 cup all-purpose flour
> 1/4 cup packed brown sugar
> 2 teaspoons seasoned salt
> 2 teaspoons pepper
> 3 tablespoons vegetable oil

1) Place salmon fillets in a large resealable plastic bag; add milk. Seal bag and turn to coat. Let stand for 10 minutes; drain.

2) Meanwhile, in a shallow bowl, combine the pecans, flour, brown sugar, seasoned salt and pepper. Coat fillets with pecan mixture, gently pressing into the fish.

3) In a large skillet, brown salmon in oil over medium-high heat. Transfer to a 15-in. x 10-in. x 1-in. baking pan coated with cooking spray. Bake at 400° for 8-10 minutes or until fish flakes easily with a fork.

Yield: 4 servings.

NUTRITION FACTS: 1 fillet equals 658 calories, 45 g fat (7 g saturated fat), 102 mg cholesterol, 778 mg sodium, 27 g carbohydrate, 3 g fiber, 38 g protein.

Seasoned Salmon Steaks

PREP/TOTAL TIME: 30 min.

Cary Winright, Medina, Texas

A flavorful basting sauce adds spark to these special salmon steaks. The moist, firm fish broils to perfection in mere minutes.

> 6 salmon steaks (1 inch thick and 6 ounces *each*)
> 1/2 cup butter, melted
> 2 teaspoons seasoned salt
> 2 teaspoons Italian seasoning
> 2 teaspoons lemon juice
> 1/2 teaspoon garlic powder
> 1/2 teaspoon grated lemon peel

Dash cayenne pepper

1) Place salmon on a greased broiler rack. Broil 4-6 in. from the heat for 8-10 minutes.

2) Meanwhile, combine the remaining ingredients. Brush some over salmon. Turn and broil 10 minutes longer or until fish flakes easily with a fork. Baste with remaining butter mixture.

Yield: 6 servings.

NUTRITION FACTS: 1 salmon steak equals 447 calories, 34 g fat (13 g saturated fat), 141 mg cholesterol, 761 mg sodium, 1 g carbohydrate, trace fiber, 34 g protein.

GRILLED TUNA WITH PINEAPPLE SALSA

Grilled Tuna with Pineapple Salsa

PREP: 25 min. + chilling **GRILL:** 10 min.

Beveylon Concha, Chesapeake, Virginia

After spending some time in Honolulu, I came upon this tropical treatment for tuna. I make the pineapple salsa for everything from grilled fish to pork and poultry.

- 1/2 medium fresh pineapple, peeled and cut into 1/2-inch slices
- 1 small onion, diced
- 2 jalapeno peppers, seeded and diced
- 2 tablespoons minced fresh cilantro
- 2 tablespoons lime juice
- 4 tuna steaks (6 ounces *each*)
- 1 tablespoon olive oil
- 1/4 teaspoon salt
- 1/4 teaspoon pepper

1) Grill pineapple slices, uncovered, over medium heat for 5-7 minutes on each side. Chill for 30 minutes. Dice the pineapple; place in a bowl. Stir in the onion, jalapenos, cilantro and lime juice. Refrigerate for 1 hour or until chilled.

2) Brush tuna steaks with oil; sprinkle with salt and pepper. Grill, covered, over medium heat for 5 minutes on each side or until fish flakes easily with a fork. Serve with pineapple salsa.

Yield: 4 servings.

Editor's Note: When cutting or seeding hot peppers, use rubber or plastic gloves to protect your hands. Avoid touching your face.

NUTRITION FACTS: 1 tuna steak with 1/2 cup salsa equals 252 calories, 5 g fat (1 g saturated fat), 77 mg cholesterol, 212 mg sodium, 10 g carbohydrate, 1 g fiber, 40 g protein.

Basil-Tomato Tuna Steaks

PREP/TOTAL TIME: 15 min.

Jan Parker, Englewood, Florida

Get ready to reel in raves when you place this fabulous fish dish on the table. It's moist and flavorful with basil, tomato and cheese.

- 4 tuna *or* salmon steaks (1 inch thick and 6 ounces *each*)
- 1 tablespoon olive oil
- 1/2 teaspoon salt
- 1/8 teaspoon pepper
- 1/3 cup loosely packed basil leaves
- 1 medium tomato, chopped
- 1/4 cup shredded part-skim mozzarella cheese

1) In a large nonstick skillet, cook tuna in oil over medium heat for 3 minutes on each side or until fish flakes easily with a fork.

2) Transfer to a broiler pan. Sprinkle fish with salt and pepper. Cover with basil leaves. Top with tomato and cheese. Broil 4-6 in. from the heat for 2 minutes or until the cheese is melted.

Yield: 4 servings.

NUTRITION FACTS: 1 serving equals 240 calories, 6 g fat (2 g saturated fat), 81 mg cholesterol, 394 mg sodium, 2 g carbohydrate, 1 g fiber, 42 g protein.

Salmon Salad

PREP/TOTAL TIME: 10 min.

Diane Benskin, Lewisville, Texas

This salad couldn't be easier. Just mix together, chill and serve!

- 2 cans (14-3/4 ounces *each*) salmon, drained and bones removed
- 2 celery ribs, sliced
- 1 large apple, peeled and chopped
- 5 green onions, sliced
- 1/2 cup mayonnaise
- 2 teaspoons snipped fresh dill *or* 3/4 teaspoon dill weed
- 3/4 teaspoon minced fresh basil *or* dash dried basil
- 1/4 teaspoon garlic salt
- 1/4 teaspoon minced fresh tarragon *or* dash dried tarragon

1) Place salmon in a large bowl and flake. Add remaining ingredients; stir gently.

2) Cover and refrigerate until serving.

Yield: 8 servings.

NUTRITION FACTS: 1 cup equals 276 calories, 19 g fat (3 g saturated fat), 51 mg cholesterol, 704 mg sodium, 4 g carbohydrate, 1 g fiber, 22 g protein.

Pierside Salmon Patties

PREP: 15 min. **BAKE:** 30 min.

Martha Conaway, Pataskala, Ohio

Dill adds flavor to the tasty sauce that tops these moist salmon patties. Baking them all at once makes this recipe a breeze to prepare!

- 2 eggs, beaten
- 1 cup milk
- 2 tablespoons lemon juice
- 3 cups coarsely crushed saltines (about 66 crackers)
- 2 teaspoons finely chopped onion
- 1/4 teaspoon salt
- 1/4 teaspoon pepper
- 2 cans (14-3/4 ounces *each*) salmon, drained, bones and skin removed

DILL SAUCE:

- 2 tablespoons butter
- 2 tablespoons all-purpose flour
- 1 teaspoon snipped fresh dill *or* 1/2 teaspoon dill weed
- 1/4 teaspoon salt

Dash pepper

Dash nutmeg

- 1-1/2 cups milk

1) In a large bowl, beat the eggs, milk, lemon juice, saltines, onion, salt and pepper. Add salmon and mix well. Shape into twelve 3-in. patties. Place in a greased 15-in. x 10-in. x 1-in. baking pan. Bake at 350° for 30-35 minutes or until lightly browned.

2) Meanwhile, melt butter in a saucepan. Stir in the flour, dill, salt, pepper and nutmeg until smooth. Gradually add milk. Bring to a boil; cook and stir for 2 minutes or until thickened. Serve with the patties.

Yield: 6 servings.

NUTRITION FACTS: 2 patties with 1/4 cup sauce equals 471 calories, 22 g fat (8 g saturated fat), 156 mg cholesterol, 1,444 mg sodium, 29 g carbohydrate, 1 g fiber, 38 g protein.

PIERSIDE SALMON PATTIES

SALMON LOAF

Salmon Loaf

PREP: 20 min. **BAKE:** 40 min. + standing

Dorothy Bateman, Carver, Massachusetts

Topping the traditional salmon loaf recipe, an olive cream sauce makes it special and unique. You can also serve the sauce on the side.

- 1 can (14-3/4 ounces) salmon, drained, bones and skin removed
- 1 small onion, finely chopped
- 1/2 cup soft bread crumbs
- 1/4 cup butter, melted
- 3 eggs, *separated*
- 2 teaspoons lemon juice
- 1 teaspoon minced fresh parsley
- 1/2 teaspoon salt
- 1/8 teaspoon pepper

OLIVE CREAM SAUCE:

- 2 tablespoons butter
- 2 tablespoons all-purpose flour
- 1-1/2 cups milk
- 1/4 cup chopped stuffed olives

1) In a large bowl, combine the salmon, onion, bread crumbs and butter. Stir in the egg yolks, lemon juice, parsley, salt and pepper.

2) In a small mixing bowl, beat the egg whites on high speed until stiff peaks form. Fold into salmon mixture.

3) Pour into a greased 8-in. x 4-in. x 2-in. loaf pan. Place loaf pan in a larger baking pan. Add 1 in. of hot water to larger pan.

4) Bake at 350° for 40-45 minutes or until a knife inserted near the center comes out clean. Let stand for 10 minutes before slicing.

5) Meanwhile, in a saucepan, melt the butter. Stir in flour until smooth; gradually add milk. Bring to a boil; cook and stir for 1 minute or until thickened. Stir in olives. Serve over salmon loaf.

Yield: 4 servings (8 slices).

NUTRITION FACTS: 2 slices with about 1/3 cup sauce equals 476 calories, 33 g fat (15 g saturated fat), 264 mg cholesterol, 1,334 mg sodium, 13 g carbohydrate, 1 g fiber, 30 g protein.

⏱ Creole Tuna

PREP/TOTAL TIME: 15 min.

Betty Bernat, Littleton, New Hampshire

This speedy recipe has been in my family for as long as I can remember. Because it relies on pantry staples, it's easy to make for dinner.

- 1/4 cup chopped green pepper
- 2 tablespoons butter
- 2 tablespoons all-purpose flour
- 1/2 teaspoon sugar
- 1/2 teaspoon salt
- 1/8 teaspoon pepper
- 1/3 cup milk
- 1 can (14-1/2 ounces) stewed tomatoes
- 1 can (6 ounces) tuna, drained and flaked
- 1 teaspoon Creole seasoning

Hot cooked rice, optional

1) In a saucepan, saute green pepper in butter until tender. Stir in the flour, sugar, salt and pepper. Gradually stir in milk. Stir in tomatoes.

2) Bring to a boil; cook and stir for 2 minutes. Add tuna and Creole seasoning; heat through. Serve over rice if desired.

Yield: 4 servings.

NUTRITION FACTS: 1 serving equals 160 calories, 7 g fat (4 g saturated fat), 31 mg cholesterol, 858 mg sodium, 13 g carbohydrate, 1 g fiber, 13 g protein.

⏱ Tuna Burgers

PREP/TOTAL TIME: 20 min.

Joann Brasington, Sumter, South Carolina

Salmon can be used in place of the tuna in this burger. My husband likes to add a slice of Swiss cheese.

- 1 can (6 ounces) tuna, drained and flaked
- 1 egg
- 1/2 cup seasoned bread crumbs
- 1/3 cup finely chopped onion
- 1/4 cup chopped celery
- 1/4 cup chopped sweet red pepper
- 1/4 cup mayonnaise
- 2 tablespoons chili sauce
- 1/2 teaspoon dill weed
- 1/4 teaspoon salt
- 1/8 teaspoon pepper

Dash hot pepper sauce

Dash Worcestershire sauce

- 4 hamburger buns, split

Tomato slices and lettuce leaves, optional

1) In a large bowl, combine the tuna, egg, bread crumbs, onion, celery, red pepper, mayonnaise, chili sauce and seasonings; mix well. Shape into four patties (mixture will be soft).

TUNA BURGERS

2) Coat a nonstick skillet with cooking spray; fry patties for 3-4 minutes on each side or until cooked through. Serve on buns with tomato and lettuce if desired.

Yield: 4 servings.

NUTRITION FACTS: 1 sandwich equals 363 calories, 16 g fat (3 g saturated fat), 71 mg cholesterol, 962 mg sodium, 36 g carbohydrate, 2 g fiber, 18 g protein.

⏱ White Bean Tuna Salad

PREP/TOTAL TIME: 30 min.

Kathleen Law, Bellingham, Washington

I adapted this recipe with a zippy Dijon dressing that adds interest to the beans, tuna, olives and onion.

- 1/4 cup red wine vinegar
- 3 garlic cloves, minced
- 2 teaspoons Dijon mustard
- 1 teaspoon sugar
- 1/2 teaspoon salt
- 1/4 teaspoon pepper
- 2 tablespoons olive oil
- 2 cans (15 ounces *each*) white kidney *or* cannellini beans, rinsed and drained
- 2 cans (6 ounces *each*) light water-packed tuna, drained and flaked
- 3/4 cup sliced ripe olives
- 1/2 cup chopped red onion

1) In a small bowl, combine vinegar, garlic, mustard, sugar, salt and pepper; gradually whisk in oil.

2) In a large bowl, combine beans, tuna, olives and onion; add dressing and toss gently. Cover and refrigerate until serving.

Yield: 6 servings.

NUTRITION FACTS: 3/4 cup equals 247 calories, 7 g fat (1 g saturated fat), 17 mg cholesterol, 754 mg sodium, 23 g carbohydrate, 6 g fiber, 20 g protein.

QUICK FIX FOR TUNA SALAD ■■■

I reduce the fishy flavor of tuna salad by sprinkling a bit of red wine vinegar on the tuna before stirring in the mayonnaise.

—*Diane A., Edgartown, Massachusetts*

FAMILY-PLEASING TUNA CASSEROLES

 CLASSIC: Tuna Mushroom Casserole is sure to bring back warm memories of your childhood. A creamy filling loaded with tuna, noodles and mushrooms contrasts nicely with the crunch from the crumb topping.

 TIME-SAVER: It's a breeze to fix Cheesy Tuna Noodles because you can assemble the ingredients while the noodles cook. Then just drain the noodles and stir into the dish. It takes only minutes to heat this mixture in the microwave.

 LIGHT: Tuna casserole gets revamped with health in mind in Hearty Tuna Bake. Lower-in-fat and lower-in-cholesterol options are featured. Plus, zucchini and tomatoes are added for color, flavor and nutrition.

 SERVES 2: A single can of tuna is used to make two individual dishes of Mini Tuna Casseroles. Crushed potato chips create a crisp topping.

TUNA MUSHROOM CASSEROLE

Tuna Mushroom Casserole

PREP: 20 min. **BAKE:** 35 min.

Connie Moore, Medway, Ohio

- 1 package (12 ounces) wide noodles, cooked and drained
- 2 cans (6 ounces *each*) tuna, drained
- 1 can (4 ounces) mushroom stems and pieces, drained
- 1 can (10-3/4 ounces) condensed cream of mushroom soup, undiluted
- 1-1/3 cups milk
- 1/2 teaspoon salt
- 1/4 teaspoon pepper
- 1/2 cup crushed saltines
- 3 tablespoons butter, melted

Paprika, tomato slices and fresh thyme, optional

1) In a large bowl, combine the noodles, tuna and mushrooms. Combine the soup, milk, salt and pepper; pour over noodle mixture and mix well. Pour into a greased 2-1/2-qt. baking dish. Combine saltines and butter; sprinkle over noodles.

2) Bake, uncovered, at 350° for 35-45 minutes or until heated through. If desired, sprinkle with paprika and garnish with tomato slices and thyme.

Yield: 6 servings.

NUTRITION FACTS: 1 cup equals 399 calories, 13 g fat (6 g saturated fat), 87 mg cholesterol, 879 mg sodium, 51 g carbohydrate, 2 g fiber, 19 g protein.

Cheesy Tuna Noodles

PREP/TOTAL TIME: 20 min.

Tamara Duggan, O'Fallon, Missouri

2-1/2 cups uncooked wide egg noodles
    1 medium onion, chopped
    2 tablespoons butter
    1 can (10-3/4 ounces) condensed cream of celery soup, undiluted
  1/3 cup milk
    1 can (6 ounces) tuna, drained and flaked
    1 cup (4 ounces) shredded cheddar cheese
  1/4 cup grated Parmesan cheese

1) Cook noodles according to package directions. Meanwhile, place onion in a greased microwave-safe 11-in. x 7-in. x 2-in. dish; dot with butter.

2) Microwave, uncovered, on high for 1 minute; stir. Microwave 1-2 minutes longer, stirring every 30 seconds.

3) In a bowl, combine soup and milk; stir in tuna and cheeses. Pour over onion. Drain noodles; add to tuna mixture and mix well. Cover and microwave on high for 3-4 minutes or until heated through and cheese is melted.

Yield: 4 servings.

NUTRITION FACTS: 1 serving equals 405 calories, 21 g fat (13 g saturated fat), 93 mg cholesterol, 1,049 mg sodium, 29 g carbohydrate, 2 g fiber, 25 g protein.

MINI TUNA CASSEROLES

2) Spoon half into a 2-qt. baking dish coated with cooking spray. Sprinkle with half of the cheese. Repeat layers. Top with tomato. Cover and bake at 350° for 30-35 minutes. Uncover and bake 5 minutes longer.

Yield: 6 servings.

NUTRITION FACTS: 3/4 cup equals 279 calories, 10 g fat (5 g saturated fat), 41 mg cholesterol, 516 mg sodium, 22 g carbohydrate, 2 g fiber, 25 g protein.

Hearty Tuna Bake

PREP: 30 min. **BAKE:** 35 min.

Jan Heshelman, Bloomfield, Indiana

    3 cups uncooked yolk-free wide noodles
    2 cans (6 ounces *each*) light water-packed tuna, drained and flaked
    1 cup shredded zucchini
  3/4 cup reduced-fat sour cream
    1 celery rib with leaves, thinly sliced
  1/4 cup chopped onion
  1/4 cup reduced-fat mayonnaise
    2 teaspoons prepared mustard
  1/2 teaspoon dried thyme
  1/4 teaspoon salt
    1 cup (4 ounces) shredded part-skim mozzarella cheese
    1 medium tomato, chopped

1) Cook noodles according to package directions; drain. In a large bowl, combine the noodles, tuna, zucchini, sour cream, celery, onion, mayonnaise, mustard, thyme and salt; mix well.

Mini Tuna Casseroles

PREP/TOTAL TIME: 30 min.

Rebecca Reese, Jacksboro, Texas

  1/2 cup chopped green onions
    2 tablespoons butter
    2 tablespoons all-purpose flour
  3/4 cup milk
    1 can (6 ounces) tuna, drained
    1 cup crushed potato chips, *divided*
  1/4 teaspoon pepper

1) In a saucepan, saute onions in butter. Stir in the flour until blended. Gradually stir in milk. Bring to a boil over medium heat; cook and stir for 2 minutes or until thickened. Remove from the heat. Stir in the tuna, 1/2 cup crushed potato chips and pepper.

2) Pour into two greased 8-oz. baking dishes. Sprinkle with remaining potato chips. Bake, uncovered, at 350° for 20-25 minutes or until hot and bubbly.

Yield: 2 servings.

NUTRITION FACTS: 1 serving equals 442 calories, 25 g fat (12 g saturated fat), 69 mg cholesterol, 619 mg sodium, 27 g carbohydrate, 2 g fiber, 28 g protein.

About Shellfish

Shellfish are divided into two general categories—mollusks and crustaceans. Mollusks have soft, unsegmented bodies; many are covered by a shell. Clams, oysters, mussels and scallops are mollusks. Crustaceans have elongated bodies with jointed external shells, which are shed periodically. Shrimp, crab and lobster are crustaceans.

CLAMS-Buying and Storing

Clams are available with hard or soft shells. Hard-shell clams are classified by size—littlenecks (small), cherry stone (medium) and chowder clams, which are usually chopped. Soft-shell clams, also called long-necks, have necks that extend out of the shell.

Hard-shell calms should be tightly closed or if slightly opened, should close when tapped. Don't purchase hard-shell clams that remain opened when tapped or have cracked shells. Soft-shell clams don't tightly close their shells; they are fresh and alive if the neck moves when lightly poked.

How to Shuck a Hard-Shell Clam

1) Scrub under cold running water with a stiff brush. Place on a tray and refrigerate for 30 minutes. They will be easier to open.

2) Protect your hand by placing the clam in a clean kitchen towel with the hinge facing out. Insert clam knife next to the hinge.

3) Slide the knife around to loosen the shells.

4) Open the top shell and cut the muscle from the top shell. Discard the top shell.

5) Use the knife to release clam from bottom shell. If desired, pour clam juice into a strainer and reserve for your recipe.

Clams are also sold shucked. Look for clams that are plump, moist and shiny. The color depends on the variety. Buy 6 to 12 clams per person.

Store live clams, mussels and oysters in a container covered with a dampened cloth. If possible, have a bed of ice in the container. It's best to use within 24 hours of purchasing. Don't store in an airtight container or fresh water, since they will die. Store shucked clams and oysters in a leakproof covered container in the refrigerator.

CLAMS-Preparing and Cooking

Scrub hard-shell clams under cold running water with a stiff brush. Soft-shell clams or steamers may have grit in them. To remove the grit before cooking, soak them in salted cold water (about 1/3 cup salt to about a gallon of water) in the refrigerator for 2 hours. Rinse off the shells before steaming.

To steam clams, bring a cup of water to a boil in a stockpot. Add clams; cover and steam for 5 to 7 minutes or until clams open. Discard any clams that do not open. Either cut or pull clam from shell. Discard sheath that connects the clam to its shell. Shucked clams are cooked when they are plump and turn opaque.

MUSSELS-Buying and Storing

Mussels are cultivated or harvested wild. Most mussels sold have blue-black shells. The cultivated mussels are sold without beards—the filament that holds the mussel to rocks. Mussels should be tightly closed or if slightly opened, should close when tapped. Don't purchase mussels that remain opened when tapped or have cracked shells. Buy 3/4 to 1 pound mussels per person. To store, see storage information for clams above.

MUSSELS-Preparing and Cooking

Scrub mussels under cold running water with a stiff brush. If the mussels have beards, remove them from the shells by pulling the beards out with your fingers. The beards should be removed just before cooking. Farm-raised mussels may not have beards. To shuck, follow directions for clams at left.

Steam mussels for 5-7 minutes or until opened. Discard any mussels that do not open. If necessary, remove from pan as they open. Shucked mussels are cooked when they are plump and turn opaque.

OYSTERS-Buying and Storing

Oysters in their shell should be tightly closed; if slightly opened, they should close when tapped. Don't purchase oysters that remain opened when tapped or have cracked shells.

Shucked oysters should be plump and generally are creamy white. Their liquid should be clear not cloudy, and the color of the liquid can range from milky white

How to Shuck Oysters

1) Scrub oysters under cold running water with a stiff brush. Place oysters on a tray and refrigerate for 1 hour. They will be easier to open.

2) Protect your hands by wrapping the oyster, bigger shell down, in a clean kitchen towel with the hinge facing out. Keep oyster level to avoid losing any juice. Insert an oyster knife next to hinge.

3) Twist the knife until you hear a snap, then pry shells open.

4) Slide the knife along the top shell to cut the oyster loose. Discard the top shell.

5) Slide knife between oyster and the bottom shell to release it. If serving in the shell, discard any bits of shell particles. If cooking shucked oysters, strain juice.

to light gray. Buy 6 oysters per person. To store, see storage information for clams at left.

OYSTERS-Preparing and Cooking

Shucked oysters can be boiled for 5 minutes or deep-fat fried at 375° for 10 minutes. Shucked oysters are cooked when they are plump, turn opaque and the edges start to curl.

SCALLOPS-Buying and Storing

The three types of scallops are sea, bay and the less commonly known calico. Sea scallops are large, about 1-1/2-in. diameter, but can be bigger. For more even cooking, cut scallops over 2-in. diameter in half or if they are very thick, cut them horizontally in half.

Bay scallops are small, about 1/2-in. diameter, and are generally found on the East Coast. They are also imported from China. They are generally available fresh in the fall and winter. Calico scallops are smaller than bay scallops, and found deep in the waters off of Florida.

Scallops vary in color from creamy white to tan and should have a sweet, fresh odor. Buy 4 ounces scallops per serving.

Store in a leakproof covered container in the refrigerator. It's best to use scallops within 24 hours of purchasing.

SCALLOPS-Preparing and Cooking

If your scallops have a crescent-shaped muscle, cut or pull off and discard. Pat dry with paper towels if they are going to be floured. Cut large scallops in half for even cooking. Scallops are frequently sauteed or pan-fried. Depending on their size, they generally take 3-4 minutes to cook and are done when they turn opaque.

SHRIMP-Buying and Storing

Shrimp are harvested in cold-water and warm-water areas. Cold-water shrimp are small and are usually sold cooked and peeled. Warm-water shrimp are large and classified by the color of their shell—white, pink and brown. Black Tiger shrimp are farm-raised shrimp that have mostly black shells with brown stripes. Rock shrimp have sweet meat and are sold with the shells off. Prawns are freshwater crustaceans that are similar to the shrimp, which live in saltwater.

Most fresh shrimp that is sold has actually been previously frozen and thawed. Fresh shrimp should have a firm texture. Avoid shrimp that have a yellow color to their meat or black spots or rings on the shells (unless they are Tiger shrimp) or meat. Shrimp in the shell (fresh or frozen) are available in different sizes (medium, large, extra large, jumbo). See the chart of shrimp sizes below. Buy 3 to 4 ounces shelled shrimp per serving. For every pound of shelled shrimp that you want, buy 1-1/4 pounds of unshelled shrimp.

SHRIMP SIZE / NAMF	COUNT
COLOSSAL	10 to 15
EXTRA JUMBO	16 to 20
JUMBO	21 to 25
EXTRA LARGE	26 to 30
LARGE	31 to 35
MEDIUM LARGE	36 to 42
MEDIUM	43 to 50
SMALL	51 to 60

Shrimp Count

Shrimp are classified and sold by size. Shrimp count indicates the number of shrimp of a certain size that are in a pound. The more shrimp it takes to make a pound the smaller they are. The terms used to describe the count are not consistent from store to store. For example, a 16-20 count may be extra jumbo in one market and extra large in another. The count is the best indication of size. (See chart on page 269.)

SHRIMP-Preparing and Cooking

Depending on their use, shrimp can be peeled and deveined before or after cooking. To cook shrimp, in a large saucepan, bring 1 quart of water and 1 teaspoon salt to a boil. Add shrimp. Reduce heat and simmer, uncovered, for 1-3 minutes or until the shrimp turn pink and opaque. Watch closely to avoid overcooking. Drain immediately. Serve warm or chilled.

CRABS-Buying and Storing

Fresh crabs are available with hard or soft shells and as crab legs from King crab. Hard-shell varieties are blue and the large Dungeness crab. Soft-shell crabs are blue crabs that have shed their shell and have not yet hardened their new shells.

Live crabs should move when touched. Buy 1 pound whole crabs per serving. Store live crabs or lobsters in

a container covered with a dampened cloth. It's best to use within 24 hours of purchase. Don't store in an airtight container or fresh water because they will die.

CRABS-Preparing and Cooking

Hard-shell crabs should be rinsed under cold running water prior to cooking. To boil hard-shell blue crabs, in a large stockpot, bring 8 to 12 quarts of water and 2 teaspoons salt to a boil. Water can also be flavored with lemon and crab boil seasoning. Add crabs. Reduce heat; cover and simmer for about 10 minutes or until crabs turn red and meat turns white.

With tongs, remove to a colander to drain. Serve with melted butter if desired. This is definitely a messy, hands-on eating activity. If desired, cover your table with newspaper before serving the crabs. When finished, roll up the newspaper with discarded shells and toss in the garbage.

LOBSTERS-Buying and Storing

Two types of lobsters are harvested in America—the spiny or rock lobster and the American or Maine lobster. The spiny lobster is harvested around warm water—Florida and California—and has no claws and is sold as a lobster tail. American lobsters are harvested around cold water—the North Atlantic coast—and are sold whole.

Live lobsters should move when touched. When picked up, a lobster should curl its tail. Lobsters are sold by weight, and the average weigh from 1 to 2-1/2 pounds. Buy 1 to 1-1/2 pounds whole lobster or 4 ounces lobster tail meat per serving. To store, see crabs storage information above.

LOBSTERS-Preparing and Cooking

Live lobsters should be purchased the same day that you plan to cook them. Rinse them under cold, running water just before cooking.

To boil live lobsters, in a large stockpot, bring enough water to cover the lobsters to a boil along with 2 to 3 teaspoons salt. Once the water has come to a boil, plunge lobster head first into the water. Start counting the cooking time once the water has returned to a boil. Reduce heat; cover and cook until a small leg or antennae can easily be removed. Lobsters will turn red immediately in water and that is *not* an indication of doneness. Remove from water with tongs and drain in a colander. Serve when cooled enough to handle. Serve with melted butter if desired.

The cooking time depends on the size of the lobster. For a 1-pound lobster, cook 10 minutes; 1-1/4-pound lobster, cook 12 minutes; 1-1/2-pound lobster, cook 15 minutes and for a 2-pound lobster, cook 18 minutes.

Defrost frozen lobster tails before cooking. Lobster tails can be boiled, broiled, grilled and cut into pieces

Cracking and Cleaning Cooked Hard-Shell Crab

1) Twist off claws and legs. Use a nutcracker or crab mallet to crack the joints and shells and pick out meat with a seafood fork.

2) Place crab upside down on its top shell. Using your hands, pull up and off the tail flap (apron) and discard.

3) Turn over and lift off and discard top shell.

4) Turn crab back on its back; scrape off feathery gills on each side, internal organs and jaw.

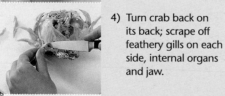

5) Break crab body in half and pick meat out with fingers or a lobster pick.

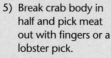

and sauteed. To boil lobster tails, in a large saucepan, bring 6 cups water and 1-1/2 teaspoons salt to a boil. Add lobster tails. Reduce heat; cover and simmer for 8-12 minutes or until meat is firm and opaque. Serve with melted butter if desired.

Cracking and Cleaning Cooked Whole Lobster

1) Twist off claws. Pull off small pincer and discard. Use a nutcracker, lobster cracker or crab mallet to crack the large claws. Remove meat.

2) Twist off the legs at body and crack shells and push out meat.

3) Twist tail and body in opposite directions to separate.

4) Turn tail, belly side up. Using scissors, cut through the membrane on both sides of shell. Lift off and discard membrane. Lift out tail meat. Discard intestinal vein. Any roe or tomalley (greenish liver) may be eaten.

Pasta with White Clam Sauce

PREP/TOTAL TIME: 30 min.

Kelli Soike, Tallahassee, Florida

Garlic and oregano enhance the flavor of this delicious main dish. An Italian friend of my mom's passed on the recipe to her, and I began preparing it when I was 14.

    12   ounces uncooked linguine
     2   garlic cloves, minced
     1   can (2 ounces) anchovies, undrained
     1   tablespoon olive oil
     1   bottle (8 ounces) clam juice
     1   can (6-1/2 ounces) minced clams, undrained
    1/3 cup water
     2   tablespoons dried oregano
     1   tablespoon minced fresh parsley
    1/4 teaspoon salt
    1/2 teaspoon pepper
     5   tablespoons shredded Parmesan cheese

1) Cook pasta according to package directions. In a saucepan, saute garlic and anchovies in oil for 3 minutes, breaking up anchovies. Stir in the clam juice, clams, water, oregano, parsley, salt and pepper. Bring to a boil.

2) Reduce heat; simmer, uncovered, for 15 minutes or until sauce is reduced by half. Drain pasta; toss with clam sauce. Sprinkle with cheese.

Yield: 5 servings.

NUTRITION FACTS: 1 cup equals 379 calories, 13 g fat (2 g saturated fat), 19 mg cholesterol, 874 mg sodium, 50 g carbohydrate, 4 g fiber, 16 g protein.

New Haven Clam Pizza

PREP: 20 min. + rising **BAKE:** 20 min.

Susan Seymour, Valatie, New York

This appetizer is the perfect start to any meal. It's always a big hit with our family and friends.

     1   package (1/4 ounce) active dry yeast
     1   cup warm water (110° to 115°)
     1   teaspoon sugar
    2-1/2 cups all-purpose flour
     1   teaspoon salt
     2   tablespoons vegetable oil
     2   cans (6-1/2 ounces *each*) chopped clams, drained
     4   bacon strips, cooked and crumbled
     3   garlic cloves, minced
     2   tablespoons grated Parmesan cheese
     1   teaspoon dried oregano
     1   cup (4 ounces) shredded part-skim mozzarella cheese

1) In a mixing bowl, dissolve yeast in warm water. Add sugar; let stand for 5 minutes. Add the flour, salt and oil; beat until smooth. Cover and let rise in a warm place until doubled, about 15-20 minutes.

2) Punch dough down. Press onto the bottom and up the sides of a greased 14-in. pizza pan; build up edges slightly. Prick dough several times with a fork.

3) Bake at 425° for 6-8 minutes. Sprinkle remaining ingredients over crust in order listed. Bake for 13-15 minutes or until crust is golden and cheese is melted. Cut into wedges.

Yield: 8 servings.

NUTRITION FACTS: 1 slice equals 252 calories, 9 g fat (3 g saturated fat), 18 mg cholesterol, 519 mg sodium, 32 g carbohydrate, 1 g fiber, 10 g protein.

Classic Crab Cakes

PREP/TOTAL TIME: 20 min.

Debbie Terenzini, Lusby, Maryland

This region is known for good seafood, and crab cakes are a traditional favorite. I learned to make them from a chef in a restaurant where they were a best-seller. The crabmeat's sweet and mild flavor is sparked by the blend of other ingredients.

- 1 pound canned crabmeat, drained, flaked and cartilage removed
- 2 to 2-1/2 cups soft bread crumbs
- 1 egg, beaten
- 3/4 cup mayonnaise
- 1/3 cup *each* chopped celery, green pepper and onion
- 1 tablespoon seafood seasoning
- 1 tablespoon minced fresh parsley
- 2 teaspoons lemon juice
- 1 teaspoon Worcestershire sauce
- 1 teaspoon prepared mustard
- 1/4 teaspoon pepper
- 1/8 teaspoon hot pepper sauce
- 2 to 4 tablespoons vegetable oil, optional

Lemon slices, optional

1) In a large bowl, combine the crab, bread crumbs, egg, mayonnaise, vegetables and seasonings.

2) Shape into eight patties. Broil patties if desired or cook in a skillet in oil for 4 minutes on each side or until golden brown. Serve with lemon if desired.

Yield: 8 servings.

NUTRITION FACTS: 1 crab cake equals 282 calories, 22 g fat (3 g saturated fat), 85 mg cholesterol, 638 mg sodium, 7 g carbohydrate, 1 g fiber, 14 g protein.

■ **Appetizer Crab Cakes:** Follow recipe as directed in step 1. Shape into 16 small crab cakes; broil or fry until golden brown on each side.

CLASSIC CRAB CAKES

Making Soft Bread Crumbs

Tear several slices of fresh white, French or whole wheat bread into 1-in. pieces. Place in a food processor or blender; cover and push pulse button several times to make coarse crumbs. One slice of bread yields about 1/2 cup crumbs.

Creamed Crab on Toast

PREP/TOTAL TIME: 10 min.

Nina De Witt, Aurora, Ohio

Marjoram and lemon juice in the sauce nicely complement the crab in this ready-in-a-jiffy dish.

- 1 can (10-3/4 ounces) condensed-cream of mushroom soup, undiluted
- 1 can (6 ounces) crabmeat, rinsed, drained, and cartilage removed
- 1 tablespoon lemon juice
- 1/4 teaspoon dried marjoram

Dash cayenne pepper

Toast *or* biscuits

1) In a 1-qt. microwave-safe dish, combine the soup, crab, lemon juice, marjoram and cayenne. Cover and microwave on high 3-4 minutes or until heated through, stirring once. Serve on toast or biscuits.

Yield: 4 servings.

NUTRITION FACTS: 1 serving (calculated without toast or biscuits) equals 133 calories, 5 g fat (2 g saturated fat), 41 mg cholesterol, 776 mg sodium, 11 g carbohydrate, 1 g fiber, 11 g protein.

Crab Salad Supreme

PREP/TOTAL TIME: 20 min.

Mrs. A. Mayer, Richmond, Virginia

This is a great take-along salad for potlucks and reunions. For a crowd, this recipe is easily doubled.

- 2 cups canned crabmeat, drained, flaked and cartilage removed
- 1/2 cup minced green onions
- 1/2 cup diced celery
- 1/2 cup finely chopped green pepper
- 1 tablespoon ground mustard
- 1/2 teaspoon salt
- 1/4 teaspoon pepper
- 2 teaspoons celery seed

SAUCE:

- 1/3 cup mayonnaise
- 1/3 cup sour cream
- 1/3 cup chili sauce

2 teaspoons lemon juice
2 cups shredded lettuce
4 hard-cooked eggs, sliced
4 medium tomatoes, cut into wedges

1) In a large bowl, combine the crab, vegetables and seasonings. For sauce, combine the mayonnaise, sour cream, chili sauce and lemon juice; pour over salad and gently toss to coat.

2) Arrange the lettuce on four individual plates or a serving plate. Top with crab salad; garnish with eggs and tomatoes. Refrigerate until serving.

Yield: 4 servings.

NUTRITION FACTS: 1 serving equals 401 calories, 26 g fat (6 g saturated fat), 292 mg cholesterol, 1,031 mg sodium, 18 g carbohydrate, 4 g fiber, 24 g protein.

Sea Shell Crab Casserole

PREP: 20 min. **BAKE:** 30 min.

Brandi Jergenson, Vaughn, Montana

This crab casserole gets color and flavor from green pepper, celery and ripe olives.

1-1/2 cups uncooked medium shell pasta
1 large onion, chopped
1 medium green pepper, chopped
3 celery ribs, chopped
3 tablespoons butter
1 can (12 ounces) evaporated milk
1/2 cup mayonnaise
1 teaspoon salt
1 teaspoon ground mustard
1 teaspoon paprika
1 teaspoon Worcestershire sauce
1 can (2-1/2 ounces) sliced ripe olives, drained
2 packages (8 ounces *each*) imitation crabmeat, flaked

1) Cook pasta according to package directions. Meanwhile, in a large skillet, saute the onion, green pepper and celery in butter until tender.

2) In a large bowl, combine milk and mayonnaise until blended. Stir in the salt, mustard, paprika and Worcestershire sauce. Drain pasta; add the pasta along with the olives, crab and vegetables to the milk mixture.

3) Transfer to a greased shallow 2-qt. baking dish. Cover and bake at 350° for 25 minutes. Uncover; bake 5-10 minutes longer or until heated through.

Yield: 6 servings.

Editor's Note: Reduced-fat or fat-free mayonnaise may not be substituted for regular mayonnaise.

NUTRITION FACTS: 1 cup equals 471 calories, 27 g fat (9 g saturated fat), 51 mg cholesterol, 1,162 mg sodium, 42 g carbohydrate, 3 g fiber, 16 g protein.

Crawfish Etouffee

PREP: 5 min. **COOK:** 1-1/2 hours

Becky Armstrong, Decatur, Alabama

Etouffee is a French word meaning to smother. This dish, featuring a tangy tomato-based sauce, is a pleasure to serve because it's attractive as well as tasty.

1/3 cup all-purpose flour
1/2 cup vegetable oil
1 large green pepper, chopped
1 large onion, chopped
1 cup chopped celery
1 can (15 ounces) tomato sauce
1 cup water
1 tablespoon Worcestershire sauce
1 teaspoon garlic powder
1 teaspoon paprika
1 teaspoon lemon juice
3/4 teaspoon Creole seasoning
2 pounds frozen cooked crawfish tails, thawed

Hot cooked rice

1) In a heavy Dutch oven, whisk the flour and oil until smooth. Cook over medium-high heat for 5 minutes, whisking constantly. Reduce heat to medium; cook and stir 10 minutes longer or until mixture is reddish-brown.

2) Add the green pepper, onion and celery; cook and stir for 5 minutes. Add tomato sauce, water, Worcestershire sauce, garlic powder, paprika, lemon juice and Creole seasoning. Bring to a boil.

3) Reduce heat; cover and simmer for 45 minutes. Add crawfish; heat through. Serve with rice.

Yield: 8 servings.

Editor's Note: The following spices may be substituted for the Creole seasoning: 1/2 teaspoon *each* paprika and garlic powder, and a pinch *each* cayenne pepper, dried thyme and ground cumin.

NUTRITION FACTS: 1 serving (calculated without rice) equals 269 calories, 15 g fat (2 g saturated fat), 155 mg cholesterol, 451 mg sodium, 11 g carbohydrate, 2 g fiber, 22 g protein.

CRAWFISH ETOUFFEE

CRAB-STUFFED PORTOBELLOS

Crab-Stuffed Portobellos
PREP/TOTAL TIME: 25 min.

Pat Ford, Southampton, Pennsylvania

Fans of portobello mushrooms will love these delectable treats. I filled them with tasty crabmeat.

- 2 **portobello mushrooms (5 ounces *each*)**
- 2 **tablespoons olive oil**
- 1 **garlic clove, minced**
- 1 **can (6 ounces) crabmeat, drained, flaked and cartilage removed**
- 5 **teaspoons mayonnaise**
- 2 **roasted sweet red pepper halves, drained**
- 2 **slices provolone cheese**

1) Remove and discard stems from mushrooms. Place caps on a greased baking sheet. Combine oil and garlic; brush over mushrooms. Broil 4-6 in. from the heat for 4-5 minutes or until tender.

2) In a small bowl, combine crab and mayonnaise. Place crab mixture and a red pepper half on each mushroom. Broil for 2-3 minutes or until heated through. Top with cheese; broil 1-2 minutes longer or until cheese is melted.

Yield: 2 servings.

NUTRITION FACTS: 1 stuffed mushroom equals 412 calories, 31 g fat (8 g saturated fat), 99 mg cholesterol, 613 mg sodium, 5 g carbohydrate, 1 g fiber, 27 g protein.

Lobster Newburg
PREP/TOTAL TIME: 25 min.

Wendy Cornell, Hudson, Maine

We like to use fresh lobster in this time-honored recipe. It can also be made with frozen, canned or imitation lobster. Guests will think you fussed.

- 3 **cups cooked lobster meat *or* canned flaked lobster meat *or* imitation lobster chunks**
- 3 **tablespoons butter**

- 1/4 **teaspoon paprika**
- 3 **cups heavy whipping cream**
- 1/2 **teaspoon Worcestershire sauce**
- 3 **egg yolks, lightly beaten**
- 1 **tablespoon sherry, optional**
- 1/4 **teaspoon salt**
- 1/3 **cup crushed butter-flavored crackers (about 8 crackers)**

1) In a large skillet, saute the lobster in butter and paprika for 3-4 minutes; set aside. In a large saucepan, bring cream and Worcestershire sauce to a gentle boil. Meanwhile, in a bowl, combine egg yolks, sherry if desired and salt.

2) Remove cream from heat; stir a small amount into egg yolk mixture. Return to the pan; stir constantly. Bring to a gentle boil; cook and stir for 5-7 minutes or until slightly thickened. Stir in lobster.

3) Divide lobster mixture between four 10-oz. baking dishes. Sprinkle with cracker crumbs. Broil 6 in. from heat 2-3 minutes or until golden brown.

Yield: 4 servings.

NUTRITION FACTS: 1 serving equals 882 calories, 81 g fat (48 g saturated fat), 505 mg cholesterol, 790 mg sodium, 12 g carbohydrate, trace fiber, 29 g protein.

Clarified Butter

To make clarified butter, melt butter over low heat without stirring. Skim off foam. Pour off clear liquid and discard milky residue in bottom of pan. Store clear liquid in an airtight container in the refrigerator for 3 to 4 weeks or freeze for up to 4 months.

Baked Lobster Tails
PREP: 20 min. **BAKE:** 20 min.

Taste of Home Test Kitchen

Lobster tails are a treat in themselves, but you can serve them with steak for an extra-special dinner!

- 4 **fresh *or* frozen lobster (8 to 10 ounces *each*), thawed**
- 1 **cup water**
- 1 **tablespoon minced fresh parsley**
- 1/8 **teaspoon salt**

Dash pepper
- 1 **tablespoon butter, melted**
- 2 **tablespoons lemon juice**

Lemon wedges and additional melted butter, optional

1) Split lobster tails in half lengthwise. With cut side up and using scissors, cut along the edge of shell to loosen the cartilage covering the tail meat from the shell; remove and discard cartilage.

2) Pour water into a 13-in. x 9-in. x 2-in. baking dish; place lobster tails in dish. Combine the

parsley, salt and pepper; sprinkle over lobster. Drizzle with butter and lemon juice.

3) Bake, uncovered, at 375° for 20-25 minutes or until meat is firm and opaque. Serve with lemon wedges and melted butter if desired.

Yield: 4 servings.

NUTRITION FACTS: 2 lobster tail halves equals 232 calories, 5 g fat (2 g saturated fat), 223 mg cholesterol, 775 mg sodium, 2 g carbohydrate, trace fiber, 43 g protein.

Perfect Scalloped Oysters
PREP: 15 min. **BAKE:** 30 min.

Alice King, Nevada, Ohio

Creamy and delicious, this dish is a real treat with fresh or canned oysters.

      2 cups crushed butter-flavored crackers (about 50)
  1/2 cup butter, melted
  1/2 teaspoon salt
Dash pepper
      1 pint shucked oysters *or* 2 cans (8 ounces *each*) whole oysters, drained
      1 cup heavy whipping cream
  1/4 teaspoon Worcestershire sauce

1) Combine cracker crumbs, butter, salt and pepper; sprinkle a third into a greased 1-1/2-qt. baking dish. Arrange half of the oysters over crumbs. Top with another third of the crumb mixture and the remaining oysters.

2) Combine cream and Worcestershire sauce; pour over oysters. Top with remaining crumb mixture. Bake, uncovered, at 350° for 30-40 minutes or until top is golden brown.

Yield: 8 servings.

NUTRITION FACTS: 1 serving equals 349 calories, 29 g fat (15 g saturated fat), 94 mg cholesterol, 508 mg sodium, 18 g carbohydrate, trace fiber, 5 g protein.

Steamed Mussels with Peppers
PREP: 30 min. **COOK:** 10 min.

Taste of Home Test Kitchen

Use the French bread to soak up the deliciously seasoned broth. If you like food zippy, add the jalapeno seeds.

      2 pounds fresh mussels, scrubbed and beards removed
      1 jalapeno pepper, seeded and chopped
      3 garlic cloves, minced
      2 tablespoons olive oil
      1 bottle (8 ounces) clam juice
  1/2 cup white wine *or* additional clam juice
  1/3 cup chopped sweet red pepper
      3 green onions, sliced
  1/2 teaspoon dried oregano

      1 bay leaf
      2 tablespoons minced fresh parsley
  1/4 teaspoon salt
  1/4 teaspoon pepper
French bread baguette, sliced, optional

1) Tap mussels; discard any that do not close. Set aside. In a skillet, saute jalapeno and garlic in oil until tender. Stir in clam juice, wine or additional juice, red pepper, onions, oregano and bay leaf.

2) Bring to a boil. Reduce heat; add mussels. Cover and simmer for 5-6 minutes or until mussels open. Discard bay leaf and any unopened mussels. Sprinkle with the parsley, salt and pepper. Serve with baguette slices if desired.

Yield: 4 servings.

Editor's Note: When cutting or seeding hot peppers, use rubber or plastic gloves to protect your hands. Avoid touching your face.

NUTRITION FACTS: 12 mussels and 1/2 cup broth (calculated without baguette) equals 293 calories, 12 g fat (2 g saturated fat), 65 mg cholesterol, 931 mg sodium, 12 g carbohydrate, 1 g fiber, 28 g protein.

Citrus Scallops
PREP/TOTAL TIME: 15 min.

Cheri Hawthorne, North Canton, Ohio

My husband and I like to eat seafood at least once a week. These scallops have a refreshing burst of flavor.

      1 medium green *or* sweet red pepper, julienned
      4 green onions, chopped
      1 garlic clove, minced
      2 tablespoons olive oil
      1 pound sea scallops
  1/2 teaspoon salt
  1/4 teaspoon crushed red pepper flakes
      2 tablespoons lime juice
  1/2 teaspoon grated lime peel
      4 medium navel oranges, peeled and sectioned
      2 teaspoons minced fresh cilantro
Hot cooked rice *or* pasta

1) In a large skillet, saute the pepper, onions and garlic in oil for 1 minute. Add scallops, salt and pepper flakes; cook for 4 minutes. Add lime juice and peel; cook for 1 minute.

2) Reduce heat. Add orange sections and cilantro; cook 2 minutes longer or until scallops are opaque. Serve with rice or pasta.

Yield: 4 servings.

NUTRITION FACTS: 1/4 pound scallops (calculated without rice or pasta) equals 240 calories, 8 g fat (1 g saturated fat), 37 mg cholesterol, 482 mg sodium, 23 g carbohydrate, 4 g fiber, 21 g protein.

⏱ Scallops and Asparagus Stir-Fry

PREP/TOTAL TIME: 20 min.

Lisa Lancaster, Tracy, California

Savory scallops, crisp-tender asparagus and juicy cherry tomatoes blend together beautifully in this fresh-tasting stir-fry. Sesame oil and soy sauce delicately accent the colorful combo that's festive enough to serve when company comes.

- 3/4 pound fresh asparagus, trimmed and cut into 2-inch pieces
- 1 tablespoon cornstarch
- 3/4 cup chicken broth
- 1 teaspoon reduced-sodium soy sauce
- 3/4 pound sea scallops, halved
- 1 cup sliced fresh mushrooms
- 1 garlic clove, minced
- 2 teaspoons canola oil
- 1 cup halved cherry tomatoes
- 2 green onions, sliced
- 1 teaspoon sesame oil
- 1/8 teaspoon pepper
- 2 cups hot cooked rice

1) Place asparagus in a saucepan and cover with water; bring to a boil. Cook, uncovered, for 3-5 minutes or until crisp-tender; drain and set aside. In a small bowl, combine the cornstarch, broth and soy sauce until smooth; set aside.

2) In a large nonstick skillet or wok, stir-fry scallops, mushrooms and garlic in canola oil until scallops are opaque and mushrooms are tender. Stir cornstarch mixture; add to skillet. Bring to a boil; cook and stir for 1-2 minutes or until sauce is thickened.

SCALLOPS AND ASPARAGUS STIR-FRY

SKILLET SEA SCALLOPS

3) Add the asparagus, tomatoes, onions, sesame oil and pepper; heat through. Serve over rice.

Yield: 4 servings.

NUTRITION FACTS: 1 cup stir-fry mixture with 1/2 cup rice equals 215 calories, 5 g fat (1 g saturated fat), 14 mg cholesterol, 314 mg sodium, 30 g carbohydrate, 2 g fiber, 11 g protein.

⏱ Skillet Sea Scallops

PREP/TOTAL TIME: 25 min.

Margaret Lowenberg, Kingman, Arizona

You'll want to keep this recipe in mind for a quick-to-fix dish when entertaining. Pasta and mixed greens nicely complement the tender, citrusy shellfish.

- 1/2 cup dry bread crumbs
- 1/2 teaspoon salt
- 1 pound sea scallops
- 2 tablespoons butter
- 1 tablespoon olive oil
- 1/4 cup white wine *or* reduced-sodium chicken broth
- 2 tablespoons lemon juice
- 1 teaspoon minced fresh parsley
- 1 garlic clove, minced

1) In a large resealable plastic bag, combine bread crumbs and salt. Add scallops, a few at a time, and shake to coat.

2) In a large skillet over medium-high heat, brown scallops in butter and oil for 1-1/2 to 2 minutes on each side or until firm and opaque. Remove and keep warm. Add the wine or broth, lemon juice, parsley and garlic to the skillet; bring to a boil. Pour over scallops. Serve immediately.

Yield: 3-4 servings.

NUTRITION FACTS: 3 scallops equals 249 calories, 11 g fat (4 g saturated fat), 52 mg cholesterol, 618 mg sodium, 14 g carbohydrate, 1 g fiber, 21 g protein.

Fiery Skewered Shrimp

PREP: 10 min. + marinating **BROIL:** 5 min.

Kara de la Vega, Santa Rosa, California

This easy entree gets its great taste from a simple yet spicy marinade. You can broil the kabobs or throw them on the grill outside. We serve them on a bed of greens.

    1 tablespoon olive oil
    2 garlic cloves, minced
1/2 to 1 teaspoon crushed red
      pepper flakes
    1 teaspoon minced fresh gingerroot
1-1/2 pounds uncooked large shrimp,
      peeled and deveined
    2 small green peppers, cut
      into 1-inch squares
    1 medium lemon, sliced

1) In a shallow bowl, combine the oil, garlic, pepper flakes and ginger. Add shrimp; stir to coat evenly. Cover and refrigerate for 2 hours.

2) Thread shrimp and green peppers alternately on metal or soaked wooden skewers. Place on a broiler pan coated with cooking spray. Broil 4-6 in. from the heat for 3 minutes. Turn; broil 2-3 minutes longer or until shrimp turn pink. Garnish with lemon slices.

Yield: 4 servings.

NUTRITION FACTS: 1 serving equals 173 calories, 5 g fat (1 g saturated fat), 252 mg cholesterol, 291 mg sodium, 4 g carbohydrate, 1 g fiber, 28 g protein.

FIERY SKEWERED SHRIMP

Coconut-Fried Shrimp

PREP/TOTAL TIME: 20 min.

Ann Atchison, O'Fallon, Missouri

The coconut coating on these crunchy shrimp adds a little sweetness, and the tangy orange marmalade and honey sauce is great for dipping.

1-1/4 cups all-purpose flour
1-1/4 cups cornstarch
6-1/2 teaspoons baking powder
  1/2 teaspoon salt
  1/4 teaspoon Cajun seasoning
1-1/2 cups cold water
  1/2 teaspoon vegetable oil
2-1/2 cups flaked coconut
    1 pound uncooked large shrimp,
      peeled and deveined
Additional oil for deep-fat frying
    1 cup orange marmalade
  1/4 cup honey

1) In a large bowl, combine the flour, cornstarch, baking powder, salt and Cajun seasoning. Stir in water and oil until smooth.

2) Place coconut in another bowl. Dip shrimp into batter, then coat with coconut. In an electric skillet or deep-fat fryer, heat oil to 375°. Fry shrimp, a few at a time, for 3 minutes or until golden brown. Drain on paper towels.

3) In a saucepan, heat marmalade and honey; stir until blended. Serve with shrimp.

Yield: 4 servings.

NUTRITION FACTS: 1/4 of the shrimp with 5 tablespoons sauce equals 1,001 calories, 36 g fat (20 g saturated fat), 168 mg cholesterol, 1,184 mg sodium, 151 g carbohydrate, 4 g fiber, 23 g protein.

Peeling and Deveining Shrimp

1) Start on the underside by the head area to remove shell from shrimp. Pull legs and first section of shell to one side. Continue pulling shell up around the top and to the other side. Pull off shell by tail if desired.

2) Remove the black vein running down the back of shrimp by making a shallow slit with a paring knife along the back from head area to tail.

3) Rinse shrimp under cold water to remove the vein.

PINEAPPLE SHRIMP KABOBS

Creamy Seafood Enchiladas

PREP: 20 min. **BAKE:** 30 min.

Evelyn Gebhardt, Kasilof, Alaska

Condensed soup helps add creaminess to the sauce in this enchilada dish. I also like that it bakes up in no time.

- 1/4 cup butter
- 1/4 cup all-purpose flour
- 1 cup chicken broth
- 1 can (10-3/4 ounces) condensed cream of chicken soup, undiluted
- 1 cup (8 ounces) sour cream
- 1/2 cup salsa
- 1/8 teaspoon salt
- 1 cup (8 ounces) small-curd cottage cheese
- 1 pound small shrimp, cooked, peeled and deveined
- 1 cup cooked *or* canned crabmeat, drained, flaked and cartilage removed
- 1-1/2 cups (6 ounces) shredded Monterey Jack cheese
- 1 can (4 ounces) chopped green chilies
- 1 tablespoon dried cilantro
- 12 flour tortillas (7 inches)

Additional salsa

1) In a saucepan over low heat, melt butter; stir in flour until smooth. Gradually stir in broth and soup until blended.

2) Bring to a boil; cook and stir for 2 minutes or until slightly thickened. Remove from the heat. Stir in sour cream, salsa and salt; set aside.

3) Place cottage cheese in a blender; cover and process until smooth. Transfer to a bowl; add the shrimp, crab, Monterey Jack cheese, chilies and cilantro.

4) Spread 3/4 cup sauce in a greased 13-in. x 9-in. x 2-in. baking dish. Place about 1/3 cup seafood mixture down the center of each tortilla. Roll up and place seam side down over sauce. Top with the remaining sauce.

5) Bake, uncovered, at 350° for 30-35 minutes or until heated through. Serve with additional salsa.

Yield: 6 servings.

NUTRITION FACTS: 2 enchiladas (calculated without additional salsa) equals 645 calories, 35 g fat (17 g saturated fat), 252 mg cholesterol, 1,812 mg sodium, 40 g carbohydrate, 2 g fiber, 42 g protein.

Pineapple Shrimp Kabobs

PREP: 30 min. + marinating **GRILL:** 10 min.

Terry Hammond, Shohola, Pennsylvania

I don't remember where I found this wonderful recipe, but my husband and I just love it. It couldn't be easier and always makes an impression on dinner guests.

- 2 cans (20 ounces *each*) pineapple chunks
- 2 cups fat-free Italian salad dressing
- 2 cans (8 ounces *each*) tomato sauce
- 1/4 cup packed brown sugar
- 2 teaspoons prepared mustard
- 2 pounds uncooked medium shrimp, peeled and deveined (about 64)
- 4 large sweet red peppers, cut into chunks
- 2 large onions, cut into chunks

1) Drain the pineapple, reserving 1/2 cup juice; refrigerate pineapple. In a small bowl, combine the salad dressing, tomato sauce, brown sugar, mustard and reserved juice.

2) Pour 3 cups into a large resealable plastic bag; add the shrimp. Seal bag and turn to coat; refrigerate for 3 hours. Cover and refrigerate remaining marinade for basting.

3) Coat grill rack with cooking spray before starting the grill. Drain and discard marinade from shrimp. On 16 metal or soaked wooden skewers, alternately thread the shrimp, red peppers, onions and pineapple.

4) Grill, covered, over medium heat for 3-5 minutes on each side or until shrimp turn pink and vegetables are tender, basting occasionally with reserved marinade.

Yield: 8 servings.

NUTRITION FACTS: 2 kabobs equals 221 calories, 2 g fat (trace saturated fat), 169 mg cholesterol, 629 mg sodium, 32 g carbohydrate, 4 g fiber, 20 g protein.

Butterflying Shrimp

After the shrimp is deveined, cut the slit deeper into the shrimp but not all the way through, leaving shrimp attached at the bottom.

SPICY SHRIMP WRAPS

Spicy Shrimp Wraps
PREP/TOTAL TIME: 20 min.

Frankie Allen Mann, Warrior, Alabama

This easy recipe is deliciously big on taste. The spicy shrimp are tucked inside a tortilla wrap, along with coleslaw and dressed-up bottled salsa.

- 1 cup salsa
- 1 medium ripe mango, peeled, pitted and diced
- 1 tablespoon ketchup
- 1 envelope reduced-sodium taco seasoning
- 1 tablespoon olive oil
- 1 pound uncooked medium shrimp, peeled and deveined
- 6 flour tortillas (10 inches), warmed
- 1-1/2 cups coleslaw mix
- 6 tablespoons reduced-fat sour cream

1) In a small bowl, combine the salsa, mango and ketchup; set aside. In a large resealable plastic bag, combine taco seasoning and oil; add shrimp. Seal bag and shake to coat.

2) In a nonstick skillet or wok, cook shrimp over medium-high heat for 2-3 minutes or until shrimp turn pink. Top tortillas with coleslaw mix, salsa mixture and shrimp.

3) Fold bottom third of tortilla up over filling; fold sides over. Serve with sour cream.

Yield: 6 servings.

NUTRITION FACTS: 1 wrap with 1 tablespoon sour cream equals 292 calories, 8 g fat (2 g saturated fat), 97 mg cholesterol, 907 mg sodium, 40 g carbohydrate, 2 g fiber, 16 g protein.

Shrimp Dijonnaise
PREP: 5 min. + marinating **BROIL:** 5 min.

Wanda Penton, Franklinton, Louisiana

This easy dish for two comes together in minutes once the shrimp have marinated. It's a refreshing departure from meat.

- 1/2 cup lemon juice
- 1/4 cup butter, melted
- 2 tablespoons vegetable oil
- 2 tablespoons Dijon mustard
- 1 tablespoon Worcestershire sauce
- 3 garlic cloves, minced
- 3/4 pound uncooked large shrimp, peeled and deveined

1) In a large resealable bag, combine the lemon juice, butter, oil, mustard, Worcestershire sauce and garlic. Add shrimp; seal bag and turn to coat.

2) Refrigerate for 4 hours, turning occasionally. Drain and discard marinade. Broil shrimp 4 in. from the heat for 4 minutes or until pink.

Yield: 2 servings.

NUTRITION FACTS: 1 serving equals 312 calories, 20 g fat (8 g saturated fat), 283 mg cholesterol, 637 mg sodium, 5 g carbohydrate, trace fiber, 28 g protein.

Garlic Butter Shrimp
PREP/TOTAL TIME: 25 min.

Sheryll Hughes-Smith, Brandon, Mississippi

Garlic and lemon lend a pleasant flavor to these speedy sauteed shrimp. I like to serve them over wild rice mix from a box.

- 1 pound uncooked medium shrimp, peeled and deveined
- 2 to 3 garlic cloves, minced
- 1/4 cup butter
- 3 tablespoons lemon juice

Hot cooked rice

1) In a large skillet, saute the shrimp and garlic in butter for 5 minutes or until shrimp turn pink. Add lemon juice; heat through. Serve with rice.

Yield: 4 servings.

NUTRITION FACTS: 1/4 pound shrimp (calculated without rice) equals 191 calories, 12 g fat (7 g saturated fat), 199 mg cholesterol, 309 mg sodium, 1 g carbohydrate, trace fiber, 18 g protein.

GARLIC BUTTER SHRIMP

CITRUS GARLIC SHRIMP

⏱ Citrus Garlic Shrimp
PREP/TOTAL TIME: 25 min.

Diane Jackson, Las Vegas, Nevada

Garlic is paired with citrus in this special shrimp and linguine combination that's pretty enough for company.

- 1 package (1 pound) linguine
- 1/2 cup olive oil
- 1/2 cup orange juice
- 1/3 cup lemon juice
- 3 to 4 garlic cloves, peeled
- 5 teaspoons grated lemon peel
- 4 teaspoons grated orange peel
- 1 teaspoon salt
- 1/4 teaspoon pepper
- 1 pound uncooked medium shrimp, peeled and deveined

Shredded Parmesan cheese and minced fresh parsley, optional

1) Cook linguine according to package directions. Meanwhile, in a blender or food processor, combine the next eight ingredients; cover and process until blended.

2) Pour into a large skillet; heat through. Add shrimp; cook for 5 minutes or until shrimp turn pink. Drain linguine; toss with shrimp mixture. Sprinkle with cheese and parsley if desired.

Yield: 6 servings.

NUTRITION FACTS: 1 cup equals 504 calories, 20 g fat (3 g saturated fat), 112 mg cholesterol, 526 mg sodium, 60 g carbohydrate, 3 g fiber, 22 g protein.

⏱ Dijon Tartar Sauce
PREP/TOTAL TIME: 5 min.

Kristen Flaherty, South Portland, Maine

Fat-free mayonnaise mixed only with pickle relish seemed so tasteless, so I began experimenting and came up with my own recipe for tartar sauce. It adds lots of flavor to fish but only a few calories.

- 1/2 cup fat-free mayonnaise
- 3 tablespoons sweet pickle relish
- 3 tablespoons chopped onion
- 4 teaspoons Dijon mustard
- 2 teaspoons lemon juice
- 1/4 teaspoon sugar
- 1/4 teaspoon salt
- 1/8 teaspoon pepper

1) In a bowl, combine all the ingredients. Store in the refrigerator for up to 1 week.

Yield: 3/4 cup.

NUTRITION FACTS: 2 tablespoons equals 31 calories, 1 g fat (trace saturated fat), 2 mg cholesterol, 392 mg sodium, 6 g carbohydrate, 1 g fiber, trace protein.

Special Spicy Seafood Sauce
PREP: 5 min. + chilling

Carolyn Chapman, Yelm, Washington

I've been serving this tangy seafood sauce for over 30 years, and I'm always asked for the recipe. Low in fat and easy to make, it's a great seafood sauce to serve with cold shrimp as an appetizer. The recipe is easy to halve or double, too.

- 1-1/2 cups ketchup
- 2 tablespoons finely chopped celery
- 2 tablespoons white wine vinegar
- 2 teaspoons finely chopped green onion
- 2 teaspoons water
- 2 teaspoons Worcestershire sauce
- 1 teaspoon prepared horseradish
- 1/2 teaspoon seasoned salt
- 1/2 teaspoon ground mustard
- 1/4 teaspoon cayenne pepper

1) In a small bowl, combine all ingredients. Cover and refrigerate for at least 1 hour before serving. Refrigerate leftovers.

Yield: 1-3/4 cups.

NUTRITION FACTS: 2 tablespoons equals 28 calories, trace fat (0 saturated fat), trace cholesterol, 445 mg sodium, 7 g carbohydrate, trace fiber, trace protein.

DIJON TARTAR SAUCE

kindness in bloom

Family nursery donates Thanksgiving dinners

For Bob Campbell, reaching the age of 91 is no reason to slow down—especially when it comes to his two loves: cooking and gardening.

Campbell's Nursery in Lincoln, Nebraska, is a family business. Bob's father founded it, Bob expanded it and, now, Bob's children and grandchildren are in charge.

For the Campbell clan, giving back to others is also a family business. For more than 12 years, the Campbell family and the nursery have been providing Thanksgiving dinner for at least eight families living at Friendship Home, a local shelter for women and their children who are victims of domestic violence.

"It's a wonderful feeling because there are so many that need help," says Bob.

He and his family have gotten their Thanksgiving routine down to a science. The family buys the turkeys and side dishes, the nursery staff donates the necessary canned goods, and Bob makes his delicious pies.

"It really is a group effort," Bob says. "Not only does the family get involved, the entire nursery staff does, too! The staff gets really excited about it."

When making his pies, Bob uses the Foolproof Pie Shells recipe given to him by his 94-year-old sister. "If they eat all the crust, I know it was good," Bob says with a laugh.

During the rest of the year, the Campbells don't forget about the women at Friendship Home. The center provides transitional housing for some women and children, and the Campbells offer their landscaping services to keep these houses looking beautiful.

Bob, who loves to cook, keeps four notebooks stuffed full of his favorite recipes. "My mom always made everything from scratch," he says. "It tastes better that way."

No doubt the families at Friendship Home would agree.

Bob Campbell

> "It really is a group effort... the staff gets really excited about it.
> ~Bob Campbell

Editor's Note: *Taste of Home learned as this book was going to press that Bob Campbell had passed away recently. At his family's request we are continuing to publish his story in hopes it will inspire others and so that his wonderful pie shell recipe will continue to be shared.*

DO YOU KNOW A COOK WHO CARES?
If you or someone you know cooks for a charitable, spiritual or other cause, tell us about it at **tasteofhome.com/CookbookBonus**

You can find Bob's pie shell recipe in the Web exclusive online at tasteofhome.com/CookbookBonus **Type in access code ICare**

Recipes

Tips

Eggs & Cheese

No two ingredients are quite as versatile and compatible in recipes as eggs and cheese. Eggs are delicious, and they are also an economical protein source. Eggs and cheese make a great combination for breakfast or a simple lunch or dinner.

Eggs also play many supporting functions in baking—they add color, flavor, texture and structure and help leaven. Egg yolks add fat and act as an emulsifier, which helps blend the shortening or oil into the liquid ingredients. Egg whites are used for their drying properties, especially for meringues.

Buying, Storing and Cooking Eggs

Brown and white eggs have the same nutritional value and they cook the same. The color of the egg is based on the breed of the chicken.

Select cartons with unbroken shells from the refrigerated case. Refrigerate them as soon as possible after purchase. Store eggs in their carton on an inside refrigerator shelf, not in a compartment on the door. The carton cushions the eggs and helps prevent moisture loss and odor absorption.

Check the grade on the egg carton; they're either AA, A or B. The higher the grade, the higher and more nicely shaped the yolk will be. Also the higher the grade, the thicker the white and the less it spreads.

Use eggs by the expiration date printed on the carton. The expiration should be no longer than 30 days past the date the eggs were packaged. Discard any eggs that have cracked or broken shells.

Don't use a recipe where the eggs will not be thoroughly cooked. Eggs are thoroughly cooked when they reach a temperature of 160°. For food safety reasons, do not leave eggs at room temperature for over 2 hours.

Pasteurized eggs have been treated with heat to destroy bacteria that may be on the shell or in the egg. These eggs are available in some markets. Due to the heat treatment, the eggs may have slightly lower amounts of heat-sensitive vitamins, such as thiamin and riboflavin.

Egg Size Equivalents

The recipes in this cookbook were tested with large eggs. The following are some guidelines for substituting other egg sizes for large eggs.

EGG SIZE	SUBSTITUTION
1 LARGE EGG	1 jumbo, 1 extra-large or 1 medium
2 LARGE EGGS	2 jumbo, 2 extra-large, 2 medium or 3 small
3 LARGE EGGS	2 jumbo, 3 extra-large, 3 medium or 4 small
4 LARGE EGGS	3 jumbo, 4 extra-large, 5 medium or 5 small
5 LARGE EGGS	4 jumbo, 4 extra-large, 6 medium or 7 small
6 LARGE EGGS	5 jumbo, 5 extra-large, 7 medium or 8 small

Beating Eggs

Lightly Beaten
Beat the egg with a fork until the yolk and white are combined.

Lemon-Colored
Beat eggs with an electric mixer on high speed for about 5 minutes. The volume of the beaten eggs will increase, the texture will go from liquid to thick and foamy, and the color will be a light yellow.

Thick and Pale Yellow
Beat eggs and sugar with an electric mixer on high speed for about 7-8 minutes or until mixture has thickened and turned a very pale yellow. Mixture will fall in ribbons from a spoon.

Soft Peaks
Beat egg whites with an electric mixer on medium speed until they are thick and white. To test for soft peaks, lift the beaters from the whites—the egg white peaks should curl down. For best results, make sure the bowl and beaters are free from oil and the egg whites contain no specks of yolk. Both will prevent the whites from reaching full volume.

Stiff Peaks
After the egg whites have reached the soft-peak stage, continue beating with an electric mixer on high speed until the volume increases more and they are thicker. To test for stiff peaks, lift the beaters from the whites—the egg white peaks should stand straight up, and if you tilt the bowl, the whites should not slide around.

Tips for Separated Eggs

Separate the eggs while they are still cold from the refrigerator, then allow the egg whites to stand at room temperature for 30 minutes before beating to obtain maximum volume.

- To store unbroken egg yolks, place in a container and cover with water. Tightly cover the container and refrigerate for 2-4 days.

- Refrigerate egg whites in a tightly covered container for up to 4 days.

- Freeze unused egg whites in a tightly covered container for up to 1 year.

- To freeze egg yolks: for each 1/4 cup of egg yolk, beat the yolks with 1/8 teaspoon salt or 1-1/2 teaspoons corn syrup. Place in a tightly covered container for up to 1 year. Make sure you label the container, noting whether salt or corn syrup was added. Use the salt-added yolks in savory dishes and the corn syrup-added yolks in sweet (dessert) recipes.

Separating Eggs
Place an egg separator over a custard cup; crack egg into the separator. As each egg is separated, place yolk in another bowl and empty egg whites into a mixing bowl. It's easier to separate eggs when they are cold.

Lightly Scrambled Eggs

PREP/TOTAL TIME: 15 min.

Patricia Kaliska, Phillips, Wisconsin

Wake up your taste buds with this fluffy entree, enhanced with sour cream, green onions and cheese. To keep it light, I use reduced-fat and fat-free ingredients.

- 9 egg whites
- 3 eggs
- 1/2 cup reduced-fat sour cream
- 1/4 cup fat-free milk
- 2 green onions, thinly sliced
- 1/4 teaspoon salt
- 1/8 teaspoon pepper
- 6 drops yellow food coloring, optional
- 3/4 cup shredded reduced-fat cheddar cheese

1) In a large bowl, whisk the egg whites and eggs. Add the sour cream, milk, onions, salt, pepper and food coloring if desired. Pour into a large nonstick skillet coated with cooking spray.

2) Cook and gently stir over medium heat until eggs are completely set. Remove from the heat. Sprinkle with cheese; cover and let stand for 5 minutes to allow cheese to melt.

Yield: 6 servings.

NUTRITION FACTS: 1/3 cup equals 135 calories, 7 g fat (4 g saturated fat), 122 mg cholesterol, 331 mg sodium, 4 g carbohydrate, 1 g fiber, 15 g protein.

Fluffy Scrambled Eggs
PREP/TOTAL TIME: 10 min.

Marjorie Carey, Alamosa, Florida

I started fixing scrambled eggs more often years ago when we raised chickens. This recipe has great taste and texture. Plus, it's easy to add extra ingredients to suit your fancy.

> 8 eggs
> 1 can (5 ounces) evaporated milk
> 2 tablespoons butter

Salt and pepper to taste

1) In a large bowl, whisk the eggs and milk. In a large skillet, heat butter until hot.

2) Add egg mixture; cook and stir over medium heat until completely set. Season with salt and pepper.

Yield: 4 servings.

NUTRITION FACTS: 1 serving (calculated without salt and pepper) equals 244 calories, 18 g fat (8 g saturated fat), 452 mg cholesterol, 218 mg sodium, 5 g carbohydrate, 0 fiber, 15 g protein.

■ **Hearty Scrambled Eggs:** In a large skillet, saute 1 cup *each* cubed fully cooked ham and sliced fresh mushrooms, 1/2 cup chopped sweet red pepper and 1/4 cup sliced green onions in 2 tablespoons butter until vegetables are tender. Remove vegetables; set aside. Whisk eggs with milk as directed; add to skillet.

Cook and stir until eggs are slightly set. Add the ham mixture and continue to cook until eggs are completely set. Remove from the heat. If desired, sprinkle top with 1 cup (4 ounces) shredded cheddar cheese; cover and let stand for 1-2 minutes or until cheese is melted.

FLUFFY SCRAMBLED EGGS

Scrambling Eggs

1) Pour beaten egg mixture into prepared skillet. As eggs begin to set, gently move a spatula across the bottom and sides of pan, allowing the uncooked eggs to flow underneath.

2) Continue to cook the eggs, stirring occasionally, until the eggs are set and no visible liquid remains.

Veggie Egg Scramble
PREP/TOTAL TIME: 20 min.

Phyllis Behringer, Defiance, Ohio

While staying with friends one weekend, we enjoyed the most wonderful eggs. I created this version to reduce the calorie and fat content. White wine turns this egg dish into a sophisticated brunch specialty.

> 6 egg whites
> 2 eggs
> 1/4 cup white wine *or* chicken broth
> 1/4 teaspoon salt
> 1/8 teaspoon pepper
> 1/8 teaspoon garlic powder
> 1/2 cup chopped green pepper
> 1/2 cup chopped onion
> 1/2 cup sliced fresh mushrooms
> 1 teaspoon butter
> 1 teaspoon olive oil
> 1/2 cup shredded reduced-fat cheddar cheese
> 2 teaspoons minced fresh basil

1) In a bowl, whisk the egg whites, eggs, wine or broth, salt, pepper and garlic powder; set aside. In a large nonstick skillet, saute the green pepper, onion and mushrooms in butter and oil for 3 minutes or until crisp-tender.

2) Reduce heat to medium. Stir in the egg mixture; cook and stir until eggs are completely set. Sprinkle with cheese and basil. Cover and remove from the heat; let stand for 5 minutes or until cheese is melted.

Yield: 3 servings.

NUTRITION FACTS: 1 cup equals 201 calories, 10 g fat (5 g saturated fat), 158 mg cholesterol, 365 mg sodium, 8 g carbohydrate, 1 g fiber, 18 g protein.

FLUFFY BREAKFAST OMELETS

 CLASSIC: If you're looking for the traditional taste of a hearty omelet but need to feed several people, try Oven Denver Omelet. It's baked in the oven, so you can serve a fresh omelet to everyone at the same time.

 TIME-SAVER: On time-crunched mornings, Omelet in a Mug is a lifesaver. The hearty one-serving breakfast cooks in the microwave in less than 2 minutes. Since it's mixed in a mug, cleanup is quick, too.

 LIGHT: The addition of egg whites to the whole eggs in Pepper Cheese Omelets creates satisfying servings that are lower in calories and fat. Part-skim mozzarella cheese and fat-free milk also help make it healthier than its classic counterpart.

 SERVES 2: Fresh Vegetable Omelet is the perfect dish for a cozy breakfast for two. After the egg mixture is cooked, simply top with cheese and sauteed veggies, fold over and cut in half.

OVEN DENVER OMELET

Omelet in a Mug

PREP/TOTAL TIME: 5 min.

Susan Adair, Somerset, Kentucky

- 2 eggs, lightly beaten
- 2 to 3 tablespoons shredded cheddar cheese
- 2 tablespoons diced fully cooked ham
- 1 tablespoon diced green pepper

Salt and pepper to taste

1) In a microwave-safe mug coated with cooking spray, combine all ingredients. Microwave, uncovered, on high for 30-40 seconds; stir. Cook 30-60 seconds longer or until eggs are completely set.

Yield: 1 serving.

NUTRITION FACTS: 1 serving equals 223 calories, 15 g fat (7 g saturated fat), 447 mg cholesterol, 449 mg sodium, 2 g carbohydrate, trace fiber, 19 g protein.

Oven Denver Omelet

PREP/TOTAL TIME: 30 min.

Ellen Bower, Taneytown, Maryland

- 8 eggs
- 1/2 cup half-and-half cream
- 1 cup (4 ounces) shredded cheddar cheese
- 1 cup finely chopped fully cooked ham
- 1/4 cup finely chopped green pepper
- 1/4 cup finely chopped onion

1) In a bowl, whisk the eggs and cream until light. Stir in the cheese, ham, green pepper and onion.

2) Pour into a greased 9-in. square baking dish. Bake at 400° for 25 minutes or until golden brown.

Yield: 6 servings.

NUTRITION FACTS: 1 piece equals 235 calories, 16 g fat (8 g saturated fat), 326 mg cholesterol, 506 mg sodium, 4 g carbohydrate, trace fiber, 17 g protein.

Pepper Cheese Omelets

PREP/TOTAL TIME: 25 min.

Susan Rekerdres, Dallas, Texas

- 2 eggs
- 4 egg whites
- 2 teaspoons fat-free milk
- 1 teaspoon paprika
- 1/4 teaspoon salt
- 1/4 teaspoon pepper
- 2 tablespoons finely chopped onion
- 2 tablespoons finely chopped sweet red pepper
- 1/4 cup shredded part-skim mozzarella cheese

1) In a small bowl, whisk the eggs, egg whites, milk, paprika, salt and pepper. Coat an 8-in. nonstick skillet with cooking spray and place over medium heat. Add half of the egg mixture. As eggs set, lift edges, letting uncooked portion flow underneath.

2) When eggs are set, sprinkle half of the onion, red pepper and cheese over one side; fold omelet over filling. Cover and let stand for 1 minute or until the cheese is melted. Repeat with the remaining ingredients.

Yield: 2 servings.

NUTRITION FACTS: 1 omelet equals 156 calories, 7 g fat (3 g saturated fat), 221 mg cholesterol, 537 mg sodium, 4 g carbohydrate, 1 g fiber, 17 g protein.

Fresh Vegetable Omelet

PREP: 30 min. **BAKE:** 10 min.

Edie DeSpain, Logan, Utah

- 4 egg whites
- 1/4 cup water
- 1/4 teaspoon cream of tartar
- 2 eggs
- 1/4 teaspoon salt
- 1 teaspoon butter
- 1 medium tomato, chopped
- 1 small zucchini, chopped
- 1 small onion, chopped
- 1/4 cup chopped green pepper
- 1/2 teaspoon Italian seasoning
- 1/3 cup shredded reduced-fat cheddar cheese

1) In a small mixing bowl, beat the egg whites, water and cream of tartar until stiff peaks form. In a large mixing bowl, beat eggs and salt until thick and lemon-colored, about 5 minutes. Fold in the whites.

2) Melt butter in a 10-in. nonstick ovenproof skillet coated with cooking spray. Add egg mixture. Cook over medium heat for 5 minutes or until

FRESH VEGETABLE OMELET

puffed and lightly browned on the bottom. Bake, uncovered, at 350° for 10-12 minutes or until a knife inserted 2 in. from edge comes out clean.

3) Meanwhile, in a skillet, saute the tomato, zucchini, onion, green pepper and Italian seasoning until tender. Carefully run a knife around edge of omelet to loosen. With a sharp knife, score center of omelet. Place vegetables on one side and sprinkle with cheese; fold other side over filling. Slide onto a serving plate; cut in half.

Yield: 2 servings.

NUTRITION FACTS: 1/2 omelet equals 222 calories, 11 g fat (5 g saturated fat), 231 mg cholesterol, 617 mg sodium, 12 g carbohydrate, 3 g fiber, 20 g protein.

Making an Omelet

1) Beat eggs, milk and any seasonings. Heat oil or butter in a 10-in. nonstick skillet over medium heat. Add eggs; cook until partially set. Lift edges, letting uncooked egg flow underneath.

2) Allow the eggs to set, and then sprinkle your favorite filling ingredients (such as ham, chopped green pepper, chopped tomato, shredded cheese or mushrooms) over half of the omelet.

3) Fold omelet in half. Proceed as recipe directs.

ASPARAGUS CRAB OMELETS

Asparagus Crab Omelets

PREP/TOTAL TIME: 30 min.

Mae Jean Damron, Sandy, Utah

These satisfying omelets are filled with a savory blend of crabmeat, asparagus, tomatoes and provolone cheese...and they're attractive enough to serve guests.

> 6 fresh asparagus spears, trimmed
> 4 eggs

Dash salt

Dash pepper

> 1/2 cup diced plum tomatoes
> 2 tablespoons butter, *divided*
> 1 can (6 ounces) crabmeat, drained, flaked and cartilage removed
> 1/2 cup (2 ounces) provolone cheese, shredded

1) Place asparagus in a steamer basket. Place in a saucepan over 1 in. of water; bring to a boil. Cover and steam for 4-5 minutes or until crisp-tender; set aside. In a small bowl, whisk the eggs, salt and pepper. Stir in tomatoes.

2) Melt 1 tablespoon butter in a small skillet over medium heat; add half of egg mixture. As eggs set, lift edges, letting uncooked portion flow underneath.

3) When the eggs are set, spoon half of the crab, asparagus and provolone cheese over one side; fold omelet over filling. Cover and let stand for 1-2 minutes or until cheese is melted. Repeat for second omelet.

Yield: 2 servings.

NUTRITION FACTS: 1 serving equals 407 calories, 27 g fat (13 g saturated fat), 541 mg cholesterol, 733 mg sodium, 6 g carbohydrate, 1 g fiber, 35 g protein.

■ **Potato Omelet:** In a small skillet, saute 1 cubed cooked medium red potato, 1/2 cup chopped fresh broccoli, 2 tablespoons chopped onion and 1/2 teaspoon dill weed in 1 tablespoon butter. Remove and keep warm.

Whisk 4 eggs with 1 tablespoon water. Cook omelets as directed in Asparagus Crab Omelets, omitting asparagus, tomatoes, crabmeat and provolone cheese. Spoon half the potato mixture over one side of each omelet; fold omelet over filling. Sprinkle each with 1/4 cup shredded cheddar *or* Swiss cheese. Cover and let stand 1-2 minutes or until cheese is melted.

Fried Eggs

PREP/TOTAL TIME: 10 min.

Taste of Home Test Kitchen

Cook slowly over medium heat to avoid overdone eggs.

> 1 to 2 tablespoons butter
> 1 to 2 eggs

1) In a 7- or 8-in. skillet or omelet pan, melt butter over medium heat. Break eggs, one at a time, into a custard cup or saucer, then gently slide into the pan. Immediately reduce heat to low. Cook slowly until the whites are completely set and the yolks begin to thicken.

2) For sunny-side-up eggs, cover pan and cook until yolk thickens but is not hard. For basted eggs, spoon butter in pan over eggs while cooking. For over-easy eggs, carefully turn eggs over to cook both sides.

Yield: 1 serving.

NUTRITION FACTS: 1 serving equals 175 calories, 16 g fat (9 g saturated fat), 243 mg cholesterol, 179 mg sodium, 1 g carbohydrate, 0 fiber, 6 g protein.

Baked Omelet Roll

PREP/TOTAL TIME: 30 min.

Susan Hudon, Fort Wayne, Indiana

This is an interesting way to serve an omelet, plus it bakes in the oven.

> 6 eggs
> 1 cup milk
> 1/2 cup all-purpose flour
> 1/2 teaspoon salt
> 1/4 teaspoon pepper
> 1 cup (4 ounces) shredded cheddar cheese

1) Place eggs and milk in a blender. Add flour, salt and pepper; cover and process until smooth. Pour into a greased 13-in. x 9-in. x 2-in. baking pan. Bake at 450° for 20 minutes or until eggs are set.

2) Sprinkle with cheese. Roll up omelet in pan, starting with a short side. Place with seam side down on a serving platter. Cut into 3/4-in. slices.

Yield: 6 servings.

NUTRITION FACTS: 2 slices equals 204 calories, 12 g fat (6 g saturated fat), 238 mg cholesterol, 393 mg sodium, 11 g carbohydrate, trace fiber, 13 g protein.

◖Asparagus Frittata

PREP/TOTAL TIME: 20 min.

James Bates, Hermiston, Oregon

You would never guess that egg substitute takes the place of eggs in this fun variation on a traditional frittata. Chock-full of fresh asparagus, this dish is perfect for a light lunch or brunch.

> 1   cup water
> 2/3 pound fresh asparagus, trimmed and cut into 1-inch pieces
> 1   medium onion, chopped
> 2   teaspoons olive oil
> 2   tablespoons minced fresh parsley
> 1-1/2 cups egg substitute
> 5   tablespoons shredded Parmesan cheese, *divided*
> 1/4 teaspoon salt
> 1/8 teaspoon pepper
> 1/4 cup shredded reduced-fat cheddar cheese

1) In a small saucepan, bring water to a boil. Add asparagus; cover and boil for 3 minutes. Drain and immediately place asparagus in ice water; drain and pat dry. In a 10-in. ovenproof skillet, saute onion in oil until tender. Add parsley and asparagus; toss to coat.

2) In a small bowl, combine the egg substitute, 3 tablespoons Parmesan cheese, salt and pepper. Pour over asparagus mixture; cover and cook over medium heat for 8-10 minutes or until eggs are nearly set. Sprinkle with remaining Parmesan.

3) Place uncovered skillet in the broiler, 6 in. from the heat, for 2 minutes or until eggs are set. Sprinkle with cheddar cheese. Cut into quarters. Serve immediately.

Yield: 4 servings.

Editor's Note: To use whole eggs, omit the egg substitute and use 6 eggs.

NUTRITION FACTS: 1 piece equals 146 calories, 5 g fat (2 g saturated fat), 8 mg cholesterol, 533 mg sodium, 9 g carbohydrate, 2 g fiber, 16 g protein.

Using Egg Substitute

Look in the refrigerated and frozen food section of grocery stores for egg substitute in cartons. Egg substitute uses egg whites and contains no cholesterol and little or no fat. One-fourth cup of egg substitute is equal to one egg.

Note that baking with egg substitute may affect the quality of your baked item. Generally, it is best to use egg substitute for only a portion of the eggs called for in a recipe. Do not use egg substitute for items such as cream puffs, popovers and sponge cakes.

SUNDAY BRUNCH CASSEROLE

Sunday Brunch Casserole

PREP: 20 min.   **BAKE:** 35 min.

Patricia Throlson, Willmar, Minnesota

My husband and sons often ask if I'll make my "egg pie," using the nickname they've given this hearty casserole. It's nice for a special brunch and versatile enough for a satisfying family supper.

> 1/2 pound sliced bacon
> 1/2 cup chopped onion
> 1/2 cup chopped green pepper
> 12   eggs
> 1   cup milk
> 1   package (16 ounces) frozen hash brown potatoes, thawed
> 1   cup (4 ounces) shredded cheddar cheese
> 1   teaspoon salt
> 1/2 teaspoon pepper
> 1/4 teaspoon dill weed

1) In a large skillet, cook bacon over medium heat until crisp. Remove to paper towels; drain, reserving 2 tablespoons drippings. Crumble bacon and set aside. In same skillet, saute onion and green pepper in drippings until tender; remove with a slotted spoon.

2) In a large bowl, whisk the eggs and milk. Stir in hash browns, cheese, salt, pepper, dill, onion mixture and reserved bacon.

3) Transfer to a greased 13-in. x 9-in. x 2-in. baking dish. Bake, uncovered, at 350° for 35-45 minutes or until a knife inserted near center comes out clean.

Yield: 8 servings.

NUTRITION FACTS: 1 piece equals 391 calories, 28 g fat (13 g saturated fat), 357 mg cholesterol, 887 mg sodium, 17 g carbohydrate, trace fiber, 18 g protein.

EYE-APPEALING FRITTATA

 CLASSIC: For breakfast, lunch or dinner, Colorful Frittata is a versatile and delicious egg dish that's hearty with ham, cheese and fresh veggies, including broccoli, mushrooms, green onions and tomatoes.

 TIME-SAVER: There's no need to turn on the oven to prepare Microwave Frittata. Like its name says, it cooks in the microwave in just a few minutes for fast, flavorful results.

 LIGHT: Portobello Spinach Frittata relies on egg substitute and fat-free ricotta to cut fat and calories. Fresh baby portobello mushrooms replace the ham found in Colorful Frittata, so this healthier version is also lower in sodium.

 SERVES 2: Red and green pepper, onion and mushrooms add great taste and color to Egg White Frittata, a tasty entree sized right for two. Because it's made with egg whites, it's lighter, too.

COLORFUL FRITTATA

Colorful Frittata

PREP/TOTAL TIME: 30 min.

Julie Watson, Anderson, Indiana

- 1 cup broccoli florets
- 3/4 cup sliced fresh mushrooms
- 2 green onions, finely chopped
- 1 tablespoon butter
- 1 cup cubed fully cooked ham
- 8 eggs
- 1/4 cup water
- 1/4 cup Dijon mustard
- 1/2 teaspoon Italian seasoning
- 1/4 teaspoon garlic salt
- 1-1/2 cups (6 ounces) shredded cheddar cheese
- 1/2 cup chopped tomatoes

1) In a large skillet, saute the broccoli, mushrooms and onions in butter until tender. Add ham; heat through. Remove from the heat and keep warm.

2) In a mixing bowl, beat the eggs, water, mustard, Italian seasoning and garlic salt until foamy. Stir in the cheese, tomatoes and broccoli mixture.

3) Pour into a greased shallow 1-1/2-qt. baking dish. Bake at 375° for 22-27 minutes or until a knife inserted in the center comes out clean.

Yield: 6 servings.

NUTRITION FACTS: 1 piece equals 277 calories, 20 g fat (10 g saturated fat), 331 mg cholesterol, 905 mg sodium, 6 g carbohydrate, 1 g fiber, 20 g protein.

Microwave Frittata

PREP/TOTAL TIME: 10 min.

Delia Kennedy, Deer Park, Washington

- 1 tablespoon butter
- 1 cup cubed fully cooked ham
- 1/2 cup chopped onion
- 1/4 cup chopped green pepper
- 4 eggs, lightly beaten

Salt and pepper to taste

1) Place butter in a microwave-safe 9-in. pie plate. Cover and microwave on high for 20-30 seconds or until melted. Add ham, onion and green pepper. Cover and cook on high for 1 minute. Stir in eggs, salt and pepper.

2) Cover and cook on high for 1-2 minutes or until a knife inserted near the center comes out clean. Let stand for 3 minutes or until completely set. Cut into wedges.

Yield: 4 servings.

NUTRITION FACTS: 1 wedge equals 163 calories, 11 g fat (4 g saturated fat), 238 mg cholesterol, 539 mg sodium, 3 g carbohydrate, trace fiber, 13 g protein.

Satisfying Sandwich

A frittata is a great choice for breakfast. But you can turn it into a hearty lunch or dinner by using the open-faced omelet as a sandwich filling. Simply cook the frittata as the recipe directs, then place a piece between two slices of substantial bakery bread, such as sourdough or foraccia. Include sliced tomato and fresh spinach leaves, if you'd like, for a quick sandwich that's sure to satisfy.

Portobello Spinach Frittata

PREP: 10 min. **BAKE:** 30 min. + standing

Irene Turner, Alma, Wisconsin

- 2 eggs
- 1/2 cup egg substitute
- 1 cup fat-free ricotta cheese
- 3/4 cup grated Parmesan cheese
- 1 package (10 ounces) frozen chopped spinach, thawed and squeezed dry
- 1/2 teaspoon salt
- 1/4 teaspoon pepper
- 3/4 cup sliced baby portobello mushrooms
- 4 green onions, chopped

1) In a large bowl, combine the eggs, egg substitute, ricotta cheese, Parmesan cheese, spinach, salt and pepper. Stir in mushrooms and onions.

2) Transfer to a 9-in. pie plate coated with cooking spray. Bake at 350° for 30-35 minutes or until a knife inserted near the center comes out clean. Let stand for 10 minutes before cutting.

Yield: 6 servings.

NUTRITION FACTS: 1 piece equals 130 calories, 5 g fat (2 g saturated fat), 85 mg cholesterol, 526 mg sodium, 7 g carbohydrate, 2 g fiber, 13 g protein.

EGG WHITE FRITTATA

Egg White Frittata

PREP/TOTAL TIME: 20 min.

Linda LaPresle, Glendora, California

- 1-1/4 cups sliced fresh mushrooms
- 1/2 medium onion, diced
- 1/2 small sweet red pepper, sliced
- 1/2 small green pepper, diced
- 1/4 teaspoon salt
- 1/4 teaspoon dried oregano

Dash pepper

- 1 tablespoon olive oil
- 8 egg whites, beaten
- 1 tablespoon grated Parmesan cheese

1) In a 10-in. ovenproof skillet, saute the mushrooms, onion, red pepper, green pepper, salt, oregano and pepper in oil until vegetables are tender. Beat egg whites until foamy; pour into skillet. Cook for 3 minutes over medium-low heat or until puffed and lightly browned on bottom. Sprinkle with cheese.

2) Bake, uncovered, at 375° for 8-10 minutes or until egg whites are set. Loosen edges and bottom of frittata with a rubber spatula. Invert onto a serving plate; cut into wedges. Serve immediately.

Yield: 2 servings

NUTRITION FACTS: 1/2 frittata equals 184 calories, 8 g fat (1 g saturated fat), 2 mg cholesterol, 565 mg sodium, 12 g carbohydrate, 2 g fiber, 17 g protein.

Cajun Corned Beef Hash

PREP/TOTAL TIME: 30 min.

Del Mason, Martensville, Saskatchewan

Neither the flavor nor the texture is "mushy" when you whip up a skillet of this tongue-tingling hash. This is an all-time favorite of mine. I created it after eating a similar variation in Texas.

- 6 cups frozen shredded hash brown potatoes, thawed
- 1/4 cup butter
- 1/2 cup *each* finely chopped green onions, sweet red pepper and green pepper
- 1 teaspoon seasoned salt
- 3/4 teaspoon Cajun seasoning
- 3/4 teaspoon chili powder
- 1/2 teaspoon pepper
- 1-1/2 cups chopped cooked corned beef
- 1 tablespoon white vinegar
- 8 eggs

Additional Cajun seasoning and hot pepper sauce, optional

1) In a large skillet, cook hash browns in butter until almost tender. Stir in onions, peppers and seasonings. Cook until hash browns are lightly browned and peppers are tender. Add corned beef; heat through.

2) Meanwhile, in a skillet with high sides, bring 2-3 in. of water and vinegar to a boil. Reduce heat; simmer gently. For each egg, break cold egg into a custard cup or saucer. Hold the cup close to the surface of the water and slip the egg into simmering water.

3) Cook 4 eggs at a time, uncovered, until whites are completely set and yolks begin to thicken, about 3-5 minutes. With a slotted spoon, remove each egg. Repeat with remaining eggs.

CAJUN CORNED BEEF HASH

4) Serve over hash mixture. Serve with additional Cajun seasoning and hot pepper sauce if desired.

Yield: 4 servings.

Editor's Note: If poaching eggs using a metal poaching insert, increase poaching time to 6-7 minutes.

NUTRITION FACTS: 1 cup equals 569 calories, 38 g fat (16 g saturated fat), 539 mg cholesterol, 1,733 mg sodium, 25 g carbohydrate, 3 g fiber, 32 g protein.

Poaching Eggs

Break cold eggs, one at a time, into a custard cup, small measuring cup or saucer. Holding the dish close to the simmering liquid's surface, slip the eggs, one at a time, into the liquid. Cook, uncovered, until the whites are completely set and the yolks begin to thicken, about 3-5 minutes.

Double-Cheese Eggs Benedict

PREP: 15 min. **COOK:** 20 min.

Megan Hakes, Wellsville, Pennsylvania

Making breakfast is my favorite part of running a bed-and-breakfast. The eggs in this recipe are served over English muffins and Canadian bacon, then topped with a simple sauce.

- 2 tablespoons butter
- 2 tablespoons plus 1-1/2 teaspoons all-purpose flour
- 1-1/2 cups milk
- 1/4 cup shredded cheddar cheese
- 2 tablespoons shredded Parmesan cheese
- 1/2 teaspoon Dijon mustard
- 1/8 teaspoon salt
- 1/8 teaspoon white pepper

POACHED EGGS:

- 1 teaspoon white vinegar
- 8 cold eggs
- 4 English muffins, split and toasted
- 8 slices Canadian bacon, warmed
- 8 bacon strips, cooked and crumbled

1) For cheese sauce, in a saucepan, melt butter. Stir in flour until smooth; gradually add the milk. Bring to a boil; cook and stir for 2 minutes or until thickened. Reduce heat to medium-low. Add the cheese, mustard, salt and pepper, stirring until cheese is melted. Cover and keep warm.

2) In a skillet with high sides, bring 2-3 in. of water and vinegar to a boil. Reduce heat; simmer gently. For each egg, break the cold egg into a custard cup or saucer. Hold the dish close to the water surface and slip the egg into simmering water.

3) Cook 4 eggs at a time, uncovered, for 3-5 minutes or until the whites are completely set and the yolks begin to thicken. With a slotted spoon, remove each egg. Repeat with remaining eggs.

4) To assemble, top each muffin half with one slice Canadian bacon, one egg, cheese sauce and bacon.

Yield: 8 servings.

Editor's Note: If poaching eggs using a metal poaching insert, increase poaching time to 6-7 minutes.

NUTRITION FACTS: 1 serving equals 301 calories, 16 g fat (7 g saturated fat), 250 mg cholesterol, 793 mg sodium, 18 g carbohydrate, 1 g fiber, 19 g protein.

■ **Asparagus Eggs Benedict:** For cheese sauce, omit the cheddar cheese, Parmesan cheese, mustard and white pepper. Stir in 6 ounces shredded Gouda to the sauce. Omit bacon strips. Trim and halve 16 asparagus spears; steam for 8-10 minutes. Prepare eggs as directed. Assemble as directed, substituting the asparagus for the bacon strips.

Stuffing Eggs Using a Pastry Bag

Mash yolks with a fork. Add remaining filling ingredients; mix well. Spoon filling into a pastry bag fitted with a #20 decorating tip. Pipe filling into egg white halves.

Hard-Cooked Eggs

PREP: 20 min. + cooling

Taste of Home Test Kitchen

This basic formula for hard-cooked eggs gives you a great end result to use in salads, sandwiches and for deviled eggs. They're terrific for snacking on, too.

6 eggs

Cold water

1) Place eggs in a single layer in a large saucepan; add enough cold water to cover by 1 in. Cover and quickly bring to a boil. Remove from the heat.

2) Let stand for 15 minutes for large eggs (18 minutes for extra-large eggs and 12 minutes for medium eggs).

3) Rinse eggs in cold water and place in ice water until completely cooled. Drain and refrigerate.

Yield: 6 servings.

NUTRITION FACTS: 1 egg equals 75 calories, 5 g fat (2 g saturated fat), 213 mg cholesterol, 63 mg sodium, 1 g carbohydrate, 0 fiber, 6 g protein.

Deviled Eggs

PREP/TOTAL TIME: 15 min.

Margaret Sanders, Indianapolis, Indiana

For variety, you can use different ingredients like the variations that follow. Or get creative and make your own versions.

6 hard-cooked eggs
2 tablespoons mayonnaise
1 teaspoon sugar
1 teaspoon white vinegar
1 teaspoon prepared mustard
1/2 teaspoon salt

Paprika

1) Slice eggs in half lengthwise; remove yolks and set whites aside. In a small bowl, mash yolks with a fork. Add next five ingredients; mix well.

2) Stuff or pipe filling into egg whites. Sprinkle with paprika. Refrigerate until serving.

Yield: 6 servings.

NUTRITION FACTS: 2 egg halves equals 114 calories, 9 g fat (2 g saturated fat), 214 mg cholesterol, 293 mg sodium, 1 g carbohydrate, trace fiber, 6 g protein.

■ **Picnic Stuffed Eggs:** To mashed yolk, add 1/4 cup mayonnaise, 2 tablespoons drained sweet pickle relish, 1-1/2 teaspoons honey mustard, 1/2 teaspoon garlic salt, 1/4 teaspoon Worcestershire sauce and 1/8 teaspoon pepper. Stuff as directed.

■ **Almond Deviled Eggs:** To mashed egg yolk, add 1/2 cup mayonnaise, 1 teaspoon Dijon mustard, 1/4 teaspoon garlic salt and 3 tablespoons finely chopped roasted almonds. Stuff as directed. Top each half with a whole roasted almond and minced fresh parsley.

■ **Crab-Stuffed Deviled Eggs:** Make 12 hard-cooked eggs. To the mashed yolks, add 1 can (6 ounces) crabmeat, drained, flaked and cartilage removed, 2/3 cup mayonnaise, 1/2 cup finely chopped celery, 1/2 cup chopped slivered almonds, 2 tablespoons finely chopped green pepper and 1/2 teaspoon salt. Stuff as directed.

DEVILED EGGS

Makeover Deviled Eggs

PREP/TOTAL TIME: 10 min.

Taste of Home Test Kitchen

If you'd like to dig in to some creamy, rich deviled eggs at your next picnic or potluck but prefer a lighter bite, go for this trimmed-down version. We made them with two-thirds less fat and saturated fat and just half the calories of the classic recipe.

- 8 hard-cooked eggs
- 1/4 cup fat-free mayonnaise
- 1/4 cup reduced-fat sour cream
- 2 tablespoons soft bread crumbs
- 1 tablespoon prepared mustard
- 1/4 teaspoon salt

Dash white pepper

- 3 stuffed olives, sliced

1) Slice eggs in half lengthwise and remove yolks; refrigerate eight yolk halves for another use. Set whites aside.

2) In a small bowl, mash remaining yolks. Stir in the mayonnaise, sour cream, bread crumbs, mustard, salt and pepper. Stuff or pipe into egg whites. Garnish with olives.

Yield: 8 servings.

NUTRITION FACTS: 2 egg halves equals 74 calories, 4 g fat (1 g saturated fat), 109 mg cholesterol, 264 mg sodium, 4 g carbohydrate, trace fiber, 6 g protein.

SIMPLER DEVILED EGGS ■■■

Instead of mixing mayonnaise and mustard with the yolks to fill deviled eggs, I simply mix the yolks with bacon ranch salad dressing. It's fast and gives the appetizers a different taste.

—*Bernice H., Plainfield, Indiana*

MAKEOVER DEVILED EGGS

GOLDENROD EGGS

Goldenrod Eggs

PREP/TOTAL TIME: 20 min.

Richard Ramsey, Eugene, Oregon

This is a classic recipe my wife had to learn to make in her high school home economics class. I've adapted and renamed it.

- 2 hard-cooked eggs
- 2 tablespoons butter
- 2 tablespoons all-purpose flour
- 1/2 teaspoon salt
- 1/8 teaspoon white pepper
- 1 cup milk
- 2 slices bread, toasted and buttered

1) Cut eggs in half; remove yolks and set aside. Chop egg whites; set aside. In a small saucepan, melt butter. Stir in the flour, salt and pepper until smooth. Gradually stir in milk. Bring to a boil; cook and stir for 1-2 minutes or until thickened.

2) Stir in egg whites; heat through. Pour over toast. Force egg yolks through a sieve to break into small pieces; sprinkle over sauce.

Yield: 2 servings.

NUTRITION FACTS: 1 serving equals 382 calories, 26 g fat (14 g saturated fat), 270 mg cholesterol, 1,001 mg sodium, 25 g carbohydrate, 1 g fiber, 13 g protein.

No-Wobble Stuffed Eggs

Here's a technique to prevent stuffed eggs from wobbling on a serving tray. After peeling the hard-cooked eggs, cut them in half the long way. Then trim a thin slice from the bottom of each half. Once they're filled, they will sit flat on a serving tray.

OLD-FASHIONED EGG SALAD

Old-Fashioned Egg Salad

PREP: 15 min. + chilling

Linda Braun, Park Ridge, Illinois

For an extra-creamy sandwich-topper, add a little cream cheese as directed in the variation that follows.

- 1/4 cup mayonnaise
- 2 teaspoons lemon juice
- 1 teaspoon dried minced onion
- 1/4 teaspoon salt
- 1/4 teaspoon pepper
- 6 hard-cooked eggs, chopped
- 1/2 cup finely chopped celery

Lettuce leaves *or* bread slices

1) In a large bowl, combine the mayonnaise, lemon juice, onion, salt and pepper. Stir in eggs and celery. Cover and refrigerate.

2) For each serving, spoon about 1/2 cup onto a lettuce leaf or spread on bread.

Yield: 3 servings.

NUTRITION FACTS: 1/2 cup (calculated without lettuce or bread) equals 294 calories, 25 g fat (5 g saturated fat), 431 mg cholesterol, 438 mg sodium, 3 g carbohydrate, trace fiber, 13 g protein.

■ **Creamy Egg Salad:** Beat 1 package (3 ounces) softened cream cheese, 1/4 cup mayonnaise, 1/2 teaspoon salt and 1/8 teaspoon pepper until smooth. Add 1/4 cup *each* finely chopped green pepper, finely chopped celery and sweet pickle relish and 2 tablespoons minced fresh parsley. Fold in 8 chopped hard-cooked eggs.
Yield: 3 cups.

FASTER EGG SALAD ■■■

To make egg salad in about half the time, use a pastry blender instead of a knife to chop the eggs. It's quick and easy!

—*Allison F., Annapolis, Maryland*

Better Than Egg Salad

PREP/TOTAL TIME: 20 min.

Lisa Renshaw, Kansas City, Missouri

Tofu duplicates the taste and texture of egg salad in this quick-to-fix sandwich.

- 1/4 cup chopped celery
- 2 green onions, chopped
- 1/4 cup reduced-fat mayonnaise
- 2 tablespoons sweet pickle relish
- 1 tablespoon Dijon mustard
- 1/4 teaspoon ground turmeric
- 1/4 teaspoon salt
- 1/8 teaspoon cayenne pepper
- 1 package (12.3 ounces) silken firm tofu, cubed
- 8 slices whole wheat bread
- 4 lettuce leaves

1) In a small bowl, combine the celery, onions, mayonnaise, relish, mustard, turmeric, salt and cayenne. Gently stir in tofu. Spread over four slices of bread; top with lettuce and remaining bread.

Yield: 4 servings.

NUTRITION FACTS: 1 sandwich equals 274 calories, 12 g fat (2 g saturated fat), 5 mg cholesterol, 734 mg sodium, 33 g carbohydrate, 5 g fiber, 13 g protein.

Egg Salad Cucumber Sandwiches

PREP/TOTAL TIME: 10 min.

Lucy Meyring, Walden, Colorado

This is a tasty variation of the traditional egg salad sandwich. The sliced cucumber and chopped onion add refreshing crunch.

- 3 hard-cooked eggs, chopped
- 1/2 cup chopped green pepper
- 1/4 cup mayonnaise
- 2 tablespoons chopped red onion
- 1/2 teaspoon lemon juice
- 1/8 teaspoon salt
- 1/8 teaspoon pepper
- 8 slices whole wheat bread
- 1 small cucumber, thinly sliced
- 4 lettuce leaves

1) In a small bowl, combine the eggs, green pepper, mayonnaise, onion, lemon juice, salt and pepper. Spread on four slices of bread.

2) Top with the cucumber and lettuce. Top with the remaining bread.

Yield: 4 servings.

NUTRITION FACTS: 1 sandwich equals 310 calories, 17 g fat (3 g saturated fat), 164 mg cholesterol, 493 mg sodium, 29 g carbohydrate, 5 g fiber, 11 g protein.

THREE-CHEESE SOUFFLES

Three-Cheese Souffles

PREP: 40 min. + cooling **BAKE:** 40 min.

Jean Ference, Sherwood Park, Alberta

No matter when I've made these—for breakfast, brunch or lunch—they have never failed. I have not had them fall once. I often get asked for the recipe.

- 1/3 cup butter
- 1/3 cup all-purpose flour
- 2 cups milk
- 1 teaspoon Dijon mustard
- 1/4 teaspoon salt
- Dash hot pepper sauce
- 1-1/2 cups (6 ounces) shredded Swiss cheese
- 1 cup (4 ounces) shredded cheddar cheese
- 1/4 cup shredded Parmesan cheese
- 6 eggs, *separated*
- 1/2 teaspoon cream of tartar

1) Melt butter in a medium saucepan. Stir in flour until smooth. Gradually add the milk, mustard, salt and hot pepper sauce. Bring to a boil; cook and stir for 2 minutes or until thickened. Reduce heat; add cheeses, stirring until cheese is melted. Remove from the heat and set aside.

2) In a small mixing bowl, beat egg yolks until thick and lemon-colored, about 5 minutes. Add 1/3 cup cheese mixture and mix well. Return all to the saucepan, stirring constantly. Return to the heat and cook for 1-2 minutes. Cool completely, about 30-40 minutes.

3) In another mixing bowl and with clean beaters, beat egg whites and cream of tartar until stiff peaks form. Fold into cheese mixture. Pour into ungreased 1-cup souffle dishes or custard cups.

4) Place in a shallow pan; add 1 in. of hot water to pan. Bake, uncovered, at 325° for 40-45 minutes

or until tops are golden brown. Serve immediately.

Yield: 8 servings.

Editor's Note: Souffles can be made ahead and frozen. Cover each dish or cup with foil and freeze. To bake, remove foil and place frozen souffles in a shallow pan; add warm water to a depth of 1 in. Bake at 325° for 60-65 minutes or until tops are golden brown.

NUTRITION FACTS: 1 serving equals 317 calories, 24 g fat (14 g saturated fat), 223 mg cholesterol, 424 mg sodium, 9 g carbohydrate, trace fiber, 17 g protein.

Florence-Inspired Souffle

PREP: 35 min. **BAKE:** 35 min.

Jenny Flake, Gilbert, Arizona

This souffle is not only absolutely delicious, but light and beautiful. Your guests will be impressed when this brunch dish is served. So grab a fork and dig in to this little taste of Florence!

- 6 egg whites
- 3/4 cup onion and garlic salad croutons
- 1 small onion, finely chopped
- 1/4 cup finely chopped sweet red pepper
- 2 ounces thinly sliced prosciutto, chopped
- 1 garlic clove, minced
- 2 teaspoons olive oil
- 2 cups fresh baby spinach
- 1/3 cup all-purpose flour
- 1/2 teaspoon salt
- 1/4 teaspoon pepper
- 1-1/4 cups fat-free milk
- 1 egg yolk, beaten
- 1/4 teaspoon cream of tartar
- 1/4 cup shredded Italian cheese blend

FLORENCE-INSPIRED SOUFFLE

1) Place egg whites in a large mixing bowl; let stand at room temperature for 30 minutes. Place croutons in a food processor; cover and process until ground. Sprinkle evenly onto the bottom and 1 in. up the sides of a 2-qt. baking dish coated with cooking spray; set aside.

2) In a large saucepan, saute the onion, red pepper, prosciutto and garlic in oil for 3-5 minutes or until vegetables are crisp-tender. Add spinach; cook just until wilted. Stir in flour, salt and pepper until blended; gradually add milk. Bring to a boil; cook and stir for 2 minutes or until thickened. Transfer to a large bowl.

3) Stir a small amount of hot mixture into egg yolk; return all to the bowl, stirring constantly. Cool slightly.

4) Add cream of tartar to egg whites; beat until stiff peaks form. Fold into vegetable mixture. Transfer to prepared dish; sprinkle with cheese. Bake at 350° for 35-40 minutes or until the top is puffed and center appears set. Serve immediately.

Yield: 4 servings.

NUTRITION FACTS: 1 serving equals 223 calories, 9 g fat (3 g saturated fat), 73 mg cholesterol, 843 mg sodium, 20 g carbohydrate, 2 g fiber, 16 g protein.

BACON QUICHE TARTS

Onion Yorkshire Puddings

PREP: 20 min. **BAKE:** 30 min.

Emily Chaney, Blue Hill, Maine

A cross between traditional Yorkshire pudding and popovers, this easy recipe makes a great complement to prime rib. We also like it with beef stew and steak. Make more than you need because everyone loves them.

> 1/2 pound yellow onions, thinly sliced
> 1 teaspoon salt, *divided*
> 1/4 teaspoon pepper
> 2 tablespoons butter
> 3/4 cup plus 2 tablespoons all-purpose flour
> 2 eggs
> 3/4 cup water
> 3/4 cup milk

1) In a large skillet, saute the onions, 1/2 teaspoon salt and pepper in butter until tender but not browned. Divide among eight 6-oz. ramekins or custard cups. Place on a baking sheet.

2) In a large bowl, combine flour and remaining salt. Whisk the eggs, water and milk; whisk into flour mixture just until blended.

3) Fill each ramekin with 1/4 cup batter. Bake at 400° for 30-35 minutes or until puffed and golden brown. Serve immediately.

Yield: 8 servings.

NUTRITION FACTS: 1 serving equals 118 calories, 5 g fat (3 g saturated fat), 63 mg cholesterol, 343 mg sodium, 14 g carbohydrate, 1 g fiber, 4 g protein

Bacon Quiche Tarts

PREP: 15 min. **BAKE:** 20 min.

Kendra Schertz, Nappanee, Indiana

Flavored with vegetables, cheese and bacon, these tarts are an impressive addition to brunch. They're also easy to make.

> 2 packages (3 ounces *each*) cream cheese, softened
> 5 teaspoons milk
> 2 eggs
> 1/2 cup shredded Colby cheese
> 2 tablespoons chopped green pepper
> 1 tablespoon finely chopped onion
> 1 tube (8 ounces) refrigerated crescent rolls
> 5 bacon strips, cooked and crumbled

1) In a small mixing bowl, beat cream cheese and milk until smooth. Add the eggs, cheese, green pepper and onion; mix well.

2) Separate dough into eight triangles; press onto the bottom and up the sides of greased muffin cups. Sprinkle half of the bacon into cups. Pour egg mixture over bacon; top with remaining bacon.

3) Bake, uncovered, at 375° for 18-22 minutes or until a knife comes out clean. Serve warm.

Yield: 8 servings.

NUTRITION FACTS: 1 serving equals 258 calories, 19 g fat (9 g saturated fat), 87 mg cholesterol, 409 mg sodium, 12 g carbohydrate, trace fiber, 8 g protein.

CHIVE-HAM BRUNCH BAKE

Chive-Ham Brunch Bake

PREP: 15 min. **BAKE:** 25 min.

Edie DeSpain, Logan, Utah

Canned ham and biscuit mix get this breakfast or brunch dish ready quickly. You can also use leftover cooked ham.

- 1/2 cup chopped onion
- 1 tablespoon butter
- 1 can (5 ounces) chunk ham, drained
- 1 medium tomato, chopped
- 2 cups biscuit/baking mix
- 1/2 cup water
- 1 cup (4 ounces) shredded Swiss *or* cheddar cheese
- 2 eggs
- 1/4 cup milk
- 1/4 teaspoon dill weed
- 1/4 teaspoon salt
- 1/8 teaspoon pepper
- 3 tablespoons minced chives

1) In a small skillet, saute onion in butter until tender. Stir in the ham and tomato; set aside.

2) In a small bowl, combine biscuit mix and water; mix well. Press onto the bottom and 1/2 in. up the sides of a greased 13-in. x 9-in. x 2-in. baking dish. Spread ham mixture over the crust; sprinkle with cheese.

3) In a bowl, beat the eggs, milk, dill, salt and pepper; pour over cheese. Sprinkle with chives. Bake, uncovered, at 350° for 25-30 minutes or until a knife inserted near the center comes out clean. Let stand for 5 minutes before cutting.

Yield: 8 servings.

NUTRITION FACTS: 1 piece equals 246 calories, 13 g fat (6 g saturated fat), 80 mg cholesterol, 749 mg sodium, 22 g carbohydrate, 1 g fiber, 11 g protein.

Testing Baked Egg Dishes for Doneness

Test egg dishes containing beaten eggs—like quiche, strata or custard—for doneness by inserting a knife near the center of the dish. If the knife comes out clean, the eggs are cooked.

Cheddar Cauliflower Quiche

PREP: 25 min. + chilling **BAKE:** 30 min. + standing

Tracy Watson, Hobson, Montana

A dear friend shared this recipe one year when we both had an abundance of cauliflower from our gardens. My husband and I enjoy this so much that I make it for breakfast, lunch and dinner!

- 1 cup all-purpose flour
- 1/4 teaspoon salt
- 1/3 cup shortening
- 3 tablespoons cold milk
- 4 cups chopped fresh cauliflower, cooked
- 1/2 cup slivered almonds, toasted
- 2 eggs
- 1/2 cup milk
- 1/2 cup mayonnaise
- 1-1/2 cups (6 ounces) shredded cheddar cheese, *divided*
- 1/8 teaspoon ground nutmeg
- 1/8 teaspoon pepper

1) In a large bowl, combine flour and salt. Cut in shortening until the mixture resembles coarse crumbs. Stir in milk until mixture forms a ball. Wrap in plastic wrap; refrigerate for 30 minutes.

2) Unwrap dough. On a floured surface, roll out to fit a 9-in. pie plate. Place in pie plate; flute edges. Line unpricked pastry with a double thickness of foil. Bake at 450° for 5 minutes. Remove foil; bake 5 minutes longer.

3) Spoon cauliflower into crust; top with almonds. In a blender, combine eggs, milk, mayonnaise, 1-1/4 cups cheese, nutmeg and pepper; cover and process until smooth. Pour over almonds; sprinkle with remaining cheese.

4) Bake, uncovered, at 350° for 30-35 minutes or until a knife inserted near the center comes out clean. Let stand for 10 minutes before cutting.

Yield: 6 servings.

Editor's Note: Reduced-fat or fat-free mayonnaise may not be substituted for regular mayonnaise in this recipe.

NUTRITION FACTS: 1 piece equals 518 calories, 41 g fat (12 g saturated fat), 111 mg cholesterol, 424 mg sodium, 24 g carbohydrate, 3 g fiber, 14 g protein.

Easter Brunch Lasagna

PREP: 30 min. **BAKE:** 40 min. + standing

Sarah Larson, La Farge, Wisconsin

Ham, broccoli and hard-cooked eggs are terrific together in this unique brunch lasagna. I created the recipe for a family gathering. Muffins and fresh fruit nicely round out the meal.

1/2 cup butter
1/3 cup all-purpose flour
1/4 teaspoon salt
Dash white pepper
3 cups milk
1/4 cup finely chopped green onions
1 teaspoon lemon juice
1/4 teaspoon hot pepper sauce
9 lasagna noodles, cooked and drained
2 cups diced fully cooked ham
3 cups frozen chopped broccoli, thawed
1/2 cup grated Parmesan cheese
3 cups (12 ounces) shredded cheddar cheese
4 hard-cooked eggs, finely chopped

1) In a heavy saucepan, melt butter over medium heat. Stir in flour, salt and pepper until smooth. Gradually add milk. Bring to a boil; cook and stir for 2 minutes or until thickened. Remove from the heat; stir in the onions, lemon juice and hot pepper sauce.

2) Spread a fourth of the white sauce in a greased 13-in. x 9-in. x 2-in. baking dish. Layer with three noodles, half of the ham and broccoli,

3 tablespoons Parmesan cheese, 1 cup cheddar cheese, half of the eggs and a fourth of the white sauce. Repeat layers. Top with the remaining noodles, white sauce and cheeses.

3) Bake, uncovered, at 350° for 40-45 minutes or until bubbly. Let stand for 15 minutes before cutting.

Yield: 12 servings.

NUTRITION FACTS: 1 serving equals 371 calories, 23 g fat (14 g saturated fat), 144 mg cholesterol, 715 mg sodium, 23 g carbohydrate, 1 g fiber, 19 g protein.

Chocolate Chip Dutch Baby

PREP/TOTAL TIME: 30 min.

Mary Thompson, LaCrosse, Wisconsin

I modified a traditional Dutch baby recipe given to me by a friend to come up with this version my family thinks is terrific. You can try it with apples or other favorite fruit.

1/4 cup miniature semisweet chocolate chips
1/4 cup packed brown sugar

DUTCH BABY:
1/2 cup all-purpose flour
2 eggs
1/2 cup half-and-half cream
1/8 teaspoon ground nutmeg
Dash ground cinnamon
3 tablespoons butter
Maple syrup and additional butter, optional

1) In a small bowl, combine chocolate chips and brown sugar; set aside. In a small mixing bowl, beat the flour, eggs, cream, nutmeg and cinnamon until smooth.

2) Place butter in a 9-in. pie plate. Heat at 425° for 4-6 minutes or until melted. Pour batter into hot pie plate. Sprinkle with chocolate chip mixture.

3) Bake for 15-20 minutes or until top edges are golden brown. Serve immediately with syrup and butter if desired.

Yield: 4 servings.

NUTRITION FACTS: 1 piece equals 313 calories, 17 g fat (10 g saturated fat), 144 mg cholesterol, 140 mg sodium, 34 g carbohydrate, 1 g fiber, 6 g protein.

■ **Apple Puff Pancake:** Omit the chips, brown sugar, nutmeg, cinnamon and 3 tablespoons butter. Mix the Dutch Baby pancake as directed but add 1/8 teaspoon salt and 1 tablespoon melted butter. Pour into a greased 8-in. square baking dish. Bake at 400° for 20-25 minutes or until lightly browned.

Meanwhile, in a small saucepan, cook 1 chopped peeled medium tart apple, 1/2 cup apply jelly and 1/8 teaspoon cinnamon until jelly is melted. Cut pancake into fourths. Serve with apple mixture.

TASTE-TEMPTING STRATA

 CLASSIC: Next time you're hosting a weekend brunch or entertaining overnight guests, add Cheese Sausage Strata to your morning menu. You put this egg dish together the night before, refrigerate it, then pop it in the oven the next morning. While the casserole bakes, you can brew some coffee and make a fresh fruit salad.

 TIME-SAVER: Even if you don't plan ahead, you can enjoy Simple Sausage Strata for breakfast. Unlike a classic strata, it doesn't need to be assembled the night before. Just toss it together when you awake...and bake!

 LIGHT: Ham and Broccoli Strata is a make-ahead morning casserole that your brunch guests can dig into without feeling guilty. It serves 12 like Cheese Sausage Strata, but it calls for fewer eggs. Plus, the recipe has ham instead of bacon, so it's lower in fat, calories and sodium.

 SERVES 2: Craving an egg casserole but not the large yield they typically make? Mozzarella Vegetable Strata is baked in a loaf pan, so it's perfectly portioned for two people to enjoy any time of the day.

CHEESE SAUSAGE STRATA

Cheese Sausage Strata

PREP: 15 min. + chilling **BAKE:** 1 hour

Teresa Marchese, New Berlin, Wisconsin

- 1-1/2 pounds bulk pork sausage
- 9 eggs, lightly beaten
- 3 cups milk
- 9 slices bread, cubed
- 1-1/2 cups (6 ounces) shredded cheddar cheese
- 1/2 pound sliced bacon, cooked and crumbled
- 1-1/2 teaspoons ground mustard

1) In a large skillet, cook sausage over medium heat until no longer pink; drain. Add the eggs, milk, bread, cheese, bacon and mustard. Transfer to a greased shallow 3-qt. baking dish. Cover and refrigerate overnight.

2) Remove from the refrigerator 30 minutes before baking. Cover and bake at 350° for 60-65 minutes or until a knife inserted near the center comes out clean. Let stand for 5 minutes before serving.

Yield: 12 servings.

NUTRITION FACTS: 1 serving equals 373 calories, 25 g fat (11 g saturated fat), 217 mg cholesterol, 1,097 mg sodium, 14 g carbohydrate, trace fiber, 23 g protein.

Simple Sausage Strata

PREP: 15 min. **BAKE:** 25 min.

Bonnie Coffman, Clarksville, Tennessee

- 6 slices bread, crusts removed
- 1 pound bulk pork sausage
- 1 teaspoon prepared mustard
- 3/4 cup shredded Swiss cheese
- 3 eggs
- 1-1/2 cups milk
- 2/3 cup half-and-half cream

Pinch pepper

1) Place bread in a greased 13-in. x 9-in. x 2-in. baking dish; set aside. In a large skillet, cook sausage over medium heat until no longer pink; drain. Stir in mustard. Sprinkle sausage and cheese evenly over bread.

2) In a large bowl, whisk eggs, milk, cream and pepper. Pour over cheese. Bake, uncovered, at 350° for 25-30 minutes or until a knife inserted near the center comes out clean. Let stand for 5 minutes before cutting into squares. Serve immediately.

Yield: 6-8 servings.

NUTRITION FACTS: 1 piece equals 286 calories, 19 g fat (9 g saturated fat), 126 mg cholesterol, 423 mg sodium, 13 g carbohydrate, trace fiber, 13 g protein.

Ham and Broccoli Strata

PREP: 15 min. + chilling **BAKE:** 35 min.

Robin Friedly, Louisville, Kentucky

- 6 cups frozen chopped broccoli, thawed and drained
- 3/4 pound thinly sliced deli ham, cut into 1/2-inch strips
- 2 cups (8 ounces) shredded Swiss cheese
- 1 loaf (8 ounces) French bread, cut into 1-inch slices
- 6 eggs
- 2 cups milk
- 3 tablespoons dried minced onion
- 3 tablespoons Dijon mustard
- 1/2 teaspoon hot pepper sauce
- 1/2 teaspoon paprika

1) In a large bowl, combine the broccoli, ham and cheese; spread half into a greased 13-in. x 9-in. x 2-in. baking dish. Arrange bread slices on top. Cover with remaining broccoli mixture. In a large bowl, whisk the eggs, milk, onion, mustard and hot pepper sauce. Pour over broccoli mixture. Sprinkle with paprika. Cover and refrigerate overnight.

2) Remove from the refrigerator 30 minutes before baking. Bake, uncovered, at 350° for 35-40 minutes or until a knife inserted near the center comes out clean. Let stand for 5 minutes.

Yield: 12 servings.

NUTRITION FACTS: 1 serving equals 224 calories, 10 g fat (5 g saturated fat), 141 mg cholesterol, 580 mg sodium, 16 g carbohydrate, 1 g fiber, 17 g protein.

MOZZARELLA VEGETABLE STRATA

Mozzarella Vegetable Strata

PREP: 20 min. **BAKE:** 30 min.

Wendy McGowan, Fontana, California

- 1/2 cup sliced zucchini
- 1/3 cup sliced fresh mushrooms
- 1/3 cup chopped onion
- 2 teaspoons vegetable oil
- 1 tablespoon minced fresh parsley *or* 1-1/2 teaspoons dried parsley flakes
- 3/4 teaspoon minced fresh basil *or* 1/4 teaspoon dried basil
- 2-3/4 cups cubed bread
- 1/2 cup shredded part-skim mozzarella cheese
- 2 eggs
- 1/2 cup 2% milk
- 1/4 teaspoon salt
- 1/8 teaspoon pepper
- 1 plum tomato, seeded and chopped

1) In a small skillet, saute the zucchini, mushrooms and onion in oil until tender; drain. Stir in parsley and basil.

2) In an 8-in. x 4-in. x 2-in. glass loaf pan coated with cooking spray, layer half of the bread cubes and mozzarella cheese. Top with vegetables and remaining bread and cheese. In a small bowl, whisk the eggs, milk, salt and pepper. Pour over cheese. Sprinkle with tomato.

3) Cover and bake at 350° for 20 minutes. Uncover; bake 10-15 minutes longer or until a knife inserted near the center comes out clean. Let stand for 5 minutes before cutting.

Yield: 2 servings.

NUTRITION FACTS: 1 piece equals 371 calories, 17 g fat (6 g saturated fat), 234 mg cholesterol, 785 mg sodium, 33 g carbohydrate, 3 g fiber, 20 g protein.

HAM AND BROCCOLI STRATA

Basic Crepes

PREP: 10 min. + standing **COOK:** 20 min.

Taste of Home Test Kitchen

For a simple breakfast, roll up crepes and drizzle with warmed honey or jelly. Any leftover crepes may be stacked with waxed paper in between and frozen for up to 2 months. Thaw in the refrigerator.

 1-1/2 cups milk
     4 eggs
     1 cup all-purpose flour
 1-1/2 teaspoons sugar
   1/8 teaspoon salt
Butter

1) In a small mixing bowl, combine milk and eggs. Combine the flour, sugar and salt; add to milk mixture and mix well. Cover and refrigerate for 1 hour.

2) Melt 1 teaspoon butter in an 8-in. nonstick skillet; pour 2 tablespoons batter into center of skillet. Lift and tilt pan to evenly coat bottom. Cook until top appears dry; turn and cook 15-20 seconds longer. Remove to a wire rack.

3) Repeat with remaining batter, adding butter to skillet as needed. When cool, stack crepes with waxed paper or paper towels in between.

Yield: 16 crepes.

NUTRITION FACTS: 1 serving equals 79 calories, 4 g fat (2 g saturated fat), 61 mg cholesterol, 65 mg sodium, 8 g carbohydrate, trace fiber, 3 g protein.

■ **Shrimp Crepes:** In a large skillet, cook 4-1/2 cups chopped fresh broccoli, 6 chopped green onions, 2 teaspoons minced garlic, 1/2 teaspoon salt, 1/4 teaspoon pepper and 1/4 teaspoon Worcestershire sauce in 3 tablespoons melted butter for 7-9 minutes or until broccoli is crisp-tender. Remove and set aside. In same skillet, saute 1 pound peeled deveined uncooked shrimp in 1/4 cup wine *or* broth until shrimp turn pink. Return broccoli to skillet and combine.

Spoon filling down center of crepes; roll up. Place in an ungreased 15-in. x 10-in. x 1-in. baking pan. Bake, uncovered, at 350° for 15-20 minutes or until heated through. Meanwhile, prepare 1 envelope bearnaise sauce according to package directions. Serve over crepes.
Yield: 8 servings.

■ **Creamy Strawberry Crepes:** In a small mixing bowl, beat 1 package (8 ounces) softened cream cheese, 1-1/4 cups confectioners' sugar, 1 tablespoon lemon juice, 1 teaspoon grated lemon peel and 1/2 teaspoon vanilla extract until smooth. Fold in 2 cups sliced fresh strawberries and 2 cups whipped cream. Spoon about 1/3 cup filling down the center of 14 crepes; roll up. Garnish with additional sliced strawberries.
Yield: 7 servings.

■ **Banana Crepes:** In a small skillet, bring 2/3 cup sugar, 2/3 cup orange juice, 1/2 cup butter and 4 teaspoons grated orange peel to a boil. Remove from the heat. Peel 6 medium firm bananas and cut in half lengthwise. Add to orange sauce; cook over medium heat until heated through, about 1 minute. Place 1 banana half in the center of a crepe; roll up. Place seam side down on a plate; drizzle with orange sauce.
Yield: 6 servings.

Cherry Cheese Blintzes

PREP: 30 min. + chilling **BAKE:** 10 min.

Jessica Vantrease, Anderson, Alaska

These elegant blintzes can be served as an attractive dessert or a brunch entree. The bright cherry sauce gives them a delightful flavor. You can try other fruits, such as raspberries, blueberries or peaches.

 1-1/2 cups milk
     3 eggs
     2 tablespoons butter, melted
   2/3 cup all-purpose flour
   1/2 teaspoon salt

FILLING:

   1 cup (8 ounces) small-curd cottage cheese
   1 package (3 ounces) cream cheese, softened
 1/4 cup sugar
 1/2 teaspoon vanilla extract

CHERRY SAUCE:

   1 pound fresh *or* frozen pitted sweet cherries
 2/3 cup plus 1 tablespoon water, *divided*
 1/4 cup sugar
   1 tablespoon cornstarch

1) In a small mixing bowl, combine the milk, eggs and butter. Combine the flour and salt; add to milk mixture and mix well. Cover and refrigerate for 2 hours.

CHERRY CHEESE BLINTZES

2) Heat a lightly greased 8-in. nonstick skillet; pour 2 tablespoons batter into the center of skillet. Lift and tilt pan to evenly coat bottom. Cook until top appears dry; turn and cook 15-20 seconds longer. Remove to a wire rack.

3) Repeat with remaining batter. When cool, stack crepes with waxed paper or paper towels in between. Wrap in foil; refrigerate.

4) In a blender, process cottage cheese until smooth. Transfer to a small mixing bowl; add cream cheese. Beat until smooth. Add sugar and vanilla; mix well. Spread about 1 rounded tablespoonful onto each crepe. Fold opposite sides of crepe over filling, forming a little bundle.

5) Place seam side down in a greased 15-in. x 10-in. x 1-in. baking pan. Bake, uncovered, at 350° for 10 minutes or until heated through.

6) Meanwhile, in a saucepan, bring the cherries, 2/3 cup water and sugar to a boil over medium heat. Reduce heat; cover and simmer for 5 minutes or until cherries are heated through.

7) Combine cornstarch and remaining water until smooth; stir into cherry mixture. Bring to a boil; cook and stir for 2 minutes or until thickened. Serve over crepes.

Yield: 9 servings.

NUTRITION FACTS: 1 serving equals 247 calories, 10 g fat (6 g saturated fat), 99 mg cholesterol, 310 mg sodium, 31 g carbohydrate, 1 g fiber, 8 g protein.

French Toast with Orange Syrup
PREP/TOTAL TIME: 15 min.

Jesse & Anne Foust, Bluefield, West Virginia

The simple orange syrup turns ordinary French toast into a real treat. You can serve the syrup over the top or on the side.

3 eggs
1 cup milk
2 tablespoons sugar
1/4 teaspoon salt
1/8 teaspoon ground cinnamon
1/8 teaspoon ground nutmeg
8 slices day-old French bread (1 inch thick)

ORANGE SYRUP:

1/2 cup orange juice
1/3 cup corn syrup
1/4 cup sugar
4 teaspoons butter
1 teaspoon grated orange peel
1/2 teaspoon orange extract

1) In a bowl, beat eggs. Beat in the milk, sugar, salt, cinnamon and nutmeg. Soak the slices of bread for 30 seconds on each side. Cook on a hot greased griddle until golden brown on both sides and cooked through.

FRENCH TOAST WITH ORANGE SYRUP

2) Meanwhile, in a saucepan, combine the orange juice, corn syrup, sugar, butter and orange peel. Bring to a boil and boil for 2 minutes, stirring constantly. Remove from the heat; stir in extract. Serve with French toast.

Yield: 4 servings.

NUTRITION FACTS: 1 serving equals 645 calories, 13 g fat (6 g saturated fat), 178 mg cholesterol, 1,076 mg sodium, 113 g carbohydrate, 4 g fiber, 18 g protein.

Overnight Caramel French Toast
PREP: 15 min. + chilling **BAKE:** 30 min.

Denise Goedeken, Platte Center, Nebraska

When guests are visiting or times are busy, you can prepare this ahead of time and refrigerate it overnight. The next day, it bakes up in no time.

1 cup packed brown sugar
1/2 cup butter
2 tablespoons light corn syrup
12 slices white *or* whole wheat bread
1/4 cup sugar
1 teaspoon ground cinnamon, *divided*
6 eggs
1-1/2 cups milk
1 teaspoon vanilla extract

1) In a small saucepan, bring the brown sugar, butter and corn syrup to a boil over medium heat, stirring constantly. Remove from the heat.

2) Pour into a greased 13-in. x 9-in. x 2-in. baking dish. Top with six slices of bread. Combine sugar and 1/2 teaspoon cinnamon; sprinkle half over the bread. Place remaining bread on top. Sprinkle with remaining cinnamon-sugar; set aside.

3) In a large bowl, beat the eggs, milk, vanilla and remaining cinnamon. Pour over bread. Cover and refrigerate for 8 hours or overnight.

4) Remove from the refrigerator 30 minutes before baking. Bake, uncovered, at 350° for 30-35 minutes.

Yield: 6 servings

NUTRITION FACTS: 1 serving equals 571 calories, 24 g fat (13 g saturated fat), 262 mg cholesterol, 539 mg sodium, 78 g carbohydrate, 1 g fiber, 13 g protein.

Cheese Basics

Cheese is classified by texture from soft to hard. When buying bulk cheese, 4 ounces equals 1 cup shredded. Check sell-by or expiration date on the package before buying and make sure it is before that date.

Check the aroma, appearance and (if possible) the flavor when purchasing from a cheese store. The aroma should be characteristic of the cheese, and the odor should not smell like sour milk or ammonia. The cheese should be free from interior cracks, discoloration and mold, unless it is a blue-veined cheese.

Wrap each type of cheese separately and store away from other foods with a strong aroma. Cheese tends to absorb the aroma and flavors of other foods, including other cheeses.

Store cheese in airtight containers, plastic bags or plastic wrap in the refrigerator. The humidity in the vegetable drawers can extend the life and quality of the cheese. Once opened, keep soft cheese for about 1 week and hard cheese for 3 to 4 weeks.

Discard any soft cheese that becomes moldy. For hard cheeses, if it has a small amount of mold, cut off a section about 1 in. around the mold and discard.

Freeze cheese for longer storage. Because the freezing process changes the cheese's texture slightly, it is best to use it in cooking or baking. Store the firmer textured cheese in the freezer for up to 6 months.

Serve fresh cheese slightly chilled. For other types of cheese to be at their flavor peak, remove from the refrigerator 30 minutes before serving.

When cooking with natural unprocessed cheese, melt at low temperatures to keep the cheese from turning tough and stringy.

Add cheese to a soup or sauce by stirring it in at the end of cooking to avoid overheating. Shredding the cheese allows it to melt faster with a minimum of heating.

Useful Definitions

Refer to the Glossary on pages 24-28 for more terms.

Fresh Cheeses: Have not been cured, such as cottage or cream cheese.

Hard Cheeses: Aged with a hard, dry texture.

Semifirm Cheese: Aged with a firm texture but are not crumbly like hard cheese.

Semisoft Cheeses: Have a sliceable soft texture, like Monterey Jack.

Three-Cheese Grilled Cheese
PREP/TOTAL TIME: 10 min.

Terri Brown, Darien, Wisconsin
My favorite combination is Swiss and cheddar with the cream cheese, but Mexican cheese is tasty, too.

  2 slices wheat, rye *or* sourdough
      bread
  2 tablespoons cream cheese,
      softened
  2 tablespoons butter, softened
  2 slices white cheese (brick,
      Monterey Jack *or* Swiss)
  2 slices yellow cheese (cheddar,
      pepper *or* taco)
  1 red onion slice
  1 tomato slice

1) For each slice of bread, spread cream cheese on one side and butter on the other. On one side of bread, with cream cheese side up, layer white cheese, yellow cheese, onion and tomato. Top with other slice of bread, cream cheese side down.

2) Toast sandwich for 2-3 minutes on each side or until bread is lightly browned. Remove from the heat; cover until cheese melts.

Yield: 1 serving.

NUTRITION FACTS: 1 sandwich equals 747 calories, 59 g fat (36 g saturated fat), 173 mg cholesterol, 1,484 mg sodium, 30 g carbohydrate, 4 g fiber, 26 g protein.

THREE-CHEESE GRILLED CHEESE

- **Raspberry Grilled Cheese:** For 2 slices of bread, spread 1-1/2 teaspoons raspberry preserves on one side of each slice and 1 tablespoon softened butter on the other sides. On one slice of bread, with raspberry side up, layer with 1 tablespoon *each* chopped pecans and sliced green onion, 2 slices Muenster *or* baby Swiss cheese. Top with the other slice of bread, raspberry side down. Toast as recipe directs.

GRILLED CHEESE FOR A CROWD ■■■

To make several grilled cheese sandwiches, prepare the sandwiches as usual, but place them on a cookie sheet instead. Bake in a 350° oven for 5-8 minutes on each side until they're golden brown.

—Sharon S., Lake Villa, Illinois

SWISS CHEESE FONDUE

Cheddar Fondue

PREP/TOTAL TIME: 15 min.

Norene Wright, Manilla, Indiana

This cheesy blend, sparked with mustard and Worcestershire sauce, is yummy at brunch or as an appetizer for a party.

- 1/4 cup butter
- 1/4 cup all-purpose flour
- 1/2 teaspoon salt, optional
- 1/4 teaspoon ground mustard
- 1/4 teaspoon pepper
- 1/4 teaspoon Worcestershire sauce
- 1-1/2 cups milk
- 2 cups (8 ounces) shredded cheddar cheese

Bread cubes, ham cubes, bite-size sausage *and/or* broccoli florets

1) In a small saucepan, melt butter; stir in flour, salt if desired, mustard, pepper and Worcestershire sauce until smooth. Gradually add milk. Bring to a boil; cook and stir for 2 minutes or until thickened. Reduce heat. Add the cheese; cook and stir until cheese is melted.

2) Transfer to a fondue pot or slow cooker; keep warm. Serve with bread, ham, sausage and/or broccoli.

Yield: 2-1/2 cups.

NUTRITION FACTS: 2 tablespoons fondue (calculated without dippers) equals 77 calories, 6 g fat (4 g saturated fat), 21 mg cholesterol, 101 mg sodium, 2 g carbohydrate, trace fiber, 3 g protein.

Swiss Cheese Fondue

PREP/TOTAL TIME: 30 min.

Taste of Home Test Kitchen

As cold winter blows outside, warm up with this rich and creamy fondue. Don't be surprised when the pot is scraped clean!

- 1 garlic clove, halved
- 2 cups white wine, chicken broth *or* unsweetened apple juice, *divided*
- 1/4 teaspoon ground nutmeg
- 7 cups (28 ounces) shredded Swiss cheese
- 2 tablespoons cornstarch

Cubed French bread

1) Rub garlic clove over the bottom and sides of a fondue pot; discard garlic and set fondue pot aside. In a large saucepan over medium-low heat, bring 1-3/4 cups wine and nutmeg to a simmer. Gradually add cheese, stirring after each addition until cheese is melted (cheese will separate from the wine).

2) Combine cornstarch and remaining wine until smooth; gradually stir into cheese mixture. Cook and stir until thickened and mixture is blended and smooth. Transfer to prepared fondue pot and keep warm. Serve with bread cubes.

Yield: about 4 cups.

NUTRITION FACTS: 1/2 cup fondue (calculated without bread cubes) equals 404 calories, 26 g fat (17 g saturated fat), 87 mg cholesterol, 249 mg sodium, 6 g carbohydrate, trace fiber, 27 g protein.

Perfect Cheese Fondue

To serve a smooth and delicious cheese fondue, keep these tips in mind. Cheese can curdle easily when overheated. So reduce the heat to low before stirring the cheese into hot liquids. Keep the heat at low while the cheese melts.

Cheese will melt faster and easier if it is shredded or cut into small cubes.

Cheese fondues are traditionally made with white wine, which not only adds flavor but helps prevent the cheese from becoming stringy. If you don't wish to use white wine, substitute broth or apple juice for the wine and add a little lemon juice.

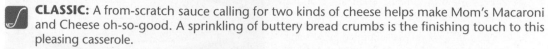

COMFORTING MAC AND CHEESE

CLASSIC: A from-scratch sauce calling for two kinds of cheese helps make Mom's Macaroni and Cheese oh-so-good. A sprinkling of buttery bread crumbs is the finishing touch to this pleasing casserole.

TIME-SAVER: When time is of the essence, turn to stovetop Three-Cheese Macaroni. Your family will ask for seconds of this quick, creamy dish that's hurried along by sliced cheese and a can of cheddar cheese soup.

LIGHT: Creamy Macaroni 'n' Cheese gets a healthy lift from reduced-fat cheddar, fat-free evaporated milk and lighter cottage cheese. Although it has fewer calories and only a third of the fat of Mom's Macaroni and Cheese, it remains rich and satisfying.

SERVES 2: You may wish for leftovers after you try this down-sized recipe of Macaroni 'n' Cheese for Two. Baked in a small dish, the hot-from-the-oven casserole is irresistible.

MOM'S MACARONI AND CHEESE

🍲 Mom's Macaroni and Cheese
PREP: 30 min. **BAKE:** 30 min.

Maria Costello, Monroe, North Carolina

1-1/2 cups uncooked elbow macaroni
    5 tablespoons butter, *divided*
    3 tablespoons all-purpose flour
  1/2 teaspoon salt
  1/4 teaspoon pepper
1-1/2 cups milk
    1 cup (4 ounces) shredded cheddar cheese
    2 ounces process cheese (Velveeta), cubed
    2 tablespoons dry bread crumbs

1) Cook macaroni according to package directions. Meanwhile, in a saucepan, melt 4 tablespoons butter over medium heat. Stir in flour, salt and pepper until smooth. Gradually add milk.

2) Bring to a boil; cook and stir for 2 minutes or until thickened. Reduce heat. Add the cheeses, stirring until cheese is melted. Drain macaroni.

3) Transfer macaroni to a greased 1-1/2-qt. baking dish. Pour cheese sauce over macaroni; mix well. Melt the remaining butter; add the bread crumbs. Sprinkle over top.

4) Bake, uncovered, at 375° for 30 minutes or until heated through and topping is golden brown.

Yield: 6 servings.

NUTRITION FACTS: 1 serving equals 309 calories, 20 g fat (13 g saturated fat), 60 mg cholesterol, 569 mg sodium, 22 g carbohydrate, 1 g fiber, 11 g protein.

🕐 Three-Cheese Macaroni
PREP/TOTAL TIME: 15 min.

Melonie Corbin, Cottage Grove, Minnesota

    1 package (7 ounces) elbow macaroni
    1 can (10-3/4 ounces) condensed cheddar cheese soup, undiluted
    2 slices process American cheese
  1/4 cup shredded Parmesan cheese
  1/4 cup milk
    1 tablespoon butter

1) Cook macaroni according to package directions. Meanwhile, in a large saucepan, combine the soup, cheeses, milk and butter. Cook and stir until cheese is melted. Drain macaroni; stir into cheese sauce.

Yield: 4 servings.

NUTRITION FACTS: 1 cup equals 320 calories, 13 g fat (7 g saturated fat), 29 mg cholesterol, 834 mg sodium, 44 g carbohydrate, 2 g fiber, 13 g protein.

CREAMY MACARONI 'N' CHEESE

Creamy Macaroni 'n' Cheese

PREP: 20 min. **BAKE:** 20 min.

Dawn Royer, Albany, Oregon

1-3/4 cups uncooked elbow macaroni

1/3 cup finely chopped onion

1/2 cup fat-free evaporated milk

1-3/4 cups 2% cottage cheese

1 teaspoon Dijon mustard

1/2 teaspoon salt

1/4 teaspoon pepper

1-3/4 cups shredded reduced-fat cheddar cheese

2 tablespoons minced fresh parsley

1) Cook macaroni according to package directions. Meanwhile, place onion in a large microwave-safe bowl. Cover and microwave onion on high for 1 to 1-1/2 minutes or until tender; drain.

2) In a small food processor, combine the milk, cottage cheese, mustard, salt and pepper; cover and process until smooth.

3) Drain macaroni; stir into onion along with cheddar cheese and parsley. Stir in cottage cheese mixture.

4) Pour into a 1-1/2-qt. baking dish coated with cooking spray. Bake, uncovered, at 350° for 20-25 minutes or until lightly browned.

Yield: 8 servings.

NUTRITION FACTS: 2/3 cup equals 229 calories, 6 g fat (1 g saturated fat), 19 mg cholesterol, 491 mg sodium, 24 g carbohydrate, 1 g fiber, 20 g protein.

TASTE TWIST ON MAC 'N' CHEESE ■■■

To make homemade macaroni and cheese more creamy and satisfying, I add either sour cream or prepared French onion dip.

—Doris E., Sheboygan Falls, Wisconsin

Macaroni 'n' Cheese for Two

PREP/TOTAL TIME: 30 min.

Mrs. O. Lick, Boyne Falls, Michigan

1/3 cup sour cream

1/3 cup milk

1 cup (4 ounces) shredded sharp cheddar cheese

3/4 cup elbow macaroni, cooked and drained

2 tablespoons chopped onion, optional

Paprika

1) In a bowl, combine sour cream and milk. Stir in the cheese, macaroni and onion if desired.

2) Transfer to a greased 2-1/2-cup baking dish; sprinkle with paprika. Cover and bake at 325° for 25 minutes or until heated through.

Yield: 2 servings.

NUTRITION FACTS: 1 serving equals 405 calories, 25 g fat (18 g saturated fat), 92 mg cholesterol, 381 mg sodium, 26 g carbohydrate, 1 g fiber, 18 g protein.

MACARONI 'N' CHEESE FOR TWO

Types of Cheese

Cheese comes in many varieties, and some are more common than others. Below are some blue-veined, fresh, hard, Pasta Filata-style (cheeses that stretch or string when cooked or melted), ripened, semifirm, semisoft and soft-ripened cheeses.

Asiago, Aged
Hard cheese. Buttery and nutty flavor. Hard granular texture. Pale yellow color. Good with pasta, grapes, apples and pears.

Bel Paese
Semisoft cheese. Mellow, delicate, buttery, tart flavor. Smooth, creamy, rich texture. Ivory color. Good with pasta, eggs, vegetables, fresh salads and pears.

Blue
Blue-veined cheese. Piquant with full, earthy flavor. Firm, crumbly texture (some are creamy). Creamy ivory color with blue or green veins. Good with pears, apples, walnuts, cashews and almonds.

Brick
Semisoft cheese. Mild, sweet flavor with a hint of nuttiness. Smooth texture. Ivory to creamy yellow color. Good with sandwiches, macaroni and cheese.

Brie
Soft-ripened cheese. Mild to pungent flavor. Rich creamy texture. Pale ivory color. Good with melons, grapes, berries and sun-dried tomatoes.

Camembert
Soft-ripened cheese. Mild to pungent flavor. Rich creamy texture. Pale ivory color. Good with melons, grapes, berries and sun-dried tomatoes.

Colby
Semifirm cheese. Mild, cheddar-like flavor. Firm, but softer than cheddar in texture. Golden color. Good with apples, pears, onions and tomatoes.

Cottage Cheese
Soft fresh cheese. Slightly acidic but delicate flavor. Smooth tender texture. Creamy white color. Good with fresh fruit, salad, vegetables and herbs.

Cheddar
Semifirm cheese. When aged, rich, nutty flavor becomes sharp and smooth, firm texture becomes granular and crumbly. White or golden color. Good with apples, pears, onions and tomatoes.

Cream Cheese
Soft fresh cheese. Rich, nutty, slightly sweet flavor. Smooth, creamy texture. Creamy white color. Good with fresh fruits, jams and jellies, fruit and nut breads and bagels.

Edam
Semifirm cheese. Light, buttery, nutty flavor. Smooth, firm texture. Pale yellow interior color. Good with peaches, melon, apricots and cherries.

Farmers
Semisoft cheese. Buttery, creamy, slightly acidic flavor. Smooth texture. Ivory to buttery in color. Good with plums, grapes, seafood and poultry.

Feta
Soft fresh cheese. Tart, salty flavor. Firm, crumbly texture. Chalk white color. Good with olives, vegetables, pasta salads, mixed green salads, seafood and chicken.

Fontina
Semisoft cheese. Slightly tart, tangy, nutty flavor. Smooth, slightly creamy texture. Pale ivory to straw yellow in color. Good with veal, crusty breads, peaches, melon and prosciutto.

Gouda
Semisoft cheese. Light, buttery flavor. Smooth, creamy texture. Pale yellow interior color. Good with peaches, melons, apricots and cherries.

Havarti
Semisoft cheese. Buttery, creamy, slightly acidic flavor. Smooth, supple texture. Pale yellow color. Good with plums, grapes, poultry and seafood.

Mascarpone
Soft fresh cheese. Rich, buttery, slightly sweet flavor. Smooth, thick, creamy texture. Creamy white color. Good with berries, shortbread and figs.

Monterey Jack
Semisoft cheese. Delicate, buttery flavor with a slight tartness. Creamy texture. Creamy white color. Good with fruit, poultry, quesadillas and Mexican-style recipes.

Mozzarella
Mild, delicate, milky flavor. Smooth, plastic texture. Creamy white color. Good with tomatoes, cured meats, pesto, roasted red peppers and black olives.

Mozzarella, fresh
Mild, delicate, milky flavor. Soft, slightly elastic texture. Creamy white color. Good with sun-dried or fresh tomatoes, cured meats, salads, sandwiches, basil and melon.

Muenster
Semisoft cheese. Mild to mellow flavor. Smooth and elastic texture. Creamy white interior color. Good with apples, grapes, whole-grain breads and sausages.

Neufchatel
Soft fresh cheese. Nutty, slightly sweet; lower in fat than cream cheese. Creamy, but slightly firmer than cream cheese. Creamy white color. Good with fresh fruit, jam, quick breads and bagels.

Parmesan
Hard cheese. Buttery, sweet, nutty flavor that intensifies with age. Granular texture. Pale yellow color. Good with pasta, rice, vegetable soups and tomato or cream sauces.

Provolone
Full flavor, can be sharp. Firm texture. Ivory to pale beige in color. Good with cured meats, tomatoes, pears, grapes and figs.

Ricotta
Soft fresh cheese. Mild flavor with a hint of sweetness. Creamy, but slightly grainy curd. Creamy white color. Good with pasta casseroles, stuffings, herbs and tomatoes.

Romano
Hard cheese. Sharp, piquant flavor. Hard, granular texture. Creamy white color. Good with apples, pears, tomatoes and olives.

Swiss
Semifirm cheese. Mellow, buttery, nutty flavor. Firm texture with eyes. Ivory color. Good with apples, pears and grapes.

An Impressive Cheese Platter

For an easy addition to an appetizer buffet, consider offering a simple cheese platter. Whether served by itself or alongside fruits, vegetables, crackers or bread, cheese appeals to people of all ages. Best of all, it requires little effort on your part. Here are a few suggestions to help you prepare a pleasing platter:

Plan on about 2 ounces of cheese per person and use four or five varieties.

Include an assortment of colors, textures and tastes. Some mild cheeses are baby Swiss, Colby, Colby-Jack, Havarti, mild cheddar and Monterey Jack. For a mellow flavor, turn to brick, Brie, Camembert, Edam, Gouda, medium cheddar and Swiss. Be sure to also include some robust varieties like Asiago, blue, Gorgonzola, Gruyere, Parmesan, provolone and sharp cheddar.

Add eye appeal by cutting cheeses into different shapes, such as rectangles, squares, triangles, cubes and sticks. (For the holidays, use small festive cutters.)

For best results, use a clean sharp knife and cut cheese while it's cold. Cutting can be done early in the day. Just wrap the cheese tightly with plastic wrap or store in airtight containers and refrigerate.

When preparing your platter for serving, it's better to serve small quantities and then refill as needed. Otherwise, the flavor and texture of the cheeses will deteriorate and the cheeses may spoil.

Nutty Fruit 'n' Cheese Tray

PREP/TOTAL TIME: 30 min.

Taste of Home Test Kitchen

Here's a simple but fun presentation for a fruit tray. Purchasing cubed cheeses makes this a snap to put together.

- 1 fresh pineapple
- 3 cups (12 ounces) cubed Colby-Monterey Jack cheese
- 3 cups (12 ounces) cubed cheddar cheese
- 3 cups (12 ounces) cubed Swiss cheese
- 3 cups (12 ounces) cubed pepper Jack cheese
- 1 pound green grapes
- 1 pound seedless red grapes
- 1 medium honeydew, peeled, seeded and cubed
- 1 medium cantaloupe, peeled, seeded and cubed
- 1 pound fresh strawberries
- 2 cups walnut halves

1) Slice pineapple in half horizontally. Cut top half of pineapple into 1-in. wedges, leaving intact. Transfer to a serving platter. Peel and cube remaining pineapple. Arrange cheeses, fruits and walnuts on platter.

Yield: 24 servings.

NUTRITION FACTS: 1 serving (6 ounces) equals 313 calories, 20 g fat (12 g saturated fat), 63 mg cholesterol, 337 mg sodium, 18 g carbohydrate, 1 g fiber, 17 g protein.

comfort for the soul

Homemade soup goes to church members in need

Nothing's quite like homemade chicken soup. A steaming bowl of it can soothe a sore throat, nourish a recuperating body and warm a soul.

It's also one of the ways the Deaconess Group at Discovery Christian Community in Salt Lake City, Utah, reaches out to help others, says Stacey Christensen, a member of the group.

Delivering homemade soup and other meals to members of the congregation who are ill, recuperating from surgery or in need has been a part of the group's ministry for years. The current program, called Meals to Go, began two years ago.

About every six months, 10-15 women gather in the church kitchen on a Saturday morning.

"It's quite a sight. Some women are making pots of chili, some are cooking whole chickens, others are chopping bags and bags of vegetables," Stacey says. "We generally use family recipes. We try to choose ones that are simple to make, cost-effective and can be frozen and reheated easily."

The group usually makes three entrees.

"We always make our Chicken Noodle Soup," says Stacey. "People say it's the best they've ever tasted. They just love it. It's really nourishing, especially for those who are sick."

The meals are stored in the church freezer. Every meal is labeled with its contents, the date it was made and directions to warm it.

"We want the meals to be easy for them," she explains, since lightening the person's burden is a goal. "They say how much of a blessing it is not to have to worry about what to feed their family or how it helped them get through a tough week on a tight budget."

Each woman in the volunteer group "has a huge, huge heart," Stacey says. "They pour their whole heart into this ministry. It blesses us as much to do it as it does the people who receive it."

The Deaconess Group

> *It's quite a sight. Some women are making pots of chili, some are cooking whole chickens, and others are chopping... vegetables.*
>
> ~Stacey Christensen

Recipes

Tips

Pasta, Grains & Beans

PASTA

Cooking with pasta gives you so many choices! You can prepare homemade pasta with a few simple ingredients or use packaged pasta to make a tasty meal in a snap.

In general, you want to select the right pasta for the sauce. A light, thin sauce should have a thin pasta, such as angel hair or vermicelli. Heavier sauces need thicker pastas, like fettuccine. For chunky or meaty sauces, choose a tubular shaped pasta like rigatoni.

Store uncooked dry pasta in a cool dry place for up to 1 year. Store fresh pasta in the refrigerator and cook or freeze by the use-by date.

To cook pasta evenly and prevent it from sticking together, always cook pasta in plenty of boiling water. To prevent a boil-over, cook pasta in a large kettle or Dutch oven.

Allow about 2 ounces of pasta per person for a main-dish serving.

For 8 ounces of pasta, bring 3 quarts water to a full rolling boil along with 1-1/2 teaspoons salt if desired. Add pasta all at once and stir. Return to a boil and cook, uncovered, stirring occasionally.

Cooking times vary with the size and variety of pasta. Fresh pasta cooks faster than dried. Thin pasta, such as angel hair, cooks faster than thicker pasta, such as spaghetti. For packaged pasta, follow the recommended cooking directions on package.

To test for doneness, use a fork to remove a single piece of pasta from the boiling water. Rinse in cold water and taste. Pasta should be cooked until al dente, which means firm yet tender. Test often while cooking to avoid overcooking, which would cause a soft or mushy texture.

If pasta will be used in a recipe that requires further cooking, such as a casserole, undercook by one-third the recommended time.

As soon as the pasta tests done, pour into a large colander to drain, minding the steam as you pour. If using the cooked pasta in a salad or at a later time, rinse it with cold water to stop cooking and remove excess starch.

Cooked pasta can be tossed with a little olive oil and refrigerated for 3 to 4 days. To reheat refrigerated pasta, place in boiling water for 1 minute, then drain and serve.

Generally, pasta should not be frozen. However, some dishes, like lasagna, stuffed shells or manicotti, can be frozen. Make the recipe as directed, then freeze for up to 2 months before baking. Thaw in the refrigerator and bake according to recipe directions until heated through.

Cooking Spaghetti

Carefully hold spaghetti in boiling water and ease it down into the water as it softens, pushing it around the edge of the pan. When fully immersed in the water, stir the spaghetti to separate strands.

How Much Pasta?

The yield for pasta will vary according to its size and shape. It is sometimes difficult to determine the amount of pasta to cook for a recipe, especially if the package is opened and partially used. For long pasta, such as spaghetti, linguine and fettuccine, 1-1/2-in. diameter bundle of the pasta is about 8 ounces. The chart at right is a guideline for uncooked, dry pasta.

TYPE OF PASTA	UNCOOKED AMOUNT	COOKED AMOUNT
ANGEL HAIR	8 oz.	4 cups
BOW TIE	4 cups/8 oz.	4 cups
EGG NOODLE	4 cups/8 oz.	4 cups
ELBOW MACARONI	2 cups/8 oz.	4 cups
FETTUCCINE	8 oz.	3-1/4 cups
LINGUINE	8 oz.	4 cups
RIGATONI	3 cups/8 oz.	4-1/2 cups
ROTINI	3 cups/8 oz.	4-1/2 cups
SHELL, MEDIUM	3 cups/8 oz.	4 cups
SPAGHETTI	8 oz.	5 cups
THIN SPAGHETTI	8 oz.	4-1/2 cups
VERMICELLI	8 oz.	4-1/2 cups
ZITI	3 cups/8 oz.	4-1/2 cups

Pasta Shapes

ANGEL HAIR   VERMICELLI   SPAGHETTI

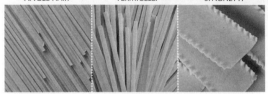

LINGUINE   FETTUCCINE   LASAGNA

SHELLS (MEDIUM)   SHELLS (JUMBO)   ELBOW MACARONI

PENNE   MANICOTTI   ROTINI (SPIRAL)

BOW TIE   EGG NOODLE   ORZO

ORECCHIETTE

Fresh Tomato Pasta Toss

PREP/TOTAL TIME: 30 min.

Cheryl Travagliante, Independence, Ohio

Dipping whole tomatoes into boiling water makes them easier to peel for this garden-fresh recipe. Parmesan or Romano cheese makes a great topper.

- 3 pounds ripe fresh tomatoes
- 1 package (16 ounces) penne pasta *or* pasta of your choice
- 2 garlic cloves, minced
- 1 tablespoon vegetable oil
- 1 tablespoon minced fresh parsley *or* 1 teaspoon dried parsley flakes
- 1 tablespoon minced fresh basil *or* 1 teaspoon dried basil
- 2 teaspoons minced fresh oregano *or* 3/4 teaspoon dried oregano
- 1 teaspoon salt
- 1/4 teaspoon sugar
- 1/8 teaspoon pepper
- 1/4 cup heavy whipping cream
- 1/4 cup shredded Parmesan *or* Romano cheese

1) To remove peels from tomatoes, fill a large saucepan with water and bring to a boil. Place tomatoes, one at a time, in boiling water for 30 seconds. Immediately plunge in ice water. Peel skins with a sharp paring knife and discard. Chop pulp; set aside.

2) Cook pasta according to package directions. Meanwhile, in a large skillet, cook garlic in oil over medium heat until golden. Add the parsley, basil, oregano, salt, sugar, pepper and reserved tomato

FRESH TOMATO PASTA TOSS

pulp; mix well. Bring to a boil; reduce heat. Add cream; heat through.

3) Drain pasta; toss with tomato sauce. Sprinkle with cheese.

Yield: 8 servings.

NUTRITION FACTS: 1 cup equals 277 calories, 7 g fat (0 saturated fat), 13 mg cholesterol, 244 mg sodium, 46 g carbohydrate, 0 fiber, 9 g protein.

Pesto Sauce

PREP/TOTAL TIME: 15 min.

Sue Jurack, Mequon, Wisconsin

I like to serve pesto over gnocchi with an extra sprinkle of Parmesan cheese. Gnocchi are little Italian potato dumplings, which are available in the pasta section of some grocery stores. You can also freeze the pesto to use later on.

2/3 cup packed fresh basil leaves
1/3 cup grated Parmesan cheese
1/3 cup olive oil
2 tablespoons pine nuts *or* sunflower kernels
1/2 teaspoon salt
1/8 teaspoon pepper
1 garlic clove, peeled

1) In a food processor, combine all ingredients; cover and process until blended. Use immediately or transfer to an airtight container. Cover and refrigerate for up to 1 week or freeze for up to 3 months.

Yield: 1/2 cup.

Editor's Note: When freezing the pesto, leave about 3/4 in. at the top of the container, then cover the top with a thin layer of olive oil so the pesto doesn't turn brown.

NUTRITION FACTS: 2 tablespoons equals 217 calories, 22 g fat (4 g saturated fat), 5 mg cholesterol, 420 mg sodium, 1 g carbohydrate, 1 g fiber, 4 g protein.

Sicilian Spaghetti Sauce

PREP/TOTAL TIME: 30 min.

Taste of Home Test Kitchen

Golden raisins and pine nuts add a new flavor twist to this southern-Italian pasta sauce.

1/2 pound lean ground beef
1/2 cup chopped onion
1 teaspoon minced garlic
1 teaspoon olive oil
2 cans (14-1/2 ounces *each*) Italian diced tomatoes, undrained
1/4 cup golden raisins
1/4 cup dry red wine *or* 1 tablespoon red wine vinegar
2 tablespoons tomato paste
1 tablespoon sugar
1 teaspoon dried basil
1/2 teaspoon salt
1/4 teaspoon pepper
8 ounces uncooked spaghetti
2 tablespoons minced fresh parsley
2 teaspoons pine nuts, toasted

1) In a large skillet, cook the beef, onion and garlic in oil over medium heat until meat is no longer pink; drain. Stir in tomatoes, raisins, wine or vinegar, tomato paste, sugar, basil, salt and pepper. Bring to a boil. Reduce heat; simmer, uncovered, for 15 minutes or until heated through.

2) Meanwhile, cook spaghetti according to package directions. Stir parsley and pine nuts into meat sauce. Drain spaghetti; top with sauce.

Yield: 4 servings.

NUTRITION FACTS: 1 cup sauce with 1 cup spaghetti equals 457 calories, 7 g fat (2 g saturated fat), 28 mg cholesterol, 1,138 mg sodium, 74 g carbohydrate, 4 g fiber, 21 g protein.

SICILIAN SPAGHETTI SAUCE

EVERYONE'S FAVORITE SPAGHETTI AND MEATBALLS

 CLASSIC: Moist homemade meatballs are baked, and then added to a slow-simmered tomato sauce to make Italian Spaghetti and Meatballs a time-honored ethnic specialty.

 TIME-SAVER: In only half an hour, you can serve up plates of Festive Spaghetti 'n' Meatballs. Fresh mushrooms, green pepper, onion and red wine perk up a jar of spaghetti sauce and a package of frozen meatballs.

 LIGHT: Broiled meatballs made with frozen spinach and lean ground turkey instead of ground beef add a light touch to Marinara Turkey Meatballs. Nicely seasoned with fresh parsley, garlic, nutmeg and allspice, the tender meatballs are quickly simmered with spaghetti sauce for a delicious pasta dinner with less fat, cholesterol, sodium and calories.

 SERVES 2: For a traditional Italian dinner for two, put Meatballs with Spaghetti Sauce on the menu. Meatballs prepared with both ground beef and pork are baked, then stirred into a made-from-scratch tomato sauce.

Italian Spaghetti and Meatballs

PREP: 30 min. **COOK:** 1-1/2 hours

Etta Winter, Pavillion, New York

- 2 cans (28 ounces *each*) diced tomatoes, undrained
- 1 can (12 ounces) tomato paste
- 1-1/2 cups water, *divided*
- 1 tablespoon sugar
- 3 tablespoons grated onion
- 1-1/2 teaspoons dried oregano
- 2-1/2 teaspoons salt, *divided*
- 1 teaspoon minced garlic, *divided*
- 3/4 teaspoon pepper, *divided*
- 1 bay leaf
- 6 slices day-old bread, torn
- 2 eggs, lightly beaten
- 1/2 cup grated Parmesan cheese
- 2 tablespoons minced fresh parsley
- 1 pound ground beef

Hot cooked spaghetti

Additional Parmesan cheese, optional

1) In a Dutch oven, combine the tomatoes, tomato paste, 1 cup water, sugar, grated onion, oregano, 1-1/2 teaspoons salt, 1/2 teaspoon garlic, 1/2 teaspoon pepper and bay leaf. Bring to a boil. Reduce the heat and simmer, uncovered, for 1-1/4 hours.

2) Meanwhile, soak bread in remaining water. Squeeze out excess moisture. In a large bowl, combine the bread, eggs, Parmesan cheese, parsley and remaining salt, garlic and pepper. Crumble beef over mixture and mix well. Shape into 1-1/2-in. meatballs (about 36 meatballs).

3) Place meatballs on a rack in a shallow baking pan. Bake, uncovered, at 400° for 20 minutes or until meat is no longer pink. Transfer to spaghetti sauce. Simmer, uncovered, until heated through,

stirring occasionally. Discard bay leaf. Serve sauce and meatballs over spaghetti with additional Parmesan if desired.

Yield: 6 servings.

NUTRITION FACTS: 1-2/3 cups (calculated without spaghetti) equals 387 calories, 14 g fat (6 g saturated fat), 126 mg cholesterol, 1,679 mg sodium, 41 g carbohydrate, 9 g fiber, 26 g protein.

■ **Italian Meatball Sandwiches:** Spoon meatballs onto split submarine, hoagie *or* French bread rolls. Place on a baking sheet, leaving sandwich open. Sprinkle each with 1/4 to 1/3 cup shredded mozzarella cheese. Bake, uncovered, at 350° for 10-15 minutes or until cheese is melted.

FESTIVE SPAGHETTI 'N' MEATBALLS

Festive Spaghetti 'n' Meatballs

PREP/TOTAL TIME: 30 min.

Mary Ann Kosmas, Minneapolis, Minnesota

- 1/2 pound sliced fresh mushrooms
- 1 large green pepper, julienned

1 large onion, halved and sliced
2 tablespoons olive oil
1/4 cup red wine *or* water
1 jar (26 ounces) meatless spaghetti sauce
1 package (12 ounces) frozen fully cooked Italian meatballs, thawed

Hot cooked spaghetti

1) In a large saucepan, saute the mushrooms, green pepper and onion in oil until crisp-tender; stir in wine or water. Bring to a boil; cook for 2 minutes. Stir in spaghetti sauce and meatballs. Return to a boil. Reduce heat; simmer, uncovered, for 10-15 minutes or until meatballs are heated through. Serve sauce and meatballs over spaghetti.

Yield: 4 servings.

NUTRITION FACTS: 1 serving (calculated without spaghetti) equals 367 calories, 18 g fat (5 g saturated fat), 71 mg cholesterol, 921 mg sodium, 30 g carbohydrate, 5 g fiber, 20 g protein.

BREAKING UNCOOKED SPAGHETTI ■■■

Are you tired of those little pieces of uncooked spaghetti scattering over the floor and stove when you try to break the spaghetti before cooking? Try wrapping the long strands in a clean dish towel. Bend the towel back and forth to break the noodles, then carefully open the towel and pour the pieces into the boiling water.

—Grace R., Wrightwood, California

Marinara Turkey Meatballs

PREP: 20 min. **COOK:** 25 min.

Taste of Home Test Kitchen

1 package (10 ounces) frozen chopped spinach, thawed and squeezed dry
1/2 cup seasoned bread crumbs
1 small onion, finely chopped
3 tablespoons minced fresh parsley
2 garlic cloves, minced
1/4 teaspoon ground nutmeg
1/4 teaspoon ground allspice
1/4 teaspoon pepper
1-1/4 pounds lean ground turkey
1 jar (26 ounces) meatless spaghetti sauce

Hot cooked spaghetti

1) In a large bowl, combine the spinach, bread crumbs, onion, parsley, garlic, nutmeg, allspice and pepper. Crumble turkey over mixture and mix well.

2) Shape into 24 meatballs. Place on a broiler pan coated with cooking spray. Broil 4-6 in. from the heat for 8 minutes. Turn; broil 3-5 minutes longer or until meat is no longer pink.

3) Transfer meatballs to a Dutch oven; add spaghetti sauce. Bring to a boil. Reduce heat; cover and simmer for 10 minutes. Serve with spaghetti.

Yield: 6 servings.

NUTRITION FACTS: 4 meatballs (calculated without spaghetti) equals 247 calories, 9 g fat (2 g saturated fat), 75 mg cholesterol, 809 mg sodium, 21 g carbohydrate, 4 g fiber, 21 g protein.

Meatballs with Spaghetti Sauce

PREP: 30 min. **BAKE:** 25 min.

Denise Linnett, Picton, Ontario

1/2 cup soft bread crumbs
1/4 cup grated Parmesan cheese
1 tablespoon 2% milk
1 egg, beaten
1-1/2 teaspoons minced fresh parsley
1/4 teaspoon garlic powder
1/8 teaspoon salt
1/8 teaspoon pepper
6 ounces lean ground beef
2 ounces ground pork

SAUCE:

1/2 cup chopped onion
1 garlic clove, minced
1 tablespoon olive oil
1 can (14-1/2 ounces) whole tomatoes, quartered
1 can (8 ounces) tomato sauce
1 can (6 ounces) tomato paste
1/2 cup water
3 tablespoons minced fresh parsley
1 teaspoon sugar
1 teaspoon dried basil
1/4 teaspoon pepper

Hot cooked spaghetti

1) In a large bowl, combine bread crumbs, Parmesan cheese, milk, egg, parsley, garlic powder, salt and pepper. Crumble the beef and pork over the mixture; mix well. Shape into 10 meatballs about 1-3/4-in. each.

2) Place meatballs on a greased rack in a shallow baking pan. Bake at 350° for 25-30 minutes or until meat is no longer pink.

3) In a large saucepan, saute onion and garlic in oil until tender. Stir in the tomatoes, tomato sauce and paste, water, parsley, sugar, basil and pepper. Bring to a boil. Reduce heat; simmer, uncovered, for 15 minutes, stirring occasionally.

4) Drain meatballs; add to sauce. Simmer 5 minutes longer or until heated through. Serve with spaghetti.

Yield: 2 servings.

NUTRITION FACTS: 1-1/2 cups sauce and 5 meatballs (calculated without spaghetti) equals 544 calories, 24 g fat (8 g saturated fat), 186 mg cholesterol, 1,445 mg sodium, 46 g carbohydrate, 9 g fiber, 37 g protein.

Pasta with Marinara Sauce

PREP/TOTAL TIME: 25 min.

Diane Hixon, Niceville, Florida

You don't have to settle for prepared sauce when this homemade marinara is so simple and tasty. Add Italian sausage links for more robust flavor.

- 2 garlic cloves, sliced
- 1/3 cup olive oil
- 1 can (28 ounces) diced tomatoes, undrained
- 3 tablespoons minced fresh parsley
- 2 tablespoons minced onion
- 2 bay leaves

Salt and pepper to taste

- 1 tablespoon chopped fresh basil

Hot cooked pasta

1) In a large saucepan, cook garlic in oil over medium heat for 3 minutes or until golden. Add the tomatoes, parsley, onion, bay leaves, salt and pepper; bring to a boil.

2) Reduce heat; cover and simmer for 15 minutes. Discard bay leaves. Add basil. Serve over pasta.

Yield: 4 servings.

NUTRITION FACTS: 3/4 cup (calculated without salt, pepper and pasta) equals 204 calories, 18 g fat (2 g saturated fat), 0 cholesterol, 254 mg sodium, 11 g carbohydrate, 3 g fiber, 2 g protein.

■ **Sausage Marinara:** In a skillet, cook 1 pound Italian sausage links over medium heat for 12-14 minutes or until browned, turning twice. When cool enough to handle, cut into slices; set aside. With the garlic, cook 1/2 pound sliced fresh mushrooms, 1 *each* chopped large onion, green pepper and sweet red pepper. Add remaining ingredients and cook as directed. Add reserved sausage and heat through.

Fettuccine Alfredo

PREP/TOTAL TIME: 20 min.

Jo Gray, Park City, Montana

A creamy and comforting cheese sauce, with a hint of pepper and nutmeg, coats fettuccine noodles in fine fashion. This is wonderful as is, but sometimes I like to add sliced fresh mushrooms and black olives that have been sauteed in butter and garlic.

- 8 ounces uncooked fettuccine
- 6 tablespoons butter, cubed
- 2 cups heavy whipping cream
- 3/4 cup grated Parmesan cheese, *divided*
- 1/2 cup grated Romano cheese
- 2 egg yolks, lightly beaten
- 1/4 teaspoon salt
- 1/8 teaspoon ground nutmeg
- 1/8 teaspoon pepper

1) Cook fettuccine according to package directions. Meanwhile, in a saucepan, melt butter over medium-low heat. Stir in the cream, 1/2 cup Parmesan cheese, Romano cheese, egg yolks, salt, pepper and nutmeg. Cook and stir over medium-low heat until a thermometer reads 160° (do not boil).

2) Drain fettuccine; toss with Alfredo sauce and remaining Parmesan cheese.

Yield: 4 servings.

NUTRITION FACTS: 1 cup equals 908 calories, 73 g fat (45 g saturated fat), 339 mg cholesterol, 821 mg sodium, 44 g carbohydrate, 2 g fiber, 23 g protein.

INDONESIAN PASTA

Indonesian Pasta

PREP/TOTAL TIME: 20 min.

Jolene Caldwell, Council Bluffs, Iowa

My family really enjoys this delectable asparagus dish. The flavors blend to create an interesting taste.

- 1/2 cup chicken broth
- 2 jalapeno peppers, seeded and chopped
- 2 tablespoons soy sauce
- 2 tablespoons peanut butter
- 1 tablespoon dried minced onion
- 1 tablespoon lemon juice
- 1/4 teaspoon brown sugar
- 18 fresh asparagus spears, trimmed and cut into 1-inch pieces
- 6 ounces uncooked angel hair pasta
- 1/2 medium sweet red pepper, julienned
- 2 teaspoons olive oil
- 1/2 cup sliced green onions

1) In a small saucepan, combine broth, jalapenos, soy sauce, peanut butter, onion, lemon juice and brown sugar. Bring to a boil, stirring constantly. Remove from the heat; keep warm.

2) Cook pasta according to package directions. Meanwhile, in a large skillet, saute asparagus and red pepper in oil for 6-8 minutes. Add green onions to the asparagus mixture; saute for 2-3 minutes or until vegetables are crisp-tender. Drain pasta; toss with vegetable mixture and reserved sauce.

Yield: 4 servings.

Editor's Note: When cutting or seeding hot peppers, use rubber or plastic gloves to protect your hands. Avoid touching your face.

NUTRITION FACTS: 1 cup equals 263 calories, 7 g fat (1 g saturated fat), 0 cholesterol, 627 mg sodium, 40 g carbohydrate, 3 g fiber, 11 g protein.

Spaghetti Carbonara

PREP: 20 min. **COOK:** 15 min.

Taste of Home Test Kitchen

A from-scratch sauce tops spaghetti in this classic recipe featuring peas and bacon.

- 8 ounces uncooked spaghetti
- 1 tablespoon cornstarch
- 4 eggs, lightly beaten
- 1 cup half-and-half cream
- 3/4 cup chopped onion
- 2 garlic cloves, minced
- 2 tablespoons olive oil
- 1 cup frozen peas
- 8 bacon strips, cooked and crumbled
- 1/2 cup grated Parmesan cheese
- 1/2 teaspoon salt
- 1/4 teaspoon white pepper

Additional Parmesan cheese, optional

1) Cook pasta according to package directions. Meanwhile, in a large bowl, combine cornstarch, eggs and cream until smooth; set aside. In a large skillet, saute onion and garlic in oil until tender. Gradually stir into egg mixture. Add peas to hot skillet; cook and stir for 1 minute or until heated through. Pour egg mixture into skillet all at once, stirring constantly.

2) Cook and stir over medium-low heat until mixture is just thick enough to coat the back of a metal spoon with a thin film and a thermometer reads 160°, about 5 minutes. Remove from the heat.

3) Drain spaghetti; toss with sauce. Sprinkle with the bacon, cheese, salt and white pepper; toss again. Serve immediately with additional Parmesan cheese if desired.

Yield: 5 servings.

NUTRITION FACTS: 1 cup equals 474 calories, 22 g fat (9 g saturated fat), 209 mg cholesterol, 658 mg sodium, 44 g carbohydrate, 3 g fiber, 21 g protein.

TUXEDO PASTA

Tuxedo Pasta

PREP/TOTAL TIME: 20 min.

Jackie Hannahs, Fountain, Michigan

With chicken and veggies, this pasta medley in a mild lemon and wine sauce is a complete meal-in-one that's a snap to assemble. I try to keep leftover chicken on hand so that I can fix this dish whenever I want.

- 2 cups uncooked bow tie pasta
- 2 cups cubed cooked chicken
- 1 medium zucchini, sliced
- 1-1/2 cups sliced fresh mushrooms
- 1/2 cup chopped sweet red pepper
- 3 tablespoons butter, *divided*
- 1/4 cup lemon juice
- 2 tablespoons white wine *or* chicken broth
- 3/4 cup shredded Parmesan cheese
- 3 tablespoons minced fresh basil *or* 1 tablespoon dried basil

1) Cook pasta according to package directions. Meanwhile, in a large skillet, saute the chicken, zucchini, mushrooms and red pepper in 2 tablespoons butter for 4-5 minutes or until vegetables are tender. Add the lemon juice and wine or broth. Bring to a boil. Reduce heat; cook and stir for 2 minutes or until heated through.

2) Drain the pasta; add to the skillet. Stir in the Parmesan cheese, basil and remaining butter.

Yield: 6 servings.

NUTRITION FACTS: 1 cup equals 243 calories, 12 g fat (6 g saturated fat), 64 mg cholesterol, 271 mg sodium, 13 g carbohydrate, 1 g fiber, 20 g protein.

REFRESHING PASTA PRIMAVERA

 CLASSIC: Broccoli, carrot, celery, sweet red pepper, peas and mushrooms add springtime flair to Garden Primavera. The colorful pasta toss is seasoned with garlic and fresh basil for family-pleasing results.

 TIME-SAVER: Refrigerated pasta and Caesar salad dressing are the savvy shortcuts that ease preparation of Tortellini Primavera. Zucchini, yellow summer squash and cherry tomatoes make this an easy entree that's eye-catching, too.

 LIGHT: You'll find a bevy of bright vegetables in every serving of Linguine Primavera. Since there's no oil in this recipe like in the classic, there are fewer calories and only half of the fat, but all of the garden-fresh flavor is still there.

 SERVES 2: A tomato-based sauce coats the veggies and your choice of pasta in Pasta Primavera, a sensational meatless main dish that serves two nicely.

GARDEN PRIMAVERA

Garden Primavera

PREP/TOTAL TIME: 30 min.

Anne Heinonen, Howell, Michigan

- 8 ounces uncooked fettuccine
- 1 cup fresh broccoli florets
- 1 medium sweet red pepper, julienned
- 1 medium carrot, sliced
- 1/2 cup sliced fresh mushrooms
- 1/4 cup sliced celery
- 1 garlic clove, minced
- 1 tablespoon olive oil
- 3/4 cup V8 juice
- 1/4 cup minced fresh basil
- 1 cup frozen peas, thawed
- 1/2 teaspoon salt

- 1/8 teaspoon pepper
- 2 tablespoons shredded Parmesan cheese

1) Cook fettuccine according to package directions. Meanwhile, in a large nonstick skillet, saute the broccoli, red pepper, carrot, mushrooms, celery and garlic in oil for 3 minutes.

2) Add V8 juice and basil; bring to a boil. Reduce heat; simmer, uncovered, for 3 minutes. Stir in the peas, salt and pepper; simmer 2 minutes longer or until peas are tender.

3) Drain fettuccine; toss with vegetable mixture. Sprinkle with Parmesan cheese.

Yield: 4 servings.

NUTRITION FACTS: 1-1/2 cups equals 310 calories, 6 g fat (1 g saturated fat), 2 mg cholesterol, 529 mg sodium, 54 g carbohydrate, 6 g fiber, 12 g protein.

Tortellini Primavera

PREP/TOTAL TIME: 20 min.

Mary Ann Dell, Phoenixville, Pennsylvania

- 1 package (9 ounces) refrigerated cheese tortellini
- 2 medium yellow summer squash, chopped
- 2 medium zucchini, chopped
- 2 teaspoons olive oil
- 1 pint cherry tomatoes, halved
- 1/2 cup chopped green onions
- 1/4 teaspoon pepper
- 1/2 cup fat-free Caesar salad dressing
- 1/4 cup shredded Parmesan cheese
- 1/4 cup sliced almonds, toasted

1) Cook tortellini according to package directions. Meanwhile, in a large skillet, saute yellow squash and zucchini in oil for 4-6 minutes or until crisp-tender.

2) Drain tortellini; transfer to a large bowl. Add the squash mixture, tomatoes, onions and pepper. Drizzle with salad dressing; toss to coat. Sprinkle with Parmesan cheese and almonds.

Yield: 6 servings.

NUTRITION FACTS: 1 cup equals 245 calories, 9 g fat (3 g saturated fat), 21 mg cholesterol, 468 mg sodium, 35 g carbohydrate, 4 g fiber, 11 g protein.

Using Part of a Package of Pasta

When a recipe calls for part of a package of long pasta, such as spaghetti or fettuccine, weighing the pasta on a kitchen scale is a great way to get the exact amount. To prevent the pasta from rolling off the scale, place a tall drinking glass on the scale, return the weight to zero and add the pasta to the glass. Keep the pasta in the glass until you are ready to add it to the boiling water.

Linguine Primavera

PREP/TOTAL TIME: 30 min.

Beverly Little, Marietta, Georgia

     8 ounces uncooked linguine
     1 medium carrot, thinly sliced
   1/2 cup chopped onion
   1/2 cup julienned sweet red pepper
   1/2 cup julienned sweet yellow pepper
     1 medium zucchini, thinly sliced
     1 medium yellow summer squash, thinly sliced
     1 cup broccoli florets
     1 pound thin fresh asparagus, cut into 3-inch pieces
   1/2 pound fresh mushrooms, sliced
   1/3 cup all-purpose flour
     2 cups cold water
     2 teaspoons chicken bouillon granules
   1/2 cup white wine *or* chicken broth
   1/4 teaspoon salt
   1/4 cup minced fresh basil
     6 tablespoons grated Parmesan cheese

1) Cook linguine according to package directions. Meanwhile, in a nonstick skillet coated with cooking spray, combine the carrot, onion, peppers, zucchini, yellow squash and broccoli. Cover and cook over medium-low heat for 10 minutes. Add asparagus and mushrooms; cook 5 minutes longer.

2) In a saucepan, combine flour and water until smooth. Add the bouillon. Bring to a boil; cook and stir for 2 minutes or until slightly thickened.

Add wine or broth and salt; stir well. Pour over vegetables.

3) Drain linguine; add to vegetable mixture. Add basil; toss to coat. Sprinkle with Parmesan cheese.

Yield: 6 servings.

NUTRITION FACTS: 1-1/2 cups equals 168 calories, 3 g fat (1 g saturated fat), 5 mg cholesterol, 614 mg sodium, 26 g carbohydrate, 4 g fiber, 9 g protein.

Pasta Primavera

PREP/TOTAL TIME: 25 min.

Clara DelVitto, Venice, Florida

     4 ounces uncooked fettuccine *or* pasta of your choice
   1/2 cup sliced onion
   1/2 cup julienned green or sweet red pepper
     2 teaspoons olive oil
   1/2 cup sliced zucchini
   1/2 cup sliced yellow summer squash
     2 medium fresh mushrooms, sliced
   3/4 cup stewed tomatoes
   1/4 to 1/2 teaspoon dried basil

Shredded Parmesan cheese, optional

1) Cook fettuccine according to package directions. Meanwhile, in a large skillet, saute onion and green pepper in oil until crisp-tender. Add the zucchini, yellow squash and mushrooms; saute for 1 minute. Add tomatoes and basil. Bring to a boil; reduce heat.

2) Cover and simmer for 8-10 minutes or until vegetables are tender. Drain fettuccine; toss with vegetable mixture. Sprinkle with Parmesan cheese if desired.

Yield: 2 servings.

NUTRITION FACTS: 1 cup equals 296 calories, 6 g fat (1 g saturated fat), 0 cholesterol, 170 mg sodium, 53 g carbohydrate, 5 g fiber, 9 g protein.

PASTA PRIMAVERA

Crab Lasagna Roll-Ups

PREP: 20 min. **BAKE:** 30 min.

Fran Rodgers, Lake Geneva, Wisconsin

A creamy, delicate filling is rolled up into lasagna noodles for a simple and satisfying main dish. Garlic bread is the perfect side!

- 12 lasagna noodles
- 2 eggs, lightly beaten
- 2 cups (16 ounces) small-curd cottage cheese
- 1/4 cup grated Parmesan cheese
- 2 tablespoons Italian seasoning
- 2 tablespoons minced fresh parsley
- 1 teaspoon dried oregano
- 1/2 teaspoon dried basil
- 1/2 teaspoon dried thyme
- 1/4 teaspoon garlic powder
- 1 package (8 ounces) imitation crabmeat, flaked
- 2 cans (8 ounces *each*) tomato sauce

1) Cook noodles according to package directions. Meanwhile, in a large bowl, combine the eggs, cheeses and seasonings. Add crab; mix well. Drain noodles. Place about 1/3 cup on each noodle; roll up.

2) Place seam side down in a greased 13-in. x 9-in. x 2-in. baking dish. Top with tomato sauce. Cover and bake at 350° for 30-40 minutes or until heated through.

Yield: 6 servings.

NUTRITION FACTS: 2 roll-ups equals 361 calories, 7 g fat (3 g saturated fat), 95 mg cholesterol, 909 mg sodium, 50 g carbohydrate, 3 g fiber, 24 g protein.

Enchilada Stuffed Shells

PREP: 20 min. **BAKE:** 30 min.

Rebecca Stout, Conroe, Texas

I served this entree to my husband, my sister and my brother-in-law, who is a hard-to-please eater. He said he liked it and even took leftovers for lunch the next day...I was thrilled!

- 15 jumbo pasta shells
- 1 pound lean ground turkey
- 1 can (10 ounces) enchilada sauce
- 1/2 teaspoon dried minced onion
- 1/4 teaspoon dried basil
- 1/4 teaspoon dried oregano
- 1/4 teaspoon ground cumin
- 1/2 cup fat-free refried beans
- 1 cup (4 ounces) shredded reduced-fat cheddar cheese

1) Cook pasta shells according to package directions. Meanwhile, in a nonstick skillet, cook turkey over medium heat until no longer pink; drain. Stir in enchilada sauce and seasonings; set aside.

ENCHILADA STUFFED SHELLS

2) Drain pasta shells. Place a rounded teaspoonful of refried beans in each pasta shell; fill with turkey mixture. Place in a greased 11-in. x 7-in. x 2-in. baking dish.

3) Cover and bake at 350° for 25 minutes. Uncover; sprinkle with cheese. Bake 5 minutes longer or until cheese is melted.

Yield: 5 servings.

NUTRITION FACTS: 3 stuffed shells equals 379 calories, 15 g fat (6 g saturated fat), 89 mg cholesterol, 591 mg sodium, 33 g carbohydrate, 2 g fiber, 28 g protein.

Creamy Tortellini and Sausage

PREP/TOTAL TIME: 30 min.

Taste of Home Test Kitchen

You don't need to spend loads of time in the kitchen creating an irresistible pasta dish. Simply jazz up a jar of store-bought Alfredo sauce.

- 1 pound bulk Italian sausage
- 1 medium onion, chopped
- 2 garlic cloves, minced
- 4 quarts water
- 1 package (19 ounces) frozen cheese tortellini
- 3 cups frozen mixed vegetables
- 1 jar (17 ounces) Alfredo sauce
- 1/4 cup minced fresh basil *or* 3 teaspoons dried basil

1) Crumble sausage into a large skillet. Add onion and garlic; cook over medium heat until the meat is no longer pink. Meanwhile, in a Dutch oven, bring water to a boil. Add tortellini and vegetables. Cook for 3-5 minutes or until pasta floats and vegetables are tender; drain.

2) Drain sausage mixture. Add pasta mixture to skillet. Pour sauce over the top. Bring to a boil, stirring occasionally. Add basil; toss to coat.

Yield: 6 servings.

NUTRITION FACTS: 1 cup equals 622 calories, 38 g fat (17 g saturated fat), 94 mg cholesterol, 1,134 mg sodium, 46 g carbohydrate, 6 g fiber, 26 g protein.

Baked Ziti

PREP: 20 min. + simmering **BAKE:** 1 hour

Kim Neer, Kalamazoo, Michigan

This comforting Italian dish has a from-scratch spaghetti sauce, ziti pasta and a generous combination of cheeses. You can easily double the recipe to serve a larger crowd.

- 1/2 pound lean ground beef
- 1 medium onion, chopped
- 2 garlic cloves, minced
- 1-3/4 cups meatless spaghetti sauce
- 1 can (14-1/2 ounces) diced tomatoes, undrained
- 1 can (6 ounces) tomato paste
- 6 tablespoons water
- 1 tablespoon minced fresh parsley
- 1-1/2 teaspoons Worcestershire sauce
- 1 teaspoon dried basil
- 3/4 teaspoon dried oregano, *divided*
- 8 ounces uncooked ziti
- 1 cup part-skim ricotta cheese
- 1 cup (4 ounces) shredded part-skim mozzarella cheese
- 1/4 cup grated Parmesan cheese, *divided*
- 1 egg, lightly beaten
- 1/4 teaspoon salt
- 1/4 teaspoon pepper

1) In a large saucepan, cook the beef, onion and garlic over medium heat until meat is no longer pink; drain. Stir in spaghetti sauce, tomatoes, tomato paste, water, parsley, Worcestershire sauce, basil and 1/2 teaspoon oregano.

2) Cover and simmer meat sauce for 3 hours, stirring occasionally. Cook pasta according to package directions; drain. In a bowl, combine the ricotta, mozzarella, 2 tablespoons Parmesan cheese, egg, salt and pepper.

3) In a greased 13-in. x 9-in. x 2-in. baking dish, spread 1 cup of meat sauce. Layer with half of the pasta, a third of the meat sauce and half of the cheese mixture. Repeat layers.

4) Top with remaining meat sauce. Sprinkle with remaining Parmesan cheese and oregano. Cover and bake at 350° for 1 hour or until heated through.

Yield: 6 servings.

NUTRITION FACTS: 1-1/3 cups equals 431 calories, 14 g fat (7 g saturated fat), 81 mg cholesterol, 818 mg sodium, 50 g carbohydrate, 6 g fiber, 27 g protein.

Roasted Pepper Chicken Penne

PREP/TOTAL TIME: 30 min.

Regina Cowles, Boulder, Colorado

My husband calls me an aerobic cook because I can make this Italian dish in just 30 minutes. No one will accuse you of cutting corners. It tastes like it's been simmering deliciously for hours.

- 1 pound boneless skinless chicken breasts, cut into 1-inch strips
- 1/4 cup balsamic vinegar
- 1 package (16 ounces) penne pasta
- 1 medium onion, sliced
- 3 garlic cloves, sliced
- 1/4 cup olive oil
- 1 can (28 ounces) crushed tomatoes
- 1 cup roasted sweet red peppers, drained and sliced
- 1 cup chicken broth
- 3 teaspoons Italian seasoning
- 1/4 teaspoon salt
- 1 cup shredded Parmesan cheese

1) Place chicken in a large resealable plastic bag; add vinegar. Seal bag and turn to coat; refrigerate for 15 minutes.

2) Cook pasta according to package directions. Meanwhile, in a large skillet, saute onion and garlic in oil for 1 minute. Drain and discard vinegar. Add chicken to skillet; cook for 4-5 minutes or until juices run clear.

3) Stir in the tomatoes, red peppers, broth, Italian seasoning and salt. Bring to a boil over medium heat; cook and stir for 4-5 minutes or until heated through. Drain pasta; toss with chicken mixture. Sprinkle with Parmesan cheese.

Yield: 8 servings.

NUTRITION FACTS: 1-1/2 cups equals 424 calories, 12 g fat (3 g saturated fat), 39 mg cholesterol, 641 mg sodium, 53 g carbohydrate, 4 g fiber, 25 g protein.

ROASTED PEPPER CHICKEN PENNE

MOUTHWATERING LASAGNA

 CLASSIC: Lasagna lovers will be requesting seconds of Traditional Lasagna, which is hearty with ground beef, pork sausage and five cheeses. Fortunately that won't be a problem, because this irresistible layered casserole serves 12.

 TIME-SAVER: There's no need to turn on the oven to get the great taste of authentic lasagna. The no-cook noodles in Saucy Skillet Lasagna are layered with meat, ricotta and a seasoned tomato sauce, then cooked on the stovetop in less than 30 minutes.

 LIGHT: Your family won't even miss the beef and sausage in Meatless Lasagna, because it's brimming with colorful zucchini, carrots, peppers and mushrooms. Eliminating the meat and using reduced-fat ricotta and part-skim mozzarella helps trim half the calories and two-thirds of the fat from this lighter version compared to Traditional Lasagna.

 SERVES 2: Start with a mere five ingredients and in less than half an hour, you can have two individual servings of Lazy Lasagna ready to eat. Cottage cheese and mozzarella make these mini noodle casseroles rich and creamy.

Traditional Lasagna

PREP: 30 min. + simmering
BAKE: 70 min. + standing

Lorri Foockle, Granville, Illinois

- 1 pound ground beef
- 3/4 pound bulk pork sausage
- 3 cans (8 ounces *each*) tomato sauce
- 2 cans (6 ounces *each*) tomato paste
- 2 garlic cloves, minced
- 2 teaspoons sugar
- 1 teaspoon Italian seasoning
- 1 teaspoon salt
- 1/2 teaspoon pepper
- 3 eggs, lightly beaten
- 3 tablespoons minced fresh parsley
- 3 cups (24 ounces) small-curd cottage cheese
- 1 cup ricotta cheese
- 1/2 cup grated Parmesan cheese
- 9 uncooked lasagna noodles
- 6 slices provolone cheese
- 3 cups (12 ounces) shredded part-skim mozzarella cheese

1) In a large skillet, cook beef and sausage over medium heat until no longer pink; drain. Add the tomato sauce, tomato paste, garlic, sugar, Italian seasoning, salt and pepper. Bring to a boil. Reduce heat; simmer, uncovered, for 1 hour, stirring occasionally.

2) Meanwhile, cook noodles according to package directions; drain. In a large bowl, combine the eggs and parsley. Stir in the cottage cheese, ricotta and Parmesan. Spread 1 cup meat sauce into an ungreased 13-in. x 9-in. x 2-in. baking dish.

3) Layer with three noodles, provolone cheese, 2 cups cottage cheese mixture, 1 cup mozzarella, three noodles, 2 cups meat sauce, remaining cottage cheese mixture and 1 cup mozzarella. Top with the remaining noodles, meat sauce and mozzarella (dish will be full).

4) Cover and bake at 375° for 50 minutes. Uncover; bake 20 minutes longer or until heated through. Let stand for 15 minutes before cutting.

Yield: 12 servings.

NUTRITION FACTS: 1 serving equals 493 calories, 27 g fat (14 g saturated fat), 143 mg cholesterol, 1,144 mg sodium, 29 g carbohydrate, 3 g fiber, 35 g protein.

Saucy Skillet Lasagna

PREP/TOTAL TIME: 30 min.

Meghan Crihfield, Ripley, West Virginia

- 1 pound ground beef
- 1 can (14-1/2 ounces) diced tomatoes, undrained
- 2 eggs, lightly beaten
- 1-1/2 cups ricotta cheese
- 4 cups Italian baking sauce
- 1 package (9 ounces) no-cook lasagna noodles
- 1 cup (4 ounces) shredded part-skim mozzarella cheese, optional

1) In a large skillet, cook beef over medium heat until no longer pink; drain. Transfer to a large bowl; stir in tomatoes. In a small bowl, combine eggs and ricotta cheese.

2) Return 1 cup meat mixture to the skillet; spread evenly. Layer with 1 cup ricotta mixture, 1-1/2 cups baking sauce and half of the noodles. Repeat layers. Top with remaining sauce.

3) Bring to a boil. Reduce heat; cover and simmer for 15-17 minutes or until noodles are tender.

SAUCY SKILLET LASAGNA

Remove from the heat. Sprinkle with mozzarella cheese if desired; let stand for 2 minutes or until cheese is melted. Serve immediately.

Yield: 6-8 servings.

Editor's Note: This recipe was tested with Barilla Al Forno Italian Baking Sauce.

NUTRITION FACTS: 1 serving equals 430 calories, 18 g fat (8 g saturated fat), 108 mg cholesterol, 750 mg sodium, 41 g carbohydrate, 4 g fiber, 27 g protein.

Meatless Lasagna

PREP: 40 min. **BAKE:** 50 min. + standing

Sharon Allen, Allentown, Pennsylvania

- 1/2 cup chopped onion
- 2 garlic cloves, minced
- 2 cups diced zucchini
- 1-1/2 cups sliced fresh mushrooms
- 1 cup thinly sliced carrots
- 1/2 cup diced green pepper
- 1/2 cup diced sweet red pepper
- 1 can (28 ounces) crushed tomatoes
- 1-1/2 cups water
- 1 can (6 ounces) tomato paste
- 1 teaspoon sugar
- 1 teaspoon dried basil
- 1/2 teaspoon salt
- 1/2 teaspoon dried rosemary, crushed
- 1/4 teaspoon pepper
- 9 uncooked lasagna noodles
- 1 carton (15 ounces) reduced-fat ricotta cheese
- 1-1/2 cups (6 ounces) shredded part-skim mozzarella cheese, *divided*
- 1/4 cup grated Romano cheese

1) In a large saucepan coated with cooking spray, saute onion and garlic for 3 minutes. Add the zucchini, mushrooms, carrots and peppers; cook and stir until tender, about 5 minutes. Stir in the tomatoes, water, tomato paste and seasonings. Bring to a boil. Reduce heat; cover and simmer for 20 minutes. Meanwhile cook noodles according to package directions; drain. Set 2 cups of sauce aside.

2) Combine the ricotta, 1 cup mozzarella and Romano cheese. In an ungreased 13-in. x 9-in. x 2-in. baking dish, layer a third of the remaining sauce, three noodles and half of the cheese mixture. Repeat layers. Top with remaining sauce and noodles. Spread reserved sauce over the top.

3) Cover and bake at 350° for 45 minutes. Uncover; sprinkle with remaining mozzarella. Bake 5-10 minutes longer or until cheese is melted. Let stand for 15 minutes before cutting.

Yield: 8 servings.

NUTRITION FACTS: 1 piece equals 244 calories, 9 g fat (5 g saturated fat), 32 mg cholesterol, 672 mg sodium, 26 g carbohydrate, 4 g fiber, 17 g protein.

Lazy Lasagna

PREP/TOTAL TIME: 30 min.

Carol Mead, Los Alamos, New Mexico

- 1-1/2 cups uncooked wide egg noodles
- 1 cup spaghetti sauce
- 3/4 cup shredded part-skim mozzarella cheese
- 1/2 cup 4% cottage cheese
- 2 tablespoons grated Parmesan cheese

1) Cook noodles according to package directions; drain. Warm the spaghetti sauce; stir in mozzarella cheese and cottage cheese. Fold in noodles. Pour into two greased 2-cup baking dishes. Sprinkle with Parmesan cheese.

2) Bake, uncovered, at 375° for 20 minutes or until bubbly.

Yield: 2 servings.

NUTRITION FACTS: 1 serving equals 399 calories, 16 g fat (8 g saturated fat), 71 mg cholesterol, 1,117 mg sodium, 36 g carbohydrate, 3 g fiber, 26 g protein.

LAZY LASAGNA

SATISFYING MANICOTTI

 CLASSIC: Entertaining is a breeze with Three-Cheese Manicotti. Two big pans of manicotti shells are stuffed with ricotta, mozzarella and Parmesan, then baked in spaghetti sauce. So you can serve a crowd of hungry guests.

 TIME-SAVER: With just five ingredients and 15 minutes, you can have Sausage Manicotti in the oven. There's no need to cook the sausage or boil the noodles first, which really cuts the prep time. Plus, the uncooked noodles are easier to fill. While they bake, you can be preparing another part of the meal.

 LIGHT: You'd never guess that Spinach Manicotti has fewer calories, only a third of the fat and about a quarter of the cholesterol of Three-Cheese Manicotti. Nutritious spinach is a tasty addition to the rich filling that's made lighter with reduced-fat sour cream, fat-free ricotta and part-skim mozzarella. Salsa adds a little zip.

 SERVES 2: Onion, green pepper and a half pound of ground beef jazz up the tomato sauce for Stuffed Manicotti. Four shells are stuffed and then draped with the meat mixture to create an oven-baked meal for two.

Three-Cheese Manicotti

PREP: 35 min. **BAKE:** 45 min.

Vikki Rebholz, West Chester, Ohio

- 20 manicotti shells
- 2 cartons (15 ounces *each*) ricotta cheese
- 5 cups (20 ounces) shredded part-skim mozzarella cheese, divided
- 1 cup grated Parmesan cheese
- 2 eggs, beaten
- 2 teaspoons dried basil
- 2 teaspoons dried oregano
- 1 teaspoon onion powder
- 1 teaspoon garlic powder
- 1 teaspoon seasoned salt
- 2 jars (26 ounces *each*) spaghetti sauce

1) Cook shells according to package directions. Meanwhile, in a large bowl, combine the ricotta cheese, 3 cups mozzarella cheese, Parmesan cheese, eggs and seasonings. Drain shells.

2) Spread 1 cup of spaghetti sauce each into two ungreased 13-in. x 9-in. x 2-in. baking dishes. Stuff manicotti shells with cheese mixture; arrange over sauce. Top with remaining sauce.

3) Cover and bake at 375° for 40 minutes. Uncover; sprinkle with remaining cheese. Bake 5-10 minutes longer or until heated through and cheese is melted.

Yield: 10 servings.

NUTRITION FACTS: 2 stuffed shells equals 574 calories, 30 g fat (16 g saturated fat), 130 mg cholesterol, 1,365 mg sodium, 45 g carbohydrate, 4 g fiber, 33 g protein.

SAUSAGE MANICOTTI

Sausage Manicotti

PREP: 15 min. **BAKE:** 65 min.

Carolyn Henderson, Maple Plain, Minnesota

- 1 pound bulk pork sausage
- 2 cups (16 ounces) 4% cottage cheese
- 1 package (8 ounces) manicotti shells
- 1 jar (26 ounces) Italian baking sauce
- 1 cup (4 ounces) shredded part-skim mozzarella cheese

1) In a large bowl, combine uncooked sausage and cottage cheese. Stuff into uncooked manicotti shells. Place in a greased 13-in. x 9-in. x 2-in. baking dish. Top with baking sauce.

2) Cover and bake at 350° for 55-60 minutes or until a meat thermometer inserted into the center of a shell reads 160°.

3) Uncover; sprinkle with mozzarella cheese. Bake 8-10 minutes longer or until cheese is melted. Let stand for 5 minutes before serving.

Yield: 7 servings.

Editor's Note: This recipe was tested with Barilla Al Forno Italian Baking Sauce.

NUTRITION FACTS: 2 stuffed shells equals 489 calories, 24 g fat (10 g saturated fat), 59 mg cholesterol, 1,232 mg sodium, 41 g carbohydrate, 3 g fiber, 27 g protein.

SPINACH MANICOTTI

Spinach Manicotti

PREP: 20 min. **BAKE:** 70 min.

Mary Steiner, West Bend, Wisconsin

- 1 carton (15 ounces) fat-free ricotta cheese
- 2 cups (8 ounces) shredded part-skim mozzarella cheese, *divided*
- 1 package (10 ounces) frozen chopped spinach, thawed and squeezed dry
- 1/2 cup reduced-fat sour cream
- 1/4 cup dry bread crumbs
- 1 tablespoon Italian seasoning
- 1 teaspoon garlic powder
- 1 teaspoon onion powder
- 2 cups tomato juice
- 1 cup chunky salsa
- 1 can (15 ounces) crushed tomatoes
- 14 uncooked manicotti shells

1) In a large bowl, combine the ricotta, 1-1/2 cups mozzarella cheese, spinach, sour cream, bread crumbs, Italian seasoning, garlic powder and onion powder.

2) Combine the tomato juice, salsa and crushed tomatoes; spread 1 cup into an ungreased 13-in. x 9-in. x 2-in. baking dish. Stuff uncooked manicotti with spinach mixture; arrange over sauce. Pour remaining sauce over manicotti.

3) Cover and bake at 350° for 55 minutes. Uncover; sprinkle with remaining mozzarella cheese. Bake 15 minutes longer or until pasta is tender.

Yield: 7 servings.

NUTRITION FACTS: 2 stuffed shells equals 345 calories, 8 g fat (5 g saturated fat), 34 mg cholesterol, 782 mg sodium, 45 g carbohydrate, 4 g fiber, 22 g protein.

Stuffed Manicotti

PREP: 30 min. **BAKE:** 25 min.

Pam Goodlet, Washington Island, Wisconsin

- 4 manicotti shells
- 1/2 pound ground beef
- 1 small onion, finely chopped
- 1/2 medium green pepper, finely chopped
- 1 can (15 ounces) tomato sauce
- 1 to 1-1/2 teaspoons dried oregano
- 1 teaspoon dried thyme
- 1 cup (4 ounces) shredded part-skim mozzarella cheese, *divided*

1) Cook shells according to package directions. Meanwhile, in a large skillet, cook the beef, onion and green pepper over medium heat until meat is no longer pink; drain. Stir in the tomato sauce, oregano and thyme; bring to a boil. Reduce heat; simmer, uncovered, for 10 minutes. Add 1/2 cup cheese; stir until melted. Drain shells.

2) Stuff half of the meat mixture into manicotti shells; arrange in a greased 8-in. square baking dish. Spoon remaining meat mixture over shells.

3) Bake, uncovered, at 325° for 20 minutes. Sprinkle with remaining cheese; bake 5-10 minutes longer or until heated through and cheese is melted.

Yield: 2 servings.

NUTRITION FACTS: 2 stuffed shells equals 533 calories, 23 g fat (12 g saturated fat), 99 mg cholesterol, 1,264 mg sodium, 42 g carbohydrate, 5 g fiber, 40 g protein.

STUFFING PASTA SHELLS ■■■

A rubber-tipped baby spoon makes quick work of filling manicotti shells. The spoon fits nicely inside the noodle, and the filling mixture doesn't stick to its rubber coating.

—Toni B., Kenosha, Wisconsin

SAUSAGE ITALIAN STEW

Sausage Italian Stew

PREP: 10 min. **COOK:** 70 min.

Nancy Cox, Martinsville, Indiana

I spice up many autumn evenings with this zippy stew. This tastes even better the next day.

  2 pounds turkey Italian sausage links, casings removed

  1 cup chopped onion

3/4 cup chopped green pepper

  3 garlic cloves, minced

  1 can (28 ounces) diced tomatoes, undrained

  1 can (15 ounces) Italian-seasoned tomato sauce

1/2 pound fresh mushrooms, sliced

  1 cup water

1/2 cup beef broth

1/2 cup red wine *or* additional beef broth

1-1/2 cups uncooked spiral pasta

1/2 cup shredded part-skim mozzarella cheese

1) Crumble sausage into a large nonstick saucepan coated with cooking spray. Add the onion, green pepper and garlic. Cook over medium heat until meat is no longer pink; drain.

2) Add the tomatoes, tomato sauce, mushrooms, water, broth and wine or additional broth. Bring to a boil. Reduce heat; cover and simmer for 1 hour.

3) Meanwhile, cook pasta according to package directions; drain. Stir into stew; heat through. Top each serving with 1 tablespoon mozzarella cheese.

Yield: 8 servings.

NUTRITION FACTS: 1-1/2 cups equals 300 calories, 12 g fat (4 g saturated fat), 65 mg cholesterol, 1,237 mg sodium, 22 g carbohydrate, 3 g fiber, 25 g protein.

Tomato Pea Couscous

PREP/TOTAL TIME: 20 min.

Sondra Ostheimer, Boscobel, Wisconsin

I modified a recipe I found in a magazine, keeping good nutrition in mind. With a hint of cumin and other mellow flavors, this is a quick-to-fix side dish that's ideal with many entrees.

1/2 cup chopped onion

  2 garlic cloves, minced

  1 tablespoon olive oil

1/2 cup ground cumin

  1 cup reduced-sodium chicken broth *or* vegetable broth

  1 cup frozen peas

1/2 cup coarsely chopped seeded tomato

3/4 cup uncooked couscous

1) In a large saucepan, saute onion and garlic in oil until tender. Stir in cumin; cook and stir for 30 seconds. Stir in the broth, peas and tomato. Cook for 1-2 minutes or until peas are almost tender.

2) Stir in couscous; cover and remove from the heat. Let stand for 5 minutes. Fluff with a fork.

Yield: 4 servings.

NUTRITION FACTS: 3/4 cup equals 184 calories, 4 g fat (1 g saturated fat), 0 cholesterol, 182 mg sodium, 31 g carbohydrate, 3 g fiber, 6 g protein.

PARMESAN NOODLES

Parmesan Noodles
PREP/TOTAL TIME: 20 min.

Elizabeth Ewan, Cleveland, Ohio

The special blend of flavors in this quick dish makes it companionable to any meal. It's a nice change of pace from regular pasta-and-cheese dishes.

- 6 cups uncooked noodles
- 2 packages (3 ounces *each*) cream cheese, softened
- 1/2 cup butter, softened, *divided*
- 2 tablespoons minced fresh parsley
- 1 teaspoon dried basil
- 1/2 teaspoon lemon-pepper seasoning
- 2/3 cup boiling water
- 1 garlic clove, minced
- 2/3 cup grated Parmesan cheese, *divided*

Additional parsley, optional

1) Cook noodle according to package directions. Meanwhile, in a small bowl, combine the cream cheese, 2 tablespoons butter, parsley, basil and lemon-pepper. Stir in water; keep warm.

2) In a saucepan, saute garlic in remaining butter until golden. Drain noodles; place in a serving bowl. Top with garlic mixture. Sprinkle with 1/3 cup Parmesan cheese; toss lightly.

3) Spoon cream sauce over noodles and sprinkle with remaining Parmesan. Garnish with parsley if desired.

Yield: 8 servings.

NUTRITION FACTS: 1 serving equals 354 calories, 21 g fat (13 g saturated fat), 59 mg cholesterol, 333 mg sodium, 31 g carbohydrate, 2 g fiber, 10 g protein.

TASTY LEFTOVER PASTA ■■■

My mother used to add beaten eggs and Parmesan cheese to leftover pasta and sauce. She cooked it in a skillet or baked it in the oven. Either way, it was delicious.

—Marie F., Pompano Beach, Florida

Garlic Parmesan Orzo
PREP/TOTAL TIME: 15 min.

Stephanie Moon-Martin, Bremerton, Washington

The buttery pasta dish calls for orzo, which cooks quickly. This recipe makes a superb side dish anytime. The garlic and Parmesan cheese really stand out.

- 2 cups uncooked orzo pasta
- 3 teaspoons minced garlic
- 1/2 cup butter, cubed
- 1/2 cup grated Parmesan cheese
- 1/4 cup milk
- 2 tablespoons minced fresh parsley
- 1 teaspoon salt
- 1/4 teaspoon pepper

1) Cook orzo according to package directions. Meanwhile, in a large skillet, saute garlic in butter until tender. Drain orzo; add to skillet. Stir in the Parmesan cheese, milk, parsley, salt and pepper; heat through.

Yield: 8 servings.

NUTRITION FACTS: 1 cup equals 321 calories, 14 g fat (8 g saturated fat), 36 mg cholesterol, 513 mg sodium, 40 g carbohydrate, 2 g fiber, 9 g protein.

GARLIC PARMESAN ORZO

Homemade Noodles

PREP: 30 min. + standing **COOK:** 5 min.

Helen Heiland, Joliet, Illinois

It's hard to beat homemade noodles in soups or as a side dish with meat and gravy. You can freeze serving-size portions to use as you need them.

> 2 to 2-1/2 cups all-purpose flour, *divided*
> 1/2 teaspoon salt
> 3 eggs, lightly beaten
> 1 tablespoon cold water
> 1 tablespoon vegetable oil

1) Place 2 cups flour and salt on a pastry surface or in a deep mixing bowl. Make a well in center of the flour; add eggs and water. Gradually mix with hands or a wooden spoon until well blended.

2) Gather into a ball and knead on a floured surface until smooth, about 10 minutes. If necessary, add remaining flour to keep dough from sticking to surface or hands.

3) Divide the dough into thirds. On a lightly floured surface, roll each section into a paper-thin rectangle. Dust top of dough with flour to prevent sticking while rolling. Trim the edges and flour both sides of dough.

4) Roll up jelly-roll style. Using a sharp knife, cut into 1/4-in. slices. Unroll noodles; dry on paper towels for at least 1 hour before cooking.

5) To cook, bring salted water to a rapid boil. Add 1 tablespoon oil to the water; drop noodles into water and cook until tender but not soft.

Yield: 10 servings.

Editor's Note: Uncooked noodles may be frozen. Divide uncooked noodles into serving-size portions. Thaw before cooking as directed in recipe.

NUTRITION FACTS: 1/2 cup equals 125 calories, 3 g fat (1 g saturated fat), 64 mg cholesterol, 373 mg sodium, 19 g carbohydrate, 1 g fiber, 4 g protein.

Broccoli Noodle Side Dish

PREP/TOTAL TIME: 20 min.

Louise Saluti, Sandwich, Massachusetts

Colorful and satisfying, this side dish cooks up quickly on the stovetop and frees up the oven for the main course.

> 6 cups uncooked wide egg noodles
> 3 to 4 garlic cloves, minced
> 1/4 cup olive oil
> 4 cups fresh broccoli florets (about 1 pound)
> 1/2 pound fresh mushrooms, thinly sliced
> 1/2 teaspoon dried thyme
> 1 teaspoon salt, optional
> 1/4 teaspoon pepper

1) Cook noodles according to package directions. Meanwhile, in a large skillet, saute garlic in oil until tender. Add broccoli; saute for 4 minutes or until crisp-tender.

2) Add the mushrooms, thyme, salt if desired and pepper; saute for 2-3 minutes. Drain noodles; add to broccoli mixture. Stir gently over low heat until heated through.

Yield: 8 servings.

NUTRITION FACTS: 3/4 cup equals 188 calories, 8 g fat (1 g saturated fat), 24 mg cholesterol, 17 mg sodium, 24 g carbohydrate, 2 g fiber, 6 g protein.

Making Homemade Noodles

1) Place flour and salt in a mixing bowl or on a floured surface. Make a well in the center; add eggs and water.

2) Mix until well blended; gather mixture into a ball. Turn onto a floured surface. Knead for about 10 minutes. Divide into thirds.

3) Roll out each portion of dough into a paper-thin rectangle. Lightly dust both sides with flour; roll up jelly-roll style. Cut into 1/4-in. slices.

4) Unroll noodles on paper towels to dry for at least 1 hour. Proceed with recipe as directed.

GNOCCHI IN SAGE BUTTER

Gnocchi in Sage Butter

PREP: 70 min. **COOK:** 5 min.

Taste of Home Test Kitchen

A buttery garlic and sage sauce adds melt-in-your-mouth flavor to these homemade potato puffs.

> 1 pound russet potatoes, peeled and quartered
> 3 quarts water
> 2/3 cup all-purpose flour
> 1 egg
> 1/2 teaspoon salt

Dash ground nutmeg

> 2 tablespoons butter
> 2 garlic cloves, thinly sliced
> 4 fresh sage leaves, thinly sliced

1) Place potatoes in a saucepan and cover with water. Bring to a boil. Reduce heat; cover and simmer for 15-20 minutes or until tender. Drain.

2) Over warm burner or very low heat, stir potatoes for 1-2 minutes or until steam is evaporated. Press through a potato ricer or strainer into a small bowl; cool slightly. In a Dutch oven, bring water to a boil.

3) Using a fork, make a well in the potatoes. Sprinkle flour over potatoes and into well. Whisk the egg, salt and nutmeg; pour into well. Stir until blended. Knead 10-12 times, forming a soft dough.

4) Divide dough into four portions. On a floured surface, roll portions into 1/2-in.-thick ropes; cut into 3/4-in. pieces. Press and roll each piece with a lightly floured fork. Cook gnocchi in boiling water in batches for 30-60 seconds or until they float. Remove with a strainer and keep warm.

5) In a large heavy saucepan, cook butter over medium heat for 3 minutes. Add garlic and sage; cook for 2-4 minutes or until butter and garlic are golden brown. Add gnocchi; stir gently to coat. Serve immediately.

Yield: 4 servings.

NUTRITION FACTS: 2/3 cup equals 232 calories, 7 g fat (4 g saturated fat), 68 mg cholesterol, 373 mg sodium, 36 g carbohydrate, 2 g fiber, 6 g protein.

Lemon Noodle Kugel

PREP: 25 min. **BAKE:** 55 min. + standing

Romaine Smith, Garden Grove, Iowa

Comforting kugel is a traditional dessert at our family's Polish Christmas Eve supper.

> 5 cups uncooked egg noodles
> 2 tablespoons butter
> 4 eggs
> 2 cups (16 ounces) sour cream
> 2 cups (16 ounces) 4% cottage cheese
> 1 cup milk
> 3/4 cup plus 1-1/2 teaspoons sugar, *divided*
> 1-1/2 teaspoons lemon extract
> 1 teaspoon vanilla extract
> 1/2 teaspoon ground cinnamon

1) Cook noodles according to package directions; drain and return to the pan. Toss with butter. In a bowl, beat the eggs, sour cream, cottage cheese, milk, 3/4 cup sugar and extracts until well blended. Stir in noodles.

2) Transfer to a greased 13-in. x 9-in. x 2-in. baking dish. Combine cinnamon and remaining sugar; sprinkle over top. Bake, uncovered, at 350° for 55-60 minutes or until a thermometer reads 200°. Let stand for 10 minutes. Refrigerate leftovers.

Yield: 12 servings.

NUTRITION FACTS: 1 serving equals 321 calories, 15 g fat (9 g saturated fat), 133 mg cholesterol, 330 mg sodium, 30 g carbohydrate, 1 g fiber, 14 g protein.

Gnocchi Know-How

1) Rice the potatoes and sprinkle with flour. Make a well and pour in egg, salt and seasonings.

2) Roll the dough into four ropes and cut each rope into 3/4-in., thimble-sized dumplings.

3) Press each piece between your thumb and a floured fork to make grooves for catching butter or sauce.

GRAINS

Common grains, which include rice, barley, wild rice, oats and hominy grits, can be found in many classic recipes. Team grains with vegetables, beans, meat or fish for hearty, nutritious and budget-conscious side-dish or main-dish fare.

 Barley is a more flavorful and chewy alternative to white rice. You can find pearl barley and quick-cooking barley in most supermarkets. Some may also carry Scotch barley. Pearl barley has had the double outer hull and bran layer removed during processing. Quick-cooking barley is pearl barley that was precooked by steaming. Scotch barley has been milled less than pearl barley and retains some of the bran layer.

In health-food stores, you may be able to find barley flakes, grits and hulled barley. Flakes and grits can be used for breakfast as a cereal. Barley flakes have been rolled and flattened. Barley grits have been toasted and cracked. Hulled barley has the hull removed, so it still has the bran and the nutrients that the bran contains. Hulled barley takes about 1-3/4 hours to cook.

Store barley in an airtight container in a cool dry place. It may also be stored in the refrigerator or freezer.

 Buckwheat is the seed of a plant related to rhubarb. It is not a wheat. The black, triangular seeds are sold as groats, grits, kasha or buckwheat flour. Groats are the kernels with the inedible black shells removed. Grits are finely ground, unroasted groats that are used for cereal. Kasha are roasted groats that have been cracked into coarse, medium or fine grain. Kasha has a toasty, nutty flavor. Buckwheat flour is ground groats used for pancakes, breads, muffins and noodles. Since buckwheat flour is gluten-free, it is usually used in combination with all-purpose flour.

Once opened, store buckwheat in an airtight container in a cool dry place. In warm climates, store in the refrigerator or freezer. Always store buckwheat flour in the refrigerator.

 Bulgur is whole wheat that is processed similar to converted rice. The whole wheat kernels are cleaned, steam-cooked, dried and cracked or ground into pieces. Bulgur is ready to eat after soaking in water or broth for about 30 minutes.

Bulgur is available in coarse, medium and fine grains. The coarse grain is used for stuffing, casserole and pilaf; medium grain for breakfast cereal, bread, stew and soup; and fine grain for tabbouleh, breakfast cereal and bread. Once opened, store bulgur in an airtight container in a cool dry place for up to 1 month. In warm climates, store in the refrigerator or freezer.

 Cornmeal is dried corn that has been hulled and finely ground. Corn can be ground between two stones, labeled stone ground, or between steel rollers. Stone-ground cornmeal is usually a coarser grind and may have some of the hull and oil-containing germ. Therefore, stone-ground cornmeal has a shorter shelf life and should be stored in an airtight container in the refrigerator for up to 4 months. The steel-ground cornmeal should be used before the use-by date on the package.

White and yellow cornmeal is available in most supermarkets. Blue cornmeal can be found in specialty markets. White and yellow may be used interchangeably. Self-rising cornmeal has baking powder and salt mixed with the cornmeal and should not be used interchangeably with plain cornmeal.

Use cornmeal for corn bread or muffins, cornmeal mush, polenta or as a coating for fried foods.

 Grits is dried corn that has been hulled and coarsely ground. The difference between cornmeal and grits is how finely it is ground. Grits are available as grits, quick-cooking grits and instant grits. Regular grits take the longest to cook. Quick-cooking grits are passed through a roller and crushed into smaller pieces. Quick-cooking grits take about 5-7 minutes to simmer. Instant grits are precooked, then dried. Instant grits are rehydrated by adding boiling water to them.

Grits are generally used for breakfast and a side dish. Grits should be used before the use-by date on the package.

 Millet is generally known as bird food. It is available in health-food stores and some supermarkets. Pearl millet is hulled and sold as a whole kernel. The color can range from pale yellow to reddish orange. A half cup of millet can be simmered in 1-1/2 cups liquid for about 25 minutes.

 Oats are one of the most popular grains and are readily available in the supermarket. Oats are usually available as old-fashioned, quick-cooking, instant and oat bran. Old-fashioned oats are made from whole oat groats that still contain the bran, endosperm and germ portion and have been flattened by rolling.

Quick-cooking oats are old-fashioned oats that are cut into smaller pieces so they cook faster. Instant oats are precooked and dried and are cut even finer than the quick-cooking variety. Oat bran is the outer bran layer, which is high in fiber.

Old-fashioned and quick-cooking oats can be used interchangeably for cookies, breads, muffins, pancakes and extenders in ground meat products. Old-fashioned oats are large and will give the product a chewier texture and more whole grain appearance. Do not substitute instant oats for old-fashioned or quick-cooking oats.

Once opened, store oats in an airtight container in a cool dry place. In warm climates, store in the refrigerator or freezer. Use oats by the use-by date on the package.

 Quinoa (pronounced "KEEN-wah") is a seed from a plant related to spinach and chard. Quinoa is a more complete protein than most other grains. The flattened, oval grains of quinoa come in a variety of colors, the most common being white, pale gold, black and red. Look for quinoa in health-food stores or large supermarkets

Rinse quinoa under cold running water before cooking to remove any residue from its naturally bitter coating. For a roasted flavor, toast in a skillet before cooking. Quinoa is done when the grains are translucent and the germ spirals out to form a tail. Quinoa has a mild taste with a light fluffy texture. The "tail" is crunchy.

Store uncooked quinoa in an airtight container in a cool dry place. In warm climates, store in the refrigerator or freezer.

Pepper-Mushroom Barley Bake

PREP: 25 min. **BAKE:** 55 min.

Shirley Doyle, Mt. Prospect, Illinois

Forget the potatoes or rice, and consider this change-of-pace dinner accompaniment. I rely on wholesome barley for this heart-smart side dish.

> 3 medium sweet red *or* green peppers, chopped
> 4 cups sliced fresh mushrooms
> 2 medium onions, chopped
> 2 tablespoons butter
> 2 cups reduced-sodium chicken broth *or* vegetable broth
> 1-1/2 cups medium pearl barley
> 1/8 teaspoon pepper

1) In a large nonstick skillet, saute the peppers, mushrooms and onions in butter for 8-10

PEPPER-MUSHROOM BARLEY BAKE

minutes or until tender. Transfer to a 13-in. x 9-in. x 2-in. baking dish coated with cooking spray. Stir in the broth, barley and pepper.

2) Cover and bake at 350° for 50 minutes. Uncover; bake 5-10 minutes longer or until barley is tender and liquid is absorbed.

Yield: 10 servings.

NUTRITION FACTS: 3/4 cup equals 157 calories, 3 g fat (2 g saturated fat), 6 mg cholesterol, 153 mg sodium, 30 g carbohydrate, 6 g fiber, 5 g protein.

Vegetable Barley Saute

PREP/TOTAL TIME: 30 min.

Taste of Home Test Kitchen

This wonderful side dish can easily be turned into a hearty entree by adding cooked chicken.

> 1/2 cup quick-cooking barley
> 2 teaspoons cornstarch
> 1/3 cup water
> 3 tablespoons soy sauce
> 1 garlic clove, minced
> 1 tablespoon vegetable oil
> 2 carrots, thinly sliced
> 1 cup cut fresh green beans (2-inch pieces)
> 2 green onions, sliced
> 1/2 cup unsalted cashews, optional

1) Prepare barley according to package directions. In a small bowl, combine the cornstarch, water and soy sauce until smooth; set aside.

2) In a large skillet or wok, saute garlic in oil for 15 seconds. Add carrots and beans; stir-fry for 1 minute. Add onions; stir-fry for 2-3 minutes.

3) Stir cornstarch mixture and stir into the skillet. Bring to a boil; cook and stir for 1 minute or until thickened. Add barley; heat through. Stir in cashews if desired.

Yield: 4 servings.

NUTRITION FACTS: 2/3 cup equals 149 calories, 4 g fat (1 g saturated fat), 0 cholesterol, 707 mg sodium, 24 g carbohydrate, 6 g fiber, 5 g protein.

Bulgur Barbecue

PREP: 25 min. **BAKE:** 50 min.

Jackie Blankenship, Sherwood, Oregon

Use this recipe to stretch ground beef into saucy and satisfying sloppy joes for a crowd. Bulgur adds a healthy measure of fiber.

2-3/4 cups water, *divided*
  2/3 cup bulgur
1-1/2 pounds lean ground beef
1-1/2 cups chopped celery
    1 large onion, chopped
    1 can (8 ounces) tomato sauce
  1/2 cup packed brown sugar
  1/2 cup ketchup
    1 tablespoon white vinegar
  1/2 teaspoon prepared mustard
  1/4 teaspoon salt
  1/4 teaspoon pepper
   12 hamburger buns, split

1) In a saucepan, bring 2 cups water to a boil. Stir in bulgur. Reduce heat; cover and simmer for 15 minutes. Remove from the heat. Drain and squeeze dry; set aside.

2) In a large nonstick skillet, cook the beef, celery and onion over medium heat until meat is no longer pink; drain. Add the tomato sauce, brown sugar, ketchup, vinegar, mustard, salt, pepper and remaining water. Stir in reserved bulgur.

3) Transfer to a 2-qt. baking dish cooked with cooking spray. Cover and bake at 350° for 50-60 minutes or until heated through. Serve on buns.

Yield: 12 servings.

NUTRITION FACTS: 1 sandwich equals 289 calories, 7 g fat (2 g saturated fat), 21 mg cholesterol, 521 mg sodium, 41 g carbohydrate, 5 g fiber, 17 g protein.

Buying Bulgur

Look for bulgur in the cereal, rice or organic food aisle of your grocery store.

Great Grain Burgers

PREP: 45 min. + chilling **COOK:** 30 min.

Pat Whitaker, Alsea, Oregon

I've experimented with countless combinations of ingredients to make a good meatless burger...and this is our favorite. These patties cook up golden brown and crispy and make delicious sandwiches.

  1/2 cup uncooked brown rice
  1/2 cup uncooked bulgur
    1 tablespoon salt-free seasoning blend
  1/4 teaspoon poultry seasoning
    2 cups water

GREAT GRAIN BURGERS

    2 cups finely chopped fresh mushrooms
  3/4 cup old-fashioned oats
    1 cup (4 ounces) shredded part-skim mozzarella cheese
  1/4 cup shredded reduced-fat cheddar cheese
  1/3 cup finely chopped onion
  1/2 cup fat-free cottage cheese
  1/4 cup egg substitute
    2 tablespoons minced fresh parsley
    1 teaspoon salt
  1/2 teaspoon dried basil
  1/8 teaspoon celery seed
    3 teaspoons canola oil, *divided*
   12 sandwich rolls, optional

Lettuce leaves and tomato slices, optional

1) In a saucepan, combine the rice, bulgur, seasoning blend, poultry seasoning and water; bring to a boil. Reduce heat; cover and simmer for 30 minutes or until rice is tender. Remove from the heat; cool completely. Transfer to a bowl; cover and refrigerate until chilled.

2) In a large bowl, combine the mushrooms, oats, mozzarella cheese, cheddar cheese and onion. In a food processor, process cottage cheese and egg substitute until smooth; add to the mushroom mixture. Stir in the parsley, salt, basil, celery seed and chilled rice mixture. Shape 1/2 cupfuls into patties.

3) In a large nonstick skillet, cook four patties in 1 teaspoon oil for 5 minutes on each side or until lightly browned and crisp. Repeat with remaining patties and oil. Serve on rolls with lettuce and tomato if desired.

Yield: 12 servings.

NUTRITION FACTS: 1 patty equals 126 calories, 4 g fat (2 g saturated fat), 8 mg cholesterol, 286 mg sodium, 15 g carbohydrate, 2 g fiber, 7 g protein.

Buckwheat Brunch Crepes

PREP: 20 min. + standing **COOK:** 15 min.

Sharon Dyck, Roxton Falls, Quebec

Try these crepes with sweet berry sauce and cream on Saturday mornings or even at suppertime with sausage and eggs. They're especially tasty with a drizzle of maple syrup.

> 5 tablespoons heavy whipping cream
> 1/2 cup sour cream
> 1/2 cup milk
> 2 eggs
> 1/3 cup all-purpose flour
> 3 tablespoons buckwheat flour *or* whole wheat flour
> 1/2 teaspoon salt

BERRY SAUCE:

> 1/2 cup sugar
> 1 tablespoon cornstarch

Dash salt

> 1/2 cup water
> 1/3 cup fresh blueberries
> 1/3 cup fresh raspberries
> 4-1/2 teaspoons butter, *divided*
> 1 teaspoon lemon juice

1) In a small mixing bowl, beat whipping cream until stiff peaks form. Place sour cream in another bowl; fold in whipped cream. Cover and refrigerate until serving.

2) In a small mixing bowl, combine milk and eggs. Combine the flours and salt; add to milk mixture and mix well. Let stand for 30 minutes.

3) Meanwhile, in a small saucepan, combine the sugar, cornstarch and salt; stir in water until smooth. Bring to a boil; cook and stir for 1-2 minutes or until thickened.

4) Add berries; cook over medium-low heat until berries burst. Add 1-1/2 teaspoons butter and lemon juice, stirring until butter is melted. Set aside and keep warm.

5) Melt 1 teaspoon butter in an 8-in. nonstick skillet; pour 2 tablespoons batter into the center of the skillet. Lift and tilt pan to evenly coat bottom. Cook until the top appears dry; turn and cook 15-20 seconds longer. Remove to a wire rack. Repeat with the remaining batter, adding more butter to the skillet as needed.

6) Stack crepes with waxed paper or paper towels in between and keep warm. Serve crepes with berry sauce and cream mixture.

Yield: about 6 crepes.

NUTRITION FACTS: 1 serving equals 782 calories, 40 g fat (24 g saturated fat), 335 mg cholesterol, 965 mg sodium, 90 g carbohydrate, 4 g fiber, 15 g protein.

Toasted Almond Granola

PREP: 15 min. **BAKE:** 20 min. + chilling

Tracy Weakly, Aloha, Oregon

I combined several granola recipes to come up with this crunchy, cranberry-and-apricot-flavored treat. The possibilities are endless when you vary the kinds of fruits and nuts.

> 3 cups old-fashioned oats
> 2 cups crisp rice cereal
> 1/2 cup wheat germ, toasted
> 1/2 cup nonfat dry milk powder
> 1/3 cup slivered almonds
> 1/4 cup packed brown sugar
> 2 tablespoons sunflower kernels
> 1/4 teaspoon salt
> 1/2 cup orange juice
> 1/4 cup honey
> 2 teaspoons canola oil
> 2 teaspoons vanilla extract
> 1/2 teaspoon almond extract
> 1 cup golden raisins
> 1 cup chopped dried apricots
> 1/2 cup dried cranberries

Fat-free plain yogurt, optional

1) In a large bowl, combine first eight ingredients. In a saucepan, combine the orange juice, honey and oil. Heat for 3-4 minutes over medium heat until honey is dissolved. Remove from heat; stir in extracts. Pour over oat mixture; stir to coat.

2) Transfer to a greased 15-in. x 10-in. x 1-in. baking pan. Bake at 350° for 20-25 minutes or until crisp; stirring every 10 minutes.

3) Cool completely on a wire rack. Stir in dried fruits. Store in an airtight container. Serve over yogurt if desired.

Yield: 8 cups.

NUTRITION FACTS: 1/2 cup equals 212 calories, 4 g fat (trace saturated fat), 0 cholesterol, 88 mg sodium, 41 g carbohydrate, 3 g fiber, 6 g protein.

TOASTED ALMOND GRANOLA

Grits Casserole

PREP: 10 min. **BAKE:** 50 min.

Georgia Johnston, Auburndale, Florida

Grits are a traditional breakfast item in the South. Here, sausage and cheese turn it into a main dish.

1 pound bulk pork sausage
4 cups water
1 teaspoon salt
1 cup quick-cooking grits
4 eggs, lightly beaten
1-1/2 cups (6 ounces) shredded sharp cheddar cheese, *divided*
1/2 cup milk
1/4 cup butter, cubed

1) Crumble sausage into a skillet. Cook over medium heat until no longer pink; drain and set aside.

2) In a saucepan, bring water and salt to a boil. Slowly stir in grits. Reduce heat; cook for 4-5 minutes, stirring occasionally. Remove from the heat. Stir a small amount of hot grits into eggs; return all to the saucepan, stirring constantly. Add sausage, 1 cup cheese, milk and butter, stirring until the butter is melted.

3) Transfer to a greased 13-in. x 9-in. x 2-in. baking dish. Sprinkle with remaining cheese. Bake, uncovered, at 350° for 50-55 minutes or until the top begins to brown.

Yield: 10 servings.

NUTRITION FACTS: 1/2 cup equals 280 calories, 20 g fat (10 g saturated fat), 133 mg cholesterol, 602 mg sodium, 14 g carbohydrate, 1 g fiber, 11 g protein.

Basil Polenta with Beans 'n' Peppers

PREP: 35 min. + cooling **COOK:** 10 min.

Kimberly Hammond, Kingwood, Texas

Basil livens up polenta and beans in this colorful meatless supper. Add a salad to complete the nice, light meal.

3 cups water
1 teaspoon salt, *divided*
1 cup yellow cornmeal
1/2 cup chopped fresh basil
1 medium green pepper, cut into strips
1 medium sweet red pepper, cut into strips
1 medium onion, thinly sliced
3 garlic cloves, minced
1 tablespoon olive oil
1 can (15 ounces) black beans, rinsed and drained
1/4 teaspoon pepper

1) In a large saucepan, bring water to a boil; add 1/2 teaspoon salt. Gradually add cornmeal, stirring constantly. Reduce heat to low. Stir in basil. Cook and stir for 10 minutes or until thick and creamy. Transfer to a greased 8-in. square dish. Cool to room temperature, about 30 minutes.

2) In a large skillet, saute the peppers, onion and garlic in oil until tender. Stir in the beans, pepper and remaining salt; keep warm.

3) Cut polenta into four squares; place on an ungreased baking sheet. Broil 4 in. from the heat for 5 minutes. Turn and broil 5-6 minutes longer or until heated through. Top with vegetable mixture.

Yield: 4 servings.

NUTRITION FACTS: 1 polenta square with 1 cup vegetables equals 276 calories, 4 g fat (1 g saturated fat), 0 cholesterol, 795 mg sodium, 50 g carbohydrate, 9 g fiber, 9 g protein.

BAKED APPLE-RAISIN STUFFING

Baked Apple-Raisin Stuffing

PREP: 15 min. **BAKE:** 45 min.

Cindy Wirtanen, Hibbing, Minnesota

After sampling a friend's turkey dressing one Thanksgiving, I was inspired to add apples, raisins and sage to my own stuffing recipe.

1/4 cup chopped onion
1 celery rib, chopped
2 tablespoons butter
1/2 cup cubed peeled tart apple
1/4 cup golden raisins
1/2 teaspoon chicken bouillon granules
1/4 teaspoon salt
1/4 teaspoon rubbed sage
1/4 teaspoon poultry seasoning
Dash to 1/8 teaspoon pepper
1/3 to 1/2 cup chicken broth
2 cups cubed day-old bread, crusts removed

1) In a small skillet, saute onion and celery in butter until tender. Add the apple, raisins, bouillon, salt, sage, poultry seasoning and pepper. Cook and stir 1-2 minutes longer. Stir in broth. Place bread cubes in a bowl; add apple mixture. Pour over bread crumbs; toss to coat.

2) Transfer to a greased 1-qt. baking dish. Cover and bake at 350° for 25 minutes. Uncover; bake 20-25 minutes longer or until golden brown.

Yield: 2 servings.

NUTRITION FACTS: 1/2 cup equals 280 calories, 13 g fat (7 g saturated fat), 31 mg cholesterol, 984 mg sodium, 39 g carbohydrate, 3 g fiber, 4 g protein.

Oyster Sausage Stuffing
PREP: 35 min. **BAKE:** 40 min.

Page Alexander, Baldwin City, Kansas

I've had this wonderful recipe for many years and always use it during the holidays. It never fails to bring raves.

  1 envelope onion soup mix
  2 cups boiling water
1/2 cup butter, cubed
 10 cups cubed day-old bread, toasted
  1 can (8 ounces) whole oysters, drained
1/2 pound bulk pork sausage, cooked and drained
1/2 cup minced fresh parsley
3/4 teaspoon poultry seasoning

1) Place soup mix in a bowl; add boiling water and let stand for 5 minutes. In a Dutch oven, melt butter. Stir in bread cubes and soup mixture. Cover and cook over low heat for 5 minutes, stirring occasionally. Gently stir in the oysters, sausage, parsley and poultry seasoning.

2) Transfer to a greased 2-1/2-qt. baking dish. Cover and bake at 375° for 40-50 minutes or until heated through.

Yield: 9 cups (enough to stuff an 8- to 10-pound turkey).

NUTRITION FACTS: 3/4 cup equals 228 calories, 13 g fat (6 g saturated fat), 38 mg cholesterol, 590 mg sodium, 22 g carbohydrate, 1 g fiber, 6 g protein.

Sausage Pecan Stuffing
PREP: 35 min. **BAKE:** 70 min.

Keri Scofield Lawson, Fullerton, California

Sweet, savory, crunchy and spicy ingredients make this a fabulous turkey stuffing. Leftover stuffing could be a meal in itself!

  1 pound bulk pork sausage
  2 large onions, chopped
  2 packages (6 ounces *each*) herb stuffing mix
  1 package (15 ounces) golden raisins
  1 cup pecan halves
  6 celery ribs, diced

1/4 teaspoon *each* salt, garlic powder, caraway seeds, curry powder, dried basil, dried oregano, poultry seasoning and pepper
2-1/2 cups chicken broth

1) In a large skillet, cook sausage and onions over medium heat until meat is no longer pink; drain. Add herb packet from the stuffing mixes. Stir in the raisins, pecans, celery and seasonings; cook for 10 minutes. Add stuffing mixes and broth; mix well. Cook and stir for 5 minutes.

2) Transfer to a greased 3-qt. baking dish. Cover and bake at 325° for 1 hour. Uncover; bake 10 minutes longer or until heated through and lightly browned.

Yield: 12 cups (enough to stuff a 12- to 14-pound turkey).

NUTRITION FACTS: 3/4 cup equals 280 calories, 11 g fat (2 g saturated fat), 10 mg cholesterol, 703 mg sodium, 40 g carbohydrate, 3 g fiber, 7 g protein.

Corn Bread Dressing
PREP: 25 min. **BAKE:** 40 min.

Norma Poole, Auburndale, Florida

Nothing gets the family hanging around like the aroma of this savory dressing baking alongside the turkey.

2-1/2 cups chopped celery
1 1/4 cups chopped onions
 10 tablespoons butter
7-1/2 cups coarsely crumbled corn bread
2-1/2 cups soft bread crumbs
  4 teaspoons rubbed sage
  4 teaspoons poultry seasoning
  2 eggs, lightly beaten
1-1/3 cups chicken broth

1) In a large skillet, saute celery and onion in butter until tender; transfer to a large bowl. Add the corn bread, bread crumbs, sage and poultry seasoning. Combine egg and broth; add to corn bread mixture, stirring gently to mix.

2) Transfer to a greased 2-qt. baking dish. Cover and bake at 325° for 30 minutes. Uncover; bake 10 minutes longer or until a thermometer reads 165° and stuffing is lightly browned.

Yield: 9 cups (enough to stuff a 8- to 10-pound turkey.)

Editor's Note: If stuffing poultry, substitute 1/2 cup egg substitute for the eggs.

NUTRITION FACTS: 3/4 cup equals 277 calories, 12 g fat (6 g saturated fat), 61 mg cholesterol, 683 mg sodium, 35 g carbohydrate, 3 g fiber, 6 g protein.

QUINOA SQUASH PILAF

🌱 Quinoa Squash Pilaf

PREP: 30 min. **COOK:** 20 min.

Annette Spiegler, Arlington Heights, Illinois

Quinoa is a grain that is native to the Andes. High in calcium and protein, it supplies many nutrients and is a unique addition to this dish.

  1 cup quinoa, rinsed
  1 can (14-1/2 ounces) vegetable
     broth
1/4 cup water
  2 medium zucchini, halved
     lengthwise and sliced
  1 medium yellow summer squash,
     halved lengthwise and sliced
  1 cup chopped leeks (white portion
     only)
  2 garlic cloves, minced
  1 tablespoon olive oil
  1 large tomato, chopped
  1 tablespoon minced fresh cilantro
1/2 teaspoon salt
1/2 teaspoon dried oregano
1/2 teaspoon ground cumin
1/2 teaspoon chili powder
1/4 teaspoon pepper
1/8 teaspoon crushed red pepper
     flakes
  2 cups fresh baby spinach, chopped

1) In a large nonstick skillet coated with cooking spray, toast the quinoa over medium heat until lightly browned, stirring occasionally.

2) In a small saucepan, bring broth and water to a boil. Add the quinoa. Reduce the heat; simmer, uncovered, for 15 minutes or until liquid is absorbed. Set aside.

3) In a large nonstick skillet, saute the zucchini, yellow squash, leeks and garlic in oil until tender. Stir in the tomato, cilantro, seasonings and quinoa; heat through. Add spinach; cook and stir until spinach is wilted.

Yield: 8 servings.

NUTRITION FACTS: 3/4 cup equals 126 calories, 3 g fat (trace saturated fat), 0 cholesterol, 377 mg sodium, 21 g carbohydrate, 3 g fiber, 5 g protein.

Millet-Stuffed Red Peppers

PREP: 40 min. **BAKE:** 55 min.

Kitty Jones, Chicago, Illinois

This vibrant alternative to tuna-filled tomatoes and stuffed green peppers has a filling made with millet.

  1/2 cup uncooked millet, rinsed
       and drained
1-1/2 cups vegetable broth
    4 medium sweet red peppers
  3/4 cup frozen corn, thawed
    1 medium onion, finely chopped
  1/3 cup finely chopped celery
  1/4 cup chopped walnuts
    1 green onion, finely chopped
    1 tablespoon chopped fresh mint
       or 1 teaspoon dried mint flakes
    2 teaspoons shredded lemon peel
1-1/2 teaspoons fresh chopped oregano
       or 1/2 teaspoon dried oregano
    1 garlic clove, minced
  1/2 teaspoon salt
  1/4 teaspoon pepper
    2 tablespoons olive oil

1) In a saucepan, bring millet and broth to a boil. Reduce heat; simmer, covered, until millet is tender and broth is absorbed, about 30-35 minutes. Transfer to a large bowl and cool.

2) Meanwhile, cut tops off peppers and remove seeds. In a large kettle, cook peppers in boiling water for 3-5 minutes. Drain and rinse in cold water; set aside.

3) With a fork, fluff cooled millet. Add the corn, onion, celery, nuts, green onion and seasonings; blend well. Spoon into sweet peppers. Drizzle with oil.

4) Place in an 11-in. x 7-in. x 2-in. baking dish coated with cooking spray. Cover and bake at 350° for 55-60 minutes or until tender.

Yield: 4 servings.

Editor's Note: Look for millet in the grains or natural food aisle of your grocery store.

NUTRITION FACTS: 1 stuffed pepper equals 281 calories, 13 g fat (1 g saturated fat), 0 cholesterol, 684 mg sodium, 37 g carbohydrate, 6 g fiber, 8 g protein.

■ **Couscous-Stuffed Peppers:** Use 1-1/2 cups cooked couscous for the millet and vegetable broth. Proceed with recipe as directed.

Storing and Cooking Rice

You can store white and wild rice in an airtight container indefinitely. Brown rice can only be stored for up to 6 months at room temperature; refrigerate or freeze to extend its storage life.

Arborio rice is a medium grain rice used for making risottos. In risottos, this rice has a creamy texture with a chewy center.

Aromatic rice, also known as fragrant rice, is rice with natural ingredients that are responsible for their aroma and fragrant taste. Each type of aromatic rice has its own cooking characteristic. Basmati, Black Japonica, Jasmine and Texmati are types of aromatic rice. The fragrance of the type of rice can vary from one growing year to the next.

Always rinse wild rice before cooking to remove any debris. It is not necessary to rinse other grains. Wild rice may become tender without absorbing all the cooking liquid. If necessary, drain before serving or combining with other recipe ingredients.

For fluffier rice, remove the saucepan from the heat after the cooking time is complete and let stand for 5 to 10 minutes. Fluff with a fork and serve.

Cooking Rice and Grains

Follow these guidelines or use the chart below to cook grains to serve as a simple side dish or to use as an ingredient in a recipe. Allow 1/2 to 3/4 cup cooked rice or wild rice for each side-dish serving.

Bring water, 1/4 teaspoon salt if desired and 1 tablespoon butter if desired to a boil in a 2-qt. saucepan. Stir in grain; return to a boil. Cover and reduce heat to simmer. Cook for the specified time or until tender.

	RICE OR GRAIN	WATER	GRAIN AMOUNT	COOKING TIME (IN MINUTES)	YIELD
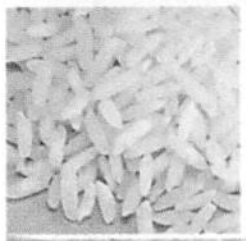	RICE, WHITE (LONG GRAIN)	2 cups	1 cup	12 to 15	3 cups
	RICE, WHITE (INSTANT)	1 cup	1 cup	5	2 cups
	RICE, WHITE (CONVERTED)	2-1/4 cups	1 cup	20	4 cups
	RICE, BROWN	2 cups	1 cup	35 to 45	3 cups
	RICE, WILD	3 cups	1 cup	45 to 60	3 cups
	BARLEY (QUICK-COOKING)	2 cups	1-1/4 cups	10 to 12	3 cups
	BARLEY (PEARL)	3 cups	3/4 cup	35 to 45	3 cups
	QUINOA	2 cups	1 cup	12 to 15	4 cups

VEGGIE BROWN RICE WRAPS

Broccoli Risotto
PREP: 10 min. **COOK:** 40 min.

George Morants, Cromwell, Connecticut

You want to add liquid to the risotto a little at a time, stirring constantly and make sure to cook just until it's creamy and the grains are tender.

> 1/4 cup olive oil, *divided*
> 1 garlic clove, thinly sliced
> 2 cups fresh broccoli florets
> 2-1/3 cups chicken broth, *divided*
> 1/4 cup chopped fresh parsley, *divided*

Salt and pepper to taste

> 1/2 small onion, chopped
> 3/4 cup uncooked long grain *or* Arborio rice
> 2/3 cup dry white wine *or* additional chicken broth
> 1 tablespoon lemon juice
> 2 tablespoons butter
> 1/4 cup grated Parmesan cheese, *divided*

1) In a skillet, heat 2 tablespoons oil. Saute garlic and broccoli until garlic is soft, about 3 minutes. Add 1/3 cup chicken broth, 3 tablespoons parsley, salt and pepper. Simmer, uncovered, just until the broccoli is tender, about 6 minutes. Keep warm.

2) In a small saucepan, heat remaining broth and keep warm. In a large saucepan, heat remaining oil. Cook onion until tender, about 3 minutes. Add rice; stir until coated. Add wine or additional broth; cook until liquid is absorbed, stirring constantly.

3) Stir 2/3 cup warm broth into rice mixture. Cook, uncovered, over medium-low heat until all of the liquid is absorbed, stirring constantly.

4) Add remaining broth, 1/3 cup at a time, stirring constantly. Allow the liquid to absorb between additions. Rice will be creamy and grains will be tender when done. (Total cooking time is about 25 minutes.)

5) Stir in the lemon juice, butter, 3 tablespoons Parmesan cheese and reserved broccoli mixture. Sprinkle with remaining Parmesan cheese and parsley. Serve immediately.

Yield: 4-6 servings.

NUTRITION FACTS: 1/2 cup (calculated without salt and pepper) equals 247 calories, 14 g fat (4 g saturated fat), 13 mg cholesterol, 473 mg sodium, 22 g carbohydrate, 1 g fiber, 5 g protein.

MORE FLAVORFUL RICE ■■■

For extra flavorful rice to serve as a bed for sweet-sour stir-fries or other entrees, I substitute pineapple juice for some of the water to cook the rice.

—Shirley S., Delphi, Indiana

Veggie Brown Rice Wraps
PREP/TOTAL TIME: 20 min.

Lisa Sullivan, St. Mary's, Ohio

Salsa gives a bit of zip to the brown rice and bean filling in these meatless tortilla wraps.

> 1 medium sweet red *or* green pepper, diced
> 1 cup sliced fresh mushrooms
> 2 garlic cloves, minced
> 1 tablespoon olive oil
> 2 cups cooked brown rice
> 1 can (16 ounces) kidney beans, rinsed and drained
> 1 cup frozen corn, thawed
> 1/4 cup chopped green onions
> 1/2 teaspoon ground cumin
> 1/2 teaspoon pepper
> 1/4 teaspoon salt
> 6 flour tortillas (8 inches), warmed
> 1/2 cup shredded reduced-fat cheddar cheese
> 3/4 cup salsa

1) In a large nonstick skillet, saute the red pepper, mushrooms and garlic in oil until tender. Add the rice, beans, corn, onions, pepper and salt. Cook and stir for 4-6 minutes or until heated through.

2) Spoon 3/4 cup onto each tortilla. Sprinkle with cheese; drizzle with salsa. Fold sides of tortilla over filling; serve immediately.

Yield: 6 servings.

NUTRITION FACTS: 1 wrap equals 371 calories, 8 g fat (2 g saturated fat), 7 mg cholesterol, 816 mg sodium, 63 g carbohydrate, 5 g fiber, 14 g protein.

Ham Fried Rice

PREP/TOTAL TIME: 25 min.

Grace Clark, Harlingen, Texas

My husband and I lived in Japan for a few years and came to love that country's ethnic foods. This dish captures the Oriental flavor better than any other recipes I've tried.

  4-1/2 teaspoons olive oil, *divided*
    2 eggs, lightly beaten
  1/4 cup chopped onion
  1/2 cup chopped celery
    2 cups cooked long grain rice
  1-1/2 cups cubed fully cooked ham
      (3/4-inch cubes)
  3/4 cup frozen peas
  3/4 cup frozen corn
    1 tablespoon soy sauce

1) In a large skillet or wok over medium-high heat, heat 2-1/4 teaspoons of oil. Pour eggs into skillet. As eggs set, lift edges, letting uncooked portion flow underneath. Remove eggs to a plate and keep warm.

2) In the same skillet, saute onion and celery in remaining oil until crisp-tender. Reduce heat. Add rice and ham; heat through. Stir in peas and corn; heat through.

3) Meanwhile, chop egg into small pieces; gently fold into rice mixture. Drizzle with soy sauce.

Yield: 5 servings.

NUTRITION FACTS: 3/4 cup equals 260 calories, 10 g fat (2 g saturated fat), 107 mg cholesterol, 784 mg sodium, 28 g carbohydrate, 2 g fiber, 14 g protein.

Confetti Rice

PREP/TOTAL TIME: 25 min.

Ruth Ann Stelfox, Raymond, Alberta

Bacon and rice make a tasty combination in this dish that gets color and crunch from peas.

    1 cup uncooked long grain rice
  1/2 pound sliced bacon, diced
    1 cup diced carrots
    1 cup diced celery
  1/2 cup fresh *or* frozen peas
Soy sauce, optional

1) Cook rice according to package directions. Meanwhile, in a large skillet, cook bacon over medium heat until crisp. Using a slotted spoon, remove to paper towels. Drain, reserving 3 tablespoon drippings.

2) In the drippings, saute carrots and celery until crisp-tender. Add the rice and peas; cook and stir until heated through. Stir in bacon. Serve with soy sauce if desired.

Yield: 8 servings.

NUTRITION FACTS: 2/3 cup equals 202 calories, 10 g fat (4 g saturated fat), 13 mg cholesterol, 198 mg sodium, 22 g carbohydrate, 1 g fiber, 5 g protein.

Vegetarian Jambalaya

PREP: 15 min. **BAKE:** 65 min.

Lynn Marie Frucci, La Center, Washington

This make-ahead meal has all the flavor and boldness of traditional jambalaya. If there's any left over, roll it up in a flour tortilla and add your favorite toppings.

    1 medium onion, finely chopped
    1 cup chopped celery
    1 cup chopped green pepper
    1 cup sliced fresh mushrooms
    2 garlic cloves, minced
    1 teaspoon olive oil
    3 cups chopped fresh tomatoes
    2 cups water
    1 cup uncooked long grain rice
    2 tablespoons reduced-sodium
      soy sauce
    1 tablespoon minced fresh parsley
  1/4 teaspoon salt
  1/4 teaspoon paprika
  1/8 teaspoon cayenne pepper
  1/8 teaspoon chili powder
  1/8 teaspoon pepper
    6 tablespoons reduced-fat
      sour cream

1) In a large nonstick skillet, saute the onion, celery, green pepper, mushrooms and garlic in oil until tender. Stir in the tomatoes, water, rice, soy sauce, parsley, salt, paprika, cayenne, chili powder and pepper.

2) Transfer to a 2-1/2-qt. baking dish coated with cooking spray. Cover and bake at 350° for 65-70 minutes or until rice is tender and liquid is absorbed. Top each serving with 1 tablespoon sour cream.

Yield: 6 servings.

NUTRITION FACTS: 1 cup equals 187 calories, 3 g fat (1 g saturated fat), 5 mg cholesterol, 339 mg sodium, 36 g carbohydrate, 3 g fiber, 5 g protein.

CONFETTI RICE

TEMPTING RICE PILAF

 CLASSIC: Round out an elegant company meal with Cranberry Rice Pilaf. Long grain rice is lightly browned in butter with celery and onion, then cooked with dried cranberries, fresh mushrooms and a little curry powder. A sprinkling of toasted pine nuts is the crunchy final touch.

 TIME-SAVER: Instant rice hurries along Almond Rice Pilaf, trimming the cooking time to just a few minutes. Although this side dish is quick and easy to make, sauteed onion and slivered almonds make it taste special.

 LIGHT: Rosemary and garlic lend fabulous flavor to Broccoli Brown Rice Pilaf, while almonds and sunflower kernels add crunch. This dish is made healthy with brown rice, reduced-sodium broth and the addition of chopped fresh broccoli.

 SERVES 2: Turn to the microwave to quickly get Tomato Rice Pilaf on a dinner table set for two. This versatile side dish gets lovely color from green onion, tomato and parsley.

Cranberry Rice Pilaf

PREP: 15 min. **COOK:** 25 min.

Carmel Patrone, Longport, New Jersey

- 3/4 cup chopped celery
- 1/2 cup chopped onion
- 2 tablespoons butter
- 1 tablespoon olive oil
- 1 cup uncooked long grain rice
- 2-1/2 cups chicken broth
- 1/2 cup chopped fresh mushrooms
- 1/2 cup dried cranberries
- 1/2 teaspoon garlic powder
- 1/2 teaspoon curry powder

Salt and pepper to taste

- 2 tablespoons minced fresh parsley
- 3 tablespoons pine nuts, toasted

1) In a large saucepan, saute celery and onion in butter and oil until tender. Add rice; cook and stir for 5 minutes or until lightly browned.

2) Add the broth, mushrooms, cranberries, garlic powder, curry powder, salt and pepper. Bring to a boil. Reduce heat; cover and simmer for 20 minutes or until liquid is absorbed and rice is tender.

3) Remove from the heat. Stir in parsley; sprinkle with pine nuts.

Yield: 4-5 servings.

NUTRITION FACTS: 3/4 cup (calculated without salt and pepper) equals 285 calories, 10 g fat (4 g saturated fat), 15 mg cholesterol, 541 mg sodium, 44 g carbohydrate, 2 g fiber, 5 g protein.

Almond Rice Pilaf

PREP/TOTAL TIME: 25 min.

Mary Jo Nikolaus, Mansfield, Ohio

- 3/4 cup chopped onion
- 1/2 cup slivered almonds
- 1 tablespoon butter
- 2 cups chicken broth
- 2 cups uncooked instant rice
- 1/2 cup frozen peas
- 1/2 teaspoon salt
- 1/4 teaspoon pepper

1) In a large skillet, saute onion and almonds in butter for 5-6 minutes or until onion is tender and almonds are golden brown.

2) Add broth. Bring to a boil. Stir in the rice, peas, salt and pepper. Cover and remove from the heat. Let stand for 6-8 minutes or until the liquid is absorbed.

Yield: 4 servings.

NUTRITION FACTS: 1 cup equals 316 calories, 10 g fat (2 g saturated fat), 8 mg cholesterol, 813 mg sodium, 48 g carbohydrate, 4 g fiber, 9 g protein.

Broccoli Brown Rice Pilaf

PREP: 5 min. **COOK:** 50 min.

Marie Condit, Brooklyn Center, Minnesota

- 1 cup uncooked brown rice
- 2-1/4 cups reduced-sodium chicken broth or vegetable broth
- 2 tablespoons minced fresh rosemary or 2 teaspoons dried rosemary, crushed
- 2 garlic cloves, minced
- 2 cups chopped fresh broccoli
- 1/4 cup slivered almonds
- 1/4 cup unsalted sunflower kernels
- 1/2 teaspoon salt
- 1/8 teaspoon pepper

1) In a large nonstick skillet coated with cooking spray, saute rice until lightly browned. Add the broth, rosemary and garlic; bring to a boil. Reduce heat; cover and simmer for 40 minutes or until rice is almost tender.

BROCCOLI BROWN RICE PILAF

2) Stir in the broccoli, almonds, sunflower kernels, salt and pepper. Cover and cook 3-5 minutes longer or until rice is tender and broccoli is crisp-tender. Fluff with a fork before serving.

Yield: 6 servings.

NUTRITION FACTS: 2/3 cup equals 202 calories, 6 g fat (1 g saturated fat), 0 cholesterol, 414 mg sodium, 31 g carbohydrate, 2 g fiber, 7 g protein.

Super Quick Pilaf

It's easy to add a bit of interest to plain rice. For each cup of uncooked jasmine, long grain white rice, brown rice or 1-1/2 cups instant rice, saute 1/2 cup each sliced celery and thinly sliced green onions in 1 tablespoon butter. Stir into cooked rice along with 1 to 1-1/2 teaspoons grated lemon peel. Season to taste with salt and pepper.

Tomato Rice Pilaf
PREP/TOTAL TIME: 25 min.
Carole Fraser, North York, Ontario

    2 teaspoons butter
  1/2 cup uncooked long grain rice
    1 small onion, sliced
1-1/4 cups chicken broth
    2 tablespoons chopped green onion
    2 tablespoons chopped tomato
    2 tablespoons minced fresh parsley

1) In a 3-cup microwave-safe dish, melt butter. Stir in the rice and onion. Microwave, uncovered, on high for 2-3 minutes or until rice is lightly browned and onion is tender, stirring once.

2) Add broth. Cover and cook on high for 13-15 minutes or until liquid is absorbed. Stir in the green onion, tomato and parsley.

Yield: 2 servings.

NUTRITION FACTS: 3/4 cup equals 216 calories, 2 g fat (1 g saturated fat), 7 mg cholesterol, 418 mg sodium, 42 g carbohydrate, 2 g fiber, 6 g protein.

TOMATO RICE PILAF

Cranberry Rice with Caramelized Onions

PREP: 5 min. **COOK:** 55 min.

Tommi Roylance, Charlo, Montana

Rice provides so many options to a creative cook—the stir-in ideas are endless. In this recipe, dried cranberries star.

- 2-1/2 cups chicken broth
- 1/2 cup uncooked wild rice
- 1/2 cup uncooked brown rice
- 3 medium onions, cut into wedges
- 2 teaspoons brown sugar
- 3 tablespoons butter
- 1 cup dried cranberries
- 1/2 teaspoon grated orange peel

1) In a large saucepan, bring broth to a boil. Add wild rice. Reduce heat. Cover; simmer for 10 minutes. Add brown rice. Cover; simmer for 45-50 minutes or until rice is tender and liquid is absorbed.

2) In a large skillet over medium heat, cook the onions and brown sugar in butter until golden, stirring frequently. Add cranberries, orange peel and rice; heat through.

Yield: 4 servings.

NUTRITION FACTS: 1 cup equals 400 calories, 10 g fat (5 g saturated fat), 23 mg cholesterol, 674 mg sodium, 74 g carbohydrate, 6 g fiber, 8 g protein.

RICE RENEWAL ■■■

Here's a tasty way to use up leftover cooked rice. In a skillet, brown some bulk sausage before stirring in the leftover rice. Then scramble a few eggs into the mixture and stir in chopped green onions. To serve, spoon onto warmed flour tortillas and top with shredded cheese. This is a favorite dish for my gang when we go camping.

—Kay Myers, Lawton, Oklahoma

CRANBERRY RICE WITH CARAMELIZED ONIONS

SPANISH RICE

Spanish Rice

PREP/TOTAL TIME: 30 min.

Sharon Donat, Kalispell, Montana

This rice recipe has been in our family for years. It's handy when you're in a hurry for a side dish to complement almost any main dish, not just Tex-Mex fare.

- 1 can (14-1/2 ounces) vegetable broth
- 1 can (14-1/2 ounces) stewed tomatoes
- 1 cup uncooked long grain rice
- 1 teaspoon olive oil
- 1 teaspoon chili powder
- 1/4 teaspoon dried oregano
- 1/4 teaspoon garlic salt

1) In a large saucepan, combine all ingredients. Bring to a boil. Reduce heat; cover and simmer for 20-25 minutes or until rice is tender and liquid is absorbed.

Yield: 6 servings.

NUTRITION FACTS: 2/3 cup equals 156 calories, 1 g fat (trace saturated fat), 0 cholesterol, 350 mg sodium, 32 g carbohydrate, 1 g fiber, 4 g protein.

VEGGIE RICE SKILLET ■■■

My wife and I enjoy medleys of steamed vegetables, such as onion, peppers, zucchini, squash and broccoli, but we frequently have leftovers. I combine them with some cooked rice and a can of diced tomatoes. Warmed in a skillet and sprinkled with grated cheese, this makes a scrumptious entree or side dish.

—Paul Toy, Little River, South Carolina

BEANS

Beans are a member of the legume family and add a tasty source of protein and fiber to the diet. With today's quicker preparation methods for dried beans and a variety of canned bean products, it's easy to make delicious bean recipes.

Soaking Methods for Dried Beans

Most dried beans need to be soaked before cooking. Select a soaking method (below) to fit your schedule. Before soaking, sort through dried beans to remove pebbles, grit or broken beans. Rinse beans with cold water in a colander.

Soaking softens and returns moisture to the beans, which helps reduce the cooking time. Soaking also helps eliminate some of the sugar molecules or oligosaccharides, which are responsible for the gas-causing effect that beans can have. The longer the beans soak, the more of the oligosaccharides are released into the water. The released sugars are discarded with the water after soaking.

Soak different kinds of beans separately. Some take longer to soak than others. Black beans can affect the color of other beans. To see if the beans have soaked long enough, slice one in half. If the center is opaque, you need to soak them longer. If you have old beans or hard water or live at a higher altitude, you may need to increase the soaking and cooking times.

Always use a large pot and plenty of water. Dried beans rehydrate to two to three times their size. After soaking, discard the soaking water (unless recipe directs otherwise); drain and rinse beans.

Quick Hot Soak

Sort and rinse beans. Place in a Dutch oven or kettle; add enough water to cover beans by 2 in. Bring to a boil; boil for 2 minutes. Remove from the heat; cover and let stand for 1 to 4 hours. Drain and rinse beans; discard liquid unless recipe directs otherwise. Proceed with recipe.

Overnight Soak

Sort and rinse beans. Place in a Dutch oven or kettle; for every cup of beans, add 3 cups of cold water. Cover and soak at room temperature for 8 hours or overnight. Drain and rinse beans; discard liquid unless recipe directs otherwise. Proceed with recipe.

Cooking Soaked Dried Beans

After soaking, beans are simmered in fresh water for about 2 hours or until tender. The time will vary, depending on the variety and size of the bean, the hardness of the water, altitude and the freshness of dried beans.

Follow recipe or package directions for the amount of water to add to beans. To reduce foaming during cooking, add 1 tablespoon oil or butter to the pot.

Salt or acidic ingredients (like tomatoes, lemon juice, mustard, molasses, wine and vinegar) inhibit the absorption of liquid and stop the softening process. So these ingredients should not be added to the beans until they are tender.

To test beans for doneness, remove a bean from the pot and place it on a cutting board. Mash the bean with the back of a spoon. If the bean mashes easily and is soft in the center, it is thoroughly cooked. Or bite into the bean to see if it is tender but not mushy.

Storing Dried Beans

Store uncooked dried beans tightly covered in a cool dry place. It is best to use dried beans within 12 months; the older the bean, the longer it takes to cook. Store cooked beans, covered, in the refrigerator for up to 5 days or freeze for up to 6 months.

- One pound packaged dried beans (uncooked) equals 2 cups dried or about 6 cups cooked and drained.
- One cup packaged dried beans (uncooked) equals about two 15-1/2-ounce cans of drained beans.
- One cup dried split peas equals about 2 cups cooked.
- One 15-1/2-ounce can of beans equals about 1-2/3 cups drained beans.
- Allow about 1/2 cup cooked beans per serving

Canned Beans

Rinse and drain canned beans before using. You will not only reduce the sodium content of the beans but also eliminate some of the gas-producing sugars.

Cooking Times for Beans

TYPE OF DRIED BEAN OR LEGUME	COOKING TIME
 BLACK BEANS	1 to 1-1/2 hours
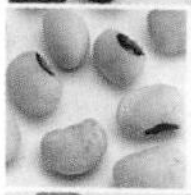 BLACK-EYED PEAS	30 min. to 1 hour
 CRANBERRY BEANS	45 min. to 1 hour
 GARBANZO BEANS	1 to 1-1/2 hours
 GREAT NORTHERN BEANS	45 min. to 1 hour
 KIDNEY BEANS	1-1/2 to 2 hours
 LENTILS, BROWN OR GREEN	20 to 30 minutes
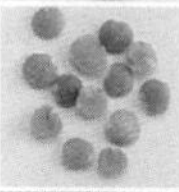 LENTILS, RED	15 minutes
 LIMA BEANS, BABY	1 hour
 LIMA BEANS, LARGE	1 to 1-1/2 hours
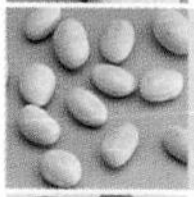 NAVY BEANS	1-1/2 to 2 hours
 PINK BEANS	1 hour
 PINTO BEANS	1-1/2 to 2 hours
 RED BEANS, SMALL	1 to 1-1/2 hours
 SPLIT PEAS	20 to 30 minutes

Three-Bean Barley Salad

PREP/TOTAL TIME: 30 min.

Pat Miller, North Fork, California

Three kinds of beans—kidney, black and garbanzo—are deliciously combined in this salad.

 2 cups water
 1 tablespoon chicken bouillon granules
 1 cup quick-cooking barley
 1 can (16 ounces) kidney beans, rinsed and drained
 1 can (15 ounces) black beans, rinsed and drained
 1 can (15 ounces) garbanzo beans *or* chickpeas, rinsed and drained
 4 green onions, thinly sliced
 1 cup honey Dijon salad dressing

1) In a saucepan, bring water and bouillon to a boil. Stir in barley. Reduce heat; cover and simmer for 11-13 minutes or until barley is tender and liquid is absorbed. Cool for 10 minutes.

2) Transfer barley to a serving bowl. Add the beans and onions. Pour dressing over top; gently stir to coat. Cover and refrigerate until serving.

Yield: 12 servings.

NUTRITION FACTS: 1/2 cup equals 224 calories, 8 g fat (1 g saturated fat), trace cholesterol, 526 mg sodium, 32 g carbohydrate, 7 g fiber, 7 g protein.

Tuscan Bean Salad

PREP: 15 min. + soaking **COOK:** 1 hour + chilling

Dixie Cannafax, Oroville, California

This marinated bean salad is a favorite of mine that is especially good alongside a pork entree.

 1 cup dried navy beans
 4 cups cold water
 1/2 cup diced red onion
 1/2 cup thinly sliced celery
 1/4 cup chopped fresh parsley
 3 tablespoons chicken broth
 2 tablespoons balsamic vinegar
 1 tablespoon olive oil
 1 teaspoon Dijon mustard
 1/2 teaspoon minced garlic
 1 teaspoon salt
 1/4 teaspoon ground oregano
 1/4 teaspoon ground thyme

1) Place beans in Dutch oven or kettle; add water to cover by 2 in. Bring to a boil; boil for 2 minutes. Remove from the heat; cover and let stand for 1-4 hours or until beans are softened.

2) Drain and rinse beans, discarding liquid. Return beans to the pan. Add cold water. Bring to a boil. Reduce the heat; cover and simmer for 50-60 minutes or until beans are tender.

3) Drain beans; place in a bowl. Add the onion, celery and parsley. In a jar with a tight-fitting lid, combine the remaining ingredients; shake well. Pour over bean mixture and stir to coat. Cover and refrigerate for at least 2 hours.

Yield: 4 servings.

NUTRITION FACTS: 3/4 cup equals 224 calories, 4 g fat (1 g saturated fat), 0 cholesterol, 682 mg sodium, 36 g carbohydrate, 14 g fiber, 12 g protein.

Meatless Hopping John
PREP/TOTAL TIME: 30 min.

Ann Buckendahl, Benton, Kansas

I traditionally make this black-eyed pea dish for New Year's celebrations. My version has more seasonings and veggies than other recipes for the classic Southern dish.

- 3/4 cup uncooked long grain rice
- 1 cup frozen corn
- 3 medium carrots, thinly sliced
- 1/2 cup *each* chopped green, sweet red and yellow pepper
- 1/4 cup chopped onion
- 4 garlic cloves, minced
- 1 tablespoon canola oil
- 1 can (15-1/2 ounces) black-eyed peas, rinsed and drained
- 1 can (14-1/2 ounces) diced tomatoes, drained
- 2 tablespoons minced fresh parsley
- 1 teaspoon dried thyme
- 1/2 teaspoon salt
- 1/4 teaspoon pepper
- 1/4 teaspoon crushed red pepper flakes

1) Cook rice according to package directions. Meanwhile, in a large nonstick skillet, saute the corn, carrots, peppers, onion and garlic in oil for 6-8 minutes or until crisp-tender.

2) Stir in the rice, peas and tomatoes; bring to a boil. Reduce heat; cover and simmer for 5 minutes or until heated through, stirring occasionally. Add the seasonings; cook 2-3 minutes longer.

Yield: 10 servings.

NUTRITION FACTS: 3/4 cup equals 149 calories, 2 g fat (trace saturated fat), 0 cholesterol, 313 mg sodium, 29 g carbohydrate, 4 g fiber, 5 g protein.

Black Bean Tortilla Casserole
PREP: 20 min. **BAKE:** 30 min.

Sue Briski, Appleton, Wisconsin

A cousin gave me this recipe because she knows my family loves Southwestern fare. This is a delicious meatless meal that we really enjoy!

- 2 large onions, chopped
- 1-1/2 cups chopped green peppers
- 1 can (14-1/2 ounces) diced tomatoes, drained
- 3/4 cup picante sauce

BLACK BEAN TORTILLA CASSEROLE

- 2 garlic cloves, minced
- 2 teaspoons ground cumin
- 2 cans (15 ounces *each*) black beans, rinsed and drained
- 8 corn tortillas (6 inches)
- 2 cups (8 ounces) shredded reduced-fat Mexican cheese blend

TOPPINGS:
- 1-1/2 cups shredded lettuce
- 1 cup chopped fresh tomatoes
- 1/2 cup thinly sliced green onions
- 1/2 cup sliced ripe olives

1) In a large saucepan, combine the onions, peppers, tomatoes, picante sauce, garlic and cumin. Bring to a boil. Reduce heat; simmer, uncovered, for 10 minutes. Stir in the beans.

2) Spread a third of the mixture into a 13-in. x 9-in. x 2-in. baking dish coated with cooking spray. Layer with four tortillas and 2/3 cup cheese. Repeat layers; top with remaining beans.

3) Cover and bake at 350° for 30-35 minutes or until heated through. Sprinkle with remaining cheese. Let stand for 5 minutes or until cheese is melted. Serve with toppings.

Yield: 9 servings.

NUTRITION FACTS: 1 serving equals 251 calories, 7 g fat (3 g saturated fat), 18 mg cholesterol, 609 mg sodium, 36 g carbohydrate, 8 g fiber, 14 g protein.

Pinto Bean Stew

PREP: 15 min. + soaking **COOK:** 1-1/2 hours

Gina Passantino, Amherst, New York

This thick, hearty stew is chock-full of beans and vegetables and makes a wonderful supper on cold winter days. It also freezes well.

- 1 cup dried pinto beans
- 2 cups cold water
- 1/2 cup chopped carrot
- 2 garlic cloves, minced
- 3/4 teaspoon chili powder
- 1/2 teaspoon salt

Dash cayenne pepper

- 1 package (16 ounces) frozen corn, thawed
- 1 large onion, chopped
- 1 medium green pepper, chopped
- 1 can (14-1/2 ounces) diced tomatoes, undrained
- 2 to 3 teaspoons balsamic vinegar
- 1/4 teaspoon sugar

1) Place the beans in a large saucepan; add water to cover by 2 in. Bring to a boil; boil for 2 minutes. Remove from the heat; cover and let stand for 1-4 hours or until beans are softened.

2) Drain and rinse beans, discarding liquid. Return beans to the pan; add cold water, carrot, garlic, chili powder, salt and cayenne. Bring to a boil. Reduce heat; cover and simmer for 45 minutes or until beans are almost tender.

3) In a nonstick skillet coated with cooking spray, saute the corn, onion and green pepper until

tender. Add to the bean mixture. Cover and cook for 45 minutes.

4) Stir in the tomatoes, vinegar and sugar. Cook 5 minutes longer or until heated through.

Yield: 6 servings.

NUTRITION FACTS: 1 cup equals 214 calories, 1 g fat (trace saturated fat), 0 cholesterol, 309 mg sodium, 45 g carbohydrate, 10 g fiber, 10 g protein.

Spicy Hummus

PREP/TOTAL TIME: 10 min.

Taste of Home Test Kitchen

Hummus is a Middle Eastern spread made from seasoned mashed chickpeas. Served with pita wedges, this is a simple and satisfying snack.

- 1/4 cup packed fresh parsley sprigs
- 2 tablespoons chopped onion
- 1 garlic clove, peeled
- 1 can (15 ounces) chickpeas *or* garbanzo beans, rinsed and drained
- 2 tablespoons sesame seeds, ground
- 2 tablespoons cider vinegar
- 2 teaspoons soy sauce
- 2 teaspoons lime juice
- 1 teaspoon honey
- 1 teaspoon Dijon mustard
- 1/4 teaspoon salt
- 1/4 teaspoon *each* ground cumin, ginger, coriander and paprika

Pita bread, cut into wedges

1) In a food processor, combine the parsley, onion and garlic; cover and process until smooth.

2) Add the chickpeas, sesame seeds, vinegar, soy sauce, lime juice, honey, mustard and seasonings; cover and process until smooth. Serve with pita bread.

Yield: 1-1/2 cups.

NUTRITION FACTS: 1/4 cup (calculated without pita bread) equals 89 calories, 3 g fat (trace saturated fat), 0 cholesterol, 316 mg sodium, 14 g carbohydrate, 3 g fiber, 4 g protein.

Hearty Red Beans and Rice

PREP: 15 min. + soaking **COOK:** 2 hours

Kathy Jacques, Chesterfield, Michigan

If you want to get the beans started ahead of time, cover them with water and let soak overnight. Drain beans and continue with the recipe as directed.

- 1 pound dried kidney beans
- 2 teaspoons garlic salt
- 1 teaspoon Worcestershire sauce
- 1/4 teaspoon hot pepper sauce
- 1 quart cold water
- 1/2 pound fully cooked ham, diced

PINTO BEAN STEW

HEARTY RED BEANS AND RICE

1/2 pound fully cooked smoked
    sausage, diced
1 cup chopped onion
1/2 cup chopped celery
3 garlic cloves, minced
1 can (8 ounces) tomato sauce
2 bay leaves
1/4 cup minced fresh parsley
1/2 teaspoon salt
1/2 teaspoon pepper
Hot cooked rice
Additional parsley, optional

1) Place beans in a Dutch oven or kettle; add water to cover by 2 in. Bring to a boil; boil for 2 minutes. Remove from the heat; cover and let stand for 1-4 hours or until beans are softened.

2) Drain and rinse beans, discarding liquid. Return to pan. Add garlic salt, Worcestershire sauce, hot pepper sauce and cold water; bring to a boil. Reduce heat; cover and simmer for 1-1/2 hours.

3) Meanwhile, in a large skillet, saute ham and sausage until lightly browned. Remove with a slotted spoon to bean mixture. Saute the onion, celery and garlic in drippings until tender; add to the bean mixture. Stir in tomato sauce and bay leaves. Cover and simmer for 30 minutes or until beans are tender.

4) Discard bay leaves. Measure 2 cups of beans; mash and return to the remaining bean mixture. Stir in the parsley, salt and pepper. Serve with rice. Garnish with parsley if desired.

Yield: 10 servings.

NUTRITION FACTS: 1 cup (calculated without rice) equals 276 calories, 9 g fat (3 g saturated fat), 27 mg cholesterol, 1,149 mg sodium, 32 g carbohydrate, 8 g fiber, 18 g protein.

Pinto Bean Chili
PREP: 20 min. + soaking **COOK:** 1-3/4 hours

Sandy Dilatush, Denver, Colorado

Cumin and chili powder season this Southwestern chili. Quesadillas on the side make it a meal.

1 pound dried pinto beans
2 pounds ground beef
1 medium onion, chopped
3 celery ribs, chopped
3 tablespoons all-purpose flour
4 cups cold water
2 tablespoons chili powder
2 tablespoons ground cumin
1/2 teaspoon sugar
1 can (28 ounces) crushed tomatoes
2 teaspoons cider vinegar
1-1/2 teaspoons salt

CHILI CHEESE QUESADILLAS:
2 cans (4 ounces *each*) chopped green chilies
12 flour tortillas (6 inches)
3 cups (12 ounces) shredded cheddar cheese
3 teaspoons vegetable oil, *divided*

1) Place beans in a Dutch oven or kettle; add water to cover by 2 in. Bring to a boil; boil for 2 minutes. Remove from the heat; cover and let stand for 1-4 hours or until beans are softened. Drain and rinse beans, discarding liquid. Set beans aside.

2) In a Dutch oven, cook the beef, onion and celery over medium heat until meat is no longer pink; drain. Stir in flour until blended. Gradually stir in cold water.

3) Add the beans, chili powder, cumin and sugar. Bring to a boil. Reduce heat; cover and simmer for 1-1/2 hours or until beans are tender. Stir in the tomatoes, vinegar and salt; heat through, stirring occasionally.

4) Meanwhile, for quesadillas, spread about 1 tablespoon of chilies on half of each tortilla. Sprinkle with 1/4 cup of cheese; fold in half.

5) In a large skillet, cook tortillas in 1 teaspoon oil over medium heat until lightly browned on each side, adding more oil as needed. Cut each quesadilla in half. Serve with chili.

Yield: 8 servings.

NUTRITION FACTS: 1-1/2 cups chili with 3 quesadilla wedges equals 787 calories, 34 g fat (15 g saturated fat), 120 mg cholesterol, 1,373 mg sodium, 72 g carbohydrate, 18 g fiber, 51 g protein.

SAUCY BAKED BEANS

 CLASSIC: The recipe for Old-Fashioned Baked Beans calls for soaking dried great northern beans for several hours, cooking them until tender, then baking them with brown sugar, molasses and bacon. The result is sweet, smoky and simply delicious.

 TIME-SAVER: Skip soaking and simmering dried beans—and save a few hours—with Like-Homemade Baked Beans. A can of pork and beans gets from-scratch flavor when quickly cooked on the stovetop with a handful of everyday ingredients.

 LIGHT: Maple Baked Beans have less than half the calories and fat of Old-Fashioned Baked Beans. These reductions are accomplished by adding less bacon and using sugar-free pancake syrup instead of brown sugar.

 SERVES 2: Starting with a small can of pork and beans keeps the yield of Hearty Baked Beans just right for two people. Kidney beans, bacon, brown sugar and ground mustard provide down-home flavor.

Old-Fashioned Baked Beans

PREP: 1-1/2 hours + soaking BAKE: 45 min.

Marjorie Thompson
West Sacramento, California

- 1 **pound dried great northern beans**
- 1 **quart cold water**
- 1/2 **teaspoon salt**
- 1 **medium onion, chopped**
- 2 **tablespoons prepared mustard**
- 2 **tablespoons brown sugar**
- 2 **tablespoons dark molasses**
- 1/2 **pound sliced bacon, cooked and crumbled**

1) Place beans in a Dutch oven or kettle; add water to cover by 2 in. Bring to a boil; boil for 2 minutes. Remove from the heat; cover and let stand for 1-4 hours or until beans are softened.

2) Drain and rinse beans, discarding liquid. Return beans to the pan. Add cold water and salt; bring to a boil. Reduce heat; cover and simmer for 1 to 1-1/4 hours or until beans are tender. Drain, reserving 2 cups cooking liquid.

3) In a greased 13-in. x 9-in. x 2-in. baking dish, combine the beans, onion, mustard, brown sugar, molasses, bacon and 1 cup of reserved cooking liquid.

4) Cover and bake at 400° for 45 minutes or until the beans have reached desired thickness, stirring occasionally (add additional reserved cooking liquid if needed).

Yield: 8 servings.

NUTRITION FACTS: 1/2 cup equals 283 calories, 5 g fat (2 g saturated fat), 8 mg cholesterol, 351 mg sodium, 44 g carbohydrate, 12 g fiber, 16 g protein.

Like-Homemade Baked Beans

PREP/TOTAL TIME: 25 min.

Sue Thomas, Casa Grande, Arizona

- 2 **bacon strips, diced**
- 1/2 **cup chopped onion**
- 1 **can (15-3/4 ounces) pork and beans**
- 2 **tablespoons brown sugar**
- 1-1/2 **teaspoons Worcestershire sauce**
- 1/2 **teaspoon ground mustard**

1) In a large skillet, cook bacon until crisp. Add onion; cook until tender.

2) Stir in the pork and beans, brown sugar, Worcestershire sauce and mustard. Reduce heat; simmer, uncovered, for 10-15 minutes or until heated through, stirring frequently.

Yield: 3 servings.

NUTRITION FACTS: 1 cup equals 259 calories, 10 g fat (3 g saturated fat), 10 mg cholesterol, 623 mg sodium, 38 g carbohydrate, 7 g fiber, 9 g protein.

OLD-FASHIONED BAKED BEANS

HEARTY BAKED BEANS

Maple Baked Beans

PREP: 10 min. **BAKE:** 40 min.

Laura Fisher, Glendale, Arizona

- 1 can (28 ounces) pork and beans
- 1/4 cup sugar-free pancake syrup
- 2 tablespoons ketchup
- 2 tablespoons prepared mustard
- 2 bacon strips, cooked and crumbled
- 1 onion slice, separated into rings

1) In a large bowl, combine the pork and beans, syrup, ketchup and mustard. Pour into an 8-in. square baking dish coated with cooking spray.

2) Sprinkle with bacon, top with onion. Bake, uncovered, at 350° for 40-45 minutes or until bubbly.

Yield: 6 servings.

NUTRITION FACTS: 1/2 cup equals 138 calories, 2 g fat (trace saturated fat), 2 mg cholesterol, 612 mg sodium, 27 g carbohydrate, 6 g fiber, 7 g protein.

Hearty Baked Beans

PREP: 20 min. **BAKE:** 25 min.

Taste of Home Test Kitchen

- 1 small onion, chopped
- 1 bacon strip, diced
- 1/4 teaspoon minced garlic
- 1 can (8 ounces) pork and beans
- 3/4 cup canned kidney beans, rinsed and drained
- 2 tablespoons brown sugar
- 1 tablespoon cider vinegar
- 1/8 teaspoon ground mustard

1) In a small skillet, saute the onion, bacon and garlic until onion is tender; drain. Stir in the pork and beans, kidney beans, brown sugar, vinegar and mustard. Cook, uncovered, for 5 minutes, stirring occasionally.

2) Transfer to a 2-cup baking dish coated with cooking spray. Cover and bake at 350° for 25-30 minutes or until bubbly.

Yield: 2 servings.

NUTRITION FACTS: 2/3 cup equals 265 calories, 3 g fat (1 g saturated fat), 3 mg cholesterol, 577 mg sodium, 52 g carbohydrate, 10 g fiber, 13 g protein.

Vegetarian Taco Salad

PREP/TOTAL TIME: 25 min.

Susan LeBrun, Sulphur, Louisiana

The cute tortilla bowls that hold this Southwestern salad are a snap to bake. To punch up the flavor, I add jalapeno peppers and hot pepper sauce.

> 4 whole wheat tortillas (8 inches)
> 6 cups shredded romaine
> 1/2 cup canned pinto beans, rinsed and drained
> 1 small tomato, chopped
> 1/4 cup shredded reduced-fat cheddar cheese
> 1/4 cup chopped green onions
> 2 tablespoons sliced ripe olives
> Sliced jalapeno peppers, optional

DRESSING:

> 1/2 cup fat-free sour cream
> 2 tablespoons prepared fat-free ranch salad dressing
> 1 teaspoon taco seasoning
> 1/4 teaspoon hot pepper sauce, optional

1) Place four 10-oz. custard cups upside down in a shallow baking pan; set aside. Place the tortillas in a single layer on ungreased baking sheets. Bake at 425° for 1 minute. Place a tortilla over each custard cup, pinching sides to form a bowl shape. Bake for 7-8 minutes or until crisp. Remove tortillas from cups to cool on wire racks.

2) In a large bowl, combine the romaine, beans, tomato, cheese, onions, olives and jalapenos if desired. In a small bowl, whisk the dressing ingredients; pour over salad and toss to coat. Serve in tortilla bowls.

Yield: 4 servings.

NUTRITION FACTS: 1 tortilla bowl with 1-1/4 cups salad equals 194 calories, 3 g fat (1 g saturated fat), 10 mg cholesterol, 489 mg sodium, 38 g carbohydrate, 5 g fiber, 10 g protein.

VEGETARIAN TACO SALAD

Lentils and Split Peas

Lentils and split peas should not be presoaked before cooking. However, just like dried beans, they should be sorted to remove any damaged lentils or peas, pebbles or grit. Rinse with cold water in a colander. Cook according to the recipe or package directions.

Lentils are available in several colors, but the most commonly available in supermarkets is the brown lentil. Look for green and red lentils in specialty markets. Brown and green lentils hold their shape well and are good for salads. Red lentils cook faster, have a softer texture and are good for pureed dishes. Green and yellow split peas are widely available.

TASTY LENTIL TACOS

Tasty Lentil Tacos

PREP: 10 min. **COOK:** 35 min.

Michelle Thomas, Bangor, Maine

My husband has to watch his cholesterol. This is a dish I found that's healthy for him and yummy for our five children.

> 1 cup finely chopped onion
> 1 garlic clove, minced
> 1 teaspoon canola oil
> 1 cup dried lentils, rinsed
> 1 tablespoon chili powder
> 2 teaspoons ground cumin
> 1 teaspoon dried oregano
> 2-1/2 cups chicken broth
> 1 cup salsa
> 12 taco shells, warmed
> 1-1/2 cups shredded lettuce
> 1 cup chopped fresh tomato
> 1-1/2 cups (6 ounces) shredded reduced-fat cheddar cheese
> 6 tablespoons fat-free sour cream

1) In a large nonstick skillet, saute the onion and garlic in oil until tender. Add the lentils, chili powder, cumin and oregano; cook and stir for 1 minute.

2) Add broth; bring to a boil. Reduce heat; cover and simmer for 25-30 minutes or until the lentils are tender. Uncover; cook for 6-8 minutes or until mixture is thickened. Mash lentils slightly.

3) Stir in salsa. Spoon about 1/4 cup lentil mixture into each taco shell. Top with lettuce, tomato, cheese and sour cream.

Yield: 6 servings.

NUTRITION FACTS: 2 tacos equals 364 calories, 11 g fat (4 g saturated fat), 17 mg cholesterol, 815 mg sodium, 45 g carbohydrate, 9 g fiber, 22 g protein.

Lemon Lentil Salad

PREP: 40 min. + chilling

Renate Kheim, St. Louis, Missouri

At first, this sounds like an odd combination. But once you try this refreshing and hearty salad, you'll want to make it again.

3 cups water
1 cup dried lentils, rinsed
1 bay leaf
5 tablespoons olive oil, *divided*
1 tablespoon lemon juice
2 teaspoons red wine vinegar
2 teaspoons sugar
1 teaspoon Dijon mustard
1/2 teaspoon dried thyme
1/4 teaspoon salt
1/4 teaspoon pepper
1 garlic clove, minced
1 large tomato, diced
1/2 cup minced fresh parsley
2 to 3 green onions, sliced

1) In a large saucepan, bring the water, lentils, bay leaf and 1 tablespoon oil to a boil. Reduce heat; simmer, uncovered, for 30 minutes. Remove from the heat. Let stand for 30 minutes.

2) For dressing, in a small bowl, combine the lemon juice, vinegar, sugar, mustard, thyme, salt, pepper, garlic and remaining oil; set aside.

3) Drain lentils if necessary. Discard bay leaf. Add the tomato, parsley, onions and dressing; mix gently. Cover and chill for at least 2 hours.

Yield: 6 servings.

NUTRITION FACTS: 1 serving equals 226 calories, 12 g fat (2 g saturated fat), 0 cholesterol, 129 mg sodium, 22 g carbohydrate, 11 g fiber, 10 g protein.

East Indian Split Pea Pilaf

PREP: 35 min. **COOK:** 30 min.

Marilyn Rodriquez, Fairbanks, Alaska

Yellow split peas, chicken broth and savory spices turn long grain rice into a piquant pilaf.

2/3 cup dried yellow split peas, rinsed
4-3/4 cups water, *divided*
1 bay leaf
3 tablespoons canola oil
1 large onion, chopped
1/2 to 1 teaspoon ground cinnamon
3/4 teaspoon ground cumin
1/2 teaspoon salt
1/4 teaspoon ground cloves
1/4 teaspoon ground turmeric
1-1/2 cups uncooked long grain rice
2-1/2 cups chicken broth

1) In a large saucepan, combine peas and 4 cups water. Bring to a boil. Reduce heat; simmer, uncovered, for 30-35 minutes or until tender. Drain and keep warm.

2) In a large nonstick skillet, cook the bay leaf in oil until golden, about 3 minutes. Add onion; saute until tender. Stir in the seasonings; saute for 30 seconds. Add the rice; cook and stir for 3 minutes. Stir in broth and remaining water.

3) Bring to a boil. Reduce heat; cover and simmer for 20-25 minutes or until rice is tender. Add peas; heat through. Discard bay leaf.

Yield: 6 servings.

NUTRITION FACTS: 1 cup equals 214 calories, 7 g fat (1 g saturated fat), 0 cholesterol, 572 mg sodium, 30 g carbohydrate, 1 g fiber, 8 g protein.

Tofu

Tofu, also known as soybean curd or bean curd, is created when soy milk is mixed with calcium or magnesium salt to create curds. The process is similar to cheese making. The more whey (liquid) that is pressed out of the curd, the firmer the tofu. Tofu has a bland flavor, but it acts as a flavor sponge and will absorb the flavors it is exposed to.

The two types of tofu, regular and silken, are available in soft, firm and extra-firm textures. Silken tofu is smoother, creamier and has a more custard-like texture.

When buying tofu, select the texture according to how you plan to use it:

- For marinating, grilling or broiling, use extra-firm tofu.
- For stir-frying or sauteing, use firm or extra-firm tofu.
- For making salad dressings, smoothies or desserts, use soft silken tofu.
- For reducing calories or fat, look for light tofu.

Check the use-by date on the package and store in the refrigerator. Store opened tofu submerged in water in a covered container for up to 1 week. Change water daily. To use tofu, drain and discard the liquid from package. Pat tofu dry with paper towels. Cut or slice according to recipe directions.

Broccoli Tofu Stir-Fry

PREP/TOTAL: 25 min.

Denise Lee, Louisville, Kentucky

I received this recipe from a friend when I wanted more meatless meals. Much to my surprise, my family doesn't mind the tofu and asks me to make it all the time.

- 1 package (12.3 ounces) silken reduced-fat extra-firm tofu, cubed
- 4 green onions, chopped
- 1 tablespoon minced fresh gingerroot
- 1 garlic clove, minced
- 1/4 teaspoon crushed red pepper flakes
- 4 teaspoons olive oil, *divided*
- 1 package (16 ounces) broccoli coleslaw mix
- 1/3 cup reduced-fat peanut butter
- 1/4 cup reduced-sodium teriyaki sauce

1) In a large nonstick skillet or wok, stir-fry the tofu, onions, ginger, garlic and pepper flakes in 3 teaspoons oil until onions are tender. Remove and set aside. In the same pan, stir-fry the coleslaw mix in remaining oil for 4-5 minutes.

2) Combine the peanut butter and teriyaki sauce; stir into coleslaw mix. Return tofu mixture to the pan. Stir-fry for 1-2 minutes or until heated through.

Yield: 4 servings.

Editor's Note: Broccoli coleslaw mix may be found in the produce section of most grocery stores.

NUTRITION FACTS: 1 cup equals 276 calories, 15 g fat (3 g saturated fat), 0 cholesterol, 526 mg sodium, 23 g carbohydrate, 5 g fiber, 16 g protein.

Tofu-Stuffed Pasta Shells

PREP: 25 min. BAKE: 35 min.

Jenni Dise, Phoenix, Arizona

Your gang won't even miss the meat in this hearty pasta dish. I jazzed up tofu with cheese, spinach and garlic for unbeatable flavor. Accented with a hint of red wine, an easy tomato sauce completes the entree.

- 15 jumbo pasta shells
- 1-1/2 cups silken firm tofu
- 3 tablespoons grated Romano cheese, *divided*
- 2 garlic cloves, peeled
- 1 package (10 ounces) frozen chopped spinach, thawed and squeezed dry
- 1 can (14-1/2 ounces) Italian diced tomatoes, drained
- 1 can (8 ounces) tomato sauce
- 1/4 cup dry red wine *or* vegetable broth
- 1/2 cup shredded part-skim mozzarella cheese

TOFU-STUFFED PASTA SHELLS

1) Cook shells according to package directions. Meanwhile, in a blender, combine the tofu, 2 tablespoons Romano cheese and garlic; cover and process until smooth. (Add 1 tablespoon of water if mixture is too thick.) Add spinach; process until blended. Drain shells and stuff with tofu mixture.

2) In a small bowl, combine the tomatoes, tomato sauce and wine or broth. Spread about 1/2 cup sauce into an 11-in. x 7-in. x 2-in. baking dish coated with cooking spray. Arrange stuffed shells over sauce. Top with remaining sauce.

3) Cover and bake at 350° for 25 minutes. Uncover; sprinkle with mozzarella and remaining Romano cheese. Bake 8-10 minutes longer or until heated through and cheese is melted.

Yield: 5 servings.

NUTRITION FACTS: 3 stuffed shells equals 262 calories, 5 g fat (2 g saturated fat), 10 mg cholesterol, 754 mg sodium, 39 g carbohydrate, 4 g fiber, 14 g protein.

TOFU-PEANUT BUTTER CONNECTION ■■■

I have a suggestion for lowering the fat content of peanut butter while increasing your soy intake. I buy reduced-fat, natural-style peanut butter and blend it in my food processor with an equal amount of low-fat silken tofu. The mixture that results is very smooth and creamy yet has just enough peanutty taste.

—*Barbara D., Lansing, Michigan*

blessings multiplied

Cafe owner's free-meal program feeds thousands

Jen Stutts

When Jen Stutts of Florence, Alabama, opened her restaurant seven years ago, she tried something that hadn't been done before in the area. On Thanksgiving Day, she invited anyone in need to enjoy a free dinner of turkey and all the fixings at her namesake business, Jen's Cafe.

What began as a small way to give back to the community has become a huge annual effort that enlists 100 volunteers and serves thousands who might not otherwise enjoy a hot meal on Thanksgiving.

"It was originally my mom and dad's idea," recalls Jen, whose mother and two sisters lend a hand at the restaurant. "They wanted to do it in Cleveland years ago, but no church in the area would host it. So when I opened Jen's Cafe in June 2002, we tried it that November.

"The first year, we didn't think it would happen. Then we started calling people, and they said, 'We'll send you this or that.' And someone else said they'd drop this off...and the churches offered to lend us some tables and chairs."

That first year, 300 people enjoyed Jen's home cooking on Thanksgiving Day. By 2008, the number had jumped to 7,500, including the 2,000 to 3,000 meals delivered before the cafe opens.

It takes a lot of preparation and manpower to make the event happen. Jen says planning starts in August when area businesses are asked for donations.

The menu changes yearly based on donations. "Last year a barbecue place smoked 45 turkeys for us last year, and a dairy donated all the milk and orange juice," she says, as examples. "Some people donate time and money, some buy to-go containers for us to use, and others donate frozen turkeys or cases of vegetables. I don't turn anything away, and I don't throw anything away."

About 100 volunteers help out over two days, doing prep work, setting up trays, moving tables and chairs, opening cans...the list goes on and on.

"It's so rewarding, knowing that you're giving back to people who are less fortunate," Jen says. "People don't understand that until they actually do it."

Recipes

Tips

Vegetables

Large grocery stores, small markets and home gardens offer abundant varieties of vegetables. This chapter highlights the most commonly available ones. For each vegetable, you'll find information about availability, buying, storing and preparation. If you purchase riper vegetables, storage life will be shorter.

The cooking chart lists recommended cooking methods and times. This information is simply a guideline. Cooking times vary depending on the size, freshness and ripeness of the vegetable you are cooking. To cook vegetables, simply follow the cooking method and times listed in the Vegetable Cooking Chart beginning on page 359. Then dress them up with a sprinkle of herbs, a dab of butter, a squirt of lemon or a drizzle of balsamic vinegar. For more variety, try the delicious flavor combinations found in the recipes in this chapter.

Veggie Toppers

Steamed, boiled or sauteed vegetables are delicious by themselves but can get a flavor boost or added crunch with these easy toppings:

- Toss with a little butter or spritz with refrigerated butter-flavored spray and sprinkle with bread crumbs.

- Sprinkle with sauteed almonds or pecans, sesame seeds or sunflower kernels.

- Saute some chopped onion, celery or garlic and stir into the cooked vegetable.

- Sprinkle with Parmesan cheese.

- Add a splash of lemon juice or balsamic vinegar.

- Season stir-fried or sauteed vegetables with a little minced fresh gingerroot, soy sauce, sherry, sesame oil or chopped green onion.

- Toss buttered vegetables with fresh herbs, like dill, basil, oregano, tarragon, marjoram, chives, rosemary or mint.

- Melt 1/4 cup butter over low heat; stir in 1/2 teaspoon garlic powder, 2 tablespoons lemon juice, 1 tablespoon slivered toasted almonds, 1 tablespoon minced chives or 1 tablespoon grated Parmesan cheese. Drizzle over cooked vegetables.

- For extra ease, prepare a packaged white, hollandaise or bearnaise sauce mix as directed and serve over your vegetable of choice.

Handling Produce

Handle vegetables gently—they bruise easily. A bruised spot will lead to decay. After purchasing, promptly refrigerate vegetables that need to be refrigerated. Don't place raw or cooked vegetables on the same surfaces that come in contact with raw meat.

Before preparing, make sure your countertops, cutting boards and utensils are clean. Wash your hands in hot, soapy water. Don't leave cooked or raw vegetables that require refrigeration at room temperature for more than 2 hours.

Rinse vegetables, including prepackaged vegetables, under cool running water. Do not wash with detergent or bleach. Some vegetables, like potatoes or carrots, should be gently scrubbed with a vegetable brush if you are going to eat the peel. Always peel vegetables with a wax coating.

Basic Cooking Methods

Blanching is used to partially cook vegetables, remove skins or stop enzymatic action before freezing. Partially cooked vegetables may be used for crudites or salads or to shorten cooking time when stir-frying.

How to Blanch

1) In a large saucepan or Dutch oven, bring a large amount of water to a boil. Boil vegetables for time given in Vegetable Cooking Chart or recipe.

2) Drain and immediately place vegetable in ice water. This step quickly stops the cooking process and helps retain the color and texture. Drain and pat dry.

Boiling can be done in 1 to 2 in. of water for vegetables such as broccoli, or it can be completely covered with water for root vegetables such as potatoes. After the water is brought to a boil, the chart will say boil, simmer or cook. When it says boil, there should be large bubbles breaking the surface of the water. For a simmer, the heat needs to be reduced to medium-low or low, and there should be tiny bubbles, frequently around the side of the pan that break the surface of the water. For cook, the heat needs to be reduced to medium, and the water will be between a boil and a simmer.

When cooking vegetables in boiling or simmering water, you can sprinkle a little salt into the cooking water before adding the vegetables if desired. However, if the vegetables are to be served in a sauce containing salt or salty ingredients, omit the salt in the cooking water.

Shallow Boiling

Place 1 to 2 in. of water in a saucepan or skillet and lightly salt if desired. Bring to a boil. Add the vegetables. Cook for the time given in the Vegetable Cooking Chart or recipe or until crisp-tender; drain.

Boiling Covered in Water

Place the vegetables in a saucepan and cover with water. Lightly salt if desired. Bring to a boil. Reduce heat; cover and cook for time given in the Vegetable Cooking Chart or recipe or until crisp-tender; drain.

Roasting and Baking are dry-heat methods of cooking that make the flavor of vegetables richer and sweeter. Root vegetables, corn, onions, garlic, eggplants and many other vegetables can be roasted.

For best results, cut vegetables into uniform sizes so they cook more evenly. If you roast a mixture of vegetables, cut the denser vegetables into smaller pieces so they will be done at the same time as the other vegetables. Roasted vegetables are generally roasted at 400° to 450°. Vegetables are baked at lower temperatures of 350° to 375°. Finally, make sure the roasting pan is not crowded. If it's too small, the vegetables will steam and not become crisp.

How to Roast

Spread vegetables in a shallow-sided roasting pan, making sure that the vegetables are not crowded. Drizzle with oil and sprinkle with herbs or seasoning; toss gently to coat. Roast, uncovered, for the time given in the Vegetable Cooking Chart or recipe or until tender, stirring occasionally.

Sauteing and Stir-Frying both quickly cook uniform pieces of food at high temperatures while stirring or moving the food. Food cooked by these methods should be golden or browned on the outside and tender and moist on the inside.

When sauteing or stir-frying, cut vegetables into uniform sizes so that they will cook more evenly. Vegetables should be dry before cooking. Heat oil over medium-high heat until hot. If cooking a variety of vegetables, add the longer-cooking vegetables first, then add the more delicate or watery vegetables, like mushrooms or zucchini. Finally, make sure the skillet or wok is not crowded. If it's too small, the vegetables will steam and not become crisp.

How to Saute or Stir-Fry

Heat oil over medium-high heat until hot. Add vegetables and cook for time given in the Vegetable Cooking Chart or recipe or until crisp-tender, stirring constantly.

Steaming uses the heat generated from the boiling water to cook the vegetables. Since the vegetables are not in the water, more of the nutrients and flavors are preserved.

How to Steam

Place the vegetables in a steamer basket. Place in a saucepan over 1 in. of water. The water should not be touching the bottom of the steamer basket. Bring to a boil. Cover and steam for time given in the Vegetable Cooking Chart or recipe or until crisp-tender. The cooking time begins when the water starts to boil.

Vegetable Cooking Chart

VEGETABLE	COOKING METHOD AND TIME (IN MINUTES)				
	BLANCHING	STEAMING	BOILING	SAUTEING/ STIR-FRYING	ROASTING/ BAKING
ARTICHOKES Baby Full-size	5 7	10 to 12 25 to 30 steam upside down	12 30 to 45 cover with water simmer covered		350° 45 to 60 with liquid and covered
ASPARAGUS	2 to 4	3 to 5	3 to 5 1/2 in. water simmer covered	3 to 4	400° 20 to 25 uncovered
BEANS Green or wax Lima	3 1 to 3	8 to 10	3 to 5, pieces 4 to 7, whole 10 to 15 cover with water boil covered	4 to 5	
BEETS			30 to 60, whole 20 to 25, cubed cover with water boil uncovered		350° 30 to 60 covered
BOK CHOY Stalks Leaves		5 to 6 2 to 3	3 to 4 1 to 1-1/2	5	
BROCCOFLOWER Florets	1 to 2	7 to 9	5 to 10 1 in. water simmer covered	5 blanch first	425° 10 to 15
BROCCOLI Florets Spears	3 5	3 to 4 5 to 8	3 to 5 5 to 8 1 in. water boil covered	5 to 7	
BROCCOLI RABE	5	3 to 4	1 to 2 1/2 in. water boil covered	3 to 5	
BRUSSELS SPROUTS	3 to 5	8 to 10	8 to 10 1/2 in. water simmer covered	10 to 12	

VEGETABLE	COOKING METHOD AND TIME (IN MINUTES)				
	BLANCHING	STEAMING	BOILING	SAUTEING/ STIR-FRYING	ROASTING/ BAKING
CABBAGE, GREEN OR RED					
Shredded	1	6 to 8	3 to 5	7 to 10	
Wedges	1-1/2	15	6 to 8 1 in. water simmer covered		
CABBAGE, NAPA				3 to 4	
CARROTS					
Slices	3	7 to 10	5 to 8		425°
Whole baby	5	12 to 15	8 to 15 1 in. water simmer covered		40 to 60 uncovered
CAULIFLOWER					
Florets	1 to 2	5 to 12	5 to 10 1 in. water simmer covered	5 blanch first	425° 15 to 20
CELERY, SLICED		5 to 7	5 to 7 1/2 in. water simmer covered	2 to 3	325° 30 to 35 with liquid, covered
CORN					
On the cob	6 to 9		3 to 5		450°
Kernels	5 to 6	4 to 5	3 to 4 cover with water cook covered		15 to 20 prepare as for grilling
CUCUMBERS		3 to 5	3 to 5 1/2 in. water or broth simmer covered	2 to 3	
EGGPLANT					
Cubed	4	5 to 7	5 to 8 cover with water boil uncovered	6 to 8	400° 30 to 40 for whole, pierce with fork; covered
FENNEL, STRIPS		6 to 8	6 to 10 1 in. water simmer covered		425° 60 wedges, uncovered
GARLIC				1 to 2	425° 30 to 35 wrapped in foil
GREENS					
Coarse (kale)			10 to 20		
Tender (Swiss chard)			8 to 10 1/2 in. water cook covered		
KOHLRABI					
Cubes or strips		6	6 to 8 1 in. water simmer covered	5	
LEEKS		13 to 15	12 to 15 cover with water boil uncovered	5	
MUSHROOMS					
Button	3 to 5	10 to 12		2 to 5	425° 20 uncovered
OKRA	3 to 5		8 to 10 1 in. water simmer covered		
ONIONS	3 to 5	10 to 12 pearl onions	8 to 10 1 in. water cook covered	5	400° 45 to 50 whole

VEGETABLE	COOKING METHOD AND TIME (IN MINUTES)				
	BLANCHING	STEAMING	BOILING	SAUTEING/ STIR-FRYING	ROASTING/ BAKING
PARSNIPS Cubes	3	8 to 10	15 cover with water boil uncovered		425° 40 to 45 cubes or pieces uncovered
PEAS, SNOW	1 to 2	1 to 2	2 to 3 1 in. water simmer covered	1 to 2	
PEAS, SUGAR SNAP	1 to 2	4	2 1 in. water simmer covered	1 blanch first	
PEAS, SWEET	1 to 2	5 to 8	5 to 8 1 in. water simmer covered		
PEPPERS Hot Sweet	2 2	6 to 7	6 to 7 1 in. water cook covered	3 to 5 3 to 5	see p. 394 see p. 394
POTATOES New, whole Medium, whole Large, whole		20 30 to 45	15 to 20 cover with water cook covered		400° 45 to 50 pierce potato with a fork
POTATOES Cubes Chunks, wedges or quarters			15 20 cover with water cook covered		425° 45 to 50 uncovered
PUMPKIN 2-in. pieces		50	25 to 30 cover with water boil uncovered		375° 60 4- to 5-in. pieces, covered
RUTABAGA Cubes	3	18 to 20	15 to 20 cover with water boil uncovered		
SPINACH	2	3 to 4	3 to 5 1/2 in. water cook covered	3 to 4	
SQUASH Summer	1 to 2	3 to 5	3 to 5 1/2 in. water cook covered	4 to 7	425° 15 to 20 uncovered
SQUASH Winter		15 to 30 quarters or rings	15 to 30 quarters or rings 1 in. water cook covered		350° 45 (1-1/2 to 2 pounds) 2 hours (3 pounds)
SWEET POTATOES Cubes or chunks Whole		20 to 25	10 to 20 25 to 40 cover with water cook covered		400° 30 to 60 uncovered
TOMATOES	30 seconds				400° 10 to 15 uncovered
TURNIPS Cubes	3	10 to 12	15 cover with water boil uncovered		

Vegetable Grilling Chart

Cut vegetables into uniform sizes. To prevent small pieces from slipping through the grill racks, use skewers or a grill basket. Grill vegetables until tender. Turn halfway through grilling time.

VEGETABLE	SLICE OR THICKNESS	HEAT	COOKING TIME
ASPARAGUS	1/2-in. thickness	Medium/Direct	6 to 8
CORN (NO HUSK)	whole	Medium/Direct	10 to 12
CORN (WITH HUSK)	whole	Medium/Direct	25 to 30
EGGPLANT	1/2-in. slices	Medium/Direct	8 to 10
FENNEL	1/4-in. slices	Medium/Direct	10 to 12
MUSHROOMS (BUTTON)	whole	Medium/Direct	8 to 10
MUSHROOMS (PORTOBELLO)	whole	Medium/Direct	12 to 15
ONIONS	1/2-in. slices	Medium/Direct	8 to 12
POTATOES	whole	Medium/Indirect	45 to 60
SWEET PEPPERS	halved or quartered	Medium/Direct	8 to 10

Artichokes

Artichokes, also known as globe artichokes, are fun to eat. The soft, meaty portion of the leaf is removed by drawing the leaf across your teeth. The heart of the artichoke is revealed after the leaves are removed and the choke, the fuzzy inedible portion over the heart, is removed. Baby artichokes have not developed the fuzzy choke and are completely edible after some trimming.

Buying

Artichokes are available year-round; peak season is March through May. Select artichokes that are heavy for their size and have leaves that are tightly closed. Slight brown discoloration may be due to frost and does not affect the quality of the artichoke. Avoid artichokes with spreading leaves and a lot of brown areas.

Storage

Store unwashed artichokes in the refrigerator for up to 4 days.

Yield: 1 medium artichoke (8 to 10 ounces)
= 1 serving

Preparing Artichokes

1) Rinse artichokes well. Cut off stem at base of artichoke. Cut 1 in. from top. With scissors, snip the tip end of each leaf. Remove outer leaves. Rub cut ends of leaves with lemon juice to help prevent browning.

2) For quarters, cut each artichoke into quarters and rub cut sides with lemon juice. With a spoon, remove and discard the center fuzzy choke.

Asparagus

Asparagus has a slender, light green stalk with a tightly closed bud at the top. White asparagus is grown underground, so it does not produce chlorophyll. Asparagus is most often served cooked as a side dish but can be enjoyed raw on vegetable platters.

Buying

Asparagus is available February through late June; peak season is April through May. Select small straight stalks with tightly closed, compact tips. Spears should be smooth and round. Green asparagus should have bright green stalks, while the tips may have a slight lavender tint. White asparagus should have straight, firm stalks.

Storage

Store unwashed asparagus in a sealed plastic bag in the refrigerator crisper drawer for up to 4 days (2 days for white asparagus). Another way to store asparagus is to cut about 1/4 inch from the bottoms of the unwashed spears. Place upright in a large glass or pitcher. Add about an inch of water. Cover with a plastic food storage bag. Store in the refrigerator. Check and change water as needed. To freeze, blanch for 2 to 4 minutes, depending on the thickness of the spears. Freeze for up to 1 year.

Yield: 1 pound asparagus = 3-1/2 cups cut

ELEGANT ARTICHOKES

Elegant Artichokes

PREP: 10 min. **COOK:** 35 min. + chilling

Pat Stevens, Granbury, Texas

Lemon not only helps retain the color but also adds wonderful flavor to the artichokes as well as the dipping sauce.

> 5 medium artichokes
>
> Lemon juice
>
> 2 medium lemons, sliced
>
> 2 garlic cloves, minced
>
> LEMON-PEPPER DIP:
>
> 1 cup vegetable oil
>
> 1/4 cup lemon juice
>
> 1/4 cup red wine vinegar
>
> 2 tablespoons spicy brown mustard
>
> 3 garlic cloves, minced
>
> 1 teaspoon salt
>
> 3/4 teaspoon pepper
>
> 1/2 cup diced green pepper
>
> 2 tablespoons sliced green onion

1) Cut off stem at base of artichoke. Cut 1 in. from top. With scissors, snip tip end of each leaf. Remove outer leaves. Rub cut ends of leaves with juice.

2) In a Dutch oven, combine the artichokes, lemon slices and garlic; cover with water. Bring to a boil. Reduce heat. Cover and simmer for 30-45 minutes or until tender. Drain; arrange on a serving platter. Refrigerate for 1 hour.

3) For dip, in a bowl, whisk the oil, lemon juice, vinegar, mustard, garlic, salt and pepper. Stir in green pepper and onion. Serve with artichokes.

Yield: 5 servings (1-3/4 cups dip).

NUTRITION FACTS: 1 artichoke with 1/3 cup dip equals 472 calories, 44 g fat (6 g saturated fat), 0 cholesterol, 667 mg sodium, 20 g carbohydrate, 7 g fiber, 5 g protein.

Preparing Asparagus

Rinse asparagus stalks well in cold water to clean. Snap off the stalk ends as far down as they will easily break when gently bent, or cut off the tough white portion. If stalks are large, use a vegetable peeler to gently peel the tough area of the stalk from the end to just below the tip. If tips are large, scrape off scales with a knife.

SESAME ASPARAGUS

⏱ Sesame Asparagus

PREP/TOTAL TIME: 20 min.

Taste of Home Test Kitchen

A simple addition of garlic and sesame seeds dresses up asparagus for a wonderful taste of spring!

- 1 pound fresh asparagus, trimmed and cut into 1-1/2-inch pieces
- 1 garlic clove, minced
- 2 tablespoons butter
- 1/2 cup chicken broth
- 1 tablespoon sesame seeds, toasted

1) In a skillet, saute the asparagus and garlic in butter for 2 minutes. Stir in broth; bring to a boil. Reduce heat; cover and simmer for 5-6 minutes or until asparagus is crisp-tender.

2) Remove to a serving dish with a slotted spoon; sprinkle with sesame seeds. Serve immediately.

Yield: 4 servings.

NUTRITION FACTS: 1/2 cup equals 78 calories, 7 g fat (4 g saturated fat), 15 mg cholesterol, 192 mg sodium, 3 g carbohydrate, 1 g fiber, 2 g protein.

⏱ Rosemary Asparagus

PREP/TOTAL TIME: 15 min.

Mavis Diment, Marcus, Iowa

Rosemary creates a nice alternative to plain asparagus in a simple and flavorful way.

- 1/2 cup chicken broth
- 1 to 2 tablespoons minced fresh rosemary *or* 1 to 2 teaspoons dried rosemary, crushed
- 1 garlic clove, halved
- 1 bay leaf
- 1 pound fresh asparagus, trimmed
- 1/3 cup chopped onion
- 1 tablespoon minced fresh parsley

1) In a large skillet, combine the broth, rosemary, garlic and bay leaf. Add asparagus and onion.

2) Bring to a boil. Reduce heat; cover and simmer for 3-5 minutes or until asparagus is crisp-tender. Discard bay leaf. Garnish with parsley.

Yield: 4 servings.

NUTRITION FACTS: 4 ounces equals 23 calories, trace fat (trace saturated fat), 0 cholesterol, 124 mg sodium, 4 g carbohydrate, 1 g fiber, 2 g protein.

Beans

Green and wax beans, also know as string beans, and lima beans are members of the legume family. Green and wax beans may be used interchangeably in recipes and are known for their mild flavor and general appeal. The pale-green lima bean is kidney shaped with a starchy texture and a mild, buttery flavor.

Buying

Green and wax beans are available year-round; peak season is from July through October. Select brightly colored, straight, smooth pods that are unblemished. Beans should be crisp and have a firm, velvety feel. Seeds inside the bean should be small.

Fresh lima beans are available from June through September. The Fordhook lima bean variety is larger than the baby lima bean. Select pods that are full, crisp and free of blemishes.

Storage

Store unwashed green and wax beans in a sealed plastic bag or covered container in the refrigerator crisper drawer for up to 3 days.

Store unwashed, unshelled lima beans in the refrigerator crisper drawer for up to 3 days.

Preparation

Snap off stem end of green or wax beans and the other end if desired. Leave whole or cut into 1-in. pieces.

Shell lima beans just before cooking. Snap off one end and split pod open. Remove beans; discard pod.

Yield: 1 pound green or wax beans = about 4 cups cut
1 pound unshelled lima beans = 2/3 cup beans

⏱ Pepper Parmesan Beans

PREP/TOTAL TIME: 15 min.

Marian Platt, Sequim, Washington

Peppers and beans get the Italian treatment with basil and Parmesan cheese in this dish.

- 1 large sweet red pepper, diced
- 1 small green pepper, diced
- 1/4 cup chopped onion
- 1 garlic clove, minced

1/4 cup olive oil

1-1/2 pounds fresh green beans, cut into 2-inch pieces

1 tablespoon minced fresh basil *or* 1 teaspoon dried basil

1 teaspoon salt

1/3 cup shredded Parmesan cheese

1) In a large skillet, saute peppers, onion and garlic in oil until vegetables are tender, about 3 minutes.

2) Add beans, basil and salt; toss to coat. Cover and cook over medium-low heat for 7-8 minutes or until beans are crisp-tender. Stir in Parmesan cheese; serve immediately.

Yield: 8 servings.

NUTRITION FACTS: 3/4 cup equals 107 calories, 8 g fat (2 g saturated fat), 2 mg cholesterol, 357 mg sodium, 8 g carbohydrate, 3 g fiber, 3 g protein.

ROASTED GREEN BEANS

Roasted Green Beans

PREP/TOTAL TIME: 30 min.

LaVonne Hegland, St. Michael, Minnesota

Red wine vinegar really perks up everyday green beans in this simply seasoned side dish. Add a sprinkling of salt and pepper to suit your family's taste.

3/4 pound fresh green beans, trimmed

1 small onion, thinly sliced and separated into rings

2 garlic cloves, thinly sliced

1 tablespoon red wine vinegar

2 teaspoons olive oil

1) Place beans in a saucepan and cover with water; bring to a boil. Cook, uncovered, for 8-10 minutes or until crisp-tender. Drain.

2) Place beans in an 11-in. x 7-in. x 2-in. baking dish cooked with cooking spray. Top with onion and garlic. Drizzle with vinegar and oil; toss to coat.

3) Bake, uncovered, at 450° for 10 minutes. Stir; bake 5 minutes longer.

Yield: 4 servings.

NUTRITION FACTS: 1 cup equals 53 calories, 2 g fat (trace saturated fat), 0 cholesterol, 5 mg sodium, 8 g carbohydrate, 3 g fiber, 2 g protein.

Garlic Green and Wax Beans

PREP: 15 min. + chilling

Marilou Robinson, Portland, Oregon

Even non-garlic lovers like this fresh-tasting salad.

1-1/2 pounds fresh green beans, trimmed

1-1/2 pounds fresh wax beans, trimmed

7 garlic cloves, minced, *divided*

1/4 cup reduced-fat sour cream

1/4 cup fat-free milk

1 teaspoon white wine vinegar

1 teaspoon olive oil

1/2 teaspoon salt

1/8 teaspoon pepper

1 cup (4 ounces) shredded part-skim mozzarella cheese

Minced fresh parsley

1) Place beans and 6 garlic cloves in a steamer basket. Place in a large saucepan over 1 in. of water; bring to a boil. Cover and steam for 8-10 minutes or until beans are crisp-tender. Transfer to a large bowl; set aside.

2) In a small bowl, combine the sour cream, milk and vinegar; let stand for 1 minute. Whisk in the oil, salt, pepper and remaining garlic.

3) Pour over beans and toss. Cover and refrigerate for at least 2 hours. Just before serving, sprinkle with mozzarella cheese and parsley.

Yield: 12 servings.

NUTRITION FACTS: 3/4 cup equals 76 calories, 2 g fat (1 g saturated fat), 7 mg cholesterol, 157 mg sodium, 9 g carbohydrate, 4 g fiber, 5 g protein.

Savory Lemon Limas

PREP/TOTAL TIME: 20 min.

Cathy Attig, Jacobus, Pennsylvania

If you are a lima bean fan like I am, this recipe just makes them even more delicious.

1/2 cup water

1 package (10 ounces) frozen lima beans

1 tablespoon butter, melted

1 tablespoon lemon juice

1 teaspoon sugar

1/2 to 3/4 teaspoon ground mustard

1/4 teaspoon salt

1) In a small saucepan, bring water to a boil. Add lima beans; return to a boil. Reduce heat; cover and simmer for 8-10 minutes or until tender. Drain.

2) Combine the butter, lemon juice, sugar, mustard and salt; pour over beans and toss to coat.

Yield: 4 servings.

NUTRITION FACTS: 1/3 cup equals 107 calories, 3 g fat (2 g saturated fat), 8 mg cholesterol, 197 mg sodium, 15 g carbohydrate, 3 g fiber, 5 g protein.

CREAMY GREEN BEAN BAKE

CLASSIC: For many families, holiday meals just wouldn't be the same without a comforting green bean dish like this one. French-style green beans, fresh mushrooms and crunchy water chestnuts are baked in a rich cheese sauce to make Mushroom Green Bean Casserole the perfect addition to a special gathering.

TIME-SAVER: By its homemade taste, you'd never guess that Microwave Corn 'n' Bean Bake takes advantage of convenience products, including frozen beans, canned corn, cream soup and butter crackers. Because it's cooked in the microwave, it's ready in minutes.

LIGHT: Fat-free evaporated milk and fat-free milk help trim down the sauce in Savory Green Bean Casserole. And a topping made from sauteed onions, bread crumbs and a little butter is lighter than typical versions. This casserole has about a third of the calories and sodium and only a fraction of the fat and cholesterol of classic Mushroom Green Bean Casserole.

SERVES 2: Mini Green Bean Casserole offers the homey taste of the traditional side dish in a size to fit a smaller household. A 2-cup baking dish holds just enough of this saucy casserole to please two palates, and it's ready to serve in 20 minutes.

MUSHROOM GREEN BEAN CASSEROLE

Mushroom Green Bean Casserole

PREP: 15 min. **BAKE:** 25 min.

Pat Richter, Lake Placid, Florida

- 1 pound fresh mushrooms, sliced
- 1 large onion, chopped
- 1/2 cup butter
- 1/4 cup all-purpose flour
- 1 cup half-and-half cream
- 1 jar (16 ounces) process cheese sauce
- 2 teaspoons soy sauce
- 1/2 teaspoon pepper

- 1/8 teaspoon hot pepper sauce
- 1 can (8 ounces) sliced water chestnuts, drained
- 2 packages (16 ounces *each*) frozen French-style green beans, thawed and well drained
- 2 to 3 tablespoons slivered almonds

1) In a large skillet, saute mushrooms and onion in butter. Stir in flour until blended. Gradually stir in cream. Bring to a boil; cook and stir for 2 minutes or until thickened.

2) Reduce heat; add the cheese sauce, soy sauce, pepper and hot pepper sauce, stirring until cheese is melted. Stir in water chestnuts.

3) Place beans in an ungreased 3-qt. baking dish. Pour cheese mixture over the top. Sprinkle with almonds. Bake, uncovered, at 375° for 25-30 minutes or until bubbly.

Yield: 14 servings.

NUTRITION FACTS: 1/2 cup equals 223 calories, 16 g fat (10 g saturated fat), 46 mg cholesterol, 654 mg sodium, 14 g carbohydrate, 3 g fiber, 7 g protein.

Microwave Corn 'n' Bean Bake

PREP/TOTAL TIME: 20 min.

Nellie Perdue, Albany, Kentucky

- 1 package (16 ounces) frozen cut green beans
- 1 can (15-1/4 ounces) whole kernel corn, drained
- 1 can (10-3/4 ounces) condensed cream of mushroom soup, undiluted
- 1 cup (4 ounces) shredded cheddar cheese, *divided*
- 1/2 cup crushed butter-flavored crackers (about 12 crackers)

1) In a large bowl, combine the beans, corn, soup and 1/2 cup cheese. Spoon into a greased 2-qt. microwave-safe dish. Cover and microwave on high for 10 minutes, stirring once.

2) Combine cracker crumbs and remaining cheese; sprinkle over the bean mixture. Microwave, uncovered, on high for 3-5 minutes or until beans are tender.

Yield: 6 servings.

NUTRITION FACTS: 3/4 cup equals 222 calories, 11 g fat (5 g saturated fat), 22 mg cholesterol, 820 mg sodium, 22 g carbohydrate, 4 g fiber, 7 g protein.

Savory Green Bean Casserole

PREP: 20 min. **BAKE:** 25 min. + standing

Taste of Home Test Kitchen

- 1 package (16 ounces) frozen cut green beans
- 1 medium onion, chopped
- 1 garlic clove, minced
- 1 teaspoon butter
- 1/2 pound fresh mushrooms, chopped
- 1 can (12 ounces) fat-free evaporated milk
- 1/4 cup all-purpose flour
- 1/2 cup fat-free milk
- 1 teaspoon reduced-sodium soy sauce
- 1/2 teaspoon salt
- 1/4 teaspoon poultry seasoning
- 1/8 to 1/4 teaspoon pepper

SAVORY GREEN BEAN CASSEROLE

TOPPING:
- 2 cups sliced onions
- 1 teaspoon butter
- 1/2 cup soft bread crumbs

1) Place beans in a microwave-safe dish. Cover and cook on high for 7-9 minutes or until tender; drain.

2) In a large nonstick skillet, cook onion and garlic in butter over medium heat until tender, about 4 minutes. Add mushrooms; cook until softened. Reduce heat to medium-low; gradually stir in evaporated milk. Combine flour and milk until smooth; gradually stir into mushroom mixture. Add the soy sauce, salt, poultry seasoning and pepper. Bring to a boil; cook and stir for 2 minutes or until thickened.

3) Stir in beans. Transfer to a 2-qt. baking dish coated with cooking spray. Bake, uncovered, at 375° for 15 minutes.

4) Meanwhile, for topping, in a small nonstick skillet, cook onions in butter over medium-low heat until golden brown. Add bread crumbs; cook until dry and golden brown. Sprinkle over casserole. Bake 7-10 minutes longer or until heated through and topping is browned. Let stand for 10 minutes before serving.

Yield: 12 servings.

NUTRITION FACTS: 1/2 cup equals 86 calories, 1 g fat (1 g saturated fat), 3 mg cholesterol, 200 mg sodium, 15 g carbohydrate, 2 g fiber, 5 g protein.

Mini Green Bean Casserole

PREP/TOTAL TIME: 20 min.

Christy Hinrichs, Parkville, Missouri

- 1/2 cup condensed cream of mushroom soup, undiluted
- 3 tablespoons 2% milk
- 1/2 teaspoon reduced-sodium soy sauce

Dash pepper

- 1-1/3 cups frozen cut green beans, thawed
- 1/2 cup french-fried onions, *divided*

1) In a small bowl, combine the soup, milk, soy sauce and pepper. Stir in green beans and 1/4 cup onions.

2) Transfer to a greased 2-cup baking dish. Sprinkle with remaining onions. Bake, uncovered, at 400° for 12-15 minutes or until bubbly.

Yield: 2 servings.

NUTRITION FACTS: 3/4 cup equals 159 calories, 8 g fat (3 g saturated fat), 3 mg cholesterol, 506 mg sodium, 17 g carbohydrate, 3 g fiber, 2 g protein.

Beets

Beets are a very deep-red, bulb-shaped root vegetable with edible dark green leaves. Beets and their greens are hearty in flavor. Beet greens can be served raw in salads or cooked. Beets are always cooked before serving and can be enjoyed whole, sliced, shredded or diced.

BEETS IN ORANGE SAUCE

Buying

Beets are available June through October; peak season is June through August. Select firm, deep-red, round beets with unwilted green tops. The skin should be smooth, unblemished and unbroken. Small and medium-sized beets are usually the most tender (maximum size should be about 2 in.). Beet greens should have a reddish tint.

Storage

Remove greens 2 in. from beets. If you plan on using the greens, store separately in a sealed plastic bag in the refrigerator for up to 3 days. Store uncooked beets in an open plastic bag in the refrigerator crisper drawer for about 2 weeks. Freeze cooked beets for up to 1 year.

Preparation

Wash beets gently. If you haven't already done so, remove greens. To help beets maintain their flavor and color after cooking, do not peel or trim them first. If you cook beets in hard water, their brilliant color fades. To prevent this, try adding a small amount of vinegar to the cooking water.

The beet color bleeds when they are cut. To protect your hands, wear plastic gloves when peeling and cutting them.

Yield: 1 pound beets = 2-1/2 cups cooked sliced or cubed

Beets in Orange Sauce
PREP: 15 min. **COOK:** 35 min.

Taste of Home Test Kitchen

To ensure your family eats their veggies, why not top beets with an irresistible orange glaze?

- 8 whole fresh beets
- 1/4 cup sugar
- 2 teaspoons cornstarch

Dash pepper

- 1 cup orange juice
- 1 medium navel orange, halved and sliced, optional
- 1/2 teaspoon grated orange peel

1) Place beets in a large saucepan; cover with water. Bring to a boil. Reduce heat; cover and cook for 25-30 minutes or until tender. Drain and cool slightly. Peel and slice; place in a serving bowl and keep warm.

2) In a small saucepan, combine the sugar, cornstarch and pepper; stir in orange juice until smooth. Bring to a boil; cook and stir for 2 minutes or until thickened.

3) Remove from the heat; stir in orange slices if desired and peel. Pour over beets.

Yield: 8 servings.

Editor's Note: A 15-ounce can of sliced beets may be substituted for the fresh beets. Omit step 1. Drain the beets and heat beets in the microwave. Proceed with step 2.

NUTRITION FACTS: 1 cup equals 63 calories, trace fat (trace saturated fat), 0 cholesterol, 39 mg sodium, 15 g carbohydrate, 1 g fiber, 1 g protein.

Roasted Beet Wedges
PREP: 15 min. **BAKE:** 1-1/4 hours

Wendy Stenman, Germantown, Wisconsin

This recipe makes ordinary beets taste delicious. They come out sweet and tender.

- 1 pound medium fresh beets, peeled
- 4 teaspoons olive oil
- 1/2 teaspoon kosher salt
- 3 to 5 fresh rosemary sprigs

1) Cut each beet into six wedges; place in a large resealable plastic bag. Add oil and salt; seal and shake to coat.

2) Place a piece of heavy-duty foil (about 12 in. long) in a 15-in. x 10-in. x 1-in. baking pan. Arrange beets on foil and top with rosemary. Fold foil around beet mixture and seal tightly.

3) Bake at 400° for 1-1/4 to 1-1/2 hours or until beets are tender. Discard rosemary sprigs.

Yield: 4 servings.

NUTRITION FACTS: 3 wedges equals 61 calories, 3 g fat (trace saturated fat), 0 cholesterol, 215 mg sodium, 8 g carbohydrate, 2 g fiber, 1 g protein.

Bok Choy

Bok choy is a cruciferous vegetable and is also known as Chinese white cabbage. Bok choy, with its large white stalks and large green leaves, more closely resembles a bunch of celery rather than a head of green cabbage. The mild-flavored white stalks are crunchy and juicy, while the leaves are tender and require less cooking time.

Buying

Bok choy is available year-round. Select bunches with firm white stalks and crisp leaves. Avoid bunches with brown spots on stalks.

Storage

Store unwashed bok choy in the crisper drawer in the refrigerator for up 4 days.

Preparation

Wash before using, not before storing. Cut leaves from stalks. Slice, chop or shred stalks. The leaves can be sliced or chopped. Bok choy may be used raw in salads or cooked in stir-fries or soups. Always start by cooking the crunchy stalk first, then add the tender leaves during the last few minutes of cooking.

Yield: 1 medium bunch (about 11 ounces) = 5-1/2 to 7 cups shredded or sliced

Sesame Bok Choy

PREP/TOTAL TIME: 25 min.

Taste of Home Test Kitchen

Mild and crunchy, bok choy makes a great base for this flavorful stir-fry that also features baby corn, snow peas and carrots.

1-1/2 teaspoons cornstarch
1/4 cup reduced-sodium chicken broth
2 tablespoons reduced-sodium soy sauce
1 tablespoon oyster sauce, optional
1/2 teaspoon sesame oil
1 bunch bok choy
2 medium carrots, thinly sliced
2 tablespoons vegetable oil
1 can (15 ounces) whole baby corn, rinsed and drained
1/2 cup fresh snow peas
4 garlic cloves, minced
2 teaspoons minced fresh gingerroot
1 teaspoon sesame seeds, toasted

1) In a small bowl, combine the cornstarch, broth, soy sauce, oyster sauce if desired and sesame oil until smooth; set aside.

2) Cut off and discard root end of bok choy, leaving stalks with leaves. Cut green leaves from stalks. Cut leaves into 1-in. slices; set aside. Cut white stalks into 1-in. pieces.

3) In a large skillet or wok, stir-fry bok choy stalks and carrots in vegetable oil for 3-5 minutes or until crisp-tender. Add the corn, peas, garlic, ginger and reserved leaves; stir-fry for 3 minutes.

4) Stir cornstarch mixture and add to the skillet. Bring to a boil; cook and stir for 1-2 minutes or until thickened. Sprinkle with sesame seeds.

Yield: 8 servings.

NUTRITION FACTS: 3/4 cup equals 76 calories, 4 g fat (1 g saturated fat), 0 cholesterol, 356 mg sodium, 7 g carbohydrate, 3 g fiber, 3 g protein.

Keeping Ginger

Peel fresh ginger with a vegetable peeler or small paring knife. To store fresh ginger, cover with dry sherry in a small jar with a tight-fitting lid in the refrigerator. After you've used the ginger, the ginger-flavored sherry makes a delicious flavor boost to any stir-fry that calls for sherry.

Broccoflower

Broccoflower is a cross between broccoli and cauliflower. It looks like a yellow-green cauliflower and has a milder flavor.

Buying

Broccoflower is available year-round; peak season is October through February. Select firm, solid heads that are heavy for their size. Avoid those with brown spots.

Storage

Place unwashed Broccoflower in an open plastic bag in the refrigerator crisper drawer for up to 4 days.

Preparation

Trim off leaves. Cut into florets or leave whole.

Yield: 1 head (1-1/4 pounds) = 4 cups florets

Broccoflower Stir-Fry

PREP/TOTAL TIME: 25 min.

Taste of Home Test Kitchen

This bright yellowish green vegetable is seasoned with Oriental flavors for a delightful side dish.

- 1 small head Broccoflower (about 1-1/4 pounds), broken into florets
- 1 tablespoon canola oil
- 1 medium sweet red pepper, chopped
- 1 tablespoon minced fresh gingerroot
- 2 garlic cloves, minced
- 2 tablespoons reduced-sodium soy sauce
- 1 teaspoon sesame oil

1) In a skillet or wok, stir-fry Broccoflower in oil for 2-3 minutes. Add the red pepper; stir-fry for 2 minutes.

2) Add ginger and garlic; stir-fry 2-3 minutes longer or until Broccoflower is crisp-tender. Drizzle with soy sauce and sesame oil.

Yield: 4 servings.

NUTRITION FACTS: 3/4 cup equals 73 calories, 5 g fat (1 g saturated fat), 0 cholesterol, 324 mg sodium, 7 g carbohydrate, 2 g fiber, 2 g protein.

Broccoli Rabe

Broccoli rabe, also known as rabe and rapini, is green with small bud clusters and resembles broccoli. It has a bitter taste that mellows during cooking.

Buying

Broccoli rabe is available year-round; peak season is fall through spring. Select bunches with crisp, bright green leaves. Avoid ones that have wilted leaves, leaves with holes or yellowed flower buds. Smaller leaves are more tender with a milder flavor.

Storage

Store unwashed broccoli rabe in an open plastic bag in the refrigerator crisper drawer for up to 3 days.

Preparation

Trim about 1/2 in. off the bottom of the stems. Discard any coarse or damaged outer leaves. Peel any thick stems. Rinse in cold water. Cut stems, leaves and tops into large pieces.

Yield: 1 bunch (1 pound) = 4 cups loosely packed

Pasta with Broccoli Rabe

PREP: 20 min. **COOK:** 20 min.

Taste of Home Test Kitchen

Orecchiette is a pasta that looks like tiny disks or "little ears," which is what the name means.

- 2-1/2 cups uncooked orecchiette *or* small tube pasta
- 1/2 pound broccoli rabe
- 4 bacon strips, diced
- 1 can (15 ounces) garbanzo beans *or* chickpeas, rinsed and drained
- 2 tablespoons chopped oil-packed sun-dried tomatoes
- 2 garlic cloves, minced
- 1/4 teaspoon salt
- 1/4 teaspoon pepper
- 2 tablespoons grated Parmesan cheese

1) Cook pasta according to package directions. Meanwhile, trim 1/4 in. off the bottoms of broccoli rabe stems; discard coarse outer leaves. Rinse broccoli rabe in cold water and cut into 2-in. pieces; set aside.

2) In a skillet, cook bacon over medium heat until crisp. Using a slotted spoon, remove to paper towels; drain, reserving 1 tablespoon drippings. Drain pasta; reserve 1 cup cooking liquid. Set aside.

3) In the bacon drippings, cook and stir garbanzo beans until lightly browned. Stir in tomatoes and garlic. Add the broccoli rabe, salt, pepper and 1/2 cup reserved cooking liquid. Bring to a boil.

4) Reduce heat; cover and simmer for 3-5 minutes or until broccoli rabe is tender. Stir in the pasta, bacon and enough remaining cooking liquid to moisten the pasta. Sprinkle with Parmesan cheese.

Yield: 4 servings.

NUTRITION FACTS: 1-1/2 cups equals 399 calories, 10 g fat (3 g saturated fat), 12 mg cholesterol, 500 mg sodium, 62 g carbohydrate, 6 g fiber, 17 g protein.

Broccoli/Broccolini

Broccoli is a member of the cauliflower family. It has pale green, thick stalks and tightly packed, dark green heads (florets) with a slight purple tint. Stalks and florets are eaten raw or cooked.

Broccolini, also known as baby broccoli, is a cross between broccoli and Chinese kale. It has slim, individual, asparagus-like stalks with broccoli-like florets. The entire stalk is edible and does not need to be peeled. Broccolini has a sweet, mild flavor with a peppery bite. It is less fibrous than broccoli or asparagus.

Buying

Broccoli is available year-round. Select firm but tender stalks of broccoli with compact, dark green or slightly purplish florets. Select firm stalks of Broccolini with compact, dark green florets.

Storage

Store unwashed broccoli or Broccolini in an open plastic bag in the refrigerator crisper drawer up to 4 days. Blanch 3-5 minutes before freezing. Freeze for up to 1 year.

Preparation

For broccoli, remove larger leaves and tough ends of lower stalks. Wash broccoli. If using whole spears, cut lengthwise into 1-in.-wide pieces; stalks may also be peeled for more even cooking. If using florets, cut 1/4 in. to 1/2 in. below heads; discard stalks. For broccolini, wash and use entire stalk.

Yield: 1 pound broccoli = 3-1/2 cups florets
1 bunch (6 ounces) Broccolini = 4 cups loosely packed or about 12 spears

BROCCOLI WITH GINGER-ORANGE BUTTER

Broccoli with Ginger-Orange Butter

PREP/TOTAL TIME: 15 min.

Taste of Home Test Kitchen

This easy-to-prepare flavored butter is a tasty topping for steamed broccoli or most any vegetable.

> 1 pound fresh broccoli, cut into spears
> 2 tablespoons orange marmalade
> 1 tablespoon butter
> 1/2 teaspoon cider vinegar
> 1/8 teaspoon ground ginger

1) In a large saucepan, bring 1 in. of water and broccoli to a boil. Reduce heat; cover and simmer for 5-8 minutes or until crisp-tender.

2) In a saucepan, combine the marmalade, butter, vinegar and ginger. Cook until marmalade is melted. Drain broccoli; drizzle with butter mixture.

Yield: 6 servings.

NUTRITION FACTS: 1 serving equals 54 calories, 2 g fat (1 g saturated fat), 5 mg cholesterol, 43 mg sodium, 8 g carbohydrate, 2 g fiber, 2 g protein.

Broccoli Corn Casserole

PREP: 5 min. **BAKE:** 30 min.

Lucille Wermes, Camp, Arkansas

I had a difficult time getting my three sons to eat vegetables when they were young. So I fooled them with this casserole that looks just like stuffing.

> 1 package (9 ounces) frozen chopped broccoli, thawed
> 1 can (14-3/4 ounces) cream-style corn
> 1 egg
> 1-1/2 cups stuffing mix
> 1/2 cup butter, melted

1) In a large bowl, combine the broccoli, corn and egg. Transfer to a greased 1-qt. baking dish. Sprinkle with stuffing mix and drizzle with butter.

2) Bake, uncovered, at 350° for 30-35 minutes or until golden brown and bubbly.

Yield: 6 servings.

NUTRITION FACTS: 1/2 cup equals 269 calories, 18 g fat (10 g saturated fat), 76 mg cholesterol, 605 mg sodium, 25 g carbohydrate, 3 g fiber, 5 g protein.

Broccolini with Shallots

PREP/TOTAL TIME: 15 min.

Taste of Home Test Kitchen

Shallots and garlic are a nice complement to the peppery bite of the Broccolini.

> 1 bunch (1/2 pound) Broccolini, trimmed
> 1/2 teaspoon salt
> 1 shallot, sliced
> 2 garlic cloves, minced
> 1 tablespoon olive oil
> 1 to 2 teaspoons lemon juice *or* white balsamic vinegar
> 1/4 teaspoon pepper

1) Place Broccolini and salt in a large skillet; cover with water. Bring to a boil. Reduce heat; cover and simmer for 5-7 minutes or until tender. Drain well. Remove and keep warm.

2) In the same skillet, saute shallot and garlic in oil until tender. Add the Broccolini, lemon juice and pepper. Saute for 1-2 minutes or until heated.

Yield: 4 servings.

NUTRITION FACTS: 1/2 cup equals 63 calories, 3 g fat (trace saturated fat), 0 cholesterol, 313 mg sodium, 6 g carbohydrate, 1 g fiber, 2 g protein.

STEAMED LEMON BROCCOLI

⃝Steamed Lemon Broccoli

PREP/TOTAL TIME: 20 min.

Michelle Hanson, Oacoma, South Dakota

I first tried this sunny side dish because it seemed to be a fresh, nutritious and easy combination. Now it's the only way my husband will eat broccoli. I love to pair it with grilled meat on hot summer days.

> 1 large bunch broccoli, cut into spears
> 1 medium onion, halved and thinly sliced
> 1 cup thinly sliced celery
> 3 garlic cloves, minced
> 3 tablespoons butter
> 2 teaspoons grated lemon peel
> 1-1/2 teaspoons lemon juice
> 1/2 teaspoon salt
> 1/4 teaspoon pepper

1) Place broccoli in a steamer basket. Place in a large saucepan over 1 in. of water; bring to a boil. Cover and steam for 5-6 minutes or until crisp-tender. Rinse in cold water; drain and set aside.

2) In a large skillet, saute the onion, celery and garlic in butter for 5 minutes or until vegetables are tender. Add the lemon peel and juice, salt, pepper and broccoli; heat through.

Yield: 4 servings.

NUTRITION FACTS: 3/4 cup equals 142 calories, 9 g fat (5 g saturated fat), 23 mg cholesterol, 451 mg sodium, 14 g carbohydrate, 6 g fiber, 6 g protein.

EASY VEGETABLE SALAD ■■■

For a tasty marinated vegetable salad, combine any leftover cooked veggies you have on hand, such as broccoli, green beans, squash and carrots. Add some minced garlic, onion, Italian seasoning and Italian or ranch dressing, then chill until serving.

—Dawn Lowenstein, Hatboro, Pennsylvania

Brussels Sprouts

A member of the cabbage family, this tiny green vegetable ranges in size from 1 to 1-1/2 in. in diameter. The name originates from Brussels, Belgium, where brussels sprouts were first grown centuries ago.

Buying

Brussels sprouts are available September through May; peak season is October through February. Select small, firm, tightly closed heads that have a bright green color.

Storage

Store unwashed brussels sprouts in an open plastic bag in the refrigerator crisper drawer for up to 3 days. Blanch 3-5 minutes before freezing. Freeze for up to 1 year.

Yield: 1 pound brussels sprouts = 22 to 28 medium sprouts or 4 cups trimmed

Preparing Brussels Sprouts

Remove any loose or yellowed outer leaves; trim stem end. Rinse sprouts. When cooking brussels sprouts, cut an X in the core end with a sharp knife. This helps the sprouts cook more quickly and evenly.

⃝Lemon-Dilled Brussels Sprouts

PREP/TOTAL TIME: 25 min.

Marlyn Duff, New Berlin, Wisconsin

Brussels sprouts get dressed up when lemon and dill season the buttery sauce and chopped walnuts add just the right crunch.

> 1-1/2 pounds fresh brussels sprouts
> 1/3 cup butter
> 2 tablespoons lemon juice
> 1 teaspoon dill weed
> 1/2 teaspoon salt
> 1/8 teaspoon pepper
> 2 tablespoons finely chopped walnuts

1) Trim brussels sprouts and cut an X in the core end of each. In a large saucepan, bring 1 in. of water and brussels sprouts to a boil. Reduce heat; cover and simmer for 10-12 minutes or until tender.

2) Meanwhile, in another saucepan, melt butter. Stir in the lemon juice, dill, salt and pepper; cook and stir for 1 minute. Drain sprouts; add to butter mixture and toss to coat. Sprinkle with walnuts.

Yield: 6-8 servings.

NUTRITION FACTS: 3/4 cup equals 117 calories, 9 g fat (5 g saturated fat), 20 mg cholesterol, 246 mg sodium, 8 g carbohydrate, 3 g fiber, 3 g protein.

Braised Brussels Sprouts

PREP/TOTAL TIME: 30 min.

Yvonne Anderson, New Philadelphia, Ohio

Bacon and caraway seeds add a bit of Old-World flavor to this recipe.

    2 pounds fresh brussels sprouts
    2 bacon strips, diced
    1 medium onion, chopped
    1 cup chicken broth
    1 teaspoon caraway seeds
  1/4 teaspoon salt
  1/8 teaspoon pepper

1) Trim brussels sprouts and cut an X in the core of each. In a large saucepan, bring 1 in. of water and brussels sprouts to a boil. Reduce heat, cover and simmer for 8-10 minutes or until crisp-tender.

2) Meanwhile, in a large skillet, cook bacon over medium heat until crisp. Using a slotted spoon, remove to paper towels to drain.

3) In the drippings, saute onion until tender. Stir in the broth, caraway seeds, salt and pepper. Bring to a boil. Reduce heat; simmer, uncovered, until liquid is almost evaporated.

4) Drain sprouts. Add sprouts and bacon to onion mixture; toss to coat.

Yield: 8 servings.

NUTRITION FACTS: 1 cup equals 91 calories, 4 g fat (1 g saturated fat), 4 mg cholesterol, 260 mg sodium, 12 g carbohydrate, 5 g fiber, 5 g protein.

Cabbage, Green or Red

Cabbage is a fleshy-leafed member of the mustard family that ranges in color from white to green to deep reddish-purple. Heads are dense and heavy. Serve raw in salads or use cooked in entrees and side dishes. Cabbage is often shredded for slaw and sliced or cut into wedges for cooking.

Buying

Cabbage is available year-round. For green cabbage, select round, compact, solid heads that are heavy for their size. Cabbage heads will vary in size, but the leaves should be tight, smooth and unblemished. Red cabbage heads are not as compact as green cabbage heads. The color should be a reddish-purple.

Storage

Store unwashed cabbage in a sealed plastic bag in the refrigerator crisper drawer for up to 2 weeks.

Preparation

Wash head. Trim center core to within 1/4 in. of leaves; remove any discolored, damaged or tough outer leaves from head. When cooking red cabbage, add a little lemon juice or vinegar to the water to help retain the red color.

Yield: 1 medium head cabbage (2-1/2 pounds)
    = 8 cups

BRAISED BRUSSELS SPROUTS

Removing Core From Cabbage

Cut cabbage in half or into quarters. Make a V-shaped cut around core and remove.

AU GRATIN CABBAGE

Au Gratin Cabbage

PREP: 10 min. **BAKE:** 30 min.

Katherine Stallwood, Richland, Washington

With my Russian heritage, I've always loved cabbage. My husband does, too, when I make it this way!

    2 cups shredded cabbage
  1/2 cup grated carrot
  1/4 cup chopped green onions
    1 egg
  1/2 cup milk
    3 tablespoons shredded Swiss cheese
  1/4 teaspoon seasoned salt
    1 tablespoon minced fresh parsley
    1 tablespoon shredded Parmesan
       cheese

1) In a large skillet coated with cooking spray, saute the cabbage, carrot and onions for 5-7 minutes or until crisp-tender. Transfer to a greased shallow 1-qt. baking dish.

2) In a bowl, combine the egg, milk, Swiss cheese and seasoned salt. Pour over the vegetables. Sprinkle with parsley and Parmesan cheese.

3) Bake, uncovered, at 350° for 30-35 minutes or until a knife inserted near the center comes out clean.

Yield: 2 servings.

NUTRITION FACTS: 3/4 cup equals 156 calories, 8 g fat (4 g saturated fat), 126 mg cholesterol, 345 mg sodium, 11 g carbohydrate, 3 g fiber, 10 g protein.

Creamy Cabbage

PREP: 25 min. **BAKE:** 15 min.

Alice Lewis, Torrance, California

This recipe, which was handed down to me from my grandmother, makes a good side dish for any meal. It's a simple way to spruce up cabbage and is happily received at potluck suppers.

    4 cups shredded cabbage
    4 bacon strips, diced
    1 tablespoon all-purpose flour

  1/2 teaspoon salt
  1/4 teaspoon paprika
  1/8 teaspoon pepper
    1 cup milk
    1 cup soft bread crumbs

1) In a large saucepan, bring 1 in. of water and cabbage to a boil. Reduce heat; cover and simmer for 3-5 minutes or until crisp-tender. Drain.

2) In a skillet, cook bacon over medium heat until crisp. Remove to paper towels; drain, reserving 1 tablespoon drippings. Stir the flour, salt, paprika and pepper into the drippings until smooth; gradually add milk. Bring to a boil; cook and stir for 1-2 minutes or until thickened.

3) Place cabbage in an ungreased 1-qt. baking dish. Top with sauce. Sprinkle bread crumbs and bacon over the top. Bake, uncovered, at 400° for 15 minutes or until heated through.

Yield: 4 servings.

NUTRITION FACTS: 1 serving equals 160 calories, 9 g fat (4 g saturated fat), 17 mg cholesterol, 518 mg sodium, 14 g carbohydrate, 2 g fiber, 6 g protein.

RED CABBAGE WITH APPLES

Red Cabbage with Apples

PREP: 15 min. **COOK:** 1 hour

Peg Schendel, Janesville, Minnesota

Cabbage and apples are simmered together in this wonderful side dish. Bacon adds color and crunch for a perfect topper.

    1 medium onion, chopped
  1/4 cup butter
    1 medium head red cabbage
       (2 pounds), shredded
    2 medium tart apples, peeled and
       chopped
    1 cup apple cider *or* juice
  1/4 cup packed brown sugar
    2 tablespoons cider vinegar
  1/2 teaspoon salt
  1/4 teaspoon pepper

2 bacon strips, cooked and
crumbled

Minced fresh parsley, optional

1) In a large skillet, saute onion in butter until golden
   and tender. Add the cabbage, apples, cider, brown
   sugar, vinegar, salt and pepper. Bring to a boil.

2) Reduce heat; cover and simmer for 1 hour or until
   cabbage and apples are tender and the liquid is
   reduced. Sprinkle with bacon and parsley if
   desired.

Yield: 6 servings.

NUTRITION FACTS: 3/4 cup equals 203 calories, 9 g fat (5 g saturated
fat), 22 mg cholesterol, 331 mg sodium, 31 g carbohydrate,
4 g fiber, 3 g protein.

Fried Cabbage

PREP/TOTAL TIME: 20 min.

Bernice Morris, Marshfield, Missouri

*Fried cabbage is so good with potatoes, deviled eggs and
corn bread. When I was young, my family grew our
own cabbage and potatoes. It was fun to put them to
use in the kitchen.*

> 2 tablespoons butter
> 1 teaspoon sugar
> 1/2 teaspoon salt
> 1/4 teaspoon crushed red pepper flakes
> 1/8 teaspoon pepper
> 6 cups coarsely chopped cabbage
> 1 tablespoon water

1) In a large skillet, melt butter over medium heat.
   Stir in the sugar, salt, pepper flakes and pepper.

2) Add the cabbage and water. Cook for 5-6 minutes
   or until tender, stirring occasionally.

Yield: 6 servings.

NUTRITION FACTS: 1 cup equals 59 calories, 4 g fat (2 g saturated
fat), 10 mg cholesterol, 251 mg sodium, 6 g carbohydrate, 2 g fiber,
1 g protein.

Cabbage, Napa

Napa cabbage, also known as Chinese cabbage, has a
mild flavor and crinkly pale green to white thin leaves.
Two common varieties of Chinese cabbage are sold
in the stores. One is more cylindrical (Michihli) and
the other is rounder (napa), but they can be used
interchangeably in recipes.

Buying

Napa cabbage is available year-round. Select heads
that are compact with crisp, fresh-looking leaves.

Storage

Store unwashed napa cabbage in an open plastic bag
in the refrigerator crisper drawer for up to 3 days.
Store away from fruits such as apples or bananas.

Preparation

Napa cabbage can be used raw or cooked. Remove
outer leaves or any wilted leaves. Rinse in cold water.
Cut according to recipe directions.

Yield: 1 head (3 pounds) = 12 cups chopped

Carrots

Carrots are long, slender
root vegetables related to the
parsnip and have a distinctive
orange color. Smaller varieties,
called baby carrots, are also available.

Buying

Carrots are available year-round. Select crisp, firm,
smooth, well-shaped carrots with deep orange color.
Smaller carrots are tender and sweet. Carrots sold in
bunches with fern-like green tops are fresher than
those sold in plastic bags but are not always available.

Storage

Trim tops and roots when present. Store unwashed,
unpeeled carrots in a sealed plastic bag in the
refrigerator crisper drawer for 1-2 weeks. Blanch
3-5 minutes before freezing. Freeze for up to 1 year.

Preparation

Young carrots may be used unpeeled if they are well
scrubbed. Larger carrots should be thinly peeled with
a vegetable peeler.

Yield: 1 pound carrots (6 to 7 medium)
= 3 to 3-1/2 cups sliced (uncooked)

HARVEST CARROTS

Harvest Carrots

PREP: 15 min. **BAKE:** 30 min.

Marty Rummel, Trout Lake, Washington

I make this dish often, and sometimes I'll add cooked turkey or chicken and turn it into a main dish.

> 4 cups sliced carrots
> 2 cups water
> 1 medium onion, chopped
> 1/2 cup butter, *divided*
> 1 can (10-3/4 ounces) condensed cream of celery soup, undiluted
> 1/2 cup shredded cheddar cheese
> 1/8 teaspoon pepper
> 3 cups seasoned stuffing croutons

1) In a large saucepan, bring carrots and water to a boil. Reduce heat; cover and simmer for 5-8 minutes or until tender. Drain. In a small skillet, saute onion in 3 tablespoons butter until tender.

2) In a large bowl, combine the carrots, onion, soup, cheese and pepper. Melt remaining butter; toss with croutons. Fold into carrot mixture.

3) Transfer to a greased 2-qt. baking dish. Cover and bake at 350° for 20 minutes. Uncover; bake 10 minutes longer or until lightly browned.

Yield: 6 servings.

NUTRITION FACTS: 3/4 cup equals 342 calories, 21 g fat (12 g saturated fat), 53 mg cholesterol, 962 mg sodium, 34 g carbohydrate, 5 g fiber, 7 g protein.

Maple-Glazed Carrots

PREP/TOTAL TIME: 15 min.

Edie DeSpain, Logan, Utah

Carrots are my favorite vegetable, so I'm always searching for different ways to prepare them. This festive dish is quick to make and nicely complements turkey or chicken.

> 12 medium carrots, julienned
> 2 tablespoons cornstarch
> 2/3 cup orange juice
> 5 tablespoons maple syrup
> 5 tablespoons butter, melted
> 1 tablespoon grated orange peel
> 3/4 teaspoon ground nutmeg
> 1/2 teaspoon salt

1) In a large saucepan, bring 1 in. of water and carrots to a boil. Reduce heat; cover and simmer for 3-5 minutes or until crisp-tender.

2) Meanwhile, in another saucepan, combine the cornstarch and orange juice until smooth. Stir in the remaining ingredients. Bring to a boil; cook and stir for 2 minutes or until thickened.

3) Drain carrots; transfer to a serving bowl. Pour glaze over carrots; gently stir to coat.

Yield: 6 servings.

Editor's Note: Two 10-ounce packages of shredded carrots can be substituted for julienned carrots.

NUTRITION FACTS: 1 cup equals 205 calories, 10 g fat (6 g saturated fat), 26 mg cholesterol, 338 mg sodium, 29 g carbohydrate, 4 g fiber, 2 g protein.

Confetti Carrot Fritters

PREP/TOTAL TIME: 30 min.

Peggy Camp, Twain, California

Crispy, sweet and savory, these delicate fritters are a fun twist on the traditional fruit-filled variety. They're yummy served with a mustard dipping sauce, but our kids enjoy them with a drizzle of warm maple syrup, too.

> 6 cups water
> 2-1/2 cups finely chopped carrots
> 1/4 cup all-purpose flour
> 1/4 teaspoon salt
> 1/4 teaspoon pepper
> 2 eggs, *separated*
> 3 tablespoons milk
> 2 tablespoons finely chopped onion
> 2 tablespoons minced fresh parsley

Vegetable oil for deep-fat frying

MUSTARD SAUCE:

> 1 tablespoon minced fresh parsley
> 1 tablespoon red wine vinegar
> 1 tablespoon Dijon mustard
> 1 teaspoon finely chopped green onion
> 1/4 cup olive oil

1) In a saucepan, bring water to a boil. Add the carrots; cover and boil for 3 minutes. Drain and immediately place carrots in ice water. Drain and pat dry.

2) In a large bowl, combine the flour, salt and pepper. Combine egg yolks and milk; stir into the flour mixture until smooth. Stir in the onion, parsley and carrots.

3) In a mixing bowl, beat egg whites on high speed until stiff peaks form; fold into batter.

4) In an electric skillet, heat 1/4 in. of oil over medium heat. Drop batter by 1/3 cupfuls into oil; press lightly to flatten. Fry until golden brown, about 2 minutes on each side.

5) For mustard sauce, in a small bowl, combine the parsley, vinegar, mustard and green onion. Slowly whisk in oil until blended. Serve with the fritters.

Yield: 9 servings.

NUTRITION FACTS: 1 serving equals 105 calories, 8 g fat (1 g saturated fat), 48 mg cholesterol, 137 mg sodium, 7 g carbohydrate, 1 g fiber, 2 g protein.

Creamed Carrots

PREP/TOTAL TIME: 25 min.

Eva Bailey, Olive Hill, Kentucky

These carrots are always a popular dish at my table. The rich sauce coats the carrots nicely and really perks up their flavor.

    1 pound carrots, sliced
    1 tablespoon butter
    1 tablespoon all-purpose flour
    2 tablespoons finely chopped onion
    2 teaspoons minced fresh basil
       or 1/2 teaspoon dried basil
  1/2 teaspoon seasoned salt
  1/8 teaspoon pepper
    1 cup evaporated milk

1) In a large saucepan, bring 1 in. of water and carrots to a boil. Reduce heat; cover and simmer for 7-9 minutes or until crisp-tender.

2) Meanwhile, in another saucepan, melt butter. Stir in the flour, onion, basil, seasoned salt and pepper until blended; gradually stir in milk. Bring to a boil; cook and stir for 2 minutes or until thickened.

3) Drain carrots and transfer to a serving bowl. Add sauce and stir to coat.

Yield: 4 servings.

NUTRITION FACTS: 3/4 cup equals 163 calories, 7 g fat (5 g saturated fat), 28 mg cholesterol, 319 mg sodium, 19 g carbohydrate, 4 g fiber, 5 g protein.

Vegetables Mornay

PREP/TOTAL TIME: 30 min.

Jo Anne Remmele, Echo, Minnesota

These saucy vegetables are a colorful and satisfying side dish we enjoy often. Our daughter earned the Reserve Grand Champion ribbon at our local county fair with this recipe.

    6 to 8 medium carrots,
       sliced 1/4 inch thick
  1/4 cup water
2-1/4 cups frozen chopped broccoli
2-1/4 cups frozen cauliflowerets
    2 jars (4-1/2 ounces *each*) whole
       mushrooms, drained
    2 tablespoons cornstarch
    1 teaspoon salt
  1/4 teaspoon pepper
1-1/2 cups milk
  1/2 cup butter, melted, *divided*
    1 cup (4 ounces) shredded Swiss
       cheese
    2 tablespoons grated Parmesan
       cheese
  1/2 cup seasoned croutons

1) Place the carrots and water in a 3-qt. microwave-safe dish. Cover and microwave on high for 2 minutes.

2) Add the broccoli and cauliflower. Cover and microwave for 6-9 minutes or until vegetables are tender; drain. Add mushrooms; set aside.

3) In another microwave-safe dish, combine the cornstarch, salt and pepper. Stir in milk and 6 tablespoons butter until smooth.

4) Cover and microwave on high for 3-5 minutes or until thickened and smooth, stirring after every minute. Add Swiss and Parmesan cheeses, stirring until melted.

5) Pour over the vegetables. Cover and microwave for 2-4 minutes or until heated through. Toss the croutons with remaining butter; stir into vegetables.

Yield: 8-10 servings.

NUTRITION FACTS: 1/2 cup equals 200 calories, 14 g fat (9 g saturated fat), 40 mg cholesterol, 538 mg sodium, 12 g carbohydrate, 3 g fiber, 7 g protein.

VEGETABLES MORNAY

Smart Shopping for Frozen Veggies

When buying bags of frozen vegetables, examine the packages for signs that they've been thawed and refrozen. Steer clear of bagged vegetables that are frozen in blocks or large chunks. If the packages are transparent, check for crystallization. Both indicate thawing and refreezing, which can diminish quality.

Cauliflower

This snowy-white vegetable has a flower-like appearance and a mild cabbage-like flavor. Cauliflower can be eaten raw or cooked.

Buying

Cauliflower is available year-round; peak season is October through March. Select firm, solid white or creamy-colored heads that are heavy for their size. The florets should be clean and tightly packed. The surrounding jacket leaves should be fresh and green. Orange, purple and green cauliflower can be handled and prepared in the same way as white cauliflower.

Storage

Store unwashed cauliflower in an open plastic bag in the refrigerator crisper drawer for up to 5 days. Blanch 1-2 minutes before freezing. Freeze for up to 1 year.

Preparation

Trim off leaves. Remove base stem at an angle so the core comes out in a cone and the head remains intact. Separate into florets if desired.

Yield: 1-1/2 pounds of cauliflower (about 1 head) trimmed = 4 cups florets

CHEESE SAUCE OVER CAULIFLOWER

Cheese Sauce over Cauliflower

PREP/TOTAL TIME: 20 min.

Ruby Zein, Monona, Wisconsin

The cheese sauce makes cauliflower hard to resist, even for picky eaters! I like to serve this dish at holidays and also for lunch along with pork sausage links.

      1 large head cauliflower
1-1/2 teaspoons salt
      3 tablespoons butter
      3 tablespoons all-purpose flour
  1/2 teaspoon dried thyme
1-1/2 cups milk
1-1/2 cups (6 ounces) shredded cheddar cheese
Paprika
Minced fresh parsley

1) In a large saucepan, bring 1 in. of water, cauliflower and salt to a boil. Reduce heat; cover and cook for 10-15 minutes or until cauliflower is crisp-tender.

2) Meanwhile, in a small saucepan, melt butter; stir in flour and thyme until blended. Gradually add milk. Bring to a boil; cook and stir for 2 minutes or until thickened. Reduce heat; add cheese, stirring until melted.

3) Drain and pat cauliflower dry; place on a serving platter. Top with cheese sauce; sprinkle with paprika and parsley. Cut into wedges.

Yield: 6 servings.

NUTRITION FACTS: 1 serving equals 237 calories, 16 g fat (11 g saturated fat), 54 mg cholesterol, 890 mg sodium, 14 g carbohydrate, 4 g fiber, 11 g protein.

Asian Cauliflower

PREP/TOTAL TIME: 20 min.

Carol Krueger, Pewaukee, Wisconsin

Every time I make this simple side dish, I get requests for the recipe. No one can believe how easy it is to make!

      1 medium head cauliflower, broken into florets
      3 tablespoons cold water, *divided*
  1/2 cup diced celery
      1 small onion, finely chopped
  1/4 cup minced fresh parsley
      1 tablespoon butter
      1 cup hot water
      1 tablespoon chicken bouillon granules
      2 tablespoons cornstarch
      1 tablespoon soy sauce
Dash pepper

1) Place cauliflower in a microwave-safe dish. Add 1 tablespoon cold water. Cover and microwave on high for 4-1/2 to 5-1/2 minutes or until tender; drain and keep warm.

2) In a 1-qt. microwave-safe bowl, combine the celery, onion, parsley and butter. Cover and microwave on high for 1 to 1-1/2 minutes or until vegetables are tender.

3) In a small bowl, combine hot water and bouillon until dissolved. Combine the cornstarch and remaining cold water until smooth. Add soy sauce, pepper and bouillon; mix well. Stir into celery mixture.

4) Microwave, uncovered, at 70% power for 2-3 minutes or until sauce comes to a boil, stirring after each minute. Pour over cauliflower.

Yield: 4-6 servings.

NUTRITION FACTS: 1 serving equals 62 calories, 2 g fat (1 g saturated fat), 5 mg cholesterol, 632 mg sodium, 9 g carbohydrate, 3 g fiber, 3 g protein.

Crumb-Topped Cauliflower

PREP/TOTAL TIME: 15 min.

Kathy Cochill, Ocqueoc, Michigan

This fast and delicious dish makes just enough tasty cauliflower for two.

- 1-1/2 cups cauliflowerets
- 1/4 cup finely chopped walnuts *or* pecans
- 3 tablespoons dry bread crumbs
- 3 tablespoons butter
- 1/4 cup chopped green onions
- 1-1/2 teaspoons minced fresh parsley
- 1 teaspoon lemon juice

1) In a saucepan, bring 1 in. of water; and cauliflower to a boil. Reduce heat; cover and simmer for 4-6 minutes or until crisp-tender.

2) Meanwhile, in a small skillet, cook nuts and bread crumbs in butter for 1 minute. Add onions and parsley; cook and stir until onions are tender and nuts and crumbs are lightly browned. Stir in lemon juice. Drain cauliflower; top with crumb mixture.

Yield: 2 servings.

Editor's Note: This recipe can be easily doubled to serve 4.

NUTRITION FACTS: 3/4 cup equals 309 calories, 27 g fat (11 g saturated fat), 46 mg cholesterol, 286 mg sodium, 14 g carbohydrate, 3 g fiber, 7 g protein.

Whipped Cauliflower

PREP/TOTAL TIME: 20 min.

Taste of Home Test Kitchen

Need a low-carb substitute for mashed potatoes? This five-ingredient dish has a mild cauliflower flavor with a smooth creamy texture.

- 1 medium head cauliflower, cut into florets
- 1/4 cup fat-free milk
- 2 tablespoons canola oil
- 1/4 teaspoon salt
- 1/8 teaspoon white pepper

1) Place cauliflower in a steamer basket; place in a saucepan over 1 in. of water. Bring to a boil; cover and steam for 8-10 minutes or until tender. Cool slightly.

2) Place milk and oil in a food processor. Add the cauliflower, salt and pepper; cover and process until blended. Transfer to a bowl. Serve immediately.

Yield: 4 servings.

NUTRITION FACTS: 1/2 cup equals 105 calories, 7 g fat (1 g saturated fat), 1 mg cholesterol, 199 mg sodium, 8 g carbohydrate, 4 g fiber, 3 g protein.

Celery

Generally, celery has a subtle flavor and a crisp, crunchy texture. The most common variety is Pascal. The root of the celery is sold as celeriac.

Buying

Celery is available year-round. Select firm, crisp ribs without any blemishes. The leaves should be green, not yellowed or wilted.

Storage

Store unwashed celery in a plastic bag in the refrigerator crisper drawer for up to 2 weeks.

Preparation

Wash ribs in cold water. Trim leaves and base from ribs before using. Outer ribs can be peeled with a vegetable peeler to remove some of the thicker strings. Leaves are good for soups, stews and garnishes.

Yield: 1 medium rib = about 1/2 cup chopped

Reviving Celery

Give limp celery a second chance to season entrees, soups and stews. Cut end from each limp stalk. Place in a jar or glass of cold water. Place in the refrigerator for several hours or overnight.

Corn

Also known as sweet corn, this vegetable has bright yellow or white kernels or a mix of both. Corn on the cob is generally served with silk and husks removed. Cooked kernels can be cut from the cob and used in recipes in place of canned or frozen corn.

Buying

Corn is available May through August; peak season is July through August. Select corn that has fresh green, tightly closed husks with dark brown, dry (but not brittle) silk. The stem should be moist but not chalky, yellow or discolored. Ears should have plump, tender, small kernels in tight rows up to the tip. Kernels should be firm enough to resist slight pressure. A fresh kernel will spurt "milk" if punctured.

Storage

Store unshucked ears in opened plastic bags in the refrigerator crisper drawer and use within 2 days. Blanch corn on the cob for 6-9 minutes and whole kernel corn for 5-6 minutes before freezing. Freeze for up to 1 year.

Preparation

If boiling or steaming, remove husk by pulling the husks down the ear; break off the undeveloped tip. Trim stem. Pull out silk between kernel rows or remove with a dry vegetable brush; rinse in cold water.

Yield: 1 ear of corn = 1/3 to 1/2 cup kernels

Cutting Kernels From Corncobs

Stand one end of the cob on a cutting board. Starting at the top, run a sharp knife down the cob, cutting deeply to remove whole kernels. One medium cob yields 1/3 to 1/2 cup kernels.

Tex-Mex Corn on the Cob
PREP/TOTAL TIME: 15 min.

Helen Jacobs, Euless, Texas

The tender ears of corn get a summery treatment seasoned with chili powder, cilantro and lime.

- 12 small ears fresh corn on the cob (about 6 inches)
- 3 tablespoons minced fresh cilantro
- 1-1/2 teaspoons chili powder
- 1-1/2 teaspoons grated lime peel
- 3/4 teaspoon salt
- 3/4 teaspoon ground cumin
- 1/4 teaspoon garlic powder

Refrigerated butter-flavored spray

1) Place corn in a Dutch oven or kettle; cover with water. Bring to a boil. Reduce heat; cover and cook for 3-5 minutes or until tender.

2) In a small bowl, combine the cilantro, chili powder, lime peel, salt, cumin and garlic powder.

3) Drain the corn. Spritz with butter-flavored spray; brush or pat seasoning mixture over corn.

Yield: 12 servings.

Editor's Note: This recipe was tested with I Can't Believe It's Not Butter Spray.

NUTRITION FACTS: 1 ear of corn equals 85 calories, 1 g fat (trace saturated fat), 20 mg cholesterol, 164 mg sodium, 20 g carbohydrate, 2 g fiber, 3 g protein.

DELICIOUS CORN PUDDING

Delicious Corn Pudding
PREP: 15 min. **BAKE:** 35 min.

Paula Marchesi, Rocky Point, New York

This comforting dish has been part of family meals for years, and it's been shared at many gatherings.

- 4 eggs, *separated*
- 2 tablespoons butter, melted and cooled
- 1 tablespoon sugar
- 1 tablespoon brown sugar

1 teaspoon salt
1/2 teaspoon vanilla extract
Dash *each* ground cinnamon and nutmeg
2 cups sweet corn (3-4 ears)
1 cup half-and-half cream
1 cup milk

1) In a large mixing bowl, beat egg yolks until lemon-colored, 5-8 minutes. Add butter, sugars, salt, vanilla, cinnamon and nutmeg; mix well. Add corn. Stir in cream and milk.

2) In a small mixing bowl, beat egg whites on high speed until stiff; fold into yolk mixture. Pour into a greased 1-1/2-qt. baking dish.

3) Bake, uncovered, at 350° for 35 minutes or until a knife inserted near the center comes out clean. Cover loosely with foil during the last 10 minutes if top browns too quickly.

Yield: 8 servings.

NUTRITION FACTS: 1 serving equals 179 calories, 10 g fat (5 g saturated fat), 133 mg cholesterol, 393 mg sodium, 16 g carbohydrate, 1 g fiber, 7 g protein.

Grilled Sweet Corn

PREP: 10 min. + soaking **GRILL:** 25 min.

Connie Lou Hollister, Lake Odessa, Michigan

We have plenty of fresh sweet corn in our area, so we use this recipe often in summer. Seasonings perfectly accent the corn's just-picked flavor.

8 large ears sweet corn in husk
6 tablespoons butter, softened
1 tablespoon minced fresh parsley
1 to 2 teaspoons chili powder
1 teaspoon garlic salt
1/2 to 1 teaspoon ground cumin

1) Carefully peel back husks from corn to within 1 in. of bottom; remove silk. Combine remaining ingredients; spread over corn.

2) Rewrap corn in husks and secure with kitchen string. Place in a large kettle; cover with cold water. Soak for 20 minutes; drain. Grill corn, covered, over medium heat, for 25-30 minutes or until tender, turning often.

Yield: 8 servings.

NUTRITION FACTS: 1 ear of corn equals 200 calories, 10 g fat (6 g saturated fat), 23 mg cholesterol, 338 mg sodium, 28 g carbohydrate, 4 g fiber, 5 g protein.

■ **Zesty Corn Packets:** Husk corn and remove silk. Place each ear on a piece of heavy-duty foil (13 in. x 12 in.). Drizzle with a mixture of, 1/3 cup melted butter, 2 tablespoons *each* prepared mustard and horseradish, 1 teaspoon Worcestershire sauce and 1/4 teaspoon lemon-pepper seasoning. Fold in edges of the foil and seal tightly. Grill over medium heat for 10-12 minutes or until corn is tender. Open foil carefully to allow steam to escape.

Three-Pepper Corn Pudding

PREP: 25 min. **BAKE:** 45 min.

Virginia Anthony, Jacksonville, Florida

Red peppers, chili peppers and jalapeno peppers liven up this comforting side dish.

1 medium sweet red pepper, chopped
6 green onions, thinly sliced
1 tablespoon olive oil
1 can (4 ounces) chopped green chilies, drained
3 medium jalapeno peppers, seeded and chopped
2 packages (10 ounces *each*) frozen corn, thawed, *divided*
1 can (12 ounces) reduced-fat evaporated milk
1/3 cup reduced-fat sour cream
1/4 cup fat-free milk
3 egg whites
2 eggs
1/4 cup cornstarch
1 teaspoon salt
1 teaspoon ground cumin
3/4 teaspoon ground thyme

1) In a nonstick skillet, saute the red pepper and onions in oil until tender. Remove from the heat. Stir in the chilies, jalapenos and half of the corn. Transfer to a 13-in. x 9-in. x 2-in. baking dish coated with cooking spray.

2) In a blender, combine the remaining ingredients; add remaining corn. Cover and process for 3 minutes or until smooth. Pour over red pepper mixture. Bake, uncovered, at 350° for 45-50 minutes or until a knife inserted near the center comes out clean.

Yield: 12 servings.

Editor's Note: When cutting or seeding hot peppers, use rubber or plastic gloves to protect your hands. Avoid touching your face.

NUTRITION FACTS: 1 piece equals 119 calories, 3 g fat (1 g saturated fat), 39 mg cholesterol, 298 mg sodium, 18 g carbohydrate, 2 g fiber, 6 g protein.

THREE-PEPPER CORN PUDDING

◖Corn Medley

PREP/TOTAL TIME: 20 min.

Ruth Andrewson, Leavenworth, Washington

With a little spark of cumin, this garden-fresh medley showcases corn in a colorful blend with tomato, green pepper and onion.

        2 cups fresh-cut sweet corn
           (3 to 4 ears)
      1/4 cup chopped onion
      1/4 cup chopped green pepper
        2 tablespoons butter
      1/2 teaspoon salt
      1/4 teaspoon ground cumin
        1 large tomato, seeded and chopped
        2 tablespoons sugar

1) In a large saucepan, combine the corn, onion, green pepper, butter, salt and cumin. Cook and stir over medium heat until butter is melted.

2) Cover and cook over low heat for 10 minutes. Stir in tomato and sugar; cook, covered, 5 minutes longer.

Yield: 5 servings.

NUTRITION FACTS: 1/2 cup equals 126 calories, 5 g fat (3 g saturated fat), 12 mg cholesterol, 295 mg sodium, 20 g carbohydrate, 2 g fiber, 3 g protein.

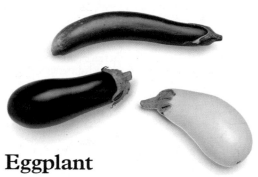

Eggplant

Eggplants that are generally found in stores have purple skin, but a white variety may be available in specialty markets. The common American eggplant is pear-shaped and 6 to 10 in. long. Italian eggplant is a smaller version of the common eggplant. Its skin is thinner and more delicate. Chinese and Japanese eggplant are thin and elongated. The Chinese eggplant is slightly larger and has a more delicate flavor than the Japanese variety.

Buying

Eggplant is available year-round; peak season is July through September. Select a firm, round or pear-shaped, heavy eggplant with a uniformly smooth color and glossy taut skin. The eggplant should be free from blemishes and rust spots with intact green caps and mold-free stems.

Storage

Store unwashed eggplant in an open plastic bag in the refrigerator crisper drawer for up to 3 days.

Preparation

Wash eggplant; cut off stem and peel if desired. Cut eggplant discolors quickly, so cut into slices, strips or cubes just before salting. Salt eggplant at least 30 minutes before cooking.

Yield: 1 medium eggplant (1 pound) = 5 cups cubes

Salting Eggplant

Salting an eggplant draws out some of the moisture, giving the flesh a denser texture. This means it will give off less moisture and absorb less fat during cooking. Salting may cut some of the bitterness from an eggplant.

To salt, place slices, cubes or strips of eggplant in a colander over a plate; sprinkle with salt and toss. Let stand for 30 minutes. Rinse, drain well and pat dry with paper towels.

Baked Ratatouille

PREP: 15 min. BAKE: 50 min.

Catherine Lee, Chandler, Arizona

Ratatouille is usually a seasoned stew made of eggplant, tomatoes, green peppers, squash and sometimes meat. Bacon and cheese make my recipe delicious.

        4 bacon strips, cut into 2-inch
           pieces
        1 cup sliced onion
        1 can (14-1/2 ounces) diced
           tomatoes, undrained
      1/3 cup tomato paste
      1/4 cup olive oil
        1 large garlic clove, minced
        1 teaspoon salt
        1 teaspoon Italian seasoning
        1 large eggplant (about 1-1/4
           pounds), peeled and cubed
        4 medium zucchini, sliced

1 large green pepper, cut into strips
8 to 12 ounces sliced Monterey
    Jack cheese

1) In a large skillet, cook bacon and onion over medium heat until bacon is crisp; drain. Stir in the tomatoes, tomato paste, oil, garlic, salt and Italian seasoning.

2) Spread half into a greased 13-in. x 9-in. x 2-in. baking dish. Layer with half of the eggplant, zucchini, green pepper and cheese. Repeat layers. Bake, uncovered, at 375° for 50-55 minutes or until hot and bubbly.

Yield: 8 servings.

NUTRITION FACTS: 1/2 cup equals 250 calories, 17 g fat (7 g saturated fat), 30 mg cholesterol, 607 mg sodium, 15 g carbohydrate, 5 g fiber, 11 g protein.

Tahini Roasted Vegetables
PREP: 25 min. **BAKE:** 25 min.

Taste of Home Test Kitchen

Hearty vegetables are flavored with honey and tahini —a thick paste made of ground sesame seeds—then roasted for this side dish. Look for tahini in the Asian section of your supermarket.

1 medium eggplant, peeled
2 medium sweet red peppers
1 medium zucchini
1 medium onion
1 tablespoon olive oil
1 tablespoon tahini
2 teaspoons rice wine vinegar
2 teaspoons honey
1/2 teaspoon salt
1/4 teaspoon pepper
2 tablespoons minced fresh parsley

1) Cut the eggplant, red peppers, zucchini and onion into 1-in. pieces. Place in a 15-in. x 10-in. x 1-in. baking pan coated with cooking spray. In a small bowl, combine the oil, tahini, vinegar, honey, salt and pepper. Drizzle over vegetables; toss to coat.

2) Bake, uncovered, at 450° for 25-30 minutes or until tender, stirring occasionally. Stir in parsley before serving.

Yield: 6 servings.

NUTRITION FACTS: 2/3 cup equals 91 calories, 4 g fat (1 g saturated fat), 0 cholesterol, 203 mg sodium, 13 g carbohydrate, 4 g fiber, 2 g protein.

Mozzarella Eggplant Bake
PREP: 25 min. + standing **BAKE:** 50 min.

Frances Sayre, Cinnaminson, New Jersey

Paired with mushrooms and tomatoes and topped with mozzarella cheese, eggplant really stars in this tasty dish.

1 medium eggplant, peeled
2 teaspoons salt
3/4 cup dry bread crumbs

MOZZARELLA EGGPLANT BAKE

3 teaspoons garlic salt
1/2 teaspoon pepper
3 eggs
3 tablespoons olive oil, *divided*
1 large green pepper, chopped
1 medium onion, chopped
1/2 pound fresh mushrooms, sliced
2 cans (14-1/2 ounces *each*) stewed tomatoes
1 package (6 ounces) sliced part-skim mozzarella cheese

1) Cut eggplant into 1/4-in.-thick slices. Place in a colander over a plate; sprinkle with salt. Let stand for 30 minutes. Rinse with cold water and pat dry with paper towels.

2) In a shallow bowl, combine the bread crumbs, garlic salt and pepper. In another shallow bowl, beat eggs. Dip eggplant slices into eggs, then coat with crumb mixture.

3) In a large skillet, cook eggplant in 2 tablespoons oil for 2 minutes on each side or until lightly browned. Transfer to an ungreased 13-in. x 9-in. x 2-in. baking dish.

4) In the same skillet, saute the green pepper, onion and mushrooms in remaining oil for 5 minutes or until pepper and onion are crisp-tender. Sprinkle over eggplant. Top with tomatoes.

5) Bake, uncovered, at 350° for 25 minutes. Uncover; place cheese slices over the top. Bake 25-30 minutes longer or until cheese is melted.

Yield: 6 servings.

NUTRITION FACTS: 1 serving equals 318 calories, 16 g fat (6 g saturated fat), 128 mg cholesterol, 1,609 mg sodium, 32 g carbohydrate, 5 g fiber, 14 g protein.

Fennel

Fennel has a celery-like texture and a sweet, mild anise-like flavor that mellows while it cooks. The bulb, stalks and feathery fronds can all be used.

Buying

Fennel is available August through April. Select fennel with creamy white bulbs, firm straight stalks and bright green fronds. Avoid withered bulbs or those with brown spots or yellowing. Smaller bulbs are more tender.

Storage

Store unwashed fennel is the refrigerator crisper drawer for up to 4 days.

Preparation

Trim off fronds and stalks. Trim base from bulb. Remove and discard any yellowed or split outer layers. Cut in half and remove core. Cut, slice or chop the bulb and stalks. Use raw or cooked. Use the fronds as you would a minced herb or for a garnish.

Yield: 1 fennel bulb (10-1/2 ounces) = 2 cups sliced

Garlic

Garlic can add zip or mellow undertones to foods depending on how it is prepared.

Buying

Garlic is available year-round. Select garlic heads that are firm and plump. Avoid those with signs of sprouting and heads that are shriveled or soft.

Storage

Store garlic in a cool, dark, well-ventilated dry place for several weeks. Do not store in the refrigerator unless it has been peeled, sliced or chopped.

Preparation

Remove individual cloves as needed from bulb. Cut the base from the cloves. Press cloves with the flat edge of a knife to lightly crush, which loosens skin, then peel. Or, cut base from clove and remove skin with fingers or a knife. If the garlic has any green sprouts, remove those before using. When using a garlic press, some garlic usually remains in the press. If you use a garlic press and like a hearty garlic flavor, you may want to increase the number of cloves you press.

The more finely chopped the garlic is, the more potent the flavor will be. The flavor mellows upon cooking to a nutty flavor. Overcooked garlic will turn bitter, so avoid letting it turn brown during cooking.

Yield: 1 garlic clove = 1/2 teaspoon minced
1 garlic bulb = 8 to 15 cloves

Preparing Garlic For Roasting

With a sharp knife, cut off the top of each head of garlic, exposing the cloves inside. Place in a small baking dish or wrap bulb in heavy-duty foil.

Greens

Greens refers to a variety of leafy produce, such as collards, dandelion greens, kale, mustard greens, Swiss chard and turnip greens.

Buying

Greens are available year-round (individual varieties have their own seasons). Select fresh crisp greens with a bright color. Avoid those with withered, yellow or blemished leaves or stems.

Collards

Cabbage-like, spicy flavor. Wide green, leathery leaves with white veins. Smaller leaves are more tender. Good for braising, boiling, stir-frying. Season: December through April. **Yield:** 1 bunch (10 ounces) = 8 cups chopped.

Dandelion Greens

Strong flavor with lemon undertones and a delicate texture. Sawtooth edges on leaves. Good for sauteing, boiling. Season: spring through summer. **Yield:** 1 bunch (1 pound) = 8 cups torn greens.

Kale

Mild cabbage flavor. Curly blue-green leaves with a thick stem; some varieties have smooth leaves and are used in salads. Good for braising, stir-frying, steaming. Season: year-round. **Yield:** 1 bunch (12 ounces) = 16 cups chopped.

Mustard Greens

Bitter flavor with a mustard bite. Ruffled, lime-green leaves; some varieties are deep red. Good for boiling. Season: December through March. **Yield:** 1 bunch (12 ounces) = 16 cups chopped.

Swiss Chard

Tangy flavor with a hint of lemon. Green leaves with a white vein and stalk. The stalk is usually removed and cooked separately. Red leaf is another variety with a red stalk. Good for braising, stir-frying, steaming. Season: June through October. **Yield:** 1 bunch (12 ounces) = 9 cups chopped.

Turnip Greens

Sharp flavor that mellows during cooking; smaller leaves are less sharp. Firm, coarse, textured green leaves. Good for boiling, stir-frying, steaming. Season: November through March. **Yield:** 1 bunch (15 ounces) = 10 cups chopped.

Storage

Remove any ties before storing greens. Discard any yellow or bruised leaves. Store in a plastic bag in the refrigerator crisper drawer for up to 3 days.

Preparation

Wash in cool water. Greens may need several changes of water to remove all the grit that gets trapped in the coarse leaves. They can be spun in a salad spinner to remove water or drained in a colander. The thick stem and vein should be removed before cooking. Fold the leaves in half at the vein and cut just along the inside of the vein, which removes both the vein and stem.

Another way to remove the vein and stem is hold the stem in one hand and run your fingers from your other hand down the stem to strip off the leaves.

Kale with Bacon

PREP: 15 min.   **COOK:** 25 min.

Margaret Wagner Allen, Abingdon, Virginia

The hearty bacon and garlic flavor makes this a great way to enjoy vitamin-rich kale.

- 2 pounds fresh kale, trimmed and torn
- 8 bacon strips, diced
- 2 large onions, chopped
- 4 garlic cloves, minced
- 1 teaspoon salt
- 1/2 teaspoon pepper

1) In a large saucepan, bring 1 in. of water to a boil. Add kale; cook for 10-15 minutes or until tender.

2) Meanwhile, in a large nonstick skillet, cook bacon over medium heat until crisp. Using a slotted spoon, remove to paper towels; drain, reserving 1 teaspoon drippings. In the drippings, saute onions and garlic until onion is tender.

3) Drain the kale; stir into onion mixture. Add the salt, pepper and bacon; heat through.

Yield: 6 servings.

NUTRITION FACTS: 1/3 cup equals 161 calories, 7 g fat (2 g saturated fat), 9 mg cholesterol, 604 mg sodium, 20 g carbohydrate, 4 g fiber, 8 g protein.

Jicama

Jicama is a beige turnip- or radish-shaped tuberous root. Its juicy, crunchy-crisp texture and slightly nutty flavor is similar to a water chestnut. Jicamas range in size from 1/2 pound to 6 pounds.

Buying

Jicamas are available year-round. Select smaller ones, as the large ones tend to be woody and fibrous. Choose firm, unblemished tubers with thin skins.

Storage

Store in the refrigerator crisper drawer for up to 2 weeks. Once cut, wrap in plastic wrap and use within 1 week.

Preparation

Wash in cold water. Peel and then cut into desired size and shape. Jicama will not discolor after cutting. It can be used in salads or stir-fries or as crudites. Jicama stays crunchy after cooking.

Yield: 1 pound = 3-1/3 cups cubed

Jicama Slaw

PREP/TOTAL TIME: 15 min.
Taste of Home Test Kitchen

For a change of pace from cabbage slaw, why not give jicama a try? The jicama adds a sweet, nutty flavor to this tasty slaw.

1/4   cup minced fresh cilantro
1/4   cup sour cream
  2   tablespoons mayonnaise
1/2   teaspoon salt
1/4   to 1/2 teaspoon pepper
  2   cups shredded peeled jicama
1/2   cup shredded carrot
1/4   cup chopped sweet red pepper

1)   In a small serving bowl, combine the cilantro, sour cream, mayonnaise, salt and pepper. Stir in the jicama, carrot and red pepper. Cover and refrigerate until serving. Stir before serving.

Yield: 4 servings.

NUTRITION FACTS: 1/2 cup equals 113 calories, 8 g fat (3 g saturated fat), 13 mg cholesterol, 350 mg sodium, 8 g carbohydrate, 4 g fiber, 1 g protein.

Kohlrabi

Kohlrabi is a pale green, bulb-shaped vegetable with white flesh and dark green leaves. Less common varieties of kohlrabi have bulbs with purple skin. Kohlrabi bulbs have a mild, turnip-like flavor. Bulbs and leaves can be enjoyed raw or cooked.

Buying

Kohlrabi is available year-round; peak season is June through July. Select small (no larger than 3 in.), firm, pale green bulbs. The bulbs should have tender skins; the leaves should appear fresh and crisp.

Storage

Trim leaves and root ends. Store unwashed kohlrabi in an open plastic bag in the refrigerator crisper drawer for up to 5 days. If using the greens, store separately in a sealed plastic bag in the refrigerator for up to 3 days.

Preparation

Cut off leaves and stems. Thinly peel bulbs. Cut into slices, strips or cubes.

Yield: 1 pound kohlrabi (without leaves)
        = 3 to 4 medium bulbs

Kohlrabi with Honey Butter

PREP/TOTAL TIME: 20 min.
Wanda Holoubek, Salina, Kansas

If you're not acquainted with kohlrabi, this recipe will serve as a pleasant introduction. Honey and lemon lend a sweet, citrusy taste to the turnip-like veggie.

  1   pound kohlrabi (4 to 5 small), peeled and cut into 1/4-inch strips
  1   medium carrot, cut into 1/8-inch strips
  1   tablespoon minced chives
  1   tablespoon lemon juice
  1   tablespoon butter, melted
  2   teaspoons honey
1/4   teaspoon grated lemon peel
1/8   teaspoon pepper

1) In a large skillet, bring 1 in. of water, kohlrabi and carrot to a boil. Reduce heat; cover and simmer for 6-10 minutes or until crisp-tender.

2) In a small bowl, combine the chives, lemon juice, butter, honey, lemon peel and pepper; mix well. Drain vegetables and transfer to a serving bowl. Drizzle with honey butter and toss to coat.

Yield: 4 servings.

NUTRITION FACTS: 1/2 cup equals 77 calories, 3 g fat (2 g saturated fat), 8 mg cholesterol, 62 mg sodium, 12 g carbohydrate, 5 g fiber, 2 g protein.

Leeks

Leeks are part of the onion family and are tasty additions to soups, casseroles or egg dishes.

Buying

Leeks are available year-round. Select young, straight, cylindrical stalks with moist, pliable green upper leaves. The white bulbs should extend 2 to 3 in. above the roots; diameter should not exceed 1-1/2 in.

Storage

Store unwashed, untrimmed leeks loosely wrapped in an open plastic bag in the refrigerator crisper drawer for up to 2 weeks.

Yield: 2 pounds leeks = 1 pound trimmed
= 4 cups chopped and 2 cups cooked

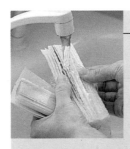

Preparing Leeks

Remove any withered outer leaves. Trim root end. Cut off and discard the green upper leaves at the point where the pale green becomes dark green. Leeks often contain sand between their many layers.

If leeks are to be sliced or chopped, cut the leek open lengthwise down one side and rinse under cold running water, separating the leaves.

If using the leek whole, cut an X about 1/4 to 1/2 in. deep in the root end. Soak for 30 minutes in water containing a splash of vinegar. Rinse under cold running water, gently opening the slit area while rinsing.

Mushrooms

Mushrooms add an earthy, nutty flavor to recipes. Mushrooms are a fungus not a vegetable, but they are treated as vegetables in cooking.

Buying

Mushrooms are available year-round (individual varieties have their own seasons). Select mushrooms with fresh, firm, smooth caps with closed gills. Avoid mushrooms with cracks, brown spots or blemishes or ones that are shriveled or moist.

Button or White

Mild mushroom flavor that intensifies on cooking. Color ranges from creamy white to beige. Comes in small (button), medium and large (used for stuffing). Season: year-round. **Yield:** 1 package (8 ounces) = about 2-1/2 cups whole or sliced.

Chanterelle

Flavor can range from nutty to fruity with a chewy texture. Color ranges from yellow to reddish orange. Resembles trumpets or inside-out umbrellas. Season: summer through fall. **Yield:** 1 package (2.5 ounces) = 1 cup whole.

Cremini or Brown

More intense earthy flavor than button. Color ranges from tan to rich brown. Resembles a button mushroom. Season: year-round. **Yield:** 1 package (8 ounces) = about 2-1/2 cups whole or sliced.

Enoki

Mild flavor with a slightly crunchy texture. Color ranges from white to golden. Tiny caps on long spaghetti-like stems. Season: year-round. **Yield:** 1 package (3-1/2 ounces) = about 2 cups whole.

Oyster

Delicate, mild flavor and a silky-chewy texture. Color ranges from pinkish white to beige to gray. Fluted shell-shaped caps. Season: year-round. **Yield:** 1 package (3-1/2 ounces) = 1-1/2 cups whole.

Portobello

Meaty flavor with firm texture. Tan caps with dark-brown gills. Available whole (as large as 6 in. diameter), sliced or as baby portobello. Season: year-round. **Yield:** 1 package (6 ounces, 2 large caps) = 2-1/2 cups sliced.

Shiitake

Woody flavor with a meaty texture. Color ranges from tan to dark brown. Has an umbrella-shaped cap. Season: year-round, peaks in spring and fall. **Yield:** 1 package (3-1/2 ounces) = 2 cups sliced.

Storage

Store unwashed, loose mushrooms in a brown paper bag in the refrigerator for up to 5-10 days, depending on the variety. Keep packaged mushrooms wrapped in their package. Moisture speeds spoilage in mushrooms.

Yield: 1/2 pound button mushrooms
= 2-1/2 cups sliced or 1 cup sauteed

Preparing Mushrooms

Gently remove dirt by rubbing with a mushroom brush or a damp paper towel. Or quickly rinse under cold water, drain and pat dry with paper towels. Do not peel mushrooms. Trim stems. For shiitake mushrooms, remove and discard stems. For enoki, trim base and separate stems. Mushrooms can be eaten raw, marinated, sauteed, stir-fried, baked, broiled or grilled.

Pickled Mushrooms

PREP: 10 min. + chilling

Linda Kelper-Quinn, Hazelton, Pennsylvania

Pennsylvania is known for its mushrooms, which are prominently featured in this recipe.

  1/2 cup red wine vinegar
  1/2 cup water
    2 bay leaves
    2 tablespoons sugar
1-1/2 teaspoons salt
    1 garlic clove, minced
    1 pound fresh mushrooms, quartered

1) In a saucepan over medium heat, combine the vinegar, water, bay leaves, sugar, salt and garlic. Add mushrooms. Bring to a boil; boil for 2 minutes. Cool slightly.

2) Transfer to a bowl; cover and refrigerate for 8 hours or overnight. Discard bay leaves before serving.

Yield: about 2-1/2 cups.

NUTRITION FACTS: 1/4 cup equals 25 calories, trace fat (trace saturated fat), 0 cholesterol, 356 mg sodium, 5 g carbohydrate, 1 g fiber, 1 g protein.

PICKLED MUSHROOMS

◖Sauteed Mushrooms

PREP/TOTAL TIME: 10 min.

Hope Meece, Ambia, Indiana

I frequently fix this speedy dish for my hungry family. Spiced carrots would be a mouthwatering companion in the pan to the mushrooms.

1/4 cup butter
1 pound fresh mushrooms, sliced
1 tablespoon lemon juice
1 tablespoon soy sauce

1) In a large skillet, melt butter. Add the mushrooms, lemon juice and soy sauce. Saute for 6-8 minutes or until mushrooms are tender.

Yield: 4 servings.

NUTRITION FACTS: 1 serving equals 132 calories, 12 g fat (7 g saturated fat), 31 mg cholesterol, 350 mg sodium, 5 g carbohydrate, 1 g fiber, 4 g protein.

Okra

Okra is a slender, ribbed edible pod with small, white seeds. This mild vegetable tastes a  little like asparagus and is known for its thickening power when cooked in gumbo, soups or stews.

Buying

Okra is available year-round in Southern states and from April to November in the North; peak season is June through November. Select young, tender, unblemished, bright green pods less than 4 in. long. The pods may be smooth or ridged, should snap easily and should not have any hard seeds. The tips should bend under slight pressure.

Storage

Store unwashed okra in a sealed plastic bag in the refrigerator crisper drawer for up to 2 days.

Preparation

Wash and remove stem ends. Leave small pods whole; cut larger pods into 1/2-in. slices.

Yield: 1 pound okra = 3 to 4 cups sliced

◖Okra Medley

PREP/TOTAL TIME: 30 min.

Nona Cheatham, McRae, Arkansas

This recipe is wonderful served with almost any entree and hot corn bread.

1 medium onion, chopped
2 tablespoons butter
2 cups sliced fresh okra

3 to 4 medium tomatoes, peeled and chopped
2 cups frozen corn
1 teaspoon sugar
1 teaspoon salt
1/4 teaspoon pepper

1) In a large saucepan, saute onion in butter until tender. Add okra; cook and stir for 5 minutes. Stir in tomatoes, corn, sugar, salt and pepper; bring to a boil. Reduce heat; cover and simmer for 10-15 minutes or until corn is tender.

Yield: 4-6 servings.

NUTRITION FACTS: 1/2 cup equals 127 calories, 5 g fat (2 g saturated fat), 10 mg cholesterol, 444 mg sodium, 22 g carbohydrate, 4 g fiber, 4 g protein.

Onions

Onions are a member of the lily family. They can be green, white, yellow or red with flavors ranging from sharp when eaten raw to mild and sweet when cooked.

Buying

Onions are available year-round (individual varieties have their own seasons). Select firm onions that have dry, papery skins with globe-shaped necks. Avoid those with soft spots, blemishes or green sprouts.

Pearl onions are small, about 1 in. in diameter, are generally white but may be yellow or red and are sold in pint containers. Red onions have a stronger flavor than yellow and are generally used raw or for grilling. Their color fades when cooked. Sweet onions are mild, sweet and juicy. They are used raw and can be cooked. Yellow onions range in size from small to large and are the common cooking onion. White onions are milder in flavor than yellow and are frequently used in Mexican cuisine.

Storage

Store onions in a dark, cool, dry, well-ventilated place for up to 3 weeks.

Preparation

Peel and cut, chop or slice as recipe directs.

Yield: 1 small onion = 1/3 cup chopped
1 medium onion = 1/2 to 3/4 cup chopped
1 large onion = 1 to 1-1/4 cups chopped

VEGETABLE-STUFFED BAKED ONIONS

Vegetable-Stuffed Baked Onions

PREP: 25 min. **BAKE:** 45 min.

Ruth Andrewson, Leavenworth, Washington

Stuffed with carrots, red pepper, diced bacon and bread crumbs, these elegant baked onions will dress up any special-occasion or company meal.

> 8 to 10 medium onions, peeled
> 4 bacon strips, diced
> 3/4 cup finely chopped carrots
> 1/2 cup finely chopped sweet red pepper
> 1-1/2 cups soft bread crumbs
> 1/3 cup minced fresh parsley
> 3 tablespoons butter, melted
> 1-1/2 teaspoons salt
> 1/2 teaspoon pepper
> 3/4 cup beef broth

1) Cut 1/2 in. off the top of each onion; trim bottom so onion sits flat. Scoop out center, leaving a 1/2-in. shell. Chop removed onion; set 1/2 cup aside (discarding remaining onion or save for another use).

2) Place onion shells in a Dutch oven or large saucepan and cover with water. Bring to a boil; reduce heat and cook for 8-10 minutes.

3) Meanwhile, in a large skillet, cook bacon over medium heat until crisp. Remove to paper towels; drain, reserving 1 teaspoon drippings.

4) In the drippings, saute the chopped onion, carrots and red pepper for 8 minutes or until tender. Remove from the heat; stir in the bread crumbs, parsley, butter, salt, pepper and bacon.

5) Drain onion shells; fill each with about 1/3 cup vegetable mixture. Place in an ungreased shallow 3-qt. baking dish. Pour broth over onions. Cover and bake at 350° for 45-50 minutes or until heated through.

Yield: 8-10 servings.

NUTRITION FACTS: 1 stuffed onion equals 155 calories, 9 g fat (4 g saturated fat), 15 mg cholesterol, 561 mg sodium, 16 g carbohydrate, 3 g fiber, 3 g protein.

Caramelized Onions

PREP: 10 min. **COOK:** 50 min.

Taste of Home Test Kitchen

The choices are endless...serve this as a topping for brats, burgers or hot dogs as well as steak.

> 1 to 2 tablespoons vegetable oil
> 6 cups thinly sliced onions (about 4 large)
> 1/4 teaspoon salt
> 1 tablespoon cider vinegar
> 2 tablespoons brown sugar

1) Heat oil in a large skillet over medium heat until hot. Add onions and sprinkle with salt. Cook and stir for 15 minutes or until moisture from onions has evaporated and onions are completely wilted.

2) Reduce heat to medium-low. Sprinkle vinegar over onions. Cook and stir for 20 minutes or until lightly golden. Stir in brown sugar; cook and stir 15-20 minutes longer or until onions are a caramel brown color. If onions begin to stick to skillet, add water, 1 tablespoon at a time, until onions no longer stick.

Yield: 1-1/2 cups.

NUTRITION FACTS: 1/4 cup equals 81 calories, 2 g fat (trace saturated fat), 0 cholesterol, 104 mg sodium, 15 g carbohydrate, 2 g fiber, 1 g protein.

Creamed Pearl Onions

PREP: 30 min. + chilling **BAKE:** 25 min.

Barbara Caserman, Lake Havasu City, Arizona

At Christmas, this was one of many recipes I relied on that can be prepared a day in advance, which gave me more time to spend with guests. Everyone expected to see this vegetable dish on the table every year.

> 6 cups water
> 50 pearl onions
> 1/4 cup butter
> 1/4 cup all-purpose flour
> 1/2 teaspoon salt

Dash pepper

> 1 cup chicken broth
> 1 cup half-and-half cream
> 1/4 cup minced fresh parsley
> 3 tablespoons grated Parmesan cheese

Pimento strips, optional

1) In a Dutch oven, bring water to a boil. Cut off root ends of onions and make an X in the core. Add onions to boiling water; boil for 10-12 minutes or until tender. Drain and rinse in cold water; peel and set aside.

2) In a saucepan, melt butter. Stir in the flour, salt and pepper until smooth. Gradually stir in broth and cream. Bring to a boil; cook and stir for 2 minutes or until thickened. Stir in the parsley, cheese and onions.

3) Pour into an ungreased 1-qt. baking dish. Cover and refrigerate overnight.

4) Remove from the refrigerator 30 minutes before baking. Cover and bake at 350° for 15 minutes. Uncover and stir. Top with pimientos if desired. Bake, 10 minutes longer or until bubbly and heated through.

Yield: 6 servings.

Editor's Note: To bake immediately instead of chilling, bake, uncovered, at 350° for 15-20 minutes or until bubbly.

NUTRITION FACTS: 3/4 cup equals 209 calories, 13 g fat (8 g saturated fat), 42 mg cholesterol, 501 mg sodium, 18 g carbohydrate, 2 g fiber, 5 g protein.

Peeling a Pearl Onion

1) Cut off the root end of each pearl onion and make an X in the core.

2) In a Dutch oven, bring 6 cups of water to a boil. Add pearl onions; boil for 3 minutes.

3) Drain and rinse in cold water; peel.

Onions, Green

Green onions, also known as scallions, are a member of the onion family. They are immature onions that were harvested before the bulb had time to develop.

Buying

Green onions are available year-round. Select green onions with bright green tops, white bulbs and short roots. Avoid ones with dry, withered or slimy greens.

Storage

Store unwashed green onions in a plastic bag in the refrigerator crisper drawer for up to 1-2 weeks.

Preparation

Trim off root end and wash in cool water. Some recipes call for just the white portion, some use the green portion or tops. When a recipe does not specify, you can use both the green and white portions. If using the tops, trim off ends along with any dry, coarse or withered portions before slicing or chopping.

Yield: 1 green onion = 2 tablespoons sliced

Parsnips

Parsnips are root vegetables that resemble a white or pale yellow carrot. Parsnips add a sweetness and nutty flavor to recipes.

Buying

Parsnips are available year-round; peak season is fall through winter. Select firm parsnips with a uniform shape. Avoid ones that have cracks and blemishes or are shriveled. Avoid large parsnips, since they might be tough.

Storage

Store unwashed parsnips in a perforated plastic bag in the refrigerator crisper drawer for up to 2 weeks.

Preparation

Wash parsnips in cool water. Trim root ends and tops, then peel skin.

Yield: 1 pound trimmed = 3 cups cubed

Baked Parsnips

PREP: 15 min. **BAKE:** 45 min.

Robert Atwood, West Wareham, Massachusetts

We enjoy parsnips in the Northeast, and I've experimented with different ways of fixing them. This is by far my favorite.

- 1-1/2 **pounds parsnips, peeled and julienned**
- 1/4 **cup butter**
- 1/4 **cup water**
- 1/2 **teaspoon dried oregano**
- 1/2 **teaspoon dried parsley flakes**
- 1/4 **teaspoon salt**
- 1/8 **teaspoon pepper**

1) Place parsnips in an ungreased 2-qt. baking dish; dot with butter. Add water. Sprinkle with the oregano, parsley, salt and pepper. Cover and bake at 350° for 45 minutes or until tender.

Yield: 4 servings.

NUTRITION FACTS: 1 cup equals 239 calories, 12 g fat (7 g saturated fat), 31 mg cholesterol, 280 mg sodium, 33 g carbohydrate, 7 g fiber, 2 g protein.

Peas, Green

Fresh green peas, sometimes called English peas, are a member of the legume family. Fresh peas are sweet and tender.

Buying

Green peas are available year-round; peak season is May through June. Select peas in their pods for maximum freshness. Choose ones that are crisp and firm and have a bright green color. Avoid large pods or those with thick skin, which indicates they are past mature.

Storage

Keep unwashed, unshelled green peas in an open plastic bag in the refrigerator crisper drawer for up to 2 days.

Yield: 1 pound unshelled green peas
= 1-1/2 cups shelled

MINTY PEAS AND ONIONS

Minty Peas and Onions
PREP/TOTAL TIME: 20 min.

Santa D'Addario, Jacksonville, Florida

With just five ingredients, you can stir up a wonderful side dish for a special dinner or any night of the week.

- 2 large onions, cut into 1/2-inch wedges
- 1/2 cup chopped sweet red pepper
- 2 tablespoons vegetable oil
- 2 packages (16 ounces *each*) frozen peas
- 2 tablespoons minced fresh mint *or* 2 teaspoons dried mint

1) In a large skillet, saute onions and red pepper in oil until onions just begin to soften.

2) Add peas; cook, uncovered, stirring occasionally, for 10 minutes or until heated through. Stir in mint and cook for 1 minute.

Yield: 8 servings.

Editor's Note: You can easily halve this recipe to make 4 servings.

NUTRITION FACTS: 1 cup equals 134 calories, 4 g fat (1 g saturated fat), 0 cholesterol, 128 mg sodium, 19 g carbohydrate, 6 g fiber, 6 g protein.

Shelling Peas

Wash pods in cool water. Snap off stem end and pull string down. Open pod by running your thumb down the length of the seam and loosening the peas. Rinse peas before cooking.

Creamed Peas
PREP/TOTAL TIME: 15 min.

Imogene Hutton, Brownwood, Texas

This recipe has been in my family for years, and we often serve it for holiday meals.

- 1 package (10 ounces) frozen peas
- 1 tablespoon butter
- 1 tablespoon all-purpose flour
- 1/4 teaspoon salt
- 1/8 teaspoon pepper
- 1/2 cup milk
- 1 teaspoon sugar

1) Cook peas according to package directions. Meanwhile, in a small saucepan, melt the butter. Stir in the flour, salt and pepper until blended; gradually add milk and sugar.

2) Bring to a boil; cook and stir for 1-2 minutes or until thickened. Drain peas; stir into the sauce and heat through.

Yield: 3-4 servings.

NUTRITION FACTS: 1/2 cup equals 110 calories, 4 g fat (2 g saturated fat), 12 mg cholesterol, 271 mg sodium, 14 g carbohydrate, 3 g fiber, 5 g protein.

French Peas
PREP/TOTAL TIME: 15 min.

Ann Nace, Perkasie, Pennsylvania

I like to dress up plain peas with green onions, lettuce and water chestnuts for this simple and tasty side dish.

- 1 package (10 ounces) frozen peas
- 2 green onions, sliced
- 1 cup finely shredded lettuce
- 1 tablespoon vegetable oil

1 teaspoon all-purpose flour
1/4 cup water
1 can (8 ounces) sliced water
  chestnuts, drained

Dash pepper

1) Cook peas according to package directions. Meanwhile, in another saucepan, cook onions and lettuce in oil over low heat for 5 minutes.

2) Combine flour with water until smooth. Stir into onion mixture; cook and stir until thickened.

3) Drain peas and add to onion mixture along with the water chestnuts and pepper; heat through.

Yield: 4 servings.

NUTRITION FACTS: 2/3 cup equals 120 calories, 4 g fat (trace saturated fat), 0 cholesterol, 86 mg sodium, 18 g carbohydrate, 5 g fiber, 5 g protein.

Peas, Snow and Sugar Snap

Snow peas and sugar snap peas are sweet, tender peas in an edible pod and are eaten whole. Snow peas have smaller peas and more translucent pods than sugar snap peas.

Buying

Snow peas are available year round. Sugar snap peas are generally available in spring and fall. Select snow peas that are flat, are about 3 in. long and have a light green color with a shiny appearance. Select sugar snap peas that have crisp, plump-looking dark green pods. Avoid dry or moldy pods.

Storage

Keep unwashed snow or sugar snap peas in an open plastic bag in the refrigerator crisper drawer for up to 2 days.

Yield: 1 pound snow peas or sugar snap peas = about 4 cups

Preparing Snow Peas

Rinse with cold water. Remove strings if desired. Cut off stem ends. Do not shell. If using raw, blanch before using.

Snow Pea Stir-Fry

PREP/TOTAL TIME: 15 min.

Sally Fitzgerald, Portland, Maine

Tired of the same ol' peas and carrots? This quick and easy recipe perks up snow peas with Dijon mustard and chopped walnuts.

1-1/2 teaspoons butter, melted
1/2 teaspoon Worcestershire sauce
1/2 teaspoon Dijon mustard
Dash salt
1 package (6 ounces) frozen snow
  peas, thawed
1 tablespoon vegetable oil
1/4 cup chopped walnuts

1) In a bowl, combine the butter, Worcestershire sauce, mustard and salt; set aside.

2) In a small skillet, stir-fry snow peas in oil for 1-2 minutes or until crisp-tender. Add walnuts; cook and stir for 1 minute.

3) Drizzle with butter mixture; toss to coat. Cover and cook for 2 minutes or until heated through.

Yield: 2 servings.

NUTRITION FACTS: 1 serving equals 232 calories, 18 g fat (3 g saturated fat), 8 mg cholesterol, 147 mg sodium, 8 g carbohydrate, 3 g fiber, 6 g protein.

Tangy Sugar Snap Peas

PREP/TOTAL TIME: 10 min.

Taste of Home Test Kitchen

This mouthwatering side dish comes together quickly in the microwave. A sweet and tangy glaze complements the crisp peas and onion.

1 pound fresh *or* frozen sugar snap
  peas, thawed
1 small onion, halved and sliced
3 tablespoons water, *divided*
4 teaspoons sugar
1 teaspoon cornstarch
1/8 teaspoon pepper
2 tablespoons cider vinegar

1) In a large microwave-safe bowl, combine the peas, onion and 2 tablespoons water. Cover and cook on high for 5-7 minutes or until crisp-tender, stirring twice; drain and keep warm.

2) In a small microwave-safe bowl, combine the sugar, cornstarch and pepper; stir in the vinegar and remaining water until smooth. Cook, uncovered, on high for 30-45 seconds or until thickened, stirring once. Pour over pea mixture; toss to coat.

Yield: 4 servings.

NUTRITION FACTS: 3/4 cup equals 75 calories, 1 g fat (0 saturated fat), 0 cholesterol, 1 mg sodium, 16 g carbohydrate, 5 g fiber, 3 g protein.

Peppers, Chili

Chili (hot) peppers come in a variety of sizes, shapes and heat levels. They generally come to a tapered point and can be either skinny or plump. Depending on the pepper, they can be green, red or yellow. Dried chili peppers are most often a black-red color.

Buying

Chili peppers are available year-round. Select peppers with firm, smooth, glossy skin. Avoid those that are shriveled or have soft spots. Heat level ranges include mild, (Anaheim, Banana or Cubanelle), moderately hot (ancho or pasilla), hot (jalapeno), hotter (serrano) and fiery (habanero).

Storage

Store unwashed, fresh chili peppers wrapped in paper towels in the refrigerator crisper drawer for up to 2 weeks.

The heat of the peppers is contained in the seeds and membranes. Use them for a spicier dish. For a milder dish, remove and discard the seeds with the tip of a spoon or knife. Not all chili peppers are the same; the heat level can vary among chilies even in the same variety. So taste-test before adding chilies to a dish. You can always add more, but you can't salvage a dish that's too hot.

Yield: (varies by size and shape)

Preparing Chilies

Chili peppers contain a skin irritant called capsaicin. When handling chili peppers, wear rubber or plastic gloves and avoid touching your eyes or face to prevent burning your skin or eyes. Wash hands and cutting surface thoroughly with hot, soapy water when finished.

Peppers, Sweet

Classified as a fruit, sweet bell peppers are used as a vegetable. They come in green, yellow, red, orange and purple-black. They have a mild flavor, although the green ones are slightly stronger.

Buying

Sweet peppers are available year-round; peak season is March through October. Select firm peppers with smooth, shiny skin and bright colors. Avoid those that are shriveled or have soft spots.

Storage

Store unwashed bell peppers in the refrigerator crisper drawer for up to 5 days.

Preparation

Rinse peppers under cold water. Remove stems, seeds and membranes (ribs). Slice or chop according to recipe directions.

Yield: 1 medium sweet pepper = 3/4 cup chopped

Roasting Peppers

1) Arrange pepper halves skin side up or whole peppers on a broiler pan coated with cooking spray. Broil on the closest rack position to the heat without the peppers touching the heat source. Broil until skins are blistered and blackened, about 10 minutes. For whole peppers, with tongs, rotate peppers a quarter turn. Broil and rotate until all sides are blistered and blackened.

2) Immediately place the peppers in a bowl; cover with plastic wrap and let stand for 15-20 minutes.

3) Peel off and discard charred skin. Remove stems and seeds from whole peppers.

Potatoes

Potatoes are tuberous vegetables that are delicious baked, boiled, mashed, fried, shredded or used in salads.

Baking potatoes, such as russet and Idaho, have a high starch content that produces a fluffy, dry texture after baking. Waxy potatoes, such as round red potatoes, have a low to medium starch content so they hold their shape after boiling. All-purpose potatoes, such as Yukon Gold, are suitable for both baking and boiling.

Buying

Potatoes are available year-round (individual varieties have their own seasons). Select well-shaped, firm potatoes that are free from cuts, decay, blemishes or green discoloration under the skin. Avoid sprouted or shriveled potatoes.

Storage

Store potatoes in a dark, cool, dry, well-ventilated place for up to 2 months. Do not store with onions or in the refrigerator.

Yield: 1 pound russet potatoes = 3 medium
      1 pound small new potatoes = 8 to 10
      1 pound potatoes = 2-1/4 cups diced or sliced

Preparing Potatoes

Scrub with a vegetable brush under cold water. Remove eyes or sprouts. When working with lots of potatoes, peel and place in cold water to prevent discoloration. Before baking a whole potato, pierce with a fork.

Keeping Fried Foods Warm

When foods need to be cooked in stages, such as potato pancakes, you'll want to keep each batch warm until the entire recipe is cooked. Drain fried foods on paper towels, then place on an ovenproof platter. Cover loosely with foil and place in a 200° oven until the entire recipe is completed.

Blue Potatoes

Blue-purple skin with dark to white flesh. Medium starch content; mild flavor. Potato will get mushy if overcooked. Use baked, boiled, fried, mashed or in salads.

Fingerlings

Finger-shaped potato with tan skin, 2-4 in. long. Waxy, firm and flavorful. Use boiled, steamed, in salads.

New Potatoes

Small potatoes with tan or red tender skin. New potatoes are fresh from the garden and have never been placed in storage. Use boiled, steamed or roasted whole.

Round Reds

Round-shaped potatoes with smooth red skin. Waxy or low starch. Use boiled, roasted, steamed, in casseroles, salads and soups.

Round Whites

Round-shaped potato with light- to medium-brown skin. Waxy or low starch. Use baked, boiled, steamed.

Russets

Oblong potato with a rough, reddish-brown skin. High starch, low moisture. Use baked, mashed, roasted, as French fries.

Yellow-Fleshed

Round potatoes with golden-colored skin and flesh that has a buttery flavor. All-purpose potato. Use baked, boiled, mashed, roasted, steamed, as French fries, in salads. Falls apart when overcooked.

FAMILY-PLEASING MASHED POTATOES

CLASSIC: For rich, creamy potatoes that will have people asking for seconds, serve up Yukon Mashed Potatoes. Yukon Gold potatoes are boiled and simply mashed with cream, butter, garlic salt and pepper.

TIME-SAVER: With their from-scratch flavor, you'd never guess that Chili-Cheese Mashed Potatoes start with mashed potato flakes. Ready in only 10 minutes, this side dish is jazzed up with minced garlic, canned green chilies and shredded Mexican cheese.

LIGHT: Fat-free cream cheese and reduced-fat sour cream add richness to Light 'n' Creamy Mashed Potatoes without the guilt of their full-fat counterparts. Seasoned with garlic powder and chives, a more generous serving of this better-for-you dish has fewer calories and a third of the fat of Yukon Mashed Potatoes.

SERVES 2: For a taste-twist on everyday mashed potatoes, try this appealing side dish that yields just enough for two. Spicy Mashed Potatoes have goat cheese, cilantro, green onion and jalapeno mixed in, then they're sprinkled with cheddar and popped in the oven to bake.

YUKON MASHED POTATOES

Yukon Mashed Potatoes

PREP/TOTAL TIME: 30 min.

Nancy Horsburgh, Everett, Ontario

- 2-3/4 to 3 pounds Yukon Gold potatoes, peeled and quartered
- 1/2 cup half-and-half cream
- 2 tablespoons butter
- 1/2 to 1 teaspoon garlic salt
- 1/8 teaspoon pepper

1) Place potatoes in a large saucepan or Dutch oven and cover with water. Bring to a boil. Reduce heat; cover and cook for 15-20 minutes or until tender. Drain.

2) In a large mixing bowl, mash potatoes. Add the cream, butter, garlic salt and pepper; beat until light and fluffy.

Yield: 6 servings.

NUTRITION FACTS: 1/2 cup equals 232 calories, 6 g fat (4 g saturated fat), 20 mg cholesterol, 212 mg sodium, 37 g carbohydrate, 2 g fiber, 6 g protein.

■ **Garlic Mashed Potatoes:** Add 4-6 peeled garlic cloves along with potatoes. Cook and mash as directed.

■ **Fancy Mashed Potatoes:** Use 1 tablespoon butter. Mash with 2 ounces softened cream cheese and 3 tablespoons minced chives.

Chili-Cheese Mashed Potatoes

PREP/TOTAL TIME: 10 min.

Peter Halferty, Corpus Christi, Texas

- 2-3/4 cups water
- 1 cup fat-free milk
- 1-1/2 teaspoons salt
- 1 tablespoon butter
- 3 garlic cloves, minced
- 3 cups mashed potato flakes
- 2 cans (4 ounces *each*) chopped green chilies
- 1 cup (4 ounces) shredded reduced-fat Mexican cheese blend

1) In a large saucepan, bring the water, milk and salt to a boil.

2) Add the butter, garlic, potato flakes and chilies; stir until thickened. Sprinkle with cheese.

Yield: 6 servings.

NUTRITION FACTS: 3/4 cup equals 215 calories, 6 g fat (3 g saturated fat), 19 mg cholesterol, 972 mg sodium, 32 g carbohydrate, 2 g fiber, 10 g protein.

SPICY MASHED POTATOES

Light 'n' Creamy Mashed Potatoes

PREP/TOTAL TIME: 30 min.

Taste of Home Test Kitchen

      6 cups quartered peeled potatoes
         (about 3 pounds)
      4 ounces fat-free cream cheese,
         cubed
    1/2 cup reduced-fat sour cream
    1/2 cup fat-free milk
    3/4 teaspoon salt
    1/4 teaspoon garlic powder
    1/4 teaspoon pepper
      1 tablespoon minced chives
Dash paprika

1) Place potatoes in a large saucepan or Dutch oven and cover with water. Bring to a boil. Reduce heat; cover and cook for 15-20 minutes or until tender. Drain.

2) In a large mixing bowl, mash the potatoes. Add the cream cheese, sour cream, milk, salt, garlic powder and pepper; beat until smooth. Stir in chives. Sprinkle with paprika.

Yield: 8 servings.

NUTRITION FACTS: 2/3 cup equals 140 calories, 2 g fat (1 g saturated fat), 6 mg cholesterol, 322 mg sodium, 26 g carbohydrate, 2 g fiber, 6 g protein.

Spicy Mashed Potatoes

PREP/TOTAL TIME: 30 min.

Laurie Balcom, Lynden, Washington

      2 medium potatoes, peeled and
         cubed
      3 tablespoons 2% milk
    1/4 cup crumbled goat cheese *or* feta
         cheese
      3 tablespoons minced fresh
         cilantro
      2 tablespoons chopped green onion
      2 tablespoons diced seeded
         jalapeno pepper
      2 garlic cloves, minced
    1/4 cup shredded cheddar cheese

1) Place the potatoes in a small saucepan and cover with water. Bring to a boil. Reduce heat; cover and cook for 10-15 minutes or until tender. Drain.

2) In a small mixing bowl, mash potatoes with milk. Beat in the goat cheese, cilantro, onion, jalapeno and garlic.

3) Spoon into a 2-cup baking dish coated with cooking spray. Sprinkle with cheddar cheese. Bake, uncovered, at 350° for 15-20 minutes or until heated through.

Yield: 2 servings.

Editor's Note: When cutting or seeding hot peppers, use rubber or plastic gloves to protect your hands. Avoid touching your face.

NUTRITION FACTS: 3/4 cup equals 341 calories, 13 g fat (9 g saturated fat), 39 mg cholesterol, 257 mg sodium, 42 g carbohydrate, 4 g fiber, 15 g protein.

COMFORTING SCALLOPED POTATOES

 CLASSIC: Chopped onion and green pepper perk up the homemade white sauce that coats tender potato slices in Scalloped Potatoes. To create the crunchy golden topping, the casserole is sprinkled with buttered bread crumbs and shredded cheddar cheese.

 TIME-SAVER: A slow cooker makes it easy to prepare Saucy Scalloped Potatoes, plus it frees up the oven for your entree or other dishes. Get the sliced potatoes and a handful of ingredients cooking in the slow cooker, stir in some chunks of ham for heartiness, then forget about this side dish until dinnertime.

 LIGHT: Light Scalloped Potatoes lets you and your family enjoy comforting potato slices without all the fat and calories. This version skips the sauce altogether, yet has plenty of flavor from chicken bouillon and Parmesan cheese. Compared to Scalloped Potatoes, one serving has a fourth less calories and significantly less fat, cholesterol and sodium.

 SERVES 2: It's easy to serve Creamy Scalloped Potatoes to two people with this recipe. Two potatoes are sliced and layered with chopped onion and a homemade cream sauce to make this savory side dish.

Scalloped Potatoes

PREP: 20 min. **BAKE:** 1-1/4 hours

Eleanore Hill, Fresno, California

- 3 tablespoons butter, *divided*
- 1 tablespoon all-purpose flour
- 1 teaspoon salt
- 1/4 teaspoon pepper
- 1-1/2 cups milk
- 4 cups thinly sliced peeled potatoes (about 2 pounds)
- 1 medium onion, finely chopped
- 1 small green pepper, finely chopped
- 1/2 cup dry bread crumbs
- 3/4 cup shredded cheddar cheese

1) In a small saucepan, melt 2 tablespoons butter; stir in flour, salt and pepper. Gradually stir in milk. Bring to a boil over medium heat; cook and stir for 2 minutes or until thickened.

2) In a greased 1-1/2-qt. baking dish, arrange half the potatoes, onion and green pepper in layers; cover with half of the sauce. Repeat layers. Cover and bake at 350° for 35 minutes.

3) Melt remaining butter; combine with bread crumbs and sprinkle over potatoes. Bake, uncovered, 40 minutes longer or until potatoes are tender. Sprinkle with cheddar cheese. Let stand for 5 minutes before serving.

Yield: 6 servings.

NUTRITION FACTS: 1/2 cup equals 250 calories, 28 g fat (8 g saturated fat), 36 mg cholesterol, 974 mg sodium, 27 g carbohydrate, 3 g fiber, 8 g protein.

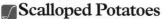

SCALLOPED POTATOES

Saucy Scalloped Potatoes

PREP: 15 min. **COOK:** 7 hours

Elaine Kane, Keizer, Oregon

- 4 cups thinly sliced peeled potatoes (about 2 pounds)
- 1 can (10-3/4 ounces) cream of celery *or* mushroom soup, undiluted
- 1 can (12 ounces) evaporated milk
- 1 large onion, sliced
- 2 tablespoons butter

SAUCY SCALLOPED POTATOES

1/2 teaspoon salt
1/4 teaspoon pepper
1-1/2 cups chopped fully cooked ham

1) In a 3-qt. slow cooker, combine the potatoes, soup, milk, onion, butter, salt and pepper; mix well. Cover and cook on high for 1 hour.

2) Stir in ham. Reduce heat to low; cook 6-8 hours longer or until potatoes are tender.

Yield: 8 servings.

NUTRITION FACTS: 1/2 cup equals 555 calories, 10 g fat (5 g saturated fat), 36 mg cholesterol, 831 mg sodium, 101 g carbohydrate, 9 g fiber, 17 g protein.

Light Scalloped Potatoes
PREP: 15 min. **BAKE:** 1-1/4 hours + standing

Tamie Foley, Thousand Oaks, California

6 medium potatoes, peeled and thinly sliced
3 cups water
4 reduced-sodium chicken bouillon cubes
1 garlic clove, minced
1/2 cup grated Parmesan cheese
Minced fresh parsley, optional

1) Place potatoes in a 2-qt. baking dish coated with cooking spray. In a small saucepan, heat the water, bouillon and garlic until bouillon is dissolved; pour over potatoes. Sprinkle with Parmesan cheese.

2) Bake, uncovered, at 350° for 1-1/4 to 1-1/2 hours or until tender. Let stand for 10 minutes before

serving. Sprinkle with parsley if desired. Serve with a slotted spoon.

Yield: 6 servings.

NUTRITION FACTS: 1/2 cup equals 175 calories, 3 g fat (0 saturated fat), 7 mg cholesterol, 168 mg sodium, 32 g carbohydrate, 0 fiber, 3 g protein.

Creamy Scalloped Potatoes
PREP: 15 min. **BAKE:** 35 min.

Mildred Stubbs, Rockingham, North Carolina

2 tablespoons butter
2 tablespoons all-purpose flour
1/2 teaspoon salt
1/8 teaspoon pepper
1-1/2 cups milk
2 large potatoes, peeled and thinly sliced
2 tablespoons finely chopped onion

1) In a small saucepan over low heat, melt butter. Stir in the flour, salt and pepper until smooth and bubbly. Gradually stir in milk. Bring to a boil; cook and stir for 2 minutes or until thickened. Remove from the heat.

2) In a greased 1-qt. baking dish, layer half of the potatoes. Top with onion and half of the white sauce. Top with remaining potatoes and white sauce. Cover and bake at 350° for 35-40 minutes or until potatoes are tender.

Yield: 2 servings.

NUTRITION FACTS: 3/4 cup equals 537 calories, 18 g fat (11 g saturated fat), 56 mg cholesterol, 818 mg sodium, 82 g carbohydrate, 6 g fiber, 15 g protein.

CREAMY SCALLOPED POTATOES

AU GRATIN POTATOES

Au Gratin Potatoes

PREP: 45 min. + chilling **BAKE:** 1 hour

Jeannine Clayton, Byron, Minnesota

You won't believe how simple it is to make this creamy and delicious dish! All it takes is a few handy ingredients, and you've got a special addition to your dinner table.

- 12 medium unpeeled red *or* white potatoes
- 1 teaspoon salt
- 1/2 teaspoon pepper
- 1/2 teaspoon garlic *or* onion salt
- 2 cups (8 ounces) shredded cheddar cheese
- 1 cup heavy whipping cream

1) Place potatoes in a large saucepan and cover with water. Bring to a boil. Reduce heat; cover and cook for 30-40 minutes or until tender. Drain; refrigerate for several hours or overnight.

2) Peel potatoes and coarsely shred. Combine the salt, pepper and garlic salt. In a greased 13-in. x 9-in. x 2-in. baking dish, layer potatoes and salt mixture. Sprinkle with cheese; pour cream over all. Bake, uncovered, at 350° for 1 hour or until golden.

Yield: 12-15 servings.

NUTRITION FACTS: 1/2 cup equals 174 calories, 10 g fat (7 g saturated fat), 38 mg cholesterol, 320 mg sodium, 15 g carbohydrate, 2 g fiber, 5 g protein.

Fried Potatoes

PREP/TOTAL TIME: 15 min.

Taste of Home Test Kitchen

Who knew a simple combination of leftover potatoes, onion, butter, salt and pepper could taste so good?

- 3 cups diced cooked potatoes
- 1/2 cup diced cooked onion
- 2 tablespoons butter

Salt and pepper to taste

1) In a large skillet, cook potatoes and onion in butter over medium heat for 10 minutes or until golden brown. Season with salt and pepper.

Yield: 3-4 servings.

NUTRITION FACTS: 3/4 cup (calculated without salt and pepper) equals 147 calories, 6 g fat (4 g saturated fat), 15 mg cholesterol, 65 mg sodium, 22 g carbohydrate, 2 g fiber, 3 g protein.

Creamy Hash Brown Casserole

PREP: 10 min. **BAKE:** 50 min.

Teresa Stutzman, Adair, Oklahoma

This versatile side dish is perfect with grilled steaks and other meats. Its creamy cheese sauce and crunchy topping is popular with my family.

- 1 package (32 ounces) frozen Southern-style hash brown potatoes, thawed
- 1 pound process cheese (Velveeta), cubed
- 2 cups (16 ounces) sour cream
- 1 can (10-3/4 ounces) condensed cream of chicken soup, undiluted
- 3/4 cup butter, melted, *divided*
- 3 tablespoons chopped onion
- 1/4 teaspoon paprika
- 2 cups cornflakes, slightly crushed

Fresh savory, optional

1) In a large bowl, combine the hash browns, cheese, sour cream, soup, 1/2 cup butter and onion. Spread into a greased 13-in. x 9-in. x 2-in. baking dish. Sprinkle with paprika. Combine cornflakes and remaining butter; sprinkle over the top.

2) Bake, uncovered, at 350° for 50-60 minutes or until heated through. Garnish with savory if desired.

Yield: 8 servings.

NUTRITION FACTS: 3/4 cup equals 663 calories, 43 g fat (27 g saturated fat), 125 mg cholesterol, 1,359 mg sodium, 49 g carbohydrate, 3 g fiber, 19 g protein.

French Fries

PREP: 20 min. + soaking **COOK:** 5 min./batch

Taste of Home Test Kitchen

You can't beat the taste of homemade french fries...they're so much better than the frozen variety.

- 1 pound russet potatoes

Oil for deep-fat frying

- 3/4 teaspoon salt

1) Cut potatoes into 1/4-in. julienned strips; soak in cold water for 30 minutes.

2) Drain potatoes; pat dry with paper towels. In an electric skillet or deep-fat fryer, heat oil to 340°. Fry potatoes in batches for 3-4 minutes or until lightly browned. Remove with a slotted spoon; drain on paper towels.

3) Increase heat of oil to 375°. Fry potatoes again in batches for 1-2 minutes or until crisp and golden

brown, turning frequently. Drain on paper towels; sprinkle with salt. Serve immediately.

Yield: 4 servings.

NUTRITION FACTS: 16 french fries equals 190 calories, 11 g fat (1 g saturated fat), 0 cholesterol, 449 mg sodium, 20 g carbohydrate, 2 g fiber, 2 g protein.

Duchess Potatoes

PREP: 35 min. **BAKE:** 20 min.

Taste of Home Test Kitchen

Potatoes get an elegant treatment when piped into pretty rosettes and baked.

> 3 medium potatoes, peeled and quartered
> 4 tablespoons butter, *divided*
> 1 to 2 tablespoons milk
> 1 egg
> 1 teaspoon minced chives

1) Place potatoes in a large saucepan and cover with water. Bring to a boil. Reduce heat; cover and cook for 15-20 minutes or until tender. Drain.

2) In a mixing bowl, beat potatoes, 2 tablespoons butter and milk on low speed just until smooth. Cool slightly. Add egg and chives; beat until fluffy.

3) Cut a small hole in the corner of a pastry or plastic bag; insert #8b open star pastry tip. Fill the bag with potato mixture. Pipe potatoes into four rosettes on a greased baking sheet.

4) Melt remaining butter; drizzle over potatoes. Bake at 350° for 20-25 minutes or until heated through.

Yield: 4 servings.

NUTRITION FACTS: 1 serving equals 197 calories, 13 g fat (8 g saturated fat), 84 mg cholesterol, 137 mg sodium, 18 g carbohydrate, 2 g fiber, 3 g protein.

Delmonico Potatoes

PREP: 55 min. + chilling **BAKE:** 50 min.

Mrs. Arnold Sonnenberg, Brookville, Ohio

After trying this magnificent dish at a restaurant, I found a way to duplicate it at home. The results are creamy, cheesy and delicious!

> 9 medium unpeeled potatoes
> 1 cup milk
> 1 cup heavy whipping cream
> 1-1/2 teaspoons salt
> 1 teaspoon ground mustard
> 1/4 teaspoon pepper
> 1/4 teaspoon ground nutmeg
> 1-1/2 pounds shredded sharp cheddar cheese

1) Place potatoes in a large saucepan and cover with water. Bring to a boil. Reduce heat; cover and cook for 30-40 minutes or until tender. Drain; refrigerate for several hours or overnight.

2) Peel potatoes and coarsely shred. In a saucepan, heat the milk, cream, salt, mustard, pepper and nutmeg over medium heat until bubbles form around sides of pan. Reduce heat; add cheese, stirring until melted.

3) Place potatoes in a greased 13-in. x 9-in. x 2-in. baking dish. Pour cheese sauce over potatoes. Bake, uncovered, at 325° for 50-55 minutes or until heated through.

Yield: 12-16 servings.

NUTRITION FACTS: 1/2 cup equals 282 calories, 19 g fat (14 g saturated fat), 72 mg cholesterol, 515 mg sodium, 16 g carbohydrate, 1 g fiber, 12 g protein.

Lemon Red Potatoes

PREP/TOTAL TIME: 20 min.

Tara Branham, Austin, Texas

Butter, lemon juice, parsley and chives enhance these potatoes. They also cook up nicely in a slow cooker.

> 1-1/2 pounds medium red potatoes
> 1/4 cup butter, melted
> 1 tablespoon lemon juice
> 3 tablespoons snipped fresh parsley
> 1 tablespoon snipped fresh chives

Salt and pepper to taste

1) Cut a strip of peel from around the middle of each potato. Place potatoes in a large saucepan and cover with water. Bring to a boil. Reduce heat; cover and cook for 15-20 minutes or until tender. Drain.

2) Combine the butter, lemon juice, parsley and chives; mix well. Pour over the potatoes and toss to coat. Season with salt and pepper.

Yield: 6 servings.

Editor's Note: The potatoes may be cooked in a slow cooker. Just place the potatoes and 1/4 cup water in a covered 3-qt. slow cooker for 2-1/2 to 3 hours on high. Then proceed as recipe directs.

NUTRITION FACTS: 1 serving (calculated without salt and pepper) equals 150 calories, 8 g fat (5 g saturated fat), 20 mg cholesterol, 85 mg sodium, 18 g carbohydrate, 2 g fiber, 2 g protein.

LEMON RED POTATOES

DELUXE TWICE-BAKED POTATOES

 CLASSIC: Stuffed Baked Potatoes are a wonderful accompaniment to steak and other meaty entrees. Butter, half-and-half cream, sour cream and cheese make these twice-baked potatoes so rich and delicious. To suit the tastes of your family, try one of the easy variations that follow the recipe.

 TIME-SAVER: Cooking the potatoes in the microwave instead of the oven cuts down the prep time dramatically for Twice-Baked Deviled Potatoes, so they're ready in half an hour. The quick-to-fix filling is jazzed up with cheese, bacon, green onions and zippy mustard.

 LIGHT: Chives, basil and dashes of cayenne and garlic powder spark the flavor of lighter Herbed Twice-Baked Potatoes. Using reduced-fat cream cheese, fat-free milk and a small amount of butter dramatically cuts the fat, calories, cholesterol and sodium in the filling for these creamy potatoes.

 SERVES 2: Have a leftover slice of cooked bacon? Put it to good use in this tempting side dish for two. Chives and cheddar cheese also lend a tasty touch to Bacon Twice-Baked Potatoes.

Stuffed Baked Potatoes

PREP: 1-1/4 hours BAKE: 20 min.

Marge Clark, West Lebanon, Indiana

- 3 large baking potatoes (1 pound *each*)
- 1-1/2 teaspoons vegetable oil, optional
- 1/2 cup sliced green onions
- 1/2 cup butter, *divided*
- 1/2 cup half-and-half cream
- 1/2 cup sour cream
- 1 teaspoon salt
- 1/2 teaspoon white pepper
- 1 cup (4 ounces) shredded cheddar cheese

Paprika

STUFFED BAKED POTATOES

1) Pierce potatoes with a fork; rub with oil if desired. Bake at 400° for 1 hour and 20 minutes or until tender.

2) When cool enough to handle, cut potatoes in half lengthwise. Scoop out the pulp, leaving a thin shell. Place pulp in a large bowl and mash.

3) In a small skillet, saute onions in 1/4 cup butter until tender. Stir into potato pulp along with cream, sour cream, salt and pepper. Fold in cheese.

4) Spoon into potato shells. Place on a baking sheet. Melt remaining butter; drizzle over the potatoes. Sprinkle with paprika. Bake at 350° for 20-30 minutes or until heated through.

Yield: 6 servings.

Editor's Note: Potatoes may be stuffed ahead of time and refrigerated or frozen. Allow additional time for reheating.

NUTRITION FACTS: 1 potato half equals 416 calories, 26 g fat (17 g saturated fat), 84 mg cholesterol, 693 mg sodium, 36 g carbohydrate, 3 g fiber, 9 g protein.

Ranch Stuffed Baked Potatoes: Stir 1 to 2 tablespoons ranch salad dressing mix into the sour cream before adding to the mashed potato pulp. Fold in 3 crumbled cooked bacon strips along with the cheese.

Tex-Mex Stuffed Baked Potatoes: Omit green onions, 1/4 cup butter and paprika. Stir in 1 can (4 ounces) drained chopped green chilies. Substitute pepper Jack for the cheddar cheese. Sprinkle with chili powder if desired.

Herb-Stuffed Baked Potatoes: Stir in 2 tablespoons each minced chives and parsley along with the green onions. Use mozzarella in place of cheddar cheese.

Making Stuffed Potatoes

Cut a lengthwise slice from the top of each potato or as recipe directs. With a spoon, scoop potato pulp from the slice and the inside of the potato, leaving a 1/4-in. shell. Discard skin from slice. Mash the pulp and spoon into shells. Bake as directed.

Twice-Baked Deviled Potatoes

PREP/TOTAL TIME: 30 min.

Karol Chandler-Ezell, Nacogdoches, Texas

 4 small baking potatoes
 1/4 cup butter, softened
 1/4 cup milk
 1 cup (4 ounces) shredded cheddar cheese
 1/3 cup real bacon bits
 2 green onions, chopped
 1 teaspoon Dijon mustard
Dash paprika

1) Scrub and pierce potatoes; place on a microwave-safe plate. Microwave on high for 7-10 minutes or until tender; turn once. Let stand for 5 minutes. Cut a thin slice off the top of each potato and discard. Scoop out pulp, leaving a thin shell.

2) In a large bowl, mash the pulp with butter and milk. Stir in the cheese, bacon, onions, mustard and paprika. Spoon into potato shells. Return to the microwave-safe plate. Microwave, uncovered, on high for 1-2 minutes or until cheese is melted.

Yield: 4 servings.

NUTRITION FACTS: 1 potato equals 396 calories, 22 g fat (14 g saturated fat), 69 mg cholesterol, 635 mg sodium, 37 g carbohydrate, 4 g fiber, 14 g protein.

Herbed Twice-Baked Potatoes

PREP: 1-1/4 hours **BAKE:** 15 min.

Ruth Andrewson, Leavensworth, Washington

 2 medium baking potatoes
 1-1/2 ounces reduced-fat cream cheese, cubed
 1 tablespoon minced chives
 1/4 teaspoon salt
 1/4 teaspoon dried basil
Dash cayenne pepper
 3 tablespoons fat-free milk
 3 teaspoons butter, melted, *divided*
Dash garlic powder
Dash paprika

1) Scrub and pierce potatoes. Bake at 375° for 1 hour or until tender. When cool enough to handle, cut potatoes in half. Scoop out pulp, leaving a thin shell.

2) In a bowl, mash the pulp with cream cheese, chives, salt, basil and cayenne. Add milk and 1-1/2 teaspoons butter; mash. Spoon into potato shells. Drizzle with remaining butter; sprinkle with garlic powder and paprika.

3) Place on a baking sheet. Bake for 15-20 minutes or until heated through.

Yield: 4 servings.

NUTRITION FACTS: 1 potato half equals 150 calories, 5 g fat (3 g saturated fat), 15 mg cholesterol, 234 mg sodium, 23 g carbohydrate, 2 g fiber, 4 g protein.

Bacon Twice-Baked Potatoes

PREP: 1-1/4 hours **BAKE:** 20 min.

Debbie Wilkerson, Lusby, Maryland

 2 medium baking potatoes
 2 tablespoons reduced-fat butter
 1/4 cup fat-free milk
 1 bacon strip, cooked and crumbled
 1 tablespoon finely chopped onion
 1 teaspoon minced chives
 1/4 teaspoon salt
Dash pepper
 1/2 cup shredded reduced-fat cheddar cheese, *divided*

1) Bake potatoes at 375° for 1 hour or until tender. When cool enough to handle, cut a thin slice off the top of each potato and discard. Scoop out pulp, leaving a thin shell.

2) In a small bowl, mash the pulp with butter. Stir in the milk, bacon, onion, chives, salt, pepper and 1/3 cup cheese. Spoon into potato shells. Top with remaining cheese.

3) Place on a baking sheet. Bake for 20-25 minutes or until cheese is melted.

Yield: 2 servings.

NUTRITION FACTS: 1 potato equals 328 calories, 14 g fat (8 g saturated fat), 39 mg cholesterol, 669 mg sodium, 42 g carbohydrate, 4 g fiber, 14 g protein.

HERBED TWICE-BAKED POTATOES

PERFECT POTATO PANCAKES

Perfect Potato Pancakes

PREP: 20 min. **COOK:** 10 min./batch

Mary Peters, Swift Current, Saskatchewan

To keep the cooked potato pancakes warm, I wrap them in foil and place them in the oven.

> 4 large potatoes (about 3 pounds)
> 2 eggs, lightly beaten
> 1/2 cup all-purpose flour
> 1/2 cup finely diced onion
> 1 teaspoon salt
> 1/8 teaspoon pepper

Oil for frying

Maple syrup *or* applesauce

1) Peel and shred potatoes; place in a bowl of cold water. Line a colander with cheesecloth or paper towels. Drain potatoes into cloth and squeeze out as much moisture as possible. In a large bowl, combine the potatoes, eggs, flour, onion, salt and pepper.

2) In an electric skillet, heat 1/4 in. of oil over medium heat. Drop batter by 1/4 cupfuls into oil, about 3 in. apart. Press lightly to flatten. Fry until golden brown, about 4 minutes on each side.

3) Drain on paper towels. Serve with syrup or applesauce.

Yield: about 16 pancakes.

NUTRITION FACTS: 2 pancakes (calculated without syrup or apple-sauce) equals 251 calories, 6 g fat (1 g saturated fat), 53 mg cholesterol, 323 mg sodium, 45 g carbohydrate, 4 g fiber, 6 g protein.

Red Potato Bundles

PREP: 10 min. **GRILL:** 40 min.

Kriss Erickson, Kalauea, Hawaii

Red potatoes just need to be scrubbed and quartered to start this side dish. You can grill or bake the packets with tasty results.

> 6 small red potatoes, quartered
> 1 small onion, thinly sliced
> 6 garlic cloves, peeled

> 2 sprigs fresh rosemary *or* 1 to 2 teaspoons dried rosemary, crushed
> 1/2 teaspoon salt

Dash pepper

> 2 tablespoons grated Parmesan cheese
> 1/4 cup olive oil

1) Place potatoes, onion and garlic on two pieces of heavy-duty foil (about 12 in. square); top with rosemary, salt, pepper and cheese. Drizzle with oil. Fold in edges of foil and seal tightly.

2) Grill, covered, over medium heat for 40-45 minutes or until potatoes are tender. Open foil carefully to allow steam to escape.

Yield: 2 servings.

Editor's Note: To bake the foil packets, place on a baking pan. Bake at 350° for 45 minutes or until potatoes are tender.

NUTRITION FACTS: 1 serving equals 390 calories, 29 g fat (5 g saturated fat), 4 mg cholesterol, 694 mg sodium, 29 g carbohydrate, 3 g fiber, 6 g protein.

Oven-Roasted Potato Wedges

PREP: 10 min. **BAKE:** 40 min.

Ellen Benninger, Greenville, Pennsylvania

This recipe is perfect for company. The potatoes get a delicious, delicate flavor from the rosemary.

> 4 unpeeled baking potatoes (2 pounds)
> 2 tablespoons olive oil
> 1 medium onion, chopped
> 2 garlic cloves, minced
> 1 tablespoon minced fresh rosemary *or* 1 teaspoon dried rosemary, crushed
> 1/2 teaspoon salt
> 1/4 teaspoon pepper

1) Cut potatoes lengthwise into wedges; place in a greased 13-in. x 9-in. x 2-in. baking pan. Drizzle with oil. Sprinkle with onion, garlic, rosemary, salt and pepper; stir to coat.

2) Bake, uncovered, at 400° for 45-50 minutes or until tender, turning once.

Yield: 8 servings.

NUTRITION FACTS: 1 serving equals 398 calories, 4 g fat (1 g saturated fat), 0 cholesterol, 176 mg sodium, 84 g carbohydrate, 8 g fiber, 10 g protein.

Making the Wedge

An apple slicer can make quick work of cutting potatoes into wedges. Cut the potatoes in half crosswise. Stand the potato half up on the cut end, then use the apple slicer to cut into wedges. Cook the center "core" along with the rest of the wedges.

Pumpkin

Pumpkins are a member of the gourd family and can be cooked like any winter squash. Varieties known as pie pumpkins are smaller than the "jack-o'-lantern" type and make flavorful puree for use in pies and cakes.

Buying

Pumpkins are available in the autumn months. Select pumpkins that have firm, blemish-free rinds and are bright orange in color.

Storage

Store in a cool, dry place for up to 1 month. A cut pumpkin may be stored in an open plastic bag in the refrigerator for up to 1 week.

Preparation

Cut off the top stem section. Remove seeds and scrape out stringy fibers.

Yield: 1 pie pumpkin (3 pounds) = about 2 cups cooked pureed.

Toasting Pumpkin Seeds

Remove fibrous strings from seeds. Place in a colander; rinse under cold water and drain. Spread out on paper towels to dry. Spread on a greased baking sheet. Bake at 250° for 1 hour. Increase heat to 400°; bake 5 minutes. Season with salt if desired.

Rutabaga

Rutabaga, also known as a Swede or Swedish turnip, is a root vegetable. It has a stronger flavor than a turnip.

Buying

Rutabaga is available year-round; peak season is fall through winter. Select a firm, solid rutabaga that feels heavy for its size. Avoid those with scars and bruises. For best flavor, select medium to small ones.

Storage

Store unwashed rutabaga in the refrigerator crisper drawer for up to 2 weeks.

Preparation

Trim top and bottom from rutabaga, then cut in half. They are coated with wax that needs to be peeled before using. Rinse with cold water after peeling.

Yield: 1 pound trimmed = 3 cups cubed

Oven-Roasted Root Vegetables

PREP: 20 min. **BAKE:** 40 min.

Mitzi Sentiff, Annapolis, Maryland

All kinds of root vegetables star in this colorful medley. Fresh thyme and sage season the mix of rutabaga, parsnips and butternut squash that's satisfying any time of year.

- 2 cups cubed peeled rutabaga
- 2 cups cubed peeled parsnips
- 2 cups cubed peeled butternut squash
- 2 medium onions, chopped
- 1 tablespoon olive oil
- 1/2 teaspoon salt
- 1/8 teaspoon pepper
- 1 tablespoon minced fresh thyme *or* 1 teaspoon dried thyme
- 1 tablespoon minced fresh sage *or* 1 teaspoon rubbed sage

1) In a large bowl, combine the rutabaga, parsnips, squash and onions. Add the oil, salt and pepper; toss to coat. Arrange in a single layer in a 15-in. x 10-in. x 1-in. baking pan coated with cooking spray.

2) Bake, uncovered, at 400° for 40-50 minutes, stirring occasionally. Sprinkle with herbs; toss to combine.

Yield: 4 servings.

NUTRITION FACTS: 3/4 cup equals 168 calories, 4 g fat (1 g saturated fat), 0 cholesterol, 319 mg sodium, 33 g carbohydrate, 9 g fiber, 3 g protein.

Triple Mashed Vegetables

PREP: 20 min. **COOK:** 25 min.

Noel Heckler, Wolcott, New York

I had trouble getting my family to eat rutabaga, until this flavor-filled recipe convinced them to try it. This is a nice variation on plain mashed potatoes.

- 1 medium rutabaga, peeled and cubed (about 3 cups)
- 6 medium potatoes, peeled and cubed (3-1/2 cups)
- 6 medium carrots, peeled and sliced (3 cups)
- 2 tablespoons butter
- 3/4 teaspoon salt
- 1/4 teaspoon pepper

1) Place vegetables in a large saucepan and cover with water. Bring to a boil. Reduce heat; cover and cook for 15-20 minutes or until very tender.

2) Drain vegetables and transfer to a mixing bowl. Mash vegetables and add the butter, salt and pepper; beat until smooth and fluffy.

Yield: 6 servings.

NUTRITION FACTS: 2/3 cup equals 162 calories, 4 g fat (2 g saturated fat), 10 mg cholesterol, 402 mg sodium, 30 g carbohydrate, 6 g fiber, 3 g protein.

Shallots

Shallots are a member of the onion family, but their appearance resembles garlic cloves.

Buying

Shallots are available year-round. Select firm, plump shallots. Avoid those with soft spots, a shriveled appearance or green sprouts.

Storage

Store in a cool, dry, well-ventilated place for up to 1 month.

Preparation

Shallots can have two or three cloves attached to one head. Each clove is a shallot. Trim base and remove papery outer skin. Mince or slice as recipe directs.

Yield: 1 package (3 ounces) = 1/2 cup chopped

Spinach

Dark green in color and tender in texture, spinach leaves can be eaten raw in salads or lightly cooked and used in soups, side dishes and main dishes.

Buying

Spinach is available year-round; peak season is late spring and early summer. Select crisp, dark green, tender leaves. Avoid yellowed or wilted spinach.

Storage

Keep unwashed spinach in a sealed plastic bag in the refrigerator crisper drawer for up to 5 days.

Preparation

Cut off the tough stems. Wash several times in cold water to remove sand; drain well and pat dry.

Yield: 1 to 1-1/2 pounds fresh spinach = 1 cup cooked

Squeezing Spinach Dry

Drain spinach in a colander. If spinach was cooked, allow to cool. With clean hands, squeeze the water out of the spinach.

Spinach Supreme

PREP/TOTAL TIME: 15 min.

Clara Coulston, Washington Court House, Ohio

Showcase spinach at its best with mushrooms, onion and crunchy walnuts.

- 1 cup sliced fresh mushrooms
- 1 medium onion, chopped
- 1/4 cup reduced-sodium chicken broth
- 8 cups chopped fresh spinach
- 1/2 teaspoon garlic powder
- 1/4 teaspoon salt
- 1/8 teaspoon pepper
- 2 tablespoons chopped walnuts, toasted

1) In a large saucepan, cook mushrooms and onion in broth over medium-low heat until tender.

2) Stir in the spinach, garlic powder, salt and pepper. Cover and cook for 2-3 minutes or until spinach is wilted. Stir in walnuts. Serve with a slotted spoon.

Yield: 2 servings.

NUTRITION FACTS: 3/4 cup equals 108 calories, 5 g fat (trace saturated fat), 0 cholesterol, 469 mg sodium, 12 g carbohydrate, 5 g fiber, 7 g protein.

Creamy Spinach Bake

PREP: 35 min. **BAKE:** 20 min.

Jennifer Bley, Austin, Texas

Artichoke hearts, Parmesan cheese and fresh dill add spark to this rich side-dish casserole. It's a nice way to use fresh spinach and ideal to serve for Thanksgiving or Christmas dinner.

- 3 packages (9 ounces *each*) fresh baby spinach
- 1 small red onion, chopped
- 1 tablespoon butter
- 1 package (8 ounces) cream cheese, cubed
- 1 cup (8 ounces) sour cream
- 1/2 cup half-and-half cream
- 1/3 cup plus 3 tablespoons grated Parmesan cheese, *divided*
- 3 garlic cloves, minced
- 1/8 teaspoon pepper
- 2 cans (14 ounces *each*) water-packed artichoke hearts, rinsed, drained and chopped
- 1 tablespoon snipped fresh dill
- 1/4 teaspoon seasoned salt
- 8 butter-flavored crackers, coarsely crushed

1) Place half of the spinach in a steamer basket; place in a large saucepan over 1 in. of water. Bring to a boil; cover and steam for 3-4 minutes or just until wilted. Transfer to a bowl. Repeat with remaining spinach; set aside.

2) In a large saucepan, saute onion in butter until tender. Reduce heat to low; stir in the cream cheese, sour cream, half-and-half, 1/3 cup Parmesan cheese, garlic and pepper. Cook and stir until cream cheese is melted. Stir in the artichokes, dill, seasoned salt and spinach.

3) Transfer to an ungreased 2-qt. baking dish. Sprinkle with cracker crumbs and remaining Parmesan cheese. Bake, uncovered, at 350° for 20-25 minutes or until edges are bubbly.

Yield: 12 servings.

NUTRITION FACTS: 1/2 cup equals 196 calories, 14 g fat (8 g saturated fat), 45 mg cholesterol, 394 mg sodium, 10 g carbohydrate, 2 g fiber, 7 g protein.

Sauteed Spinach and Peppers
PREP/TOTAL TIME: 15 min.

Mary Lou Moon, Beaverton, Oregon

We often steam our fresh spinach and eat it plain. But this version is a nice change.

 1 large sweet red pepper, coarsely chopped
 1 tablespoon olive oil
 1 small red onion, finely chopped
 3 garlic cloves, minced
 8 cups packed fresh spinach
 1/2 teaspoon salt
 1/4 teaspoon pepper
 1/8 teaspoon sugar

1) In a large nonstick skillet, saute red pepper in oil for 1 minute. Add onion and garlic; saute until tender, about 1-1/2 minutes longer.

SAUTEED SPINACH AND PEPPERS

2) Stir in the spinach, salt, pepper and sugar; saute for 1-2 minutes or until spinach is wilted and tender. Serve with a slotted spoon.

Yield: 4 servings.

NUTRITION FACTS: 1/2 cup equals 65 calories, 4 g fat (1 g saturated fat), 0 cholesterol, 342 mg sodium, 7 g carbohydrate, 3 g fiber, 2 g protein.

Squash, Summer

Summer squash are members of the gourd family. Their skin and seeds are completely edible. Summer squash may be used raw or cooked.

Buying

Summer squash are available year-round; peak season is late summer through early fall. Select firm, plump squash with bright, smooth skin. Baby squash are a smaller version of their counterparts and are harvested when they are young.

Zucchini is available with green and yellow skin. Yellow summer squash is available with a crookneck (one end is narrower and has a slight bend) or straight neck. Pattypan is a small, round, squat squash with a scalloped edge; generally they are pale green or white. Sunburst is a bright yellow pattypan with a green stem.

Storage

Store unwashed summer squash in the refrigerator crisper drawer for up to 4 days.

Preparation

Wash summer squash but do not peel unless squash is mature. Remove stem and blossom ends. Serve pattypan squash whole. Cut zucchini and summer squash into 1/2-in. slices.

Yield: 1 pound = 4 cups grated or 3-1/2 cups sliced

Stuffed Zucchini

PREP/TOTAL TIME: 30 min.

Vonnie Elledge, Pinole, California

Zucchini makes a great shell for a filling of squash, bread crumbs, Parmesan cheese and onion.

- 4 medium zucchini
- 8 cups water
- 1/4 teaspoon salt
- 1 small onion, minced
- 2 tablespoons vegetable oil
- 2 eggs, lightly beaten
- 1/2 cup dry bread crumbs
- 1/4 cup grated Parmesan cheese
- 2 tablespoons minced fresh parsley

Salt and pepper to taste

1) Cut zucchini in half lengthwise. Scoop out pulp, leaving a 3/8-in. shell. Reserve pulp.

2) In a large saucepan, bring water and salt to a boil. Add zucchini shells; cover and boil for 2 minutes. Drain and set aside. Chop zucchini pulp.

3) In a large skillet, saute the onion and chopped zucchini in oil until tender. Remove from the heat. Stir in the eggs, bread crumbs, cheese, parsley, salt and pepper. Fill shells.

4) Place in a greased baking dish. Bake, uncovered, at 375° for 15 minutes or until filling reaches 160° and is heated through.

Yield: 4 servings.

NUTRITION FACTS: 2 zucchini halves (calculated without salt and pepper) equals 208 calories, 12 g fat (3 g saturated fat), 110 mg cholesterol, 396 mg sodium, 18 g carbohydrate, 3 g fiber, 9 g protein.

Zucchini Fries

PREP/TOTAL TIME: 30 min.

Debbie Brunssen, Randolph, Nebraska

These flavorful fries are the first thing we make when the zucchini in our garden is ready.

- 1 medium zucchini
- 1/2 cup all-purpose flour
- 1 teaspoon onion salt
- 1 teaspoon dried oregano
- 1/2 teaspoon garlic powder
- 1 egg, lightly beaten
- 1/3 cup milk
- 1 teaspoon vegetable oil
- 4 cups Corn Chex, crushed

Oil for deep-fat frying

1) Cut zucchini in half widthwise, then cut each half lengthwise into eight wedges; set aside. In a bowl, combine the flour, onion salt, oregano and garlic powder.

2) Combine the egg, milk and oil; stir into the dry ingredients just until blended. Dip zucchini wedges in batter, then roll in crushed cereal.

3) In an electric skillet or deep-fat fryer, heat oil to 375°. Fry zucchini wedges, a few at a time, for 3-4 minutes or until golden brown. Drain on paper towels; keep warm.

Yield: 4 servings.

NUTRITION FACTS: 4 zucchini fries equals 250 calories, 7 g fat (1 g saturated fat), 56 mg cholesterol, 769 mg sodium, 41 g carbohydrate, 2 g fiber, 7 g protein.

Grilled Vegetable Skewers

PREP/TOTAL TIME: 20 min.

Susan Bourque, Danielson, Connecticut

We love to eat vegetables the most flavorful way —grilled! Seasoned with fresh herbs, these colorful kabobs showcase the best of summer's bounty.

- 1 medium ear fresh *or* frozen sweet corn, thawed and quartered
- 1 small zucchini, quartered
- 1/4 small red onion, halved
- 4 cherry tomatoes
- 1/4 teaspoon dried basil
- 1/4 teaspoon dried rosemary, crushed
- 1/4 teaspoon dried thyme
- 1/8 teaspoon garlic powder
- 1/8 teaspoon salt
- 1/8 teaspoon pepper

1) Place the corn on a microwave-safe plate. Cover with waxed paper. Microwave on high for 2 minutes.

2) Coat grill rack with cooking spray before starting the grill. On two metal or soaked wooden skewers, alternately thread the corn, zucchini, onion and tomatoes.

GRILLED VEGETABLE SKEWERS

3) Lightly coat vegetables with cooking spray. In a small bowl, combine the seasonings; sprinkle over vegetables.

4) Grill, covered, over medium heat for 3 minutes or until vegetables are tender.

Yield: 2 servings.

Editor's Note: To broil the kabobs, place on a broiler pan coated with cooking spray. Broil 4-6 in. from the heat for 3 minutes on each side.

NUTRITION FACTS: 1 kabob equals 69 calories, 1 g fat (trace saturated fat), 0 cholesterol, 131 mg sodium, 16 g carbohydrate, 3 g fiber, 3 g protein.

Summer Garden Medley

PREP/TOTAL TIME: 15 min.

Elaine Nelson, Fresno, California

This side dish brings back memories of the corn-and-tomato dish my mother often prepared. Farmers in our area supply us with eggplant, so I sometimes substitute them for the zucchini.

> 2 medium zucchini, halved lengthwise and cut into 1/4-inch slices
> 1 cup fresh *or* frozen corn, thawed
> 3/4 cup diced green pepper
> 1 medium leek (white portion only), sliced
> 1/2 teaspoon seasoned salt
> 1 tablespoon olive oil
> 2 medium tomatoes, seeded and diced

1) In a large nonstick skillet, saute the zucchini, corn, green pepper, leek and seasoned salt in oil until vegetables are tender. Stir in the tomatoes; heat through.

Yield: 4 servings.

NUTRITION FACTS: 1 cup equals 113 calories, 4 g fat (1 g saturated fat), 0 cholesterol, 202 mg sodium, 19 g carbohydrate, 3 g fiber, 3 g protein.

Roasted Veggie Chili

PREP: 30 min. **COOK:** 40 min.

C.J. Counts, Murphy, North Carolina

You're sure to get a kick out of this good-for-you chili that uses a bounty of veggies.

> 2 cups fresh *or* frozen corn
> 2 cups *each* cubed zucchini, yellow summer squash and eggplant
> 2 *each* medium green and sweet red peppers, cut into 1-inch pieces
> 2 large onions, chopped
> 1/2 cup garlic cloves, peeled
> 1/4 cup olive oil
> 4 quarts chicken broth
> 2 cans (14-1/2 ounces *each*) stewed tomatoes

ROASTED VEGGIE CHILI

> 2 cans (14-1/2 ounces *each*) tomato puree
> 1/4 cup lime juice
> 4 teaspoons chili powder
> 1-1/4 teaspoons cayenne pepper
> 1 teaspoon ground cumin
> 1/2 cup butter
> 1/2 cup all-purpose flour
> 3 cans (15 ounces *each*) white kidney *or* cannellini beans, rinsed and drained
> 1/2 cup minced fresh cilantro

1) Place the vegetables and garlic in a roasting pan. Drizzle with oil; toss to coat. Cover and bake at 400° for 20-30 minutes or until vegetables are tender; cool slightly. Remove and chop garlic.

2) In a Dutch oven or soup kettle, combine the broth, tomatoes, tomato puree, lime juice, chili powder, cayenne and cumin. Bring to a boil. Reduce heat; simmer, uncovered, for 25-35 minutes or until mixture is reduced by a quarter.

3) In a large saucepan or Dutch oven, melt butter; stir in flour until smooth. Cook and stir until bubbly and starting to brown. Slowly whisk into tomato mixture. Add roasted vegetables, garlic, beans and cilantro; mix well.

4) Simmer, uncovered, until chili reaches desired thickness.

Yield: 24 servings (6 quarts).

NUTRITION FACTS: 1 cup equals 168 calories, 7 g fat (3 g saturated fat), 10 mg cholesterol, 802 mg sodium, 22 g carbohydrate, 4 g fiber, 6 g protein.

Making Zucchini Ribbons

Trim ends from zucchini. Use a vegetable peeler to make long thin strips from the zucchini.

Steamed Vegetable Ribbons

PREP/TOTAL TIME: 20 min.

Taste of Home Test Kitchen

These extra-thin slices of zucchini and carrot will add a pretty touch to a dinner plate.

4 large carrots, peeled
8 small zucchini
4 teaspoons lemon juice
2 teaspoons olive oil
1 teaspoon salt
1/8 to 1/4 teaspoon pepper

1) Trim ends from the carrots and zucchini. Use a vegetable peeler to make long thin strips down the length of each carrot and zucchini, making long ribbons.

2) Place carrots in a steamer basket. Place in a large saucepan over 1 in. of water; bring to a boil. Cover and steam for 2 minutes.

3) Add zucchini; cover and steam 2-3 minutes longer or until vegetables are tender. Transfer vegetables to a bowl. Add the lemon juice, oil, salt and pepper; toss to coat.

Yield: 8 servings.

NUTRITION FACTS: 1/2 cup equals 43 calories, 1 g fat (trace saturated fat), 0 cholesterol, 309 mg sodium, 7 g carbohydrate, 3 g fiber, 2 g protein.

STEAMED VEGETABLE RIBBONS

Rosemary Peas 'n' Squash

PREP/TOTAL TIME: 15 min.

Emily Chaney, Blue Hill, Maine

When you have a bounty of squash from your garden, here's a great way to use it up!

1 tablespoon butter
1 medium yellow summer *or* pattypan squash, cut into 1-inch chunks

ROSEMARY PEAS 'N' SQUASH

1 medium zucchini, cut into 1-inch chunks
1/4 pound fresh *or* frozen sugar snap peas
1 tablespoon minced fresh rosemary *or* 1 teaspoon dried rosemary, crushed

Salt and pepper to taste

1) In a large skillet, melt butter. Saute squash, peas and rosemary for 5 minutes or until vegetables are crisp-tender. Sprinkle with salt and pepper.

Yield: 4 servings.

NUTRITION FACTS: 1 serving (calculated without salt and pepper) equals 55 calories, 3 g fat (2 g saturated fat), 8 mg cholesterol, 33 mg sodium, 6 g carbohydrate, 2 g fiber, 2 g protein.

Squash, Winter

Winter squash is a member of the gourd family. It has a hard, inedible shell and fully mature seeds.

Buying

Winter squash is available year-round; peak season is October through December. Select squash that is heavy for its size. The shells should be hard with a deep color. Avoid those with cracks or soft spots.

Storage

Store unwashed winter squash in a cool, dry, well-ventilated place for up to 4 weeks.

Yield: 1-3/4 pounds winter squash = 1-3/4 cups cooked mashed

Acorn Squash

Resembles an acorn. Its ridged shell can be dark green, golden/orange or cream colored. The orange flesh is mild.

Buttercup Squash

Has a cap or turban on one end of its green shell. The orange flesh has a sweet, classic squash flavor and creamy texture.

Butternut Squash

Is bell-shaped with a pale tan shell. The shell can be peeled before cooking. The orange flesh is sweet and flavorful.

Delicata Squash

Is cylindrical and has a yellow shell with green stripes. Its pale yellow flesh is sweet and is sometimes compared to a sweet potato.

Hubbard Squash

Is a larger squash (can grow to 25 pounds) and is sometimes sold in pieces because of its size. Its hard, bumpy shell can be orange, gray-blue or green. The orange flesh is sweet and rich.

Spaghetti Squash

Is watermelon-shaped with a thin, yellow shell. Once cooked, its mild and slightly nutty-flavored flesh separates into spaghetti-like strands.

Sweet Dumpling

Is a small, pumpkin-shaped squash with a yellow shell that has green stripes like the Delicata squash. Its fine-textured yellow flesh is sweet and is sometimes said to have a mild corn flavor.

Turban Squash

Has a large cap or turban on one end of its shell. The hard-to-remove shell comes in green, orange or white. Its yellow, mealy flesh has a nutty flavor.

Halving a Winter Squash

With their hard shells, winter squashs can be difficult to cut in half. Here's a method that doesn't rely just on strength. Use a rubber mallet and a large knife, such as a French chef's knife. Cover mallet with a food storage bag and secure to the handle with a rubber band or twist tie. Insert the knife lengthwise into the middle of the squash. Hold the knife handle with one hand and hit the top of the blade by the handle with the mallet. Continue hitting the knife with the mallet until the squash is cut in half.

Honey-Spice Acorn Squash

PREP: 15 min. **BAKE:** 70 min.

Alpha Wilson, Roswell, New Mexico

Cinnamon and ginger give a nice spiced flavor to the moist, tender squash halves.

- 3 tablespoons honey
- 2 tablespoons butter, melted
- 1/4 teaspoon salt
- 1/8 teaspoon ground cinnamon
- 1/8 teaspoon ground ginger
- 2 medium acorn squash

1) In a small bowl, combine the honey, butter, salt, cinnamon and ginger. Cut squash in half; discard the seeds. With a sharp knife, cut a thin slice from bottom of squash to allow it to sit flat.

2) Place cavity side up in a greased 15-in. x 10-in. x 1-in. baking pan. Fill squash halves with butter mixture.

3) Cover and bake at 375° for 1 hour. Uncover; bake 10 minutes longer or until squash is tender.

Yield: 4 servings.

NUTRITION FACTS: 1 serving equals 185 calories, 6 g fat (4 g saturated fat), 15 mg cholesterol, 212 mg sodium, 36 g carbohydrate, 3 g fiber, 2 g protein.

RUSTIC SQUASH TARTS

Rustic Squash Tarts

PREP: 30 min. **BAKE:** 35 min.

Ann Marie Moch, Kintyre, North Dakota

The rustic-looking pastry shells of this unique side dish hold a sweet and spicy pecan layer under the slices of butternut and acorn squash slices.

- 1 medium butternut squash, peeled, seeded and cut into 1/8-inch slices
- 1 medium acorn squash, peeled, seeded and cut into 1/8-inch slices
- 2 tablespoons water
- 1/4 cup olive oil
- 1 tablespoon minced fresh thyme
- 1 tablespoon minced fresh parsley
- 1/2 teaspoon salt
- 1/4 teaspoon pepper
- 1/2 cup all-purpose flour
- 1/2 cup ground pecans
- 6 tablespoons sugar
- 1/2 teaspoon ground nutmeg
- 1/2 teaspoon ground cinnamon
- 1 package (17.3 ounces) frozen puff pastry, thawed
- 1 egg, lightly beaten
- 2 tablespoons butter

1) In a large microwave-safe bowl, combine squash and water. Cover and microwave on high for 5 minutes or until crisp-tender. Drain; transfer to a large resealable plastic bag.

2) Add the oil, thyme, parsley, salt and pepper; seal bag and shake to coat. Set aside. In a small bowl, combine the flour, pecans, sugar, nutmeg and cinnamon; set aside.

3) Unfold pastry sheets on a lightly floured surface. Roll each pastry to 1/8-in. thickness; transfer each to an ungreased baking sheet. Sprinkle with pecan mixture. Arrange squash slices to within 1-1/2 in. of edges, alternating slices of butternut and acorn squash.

4) Fold up edges of pastry over filling, leaving centers uncovered. Brush pastry with egg. Dot

squash with butter. Bake at 375° for 35-40 minutes or until golden brown.

Yield: 2 tarts (8 servings each).

NUTRITION FACTS: 1 tart piece equals 279 calories, 15 g fat (4 g saturated fat), 17 mg cholesterol, 196 mg sodium, 34 g carbohydrate, 5 g fiber, 4 g protein.

Spaghetti Squash with Sweet Peppers

PREP/TOTAL TIME: 25 min.

Julie Vaniek, Box Elder, South Dakota

For a dish with harvesttime appeal, you can't go wrong with this veggie medley I created. It makes a satisfying main dish or a hearty side.

- 1 medium spaghetti squash (2 pounds)
- 1/2 medium green pepper, sliced
- 1/2 medium sweet red pepper, sliced
- 4 medium fresh mushrooms, sliced
- 1 small onion, chopped
- 1 tablespoon olive oil
- 2 medium tomatoes, quartered
- 1 garlic clove, minced
- 1/2 cup chicken broth
- 1/4 teaspoon salt
- 3 tablespoons shredded Parmesan cheese

1) Cut squash in half lengthwise; discard seeds. Place squash cut side down on a microwave-safe plate. Microwave, uncovered, on high for 10-12 minutes or until tender.

2) Meanwhile, in a large nonstick skillet, saute the peppers, mushrooms and onion in oil until tender. Add tomatoes and garlic; saute 4-5 minutes longer. Add broth and salt; simmer, uncovered, for 3-4 minutes.

3) When squash is cool enough to handle, use a fork to separate strands. Place squash on a serving platter or individual plates; top with the pepper mixture. Sprinkle with Parmesan cheese.

Yield: 4 servings.

NUTRITION FACTS: 1/2 cup equals 110 calories, 5 g fat (1 g saturated fat), 4 mg cholesterol, 372 mg sodium, 13 g carbohydrate, 3 g fiber, 4 g protein.

Cooking Spaghetti Squash

Halve the squash; discard seeds. Place cut side down in a greased baking dish; bake at 350° for 45-60 minutes or until shell can be pierced easily with a fork. Cool slightly. Use a fork to separate squash into strands, resembling spaghetti.

Sweet Potatoes

Sweet potatoes are sometimes referred to as yams, but they are not. Yams are grown in more tropical areas, like South America and Africa.

Buying

Sweet potatoes are available year-round; peak season is November. Select sweet potatoes with a thin, smooth skin and tapered ends that are heavy for their size. Avoid ones with shriveled skin, soft spots or bruises. Handle gently to avoid bruising.

There are two main types of sweet potatoes. The familiar, moist, orange-fleshed sweet potato and the starchier, drier, yellow-fleshed sweet potato.

Storage

Store sweet potatoes in a dark, cool, dry, well-ventilated place for up to 1 week.

Preparing Sweet Potatoes

Scrub with a vegetable brush under cold water. Depending on use, they may be peeled before or after cooking.

Yield: 1 pound = 2 cups cooked mashed

Sweet Potatoes with Apples

PREP: 40 min. **BAKE:** 35 min.

Jean Winfree, Wausau, Wisconsin

This dish is very welcome at any meal at our house, especially on holidays. The tart apple slices taste so good baked on top of the mild sweet potatoes.

> 3 to 3-1/2 pounds sweet potatoes
> 2 tart apples, peeled, cored and cut into 1/4-inch rings
> 1/2 cup orange juice

SWEET POTATOES WITH APPLES

> 1/4 cup packed brown sugar
> 1/4 teaspoon ground ginger
> 1/4 teaspoon ground cinnamon
> 2 tablespoons butter

1) Place sweet potatoes in a large saucepan and cover with water. Bring to a boil. Reduce heat; cover and cook for 30 minutes or until just tender. Drain and cool slightly. Peel and cut into 1/4-in. slices.

2) In a greased 13-in. x 9-in. x 2-in. baking dish, alternately layer potatoes and apples. Pour orange juice over top. Combine the brown sugar, ginger and cinnamon; sprinkle over potatoes and apples. Dot with butter.

3) Bake, uncovered, at 350° for 35-45 minutes or until heated through and apples are tender.

Yield: 8 servings.

NUTRITION FACTS: 1 cup equals 225 calories, 3 g fat (2 g saturated fat), 8 mg cholesterol, 106 mg sodium, 48 g carbohydrate, 5 g fiber, 2 g protein.

Dijon Scalloped Potatoes

PREP: 25 min. **BAKE:** 50 min. + standing

Carolyn Putnam, Norwalk, Ohio

My family loves this creamy and colorful dish. What's not to love? It has both sweet and white potatoes, lots of buttery, cheesy flavor and a pretty, golden-crumb topping.

> 2/3 cup chopped onion
> 2 teaspoons vegetable oil
> 1 can (14-1/2 ounces) chicken broth
> 2 packages (3 ounces *each*) cream cheese, cubed
> 1 tablespoon Dijon mustard
> 3 medium russet potatoes, peeled and thinly sliced
> 2 medium sweet potatoes, peeled and thinly sliced
> 1-1/2 to 2 cups crushed butter-flavored crackers
> 3 tablespoons grated Parmesan cheese
> 2 tablespoons butter, melted
> 2 teaspoons minced fresh parsley

1) In a Dutch oven, saute onion in oil until tender. Reduce heat to medium; stir in the broth, cream cheese and mustard until blended. Remove from the heat. Stir in the potatoes.

2) Transfer to a greased 13-in. x 9-in. x 2-in. baking dish. Combine the crushed crackers, Parmesan cheese and butter; sprinkle over the top.

3) Bake, uncovered, at 350° for 50-60 minutes or until potatoes are tender. Sprinkle with parsley. Let stand for 10 minutes before serving.

Yield: 8 servings.

NUTRITION FACTS: 3/4 cup equals 293 calories, 16 g fat (8 g saturated fat), 34 mg cholesterol, 524 mg sodium, 32 g carbohydrate, 2 g fiber, 6 g protein.

HOLIDAY SWEET POTATO BAKE

 CLASSIC: Tender sweet potatoes are mashed with brown sugar, cinnamon, allspice and nutmeg to make the base for Old-Fashioned Sweet Potato Casserole. But it's the puffy, golden marshmallow topping that makes this holiday side dish so memorable.

 TIME-SAVER: Cranberry-Apple Sweet Potatoes lets you add a sweet potato casserole to your holiday buffet without all the work. A few canned goods are layered and baked in less than half an hour for fast, fruity results.

 LIGHT: To put a healthier spin on tradition, Citrus Sweet Potatoes does not call for butter, egg or marshmallows. Instead, cooked sweet potato slices are baked in a sauce made with orange juice concentrate, grated lemon peel and a little brown sugar. A serving of this lighter side dish has a third of the calories and none of the fat or cholesterol of Old-Fashioned Sweet Potato Casserole.

 SERVES 2: One sweet potato serves two quite nicely when it's cooked and mashed with raisins, orange peel and homey spices. A sprinkling of coconut is added right before Mini Sweet Potato Casserole is baked.

Old-Fashioned Sweet Potato Casserole

PREP: 25 min. **BAKE:** 45 min.

Taste of Home Test Kitchen

- 4 pounds sweet potatoes (about 5 large), peeled and cubed
- 1 cup milk
- 1/2 cup packed brown sugar
- 6 tablespoons butter, softened
- 1 egg, lightly beaten
- 1-1/2 teaspoons ground cinnamon
- 1-1/2 teaspoons vanilla extract
- 3/4 teaspoon ground allspice
- 1/2 teaspoon salt
- 1/4 teaspoon ground nutmeg
- 18 large marshmallows

1) Place sweet potatoes in a large saucepan; cover with water. Bring to a boil. Reduce heat; cover and cook for 15-20 minutes or until tender. Drain.

2) In a large mixing bowl, mash the potatoes. Add the milk, brown sugar, butter, egg, cinnamon, vanilla, allspice, salt and nutmeg; beat until smooth. Transfer to a greased shallow 2-1/2-qt. baking dish. Bake, uncovered, at 350° for 40-45 minutes or until heated through.

3) Top with marshmallows. Bake 5-10 minutes longer or just until marshmallows begin to brown.

Yield: 10 servings.

NUTRITION FACTS: 3/4 cup equals 282 calories, 8 g fat (5 g saturated fat), 43 mg cholesterol, 227 mg sodium, 50 g carbohydrate, 4 g fiber, 4 g protein.

■ **Crunchy-Topped Sweet Potato Casserole:** Omit marshmallows and reduce brown sugar in sweet potato mixture to 1/4 cup. Before baking, combine 3/4 cup all-purpose flour, 3/4 cup packed brown sugar, 3/4 cup chopped pecans and 1/2 cup melted butter in a small bowl. Sprinkle over the mashed sweet potato mixture. Bake, uncovered, at 350° for 50-55 minutes or until heated through and topping is browned.

Cranberry-Apple Sweet Potatoes

PREP/TOTAL TIME: 30 min.

Nella Parker, Hersey, Michigan

- 1 can (21 ounces) apple pie filling
- 1 can (2 pounds 8 ounces) cut sweet potatoes, drained and sliced
- 3/4 cup whole-berry cranberry sauce
- 2 tablespoons apricot preserves
- 2 tablespoons orange marmalade

1) Spread apple pie filling into a greased 8-in. square baking dish. Top with sweet potato slices. In a small bowl, combine the cranberry sauce, preserves and marmalade; spread over potatoes.

2) Cover and bake at 350° for 20-25 minutes or until heated through.

Yield: 6-8 servings.

NUTRITION FACTS: 1/2 cup equals 263 calories, trace fat (trace saturated fat), 0 cholesterol, 106 mg sodium, 65 g carbohydrate, 5 g fiber, 2 g protein.

A TOUCH OF ORANGE ■■■

I've always added grated orange peel to my mashed sweet potatoes. To save time and mess, I now just cut a 2- to 3-inch strip of orange peel and add it to the boiling potatoes. Later, I mash the softened peel with the potatoes for fresh wonderful flavor.

—*Pat W., New Bloomfield, Missouri*

CITRUS SWEET POTATOES

Citrus Sweet Potatoes

PREP: 1 hour **BAKE:** 30 min.

Pauline Kelley, St. Peters, Missouri

- 6 medium sweet potatoes, peeled
- 1/3 cup packed brown sugar
- 1 tablespoon cornstarch
- 1 cup orange juice concentrate
- 2 teaspoons grated lemon peel
- 1/2 cup chopped pecans, optional

1) Place sweet potatoes in a large saucepan and cover with water. Bring to a boil. Reduce heat; cover and cook for 30-40 minutes or until tender.

2) Drain and cool. Cut potatoes into 1/2-in. slices. Place in a greased 13-in. x 9-in. x 2-in. baking dish.

3) In a small saucepan, combine brown sugar and cornstarch. Whisk in orange juice concentrate and lemon peel. Bring to a boil; cook and stir for 1-2 minutes or until thickened. Pour over sweet potatoes. Sprinkle with pecans if desired.

4) Bake, uncovered, at 325° for 30-35 minutes or until sweet potatoes are heated through and sauce is bubbly.

Yield: 12 servings.

NUTRITION FACTS: 3/4 cup equals 93 calories, trace fat (trace saturated fat), 0 cholesterol, 8 mg sodium, 23 g carbohydrate, 2 g fiber, 1 g protein.

Mini Sweet Potato Casserole

PREP: 35 min. **BAKE:** 25 min.

Bob Breno, Strongsville, Ohio

- 1 medium sweet potato
- 2 tablespoons butter, melted, *divided*
- 1 tablespoon raisins
- 1/2 teaspoon grated orange peel
- 1/8 teaspoon salt
- 1/8 teaspoon ground cinnamon

Dash ground nutmeg

- 2 tablespoons flaked coconut

1) Place the sweet potato in a saucepan; cover with water. Bring to a boil. Reduce heat; cover and cook for 30-40 minutes or just until tender.

2) Drain; cool slightly and peel. Place in a bowl; mash. Stir in 1 tablespoon butter, raisins, orange peel, salt, cinnamon and nutmeg.

3) Transfer to a greased 1-1/2-cup baking dish. Toss coconut with remaining butter; sprinkle over the top. Bake, uncovered, at 350° for 25-30 minutes or until golden brown.

Yield: 2 servings.

NUTRITION FACTS: 1/2 cup equals 203 calories, 14 g fat (9 g saturated fat), 31 mg cholesterol, 285 mg sodium, 20 g carbohydrate, 2 g fiber, 1 g protein.

Sweet Potato Orange Cups

PREP: 30 min. **BAKE:** 20 min.

Melonie Bowers, Sugarcreek, Ohio

Mashed sweet potatoes can be spooned or piped into the orange halves for a special presentation.

- 3 large sweet potatoes (2 to 2-1/2 pounds), peeled and cubed
- 1 can (6 ounces) frozen orange juice concentrate, thawed
- 1/4 cup packed brown sugar
- 1/4 cup half-and-half cream
- 2 tablespoons butter, softened
- 3/4 cup miniature marshmallows
- 1/4 cup chopped pecans
- 4 large oranges, halved
- 32 additional miniature marshmallows

1) Place sweet potatoes in a large saucepan or Dutch oven; cover with water. Bring to a boil. Reduce heat; cover and cook for 15-25 minutes or just until tender. Drain.

2) In a large mixing bowl, beat the sweet potatoes, orange juice concentrate, brown sugar, cream and butter on low speed until smooth. Stir in 3/4 cup marshmallows and pecans; set aside.

3) Remove pulp from oranges, leaving a shell. (Discard pulp or save for another use.) Spoon sweet potato mixture into shells. Place four marshmallows on top of each.

4) Place in a greased 15-in. x 10-in. x 1-in. baking pan. Bake, uncovered, at 350° for 20 minutes or until heated through.

Yield: 8 servings.

NUTRITION FACTS: 1 orange cup equals 401 calories, 7 g fat (3 g saturated fat), 11 mg cholesterol, 51 mg sodium, 83 g carbohydrate, 9 g fiber, 6 g protein.

Tomatoes

Classified as a fruit but used as a vegetable, tomatoes are smooth-skinned, round or pear-shaped. They are bright red or yellow when ripe and are eaten raw or cooked.

Buying

Tomatoes are available year-round; peak season is summer through early fall.

Storage

Keep unwashed tomatoes at room temperature until ripe. Store out of direct sunlight. Tomatoes can be kept in the refrigerator for up to 3 days.

Yield: 1 pound of tomatoes (about 2-3 medium)
= 1-1/2 to 1-3/4 cups chopped
1 pound plum tomatoes (5 medium)
= about 2-1/2 cups chopped
1 pint cherry or grape tomatoes
= 2 cups halved

SWEET POTATO ORANGE CUPS

Peeling Tomatoes

1) Wash and core tomatoes. Place tomato in boiling water for 30 seconds. Immediately plunge in ice water.

2) Remove skin with a sharp paring knife.

Beefsteak Tomatoes

Are large, round tomatoes with a slightly flattened top. They are juicy and readily available. Use raw or cooked.

Cherry Tomatoes

May be red or yellow and are primarily used for salads or garnishes.

Grape Tomatoes

Are grape-shaped, and they are sweeter and firmer than cherry tomatoes. Use for salads, crudites, garnishes or snacking.

Plum/Roma Tomatoes

Are meaty tomatoes with small seeds. These short, elongated, tomatoes are usually red, but yellow are available. Use for cooking, sauces or salads.

Sun-Dried Tomatoes

Are dehydrated tomatoes with a leathery texture and intense flavor. They are available in cellophane packages or oil-packed in jars. To rehydrate packaged sun-dried tomatoes, place in a heatproof bowl and cover with boiling water. Let stand for about 10 minutes, then drain.

Broiled Parsley Tomatoes

PREP/TOTAL TIME: 10 min.

Howie Wiener, Spring Hill, Florida

I get loads of compliments on this recipe for my mother's tomato side dish. She loved to make great-tasting meals but preferred spending time with us rather than in the kitchen.

- 4 large plum tomatoes, halved lengthwise
- 3 tablespoons butter, melted
- 2 teaspoons minced fresh parsley
- 1/4 teaspoon salt
- 1/4 teaspoon pepper

1) With a knife, make deep cuts in the cut surface of each tomato. Place cut side up on a greased baking sheet.
2) In a small bowl, combine the butter, parsley, salt and pepper; spoon over tomatoes. Broil 3-4 in. from the heat for 3-4 minutes or until tops are lightly browned.

Yield: 4 servings.

NUTRITION FACTS: 1 serving equals 89 calories, 9 g fat (5 g saturated fat), 23 mg cholesterol, 240 mg sodium, 3 g carbohydrate, 1 g fiber, 1 g protein.

Seeding a Tomato

To seed a tomato, cut it in half. Using a teaspoon, scrape out the seeds.

Scalloped Tomatoes

PREP: 20 min. **BAKE:** 35 min.

Norma Piper, West Salem, Wisconsin

Warm and comforting, this old-fashioned side dish is a great way to use up garden bounty. I lightened the original recipe by using less butter and flour and only a bit of honey.

- 1/2 cup chopped onion
- 1/2 cup chopped celery
- 1 tablespoon butter
- 1 tablespoon all-purpose flour
- 1 tablespoon honey
- 2 teaspoons prepared mustard
- 1/2 teaspoon salt
- 1/4 teaspoon pepper
- 2 slices whole wheat bread, toasted and cubed
- 4 cups chopped fresh tomatoes

1) In a nonstick skillet, cook onion and celery in butter until tender. Stir in the flour until blended; cook 1 minute longer. Stir in the honey, mustard, salt and pepper until blended. Stir in bread cubes and tomatoes.
2) Transfer to an 8-in. square baking dish coated with cooking spray. Bake, uncovered, at 350° for 35-40 minutes or until bubbly.

Yield: 6 servings.

NUTRITION FACTS: 3/4 cup equals 88 calories, 3 g fat (1 g saturated fat), 5 mg cholesterol, 304 mg sodium, 15 g carbohydrate, 2 g fiber, 2 g protein.

FAST CORED TOMATOES ■■■

A quick way to core tomatoes is to slice off the end and use a grapefruit spoon to scoop out the core.

—Nancy Johnson, Lombard, Illinois

Tomatillos

Tomatillos are green, tomato-like fruit with a papery outer husk. They have lemon-herb flavor and are used in Mexican and Southwestern cooking.

Buying

Tomatillos are available year-round. Select firm, dry, green tomatillos with husks that tightly surround the fruit.

Storage

Store in a paper bag in the refrigerator crisper drawer for up to 3 weeks.

Preparation

Remove and discard papery husk. Rinse under cold water and seed. Can be used raw or cooked.

Yield: 1 pound = 12 tomatillos = 3 cups sliced

Salsa Verde

PREP: 15 min. + chilling

Nanette Hilton, Las Vegas, Nevada

Green salsa is a fun change from the typical red varieties. If you like your salsa hot, don't remove the seeds from the jalapeno.

- 4 cups water
- 8 tomatillos, husks removed and rinsed
- 1 medium ripe avocado, peeled and pitted
- 1 small onion, halved
- 1 jalapeno pepper, seeded
- 1/3 cup fresh cilantro leaves
- 1/2 teaspoon salt
  Tortilla chips

1) In a large saucepan, bring water to a boil; add tomatillos. Reduce heat; simmer, uncovered, for 5 minutes. Drain.

2) Place the tomatillos, avocado, onion, jalapeno, cilantro and salt in a food processor; cover and process until blended. Transfer to a bowl. Refrigerate for 1 hour. Serve with tortilla chips.

Yield: 2-1/2 cups.

Editor's Note: When cutting or seeding hot peppers, use rubber or plastic gloves to protect your hands. Avoid touching your face.

NUTRITION FACTS: 1/4 cup (calculated without chips) equals 42 calories, 3 g fat (trace saturated fat), 0 cholesterol, 121 mg sodium, 3 g carbohydrate, 2 g fiber, 1 g protein.

Turnips

Turnips are a root vegetable with a mild, sweet flavor.

Buying

Turnips are available year-round; peak season is fall through winter. Select turnips that are firm, unblemished and heavy for their size. Light ones may be woody. Any attached greens should be bright and fresh looking. Greens can be removed and cooked separately.

Storage

Store unwashed turnips in the refrigerator crisper drawer for up to 1 week.

Preparation

Scrub young (small) turnips under cold running water. Peel larger turnips. Trim both ends.

Yield: 1 pound trimmed = 3 cups cubed

Turnip Casserole

PREP: 25 min. **BAKE:** 20 min.

Doris Hubert, East Killingly, Connecticut

Turnips are good alone or with other vegetables. Try chopping them to add texture and flavor to soups and stews.

- 4 medium turnips, peeled and cubed
- 1 cup water
- 1 egg, beaten
- 1/3 cup sugar
- 3 tablespoons butter
- 1/2 teaspoon salt
- 1/4 teaspoon ground cinnamon

1) Place turnips in a large saucepan and cover with water. Bring to a boil. Reduce heat; cover and cook for 15 minutes or until tender. Drain.

2) Transfer turnips to a bowl and mash. Add the egg, sugar, butter and salt; mix well. Transfer to a greased 1-qt. baking dish; sprinkle with cinnamon.

3) Cover and bake at 350° for 20-25 minutes or until a thermometer reads 160° and mixture is heated through.

Yield: 4 servings.

NUTRITION FACTS: 3/4 cup equals 192 calories, 10 g fat (6 g saturated fat), 76 mg cholesterol, 479 mg sodium, 25 g carbohydrate, 2 g fiber, 3 g protein.

a little bit of heaven

Tasty treats benefit shelters & youth programs

Church volunteers

> A plump apple dumpling, swimming in a sea of cinnamon and served in a soup bowl—that's one of autumn's pure pleasures!
>
> ~Carolyn Weaver

Apples have proven tempting since biblical times, but for folks around Beaver Falls, Pennsylvania, one bite isn't forbidden…it's heavenly!

"This is the 16th year our church will sell apple dumplings, home-made by our Women's Association," says Carolyn Weaver, a member of the College Hill Presbyterian Church. Annually, they roll out 900 of the yummy moneymakers—tart apples wrapped in tender pie dough.

Come September, area fruit trees are dripping with all manner of apples.

"We order 10 bushels from a local orchard," Carolyn says. "MacIntosh and Rome are our favorite varieties because they bake up so nice and juicy.

"Our crew of 10 volunteers meets in the church hall in mid-October for a number of dumpling workdays. Young mothers, retired women and even some husbands pitch in. Soon we have an assembly line going."

The process begins with a vintage, hand-cranked peeler. From there, the fruit moves to a coring station. Next, a team of seasoners adds cinnamon, sugar and butter to each apple. Pastry makers roll dough into squares to wrap around each apple. Finally, the crew flash-freezes the dumplings, bags them and stores them in the freezer until sale day.

"Word of mouth is our best advertisement. The congregation tells family and friends, and soon orders are pouring in," says Carolyn. On sale day, the Saturday before Thanksgiving, customers from town and surrounding counties come to church and pick up their apple dumplings—either baked or frozen.

The fruits of the dedicated dumpling gang's labor support several worthy causes. Profits go to the Salvation Army, a soup kitchen, a rescue mission, a women's center, youth programs and more.

"Besides that," Carolyn adds, "apple dumplings have become a delicious and comforting tradition for families all around here.

"A plump apple dumpling, swimming in a sea of cinnamon and served in a soup bowl—that's one of autumn's pure pleasures!"

You can find the group's Apple Dumpling recipe in the Web exclusive online at tasteofhome.com/CookbookBonus **Type in access code ICare**

DO YOU KNOW A COOK WHO CARES?
If you or someone you know cooks for a charitable, spiritual or other cause, tell us about it at **tasteofhome.com/CookbookBonus**

FRUIT

Recipes

Tips

FRUIT

Fruit

Fresh fruits can be eaten alone, with salads, in desserts or sauces and sometimes even as accompaniments to meats and poultry. This chapter features many delightful recipes to showcase them.

Each fruit listed has information about availability, buying and storing. If you purchase a fruit that is over ripe, its storage life will be shorter than the times suggested here.

Handle fruits gently—they bruise easily. A bruised spot will lead to decay. After purchasing, promptly refrigerate fruits that require refrigeration.

Many types of underripe fruits such as apricots, nectarines, plums and pears can be placed in a closed paper bag and left at room temperature to ripen. Other fruits such as bananas, mangoes, melons and papayas can be placed in a bowl out of direct sunlight to ripen at room temperature.

Before preparing fruit, make sure the countertops, cutting boards and utensils are clean. Wash your hands in hot, soapy water.

Apples

Apples range in flavor from sweet to tart, depending on the variety. They make great snacks but are also good for salads, sauces, breads, muffins, cakes, pies and baking. Refer to the types of apples on page 422 for the best uses of individual varieties.

Buying

Apples are available year-round (individual varieties have their own peak seasons, see page 422). Select apples that are firm and have a smooth, unblemished skin that is free of any bruises. Handle gently to prevent bruising.

Storage

Store unwashed apples in the refrigerator away from other vegetables with strong aromas. Apples can be refrigerated for up to 6 weeks. Wash before using.

Yield: 1 pound (3 medium) = 2-3/4 cups sliced

Coring an Apple

1) Use an apple corer to core a whole apple. Push apple corer down into center of a washed apple. Twist and remove the center seeds and membranes.

2) Core an apple quarter by cutting out the core with a sharp knife.

Types of Apples

Braeburn
Sweet-tart flavor with a hint of spice. Crisp, firm apple. Good for eating, baking and using in salads and sauces. Season: October through April.

Granny Smith
Tart flavor. Crisp apple; good for eating, baking and using in pies, salads and sauces. Season: year-round.

Cortland
Sweet with a hint of tartness. Juicy and tender apple that resists browning. Good for eating, baking and using in pies, salads and sauces. Season: September through April.

Jonathan
Tart flavor with a hint of spice. Moderately tender apple. Good for eating, baking and using in pies, salads and sauces. Season: September through April.

Empire
Sweet-tart flavor. Juicy, crisp apple. Good for eating, baking and using in pies, salads and sauces. Season: September through July.

McIntosh
Tart, tangy flavor. Juicy, tender apple. Good for eating and using in pies, salads and sauces. Season: September through May.

Fuji
Very sweet flavor. Juicy, crisp apple. Good for eating and using in salads and sauces. Season: October through June.

Pink Lady
Sweet-tart flavor. Crisp apple. Good for eating, baking and using in salads. Season: October through June.

Gala
Sweet flavor. Juicy, crisp apple. Good for eating and using in salads. Season: August through December.

Red Delicious
Sweet flavor. Crisp apple. Good for eating and using in salads. Season: year-round.

Golden Delicious
Mild sweet flavor. Juicy, crisp, all-purpose apple with yellow flesh. Good for eating, baking and using in pies, salads and sauces. Season: year-round.

Rome Beauty
Mildly tart flavor. Firm apple. Good for baking and using in sauces and pies. Season: October through May.

Cider Apple Bake

PREP: 10 min. **BAKE:** 50 min.

Shelly Schierman, Louisburg, Kansas

This is a warm and wonderful way to use up apples. You can serve it as part of a brunch or top it with cream for dessert.

> 6 large tart apples, peeled and sliced
> 2 cups apple cider *or* juice
> 1/3 cup packed brown sugar
> 1/4 teaspoon ground cinnamon
> 1 cup half-and-half *or* heavy whipping cream

1) Place apples in a greased 2-qt. baking dish. Combine the cider and brown sugar; pour over the apples.

2) Bake, uncovered, at 350° for 50-60 minutes or until apples are tender, stirring once. Sprinkle with cinnamon. Cool slightly. Serve warm with cream.

Yield: 6 servings.

NUTRITION FACTS: 1 serving equals 265 calories, 5 g fat (3 g saturated fat), 20 mg cholesterol, 33 mg sodium, 56 g carbohydrate, 6 g fiber, 2 g protein.

Glazed Apple Rings

PREP/TOTAL TIME: 20 min.

Mary Jane Ruther, Trenton, New Jersey

Four ingredients and a skillet are all you'll need to make these delightful apple rings. They make a sweet side dish alongside pork or a simple dessert.

> 2 tablespoons butter
> 2 tablespoons sugar
> 3 teaspoons lemon juice
> 2 medium apples, peeled and cored

1) In a large skillet, melt butter over medium heat. Stir in sugar and lemon juice. Cut each apple into four rings; add to skillet. Reduce heat.

2) Cover and simmer for 10-15 minutes or until apples are tender, turning frequently. Serve warm.

Yield: 4 servings.

NUTRITION FACTS: 2 apple rings equals 107 calories, 6 g fat (4 g saturated fat), 15 mg cholesterol, 58 mg sodium, 15 g carbohydrate, 1 g fiber, trace protein.

Cinnamon Apples

PREP: 20 min. + chilling

Alma Dinsmore, Lebanon, Indiana

Older kids will have fun melting the red cinnamon candies that give bright color to these tender apples. Serve this as a salad or a side dish to accompany pork.

> 2 cups water
> 3/4 cup red-hot candies
> 1/3 cup sugar
> 6 medium tart apples, peeled and quartered

CINNAMON APPLES

1) In a large saucepan, bring the water, candies and sugar to a boil over medium heat; boil and stir until candies and sugar are dissolved. Reduce the heat and carefully add apples. Cook, uncovered, until apples are tender. Cool slightly.

2) With a slotted spoon, transfer apples to a serving dish; pour sugar syrup over apples. Cool slightly. Cover and refrigerate for at least 3 hours.

Yield: 6 servings.

NUTRITION FACTS: 3/4 cup equals 209 calories, 1 g fat (trace saturated fat), 0 cholesterol, 4 mg sodium, 51 g carbohydrate, 2 g fiber, trace protein.

Apple Cranberry Crumble

PREP: 15 min. **BAKE:** 55 min.

Teri Roberts, Hilliard, Ohio

When I first took this dessert to Thanksgiving dinner, it quickly became a tradition. We enjoy it for breakfast, lunch, dinner and snack time!

> 3 cups chopped peeled apples
> 2 cups fresh *or* frozen cranberries
> 3/4 cup sugar
> 1 cup old-fashioned *or* quick-cooking oats
> 3/4 cup packed brown sugar
> 1/3 cup all-purpose flour
> 1/2 cup butter, melted
> 1/2 cup chopped pecans, optional

1) In a greased 8-in. square baking dish, combine apples and cranberries; sprinkle with sugar. In another bowl, combine the oats, brown sugar, flour and butter; sprinkle over cranberry mixture.

2) Top with pecans if desired. Bake, uncovered, at 350° for 55-60 minutes or until browned and bubbly. Serve warm.

Yield: 6 servings.

NUTRITION FACTS: 1 cup equals 456 calories, 16 g fat (10 g saturated fat), 41 mg cholesterol, 166 mg sodium, 78 g carbohydrate, 4 g fiber, 3 g protein.

■ **Pear Cranberry Crumble:** Substitute 3 cups chopped peeled pears for the apples.

DOWN-HOME APPLESAUCE

 CLASSIC: Chunky Applesauce is a simple dish that's sure to please the whole family. Chopped apples are lightly spiced, simmered on the stovetop until tender and mashed to your liking.

 TIME-SAVER: When there's no time to peel and cook apples but you want a homemade taste, try Dressed-Up Applesauce. Like its name says, applesauce is dressed up with lemon juice, rum extract and a handful of spices. Served warm, it's ready in 10 minutes.

 LIGHT: A bounty of fresh fruit—apples, rhubarb, strawberries, blueberries and cranberries—adds bright color and flavor to Mishmash Applesauce. Sugar-free gelatin replaces the sweetness from the sugar in the classic Chunky Applesauce. So this lighter, fruity sauce has half the calories and less than half the carbohydrates, making it a suitable choice for diabetics.

SERVES 2: There's no need to turn on the stove to serve up Fresh Applesauce. Just process apples with juice, honey and cinnamon for two tasty servings of the freshest applesauce around. This downsized recipe is quick, too—it's ready in just 5 minutes.

Chunky Applesauce
PREP: 15 min. **COOK:** 30 min.

Deborah Amrine, Grand Haven, Michigan

- 8 cups chopped peeled tart cooking apples (about 3-1/2 pounds)
- 1/2 cup packed brown sugar
- 2 teaspoons vanilla extract
- 1 teaspoon ground cinnamon

CHUNKY APPLESAUCE

1) In a Dutch oven, combine all the ingredients. Cover and cook over medium-low heat for 30-40 minutes or until apples are tender, stirring occasionally.

2) Remove from the heat; mash the apples (a potato masher works well) until sauce reaches desired consistency. Serve warm or chilled.

Yield: about 3-1/2 cups.

NUTRITION FACTS: 1/2 cup equals 157 calories, trace fat (trace saturated fat), 0 cholesterol, 7 mg sodium, 40 g carbohydrate, 3 g fiber, trace protein.

APPLESAUCE WITH A KICK ■■■

When I serve guests applesauce with pork for a meal, I add a touch of prepared horseradish. It lends a grown-up touch.

—*Carol Donarski, Seminole, Florida*

Dressed-Up Applesauce
PREP/TOTAL TIME: 10 min.

Therian Mendelsohn, Cincinnati, Ohio

- 2 cups unsweetened applesauce
- 1/4 cup sugar
- 1-1/2 teaspoons lemon juice
- 1/2 teaspoon rum extract
- 1/4 teaspoon ground cinnamon
- 1/4 teaspoon ground allspice
- 1/8 to 1/4 teaspoon ground cloves
- 1/8 teaspoon ground ginger

1) In a large saucepan, combine all ingredients. Bring to a boil. Cook, uncovered, for 1 minute. Serve warm or chilled.

Yield: 4 servings.

NUTRITION FACTS: 1/2 cup equals 105 calories, trace fat (trace saturated fat), 0 cholesterol, 3 mg sodium, 27 g carbohydrate, 2 g fiber, trace protein.

MISHMASH APPLESAUCE

Mishmash Applesauce

PREP: 30 min. **COOK:** 30 min. + standing

Beverly Rice, Elm Grove, Wisconsin

- 3 pounds tart apples, chopped
- 2 cups chopped fresh *or* frozen rhubarb
- 1 cup chopped fresh *or* frozen strawberries
- 1 cup fresh *or* frozen blueberries
- 1 cup fresh *or* frozen cranberries
- 1 cup orange juice
- 2 packages (.3 ounce *each*) sugar-free strawberry gelatin

1) In a Dutch oven, combine the apples, rhubarb, berries and orange juice. Bring to a boil over medium heat, stirring frequently. Sprinkle gelatin over fruit mixture; stir until combined. Reduce heat; cover and simmer for 15-20 minutes or until apples are tender.

2) Remove from the heat; mash fruit. Let stand for 15 minutes. Serve warm or chilled.

Yield: 8 cups.

NUTRITION FACTS: 1/2 cup equals 75 calories, trace fat (trace saturated fat), 0 cholesterol, 24 mg sodium, 18 g carbohydrate, 3 g fiber, 1 g protein.

Fresh Applesauce

PREP/TOTAL TIME: 5 min.

Mary Ann Gove, Cottonwood, Arizona

- 1/3 cup unsweetened apple juice
- 3/4 pound tart apples, peeled and quartered
- 1 tablespoon honey
- 1/4 teaspoon ground cinnamon

1) In a food processor, combine all ingredients; cover and process until smooth. Transfer to a small bowl. Cover and refrigerate until serving.

Yield: 2 servings.

NUTRITION FACTS: 2/3 cup equals 153 calories, 1 g fat (trace saturated fat), 0 cholesterol, 2 mg sodium, 40 g carbohydrate, 5 g fiber, trace protein.

◐ Apple-Nut Tossed Salad

PREP/TOTAL TIME: 10 min.

Maureen Reubelt, Gales Ferry, Connecticut

When you want an alternative to a plain green salad, give this a try. A light dressing tops apples, walnuts, lettuce and blue cheese.

  3 tablespoons olive oil
  1 teaspoon Dijon mustard
3/4 teaspoon sugar
Salt and pepper to taste
1/2 cup chopped apple
  1 tablespoon chopped green onion
  3 cups torn Bibb lettuce
  1 to 2 tablespoons chopped walnuts
  1 to 2 tablespoons crumbled blue cheese

1) In a large bowl, whisk the oil, mustard, sugar, salt and pepper. Add apple and onion; toss to coat. Add lettuce, walnuts and blue cheese; toss gently. Serve immediately.

Yield: 4 servings.

NUTRITION FACTS: 3/4 cup (calculated without salt and pepper) equals 128 calories, 12 g fat (2 g saturated fat), 2 mg cholesterol, 63 mg sodium, 5 g carbohydrate, 1 g fiber, 2 g protein.

Sweet Shoppe Caramel Apples

PREP: 35 min. **COOK:** 1 hour + chilling

Mary Bilyeu, Ann Arbor, Michigan

My hand-dipped apples are as beautiful as the ones you'll find at fancy candy counters, only they're fresher and more economical. Make some for Halloween or your next party.

    6 large McIntosh apples
    6 Popsicle sticks
    2 cups sugar
    2 cups half-and-half cream
    1 cup light corn syrup
  1/2 cup butter, cubed
1-1/4 cups English toffee bits *or* almond brickle chips
    1 cup semisweet chocolate chips
    1 cup vanilla *or* white chips

1) Line a baking sheet with waxed paper and grease the paper; set aside. Wash and thoroughly dry apples. Insert a Popsicle stick into each; place on prepared pan. Chill.

2) In a heavy 3-qt. saucepan, combine the sugar, cream, corn syrup and butter; bring to a boil over medium-high heat. Cook and stir until a candy thermometer reads 245°, about 1 hour.

3) Remove from the heat. Working quickly, dip each apple into hot caramel mixture to completely coat, then dip the bottom into toffee bits. Return to baking sheet; chill.

4) In a small microwave-safe bowl, microwave chocolate chips at 50% power for 1-2 minutes or

SWEET SHOPPE CARAMEL APPLES

until melted; stir until smooth. Transfer to a small heavy-duty resealable plastic bag; cut a small hole in a corner of bag. Drizzle over apples.

5) Repeat with vanilla chips. Chill until set. Remove from the refrigerator 5 minutes before serving.

Yield: 6 servings.

Editor's Note: We recommend that you test your candy thermometer before each use by bringing water to a boil; the thermometer should read 212°. Adjust your recipe temperature up or down based on your test.

NUTRITION FACTS: 1 caramel apple equals 1,331 calories, 58 g fat (32 g saturated fat), 103 mg cholesterol, 573 mg sodium, 208 g carbohydrate, 7 g fiber, 6 g protein.

Hot Caramel Apples

PREP: 15 min. **COOK:** 4 hours

Pat Sparks, St. Charles, Missouri

This old-time favorite goes together quickly, and it's such a treat to come home to the aroma of cinnamony baked apples just like Mom used to make.

    4 large tart apples, cored
  1/2 cup apple juice
  1/2 cup packed brown sugar
   12 red-hot candies
    4 tablespoons butter
    8 caramels
  1/4 teaspoon ground cinnamon
Whipped cream, optional

1) Peel about 3/4 in. off the top of each apple; place in a 3-qt. slow cooker. Pour juice over apples. Fill the center of each apple with 2 tablespoons of brown sugar, three red-hots, 1 tablespoon butter and two caramels. Sprinkle with cinnamon.

2) Cover and cook on low for 4-6 hours or until the apples are tender. Serve immediately with whipped cream if desired.

Yield: 4 servings.

NUTRITION FACTS: 1 caramel apple equals 424 calories, 14 g fat (9 g saturated fat), 32 mg cholesterol, 177 mg sodium, 79 g carbohydrate, 6 g fiber, 1 g protein.

New Waldorf Salad
PREP/TOTAL TIME: 20 min.

Marie Engwall, Willmar, Minnesota

A nice blend of colorful fruits and nuts gives this refreshing salad a great flavor and texture. The citrusy topping dresses it up perfectly.

- 1 medium unpeeled red apple, chopped
- 1 medium unpeeled green apple, chopped
- 1 medium unpeeled pear, chopped
- 1/2 cup green grapes
- 1/4 cup raisins
- 1/4 cup slivered almonds, toasted
- 1 carton (6 ounces) reduced-fat lemon yogurt
- 2 teaspoons lemon juice
- 2 teaspoons orange juice
- 2 teaspoons honey
- 1 teaspoon grated orange peel

1) In a large bowl, combine the apples, pear, grapes, raisins and almonds. In a small bowl, combine the yogurt, lemon and orange juices, honey and orange peel. Pour over fruit mixture and stir to coat. Serve immediately.

Yield: 4 servings.

NUTRITION FACTS: 1 cup equals 193 calories, 5 g fat (1 g saturated fat), 2 mg cholesterol, 33 mg sodium, 35 g carbohydrate, 4 g fiber, 5 g protein.

NEW WALDORF SALAD

APPLE DUMPLINGS

Apple Dumplings
PREP: 20 min. **BAKE:** 55 min.

Jody Fisher, Stewartstown, Pennsylvania

The golden dumplings in this dessert are filled with apples and topped with a sweet caramel sauce. A scoop of ice cream adds the perfect touch.

- 2 cups all-purpose flour
- 1 teaspoon salt
- 2/3 cup shortening
- 4 to 5 tablespoons cold water
- 2 cups chopped peeled tart apples
- 2 cups packed brown sugar
- 1 cup water
- 1/4 cup butter, cubed

Vanilla ice cream

1) In a large bowl, combine the flour and salt; cut in shortening until crumbly. Gradually add water, tossing with a fork until dough forms a ball. On a lightly floured surface, roll out dough into a 12-in. x 18-in. rectangle. Cut into six squares.

2) Place 1/3 cup chopped apples in the center of each square. Brush edges of dough with water; fold up corners to center and pinch to seal. Place in a greased 13-in. x 9-in. x 2-in. baking dish. Bake, uncovered, at 350° for 30 minutes.

3) In a small saucepan, combine the brown sugar, water and butter; bring to a boil, stirring constantly. Remove from the heat. Pour over the dumplings. Bake 25-30 minutes longer or until apples are tender. Serve warm with ice cream.

Yield: 6 servings.

NUTRITION FACTS: 1 dumpling (calculated without ice cream) equals 711 calories, 29 g fat (10 g saturated fat), 20 mg cholesterol, 500 mg sodium, 109 g carbohydrate, 2 g fiber, 4 g protein.

Apricots

Apricots are a dense, sweet fruit with a smooth skin. Fresh apricots are used for eating and for salads and desserts.

Buying

Apricots are available May through August. Select apricots that are plump and fairly firm, not hard, and are orange-yellow to orange in color. Avoid apricots that have blemishes or soft spots or that have a pale-yellow or greenish-yellow color.

Storage

Store firm apricots at room temperature. Once the fruit yields to gentle pressure, store in the refrigerator for 2-3 days.

Yield: 1 pound (8 to 12 medium) = 2-1/2 cups sliced

Stewed Holiday Fruit

PREP: 15 min. + chilling
COOK: 10 min. + cooling

Taste of Home Test Kitchen

Bananas, dried apricots and plums are drizzled with a sweet cider and marmalade sauce in this fruity concoction. Hints of cinnamon and citrus lend zest to each cool spoonful. Serve a bowlful for breakfast, snack time or dessert.

> 12 dried apricots
> 12 dried plums
> 1-1/2 cups apple cider *or* juice
> 2 cinnamon sticks (3 inches)
> 8 whole cloves
> 2 whole allspice
> 1/4 cup orange marmalade
> 2 teaspoons lemon juice
> 1 teaspoon butter
> 2 medium firm bananas, sliced
> 2 tablespoons sliced almonds, toasted

1) In a small saucepan, combine the apricots, plums, cider, cinnamon, cloves and allspice. Bring to a boil. Remove from the heat; transfer to a bowl. Cover and refrigerate overnight.

2) Strain cider, reserving liquid; set apricots and plums aside. Discard spices. In a small saucepan, combine the marmalade, lemon juice, butter and the reserved cider. Bring to a boil, stirring occasionally. Cool.

3) Divide apricots, plums and bananas among serving dishes; drizzle with cooled sauce. Sprinkle with almonds.

Yield: 4 servings.

NUTRITION FACTS: 3/4 cup fruit with 1/4 cup sauce equals 259 calories, 3 g fat (1 g saturated fat), 3 mg cholesterol, 26 mg sodium, 61 g carbohydrate, 5 g fiber, 2 g protein.

Spiced Hot Fruit

PREP: 15 min. **BAKE:** 30 min.

Irene Howard, Shenandoah, Iowa

This recipe takes advantage of convenient canned fruit. Assembled in a flash, the crowd-pleasing compote is sparked with cinnamon and ginger.

> 2 cans (one 20 ounces, one 8 ounces) pineapple chunks
> 2 cans (15-1/4 ounces *each*) apricots, drained and quartered
> 1 can (29 ounces) sliced peaches, drained
> 1 can (29 ounces) pear halves, drained and quartered
> 3/4 cup packed brown sugar
> 1/4 cup butter
> 2 cinnamon sticks (3 inches)
> 1/2 teaspoon ground ginger

1) Drain pineapple, reserving juice. In an ungreased shallow 3-1/2-qt. baking dish, combine the pineapple, apricots, peaches and pears; set aside.

2) In a saucepan, combine brown sugar, butter, cinnamon, ginger and reserved pineapple juice; bring to a boil. Reduce heat; simmer for 5 minutes. Discard cinnamon. Pour sauce over fruit.

3) Bake, uncovered, at 350° for 30 minutes or until heated through. Serve warm.

Yield: 10 cups.

NUTRITION FACTS: 1/2 cup equals 131 calories, 2 g fat (0 saturated fat), 0 cholesterol, 38 mg sodium, 29 g carbohydrate, 0 fiber, 1 g protein.

SPICED HOT FRUIT

Bananas

Bananas have a soft to tender texture and a sweet taste.

Buying

Bananas are available all year-round. Select plump bananas that are free from bruises. The banana skin goes from green to yellow to yellow with speckles to black, depending on ripeness and how it's stored.

Storage

Store at room temperature until ripe, then store in the refrigerator or freeze. The skin will turn black in the refrigerator. Brush cut bananas with lemon, lime, orange or pineapple juice to prevent browning.

Cooking

Use firm bananas with yellow skins and green tips for cooking. Use firm but ripe bananas for salads, and use ripe bananas for baking.

Yield: 1 pound (3 medium) = 1-1/3 cups mashed or 1-1/2 to 2 cups sliced

Cavendish
The most readily available banana in the supermarket.

Finger Bananas
A smaller version of the Cavendish and are considered to be sweeter.

Red Bananas
Short, chunky bananas and have a red skin that turns purplish-red when ripe. The pink flesh is sweet and creamy. Some say the banana has a hint of berry flavor to it.

Plantains
A starchy fruit used for cooking and served as a side dish or dessert.

Banana Nut Salad

PREP/TOTAL TIME: 15 min.

Sharon Mensing, Greenfield, Iowa

I combine two kid-friendly flavors in this speedy salad, and the children can help by arranging the bananas. Then just stir up the dressing and serve in minutes.

    2 medium ripe bananas, sliced
Leaf lettuce
  1/4 cup mayonnaise
    1 tablespoon peanut butter
    1 tablespoon honey
  1/4 cup chopped peanuts

1) Place bananas on lettuce-lined salad plates. In a small bowl, combine the mayonnaise, peanut butter and honey. Spoon over bananas; sprinkle with peanuts.

Yield: 4 servings.

NUTRITION FACTS: 1 serving equals 242 calories, 17 g fat (3 g saturated fat), 5 mg cholesterol, 95 mg sodium, 21 g carbohydrate, 2 g fiber, 4 g protein.

Layered Banana Pudding

PREP: 30 min. + chilling

Esther Matteson, South Bend, Indiana

This old-fashioned favorite is satisfying and beats any comparison to instant pudding mixes.

  1/2 cup all-purpose flour
  2/3 cup packed brown sugar
    2 cups milk
    2 egg yolks, beaten
    2 tablespoons butter
    1 teaspoon vanilla extract
    1 cup heavy whipping cream, whipped
 4 to 6 medium firm bananas, sliced
Chopped walnuts, optional

1) In a large saucepan, combine the flour and brown sugar. Stir in milk until smooth. Cook and stir over medium-high heat until thickened and bubbly. Reduce heat; cook and stir 2 minutes longer.

2) Remove from the heat. Stir a small amount of hot filling into egg yolks; return all to pan, stirring constantly. Bring to a gentle boil; cook and stir 2 minutes longer.

3) Remove from the heat; stir in butter and vanilla. Cool to room temperature without stirring. Fold in the whipped cream.

4) Layer a third of the pudding in a 2-qt. glass bowl; top with half of the bananas. Repeat layers. Top with remaining pudding. Sprinkle with nuts if desired. Cover and refrigerate for at least 1 hour before serving.

Yield: 8 servings.

NUTRITION FACTS: 1 serving equals 333 calories, 18 g fat (10 g saturated fat), 110 mg cholesterol, 80 mg sodium, 41 g carbohydrate, 2 g fiber, 5 g protein.

Banana Fruit Compote

PREP: 20 min. + chilling

Maxine Otis, Hobson, Montana

My mother used to make this recipe when I was a child. My four kids always ate more fruit when I dressed it up this way.

    1   cup apricot nectar, *divided*
Dash to 1/8 teaspoon ground cloves
Dash to 1/8 teaspoon ground cinnamon
    1   tablespoon cornstarch
    2   tablespoons lemon juice
    1   firm banana, cut into 1/2-inch slices
    4   fresh strawberries, sliced
    1   kiwifruit, halved and thinly sliced

1) In a small saucepan, bring 3/4 cup apricot nectar, cloves and cinnamon to a boil. Combine the cornstarch and remaining apricot nectar until smooth; gradually whisk into the pan. Return to a boil; cool and stir for 1-2 minutes or until thickened and bubbly. Remove from the heat; stir in lemon juice. Cool.

2) Stir in the banana, strawberries and kiwi. Cover and refrigerate for at least 1 hour before serving.

Yield: 2 servings.

NUTRITION FACTS: 1 cup equals 174 calories, 1 g fat (trace saturated fat), 0 cholesterol, 7 mg sodium, 44 g carbohydrate, 4 g fiber, 2 g protein.

BANANA FRUIT COMPOTE

    1   tablespoon honey
    1   tablespoon flaked coconut
1-1/2   teaspoons grated lime peel

1) In a small bowl, toss bananas with lime juice. Add peanuts and honey; mix well. Spoon into individual dishes. Sprinkle with coconut and lime peel. Serve immediately.

Yield: 2 servings.

NUTRITION FACTS: 1 cup equals 210 calories, 6 g fat (2 g saturated fat), 0 cholesterol, 48 mg sodium, 40 g carbohydrate, 4 g fiber, 4 g protein.

Tropical Bananas

PREP/TOTAL TIME: 10 min.

Kathleen Jones, Chicago, Illinois

Lime provides the refreshing twist to this exotic-tasting dessert that's healthy, quick and delicious. I sometimes like to serve it as a midday snack.

    2   medium firm bananas, sliced
    1   tablespoon lime juice
    2   tablespoons salted peanuts

TROPICAL BANANAS

Berries

Berries come in many varieties; please refer to the individual listings for more information about each.

Buying

Individual varieties have their own peak seasons. Select berries that are plump. Avoid those that are bruised, mushy or moldy. Avoid packages with juice-stained bottoms.

Storage

Berries are fragile and very perishable. Before refrigerating, sort through and discard any crushed, mushy or moldy fruit.

Store unwashed berries in their container for 1-2 days. For longer storage, refer to the information on individual berries. To freeze, arrange in a single layer on a plastic wrap-lined baking sheet. Once frozen, transfer to a freezer container or bag. Freeze for up to 1 year. Gently wash berries before using.

Yield: 1 pint = 1-1/2 to 2 cups

Blackberries

This is a sweet and juicy, purplish-black fruit. Peak season is May through September. Boysenberries are a cross between a blackberry and a red raspberry, and they can be substituted for blackberries. Refrigerate a single layer on a paper towel-lined baking sheet covered with a paper towel for 2 days. Freeze up to 1 year.

Raspberries

Sweet and juicy raspberries come in red, black and golden colors. The black raspberry has a sweet-tart flavor. Peak seasons are from June through July and September through October. Refrigerate a single layer on a paper towel-lined baking sheet covered with a paper towel for 3 days. Freeze up to 1 year.

Blueberries

This sweet-tart blue fruit has a silvery sheen. Peak season is May through October. Refrigerate blueberries in their container or tightly covered for up to 1 week. Freeze up to 1 year.

Strawberries

Strawberries are a sweet and juicy red fruit; pale white fruit is unripe. Strawberries do not continue to ripen after they are picked. Available year-round; peak season is April through June. Refrigerate in a paper towel-lined, moisture-proof container for 2-3 days. Freeze up to 1 year.

Cranberries

Tart, firm, red cranberries have a peak season from October through December. Refrigerate in their bag for 1-2 months. Freeze in their bag for up to 1 year.

Yield: 12 ounces = 3 cups whole, 2-1/2 cups finely chopped

Currants

This tart, tiny, glossy fruit grows in a cluster like grapes and comes in red, black and white varieties. Generally they are used in jams and jellies. Peak season is June through August. Refrigerate on paper towels for up to 3 days.

Yield: 4 ounces = 1-1/4 cups

Gooseberries

Tart, translucent gooseberries come in green, white and purple varieties. Peak season is summer. Refrigerate for up to 2 weeks. Freeze up to 1 year. Remove stem and top before using.

Yield: 1 package (6 ounces) = 1 cup

Making a Strawberry Fan

1) Place firm ripe berries with stem down on a cutting board. With a sharp knife, make cuts 1/8 in. apart through the berry to within 1/8 in. of the stem.

2) Use your fingers to gently spread apart slices to form a fan.

3) Add further appeal with fresh mint, if available. After carefully removing the berry leaves with the knife point, replace them with a sprig of mint.

Hulling Strawberries

Use a strawberry huller or the tip of a serrated grapefruit spoon to easily remove the stem/hull. Just insert the tip of the spoon into the strawberry next to the stem and cut around the stem.

Summer Berry Salsa

PREP: 10 min. + chilling

Diane Hixon, Niceville, Florida

Other fruits are often used in relishes and sauces, but I decided to make one with my favorites. I get rave reviews when I serve this fruity, distinctive salsa over chicken, pork or fish. It's also delicious atop a spinach or lettuce salad.

1 pint fresh blueberries
1 pint fresh strawberries, chopped
1/4 cup sugar
2 tablespoons finely chopped onion
1 tablespoon lemon juice
1/2 teaspoon pepper
2 drops hot pepper sauce
1/4 cup slivered *or* sliced almonds, toasted

1) In a large bowl, combine the berries, sugar, onion, lemon juice, pepper and hot pepper sauce. Cover and refrigerate for 1 hour. Just before serving, stir in almonds.

Yield: 4 cups.

NUTRITION FACTS: 1/4 cup equals 42 calories, 1 g fat (0 saturated fat), 0 cholesterol, 2 mg sodium, 8 g carbohydrate, 0 fiber, 1 g protein.

SUMMER BERRY SALSA

Cranberry Ice

PREP: 30 min. + freezing

Carolyn Butterworth, Spirit Lake, Iowa

This was a traditional Christmastime dessert in my family. My grandmother first made it, then she handed down the recipe to my mother, who later shared it with me and my sisters. The cold, tart, rosy-red treat is refreshing after a hearty turkey dinner.

3 cups fresh *or* frozen cranberries
2 cups water
1 teaspoon unflavored gelatin
1/2 cup cold water
1-1/2 cups sugar
1/2 cup lemon juice

1) In a large saucepan, bring cranberries and water to a boil. Cook over medium heat until the berries pop, about 10 minutes. Remove from the heat; cool slightly. Press mixture through a sieve or food mill, reserving juice. Discard skins and seeds.

2) In a small bowl, sprinkle gelatin over cold water; set aside. In a saucepan, combine cranberry mixture and sugar; cook and stir until sugar is dissolved and mixture just begins to boil. Remove from the heat. Stir in gelatin mixture until gelatin is dissolved. Add lemon juice.

3) Transfer to a shallow 1-qt. freezer container. Cover and freeze until ice begins to form around the edges of container, about 1 hour; stir mixture. Freeze until slushy, stirring occasionally.

Yield: 8 servings.

NUTRITION FACTS: 1 cup equals 167 calories, trace fat (trace saturated fat), 0 cholesterol, 1 mg sodium, 43 g carbohydrate, 2 g fiber, trace protein.

Washing Berries

To wash berries, place a few at a time in a colander. Gently spray with sink sprayer. Then spread out on paper towels and pat dry.

Poppy Seed Fruit Salad

PREP/TOTAL TIME: 15 min.

Edie DeSpain, Logan, Utah

Almonds add a nice crunch to this pretty salad that's always a hit when I serve it. It goes with just about anything. The dressing can be used with any combination of fruit.

1/4 cup honey
1/4 cup limeade concentrate
2 teaspoons poppy seeds
1 cup halved fresh strawberries
1 cup cubed fresh pineapple
1 cup fresh blueberries

1 cup cubed seedless watermelon
1/4 cup slivered almonds, toasted

1) In a small bowl, combine the honey, limeade concentrate and poppy seeds. In a serving bowl, combine the fruit. Drizzle with dressing; toss to coat. Sprinkle with almonds. Serve with a slotted spoon.

Yield: 6 servings.

NUTRITION FACTS: 3/4 cup equals 111 calories, 1 g fat (trace saturated fat), 0 cholesterol, 2 mg sodium, 29 g carbohydrate, 2 g fiber, 1 g protein.

Cherries

Cherries are available in sweet and tart varieties, which are frequently used for pies. Bing (dark red) and Royal Ann (golden) are sweet cherries while the Montmorency is tart.

Buying

Sweet cherries are available May through July. Peak season for tart cherries is June through July. Select cherries that are plump and firm with a shiny skin. Avoid soft, bruised, shriveled fruit or fruit that has browned around the stem area.

Storage

Before refrigerating, sort through and discard any crushed, mushy or moldy fruit. Store unwashed cherries in a closed plastic bag in the refrigerator away from other vegetables with strong aromas for 1-2 days. To freeze, arrange in a single layer on a plastic wrap-lined baking sheet. Once frozen, transfer to a freezer container or bag. Freeze up to 1 year.

Preparation

Gently wash cherries before using, not before refrigeration. Use a cherry pitter or tip of a vegetable peeler to remove the pit.

Yield: 1 pound = 3 cups whole or 3-1/2 cups halved

Northern Cherry Puffs

PREP: 25 min. **BAKE:** 20 min. + cooling

Barbara Hanmer, Benzonia, Michigan

Michigan is a cherry-producing state, and that delightful fruit is highlighted in this classic recipe. Try it topped with whipped cream or ice cream.

1 cup fresh *or* frozen pitted dark sweet cherries, thawed and drained
1 tablespoon lemon juice
1-1/2 teaspoons almond extract, *divided*

1/4 teaspoon red food coloring, optional
1/3 cup shortening
2/3 cup sugar
1 egg
1 cup all-purpose flour
1/2 teaspoon baking powder
1/2 teaspoon salt
1/3 cup milk

SAUCE:
1/2 cup sugar
4-1/2 teaspoons cornstarch
1/4 cup water
2 cups fresh *or* frozen pitted dark sweet cherries
1/4 teaspoon red food coloring, optional

Whipped cream *or* vanilla ice cream

1) In a small bowl, combine cherries, lemon juice, 1/2 teaspoon extract and food coloring if desired; toss to coat. Spoon into four greased 10-oz. custard cups or ramekins.

2) In a small mixing bowl, cream shortening and sugar. Beat in the egg and remaining extract. Combine flour, baking powder and salt; add to the creamed mixture alternately with milk. Spoon over cherry mixture. Bake, uncovered, at 375° for 20-25 minutes or until golden brown. Cool for 10 minutes.

3) Meanwhile, in a saucepan, combine sugar and cornstarch. Stir in water until blended. Add cherries and food coloring if desired. Bring to a boil over medium heat; cook and stir for 2 minutes or until thickened. Invert puffs onto dessert plates; top with warm cherry sauce and whipped cream.

Yield: 4 servings.

NUTRITION FACTS: 1 serving (calculated without whipped cream or ice cream) equals 608 calories, 19 g fat (5 g saturated fat), 56 mg cholesterol, 372 mg sodium, 104 g carbohydrate, 3 g fiber, 7 g protein.

NORTHERN CHERRY PUFFS

George Washington Cherry Cobbler

PREP: 20 min. **BAKE:** 30 min.

Juanita Sherwood, Charleston, Illinois

Since Dad loved fruit, my mother prepared this dessert often in different ways. You can try it with blackberries or blueberries, too.

    1/2 cup sugar
      2 tablespoons cornstarch
    1/4 teaspoon ground cinnamon
    3/4 cup water
      1 package (12 ounces) frozen pitted
         dark sweet cherries, thawed
      1 tablespoon butter

TOPPING:

      1 cup all-purpose flour
      4 tablespoons sugar, *divided*
      2 teaspoons baking powder
    1/2 teaspoon salt
      3 tablespoons shortening
    1/2 cup milk

Ice cream, optional

1) In a large saucepan, combine sugar, cornstarch and cinnamon. Stir in water until smooth. Add the cherries and butter. Bring to a boil over medium heat; cook and stir for 2 minutes or until thickened. Pour into an 8-in. square baking dish; set aside.

2) In a bowl, combine the flour, 2 tablespoons sugar, baking powder and salt. Cut in shortening until mixture resembles coarse crumbs. Stir in milk just until moistened. Drop by spoonfuls over the cherries; sprinkle with remaining sugar.

3) Bake at 400° for 30-35 minutes or until golden brown. Serve warm with ice cream if desired.

Yield: 8 servings.

NUTRITION FACTS: 1 serving equals 231 calories, 7 g fat (2 g saturated fat), 6 mg cholesterol, 270 mg sodium, 40 g carbohydrate, 1 g fiber, 3 g protein.

Citrus Fruit

Citrus fruit comes in many varieties; please refer to the individual listings for more information about each.

Buying

Citrus fruit is available year-round (individual varieties have their own peak seasons). Select citrus fruit that is firm, heavy for its size and has a bright color. Avoid fruit with bruises or wrinkles. Weather conditions during the growing season can affect the thickness of the peel.

Storage

Store most citrus fruit at room temperature for about 3 days. For longer storage, store in the crisper drawer in the refrigerator for 2-3 weeks. Juice or grated peel may be frozen for up to 1 year.

Grapefruit

Has a white, pink or red flesh and a refreshing, sweet-tart flavor.

Yield: 1 medium = 3/4 cup juice or 1-1/2 cups segments

Lemon

Is a tart-tangy fruit with sunny yellow flesh. The two major varieties, Libson and Eureka, look similar.

Yield: 1 medium = 3 tablespoons juice or 2 teaspoons grated peel

Lime

A tart fruit with a light green flesh. Persian limes are most commonly sold and are a bright green color. They may have some small brown patches on their skin. Key limes grown in the Florida Keys have a limited season. They are smaller in size, have a yellow-green skin and are more tart. The juice is used for Key Lime Pie.

Yield: 1 medium Persian lime = 2 tablespoons juice or 1-1/2 teaspoons grated peel

Orange

Oranges are divided into three groups: sweet, loose-skinned and bitter. Sweet oranges are the seedless navel, juicy Valencia and the red-flesh blood orange.

Valencia oranges may have some green color on their skin; this is a natural occurrence and is not a sign that the orange is underripe. Small brown patches on the skin sometimes occur and that does not affect the quality of the orange.

Loose-skinned oranges are very easy to peel and separate the fruit into segments. Loose-skinned oranges generally fall into the mandarin family. Tangerines, temple oranges, clementines and Minneola tangelos are examples of loose-skinned oranges. Bitter oranges, such as Seville, are used for cooking or marmalade.

Yield: 1 medium = 1/3 to 1/2 cup juice or 4 teaspoons grated peel

Tangy Texas Salsa

PREP: 15 min. + chilling

Lois Kildahl, McAllen, Texas

This is one way to work citrus into a main dish. The combination of tangy fruit, spicy jalapeno and distinctive cilantro is perfect over any meat, poultry or fish. We also dip into it with chips.

- 1 medium grapefruit
- 1 large navel orange
- 1 *each* medium green, sweet red and yellow pepper, chopped
- 1 medium tomato, seeded and chopped
- 1 jalapeno pepper, seeded and chopped
- 3 tablespoons chopped red onion
- 1 tablespoon minced fresh oregano
- 1-1/2 teaspoons sugar
- 1/2 teaspoon salt

1) To section grapefruit and orange, cut a thin slice off the bottom and top of each. Place each fruit cut side down on a cutting board. With a sharp knife, remove peel and white pith. Slice between the membrane of each section and the fruit until the knife reaches the center; remove sections.

2) Place grapefruit and orange sections in a large bowl; add the remaining ingredients and mix well. Cover and refrigerate for at least 2 hours.

Yield: about 5 cups.

Editor's Note: When cutting or seeding hot peppers, use rubber or plastic gloves to protect your hands. Avoid touching your face.

NUTRITION FACTS: 1/4 cup equals 17 calories, trace fat (trace saturated fat), 0 cholesterol, 60 mg sodium, 4 g carbohydrate, 1 g fiber, trace protein

Orange Rose

1) Cut a very thin slice from bottom of orange and discard. Starting at the top of the orange, use a vegetable peeler or sharp knife to cut a continuous narrow strip of peel in a spiral fashion around the entire orange.

2) Beginning at the end of the strip where you started, wrap the strip around itself to form a coil. Insert one or two toothpicks horizontally into the base to secure.

Lemon Wheels

Use a citrus stripper or large zester to make evenly spaced vertical strips around a lemon. Cut the lemon into 1/8-in. slices. Make one cut from the center of each slice through the peel to place over the rim of a glass.

Sweet Broiled Grapefruit

PREP/TOTAL TIME: 10 min.

Terry Bray, Auburndale, Florida

I was never a fan of grapefruit until I had it broiled at a restaurant. It was so tangy and delicious! I finally got the recipe and now make it often for my husband, children and grandchildren.

- 1 large grapefruit
- 2 tablespoons butter, softened
- 2 tablespoons sugar
- 1/2 teaspoon ground cinnamon

1) Cut each grapefruit in half. With a sharp knife, cut around the membrane in the center of each half and discard. Cut around each section to loosen the fruit.

2) Place 1 tablespoon butter in the center of each half. Combine sugar and cinnamon; sprinkle over each. Place on a baking pan.

3) Broil 4 in. from the heat until butter is melted and sugar is bubbly. Serve immediately.

Yield: 2 servings.

NUTRITION FACTS: 1 serving equals 203 calories, 12 g fat (7 g saturated fat), 31 mg cholesterol, 116 mg sodium, 26 g carbohydrate, 2 g fiber, 1 g protein

SWEET BROILED GRAPEFRUIT

Grapefruit Alaska

PREP/TOTAL TIME: 30 min.

Peg Atzen, Hackensack, Minnesota

You'll easily impress guests with this dessert. Every time I serve it, I get rave reviews.

- 4 large grapefruit
- 2 teaspoons rum extract
- 1/2 cup heavy whipping cream, whipped
- 3 egg whites
- 1 teaspoon cornstarch
- 1/4 teaspoon cream of tartar
- 1/4 cup sugar
- 8 maraschino cherries

1) Halve grapefruit and cut into sections; remove membranes. Return grapefruit sections to grapefruit halves. Drizzle 1/4 teaspoon rum extract over each.

2) Top each grapefruit half with 1 rounded tablespoon of whipped cream. Place on an ungreased foil-lined baking sheet.

3) In a large mixing bowl, beat the egg whites, cornstarch and cream of tartar on medium speed until soft peaks form. Gradually beat in sugar, 1 tablespoon at a time, on high until stiff glossy peaks form and sugar is dissolved.

4) Mound 1/2 cup on each grapefruit half; spread meringue to edges to seal. Bake at 350° for 15 minutes or until meringue is browned. Top each with a cherry. Serve immediately.

Yield: 8 servings.

NUTRITION FACTS: 1 serving equals 152 calories, 6 g fat (3 g saturated fat), 20 mg cholesterol, 26 mg sodium, 24 g carbohydrate, 2 g fiber, 3 g protein.

Cinnamon-Honey Grapefruit

PREP/TOTAL TIME: 10 min.

Mrs. Carson Sadler, Souris, Manitoba

Naturally delicious grapefruit gains even more great flavor with this recipe. I often like to prepare this as a breakfast on its own. But it also makes an appealing addition to your morning meal.

- 1 medium grapefruit
- 2 teaspoons honey

Dash ground cinnamon

1) Cut the grapefruit in half. With a sharp knife, cut around each section to loosen fruit. Place cut side up in a small baking pan.

2) Drizzle each half with 1 teaspoon honey; sprinkle with cinnamon. Broil 4 in. from the heat for 2-3 minutes or until bubbly. Serve warm.

Yield: 2 servings.

NUTRITION FACTS: 1/2 grapefruit equals 63 calories, trace fat (trace saturated fat), 0 cholesterol, trace sodium, 16 g carbohydrate, 1 g fiber, 1 g protein.

AVOCADO CITRUS TOSS

Avocado Citrus Toss

PREP/TOTAL TIME: 20 min.

Marie Hattrup, Moro, Oregon

The light dressing doesn't mask the goodness of sweet citrus sections, crisp lettuce, crunchy almonds and mellow avocados.

- 6 cups torn salad greens
- 2 medium grapefruit, peeled and sectioned
- 3 navel oranges, peeled and sectioned
- 1 ripe avocado, peeled and sliced
- 1/4 cup slivered almonds, toasted

DRESSING:

- 1/2 cup vegetable oil
- 1/3 cup sugar
- 3 tablespoons white vinegar
- 2 teaspoons poppy seeds
- 1 teaspoon finely chopped onion
- 1/2 teaspoon ground mustard
- 1/2 teaspoon salt

1) In a large salad bowl, toss the greens, grapefruit, oranges, avocado and almonds.

2) In a jar with tight-fitting lid, combine the dressing ingredients; shake well. Drizzle over salad and toss to coat. Serve immediately.

Yield: 6 servings.

NUTRITION FACTS: 1 cup equals 355 calories, 26 g fat (3 g saturated fat), 0 cholesterol, 215 mg sodium, 31 g carbohydrate, 6 g fiber, 4 g protein.

Grating Citrus Fruit

The peel from citrus fruit adds a burst of flavor to recipes and color to garnishes. Citrus peel, also called zest, can be grated into fine shreds with a Microplane grater. For slightly thicker and longer shreds, use a zester; for long, continuous strips, use a stripper. Remove only the colored portion of the peel, not the bitter white pith.

Almond Sunshine Citrus

PREP: 30 min. + chilling

Geri Barr, Calgary, Alberta

I adapted this recipe from one I found in a newspaper. The tangy combination of citrus fruits is welcome as a light dessert after a big meal or as a refreshing addition to a brunch.

> 3 large navel oranges
> 1 medium red grapefruit
> 1 medium white grapefruit
> 1 small lemon
> 1 small lime
> 1/3 cup sugar
> 1/8 teaspoon almond extract
> 2 tablespoons sliced almonds, toasted

1) Grate enough peel from the oranges, grapefruit, lemon and lime to measure 1 tablespoon of mixed citrus peel; set peel aside.

2) To section citrus fruit, cut a thin slice off the bottom and top of the oranges, grapefruit, lemon and lime. Place each fruit cut side down on a cutting board. With a sharp knife, remove peel and white pith. Holding fruit over a bowl, slice between the membrane of each section and the fruit until the knife reaches the center; remove sections and place in a glass bowl. Set 1/2 cup juice aside.

3) In a small saucepan, combine the sugar and reserved peel and juice. Bring to a boil. Reduce heat; simmer, uncovered for 10 minutes.

4) Cool; stir in extract. Pour over fruit. Refrigerate overnight. Just before serving, sprinkle with almonds.

Yield: 4 servings.

NUTRITION FACTS: 3/4 cup equals 197 calories, 2 g fat (trace saturated fat), 0 cholesterol, 1 mg sodium, 47 g carbohydrate, 6 g fiber, 3 g protein.

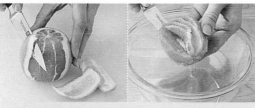

Sectioning Citrus Fruit

1) Cut a thin slice off the bottom and top of the fruit. Rest the fruit, cut side down, on a cutting board. With a sharp paring knife, remove peel and white pith from fruit.

2) Hold fruit over a bowl and slice between the membrane of a section and the fruit until the knife reaches the center. Turn the knife and follow the membrane so the fruit is released. Repeat until all sections are removed.

Dates

Dates have a high sugar content, which is even more concentrated when dried.

Buying

Dried dates are available year-round. Peak season for fresh dates is late summer to mid-fall. Select fresh dates that are plump with a smooth shiny skin.

Storage

Store in the refrigerator in a plastic bag for up to 2 weeks. Remove pits before using.

Yield: 1 pound dried dates = 2-3/4 cups pitted and chopped
1 package (10 ounces) dried pitted dates = 1-1/4 cups chopped

Date Nut Bars

PREP: 10 min. **BAKE:** 20 min. + cooling

Margaret Asselin, Port Huron, Michigan

Even those who aren't usually fond of nuts or dates enjoy these bars. They freeze well in airtight containers.

> 2 cups sugar
> 2 cups all-purpose flour
> 2 teaspoons baking powder
> 1/4 teaspoon salt
> 2 cups chopped dates
> 2 cups chopped walnuts *or* pecans
> 4 eggs, lightly beaten
> 2 tablespoons butter, melted
> 1 teaspoon vanilla extract

Confectioners' sugar

1) In a large bowl, combine the first six ingredients. Add the eggs, butter and vanilla; stir just until dry ingredients are moistened (batter will be very stiff).

2) Spread into a greased 15-in. x 10-in. x 1-in. baking pan. Bake at 350° for 20-25 minutes or until golden brown. Cool on a wire rack. Dust with confectioners' sugar.

Yield: 5 dozen.

NUTRITION FACTS: 2 bars (calculated without confectioners' sugar) equals 182 calories, 6 g fat (1 g saturated fat), 30 mg cholesterol, 63 mg sodium, 30 g carbohydrate, 2 g fiber, 4 g protein.

DATE PUDDING

Date Pudding

PREP: 10 min. **BAKE:** 30 min.

Opal Hamer, St. Petersburg, Florida

This pudding has been our family's favorite holiday dessert for years. At Christmas, I top each with green-tinted whipped cream and a red maraschino cherry.

3/4 cup chopped dates
1/2 cup chopped walnuts
6 tablespoons sugar
1 egg
2 tablespoons milk
1/2 teaspoon vanilla extract
2 tablespoons all-purpose flour
1/2 teaspoon baking powder
Dash salt
1 tablespoon butter
Whipped cream

1) In a bowl, combine the dates, walnuts and sugar. In another bowl, beat egg, milk and vanilla. Add to date mixture; mix well.

2) Combine flour, baking powder and salt; add to the date mixture. Spread into a greased 1-qt. baking dish; dot with butter.

3) Bake at 325° for 30 minutes or until a knife inserted near the center comes out clean. Serve warm with whipped cream.

Yield: 2 servings.

NUTRITION FACTS: 1/2 cup (calculated without whipped cream) equals 646 calories, 27 g fat (6 g saturated fat), 124 mg cholesterol, 273 mg sodium, 97 g carbohydrate, 7 g fiber, 13 g protein.

Festive Stuffed Dates

PREP: 15 min. + chilling

Diana Debruyn, Cincinnati, Ohio

Four ingredients are all you need for these change-of-pace treats. By the way, just 1/2 cup dates contains more potassium than a medium banana.

3 ounces reduced-fat cream cheese
1/4 cup confectioners' sugar
2 teaspoons grated orange peel
30 pitted dates

1) In a small mixing bowl, beat the cream cheese, confectioners' sugar and orange peel until blended.

2) Carefully make a slit in the center of each date; fill with cream cheese mixture. Cover and refrigerate for at least 1 hour before serving.

Yield: 10 servings.

NUTRITION FACTS: 3 stuffed dates equals 102 calories, 2 g fat (1 g saturated fat), 6 mg cholesterol, 37 mg sodium, 22 g carbohydrate, 2 g fiber, 1 g protein.

Make a Date with Dates

Dates are high in fiber and contain iron and potassium. They are also one of the sweetest of fruits—70% of their weight can be made up of sugar. To prevent sticking when slicing or chopping dates, spray your scissors or knife with cooking spray, or frequently dip in cold water. Dried dates stay fresh for 1 year in the refrigerator and for up to 5 years in the freezer.

Figs

The many varieties of figs include Black Mission, Calimyrna and Kadota. Depending on the variety, the skin may be green, brown or purplish-black; the seed-filled sweet pulp can be white, pink or purple.

Buying

Figs are available June through October. Select plump, firm fruit that is heavy for its size and gives slightly when gently pressed. Avoid bruised, soft fruit or fruit with a sour aroma. Handle carefully as figs bruise easily.

Storage

Store unwashed figs in the refrigerator and use within 2 days. Dried figs can be stored in an airtight container for up to 6 months.

Yield: 1 package (8 ounces) Black Mission Figs = 1-1/2 cups sliced

Grapes

Flavors of grapes vary from sweet to sweet-tart. They are available seedless and with seeds. Grapes are divided by their color (green or white, red and black) and their use (table, wine or commercial).

The grapes available in the store are table grapes. The most common green grapes are Thompson seedless and Perlette seedless. The most common red grapes are Flame and Ruby (both seedless) and Red Globe. Beauty or Black seedless black grapes may be available in your market.

Buying

Green grapes are available year-round (individual varieties have their own peak seasons). Select grapes that are plump, firmly attached to the stem and have good color for their variety. Avoid grapes that have bruises, soft spots or mold.

Storage

Store unwashed grapes in the refrigerator in a perforated plastic bag for about 1 week. Wash before using, not before refrigeration.

Grapes can be frozen and stored in an airtight container. Frozen grapes make a refreshing treat in the summer.

Yield: 1 pound = 3 cups

Layered Fruit Salad

PREP: 20 min. + chilling

Page Alexander, Baldwin City, Kansas

Fresh fruit is layered into an eye-catching salad that's a welcome side dish all summer long.

- 1/2 cup orange juice
- 1/4 cup lemon juice
- 1/4 cup packed brown sugar
- 1/2 teaspoon grated orange peel
- 1/2 teaspoon grated lemon peel
- 1 cinnamon stick (3 inches)
- 2 cups fresh *or* drained canned pineapple chunks
- 1 cup seedless red grapes
- 2 medium firm bananas, sliced
- 2 medium oranges, sectioned
- 1 medium grapefruit, sectioned
- 1 pint fresh strawberries, sliced
- 2 medium kiwifruit, peeled and sliced

1) In a large saucepan, combine the juices, brown sugar, peels and cinnamon stick; bring to a boil. Reduce heat; simmer, uncovered, for 5 minutes. Remove from the heat; cool completely.

2) Meanwhile, layer fruit in a glass serving bowl. Remove cinnamon stick from sauce; pour over fruit. Cover and refrigerate for several hours.

Yield: 8 servings.

NUTRITION FACTS: 1 cup equals 137 calories, 1 g fat (trace saturated fat), 0 cholesterol, 5 mg sodium, 34 g carbohydrate, 3 g fiber, 1 g protein.

Sparkling Fruit Salad

PREP: 10 min. + chilling

Taste of Home Test Kitchen

Pineapple chunks, mandarin oranges, strawberries and grapes are treated to a dressing of wine and sparkling club soda in this delightful salad. Serve in dessert dishes or set the whole bowl on the table for a fetching presentation.

- 1 fresh pineapple, peeled and cut into chunks
- 1 can (11 ounces) mandarin oranges, drained
- 1 cup halved fresh strawberries
- 1 cup halved green grapes
- 1 cup white wine *or* white grape juice
- 1/2 cup chilled club soda

1) In a large bowl, combine the pineapple, oranges, strawberries and grapes. Combine wine or grape juice and club soda; pour over fruit.

2) Cover and refrigerate for at least 2 hours, stirring occasionally. Serve with a slotted spoon.

Yield: 8 servings.

NUTRITION FACTS: 1 cup equals 87 calories, trace fat (trace saturated fat), 0 cholesterol, 6 mg sodium, 16 g carbohydrate, 1 g fiber, 1 g protein.

LAYERED FRUIT SALAD

OLD-FASHIONED FRUIT CRISPS

 CLASSIC: Raspberries and blueberries are showcased in delectable Double-Berry Crisp. An amazing topping made with oats, cornflakes, brown sugar, cinnamon and butter gives traditional flavor to this warm, homey dessert.

 TIME-SAVER: Don't bother preheating your oven! Microwave Apple Crisp uses the handy appliance to finish this nicely spiced dessert in minutes. Graham cracker crumbs are a different addition to the topping.

 LIGHT: Less sugar in the fruit filling helps trim down Raspberry Pear Crisp, and the better-for-you topping uses less butter and replaces the sugar with honey. That's why one serving has fewer calories and only a third of the fat of Double-Berry Crisp and none of its cholesterol.

 SERVES 2: You'll need just two juicy peaches to make tempting Peach Crisp Cups. These individual baked desserts have a sweet and buttery crumb topping of oats and almonds.

DOUBLE-BERRY CRISP

Double-Berry Crisp

PREP: 20 min. **BAKE:** 25 min. + cooling

Bernadette Beaton
Goose River, Prince Edward Island

- 1 cup sugar
- 1/4 cup cornstarch
- 2 tablespoons orange juice
- 1 teaspoon grated orange peel
- 2 cups fresh *or* frozen raspberries
- 2 cups fresh *or* frozen blueberries
- 1 cup old-fashioned oats
- 1/2 cup cornflakes
- 1/2 cup packed brown sugar

- 1/2 teaspoon ground cinnamon
- 1/4 teaspoon salt
- 1/4 cup butter, melted

1) In a large saucepan, combine sugar, cornstarch, the orange juice, orange peel and berries until blended. Bring to a boil; cook and stir for 2 minutes or until thickened and bubbly. Pour into a greased 8-in. square baking dish.

2) In a bowl, combine the oats, cornflakes, brown sugar, cinnamon and salt; stir in butter. Sprinkle over berry mixture.

3) Bake at 350° for 25-30 minutes or until filling is bubbly. Cool for 10 minutes before serving.

Yield: 6 servings.

NUTRITION FACTS: 1 serving equals 394 calories, 9 g fat (5 g saturated fat), 20 mg cholesterol, 201 mg sodium, 79 g carbohydrate, 5 g fiber, 3 g protein.

Microwave Apple Crisp

PREP/TOTAL TIME: 30 min.

Suzie Salle, Renton, Washington

- 1 cup graham cracker crumbs (about 16 squares)
- 1/2 cup all-purpose flour
- 1/2 cup packed brown sugar
- 1 teaspoon ground cinnamon
- 1/2 teaspoon ground nutmeg
- 1/2 cup butter, melted
- 8 medium tart apples, peeled and sliced

Whipped topping *or* ice cream

1) In a large bowl, combine the cracker crumbs, flour, brown sugar, cinnamon, nutmeg and butter. Place apples in a greased microwave-safe 2-1/2-qt. baking dish. Top with crumb mixture.

2) In a bowl, combine the oats, honey, margarine, cinnamon and nutmeg. Sprinkle over fruit. Bake at 350° for 30-35 minutes or until pears are tender and mixture is bubbly.

Yield: 8 servings.

NUTRITION FACTS: 1 serving equals 151 calories, 3 g fat (1 g saturated fat), 0 cholesterol, 46 mg sodium, 30 g carbohydrate, 5 g fiber, 2 g protein.

Peach Crisp Cups

PREP: 10 min. **BAKE:** 30 min.

Aida Von Babbel, Coquitlam, British Columbia

- 2 medium fresh peaches, peeled and sliced
- 2 teaspoons sugar
- 2 tablespoons quick-cooking oats
- 2 tablespoons all-purpose flour
- 1 tablespoon brown sugar
- 2 teaspoons chopped almonds
- 5 teaspoons cold butter
- 1/4 teaspoon almond extract

1) In a bowl, combine peaches and sugar. Transfer to two greased 6-oz. baking dishes. Combine the oats, flour, brown sugar and almonds. Cut in butter until mixture resembles coarse crumbs. Sprinkle with almond extract; toss.

2) Sprinkle over peaches. Bake at 375° for 30 minutes or until bubbly and golden brown.

Yield: 2 servings.

NUTRITION FACTS: 1 serving equals 234 calories, 11 g fat (6 g saturated fat), 26 mg cholesterol, 99 mg sodium, 32 g carbohydrate, 3 g fiber, 3 g protein.

■ **Apple Crisp Cups:** Use 2 medium tart apples in place of the peaches. If desired, mix 1/8 teaspoon ground cinnamon with the sugar before sprinkling it over the apples.

MICROWAVE APPLE CRISP

2) Microwave, uncovered, on high for 8-9 minutes or until apples are tender. Serve warm with whipped topping or ice cream.

Yield: 8 servings.

NUTRITION FACTS: 1 cup (calculated without whipped topping or ice cream) equals 289 calories, 13 g fat (7 g saturated fat), 30 mg cholesterol, 150 mg sodium, 44 g carbohydrate, 3 g fiber, 2 g protein.

REDUCING SUGAR IN FRUIT CRISPS ■■■

I was intrigued by an article about reducing sugar in fruit crisps, pies and cobblers. It said to cut the amount of sugar called for in half, then add a little baking soda. The baking soda, according to the article, neutralizes the acid content and allows the sweetness level to remain the same. I put this to the test by making two mixed-fruit crisps using strawberries, apples, rhubarb and blackberries. I added a teaspoon of baking soda and half the sugar to one and made the other as usual. My family and some co-workers tried both and found the one made with baking soda tasted slightly sweeter!

—*Shirley S., Indianapolis, Indiana*

Raspberry Pear Crisp

PREP: 15 min. **BAKE:** 30 min.

Ruby Williams, Bogalusa, Louisiana

- 2 medium ripe pears, peeled and thinly sliced
- 3 cups fresh raspberries
- 2 tablespoons sugar
- 1 cup quick-cooking oats
- 1/4 cup honey
- 3 tablespoons stick margarine, melted
- 1 teaspoon ground cinnamon
- 1/2 teaspoon ground nutmeg

1) Place pears in an 8-in. square baking dish coated with cooking spray. Sprinkle with raspberries and sugar.

RASPBERRY PEAR CRISP

Kiwifruit

Kiwifruit has a unique, sweet-tart flavor with tones of pineapple, strawberry and citrus. The two varieties of kiwifruit available in stores are green and golden. The green kiwi is egg-shaped with a fuzzy brown exterior, and it has emerald-green flesh with tiny black edible seeds. The golden kiwi is sweeter than the green. It has a pointed end, smooth brown skin and golden flesh with tiny black edible seeds.

Buying

Green kiwifruit is available year-round; peak season for golden kiwifruit is June through November. Select plump fruit that yields to gentle pressure. Avoid fruit with soft spots or a shriveled skin. Firm fruit will still need to ripen.

Storage

Store unripened kiwifruit at room temperature. To speed the ripening process, store in a paper bag with an apple or banana. Once ripened, store in the refrigerator for 2-3 days.

To eat, just cut in half and scoop the fruit out with a spoon. Or peel skin and cut into slices or cubes.

Do not add fresh kiwifruit to gelatin salads or desserts. It contains an enzyme that prevents gelatin from setting up.

Yield: 1 medium kiwifruit (3 ounces) = 5 to 6 slices or 1/3 cup slices

Peeling a Kiwifruit

1) For eating, cut an end off fruit or cut in half. Using a spoon, scoop out flesh.

2) Cut both ends from fruit. Using a vegetable peeler, peel off fuzzy brown skin. Cut into slices, wedges or cubes with a sharp knife.

Simply Fruit

PREP/TOTAL TIME: 10 min.

Taste of Home Test Kitchen

Young and old alike will enjoy this fun fruit medley featuring banana, kiwifruit, oranges and grapes. A dollop of yogurt with brown sugar tops off this nourishing sweet treat.

- 2 medium navel oranges, peeled and sliced
- 2 kiwifruit, peeled and cubed
- 1 medium firm banana, sliced
- 1 cup seedless red grapes
- 1/2 cup reduced-fat vanilla yogurt
- 2 tablespoons plus 2 teaspoons brown sugar

1) In a large bowl, combine the oranges, kiwi, banana and grapes. Divide among six serving bowls.

2) Combine yogurt and brown sugar; dollop over fruit. Serve immediately.

Yield: 6 servings.

NUTRITION FACTS: 2/3 cup equals 107 calories, 1 g fat (trace saturated fat), 1 mg cholesterol, 15 mg sodium, 27 g carbohydrate, 4 g fiber, 2 g protein.

Kiwi Ice

PREP: 20 min. + freezing

Shirley Glaab, Hattiesburg, Mississippi

All you need are five ingredients to blend together this tart, refreshing frozen treat. A serving is especially pretty garnished with kiwi and orange slices.

- 2 cups unsweetened apple juice
- 1 tablespoon lemon juice
- 4 medium kiwifruit, peeled and sliced

Sugar substitute equivalent to 6 teaspoons sugar

- 1/2 teaspoon grated orange peel

Sliced orange and additional kiwifruit, optional

1) In a blender, combine the juices and kiwi; cover and process just until smooth. Add the sugar substitute and orange peel. Pour mixture into an ungreased 8-in. square dish. Cover and freeze for 1-1/2 to 2 hours or until partially set.

2) Transfer to a large mixing bowl; beat on medium speed for 1-1/2 minutes. Return to pan; freeze for 2-3 hours or until firm.

3) Remove from the freezer 10 minutes before serving. Spoon into small bowls; garnish with orange slices and additional kiwi if desired.

Yield: 8 servings.

Editor's Note: This recipe was tested with Splenda No Calorie Sweetener.

NUTRITION FACTS: 1/2 cup equals 56 calories, trace fat (0 saturated fat), 0 cholesterol, 2 mg sodium, 14 g carbohydrate, 0 fiber, 1 g protein.

Kumquats

Kumquats are a member of the citrus family. This egg-shaped orange fruit has a sweet skin and tart flesh. It can be sliced and eaten, skin and all.

Buying

Kumquats are available November through March. Select fruit that is completely orange with firm and glossy skin. Avoid bruised, soft or shriveled fruit.

Storage

Store unwashed kumquats in the refrigerator for about 2 weeks.

Yield: 1 kumquat (1/2 ounce)
3 kumquats = scant 1/4 cup slices

Mangoes

This juicy, tropical fruit has a sweet-sour flavor.

Buying

Mangoes are available most of the year. Select plump fruit with a sweet, fruity aroma. Avoid very soft or bruised fruit. The skin of a ripe mango is green to yellow in color with a tinge of red. It should yield slightly when pressed and have a fruity aroma at the stem end.

Storage

Store unwashed mangoes in the refrigerator away from other fruits and vegetables with strong aromas. Keep green mangoes at room temperature out of direct sunlight until ripened.

Yield: 1 medium mango (9 ounces) = 1 cup chopped

🌿 Minty Mango Salsa

PREP: 10 min. + chilling

Diane Thompson, Nutrioso, Arizona

My husband often likes to prepare a whole smoked turkey, and I make this colorful salsa with fresh mint to accompany it.

    1 large ripe mango, peeled and diced
    1 medium sweet red pepper, diced
    1 can (4 ounces) chopped green chilies
1/4 cup chopped green onions
    1 tablespoon lime juice
    2 teaspoons minced fresh mint
1/4 teaspoon ground ginger
Tortilla chips

1) In a small bowl, combine the mango, red pepper, chilies, onions, lime juice, mint and ginger. Cover and refrigerate for at least 8 hours. Serve with tortilla chips.

Yield: about 2-1/2 cups.

NUTRITION FACTS: 1/4 cup (calculated without chips) equals 20 calories, trace fat (trace saturated fat), 0 cholesterol, 43 mg sodium, 5 g carbohydrate, 1 g fiber, trace protein.

MINTY MANGO SALSA

Dicing a Mango

1) Wash fruit. Lay fruit on the counter, then turn so the top and bottom are now the sides. Using a sharp knife, make a lengthwise cut as close to the long, flat seed as possible to remove each side of the fruit. Trim fruit away from the seed.

2) Score each side of the fruit lengthwise and widthwise, without cutting through the skin.

3) Using your hand, push the skin up, turning the fruit out. Cut fruit off at the skin with a knife.

Melons

Melons are in the same family as squash, cucumber and gourds. Melons have hard rinds and a hollow, seed-filled center. Muskmelons, which are also called cantaloupes, have a musky fragrance and netted (webbed) rind. Winter melons lack the musky fragrance, typically lack the netted rind and are oblong in shape. (Watermelons are on page 459.)

Buying

Melons are available year-round (individual varieties have their own peak seasons). Select melons that are heavy for their size and have no cracks or dents in the skin. A ripe melon should have a fruity, pleasant aroma. Avoid melons that are bruised or have a strong aroma, which indicates they are overripe.

Storage

Store underripe melons at room temperature for 2-3 days. Store ripe melons in the refrigerator for 1 week. Store cut melon, wrapped in plastic wrap or in an airtight container, in the refrigerator.

Cantaloupe
Has a heavy netting over its cream-colored rind. Its orange flesh is sweet. Available year-round; peak season is June through October.

Yield: 1 medium cantaloupe (3 pounds) = 4-1/2 cups cubed

Crenshaw
Has a smooth but ribbed rind, is a golden yellow when ripe and is pointed at one end. A ripe Crenshaw has sweet pink flesh with a spicy rich fragrance. Available June through October. Peak season is July.

Yield: 1 Crenshaw (about 5-1/2 pounds) = 9 cups cubed

Honeydew
Has a smooth, creamy white rind. Most honeydews have a pale green flesh and mild pleasant flavor. Available year-round; peak season is May through October.

Yield: 1 medium honeydew (4-5 pounds) = 4 cups cubed

Persian
Resembles a cantaloupe, but the netting on the rind is more delicate. It's also slightly larger. The skin turns to a lighter green when ripe. The salmon-colored flesh is sweet. Peak season is June through November.

Yield: 1 medium Persian (about 4 pounds) = 8 cups cubed

Melon Ambrosia

PREP: 20 min. + chilling

Edie DeSpain, Logan, Utah

Each time I serve this light and refreshing dessert, it gets rave reviews. With three kinds of melon, it's lovely and colorful but so simple to prepare.

  1 cup watermelon balls *or* cubes
  1 cup cantaloupe balls *or* cubes
  1 cup honeydew balls *or* cubes
1/3 cup lime juice
  2 tablespoons sugar
  2 tablespoons honey
1/4 cup flaked coconut, toasted
Fresh mint, optional

1) In a small bowl, combine the melon balls. In another bowl, combine the lime juice, sugar and honey; pour over melon and toss to coat. Cover and refrigerate for at least 1 hour. Sprinkle with coconut. Garnish with mint if desired.

Yield: 4 servings.

NUTRITION FACTS: 3/4 cup equals 137 calories, 4 g fat (3 g saturated fat), 0 cholesterol, 12 mg sodium, 29 carbohydrate, 2 g fiber, 1 g protein.

Chilly Melon Cups

PREP: 20 min. + freezing

Katie Koziolek, Hartland, Minnesota

This cool treat is stored in the freezer so it's always handy. It's a great way to use what's left from a fruit platter or melon boat.

  1 cup water
  1 cup sugar
1/2 cup lemonade concentrate

1/2 cup orange juice concentrate
4 cups watermelon balls *or* cubes
2 cups cantaloupe balls *or* cubes
2 cups honeydew balls *or* cubes
2 cups pineapple chunks
2 cups fresh raspberries

1) In a large bowl, combine the water, sugar and concentrates; stir until the sugar is dissolved. Add fruit and stir gently to coat. Spoon into foil-lined muffin cups or 3-oz. plastic cups. Freeze for up to 3 months.

2) Before serving, thaw overnight in the refrigerator or let stand at room temperature for 30-45 minutes until mixture is slushy.

Yield: 12-14 servings.

NUTRITION FACTS: 1 serving equals 152 calories, trace fat (trace saturated fat), 0 cholesterol, 7 mg sodium, 38 g carbohydrate, 2 g fiber, 1 g protein.

Gingered Melon

PREP/TOTAL TIME: 15 min.

Patricia Richardson, Verona, Ontario

When I have guests, I like to let them spoon melon from a large serving bowl and add their own toppings. You can also combine the fruit with ice cream or frozen yogurt and ginger ale to make a melon float!

1/2 medium honeydew, cut into 1-inch cubes
1/4 cup orange juice
1-1/2 teaspoons ground ginger
1/2 to 1 cup whipped cream
1/4 cup fresh *or* frozen raspberries

1) In a small bowl, combine the melon, orange juice and ginger. Cover and refrigerate for 5-10 minutes. Spoon into tall dessert glasses or bowls. Top with whipped cream and raspberries.

Yield: 4 servings.

NUTRITION FACTS: 1 cup equals 76 calories, 2 g fat (1 g saturated fat), 6 mg cholesterol, 22 mg sodium, 15 g carbohydrate, 1 g fiber, 1 g protein.

Fresh Fruit Bowl

PREP: 15 min. + chilling

Marion Kirst, Troy, Michigan

The glorious colors make this a great summer salad. Slightly sweet and chilled, it's a nice accompaniment to a grilled entree.

8 to 10 cups fresh melon cubes
1 to 2 tablespoons light corn syrup
1 pint fresh strawberries
2 cups fresh pineapple chunks
2 oranges, sectioned
Fresh mint leaves, optional

1) In a large bowl, combine melon cubes and corn syrup. Cover and refrigerate overnight. Just before

serving, stir in remaining fruit. Garnish with mint if desired.

Yield: 16 servings.

NUTRITION FACTS: 3/4 cup equals 55 calories, trace fat (trace saturated fat), 0 cholesterol, 9 mg sodium, 13 g carbohydrate, 2 g fiber, 1 g protein.

Melon with Raspberry Sauce

PREP/TOTAL TIME: 20 min.

Taste of Home Test Kitchen

Refreshing melon slices fanned out in a pretty pool of raspberry sauce create a light but elegant ending to any special-occasion meal.

2-2/3 cups fresh raspberries
3 tablespoons honey
1 teaspoon lemon juice
1/2 teaspoon minced fresh gingerroot
1/2 large cantaloupe
1/2 medium honeydew

1) Set aside a few raspberries for garnish. Place the remaining berries in a blender; cover and process until pureed. Add the honey, lemon juice and ginger; cover and process until combined. Strain and discard seeds; set sauce aside.

2) Cut the cantaloupe and honeydew into three wedges; cut each wedge widthwise in half. Remove seeds and rind. Slice each piece of melon lengthwise toward narrow end without cutting completely to the end. Open into a fan shape.

3) On each dessert plate, place 2 tablespoons of raspberry sauce, a cantaloupe fan and a honeydew fan. Garnish with reserved raspberries.

Yield: 6 servings.

NUTRITION FACTS: 1 serving equals 130 calories, 1 g fat (1 g saturated fat), 0 cholesterol, 19 mg sodium, 33 g carbohydrate, 5 g fiber, 2 g protein.

MELON WITH RASPBERRY SAUCE

Nectarines and Peaches

Nectarines and peaches are used interchangeably in recipes. Nectarines have a smooth, thin skin; peaches have a fuzzy skin. Peaches are classified as freestone when the pit falls away from the flesh, and clingstone when the pit clings to the flesh.

Buying

Both fruits are available May through November. Select plump fruit. Avoid fruit with bruises, soft spots or cuts. Avoid peaches with a green background as these will not ripen or be sweet. Ripe nectarines and peaches will give slightly when gently pressed and have a sweet aroma.

Storage

Store ripe fruit in the refrigerator for 3-5 days. Store firm fruit at room temperature until ripened. To ripen more quickly, place fruit in a paper bag at room temperature. Freeze for up to 1 year.

Yield: 1 pound nectarines (3 medium) = 3 cups sliced
1 pound peaches (4 medium) = 2-3/4 cups sliced

Pitting Peaches

1) Cut peach in half, cutting around the pit and using the indentation as a guide.

2) Twist halves in opposite directions to separate. Using a sharp knife, loosen and remove pit. Treat cut surfaces with lemon juice to avoid discoloration.

COCONUT PEACH DESSERT

Coconut Peach Dessert

PREP: 15 min. **BAKE:** 20 min. + chilling

Inez Orsburn, Demotte, Indiana

If you enjoy peaches and coconut, you're sure to like this sweet fruit pizza-style treat. It is also great on an appetizer table or for a potluck.

1-1/3   cups flaked coconut
 1/2   cup chopped almonds
 1/3   cup sugar
   2   tablespoons all-purpose flour
 1/8   teaspoon salt
   2   egg whites, lightly beaten
 1/2   teaspoon almond extract

TOPPING:

   2   cups heavy whipping cream, whipped
   4   cups sliced fresh *or* frozen peaches, thawed
 1/2   cup sugar *or* honey

1) In a small bowl, combine the coconut, almonds, sugar, flour and salt. Stir in egg whites and extract. Line a baking sheet with foil; grease foil well. Spread the coconut mixture into a 9-in. circle on foil.

2) Bake at 325° for 20-25 minutes or until lightly browned. Cool on a wire rack. Refrigerate overnight.

3) Place the crust on a serving plate; spread with whipped cream. Combine peaches and sugar; spoon over cream. Cut into wedges; serve.

Yield: 8 servings.

NUTRITION FACTS: 1 wedge equals 358 calories, 21 g fat (12 g saturated fat), 41 mg cholesterol, 103 mg sodium, 42 g carbohydrate, 3 g fiber, 4 g protein.

Mixed Fruit Cobbler

PREP: 20 min. **BAKE:** 35 min.

Mary Katherine Pitts, Ambia, Indiana

The corn bread topping gives this old-fashioned fruit cobbler a brand-new taste. You can use most any combination of fruits to make it. A scoop of ice cream makes it extra special.

- 4 medium ripe apricots, peeled and sliced
- 2 large ripe nectarines, peeled and sliced
- 2 large ripe peaches, peeled and sliced
- 2/3 cup sugar, *divided*
- 2 tablespoons cornstarch
- 1 tablespoon cold butter, cut into small pieces
- 1 cup all-purpose flour
- 1/2 cup cornmeal
- 2 teaspoons baking powder
- 1/4 teaspoon ground cinnamon
- 1/8 teaspoon salt
- 1/2 cup milk
- 1/4 cup vegetable oil

1) In a large bowl, combine the fruit, 1/3 cup sugar and cornstarch. Spoon into a greased 8-in. square baking dish. Dot with butter.

2) In another bowl, combine the flour, cornmeal, baking powder, cinnamon, salt and remaining sugar. Stir in milk and oil just until moistened. Spread over fruit mixture.

3) Bake at 375° for 35-40 minutes or until bubbly and top is golden brown. Serve warm.

Yield: 9 servings.

NUTRITION FACTS: 1 serving equals 247 calories, 8 g fat (2 g saturated fat), 5 mg cholesterol, 109 mg sodium, 41 g carbohydrate, 2 g fiber, 3 g protein.

MIXED FRUIT COBBLER

Peeling Peaches

1) Place peaches in a large pot of boiling water for 10-20 seconds or until the skin splits.

2) Remove with a slotted spoon. Immediately place in an ice-water bath to cool fruit and stop the cooking process.

3) Use a paring knife to peel the skin, which should easily peel off. If stubborn areas of skin won't peel off, just return fruit to the boiling water for a few more seconds.

Roasted Rosemary Fruit Topping

PREP/TOTAL TIME: 25 min.

Mildred Sherrer, Fort Worth, Texas

While it seems odd to combine roasted rosemary and fruit, I think you'll find the unique flavors are perfect toppers for ice cream or frozen yogurt.

- 1 medium fresh peach
- 1 medium fresh plum
- 2 cups fresh *or* frozen pitted tart cherries, thawed
- 2 tablespoons butter, melted
- 2 tablespoons sugar
- 1 tablespoon lime juice
- 1 to 2 teaspoons minced fresh rosemary
- 2 cups reduced-fat vanilla ice cream *or* frozen yogurt

1) Prick the skin of the peach and plum with a fork. Cut in half; remove pits. Cut each half into eight slices. Place in a greased 15-in. x 10-in. x 1-in. baking pan. Add the cherries.

2) In a small bowl, combine the butter, sugar, lime juice and rosemary. Spoon over fruit. Bake at 400° for 13-15 minutes or until fruit is tender, stirring occasionally. Serve over ice cream or frozen yogurt. Drizzle with pan juices.

Yield: 4 servings.

NUTRITION FACTS: 1/2 cup topping with 1/2 cup ice cream equals 227 calories, 9 g fat (5 g saturated fat), 25 mg cholesterol, 117 mg sodium, 36 g carbohydrate, 2 g fiber, 4 g protein.

Pears

This sweet-and-juicy fruit is readily available in many varieties. Depending on the variety, the skin color can be green, yellow, red or a combination of colors.

Buying

Pears are available year-round. Peak season is July through January. Select pears that are plump. Avoid those with bruises, soft spots or cuts. For some varieties, the color of the skin will change as the pear ripens. Select firm pears for baking. For eating, select pears that give slightly when gently pressed.

Papayas

This pear-shaped, tropical fruit has a sweet-tart flavor and smooth flesh. The variety that's most commonly sold in America is the Solo, which weighs 1 to 2 pounds. Mexican-type papayas are larger (can be up to 20 pounds) with deep-red flesh.

Buying

Papayas are available year-round. Select papayas that have a golden yellow skin. Ripe fruit will give slightly when gently pressed and have a sweet aroma. Avoid bruised, soft or shriveled fruit.

Storage

Store ripe fruit in the refrigerator for 3-4 days. Store fruit that has slightly green skin or firm fruit at room temperature until ripened.

Yield: 1 pound (1 medium) = 1-3/4 cups sliced or cubed

Anjou
Sweet, spicy flavor. Tender, egg-shaped pear. Good for eating, cooking and in salads. Season: October through May.

Barlett
Sweet flavor. Tender, bell-shaped pear available with yellow and red skin. Good for eating, cooking and in salads. Season: August through January.

Bosc
Sweet, spicy flavor. Dense, bell-shaped pear with golden brown skin. Good for eating, poaching and cooking. Season: September through May.

Comice
Sweet with a fruity aroma. Smooth texture, yellow skin when ripe. Good for eating. Season: October through February.

Preparing Papaya

1) Wash fruit. Slice lengthwise in half. Scoop out seeds. The peppery seeds are edible but are generally discarded.

2) Peel papaya and slice or cube.

Seckel
Sweet, spicy flavor. Firm, grainy-textured, bell-shaped pear with olive-green skin with red blush. Good for cooking. Season: August through December.

Storage

Store unwashed ripe pears in the refrigerator away from other fruits and vegetables with strong aromas for 3-5 days. To ripen firm pears, place in a paper bag at room temperature for 2-3 days. Cut pears should be brushed with lemon, lime, orange or pineapple juice to prevent browning. Freeze for up to 1 year.

Yield: 1 pound (3 medium) = 3 cups sliced

Gorgonzola Pear Salad

PREP: 15 min. **BAKE:** 25 min.

Melinda Singer, Tarzana, California

Tired of tossed salads? Here's an irresistible variation featuring pears that makes an attractive and tasty first course. The cheese and pecans are nice additions. You'll appreciate how easy it is.

>   3 medium pears, cored and halved
>   3 tablespoons olive oil
> 1/2 teaspoon salt
>   6 cups spring mix salad greens
>   2 plum tomatoes, seeded and chopped
>   1 cup crumbled Gorgonzola cheese
> 1/2 cup pecan halves, toasted
> 3/4 cup balsamic vinaigrette

1) Place pears in an ungreased 13-in. x 9-in. x 2-in. baking dish. Drizzle with oil and sprinkle with salt. Bake, uncovered, at 400° for 25-30 minutes, basting occasionally with cooking juices.

2) In a large salad bowl, combine the greens, tomatoes, cheese and pecans. Drizzle with vinaigrette and toss to coat. Divide among six serving plates; top each with a pear half.

Yield: 6 servings.

NUTRITION FACTS: 1 serving equals 311 calories, 24 g fat (6 g saturated fat), 17 mg cholesterol, 716 mg sodium, 21 g carbohydrate, 5 g fiber, 6 g protein.

GORGONZOLA PEAR SALAD

Ruby Pears

PREP: 15 min. **BAKE:** 25 min.

Kathy Ginn, Washington Court House, Ohio

Cranberry sauce gives a sweet-tart taste to pear halves in this spiced side dish that's perfect for fall. It's excellent with chicken or pork dishes and can be enjoyed warm or chilled.

>   1 can (29 ounces) pear halves, drained
>   1 can (16 ounces) whole-berry cranberry sauce
> 1/4 cup sugar
>   2 tablespoons lemon juice
> 1/4 teaspoon ground cinnamon

1) Place pears cut side up in a greased 8-in. square baking dish. In a saucepan, combine cranberry sauce, sugar, lemon juice and cinnamon. Cook and stir until sugar is dissolved and mixture is heated through.

2) Spoon sauce over pears. Bake, uncovered, at 350° for 25-30 minutes or until heated through.

Yield: 5-6 servings.

NUTRITION FACTS: 1 serving equals 243 calories, trace fat (trace saturated fat), 0 cholesterol, 23 mg sodium, 63 g carbohydrate, 3 g fiber, trace protein.

Caramel Pear Crumble

PREP: 15 min. **BAKE:** 30 min.

Karen Ann Bland, Gove, Kansas

This is the first recipe I turn to after my mother shares juicy pears from her orchard. Its crumbly topping and hint of caramel keep friends asking for more.

> 1-1/4 cups all-purpose flour
>   1 cup quick-cooking oats
>   1 cup packed brown sugar
>   1 teaspoon ground cinnamon
> 1/2 cup butter, melted
>   20 caramels
>   1 tablespoon milk
>   3 medium pears, peeled and sliced

1) In a small bowl, combine the flour, oats, brown sugar and cinnamon. Stir in butter (mixture will be crumbly); set aside 1 cup. Press the remaining oat mixture into an ungreased 8-in. square baking dish.

2) In a small saucepan over low heat, cook and stir caramels and milk until caramels are melted and mixture is smooth. Remove from the heat.

3) Arrange pears over crust; spoon caramel mixture over pears. Sprinkle with the reserved crumb mixture.

4) Bake at 350° for 30-35 minutes or until pears are tender and top is golden brown. Serve warm.

Yield: 6 servings.

NUTRITION FACTS: 1 serving equals 598 calories, 19 g fat (12 g saturated fat), 44 mg cholesterol, 253 mg sodium, 103 g carbohydrate, 5 g fiber, 7 g protein.

ELEGANT POACHED PEARS

 CLASSIC: Pomegranate juice and red wine give the rosy hue to Pomegranate Poached Pears. This impressive company dessert is presented with an orange slice, rich Mascarpone cheese and a drizzle of the reduced poaching liquid spiced with orange peel, rosemary and cinnamon.

 TIME-SAVER: End your next meal with delightful Dessert Pears, a treat that's ready in minutes but looks like you fussed. Only four ingredients are needed to fix these fruity pears, which are cooked in the microwave to save time.

 LIGHT: Chinese five-spice powder, cinnamon and honey give a sweet and spicy touch to these lightened-up poached pears. Compared to Pomegranate Poached Pears, each serving of Spiced Honey Pears has 324 fewer calories, 1 gram of fat, no cholesterol and a trace of sodium.

 SERVES 2: Surprise someone special with Chocolate Pears in Caramel Sauce, a decadent dessert sized right for two. Tender baked pears are placed in a pool of caramel and macadamia nuts, then drizzled with a rich chocolate sauce for a restaurant-worthy presentation.

POMEGRANATE POACHED PEARS

Pomegranate Poached Pears

PREP: 20 min. **COOK:** 1 hour 25 min.

Bev Jones, Brunswick, Missouri

- 3 cups dry red wine *or* red grape juice
- 1 bottle (16 ounces) pomegranate juice
- 1 cup water
- 1/2 cup sugar
- 1/4 cup orange juice
- 2 tablespoons grated orange peel
- 3 fresh rosemary sprigs (4 inches)
- 1 cinnamon stick (3 inches)
- 6 medium pears
- 6 orange slices
- 6 tablespoons Mascarpone cheese

1) In a Dutch oven, combine the wine or grape juice, pomegranate juice, water, sugar, orange juice and peel, rosemary and cinnamon. Core pears from the bottom, leaving stems intact. Peel pears; place on their sides in the Dutch oven. Bring to a boil. Reduce heat; cover and simmer for 25-30 minutes or until pears are almost tender.

2) Remove pears with a slotted spoon; cool. Strain poaching liquid and return to the pan. Bring to a boil; cook until reduced to 1 cup, about 45 minutes.

3) Discard rosemary and cinnamon. Place an orange slice on each serving plate; top with 1 tablespoon cheese and a pear. Drizzle with poaching liquid.

Yield: 6 servings.

NUTRITION FACTS: 1 serving equals 443 calories, 13 g fat (7 g saturated fat), 35 mg cholesterol, 32 mg sodium, 61 g carbohydrate, 6 g fiber, 3 g protein.

Dessert Pears

PREP/TOTAL TIME: 15 min.

Terri Casteel, Fairfax, Virginia

- 4 medium pears, peeled, halved and cored
- 1/4 cup cranberry juice
- 1/4 cup strawberry preserves
- 1/2 teaspoon vanilla extract

1) Place pears in a 9-in. square microwave-safe dish. Combine the cranberry juice, preserves and vanilla; pour over pears. Cover and microwave on high for 7-9 minutes or until pears are tender. Serve warm.

Yield: 4 servings.

NUTRITION FACTS: 1 pear equals 156 calories, 1 g fat (trace saturated fat), 0 cholesterol, trace sodium, 40 g carbohydrate, 4 g fiber, 1 g protein.

Spiced Honey Pears

PREP/TOTAL TIME: 15 min.

Taste of Home Test Kitchen

- 6 medium ripe pears
- 2 tablespoons honey
- 1/4 to 1/2 teaspoon Chinese five-spice powder
- 1/4 to 1/2 teaspoon ground cinnamon

1) Cut a 3/4-in. slice off the top of each pear, reserving tops. Core pears, leaving bottoms intact. If necessary, cut 1/8 in. from bottoms to level. Drizzle inside of each pear with 1 teaspoon of honey. Combine the five-spice powder and cinnamon; sprinkle inside pears. Replace the pear tops.

2) Arrange pears upright in a shallow 2-qt. microwave-safe dish. Microwave, uncovered, on high for 4-7 minutes or until pears are tender, turning every 2 minutes. Serve warm with juices spooned over pears.

Yield: 6 servings.

NUTRITION FACTS: 1 pear equals 119 calories, 1 g fat (trace saturated fat), 0 cholesterol, trace sodium, 31 g carbohydrate, 4 g fiber, 1 g protein.

Coaring Pears Like a Pro

To core a fresh whole pear, insert an apple corer into the bottom of the pear to within 1-in. of its top. Twist the corer to cut around the core, then slowly pull the corer out of the pear to remove the core. If you don't have an apple corer, use a sharp knife or vegetable peeler to cut the core from the bottom of the pear.

For fresh pear halves, a melon baller is the perfect tool for removing the core.

CHOCOLATE PEARS IN CARAMEL SAUCE

Chocolate Pears in Caramel Sauce

PREP: 15 min. **BAKE:** 25 min.

Margaret Pache, Mesa, Arizona

- 2 medium ripe pears
- 1-1/2 teaspoons lemon juice
- 3 tablespoons butter, melted, *divided*
- 1 tablespoon sugar
- 2 squares (1 ounce *each*) semisweet chocolate
- 1-1/2 teaspoons heavy whipping cream
- 6 tablespoons caramel ice cream topping
- 1/4 cup chopped macadamia nuts, toasted

1) Core pears from bottom, leaving stems intact. Peel pears. If necessary, cut 1/4 in. from bottom to level. Place in a small baking dish. Brush pears with lemon juice and 1 tablespoon butter. Sprinkle with sugar. Bake, uncovered, at 375° for 25 minutes or until tender, basting occasionally.

2) In a small saucepan, combine the chocolate, cream and remaining butter. Heat over low heat until smooth, stirring occasionally. Combine caramel topping and macadamia nuts; spoon onto dessert plates. Place pears upright on plates; spoon chocolate sauce over pears.

Yield: 2 servings.

NUTRITION FACTS: 1 serving equals 632 calories, 36 g fat (16 g saturated fat), 52 mg cholesterol, 434 mg sodium, 83 g carbohydrate, 7 g fiber, 4 g protein.

Baked Stuffed Pears

PREP: 15 min. **BAKE:** 30 min.

Marie Labanowski, New Hampton, New York

This simple dessert is a tasty ending to our Thanksgiving meal of roast turkey or pork. Pears are a yummy change from the typical apples.

- 4 medium ripe pears
- 2 tablespoons lemon juice, *divided*
- 1/3 cup coarsely chopped walnuts
- 1/4 cup golden raisins
- 2 tablespoons maple syrup
- 2 teaspoons brown sugar
- 1 teaspoon grated lemon peel
- 1/8 teaspoon ground cinnamon
- 1 tablespoon butter
- 2/3 cup apple juice

1) Core pears and peel 1 in. down from the top on each. Brush peeled portion with some of the lemon juice. Place in a greased 1-qt. baking dish.

2) In a bowl, combine the walnuts, raisins, syrup, brown sugar, lemon peel, cinnamon and remaining lemon juice. Spoon into pears. Dot with butter. Pour apple juice around pears.

3) Bake, uncovered, at 350° for 30-40 minutes or until pears are tender, basting several times.

Yield: 4 servings.

NUTRITION FACTS: 1 serving equals 707 calories, 12 g fat (2 g saturated fat), 8 mg cholesterol, 33 mg sodium, 160 g carbohydrate, 23 g fiber, 6 g protein.

Pears with Raspberry Sauce

PREP: 10 min. **BAKE:** 1-1/2 hours

Florence Palmer, Marshall, Illinois

Pears and raspberries are two seasonal favorites showcased in this simple recipe.

- 6 medium ripe pears
- 2 tablespoons honey
- 2 tablespoons lemon juice
- 1/4 cup reduced-sugar raspberry fruit spread
- 2 tablespoons cider vinegar
- 2 cups fresh *or* frozen raspberries

1) Core pears from bottom. Cut 1/4 in. from bottom to level if necessary. Set upright in an 8-in. square baking dish. Combine honey and lemon juice; pour over pears. Cover and bake at 350° for 1-1/2 hours or until pears are tender, basting occasionally.

2) In a saucepan, combine fruit spread and vinegar; stir in berries. Cook over medium-low heat until heated through; spoon over pears. Serve warm.

Yield: 6 servings.

NUTRITION FACTS: 1 serving equals 166 calories, 1 g fat (0 saturated fat), 0 cholesterol, 4 mg sodium, 42 g carbohydrate, 0 fiber, 1 g protein.

PEAR 'N' APPLE COBBLER

Pear 'n' Apple Cobbler

PREP: 20 min. **BAKE:** 35 min.

Shirley Brown, Chubbuck, Idaho

Nutmeg lends a homey touch to apple pie filling and canned pears topped with tender biscuits. I've received many great comments about this dessert from my family and friends. Vanilla ice cream would make a wonderful addition to it.

- 2 teaspoons cornstarch
- 1/4 teaspoon plus 1/8 teaspoon ground nutmeg, *divided*
- 2/3 cup orange juice
- 1 can (21 ounces) apple pie filling
- 1 can (15-1/4 ounces) sliced pears, drained
- 1-1/2 cups biscuit/baking mix
- 2 tablespoons plus 2 teaspoons sugar, *divided*
- 1/2 cup milk
- 2 tablespoons butter, melted

1) In a large saucepan, combine the cornstarch, 1/4 teaspoon of nutmeg and orange juice until smooth. Gently stir in pie filling and pears. Bring to a boil; cook and stir for 1-2 minutes or until thickened. Keep warm.

2) In a small bowl, combine biscuit mix, 2 tablespoons sugar, milk and butter just until blended. Pour hot filling into an ungreased 11-in. x 7-in. x 2-in. baking dish.

3) Drop batter in six mounds onto fruit mixture. Combine the remaining sugar and nutmeg; sprinkle over the top.

4) Bake at 350° for 35-40 minutes or until fruit mixture is bubbly and a toothpick inserted in a biscuit comes out clean. Serve warm.

Yield: 6 servings.

NUTRITION FACTS: 1 serving equals 352 calories, 9 g fat (4 g saturated fat), 13 mg cholesterol, 476 mg sodium, 66 g carbohydrate, 2 g fiber, 4 g protein.

Persimmons

The two varieties available are the Hachiya and Fuyu. The Hachiya is heart-shaped and deep orange; it must be fully ripened before eating or it becomes astringent. Fuyu persimmons are pale orange and look somewhat like a squashed tomato.

Buying

Persimmons are available October through February. Select plump, slightly firm fruit with smooth, glossy skin; the cap end should still be attached. Avoid fruit that is bruised or has cuts in the skin.

Storage

Store ripe fruit in the refrigerator for up to 3 days. To ripen, place in a paper bag at room temperature for 1-3 days. The pulp from the Hachiya persimmon may be frozen in an airtight container.

Hachiya is ripe when it is soft. To use, cut in half and scoop out pulp with a spoon. Discard seeds. Puree pulp if desired. Use for eating and cooking. Fuyu is still firm but not hard when it is ripe. To use, peel, core and slice. Use for eating and making salads.

Yield: 1 medium (4-3/4 ounces) Fuyu = 2/3 cup sliced
1 large (9 ounces) Hachiya = 2/3 cup pulp

PERSIMMON NUT ROLL

Persimmon Nut Roll

PREP: 25 min. **BAKE:** 15 min. + cooling

Nancy Wilson, Van Nuys, California

For holiday gift-giving, I make a dozen or so of these cake rolls to share with friends and neighbors. They slice nicely straight from the freezer.

    3 eggs
    1 cup sugar
  2/3 cup mashed ripe persimmon pulp
    1 teaspoon lemon juice
    1 cup self-rising flour
    2 teaspoons ground cinnamon
    1 teaspoon baking powder
    1 teaspoon ground ginger
  1/2 teaspoon salt
  1/2 teaspoon ground nutmeg
    1 cup chopped pecans
FILLING:
    1 package (8 ounces) cream cheese, softened
  1/4 cup butter, softened
    1 cup confectioners' sugar
    1 teaspoon vanilla extract
Additional confectioners' sugar

1) Line a 15-in. x 10-in. x 1-in. baking pan with waxed paper and grease the paper; set aside. In a large mixing bowl, beat eggs for 5 minutes on medium speed or until lemon-colored. Gradually add the sugar, persimmon pulp and lemon juice; beat for 3 minutes.

2) Combine the flour, cinnamon, baking powder, ginger, salt and nutmeg; add to egg mixture and beat well. Spread batter evenly in prepared pan; sprinkle with pecans. Bake at 375° for 15 minutes or until lightly browned. Cool in pan for 5 minutes.

3) Turn cake onto a kitchen towel dusted with confectioners' sugar. Gently peel off waxed paper. Roll up cake in the towel jelly-roll style, starting with a short side. Cool completely on a wire rack.

4) For filling, in a small mixing bowl, beat cream cheese and butter until smooth. Beat in the confectioners' sugar and vanilla. Unroll cake and spread filling evenly over cake to within 1/2 in. of edges. Roll up again.

5) Cover and refrigerate until serving. Dust with additional confectioners' sugar. Refrigerate or freeze leftovers.

Yield: 10 servings.

Editor's Note: As a substitute for self-rising flour, place 1-1/2 teaspoons baking powder and 1/2 teaspoon salt in a measuring cup. Add all-purpose flour to measure 1 cup.

NUTRITION FACTS: 1 slice (calculated without additional confectioners' sugar) equals 402 calories, 23 g fat (9 g saturated fat), 101 mg cholesterol, 435 mg sodium, 47 g carbohydrate, 2 g fiber, 6 g protein.

Glazed Persimmon Bars

PREP: 15 min. **BAKE:** 20 min. + cooling

Delores Leach, Penn Valley, California

Persimmons are an excellent source of vitamins A and C and are rich in fiber. They star in these dessert bars along with dates and nuts.

- 1 cup mashed ripe persimmon pulp
- 1 cup sugar
- 1/2 cup vegetable oil
- 1 egg
- 1-1/2 teaspoons lemon juice
- 1-3/4 cups all-purpose flour
- 1 teaspoon baking soda
- 1 teaspoon salt
- 1 teaspoon ground cinnamon
- 1 teaspoon ground nutmeg
- 1/4 teaspoon ground cloves, optional
- 1-1/2 cups chopped dates *or* raisins
- 1 cup chopped nuts

GLAZE:
- 1 cup confectioners' sugar
- 2 tablespoons lemon juice

1) In a large mixing bowl, combine the persimmon pulp, sugar, oil, egg and lemon juice. Combine the flour, baking soda, salt, cinnamon, nutmeg and cloves if desired; add to sugar mixture. Stir in dates and nuts.

2) Spread into a greased 15-in. x 10-in. x 1-in. baking pan. Bake at 350° for 20-25 minutes or until a toothpick inserted near the center comes out clean. Cool on a wire rack. Combine glaze ingredients; spread over cooled bars.

Yield: 4 dozen.

NUTRITION FACTS: 1 bar equals 99 calories, 4 g fat (trace saturated fat), 4 mg cholesterol, 77 mg sodium, 16 g carbohydrate, 1 g fiber, 1 g protein.

Pineapple

This sweet-tangy, juicy, fibrous fruit has a bumpy diamond-shaped pattern on its skin. It must be picked ripe, as it will not get sweeter after it's been picked.

Buying

Pineapple is available year-round. Select pineapple that is plump and fresh looking, is slightly soft and has a sweet fragrance. Avoid fruit with dry or brown leaves, bruises and soft spots.

Storage

Store ripe fruit in the refrigerator for up to 4 days. Refrigerate cut fruit in an airtight container for up to 3 days.

Cutting Up Fresh Pineapple

1) Cut off crown of the fruit. Stand pineapple upright and cut off the rind using a sharp knife. Cut off the base.

2) Follow the pattern of the eyes to cut diagonal wedge-shaped grooves in pineapple. Remove the wedges.

3) Stand pineapple upright and cut off fruit next to, but not through, the core. Cut pieces into chunks or spears.

Pineapple Cobbler

PREP: 10 min. **BAKE:** 40 min.

Aljene Wendling, Seattle, Washington

I think of our trip to Hawaii every time I taste this favorite. It's made with juicy fresh pineapple, which is a nice change from the usual cobbler ingredients.

- 1 cup sugar
- 1/3 cup biscuit/baking mix
- 1 teaspoon grated lemon peel
- 4 cups fresh pineapple chunks

TOPPING:

- 3/4 cup biscuit/baking mix
- 2/3 cup sugar
- 1 egg, beaten
- 1/4 cup butter, melted

Vanilla ice cream, optional

1) In a large bowl, combine the sugar, biscuit mix and lemon peel; stir in pineapple. Pour into a greased 9-in. square baking dish.

2) Combine biscuit mix, sugar and egg; sprinkle over pineapple mixture. Drizzle with butter. Bake at 350° for 40-45 minutes or until browned. Serve warm with ice cream if desired.

Yield: 9 servings.

NUTRITION FACTS: 1 serving equals 289 calories, 8 g fat (4 g saturated fat), 37 mg cholesterol, 241 mg sodium, 55 g carbohydrate, 1 g fiber, 2 g protein.

HEALTHIER FRUIT SALAD ■■■

When making fruit salad, I sometimes use fat-free whipped topping mixed with vanilla yogurt. Everyone seems to enjoy it just as much as the traditional version, but it has fewer calories and less fat.

—*Marie R., Lake Charles, Louisiana*

Hawaiian Fruit Salad

PREP/TOTAL TIME: 30 min.

Taste of Home Test Kitchen

A simple dressing made with flavored yogurt coats this refreshing combination of fresh and canned fruit. It looks spectacular when presented in a pineapple boat and sprinkled with coconut.

- 1 whole fresh pineapple
- 1 can (15 ounces) mandarin oranges, drained
- 1-1/2 cups sliced fresh strawberries
- 1-1/2 cups green grapes, halved
- 1-1/4 cups pina colada-flavored *or* vanilla yogurt
- 1/2 cup flaked coconut, toasted, *divided*
- 1/4 to 1/2 teaspoon coconut *or* vanilla extract

1) Stand the pineapple upright and vertically cut a third from one side, leaving the leaves attached. Set cut piece aside.

HAWAIIAN FRUIT SALAD

2) Using a paring or grapefruit knife, remove strips of pineapple from large section, leaving a 1/2-in. shell; discard core. Cut the strips into bite-size chunks. Invert shell onto paper towels to drain.

3) Remove fruit from the small pineapple piece and cut into chunks; discard peel. Place shell in a serving basket or bowl.

4) In another bowl, combine the pineapple chunks, oranges, strawberries and grapes. Combine the yogurt, 1/4 cup coconut and extract; spoon over fruit and stir gently. Spoon into pineapple shell. Sprinkle with remaining coconut.

Yield: 6 servings.

NUTRITION FACTS: 1 serving equals 203 calories, 5 g fat (4 g saturated fat), 5 mg cholesterol, 55 mg sodium, 38 g carbohydrate, 3 g fiber, 4 g protein.

Spiced Pineapple

PREP/TOTAL TIME: 25 min.

Chris Nash, Berthoud, Colorado

This is a nice complement to lamb chops or ham. It's a no-fuss side dish that really makes a meal stand out.

- 2 cans (one 20 ounces, one 8 ounces), unsweetened pineapple chunks
- 1-1/4 cups sugar
- 1/2 cup cider vinegar
- 1 cinnamon stick (3 inches)
- 6 to 8 whole cloves

Dash salt

1) Drain pineapple, reserving 1 cup juice. In a saucepan, combine the sugar, vinegar, cinnamon, cloves, salt and reserved juice. Bring to a boil. Reduce heat; cover and simmer for 10 minutes.

2) Discard cinnamon and cloves. Add pineapple. Return to a boil; cook and stir for 2-3 minutes. Serve warm with a slotted spoon.

Yield: 4-6 servings.

NUTRITION FACTS: 3/4 cup equals 229 calories, 0 fat (0 saturated fat), 0 cholesterol, 36 mg sodium, 59 g carbohydrate, 1 g fiber, 0 g protein.

Hot Pineapple Side Dish

PREP: 10 min. **BAKE:** 30 min.

Alice Blackley, Elkin, North Carolina

The first time I passed along this treasured recipe was to Taste of Home. It's handed down from my mother, and it's always been special to me.

- 1 can (20 ounces) pineapple chunks
- 1/2 cup sugar
- 3 tablespoons all-purpose flour
- 1/4 cup butter, melted
- 1-1/2 cups (6 ounces) shredded cheddar cheese, *divided*
- 2/3 cup coarsely crushed saltines (14 crackers)

1) Drain the pineapple, reserving 1/4 cup juice; set aside. In a small bowl, combine sugar and flour. Add the butter and 1 cup cheese; mix well. Gently stir in pineapple.

2) Pour into a greased 1-1/2-qt. baking dish. Sprinkle crushed crackers on top; drizzle with reserved pineapple juice.

3) Bake, uncovered, at 350° for 30-35 minutes or until bubbly around edges. Remove from the oven and sprinkle with the remaining cheese.

Yield: 6 servings.

NUTRITION FACTS: 1/2 cup equals 330 calories, 16 g fat (11 g saturated fat), 50 mg cholesterol, 335 mg sodium, 40 g carbohydrate, 1 g fiber, 8 g protein.

FRUIT SALSA WITH GINGER CHIPS

Fruit Salsa with Ginger Chips

PREP: 15 min. + chilling **BAKE:** 5 min. + cooling

Christy Johnson, Columbus, Ohio

This combination of fruity salsa and crisp gingery chips is wonderful on a hot day. I like to serve this with pineapple iced tea, which I make by simply adding some of the drained pineapple juice from this recipe to a pitcher of tea.

- 1 can (20 ounces) unsweetened crushed pineapple
- 1 large mango *or* 2 medium peaches, peeled and chopped
- 2 medium kiwifruit, peeled and chopped
- 1/4 cup chopped macadamia nuts
- 4-1/2 teaspoons brown sugar
- 4-1/2 teaspoons flaked coconut
- 8 flour tortillas (8 inches)
- 1 tablespoon water
- 1/4 cup sugar
- 1 to 2 teaspoons ground ginger

1) Drain pineapple, reserving 3 tablespoons juice. In a large bowl, combine the pineapple, mango, kiwi, nuts, brown sugar, coconut and reserved juice. Cover and refrigerate for at least 1 hour.

2) For chips, lightly brush one side of each tortilla with water. Combine sugar and ginger; sprinkle over the moistened side of tortillas. Cut each into six wedges. Place in a single layer on ungreased baking sheets. Bake at 400° for 5-7 minutes or until golden brown and crisp. Cool on wire racks. Serve with salsa.

Yield: 12 servings.

NUTRITION FACTS: 1/4 cup salsa with 4 chips equals 190 calories, 4 g fat (1 g saturated fat), 0 cholesterol, 173 mg sodium, 35 g carbohydrate, 1 g fiber, 3 g protein.

Warm Fruit Compote

PREP/TOTAL TIME: 15 min.

Page Alexander, Baldwin City, Kansas

This sunny-colored medley smells so good while it cooks. The cream cheese topping adds a touch of elegance.

- 1/4 cup packed brown sugar
- 1 teaspoon cornstarch
- 1/4 cup water
- 1/4 cup orange juice concentrate
- 2 tablespoons butter
- 1 can (20 ounces) pineapple chunks, drained
- 1 can (15-1/4 ounces) sliced pears, drained and halved
- 1 can (15 ounces) mandarin oranges, drained

TOPPING:

- 1 package (3 ounces) cream cheese, softened
- 1 tablespoon sugar
- 1 tablespoon orange juice concentrate

1) In a large saucepan, combine the brown sugar and cornstarch. Stir in the water and orange juice concentrate until smooth.

2) Add butter. Bring to a boil; cook and stir for 2 minutes or until thickened. Reduce heat. Add the fruit; heat through.

3) In a small mixing bowl, beat all of the topping ingredients until smooth. Dollop over fruit.

Yield: 6 servings.

NUTRITION FACTS: 1 serving equals 263 calories, 9 g fat (5 g saturated fat), 26 mg cholesterol, 94 mg sodium, 45 g carbohydrate, 1 g fiber, 3 g protein.

Plums

Many varieties of plums are available, including Santa Rosa, Kelsey, mirabelle and greengage, to name a few. The skin may be red, purple, yellow, green and blue. The flavor may be sweet or tart. Plums must be picked ripe, as they will not get sweeter after they've been picked.

Buying

Plums are available June through November. Select plump fruit. Ripe plums will give slightly when gently pressed and have a fruity aroma. Avoid hard, bruised, soft or shriveled fruit.

Storage

Store unwashed ripe plums in the refrigerator for 3-5 days. To ripen, place in a paper bag at room temperature for 1-3 days.

Yield: 1 pound (4-5 medium) = 2 to 2-1/2 cups halved or 2-1/2 cups sliced

Spiced Dried Plums

PREP: 10 min. + cooling

Alcy Thorne, Los Molinos, California

We harvest 42 acres of plums on our ranch. I like to serve these plums along with meats or cottage cheese salad. They also make a nice breakfast fruit.

- 1 pound pitted dried plums
- 2 cups water
- 1 teaspoon ground cinnamon
- 1 teaspoon ground cloves
- 1/2 teaspoon ground ginger
- 3 tablespoons lemon juice

1) In a saucepan over medium heat, combine the plums, water, cinnamon, cloves and ginger; bring to a boil.

2) Remove from the heat; cover and let stand until cool. Stir in lemon juice. Store, covered, in the refrigerator.

Yield: 8 servings.

NUTRITION FACTS: 1 serving equals 159 calories, trace fat (trace saturated fat), 0 cholesterol, 8 mg sodium, 38 g carbohydrate, 3 g fiber, 1 g protein.

Pretty Plum Parfaits

PREP: 30 min. + chilling

Norma Reynolds, York, Pennsylvania

This is a refreshing way to use garden-fresh plums. Red or purple varieties both work well.

- 9 to 12 medium ripe red *or* purple plums (2 pounds), sliced
- 1/2 cup red currant jelly
- 1/2 cup packed brown sugar
- 1 orange peel strip (1 to 3 inches)
- 1 cinnamon stick (3 inches)
- 1 cup heavy whipping cream
- 1 tablespoon confectioners' sugar
- 1/2 teaspoon vanilla extract

Pirouette cookies and additional whipped cream and plum slices, optional

1) In a large heavy saucepan, combine the plums, jelly, brown sugar, orange peel and cinnamon stick. Bring to a boil. Reduce heat; simmer, uncovered, for 10-15 minutes or until plums are tender, stirring occasionally.

2) Remove from the heat; cool slightly. Discard orange peel and cinnamon stick; coarsely mash plums. Cover and refrigerate.

3) Just before serving, in a small mixing bowl, beat cream until it begins to thicken. Add the confectioners' sugar and vanilla; beat until stiff peaks form.

4) Place about 1/4 cup plum mixture into each of four chilled parfait glasses; top with 1/4 cup whipped cream. Repeat layers. Top with the remaining plum mixture. Garnish with a cookie, a dollop of whipped cream and a plum slice if desired.

Yield: 4 servings.

NUTRITION FACTS: 1 parfait equals 499 calories, 23 g fat (14 g saturated fat), 82 mg cholesterol, 33 mg sodium, 76 g carbohydrate, 2 g fiber, 2 g protein.

PRETTY PLUM PARFAITS

Plum Bumble

PREP: 10 min. **BAKE:** 45 min.

Arlis Enburg, Rock Island, Illinois

I've served this recipe numerous times to family and friends. Similar to a cobbler, it is always a favorite.

- 1 cup plus 5 teaspoons sugar, *divided*
- 1/4 cup cornstarch
- 3 cups sliced fresh plums (about 1-1/4 pounds)
- 3/4 cup pineapple tidbits
- 2 tablespoons butter, *divided*
- 1/2 teaspoon ground cinnamon
- 1 tube (7-1/2 ounces) refrigerated buttermilk biscuits, separated and quartered

1) In a large bowl, combine 1 cup sugar, cornstarch, plums and pineapple. Transfer to a greased shallow 2-qt. baking dish; dot with 1 tablespoon butter. Bake, uncovered, at 400° for 15 minutes.

2) Meanwhile, melt remaining butter. In a small bowl, combine cinnamon and remaining sugar. Place biscuit pieces over hot plum mixture; brush with butter and sprinkle with cinnamon-sugar. Bake 25-30 minutes longer or until biscuits are golden brown. Serve warm.

Yield: 6 servings.

NUTRITION FACTS: 1 serving 344 calories, 5 g fat (3 g saturated fat), 10 mg cholesterol, 343 mg sodium, 74 g carbohydrate, 2 g fiber, 4 g protein.

Pomegranates

Pomegranates are about the size of an apple and have a deep red to purplish-red leathery rind. The only part of the pomegranate that is edible are the sweet-tart seeds and their surrounding juice sacs (arils). The fruit can cause permanent stains. Eat the seeds as a fruit or use as a garnish for salads and desserts.

Buying

Pomegranates are available September through January. Select fruit that is heavy for its size and is fresh looking. Avoid bruised, soft or shriveled fruit.

Storage

Store at room temperature out of direct sunlight for several weeks. Refrigerate for up to 3 months. The seeds may be frozen in an airtight container.

Yield: 1 medium (8 ounces) = 3/4 cup arils

Opening a Pomegranate

1) Cut off the crown of the fruit and score in quarters, taking care not to cut into the red juice sacs (arils).

2) Place the sections in a bowl of water and soak for 5 minutes. Break sections open with your finger and gently push out the seed clusters with your fingers. Discard skin and white membrane. Drain water, reserving arils. Dry on paper towels. The arils may be eaten whole, seeds and all.

Pomegranate Gelatin

PREP: 15 min. + chilling

Deidre Hobbs, Redding, California

As a former home economics teacher, I like to surprise dinner guests with recipes that are a little more special. This salad combines sweet and tart tastes.

- 2 packages (3 ounces *each*) raspberry gelatin
- 2 cups boiling water
- 1 cup cold water
- 1-1/2 cups pomegranate arils/juice sacs (about 2 pomegranates)
- 1 can (8 ounces) crushed pineapple, drained
- 1/2 cup sour cream
- 1/2 cup mayonnaise

1) In a large bowl, dissolve gelatin in boiling water. Stir in the cold water, pomegranate arils and pineapple. Pour into an 11-in. x 7-in. x 2-in. dish. Refrigerate until firm.

2) Combine sour cream and mayonnaise; spread over gelatin. Refrigerate until serving.

Yield: 10 servings.

NUTRITION FACTS: 1 cup equals 194 calories, 11 g fat (3 g saturated fat), 12 mg cholesterol, 106 mg sodium, 22 g carbohydrate, trace fiber, 2 g protein.

ZESTY FRUIT SALAD ■■■

To ordinary fruit salad (cut-up apples, oranges, bananas, grapes), I sprinkle in powdered lemonade mix to taste. It adds a sweet tang to the fruit.

—Merilee Nevins, Lawton, Oklahoma

Rhubarb

The stalks of rhubarb vary in color from pale pink to cherry red. Its tart flavor lends itself to sugar-enhanced pies, desserts, sauces, relishes and jams.

Buying

Rhubarb is available April through June. Select rhubarb that is firm and crisp. Avoid limp stalks.

Storage

Store unwashed rhubarb in the refrigerator for up to 1 week. Sliced rhubarb can be frozen for 9 months.

Preparation

Always trim and discard any leaves, which contain oxalic acid and are toxic. Thick stalks can be peeled with a vegetable peeler to remove the fibrous strings.

Yield: 1 pound = 3 cups chopped raw or 2 cups cooked

Easy Rhubarb Dessert

PREP: 10 min. **BAKE:** 35 min.

Deb Jesse, Storm Lake, Iowa

I start with a cake mix and add fresh rhubarb, sugar and cream to create this dessert in a jiffy.

> 1 package (18-1/2 ounces) yellow cake mix
> 5 cups diced fresh *or* frozen rhubarb
> 1 cup sugar
> 1 cup heavy whipping cream

1) Prepare the cake batter according to package directions. Pour into a greased 13-in. x 9-in. x 2-in. baking pan. Spread rhubarb over batter. Sprinkle with sugar; pour cream over the top. Do not mix.

2) Bake at 350° for 35-40 minutes or until a toothpick inserted into the cake comes out clean. Serve warm or cooled.

Yield: 16 servings.

NUTRITION FACTS: 1 piece equals 245 calories, 9 g fat (5 g saturated fat), 20 mg cholesterol, 213 mg sodium, 41 g carbohydrate, 1 g fiber, 2 g protein.

Star Fruit

When the five-ribbed carambola is sliced, it forms a star shape, hence its common name of star fruit. The sweet-tart flavor of this fruit seems to combine plums, grapes, apples, pineapple and citrus.

Buying

Star fruit is available from late summer to midwinter. Select plump fruit with glossy, golden-yellow skin. Choose fruit with wider-spaced ribs, which are said to be sweeter than the narrower-spaced ribs. Avoid fruit with browned ribs.

Storage

Refrigerate unwashed ripe fruit for up to 2 weeks. Fruit with green-tipped ribs is unripe. Keep at room temperature until it's yellow and has a fruity fragrance.

Preparation

Wash before using. Cut into slices. It's good for eating, using in salads and desserts or garnishing.

Yield: 1 medium (3-3/4 ounces) = 1 cup sliced

Watermelon

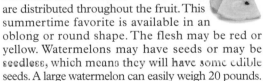

Watermelon belongs to the gourd family, which also includes squash and cucumbers, but more closely resembles a cucumber since the seeds are distributed throughout the fruit. This summertime favorite is available in an oblong or round shape. The flesh may be red or yellow. Watermelons may have seeds or may be seedless, which means they will have some edible seeds. A large watermelon can easily weigh 20 pounds.

Buying

Watermelon is available year-round. Peak season is May through September. Select watermelons with a hard, green rind that has a dull appearance. The part that rested on the ground will be creamy yellow or white color. To test for ripeness, slap the side with the palm of your hand. A deep thump means it is ripe.

Storage

Store in the refrigerator for up to 1 week. Store cut melon, wrapped in plastic wrap or in an airtight container, in the refrigerator.

Yield: 1 pound = about 1 cup cubes

TANGY WATERMELON SALAD

Melon Cucumber Medley

PREP: 15 min. + chilling

Edie DeSpain, Logan, Utah

A light, lemony dressing complements a beautiful mixture of melons and sliced cucumbers. This delightful summer salad is especially good served at a brunch or luncheon.

> 1/2 cup vegetable oil
> 1/4 cup lemon juice
> 1 teaspoon sugar
> 1/2 teaspoon salt

Dash pepper

> 6 cups melon balls *or* cubes (cantaloupe, honeydew *and/or* watermelon)
> 3 medium cucumbers, peeled and thinly sliced

Lettuce leaves, optional

1) In a jar with a tight-fitting lid, combine the oil, lemon juice, sugar, salt and pepper; shake until sugar is dissolved.

2) In a large bowl, combine melon and cucumbers; drizzle with dressing and gently toss to coat. Cover and refrigerate for at least 1 hour. Serve in a lettuce-lined bowl if desired.

Yield: 12 servings.

NUTRITION FACTS: 3/4 cup equals 119 calories, 9 g fat (1 g saturated fat), 0 cholesterol, 100 mg sodium, 9 g carbohydrate, 1 g fiber, 1 g protein.

Tangy Watermelon Salad

PREP: 35 min. + chilling

Alisha Duncan, Blanchard, Oklahoma

I rely on this refreshing blend of watermelon, onion and a splash of citrus to serve at summer picnics and potlucks. I like to prepare it a day ahead so the flavors have a chance to blend, and after scooping out the melon, I like to keep the rind for a colorful serving bowl. To save time, you can substitute any bottled citrus vinaigrette for the homemade dressing.

> 14 cups cubed seedless watermelon
> 1 medium red onion, halved and thinly sliced
> 1 cup chopped green onions
> 3/4 cup orange juice
> 5 tablespoons red wine vinegar
> 2 tablespoons plus 1-1/2 teaspoons honey
> 1 tablespoon finely chopped sweet red pepper
> 1/2 teaspoon salt
> 1/4 teaspoon onion powder
> 1/4 teaspoon garlic powder
> 1/4 teaspoon ground mustard
> 1/4 teaspoon pepper
> 3/4 cup vegetable oil

1) In a large bowl, combine the watermelon and onions. In a small bowl, combine the orange juice, vinegar, honey, red pepper and seasonings; slowly whisk in the oil.

2) Pour over watermelon mixture; toss gently to coat. Cover and refrigerate for at least 2 hours, stirring occasionally. Serve with a slotted spoon.

Yield: 16 servings.

NUTRITION FACTS: 3/4 cup equals 147 calories, 10 g fat (1 g saturated fat), 0 cholesterol, 80 mg sodium, 17 g carbohydrate, 1 g fiber, 1 g protein.

MELON CUCUMBER MEDLEY

food, fellowship and growth

Recipes capture the attention of young cooks

Age doesn't matter when it comes to enjoying good food. But, let's face it, those with extra years under their belts usually have more expertise in the kitchen.

A lifelong passion for young people, plus a collection of tried-and-true *Taste of Home* recipes, led West Bend, Wisconsin, residents Diane Fechter and RuthAnn Phaneuf to host an "Apples of Gold" program for young women in their community.

Apples of Gold is a 6-week-long mentoring program that combines Bible lessons with live cooking demonstrations and shared meals.

As the program puts it, it teaches young women how to be godly wives and mothers, while emphasizing the importance of hospitality in the home.

"The older women teach the younger women life skills, including how to prepare home-cooked meals," says Diane. "Young people like good food just as much as we do, and they don't always want to use a microwave in the process."

The leaders use primarily *Taste of Home* recipes for their demos. At one meeting, Diane and RuthAnn (with some help from a few of the older members) prepared six recipes, ranging from Creamy Turkey Soup to Tiramisu Toffee Torte.

"We use *Taste of Home* recipes because they're delicious, they're easy to make and they always turn out," says RuthAnn. "We show the girls that having friends over for a wonderful meal doesn't have to be very difficult or scary."

Apples of Gold members

> *"The older women teach the younger women life skills, including how to prepare home-cooked meals."*
>
> ~Diane Fechter

DO YOU KNOW A COOK WHO CARES?
If you or someone you know cooks for a charitable, spiritual or other cause, tell us about it at **tasteofhome.com/CookbookBonus**

You can find recipes taught by Apples of Gold in the Web exclusive online at tasteofhome.com/CookbookBonus **Type in access code ICare**

Recipes

Tips

Salads & Salad Dressings

Common Types of Lettuce

Salads are more than just greens topped with a dressing. They can tease the appetite, round out a meal or become the entire meal itself. There are also coleslaws, potato salads, pasta salads, vegetable salads and gelatin salads.

For traditional tossed salads, select the freshest greens and ingredients. Look for lettuce that is crisp, is free of yellowing or rust spots (browning) and is not slimy. Lettuce, such as iceberg, should feel heavy for its size. Wash greens and thoroughly dry before using. Wet greens can make the salad soggy.

Select a dressing that is appropriate for the green. A sturdy lettuce like iceberg or romaine can hold a creamy blue cheese or Thousand Island dressing, while a lighter vinaigrette would be suitable for Bibb or Boston lettuce.

Just before serving, tear greens into bite-size pieces or use a plastic lettuce knife. Cutting greens with a metal knife will turn the edges brown with time. Allow greens to stand at room temperature no longer than 15 minutes before serving.

Toss greens with salad dressing in a large bowl and serve immediately, or place greens in a salad bowl and pass the dressing at the table. Adding too much dressing will make a salad soggy and limp.

A green salad doesn't just mean iceberg lettuce. The combination of flavors (mild, sweet lettuce with bitter greens), textures (buttery, tender, crisp and crunchy) and colors (shades of green, red and white) make a salad that appeals to the eyes as well as the palate.

Crisphead
Has a round compact head with pale green leaves. Mild-flavored, crispy iceberg lettuce is a crisphead.

Butterhead
Has small, loosely formed heads with tender, silky, soft leaves. Bibb lettuce has tender leaves with a sweet, subtle flavor. Boston lettuce has tender, buttery leaves with a mild sweet flavor.

Leaf or Looseleaf
Has leaves that branch out from a stalk. Green and red leaf lettuce are flavorful with crisp, curly-edged leaves. The red leaf has red-tipped leaves.

Romaine or Cos
Has a long, cylindrical head with large, crisp, green outer leaves that are slightly bitter.

Common Salad Greens

The variety of greens suitable for salads seems almost endless. Bok choy, cabbage, collard greens, kale, mustard greens, spinach and Swiss chard are suitable for salads. You can find information about these greens in the Vegetable Chapter. The following is a brief description of some commonly available greens.

Arugula
Is also known as rocket and is a tender, bitter green that resembles a radish leaf.

Belgian Endive
Has white leaves with pale yellow-green tips. Its bitter leaves are crunchy.

Curly Endive
Is also known as chicory, has curly leaves that are tough, chewy and bitter. It's best used as an accent flavor in a salad. Its flavor mellows when cooked.

Escarole
Has slightly bitter, firm, lettuce-like leaves.

Frisee
Gets a feathery appearance from its delicate curly leaves. This mildly bitter green ranges in color from yellow-white to yellow-green.

Radicchio
Has satiny, red, bitter-tasting leaves.

Sorrel
Has tender, green leaves with a tart, acidic flavor.

Watercress
Has delicate, small, deep-green leaves with a slightly bitter, peppery bite.

Washing and Storing

Remove rubber bands or ties from lettuce or greens. Remove and discard any brown, wilted or damaged outer leaves. Cut off or cut out core from lettuce. Separate leaves, except for iceberg.

Greens such as arugula or escarole may be sandy or dirty, and should be swished in a sink or bowl of cold water. Lift greens out, allowing the sand and grit to sink to the bottom. Repeat in clean water if necessary. Rinse other greens gently in cool water.

Greens need to be dried because they do not keep well in the refrigerator if they are wet. Pat them dry with a clean towel or paper towel. A salad spinner is an easy way to remove the water (fill only half to two-thirds full). Greens can also be stored in some salad spinners.

Store in a covered container or plastic bag and refrigerate for at least 30 minutes before serving to crisp the greens. Place a piece of paper towel in the bottom of the container or bag to absorb excess moisture. Store in the refrigerator crisper drawer for about 1 week.

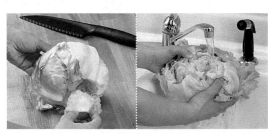

For iceberg lettuce, cut out the core with a paring knife or plastic lettuce knife. Or grasp the head in your hand and hit the core area against the countertop; lift out the core. Rinse the head under running water and drain, core side down, in a colander in the sink.

Ready-to-use salad mixes are available in the produce section. These are already washed and torn. Store in their plastic bag in the refrigerator crisper drawer. Once opened, tightly close the bag. Follow the "use-by" date stamped on the package.

Salad Ingredients

Avocados

Most avocados have a buttery texture and a rich, slightly nutty flavor. The two most common types of avocados are the Hass and Florida.

The Hass avocado is grown in California, weighs about 1/2 pound, has a pebbly skin that goes from green to black as it ripens, and is available year-round.

The Florida avocado is grown in Florida, is larger than the Hass and has a shiny medium-green skin that doesn't change color as it ripens. It has more water and, ounce for ounce, has less fat and calories. It is available early fall through winter.

Select avocados that are heavy for their size and have no blemishes. If the avocado is hard, it will need to ripen before using. If it yields to gentle pressure, it is ready to slice. If the avocado has a small dent after pressing, then it is too soft to slice but is suitable for mashing. If there is a large dent after pressing, then it is overripe and the flesh is spoiled.

To ripen avocados, place in a brown paper bag and leave at room temperature for a few days. To hasten ripening, add an apple or banana to the bag.

Removing an Avocado Pit

1) Wash avocado. Cut in half lengthwise, cutting around the seed. Twist halves in opposite directions to separate.

2) Slip a tablespoon under the seed to loosen it from the fruit.

3) To remove avocado flesh from the skin, loosen it from the skin with a large spoon and scoop out.

4) Slice the peeled avocado as desired. Or cut into unpeeled wedges and slice between the flesh and the skin.

Ripe avocados should be stored in the refrigerator for up to 3 days. Cut avocados should be brushed with lemon or lime juice to help prevent the flesh from darkening. Place in an airtight container and eat within 2 days.

Cucumbers

The most popular cucumber is just classified as the common cucumber. It was bred to have a thicker skin than other cucumbers to protect it during shipping. This cucumber generally has a waxed coating on the skin to keep it fresher longer.

The Kirby cucumber is shorter and has bumpy skin. The Kirby was originally used for pickling but can be used in place of the common cucumber in recipes. The English cucumber, also know as Burpless or Hothouse cucumber, is narrow and about 2 feet long. This seedless cucumber is found in stores wrapped in plastic.

Select firm cucumbers with round ends. Avoid those with soft spots, bulging middles or withered ends. Store unwashed cucumbers in the refrigerator crisper drawer for up to 1 week. Avoid cold areas of the refrigerator where the cucumber might freeze. Wash before using. Peel waxed cucumbers and seed if desired.

Seeding a Cucumber

Peel or score cucumber if desired. Cut lengthwise in half. Using a teaspoon, run the tip under the seeds to loosen and remove.

Radishes

The most commonly available radish is the red radish, which is round or oval. Radishes have a peppery flavor that can range from mild to fiery. White icicle radishes have a flavor similar to the red but are elongated and carrot-shaped. The Japanese daikon radishes are large, white radishes that can weigh around 2 pounds.

Select firm, well-formed radishes. Avoid those with cracks or blemishes. Store in the refrigerator crisper drawer for 1 week. Store daikon radishes only 3 days. Wash or scrub with a vegetable brush before using.

CHERRY BRIE TOSSED SALAD

◐ Cherry Brie Tossed Salad

PREP/TOTAL TIME: 20 min.

Toni Borden, Wellington, Florida

Draped in a light vinaigrette and sprinkled with almonds, this pretty salad is a variation of a recipe that's been passed around at school and church functions and even birthday parties. Everyone wants the recipe. You can also try different cheeses.

DRESSING:

1	cup cider vinegar
1/2	cup sugar
1/4	cup olive oil
1	teaspoon ground mustard
1-1/2	teaspoons poppy seeds

SALAD:

2	tablespoons butter
3/4	cup sliced almonds
3	tablespoons sugar
8	cups torn romaine
8	ounces Brie *or* Camembert, rind removed, cubed
1	package (6 ounces) dried cherries

1) In a jar with a tight-fitting lid, combine the dressing ingredients; shake until sugar is dissolved.

2) For salad, in a heavy skillet, melt butter over medium heat. Add almonds; cook and stir until nuts are toasted, about 4 minutes. Sprinkle with sugar; cook and stir until sugar is melted, about 3 minutes. Spread on foil to cool; break apart.

3) In a large salad bowl, combine the romaine, cheese and cherries. Shake dressing; drizzle over salad. Sprinkle with sugared almonds and toss to coat.

Yield: 10 servings.

Editor's Note: Swiss cheese can be used in place of the Brie or Camembert.

NUTRITION FACTS: 1 serving equals 309 calories, 18 g fat (6 g saturated fat), 29 mg cholesterol, 171 mg sodium, 32 g carbohydrate, 2 g fiber, 8 g protein.

Layered Lettuce Salad

PREP: 15 min. + chilling

Julia Burkholder, Robesonia, Pennsylvania

I often make the dressing to use on other salads, especially when I have fresh basil. It's so flavorful.

1	medium head lettuce, torn
1	cup minced fresh parsley
4	hard-cooked eggs, sliced
2	large tomatoes, chopped
1	package (10 ounces) frozen peas, thawed and patted dry
6	bacon strips, cooked and crumbled
1	cup (4 ounces) shredded cheddar cheese
1	small red onion, chopped

DRESSING:

1-1/2	cups mayonnaise
1/2	cup sour cream
1	teaspoon dill weed
3/4	teaspoon dried basil
1/2	teaspoon salt
1/8	teaspoon pepper

Fresh dill sprigs, optional

1) In a large salad bowl, layer the lettuce, parsley, eggs, tomatoes, peas, bacon, cheese and onion in the order listed.

2) In a small bowl, combine the mayonnaise, sour cream, dill, basil, salt and pepper. Carefully spread on top of salad.

3) Cover and refrigerate for several hours or overnight. Garnish with dill sprigs if desired.

Yield: 12 servings.

NUTRITION FACTS: 1 cup equals 335 calories, 30 g fat (7 g saturated fat), 101 mg cholesterol, 423 mg sodium, 7 g carbohydrate, 2 g fiber, 8 g protein.

LAYERED LETTUCE SALAD

GREENS WITH CREAMY HERBED SALAD DRESSING

Greens with Creamy Herbed Salad Dressing

PREP/TOTAL TIME: 10 min.

Janet Les, Chilliwack, British Columbia

If you're looking for a way to spice up everyday greens, try this salad dressing. With its thick consistency, it also makes a delectable veggie dip.

- 1/2 cup fat-free mayonnaise
- 2 tablespoons plus 2 teaspoons fat-free milk
- 4 teaspoons white vinegar
- 1 teaspoon dried oregano
- 1/2 teaspoon dried basil
- 1/4 teaspoon sugar
- 1/4 teaspoon salt
- 1/4 garlic powder
- 1/4 teaspoon pepper
- 5 cups mixed salad greens

1) In a small bowl, whisk the mayonnaise, milk and vinegar until combined. Whisk in the oregano, basil, sugar, salt, garlic powder and pepper. Serve over salad greens.

Yield: 5 servings.

NUTRITION FACTS: 1 cup greens with 2 tablespoons dressing equals 33 calories, 1 g fat (trace saturated fat), 3 mg cholesterol, 328 mg sodium, 6 g carbohydrate, 2 g fiber, 1 g protein.

Artichoke Tossed Salad

PREP/TOTAL TIME: 20 min.

Karin Graw, Hudson, Wisconsin

It's a cinch to mix together this zesty salad for a potluck. It'll feed a crowd and then some. For a lighter version, I use less oil and a sugar substitute for the dressing and toss in turkey bacon.

- 1 bunch romaine (1 pound), torn
- 1/2 pound sliced bacon, cooked and crumbled
- 1 jar (4-1/2 ounces) marinated artichoke hearts, drained and sliced
- 1/2 cup crumbled blue cheese
- 1/2 cup sliced celery

- 1/2 cup chopped sweet red pepper
- 1/2 cup chopped sweet yellow pepper
- 3 tablespoons cider vinegar
- 2 tablespoons chopped onion
- 2 teaspoons brown sugar
- 2 teaspoons spicy brown mustard
- 1/2 teaspoon salt
- 1/4 teaspoon pepper
- 2 tablespoons vegetable oil

1) In a large salad bowl, combine the romaine, bacon, artichoke hearts, cheese, celery and sweet peppers. Cover; refrigerate until serving.

2) In a blender or food processor, combine the vinegar, onion, brown sugar, mustard, salt and pepper; cover and process until smooth.

3) While processing, add oil in a steady stream; blend until thickened. Drizzle over salad; toss gently to coat. Serve immediately.

Yield: 10-12 servings.

NUTRITION FACTS: 1 cup equals 107 calories, 9 g fat (3 g saturated fat), 10 mg cholesterol, 333 mg sodium, 4 g carbohydrate, 1 g fiber, 4 g protein.

Autumn Salad

PREP: 20 min. + chilling

Pat Schmeling, Germantown, Wisconsin

This recipe is a perfect accompaniment to a holiday dinner. The vinaigrette adds a wonderfully fresh flavor.

- 1/4 cup white wine vinegar
- 2 teaspoons Dijon mustard
- 1/2 teaspoon dill weed
- 1/2 teaspoon ground nutmeg
- 1/8 teaspoon kosher salt
- 1/8 teaspoon pepper
- 1/2 cup olive oil
- 3 large unpeeled Red Delicious apples, thinly sliced
- 1/3 cup crumbled blue cheese
- 1/4 cup walnut halves, toasted
- 1 bunch romaine, torn
- 1 bunch watercress, trimmed

1) In a small bowl, whisk the vinegar, mustard, dill, nutmeg, salt and pepper. Slowly add oil while whisking. In a large bowl, combine the apples, cheese, walnuts and 3 tablespoons dressing; toss to coat. Cover and refrigerate for up to 4 hours. Cover and refrigerate remaining dressing.

2) Place romaine and watercress in a large salad bowl; drizzle with remaining dressing; toss to coat. Arrange romaine mixture and apple mixture on serving plates. Serve immediately.

Yield: 8 servings.

NUTRITION FACTS: 3/4 cup equals 219 calories, 18 g fat (3 g saturated fat), 4 mg cholesterol, 147 mg sodium, 15 g carbohydrate, 3 g fiber, 3 g protein.

ITALIAN BREAD SALAD

Italian Bread Salad

PREP/TOTAL TIME: 25 min.

Kathleen Williams, St. Albans, West Virginia

For a fresh-tasting side dish, I serve this pretty blend that's a snap to prepare. For variety, add whatever vegetables you like, such as green or yellow peppers, zucchini, summer squash or sliced olives.

- 4 slices Italian *or* French bread (1 inch thick)
- 2 tablespoons olive oil, *divided*
- 2 plum tomatoes, halved lengthwise and sliced
- 1 medium cucumber, seeded and chopped
- 2 to 3 green onions, sliced
- 2 tablespoons shredded Parmesan cheese

Lettuce leaves

- 3 tablespoons red wine vinegar
- 1 garlic clove, minced
- 1/4 teaspoon dried basil

1) Brush both sides of bread with 1 tablespoon of oil. Place on a baking sheet. Broil 5 in. from the heat for 1-2 minutes on each side or until lightly browned. Cut into 1/2-in. cubes.

2) In a bowl, gently toss the bread cubes, tomatoes, cucumber, onions and Parmesan cheese. Divide among four lettuce-lined salad plates.

3) In a small bowl, whisk the vinegar, garlic, basil and remaining oil. Drizzle over salads. Serve immediately.

Yield: 4 servings.

NUTRITION FACTS: 1 cup equals 176 calories, 9 g fat (2 g saturated fat), 2 mg cholesterol, 222 mg sodium, 20 g carbohydrate, 2 g fiber, 5 g protein.

Chef's Salad

PREP/TOTAL TIME: 15 min.

Katie Anderson, Cheney, Washington

Pair this smaller-sized version of an all-time classic with breadsticks for lunch.

- 2 cups torn salad greens
- 2 green onions, chopped
- 1/4 cup chopped celery
- 4 ounces deli ham, julienned
- 4 ounces deli turkey, julienned
- 4 ounces Swiss cheese, julienned
- 1 hard-cooked egg, sliced
- 4 pitted ripe olives

Salad dressing of your choice

1) On two serving plates, arrange the salad greens, onion, celery, ham, turkey, cheese, egg and olives. Serve with dressing.

Yield: 2 servings.

NUTRITION FACTS: 1 serving (calculated without salad dressing) equals 413 calories, 24 g fat (12 g saturated fat), 210 mg cholesterol, 1,783 mg sodium, 9 g carbohydrate, 2 g fiber, 41 g protein.

■ **Mix-and-Match Chef's Salad:** Use 4 ounces julienned deli roast beef, corned beef or salami for any of the meat listed and use 4 ounces julienned cheddar, provolone, Monterey Jack, pepper Jack, Muenster or Colby cheese for the Swiss cheese.

Classic Cobb Salad

PREP/TOTAL TIME: 15 min.

Patty Kile, Elizabethtown, Pennsylvania

Suit your tastes by using different meats or veggies.

- 6 cups torn lettuce
- 2 medium tomatoes, chopped
- 1 medium ripe avocado, peeled and chopped
- 3/4 cup diced fully cooked ham
- 2 hard-cooked eggs, chopped
- 3/4 cup diced cooked turkey
- 1-1/4 cups sliced fresh mushrooms
- 1/2 cup crumbled blue cheese

Red onion rings, lemon wedges and sliced ripe olives, optional

Salad dressing of your choice

1) Arrange lettuce in a large bowl. Place tomatoes across the center, dividing the bowl in half. On one half, arrange the avocado, ham and eggs in sections. On the other half, arrange the turkey, mushrooms and blue cheese.

2) Garnish with onion, lemon and olives if desired. Serve with salad dressing.

Yield: 12 servings.

NUTRITION FACTS: 3/4 cup (calculated without salad dressing) equals 98 calories, 6 g fat (2 g saturated fat), 51 mg cholesterol, 213 mg sodium, 3 g carbohydrate, 1 g fiber, 7 g protein.

ROMAINE CAESAR SALAD

Romaine Caesar Salad

PREP: 10 min. + chilling

Marie Hattrup, Moro, Oregon

After tasting this terrific salad my daughter made, I was eager to get the recipe and try it myself. The dressing is easy to mix up in the blender.

>   2   hard-cooked eggs
>   1/4   cup lemon juice
>   2   tablespoons balsamic vinegar
>   1   anchovy fillet
>   1   tablespoon Dijon mustard
>   2   garlic cloves, peeled
>   1   teaspoon Worcestershire sauce
>   1   teaspoon pepper
>   3/4   teaspoon salt
>   1/2   cup olive oil
>   1   bunch romaine, torn
>   1   cup (4 ounces) shredded
>   Parmesan cheese
>   1   cup Caesar salad croutons

1) Slice eggs in half; remove yolks. Refrigerate whites for another use. In a blender or food processor, combine the lemon juice, vinegar, anchovy, mustard, garlic, Worcestershire sauce, pepper, salt and egg yolks; cover and process until blended. While processing, gradually add oil in a steady stream. Cover and refrigerate for 1 hour.

2) In a salad bowl, combine the romaine, Parmesan cheese and croutons. Drizzle with dressing; toss to coat. Serve immediately.

Yield: 8 servings.

NUTRITION FACTS: 1 cup equals 238 calories, 20 g fat (5 g saturated fat), 64 mg cholesterol, 617 mg sodium, 7 g carbohydrate, 1 g fiber, 9 g protein.

■ **Chicken Caesar Salad:** Grill or broil 8 chicken breast halves seasoned with salt and pepper. Cut each chicken breast half into strips. Top each individual salad with a cooked chicken breast half.

Keeping Clean While Processing

Adding oil through the hole in the blender lid while running the blender gives a thick and well-blended dressing. It can also leave you and the kitchen a little messy. To cut down on splatter, place a funnel in the lid hole and pour the oil through the funnel.

Two-Cabbage Slaw

PREP/TOTAL TIME: 15 min.

Carol Gaus, Itasca, Illinois

If you'd like to make a summer barbecue festive, bring out this eye-catching side dish. It's a great way to use up homegrown produce.

>   4   cups shredded green cabbage
>   1   cup shredded red cabbage
>   1   medium green pepper, chopped
>   1   medium sweet red pepper,
>   chopped
>   4   green onions, finely chopped

DRESSING:

>   1   cup (8 ounces) reduced-fat sour
>   cream
>   3   tablespoons tarragon vinegar *or*
>   cider vinegar
>   1   tablespoon sugar
>   1   teaspoon salt
>   3/4   teaspoon celery seed
>   1/4   teaspoon white pepper

1) In a large bowl, combine the first five ingredients. In a small bowl, combine the dressing ingredients. Pour over cabbage mixture and stir to coat. Serve immediately.

Yield: 6 servings.

NUTRITION FACTS: 1 cup equals 140 calories, 4 g fat (3 g saturated fat), 13 mg cholesterol, 465 mg sodium, 21 g carbohydrate, 6 g fiber, 6 g protein.

■ **Carrot Two-Cabbage Slaw:** Use 3 shredded large carrots in place of the peppers.

Shredding Cabbage

To shred cabbage by hand, cut cabbage into wedges. Place cut side down on a cutting board. With a large sharp knife, cut into thin slices.

TANGY COLESLAW

Tangy Coleslaw

PREP/TOTAL TIME: 30 min.

Pat Cole, Polebridge, Montana

The fresh flavor and crunchy texture of garden vegetables star in this tart, colorful coleslaw. Lightly dressed with vinegar and oil, it's a refreshing summer salad. My mom fixed it often when I was growing up.

- 6 cups shredded cabbage
- 4 medium carrots, shredded
- 4 celery ribs, chopped
- 1/2 cup finely chopped green pepper
- 1/2 cup finely chopped onion
- 1/2 cup cider vinegar
- 1/4 cup vegetable oil
- 1/4 cup sugar
- 1-1/2 teaspoons salt
- 1/4 teaspoon pepper
- 1/4 teaspoon paprika

1) In a large bowl, combine the first five ingredients. In a jar with a tight-fitting lid, combine the vinegar, oil, sugar, salt, pepper and paprika; shake well.

2) Pour over cabbage mixture and toss to coat. Cover and refrigerate until serving.

Yield: 10 servings.

NUTRITION FACTS: 1 cup equals 97 calories, 6 g fat (1 g saturated fat), 0 cholesterol, 385 mg sodium, 12 g carbohydrate, 2 g fiber, 1 g protein.

'GRAPE' ADDITION TO COLESLAW ■■■

I've found that seedless grapes tossed into my coleslaw make this salad a real winner at family meals.

—*Ann C., Watsonville, California*

Wilted Lettuce Salad

PREP/TOTAL TIME: 15 min.

Alberta McKay, Bartlesville, Oklahoma

This salad looks and tastes great! I've used both leaf lettuce and spinach with wonderful results.

- 8 cups torn leaf lettuce *or* spinach
- 1/4 cup sliced green onions

Pepper to taste

- 3 bacon strips, diced
- 1 tablespoon white wine vinegar
- 2 teaspoons lemon juice
- 1/2 teaspoon sugar
- 1/4 teaspoon salt
- 1 hard-cooked egg, chopped

1) In a large bowl, combine lettuce and onions. Sprinkle with pepper; set aside.

2) In a large skillet, cook bacon over medium heat until crisp. Stir the vinegar, lemon juice, sugar and salt into drippings. Pour over lettuce and toss gently until well coated. Top with hard-cooked egg. Serve immediately.

Yield: 6 servings.

NUTRITION FACTS: 1 cup equals 93 calories, 8 g fat (3 g saturated fat), 43 mg cholesterol, 199 mg sodium, 4 g carbohydrate, 2 g fiber, 3 g protein.

Apple-Brie Spinach Salad

PREP/TOTAL TIME: 30 min.

Rhonda Crowe, Victoria, British Columbia

In the summer, I don't like to prepare or eat large meals, so I often make salads. I'm always on the lookout for new and interesting recipes, and this one is a winner that I like to make for company.

- 4 large apples, cut into 1/2-inch wedges
- 4 tablespoons maple syrup, *divided*
- 8 cups fresh baby spinach
- 1 round (8 ounces) **Brie** *or* **Camembert cheese**, rind removed and cubed
- 1/2 cup pecan halves, toasted

DRESSING:

- 1/4 cup apple cider *or* juice
- 1/4 cup vegetable oil
- 3 tablespoons cider vinegar
- 1 teaspoon Dijon mustard
- 1 garlic clove, minced

1) Place apples on an ungreased baking sheet; brush with 2 tablespoons syrup. Broil 3-4 in. from the heat for 3 minutes. Turn; brush with remaining syrup. Broil 3-5 minutes longer or until crisp-tender.

APPLE-BRIE SPINACH SALAD

2) In a large salad bowl, combine the spinach, cheese, pecans and apples. In a small saucepan, combine the dressing ingredients; bring to a boil. Pour over salad; toss to coat. Serve immediately.

Yield: 10 servings.

NUTRITION FACTS: 3/4 cup equals 242 calories, 16 g fat (5 g saturated fat), 23 mg cholesterol, 176 mg sodium, 21 g carbohydrate, 3 g fiber, 6 g protein.

Potato Salads

Generally, potatoes with a waxy texture, such as round red potatoes and round white potatoes, or an all-purpose potato like Yukon Gold, are recommended for potato salad. Russets are mealy and crumbly.

If cooked whole with the skin on, potatoes absorb less water but take longer to cook. So you may want to peel them when they are warm, then cube or slice. It's best to wear rubber gloves when doing this to protect your hands. If uncooked potatoes are cubed, it is a matter of preference if they're peeled or not. Unpeeled cubed potatoes give the salad a rustic or country feel.

Scrub the potatoes with a brush and remove any eyes or sprouts. Peel and cube if desired. Place potatoes in a Dutch oven or large kettle. Cover with cold water; add about 1/2 to 1 teaspoon salt for each quart of water. Bring to a boil. Cover and cook until just fork-tender yet firm. Do not overcook; the potatoes might fall apart in the salad and result in a mushy texture.

Cooking times vary greatly with size and variety—small whole potatoes may cook in 15 minutes while larger whole potatoes may need 30 minutes. Cubed potatoes may take 10-20 minutes. Drain potatoes.

Hot potatoes absorb more flavors than cold potatoes. Prepare a dressing in a separate bowl, then pour over the potatoes. Gently stir to coat potatoes; avoid overmixing since the potatoes may crumble.

Dress up a classic potato salad recipe by adding diced seeded cucumber, sliced green onions, chopped radishes, chopped shallots, crumbled feta cheese, chopped fully cooked ham or cooked tiny shrimp.

Tangy German Potato Salad

PREP: 5 min. **COOK:** 35 min.

Thelma Waggoner, Hopkinsville, Kentucky

This recipe has been a handed-down favorite in my family for years. It's delicious every time I make it.

- 7 medium potatoes (about 1-3/4 pounds)
- 8 bacon strips
- 1 small onion, chopped
- 1/2 cup diced celery
- 3 tablespoons all-purpose flour
- 3 tablespoons sugar
- 1/4 to 1/2 teaspoon salt

Pepper to taste

- 3/4 cup water
- 1/2 to 3/4 cup vinegar

1) Peel potatoes; place in a large saucepan and cover with water. Bring to a boil. Reduce heat; cover and cook for 30-40 minutes or until tender but firm.

2) Meanwhile, in a large skillet, cook bacon over medium heat until crisp. Remove to paper towels; drain, reserving 3 tablespoons drippings. When cool enough to handle, crumble bacon; set aside.

3) In the drippings, saute onion and celery until tender. Stir in flour, sugar, salt and pepper until blended. Add water and vinegar. Bring to a boil; cook and stir for 2 minutes or until thickened.

4) Drain potatoes; slice and place in a large bowl. Add the bacon and sauce; toss gently to coat. Serve warm or at room temperature.

Yield: 6 servings.

NUTRITION FACTS: 1/2 cup equals 273 calories, 11 g fat (5 g saturated fat), 14 mg cholesterol, 286 mg sodium, 38 g carbohydrate, 3 g fiber, 6 g protein.

TANGY GERMAN POTATO SALAD

DRESSED-UP POTATO SALAD

 CLASSIC: Potatoes are teamed up with bacon in Potato Salad with Bacon. This salad is dressed with a creamy, but zippy mixture of mayonnaise and sour cream.

 TIME-SAVER: Who would guess that Lazy Days Potato Salad can be ready in just 20 minutes? Canned potatoes are the key to quickness in this tasty salad that's brightened with shredded carrot and sliced celery.

 LIGHT: Fat-free mayonnaise lightens the dressing for Healthy Potato Salad, which has only 110 calories and one gram of fat in each serving. Although the recipe calls for five hard-cooked eggs, the yolks are discarded to cut the cholesterol to just 2 milligrams per serving.

 SERVES 2: Four small red potatoes and one hard-cooked egg are needed to stir together this small batch of Creamy Potato Salad. Fresh carrot, celery and red onion add color and crunch.

POTATO SALAD WITH BACON

Potato Salad with Bacon

PREP: 45 min. + chilling

Collette Reynolds, Raleigh, North Carolina

- 3 pounds red potatoes (about 12 medium)
- 4 hard-cooked eggs
- 3/4 cup sour cream
- 2/3 cup mayonnaise
- 1 teaspoon salt
- 1 teaspoon prepared mustard
- 1/2 teaspoon garlic powder
- 1/4 teaspoon pepper
- 11 bacon strips, cooked and crumbled

- 1/2 cup chopped celery
- 1/4 cup chopped green onions
- 1/4 cup Italian salad dressing

1) Cut potatoes into 1/2-in. cubes; place in a Dutch oven and cover with water. Bring to a boil. Reduce heat; cover and simmer for 10-15 minutes or until tender. Drain and cool to room temperature.

2) Cut eggs in half; chop egg whites and set aside. In a bowl, mash egg yolks. Stir in the sour cream, mayonnaise, salt, mustard, garlic powder and pepper; set aside.

3) In a large bowl, combine the potatoes, bacon, egg whites, celery, onions and Italian dressing. Fold in mayonnaise mixture. Cover and refrigerate for at least 2 hours before serving.

Yield: 16 servings.

NUTRITION FACTS: 3/4 cup equals 216 calories, 14 g fat (4 g saturated fat), 68 mg cholesterol, 363 mg sodium, 16 g carbohydrate, 2 g fiber, 5 g protein.

Lazy Days Potato Salad

PREP/TOTAL TIME: 20 min.

Margaret Wilson, Hemet, California

- 1 can (14-1/2 ounces) sliced potatoes, drained
- 1/4 cup thinly sliced celery
- 1/4 cup sliced green onions
- 1/4 cup shredded carrot
- 1 can (2-1/4 ounces) sliced ripe olives, drained
- 2 tablespoons chopped dill pickle
- 1/2 cup fat-free mayonnaise
- 1 to 2 tablespoons Dijon mustard
- 1/4 teaspoon garlic powder
- 1/4 teaspoon pepper

1) In a large bowl, combine the potatoes, celery, onions, carrot, olives and pickle. In a small bowl, combine the mayonnaise, mustard, garlic powder

HEALTHY POTATO SALAD

and pepper. Drizzle over potato mixture; toss to coat. Cover and refrigerate until serving.

Yield: 4 servings.

NUTRITION FACTS: 2/3 cup equals 70 calories, 2 g fat (trace saturated fat), 0 cholesterol, 537 mg sodium, 12 g carbohydrate, 2 g fiber, 1 g protein.

Healthy Potato Salad

PREP: 25 min. + chilling

Pat Potter, Calumet City, Illinois

- 2 pounds small red potatoes, quartered
- 5 hard-cooked eggs
- 3/4 cup fat-free mayonnaise
- 2 teaspoons cider vinegar
- 1 teaspoon sugar
- 1 teaspoon ground mustard
- 1/2 teaspoon salt
- 1/4 teaspoon pepper
- 1 large sweet onion, chopped
- 2 celery ribs, chopped
- 1/2 cup chopped green onions
- 1/2 cup julienned sweet red pepper
- 1/4 cup minced fresh parsley

1) Place the potatoes in a saucepan and cover with water. Bring to a boil. Reduce heat; cover and simmer for 12-14 minutes or until tender. Drain; cool for 30 minutes.

2) Slice eggs in half (discard yolks or save for another use). Cut the whites into 1/2-in. pieces.

3) In a large bowl, combine the mayonnaise, vinegar, sugar, mustard, salt and pepper. Add the potatoes,

egg whites, onion, celery, green onions, red pepper and parsley; toss to coat. Cover and refrigerate for 2 hours or until chilled.

Yield: 10 servings.

NUTRITION FACTS: 3/4 cup equals 110 calories, 1 g fat (trace saturated fat), 2 mg cholesterol, 305 mg sodium, 22 g carbohydrate, 3 g fiber, 4 g protein.

Creamy Potato Salad

PREP/TOTAL TIME: 15 min.

Caron Osberg, Urbandale, Iowa

- 4 small red potatoes, cubed
- 1/4 cup water
- 1/3 cup fat-free mayonnaise
- 1 hard-cooked egg, chopped
- 2 tablespoons chopped celery
- 2 tablespoons chopped carrot
- 2 tablespoons chopped red onion
- 2 teaspoons sweet pickle relish
- 1/8 teaspoon salt
- 1/8 teaspoon pepper

1) Place the potatoes in a microwave-safe bowl; add water. Cover and microwave on high for 4-5 minutes or until tender; drain and rinse in cold water.

2) In a large bowl, combine remaining ingredients. Add potatoes; gently toss to coat. Cover and refrigerate until chilled.

Yield: 2 servings.

NUTRITION FACTS: 1 cup equals 227 calories, 4 g fat (1 g saturated fat), 110 mg cholesterol, 563 mg sodium, 41 g carbohydrate, 5 g fiber, 7 g protein.

Pasta Salads

For pasta salads, choose a pasta shape that can hold up well in the salad and can compete with the shape and texture of the other foods in the salad. Elbow macaroni, shell, rotini, bow ties, wagon wheels, tortellini and radiatore are good choices for salads.

Cook pasta according to package directions until just tender and firm or al dente. Do not overcook or the pasta may fall apart in the salad.

Drain, rinse with cold water and drain again. Transfer to a bowl and, if desired, toss with a little olive oil. Cool and add other ingredients; toss to coat with dressing. Pasta salads should chill for a few hours to allow flavors to blend.

Antipasto Pasta Salad

PREP/TOTAL TIME: 30 min.

Bernadette Nelson, Arcadia, California

This combination of beans, sausage, cheese and pasta is a hearty complement to any meal. It's also a hit at potlucks and picnics.

- 1 package (16 ounces) penne pasta
- 1 can (15 ounces) garbanzo beans *or* chickpeas, rinsed and drained
- 1 medium sweet red *or* green pepper, julienned
- 1 bunch green onions, sliced
- 2 plum tomatoes, halved lengthwise and sliced
- 4 ounces Monterey Jack cheese, julienned
- 4 ounces part-skim mozzarella cheese, juilienned
- 4 ounces brick *or* provolone cheese, julienned
- 4 ounces thinly sliced hard salami, julienned
- 3 ounces thinly sliced pepperoni

ANTIPASTO PASTA SALAD

- 1 can (2-1/4 ounces) sliced ripe olives, drained
- 1 to 2 tablespoons minced chives

BASIL VINAIGRETTE:
- 2/3 cup vegetable oil
- 1/3 cup red wine vinegar
- 3 tablespoons minced fresh basil *or* 1 tablespoon dried basil
- 1 garlic clove, minced
- 1/4 teaspoon salt

1) Cook pasta according to package directions; rinse with cold water and drain. In a large bowl, combine the pasta, beans, vegetables, cheeses, meats, olives and chives.

2) In a small bowl, whisk together the vinaigrette ingredients. Pour over salad; toss to coat. Cover and refrigerate until serving. Toss again before serving.

Yield: 18 servings.

NUTRITION FACTS: 1 cup equals 248 calories, 18 g fat (5 g saturated fat), 24 mg cholesterol, 431 mg sodium, 13 g carbohydrate, 2 g fiber, 9 g protein.

Vegetable Pasta Salad

PREP: 15 min. + chilling

Helen Phillips, Horseheads, New York

It's fun to incorporate our garden's bounty into different dishes. This salad not only does that, it looks and tastes great.

- 2 cups broccoli florets
- 4 cups cooked spiral pasta
- 2 medium carrots, julienned
- 1/2 cup frozen peas, thawed
- 1/2 cup cubed fully cooked ham
- 1/2 cup cubed cheddar cheese
- 1/3 cup sliced green onions

DRESSING:
- 3/4 cup mayonnaise
- 2 tablespoons cider vinegar
- 1 tablespoon Dijon mustard
- 1 garlic clove, minced
- 1 teaspoon dill weed
- 1/4 teaspoon pepper

1) Place 1 in. of water in a small saucepan; add broccoli. Bring to a boil. Reduce heat; cover and simmer for 2-3 minutes. Rinse in cold water and drain.

2) In a large bowl, combine the broccoli, pasta, carrots, peas, ham, cheese and onions. In another bowl, combine the dressing ingredients. Pour over salad and toss to coat. Cover and refrigerate for at least 1 hour.

Yield: 10 servings.

NUTRITION FACTS: 1 cup equals 252 calories, 17 g fat (3 g saturated fat), 17 mg cholesterol, 276 mg sodium, 19 g carbohydrate, 2 g fiber, 7 g protein.

BLUE CHEESE ORZO SALAD

Blue Cheese Orzo Salad

PREP/TOTAL TIME: 30 min.

Helen Conwell, Fairhope, Alabama

The crunch of walnuts and bacon is a pleasant contrast to the creamy rice-shaped pasta. The blue cheese and arugula lend a satisfying, savory quality.

3/4 cup uncooked orzo pasta
  3 cups fresh arugula, torn
  5 bacon strips, cooked and crumbled
3/4 cup crumbled blue cheese
1/4 cup sliced green onions
1/4 cup chopped walnuts, toasted

WALNUT VINAIGRETTE:

  2 tablespoons red wine vinegar
  1 garlic clove, peeled
  1 teaspoon Creole *or* whole grain mustard
1/2 teaspoon salt
1/2 teaspoon brown sugar
1/4 cup chopped walnuts, toasted
1/4 cup olive oil

1) Cook orzo according to package directions; drain and place in a large bowl. Add the arugula, bacon, blue cheese, onions and walnuts.

2) In a blender, combine the first six vinaigrette ingredients; cover and process until smooth. While processing, gradually add oil in a steady stream. Drizzle over salad; toss to coat. Serve immediately.

Yield: 5 servings.

NUTRITION FACTS: 3/4 cup equals 397 calories, 27 g fat (7 g saturated fat), 22 mg cholesterol, 692 mg sodium, 26 g carbohydrate, 2 g fiber, 14 g protein.

Bacon Macaroni Salad

PREP: 20 min. + chilling

Norene Wright, Manilla, Indiana

If you like BLT sandwiches, you'll like this pleasing pasta salad draped in a tangy mayonnaise and vinegar dressing.

  2 cups uncooked elbow macaroni
  5 green onions, finely chopped
  1 large tomato, diced
1-1/4 cups diced celery
1-1/4 cups mayonnaise
  5 teaspoon white vinegar
1/4 teaspoon salt
1/8 to 1/4 teaspoon pepper
  1 pound sliced bacon, cooked and crumbled

1) Cook macaroni according to package directions; drain and rinse in cold water. In a large bowl, combine the macaroni, green onions, tomato and celery.

2) In a small bowl, combine the mayonnaise, vinegar, salt and pepper. Pour over macaroni mixture and toss to coat. Cover and refrigerate for at least 2 hours. Just before serving, add bacon.

Yield: 12 servings.

NUTRITION FACTS: 3/4 cup equals 290 calories, 25 g fat (5 g saturated fat), 19 mg cholesterol, 387 mg sodium, 11 g carbohydrate, 1 g fiber, 6 g protein.

Tabbouleh

PREP: 40 min. + chilling

Wanda Watson, Irving, Texas

Tabbouleh is a Mediterranean dish featuring bulgur. This cool, refreshing salad is perfect to serve in warm weather.

  1 cup bulgur
  2 cups boiling water
  3 tablespoons lemon juice
  2 tablespoons olive oil
  2 tablespoons sliced green onions (tops only)
  1 tablespoon minced fresh parsley
  1 teaspoon salt
  1 teaspoon minced fresh mint
  1 medium tomato, seeded and diced
  6 romaine leaves

1) Place bulgur in a bowl; stir in water. Cover and let stand for 30 minutes or until liquid is absorbed. Drain and squeeze dry. Stir in the lemon juice, oil, onions, parsley, salt and mint.

2) Cover; refrigerate for 1 hour. Just before serving, stir in tomato. Serve in a lettuce-lined bowl.

Yield: 6 servings.

NUTRITION FACTS: 3/4 cup equals 129 calories, 5 g fat (1 g saturated fat), 0 cholesterol, 399 mg sodium, 20 g carbohydrate, 5 g fiber, 3 g protein.

Corn Bread Layered Salad

PREP: 20 min. **BAKE:** 20 min. + cooling

Jody Miller, Oklahoma City, Oklahoma

My corn bread salad is so complete, it can be a meal in itself. The recipe has been in our family for years.

- 1 package (8-1/2 ounces) corn bread/muffin mix
- 6 green onions, chopped
- 1 medium green pepper, chopped
- 1 can (15-1/4 ounces) whole kernel corn, drained
- 1 can (15 ounces) pinto beans, rinsed and drained
- 3/4 cup mayonnaise
- 3/4 cup sour cream
- 2 medium tomatoes, seeded and chopped
- 1/2 cup shredded cheddar cheese

1) Prepare and bake corn bread according to package directions. Cool on a wire rack.

2) Crumble corn bread into a 2-qt. glass serving bowl. Layer with onions, green pepper, corn and beans.

3) In a small bowl, combine mayonnaise and sour cream; spread over the vegetables. Sprinkle with tomatoes and cheese. Refrigerate until serving.

Yield: 6-8 servings.

NUTRITION FACTS: 1 serving equals 458 calories, 27 g fat (8 g saturated fat), 65 mg cholesterol, 652 mg sodium, 41 g carbohydrate, 4 g fiber, 10 g protein.

Brown and Wild Rice Salad

PREP/TOTAL TIME: 15 min.

Taste of Home Test Kitchen

Tangy raspberry vinegar complements the nutty flavor of the rice in this side dish, while dried cranberries provide unexpected bursts of sweetness.

- 1 cup brown rice, cooked
- 1 cup wild rice, cooked
- 6 green onions, chopped
- 3/4 cup dried cranberries
- 1/3 cup coarsely chopped pecans, toasted
- 2 tablespoons chopped fresh parsley
- 1/4 cup olive oil
- 6 tablespoons raspberry vinegar
- 2 tablespoons honey
- 1-1/2 teaspoons salt
- 1/2 teaspoon pepper

1) In a large bowl, combine the rice, onions, cranberries, pecans and parsley. In a small bowl, whisk together the oil, vinegar, honey, salt and pepper. Pour over salad and toss to coat.

Yield: 8 servings.

NUTRITION FACTS: 1 cup equals 343 calories, 12 g fat (1 g saturated fat), 0 cholesterol, 450 mg sodium, 55 g carbohydrate, 5 g fiber, 6 g protein.

Asian Crunch Salad

PREP: 15 min. + chilling

Linda Kees, Boise, Idaho

A bright assortment of crisp, fresh vegetables is lightly coated with a dressing of soy sauce, cider vinegar and sesame oil. You can also add sliced carrots for more color.

- 1 cup fresh broccoli florets
- 1 cup fresh cauliflowerets
- 1 cup cherry tomatoes
- 1/2 cup fresh snow peas
- 2 green onions, thinly sliced
- 1/2 cup sliced water chestnuts, drained
- 4-1/2 teaspoons reduced-sodium soy sauce
- 1 tablespoon cider vinegar
- 1 tablespoon sesame oil
- 3/4 teaspoon sugar
- 1/2 teaspoon sesame seeds, toasted
- 1/2 teaspoon olive oil

Dash pepper

1) In a large bowl, combine the broccoli, cauliflower, tomatoes, peas and onions. Stir in water chestnuts. In a small bowl, whisk the soy sauce, vinegar, sesame oil, sugar, sesame seeds, olive oil and pepper. Pour over vegetables and stir to coat. Cover and refrigerate until chilled.

Yield: 4 servings.

NUTRITION FACTS: 1 cup equals 82 calories, 4 g fat (1 g saturated fat), 0 cholesterol, 246 mg sodium, 10 g carbohydrate, 3 g fiber, 2 g protein.

ASIAN CRUNCH SALAD

Fresh Mozzarella Tomato Salad

PREP/TOTAL TIME: 15 min.

Regina Wood, Mackenzie, British Columbia

It will only take you a few minutes to prepare this attractive salad and have it ready when a hungry bunch is coming to eat. Basil is the finishing touch.

- 3 medium tomatoes, sliced
- 8 ounces fresh mozzarella cheese, thinly sliced
- 1/4 cup olive oil
- 2 tablespoons minced fresh basil
- 1/4 teaspoon salt
- 1/4 teaspoon coarsely ground pepper

1) Alternate tomato and cheese slices on a platter. Drizzle with oil; sprinkle with the basil, salt and pepper. Serve immediately.

Yield: 6 servings.

NUTRITION FACTS: 3/4 cup equals 204 calories, 17 g fat (7 g saturated fat), 30 mg cholesterol, 159 mg sodium, 4 g carbohydrate, 1 g fiber, 7 g protein.

Dilled Cucumbers

PREP/TOTAL TIME: 20 min.

Betty Claycomb, Alverton, Pennsylvania

Simple and classic, these dilled cucumbers are a perfect side for a summer picnic or potluck. We like them alongside grilled hamburgers.

- 2 medium cucumbers, peeled and thinly sliced
- 1/2 teaspoon salt
- 1/2 cup sour cream
- 1 tablespoon lemon juice
- 2 tablespoons finely chopped green onion

- 1/8 teaspoon pepper
- 1/4 teaspoon sugar
- 1/2 teaspoon dried dill weed

1) In a small bowl, toss cucumbers with salt. Allow to stand for 10 minutes. Meanwhile, combine all of the remaining ingredients.

2) Drain cucumbers and combine with sour cream mixture. Cover; refrigerate until serving.

Yield: 6 servings.

NUTRITION FACTS: 1 cup equals 57 calories, 3 g fat (2 g saturated fat), 13 mg cholesterol, 207 mg sodium, 4 g carbohydrate, 1 g fiber, 2 g protein.

Carrot Raisin Salad

PREP/TOTAL TIME: 10 min.

Denise Baumert, Jameson, Missouri

This traditional salad is fun to eat because of its crunchy texture and slightly sweet flavor.

- 4 cups shredded carrots (about 4 to 5 large)
- 3/4 to 1-1/2 cups raisins
- 1/4 cup mayonnaise
- 2 tablespoons sugar
- 2 to 3 tablespoons milk

1) Place carrots and raisins in a large bowl. In a small bowl, whisk together the mayonnaise, sugar and enough milk to achieve the consistency of a creamy salad dressing. Pour over carrot mixture and toss to coat.

Yield: 8 servings.

NUTRITION FACTS: 1/2 cup equals 129 calories, 6 g fat (1 g saturated fat), 3 mg cholesterol, 60 mg sodium, 20 g carbohydrate, 2 g fiber, 1 g protein.

TANGY FOUR-BEAN SALAD

🌿 Tangy Four-Bean Salad

PREP: 20 min. + chilling

Sharon Cain, Revelstoke, British Columbia

Canned beans make this colorful salad easy to fix, while a no-fuss dressing lends sweet-and-sour flair. Green pepper and mushrooms help it stand out from other bean medleys.

- 1 can (16 ounces) kidney beans, rinsed and drained
- 1 can (15 ounces) garbanzo beans *or* chickpeas, rinsed and drained
- 1 can (14-1/2 ounces) cut green beans, drained
- 1 can (14-1/2 ounces) cut wax beans, drained
- 1 cup sliced fresh mushrooms
- 1 cup chopped green pepper
- 1 cup chopped onion

DRESSING:

- 1/2 cup cider vinegar
- 1/3 cup sugar
- 1/4 cup canola oil
- 1 teaspoon celery seed
- 1/2 teaspoon pepper
- 1/4 teaspoon salt
- 1/8 teaspoon dried basil
- 1/8 teaspoon dried oregano

1) In a large bowl, combine the beans, mushrooms, green pepper and onion. In a jar with a tight-fitting lid, combine the dressing ingredients; shake well.

2) Pour dressing over bean mixture and stir to coat. Cover and refrigerate for at least 4 hours. Serve with a slotted spoon.

Yield: 12 servings.

NUTRITION FACTS: 3/4 cup equals 162 calories, 6 g fat (trace saturated fat), 0 cholesterol, 366 mg sodium, 24 g carbohydrate, 5 g fiber, 5 g protein.

Summer Squash Salad

PREP: 15 min. + chilling

Diane Hixon, Niceville, Florida

The flavors from the dressing in this salad get even better with time. My family loves this, and I love that it uses up fresh summer produce.

- 2 cups julienned zucchini
- 2 cups julienned yellow summer squash
- 1 cup sliced radish
- 1/2 cup vegetable oil
- 2 tablespoons plus 2 teaspoons cider vinegar
- 1 tablespoon Dijon mustard
- 1 tablespoon minced fresh parsley
- 3/4 teaspoon salt
- 1/2 teaspoon dill weed
- 1/4 teaspoon pepper

1) In a large bowl, toss the zucchini, squash and radishes. In a small bowl or jar with a tight-fitting lid, combine remaining ingredients; shake well. Pour over vegetables. Cover and refrigerate for at least 2 hours.

Yield: 6-8 servings.

NUTRITION FACTS: 3/4 cup equals 137 calories, 14 g fat (2 g saturated fat), 0 cholesterol, 274 mg sodium, 3 g carbohydrate, 1 g fiber, 1 g protein.

SUMMER SQUASH SALAD

Creamy Corn Salad

PREP: 25 min. + chilling

Esther Horst, Monterey, Tennessee

I remember enjoying a salad similar to this when I was a girl. I never got the recipe, but I think I was able to duplicate it pretty well. We enjoy it alongside rice and beans.

- 6 cups frozen corn, thawed
- 3 cups chopped seeded tomatoes
- 1 cup cubed avocado
- 2/3 cup julienned sweet red pepper
- 2/3 cup julienned green pepper
- 1/2 cup chopped onion

CREAMY CORN SALAD

DRESSING:

- 1 cup mayonnaise
- 2 tablespoons red wine vinegar
- 2 tablespoons Dijon mustard
- 1 teaspoon salt
- 1/8 teaspoon pepper

1) In a large bowl, combine the corn, tomatoes, avocado, peppers and onion. In a small bowl, whisk the dressing ingredients. Pour over salad; toss to coat. Cover and refrigerate for 30 minutes or until chilled.

Yield: 12 servings.

NUTRITION FACTS: 3/4 cup equals 242 calories, 17 g fat (2 g saturated fat), 7 mg cholesterol, 363 mg sodium, 22 g carbohydrate, 3 g fiber, 3 g protein.

FRESH MARSHMALLOWS ■■■

To keep marshmallows from turning hard, store them in the freezer. When thawed, they're like fresh.

—Lyn C., Provo, Utah

Ambrosia Salad

PREP: 10 min. + chilling

Judi Bringegar, Liberty, North Carolina

This salad is great for last-minute planning because it's easy to prepare.

- 1 can (11 ounces) mandarin oranges, drained
- 1 can (8 ounces) pineapple chunks, drained
- 1 cup miniature marshmallows
- 1 cup flaked coconut
- 1 cup (8 ounces) sour cream

1) In a large bowl, combine the oranges, pineapple, marshmallows and coconut. Add sour cream and toss to mix. Cover; refrigerate for several hours.

Yield: 4 servings.

NUTRITION FACTS: 1 cup equals 332 calories, 18 g fat (14 g saturated fat), 40 mg cholesterol, 99 mg sodium, 37 g carbohydrate, 1 g fiber, 4 g protein.

Taffy Apple Salad

PREP: 20 min. + chilling

Cathy LaReau, Lowell, Indiana

When you take a bite of this salad, you may think you're eating a candied apple. It's delicious!

- 1 can (20 ounces) crushed pineapple
- 4 cups miniature marshmallows
- 1 egg, lightly beaten
- 1/2 cup sugar
- 1/4 cup packed brown sugar
- 1 tablespoon all-purpose flour
- 4-1/2 teaspoons cider vinegar
- 1 carton (8 ounces) frozen whipped topping, thawed
- 3 cups diced unpeeled apples
- 1-1/2 cups lightly salted peanuts, coarsely chopped

1) Drain pineapple, reserving juice. In a large bowl, combine pineapple and marshmallows; cover and refrigerate for several hours.

2) In a saucepan, combine the egg, sugars, flour, vinegar and reserved pineapple juice; cook and stir until mixture thickens and reaches 160°. Remove from heat; cool. Cover and refrigerate.

3) Fold whipped topping into the chilled dressing. Add the apples and peanuts to the pineapple and marshmallows. Fold dressing into fruit mixture. Refrigerate leftovers.

Yield: 10-12 servings.

NUTRITION FACTS: 3/4 cup equals 315 calories, 13 g fat (5 g saturated fat), 18 mg cholesterol, 93 mg sodium, 47 g carbohydrate, 3 g fiber, 6 g protein.

TAFFY APPLE SALAD

Better Gelatin Salads

Always use canned or cooked pineapple in gelatin salads. Fresh pineapple, kiwifruit, papaya, guava, figs or gingerroot will prevent the salad from setting.

For easy removal of gelatin salads from the mold, coat mold with cooking spray before filling. To avoid spilling when transferring the mold into the refrigerator, place mold on a baking sheet or tray in the refrigerator and then fill with the gelatin mixture.

To prevent fruits or vegetables from floating or sinking in the mold, add them when the gelatin is slightly thickened. If the gelatin is too thin, the fruit will sink; too thick, and the fruit will float.

If your gelatin mixture sets too fast and you've passed the "partially set" step, place the bowl of gelatin in a pan of warm water and stir until the gelatin has softened. Chill again until the mixture is the consistency of unbeaten raw egg whites.

For a layered mold, always start and end with gelatin mixture since the creamy layer might not be sturdy enough to support the gelatin mixture. Add the creamy layer when the gelatin layer sticks to a finger when touched. If the gelatin layer is too set up, the layers may slip apart when unmolded.

Before unmolding, make sure the gelatin mixture has completely set up. The gelatin should not feel sticky and should not move when the mold is tilted. When unmolding a large salad, rinse the serving platter with cold water before turning the gelatin out. The moisture helps allow the salad to be centered on the platter.

Unmolding Gelatin Salads

1) Loosen the gelatin from the top edge of mold by gently pulling the gelatin away from edge with a moistened finger. Then dip the mold up to its rim in a sink or large pan of warm water for a few seconds or until edges begin to release from the side of the mold.

2) Place a plate over the mold and invert. Carefully lift the mold from the salad.

APRICOT GELATIN SALAD

Apricot Gelatin Salad

PREP: 15 min. + chilling

Neva Jane Upp, Hutchinson, Kansas

A family who usually passes up molded salads will hunt for this fruity version at our covered dish buffet. Not only is it delicious, it adds color to any meal.

> 2 cans (16 ounces *each*) apricot halves

Dash salt

> 2 packages (3 ounces *each*) orange gelatin
> 1 can (6 ounces) frozen orange juice concentrate, thawed
> 1 tablespoon lemon juice
> 1 cup lemon-lime soda

1) Drain the apricots, reserving 1-1/2 cups juice; set apricots aside. In a small saucepan, bring apricot juice and salt to a boil over medium heat. Remove from the heat; add gelatin, stirring until gelatin is dissolved.

2) In a blender, combine orange juice concentrate, lemon juice and reserved apricots; cover and process until smooth. Add to gelatin mixture along with soda; mix well.

3) Pour into a 6-cup mold coated with cooking spray. Cover and refrigerate until firm. Unmold and transfer to a serving plate.

Yield: 10 servings.

NUTRITION FACTS: 1 piece equals 181 calories, trace fat (trace saturated fat), 0 cholesterol, 60 mg sodium, 45 g carbohydrate, 2 g fiber, 3 g protein.

MORE NUTRITIOUS GELATIN SALAD ■■■

When I make a 3-ounce package of gelatin, I add 6 ounces of yogurt and 1 cup orange juice instead of the cold water. It's a nutritious and refreshing salad.

—Donna C., Olympia, Washington

Cherry Ribbon Salad

PREP: 10 min. + chilling

Virginia Luke, Red Level, Alabama

Filled with pineapple, pecans and cherry pie filling, this colorful salad mold adds fun, fruity flavor to any potluck menu.

- 1 package (3 ounces) cherry gelatin
- 2-1/4 cups boiling water, *divided*
- 1 can (21 ounces) cherry pie filling
- 1 package (3 ounces) orange gelatin
- 1 can (8 ounces) crushed pineapple, undrained
- 1 cup whipped topping
- 1/3 cup mayonnaise
- 1/4 cup chopped pecans, optional

1) In a large bowl, dissolve cherry gelatin in 1-1/4 cups boiling water. Stir in pie filling. Pour into a 7-cup ring mold coated with cooking spray; chill for about 1 hour or until set but not firm.

2) In a large bowl, dissolve orange gelatin in remaining boiling water. Stir in pineapple. Chill for about 1 hour or until thickened but not set.

3) Combine the whipped topping, mayonnaise and pecans if desired; fold into orange mixture. Spoon over cherry layer. Refrigerate for at least 1 hour or until firm. Unmold onto a serving plate.

Yield: 12 servings.

NUTRITION FACTS: 1 slice equals 184 calories, 6 g fat (2 g saturated fat), 2 mg cholesterol, 75 mg sodium, 31 g carbohydrate, trace fiber, 2 g protein.

NO-MELT GELATIN MOLDS ▪▪▪

During summer, I love to serve cool gelatin salads, but they seem to sag and wilt in the heat. I discovered if I add one envelope of unflavored gelatin (but no extra liquid), along with the flavored gelatin called for in the recipe, my salad "stands" until the very last spoonful!

—Cynthia Linton, Sister Bay, Wisconsin

Orange Gelatin Pretzel Salad

PREP: 30 min. + chilling

Peggy Boyd, Northport, Alabama

The pretzels give the refreshing layered salad a nice crunch. It's a favorite in our family.

- 2 cups crushed pretzels
- 3 teaspoons plus 3/4 cup sugar, *divided*
- 3/4 cup butter, melted
- 2 packages (3 ounces *each*) orange gelatin
- 2 cups boiling water
- 2 cans (8 ounces *each*) crushed pineapple, drained
- 1 can (11 ounces) mandarin oranges, drained
- 1 package (8 ounces) cream cheese, softened
- 2 cups whipped topping

Additional whipped topping, optional

1) In a small bowl, combine pretzels and 3 teaspoons sugar; stir in butter. Press into an ungreased 13-in. x 9-in. x 2-in. baking dish. Bake at 350° for 10 minutes. Cool on a wire rack.

2) In a large bowl, dissolve gelatin in boiling water. Add pineapple and oranges. Chill until partially set, about 30 minutes.

3) In a small mixing bowl, beat cream cheese and remaining sugar until smooth. Fold in whipped topping. Spread over crust. Gently spoon gelatin mixture over cream cheese layer. Cover and refrigerate for 2-4 hours or until firm.

4) Cut into squares. Garnish with additional whipped topping if desired.

Yield: 15 servings.

NUTRITION FACTS: 1 piece equals 286 calories, 16 g fat (11 g saturated fat), 41 mg cholesterol, 326 mg sodium, 33 g carbohydrate, 1 g fiber, 3 g protein.

ORANGE GELATIN PRETZEL SALAD

Salad Dressings

If you plan on serving a vinegar and oil dressing right away, you can combine all ingredients in a jar with a tight-fitting lid and shake well. The mixture will separate upon standing; simply shake before serving. To mix a vinegar and oil dressing that will stand for an hour or two without separating, see Whisking Vinegar and Oil Dressings (below right). Also use this method for dressings with mayonnaise or prepared mustard.

Homemade salad dressings made with olive oil will thicken during refrigeration. Remove the dressing 30 minutes before using to allow the olive oil to warm up.

By experimenting with a basic vinaigrette, you can create a variety of dressings to complement different salads. Try substituting an herb-, fruit- or wine-flavored vinegar for white or cider vinegar. Use citrus juice for part or all of the vinegar. Use nut-flavored oil for vegetable oil or add a drop or two of dark sesame oil. Finally, vary the herbs to best match the flavor of foods being dressed.

Citrus Vinaigrette

PREP/TOTAL TIME: 5 min.

Taste of Home Test Kitchen

Tart, tangy and citrusy flavors abound in this vinaigrette. Quickly whisk it together any night of the week.

- 1/4 cup orange juice
- 3 tablespoons red wine vinegar
- 2 teaspoons honey
- 1-1/2 teaspoons Dijon mustard
- 1 tablespoon olive oil

1) In a small bowl, whisk together all the ingredients. Store in the refrigerator.

Yield: 1/2 cup.

NUTRITION FACTS: 2 tablespoons equals 53 calories, 4 g fat (trace saturated fat), 0 cholesterol, 47 mg sodium, 5 g carbohydrate, trace fiber, trace protein.

Raspberry Vinaigrette

PREP: 10 min. + chilling

Valerie Jordan, Kingmont, West Virginia

My family requests this light, fruity dressing all year. I especially like it in the summer as an alternative to heavier, cream-based dressings.

- 1/2 cup raspberry vinegar
- 1/3 cup sugar
- 3/4 cup olive oil
- 1/2 teaspoon Dijon mustard
- 1/8 teaspoon pepper

1) In a small saucepan, cook and stir vinegar and sugar over low heat until sugar is dissolved. Cool slightly. Pour into a jar with tight-fitting lid. Add remaining ingredients; cover and shake well. Refrigerate until chilled. Shake before using. Refrigerate leftovers.

Yield: 1-1/4 cups.

NUTRITION FACTS: 2 tablespoons equals 173 calories, 16 g fat (2 g saturated fat), 0 cholesterol, 6 mg sodium, 7 g carbohydrate, trace fiber, trace protein.

Poppy Seed Dressing

PREP/TOTAL TIME: 20 min.

Andra Kunkle, Lenoir, North Carolina

We especially love this sweet dressing on an assortment of fresh fruit.

- 2 cups sugar
- 3/4 teaspoon salt
- 3/4 teaspoon onion powder
- 3/4 teaspoon ground mustard
- 3/4 cup cider vinegar
- 1 cup vegetable oil
- 3/4 teaspoon poppy seeds

1) In a small mixing bowl, combine the sugar, salt, onion powder and mustard. Add the vinegar and beat for 4 minutes.

2) Add the oil; beat for 10 minutes. Add the poppy seeds; beat for 5 minutes. Store in the refrigerator.

Yield: 2-3/4 cups.

NUTRITION FACTS: 2 tablespoons equals 159 calories, 10 g fat (1 g saturated fat), 0 cholesterol, 81 mg sodium, 18 g carbohydrate, trace fiber, trace protein.

Whisking Vinegar and Oil Dressings

In a small bowl, combine all ingredients except oil. Slowly add oil while mixing vigorously with a wire whisk.

CREAMY FRENCH DRESSING

⏱Creamy French Dressing
PREP/TOTAL TIME: 10 min.

Taste of Home Test Kitchen

You'll need just a few ingredients from your pantry to blend together this mild dressing. It's thick, creamy and perfect on tossed salad greens.

- 1 cup ketchup
- 1/2 cup reduced-fat mayonnaise
- 3 tablespoons cider vinegar
- 3 tablespoons honey
- 2 tablespoons water
- 1 tablespoon olive oil
- 1 teaspoon lemon juice
- 1/2 teaspoon ground mustard
- 1/4 teaspoon salt

1) In a blender or food processor, combine all of the ingredients; cover and process until blended. Store in the refrigerator.

Yield: 1-3/4 cups.

NUTRITION FACTS: 2 tablespoons equals 70 calories, 4 g fat (1 g saturated fat), 3 mg cholesterol, 318 mg sodium, 10 g carbohydrate, 1 g fiber, 1 g protein.

Caesar Dressing
PREP: 15 min. + chilling

Taste of Home Test Kitchen

Looking for a new and different salad dressing you can whisk up in minutes for special occasions? You can't miss with this light, savory Caesar blend. It really dresses up fresh greens!

- 2/3 cup reduced-fat mayonnaise
- 1/2 cup reduced-fat sour cream
- 1/2 cup buttermilk
- 1 tablespoon red wine vinegar
- 1 tablespoon stone-ground mustard
- 1-1/2 teaspoons lemon juice
- 1-1/2 teaspoons Worcestershire sauce

- 1/3 cup grated Parmigiano-Reggiano cheese
- 2 anchovy fillets, minced
- 2 garlic cloves, minced
- 1/2 teaspoon coarsely ground pepper

1) In a small bowl, whisk the mayonnaise, sour cream, buttermilk, vinegar, mustard, lemon juice and Worcestershire sauce. Stir in the cheese, anchovies, garlic and pepper. Cover and refrigerate for at least 1 hour.

Yield: 1-2/3 cups.

NUTRITION FACTS: 2 tablespoons equals 71 calories, 6 g fat (2 g saturated fat), 10 mg cholesterol, 205 mg sodium, 3 g carbohydrate, trace fiber, 2 g protein.

⏱Blue Cheese Salad Dressing
PREP/TOTAL TIME: 10 min.

Christy Freeman, Central Point, Oregon

This distinctively flavored dressing makes a great accompaniment to a mix of fresh greens. The thick, creamy dressing does double duty at our house—I often serve it as a dip with vegetables.

- 2 cups mayonnaise
- 1 cup (8 ounces) sour cream
- 1/4 cup white wine vinegar
- 1/4 cup minced fresh parsley
- 1 garlic clove, crushed
- 1/2 teaspoon ground mustard
- 1/2 teaspoon salt
- 1/4 teaspoon pepper
- 4 ounces crumbled blue cheese

1) Place all the ingredients in a blender; cover and process until smooth. Store in the refrigerator.

Yield: 3 cups.

NUTRITION FACTS: 2 tablespoons equals 172 calories, 18 g fat (4 g saturated fat), 17 mg cholesterol, 220 mg sodium, 1 g carbohydrate, trace fiber, 1 g protein.

BLUE CHEESE SALAD DRESSING

CRACKED PEPPER SALAD DRESSING

Cracked Pepper Salad Dressing

PREP: 15 min. + chilling

Millie Vickery, Lena, Illinois

The pepper is bold but not too sharp in this creamy dressing that will complement your favorite salad ingredients. It's easy to mix up and great to have on hand.

- 2 cups mayonnaise
- 1/4 cup water
- 1/4 cup milk
- 1/4 cup buttermilk
- 2 tablespoons grated Parmesan cheese
- 1 tablespoon coarsely ground pepper
- 2 teaspoons finely chopped green onion
- 1 teaspoon lemon juice
- 1/2 teaspoon garlic salt
- 1/2 teaspoon garlic powder

1) In a small bowl, whisk all ingredients until blended. Cover and chill for at least 1 hour. May be stored in the refrigerator for up to 2 weeks.

Yield: 2-1/2 cups.

NUTRITION FACTS: 2 tablespoons equals 167 calories, 18 g fat (3 g saturated fat), 9 mg cholesterol, 179 mg sodium, 1 g carbohydrate, trace fiber, trace protein.

Tangy Bacon Salad Dressing

PREP/TOTAL TIME: 10 min.

Barbara Birk, St. George, Utah

You can serve this over salad greens or spinach, and you can add different berries, radishes or tomatoes for color.

- 3/4 cup sugar
- 1/3 cup white vinegar
- 1/3 cup ketchup
- 1 teaspoon Worcestershire sauce
- 1/2 cup vegetable oil
- 8 bacon strips, cooked and crumbled
- 1 small onion, finely chopped

1) In a small bowl, whisk together the sugar, vinegar, ketchup and Worcestershire sauce. Gradually whisk in the oil in a steady stream. Stir in bacon and onion. Store in the refrigerator.

Yield: about 2 cups.

NUTRITION FACTS: 2 tablespoons equals 122 calories, 8 g fat (1 g saturated fat), 3 mg cholesterol, 113 mg sodium, 11 g carbohydrate, trace fiber, 1 g protein.

Seasoned Croutons

PREP/TOTAL TIME: 30 min.

Shelley McKinney, New Castle, Indiana

You can use these croutons as a topping for salads, soups or some of your favorite side-dish casseroles.

- 2 tablespoons butter
- 1 tablespoon olive oil
- 1/4 teaspoon garlic powder
- 1/4 teaspoon onion powder
- 1/4 teaspoon dried oregano
- 1/4 teaspoon dried basil

Pinch salt

- 6 slices day-old bread, cubed

1) In an ungreased 13-in. x 9-in. x 2-in. baking pan, combine the butter, oil and seasonings. Heat in a 300° oven until butter is melted. Remove from the oven; stir to combine.

2) Add bread cubes and toss to coat. Bake for 10-15 minutes or until lightly browned, stirring frequently. Cool. Store in the refrigerator in an airtight container.

Yield: 3 cups.

NUTRITION FACTS: 1/4 cup equals 61 calories, 3 g fat (1 g saturated fat), 5 mg cholesterol, 99 mg sodium, 6 g carbohydrate, trace fiber, 1 g protein.

■ **Lighter Seasoned Croutons:** Omit butter and oil. Spray bread cubes with butter-flavored cooking spray. Sprinkle with seasonings and bake as directed.

■ **Dilly Croutons:** Omit seasonings and use 1 teaspoon dill weed. Bake as directed.

HOMESPUN FAT-FREE DRESSING ■■■

I don't care for bottled fat-free dressings, so I make my own. I start with a packet of ranch salad dressing mix and fat-free milk and mayonnaise in place of the regular milk and mayonnaise called for on the package. It's so good you won't think it's fat-free.

—*Leticia S., Fort Huachuca, Arizona*

a passion for peppers

Business profits may help find a cure for MS

Kristen and Steve Cummins

> " When we started the business, one of our goals was to donate a portion of the profits to the National MS Society. "
>
> ~Kristen Cummins

Soon after Kristen Cummins met her husband, Steve, she knew they had been brought together for a reason—to start a pickled pepper business. On one of the couple's early dates, Steve asked her to help can pickled peppers using a recipe that had been handed down from his grandmother and tweaked to add his own twist.

"It was right then and there that I got a clear view on how great the peppers were," Kristen recalls from the family's farm near Rootstown, Ohio. "Our peppers are different because they're cold-packed, which makes them extra flavorful and crunchy.

"Nobody else makes a pepper like this, I thought. And if God hadn't brought us together, I don't think Steve would have done anything with the recipe. So I was sure He had brought us together to start this business," Kristen says.

She was convinced the public would buy them, so the couple went into business in 2004, producing both a hot and mild variety.

"Our teenagers, Craig, Dana and Clark, are a huge help with planting, picking and deliveries," says Kristen. "We rent a commercial kitchen in town, and aunts, uncles,

cousins, parents and friends form an assembly line, with each member assigned a job to do."

About 1-1/2 years after launching Stevereno's Peppers, Kristen was diagnosed with multiple sclerosis and realized the much bigger purpose behind God's plan— to help find a cure for MS.

"We've supported the National MS Society for years," she explains. In 1987 Kristen's father was diagnosed with MS, a chronic neurological disease that affects the central nervous system; her younger sister was diagnosed in 1996.

"We always participated in the MS fund-raising walks, and we chose to live across the street from my parents so we would always be there to help Dad," Kristen says. "When we started the business, one of our goals was to donate a portion of the profits to the National MS Society." Kristen is more passionate about that goal than ever.

"Our products have been successful, thanks to the Lord's support. And it's part of His plan that we use them to help others," she says. "As we say in our family—if you want to spice up life...just add peppers!"

DO YOU KNOW A COOK WHO CARES?

If you or someone you know cooks for a charitable, spiritual or other cause, tell us about it at **tasteofhome.com/CookbookBonus**

Recipes

Tips

Sauces & Condiments

Sauces and condiments enhance other foods with sweet or savory flavors. Sauces help dress up meat or vegetables. Condiments are served along with a meal and include everything from jams and jellies to relishes, pickled vegetables, chutneys and salsas.

White Sauces

White sauces can be used as a base for a casserole or flavored as a topping for vegetables or meats. White sauce typically starts with a roux, which is a smooth mixture of equal parts butter and flour. The amount of butter and flour per 1 cup of liquid determines the thickness of the white sauce.

- Thin sauce: 1 tablespoon *each* butter and flour.
- Medium sauce: 2 tablespoons *each* butter and flour.
- Thick sauce: 3 tablespoons *each* butter and flour.

Basic White Sauce

PREP/TOTAL TIME: 10 min.

Lois Gelzer, Oak Bluffs, Massachusetts

For years I have used this smooth sauce to make many dishes. The recipe can easily be doubled.

> 2 tablespoons butter
> 2 tablespoons all-purpose flour
> 1/8 teaspoon salt
> Dash white pepper
> 1 cup milk

1) In a saucepan, melt butter over medium heat. Whisk in the flour, salt and pepper until smooth. Gradually whisk in the milk.

2) Bring to a boil; cook and stir for 2 minutes or until thickened. Use immediately or refrigerate.

Yield: 1 cup.

NUTRITION FACTS: 2 tablespoons equals 51 calories, 4 g fat (2 g saturated fat), 12 mg cholesterol, 81 mg sodium, 3 g carbohydrate, trace fiber, 1 g protein.

- **Cheese Sauce:** Prepare Basic White Sauce as directed. Reduce the heat; stir in 1/2 to 3/4 cup shredded cheddar cheese. Continue to stir just until cheese is melted.

- **Curry Sauce:** Add 1/2 teaspoon curry powder and a dash of ground ginger along with the salt and pepper. Prepare as directed.

- **Mornay Sauce:** Prepare Basic White Sauce as directed. Reduce heat; stir in 1/4 cup shredded Swiss cheese, Parmesan cheese *or* a combination of both and a dash of ground nutmeg. Continue to stir just until cheese is melted.

- **Mustard Sauce:** Stir in 1 tablespoon Dijon mustard into finished Basic White Sauce.

- **Brown Sauce:** Use 1 cup beef broth in place of the milk. Prepare as directed. For a richer color, add a dash of browning sauce.

- **Veloute Sauce:** Use 1 cup chicken, turkey or fish broth in place of the milk. Prepare as directed.

Making a White Sauce

1) Start a white sauce by whisking flour into melted butter over medium heat until mixture becomes smooth.

2) Gradually whisk milk into mixture until blended. Bring mixture to a boil; cook and stir 2 minutes or until thickened.

☼Pan Gravy

PREP/TOTAL TIME: 15 min.

Taste of Home Test Kitchen

Use this recipe to make gravy from meats and poultry roasted in an uncovered roasting pan.

Roasted meat drippings
  1/4 cup all-purpose flour
Chicken broth *or* water
Salt, pepper and browning sauce,
  optional

1) Pour pan drippings into a measuring cup. Loosen the browned bits from the roasting pan and add to drippings. Skim fat.

2) Reserve 1/4 cup fat and transfer to a saucepan; whisk in flour until smooth. Add enough broth or water to pan drippings to measure 2 cups.

3) Gradually stir into flour mixture in saucepan. Bring to a boil; cook and stir for 2 minutes or until thickened. Season with salt, pepper and browning sauce if desired.

Yield: 2 cups.

NUTRITION FACTS: 2 tablespoons equals 40 calories, 4 g fat (2 g saturated fat), 4 mg cholesterol, 121 mg sodium, 2 g carbohydrate, trace fiber, trace protein.

Making Pan Gravy

1) Pour pan drippings into a heat-resistant measuring cup along with any browned bits scraped from roasting pan. Skim fat.

2) Reserve 1/4 cup fat and place in a saucepan. Whisk in flour until smooth.

3) Add enough broth or water to reserved pan drippings to equal 2 cups. Add all at once to flour mixture. Cook and stir over medium-high heat until mixture comes to a boil; cook and stir 2 minutes longer.

Reducing Pan Juices for Gravy

To thicken pan juices without flour, remove the meat to a warm serving platter. Transfer pan juices along with browned bits to a saucepan. Bring to a boil; cook, uncovered, until the liquid evaporates enough that it thickens to a gravy consistency.

☼ Makeover Home-Style Gravy

PREP: 15 min. **COOK:** 45 min.

Taste of Home Test Kitchen

Thinking of skipping the gravy at the holidays because it's "bad" for you? Don't even think of it! We've created this low-cal, low-fat gravy you won't believe.

  1 large onion, chopped
  1 medium carrot, chopped
  1 celery rib, chopped
  2 teaspoons canola oil
1/2 cup sherry *or* unsweetened
       apple juice
2-1/2 cups water
1/2 cup packed fresh parsley sprigs
  2 bay leaves
1/4 cup all-purpose flour
  1 can (14-1/2 ounces) reduced-
       sodium chicken broth
  1 tablespoon turkey drippings
  1 teaspoon rubbed sage
1/2 teaspoon browning sauce,
       optional
1/4 teaspoon salt
1/4 teaspoon pepper

1) In a large saucepan, saute the onion, carrot and celery in oil until tender. Add sherry or apple juice; cook and stir 1 minute longer. Add the water, parsley and bay leaves; bring to a boil. Reduce heat; simmer, uncovered, for 30 minutes or until liquid is nearly reduced by half.

2) Strain and discard vegetables and herbs; set liquid aside (liquid should measure 1-1/2 cups). In a small saucepan, combine flour and broth until smooth. Stir in the drippings, sage, browning sauce if desired, salt, pepper and reserved liquid. Bring to a boil; cook and stir for 2 minutes or until thickened.

Yield: 3 cups.

NUTRITION FACTS: 1/4 cup equals 31 calories, 2 g fat (1 g saturated fat), 1 mg cholesterol, 146 mg sodium, 3 g carbohydrate, trace fiber, 1 g protein.

BETTER-FOR-YOU GRAVY ■■■

To make a healthier gravy, brown flour in a skillet. Cool slightly, then add some instant chicken, beef or vegetable bouillon granules and warm water. Cook and stir until thickened, then add salt and pepper if necessary.

—Elva G., Detroit, Michigan

HOLLANDAISE SAUCE

Hollandaise Sauce

Hollandaise is a lemony, butter sauce that uses egg yolks rather than flour as the thickener. Hollandaise sauce can be tricky to make, so follow these pointers:

- Heat egg yolks over low heat. If the heat is too high, it will result in scrambled eggs.

- So the sauce thickens properly, allow the yolks to absorb a little butter at a time. Gradually add the butter in small amounts and completely incorporate into the yolks.

- Beat a tablespoon of cold water into the finished sauce if it starts to separate.

Hollandaise Sauce

PREP/TOTAL TIME: 30 min.

Taste of Home Test Kitchen

This traditional sauce adds an elegant touch to fresh steamed asparagus. The rich, lemony mixture is the typical sauce for eggs Benedict and is also delicious served over broccoli.

 3 egg yolks
1/4 cup water
 2 tablespoons lemon juice
1/2 cup cold butter, cut into 8 pieces
1/8 teaspoon salt
1/8 teaspoon paprika
Dash white pepper

1) In a small heavy saucepan or double boiler, whisk together the egg yolks, water and lemon juice. Cook and stir over low heat until mixture begins to thicken, bubbles around edges and reaches 160°, about 20 minutes.

2) Add butter to yolk mixture, one piece at a time, whisking after each addition until butter is melted. Remove from the heat; stir in the salt, paprika and pepper. Serve immediately.

Yield: 1 cup.

Editor's Note: To make a double boiler, place a stainless-steel mixing bowl in a saucepan. The bowl should only partially fit into the saucepan. Fill the saucepan with enough water so that when the bowl rests in the saucepan the water does not touch the bottom of the bowl. Bring the water to a simmer. Add the ingredients to the bowl and place the bowl in the saucepan.

NUTRITION FACTS: 2 tablespoons equals 124 calories, 13 g fat (8 g saturated fat), 110 mg cholesterol, 155 mg sodium, trace carbohydrate, trace fiber, 1 g protein.

Bearnaise Sauce

PREP/TOTAL TIME: 30 min.

Taste of Home Test Kitchen

This is a smooth, creamy sauce that makes a tangy accompaniment to roast beef.

1/4 cup white wine vinegar
1/4 cup white wine *or* chicken broth
1/4 cup minced shallot
 3 tarragon sprigs
1/4 teaspoon pepper
 4 egg yolks
 2 tablespoons cold water
1/4 teaspoon salt
1/8 teaspoon white pepper
1/2 cup butter, melted and cooled
 2 tablespoons minced fresh tarragon
 1 tablespoon minced fresh parsley

1) In a small saucepan, combine the vinegar, wine or broth, shallot, tarragon sprigs and pepper; bring to a boil. Reduce heat; simmer for 10 minutes or until mixture is reduced by half. Strain and set liquid aside; discard solids.

2) In a small heavy saucepan, whisk together the egg yolks, water, salt, white pepper and reserved vinegar liquid. Cook and stir over low heat until the mixture begins to thicken, bubbles around the edges and reaches 160°.

3) Gradually whisk in butter. Remove from the heat; stir in tarragon and parsley. Serve immediately.

Yield: 1 cup.

NUTRITION FACTS: 2 tablespoons equals 142 calories, 14 g fat (8 g saturated fat), 137 mg cholesterol, 194 mg sodium, 2 g carbohydrate, trace fiber, 2 g protein.

Dijon Sauce for Veggies

PREP/TOTAL TIME: 20 min.

Jan Allen, Lander, Wyoming

Here's a deliciously different way to serve good-for-you vegetables to your family. The creamy, trimmed-down sauce with its subtle Dijon flavor drapes nicely over cauliflower, carrots or just about any vegetable. I like to blanch broccoli florets and toss them with the sauce.

- 1/2 cup finely chopped onion
- 2 garlic cloves, minced
- 1 teaspoon olive oil
- 2-1/2 cups fat-free milk
- 3 tablespoons cornstarch
- 1/4 cup vegetable broth
- 2 ounces reduced-fat cream cheese, cubed
- 2 tablespoons Dijon mustard
- 1/4 teaspoon salt
- 1/8 teaspoon pepper

Dash ground nutmeg

1) In a small nonstick saucepan, saute the onion and garlic in oil until tender. Stir in milk. Combine cornstarch and broth until smooth; stir into the pan. Bring to a boil; cook and stir for 1 minute or until thickened.

2) Remove from the heat. Whisk in cream cheese until melted. Stir in the mustard, salt, pepper and nutmeg. Serve with vegetables.

Yield: 2-1/2 cups.

NUTRITION FACTS: 1/4 cup equals 58 calories, 2 fat (1 saturated fat), 6 mg cholesterol, 212 mg sodium, 7 g carbohydrate, trace fiber, 3 g protein.

DIJON SAUCE FOR VEGGIES

Herb Butter

PREP/TOTAL TIME: 5 min.

Donna Smith, Victor, New York

We love to use this savory butter on fresh corn on the cob, but it is also yummy on many fresh vegetables.

- 1/2 cup butter, softened
- 1 tablespoon minced fresh chives
- 1 tablespoon minced fresh dill
- 1 tablespoon minced fresh parsley
- 1/2 teaspoon dried thyme
- 1/4 teaspoon salt

Dash garlic powder

Dash cayenne pepper

Hot cooked vegetables

1) In a small bowl, combine all the ingredients. Serve over vegetables. Refrigerate leftovers.

Yield: 2/3 cup.

NUTRITION FACTS: 1 tablespoon equals 203 calories, 10 g fat (6 g saturated fat), 25 mg cholesterol, 158 mg sodium, 29 g carbohydrate, 4 g fiber, 4 g protein.

Pecan Barbecue Sauce

PREP/TOTAL TIME: 30 min.

Vickie Patterson, Vinta, Oklahoma

After years of making this delicious sauce, I haven't found anything that this sauce doesn't taste great on.

- 1 can (12 ounces) tomato paste
- 1 cup ground pecans
- 3/4 cup water
- 1/3 cup packed brown sugar
- 1/4 cup cider vinegar
- 1/4 cup chopped onion
- 1/4 cup honey
- 2 tablespoons lemon juice
- 1 tablespoon prepared mustard
- 1 teaspoon seasoned salt
- 2 garlic cloves, minced

1) In a large saucepan, combine all the ingredients. Bring to a boil. Reduce heat; simmer, uncovered, for 20 minutes or until thickened, stirring occasionally. Cool. Store in the refrigerator.

Yield: 3 cups.

NUTRITION FACTS: 2 tablespoons equals 59 calories, 2 g fat (trace saturated fat), 0 cholesterol, 83 mg sodium, 10 g carbohydrate, 1 g fiber, 1 g protein.

Jamaican Barbecue Sauce

PREP/TOTAL TIME: 20 min.

Lee Ann Odell, Erie, Colorado

Since visiting Jamaica, I've become a big fan of jerk chicken and fish. I came up with my own version of that zesty island flavoring. It's a great sauce for ribs.

- 1 bacon strip, halved
- 1/2 cup chopped onion

2 tablespoons chopped green onion

1 tablespoon chopped jalapeno pepper

1 cup ketchup

1/2 cup chicken broth

1/2 cup molasses

2 tablespoons cider vinegar

2 tablespoons lemon juice

1 tablespoon minced fresh thyme

1 tablespoon soy sauce

1 tablespoon Worcestershire sauce

1 tablespoon prepared mustard

1 teaspoon salt

1/2 teaspoon pepper

1/4 to 1/2 teaspoon ground cinnamon

1/4 to 1/2 teaspoon ground nutmeg

1) In a saucepan, cook bacon over medium heat until crisp. Discard bacon or save for another use.

2) In the drippings, saute the onions and jalapeno until tender. Stir in the remaining ingredients. Bring to a boil. Remove from the heat; cool. Store in the refrigerator.

Yield: 2 cups.

Editor's Note: When cutting or seeding hot peppers, use rubber or plastic gloves to protect your hands. Avoid touching your face.

NUTRITION FACTS: 2 tablespoons equals 61 calories, 1 g fat (1 g saturated fat), 1 mg cholesterol, 450 mg sodium, 12 g carbohydrate, trace fiber, 1 g protein.

Summertime Barbecue Sauce

PREP: 15 min. **COOK:** 25 min. + chilling

Diane Shipley, Mentor, Ohio

Friends and family love this sauce on pork chops or ribs. Every time I make it, someone asks for the recipe!

4 cups finely chopped onions

4 garlic cloves, minced

1 cup vegetable oil

4 cups water

3 cups ketchup

1-1/3 cups lemon juice

3/4 cup sugar

1/2 cup Worcestershire sauce

1/4 cup prepared mustard

2 tablespoons salt

2 tablespoons steak sauce

2 tablespoons Liquid Smoke, optional

1 teaspoon hot pepper sauce, optional

1) In a Dutch oven, saute onions and garlic in oil for 8-10 minutes or until tender. Stir in the remaining ingredients. Bring to a boil. Reduce heat; simmer, uncovered, for 15 minutes. Cool. Transfer to

SUMMERTIME BARBECUE SAUCE

storage containers; cover and refrigerate overnight. Refrigerate for up to 5 days. Freeze up to 6 months.

Yield: 3 quarts.

NUTRITION FACTS: 1 serving (1/4 cup) equals 78 calories, 5 g fat (1 g saturated fat), 0 cholesterol, 527 mg sodium, 10 g carbohydrate, 1 g fiber, trace protein.

Spicy Mustard

PREP: 15 min. **COOK:** 5 min. + standing

Joyce Lonsdale, Unionville, Pennsylvania

I like to make this using fresh horseradish from my garden and vinegar seasoned with homegrown tarragon. It's a delightful dipper for pretzel rods or as a sandwich spread.

1/2 cup tarragon *or* cider vinegar

1/2 cup water

1/4 cup olive oil

2 tablespoons prepared horseradish

1/2 teaspoon lemon juice

1 cup ground mustard

1/2 cup sugar

1/2 teaspoon salt

1) In a blender or food processor, combine all ingredients; cover and process for 1 minute. Scrape down the sides of the container and process for 30 seconds.

2) Transfer to a small saucepan and let stand for 10 minutes. Cook over low heat until bubbly, stirring constantly. Cool completely. If a thinner mustard is desired, stir in an additional 1-2 tablespoons water.

3) Pour into small containers with tight-fitting lids. Store in the refrigerator.

Yield: 1-1/2 cups.

NUTRITION FACTS: 1 tablespoon equals 67 calories, 4 g fat (trace saturated fat), 0 cholesterol, 54 mg sodium, 6 g carbohydrate, 1 g fiber, 2 g protein.

LEMON CURD

1) In a small saucepan, combine sugar, cornstarch and salt. Gradually stir in water until smooth.

2) Bring to a boil; cook and stir for 15 minutes until smooth, thickened and clear. Remove from heat; stir in vanilla and butter. Serve warm over cake.

Yield: 1 cup.

NUTRITION FACTS: 2 tablespoons equals 155 calories, 6 g fat (4 g saturated fat), 15 mg cholesterol, 206 mg sodium, 27 g carbohydrate, trace fiber, trace protein.

Grandma's Chunky Peanut Butter

PREP: 10 min. + chilling

Noble Winstead, Tuscaloosa, Alabama

I think this creamy peanut butter with just a hint of orange flavor is truly special. I even give it as a gift during the holidays.

> 1-3/4 cups peanuts
> 1/4 teaspoon salt, optional
> 1/4 teaspoon grated orange peel, optional

1) Chop 1/4 cup peanuts and set aside. Place remaining peanuts in a blender. Cover and process for 5 minutes or until smooth and spreadable, occasionally scraping sides of bowl. Stir in the chopped peanuts. Add salt and orange peel if desired. Cover and refrigerate for 1 hour. May be refrigerated for up to 1 month.

Yield: 1 cup.

NUTRITION FACTS: 2 tablespoons equals 183 calories, 16 g fat (2 g saturated fat), 0 cholesterol, 136 mg sodium, 6 g carbohydrate, 3 g fiber, 8 g protein.

Cherry Sauce

PREP/TOTAL TIME: 10 min.

Kathy Emberton, Cicero, Indiana

Served warm, this sauce makes a wonderful topping for sponge cake, pound cake or ice cream. Or try it as a filling for crepes or blintzes.

> 1 can (16 ounces) pitted tart red cherries
> 1/4 cup sugar
> 2 tablespoons cornstarch
> 1 tablespoon butter
> 1/4 teaspoon vanilla extract

Few drops red food coloring, optional

1) Drain cherries, reserving juice. Set cherries aside. Add enough water to juice to equal 1-1/4 cups.

2) In a saucepan, combine sugar and cornstarch. Stir in juice. Bring to a boil; cook and stir for 2 minutes or until thickened.

3) Remove from the heat. Stir in the butter, vanilla, cherries and food coloring if desired.

Yield: 4-6 servings.

NUTRITION FACTS: 1 serving equals 116 calories, 2 g fat (1 g saturated fat), 5 mg cholesterol, 25 mg sodium, 25 g carbohydrate, 1 g fiber, 1 g protein.

Lemon Curd

PREP/TOTAL TIME: 20 min.

Taste of Home Test Kitchen

Lemon curd is a scrumptious spread for scones, biscuits, English muffins or other baked goods. You can find it in larger grocery stores alongside jams and jellies or with baking supplies, but you may enjoy making it from scratch with this recipe.

> 3 eggs
> 1 cup sugar
> 1/2 cup lemon juice (about 2 lemons)
> 1/4 cup butter, melted
> 1 tablespoon grated lemon peel

1) In a heavy saucepan, beat eggs and sugar. Stir in the lemon juice, butter and lemon peel.

2) Cook and stir over medium-low heat for 15 minutes or until mixture is thickened and reaches 160°. Cover; store in refrigerator for up to 1 week.

Yield: 1-2/3 cups.

NUTRITION FACTS: 2 tablespoons equals 110 calories, 5 g fat (3 g saturated fat), 58 mg cholesterol, 50 mg sodium, 16 g carbohydrate, trace fiber, 2 g protein.

Hard Sauce for Cake

PREP/TOTAL TIME: 20 min.

Deb Brass, Cedar Falls, Iowa

My grandmother used to make this sauce to dress up plain cake. It's also good over gingerbread.

> 1 cup sugar
> 2 tablespoons cornstarch
> 1/2 teaspoon salt
> 2 cups boiling water
> 1/2 teaspoon vanilla extract
> 1/4 cup butter

Strawberry Syrup

PREP/TOTAL TIME: 20 min.

Nancy Dunaway, Springfield, Illinois

This recipe is a spin-off of my dad's homemade syrup. Our son requests it with pancakes, waffles or ice cream.

- 1 cup sugar
- 1 cup water
- 1-1/2 cups mashed unsweetened strawberries

1) In a saucepan, bring sugar and water to a boil. Gradually add strawberries; return to a boil. Reduce heat; simmer, uncovered, for 10 minutes, stirring occasionally.

Yield: about 2-1/2 cups.

NUTRITION FACTS: 2 tablespoons equals 57 calories, trace fat (0 saturated fat), 0 cholesterol, trace sodium, 15 g carbohydrate, trace fiber, trace protein.

Cinnamon Apple Syrup

PREP/TOTAL TIME: 15 min.

Alberta McKay, Bartlesville, Oklahoma

Cinnamon and vanilla take center stage in this no-fuss syrup. Try it warm over pancakes or crepes.

- 2 tablespoons cornstarch
- 1/2 teaspoon ground cinnamon
- 1/8 teaspoon salt
- 1 cup water
- 3/4 cup unsweetened apple juice concentrate
- 1/2 teaspoon vanilla extract

1) In a small saucepan, combine the cornstarch, cinnamon and salt. Gradually stir in water and apple juice concentrate until smooth. Bring to a boil; cook and stir for 2 minutes or until thickened.

2) Remove from the heat; stir in vanilla. Serve warm. Refrigerate leftovers.

Yield: 1-1/2 cups.

NUTRITION FACTS: 2 tablespoons equals 35 calories, trace fat (trace saturated fat), 0 cholesterol, 29 mg sodium, 9 g carbohydrate, trace fiber, trace protein.

Seasoned Salt

PREP/TOTAL TIME: 5 min.

Rene Ammundsen, Victoria, British Columbia

Our family likes to make things from scratch—including spices and seasonings. The kids jostle for a turn to mix up Seasoned Salt.

- 2/3 cup fine sea salt
- 1/2 cup sugar
- 4-1/2 teaspoons paprika
- 1 tablespoon onion powder
- 1 tablespoon garlic powder
- 1 teaspoon ground turmeric
- 1/4 teaspoon dried thyme
- 1/4 teaspoon dried marjoram

1) In a small bowl, combine all ingredients. Store in an airtight container for up to 1 year.

Yield: 1-1/4 cups.

NUTRITION FACTS: 1 teaspoon equals 8 calories, trace fat (trace saturated fat), 0 cholesterol, 1,259 mg sodium, 2 g carbohydrate, trace fiber, trace protein.

Zesty Salt Substitute

PREP/TOTAL TIME: 5 min.

Peggy Key, Grant, Alabama

Folks on a low-sodium diet will fall for this salt substitute. It beautifully seasons a variety of foods.

- 5 teaspoons onion powder
- 3 teaspoons garlic powder
- 3 teaspoons ground mustard
- 3 teaspoons paprika
- 1/2 teaspoon celery seed
- 1/2 teaspoon white pepper

1) In a small bowl, combine all ingredients. Store in an airtight container for up to 6 months.

Yield: about 1/4 cup.

NUTRITION FACTS: 1 teaspoon equals 10 calories, trace fat (trace saturated fat), 0 cholesterol, 1 mg sodium, 2 g carbohydrate, trace fiber, trace protein.

Using Rubs

Rubs are a combination of herbs and spices that are rubbed onto meat, fish or poultry. They are quick to make and an easy way to add a flavor boost to a plain piece of meat without adding fat. Try one of these the next time you want to add a little zip to grilled food.

- **Zippy Dry Rub:** Combine 1 tablespoon salt, 1 teaspoon *each* mustard seed, chili powder, paprika and pepper, 1/2 teaspoon *each* ground cumin and dried coriander and 1/4 teaspoon garlic powder. Store in an airtight container. Rub onto meat or poultry and refrigerate for at least 4 hours before grilling. —*Gaynelle Fritsch Welches, Oregon*

- **Savory Steak Rub:** Combine 1 tablespoon *each* dried marjoram and basil, 2 teaspoons *each* dried thyme and rosemary, crushed and 3/4 teaspoon dried oregano. Store in an airtight container. Rub over steaks just before grilling. —*Donna Brockett Kingfisher, Oklahoma*

- **Barbecue Seasoning Rub:** Combine 1/4 cup *each* beef bouillon granules, chili powder and paprika, 1 tablespoon *each* sugar, garlic salt and onion salt, 1 teaspoon *each* celery salt, cayenne papper and black pepper, and 1/2 teaspoon *each* curry powder and dried oregano. Rub over ribs, chicken or pork before grilling. —*Rose Rainier Sheridan, Wyoming*

Using Marinades

Marinades add flavor and can tenderize meat. However, marinades only penetrate about 1/2 in. deep, so the flavor is on the outer surface of the food. Meat and poultry need at least 1 to 4 hours to marinate; many cuts can be marinated overnight. You can make up the marinade one evening and marinate the food until the next night, or add the food in the morning and marinate until you are ready cook it that night.

Most fish and seafood only need 15 to 30 minutes and can be marinating while you prepare other items for dinner. Marinating too long may cause the meat texture to break down and become mushy.

An easy way to marinate is to use a resealable plastic bag. Pour the marinade into the bag, add the meat or vegetables and partially seal the bag. Squeeze out as much air as possible, then completely seal the bag. Place on a tray to contain any leakage. Any food marinated for more than 30 minutes must be placed in the refrigerator.

For food safety reasons, if you want to use some of the marinade for basting or for a dipping sauce, set aside some of the fresh marinade for this purpose. Any marinade that came in contact with uncooked meat, poultry or seafood should be discarded.

Here are some easy marinade recipes you can put together in mere minutes.

- **Kentucky Marinade:** Combine 1/2 cup cider vinegar, 1/4 cup vegetable oil, 2-1/2 teaspoons Worcestershire sauce, 2 teaspoons hot pepper sauce and 1 teaspoon salt. Reserve 1/4 cup for basting if desired. Marinate meat in remaining marinade for up to 4 hours. (Enough to marinate about 3 pounds of meat or poultry.) —*Jill Evely Wilmore, Kentucky*

- **Rosemary Orange Marinade:** Combine 1 cup orange juice, 1/4 cup olive oil, 3 minced garlic cloves and 1 tablespoon *each* dried thyme and rosemary, crushed. Reserve 1/2 cup for basting if desired. Marinate meat in remaining marinade for up to 4 hours. (Enough to marinate about 2 pounds of poultry or pork.) —*Marcia Morgan Chevy Chase, Maryland*

- **Lemonade Marinade:** Combine 1 can (12 ounces) frozen lemonade concentrate (thawed), 2 tablespoons *each* brown sugar and soy sauce, 1 teaspoon garlic powder and 1/4 teaspoon dried mint flakes. Reserve 3/4 cup for basting if desired. Marinate meat in remaining marinade for up to 4 hours. (Enough to marinate about 4 pounds of poultry, pork or fish.) —*Olivia Logan Delphi, Indiana*

Refrigerator & Freezer Jellies and Jams

When making jam, use firm, ripe fruit. Overripe fruit will cause the jelly or jam to be soft and watery, while underripe fruit will make it too firm and hard to spread. Make sure frozen fruit is thawed before using.

Do not reduce the sugar in recipes or use sugar substitutes. If you do, the jelly or jam will not properly set up. To make a reduced-sugar jelly or jam, look for pectin specifically designed for lower sugar recipes and follow recommended sugar amounts on the pectin box.

Do not double recipes because the spread may not properly set. If a larger yield is desired, make two separate batches.

Use containers that are no larger than 1 pint (2 cups) and are suitable for the refrigerator or freezer. Store in the refrigerator for up to 3 weeks or freeze up to 1 year. If frozen, thaw in the refrigerator and use within 3 weeks. Recipes that use gelatin do not freeze well and may become thin after thawing.

Pretty Peach Jam
PREP: 20 min. **COOK:** 20 min. + cooling
Theresa Beckman, Inwood, Iowa
This has been a favorite jam in my family for as long as I can remember. It's a delicious medley of peaches, cherries, pineapple and orange.

>   8   medium peaches, peeled and cut into wedges
>   1   small unpeeled navel orange, cut into wedges
>   2   cans (8 ounces *each*) crushed pineapple, undrained
>   12   maraschino cherries
>   3   tablespoons maraschino cherry juice
>   2   packages (1-3/4 ounces *each*) powdered fruit pectin
>   10   cups sugar

1) In a blender or food processor, cover and process fruits and cherry juice in batches until smooth. Transfer to a large kettle; stir in pectin and bring to a rolling boil over high heat, stirring frequently. Add sugar and return to a rolling boil. Boil for 2 minutes, stirring constantly.

2) Remove from the heat. Pour into jars or plastic containers. Cover and let stand overnight or until set, but not longer than 24 hours. Refrigerate for up to 3 weeks or freeze for up to 1 year.

Yield: 13 cups.

NUTRITION FACTS: 2 tablespoons equals 88 calories, trace fat (trace saturated fat), 0 cholesterol, trace sodium, 22 g carbohydrate, trace fiber, trace protein.

Orange Pear Jam

PREP: 20 min. **COOK:** 20 min. + standing

Delores Ward, Decatur, Indiana

Orange gelatin brings bright citrus flavor to the pear and pineapple combination in this jam. It's great on toasted homemade bread.

　　7　cups sugar
　　5　cups chopped peeled fresh pears
　　1　cup crushed pineapple, drained
　　2　tablespoons lemon juice
　　2　packages (3 ounces *each*) orange gelatin

1) In a Dutch oven or large kettle, combine sugar, pears, pineapple and lemon juice. Bring to a full rolling boil over high heat, stirring constantly.

2) Reduce heat; simmer for 15 minutes, stirring frequently. Remove from the heat; stir in gelatin until dissolved.

3) Pour into jars or containers; cool to room temperature, about 1 hour. Cover and let stand overnight or until set, but no longer than 24 hours. Refrigerate for up to 3 weeks.

Yield: about 7 cups.

NUTRITION FACTS: 2 tablespoons equals 119 calories, trace fat (trace saturated fat), 0 cholesterol, 7 mg sodium, 31 g carbohydrate, trace fiber, trace protein.

CINNAMON BLUEBERRY JAM, ORANGE PEAR JAM AND RASPBERRY PLUM JAM

Cinnamon Blueberry Jam

PREP: 15 min. **PROCESS:** 15 min. + standing

Barbara Burns, Phillipsburg, New Jersey

I was surprised to discover that the cinnamon-blueberry combination was so delightful.

　　1　pound fresh *or* frozen blueberries (about 1 quart)
3-1/2　cups sugar
　　1　tablespoon lemon juice
　1/4　teaspoon ground cinnamon
　1/8　teaspoon ground cloves
　　1　pouch (3 ounces) liquid fruit pectin

1) Crush blueberries; measure 2-1/2 cups and place in a large saucepan. Add the sugar, lemon juice, cinnamon and cloves; bring to a full rolling boil over high heat.

2) Quickly stir in the pectin. Return to a boil; boil for 1 minute, stirring constantly.

3) Remove from the heat. Skim off foam. Pour hot into hot sterilized jars, leaving 1/4-in. headspace. Adjust caps. Process for 15 minutes in a boiling-water bath.

Yield: 4 half-pints.

NUTRITION FACTS: 2 tablespoons equals 93 calories, trace fat (trace saturated fat), 0 cholesterol, 1 mg sodium, 24 g carbohydrate, trace fiber, trace protein.

Raspberry Plum Jam

PREP: 25 min. **PROCESS:** 15 min. + standing

Arlene Loker, Craigville, Indiana

Raspberries and plums are deliciously combined in this jam, which you can serve on warm bread, rolls or scones.

4-1/2　cups chopped *or* coarsely ground peeled pitted fresh plums (2-1/2 pounds)
　　2　packages (10 ounces *each*) frozen sweetened raspberries
　10　cups sugar
　1/2　cup lemon juice
　　2　pouches (3 ounces *each*) liquid fruit pectin

1) In a large kettle, combine the plums, raspberries, sugar and lemon juice. Bring to a full rolling boil over high heat, stirring constantly.

2) Quickly stir in pectin; return to a full rolling boil. Boil for 1 minute, stirring constantly.

3) Remove from the heat; skim off foam. Pour hot liquid into hot sterilized jars, leaving 1/4-in. headspace. Adjust caps. Process for 15 minutes in a boiling-water bath.

Yield: 6 pints.

NUTRITION FACTS: 2 tablespoons equals 91 calories, trace fat (trace saturated fat), 0 cholesterol, trace sodium, 24 g carbohydrate, trace fiber, trace protein.

Boiling-Water-Bath Basics

1) Wash jars and two-piece caps in hot, soapy water; rinse thoroughly. Dry bands on a towel. Put jars in a large kettle with enough water to cover; simmer to 180°. Remove from heat. Place lids in a small saucepan and cover with water; simmer to 180°. Remove from the heat.

2) Place rack in canner. Add several inches of water; bring to a simmer. Meanwhile, prepare recipe. Ladle or pour hot mixture into hot jars, leaving the recommended amount of headspace for expansion during processing.

3) Wipe threads and rim of jar with a clean damp cloth. Place warm lids on jars with sealing compound next to the glass. Screw band onto the jars just until resistance is met.

4) Immediately after filling each jar, use a jar lifter to place the jar onto the rack in the canner, making sure the jars are not touching. Lower rack when filled. If necessary, add enough boiling water to canner to cover jar lids by 1 to 2 in. Cover canner with its lid. Adjust heat to hold a steady rolling boil. Start counting the processing time when the water returns to a boil. If the water level decreases while processing, add additional boiling water.

5) When the processing time has ended, remove jars from the canner with jar lifter. Stand upright on a towel, out of drafts, leaving 1-2 in. of space around each jar.

After 12 to 24 hours, test each of the lids to determine if they have sealed by pressing the center of the lid. If it is concave (indented), remove the band and try to lift the lid. If lid is secure, the jar is vacuum-sealed. Wipe jars to remove any food. Label and date jars.

Caramelized Onion Jam

PREP: 50 min. **PROCESS:** 10 min. + standing

Vanessa Lambert, Sioux Falls, South Dakota

This savory jam is very good served with meats—we especially like it with venison. People who enjoy garlic and onions think it's terrific.

4	whole garlic bulbs
1	teaspoon vegetable oil
5	cups chopped sweet onions (1-1/2 pounds)
1/4	cup butter, cubed
3/4	cup cider vinegar
1/2	cup lemon juice
1/4	cup balsamic vinegar
1-1/2	teaspoons ground mustard
1	teaspoon salt
3/4	teaspoon white pepper
1/2	teaspoon ground ginger
1/4	teaspoon ground cloves
6	cups sugar
1	pouch (3 ounces) liquid fruit pectin

1) Remove papery outer skin from garlic (do not peel or separate cloves). Cut top off garlic bulbs; brush with oil. Wrap each bulb in heavy-duty foil. Bake at 425° for 30-35 minutes or until softened. Cool for 10-15 minutes.

2) In a Dutch oven, saute onions in butter for 30-40 minutes or until lightly browned. Squeeze softened garlic into pan. Stir in the cider vinegar, lemon juice, balsamic vinegar, mustard, salt, pepper, ginger and cloves. Bring to a rolling boil. Gradually add sugar, stirring constantly. Return to a boil for 3 minutes.

3) Add pectin; bring to a full rolling boil. Boil for 1 minute, stirring constantly. Remove from the heat; let stand for 3 minutes. Skim off foam. Pour hot mixture into hot jars, leaving 1/2-in. headspace. Adjust caps. Process for 10 minutes in a boiling-water bath.

Yield: about 3-1/2 pints.

NUTRITION FACTS: 2 tablespoons equals 103 calories, 1 g fat (1 g saturated fat), 2 mg cholesterol, 52 mg sodium, 24 g carbohydrate, trace fiber, trace protein.

CARAMELIZED ONION JAM

TEXAS JALAPENO JELLY

Texas Jalapeno Jelly

PREP: 15 min. **PROCESS:** 10 min. + standing

Lori McMullen, Victoria, Texas

A jar of this jelly is always warmly received. I like to trim the lid with a bandanna.

- 2 jalapeno peppers, seeded and chopped
- 3 medium green peppers, cut into 1-inch pieces, *divided*
- 1-1/2 cups white vinegar, *divided*
- 6-1/2 cups sugar
- 1/2 to 1 teaspoon cayenne pepper
- 2 pouches (3 ounces *each*) liquid fruit pectin

About 6 drops green food coloring, optional

Cream cheese and crackers, optional

1) In a blender or food processor, place the jalapenos, half of the green peppers and 1/2 cup vinegar; cover and process until pureed.

2) Transfer to a large Dutch oven or kettle. Repeat with remaining green peppers and another 1/2 cup vinegar. Add sugar, cayenne and remaining vinegar to pan. Bring to a rolling boil over high heat, stirring constantly.

3) Quickly stir in pectin. Return to a rolling boil; boil for 1 minute, stirring constantly.

4) Remove from the heat. Skim off foam. Add food coloring if desired. Ladle hot liquid into hot jars, leaving 1/4-in. headspace. Adjust caps. Process for 10 minutes in a boiling-water bath. Serve over cream cheese with crackers if desired.

Yield: 7 half-pints.

Editor's Note: When cutting or seeding hot peppers, use rubber or plastic gloves to protect your hands. Avoid touching your face.

NUTRITION FACTS: 2 tablespoons equals 92 calories, trace fat (trace saturated fat), 0 cholesterol, 1 mg sodium, 24 g carbohydrate, trace fiber, trace protein.

Reprocessing Unsealed Jars

If a lid does not seal within 24 hours, the product must either be stored in the refrigerator and used within several days or reprocessed. To reprocess:

Remove and discard the lid. The band may be reused if in good condition. Don't reuse a jar with chips or cracks.

Reheat the product. Ladle or pour hot mixture into a hot clean jar, leaving the recommended amount of headspace. Adjust cap.

Process in a boiling-water bath as recipe directs.

Caramel Apple Jam

PREP: 30 min. **PROCESS:** 10 min. + standing

Robert Atwood, West Wareham, Massachusetts

The flavor of apples, brown sugar, cinnamon and nutmeg come together in this spreadable treat. It's a must-have at our breakfast table.

- 6 cups diced peeled apples (1/8-inch cubes)
- 1/2 cup water
- 1/2 teaspoon butter
- 1 package (1-3/4 ounces) powdered fruit pectin
- 3 cups sugar
- 2 cups packed brown sugar
- 1/2 teaspoon ground cinnamon
- 1/4 teaspoon ground nutmeg

1) In a large kettle, combine the apples, water and butter. Cook and stir over low heat until apples are soft.

2) Stir in pectin and bring to a rolling boil, stirring constantly. Add the sugars, cinnamon and nutmeg; return to a rolling boil. Boil for 1 minute, stirring constantly.

3) Remove from the heat and skim off any foam. Ladle hot jam into hot sterilized jars, leaving 1/4-in. headspace. Adjust caps. Process for 10 minutes in a boiling-water bath.

Yield: 7 half-pints.

NUTRITION FACTS: 2 tablespoons equals 83 calories, trace fat (trace saturated fat), trace cholesterol, 4 mg sodium, 21 g carbohydrate, trace fiber, trace protein.

Skimming Foam from Jellies and Jams

Remove kettle from the heat and skim off foam with a large spoon. Proceed with recipe.

EASY REFRIGERATOR PICKLES

1) In a chilled small mixing bowl, beat cream until stiff peaks form. Fold in the horseradish, mustard and salt. Cover and refrigerate for 15 minutes before serving.

Yield: 6 servings.

NUTRITION FACTS: 2 tablespoons equals 75 calories, 7 g fat (5 g saturated fat), 27 mg cholesterol, 117 mg sodium, 2 g carbohydrate, trace fiber, 1 g protein.

Making Vegetable Relishes

If you plan to prepare a lot of relish, make the chopping easier by using a food processor or a food grinder with a coarse grinding blade. Seed large zucchini or cucumbers before chopping.

Use fresh spices for maximum flavor. Spices older than 1 year begin to lose their strength.

Pomadoro Sauce

PREP: 25 min. + standing

JoAnn Renze, Omaha, Nebraska

This can be used like bruschetta—to top slices of Italian or French bread. Or, toss it with pasta or serve with grilled or roasted poultry, fish or pork.

- 4 large tomatoes, seeded and chopped
- 1/4 cup olive oil
- 4 garlic cloves, minced
- 3 tablespoons minced fresh basil
- 1/2 teaspoon salt

Freshly ground pepper to taste

Thinly sliced French bread, toasted, optional

1) In a small bowl, combine the tomatoes, oil, garlic, basil, salt and pepper. Cover and let stand at room temperature for 20 minutes. Serve as topping on French bread if desired or as a sauce.

Yield: 3 cups.

NUTRITION FACTS: 1/4 cup equals 54 calories, 5 g fat (1 g saturated fat), 0 cholesterol, 104 mg sodium, 3 g carbohydrate, 1 g fiber, 1 g protein.

Easy Refrigerator Pickles

PREP: 20 min. + chilling

Catherine Seibold, Elma, New York

When you have an abundance of cucumbers and onions from your garden, this is a great way to use them up!

- 6 cups thinly sliced cucumbers
- 2 cups thinly sliced onions
- 1-1/2 cups sugar
- 1-1/2 cups cider vinegar
- 1/2 teaspoon salt
- 1/2 teaspoon mustard seed
- 1/2 teaspoon celery seed
- 1/2 teaspoon ground turmeric
- 1/2 teaspoon ground cloves

1) Place cucumbers and onions in a large bowl; set aside. Combine remaining ingredients in a saucepan; bring to a boil. Cook and stir just until the sugar is dissolved.

2) Pour over cucumber mixture; cool. Cover tightly and refrigerate for at least 24 hours before serving.

Yield: 6 cups.

NUTRITION FACTS: 1/4 cup equals 58 calories, trace fat (trace saturated fat), 0 cholesterol, 50 mg sodium, 15 g carbohydrate, trace fiber, trace protein.

Horseradish Spread

PREP: 10 min. + chilling

Mark Morgan, Waterford, Wisconsin

I like to serve this with tenderloin or rib roast. The light-textured spread also tastes terrific on sandwiches.

- 1/2 cup heavy whipping cream
- 1/4 cup fresh grated horseradish root
- 1/2 teaspoon Dijon mustard
- 1/4 teaspoon salt

POMADORO SAUCE

Old-Fashioned Corn Relish

PREP/TOTAL TIME: 30 min.

Jean Peterson, Mulliken, Michigan

This was the first recipe I received after moving away from the city—a farm wife neighbor shared it. Made with garden-fresh ingredients, you can serve it with your favorite meat.

    2   cups fresh *or* frozen corn
    2   cups chopped onions
    2   cups chopped tomatoes
    2   cups chopped seeded cucumber
    1   large green pepper, chopped
    1   cup sugar
    1   cup cider vinegar
1-1/2   teaspoons celery seed
1-1/2   teaspoons mustard seed
    1   teaspoon salt
  1/2   teaspoon ground turmeric

1) In a large saucepan, combine all ingredients. Bring to a boil. Reduce heat; simmer, uncovered, for 20-30 minutes or until thickened. Store in the refrigerator for up to 3 weeks.

Yield: 6-1/2 cups.

NUTRITION FACTS: 2 tablespoons equals 27 calories, trace fat (trace saturated fat), 0 cholesterol, 47 mg sodium, 6 g carbohydrate, trace fiber, trace protein.

Chipotle Rhubarb Sauce

PREP/TOTAL TIME: 30 min.

Deborah Clayton, Squamish, British Columbia

Folks are surprised to hear that rhubarb is this sauce's secret. Chipotle peppers add a little kick. It's great on meat or chicken.

    2   cups chopped fresh *or* frozen rhubarb
    1   cup ketchup
  1/2   cup water
    1   small onion, chopped
  1/4   cup packed brown sugar
    2   tablespoons cider vinegar
    2   tablespoons Dijon mustard
    2   tablespoons chopped chipotle peppers in adobo sauce
    2   teaspoons Worcestershire sauce
    2   garlic cloves, peeled
  1/2   teaspoon salt

1) In a large saucepan, combine all ingredients. Bring to a boil. Reduce heat; simmer, uncovered, for 18-22 minutes or until rhubarb is tender.

2) Cool rhubarb mixture slightly. In a blender, cover and process the sauce until smooth. Serve warm.

Yield: 3 cups.

NUTRITION FACTS: 1/4 cup equals 51 calories, trace fat (trace saturated fat), 0 cholesterol, 427 mg sodium, 12 g carbohydrate, 1 g fiber, 1 g protein.

COLORFUL APRICOT CHUTNEY

Colorful Apricot Chutney

PREP: 10 min. **COOK:** 25 min. + chilling

Lucile Cline, Wichita, Kansas

You can use this chutney as an appetizer on crackers or mixed with cream cheese for a spread. It's also a nice condiment with pork or poultry.

    3   large sweet red peppers, diced
   12   ounces dried apricots, diced
    1   cup raisins
    1   cup sugar
    1   large onion, finely chopped
  3/4   cup red wine vinegar
    5   garlic cloves, minced
1-1/2   teaspoons salt
1-1/2   teaspoons crushed red pepper flakes
  1/4   teaspoon ground ginger
  1/4   teaspoon ground cumin
  1/4   teaspoon ground mustard

1) In a large heavy saucepan, combine all the ingredients; bring to a boil. Reduce heat; simmer, uncovered, for 25-30 minutes or until thickened, stirring occasionally. Cover and refrigerate.

2) Serve as an accompaniment to pork or chicken. Chutney may be stored in the refrigerator for up to 1 month.

Yield: 4 cups.

NUTRITION FACTS: 1/4 cup equals 144 calories, trace fat (trace saturated fat), 0 cholesterol, 226 mg sodium, 37 g carbohydrate, 3 g fiber, 1 g protein.

Teapot Cranberry Relish

PREP: 5 min. **COOK:** 25 min. + chilling

Carolyn Huston, Jamesport, Missouri

A Christmas party at the tearoom we operate inspired my friend and me to create this relish. It was an instant hit that turned many into cranberry lovers.

- 1 package (12 ounces) fresh *or* frozen cranberries
- 2 cups sugar
- 1/2 cup orange juice
- 1/2 cup cranberry juice
- 2 cups dried cherries *or* golden raisins
- 1 teaspoon grated orange peel

1) In a large saucepan, cook the cranberries, sugar and juices over medium heat until the berries pop, about 15 minutes.

2) Add the cherries and orange peel. Simmer, uncovered, for 10 minutes. Cool slightly. Transfer to a bowl; cover and refrigerate until serving.

Yield: 4 cups.

NUTRITION FACTS: 1/4 cup equals 165 calories, trace fat (trace saturated fat), 0 cholesterol, 1 mg sodium, 42 g carbohydrate, 1 g fiber, 1 g protein.

Garden Salsa

PREP/TOTAL TIME: 15 min.

Michelle Beran, Caflin, Kansas

Ripe garden ingredients and subtle seasonings make this a real summer treat.

- 6 medium tomatoes, finely chopped
- 3/4 cup finely chopped green pepper
- 1/2 cup finely chopped onion
- 1/2 cup thinly sliced green onions
- 6 garlic cloves, minced
- 2 teaspoons cider vinegar
- 2 teaspoons lemon juice
- 2 teaspoons olive oil
- 1 to 2 teaspoons minced jalapeno pepper
- 1 to 2 teaspoons ground cumin
- 1/2 teaspoon salt
- 1/4 to 1/2 teaspoon cayenne pepper

Tortilla chips

1) In a large bowl, combine the first 12 ingredients. Cover; refrigerate until serving. Serve with chips.

Yield: 5 cups.

NUTRITION FACTS: 2 tablespoons salsa (calculated without chips) equals 17 calories, trace fat (0 saturated fat), 0 cholesterol, 62 mg sodium, 3 g carbohydrate, trace fiber, trace protein.

■ **Three-Pepper Garden Salsa:** Broil 6 Anaheim chilies 4 in. from heat until skins blister, about 2 minutes. With tongs, rotate peppers a quarter turn. Broil and rotate until all sides blister and blacken. Immediately place chilies in a bowl. Cover; let stand 15-20 minutes. Peel off and discard charred skin; remove stems and seeds. Finely chop peppers. Add to salsa.

Peppery Black Bean Salsa

PREP: 15 min. + standing
BROIL: 10 min. + chilling

Gary Maly, West Chester, Ohio

I love foods that surprise the senses. Use this as a topping for grilled meats or serve it as a relish.

- 4 jalapeno peppers
- 2 cans (15 ounces *each*) black beans, rinsed and drained
- 2 cups fresh *or* frozen corn
- 1 medium sweet red pepper, diced
- 1 cup chopped seeded tomato
- 1 medium red onion, chopped
- 1/3 cup lime juice
- 2 tablespoons minced fresh cilantro
- 1 garlic clove, minced

1) Place jalapenos on a broiler pan; broil 4 in. from the heat until skins blister, about 2 minutes. With tongs, rotate jalapenos a quarter turn. Broil and rotate until all sides are blistered and blackened.

2) Immediately place peppers in a bowl; cover for 15-20 minutes. Peel off and discard charred skin. Remove stems and seeds. Finely chop peppers. In a bowl, combine remaining ingredients. Add jalapenos. Cover; chill several hours.

Yield: 12 servings.

Editor's Note: When cutting or seeding hot peppers, use rubber or plastic gloves to protect your hands. Avoid touching your face.

NUTRITION FACTS: 1/2 cup equals 93 calories, trace fat (trace saturated fat), 0 cholesterol, 137 mg sodium, 19 g carbohydrate, 4 g fiber, 5 g protein.

dinner from the heart

Feeding those in need is a Christmas tradition

Sue Ross

> Everyone always talks about Christmas being for children, but this is for Grandma or Grandpa or aunts and uncles who have no one.
>
> ~Sue Ross

When she observed that homeless and homebound elderly in her community were overlooked on Christmas, Sue Ross of Casa Grande, Arizona, took it upon herself to start a program to feed them.

Since 1994 she has baked, cooked and served meals on Christmas. She is backed by many volunteers, including her husband Paul, and the support of local food stores and Seeds of Hope—a local nonprofit agency focused on breaking the cycle of poverty and strengthening communities.

"Everyone always talks about Christmas being for children, but this is for Grandma or Grandpa or aunts and uncles who have no one. There's more than we know," says Sue, who is a *Taste of Home* field editor.

Last year, in addition to serving about 60 people at their host site, Calvary Southern Baptist Church, the volunteers delivered 126 meals to the homebound. People coming to the church for Christmas dinner also received a sack lunch to take with them and a gift-wrapped box of personal and hygienic items.

The dinner typically includes turkey, mashed potatoes, sweet potatoes, green beans, corn, cranberry sauce, rolls, coleslaw and pie.

Sue asks for monetary contributions for food from local stores. A Mormon church in the area supplies 30 pies, and volunteers from other churches make cookies.

And everything is homemade.

"It comes from the heart when you make it yourself, and it tastes so much better than when you buy it semi-prepared." Sue says. "I'm from Iowa and my hometown has a large Amish population, so I know how much those people care and I think some of that rubbed off on me."

Refusing to serve instant mashed potatoes, Sue peeled 100 pounds of potatoes the first six years of the program. She has since passed potato duty to another volunteer.

The day would not run so smoothly if it were not for those dedicated volunteers, she says.

"A lot of kids come with their parents to help out," Sue notes. "We serve family-style, so we like to have the teenagers serve at the tables."

"I really look forward to this tradition," Sue adds. "I start counting down the days until Christmas at 364!"

tasteofhome
cooks who care

DO YOU KNOW A COOK WHO CARES?
If you or someone you know cooks for a charitable, spiritual or other cause, tell us about it at **tasteofhome.com/CookbookBonus**

Recipes

Tips

Quick Breads

Quick breads can be sweet or savory breads and loaves, but they're also muffins, scones, biscuits, breadsticks, popovers, pancakes and waffles.

The convenience of quick breads comes from the fact that they're leavened with baking powder and/or baking soda, not yeast. So you can mix, bake and enjoy these baked goods in less time than traditional yeast breads.

Baking Powder and Baking Soda

Baking powder and baking soda are leaveners that cause baked goods to rise and have a light texture.

Baking powder is available in single-acting and double-acting varieties. Double-acting baking powder is the most readily available type and is the type used in this cookbook. Double-acting baking powder produces carbon dioxide gas in two stages: when it is mixed with liquid and when it is heated. Single-acting baking powder creates carbon dioxide gas only when it is mixed with liquid. Baking powder can lose its ability to leaven. Discard any baking powder that is past the expiration date on the package.

Baking soda is an alkaline substance used in batters that have acidic ingredients such as buttermilk, molasses and sour cream. When the baking soda is mixed with the acidic ingredient, there is an immediate release of carbon dioxide gas. Batter and dough that use only baking soda as a leavening agent should be baked immediately. Otherwise, the baked product might not rise as high and the texture won't be as light.

Be sure your baking powder and baking soda are fresh. Always check the expiration date on the packages before using. To test baking powder for freshness, mix 1 teaspoon of baking powder and 1/3 cup hot water. For baking soda, mix 1/4 teaspoon baking soda and 2 teaspoons vinegar. If bubbling occurs, the products are still fresh. If not, they should be replaced.

Quick Bread Tips

Arrange the oven racks before preheating so that the bread will bake in the center of the oven. Preheat the oven for 10-15 minutes before baking.

Use fats such as butter, stick margarine (with at least 80% oil) or shortening. For best results, do not use whipped, tub, soft, liquid or reduced-fat products. The fat should be softened (at room temperature), meaning it is pliable when touched. Measure ingredients accurately.

Mix the liquid and dry ingredients together only until moistened. A few lumps in the batter are fine. Overmixing causes the gluten in the flour to develop and the texture to be coarse and tough.

Aluminum baking pans and sheets that have a dull rather than shiny or dark finish will give the best results. Grease pans if directed in recipe. Fill pans two-thirds full.

Bake most quick breads shortly after combining the dry ingredients and liquid ingredients because the leaveners will begin producing gas once they are moistened. If allowed to stand too long before baking, the bread may have a sunken center.

Leave at least 1 in. of space between all pans and between pans and sides of oven to allow for good air circulation while baking. Switch pan positions and rotate pans halfway through the baking time.

Cool in the pan for 10 minutes, unless recipe directs otherwise. Turn loaves out onto a wire rack to cool. Most quick breads should be cooled completely before slicing to prevent crumbling.

MOIST BANANA BREAD

 CLASSIC: A slice of Special Banana Nut Bread makes a great breakfast treat or afternoon snack. Eggs and cream cheese add richness to these attractive loaves, which are packed with pecans and drizzled with an orange glaze.

 TIME-SAVER: Easy Banana Nut Bread starts with a convenient yellow cake mix. Add a few other ingredients, and you can have two tasty loaves ready to share in the time it takes the classic version of this quick bread to bake.

 LIGHT: Dried cherries and cocoa add flavor to Chocolate-Cherry Banana Bread. Using fat-free sour cream and one egg with two whites, a slice has 70 fewer calories, a third less cholesterol and less than half the fat of one slice of Special Banana Nut Bread.

 SERVES 2: A small loaf pan is just the right size for Mini Banana Nut Bread. With a large ripe banana, a few tablespoons of chopped walnuts and a handful of pantry staples, you can stir up the batter to make eight slices of this appealing bread. Leftovers can be frozen.

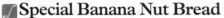

Special Banana Nut Bread

PREP: 25 min. **BAKE:** 1 hour + cooling

Beverly Sprague, Catonsville, Maryland

- 3/4 cup butter, softened
- 1 package (8 ounces) cream cheese, softened
- 2 cups sugar
- 2 eggs
- 1-1/2 cups mashed ripe bananas (about 4 medium)
- 1/2 teaspoon vanilla extract
- 3 cups all-purpose flour
- 1/2 teaspoon baking powder
- 1/2 teaspoon baking soda
- 1/2 teaspoon salt
- 2 cups chopped pecans, *divided*

ORANGE GLAZE:
- 1 cup confectioners' sugar
- 3 tablespoons orange juice
- 1 teaspoon grated orange peel

1) In a large mixing bowl, cream the butter, cream cheese and sugar until light and fluffy. Add eggs, one at a time, beating well after each addition. Beat in bananas and vanilla. Combine the flour, baking powder, baking soda and salt; add to creamed mixture. Fold in 1 cup pecans.

2) Transfer to two greased 8-in. x 4-in. x 2-in. loaf pans. Sprinkle with remaining pecans. Bake at 350° for 1 to 1-1/4 hours or until a toothpick inserted near the center comes out clean.

3) In a small bowl, whisk the glaze ingredients; drizzle over loaves. Cool for 10 minutes before removing from pans to wire racks to cool completely.

Yield: 2 loaves (12 slices each).

NUTRITION FACTS: 1 slice equals 234 calories, 13 g fat (5 g saturated fat), 32 mg cholesterol, 119 mg sodium, 29 g carbohydrate, 1 g fiber, 3 g protein.

SPECIAL BANANA NUT BREAD

Easy Banana Nut Bread

PREP: 10 min. **BAKE:** 40 min. + cooling

Marie Davis, Pendleton, South Carolina

- 1 package (18-1/4 ounces) yellow cake mix
- 1 egg
- 1/2 cup milk
- 1 cup mashed ripe bananas (about 2 medium)
- 1/2 cup chopped pecans

1) In a large mixing bowl, combine the cake mix, egg and milk. Add bananas; beat on medium speed for 2 minutes. Stir in pecans.

2) Transfer to two greased 8-in. x 4-in. x 2-in. loaf pans. Bake at 350° for 40-45 minutes or until a toothpick inserted near the center comes out clean. Cool for 10 minutes before removing from pans to wire racks to cool completely.

Yield: 2 loaves (12 slices each).

NUTRITION FACTS: 1 slice equals 117 calories, 4 g fat (1 g saturated fat), 9 mg cholesterol, 145 mg sodium, 20 g carbohydrate, trace fiber, 1 g protein.

Chocolate-Cherry Banana Bread

PREP: 30 min. **BAKE:** 45 min. + cooling

Cindy Beberman, Orland Park, Illinois

- 1 cup boiling water
- 2/3 cup dried cherries
- 1/4 cup butter, softened
- 3/4 cup sugar
- 2 egg whites
- 1 egg
- 1/2 cup mashed ripe banana (about 1 large)
- 1/2 cup fat-free sour cream
- 2 teaspoons vanilla extract
- 1-1/2 cups all-purpose flour
- 1/3 cup baking cocoa
- 1 teaspoon baking powder
- 1/2 teaspoon baking soda
- 1/2 teaspoon ground cinnamon
- 1/4 teaspoon salt
- 1/4 cup chopped pecans

1) In a small bowl, pour water over cherries; let stand for 15 minutes. Meanwhile, in a large mixing bowl, beat butter and sugar for 2 minutes or until light and fluffy. Add the egg whites and egg, one at a time, beating well after each addition.

2) Combine the banana, sour cream and vanilla. Combine the flour, cocoa, baking powder, baking soda, cinnamon and salt; add to creamed mixture alternately with banana mixture. Drain cherries and coarsely chop; fold into batter with pecans.

3) Transfer to a 9-in. x 5-in. x 3-in. loaf pan coated with cooking spray. Bake at 350° for 45-50 minutes or until a toothpick inserted near the center comes out clean. Cool for 10 minutes before removing from pan to a wire rack to cool completely.

Yield: 1 loaf (16 slices).

NUTRITION FACTS: 1 slice equals 164 calories, 5 g fat (2 g saturated fat), 22 mg cholesterol, 148 mg sodium, 27 g carbohydrate, 1 g fiber, 3 g protein.

CHOCOLATE-CHERRY BANANA BREAD

MINI BANANA NUT BREAD

Mini Banana Nut Bread

PREP: 15 min. **BAKE:** 50 min. + cooling

Anna Marie Moore, Aurora, Nebraska

- 3 tablespoons shortening
- 1/3 cup sugar
- 1 egg
- 1/4 teaspoon vanilla extract
- 2/3 cup all-purpose flour
- 1/4 teaspoon baking soda
- 1/8 teaspoon salt
- 1/2 cup mashed ripe banana (about 1 large)
- 3 tablespoons chopped walnuts

1) In a small mixing bowl, cream shortening and sugar. Beat in egg and vanilla. Combine the flour, baking soda and salt; add to creamed mixture alternately with banana. Fold in walnuts.

2) Transfer to a 5-3/4-in. x 3-in. x 2-in. loaf pan coated with cooking spray. Bake at 325° for 50-55 minutes or until a toothpick inserted near the center comes out clean. Cool for 10 minutes before removing from pan to a wire rack to cool completely.

Yield: 1 loaf (8 slices).

NUTRITION FACTS: 1 slice equals 151 calories, 7 g fat (1 g saturated fat), 26 mg cholesterol, 85 mg sodium, 20 g carbohydrate, 1 g fiber, 3 g protein.

SLICING QUICK BREADS EVENLY ■■■

When making banana bread or other quick breads, I use this handy trick to help me cut even slices. When I transfer the warm loaf from the pan onto a wire rack to cool, I press down slightly on the top of the loaf. After the bread has completely cooled, I turn the loaf over, and the pressure has perfectly marked my cutting lines on the bottom.

—Sherry B., Four States, West Virginia

ORANGE NUT BREAD

Orange Nut Bread

PREP: 15 min. **BAKE:** 50 min. + cooling

Helen Luksa, Las Vegas, Nevada

A friend shared this recipe years ago, and it has withstood the test of time. The bread is delicious for breakfast or with a salad.

4-1/2	cups all-purpose flour
1-3/4	cups sugar
4	teaspoons baking powder
1-1/2	teaspoons salt
1	teaspoon baking soda
1-1/2	cups chopped walnuts
1	to 2 tablespoons grated orange peel
2	eggs
1	cup milk
1	cup orange juice
1/4	cup butter, melted

1) In a large bowl, combine the flour, sugar, baking powder, salt and baking soda. Stir in nuts and orange peel.

2) In a small bowl, beat the eggs, milk, orange juice and butter. Stir into dry ingredients just until moistened. Pour into two greased 8-in. x 4-in. x 2-in. loaf pans.

Test for Doneness

Check for doneness 10-15 minutes before the end of the recommended baking time. If a toothpick inserted near the center comes out clean, the bread is done. If it is not done, test again in a few more minutes. The bread may have a split in the center, which is typical of a quick bread.

3) Bake at 350° for 50-60 minutes or until a toothpick inserted near the center comes out clean. Cool for 10 minutes before removing from pans to wire racks to cool completely.

Yield: 2 loaves (12 slices each).

NUTRITION FACTS: 1 slice equals 223 calories, 7 g fat (2 g saturated fat), 24 mg cholesterol, 297 mg sodium, 35 g carbohydrate, 1 g fiber, 5 g protein.

Zucchini Bread

PREP: 15 min. **BAKE:** 55 min. + cooling

Kevin Bruckerhoff, Columbia, Missouri

I like this bread because it's lighter and fluffier than most zucchini breads. Plus, it's a great way to put that abundant vegetable to good use!

3	cups all-purpose flour
2	cups sugar
1	teaspoon salt
1	teaspoon baking soda
1/4	teaspoon baking powder
3	eggs
1	cup vegetable oil
2	teaspoons vanilla extract
1	teaspoon ground cinnamon
1	teaspoon grated lemon peel
2	cups shredded zucchini (about 2 medium)
1/2	cup chopped nuts

1) In a large bowl, combine the flour, sugar, salt, baking soda and baking powder. In a small bowl, whisk the eggs, oil, vanilla, cinnamon and lemon peel. Stir into dry ingredients just until moistened. Stir in zucchini and nuts.

2) Transfer to two greased 8-in. x 4-in. x 2-in. loaf pans. Bake at 350° for 55-65 minutes or until a toothpick inserted near the center comes out clean. Cool for 10 minutes before removing from pans to wire racks to cool completely.

Yield: 2 loaves (12 slices each).

NUTRITION FACTS: 1 slice equals 229 calories, 11 g fat (1 g saturated fat), 26 mg cholesterol, 165 mg sodium, 29 g carbohydrate, 1 g fiber, 3 g protein.

■ **Chocolate Zucchini Bread:** Omit lemon peel and nuts. Reduce flour to 2-3/4 cups. Add 1/3 cup baking cocoa to flour mixture. Stir in 1 cup semisweet chocolate chips with zucchini. Bake as directed.

■ **Zucchini Apple Bread:** Omit lemon peel. Reduce sugar to 1 cup and add 1 cup brown sugar. Add 1/4 teaspoon ground nutmeg with cinnamon. Reduce zucchini to 1-1/2 cups. Add 1 cup grated peeled tart apple with zucchini and nuts. Bake as directed.

■ **Mini Zucchini Loaves:** Use four greased 5-3/4-in. x 3-in. x 2-in. loaf pans. Bake at 350° for 35-40 minutes or until a toothpick comes out clean. Cool as directed.

GOLDEN LEMON BREAD

Golden Lemon Bread

PREP: 20 min. **BAKE:** 40 min. + cooling

Marjorie Rose, Albuquerque, New Mexico

This wonderful bread, made from my grandmother's recipe, won Best of Show at the New Mexico State Fair. It's so good! My grandchildren love it, too.

     1/2 cup shortening
     3/4 cup sugar
       2 eggs
  1-1/2 cups all-purpose flour
  1-1/2 teaspoons baking powder
     1/2 teaspoon salt
     3/4 cup milk

GLAZE:
     1/2 cup confectioners' sugar
       2 teaspoons grated lemon peel
       2 to 3 tablespoons lemon juice

1) In a large mixing bowl, cream shortening and sugar. Add eggs, one at a time, beating well after each addition. Combine flour, baking powder and salt; add to creamed mixture alternately with milk.

2) Pour into a greased 9-in. x 5-in. x 3-in. loaf pan. Bake at 350° for 40-45 minutes or until a toothpick inserted near the center comes out clean. Place pan on a wire rack.

3) Combine the glaze ingredients; immediately pour over warm bread. Cool completely before removing from pan.

Yield: 1 loaf (16 slices).

NUTRITION FACTS: 1 slice equals 165 calories, 7 g fat (2 g saturated fat), 28 mg cholesterol, 125 mg sodium, 23 g carbohydrate, trace fiber, 2 g protein.

MAKE QUICK BREADS QUICKER ■■■

I make zucchini bread and other quick breads every week for snacks and lunches. To save time, I premeasure four batches of dry ingredients from my favorite recipes and store them in small containers. When I make a loaf, all I need to do is grab a premeasured mix and add the remaining ingredients.

—*Kathy S., Hungtingtown, Maryland*

Date Pecan Tea Bread

PREP: 20 min. **BAKE:** 65 min.

Carole Resnick, Cleveland, Ohio

This moist and nicely sweet bread is excellent on its own and even better topped with the chunky cream cheese spread.

  2-1/2 cups chopped dates
  1-1/2 cups boiling water
  1-1/2 teaspoons baking soda
  1-3/4 cups all-purpose flour
     1/4 teaspoon *each* ground cloves, cinnamon, ginger and nutmeg
       2 tablespoons butter, softened
  1-1/4 cups sugar
       1 egg, lightly beaten
       2 teaspoons vanilla extract
  1-1/2 cups coarsely chopped pecans

SPREAD:
       1 package (3 ounces) cream cheese, softened
       2 tablespoons chopped dates
       2 tablespoons coarsely chopped pecans
       1 tablespoon milk

1) Place dates in a bowl. Combine boiling water and baking soda; pour over dates. Combine the flour, cloves, cinnamon, ginger and nutmeg; set aside.

2) In a mixing bowl, beat butter and sugar until crumbly. Beat in egg and vanilla. Add flour mixture alternately with date mixture. Stir in pecans.

3) Pour into a greased 9-in. x 5-in. x 3-in. loaf pan. Bake at 350° for 65-75 minutes or until a toothpick inserted near the center comes out clean. Cool for 10 minutes before removing from pan to a wire rack to cool completely.

4) In a small bowl, combine all of the spread ingredients. Cover and refrigerate for 1 hour. Serve with bread.

Yield: 1 loaf (16 slices) and 1/2 cup spread.

NUTRITION FACTS: 1 slice with 1-1/2 teaspoons spread equals 312 calories, 13 g fat (3 g saturated fat), 23 mg cholesterol, 154 mg sodium, 50 g carbohydrate, 4 g fiber, 4 g protein.

DATE PECAN TEA BREAD

GOLDEN CORN BREAD

 CLASSIC: Warm squares of Sweet Corn Bread are a fabulous way to round out many meals, from fried chicken to zippy chili. Don't miss the details that follow the recipe for baking the batter into muffins and for two flavorful variations.

 TIME-SAVER: When there's a need for speed, golden-brown wedges of Skillet Corn Bread are the answer. The from-scratch batter is cooked in a skillet on the stovetop and is ready in 15 minutes.

 LIGHT: Enjoy all the old-fashioned goodness of corn bread without the guilt. Low-Fat Corn Bread calls for applesauce, egg whites and fat-free milk, so it has less than half the calories of classic Sweet Corn Bread and virtually no fat or cholesterol.

 SERVES 2: Bake Tennessee Corn Bread in a 6-inch skillet or baking dish, and you'll have the right amount to share with a second person. Mayonnaise and buttermilk add moistness.

SWEET CORN BREAD

■ **Sweet Corn Bread Muffins:** Follow recipe as directed, except fill greased muffin cups two-thirds full. Bake at 400° for 15-18 minutes or until a toothpick inserted near the center comes out clean. Serve warm.
Yield: about 15 muffins.

■ **Colorful Corn Bread:** Add 2 tablespoons diced pimientos and 1 teaspoon minced dried onion to the batter. Proceed as directed in recipe.

■ **Tex-Mex Corn Bread:** Fold in 1 cup (4 ounces) shredded Mexican cheese blend and 1 can (4 ounces) drained chopped green chilies to batter. Proceed as directed.

Sweet Corn Bread

PREP/TOTAL TIME: 30 min.

Virginia Hanker, Essex Junction, Vermont

- 1 cup all-purpose flour
- 1 cup cornmeal
- 1/4 cup sugar
- 1/2 teaspoon baking powder
- 1/2 teaspoon baking soda
- 1/2 teaspoon salt
- 1 egg, lightly beaten
- 1 cup (8 ounces) sour cream
- 1/3 cup milk
- 1/4 cup butter, melted

1) In a large bowl, combine the flour, cornmeal, sugar, baking powder, baking soda and salt. Combine the egg, sour cream, milk and butter; stir into dry ingredients just until moistened.

2) Pour into a greased 8-in. square baking dish. Bake at 400° for 20-25 minutes or until a toothpick comes out clean. Serve warm.

Yield: 9 servings.

NUTRITION FACTS: 1 piece equals 240 calories, 11 g fat (7 g saturated fat), 56 mg cholesterol, 300 mg sodium, 29 g carbohydrate, 2 g fiber, 5 g protein.

Skillet Corn Bread

PREP/TOTAL TIME: 15 min.

Kathy Teela, Tucson, Arizona

- 1/4 cup all-purpose flour
- 1/4 cup cornmeal
- 1/2 teaspoon baking powder
- 1/4 teaspoon salt
- 1 egg
- 1/4 cup milk
- 4 teaspoons vegetable oil, *divided*

1) In a small bowl, combine the flour, cornmeal, baking powder and salt. In another small bowl, whisk the egg, milk and 3 teaspoons oil; stir into dry ingredients just until moistened.

2) Heat remaining oil in a heavy 8-in. skillet over low heat. Pour batter into the hot skillet; cover and cook for 4-5 minutes. Turn and cook 4 minutes longer or until golden brown.

Yield: 4 servings.

NUTRITION FACTS: 1 piece equals 127 calories, 6 g fat (1 g saturated fat), 54 mg cholesterol, 222 mg sodium, 13 g carbohydrate, 1 g fiber, 4 g protein.

SKILLET CORN BREAD

Low-Fat Corn Bread

PREP/TOTAL TIME: 30 min.

Heather Andersen, Tuscon, Arizona

- 1 cup all-purpose flour
- 1 cup cornmeal
- 2 tablespoons sugar
- 2 teaspoons baking powder
- 1/2 teaspoon salt
- 2 egg whites
- 1 cup fat-free milk
- 1/4 cup unsweetened applesauce

1) In a large bowl, combine the flour, cornmeal, sugar, baking powder and salt. In a small bowl, combine the egg whites, milk and applesauce. Stir into dry ingredients just until moistened.

Storing and Serving Quick Breads

While corn breads, coffee cakes and muffins are best served warm, other quick breads (such as banana, zucchini and cranberry) slice and taste best a day after baking. Wrap the cooled bread in foil or plastic wrap; leave at room temperature overnight.

Use a sawing motion and a thin, sharp knife to cut loaves. Use a serrated knife for quick breads that have fruits and/or nuts.

If made with cheese, cream cheese or other perishable foods, quick breads and muffins should be refrigerated. For longer storage, place in heavy-duty resealable plastic bags and freeze quick breads for 3 months and muffins for up to 1 month.

2) Pour into a 9-in. square baking pan coated with cooking spray. Bake at 400° for 15-20 minutes or until a toothpick inserted near the center comes out clean. Serve warm.

Yield: 12 servings.

NUTRITION FACTS: 1 piece equals 100 calories, trace fat (trace saturated fat), trace cholesterol, 183 mg sodium, 21 g carbohydrate, 1 g fiber, 3 g protein.

Tennessee Corn Bread

PREP/TOTAL TIME: 30 min.

Betty Kaytis, Elizabethton, Tennessee

- 1 egg
- 1/4 cup mayonnaise
- 1/4 cup buttermilk
- 1 tablespoon vegetable oil
- 1 cup yellow cornmeal
- 1/4 cup sugar
- 1-1/2 teaspoons baking powder
- 1/2 teaspoon salt

1) In a large mixing bowl, beat the egg, mayonnaise, buttermilk and oil until smooth. Combine the cornmeal, sugar, baking powder and salt; add to egg mixture and beat just until combined.

2) Grease an ovenproof 6-in. skillet or round baking dish; dust with cornmeal. Add batter. Bake at 425° for 18-20 minutes or until a toothpick inserted near the center comes out clean.

Yield: 2 servings.

Editor's Note: Reduced-fat or fat-free mayonnaise is not recommended for this recipe.

NUTRITION FACTS: 1 serving equals 659 calories, 33 g fat (5 g saturated fat), 117 mg cholesterol, 1,106 mg sodium, 80 g carbohydrate, 5 g fiber, 10 g protein.

TENNESSEE CORN BREAD

DELICIOUS PUMPKIN BREAD

Poppy Seed Cranberry Bread

PREP: 15 min. **BAKE:** 55 min. + cooling

Cindy Harmon, Stuarts Draft, Virginia

I make poppy seed bread about once a month. So one Christmas, I decided to make it a little more festive by stirring in some cranberries. My family loved the colorful addition.

- 2-1/2 cups all-purpose flour
- 3/4 cup sugar
- 2 tablespoons poppy seeds
- 3 teaspoons baking powder
- 1/2 teaspoon salt
- 1 egg
- 1 cup milk
- 1/3 cup butter, melted
- 2 teaspoons vanilla extract
- 2 teaspoons grated lemon peel
- 1 cup fresh *or* frozen cranberries, thawed and chopped

ICING:
- 1/2 cup confectioners' sugar
- 2 teaspoons milk

1) In a large bowl, combine the flour, sugar, poppy seeds, baking powder and salt. In a small bowl, beat the egg, milk, butter, vanilla and lemon peel.

2) Stir into dry ingredients just until moistened. Fold in cranberries. Pour into a greased 8-in. x 4-in. x 2-in. loaf pan.

3) Bake at 350° for 55-60 minutes or until a toothpick inserted near the center comes out clean. Cool for 10 minutes before removing from pan to a wire rack to cool completely. Combine icing ingredients; drizzle over cooled loaf.

Yield: 1 loaf (12 slices).

NUTRITION FACTS: 1 slice equals 239 calories, 7 g fat (4 g saturated fat), 34 mg cholesterol, 266 mg sodium, 40 g carbohydrate, 1 g fiber, 4 g protein.

Delicious Pumpkin Bread

PREP: 15 min. **BAKE:** 50 min. + cooling

Linda Burnett, Prescott, Arizona

An enticing aroma wafts through my house when this tender, cake-like bread is in the oven. I bake extra loaves to give as holiday gifts.

- 5 eggs
- 1-1/4 cups vegetable oil
- 1 can (15 ounces) solid-pack pumpkin
- 2 cups all-purpose flour
- 2 cups sugar
- 2 packages (3 ounces *each*) cook-and-serve vanilla pudding mix
- 1 teaspoon baking soda
- 1 teaspoon ground cinnamon
- 1/2 teaspoon salt

1) In a large mixing bowl, beat the eggs. Add oil and pumpkin; beat until smooth. Combine all of the remaining ingredients; gradually beat into the pumpkin mixture.

2) Pour into five greased 5-3/4-in. x 3-in. x 2-in. loaf pans. Bake at 325° for 50-55 minutes or until a toothpick inserted near the center comes out clean. Cool for 10 minutes before removing from pans to wire racks to cool completely.

Yield: 5 mini loaves (8 slices each).

NUTRITION FACTS: 1 slice equals 150 calories, 8 g fat (1 g saturated fat), 27 mg cholesterol, 96 mg sodium, 20 g carbohydrate, 1 g fiber, 2 g protein.

CARAWAY BEER BREAD

Caraway Beer Bread

PREP: 10 min. **BAKE:** 40 min. + cooling

Janet Newmyer, Wilber, Nebraska

This moist and tender loaf boasts a mild beer and caraway flavor that can hold its own with hearty soups and chili.

- 2-1/2 cups biscuit/baking mix
- 2 tablespoons sugar
- 1 teaspoon caraway seeds
- 2 eggs
- 1 cup beer *or* nonalcoholic beer
- 3 tablespoons butter, melted

1) In a large bowl, combine the biscuit mix, sugar and caraway seeds. In a small bowl, whisk the eggs, beer and butter until smooth. Stir into dry ingredients just until moistened.

2) Pour into a greased 9-in. x 5-in. x 3-in. loaf pan. Bake at 350° for 40-45 minutes or until a toothpick inserted near the center comes out clean. Cool for 10 minutes before removing to a wire rack to cool completely.

Yield: 1 loaf (16 slices).

NUTRITION FACTS: 1 slice equals 156 calories, 7 g fat (3 g saturated fat), 43 mg cholesterol, 347 mg sodium, 18 g carbohydrate, 1 g fiber, 3 g protein.

IRISH SODA BREAD

Irish Soda Bread

PREP: 15 min. **BAKE:** 40 min. + cooling

Kerry Barnett-Amundson, Ocean Park, Washington

This is the best Irish soda bread I've ever had. It's lighter and softer than most others I've tried. We like slices spread with whipped butter.

3-1/2 cups all-purpose flour
1/2 cup sugar
2 tablespoons caraway seeds
2 teaspoons baking powder
1 teaspoon salt
1/2 teaspoon baking soda
2 eggs
2 cups (16 ounces) sour cream
3/4 cup raisins

1) In a large bowl, combine the flour, sugar, caraway seeds, baking powder, salt and baking soda. In a small bowl, whisk eggs and sour cream. Stir into dry ingredients just until moistened. Fold in raisins.

2) Transfer to a greased 9-in. springform pan. Bake at 350° for 40-45 or until a toothpick inserted near the center comes out clean. Cool on a wire rack for 10 minutes before removing sides of pan. Cut into wedges; serve warm.

Yield: 1 loaf (12 slices).

NUTRITION FACTS: 1 slice equals 359 calories, 14 g fat (9 g saturated fat), 86 mg cholesterol, 355 mg sodium, 46 g carbohydrate, 2 g fiber, 8 g protein.

Hearty Brown Quick Bread

PREP: 15 min. **BAKE:** 50 min. + cooling

Susan Lane, Waukesha, Wisconsin

Even though this bread is low in fat, it is also moist, rich, delicious and filling with sweet raisins and crunchy pecans.

4 cups whole wheat flour
2 cups all-purpose flour
2 cups packed brown sugar
1/2 cup sugar
2 teaspoons baking soda
1 teaspoon salt
3 cups 1% buttermilk
2 eggs, lightly beaten
1 cup raisins
1/2 cup chopped pecans

1) In a large bowl, combine the flours, sugars, baking soda and salt. Stir in buttermilk and eggs just until moistened. Fold in raisins and pecans.

2) Pour into two 9-in. x 5-in. x 3-in. loaf pans coated with cooking spray. Bake at 350° for 50-60 minutes or until a toothpick inserted near the center comes out clean. Cool for 10 minutes before removing from pans to wire racks.

Yield: 2 loaves (16 slices each).

NUTRITION FACTS: 1 slice equals 183 calories, 2 g fat (trace saturated fat), 14 mg cholesterol, 187 mg sodium, 38 g carbohydrate, 2 g fiber, 4 g protein.

Batters for Quick Breads

Creamed Batter

When a quick bread is made with solid fat, like softened butter or shortening, the fat and sugar are creamed together just like when making a cake. Then the eggs, dry ingredients and any liquid are added. This method incorporates air bubbles into the fat, resulting in a cake-like texture. Ingredients such as nuts, chocolate chips and dried or fresh fruit are folded in at the end.

Stirred Batter

When a quick bread is made with liquid fat (melted butter or oil), the fat, eggs and liquid are first combined, then stirred into the dry ingredients just until moistened, leaving a few lumps. Overmixing will result in a tough baked product. Ingredients such as nuts, chocolate chips and dried or fresh fruit are folded in at the end.

INVITING COFFEE CAKES

 CLASSIC: If you like something sweet with your coffee, you'll love a slice of Sour Cream Coffee Cake. Made with butter and sour cream, the tender cake has a sweet filling of pecans, sugar and cinnamon tucked inside. Confectioners' sugar glaze adds the finishing touch.

 TIME-SAVER: Eliminate the step of measuring several dry ingredients by stirring up Coconut-Chip Coffee Cake, which relies on biscuit/baking mix instead. With a swirl of melted chocolate and a cocnut-walnut topping, this breakfast treat is both quick and delicious.

 LIGHT: You can feel free to indulge in Blueberries 'n' Cheese Coffee Cake. Thanks to egg whites, applesauce, canola oil, buttermilk and reduced-fat cream cheese, one piece has a third of the calories and less than half the fat and cholesterol of a serving of classic Sour Cream Coffee Cake.

 SERVES 2: When you don't need to serve a crowd, turn to Raspberry Coffee Cake. A nutty crumb topping accents the raspberry-swirled batter, which is baked in a loaf pan.

Sour Cream Coffee Cake

PREP: 20 min. **BAKE:** 45 min. + cooling

Doris Rice, Storm Lake, Iowa

- 1 cup butter, softened
- 1-1/2 cups sugar
- 3 eggs
- 1 teaspoon *each* almond, lemon and vanilla extract
- 2-1/2 cups all-purpose flour
- 2 teaspoons baking powder
- 1 teaspoon baking soda
- 1 cup (8 ounces) sour cream

FILLING:

- 1/3 cup chopped pecans
- 3 tablespoons sugar
- 3 teaspoons ground cinnamon

GLAZE:

- 1 cup confectioners' sugar
- 2 tablespoons milk

1) In a large mixing bowl, cream butter and sugar. Add eggs, one at a time, beating well after each addition. Beat in extracts. Combine the flour, baking powder and baking soda; add to creamed mixture alternately with sour cream.

2) Spread half of the batter in a greased and floured 10-in. fluted tube pan. Make a well in the center of the batter. Combine filling ingredients; sprinkle into well. Carefully cover with remaining batter.

3) Bake at 350° for 45-50 minutes or until a toothpick inserted near the center comes out clean. Cool for 10 minutes before removing from pan to a wire rack. Combine glaze ingredients; drizzle over warm cake.

Yield: 16 servings.

NUTRITION FACTS: 1 piece equals 349 calories, 17 g fat (9 g saturated fat), 81 mg cholesterol, 265 mg sodium, 45 g carbohydrate, 1 g fiber, 4 g protein.

Coconut-Chip Coffee Cake

PREP: 15 min. **BAKE:** 25 min. + cooling

Pauletta Bushnell, Lebanon, Oregon

- 2 cups biscuit/baking mix
- 1/2 cup sugar, *divided*
- 1 egg
- 3/4 cup milk
- 3 tablespoons butter, melted, *divided*
- 1/3 cup semisweet chocolate chips, melted
- 1/3 cup flaked coconut
- 1/4 cup chopped walnuts

1) In a large bowl, combine biscuit mix and 1/4 cup sugar. Whisk egg, milk and 2 tablespoons butter; stir into dry ingredients just until moistened.

2) Pour into a greased 8-in. square baking dish. Pour chocolate over the batter; cut through batter with a knife to swirl the chocolate.

3) Combine the coconut, walnuts, and remaining sugar and butter; sprinkle over the top. Bake at 400° for 25-30 minutes or until a toothpick comes out clean. Cool on a wire rack.

Yield: 9 servings.

NUTRITION FACTS: 1 piece equals 274 calories, 14 g fat (6 g saturated fat), 37 mg cholesterol, 401 mg sodium, 35 g carbohydrate, 1 g fiber, 4 g protein.

COCONUT-CHIP COFFEE CAKE

Blueberries 'n' Cheese Coffee Cake

PREP: 25 min. **BAKE:** 30 min.

Shirley Wilder, Marietta, Georgia

- 2 tablespoons butter, softened
- 3/4 cup sugar
- 1 egg
- 2 egg whites
- 1/4 cup unsweetened applesauce
- 2 tablespoons canola oil
- 1 teaspoon grated lemon peel
- 2-1/4 cups all-purpose flour, *divided*
- 1-1/4 teaspoons baking powder
- 1 teaspoon salt
- 1/2 teaspoon baking soda
- 1 cup buttermilk
- 2 cups fresh *or* frozen blueberries
- 1 package (8 ounces) reduced-fat cream cheese, diced

TOPPING:
- 1/4 cup all-purpose flour
- 1/4 cup sugar
- 1 teaspoon grated lemon peel
- 2 tablespoons cold butter

RASPBERRY COFFEE CAKE

1) In a large mixing bowl, beat the butter and sugar until light and crumbly. Beat in egg, egg whites, applesauce, oil and lemon peel. Combine 2 cups flour, baking powder, salt and baking soda; add to sugar mixture alternately with buttermilk.

2) In a bowl, toss blueberries with remaining flour; fold into batter along with cream cheese. Pour into a 13-in. x 9-in. x 2-in. baking dish coated with cooking spray.

3) For topping, combine the flour, sugar and lemon peel in a bowl; cut in butter until mixture is crumbly. Sprinkle over batter.

4) Bake at 375° for 30-35 minutes or until a toothpick comes out clean. Cool on a wire rack.

Yield: 15 servings.

Editor's Note: If using frozen blueberries, do not thaw before adding to batter.

NUTRITION FACTS: 1 piece equals 224 calories, 8 g fat (4 g saturated fat), 31 mg cholesterol, 346 mg sodium, 34 g carbohydrate, 1 g fiber, 5 g protein.

Raspberry Coffee Cake

PREP: 25 min. **BAKE:** 35 min. + cooling

Mary Ross, Washburn, Wisconsin

- 1-1/2 cups all-purpose flour
- 1/2 cup sugar
- 1-1/2 teaspoons baking powder
- 1/2 teaspoon salt
- 1/2 teaspoon ground cinnamon
- 1/8 teaspoon ground mace, optional
- 1/2 cup cold butter
- 1 egg
- 1/2 cup 2% milk
- 1/2 teaspoon vanilla extract

FILLING:
- 1/2 cup sugar
- 2 tablespoons cornstarch
- 6 tablespoons water
- 1 cup fresh raspberries
- 1-1/2 teaspoons lemon juice

TOPPING:
- 1/3 cup all-purpose flour
- 3 tablespoons sugar
- 4-1/2 teaspoons cold butter
- 3 tablespoons chopped walnuts

1) In a bowl, combine the flour, sugar, baking powder, salt, cinnamon and mace if desired. Cut in butter until mixture resembles coarse crumbs. Whisk egg, milk and vanilla; stir into crumb mixture just until moistened. Spoon into a greased 9-in. x 5-in. x 3-in. loaf pan.

2) In a small saucepan, combine sugar and cornstarch; stir in water until smooth. Add raspberries and lemon juice. Bring to a boil; cook and stir for 1-2 minutes or until thickened. Pour over batter; cut through with a knife to swirl.

3) In a small bowl, combine flour and sugar. Cut in butter until crumbly. Sprinkle over batter; top with nuts. Bake at 350° for 35-40 minutes or until a toothpick comes out clean. Cool on a wire rack.

Yield: 6 servings.

NUTRITION FACTS: 1 piece equals 519 calories, 22 g fat (12 g saturated fat), 85 mg cholesterol, 502 mg sodium, 75 g carbohydrate, 3 g fiber, 7 g protein.

CHERRY CREAM CHEESE COFFEE CAKE

Cherry Cream Cheese Coffee Cake

PREP: 25 min. **BAKE:** 50 min. + cooling

Linda Guiles, Belvidere, New Jersey

In this tender coffee cake, the sour cream pairs well with the cherries, and the crunchy almonds make a nice accent. With a sweet streusel topping, it's hard to eat only one slice!

- 2-1/4 cups all-purpose flour
- 3/4 cup sugar
- 3/4 cup cold butter, cubed
- 1/2 teaspoon baking powder
- 1/2 teaspoon baking soda
- 1/2 teaspoon salt
- 1 egg, lightly beaten
- 3/4 cup sour cream
- 1 teaspoon almond extract

FILLING:

- 1 package (8 ounces) cream cheese, softened
- 1/4 cup sugar
- 1 egg, lightly beaten
- 1 can (21 ounces) cherry pie filling
- 1/2 cup slivered almonds

1) In a large bowl, combine the flour and sugar. Cut in butter until crumbly. Set aside 3/4 cup crumb mixture. Add the baking powder, baking soda and salt to remaining crumb mixture. Stir in the egg, sour cream and almond extract until blended.

2) Press onto the bottom and 1 in. up the sides of an ungreased 9-in. springform pan. Place on a baking sheet.

3) For filling, in a large mixing bowl, beat cream cheese and sugar for 1 minute. Add egg; beat just until combined. Spread over crust. Carefully top with pie filling. Sprinkle with almonds and reserved crumb mixture.

4) Bake at 350° for 50-60 minutes or until center is set. Cool on a wire rack. Carefully run a knife around edge of pan to loosen; remove sides of pan. Store in the refrigerator.

Yield: 8-10 servings.

NUTRITION FACTS: 1 piece equals 532 calories, 29 g fat (16 g saturated fat), 116 mg cholesterol, 440 mg sodium, 61 g carbohydrate, 2 g fiber, 8 g protein.

■ **Apple Cream Cheese Coffee Cake:** Use 1 can (21 ounces) apple pie filling and 1/2 cup chopped pecans *or* walnuts for the cherry pie filling and almonds. Proceed as directed.

■ **Blueberry Cream Cheese Coffee Cake:** Use 1 can (21 ounces) blueberry pie filling for the cherry pie filling. Proceed as directed.

Lemon Curd Coffee Cake

PREP: 20 min. **BAKE:** 55 min. + cooling

Anne Wickman, Endicott, New York

I tried this recipe for my son's birthday years ago and fell in love with the tart lemon filling, powdered sugar glaze and coconut topping.

- 1/2 cup all-purpose flour
- 1/3 cup sugar
- 3 tablespoons cold butter
- 1/2 cup flaked coconut

BATTER:

- 2-1/4 cups all-purpose flour
- 1/2 teaspoon salt
- 1/2 teaspoon baking powder
- 1/2 teaspoon baking soda
- 3/4 cup cold butter
- 2/3 cup vanilla yogurt
- 1 tablespoon lemon juice
- 2 teaspoons grated lemon peel
- 1 egg
- 1 egg yolk
- 1/2 cup lemon curd

GLAZE:

- 1/2 cup confectioners' sugar
- 1 teaspoon water
- 1 teaspoon lemon juice

1) In a small bowl, combine the flour and sugar. Cut in butter until mixture resembles coarse crumbs. Stir in coconut; set aside.

2) For batter, in a large bowl, combine the flour, salt, baking powder and baking soda. Cut in butter until mixture resembles coarse crumbs. Combine the yogurt, lemon juice, peel, egg and egg yolk; stir into crumb mixture just until moistened (batter will be stiff).

3) Spread 2 cups of the batter into a greased 9-in. springform pan; sprinkle with 3/4 cup of coconut mixture. Drop 1/2 teaspoonfuls of lemon curd over the top to within 1/2 in. of edges. Carefully spoon remaining batter over lemon curd; sprinkle with remaining coconut mixture.

4) Place pan on a baking sheet. Bake at 350° for 55-60 minutes or until a toothpick inserted near the center comes out clean. Cool for 10 minutes. Carefully run a knife around the edge of pan to loosen; remove sides of pan. Combine glaze ingredients; drizzle over warm coffee cake.

Yield: 12 servings.

Editor's Note: A recipe for Lemon Curd can be found on page 492.

NUTRITION FACTS: 1 slice equals 362 calories, 18 g fat (11 g saturated fat), 85 mg cholesterol, 347 mg sodium, 46 g carbohydrate, 1 g fiber, 5 g protein.

Cinnamon-Walnut Coffee Cake

PREP: 15 min. **BAKE:** 35 min.

Jill Hanselman, Lexington, North Carolina

My husband and I work outside the home, so we only have time for from-scratch breakfasts on the weekends.

  1-1/2 cups chopped walnuts
  1-1/2 cups sugar, *divided*
      3 teaspoons ground cinnamon
      2 cups all-purpose flour
    3/4 teaspoon baking soda
    1/2 teaspoon salt
      1 cup buttermilk
    1/4 cup vegetable oil
      1 egg
      1 teaspoon vanilla extract

GLAZE:
    1/3 cup confectioners' sugar
      2 to 2-1/2 teaspoons milk

1) In a small bowl, combine the walnuts, 3/4 cup sugar and cinnamon; set aside. Combine the flour, baking soda and salt; set aside. In a large mixing bowl, combine the buttermilk, oil, egg, vanilla and remaining sugar. Add flour mixture; beat just until moistened.

2) Spread half of the batter into a greased 8-in. square baking dish. Sprinkle with 1-1/2 cups walnut mixture. Spread with remaining batter; top with remaining walnut mixture. Cut through batter with a knife to swirl.

3) Bake at 350° for 35-40 minutes or until a toothpick inserted near the center comes out clean. Combine glaze ingredients; drizzle over coffee cake. Serve warm if desired or cool on a wire rack.

Yield: 9 servings.

NUTRITION FACTS: 1 piece equals 450 calories, 19 g fat (2 g saturated fat), 25 mg cholesterol, 273 mg sodium, 64 g carbohydrate, 2 g fiber, 10 g protein.

Apricot Coffee Cake

PREP: 15 min. **BAKE:** 40 min. + cooling

Taste of Home Test Kitchen

Are you having friends over for coffee? Serve them this scrumptious cake...they'll never guess it's light!

      1 jar (10 ounces) 100% apricot spreadable fruit, *divided*
    3/4 cup chopped pecans
Sugar substitute equivalent to 1/3 cup sugar
      4 teaspoons ground cinnamon

CAKE:
  3-1/4 cups reduced-fat biscuit/baking mix
Sugar substitute equivalent to 3/4 cup sugar
    1/8 teaspoon ground cardamom
      2 eggs
      1 cup fat-free milk
    2/3 cup reduced-fat sour cream
      1 tablespoon butter, melted

1) Place 3 tablespoons spreadable fruit in a small microwave-safe bowl; cover and refrigerate. In another bowl, combine the pecans, sugar substitute, cinnamon and remaining spreadable fruit; set aside.

2) For cake, in a large bowl, combine the biscuit mix, sugar substitute and cardamom. Combine the eggs, milk, sour cream and butter; stir into dry ingredients just until moistened.

3) Spread a third of the batter into a 10-in. fluted tube pan coated with cooking spray. Spread with half of the pecan mixture. Repeat layers. Top with remaining batter.

4) Bake at 350° for 40-45 minutes or until a toothpick inserted near the center comes out clean. Cool for 15 minutes before removing from pan to a wire rack. In a microwave, warm the reserved spreadable fruit; brush over warm cake. Cool completely.

Yield: 16 servings.

Editor's Note: This recipe was tested with Splenda No Calorie Sweetener.

NUTRITION FACTS: 1 slice equals 213 calories, 8 g fat (2 g saturated fat), 32 mg cholesterol, 313 mg sodium, 32 g carbohydrate, 1 g fiber, 4 g protein.

Making a Streusel-Filled Coffee Cake

Spoon about a third of the batter into greased pan. Sprinkle with a third of the streusel mixture. Repeat layers twice. Or, layer as stated in recipe. Bake as directed.

Royal Rhubarb Coffee Cake

PREP: 15 min. **BAKE:** 45 min. + cooling

Lorraine Robinson, Stony Plain, Alberta

For another twist, you can use raspberries and blueberries in place of the rhubarb with equally delicious results.

- 1/3   cup butter, softened
- 1   cup sugar
- 1   egg
- 1   teaspoon vanilla extract
- 2   cups all-purpose flour
- 3   teaspoons baking powder
- 1/2   teaspoon salt
- 1   cup milk
- 3-1/2   cups chopped fresh *or* frozen rhubarb

TOPPING:

- 3/4   cup packed brown sugar
- 1/4   cup butter, melted
- 1   teaspoon ground cinnamon

1) In a large mixing bowl, cream butter and sugar until light and fluffy. Add egg and vanilla; beat well. Combine the flour, baking powder and salt; add to creamed mixture alternately with milk.

2) Transfer to a greased 13-in. x 9-in. x 2-in. baking dish. Spoon rhubarb over top to within 1/2 in. of edges. Combine topping ingredients; sprinkle over rhubarb.

3) Bake at 350° for 45-55 minutes or until a toothpick inserted near the center comes out clean. Cool on a wire rack.

Yield: 15 servings.

Editor's Note: If using frozen rhubarb, measure rhubarb while frozen, then thaw completely. Drain in a colander, but do not press liquid out.

NUTRITION FACTS: 1 serving equals 238 calories, 8 g fat (5 g saturated fat), 35 mg cholesterol, 249 mg sodium, 39 g carbohydrate, 1 g fiber, 3 g protein.

Surprise Monkey Bread

PREP: 25 min. **BAKE:** 40 min.

Lois Rutherford, Elkton, Florida

When my neighbor hosts her Christmas brunch, this is one recipe that's always requested.

- 1   cup packed brown sugar
- 1/2   cup butter, cubed
- 2   tubes (12 ounces *each*) refrigerated flaky buttermilk biscuits
- 1/2   cup sugar
- 1   tablespoon ground cinnamon
- 1   package (8 ounces) cream cheese, cut into 20 cubes
- 1-1/2   cups chopped walnuts

1) In a small microwave-safe bowl, heat brown sugar and butter on high for 1 minute or until sugar is dissolved; set aside.

2) Flatten each biscuit into a 3-in. circle. Combine sugar and cinnamon; sprinkle 1/2 teaspoon in the center of each biscuit. Top with a cream cheese cube. Fold dough over filling; pinch edges to seal tightly.

3) Sprinkle 1/2 cup walnuts into a greased 10-in. fluted tube pan. Layer with half of the biscuits, about 2 tablespoons cinnamon-sugar, half of the butter mixture and 1/2 cup walnuts. Repeat layers.

4) Bake at 350° for 40-45 minutes or until golden brown. Immediately invert onto a serving platter. Serve warm. Refrigerate leftovers.

Yield: 1 loaf (12 slices).

NUTRITION FACTS: 1 slice equals 467 calories, 24 g fat (10 g saturated fat), 41 mg cholesterol, 625 mg sodium, 56 g carbohydrate, 1 g fiber, 10 g protein.

Muffins

Standard muffin pans come in different sizes, which affect baking time. The muffin pans used by the Taste of Home Test Kitchen measure 2-1/2 in. across.

Fill greased or paper-lined muffin cups about two-thirds to three-fourths full, wiping off any spills. To quickly fill muffin cups with little mess, use an ice cream scoop with a quick release. Or pour the batter from a measuring cup. If your muffin recipe does not fill all the cups in your pan, fill the empty cups with water. The muffins will bake more evenly.

Unless directed otherwise, muffins should go into the oven as soon as the batter is mixed.

Use a kitchen timer. Check for doneness 5-7 minutes before the end of the recommended baking time to avoid overbaking.

Muffins are done when a toothpick inserted near the center comes out clean. For muffins with a filling, make sure the toothpick is inserted into the muffin and not the filling.

Cool in the pan for 5 minutes, unless the recipe directs otherwise. Muffins are best served warm, fresh from the oven.

ADD SOME FLAXSEED ■■■

Milled flaxseed is packed with heart-healthy oils and is a good source of fiber. Besides sprinkling it on cereal or blending it into smoothies, it can be substituted for some of the fat in breads and muffins. Try using 3 tablespoons of milled flaxseed instead of 1 tablespoon butter or oil called for in a recipe. Be sure to use the milled or ground flaxseed to enjoy all of its wholesome benefits.

—*Karen K., New Berlin, Pennsylvania*

Brown Sugar Oat Muffins

PREP/TOTAL TIME: 30 min.

Regina Stock, Topeka, Kansas

With Kansas being one of the top wheat-producing states, it seems only fitting to share a recipe containing whole wheat flour. These are great muffins to have for breakfast. We enjoy them fresh out of the oven.

    1   cup old-fashioned oats
    1   cup whole wheat flour
  1/2   cup all-purpose flour
  3/4   cup packed brown sugar
    2   teaspoons baking powder
  1/2   teaspoon salt
    2   eggs
  3/4   cup milk
  1/4   cup vegetable oil
    1   teaspoon vanilla extract

1) In a small bowl, combine the oats, flours, brown sugar, baking powder and salt. In another small bowl, whisk the eggs, milk, oil and vanilla. Stir into the dry ingredients just until moistened.

2) Fill greased or paper-lined muffin cups two-thirds full. Bake at 400° for 15-17 minutes or until a toothpick comes out clean. Cool for 5 minutes before removing from pan to a wire rack. Serve warm.

Yield: 1 dozen.

NUTRITION FACTS: 1 muffin equals 192 calories, 7 g fat (1 g saturated fat), 37 mg cholesterol, 189 mg sodium, 30 g carbohydrate, 2 g fiber, 4 g protein.

Lemon Pound Cake Muffins

PREP: 15 min. **BAKE:** 20 min.

Lola Baxter, Winnebago, Minnesota

I make these lemony muffins for all kinds of occasions. My family asks for them often. They're so good!

  1/2   cup butter, softened
    1   cup sugar
    2   eggs
    1   teaspoon vanilla extract
  1/2   teaspoon lemon extract
 1-3/4 cups all-purpose flour
  1/2   teaspoon salt
  1/4   teaspoon baking soda
  1/2   cup sour cream

GLAZE:

    2   cups confectioners' sugar
    3   tablespoons lemon juice

1) In a large mixing bowl, cream butter and sugar until light and fluffy. Beat in eggs and extracts. Combine the flour, salt and baking soda; add to creamed mixture alternately with sour cream.

2) Fill greased or paper-lined muffin cups three-fourths full. Bake at 400° for 18-20 minutes or until a toothpick comes out clean. Cool for 5 minutes before removing from pan to a wire rack.

3) Combine the glaze ingredients; drizzle over cooled muffins.

Yield: 1 dozen.

NUTRITION FACTS: 1 muffin equals 311 calories, 10 g fat (6 g saturated fat), 63 mg cholesterol, 218 mg sodium, 51 g carbohydrate, 1 g fiber, 3 g protein.

EYE-OPENING MUFFINS

 CLASSIC: You can bake a batch of warm Berry Cream Muffins any time of year because they call for fresh or frozen raspberries or blueberries. For more delicious options, be sure to take a look at the two variations that follow the recipe.

 TIME-SAVER: For homemade taste without the effort, turn to Cranberry Bran Muffins. Simply stir crushed bran cereal, dried cranberries and some milk into apple cinnamon muffin mix to bake up six nutritious muffins that make a great on-the-go breakfast.

 LIGHT: After one bite of Orange Yogurt Muffins, you can't help but notice the citrusy taste from grated orange peel in the batter and sweet glaze. Plain yogurt and 2% milk help lighten these muffins, so they have fewer calories, a third of the fat, and less cholesterol and sodium than classic Berry Cream Muffins.

 SERVES 2: You may wish you doubled the recipe for I Want S'more Muffins after trying these treats. Graham cracker crumbs, milk chocolate chips and marshmallow creme lend a sweet, distinctive flavor to this small batch.

Berry Cream Muffins

PREP: 15 min. **BAKE:** 20 min.

Linda Gilmore, Hampstead, Maryland

- 2 cups all-purpose flour
- 1 cup sugar
- 1/2 teaspoon baking powder
- 1/2 teaspoon baking soda
- 1/2 teaspoon salt
- 1-1/2 cups fresh *or* frozen raspberries *or* blueberries
- 2 eggs, lightly beaten
- 1 cup (8 ounces) sour cream
- 1/2 cup vegetable oil
- 1/2 teaspoon vanilla extract

BERRY CREAM MUFFINS

1) In a large bowl, combine the flour, sugar, baking powder, baking soda and salt; add berries and toss gently. Combine the eggs, sour cream, oil and vanilla; mix well. Stir into dry ingredients just until moistened.

2) Fill greased muffin cups two-thirds full. Bake at 400° for 18-22 minutes or until a toothpick comes out clean. Cool for 5 minutes before removing from pan to a wire rack. Serve warm.

Yield: about 1 dozen.

Editor's Note: If using frozen berries, do not thaw before adding to the batter.

NUTRITION FACTS: 1 serving equals 241 calories, 12 g fat (3 g saturated fat), 42 mg cholesterol, 162 mg sodium, 30 g carbohydrate, 1 g fiber, 3 g protein.

■ **Berry Cream Lemon Muffins:** Prepare muffin recipe as directed, except substitute 1 cup lemon yogurt for the sour cream and add 2 teaspoons grated lemon peel with the vanilla.

■ **Berry Streusel Muffins:** Prepare muffin recipe as directed. For topping, combine 3 tablespoons each all-purpose flour and quick-cooking oats, 2 tablespoons sugar and 1/8 teaspoon ground cinnamon. Cut in 2 tablespoons cold butter until crumbly. Sprinkle over muffins before baking.

Cranberry Bran Muffins

PREP/TOTAL TIME: 25 min.

Taste of Home Test Kitchen

- 1 package (8.1 ounces) apple cinnamon muffin mix
- 1/2 cup All-Bran, crushed
- 1/2 cup dried cranberries
- 1/2 cup milk

1) In a large bowl, combine the muffin mix, bran and cranberries. Stir in milk just until moistened. Fill greased or paper-lined muffin cups three-fourths full.

2) Bake at 450° for 15-20 minutes or until a toothpick comes out clean. Cool for 5 minutes before removing from pan to a wire rack. Serve warm.

Yield: 6 muffins.

NUTRITION FACTS: 1 muffin equals 210 calories, 5 g fat (1 g saturated fat), 4 mg cholesterol, 567 mg sodium, 41 g carbohydrate, 2 g fiber, 3 g protein.

Orange Yogurt Muffins

PREP/TOTAL TIME: 30 min.

Anne Prince, Courtland, Virginia

- 1/2 cup sugar, *divided*
- 2 tablespoons grated orange peel
- 2 tablespoons water
- 5 tablespoons butter, cubed
- 2 cups all-purpose flour
- 1 teaspoon baking powder
- 1 teaspoon baking soda
- 1/2 teaspoon salt
- 2 eggs
- 3/4 cup plain yogurt
- 3/4 cup 2% milk

GLAZE:
- 1 cup confectioners' sugar
- 2 tablespoons orange juice
- 1 teaspoon grated orange peel

1) In a small saucepan, combine 1/4 cup sugar, orange peel and water. Cook and stir over low heat for 3-5 minutes or until sugar is dissolved. Add butter; stir until melted. Remove from the heat; set aside.

2) In a large bowl, combine the flour, baking powder, baking soda, salt and remaining sugar. In another bowl, whisk the eggs, yogurt, milk and reserved butter mixture. Stir into dry ingredients just until moistened.

3) Coat muffin cups with cooking spray; fill each with a scant 1/4 cup of batter. Bake at 375° for 13-18 minutes or until a toothpick comes out clean.

4) Combine glaze ingredients; spoon about 1-1/2 teaspoons over each warm muffin. Remove from pans to wire racks. Serve warm.

Yield: 1-1/2 dozen.

NUTRITION FACTS: 1 muffin equals 147 calories, 4 g fat (2 g saturated fat), 34 mg cholesterol, 207 mg sodium, 24 g carbohydrate, trace fiber, 3 g protein.

I Want S'more Muffins

PREP: 20 min. **BAKE:** 15 min.

Sally Sibthorpe, Shelby Township, Michigan

- 3 tablespoons butter, softened
- 1/4 cup packed brown sugar
- 4 teaspoons sugar
- 1 egg
- 1/3 cup sour cream
- 2/3 cup all-purpose flour
- 1/2 cup graham cracker crumbs
- 1/4 teaspoon salt
- 1/4 teaspoon baking powder
- 1/4 teaspoon ground cinnamon
- 1/8 teaspoon baking soda
- 3 tablespoons 2% milk
- 1/3 cup milk chocolate chips
- 6 tablespoons marshmallow creme

1) In a small mixing bowl, cream butter and sugars until light and fluffy. Beat in egg. Stir in sour cream. Combine the flour, graham cracker crumbs, salt, baking powder, cinnamon and baking soda; add to creamed mixture alternately with milk just until moistened. Fold in chocolate chips.

2) Coat six muffin cups with cooking spray; fill one-fourth full with batter. Spoon 1 tablespoon marshmallow creme into each muffin cup. Top with remaining batter.

3) Bake at 400° for 14-16 minutes or until a toothpick comes out clean. Cool for 5 minutes before removing from pan to a wire rack. Serve warm.

Yield: 6 muffins.

Editor's Note: Fill empty muffin cups halfway with water before baking.

NUTRITION FACTS: 1 muffin equals 287 calories, 13 g fat (7 g saturated fat), 62 mg cholesterol, 279 mg sodium, 39 g carbohydrate, 1 g fiber, 4 g protein.

I WANT S'MORE MUFFINS

CARAWAY RYE MUFFINS

☙ Caraway Rye Muffins

PREP/TOTAL TIME: 30 min.

Jean Tyner, Darlington, South Carolina

The distinctive taste of caraway abounds in this recipe, which also features rye flour for a change of pace.

    1   cup rye flour
  3/4   cup all-purpose flour
  1/4   cup sugar
2-1/2   teaspoons baking powder
  1/2   teaspoon salt
  1/2   teaspoon caraway seeds
  3/4   cup shredded cheddar cheese
    1   egg, beaten
  3/4   cup milk
  1/3   cup vegetable oil

1) In a large bowl, combine the flours, sugar, baking powder, salt and caraway seeds. Stir in cheese. Combine the egg, milk and oil; stir into the dry ingredients just until moistened.

2) Fill greased or paper-lined muffin cups two-thirds full. Bake at 400° for 20-23 minutes or a toothpick comes out clean. Cool for 5 minutes before removing from pan to a wire rack. Serve warm.

Yield: 10 muffins.

NUTRITION FACTS: 1 muffin equals 203 calories, 11 g fat (3 g saturated fat), 33 mg cholesterol, 285 mg sodium, 21 g carbohydrate, 2 g fiber, 5 g protein.

Changing Muffin Size

When baking mini or jumbo muffins, the oven temperature generally will not need to be adjusted, but the baking time will most likely need to be altered. Mini muffins will take anywhere from 10-15 minutes while jumbo muffins will bake from 20-40 minutes. Check jumbo muffins for doneness after 20 minutes, then every 5-10 minutes. Keep in mind that the baking time will vary according to the recipe. The variation is due to the oven temperature and the amount of batter in each muffin cup.

☙ Cracked Pepper Cheddar Muffins

PREP: 15 min. **BAKE:** 25 min.

Susan Kelm, Mineral Point, Wisconsin

Served warm, these golden muffins make a great accompaniment to soup, stew or any other cold-weather entree. My family loves the cheese and pepper flavor.

    2   cups all-purpose flour
    1   tablespoon sugar
    3   teaspoons baking powder
  1/2   teaspoon coarsely ground pepper
    1   egg

☙ Best Bran Muffins

PREP: 15 min. **BAKE:** 20 min.

Karen Hill, Sheridan, Oregon

These hearty muffins were a staple with my twin sister and me all through high school. Raisins or dried cranberries can make a nice addition.

1-1/2   cups old-fashioned oats
    1   cup All-Bran
    1   cup boiling water
  1/2   cup sugar
  1/2   cup packed brown sugar
  1/2   cup butter, melted
    2   eggs, beaten
  1/4   cup toasted wheat germ
2-1/2   cups all-purpose flour
2-1/2   teaspoons baking soda
  1/2   teaspoon salt
    2   cups buttermilk

1) Place oats and cereal in a bowl; cover with boiling water. Let stand for 5 minutes. Stir in the sugars, butter, eggs and wheat germ; mix well.

2) Combine the flour, baking soda and salt; stir into oat mixture alternately with buttermilk just until moistened.

3) Fill greased muffin cups two-thirds full. Bake at 375° for 18-20 minutes or until a toothpick comes out clean. Cool for 5 minutes before removing from pans to wire racks. Serve warm.

Yield: 2 dozen.

NUTRITION FACTS: 1 muffin equals 158 calories, 5 g fat (3 g saturated fat), 29 mg cholesterol, 254 mg sodium, 25 g carbohydrate, 2 g fiber, 4 g protein.

1-1/4 cups milk
2 tablespoons vegetable oil
1 cup (4 ounces) shredded cheddar cheese

1) In a large bowl, combine the flour, sugar, baking powder and pepper. In another bowl, whisk the egg, milk and oil. Stir into dry ingredients just until moistened. Fold in cheese.

2) Fill greased muffin cups two-thirds full. Bake at 375° for 25-30 minutes or until a toothpick comes out clean. Cool for 5 minutes before removing from pan to a wire rack. Serve warm.

Yield: 1 dozen.

NUTRITION FACTS: 1 muffin equals 155 calories, 6 g fat (3 g saturated fat), 30 mg cholesterol, 173 mg sodium, 19 g carbohydrate, 1 g fiber, 6 g protein.

CRACKED PEPPER CHEDDAR MUFFINS

Biscuits and Scones

Use cold butter, cold stick margarine (with at least 80% oil) or shortening. Cut in the butter, margarine or shortening only until mixture resembles coarse crumbs.

Biscuits and scones are done when they're golden brown on the top and bottom. The sides will always be a little light. Remove to wire racks. Biscuits are best served fresh from the oven or eaten the day they are made. Scones are best on the day they are made.

If you have leftover biscuits or scones, store in an airtight container at room temperature for up to 2 days. If made with cheese, cream cheese or other perishable foods, they should be stored in the refrigerator. You can freeze biscuits and scones for up to 3 months.

Cornmeal Drop Biscuits
PREP: 10 min. **BAKE:** 30 min.

Rhonda McKee, Greensburg, Kansas
I like to stir up a batch of these light, golden biscuits.

1-1/3 cups all-purpose flour
1/2 cup cornmeal
2-1/2 teaspoons baking powder
1/2 teaspoon salt
1/2 teaspoon ground mustard
1/2 cup shortening
1/2 cup shredded cheddar cheese
1 cup milk

1) In a bowl, combine flour, cornmeal, baking powder, salt and mustard; cut in shortening until crumbly. Stir in cheese and milk just until moistened.

2) Drop by 1/4 cupfuls 2 in. apart onto a greased baking sheet. Bake at 375° for 26-28 minutes or until golden brown. Serve warm.

Yield: 10 biscuits.

NUTRITION FACTS: 1 biscuit equals 210 calories, 12 g fat (4 g saturated fat), 9 mg cholesterol, 265 mg sodium, 19 g carbohydrate, 1 g fiber, 4 g protein.

Cherry Chip Scones
PREP: 15 min. **BAKE:** 20 min.

Pamela Brooks, South Berwick, Maine
These flaky scones dotted with dried cherries are a real treat.

3 cups all-purpose flour
1/2 cup sugar
2-1/2 teaspoons baking powder
1/2 teaspoon baking soda
6 tablespoons cold butter
1 cup (8 ounces) vanilla yogurt
1/4 cup plus 2 tablespoons milk, *divided*
1-1/3 cups dried cherries
2/3 cup vanilla *or* white chips

1) In a bowl, combine flour, sugar, baking powder and baking soda. Cut in butter until crumbly. Combine yogurt and 1/4 cup milk; stir into the crumb mixture just until moistened. Knead in the cherries and chips.

2) On a greased baking sheet, pat the dough into a 9-in. circle. Cut into eight wedges; separate wedges. Brush with the remaining milk. Bake at 400° for 20-25 minutes or until golden brown. Serve warm.

Yield: 8 scones.

NUTRITION FACTS: 1 scone equals 543 calories, 23 g fat (14 g saturated fat), 52 mg cholesterol, 410 mg sodium, 77 g carbohydrate, 2 g fiber, 8 g protein.

■ **Cranberry Chip Scones:** Use 1-1/3 cups dried cranberries instead of the dried cherries. Use vanilla *or* semisweet chocolate chips.

■ **Blueberry Chip Scones:** Use 1-1/3 cups dried blueberries instead of the dried cherries.

HOT HOMEMADE BISCUITS

 CLASSIC: You need only seven pantry ingredients to make Fluffy Biscuits. In 30 minutes, you can knead, cut and bake a dozen of these tender biscuits to accompany most any meal. Served warm with butter, they're irresistible.

 TIME-SAVER: Skip the kneading, rolling and cutting! Potato Drop Biscuits are stirred together with biscuit/baking mix and three other ingredients, then dropped from a spoon onto the pan. They bake in 10 minutes, so you can have them on the table quickly.

 LIGHT: Green onions and onion powder provide the savory flavor in these better-for-you biscuits. Because the recipe for Green Onion Biscuits calls for canola oil and butter-flavored spray but no egg, each biscuit has almost half the calories and sodium and a third of the fat of Fluffy Biscuits, with only a whisper of cholesterol.

SERVES 2: When a dozen is simply too many biscuits, turn to the recipe for Touch of Honey Biscuits. It yields four from-scratch biscuits that are lightly sweetened with honey and baked until golden.

FLUFFY BISCUITS

Fluffy Biscuits

PREP/TOTAL TIME: 30 min.

Nancy Horsburgh, Everett, Ontario

- 2 cups all-purpose flour
- 4 teaspoons baking powder
- 3 teaspoons sugar
- 1/2 teaspoon salt
- 1/2 cup shortening
- 1 egg
- 2/3 cup milk

1) In a small bowl, combine the flour, baking powder, sugar and salt. Cut in shortening until the mixture resembles coarse crumbs. Beat egg with milk; stir into dry ingredients just until moistened.

2) Turn onto a well-floured surface; knead 20 times. Roll to 3/4-in. thickness; cut with a floured 2-1/2-in. biscuit cutter.

3) Place on a lightly greased baking sheet. Bake at 450° for 8-10 minutes or until golden brown. Serve warm.

Yield: 1 dozen.

NUTRITION FACTS: 1 biscuit equals 168 calories, 9 g fat (2 g saturated fat), 20 mg cholesterol, 244 mg sodium, 18 g carbohydrate, 1 g fiber, 3 g protein.

■ **Italian Biscuits:** Add 1 teaspoon of Italian seasoning to the flour mixture.

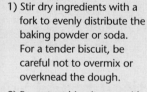

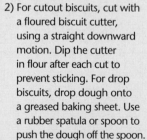

Making Biscuits

1) Stir dry ingredients with a fork to evenly distribute the baking powder or soda. For a tender biscuit, be careful not to overmix or overknead the dough.

2) For cutout biscuits, cut with a floured biscuit cutter, using a straight downward motion. Dip the cutter in flour after each cut to prevent sticking. For drop biscuits, drop dough onto a greased baking sheet. Use a rubber spatula or spoon to push the dough off the spoon.

3) When reworking biscuit trimmings, handle the dough as little as possible and use as little additional flour as needed. Overworking the dough or using too much flour will result in a tough, dry product.

Potato Drop Biscuits
PREP/TOTAL TIME: 20 min.

Roberta Strohmaier, Lebanon, New Jersey

- 2-1/4 cups biscuit/baking mix
- 1/3 cup mashed potato flakes
- 2/3 cup milk
- 2 tablespoons sour cream

1) In a large bowl, combine biscuit mix and potato flakes. In a small bowl, whisk milk and sour cream. Stir into the dry ingredients just until moistened.

2) Drop by heaping tablespoonfuls onto a greased baking sheet. Bake at 400° for 10-12 minutes or until tops begin to brown. Serve warm.

Yield: 1 dozen.

NUTRITION FACTS: 1 biscuit equals 112 calories, 4 g fat (1 g saturated fat), 4 mg cholesterol, 295 mg sodium, 16 g carbohydrate, trace fiber, 2 g protein.

GREEN ONION BISCUITS

Green Onion Biscuits
PREP/TOTAL TIME: 25 min.

Taste of Home Test Kitchen

- 2 cups all-purpose flour
- 1 teaspoon baking powder
- 1/2 teaspoon salt
- 1/4 teaspoon baking soda
- 1/4 teaspoon onion powder
- 1 cup buttermilk
- 1/2 cup finely chopped green onions
- 3 tablespoons canola oil

Refrigerated butter-flavored spray

1) In a large bowl, combine the flour, baking powder, salt, baking soda and onion powder. Combine the buttermilk, onions and oil; stir into dry ingredients just until moistened.

2) Drop by heaping teaspoonfuls 2 in. apart onto baking sheets coated with cooking spray. Spritz tops with butter-flavored spray. Bake at 400° for 14-18 minutes or until golden brown. Serve warm.

Yield: 16 biscuits.

Editor's Note: This recipe was tested with I Can't Believe It's Not Butter Spray.

NUTRITION FACTS: 1 biscuit equals 85 calories, 3 g fat (trace saturated fat), 1 mg cholesterol, 124 mg sodium, 12 g carbohydrate, 1 g fiber, 2 g protein.

LESS-MESS KNEADED BISCUITS ■■■

When making kneaded biscuits, I knead, pat out the dough, cut the biscuits and bake them all on the same round pizza pan. This really helps keep the mess to a minimum.

—*Judy B., Goshen, Indiana*

Touch of Honey Biscuits
PREP/TOTAL TIME: 25 min.

Donna Jeffers, Petersburg, West Virginia

- 1 cup all-purpose flour
- 1-1/2 teaspoons baking powder
- 1/4 teaspoon salt
- 1/4 teaspoon cream of tartar
- 1/4 cup cold butter, cubed
- 1/3 cup milk
- 1 teaspoon honey

1) In a large bowl, combine the flour, baking powder, salt and cream of tartar; cut in butter until crumbly. Stir in milk and honey just until moistened.

2) Turn onto a floured surface; knead gently 8-10 times. Roll out to 3/4-in. thickness; cut with a floured 2-1/2-in. biscuit cutter.

3) Place 1 in. apart on a greased baking sheet. Bake at 450° for 10-15 minutes or until golden brown. Serve warm.

Yield: 4 biscuits.

NUTRITION FACTS: 1 biscuit equals 232 calories, 12 g fat (8 g saturated fat), 33 mg cholesterol, 424 mg sodium, 26 g carbohydrate, 1 g fiber, 4 g protein.

TOUCH OF HONEY BISCUITS

FRESH-FROM-THE-OVEN SCONES

 CLASSIC: Butter, eggs and heavy cream lend traditional taste and texture to British Scones. Brushed with additional cream for a pretty look after baking, these treats are wonderful with a pot of tea or coffee.

 TIME-SAVER: Using an all-in-one biscuit/baking mix instead of measuring a bunch of dry ingredients cuts your prep time for Parmesan Sage Scones. Topped with fresh sage leaves, the savory wedges are ready from start to finish in 25 minutes.

 LIGHT: Buttermilk and orange juice instead of heavy cream help lighten Festive Poppy Seed Scones. Dried cranberries, orange peel and quick-cooking oats add interest to these treats, which are lower in fat, calories, cholesterol and sodium than classic British Scones.

 SERVES 2: Citrus peel and dried currants accent the flavor of Afternoon Tea Scones. Since it makes a small batch of six, you can enjoy a few and share a few without lots of leftovers.

British Scones

PREP/TOTAL TIME: 30 min.

Carole Jasier, Albuquerque, New Mexico

- 2 cups all-purpose flour
- 1 tablespoon sugar
- 2 teaspoons baking powder
- 1/2 teaspoon salt
- 6 tablespoons cold butter
- 2 eggs, lightly beaten
- 1/3 cup plus 1 tablespoon heavy whipping cream, *divided*
- 1/2 teaspoon vanilla extract

1) In a large bowl, combine the flour, sugar, baking powder and salt. Cut in butter until mixture resembles coarse crumbs. Combine the eggs, 1/3 cup cream and vanilla; add to crumb mixture and stir until a soft dough forms.

2) Turn onto a floured surface; gently knead 6-8 times. Pat dough into a 6-in. circle. Cut into eight wedges. Separate wedges and place 1 in. apart on an ungreased baking sheet. Brush tops with remaining cream.

3) Bake at 400° for 12-14 minutes or until browned. Serve warm.

Yield: 8 scones.

NUTRITION FACTS: 1 scone equals 254 calories, 14 g fat (9 g saturated fat), 92 mg cholesterol, 331 mg sodium, 26 g carbohydrate, 1 g fiber, 5 g protein.

■ **Cheese Scones:** Omit vanilla and decrease sugar to 1-1/2 teaspoons. Increase salt to 3/4 teaspoon. Stir 1 cup (4 ounces) shredded cheddar cheese and 1/4 teaspoon dill weed into flour mixture. Proceed as directed.

■ **Currant Hazelnut Scones:** Increase salt to 3/4 teaspoon. Add 1/2 cup toasted chopped hazelnuts and 1/3 cup dried currants to dough; gently knead 6-8 times. Proceed as directed.

PARMESAN SAGE SCONES

Parmesan Sage Scones

PREP/TOTAL TIME: 25 min.

Taste of Home Test Kitchen

- 2-1/4 cups biscuit/baking mix
- 1/4 cup grated Parmesan cheese
- 1-3/4 teaspoons minced fresh sage
- 1/4 teaspoon pepper
- 1/2 cup plus 1 tablespoon half-and-half cream, *divided*
- 8 fresh sage leaves

1) In a large bowl, combine the biscuit mix, Parmesan cheese, minced sage and pepper. Stir in 1/2 cup cream. Turn onto a floured surface; knead 5 times.

2) Transfer dough to a greased baking sheet. Pat into a 6-in. circle. Cut into eight wedges, but do not separate. Brush remaining cream over dough. Press a sage leave onto the top of each wedge.

3) Bake at 375° for 10-15 minutes or edges are until golden brown. Serve warm.

Yield: 8 scones.

NUTRITION FACTS: 1 scone equals 172 calories, 8 g fat (3 g saturated fat), 10 mg cholesterol, 480 mg sodium, 22 g carbohydrate, 1 g fiber, 4 g protein.

⚜ Festive Poppy Seed Scones

PREP: 20 min. **BAKE:** 15 min.

Lisa Varner, Greenville, South Carolina

- 2 cups all-purpose flour
- 1/2 cup sugar
- 1/2 cup quick-cooking oats
- 1 tablespoon poppy seeds
- 2 teaspoons baking powder
- 1/2 teaspoon salt
- 1/4 teaspoon baking soda
- 1/3 cup cold butter
- 1 egg
- 1/2 cup orange juice
- 3 tablespoons buttermilk
- 1/2 cup dried cranberries
- 1 teaspoon grated orange peel

1) In a large bowl, combine the flour, sugar, oats, poppy seeds, baking powder, salt and baking soda. Cut in the butter until mixture resembles coarse crumbs. In a small bowl, whisk the egg, orange juice and buttermilk; add to the crumb mixture just until moistened. Stir in cranberries and orange peel.

2) Turn onto a lightly floured surface; gently knead 6-8 times. Divide dough in half. Pat each portion into a 6-in. circle. Place on a baking sheet coated with cooking spray. Cut each circle into six wedges, but do not separate.

3) Bake at 375° for 15-20 minutes or until golden brown. Serve warm.

Yield: 1 dozen.

NUTRITION FACTS: 1 scone equals 197 calories, 6 g fat (3 g saturated fat), 31 mg cholesterol, 253 mg sodium, 32 g carbohydrate, 1 g fiber, 4 g protein.

AFTERNOON TEA SCONES

▧ Afternoon Tea Scones

PREP/TOTAL TIME: 30 min.

Ruth Ann Stelfox, Raymond, Alberta

- 1-3/4 cups all-purpose flour
- 1/4 cup sugar
- 2 teaspoons baking powder
- 3/4 teaspoon baking soda
- 1/2 teaspoon salt
- 2 tablespoons cold butter
- 1 egg, lightly beaten
- 3/4 cup sour cream
- 1/2 cup dried currants *or* raisins
- 1 teaspoon grated lemon peel
- 1 teaspoon grated orange peel
- 1 egg yolk
- 2 tablespoons water

1) In a large bowl, combine the flour, sugar, baking powder, baking soda and salt; cut in butter until mixture resembles coarse crumbs. Stir in egg, sour cream, currants, lemon peel and orange peel.

2) Turn onto a well-floured surface. Roll into a 7-in. circle. In a small bowl, beat egg yolk and water. Brush over dough. Cut into six wedges.

3) Transfer to a greased baking sheet. Bake at 400° for 15 minutes or until golden brown. Serve warm.

Yield: 6 scones.

NUTRITION FACTS: 1 scone equals 295 calories, 8 g fat (5 g saturated fat), 91 mg cholesterol, 559 mg sodium, 47 g carbohydrate, 2 g fiber, 8 g protein.

FESTIVE POPPY SEED SCONES

⬤ Sage Breadsticks

PREP/TOTAL TIME: 30 min.

Sue Wagner, West Farmington, Ohio

Sage is subtle but wonderful in these cheesy-crisp breadsticks. Try them as a snack or alongside soup or salad.

> 1 cup all-purpose flour
> 1-1/2 teaspoons baking powder
> 1 teaspoon rubbed sage
> 1/2 teaspoon salt
> 1/2 cup finely shredded cheddar cheese
> 2 tablespoons cold butter
> 1/3 cup cold water

1) In a small bowl, combine the flour, baking powder, sage and salt; stir in cheese. Cut in butter until mixture resembles coarse crumbs. Gradually add water, tossing with a fork until dough forms a ball.

2) On a lightly floured surface, roll dough into a 12-in. x 10-in. rectangle. Cut in half lengthwise; cut each half widthwise into 1-in. strips. Twist each strip two to three times.

3) Place 1 in. apart on baking sheets coated with cooking spray. Bake at 425° for 8-10 minutes or until golden brown. Serve warm.

Yield: 2 dozen.

NUTRITION FACTS: 2 breadsticks equals 71 calories, 3 g fat (2 g saturated fat), 10 mg cholesterol, 196 mg sodium, 8 g carbohydrate, trace fiber, 2 g protein.

⬤ Cheddar Bread Twists

PREP/TOTAL TIME: 25 min.

Tracy Travers, Fairhaven, Massachusetts

These quick-to-fix breadsticks are light and flaky, with a little crunch. Serve the cheesy twists as a side dish or even as an appetizer with dip.

> 1 sheet frozen puff pastry, thawed
> 1 egg white
> 1 tablespoon cold water
> 1/2 cup shredded cheddar cheese

Dash salt

1) Place the puff pastry on a greased baking sheet. In a small bowl, beat the egg white and water; brush over pastry. Sprinkle with cheese and salt.

2) Cut into ten 1-in. strips; twist each strip three times. Bake at 400° for 10-13 minutes or until golden brown.

Yield: 10 breadsticks.

NUTRITION FACTS: 1 breadstick equals 142 calories, 8 g fat (3 g saturated fat), 6 mg cholesterol, 135 mg sodium, 14 g carbohydrate, 2 g fiber, 3 g protein.

Popovers and Puffs

For popovers, place oven rack in lowest position. Generously grease the muffin pan cups, custard cups or popover pan cups. Mix batter until smooth. Batter may be refrigerated for up to 1 day. Pour into cups.

Bake according to recipe directions. Don't open the oven door during baking or popovers will fall. After removing popovers from the oven, prick with the point of a sharp knife to allow steam to escape. Popovers are best served warm, fresh from the oven.

⬤ Baked Herb Puffs

PREP: 20 min. **BAKE:** 25 min.

Dorothy Smith, El Dorado, Arkansas

Ground mustard, parsley and green onions make these puffs a nice addition to any meal. I often freeze them, then reheat for a few minutes in the oven.

> 1 cup water
> 1/2 cup butter
> 1 teaspoon ground mustard
> 1/4 teaspoon salt
> 1/8 teaspoon pepper
> 1 cup all-purpose flour
> 4 eggs
> 1/3 cup minced fresh parsley
> 1/4 cup chopped green onions

1) In a large saucepan, bring the water, butter, mustard, salt and pepper to a boil. Add flour all at once and stir until a smooth ball forms. Remove from the heat; let stand for 5 minutes.

2) Add eggs, one at a time, beating well after each addition. Continue beating until mixture is smooth and shiny. Add parsley and green onions; mix well.

BAKED HERB PUFFS

3) Drop by 2 tablespoonfuls 2 in. apart onto baking sheets coated with cooking spray. Bake at 400° for 18-20 minutes or until golden brown. Cut a slit in each to allow steam to escape; bake 5 minutes longer. Serve warm.

Yield: 1-1/2 dozen.

NUTRITION FACTS: 1 puff equals 88 calories, 6 g fat (3 g saturated fat), 61 mg cholesterol, 99 mg sodium, 6 g carbohydrate, trace fiber, 2 g protein.

Christmas Morning Popovers

PREP: 15 min. **BAKE:** 35 min.

Sue Jurack, Mequon, Wisconsin

Popovers are a Christmas morning tradition that my father-in-law started years ago. Now I get up early to make the popovers, then wake the family to begin opening gifts.

  1-1/4 **cups milk**
     1 **tablespoon butter, melted and cooled**
     1 **cup all-purpose flour**
  1/4 **teaspoon salt**
     2 **eggs**

1) In a small mixing bowl, beat the milk, butter, flour and salt until blended. Add the eggs, one at a time, beating well after each addition. Fill the buttered popover pans or large custard cups three-fourths full.

2) Bake at 450° for 15 minutes. Reduce heat to 350°; bake 20 minutes longer or until very firm. Remove from the oven; prick each popover with a sharp knife to allow steam to escape. Serve immediately.

Yield: 9 popovers.

NUTRITION FACTS: 1 popover equals 99 calories, 4 g fat (2 g saturated fat), 55 mg cholesterol, 109 mg sodium, 12 g carbohydrate, trace fiber, 4 g protein.

Orlando Orange Fritters

PREP: 15 min. **COOK:** 5 min./batch

Floyce Thomas-Larson, Silver Spring, Maryland

When grandchildren came to visit, my mother served them this version of her Heartland fried cakes.

     2 **cups all-purpose flour**
  1/2 **cup sugar**
     2 **teaspoons baking powder**
  1/2 **teaspoon salt**
     2 **eggs**
  1/2 **cup orange juice**
     2 **tablespoons butter, melted**
     1 **tablespoon grated orange peel**
Oil for deep-fat frying
Confectioners' sugar

1) In a small bowl, combine the flour, sugar, baking powder and salt. Combine the eggs, orange juice, butter and orange peel; stir into dry ingredients just until moistened.

ORLANDO ORANGE FRITTERS

2) In an electric skillet or deep-fat fryer, heat oil to 375°. Drop batter by rounded tablespoonfuls, a few at a time, into hot oil. Fry until golden brown, about 1-1/2 minutes on each side. Drain on paper towels. Dust with confectioners' sugar.

Yield: 20 fritters.

NUTRITION FACTS: 2 fritters (calculated without confectioners' sugar) equals 277 calories, 16 g fat (3 g saturated fat), 48 mg cholesterol, 229 mg sodium, 31 g carbohydrate, 1 g fiber, 4 g protein.

French Breakfast Puffs

PREP: 20 min. **BAKE:** 20 min.

Kimberly Flora, Peru, Indiana

Rather than serve typical pastries, I like to prepare these light and tender treats when I have guests. Everyone enjoys the cinnamon-sugar coating.

  1/3 **cup shortening**
     1 **cup sugar,** *divided*
     1 **egg**
  1-1/2 **cups all-purpose flour**
  1-1/2 **teaspoons baking powder**
  1/2 **teaspoon salt**
  1/4 **teaspoon ground nutmeg**
  1/2 **cup milk**
     1 **teaspoon ground cinnamon**
     6 **tablespoons butter, melted**

1) In a small mixing bowl, beat shortening, 1/2 cup sugar and egg until smooth. Combine the flour, baking powder, salt and nutmeg; add to the sugar mixture alternately with milk.

2) Fill greased muffin cups two-thirds full. Bake at 350° for 20 minutes or until a toothpick inserted near the center comes out clean. Cool for 5 minutes.

3) Meanwhile, combine cinnamon and remaining sugar in a shallow bowl. Remove puffs from pan; roll in butter, then in cinnamon-sugar. Serve immediately.

Yield: 1 dozen.

NUTRITION FACTS: 1 puff equals 234 calories, 12 g fat (5 g saturated fat), 34 mg cholesterol, 217 mg sodium, 29 g carbohydrate, 1 g fiber, 3 g protein.

SUNDAY MORNING PANCAKES

 CLASSIC: Start your family's day in a delicious way with Buttermilk Blueberry Pancakes. These from-scratch pancakes get their tender, fluffy texture from creamy buttermilk and their great fruit flavor from a sprinkling of blueberries.

 TIME-SAVER: Kids of all ages won't have to wait long to enjoy Peanut Butter Pancakes. The batter is hurried along by pancake mix, so it's stirred up in minutes. While the pancakes sizzle on the griddle, combine butter and honey for a sweet, rich topping.

 LIGHT: You'll enjoy the sunny flavor of Orange Whole Wheat Pancakes so much, you won't even realize that whole wheat flour and applesauce make them more nutritious. Compared to Buttermilk Blueberry Pancakes, these have fewer calories, virtually no fat and no cholesterol.

 SERVES 2: For a filling breakfast for two, mix up a batch of Multigrain Pancakes. Four hearty pancakes made with quick-cooking oats and whole wheat flour are sure to satisfy.

Buttermilk Blueberry Pancakes

PREP/TOTAL TIME: 30 min.

Ann Moran, Islesford, Maine

- 2 cups all-purpose flour
- 1 tablespoon sugar
- 1/2 teaspoon baking soda
- 1/4 teaspoon salt
- 1/8 teaspoon baking powder
- 2 eggs
- 2 cups buttermilk
- 1 tablespoon vegetable oil
- 1 cup fresh *or* frozen blueberries

Butter and syrup, optional

1) In a large bowl, combine the flour, sugar, baking soda, salt and baking powder. In a small bowl, beat the eggs, buttermilk and oil. Stir into flour mixture just until moistened.

2) Pour batter by 1/4 cupfuls onto a greased hot griddle. Sprinkle about 1 tablespoon of blueberries on each pancake. Turn pancakes when bubbles form on top; cook until second side is golden brown. Serve with butter and syrup if desired.

Yield: 12 pancakes.

Editor's Note: If using frozen blueberries, do not thaw before adding to the batter.

NUTRITION FACTS: 2 pancakes equals 250 calories, 5 g fat (1 g saturated fat), 74 mg cholesterol, 322 mg sodium, 41 g carbohydrate, 2 g fiber, 9 g protein.

■ **Buttermilk Pancakes:** Omit the blueberries. Proceed as directed.

HOMEMADE PANCAKES FROM A MIX ■■■

To give homemade taste to pancakes from a mix, simply add one of the following to the batter: ground cinnamon, ginger or nutmeg, orange extract or chocolate chips.

—*Kathleen S., Narvon, Pennsylvania*

PEANUT BUTTER PANCAKES

Peanut Butter Pancakes

PREP/TOTAL TIME: 15 min.

Dorothy Pritchett, Wills Point, Texas

- 1 cup pancake mix
- 2 tablespoons sugar
- 1 egg
- 1/3 cup peanut butter
- 1 can (5 ounces) evaporated milk
- 1/3 cup water

HONEY BUTTER:

- 1/4 cup butter, softened
- 2 tablespoons honey

1) In a large bowl, combine pancake mix and sugar. In a small bowl, beat egg and peanut butter; add milk and water. Stir into dry ingredients just until moistened.

Preparing Pancakes

1) Pour batter by 1/4 cupfuls (or as recipe directs) onto a hot griddle or skillet, making sure to leave enough room between pancakes for expansion.

2) Turn pancakes over when edges become dry and bubbles that appear on top begin to pop. Continue cooking until bottom is golden brown.

2) Pour batter by 1/4 cupfuls onto a lightly greased medium-hot griddle. Turn when bubbles form on top; cook until second side is golden brown. In a small bowl, combine honey butter ingredients. Serve with pancakes.

Yield: 10 pancakes.

Editor's Note: Reduced-fat or generic brands of peanut butter are not recommended for this recipe.

NUTRITION FACTS: 3 pancakes with 2 tablespoons honey butter equals 595 calories, 35 g fat (15 g saturated fat), 127 mg cholesterol, 843 mg sodium, 58 g carbohydrate, 4 g fiber, 16 g protein.

Orange Whole Wheat Pancakes
PREP/TOTAL TIME: 25 min.

Earl Brunner, Las Vegas, Nevada

- 3 egg whites
- 1 cup orange juice
- 1/3 cup unsweetened applesauce
- 1/4 teaspoon orange extract
- 1-1/4 cups whole wheat flour
- 2 tablespoons sugar
- 2 teaspoons baking powder
- 1/2 teaspoon salt
- 1/2 cup orange marmalade

1) Place the egg whites, orange juice, applesauce and extract in a blender; cover and process until smooth. In a bowl, combine the flour, sugar, baking powder and salt; make a well in the center. Add the orange juice mixture; stir just until moistened.

2) Pour batter by 2 tablespoonfuls onto a hot griddle coated with cooking spray. Turn when bubbles form on top; cook until second side is golden brown. Serve with marmalade.

Yield: 16 pancakes.

NUTRITION FACTS: 2 pancakes with 1 tablespoon marmalade equals 150 calories, trace fat (trace saturated fat), 0 cholesterol, 238 mg sodium, 35 g carbohydrate, 3 g fiber, 4 g protein.

Multigrain Pancakes
PREP/TOTAL TIME: 20 min.

Jeri Tirmenstein, Apache Junction, Arizona

- 1/4 cup all-purpose flour
- 1/4 cup whole wheat flour
- 1/4 cup quick-cooking oats
- 1 tablespoon brown sugar
- 1 teaspoon baking powder
- 1/4 teaspoon salt
- 1/2 cup plus 1 tablespoon fat-free milk
- 2 tablespoons egg substitute
- 2 teaspoons canola oil

1) In a bowl, combine the flours, oats, brown sugar, baking powder and salt. Combine the milk, egg substitute and oil; stir into dry ingredients just until moistened.

2) Pour batter by 1/4 cupfuls onto a greased hot griddle. Turn when bubbles form on top; cook until second side is golden brown.

Yield: 4 pancakes.

NUTRITION FACTS: 2 pancakes equals 243 calories, 6 g fat (1 g saturated fat), 1 mg cholesterol, 559 mg sodium, 40 g carbohydrate, 3 g fiber, 9 g protein.

- **Vanilla Pancakes:** Omit whole wheat flour and oats. Use 3/4 cup all-purpose flour. Add 3/4 teaspoon vanilla extract to milk mixture. Proceed as directed.

MULTIGRAIN PANCAKES

WAFFLES FROM SCRATCH

⬡ Waffles from Scratch

PREP/TOTAL TIME: 20 min.

Florence Dean, Towson, Maryland

My mom always made these. They're wonderful topped with fruit or maple syrup.

- 1-1/2 cups all-purpose flour
- 1 teaspoon baking powder
- 1/2 teaspoon salt
- 2 eggs, *separated*
- 1 cup milk
- 1/4 cup butter, melted

Confectioners' sugar and fresh fruit *or* maple syrup

1) In a small bowl, combine the flour, baking powder and salt. Combine egg yolks, milk and butter; stir into dry ingredients just until moistened.

2) In a small mixing bowl, beat egg whites on medium speed until soft peaks form; gently fold into batter.

3) Bake in a preheated waffle iron according to manufacturer's directions until golden brown. Top with confectioners' sugar and fruit or serve with syrup.

Yield: 4 waffles (about 6 inches).

NUTRITION FACTS: 2 waffles (calculated without confectioners' sugar, fruit or syrup) equals 691 calories, 33 g fat (18 g saturated fat), 290 mg cholesterol, 1,146 mg sodium, 78 g carbohydrate, 3 g fiber, 20 g protein.

- ■ **Oat Waffles:** Add 1/4 cup old-fashioned oats to flour mixture. Add an extra tablespoon of milk. Stir 1/2 teaspoon vanilla extract into egg yolk mixture. Proceed as directed.

- ■ **Spice Waffles:** Stir 1/2 teaspoon of ground cinnamon and 1/8 teaspoon *each* ground nutmeg and cloves into flour mixture. Fold 1/3 cup grated carrot, apple *or* zucchini into batter. Proceed as directed.

Buttermilk Doughnuts

PREP: 20 min. + chilling **COOK:** 5 min./batch

Betty Rauschendorfer, Sidney, Montana

Whether you serve these at breakfast or brunch, they're sure to disappear fast.

- 4 eggs
- 2 cups sugar
- 1/3 cup butter, melted
- 1 teaspoon vanilla extract
- 5-1/2 to 6 cups all-purpose flour
- 2 teaspoons baking powder
- 2 teaspoons baking soda
- 1 teaspoon salt
- 1 teaspoon ground nutmeg
- 2 cups buttermilk

Oil for deep-fat frying

Additional sugar, cinnamon-sugar *or* confectioners' sugar, optional

1) In a large mixing bowl, beat eggs and sugar until light and lemon-colored. Add butter and vanilla; mix well. Combine flour, baking powder, baking soda, salt and nutmeg; add to egg mixture alternately with buttermilk. Cover and refrigerate for 2-3 hours.

2) On a lightly floured surface, roll dough to 1/2-in. thickness. Cut with a floured 3-in. doughnut cutter.

3) In an electric skillet or deep-fat fryer, heat oil to 375°. Fry doughnuts, a few at a time, for 1 minute on each side or until golden. Drain on paper towels. Roll in additional sugar if desired.

Yield: 4 dozen.

NUTRITION FACTS: 1 doughnut equals 140 calories, 6 g fat (1 g saturated fat), 21 mg cholesterol, 144 mg sodium, 20 g carbohydrate, trace fiber, 2 g protein.

BUTTERMILK DOUGHNUTS

raising 'bread' for charity

Fund-raiser helps build new homes in Nicaragua

Merle Dyck helped bake up a successful fund-raiser in her hometown of Elkford—a coal-mining town of about 3,500 people in British Columbia.

Merle heard about the nonprofit organization Bridges to Community from co-workers. Employees from the 11 branches of Falkins Insurance Group in the Kootenays of British Columbia are working to raise enough money to build 100 homes in developing countries within five years.

Merle and her officemates wanted to help raise money for two employees to participate in the program.

Cyndal Dobson and Deanna Lacasse were chosen to go to Nicaragua because of essays they had written describing why they wanted to take part in the charity. The co-workers needed to raise $4,000 to build a 16- by 20-foot concrete shell for a home and $2,500 to cover expenses and flights.

Nicaragua is one of the poorest countries in the world; most farm laborers live on less than $1 per day.

"Some recipients have been on a waiting list for years," shares Merle. "And they have to make monthly payments on the home once it has been built."

This company knows how to put the "fun" in fund-raising! For example, the CEO had to name each of the 100 employees during a company retreat. He then paid $5 for each name he missed.

Inspired by this idea, Merle and her co-workers came up with their own creative ways to raise money.

"Another office coordinated a cookbook, which we all contributed recipes to and sold," she explains. "Our office held a coffee, muffin and used-book sale where we raffled off a Busy Bakers Big Basket of treats."

Merle says she and her co-workers were overwhelmed by the support of their small community, which raised $600 toward the trip.

In addition to the money from Merle's office, the rest of the company raised enough for Cyndal and Deanna's trip. They built two homes in Nicaragua and were able to contribute additional money toward 15 more homes.

"We built homes with a future for them, and in return we gained a better understanding of how truly blessed we are," Deanna and Cyndal said in a thank-you note to co-workers.

Merle Dyck, second from left, and other bakers

> *This effort made us all appreciate how fortunate we are to have what we have and live where we live.*
>
> ~Merle Dyck

You can find some of Busy Bakers' recipes in the Web exclusive online at tasteofhome.com/ CookbookBonus **Type in access code ICare**

taste of home
cooks who care

DO YOU KNOW A COOK WHO CARES?

If you or someone you know cooks for a charitable, spiritual or other cause, tell us about it at **tasteofhome.com/CookbookBonus**

Recipes

Tips

Yeast Breads

Yeast breads are divided into two kinds: kneaded breads and batter breads. They can be savory or sweet.

Kneaded yeast breads are usually mixed, kneaded, allowed to rise, shaped, allowed to rise again and then baked. Bread machine breads are also kneaded breads.

Batter breads aren't kneaded. Rather, ingredients are beaten, allowed to rise once or twice and then baked. Batter breads have a coarser texture and rugged crust.

Baking Hints

Use butter, stick margarine (with at least 80% oil) or shortening. Do not use light or whipped butter, diet spread or tub margarine. Measure ingredients accurately. Check temperature of liquid ingredients with an instant read thermometer.

Arrange the oven racks so that the bread will bake in the center of the oven. Preheat oven for 10 to 15 minutes before baking.

When mixing dough, always start with a minimum amount of flour until dough reaches desired consistency (soft, sticky, stiff or firm). Knead dough only until it does not tear easily when stretched. Let dough rise in a warm (80° to 85°), draft-free area. Proper rising helps in the development of the bread texture.

Use aluminum pans with a dull rather than shiny or dark finish. Glass baking dishes and dark finishes will produce darker crusts. To allow for good air circulation while baking, leave at least 1 in. of space between pans and between pans and sides of oven.

Use a kitchen timer and test for doneness at the minimum recommended baking time. Bread is done when it is golden brown and sounds hollow when

tapped on the bottom. Or, insert an instant-read thermometer in the thickest part of the loaf. The bread is done when the thermometer reads 200°.

Remove breads from pans and cool on wire racks. Let breads cool for at least 20 minutes before slicing. Use a serrated knife and a sawing motion when cutting.

Bread Ingredients

The ingredients used in bread making will affect the texture, density and crust. Lean breads (like French bread) are made with yeast, flour, water, salt and a minimal amount of sugar to produce a dense, chewy bread with a crisp crust. Rich or short breads (like Brioche) are made with fat such as butter or shortening, eggs and/or milk to produce a tender bread with a soft crust.

Fats and Eggs: They tenderize, add moisture, carry flavors and give a richness to the bread.

Flours: Wheat flour, the most commonly used flour, contains gluten—an elastic protein. Kneading the dough develops the gluten. During the rise time, the yeast produces carbon dioxide gas, which becomes trapped in the dough. As the gases push against the protein, the dough rises. During baking, the protein is set by the heat and gives the baked good its structure.

The terms soft and hard wheat refer to the amount of protein (gluten) in the flour—soft has less and hard has more. The amount of gluten will affect the texture of the bread.

High-gluten flours, such as all-purpose or bread flour, are used for the best yeast bread results. Whole wheat and rye flours contain less gluten, and the bread would be heavy and dense bread without the addition of all-purpose or bread flour.

Liquids: Most breads are prepared with water, milk or water reserved from cooking potatoes. Breads prepared with water will yield a crunchy crust. Those made with milk will produce a softer crust and a tender crumb. All liquids need to be warmed to the temperature required by the yeast and mixing method.

Salt: This helps round out flavors and controls the growth of the yeast. Too much or too little salt will affect the final product. For best results, use the amount of salt listed in the recipe and never omit it.

Sugars and Other Sweeteners: Used in small amounts, sugars feed the yeast. Sugars and other sweeteners tenderize, add sweetness and flavor, promote browning and enhance the keeping quality. Depending on the recipe, you may use white or brown sugar, molasses or honey to sweeten and flavor your bread.

Yeast: This microorganism becomes activated when combined with warm water and sugar. It consumes the sugars in sweeteners and flours and produces carbon dioxide gas that helps give bread its light, airy texture. There are several different types of yeast, which are all handled differently. Check the expiration date on the package before using and discard yeast if it is past the date.

Active dry yeast is available in 1/4-ounce foil packages or 4-ounce jars. With the Traditional Mixing Method for Yeast Breads at right, the active yeast is dissolved in liquid that has been warmed to 110° to 115°. If the liquid temperature is too low, the yeast will not be activated. If the liquid temperature is too high, the yeast will be killed, preventing the bread from rising.

With the Rapid Mixing Method for Yeast Breads on page 542, the active dry yeast is added directly to the flour and other dry ingredients. Then warm liquid (120° to 130°) is added.

Quick-rise yeast is available in 1/4-ounce foil packages or 4-ounce jars. Quick-rise yeast is finely granulated and should only be combined with the other ingredients using the Rapid Mixing Method for Yeast Breads on page 542. Quick-rise yeast will raise bread dough in about a third to half the traditional time.

Bread machine yeast is available in 4-ounce jars. This is an instant yeast with finer granules. The smaller granules allow the yeast to mix into the dough more evenly.

Fresh or cake yeast is most commonly available in 2-ounce cakes, which is equivalent to three 1/4-ounce packages of active dry yeast. A third of the fresh yeast cake (about 0.6 ounce) is equal to one packet of active dry yeast. Some older bread recipes often call for a "cake" of yeast. Cake yeast is a fresh product found in your grocer's dairy case. It should be used within

10 days of purchase. To use, crumble the yeast into the dry ingredients or soften in tepid water (70° to 80°).

Make sure the active dry yeast (not the quick-rise yeast) is alive and active. You proof it by dissolving one package of yeast and 1 teaspoon sugar in 1/4 cup warm water (110° to 115°). Let stand for 5 to 10 minutes. If the mixture foams up, the yeast mixture can be used because the yeast is active. If it does not foam, the yeast should be discarded.

Traditional Mixing Method for Yeast Breads

1) Heat liquid to 110° to 115°, using a thermometer. Measure liquid, then pour into a large mixing bowl. Add active dry yeast; stir until dissolved.

2) Add sugar, salt, fat, eggs (if using) and about half of the flour. Beat with an electric mixer or by hand until smooth.

3) Gradually stir in enough of the remaining flour by hand to form a dough of the consistency stated in the recipe.

Kneading, Shaping and Baking Yeast Breads

1) Turn dough onto a lightly floured surface; shape into a ball. Fold top of dough toward you. With palms, push with a rolling motion away from you. Turn dough a quarter turn; repeat motion until dough is smooth and elastic. Add flour to surface only as needed.

2) Place the dough in a bowl greased with butter, oil or cooking spray. Turn dough over to grease the top. This prevents the dough from drying out while rising.

3) Cover with a clean towel or plastic wrap. Place covered dough in a warm, draft-free area (80° to 85°) until dough has doubled. (Place covered bowl on the top rack in a cold oven with a pan of steaming, hot water underneath. Or turn your oven to its lowest setting for no longer than 40 to 50 seconds. Turn off and let dough rise in the oven.)

4) Press two fingers 1/2 in. into the dough. If the dents remain, the dough is doubled in size and ready to punch down.

5) To punch dough down, make a fist and push it into the center. Gather the dough to the center and shape into a ball. Place on a floured surface.

6) Divide the dough if the recipe directs; shape into balls. Roll each ball into a 12-in. x 8-in. rectangle. You will hear air bubbles "popping" as you roll the dough.

7) Dust off any loose flour that might cling to the dough. Beginning at the short end, roll up each rectangle firmly. If it's too loose, you'll see air pockets when the bread is cut. If it's too tight, the bread will crack while baking.

8) Pinch seam and each end to seal. Place seam side down in a greased pan; cover with a towel and allow to double in size in a warm, draft-free area.

9) When dough has doubled, remove towel; place pans several inches apart in the center of the preheated oven.

10) When bread is golden brown, test for doneness by carefully removing loaves from pans and tapping the bottom crusts. If it sounds hollow, the bread is done. You can also use a thermometer to check that bread reaches 200°. If the bread is browning too fast and it's not done, tent with foil and continue baking. Unless recipe directs otherwise, immediately remove breads from pans. Cool completely on a wire rack.

Baking at High Altitudes

High altitude (over 3,000 feet) affects bread baking because the lower air pressure allows the yeast to rise 25 to 50 percent faster, and the drier air makes the flour drier. If the dough over-rises, the results might be a heavy, dry loaf or a misshapen or collapsed loaf. Make these adjustments when baking bread at high altitudes:

- Start checking the dough halfway through the recommended rise time to see if it has doubled. If the dough has over-risen, punch it down and allow it to rise again.

- Use about a third less yeast. If a recipe calls for one package of active dry yeast (2-1/4 teaspoons), you would need to use about 1-1/2 teaspoons.

- Add flour slowly when mixing the dough and use only enough to make the dough easy to handle. If the dough is sticky, use greased rather than floured hands for kneading.

- Oil the dough and cover with greased plastic wrap to prevent it from drying out while using.

- Check for doneness a few minutes before the minimum recommended baking time. Tent with foil if it's browning too quickly.

Dressing Up French Bread

Spread one of these flavorful toppings on French bread for a welcome treat at dinner. For each topping, cut a 1-pound loaf in half lengthwise and spread over the cut sides.

- **Golden Garlic Bread:** Combine 1/3 cup softened butter with 1/4 cup grated Parmesan cheese, 1 to 2 minced garlic cloves and 1 teaspoon dried basil. Broil 4 in. from the heat for 3-4 minutes or until golden brown.   —*Annette Self Junction City, Ohio*

- **Olive Cheese Bread:** Combine 1/2 cup melted butter, 1/2 cup mayonnaise, 1 can (2-1/4 ounces) drained sliced ripe olives, 2 chopped green onions and 1-1/2 cups shredded Monterey Jack cheese. Bake at 350° for 15-20 minutes or until cheese is melted.   —*Nancy McWhorter, Bridge City, Texas*

- **Ranch Garlic Bread:** Combine 1 cup softened butter with 2 to 3 tablespoons ranch salad dressing mix and 2 teaspoons garlic powder. Broil 4 in. from the heat for 3-4 minutes or until golden brown.   —*John Palmer, Cottonwood, California*

Crusty French Bread

PREP: 20 min. + rising **BAKE:** 25 min. + cooling

Deanna Naivar, Temple, Texas

A delicate texture makes this bread absolutely wonderful. I also use the dough to make breadsticks brushed with melted butter and garlic powder.

- 1 package (1/4 ounce) active dry yeast
- 1 cup warm water (110° to 115°)
- 2 tablespoons sugar
- 2 tablespoons vegetable oil
- 1-1/2 teaspoons salt
- 3 to 3-1/4 cups all-purpose flour

Cornmeal

- 1 egg white
- 1 teaspoon cold water

1) In a large mixing bowl, dissolve yeast in warm water. Add the sugar, oil, salt and 2 cups flour. Beat until blended. Stir in enough remaining flour to form a stiff dough.

2) Turn onto a floured surface; knead until smooth and elastic, about 6-8 minutes. Place in a greased bowl, turning once to grease top.

3) Cover and let rise in a warm place until doubled, about 1 hour. Punch dough down; return to bowl. Cover and let rise for 30 minutes.

4) Punch dough down. Turn onto a lightly floured surface. Shape into a loaf 16 in. long x 2-1/2 in. wide with tapered ends. Sprinkle a greased baking sheet with cornmeal and place loaf on baking sheet. Cover and let rise until doubled, about 25 minutes.

5) Beat egg white and cold water; brush over dough. With a sharp knife, make diagonal slashes 2 in. apart across top of loaf. Bake at 375° for 25-30 minutes or until golden brown. Remove from pan to a wire rack to cool.

Yield: 1 loaf (16 slices).

NUTRITION FACTS: 1 slice equals 109 calories, 2 g fat (trace saturated fat), 0 cholesterol, 225 mg sodium, 20 g carbohydrate, 1 g fiber, 3 g protein.

Making Slashes

Slashing or scoring the top of a bread loaf allows steam to vent, helps prevent cracking and gives bread a decorative appearance. With a sharp knife, make shallow slashes across top of loaf.

ROUND WHOLE WHEAT LOAVES

🌾 Round Whole Wheat Loaves

PREP: 30 min. + rising **BAKE:** 30 min. + cooling

Genny Monchamp, Redding, California

Honey lends a mildly sweet taste to this hearty golden-brown bread that everyone enjoys.

- 4-1/2 cups all-purpose flour
- 1-1/2 cups whole wheat flour
  - 2 packages (1/4 ounce *each*) active dry yeast
  - 3/4 cup warm water (110° to 115°)
  - 1 cup warm milk (110° to 115°)
  - 3/4 cup shortening
  - 1/2 cup honey
  - 2 teaspoons salt
  - 3 eggs
  - 1 teaspoon butter, melted

1) In a large bowl, combine the flours; set aside. In a large mixing bowl, dissolve yeast in warm water. Add milk, shortening, honey, salt and eggs. Beat in half of the flour mixture until smooth. Stir in enough remaining flour mixture to form a soft dough.

2) Turn onto a floured surface; knead until smooth and elastic, about 6-8 minutes. Place in a greased bowl, turning once to grease top. Cover and let rise in a warm place until doubled, about 1 hour.

3) Punch dough down. Turn onto a lightly floured surface; divide in half. Shape into round loaves. Place each loaf on a greased baking sheet. Cover and let rise until doubled, about 35 minutes.

4) With a sharp knife, make a deep X on top of each loaf. Bake at 375° for 30-35 minutes or until golden brown. Remove from pans to wire racks; brush with butter. Cool completely.

Yield: 2 loaves (16 slices each).

NUTRITION FACTS: 1 slice equals 154 calories, 6 g fat (2 g saturated fat), 21 mg cholesterol, 159 mg sodium, 22 g carbohydrate, 1 g fiber, 4 g protein.

🌾 Rosemary Focaccia

PREP: 30 min. + rising **BAKE:** 25 min. + cooling

Debrah Peoples, Calgary, Alberta

The savory aroma of rosemary as this classic bread bakes is irresistible. Try this bread as a side with any meal, as a snack or as a pizza crust.

- 2 medium onions, chopped
- 1/4 cup olive oil plus 3 tablespoons olive oil, *divided*
- 1-1/2 teaspoons active dry yeast
- 1-1/2 cups warm water (110° to 115°), *divided*
- 1/2 teaspoon sugar
- 1/2 teaspoon salt
- 3 to 4 cups all-purpose flour
- 2 tablespoons snipped fresh rosemary *or* 2 teaspoons dried rosemary, crushed, *divided*

Cornmeal

Coarse salt

1) In a large skillet, saute onions in 1/4 cup oil until tender; cool. In a large mixing bowl, dissolve yeast in 1/4 cup warm water. Add sugar and let stand for 5 minutes.

2) Add 2 tablespoons oil, salt and remaining water. Add 2 cups flour. Beat until smooth. Stir in enough remaining flour to form a soft dough.

3) Turn onto a floured surface; knead until smooth and elastic, about 6-8 minutes. Add onions and half of the rosemary. Knead 1 minute longer. Place in a greased bowl, turning once to grease top. Cover and let rise in a warm place until doubled, about 40 minutes.

4) Punch dough down. Turn onto a lightly floured surface; divide in half. Pat each piece flat. Let rest for 5 minutes. Grease two baking sheets and sprinkle with cornmeal. Stretch each portion of dough into a 10-in. circle on prepared pans. Cover and let rise until doubled, about 40 minutes.

5) Brush with remaining oil. Sprinkle with coarse salt and remaining rosemary. Bake at 375° for 25-30 minutes or until golden brown. Remove from pans to wire racks to cool.

Yield: 2 loaves (8 wedges each).

NUTRITION FACTS: 1 wedge (calculated without coarse salt) equals 147 calories, 6 g fat (1 g saturated fat), 0 cholesterol, 75 mg sodium, 20 g carbohydrate, 1 g fiber, 3 g protein.

■ **Parmesan Rosemary Focaccia:** Sprinkle 1 tablespoon Parmesan cheese over each focaccia before baking.

■ **Rosemary Olive Focaccia:** Prepare dough as directed, omitting sauteed onions. Knead as directed, adding 1/3 cup well-drained sliced ripe olives along with half of the rosemary. Sprinkle 1 tablespoon Parmesan cheese over each focaccia before baking.

WARM, HOMEMADE BREAD

CLASSIC: Get back to the basics with Simple White Bread, and you can enjoy the wonderful aroma of old-fashioned, home-baked bread wafting from the oven. The two golden-brown loaves are brushed with melted butter to keep them soft.

TIME-SAVER: You can serve your family warm slices of Italian Herb Bread even if you have a busy day ahead of you. Just add the ingredients to the bread machine after lunch and go. It does the work while you do other things, so a nicely seasoned loaf is ready by dinnertime.

LIGHT: For a healthier home-baked loaf, try Traditional Whole Wheat Bread. Whole wheat flour, toasted wheat germ and mashed potato flakes are included in these loaves, so they have double the fiber, half the fat and 50 fewer calories a slice than Simple White Bread.

SERVES 2: Yielding eight slices, Mini Challah is just the right size when a large loaf of bread is too much for your small household. This pretty braided bread is brushed with egg and sprinkled with sesame or poppy seeds before baking.

SIMPLE WHITE BREAD

Simple White Bread

PREP: 20 min. + rising BAKE: 35 min. + cooling

Ruth VonLienen, Marengo, Iowa

- 2 packages (1/4 ounce *each*) active dry yeast
- 2-1/2 cups warm water (110° to 115°), *divided*
- 1/2 cup nonfat dry milk powder
- 1/2 cup vegetable oil
- 2 tablespoons sugar
- 1 tablespoon salt
- 8-1/2 to 9 cups all-purpose flour
- 1 tablespoon butter, melted

1) In a large mixing bowl, dissolve yeast in 1/2 cup warm water. Add the milk powder, oil, sugar, salt, 3 cups flour and remaining water. Beat on medium speed for 3 minutes or until smooth. Stir in enough remaining flour to form a soft dough.

2) Turn onto a floured surface; knead until smooth and elastic, about 6-8 minutes. Place in a greased

bowl, turning once to grease top. Cover and let rise in a warm place until doubled, about 1 hour.

3) Punch dough down. Divide in half; shape into loaves. Place in two greased 9-in. x 5-in. x 3-in. loaf pans. Cover and let rise until doubled, about 1 hour.

4) Bake at 375° for 35 minutes or until golden brown. Remove from pans to wire racks to cool. Brush with butter.

Yield: 2 loaves (16 slices each).

NUTRITION FACTS: 1 slice equals 165 calories, 4 g fat (1 g saturated fat), 1 mg cholesterol, 236 mg sodium, 27 g carbohydrate, 1 g fiber, 4 g protein.

Italian Herb Bread

PREP: 5 min. BAKE: 3 hours + cooling

Dolores Bell, Belleview, Florida

- 1 cup water (70° to 80°)
- 3 tablespoons butter
- 1 egg, lightly beaten
- 2 tablespoons sugar
- 1 teaspoon salt
- 1 teaspoon garlic powder
- 1 teaspoon dried oregano
- 1/2 teaspoon dried basil
- 1/4 teaspoon dried tarragon
- 1/4 teaspoon dill weed
- 1/8 teaspoon dried thyme
- 2/3 cup grated Parmesan cheese
- 3 cups bread flour
- 2-1/4 teaspoons active dry yeast

1) In bread machine pan, place all ingredients in order suggested by manufacturer. Select basic bread setting. Choose crust color and loaf size if available.

2) Bake according to bread machine directions (check dough after 5 minutes of mixing; add 1 to 2 tablespoons of water or flour if needed).

Yield: 1 loaf (1-1/2 pounds, 16 slices).

NUTRITION FACTS: 1 slice equals 123 calories, 3 g fat (2 g saturated fat), 22 mg cholesterol, 236 mg sodium, 19 g carbohydrate, 1 g fiber, 5 g protein.

■ **White Bread:** Omit the garlic powder, oregano, basil, tarragon, dill weed, thyme and Parmesan cheese. Increase flour to 3-1/4 cups. Proceed as directed.

MINI CHALLAH

Traditional Whole Wheat Bread

PREP: 30 min. + rising **BAKE:** 35 min. + cooling

Carol Forcum, Marion, Illinois

- 3 cups whole wheat flour
- 1/2 cup toasted wheat germ
- 1/4 cup mashed potato flakes
- 1/4 cup nonfat dry milk powder
- 2 tablespoons sugar
- 2 packages (1/4 ounce *each*) active dry yeast
- 2 teaspoons salt
- 2 cups water
- 3 tablespoons vegetable oil
- 3 eggs
- 3 to 3-1/2 cups all-purpose flour

1) In a large mixing bowl, combine the whole wheat flour, wheat germ, potato flakes, milk powder, sugar, yeast and salt. In a small saucepan, heat water and oil to 120°-130°. Add to dry ingredients; beat until blended. Beat in eggs until smooth. Stir in enough all-purpose flour to form a soft dough.

2) Turn onto a floured surface; knead until smooth and elastic, about 8-10 minutes. Place in a greased bowl, turning once to grease top. Cover and let rise in a warm place until doubled, about 1 hour.

3) Punch dough down. Turn onto a lightly floured surface; divide in half. Shape into loaves. Place in two greased 9-in. x 5-in. x 3-in. loaf pans. Cover and let rise until doubled, about 45 minutes.

4) Bake at 375° for 35-40 minutes or until golden brown. Remove from pans to wire racks to cool.

Yield: 2 loaves (16 slices each).

NUTRITION FACTS: 1 slice equals 114 calories, 2 g fat (trace saturated fat), 20 mg cholesterol, 161 mg sodium, 20 g carbohydrate, 2 g fiber, 4 g protein.

Mini Challah

PREP: 30 min. + rising **BAKE:** 20 min. + cooling

Taste of Home Test Kitchen

- 1-1/4 teaspoons active dry yeast
- 1/4 cup warm water (110° to 115°)
- 2 tablespoons vegetable oil
- 4 teaspoons sugar
- 3/4 teaspoon salt
- 1 egg
- 1-1/2 to 1-2/3 cups all-purpose flour

TOPPING:
- 1 tablespoon beaten egg
- 1/4 teaspoon cold water
- 3/4 teaspoon sesame *or* poppy seeds, optional

1) In a small mixing bowl, dissolve yeast in warm water. Add the oil, sugar, salt, egg and 1 cup flour. Beat until smooth. Stir in enough remaining flour to form a soft dough.

2) Turn onto a floured surface; knead until smooth and elastic, about 6-8 minutes. Place in a bowl coated with cooking spray, turning once to coat top. Cover and let rise in a warm place until doubled, about 1 hour.

3) Punch dough down. Turn onto a lightly floured surface; divide into thirds. Shape each portion into an 8-in. rope. Place ropes on a baking sheet coated with cooking spray and braid; pinch ends to seal and tuck under. Cover and let rise until doubled, about 45 minutes.

4) Beat egg and water; brush over braid. Sprinkle with sesame or poppy seeds if desired. Bake at 350° for 20-25 minutes or until golden brown. Remove to a wire rack to cool.

Yield: 1 loaf (8 slices).

NUTRITION FACTS: 1 slice equals 137 calories, 4 g fat (1 g saturated fat), 35 mg cholesterol, 232 mg sodium, 20 g carbohydrate, 1 g fiber, 4 g protein.

Making Mini Loaves

If you are baking for two, you can turn full-size yeast bread recipes into mini loaves. A recipe that uses about 3 cups of flour and makes 1 loaf of bread can be baked in two 5-3/4-in. x 3-in. x 2-in. loaf pans. For a recipe that uses 5-6 cups of flour use four pans. Bake as directed, but check for doneness about 10 minutes sooner. Enjoy one loaf and cool the remaining loaves. Wrap individually and freeze for up to 3 months.

BRAIDED EGG BREAD

🍞 Braided Egg Bread

PREP: 30 min. + rising **BAKE:** 25 min. + cooling

Marlene Jeffery, Holland, Manitoba

*I first made this bread a few years ago, and I already
know it's one recipe I'll pass down to future generations.*

- 3-1/4 to 3-3/4 cups all-purpose flour
- 1 tablespoon sugar
- 1 package (1/4 ounce) active
  dry yeast
- 3/4 teaspoon salt
- 3/4 cup water
- 3 tablespoons vegetable oil
- 2 eggs

TOPPING:

- 1 egg
- 1 teaspoon water
- 1/2 teaspoon poppy seeds

1) In a large mixing bowl, combine 2-1/2 cups flour,
sugar, yeast and salt. In a saucepan, heat water
and oil to 120°-130°. Add to the dry ingredients
along with eggs. Beat on medium speed for
3 minutes. Stir in enough remaining flour to form
a soft dough.

2) Turn onto a floured surface; knead until smooth
and elastic, about 6-8 minutes. Place in a greased
bowl, turning once to grease top. Cover and let
rise in a warm place until doubled, about 1-1/2
hours.

3) Punch dough down. Turn onto a lightly floured
surface. Set a third of the dough aside. Divide
remaining dough into three pieces. Shape each
into a 13-in. rope. Place ropes on a greased baking
sheet and braid; pinch ends to seal and tuck
under.

4) Divide reserved dough into three equal pieces;
shape each into a 14-in. rope. Braid ropes. Center
14-in. braid on top of the shorter braid. Pinch
ends to seal and tuck under. Cover and let rise
until doubled, about 30 minutes.

5) Beat egg and water; brush over dough. Sprinkle
with poppy seeds. Bake at 375° for 25-30 minutes
or until golden brown. Cover with foil during the
last 15 minutes of baking. Remove from pan to a
wire rack to cool.

Yield: 1 loaf (16 slices).

NUTRITION FACTS: 1 slice equals 134 calories, 4 g fat (1 g saturated
fat), 40 mg cholesterol, 123 mg sodium, 20 g carbohydrate, 1 g fiber,
4 g protein.

Braiding Breads

1) Place three ropes
almost touching on a
baking sheet. Starting
in the middle, loosely
bring left rope under
center rope. Bring
right rope under
new center rope and
repeat until you
reach the end.

2) Turn the pan and
repeat braiding.

3) Press each end to
seal; tuck ends under.

Freezing Yeast Dough

Yeast dough is best frozen after it is kneaded and
before the first rise. To freeze dough, divide it into
the desired amounts and flatten into disks that are
about 1 inch thick. Place flattened dough on baking
sheets and freeze for 1 hour or until dough is frozen.
Remove from the freezer; wrap tightly with either
plastic wrap or aluminum foil. Then place in
resealable plastic bags and return to the freezer.
Dough can be kept frozen for up to 4 weeks.

For even thawing, place in the refrigerator overnight.
When ready to use, place dough on your kitchen
counter; cover it lightly and let it come to room
temperature (first rise). Punch the dough down.
Proceed as usual with shaping and the second rising.

Roasted Garlic Bread

PREP: 45 min. + rising **BAKE:** 20 min. + cooling

Barb Alexander, Princeton, New Jersey

I came up with this bread recipe one very stormy morning when we lived on the beach in the Florida Panhandle. While lightning blinked over the Gulf and rain tap-tap-tapped on our balcony, the wonderful aroma of this bread baking gave me such a cozy feeling.

- 2 medium whole garlic bulbs
- 2 teaspoons olive oil
- 1 package (1/4 ounce) active dry yeast
- 1 cup warm water (110° to 115°)
- 1 tablespoon sugar
- 1 teaspoon salt
- 2-1/2 to 3 cups all-purpose flour
- 2 tablespoons minced fresh sage *or* 2 teaspoons rubbed sage
- 2 teaspoons minced fresh marjoram *or* 3/4 teaspoon dried marjoram
- 1 teaspoon minced fresh rosemary *or* 1/2 teaspoon dried rosemary, crushed
- 2 tablespoons grated Parmesan cheese
- 1 tablespoon butter, melted

ROASTED GARLIC BREAD

1) Remove papery outer skin from garlic (do not peel or separate cloves). Cut top off garlic bulbs; brush with oil. Wrap each bulb in heavy-duty foil. Bake at 425° for 30-35 minutes or until softened. Cool for 10-15 minutes. Squeeze softened garlic into a small bowl; set aside.

2) In a large mixing bowl, dissolve yeast in warm water. Add the sugar, salt and 1 cup flour; beat until smooth. Stir in enough remaining flour to form a soft dough.

3) Turn onto a lightly floured surface; knead until smooth and elastic, about 6-8 minutes. Place in a bowl coated with cooking spray, turning once to coat top. Cover and let the dough rise in a warm place until doubled, about 45 minutes. Meanwhile, add the sage, marjoram and rosemary to the reserved roasted garlic.

4) Punch dough down. Turn onto a lightly floured surface; divide in half. Roll each portion into a 10-in. x 8-in. rectangle. Spread each with half the garlic mixture to within 1/2 in. of edges. Sprinkle each with 1 tablespoon Parmesan cheese. Roll up jelly-roll style, starting with a long side; pinch seam and ends to seal.

5) Coat a baking sheet with cooking spray. Place loaves seam side down on pan; tuck ends under. With a sharp knife, make several slashes across the top of each loaf. Cover and let rise until doubled, about 30 minutes.

6) Bake at 375° for 20-25 minutes or until golden brown. Remove from pans to wire racks to cool; brush with butter.

Yield: 2 loaves (10 slices each).

NUTRITION FACTS: 1 slice equals 84 calories, 1 g fat (1 g saturated fat), 2 mg cholesterol, 136 mg sodium, 15 g carbohydrate, 1 g fiber, 2 g protein.

Basic Pizza Crust

PREP: 10 min. + resting **BAKE:** 25 min.

Beverly Anderson, Sinclairville, New York

I like to double this recipe and keep one baked crust in the freezer for a quick snack or meal later.

- 1 package (1/4 ounce) active dry yeast
- 1 cup warm water (110° to 115°)
- 2 tablespoons vegetable oil
- 1 teaspoon sugar
- 1/4 teaspoon salt
- 2-1/2 to 2-3/4 cups all-purpose flour
- Cornmeal
- Pizza toppings of your choice

1) In a large mixing bowl, dissolve yeast in warm water. Add the oil, sugar, salt and 1-1/2 cups flour. Beat until smooth. Stir in enough remaining flour to form a firm dough. Turn onto a floured surface; cover and let rest for 10 minutes.

2) Roll into a 13-in. circle. Grease a 12-in. pizza pan and sprinkle with cornmeal. Transfer dough to prepared pan, building up edges slightly. Do not let rise.

3) Bake at 425° for 12-15 minutes or until browned. Add toppings; bake 10-15 minutes longer.

Yield: 1 pizza crust (6 wedges).

NUTRITION FACTS: 1 wedge (calculated without toppings) equals 236 calories, 5 g fat (1 g saturated fat), 0 cholesterol, 100 mg sodium, 41 g carbohydrate, 2 g fiber, 6 g protein.

SWEDISH RYE LOAVES

◎ Swedish Rye Loaves

PREP: 20 min. + rising **BAKE:** 25 min. + cooling

Iola Egle, Bella Vista, Arkansas

Oats, brown sugar and molasses make these down-home loaves the best-tasting rye bread I've ever had.

- 1/4 cup old-fashioned oats
- 1/3 cup packed brown sugar
- 1/4 cup molasses
- 5 tablespoons butter, *divided*
- 2 teaspoons salt
- 2 cups boiling water
- 3 cups bread flour
- 2 packages (1/4 ounce *each*) active dry yeast
- 3 cups rye flour
- 1 teaspoon caraway seeds

1) In a large bowl, combine the oats, brown sugar, molasses, 4 tablespoons butter and salt; stir in boiling water. Let stand until mixture cools to 120°-130°, stirring occasionally. In a large mixing bowl, combine 2 cups bread flour and yeast. Add the molasses mixture just until moistened. Stir in rye flour and enough of the remaining bread flour to form a medium stiff dough.

2) Turn onto a floured surface; knead until smooth and elastic, about 6-8 minutes. Place in a large bowl coated with cooking spray, turning once to coat top. Cover and let rise in a warm place until doubled, about 1 hour.

3) Punch dough down; cover and let rise in a warm place until doubled, about 30 minutes. Punch down. Turn onto a lightly floured surface; divide into three portions. Shape into loaves. Place on baking sheets coated with cooking spray. Cover and let rise until doubled, about 30 minutes.

4) Bake at 375° for 25-30 minutes or until golden brown. Remove from pans to wire racks. Melt remaining butter; brush over loaves. Sprinkle with caraway seeds. Cool.

Yield: 3 loaves (12 slices each).

NUTRITION FACTS: 1 slice equals 102 calories, 2 g fat (1 g saturated fat), 4 mg cholesterol, 149 mg sodium, 19 g carbohydrate, 2 g fiber, 2 g protein.

◎ Hawaiian Sweet Bread

PREP: 20 min. + rising **BAKE:** 20 min. + cooling

Ruthie Banks, Prescot, Arizona

Pineapple juice sweetens these three delicious loaves.

- 7 to 7-1/2 cups all-purpose flour
- 3/4 cup mashed potato flakes
- 2/3 cup sugar
- 2 packages (1/4 ounce *each*) active dry yeast
- 1 teaspoon salt
- 1/2 teaspoon ground ginger
- 1 cup milk
- 1/2 cup water
- 1/2 cup butter, softened
- 1 cup pineapple juice
- 3 eggs
- 2 teaspoons vanilla extract

1) In a large mixing bowl, combine 3 cups flour with the next five ingredients. In a small saucepan, heat milk, water, butter and juice to 120°-130°. Add to dry ingredients; beat just until moistened. Add eggs; beat until smooth. Beat in vanilla. Stir in enough remaining flour to form a soft dough.

2) Turn onto a floured surface; knead until smooth and elastic, about 6-8 minutes. Place in a greased bowl, turning once to grease the top. Cover; let rise in a warm place until doubled, about 1-1/4 hours.

3) Punch dough down. Turn onto a lightly floured surface; divide into thirds. Shape each into a ball. Place in three greased 9-in. round baking pans. Cover; let rise until doubled, about 45 minutes.

Rapid Mixing Method for Yeast Breads

1) In a mixing bowl, combine flour (about 2 cups), sugar, active dry or quick-rise yeast, salt and any seasonings.

2) In a saucepan, heat liquid ingredients (water, milk, honey, molasses and butter or oil) to 120°-130°. Add to dry ingredients; beat just until moistened.

3) Add any eggs; beat until smooth. Gradually stir in enough of the remaining flour to form a dough of the desired consistency.

4) Bake at 375° for 20-25 minutes or until golden brown. Cover loosely with foil if top browns too quickly. Remove from pans to wire racks to cool.

Yield: 3 loaves (12 wedges each).

NUTRITION FACTS: 1 wedge equals 146 calories, 3 g fat (2 g saturated fat), 25 mg cholesterol, 103 mg sodium, 25 g carbohydrate, 1 g fiber, 4 g protein.

Cinnamon Spiral Bread

PREP: 30 min. + rising **BAKE:** 35 min. + cooling

Sharon Moeller, Ceresco, Nebraska

Delicate swirls of cinnamon make this sweet bread a treat anytime of day. Thick slices are wonderful when toasted and topped with cream cheese.

5-1/4 to 5-1/2 cups all-purpose flour
    2 cups quick-cooking oats
  2/3 cup nonfat dry milk powder
  1/4 cup packed brown sugar
    2 packages (1/4 ounce *each*) active dry yeast
    3 teaspoons salt
2-1/2 cups water
    2 tablespoons butter
    1 egg
    1 cup raisins
  1/2 cup sugar
    2 teaspoons ground cinnamon

1) In a large mixing bowl, combine 2 cups flour, oats, milk powder, brown sugar, yeast and salt. In a small saucepan, heat water and butter to 120°-130°. Add to dry ingredients; beat just until moistened. Add egg; beat until smooth. Stir in enough remaining flour to form a firm dough. Stir in raisins.

2) Turn onto a floured surface; knead until smooth and elastic, about 6-8 minutes. Place in a greased bowl, turning once to grease top. Cover and let rise in a warm place until doubled, about 1 hour.

3) Punch dough down. Turn onto a lightly floured surface; divide in half. Roll each portion into an 18-in. x 9-in. rectangle. Combine sugar and cinnamon. Set aside 2 tablespoons for topping. Sprinkle remaining cinnamon-sugar over rectangles to within 1/2 in. of edges. Roll up jelly-roll style, starting with a short side; pinch seam to seal.

4) Place seam side down in two greased 9-in. x 5-in. x 3-in. loaf pans. Cover and let rise until doubled, about 30 minutes. Sprinkle with reserved cinnamon-sugar.

5) Bake at 375° for 35-40 minutes or until golden brown. Cover loosely with foil if tops brown too quickly. Cool for 10 minutes before removing from pans to wire racks.

Yield: 2 loaves (16 slices each).

NUTRITION FACTS: 1 slice equals 145 calories, 1 g fat (1 g saturated fat), 9 mg cholesterol, 244 mg sodium, 29 g carbohydrate, 1 g fiber, 4 g protein.

Batter Breads

Batter bread is beaten with an electric mixer to help develop the gluten faster and to give the bread a better texture. Because these breads are not kneaded, it is important to beat them until the batter comes away from the bowl and appears to be stringy.

Stir in the remaining flour with a sturdy wooden spoon until you have a stiff batter. Since less flour is used for batter breads, it forms a batter rather than a dough and is stickier than a kneaded dough.

Most batter breads are spooned or spread into a baking pan or dish. Push batter evenly to the edge of pan or into corners with a rubber spatula. Some batter breads can be shaped.

Follow the directions given for rising in each recipe. Batter breads rise until doubled or almost doubled—they don't rise to the top of the pan. If left to rise too long, they may fall during baking. Batter breads are best served the day they are made.

Honey Oatmeal Bread

PREP: 25 min. + rising **BAKE:** 40 min. + cooling

Janice Dancer, Williamstown, Vermont

If the kneading step in making bread is what has prevented you from baking, then try this recipe.

    2 cups water, *divided*
    1 cup rolled oats
  1/3 cup butter, softened
  1/3 cup honey
    1 tablespoon salt
    2 packages (1/2 ounce *each*) active dry yeast
    1 egg
    4 to 5 cups all-purpose flour, *divided*
Melted butter, optional

1) In a small saucepan, heat 1 cup water to boiling. Stir in the oats, butter, honey and salt. Let stand until mixture cools to 110°-115°, stirring occasionally. Heat remaining water to 110°-115°.

2) In a large mixing bowl, dissolve yeast in warm water. Add the egg, oat mixture and 2 cups flour. Beat until smooth. Stir in enough remaining flour to form a stiff dough.

3) Spread batter evenly into two greased 8-in. x 4-in. x 2-in. loaf pans. Smooth tops of loaves. Cover and let rise in a warm place until doubled, about 35-40 minutes.

4) Bake at 375° for 40-45 minutes. Remove from pans to wire racks to cool. Brush with melted butter if desired.

Yield: 2 loaves (12 slices each).

NUTRITION FACTS: 1 slice equals 132 calories, 3 g fat (2 g saturated fat), 16 mg cholesterol, 325 mg sodium, 22 g carbohydrate, 1 g fiber, 3 g protein.

Cheddar Batter Bread

PREP: 20 min. + rising **BAKE:** 35 min. + cooling

Debbie Keslar, Utica, Nebraska

I love batter breads because I can offer my family delicious homemade bread without the hassle of kneading and shaping the dough. This loaf is terrific with chili.

- 2 cups all-purpose flour
- 2 tablespoons sugar
- 1 package (1/4 ounce) active dry yeast
- 1/4 teaspoon onion powder
- 1/4 teaspoon salt
- 1/4 teaspoon pepper
- 1 cup milk
- 2 tablespoons butter
- 1 egg
- 1/2 cup cornmeal
- 3/4 cup shredded cheddar cheese

Additional cornmeal

1) In a large mixing bowl, combine 1-1/2 cups flour, sugar, yeast, onion powder, salt and pepper. In a small saucepan, heat milk and butter to 120°-130°. Add to dry ingredients; beat until moistened. Add egg; beat on low speed for 30 seconds. Beat on high for 3 minutes.

2) Stir in cornmeal and remaining flour. Stir in cheese (batter will be thick). Do not knead. Cover and let rise in a warm place until doubled, about 20 minutes.

3) Stir dough down. Grease a 9-in. x 5-in. x 3-in. loaf pan and sprinkle with additional cornmeal. Spoon batter into prepared pan. Cover and let rise in a warm place until doubled, about 30 minutes.

4) Bake at 350° for 35-40 minutes or until golden brown. Cool for 10 minutes before removing

CHEDDAR BATTER BREAD

from pan to a wire rack. Store in the refrigerator.

Yield: 1 loaf (16 slices).

NUTRITION FACTS: 1 slice equals 125 calories, 4 g fat (2 g saturated fat), 24 mg cholesterol, 90 mg sodium, 18 g carbohydrate, 1 g fiber, 4 g protein.

■ **Dill-Onion Batter Bread:** Omit the onion powder, pepper, cornmeal, cheese and additional cornmeal. Increase flour to 2-1/2 cups and salt to 1/2 teaspoon. Add 2 teaspoons *each* dill seed and dried minced onion to flour mixture. Proceed as directed. Bake at 350° for 30-35 minutes (cover loosely with foil if top browns too quickly). Store at room temperature.

Blue-Ribbon Herb Rolls

PREP: 20 min. + rising **BAKE:** 15 min.

Mary Ann Evans, Tarpon Springs, Florida

I developed these rolls using several ideas and techniques that I picked up while learning the art of bread making. They are savory and slightly sweet, and they won a blue ribbon at a county fair.

- 2 packages (1/4 ounce *each*) active dry yeast
- 2-3/4 cups warm water (110° to 115°), *divided*
- 1/3 cup vegetable oil
- 1/4 cup honey *or* molasses
- 1 tablespoon salt
- 2 teaspoons dill weed
- 2 teaspoons dried thyme
- 2 teaspoons dried basil
- 1 teaspoon onion powder
- 1 egg, beaten
- 4 cups whole wheat flour
- 4 to 4-1/2 cups all-purpose flour

1) In a large mixing bowl, dissolve yeast in 1/2 cup warm water. Add the oil, honey, salt, seasonings, egg, whole wheat flour and remaining water. Beat until smooth. Stir in enough all-purpose flour to form a soft dough.

2) Turn onto a floured surface; knead until smooth and elastic, 6-8 minutes. Place in a greased bowl, turning once to grease top. Cover and let rise in a warm place until doubled, about 1 hour.

3) Punch dough down. Turn onto a lightly floured surface; divide into six portions. Divide each into 24 pieces. Shape each into a 1-in. ball; place three balls in each greased muffin cup. Cover and let rise until doubled, 20-25 minutes. Bake at 375° for 12-15 minutes or until tops are golden brown. Remove from pans to wire racks.

Yield: 4 dozen.

NUTRITION FACTS: 1 roll equals 94 calories, 2 g fat (trace saturated fat), 4 mg cholesterol, 150 mg sodium, 17 g carbohydrate, 2 g fiber, 3 g protein.

Shaping Dinner Rolls

Plain Rolls
Divide dough into equal pieces as recipe directs. Shape each piece into a ball, pulling edges under to smooth top. Place 1 in. to 2 in. apart on greased baking sheets. For pan rolls, place eight balls in a greased 9-in. round baking pan or 12 balls in a greased 13-in. x 9-in. x 2-in. baking pan.

Cloverleaf Rolls
Divide dough into 1-1/2-in. balls. Make each ball smooth by pulling the edges under. Place three balls smooth side up in each greased muffin cup.

S-Shaped Rolls
Divide dough into 2-in. balls. Shape each ball into a 10-in. rope. On a greased baking sheet, coil each end in opposite directions until it touches the center and forms an S-shape.

Knot-Shaped Rolls
Divide dough into 3-in. balls. Roll each ball into a 10-in. rope; tie into a knot. Tuck and pinch ends under.

Crescent Rolls
Roll a portion of the dough into a 10-in. to 12-in. circle. Cut into 12-in. wedges and roll up, beginning at the wide end. Place pointed side down 2 in. apart on greased baking sheets. Curve ends to form crescent shape.

Three-Grain Pan Rolls
PREP: 40 min. rising **BAKE:** 20 min.

Montserrat Wadsworth, Winnemucca, Nevada

The first time I made these rolls, I was a little worried that my husband wouldn't like them. But he loved them! The seeds on top add flavor and fun crunch.

- 2 cups water
- 1/2 cup bulgur
- 1 package (1/4 ounce) active dry yeast
- 1 cup warm milk (110° to 115°)
- 1/2 cup quick-cooking oats
- 1/3 cup honey
- 2 eggs
- 2 teaspoons salt
- 3/4 teaspoon pepper
- 1-1/2 cups whole wheat flour
- 2-1/2 to 3-1/2 cups all-purpose flour
- 2 tablespoons olive oil
- 2 teaspoons *each* celery seed, fennel seed and sesame seeds
- 1 teaspoon poppy seeds

1) In a saucepan, bring water to a boil. Stir in bulgur. Reduce heat; cover and simmer for 15 minutes or until tender. Drain.

2) In a large mixing bowl, dissolve yeast in warm milk. Add the oats, honey, eggs, salt, pepper, cooked bulgur and whole wheat flour; beat until smooth. Stir in enough all-purpose flour to form a soft dough.

3) Turn onto a lightly floured surface; knead until elastic, about 6-8 minutes (mixture will be lumpy). Place in a bowl coated with cooking spray, turning once to coat top. Cover and let rise in a warm place until doubled, about 1-1/4 hours.

4) Punch dough down. Turn onto a lightly floured surface; divide into 22 pieces. Roll each into a ball. Brush two 9-in. round baking pans with some of the oil. Arrange 11 balls in each pan; brush tops with remaining oil.

5) Combine the celery seed, fennel seed, sesame seeds and poppy seeds; sprinkle over rolls. Cover and let rise in a warm place until doubled, about 40 minutes. Bake at 375° for 18-22 minutes or until golden brown. Remove from pans to wire racks.

Yield: 22 rolls.

NUTRITION FACTS: 1 roll equals 157 calories, 3 g fat (1 g saturated fat), 21 mg cholesterol, 227 mg sodium, 29 g carbohydrate, 2 g fiber, 5 g protein.

MELT-IN-YOUR-MOUTH ROLLS

 CLASSIC: Please a hungry crowd with this recipe for Soft Yeast Pan Rolls. The homemade dough makes three pans of tender, golden rolls, so you can round out your dinner menu with one pan and share the extras with friends or neighbors.

 TIME-SAVER: With French Onion Pan Rolls, you can serve up fresh-baked rolls without all the time it takes to make the dough from scratch. Frozen bread dough is thawed, shaped into balls, coated in melted butter and deliciously dressed up with Parmesan cheese and dry onion soup mix. For even quicker prep, start with frozen dinner rolls.

 LIGHT: Like the name says, Whole Wheat Buttermilk Rolls get their healthy spin from whole wheat flour. But with their irresistible flavor, you'd never guess they're better for you. Compared to Soft Yeast Pan Rolls, one of these rolls has 90 fewer calories, about a third of the fat and almost no cholesterol.

 SERVES 2: Garlic powder, oregano, basil and Parmesan cheese provide the wonderful seasoning in Garlic Herb Rolls. Baked in a muffin tin, the six rolls are so appealing they'll disappear in no time.

Soft Yeast Pan Rolls
PREP: 30 min. + rising **BAKE:** 20 min.
Angie Price, Bradford, Tennessee

- 2 packages (1/4 ounce *each*) active dry yeast
- 1 teaspoon plus 2/3 cup sugar, *divided*
- 1 cup warm water (110° to 115°)
- 1/2 cup butter, softened
- 1/2 cup shortening
- 1 teaspoon salt
- 1 cup boiling water
- 2 eggs
- 7 to 7-1/2 cups all-purpose flour

1) In a large mixing bowl, dissolve yeast and 1 teaspoon sugar in warm water; let stand for 5 minutes. Add the butter, shortening, salt and remaining sugar. Add boiling water; cool to 110°-115°. Add yeast mixture and eggs. Beat on medium speed until smooth. Stir in enough remaining flour to form a soft dough.

2) Turn onto a floured surface; knead until smooth and elastic, about 6-8 minutes. Place in a greased bowl, turning once to grease top. Cover and let rise in a warm place until doubled, about 1 hour.

3) Punch dough down. Turn onto a lightly floured surface; divide into thirds. Divide each portion into nine pieces; shape into balls. Place in three greased 9-in. round baking pans. Cover and let rise until doubled, about 30 minutes.

4) Bake at 350° for 20-25 minutes or until golden brown. Serve warm.

Yield: 27 rolls.

NUTRITION FACTS: 1 roll equals 206 calories, 8 g fat (3 g saturated fat), 25 mg cholesterol, 127 mg sodium, 30 g carbohydrate, 1 g fiber, 4 g protein.

FRENCH ONION PAN ROLLS

French Onion Pan Rolls
PREP: 15 min. + rising **BAKE:** 30 min.
Anne Prince, Elkhorn, Wisconsin

- 2 loaves (1 pound *each*) frozen bread dough, thawed
- 1 cup grated Parmesan cheese
- 1 envelope onion soup mix
- 1/2 cup butter, melted

1) Divide the bread dough into 20 portions; shape each into a ball. In a shallow bowl, combine the Parmesan cheese and soup mix. Place butter in another shallow bowl. Roll each ball in butter, then in the cheese mixture.

2) Arrange in a greased 13-in. x 9-in. x 2-in. baking dish. Cover and let rise in a warm place until doubled, about 45 minutes.

3) Bake at 350° for 30-35 minutes or until golden brown. Remove from pan to a wire rack. Serve warm.

Yield: 20 rolls.

NUTRITION FACTS: 1 roll equals 188 calories, 8 g fat (4 g saturated fat), 16 mg cholesterol, 471 mg sodium, 23 g carbohydrate, 2 g fiber, 6 g protein.

Whole Wheat Buttermilk Rolls

PREP: 35 min. + rising **BAKE:** 10 min.

Irene Cliett, Cedar Bluff, Mississippi

- 1-1/2 cups self-rising flour
- 1-1/2 cups whole wheat flour
- 1/3 cup sugar
- 1 package (1/4 ounce) quick-rise yeast
- 1 cup buttermilk
- 1/4 cup canola oil

1) In a large mixing bowl, combine the self-rising flour, 3/4 cup whole wheat flour, sugar and yeast. In a small saucepan, heat buttermilk and oil to 120°-130° (mixture will appear curdled). Add to dry ingredients; beat just until smooth. Stir in remaining whole wheat flour.

2) Turn onto a lightly floured surface; knead until smooth and elastic, about 6-8 minutes. Cover and let rest for 10 minutes.

3) Roll dough to 1/2-in. thickness; cut with a floured 2-1/2-in. biscuit cutter. Place 2 in. apart on baking sheets coated with cooking spray. Cover and let rise in a warm place until doubled, about 35-40 minutes.

4) Bake at 375° for 8-12 minutes or until golden brown. Remove from pans to wire racks. Serve warm.

Yield: 1-1/2 dozen.

Editor's Note: As a substitute for 1-1/2 cups self-rising flour, place 2-1/4 teaspoons baking powder and 3/4 teaspoon salt in a measuring cup. Add all-purpose flour to measure 1 cup. Combine with an additional 1/2 cup all-purpose flour.

NUTRITION FACTS: 1 roll equals 116 calories, 3 g fat (trace saturated fat), 1 mg cholesterol, 135 mg sodium, 19 g carbohydrate, 1 g fiber, 3 g protein.

GARLIC HERB ROLLS

Garlic Herb Rolls

PREP: 15 min. + rising **BAKE:** 10 min.

Virginia Lapierre, Greensboro Bend, Vermont

- 1 teaspoon active dry yeast
- 1/4 teaspoon sugar
- 1/4 cup warm water (110° to 115°)
- 1/2 cup plus 2 tablespoons all-purpose flour
- 1-1/2 teaspoons vegetable oil
- 1/4 teaspoon salt
- 1 tablespoon butter, softened
- 3/4 teaspoon garlic powder
- 3/4 teaspoon grated Parmesan cheese
- 1/4 teaspoon dried oregano
- 1/4 teaspoon dried basil

1) In a small mixing bowl, dissolve yeast and sugar in warm water. Beat in the flour, oil and salt until smooth. Turn onto a heavily floured surface; knead until smooth and elastic, about 6-8 minutes. Place in a bowl coated with cooking spray, turning once to coat top. Cover and let rise in a warm place until doubled, about 30 minutes.

2) Grease six muffin cups with the butter. Combine garlic powder, Parmesan cheese, oregano and basil; sprinkle into cups. Punch dough down; divide into six portions. Shape each into a ball; place in prepared cups, turning once to coat. Cover and let rise until doubled, about 30 minutes.

3) Bake at 425° for 10-15 minutes or until golden brown. Remove from pan to a wire rack. Serve warm.

Yield: 6 rolls.

NUTRITION FACTS: 1 roll equals 79 calories, 3 g fat (1 g saturated fat), 5 mg cholesterol, 122 mg sodium, 11 g carbohydrate, 1 g fiber, 2 g protein.

Handy Bench Knife

If you are a yeast bread baker, a bench knife is a great addition to your collection of kitchen tools. Use a bench knife to scrape yeast dough bits from the work surface, to help turn sticky doughs when kneading and to cut dough into halves for loaves or into pieces for rolls.

Parker House Rolls

PREP: 30 min. + rising **BAKE:** 10 min.

Sandra Melnychenko, Grandview, Manitoba

These tender rolls were created at Boston's Parker House Hotel in the 1870s. The folded shape makes them unique.

- 2 packages (1/4 ounce *each*) active dry yeast
- 1 teaspoon plus 6 tablespoons sugar, *divided*
- 1 cup warm water (110° to 115°), *divided*
- 1 cup warm milk (110° to 115°)
- 2 teaspoons salt
- 1 egg
- 2 tablespoons plus 2 teaspoons vegetable oil
- 5-1/2 to 6 cups all-purpose flour
- 3 tablespoons butter, melted, optional

1) In a large mixing bowl, dissolve yeast and 1 teaspoon sugar in 1/2 cup water; let stand for 5 minutes. Add the milk, salt, egg, oil and remaining sugar and water.

2) Gradually add 2 cups warm flour; beat until smooth. Stir in enough remaining flour to make a soft dough.

3) Turn onto a floured surface; knead until smooth and elastic, about 6-8 minutes. Place in a greased bowl, turning once to grease top. Cover and let rise in a warm place until doubled, about 45 minutes.

4) Punch dough down. Turn onto a lightly floured surface; divide in half. Roll out each piece to 1/3-in. or 1/2-in. thickness. Cut with a floured 2-1/2-in. round cutter. Brush with butter if desired.

5) Using the dull edge of a table knife, make an off-center crease in each roll. Fold along crease so the large half is on top; press along folded edge. Place 2 in. apart on greased baking sheets. Cover and let rise until doubled, about 30 minutes.

6) Bake at 375° for 10-15 minutes or until golden brown. Remove from pans to wire racks.

Yield: 2-1/2 dozen.

NUTRITION FACTS: 1 roll equals 113 calories, 2 g fat (trace saturated fat), 8 mg cholesterol, 164 mg sodium, 21 g carbohydrate, 1 g fiber, 3 g protein.

Forming Parker House Rolls

Roll out to 1/2-in. thickness. Cut with a floured 2-1/2-in. biscuit cutter. Brush with melted butter. Using the dull edge of a table knife, make an off-center crease in each roll. Fold along crease so the large half is on top.

Brioche

PREP: 30 min. + rising **BAKE:** 15 min.

Wanda Kristoffersen, Owatonna, Minnesota

At 10 o'clock every morning, it's coffee time at our house. Friends, neighbors and relatives stop by just to see what's baking in my oven.

- 3-1/2 cups all-purpose flour
- 1/2 cup sugar
- 2 packages (1/4 ounce *each*) active dry yeast
- 1 teaspoon grated lemon peel
- 1/2 teaspoon salt
- 2/3 cup butter
- 1/2 cup milk
- 5 eggs

1) In a large mixing bowl, combine 1-1/2 cups flour, sugar, yeast, lemon peel and salt. In a saucepan, heat butter and milk to 120°-130°. Add to dry ingredients; beat until moistened. Add 4 eggs; beat on medium speed for 2 minutes. Add 1 cup flour.

2) Beat until smooth. Stir in the remaining flour. Do not knead. Spoon into greased bowl. Cover; let rise in a warm place until doubled, about 1 hour. Stir dough down. Cover and refrigerate overnight.

3) Punch dough down. Turn onto a lightly floured surface. Cover with a bowl; let rest for 15 minutes. Cut one-sixth from the dough; set aside. Shape remaining dough into 12 balls (about 2-1/2 in.); place in well-greased muffin cups. Divide reserved dough into 12 small balls.

4) Make an indentation in the top of each large ball; place a small ball in each indentation. Cover and

PARKER HOUSE ROLLS

let rise in a warm place until doubled, about 1 hour. Beat remaining egg; brush over rolls. Bake at 375° for 15-20 minutes or until golden brown. Remove from pan to wire racks.

Yield: 1 dozen.

NUTRITION FACTS: 1 roll equals 295 calories, 13 g fat (7 g saturated fat), 117 mg cholesterol, 234 mg sodium, 37 g carbohydrate, 1 g fiber, 7 g protein.

SOUR CREAM FAN ROLLS

Sour Cream Fan Rolls

PREP: 30 min. + rising **BAKE:** 20 min.

Carrie Ormsby, West Jordan, Utah

I received this recipe from an E-mail pen pal in Canada. The dough is so easy to work with, and it makes the lightest yeast rolls. I haven't used another white bread recipe since I started making this one.

> 2 tablespoons active dry yeast
> 1 cup warm water (110° to 115°)
> 2 tablespoons plus 1/2 cup sugar, *divided*
> 2 cups warm sour cream (110° to 115°)
> 2 eggs, lightly beaten
> 6 tablespoons butter, melted
> 1-1/2 teaspoons salt
> 1/4 teaspoon baking powder
> 7 to 8 cups all-purpose flour

1) In a bowl, dissolve yeast in warm water. Add 2 tablespoons sugar; let stand for 5 minutes. In a large mixing bowl, combine the sour cream, eggs, butter, salt and remaining sugar.

2) Stir in baking powder, yeast mixture and 4 cups of flour until smooth. Stir in enough remaining flour to form a soft dough.

3) Turn onto a floured surface; knead until smooth and elastic, about 6-8 minutes. Place in a greased

bowl, turning once to grease top. Cover and let rise in a warm place until doubled, about 1 hour.

4) Punch dough down. Turn onto a lightly floured surface; divide in half. Roll each portion into a 23-in. x 9-in. rectangle.

5) Cut into 1-1/2-in. strips. Stack five strips together; cut into 1-1/2-in. pieces and place cut side up in a greased muffin cup. Cover and let rise until doubled, about 20 minutes. Bake at 350° for 20-25 minutes or until golden brown. Remove from pans to wire racks.

Yield: about 2-1/2 dozen.

NUTRITION FACTS: 1 roll equals 182 calories, 6 g fat (3 g saturated fat), 31 mg cholesterol, 158 mg sodium, 27 g carbohydrate, 1 g fiber, 4 g protein.

Sour Cream Crescents

PREP: 15 min. + rising **BAKE:** 15 min.

Judie Anglen, Riverton, Wyoming

I don't mind that my family insists on having these for holiday dinners because they can be made ahead and frozen!

> 3 teaspoons active dry yeast
> 1/3 cup warm water (110° to 115°)
> 1/2 cup sugar
> 1/2 teaspoon salt
> 1 cup butter, softened
> 1 cup (8 ounces) sour cream
> 2 eggs
> 4 cups all-purpose flour

1) In a large mixing bowl, dissolve yeast in warm water. Add the sugar, salt, butter, sour cream and eggs. Beat until smooth. Add 3 cups flour; mix well. Stir in the remaining flour. Cover and refrigerate for 6 hours or overnight.

2) Punch dough down. Turn onto a floured surface; divide into four pieces. Roll each into a 10-in. circle; cut each circle into 12 wedges.

3) Roll up wedges from the wide end and place point side down 3 in. apart on greased baking sheets. Curve ends to form a crescent. Cover and let rise in a warm place until doubled, about 1-1/2 hours. Bake at 375° for 15 minutes or until golden brown. Remove from pans to wire racks.

Yield: 4 dozen.

NUTRITION FACTS: 1 roll equals 93 calories, 5 g fat (3 g saturated fat), 22 mg cholesterol, 68 mg sodium, 10 g carbohydrate, trace fiber, 2 g protein.

SAVE LEFTOVER BREAD FOR CRUMBS ■■■

I keep the heels of bread in a heavy-duty resealable plastic bag in the freezer. When the bag is full, I use my food processor to turn the heels into bread crumbs. This way I don't have to process a few heels at a time, and I always have a supply of soft bread crumbs available to use in recipes.

—*Debbie Valentine, Blanchester, Ohio*

SAVORY BREADSTICKS

 CLASSIC: Round out most any meal in a tasty way with Bacon Onion Breadsticks. Cooked bacon and sauteed onion are kneaded into the homemade dough, which is brushed with egg and lightly sprinkled with coarse salt for family-pleasing results.

 TIME-SAVER: When you want breadsticks in a flash, turn to this recipe for Pesto Breadsticks. A tube of refrigerated breadsticks is brushed with store-bought pesto and garlic pepper, then topped with Parmesan cheese. So these twists are ready in a fraction of the time it takes to make breadsticks from scratch.

 LIGHT: You can enjoy the rich, savory flavor of Soft Onion Breadsticks without feeling the least bit guilty. Compared to Bacon Onion Breadsticks, each of these lovely, seed-topped breadsticks has about 50 fewer calories and 2 grams less fat.

 SERVES 2: Once you sample Breadsticks for Two, you'll be sure to keep frozen dinner rolls handy in the freezer to make this recipe whenever you want. Roll out four thawed rolls to bake these tasty twists that are dressed up with basil, garlic and Parmesan.

Bacon Onion Breadsticks

PREP: 30 min. + rising **BAKE:** 15 min.

Michelle Buerge, Ithaca, Michigan

- 2 **tablespoons active dry yeast**
- 2 **cups warm milk (110° to 115°),** *divided*
- 1 **teaspoon sugar**
- 1/2 **cup butter, melted**
- 1-1/4 **teaspoons salt,** *divided*
- 5-1/2 **to 6 cups all-purpose flour**
- 1 **pound sliced bacon, diced**
- 1 **medium onion, chopped**
- 1/4 **teaspoon pepper**
- 1 **egg, beaten**

Coarse salt

1) In a large mixing bowl, dissolve yeast in 1 cup warm milk. Add sugar; let stand for 5 minutes. Add butter, 1 teaspoon salt and remaining milk. Beat until smooth. Stir in enough flour to form a soft dough.

2) Turn onto a floured surface; knead until smooth and elastic, about 6-8 minutes. Place in a greased bowl, turning once to grease top. Cover and let rise in a warm place until doubled, about 1-1/2 hours.

3) Meanwhile, in a large skillet, cook bacon and onion until bacon is crisp; drain. Add pepper and remaining salt. Cool completely. Punch dough down. Turn onto a floured surface; knead bacon mixture into dough.

4) Roll dough into a 14-in. square. Brush with egg; sprinkle with coarse salt. Cut dough in half lengthwise and in thirds widthwise. Cut each section into six strips. Place 2 in. apart on greased baking sheets. Cover and let rise in a warm place until doubled, about 30 minutes.

5) Bake at 375° for 15-20 minutes or until golden brown. Remove from pans to wire racks. Serve warm.

Yield: 3 dozen.

NUTRITION FACTS: 1 breadstick equals 130 calories, 5 g fat (3 g saturated fat), 18 mg cholesterol, 183 mg sodium, 16 g carbohydrate, 1 g fiber, 4 g protein.

Pesto Breadsticks

PREP/TOTAL TIME: 20 min.

Taste of Home Test Kitchen

- 1 **tube (11 ounces) refrigerated breadsticks**
- 2 **tablespoons prepared pesto**
- 1/4 **teaspoon garlic pepper blend**

PESTO BREADSTICKS

1 tablespoon butter, melted
2 tablespoons shredded Parmesan
cheese

1) Unroll and separate breadsticks; place on an
ungreased baking sheet. Combine pesto and
garlic pepper; brush over breadsticks. Twist each
breadstick three times.

2) Brush with butter; sprinkle with Parmesan cheese.
Bake at 375° for 10-13 minutes or until golden
brown. Serve warm.

Yield: 1 dozen.

NUTRITION FACTS: 1 breadstick equals 95 calories, 4 g fat (2 g
saturated fat), 4 mg cholesterol, 231 mg sodium, 13 g carbohydrate,
trace fiber, 3 g protein.

Soft Onion Breadsticks

PREP: 30 min. + rising **BAKE:** 20 min.

Maryellen Hays, Wolcottville, Indiana

3/4 cup chopped onion
1 tablespoon vegetable oil
2-1/4 teaspoons active dry yeast
1/2 cup warm water (110° to 115°)
1/2 cup warm milk (110° to 115°)
2 eggs
1/4 cup butter, softened
1 tablespoon sugar
1-1/2 teaspoons salt
3-1/2 to 4 cups all-purpose flour
2 tablespoons cold water
2 tablespoons sesame seeds
1 tablespoon poppy seeds

1) In a skillet, saute onion in oil until tender; cool. In
a large mixing bowl, dissolve yeast in warm water.
Add the milk, 1 egg, butter, sugar, salt and 1 cup
flour. Beat on medium speed for 2 minutes.

2) Stir in onion and enough remaining flour to form
a soft dough. Turn onto a floured surface; knead
until smooth and elastic, 6-8 minutes.

3) Place in a greased bowl, turning once to grease
top. Cover and let rise in a warm place until
doubled, about 1 hour.

4) Punch dough down. Let stand for 10 minutes.
Turn onto a lightly floured surface; divide into
32 pieces. Shape each piece into an 8-in. rope.
Place 2 in. apart on greased baking sheets. Cover
and let rise for 15 minutes.

5) Beat cold water and remaining egg; brush over
breadsticks. Sprinkle half with sesame seeds and half
with poppy seeds. Bake at 350° for 16-22 minutes
or until golden brown. Remove to wire racks.

Yield: 32 breadsticks.

NUTRITION FACTS: 1 breadstick equals 81 calories, 3 g fat (1 g
saturated fat), 18 mg cholesterol, 132 mg sodium, 12 g carbohydrate,
1 g fiber, 2 g protein.

SOFT ONION BREADSTICKS

■ **Garlic Parmesan Breadsticks:** Prepare the
recipe as directed except omit brushing with the
egg mixture and sprinkling with sesame and
poppy seeds. Brush with 1/4 cup melted butter
and sprinkle with garlic salt and grated Parmesan
cheese. Bake as directed.

Breadsticks for Two

PREP: 15 min. + rising **BAKE:** 15 min.

Taste of Home Test Kitchen

1/3 cup grated Parmesan cheese
1/2 teaspoon dried basil
1/4 teaspoon garlic powder
1 egg white
1 teaspoon water
4 frozen bread dough dinner rolls,
thawed

1) In a shallow bowl, combine the Parmesan cheese,
basil and garlic powder. In another bowl, whisk egg
white and water. Roll each dough ball into an 8-in.
rope. Dip in egg white mixture, then roll in cheese
mixture. Twist each rope three or four times.

2) Place on a greased baking sheet. Cover and let rise
in a warm place until doubled, about 20 minutes.
Bake at 350° for 12-16 minutes or until golden
brown. Serve warm.

Yield: 4 breadsticks.

NUTRITION FACTS: 1 breadstick equals 132 calories, 4 g fat (1 g
saturated fat), 6 mg cholesterol, 313 mg sodium, 19 g carbohydrate,
1 g fiber, 7 g protein.

Shaping Breadsticks

Divide dough as recipe
directs. Shape each piece
into a ball. Roll each ball
back and forth with both
hands until they are shaped
into a rope.

Sweet Yeast Breads

Sweet yeast breads fall into two basic categories: sweet loaves and sweet rolls. The dough can be made by hand or in a bread machine.

Sweet breads include fruit-filled breads and a variety of coffee cakes. Sweet rolls refer to fruit-filled rolls, sticky buns, cinnamon rolls, doughnuts, kolachkes and individual Danishes.

After punching down the dough, let it rest for 10 minutes. This allows the dough to relax, which makes it easier to roll out.

Roll up dough firmly. If it's too loose, you'll see air pockets or large gaps when cut. If it's too tight, the bread will crack.

A simple way to slice the dough for cinnamon rolls or sticky buns is to place a piece of unflavored dental floss or heavy-duty thread under the rolled dough, 1 in. from the end. Bring the floss up around the dough and cross it over the top, cutting through the dough and filling. Repeat at 1-in. intervals.

Evenly space the cut rolls in the pan, leaving room around each to allow for the final rising.

Raspberry Swirl Coffee Cake
PREP: 40 min. + rising **BAKE:** 15 min.

Mary Bergman, Navarra, Spain

My husband and I and our three children are missionaries in northern Spain. Special treats like this flavorful swirled bread are truly a taste of home for us.

- 1 tablespoon active dry yeast
- 1/3 cup warm water (110° to 115°)
- 1/2 cup warm sour cream (110° to 115°)
- 1/4 cup butter, melted
- 1/4 cup sugar
- 1 teaspoon salt
- 1 egg
- 2-1/4 to 2-1/2 cups all-purpose flour

FILLING:
- 1 package (8 ounces) cream cheese, softened
- 1 egg
- 1/2 cup sugar
- 1 teaspoon vanilla extract
- 1/8 teaspoon salt
- 1/2 cup raspberry jam

GLAZE:
- 1-1/4 cups confectioners' sugar
- 1 teaspoon vanilla extract
- 2 tablespoons milk

1) In a large bowl, dissolve yeast in warm water. Stir in sour cream, butter, sugar, salt and egg. Stir in enough flour to form a soft dough.

2) Turn onto a floured surface; knead 20 times or until smooth. Place in a greased bowl, turning once to grease top. Cover and let rise in a warm place until doubled, about 1-1/4 hours.

3) In a small mixing bowl, beat the cream cheese, egg, sugar, vanilla and salt until smooth; set aside. Punch dough down. Turn onto a lightly floured surface; divide in half.

4) Roll each piece into a 12-in. x 8-in. rectangle. Spread filling to within 1/2 in. of edges. Spoon jam lengthwise over half of the filling. Roll up jelly-roll style, starting with the long side with the jam. Pinch seams to seal; tuck ends under.

5) Place loaves seam side down on a greased baking sheet. With a sharp knife, cut shallow slashes across the top of each. Cover and let rise until doubled, about 30 minutes.

6) Bake at 375° for 15-20 minutes or until golden brown. Remove from pan to a wire rack. Combine glaze ingredients; drizzle over warm coffee cakes.

Yield: 2 loaves (10 slices each).

NUTRITION FACTS: 1 slice equals 212 calories, 8 g fat (5 g saturated fat), 44 mg cholesterol, 200 mg sodium, 32 g carbohydrate, 1 g fiber, 3 g protein.

■ **Peach Swirl Coffee Cake:** Use 1/2 cup of peach preserves for the raspberry jam.

RASPBERRY SWIRL COFFEE CAKE

Reheating Coffee Cakes
If you make a coffee cake in advance but want fresh-from-the-oven flavor when you serve it to guests, try this trick. Wrap an unfrosted coffee cake in foil. Reheat at 350° for a few minutes or until warm.

APRICOT TEA RINGS

Apricot Tea Rings

PREP: 45 min. + rising **BAKE:** 25 min. + cooling

Dot Christiansen, Orion, Illinois

This coffee cake is a favorite of mine. It's attractive, delicious and cuts like a dream. Sometimes I use canned pie filling when I'm pressed for time.

> 4-1/4　cups all-purpose flour
> 1/4　cup sugar
> 2　packages (1/4 ounce *each*) active dry yeast
> 1　teaspoon salt
> 1/4　teaspoon ground nutmeg
> 1　cup milk
> 1/4　cup water
> 1/4　cup butter, cubed
> 2　eggs

FILLING:

> 12　ounces dried apricots, diced
> 2　cups water
> 6　tablespoons brown sugar
> 4　teaspoons orange juice
> 1/2　cup chopped pecans

GLAZE:

> 1　cup confectioners' sugar
> 2　to 3 tablespoons milk

1) In a large mixing bowl, combine the flour, sugar, yeast, salt and nutmeg. In a saucepan, heat the milk, water and butter to 120°-130°. Add to dry ingredients; beat until moistened. Beat in eggs until smooth. Cover and refrigerate overnight.

2) In a saucepan, combine the apricots and water. Cook over medium heat for 30 minutes or until the water is absorbed and apricots are tender.

Remove from the heat; stir in the brown sugar, juice and nuts. Cool.

3) Punch dough down. Turn onto a lightly floured surface; divide in half. Roll each into an 18-in. x 12-in. rectangle.

4) Spread half of the filling over each rectangle to within 1/2 in. of edges. Roll up each jelly-roll style, starting with a long side; pinch seam to seal. Place seam side down on greased baking sheets; pinch ends of each together to form a ring.

5) With scissors, cut each from outside edge two-thirds toward center of ring at 1 in. intervals. Separate strips slightly; twist so filling shows, slightly overlapping with previous piece. Cover and let rise in a warm place until doubled, about 1 hour.

6) Bake at 375° for 25-28 minutes or until golden brown. Remove from pans to wire racks to cool. Combine glaze ingredients; drizzle over warm tea rings.

Yield: 2 rings (12 slices each).

NUTRITION FACTS: 1 slice equals 205 calories, 5 g fat (2 g saturated fat), 24 mg cholesterol, 132 mg sodium, 37 g carbohydrate, 2 g fiber, 4 g protein.

Shaping a Coffee Cake Ring

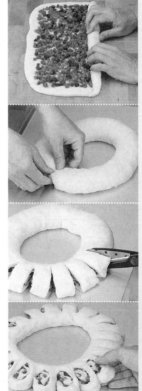

1) Roll into a rectangle. Spread filling evenly over dough to within 1/2 in. of edges. Roll up jelly-roll style, starting with a long side; pinch seam to seal.

2) Place seam side down on a greased baking sheet; pinch ends together to form a ring.

3) With scissors, cut from outside edge to two-thirds of the way toward center of ring at 1-in. intervals.

4) Separate the cut pieces slightly, twisting each individually to allow filling to show.

Orange Bubble Bread

PREP: 35 min. + rising **BAKE:** 40 min.

Cyndie Wowchuk, Saskatoon, Saskatchewan

This sweet version of bubble bread gets great flavor from raisins, coconut and an orange glaze.

- 1 package (1/4 ounce) active dry yeast
- 1 teaspoon plus 1/4 cup sugar, *divided*
- 1 cup warm milk (110° to 115°)
- 3-1/2 to 4 cups all-purpose flour
- 1 teaspoon salt
- 1/2 cup cold butter
- 2 eggs, lightly beaten

ORANGE SYRUP:
- 3/4 cup orange juice
- 3/4 cup orange marmalade
- 4 to 5 tablespoons sugar
- 2 tablespoons plus 1 teaspoon butter
- 3/4 teaspoon grated orange peel
- 1 cup flaked coconut, toasted, *divided*
- 1/2 cup golden raisins

1) In a small bowl, dissolve yeast and 1 teaspoon sugar in warm milk; set aside. In a large bowl, combine 3-1/2 cups flour, salt and remaining sugar.

2) Cut in butter until crumbly. Stir in eggs. Stir in yeast mixture and enough remaining flour until mixture forms a firm ball (mixture will be slightly sticky).

3) Turn onto a floured surface; knead until smooth and elastic, about 6-8 minutes. Place in a greased bowl, turning once to grease top. Cover and let rise in a warm place until doubled, about 1-1/4 hours.

4) Meanwhile, for syrup, combine the orange juice, marmalade, sugar, butter and orange peel in a saucepan. Cook and stir until mixture comes to a boil. Reduce heat; simmer, uncovered, for 5 minutes. Cool to room temperature. Place 1/2 cup syrup and 1/2 cup coconut on the bottom of a greased 10-in. tube pan.

5) Punch dough down. Turn onto a lightly floured surface; divide into 32 pieces. Roll each into a 1-in. ball. Dip each into remaining orange syrup.

6) Place 16 balls in prepared pan. Sprinkle with half of the raisins and 1/4 cup coconut. Top with remaining balls, raisins and coconut. Cover and let rise until doubled, about 45 minutes.

7) Bake at 350° for 40-50 minutes or until golden brown. Cool for 5 minutes before inverting bread onto a serving plate.

   Yield: 1 loaf (16 servings).

   NUTRITION FACTS: 2 balls equal 294 calories, 11 g fat (7 g saturated fat), 48 mg cholesterol, 263 mg sodium, 46 g carbohydrate, 1 g fiber, 5 g protein.

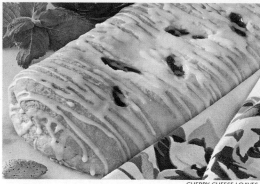

CHERRY CHEESE LOAVES

Cherry Cheese Loaves

PREP: 1-1/2 hours + chilling
BAKE: 20 min. + cooling

Carolyn Gregory, Hendersonville, Tennessee

This has become my "trademark" dessert. I'm asked to take it everywhere I go!

- 2 packages (1/4 ounce *each*) active dry yeast
- 1/2 cup warm water (110° to 115°)
- 1 cup (8 ounces) sour cream
- 1/2 cup butter, cubed
- 1/2 cup sugar
- 2 eggs
- 4 cups all-purpose flour

FILLING:
- 2 packages (one 8 ounces, one 3 ounces) cream cheese, softened
- 1/2 cup sugar
- 1 egg
- 1 teaspoon almond extract
- 1 can (21 ounces) cherry pie filling

GLAZE:
- 2 cups confectioners' sugar
- 1/4 cup milk
- 1 teaspoon almond extract

1) In a large mixing bowl, dissolve yeast in warm water. In a saucepan, heat sour cream and butter to 110°-115°. Add to yeast mixture. Add sugar and eggs; mix well. Gradually add flour; mix well. Do not knead. Cover and refrigerate overnight.

2) For filling, in a small mixing bowl, beat the cream cheese, sugar, egg and extract until smooth; set aside. Turn dough onto a lightly floured surface; divide into four portions. Roll each into a 12-in. x 8-in. rectangle.

3) Spread a fourth of the cream cheese mixture down the center of each rectangle. Spoon a fourth of the pie filling over the cream cheese. Fold lengthwise into thirds; pinch side seam and ends to seal. Place seam side down on greased baking sheets.

4) With a sharp scissors, make several 1-in. diagonal cuts near the center of loaves. Cover and let rise in a warm place until doubled, about 1 hour.

5) Bake at 375° for 20-25 minutes or until lightly browned. Combine glaze ingredients; drizzle over warm loaves. Cool on wire racks. Refrigerate leftovers.

Yield: 4 loaves (10 slices each).

NUTRITION FACTS: 1 slice equals 173 calories, 7 g fat (4 g saturated fat), 35 mg cholesterol, 58 mg sodium, 25 g carbohydrate, 1 g fiber, 3 g protein.

Lemon-Twist Loaves

PREP: 30 min. + rising **BAKE:** 25 min.

Audrey Thibodeau, Gilbert, Arizona

This mouthwatering bread has a tangy twist and pretty glaze.

   2 packages (1/4 ounce *each*) active dry yeast
   2 cups warm water (110° to 115°), *divided*
   3 cups sugar, *divided*
   1 cup butter, melted and cooled, *divided*
3/4 teaspoon salt
   1 egg
   1 egg yolk
   7 cups all-purpose flour
   1 cup sliced almonds, chopped
   3 tablespoons grated lemon peel

GLAZE:
   3 cups confectioners' sugar
   3 tablespoons grated lemon peel
   1 teaspoon lemon extract
   3 to 4 tablespoons milk
   1 cup sliced almonds, toasted

1) In a large mixing bowl, dissolve yeast in 1/2 cup warm water. Add 1 cup sugar, 1/2 cup butter, salt, egg, egg yolk and remaining water. Beat until blended. Add 4 cups flour. Beat until smooth. Stir in enough remaining flour to form a soft dough.

2) Turn onto a floured surface; knead until smooth and elastic, 6-8 minutes. Place in a greased bowl, turning once to grease top. Cover and refrigerate for 8 hours.

3) Punch dough down. Turn onto a lightly floured surface; divide into thirds. Roll each piece into a 16-in. x 10-in. rectangle. Spread remaining melted butter over dough.

4) Combine the chopped almonds, lemon peel and remaining sugar; sprinkle over butter. Roll up jelly-roll style, starting with a long side; pinch seams and ends to seal. Place seam side down on greased baking sheets. With a knife, cut loaves in half lengthwise to within 1 in. of one end. Holding

the uncut end, loosely twist strips together. Cover and let rise until doubled, about 1-1/2 hours.

5) Bake at 350° for 25-30 minutes until bread sounds hollow when tapped. Remove from pans to wire racks.

6) Combine the confectioners' sugar, lemon peel, extract and enough milk to achieve spreading consistency; spread over warm bread. Sprinkle with toasted almonds.

Yield: 3 loaves (12 slices each).

NUTRITION FACTS: 1 slice equals 274 calories, 8 g fat (4 g saturated fat), 26 mg cholesterol, 104 mg sodium, 47 g carbohydrate, 1 g fiber, 4 g protein.

Almond Coffee Cake

PREP: 35 min. + rising **BAKE:** 20 min. + cooling

Mary Shivers, Ada, Oklahoma

This cake is doubly delicious due to the cream cheese and vanilla chip filling. One piece leads to another!

   1 loaf (1 pound) frozen bread dough, thawed
   1 package (8 ounces) cream cheese, softened
1/4 cup sugar
   1 egg
1/2 teaspoon almond extract
3/4 cup vanilla *or* white chips
   1 tablespoon milk

GLAZE:
   1 cup confectioners' sugar
1/4 teaspoon almond extract
   1 to 2 tablespoons milk
1/2 cup slivered almonds, toasted

1) On a lightly floured surface, roll dough into a 15-in. x 9-in. rectangle. Transfer to a lightly greased baking sheet.

2) In a small mixing bowl, beat cream cheese and sugar until smooth. Add egg and extract; mix well (filling will be soft). Spread down center of rectangle; sprinkle with chips. On each long side, cut 1-in.-wide strips, about 1/2 in. from filling. Starting at one end, fold alternating strips at an angle across filling. Seal ends. Cover and let rise in a warm place until doubled, about 1 hour.

3) Brush with milk. Bake at 350° for 20-30 minutes or until golden brown. Cool on a wire rack.

4) For glaze, in a small bowl, combine confectioners' sugar and extract. Stir in enough milk to achieve desired consistency. Drizzle over coffee cake. Sprinkle with almonds.

Yield: 8-10 servings.

NUTRITION FACTS: 1 slice equals 382 calories, 17 g fat (8 g saturated fat), 49 mg cholesterol, 339 mg sodium, 50 g carbohydrate, 2 g fiber, 9 g protein.

NUT ROLL COFFEE CAKES

time, on high until stiff glossy peaks form and sugar is dissolved. Fold in walnuts; set aside.

3) Turn dough onto a lightly floured surface. Let stand for 10 minutes or until easy to handle. Divide into thirds. Roll each portion into a 15-in. x 13-in. rectangle. Spread filling over rectangles to within 1/2 in. of edges. Roll up jelly-roll style, starting with a long side; pinch seam to seal.

4) Place seam side down on greased baking sheets. Cover and let rise until doubled, about 45 minutes.

5) Bake at 350° for 20-25 minutes or until golden brown. Remove from pans to wire racks to cool. Combine icing ingredients; drizzle over coffee cakes.

Yield: 3 loaves (15 slices each).

NUTRITION FACTS: 1 slice equals 124 calories, 7 g fat (3 g saturated fat), 26 mg cholesterol, 74 mg sodium, 13 g carbohydrate, 1 g fiber, 2 g protein.

Nut Roll Coffee Cakes

PREP: 45 min. + chilling
BAKE: 20 min. + cooling

Louise Gasper, Northville, Michigan

I especially love preparing povatica (a Croatian speciality bread) with ground-up walnuts. The bread is tender with a golden brown crust and a nutty filling that's flavorful but not too sweet. With a drizzle of white icing and a sprinkle of walnuts on top, this bread becomes a festive dessert.

 1 package (1/4 ounce) active dry yeast
1/4 cup warm water (110° to 115°)
 1 cup butter, melted and cooled
1/2 cup warm milk (110° to 115°)
 3 egg yolks
 2 tablespoons sugar
1/2 teaspoon salt
 3 cups all-purpose flour

FILLING:
 3 egg whites
 1 teaspoon vanilla extract
3/4 cup sugar
2-1/4 cups ground walnuts

ICING:
3/4 cup confectioners' sugar
 1 teaspoon butter, softened
 1 teaspoon vanilla extract
 3 to 4 teaspoons milk

1) In a large mixing bowl, dissolve yeast in warm water. Add the butter, milk, egg yolks, sugar, salt and flour; beat until smooth. Do not knead. Cover and refrigerate overnight.

2) For filling, in a small mixing bowl, beat egg whites and vanilla on medium speed until soft peaks form. Gradually beat in sugar, 1 tablespoon at a

Pecan Peach Coffee Cakes

PREP: 35 min. + rising **BAKE:** 25 min. + cooling

Barbara Gerriets, Emporia, Kansas

With a filling of peach preserves and pecans, this special coffee cake is nice for holiday celebrations and family gatherings. The recipe makes two, so you can serve a crowd.

 2 packages (1/4 ounce *each*) active dry yeast
1/2 cup warm water (110° to 115°)
1/2 cup warm milk (110° to 115°)
1/2 cup butter, softened
1/2 cup sugar
 2 teaspoons salt
 3 eggs
 5 to 5-1/2 cups all-purpose flour

FILLING:
1/4 cup butter, melted
1-1/2 cups peach preserves
 1 cup chopped pecans
2/3 cup sugar
 2 teaspoons ground cinnamon

GLAZE:
1-1/2 cups confectioners' sugar
1-1/2 teaspoons vanilla extract
 2 to 3 tablespoons milk

1) In a large mixing bowl, dissolve yeast in water. Add the milk, butter, sugar, salt, eggs and 2 cups flour; beat on low speed for 3 minutes. Stir in enough remaining flour to form a soft dough.

2) Turn onto a floured surface; knead until smooth and elastic, about 6-8 minutes. Place in a greased bowl, turning once to grease top. Cover and let rise in a warm place until doubled, about 1 hour.

3) Punch dough down. Turn onto a lightly floured surface; divide in half. Roll each portion into a

20-in. x 10-in. rectangle. Spread with butter; top with preserves and pecans. Combine sugar and cinnamon; sprinkle over the top.

4) Roll up jelly-roll style, starting with a long side. Pinch seams to seal and tuck ends under. Place seam side down on a greased baking sheet, curving ends to make a U shape. With scissors, make cuts every 1-1/2 in. Cover and let rise in a warm place for 45 minutes.

5) Bake at 350° for 25-30 minutes or until golden brown. Remove from pans to wire racks. Combine the glaze ingredients; drizzle over warm coffee cakes. Cool.

Yield: 2 coffee cakes (16 slices each).

NUTRITION FACTS: 1 slice equals 233 calories, 8 g fat (3 g saturated fat), 32 mg cholesterol, 200 mg sodium, 39 g carbohydrate, 1 g fiber, 3 g protein.

Braiding a Filled Bread

1) Spread filling down center of rectangle. On each long side, cut 1-in.-wide strips, about 1/2 in. from filling.

2) Starting at one end, fold alternating strips at an angle across filling. Seal ends.

Apple Ladder Loaves

PREP: 70 min. + chilling **BAKE:** 30 min.

Norma Foster, Compton, Illinois

This pretty filled bread makes a nice breakfast pastry or—with a scoop of ice cream—a lovely dessert. If you don't have time to make the dough from scratch, thaw a 1-pound loaf of frozen bread dough and use that instead of the first eight ingredients.

　　2　packages (1/4 ounce *each*) active dry yeast
　1/4　cup warm water (110° to 115°)
　1/2　cup warm milk (110° to 115°)
　1/2　cup butter, softened
　1/3　cup sugar
　　4　eggs
　　1　teaspoon salt
4-1/2　to 4-3/4 cups all-purpose flour

FILLING:
　1/4　cup butter, softened
　1/3　cup packed brown sugar
　　2　tablespoons all-purpose flour
1-1/4　teaspoons ground cinnamon

　1/2　teaspoon ground nutmeg
　1/8　teaspoon ground allspice
　　4　cups thinly sliced peeled tart apples

ICING:
　　1　cup confectioners' sugar
　1/4　teaspoon vanilla extract
　　1　to 2 tablespoons orange juice

1) In a large mixing bowl, dissolve yeast in warm water. Add the milk, butter, sugar, eggs, salt and 2 cups flour. Beat on low speed for 3 minutes. Stir in enough remaining flour to form a soft dough.

2) Turn onto a lightly floured surface; knead until smooth and elastic, about 6-8 minutes. Place in a greased bowl, turning once to grease top. Cover and refrigerate for 1-2 hours; punch dough down. Cover and refrigerate overnight.

3) Punch dough down. Turn onto a lightly floured surface; divide in half. Roll each portion into a 12-in. x 9-in. rectangle. Place each on a greased baking sheet. Spread with butter. In a large bowl, combine the brown sugar, flour, cinnamon, nutmeg and allspice; add apples and toss to coat. Spread down the center third of each rectangle.

4) On each long side, cut 1-in.-wide strips about 3 in. into center. Starting at one end, fold alternating strips at an angle across filling; seal ends. Cover and let rise until nearly doubled, about 45-60 minutes.

5) Bake at 350° for 30-40 minutes or until golden brown. For icing, combine confectioners' sugar, vanilla and enough orange juice to achieve drizzling consistency; drizzle over warm loaves. Serve warm or at room temperature. Store in the refrigerator.

Yield: 2 loaves (10 slices each).

NUTRITION FACTS: 1 slice equals 250 calories, 8 g fat (5 g saturated fat), 62 mg cholesterol, 205 mg sodium, 39 g carbohydrate, 1 g fiber, 5 g protein.

APPLE LADDER LOAVES

BLACK RASPBERRY BUBBLE RING

Black Raspberry Bubble Ring

PREP: 35 min. + rising **BAKE:** 25 min.

Kila Frank, Reedsville, Ohio

I first made this pretty bread years ago for a 4-H project. It helped me win Grand Champion for my county and took me to the Ohio State Fair. It takes some time to make, but I pull out this recipe any time I want a breakfast or dessert that will really impress.

- 1 package (1/4 ounce) active dry yeast
- 1/4 cup warm water (110° to 115°)
- 1 cup warm milk (110° to 115°)
- 1/4 cup plus 2 tablespoons sugar, *divided*
- 1/2 cup butter, melted, *divided*
- 1 egg
- 1 teaspoon salt
- 4 cups all-purpose flour
- 1 jar (10 ounces) seedless black raspberry preserves

SYRUP:

- 1/3 cup corn syrup
- 2 tablespoons butter, melted
- 1/2 teaspoon vanilla extract

1) In a large mixing bowl, dissolve yeast in warm water. Add the milk, 1/4 cup sugar, 1/4 cup butter, egg, salt and 3-1/2 cups flour. Beat until smooth. Stir in enough remaining flour to form a soft dough.

2) Turn onto a floured surface; knead until smooth and elastic, about 6-8 minutes. Place in a greased bowl, turning once to grease top. Cover and let rise in a warm place until doubled, about 1-1/4 hours.

3) Punch dough down. Turn onto a lightly floured surface; divide into 32 pieces. Flatten each into a 3-in. disk. Place about 1 teaspoon of preserves on the center of each piece; bring edges together and seal.

4) Place 16 dough balls in a greased 10-in. fluted tube pan. Brush with half of the remaining butter; sprinkle with 1 tablespoon sugar. Top with remaining balls, butter and sugar. Cover and let rise until doubled, about 35 minutes.

5) Bake at 350° for 25-30 minutes or until golden brown. Combine syrup ingredients; pour over warm bread. Cool for 5 minutes before inverting onto a serving plate.

Yield: 1 loaf (16 slices).

NUTRITION FACTS: 1 slice equals 274 calories, 8 g fat (5 g saturated fat), 34 mg cholesterol, 220 mg sodium, 46 g carbohydrate, 1 g fiber, 4 g protein.

Cranberry Kuchen

PREP: 30 min. + rising **BAKE:** 25 min.

Linda Bright, Wichita, Kansas

This German coffee cake has been served at family breakfasts for more than five generations. There is no recipe requested more by our large family.

- 2 packages (1/4 ounce *each*) active dry yeast
- 1/4 cup warm water (110° to 115°)
- 1 cup warm milk (110° to 115°)
- 1/4 cup butter, softened
- 1/4 cup sugar
- 1 teaspoon salt
- 1 egg
- 3-1/2 to 4 cups all-purpose flour

CRANBERRY SAUCE:

- 2 cups water
- 1-1/2 cups sugar
- 4 cups fresh *or* frozen cranberries

EGG MIXTURE:

- 8 eggs
- 3/4 cup evaporated milk
- 3/4 cup sugar

TOPPING:

- 2 cups all-purpose flour
- 2 cups sugar
- 1 cup cold butter

1) In a large mixing bowl, dissolve yeast in a warm water. Add the milk, butter, sugar, salt, egg and 2 cups flour. Beat until smooth.

2) Stir in enough remaining flour to form a soft dough. Do not knead. Cover and let rise in a warm place until doubled, about 1 hour.

3) For cranberry sauce, in a saucepan, bring water and sugar to a boil. Add cranberries. Reduce heat; cover and simmer for 10 minutes. Remove from the heat; set aside.

4) For egg mixture, in a bowl, combine the eggs, evaporated milk and sugar; beat well. Divide half of the egg mixture between two greased 13-in. x 9-in. x 2-in. baking pans; set remaining egg mixture aside.

5) Punch dough down. Divide in half. Pat each portion over egg mixture in pans. Spoon cranberry sauce over dough. Drizzle with remaining egg mixture.

6) For topping, combine flour and sugar in a bowl. Cut in butter until crumbly; sprinkle over the top.

7) Bake at 350° for 25-30 minutes or until lightly browned. Cool on a wire rack. Serve warm.

Yield: 2 kuchens (12 slices each).

NUTRITION FACTS: 1 slice equal 387 calories, 13 g fat (7 g saturated fat), 109 mg cholesterol, 232 mg sodium, 63 g carbohydrate, 2 g fiber, 7 g protein.

Buttery Croissants

PREP: 1 hour + chilling **BAKE:** 15 min./batch

Loraine Meyer, Bend, Oregon

A traditional dinner roll like this is always welcome at holiday dinners. The recipe makes a big batch, so it's great when you're entertaining.

- 1-1/2 cups butter, softened
- 1/3 cup all-purpose flour

DOUGH:
- 1 package (1/4 ounce) active dry yeast
- 1/4 cup warm water (110° to 115°)
- 1 cup warm milk (110° to 115°)
- 1/4 cup sugar
- 1 egg
- 1 teaspoon salt
- 3-1/2 to 3-3/4 cups all-purpose flour

1) In a small mixing bowl, beat butter and flour until combined; spread into a 12-in. x 6-in. rectangle on a piece of waxed paper. Cover with another piece of waxed paper; refrigerate for at least 1 hour.

2) In a large mixing bowl, dissolve yeast in warm water. Add the milk, sugar, egg, salt and 2 cups flour; beat until smooth. Stir in enough remaining flour to form a soft dough. Turn onto a floured surface; knead until smooth and elastic, about 6-8 minutes.

3) Roll dough into a 14-in. square. Remove top sheet of waxed paper from butter; invert onto half of dough. Remove waxed paper. Fold dough over butter; seal edges. Roll into a 20-in. x 12-in. rectangle. Fold into thirds. Repeat rolling and folding twice. (If butter softens, chill after folding.) Wrap in plastic wrap; refrigerate overnight.

4) Unwrap dough. On a lightly floured surface, roll into a 25-in. x 20-in. rectangle. Cut into 5-in. squares. Cut each square diagonally in half, forming two triangles. Roll up triangles from the wide end; place 2 in. apart point side down on ungreased baking sheets. Curve ends to form crescents.

5) Cover and let rise until doubled, about 45 minutes. Bake at 375° for 12-14 minutes or until golden brown. Remove to wire racks. Serve warm.

Yield: about 3 dozen.

NUTRITION FACTS: 1 croissant equals 115 calories, 7 g fat (4 g saturated fat), 25 mg cholesterol, 133 mg sodium, 11 g carbohydrate, trace fiber, 2 g protein.

Overnight Yeast Waffles

PREP: 15 min. + chilling **COOK:** 5 min./batch

Mary Balcomb, Florence, Oregon

These light, crisp waffles are a great way to start the day. Freeze the extras to enjoy on a hurried morning.

- 1 package (1/4 ounce) active dry yeast
- 1/2 cup warm water (110° to 115°)
- 1 teaspoon sugar
- 2 cups warm fat-free milk (110° to 115°)
- 2 eggs, *separated*
- 2 tablespoons butter, melted
- 1 tablespoon canola oil
- 1-3/4 cups all-purpose flour
- 1 teaspoon salt

1) In a large mixing bowl, dissolve yeast in warm water. Add sugar; let stand for 5 minutes. Add the milk, egg yolks, butter and oil (refrigerate egg whites). Combine flour and salt; stir into milk mixture. Cover and refrigerate overnight.

2) Place egg whites in a small mixing bowl; let stand at room temperature for 30 minutes. Beat until stiff peaks form. Stir batter; fold in egg whites.

3) Pour batter by 1/4 cupfuls onto a preheated waffle iron; bake according to manufacturer's directions until golden brown.

Yield: 10 servings.

NUTRITION FACTS: 2 waffles equals 148 calories, 5 g fat (2 g saturated fat), 50 mg cholesterol, 298 mg sodium, 20 g carbohydrate, 1 g fiber, 5 g protein.

OVERNIGHT YEAST WAFFLES

CINNAMON CRISPS

3) Turn onto a floured surface; knead until smooth and elastic, about 6-8 minutes. Place in a greased bowl, turning once to grease top. Cover and let rise in a warm place until doubled, about 1 hour.

4) Meanwhile, combine filling ingredients and set aside. For topping, combine sugar, cinnamon and pecans; set aside. Punch dough down. Turn onto a lightly floured surface; divide in half.

5) Roll each piece into a 12-in. square. Spread each with half of the filling. Roll up tightly jelly-roll style and pinch to seal.

6) Cut into 1-in. slices and place on greased baking sheets (four slices per sheet). Cover with waxed paper; flatten slices with palm of hand into 3-in. circles. Cover and let rise until doubled, about 30 minutes. Cover with waxed paper and flatten or roll to 5-in. diameter.

7) Brush with butter; sprinkle with topping. Cover with waxed paper; roll or flatten again. Discard waxed paper. Bake at 400° for 10-12 minutes or until browned.

Yield: 2 dozen.

NUTRITION FACTS: 1 crisp equals 231 calories, 8 g fat (3 g saturated fat), 21 mg cholesterol, 148 mg sodium, 36 g carbohydrate, 1 g fiber, 3 g protein.

Cinnamon Crisps
PREP: 30 min. + rising **BAKE:** 10 min.

Sarah Bueckert, Austin, Manitoba

Are they a cookie or a bread? Either way, these crispy treats are tasty and delicious. They make a great gift for a housewarming or holiday.

      4 cups all-purpose flour
      1 package (1/4 ounce) active dry yeast
  1-1/4 cups warm milk (120° to 130°)
    1/4 cup shortening
    1/4 cup sugar
      1 teaspoon salt
      1 egg

FILLING:
    1/2 cup packed brown sugar
    1/2 cup sugar
    1/4 cup butter, melted
      1 teaspoon ground cinnamon

TOPPING:
      1 cup sugar
      1 teaspoon ground cinnamon
    1/2 cup chopped pecans
    1/4 cup butter, melted

1) In a large mixing bowl, combine 2 cups flour and yeast. Combine the milk, shortening, sugar and salt; add to flour mixture and beat for 1 minute.

2) Add egg; beat on low speed for 1 minute. Beat on medium for 3 minutes. Stir in enough remaining flour to form a soft dough.

Glazed Doughnuts
PREP: 25 min. + rising **COOK:** 5 min./batch

Pat Siebenaler, Random Lake, Wisconsin

The coffee-flavored glaze on these moist and tasty doughnuts makes them a perfect way to start off a morning. They're also good with a cinnamon-sugar topping.

      2 packages (1/4 ounce *each*) active dry yeast
    1/4 cup warm water (110° to 115°)
      2 cups warm milk (110° to 115°)
    1/2 cup butter
      1 cup hot mashed potatoes (without added milk and butter)
      3 eggs
    1/2 teaspoon lemon extract, optional
      1 cup sugar
  1-1/2 teaspoons salt
    1/2 teaspoon ground cinnamon
  9-1/4 to 9-3/4 cups all-purpose flour

COFFEE GLAZE:
      6 to 8 tablespoons cold milk
      1 tablespoon instant coffee granules
      2 teaspoons vanilla extract
    3/4 cup butter, softened
      6 cups confectioners' sugar
    1/2 teaspoon ground cinnamon
Dash salt
Oil for deep-fat frying

1) In a large mixing bowl, dissolve yeast in warm water. Add the milk, butter, potatoes, eggs and extract if desired. Add the sugar, salt, cinnamon and 3 cups flour. Beat until smooth.

2) Stir in enough remaining flour to form a soft dough. Cover and let rise in a warm place until doubled, about 1 hour.

3) Stir down dough. On a well-floured surface, roll out to 1/2-in. thickness. Cut with a floured 2-1/2-in. doughnut cutter. Place on greased baking sheets; cover and let rise for 45 minutes.

4) Meanwhile, for glaze, combine 6 tablespoons milk, coffee and vanilla; stir to dissolve coffee. In a mixing bowl, beat the butter, sugar, cinnamon and salt. Gradually add milk mixture; beat until smooth, adding additional milk to make a dipping consistency.

5) In an electric skillet or deep-fat fryer, heat oil to 375°. Fry doughnuts, a few at a time, about 1-1/2 minutes per side or until golden. Drain on paper towels. Dip tops in glaze while warm.

Yield: about 4 dozen.

NUTRITION FACTS: 1 doughnut equals 231 calories, 7 g fat (3 g saturated fat), 28 mg cholesterol, 137 mg sodium, 39 g carbohydrate, 1 g fiber, 4 g protein.

■ **Cinnamon-Sugar Doughnuts:** Prepare recipe as directed except omit the glaze. Gently roll the warm doughnuts in a mixture of 2 cups sugar and 1 teaspoon ground cinnamon.

GLAZED DOUGHNUTS

Chocolate Pinwheel Bread

PREP: 30 min. + rising **BAKE:** 40 min. + cooling

Dawn Onuffer, Freeport, Florida

This swirled yeast bread is chock-full of chocolate chips. The sweet slices don't need any butter. Keep one loaf for your family and share the other with a neighbor.

- 1 package (1/4 ounce) active dry yeast
- 1 cup warm milk (110° to 115°)
- 1/4 cup sugar
- 1 teaspoon salt
- 2 eggs
- 4 ounces cream cheese, softened
- 4 to 4-1/2 cups bread flour

FILLING:

- 4 ounces cream cheese, softened
- 1/2 cup confectioners' sugar
- 2 tablespoons baking cocoa
- 1 cup (6 ounces) semisweet chocolate chips
- 1 egg, beaten

1) In a large mixing bowl, dissolve yeast in warm milk. Add the sugar, salt, eggs, cream cheese and 2 cups flour; beat until smooth. Stir in enough remaining flour to form a soft dough.

2) Turn onto a floured surface; knead until smooth and elastic, about 6-8 minutes. Place in a greased bowl, turning once to grease top. Cover and let rise in a warm place until doubled, about 1 hour.

3) Punch dough down. Turn onto a floured surface; divide in half. Roll each portion into a 12-in. x 8-in. rectangle. In a small mixing bowl, beat cream cheese, confectioners' sugar and cocoa until smooth. Spread over each rectangle to within 1/2 in. of edges. Sprinkle with chocolate chips.

4) Roll up jelly-roll style, starting with a short side; pinch seam to seal. Place seam side down in two greased 9-in. x 5-in. x 3-in. loaf pans. Cover and let rise until doubled, about 45 minutes.

5) Brush tops of loaves with egg. Bake at 350° for 25 minutes. Cover loosely with foil. Bake 15-20 minutes longer or until loaves sound hollow when tapped. Remove from pans to wire racks to cool.

Yield: 2 loaves (16 slices each).

NUTRITION FACTS: 1 slice equals 127 calories, 5 g fat (3 g saturated fat), 29 mg cholesterol, 105 mg sodium, 19 g carbohydrate, 1 g fiber, 4 g protein.

Storing Coffee Cakes and Sweet Rolls

Cool coffee cakes and sweet rolls completely. Place in an airtight container or plastic bag; keep at room temperature for 2 to 3 days. Breads containing perishable items should be refrigerated.

For longer storage, unfrosted sweet breads can be frozen for up to 3 months. Thaw at room temperature, then frost or glaze as desired.

SCRUMPTIOUS BREAKFAST ROLLS

CLASSIC: For an over-the-top morning treat, you can't go wrong with Caramel-Pecan Sticky Buns. Sugar and cinnamon are rolled up in sweet yeast dough, which is sliced to form spirals. The rolls bake to ooey-gooey goodness in a rich caramel topping made with brown sugar, whipping cream and plenty of pecans.

TIME-SAVER: A loaf of frozen bread dough and five additional ingredients make it a snap to prepare Orange Marmalade Sweet Rolls. Marmalade rolled inside and a simple orange glaze on top add lively citrus flavor to these raisin-studded sweet rolls that are not only quick, but light, too.

LIGHT: With a name like Best-Ever Cinnamon Rolls, you wouldn't expect these treats to be healthier. But thanks to fat-free milk, whole wheat flour and a lighter powdered sugar glaze, these rolls have less than half the calories, about a quarter of the fat and cholesterol, and a third of the carbohydrates of Caramel-Pecan Sticky Buns.

SERVES 2: Don't want to be tempted by a big pan of enticing sweet rolls? Then you'll appreciate this small batch of Chocolate Chip Cinnamon Rolls. It makes six breakfast rolls, so the two of you can satisfy your sweet tooth and freeze a few to enjoy later.

Caramel-Pecan Sticky Buns

PREP: 30 min. + rising **BAKE:** 30 min.

Judy Powell, Star, Idaho

- 1 package (1/4 ounce) active dry yeast
- 3/4 cup warm water (110° to 115°)
- 3/4 cup warm milk (110° to 115°)
- 1/4 cup sugar
- 3 tablespoons vegetable oil
- 2 teaspoons salt
- 3-3/4 to 4-1/4 cups all-purpose flour

FILLING:

- 1/4 cup butter, softened
- 1/4 cup sugar
- 3 teaspoons ground cinnamon
- 3/4 cup packed brown sugar
- 1/2 cup heavy whipping cream
- 1 cup coarsely chopped pecans

1) In a large mixing bowl, dissolve yeast in warm water. Add the milk, sugar, oil, salt and 1-1/4 cups flour. Beat on medium speed for 2-3 minutes or until smooth. Stir in enough remaining flour to form a soft dough.

2) Turn onto a floured surface; knead until smooth and elastic, about 6-8 minutes. Place in a greased bowl, turning once to grease top. Cover and let rise in a warm place until doubled, about 1 hour.

3) Punch dough down. Turn onto a lightly floured surface. Roll into an 18-in. x 12-in. rectangle. Spread butter to within 1/2 in. of edges. Combine sugar and cinnamon; sprinkle over butter. Roll up jelly-roll style, starting with a long side; pinch seam to seal. Cut into 12 slices.

4) Combine brown sugar and cream; pour into a greased 13-in. x 9-in. x 2-in. baking pan. Sprinkle

with pecans. Place rolls cut side down over pecans. Cover; let rise until doubled, about 1 hour.

5) Bake at 350° for 30-35 minutes or until well browned. Cool for 1 minute before inverting onto a serving platter.

Yield: 1 dozen.

NUTRITION FACTS: 1 bun equals 405 calories, 19 g fat (6 g saturated fat), 26 mg cholesterol, 450 mg sodium, 55 g carbohydrate, 2 g fiber, 6 g protein.

Orange Marmalade Sweet Rolls

PREP: 15 min. + rising **BAKE:** 15 min.

Lacey Griffin, Fredonia, Pennsylvania

- 1 loaf (1 pound) frozen bread dough, thawed
- 1/3 cup 100% orange marmalade spreadable fruit
- 2 tablespoons raisins
- 1/3 cup confectioners' sugar
- 1/2 teaspoon grated orange peel
- 2 teaspoons orange juice

1) On a floured surface, roll dough into a 12-in. x 8-in. rectangle; brush with spreadable fruit. Sprinkle with raisins. Roll up jelly-roll style, starting with a long side; pinch seam to seal.

2) Cut into 12 slices. Place cut side down in muffin cups coated with cooking spray. Cover and let rise until doubled, about 45 minutes.

3) Bake at 350° for 15-20 minutes or until golden brown. Immediately invert onto serving plates. Combine the confectioners' sugar, orange peel and orange juice; drizzle over warm rolls.

Yield: 12 servings.

NUTRITION FACTS: 1 roll equals 140 calories, 2 g fat (trace saturated fat), 0 cholesterol, 211 mg sodium, 28 g carbohydrate, 1 g fiber, 4 g protein.

Best-Ever Cinnamon Rolls

PREP: 35 min. + rising **BAKE:** 25 min.

Traci Rose, Eugene, Oregon

- 1 package (1/4 ounce) active dry yeast
- 1 cup warm fat-free milk (110° to 115°)
- 2 egg whites
- 1/3 cup sugar
- 3 tablespoons vegetable oil
- 1/2 teaspoon salt
- 2-1/2 to 2-3/4 cups all-purpose flour
- 1 cup whole wheat flour
- 1/4 cup butter, softened
- 1/3 cup packed brown sugar
- 1 teaspoon ground cinnamon
- 1 cup confectioners' sugar
- 4 to 5 teaspoons orange juice

1) In a large mixing bowl, dissolve yeast in warm milk. Add the egg whites, sugar, oil, salt, 1 cup all-purpose flour and whole wheat flour; beat until smooth. Stir in enough remaining all-purpose flour to form a firm dough.

2) Turn onto a lightly floured surface; knead until smooth and elastic, about 6-8 minutes. Place in a bowl coated with cooking spray, turning once to coat top. Cover and let rise in a warm place until doubled, about 1 hour.

3) Punch dough down. Turn onto a lightly floured surface; divide in half. Roll each portion into a 12-in. x 9-in. rectangle; spread with butter. Combine brown sugar and cinnamon; sprinkle over dough to within 1/2 in. of edges. Roll up jelly-roll style, starting with a long side; pinch seams to seal.

4) Cut each portion into nine slices; place cut side down in two 9-in. round baking pans coated with cooking spray. Cover and let rise until doubled, about 40 minutes.

5) Bake at 350° for 25-30 minutes or until golden brown. Combine confectioners' sugar and orange juice; drizzle over rolls. Serve warm.

Yield: 1-1/2 dozen.

NUTRITION FACTS: 1 roll equals 193 calories, 5 g fat (2 g saturated fat), 7 mg cholesterol, 107 mg sodium, 33 g carbohydrate, 1 g fiber, 4 g protein.

Chocolate Chip Cinnamon Rolls

PREP: 20 min. + chilling **BAKE:** 15 min.

Cindy Padgett, Galvin, Washington

- 3/4 teaspoon active dry yeast
- 1 tablespoon warm water (110° to 115°)
- 1 cup plus 2 tablespoons all-purpose flour
- 2 tablespoons sugar, *divided*
- 1/4 teaspoon salt

CHOCOLATE CHIP CINNAMON ROLLS

- 3 tablespoons cold butter, *divided*
- 1/4 cup warm milk (110° to 115°)
- 1 egg yolk
- 2 tablespoons brown sugar
- 1/4 teaspoon ground cinnamon
- 1/3 cup miniature semisweet chocolate chips

GLAZE:

- 1/3 cup confectioners' sugar
- 1-1/2 teaspoons butter, softened
- 1/4 teaspoon vanilla extract
- 1-1/2 to 2 teaspoons hot water

1) In a small bowl, dissolve yeast in warm water. In a large bowl, combine the flour, 1 tablespoon sugar and salt. Cut in 2 tablespoons butter until crumbly. Add the milk, egg yolk and yeast mixture; stir well. Cover with plastic wrap; refrigerate for at least 4 hours or overnight.

2) Turn dough onto a lightly floured surface. Roll into a 10-in. x 6-in. rectangle. Melt remaining butter; brush over dough to within 1/2 in. of edges. Combine the brown sugar, cinnamon and remaining sugar; sprinkle over dough. Sprinkle with chocolate chips.

3) Roll up jelly-roll style, starting with a short side; pinch seam to seal. Cut into 1-in. slices; place cut side down in a greased 8-in. square baking dish. Cover and let rise in a warm place until doubled, about 1-1/2 hours.

4) Bake at 375° for 15-18 minutes or until golden brown. In a small bowl, combine confectioners' sugar, butter, vanilla and enough water to achieve drizzling consistency; drizzle over rolls. Serve warm.

Yield: 6 rolls.

Editor's Note: Baked rolls may be frozen for up to 2 months. Reheat in the microwave before serving if desired.

NUTRITION FACTS: 1 roll equals 267 calories, 11 g fat (6 g saturated fat), 55 mg cholesterol, 176 mg sodium, 40 g carbohydrate, 1 g fiber, 4 g protein.

Danish Kringle

PREP: 30 min. + rising **BAKE:** 20 min. + cooling

Jeanne Hardaker, Harrisonburg, Virginia

Everyone agrees that no store-bought kringle can top my version. The nut filling and sweet glaze give this spectacular coffee cake great flavor.

- 2 cups all-purpose flour
- 1 tablespoon sugar
- 1/2 teaspoon salt
- 1/2 cup cold butter
- 1 package (1/4 ounce) active dry yeast
- 1/4 cup warm water (110° to 115°)
- 1/2 cup warm milk (110° to 115°)
- 1 egg, beaten

FILLING:
- 1-1/2 cups finely chopped pecans
- 1 cup packed brown sugar
- 1/2 cup butter, softened

GLAZE:
- 1 cup confectioners' sugar
- 4 teaspoons water
- 1/2 teaspoon vanilla extract
- 2 tablespoons chopped pecans

1) In a large mixing bowl, combine the flour, sugar and salt; cut in butter until mixture resembles fine crumbs. Dissolve yeast in warm water; stir into flour mixture with warm milk and egg. Beat until smooth (dough will be very soft). Cover; refrigerate at least 2 hours but not more than 24 hours.

DANISH KRINGLE

2) Punch dough down. Divide dough in half; refrigerate one half. On a well-floured surface, roll remaining half into a 15-in. x 6-in. rectangle.

3) Combine filling ingredients. Spread half of the filling down center of rectangle in a 2-in. strip. Fold sides of dough over filling; overlapping 1-1/2-in.; pinch edges to seal. Shape into an oval; pinch ends together.

4) Place seam side down on a greased 15-in. x 10-in. x 1-in. baking pan. Repeat with remaining dough and filling. Cover and let rise in a warm place for 30 minutes.

5) Bake at 375° for 20-25 minutes or until golden brown. Cool for 15 minutes. Combine the confectioners' sugar, water and vanilla; spread over the kringles. Sprinkle with nuts.

Yield: 2 kringles (10 slices each).

NUTRITION FACTS: 1 slice equals 268 calories, 17 g fat (6 g saturated fat), 36 mg cholesterol, 162 mg sodium, 29 g carbohydrate, 1 g fiber, 3 g protein.

Nut-Filled Butterhorns

PREP: 1 hour + chilling
BAKE: 20 min./batch + cooling

Michael Engerson, Hustisford, Wisconsin

These rich, flaky butterhorns were made on Good Friday morning or Christmas Eve morning when I was growing up. We used them to celebrate the joy of family and friends coming together. They're so special and are worth the bit of extra effort.

- 3 packages (1/4 ounce *each*) active dry yeast
- 1/4 cup warm milk (110° to 115°)
- 2 tablespoons sugar
- 2 cups butter, softened
- 1 package (8 ounces) cream cheese, softened
- 1 cup heavy whipping cream
- 1 cup (8 ounces) sour cream
- 7 egg yolks
- 1/8 teaspoon salt
- 8 to 8-1/2 cups all-purpose flour

FILLING:
- 6 egg whites
- 1 teaspoon cream of tartar
- 1 cup sugar, *divided*
- 3 cups ground walnuts *or* pecans
- 2 teaspoons ground cinnamon, optional

ICING:
- 3 cups confectioners' sugar
- 2 tablespoons butter, softened
- 1/2 teaspoon almond *or* vanilla extract, optional
- 5 to 7 tablespoons milk

NUT-FILLED BUTTERHORNS

1) In a large mixing bowl, dissolve yeast in warm milk. Add sugar; let stand for 5 minutes. Add the butter, cream cheese, cream, sour cream, egg yolks, salt and 2-1/2 cups flour. Beat until smooth. Stir in enough remaining flour to form a soft dough.

2) Turn onto a floured surface; knead until smooth and elastic, about 6-8 minutes. Place in a greased bowl, turning once to grease top. Cover and refrigerate overnight.

3) In a mixing bowl, beat egg whites and cream of tartar on medium speed until soft peaks form. Gradually add 2 tablespoons sugar, beating until glossy stiff peaks form. Fold in nuts.

4) Turn dough onto a lightly floured surface; divide into fourths. Roll each portion into a 12-in. circle; spread a fourth of the filling over each circle. Add cinnamon if desired to remaining sugar; sprinkle over filling.

5) Cut each into 12 wedges. Roll up wedges from the wide end; place point side down 3 in. apart on greased baking sheets. Curve ends to form a crescent shape. Bake at 350° for 17-20 minutes or until golden brown. Remove from pans to wire racks to cool.

6) For the icing, in a large bowl, combine the confectioners' sugar, butter, extract if desired and enough milk to achieve drizzling consistency. Drizzle over rolls.

Yield: 4 dozen.

NUTRITION FACTS: 1 roll equals 285 calories, 17 g fat (8 g saturated fat), 68 mg cholesterol, 117 mg sodium, 30 g carbohydrate, 1 g fiber, 5 g protein.

Hot Cross Buns

PREP: 40 min. + rising **BAKE:** 15 min. + cooling

Lorri Bailey, Pulaski, Iowa

These golden buns, with a light seasoning from cinnamon and allspice, were a family Easter tradition. My mom made them only once a year using her mother's recipe.

- 2 packages (1/4 ounce *each*) active dry yeast
- 1/4 cup warm water (110° to 115°)
- 1 cup warm milk (110° to 115°)
- 1/2 cup sugar
- 1/4 cup shortening
- 2 eggs
- 2 teaspoons salt
- 1 teaspoon ground cinnamon
- 1/4 teaspoon ground allspice
- 4-1/2 to 5 cups all-purpose flour
- 1 cup dried currants
- 1 egg white, lightly beaten

ICING:

- 1-3/4 cups confectioners' sugar
- 1/2 teaspoon vanilla extract
- 4 to 6 teaspoons milk

1) In a large mixing bowl, dissolve yeast in warm water. Add the milk, sugar, shortening, eggs, salt, cinnamon, allspice and 3 cups flour. Beat until smooth. Stir in currants and enough remaining flour to form a soft dough.

2) Turn onto a floured surface; knead until smooth and elastic, about 6-8 minutes. Place in a greased bowl, turning once to grease top. Cover and let rise in a warm place until doubled, about 1 hour.

3) Punch dough down. Cover and let rest for 10 minutes. On a lightly floured surface, roll out to 1/2-in. thickness. Cut with a floured 2-1/2-in. biscuit cutter. Place 2 in. apart on lightly greased baking sheets. Cover and let rise until doubled, about 30 minutes.

4) Brush with egg white. Bake at 350° for 12-15 minutes or until golden brown. Remove from pans to wire racks to cool.

5) For icing, combine the confectioners' sugar, vanilla and enough milk to achieve piping consistency. Pipe a cross on top of each bun.

Yield: 2 dozen.

NUTRITION FACTS: 1 bun equals 187 calories, 3 g fat (1 g saturated fat), 19 mg cholesterol, 211 mg sodium, 36 g carbohydrate, 1 g fiber, 4 g protein.

SWEET DOUGH ■■■

I used to work in the kitchen of a school cafeteria, and my supervisor taught me to add just a little vanilla to sweet roll dough. It adds a subtle flavor boost to plain yeast rolls or breads.

—Vaunda Box, American Fork, Utah

Mashed Potato Kolachkes

PREP: 45 min. + rising **BAKE:** 10 min.

Jan Wagner-Cuda, Deer Park, Washington

My husband's Bohemian mother brought a kolachke recipe with her when she came to America. So these rolls are a part of our family's heritage. Other traditional fillings are prune, poppy seed and cottage cheese.

> 1 medium potato, peeled and cubed
> 1-1/4 teaspoons active dry yeast
> 2 tablespoons warm water (110° to 115°)
> 3/4 cup sugar
> 1/2 cup warm milk (110° to 115°)
> 1/4 cup shortening
> 6 tablespoons butter, softened, *divided*
> 1 egg, lightly beaten
> 3/4 teaspoon salt
> 3 to 4 cups all-purpose flour
> 1/3 cup apricot filling
> 1/3 cup raspberry filling
> 2/3 cup confectioners' sugar
> 4 teaspoons milk

1) Place potato in a saucepan and cover with water. Bring to a boil. Reduce heat; cover and cook for 15-20 minutes or until tender. Drain, reserving 1/2 cup cooking liquid. Mash potato; set aside 1/2 cup (discard remaining potato or save for another use).

2) In a large mixing bowl, dissolve yeast in warm water. Add sugar, milk, shortening, 4 tablespoons butter, egg, salt, reserved cooking liquid and mashed potato. Beat in 2 cups flour until smooth. Stir in enough of the remaining flour to form a soft dough.

3) Turn onto a floured surface; knead until smooth and elastic, about 6-8 minutes. Place in a greased bowl, turning once to grease top. Cover and let rise in a warm place until doubled, about 45 minutes.

4) Turn onto a well-floured surface. Shape into 1-1/2-in. balls; place 2 in. apart on greased baking sheets. Flatten to 1/2-in. thickness. Cover and let rise for 15 minutes or until almost doubled. Melt the remaining butter.

5) Using the end of a wooden spoon handle, make an indentation in the center of each ball; brush with butter and fill with a rounded teaspoon of filling. Bake at 400° for 10-15 minutes or until lightly browned. Remove from pans to wire racks. Combine confectioners' sugar and milk; drizzle over rolls.

Yield: about 2 dozen.

Editor's Note: This recipe was tested with Solo apricot and raspberry fillings.

NUTRITION FACTS: 1 kolachke equals 161 calories, 5 g fat (2 g saturated fat), 17 mg cholesterol, 110 mg sodium, 26 g carbohydrate, 1 g fiber, 2 g protein.

Using Bread Machines

Before beginning, carefully read your bread machine owner's manual.

All liquid ingredients should be at room temperature (70° to 80°). This includes water, milk, yogurt, juice, cottage cheese, eggs and applesauce.

Measure ingredients accurately before adding to your machine. Then add in the order suggested by your bread machine manufacturer.

For best results, use bread flour. While either active dry yeast or bread machine yeast can be used in bread machines, bread machine yeast is a little finer, which allows for better dispersion during mixing and kneading. For 1 cup flour, it is generally recommended to use 3/4 teaspoon active dry yeast or 1/2 teaspoon bread machine yeast.

Check dough after 5 minutes of mixing. The dough should feel smooth, soft and slightly tacky. If it's moist or sticky, add 1 tablespoon flour and check again after a few more minutes of mixing. If it's dry and crumbly, add 1 tablespoon liquid, then check again.

Recipes containing eggs, milk, sour cream, cottage cheese and other dairy or perishable products should be baked immediately and not placed on a "timed-bake" cycle.

Converting Recipes for Bread Machines

Converting a traditional yeast bread recipe for the bread machine will require some experimentation. First, determine the size of your bread machine. Look at the recipes that came with your bread machine and note the amount of flour and liquid called for in most of those recipes.

Flour includes dry ingredients such as any type of flour, oats, cereal and cornmeal. Liquid includes milk, water, yogurt, sour cream, applesauce, eggs (1/4 cup liquid per egg), cottage cheese, etc. Sugar also includes sweeteners such as honey, molasses or brown sugar. Fat includes shortening, butter, margarine and oil.

It's best to start with a bread recipe you are familiar with and have successfully made. Once you master those familiar recipes, look for other bread recipes that use the amount of flour your bread machine needs. Or look for a recipe that makes two loaves and can be easily divided in half. Avoid recipes for sourdough, those that require refrigerating the dough or those that have a high ratio of fat. These types of recipes won't be successful in the bread machine.

For breads with toppings or fillings as well as ones that require special shapes or rolls—just mix, knead and proof the dough in the bread machine. Punch the dough down, fill and/or shape. Then follow the original recipe to finish the bread.

Make notes on your recipe for reference. If it wasn't quite right, make an adjustment in one ingredient and try again.

The chart below is a guideline for the ratio of ingredients for bread machines yielding 1-pound, 1-1/2-pound and 2-pound loaves.

Ingredient Guidelines for Bread Machines

BREAD MACHINE SIZE:	1 pound	1-1/2 pounds	2 pounds
FLOUR:	2 to 2-1/2 cups	3 to 3-1/2 cups	4 to 4-1/2 cups
LIQUID:	2/3 cup	1 cup	1-1/3 cups
ACTIVE DRY YEAST:	1-1/2 teaspoons	2-1/2 teaspoons	3 teaspoons
SUGAR:	2 tablespoons	3 tablespoons	4 tablespoons
SALT:	1 teaspoon	1-1/2 teaspoons	2 teaspoons
FAT:	4 teaspoons	6 teaspoons	8 teaspoons

Home-Style White Bread

PREP: 5 min. **BAKE:** 3 hours + cooling

Yvonne Nave, Lyons, Kansas

Serve this basic white bread with butter and jam, or slice and assemble your favorite sandwiches.

  1 cup water (70° to 80°)
  2 tablespoons butter, softened
  1 teaspoon salt
  2 tablespoons sugar
  2 tablespoons nonfat dry milk powder
  3 cups bread flour
  2 teaspoons active dry yeast

1) In bread machine pan, place all ingredients in order suggested by manufacturer. Select basic bread setting. Choose crust color and loaf size if available. Bake according to bread machine directions (check dough after 5 minutes of mixing; add 1 to 2 tablespoons water or flour if needed).

Yield: 1 loaf (about 1-1/2 pounds, 16 slices).

NUTRITION FACTS: 1 slice equals 98 calories, 1 g fat (1 g saturated fat), 4 mg cholesterol, 167 mg sodium, 19 g carbohydrate, 1 g fiber, 4 g protein.

Honey Wheat Breadsticks

PREP: 30 min. + rising **BAKE:** 10 min.

Ted Van Schoick, Jersey Shore, Pennsylvania

Whole wheat flour and a little honey help give these breadsticks a wholesome taste and keep them on the healthy side.

1-1/3 cups water (70° to 80°)
   3 tablespoons honey
   2 tablespoons vegetable oil
1-1/2 teaspoons salt
   2 cups bread flour
   2 cups whole wheat flour
   3 teaspoons active dry yeast

1) In bread machine pan, place all ingredients in order suggested by manufacturer. Select dough setting (check dough after 5 minutes of mixing; add 1 to 2 tablespoons of water or flour if needed).

2) When cycle is completed, turn dough onto a lightly floured surface. Divide into 16 portions; shape each into a ball. Roll each into an 8-in. rope. Place 2 in. apart on greased baking sheets.

3) Cover and let rise in a warm place until doubled, 30 minutes. Bake at 375° for 10-12 minutes or until golden brown. Remove from pans to wire racks.

Yield: 16 breadsticks.

NUTRITION FACTS: 1 breadstick equals 131 calories, 2 g fat (trace saturated fat), 0 cholesterol, 222 mg sodium, 25 g carbohydrate, 2 g fiber, 4 g protein.

HONEY WHEAT BREADSTICKS

Dough Cycles

Yeast breads that are shaped, such as cinnamon rolls or breadsticks, are removed from the bread machine after the first rise. The dough is then shaped and allowed to rise one last time before baking. Most bread machines have a dough setting that will stop or beep at the end of the cycle, signaling that the first rise is completed and the dough is ready to be removed. If your bread machine does not have this option, you will need to keep a close eye on it and remove the dough after the first rise or refer to your owner's manual to determine when the first rise ends.

Herbed Onion Bread

PREP: 5 min. **BAKE:** 3 hours + cooling

Sue Call, Beech Grove, Indiana

I enjoy the convenience of my bread machine and use it often. This is one of my best recipes.

- 1 cup plus 1 tablespoon water (70° to 80°)
- 2 tablespoons butter, softened
- 1-1/4 teaspoons salt
- 3 cups bread flour
- 2 teaspoons dried minced onion
- 1-1/2 teaspoons dill weed
- 1 teaspoon poppy seeds
- 2 tablespoons nonfat dry milk powder
- 2 tablespoons sugar
- 1-1/2 teaspoons active dry yeast

1) In bread machine pan, place all ingredients in order suggest by manufacturer. Select basic bread setting. Choose crust color and loaf size if available. Bake according to bread machine directions (check dough after 5 minutes of mixing; add 1 to 2 tablespoons water or flour if needed).

Yield: 1 loaf (1-1/2 pounds, 16 slices).

NUTRITION FACTS: 1 slice equals 100 calories, 2 g fat (1 g saturated fat), 4 mg cholesterol, 204 mg sodium, 19 g carbohydrate, 1 g fiber, 4 g protein.

Rosemary Potato Rolls

PREP: 15 min. + rising **BAKE:** 15 min.

Mary Dixson, Decatur, Alabama

You can choose sesame seeds or poppy seeds to sprinkle over these golden rolls.

- 1 cup plus 2 tablespoons water (70° to 80°)
- 2 tablespoons olive oil
- 1/2 cup mashed potato flakes
- 2 tablespoons nonfat dry milk powder
- 1 tablespoon sugar
- 1 teaspoon dried rosemary, crushed
- 1 to 1-1/2 teaspoons salt
- 3 cups bread flour
- 2-1/4 teaspoons active dry yeast
- 1 egg, lightly beaten

Sesame seeds *or* poppy seeds

1) In bread machine pan, place first nine ingredients in order suggested by manufacturer. Select dough setting (check dough after 5 minutes of mixing; add 1 to 2 tablespoons of water or flour if needed).

2) When cycle is completed, turn dough onto a lightly floured surface. Punch down and let stand for 10 minutes.

3) Divide dough into 12 portions. Shape each into a 10-in. rope. Holding one end of rope, loosely form into a coil. Tuck end under; pinch to seal. Place 2 in. apart on a greased baking sheet. Cover and let rise in a warm place until doubled, about 30 minutes.

4) Brush tops with egg. Sprinkle with sesame or poppy seeds. Bake at 375° for 13-16 minutes or until golden. Remove from pan to a wire rack.

Yield: 1 dozen.

NUTRITION FACTS: 1 roll (calculated without sesame seeds or poppy seeds) equals 147 calories, 3 g fat (trace saturated fat), 18 mg cholesterol, 215 mg sodium, 26 g carbohydrate, 1 g fiber, 6 g protein.

Maple Oatmeal Bread

PREP: 10 min. **BAKE:** 3 hours + cooling

Kathy Morin, Haverhill, Massachusetts

Maple syrup gives this bread its delicate flavor. Slices taste terrific when toasted.

- 3/4 cup plus 2 tablespoons water (70° to 80°)
- 1/3 cup maple syrup
- 1 tablespoon vegetable oil
- 1 teaspoon salt
- 3/4 cup quick-cooking oats
- 2-1/2 cups bread flour
- 2-1/4 teaspoons active dry yeast

1) In bread machine pan, place all ingredients in order suggested by manufacturer. Select basic bread setting. Choose crust color and loaf size if available.

2) Bake according to bread machine directions (check dough after 5 minutes of mixing; add 1 to 2 tablespoons of water or flour if needed).

Yield: 1 loaf (1-1/2 pounds, 16 slices).

NUTRITION FACTS: 1 slice equals 104 calories, 1 g fat (trace saturated fat), 0 cholesterol, 148 mg sodium, 21 g carbohydrate, 1 g fiber, 3 g protein.

MAPLE OATMEAL BREAD

pies & tarts

'net worth' in mosquito country

12-year-old's efforts stretch from Iowa to Africa

Miranda Walters

A video shown at church inspired Miranda Walters to make a difference halfway around the globe.

She saw the faces of children dying from malaria thousands of miles from her Cedar Falls, Iowa, home and knew she couldn't ignore them.

A $10 mosquito net dramatically reduces the risk African children face of contracting malaria, an often-fatal infectious disease transmitted through mosquito bites. So Miranda, 12, gave herself a goal: Raise $100, enough to buy 10 nets for the nonprofit organization Nothing But Nets.

"After seeing the video, I told my grandma I wanted to do something to help them," Miranda says. "She suggested a bake sale. So we talked to people at church, made posters and baked some things."

She and her grandmother, Jill Rechkemmer, also of Cedar Falls, made Caramel-Pecan Cheesecake Pie and Caramel-Pecan Apple Pie, both from *Taste of Home*. They also invited others from the congregation to help with the baking.

"At first I worried we wouldn't get enough baked goods," says grandma Jill. "But there were so many!"

The bake sale raised $640, enough to buy 64 nets.

Miranda encourages other kids to think about raising money for a cause.

"It's possible no matter how busy you are," she says. "It feels good to do something to make a difference."

Recipes

Tips

Pies & Tarts

While pies conjure up a homey image and tarts feel a little more elegant, they both have a sweetened filling. The main difference is that tarts are more shallow than pies (typically about 1 in. high). Tarts can be full-size, individual or bite-size.

Pie Pastry

Classic pie pastry recipes are prepared with solid shortening. Lard or butter-flavored shortening can be substituted for plain shortening if desired.

Measure all ingredients accurately. Combine flour and salt thoroughly before adding the shortening and water. Be sure to use ice-cold water. Add an ice cube to water and measure before adding to the flour mixture.

To produce a flaky crust, avoid overmixing when adding the water to the flour and shortening mixture. Overmixing develops the gluten in the flour, causing the pastry to become tough.

A floured surface is essential to prevent sticking when rolling out pastry. A pastry cloth and rolling pin cover are good investments—they keep the pastry from sticking and minimize the amount of flour used. The less flour you add while rolling, the flakier and lighter the pastry will be.

Chill pie pastry dough for 30 minutes before rolling to make it easier to handle.

Choose dull-finish aluminum or glass pie plates for crisp, golden crusts. Shiny pans can produce soggy crusts. Because of the high fat content in a pastry, do not grease the pie plate unless the recipe directs.

Never prick the bottom of a pastry crust when the filling and crust are to be baked together.

Arrange the oven racks so that the pie will bake in the center of the oven. Preheat the oven for 10-15 minutes before baking.

Finishing Touches for Pie Crusts

To top off double-crust pies before baking, use a pastry brush to lightly and evenly apply one of the following washes to the top crust, avoiding the edges.

- For a shine and a light browning, brush with an egg white that was lightly beaten with 1 teaspoon of water.

- For a glossy golden appearance, brush with an egg yolk that was beaten with 1 teaspoon of water.

- For a slight shine, brush with half-and-half cream or heavy whipping cream.

- For a crisp, brown crust, brush with water.

- For a little sparkle, sprinkle with sugar or decorator sugar after brushing with one of the washes.

To give a little more shine to a baked double-crust pie, warm 1 tablespoon of light corn syrup. Gently brush over the warm baked crust.

Making and Shaping Single- and Double-Crust Pie Pastry

1) Combine flour and salt in a bowl. With a pastry blender or two knives, cut in shortening until the mixture resembles coarse crumbs (the size of small peas).

2) Sprinkle 1 tablespoon of cold water over the mixture and toss gently with a fork. Repeat until dry ingredients are moist and mixture forms a ball. Use only as much water as necessary.

3) Shape into a ball. (For a double-crust pie, divide pastry in half so that one ball is slightly larger than the other.) On a floured surface or floured pastry cloth, flatten the ball (the larger one, if making a double-crust pie) into a circle, pressing together any cracks or breaks.

4) Roll with a floured rolling pin from the center of the pastry to the edges, forming a circle 2 in. larger than the pie plate. The pastry should be about 1/8 in. thick.

5) To move pastry to the pie plate, roll up onto the rolling pin. Position over the edge of pie plate and unroll. Let the pastry ease into the plate. Do not stretch the pastry to fit. For a single-crust pie, trim pastry with a scissors to 1/2 in. beyond the plate edge; turn under and flute as in step 8. Either bake the shell or fill according to recipe directions. For a double-crust pie, trim pastry even with the edge of the plate. For a lattice-crust pie, trim pastry to 1 in. beyond the plate edge.

6) For a double-crust pie, roll out second ball into a 12-in. circle about 1/8 in. thick. Roll up pastry onto rolling pin; position over filling. With a knife, cut slits in top to allow steam to escape while baking.

7) With scissors, trim top pastry to 1 in. beyond plate edge. Fold top pastry over bottom pastry.

8) To flute the edge, position your thumb on the inside of the crust. Place the thumb and index finger of your other hand on the outside edge and pinch pastry around the thumb to form a V-shape and seal dough together. Continue around the edge.

FREEZING PIE CRUST DOUGH ■■■

I like to bake pies for the potluck suppers I attend. To save time, I make the dough for several pie crusts at once, then store it in the freezer. I found that if I form the pastry dough into balls, I save more freezer space than by storing it in separate pie tins. I freeze a 9-ounce ball of dough for a 10-inch pie and a 7-ounce ball for a 9-inch pie. For a top crust, a 5-ounce ball of dough works fine. The dough thaws overnight in the refrigerator.

—*Laurene Rice, Kennedy, New York*

Classic Pie Pastry

PREP: 15 min. + chilling

Taste of Home Test Kitchen

Just four ingredients are all you need to create a fabulous, flaky pie crust. The double-crust recipe should be used when making a lattice-topped pie.

INGREDIENTS FOR SINGLE-CRUST PIE:

1-1/4 cups all-purpose flour
1/2 teaspoon salt
1/3 cup shortening
4 to 5 tablespoons cold water

INGREDIENTS FOR DOUBLE-CRUST PIE:

2 cups all-purpose flour
3/4 teaspoon salt
2/3 cup shortening
6 to 7 tablespoons cold water

1) In a small bowl, combine the flour and salt; cut in the shortening until mixture is crumbly. Gradually add water, tossing with a fork until a ball forms. Cover and refrigerate for 30 minutes or until easy to handle.

2) For a single crust, roll out pastry on a lightly floured surface to fit a 9-in. or 10-in. pie plate. Transfer pastry to pie plate. Trim pastry to 1/2 in. beyond edge of pie plate; flute edges. Fill or bake shell according to recipe directions.

3) For a double crust, divide dough in half so that one ball is slightly larger than the other. Roll out larger ball on a lightly floured surface to fit a 9-in. or 10-in. pie plate. Transfer pastry to pie plate. Trim pastry even with edge of plate. Add filling. Roll out remaining pastry to fit top of pie; place over filling. Trim, seal and flute edges. Cut slits in top. Bake according to recipe directions.

Yield: 1 pastry for a single- or double-crust pie (9 or 10 inches).

NUTRITION FACTS: 1/8 of single pie pastry equals 144 calories, 8 g fat (2 g saturated fat), 0 cholesterol, 148 mg sodium, 15 g carbohydrate, 1 g fiber, 2 g protein.

Never-Fail Pie Crust

PREP: 10 min. + chilling

Ruth Gritter, Grand Rapids, Michigan

Even novice bakers can't go wrong with this recipe. It is easy to roll out and produces a perfect crust every time.

INGREDIENTS FOR SINGLE-CRUST PIE:

1 cup all-purpose flour
1/4 teaspoon salt
1/3 cup shortening
1-1/2 teaspoons white vinegar
2 to 3 tablespoons milk

INGREDIENTS FOR DOUBLE-CRUST PIE:

2 cups all-purpose flour
1/2 teaspoon salt
2/3 cup shortening
1 tablespoon white vinegar
5 to 6 tablespoons milk

1) In a small bowl, combine the flour and salt; cut in shortening until mixture is crumbly. Sprinkle with vinegar. Gradually add the milk, tossing with a fork until a ball is formed. Cover and refrigerate for 30 minutes or until easy to handle.

2) For a single crust, roll out pastry on a lightly floured surface to fit a 9-in. or 10-in. pie plate. Transfer pastry to pie plate. Trim pastry 1/2 in. beyond edge of plate; flute edges. Fill or bake shell according to recipe directions.

3) For a double crust, divide pastry in half so that one ball is slightly large than the other. Roll out large ball on a lightly floured surface to fit a 9-in. or 10-in. pie plate. Transfer pastry to pie plate. Trim pastry even with edge of plate. Add filling. Roll out remaining pastry to fit top of pie; place over filling. Trim, seal and flute edges. Cut slits in top. Bake according to recipe directions.

Yield: 1 pastry for a single- or double-crust pie (9 or 10 inches).

NUTRITION FACTS: 1/8 of single pie pastry equals 132 calories, 8 g fat (2 g saturated fat), 1 mg cholesterol, 76 mg sodium, 12 g carbohydrate, trace fiber, 2 g protein.

Baking and Storing Pies

A pastry shell is thoroughly baked when it is a light golden brown. Fruit pies are done when the filling bubbles and the crust is light golden brown. (The filling should be clear, not cloudy.) Meringues are properly baked when the top has set and the tips of the meringue peaks are light golden brown. Custard pies are done when a knife inserted near the center comes out clean. A small area in the center of pie should still be soft. The center will continue to cook and set up during cooling.

Cool fruit pies for at least 1 hour before serving. They can be kept at room temperature for 1 day. For longer storage, cover and refrigerate for up to 5 days. Cool meringue-topped and custard pies on a wire rack for 1 hour, then chill for at least 3 hours before serving. Store custard and cream pies in the refrigerator for up to 3 days.

Decorative Pie Crust Edges

Ruffle Edge

Used for a single- or double-crust pie. Trim pastry 1/2 in. beyond edge of pie plate (1 in. for a double-crust pie). Turn the overhanging pastry under to form the rolled edge.

Position your thumb and index finger about 1 in. apart on the edge of the crust and point out. Position the index finger on your other hand between the thumb and index finger and gently push the pastry toward the center in an upward direction. Continue around the edge.

Rope Edge

Used for a single- or double-crust pie. Trim pastry 1/2 in. beyond edge of pie plate (1 in. for a double-crust pie). Turn the overhanging pastry under to form the rolled edge. Make a fist with one hand and press your thumb at an angle into the pastry. Pinch some of the pastry between your thumb and index finger. Repeat at about 1/2-in. intervals around the crust. For a looser-looking rope, position your thumb at a wider angle and repeat at 1-in. intervals.

Leaf Trim

Used for a single-crust pie. Make enough pastry for a double crust. Line a 9-in. pie plate with the bottom pastry and trim pastry even with edge of pie plate. Roll out remaining pastry to 1/8-in. thickness.

Cut out leaf shapes, using 1-in. to 1-1/2-in. cookie cutters. With a sharp knife, score leaf shapes to create leaf veins. Brush bottom of each leaf with water. Place one or two layers of leaves around the edge of crust; press lightly to secure. Cover with foil to protect edges from overbrowning.

You can also use this technique with other cookie cutter designs such as hearts and apples. Vary them to suit the occasion or season you are celebrating.

Making Pastry Cutouts for a Pie

Pastry cutouts can be used for a single- or double-crust pie. Make enough pastry for a double-crust. Prepare bottom pastry as recipe directs. To make cutouts, roll out dough to 1/8-in. thickness. Cut out with 1-in. to 1-1/2-in. cookie cutters of desired shape. With a sharp knife, score designs (if desired) on cutouts.

For a single-crust pie, bake cutouts on an ungreased baking sheet at 400° for 6-8 minutes or until golden brown. Remove to a wire rack to cool. Arrange over cooled baked pie.

For a double-crust pie, brush bottom of each unbaked cutout with water or milk and arrange over top crust of an unbaked pie. Press lightly to secure. Bake pie as recipe directs.

APPLE PIE JUST LIKE MOM'S ■■■

My mother makes the best apple pie. Her secret is to use half light brown sugar and half white sugar instead of all white sugar mixed with the apples and cinnamon.

—Beverly O., Alpena, Michigan

Pie Thickeners

Thickeners help prevent fruit pies from being too runny. All-purpose flour, cornstarch and quick-cooking tapioca are the thickeners commonly used in fruit pies. Flour gives the filling an opaque appearance, cornstarch gives a clear appearance and tapioca gives a clear to almost gel-like appearance.

One thickener can be substituted for another; however, the thickening power of each is different and you may need to make adjustments. Equal amounts of quick-cooking tapioca and cornstarch can be substituted for each other. When replacing flour in a recipe, use half the amount of cornstarch or use 2 teaspoons of quick-cooking tapioca for every 1 tablespoon of flour.

When using tapioca, mix it with the filling ingredients and allow the mixture to stand for 15 minutes before proceeding with the recipe.

Homemade Crumb Crusts

In a mixing bowl, combine the crumbs and sugar; add the melted butter and blend well. Press the mixture onto the bottom and up the sides of an ungreased 9-in. pie plate. Refrigerate for 30 minutes before filling, or bake at 375° for 8-10 minutes or until the crust is lightly browned. Cool on a wire rack before filling.

TYPE OF CRUST	CRUMBS	SUGAR	BUTTER, MELTED
GRAHAM CRACKER	1-1/2 cups (24 squares)	1/4 cup	1/3 cup
CHOCOLATE WAFER	1-1/4 cups (20 wafers)	1/4 cup	1/4 cup
VANILLA WAFER	1-1/2 cups (30 wafers)	none	1/4 cup
CREAM-FILLED CHOCOLATE	1-1/2 cups (15 cookies)	none	1/4 cup
GINGERSNAP	1-1/2 cups (24 cookies)	none	1/4 cup
MACAROON	1-1/2 cups	none	1/4 cup
PRETZEL (use a greased pie plate)	1-1/4 cups	1/4 cup	1/2 cup

Editor's Note: For desserts made in a 9-in. springform pan (such as cheesecakes), you may need to add 1/4 to 1/2 cup crumbs and 1 tablespoon butter.

Protecting Pastry Edges From Overbrowning

The edges of a pie pastry often brown before the rest of the pie is thoroughly baked. To protect the edges, fold a 12-in. piece of foil in quarters. Place the folded corner toward you. Measure 3-3/4 in. up each adjacent side and cut out an arc joining the two sides. Discard the center.

Unfold the remaining foil and place it over the unbaked pie. Trim corners if necessary. Gently crimp foil around edge of crust to secure. Bake the pie for 20 to 30 minutes before removing the foil. Or add during the final 10 to 20 minutes of baking.

Apple Crumb Pie

PREP: 15 min. **BAKE:** 45 min.

Ardis Rollefson, Jackson Hole, Wyoming

I often brown the topping for this special-occasion pie under the broiler to give it extra eye appeal. Watch it carefully, though, because you don't want to burn Thanksgiving dessert!

Pastry for single crust pie (9 inches)

- 6 cups chopped peeled tart apples (about 6 medium)
- 2 tablespoons butter, melted
- 2 tablespoons sour cream
- 4 teaspoons lemon juice
- 1/2 cup sugar
- 1 tablespoon all-purpose flour
- 1/2 teaspoon ground cinnamon
- 1/2 teaspoon ground nutmeg

TOPPING:
- 1/2 cup all-purpose flour
- 1/2 cup sugar
- 1/4 cup cold butter

1) Line a 9-in. pie plate with pastry; flute edges. In a large bowl, combine the next eight ingredients. Spoon into pastry shell.

2) For topping, combine flour and sugar in a bowl; cut in butter until mixture resembles coarse crumbs. Sprinkle over filling. Bake at 375° for 45-50 minutes or until the filling is bubbly and the apples are tender. Cool on a wire rack.

Yield: 8 servings.

NUTRITION FACTS: 1 piece equals 380 calories, 17 g fat (9 g saturated fat), 30 mg cholesterol, 189 mg sodium, 57 g carbohydrate, 2 g fiber, 2 g protein.

DOWN-HOME APPLE PIE

 CLASSIC: The irresistible aroma of apples and cinnamon wafting from the oven will make mouths water when you bake German Apple Pie. A from-scratch pie crust is filled with fresh sliced apples along with heavy whipping cream for added richness.

 TIME-SAVER: When time is tight, enjoy All-Star Apple Pie—it can be made from start to finish in less than 30 minutes. A prepared pie shell and a can of apple pie filling hurry along the dessert, which is jazzed up with a crunchy, golden topping of brown sugar, pecans, oats and coconut.

 LIGHT: With its homemade crust, cream cheese filling and pretty apple slices, no one will guess that Bavarian Apple Tart is lighter. One slice has less than half the calories, about half the carbohydrates and close to a third of the fat of classic German Apple Pie.

 SERVES 2: Butterscotch chips melted into the topping give special flavor to Apple Butterscotch Crumb Pie. The recipe makes two little individual pies, so it's a nice treat for two.

GERMAN APPLE PIE

🥧 German Apple Pie
PREP: 20 min. **BAKE:** 1 hour 5 min.

Mrs. Woodrow Taylor, Adams Center, New York

1-1/2 cups all-purpose flour
1/2 teaspoon salt
1/2 cup shortening
1 teaspoon vanilla extract
2 to 3 tablespoons ice water

FILLING:
1 cup sugar
1/4 cup all-purpose flour
2 teaspoons ground cinnamon
6 cups sliced peeled tart apples
1 cup heavy whipping cream
Whipped cream, optional

1) In a small bowl, combine flour and salt; cut in the shortening until crumbly. Add vanilla. Gradually add water, tossing with a fork until dough forms a ball. Roll out pastry to fit a 9-in. pie plate. Transfer pastry to pie plate. Trim pastry to 1/2 in. beyond edge of pie plate; flute edges.

2) For filling, combine the sugar, flour and the cinnamon; sprinkle 3 tablespoons into crust. Layer with half of the apples, then sprinkle with half of the remaining sugar mixture. Repeat layers. Pour cream over all.

3) Bake at 450° for 10 minutes. Reduce heat to 350°; bake for 55-60 minutes or until apples are tender. Cool on a wire rack. Store in the refrigerator. Serve with whipped cream if desired.

Yield: 8 servings.

NUTRITION FACTS: 1 piece equals 459 calories, 24 g fat (10 g saturated fat), 41 mg cholesterol, 160 mg sodium, 59 g carbohydrate, 3 g fiber, 4 g protein.

🕐 All-Star Apple Pie
PREP: 10 min. **BAKE:** 15 min. + cooling

Cindy Glick, Bradford, New York

1 can (21 ounces) apple pie filling
1 tablespoon lemon juice
1/4 teaspoon ground cinnamon
1 pastry shell (9 inches), baked
1/4 cup all-purpose flour
1/4 cup packed brown sugar
2 tablespoons cold butter
1/4 cup chopped pecans *or* walnuts
1/4 cup quick-cooking oats
2 tablespoons flaked coconut

1) In a large bowl, combine pie filling, lemon juice and cinnamon; spoon into pastry shell. In a small bowl, combine the flour and brown sugar; cut in butter until crumbly. Stir in nuts, oats and coconut; sprinkle over pie filling.

ALL-STAR APPLE PIE

2) Bake at 400° for 12-15 minutes or until topping is golden brown, covering edges loosely with foil to prevent overbrowning if necessary. Cool on a wire rack.

Yield: 6-8 servings.

NUTRITION FACTS: 1 piece equals 304 calories, 13 g fat (6 g saturated fat), 13 mg cholesterol, 160 mg sodium, 45 g carbohydrate, 2 g fiber, 2 g protein.

Bavarian Apple Tart

PREP: 25 min. **BAKE:** 40 min. + cooling

Mary Anne Engel, West Allis, Wisconsin

1/3 cup butter, softened
1/3 cup sugar
1/2 teaspoon vanilla extract
1 cup all-purpose flour
1/8 teaspoon ground cinnamon

FILLING:

1 package (8 ounces) reduced-fat cream cheese
1/4 cup sugar
1 egg
1-1/2 teaspoons vanilla extract

TOPPING:

4 cups thinly sliced peeled Granny Smith *or* other tart apples (about 2 medium)
1/3 cup sugar
3/4 teaspoon ground cinnamon

1) In a large mixing bowl, cream butter and sugar. Add the vanilla, flour and cinnamon. Press onto the bottom and 1 in. up the sides of a 9-in springform pan coated with cooking spray.

2) In a large mixing bowl, beat the cream cheese and sugar until smooth. Beat in egg and vanilla just until combined. Spread over crust.

3) In another bowl, toss the apples, sugar and cinnamon; arrange over filling. Bake at 400° for 40 minutes or until apples are tender and crust is golden brown. Cool on a wire rack. Store in the refrigerator.

Yield: 12 servings.

NUTRITION FACTS: 1 piece equals 213 calories, 9 g fat (5 g saturated fat), 42 mg cholesterol, 113 mg sodium, 30 g carbohydrate, 1 g fiber, 4 g protein.

Apple Butterscotch Crumb Pie

PREP: 20 min. + chilling **BAKE:** 30 min. + cooling

Kathryn Sievers, Bertram, Texas

1/2 cup all-purpose flour
1/8 teaspoon salt
3 tablespoons shortening
4 teaspoons cold water

FILLING:

1 cup thinly sliced peeled tart apples
1/2 teaspoon lemon juice
2 tablespoons all-purpose flour
2 tablespoons sugar
1/4 teaspoon ground cinnamon
1/8 teaspoon salt

TOPPING:

1/2 cup butterscotch chips
1 tablespoon butter
2 tablespoons all-purpose flour

1) In a small bowl, combine the flour and salt; cut in shortening until crumbly. Gradually add water, tossing with a fork until dough forms a ball. Cover and refrigerate for at least 30 minutes.

2) Shape into two balls; roll into two 6-in. circles. Transfer to two 4-1/2-in. pie plates. Trim pastry to 1/2 in. beyond edge of plate; flute edges. Set aside.

3) Place apples in a small bowl; sprinkle with the lemon juice, flour, sugar, cinnamon and salt. Toss to combine. Spoon into pastry shells. Bake at 375° for 15 minutes. Remove from the oven.

4) For topping, melt butterscotch chips and butter in a small saucepan over low heat, stirring constantly. Remove from the heat; stir in flour with a fork until crumbly. Sprinkle over apple mixture. Bake 15-20 minutes longer or until apples are tender. Cool on a wire rack.

Yield: 2 individual pies.

NUTRITION FACTS: 1 pie equals 791 calories, 42 g fat (24 g saturated fat), 19 mg cholesterol, 401 mg sodium, 95 g carbohydrate, 3 g fiber, 7 g protein.

MY BEST PIE CRUST ■■■

My husband never liked pie crust until he tried my mother's. She adds a little sugar...and now I do, too.

—Heidi H., Basalt, Colorado

SIMPLE APRICOT TART

Simple Apricot Tart

PREP: 15 min. **BAKE:** 35 min. + cooling

Taste of Home Test Kitchen

Apricots and pumpkin pie spice come together beautifully in this special tart.

> 1/4 cup plus 1 teaspoon sugar, *divided*
> 2 tablespoons cornstarch
> 1/2 teaspoon pumpkin pie spice
> 3 cans (15 ounces *each*) reduced-sugar apricot halves, drained

Pastry for single-crust pie (9 inches)

> 1 egg white, beaten
> 2 tablespoons sliced almonds
> 1 tablespoon fat-free milk

1) In a bowl, combine 1/4 cup sugar, cornstarch and pumpkin pie spice. Add apricots and toss to coat.

2) Place pastry on a parchment paper-lined 12-in. pizza pan. Brush with egg white to within 1-1/2 in. of edges. Spoon apricot mixture over egg white; sprinkle with almonds. Fold up edges of pastry over filling, leaving center uncovered. Brush folded pastry with milk; sprinkle with remaining sugar.

3) Bake at 375° for 35-40 minutes or until crust is golden and filling is bubbly. Use parchment paper to slide tart onto a wire rack to cool.

Yield: 6 servings.

NUTRITION FACTS: 1 piece equals 278 calories, 11 g fat (4 g saturated fat), 7 mg cholesterol, 151 mg sodium, 43 carbohydrate, 1 g fiber, 4 g protein.

Country Fair Cherry Pie

PREP: 20 min. **BAKE:** 55 min. + cooling

Taste of Home Test Kitchen

A homemade cherry filling peeks out from a star-shaped pastry top. You can try different shapes for other occasions.

> 1-1/4 cups sugar
> 2 tablespoons cornstarch

Dash salt

> 4 cups pitted unsweetened sour cherries

Pastry for double-crust pie (9 inches)

Star cookie cutters (1/2 inch and 2 inches)

Confectioners' sugar

1) In a saucepan, combine sugar, cornstarch and salt; stir in cherries. Let stand for 30 minutes. Bring to a boil over medium heat; cook and stir for 2 minutes or until thickened. Set aside.

2) Line a 9-in. pie plate with bottom crust; trim pastry even with edge. Fill with cherry filling. Bake at 375° for 45 minutes or until crust is golden brown and filling is bubbly. Cover edges during the last 20 minutes to prevent overbrowning. Cool on a wire rack.

3) Meanwhile, roll out remaining pastry to 1/8-in. thickness. Cut into 12-14 large stars and 16-18 small stars; place on an ungreased baking sheet. Bake at 375° for 8-10 minutes or until golden brown. Remove to a wire rack to cool.

4) Sprinkle stars with confectioners' sugar. Place stars randomly over cooled pie. Sprinkle edges of pie with confectioners' sugar.

Yield: 8 servings.

NUTRITION FACTS: 1 piece (calculated without confectioners' sugar) equals 426 calories, 14 g fat (6 g saturated fat), 10 mg cholesterol, 220 mg sodium, 74 g carbohydrate, 2 g fiber, 3 g protein.

■ **Cherry Almond Pie:** Once the pie filling has been removed from the heat, stir in 1/4 teaspoon almond extract.

Walnut Mincemeat Pie

PREP: 15 min. **BAKE:** 50 min. + cooling

Laverne Kamp, Kutztown, Pennsylvania

As a cold and tasty finishing touch, put a scoop of vanilla ice cream on top of each slice.

> 2 eggs
> 1 cup sugar
> 2 tablespoons all-purpose flour
> 1/8 teaspoon salt
> 2 cups prepared mincemeat
> 1/2 cup chopped walnuts
> 1/4 cup butter, melted
> 1 unbaked pastry shell (9 inches)

1) In a small mixing bowl, lightly beat eggs. Combine the sugar, flour and salt; gradually add to eggs. Stir in mincemeat, nuts and butter; pour into pie shell.

2) Bake at 400° for 15 minutes. Reduce heat to 325°; bake 35-40 minutes or until a knife inserted near the center comes out clean. Cool completely. Store in the refrigerator.

Yield: 8 servings.

NUTRITION FACTS: 1 piece equals 440 calories, 18 g fat (7 g saturated fat), 73 mg cholesterol, 231 mg sodium, 65 g carbohydrate, 2 g fiber, 5 g protein.

Rhubarb-Strawberry Pie

PREP: 15 min. + standing **BAKE:** 50 min.

Sandy Brown, Lake Worth, Florida

Strawberries, rhubarb and a hint of orange make a winning combination in this pie recipe.

- 1/2 to 3/4 cup sugar
- 4-1/2 tablespoons instant tapioca
- 3 cups sliced fresh *or* frozen rhubarb, thawed (1/4-inch pieces)
- 3 cups sliced fresh *or* frozen unsweetened strawberries, thawed
- 1/3 cup fresh orange juice
- 4-1/2 teaspoons orange marmalade, optional
- 1/4 teaspoon grated orange peel

Pastry for double-crust pie (9 inches)

1) In a large bowl, combine sugar and tapioca. Add fruit; toss to coat. Gently stir in the juice, marmalade if desired and orange peel. Let stand for 15 minutes.

2) Line a deep-dish 9-in. pie plate with bottom crust; trim pastry 1 in. beyond edge. Fill with fruit filling. Roll out remaining pastry; make a lattice crust. Trim, seal and flute edges.

3) Bake at 400° for 20 minutes. Reduce heat to 375°; bake 30 minutes more or until filling is bubbly and rhubarb is tender. Cool on a wire rack. Store in the refrigerator.

Yield: 8 servings.

NUTRITION FACTS: 1 piece equals 329 calories, 14 g fat (6 g saturated fat), 10 mg cholesterol, 203 mg sodium, 48 g carbohydrate, 2 g fiber, 3 g protein.

Ozark Mountain Berry Pie

PREP: 15 min. **BAKE:** 45 min. + cooling

Elaine Moody, Clever, Missouri

I taste the berries or filling before adding to the pie crust to make sure it's sweet enough.

- 1 cup sugar
- 1/4 cup cornstarch
- 1/2 teaspoon ground cinnamon, optional

Dash salt

OZARK MOUNTAIN BERRY PIE

- 1/2 cup water
- 2 tablespoons lemon juice
- 1 cup blueberries
- 1 cup strawberries
- 3/4 cup blackberries
- 3/4 cup red raspberries

Pastry for double-crust pie (9 inches)

- 2 tablespoons butter

1) In a large saucepan, combine the sugar, cornstarch, cinnamon if desired and salt. Stir in the water and lemon juice. Add the berries. Cook and gently stir over medium heat until mixture just comes to a boil.

2) Line a 9-in. pie plate with bottom crust; trim pastry even with edge of plate. Add filling, dot with butter. Roll out remaining pastry; make a lattice crust. Trim, seal and flute edges.

3) Bake at 350° for about 45-50 minutes or until crust is golden. Serve warm or chilled. Cool on a wire rack. Store in the refrigerator.

Yield: 8 servings.

NUTRITION FACTS: 1 piece equals 406 calories, 17 g fat (8 g saturated fat), 18 mg cholesterol, 248 mg sodium, 62 g carbohydrate, 2 g fiber, 3 g protein.

Creating a Lattice-Topped Pie

1) Make pastry for a double-crust pie. Line a 9-in. pie plate with the bottom pastry and trim to 1 in. beyond edge of plate. Roll out remaining pastry to a 12-in. circle. With a fluted pastry wheel, pizza cutter or sharp knife, cut pastry into 1/2-in.- to 1-in.-wide strips. Lay strips in rows about 1/2 in. to 3/4 in. apart. (Use longer strips for the center of the pie and shorter strips for the sides.) Fold every other strip halfway back. Starting at the center, add strips at right angles, lifting every other strip as the cross strips are put down.

2) Continue to add strips, lifting and weaving until lattice top is completed.

3) Trim strips even with pastry edge. Fold bottom pastry up and over ends of strips and seal. Flute edges.

LUSCIOUS PEACH PIE

 CLASSIC: Peach Pie shines the spotlight on fresh, juicy peaches in season. Almond extract accents the flavor of the fruit filling while a lattice top gives the home-baked pie a pretty appearance.

 TIME-SAVER: It takes just 10 minutes to assemble Peach Strawberry Pie, because it starts with convenience items, including a store-bought graham cracker crust, canned peaches and prepared strawberry glaze. With layers of sweetened cream cheese and fresh berries, there's no baking required—just pop it in the fridge to chill.

 LIGHT: Country Peach Tart has wonderful peach flavor with an appealing rustic look and healthier nutritional numbers. It has only half the calories, fat and carbohydrates of classic Peach Pie, plus an extra gram of fiber per slice, thanks to whole wheat flour in the crust.

 SERVES 2: Seasoned with cinnamon, orange peel and a dash of cloves, the filling in Mini Peach Pie is nicely spiced. The pie is baked in a 7-inch pie plate and yields four servings, so you can share it with another couple or enjoy the leftovers the next day.

Peach Pie

PREP: 15 min. + standing
BAKE: 40 min. + cooling

Annie Tompkins, Deltona, Florida

Pastry for double-crust pie (9 inches)
- 5 cups sliced peeled fresh peaches
- 1 tablespoon lemon juice
- 1/2 teaspoon almond extract
- 1 cup sugar
- 1/4 cup quick-cooking tapioca
- 1/4 teaspoon salt
- 2 tablespoons butter

1) Line a 9-in. pie plate with bottom crust. Trim pastry to 1 in. beyond edge of plate; set aside.

2) In a large bowl, combine the peaches, lemon juice and extract. Add sugar, tapioca and salt; toss gently. Let stand for 15 minutes.

3) Pour filling into crust; dot with butter. Roll out remaining pastry; make a lattice crust. Trim, seal and flute edges.

4) Cover edges loosely with foil. Bake at 425° for 20 minutes. Remove foil; bake 20-30 minutes longer or until crust is golden brown and filling is bubbly. Cool on a wire rack.

Yield: 6-8 servings.

NUTRITION FACTS: 1 piece equals 425 calories, 17 g fat (8 g saturated fat), 18 mg cholesterol, 294 mg sodium, 66 g carbohydrate, 2 g fiber, 3 g protein.

■ **Blueberry Peach Pie:** Omit almond extract. Reduce sugar to 2/3 cup. Add a dash of ground nutmeg to sugar mixture. Sprinkle 3 tablespoons red-hot candies over filling, then dot with butter. Cover with top crust or lattice crust. Bake as directed.

PEACH STRAWBERRY PIE

Peach Strawberry Pie

PREP: 10 min. + chilling

Judy Long, Limestone, Tennessee
- 1 package (8 ounces) cream cheese, softened
- 1/4 cup sugar
- 1 tablespoon milk
- 1 graham cracker crust (9 inches)
- 1 can (15-1/4 ounces) sliced peaches, well drained
- 3 cups sliced fresh strawberries
- 1 carton (16 ounces) strawberry glaze

1) In a small mixing bowl, beat the cream cheese, sugar and milk until smooth. Spread over the bottom and up the sides of the crust.

2) Cut peach slices in half if desired. Arrange over cream cheese. Combine the strawberries and glaze; spoon over peaches. Refrigerate for up to 4 hours before serving.

Editor's Note: This pie is best the day it's prepared.

Yield: 6-8 servings.

NUTRITION FACTS: 1 piece equals 344 calories, 15 g fat (7 g saturated fat), 31 mg cholesterol, 268 mg sodium, 47 g carbohydrate, 2 g fiber, 4 g protein.

Country Peach Tart

PREP: 20 min. + chilling
BAKE: 25 min. + cooling

Taste of Home Test Kitchen

3/4 cup cake flour
1/2 cup whole wheat flour
6 tablespoons sugar, *divided*
1/2 teaspoon salt
4 tablespoons cold butter
1 tablespoon canola oil
3 tablespoons cold water
2 tablespoons buttermilk
2 tablespoons all-purpose flour
4 cups fresh *or* frozen peeled sliced peaches, thawed
1 tablespoon fat-free milk

1) In a small bowl, combine the cake flour, whole wheat flour, 2 tablespoons sugar and salt. Cut in

COUNTRY PEACH TART

butter until crumbly. Add oil and toss with a fork. Gradually add water and buttermilk, tossing with a fork until mixture sticks together. Shape dough into a ball; flatten dough. Wrap in plastic wrap and refrigerate for at least 1 hour.

2) On a lightly floured surface, roll out dough into a 14-in. circle. Transfer to a parchment paper-lined baking sheet. In a large bowl, combine 3 tablespoons sugar and all-purpose flour; add peaches and toss to coat. Spoon over pastry to within 2 in. of edges. Fold edges of pastry over peaches, leaving center uncovered. Brush folded edge with milk; sprinkle with remaining sugar.

3) Bake at 400° for 25-30 minutes or until the crust is golden brown and filling is bubbly. Use parchment paper to slide tart onto a wire rack to cool.

Yield: 8 servings.

NUTRITION FACTS: 1 piece equals 215 calories, 8 g fat (4 g saturated fat), 16 mg cholesterol, 210 mg sodium, 35 g carbohydrate, 3 g fiber, 3 g protein.

Mini Peach Pie

PREP: 20 min. **BAKE:** 40 min. + cooling

Taste of Home Test Kitchen

1/4 cup sugar
1 tablespoon quick-cooking tapioca
1/4 teaspoon ground cinnamon
1/4 teaspoon grated orange peel
1/8 teaspoon salt
Dash ground cloves
3 cups frozen unsweetened sliced peaches, thawed
1 refrigerated pie pastry
1 egg white, beaten
1 teaspoon coarse sugar
Additional ground cinnamon

1) In a large bowl, combine the sugar, tapioca, cinnamon, orange peel, salt and cloves. Add peaches; toss gently to coat. Let stand for 15 minutes.

2) Cut pastry sheet in half. On a lightly floured surface, roll out one half into an 8-in. circle. Transfer to a 7-in. pie plate; trim pastry even with edge of plate. Add filling.

3) Roll out remaining pastry to fit top of pie. Place over filling. Trim, seal and flute edges. Cut slits in pastry. Brush with egg white; sprinkle with coarse sugar and additional cinnamon.

4) Bake at 400° for 40-45 minutes or until crust is golden brown and filling is bubbly. Cool on a wire rack.

Yield: 4 servings.

NUTRITION FACTS: 1 piece equals 343 calories, 14 g fat (6 g saturated fat), 10 mg cholesterol, 288 mg sodium, 50 g carbohydrate, 1 g fiber, 4 g protein.

FESTIVE FRUIT TART

Festive Fruit Tart

PREP: 30 min. + cooling

Nancy Adams, Hancock, New Hampshire

"Wow!" is what you'll hear when you serve this impressive dessert to company. The tart is not only pretty, it's also easy to make. Try it with your favorite fresh fruit.

Pastry for single-crust pie (9 inches)
- 1 package (8 ounces) cream cheese, softened
- 3 tablespoons sugar
- 1 teaspoon vanilla extract
- 3/4 teaspoon almond extract, *divided*
- 1 cup fresh blueberries
- 1 cup fresh raspberries
- 1 medium ripe peach *or* nectarines, peeled and sliced
- 2 tablespoons apricot preserves

1) Press pastry onto the bottom and up the sides of an ungreased 9-in. tart pan with a removable bottom; trim edges. Generously prick the bottom with a fork. Bake at 450° for 10-12 minutes or until golden brown. Cool completely on a wire rack.

2) In a small mixing bowl, beat the cream cheese, sugar, vanilla and 1/2 teaspoon almond extract until smooth; spread over crust. Arrange fruit over cream cheese mixture.

3) In a small microwave-safe bowl, combine apricot preserves and the remaining almond extract. Microwave, uncovered, on high for 20-30 seconds or until warm; brush over fruit. Store in the refrigerator.

Yield: 12 servings.

NUTRITION FACTS: 1 piece equals 264 calories, 16 g fat (8 g saturated fat), 27 mg cholesterol, 191 mg sodium, 27 g carbohydrate, 1 g fiber, 3 g protein.

Cranberry Walnut Tart

PREP: 30 min. + chilling **BAKE:** 20 min. + cooling

Patricia Harmon, Baden, Pennsylvania

Both attractive and delicious, this flaky tart combines a tender crust with a sweet filling that might remind you of baklava. It's a holiday favorite at our house.

- 2-1/2 cups all-purpose flour
- 1 cup cold butter, cubed
- 1/4 cup sugar
- 2 egg yolks
- 3 tablespoons cold water
- 1 tablespoon lemon juice
- 1/2 teaspoon grated lemon peel

FILLING:
- 1 cup sugar
- 1/4 cup butter, cubed
- 1/4 cup water
- 2/3 cup heavy whipping cream
- 3 tablespoons honey
- 1/2 teaspoon salt
- 2 cups chopped walnuts
- 1/2 cup dried cranberries
- 1 egg white, beaten
- 1 teaspoon coarse sugar

1) Place flour, butter and sugar in a food processor; cover and process until mixture resembles coarse crumbs. Add egg yolks, water, lemon juice and peel; cover and process until dough forms a ball. Divide dough in half; wrap in plastic wrap. Refrigerate for 1 hour or until firm.

2) In a small saucepan, bring the sugar, butter and water to a boil; cook and stir for 1 minute. Cook, without stirring, until mixture turns a golden amber color, about 7 minutes.

3) Remove from the heat; gradually stir in cream. Return to heat; stir in honey and salt until smooth. Stir in walnuts and cranberries. Bring to a boil. Reduce heat; simmer, uncovered, for 5 minutes. Remove from the heat; cool to room temperature.

4) On a lightly floured surface, roll out one portion of dough into an 11-in. circle. Transfer to an ungreased 9-in. fluted tart pan with a removable bottom; trim pastry even with edge. Add filling. Roll out remaining dough to fit top of tart; place over filling. Trim and seal edges. Cut slits in pastry.

5) Brush with egg white; sprinkle with coarse sugar. Bake at 400° for 20-25 minutes or until filling is bubbly. Cool on a wire rack.

Yield: 10-12 servings.

NUTRITION FACTS: 1 piece equals 558 calories, 37 g fat (16 g saturated fat), 102 mg cholesterol, 245 mg sodium, 53 g carbohydrate, 2 g fiber, 9 g protein.

German Plum Tart

PREP: 10 min. **BAKE:** 35 min.

Helga Schlape, Florham Park, New Jersey

The buttery crust of this fruit-filled treat melts in your mouth. You can substitute sliced apples or peaches for the plums with great results. I've used this crust with blueberries, too.

    1/2 cup butter, softened
      4 tablespoons sugar, *divided*
      1 egg yolk
    3/4 to 1 cup all-purpose flour
      2 pounds plums, quartered
         (about 4 cups)

1) In a small mixing bowl cream butter and 3 tablespoons sugar until light and fluffy. Beat in egg yolk. Gradually add flour, 1/4 cup at a time, until mixture forms a soft dough. Press onto the bottom and up the sides of a 10-in. pie plate.

2) Arrange the plums in crust skin side up with edges overlapping; sprinkle with remaining sugar. Bake at 350° for 35-45 minutes or until crust is golden brown and fruit is tender.

Yield: 6-8 servings.

NUTRITION FACTS: 1 piece equals 237 calories, 13 g fat (7 g saturated fat), 57 mg cholesterol, 117 mg sodium, 30 g carbohydrate, 2 g fiber, 3 g protein.

Rustic Pear Tart

PREP: 25 min. **BAKE:** 45 min. + cooling

Taste of Home Test Kitchen

In this delightful pie, the pastry makes a "pouch" for a pleasant pear filling. For even more flavor, top with a powdered sugar glaze and toasted almonds.

    1-1/3 cups all-purpose flour
        3 tablespoons sugar
      1/4 teaspoon salt
        7 tablespoons cold butter, cubed
        2 to 3 tablespoons cold water

FILLING:
      3/4 cup sugar
      1/4 cup slivered almonds, toasted
      1/4 cup all-purpose flour
    1-1/2 teaspoons dried grated lemon peel
      1/2 to 3/4 teaspoon ground cinnamon
        4 medium ripe pears, peeled and sliced
        1 tablespoon butter

TOPPING (optional):
        1 egg white
        1 tablespoon water

Coarse sugar

GLAZE (optional):
      1/4 cup confectioners' sugar
    1-1/2 teaspoons milk
      1/4 teaspoon vanilla extract
      1/4 cup slivered almonds, toasted

1) In a bowl, combine flour, sugar and salt; cut in butter until crumbly. Gradually add water, tossing with a fork until dough forms a ball. Roll out to a 14-in. circle. Transfer pastry to a 14-in. pizza pan.

2) In a large bowl, combine the sugar, almonds, flour, lemon peel and cinnamon. Add pears; toss to coat. Spoon over the pastry to within 2 in. of edges; dot with butter. Fold edges of pastry over pears, leaving center uncovered.

3) For topping, beat egg white and water. Brush over crust. Sprinkle with coarse sugar. Bake at 375° for 45-50 minutes or until golden brown.

4) For glaze, combine the confectioners' sugar, milk and vanilla. Drizzle over warm tart. Sprinkle with almonds. Cool on a wire rack. Store in refrigerator.

Yield: 10 servings.

NUTRITION FACTS: 1 piece equals 314 calories, 12 g fat (6 g saturated fat), 24 mg cholesterol, 131 mg sodium, 49 g carbohydrate, 3 g fiber, 4 g protein.

RUSTIC PEAR TART

CHERRY MERINGUE PIE

Cherry Meringue Pie

PREP: 20 min. **BAKE:** 15 min. + chilling

Susan Card, Franklin, New Jersey

People are surprised to hear this pie's meringue crust features saltines. The cherry-cream cheese filling makes this dessert special.

     3 egg whites
     1 teaspoon white vinegar
     1 cup sugar
   1/2 cup crushed saltines (about 12
        crackers)
   1/2 cup finely chopped pecans
     1 teaspoon baking powder
     1 teaspoon vanilla extract

TOPPING:

     1 package (3 ounces) cream cheese,
        softened
   1/2 cup confectioners' sugar
     1 teaspoon vanilla extract
   1/2 cup heavy whipping cream,
        whipped
     1 can (21 ounces) cherry pie filling

1) In a large mixing bowl, beat egg whites and vinegar on medium speed until soft peaks form. Gradually beat in sugar, 1 tablespoon at a time, on high until stiff glossy peaks form and sugar is dissolved. Fold in the cracker crumbs, pecans, baking powder and vanilla.

2) Spread onto the bottom and up the sides of a greased deep-dish 9-in. pie plate. Bake at 350° for 14-18 minutes or until lightly browned. Cool on wire rack (meringue shell will fall in center).

3) In a mixing bowl, beat cream cheese, confectioners' sugar and vanilla until fluffy. Fold in whipped cream. Spoon into meringue shell. Top with pie filling. Chill for at least 2 hours before serving.

Yield: 8-10 servings.

NUTRITION FACTS: 1 piece equals 280 calories, 10 g fat (4 g saturated fat), 18 mg cholesterol, 134 mg sodium, 46 g carbohydrate, 1 g fiber, 3 g protein.

■ **Favorite Meringue Pie:** Replace the cherry pie filling with the pie filling of your choice.

Creamy Banana Pie

PREP: 30 min. + chilling

Rita Pribyl, Indianapolis, Indiana

When friends ask me to share a recipe using bananas, I know instantly this is the best dessert to pass along. Everyone who tastes a slice enjoys its delicious old-fashioned flavor.

       1 envelope unflavored gelatin
     1/4 cup cold water
     3/4 cup sugar
     1/4 cup cornstarch
     1/2 teaspoon salt
   2-3/4 cups milk
       4 egg yolks, beaten
       2 tablespoons butter
       1 tablespoon vanilla extract
       4 medium firm bananas, *divided*
       1 cup heavy whipping cream,
          whipped
       1 pastry shell (10 inches), baked

Juice and grated peel of 1 lemon
     1/2 cup apple jelly

1) Soften gelatin in cold water; set aside. In a saucepan, combine the sugar, cornstarch and salt. Whisk in the milk until smooth. Cook and stir over medium-high heat until thickened and bubbly. Reduce heat; cook and stir 2 minutes longer. Remove from the heat.

2) Stir a small amount of hot filling into yolks. Return all to the pan, stirring constantly. Bring to a gentle boil. Cook and stir 2 minutes longer. Remove from the heat; stir in softened gelatin until dissolved. Stir in butter and vanilla. Cover the surface of custard with plastic wrap and chill until no longer warm.

3) Slice 3 bananas; fold into custard along with whipped cream. Spoon into pie shell. Cover and refrigerate until set, about 4-5 hours.

4) Just before serving, place lemon juice in a small bowl and slice the remaining banana into it. Melt jelly in a saucepan over low heat.

5) Drain banana; pat dry and arrange over filling. Brush banana with the jelly. Sprinkle with grated lemon peel. Serve immediately. Refrigerate leftovers.

Yield: 8 servings.

NUTRITION FACTS: 1 piece equals 478 calories, 21 g fat (11 g saturated fat), 151 mg cholesterol, 330 mg sodium, 67 g carbohydrate, 1 g fiber, 7 g protein.

TASTY TRICK FOR CHERRY PIE ■■■

When I make a homemade cherry pie, I mix a small package of cherry gelatin into the filling. I think it gives the pie better flavor and a rich, appetizing color that brings people back for a second slice. I use raspberry gelatin when I make a berry pie.

—*Ruth K., Grand Rapids, Michigan*

Topping a Pie With Meringue

Spread meringue over hot filling to minimize "weeping" (the watery layer between the meringue and filling) and seal to the edges of pastry. Cool the pie away from drafts on a wire rack at room temperature for 1 hour. Refrigerate for at least 3 hours before cutting and serving. Store leftovers in the refrigerator.

Coconut Cream Meringue Pie

PREP: 30 min. + chilling **BAKE:** 15 min. + cooling

Betty Sitzman, Wary, Colorado

We usually have a good selection of pies at our neighborhood get-togethers, but I always come home with an empty pan when I bring this classic.

  2/3 cup sugar
  1/4 cup cornstarch
  1/4 teaspoon salt
    2 cups milk
    3 egg yolks, lightly beaten
    1 cup flaked coconut, finely chopped
    2 tablespoons butter
  1/2 teaspoon vanilla extract
    1 pastry shell (9 inches), baked

MERINGUE:

    3 egg whites
  1/4 teaspoon cream of tartar
    6 tablespoons sugar
  1/2 cup flaked coconut

1) In a small saucepan, combine the sugar, cornstarch and salt. Stir in milk until smooth. Cook and stir over medium-high heat until thickened and bubbly. Reduce heat; cook and stir 2 minutes longer. Remove from the heat.

2) Stir a small amount of hot filling into egg yolks; return all to pan, stirring constantly. Bring to a gentle boil; cook and stir 2 minutes longer. Remove from the heat. Gently stir in chopped coconut, butter and vanilla until butter is melted. Pour hot filling into crust.

3) For meringue, in a small mixing bowl, beat egg whites and cream of tartar on medium speed until soft peaks form. Gradually beat in the sugar, 1 tablespoon at a time, on high until stiff glossy peaks form and sugar is dissolved. Spread evenly over hot filling, sealing edges to crust.

4) Sprinkle with flaked coconut. Bake at 350° for 12-15 minutes or until the meringue is golden. Cool on a wire rack for 1 hour. Refrigerate at least 3 hours before serving. Refrigerate leftovers.

Yield: 8 servings

NUTRITION FACTS: 1 piece equals 415 calories, 20 g fat (12 g saturated fat), 101 mg cholesterol, 302 mg sodium, 54 g carbohydrate, 1 g fiber, 6 g protein.

Prebaking a Pastry Shell

1) After placing pastry in the pie plate and fluting edges, line unpricked shell with a double thickness of heavy-duty foil. If desired, fill with dried beans, uncooked rice or pie weights. The weight will keep the crust from puffing up, shrinking and slipping down the pie plate while baking.

2) Bake at 450° for 8 minutes. With oven mitts, carefully remove foil and beans, rice or weights. Bake 5-6 minutes longer or until light golden brown. Cool on a wire rack. Let beans or rice cool; store (they may be reused for pie weights but cannot be cooked and used in recipes).

COCONUT CREAM MERINGUE PIE

SWEET AND TANGY LEMON MERINGUE

 CLASSIC: A cup of fresh lemon juice adds zest to the cooked filling in Very Lemony Meringue Pie. A light, golden meringue is the crowning touch to this delightful dessert.

 TIME-SAVER: Five ingredients, including a convenient can of lemon pie filling, make creamy Layered Lemon Pie a snap to assemble. It needs to chill for only a few minutes, so it's ready to serve in less than half an hour.

 LIGHT: Lemon Yogurt Cream Pie gets its fabulous flavor from lemon juice, grated lemon peel and fat-free lemon yogurt. Using sugar substitute, reduced-fat whipped topping and a reduced-fat graham cracker crust helps trim down this dessert. Each slice has 150 fewer calories and about half the fat and carbohydrates of Very Lemony Meringue Pie and almost no cholesterol.

 SERVES 2: Best Lemon Meringue Pie is the result of downsizing a traditional pie to proportions for a pair. It's made in a 5-inch pie plate, so it's perfectly sized for two.

Very Lemony Meringue Pie

PREP: 25 min. **BAKE:** 20 min. + chilling

Betty Bradley, Sebring, Florida

- 1-1/4 cups sugar
- 1/3 cup cornstarch
- 1 cup cold water
- 3 egg yolks
- 1 cup lemon juice
- 3 tablespoons butter
- 1 pastry shell (9 inches), baked

MERINGUE:

- 1 tablespoon cornstarch
- 1/3 cup cold water
- 3 egg whites
- 1 teaspoon vanilla extract

Dash salt

- 6 tablespoons sugar

1) In a saucepan, combine sugar and cornstarch. Stir in water until smooth. Cook and stir over medium heat until thickened and bubbly. Reduce heat; cook and stir 2 minutes longer. Remove from heat.

2) Stir in a small amount of hot filling into egg yolks. Return all to the pan, stirring constantly. Bring to a gentle boil; cook and stir 2 minutes longer.

3) Remove from the heat. Add lemon juice and butter; stir until butter is melted and mixture is blended. Pour hot filling into pastry shell.

4) In a saucepan, combine cornstarch and water until smooth. Cook and stir over medium-low heat until mixture is thickened, about 2 minutes. Remove from the heat.

5) In a mixing bowl, beat egg whites, vanilla and salt until foamy. Gradually beat in sugar, 1 tablespoon at a time, on medium speed until soft peaks form and sugar is dissolved. Gradually beat in cornstarch mixture, 1 tablespoon at a time, on high until stiff peaks form.

6) Spread evenly over hot filling, sealing edges to crust. Bake at 325° for 18-20 minutes or until meringue is golden. Cool on a wire rack for 1 hour. Refrigerate pie for at least 3 hours before serving. Refrigerate leftovers.

Yield: 8 servings.

NUTRITION FACTS: 1 piece equals 376 calories, 13 g fat (6 g saturated fat), 96 mg cholesterol, 186 mg sodium, 62 g carbohydrate, trace fiber, 4 g protein.

Layered Lemon Pie

PREP/TOTAL TIME: 25 min.

Elizabeth Yoder, Belcourt, North Dakota

- 1 package (8 ounces) cream cheese, softened
- 1/2 cup sugar
- 1 can (15-3/4 ounces) lemon pie filling
- 1 carton (8 ounces) frozen whipped topping, thawed
- 1 graham cracker crust (9 inches)

LAYERED LEMON PIE

1) In a large mixing bowl, beat cream cheese and sugar until smooth. Beat in half of the pie filling. Fold in the whipped topping. Spoon into crust. Spread remaining pie filling over cream cheese layer. Refrigerate for 15 minutes or until serving. Refrigerate leftovers.

Yield: 8 servings.

NUTRITION FACTS: 1 piece equals 526 calories, 24 g fat (13 g saturated fat), 104 mg cholesterol, 251 mg sodium, 72 g carbohydrate, 1 g fiber, 6 g protein.

BEST LEMON MERINGUE PIE

Lemon Yogurt Cream Pie

PREP: 15 min. + chilling

Susan Kostecke, St. Louis, Missouri

- 1 envelope unflavored gelatin
- 1/4 cup cold water

Sugar substitute equivalent to 1/3 cup sugar

- 1/3 cup lemon juice
- 2 cartons (6 ounces *each*) fat-free lemon yogurt
- 1 teaspoon grated lemon peel
- 1 carton (8 ounces) frozen reduced-fat whipped topping, thawed
- 1 reduced-fat graham cracker crust (8 inches)

Lemon slices and mint, optional

1) In a microwave-safe bowl, sprinkle gelatin over cold water; let stand for 1 minute. Microwave, uncovered, on high for 20 seconds. Stir in sugar substitute and lemon juice. Add yogurt and lemon peel; mix well. Fold in whipped topping; spoon into crust.

2) Cover and refrigerate for 8 hours or overnight. Garnish with lemon slices and mint if desired.

Yield: 8 servings.

Editor's Note: This recipe was tested with Splenda No Calorie Sweetener.

NUTRITION FACTS: 1 piece equals 226 calories, 6 g fat (4 g saturated fat), 1 mg cholesterol, 130 mg sodium, 33 g carbohydrate, trace fiber, 7 g protein.

Best Lemon Meringue Pie

PREP: 45 min. **BAKE:** 10 min. + chilling

Sherie Snitker, Wichita, Kansas

- 1/2 cup all-purpose flour
- 1/8 teaspoon salt
- 2 tablespoons shortening
- 2 tablespoons water

FILLING:

- 1/2 cup sugar
- 2 tablespoons cornstarch
- 1/8 teaspoon salt
- 1/2 cup water

- 2 egg yolks, beaten
- 2 teaspoons butter
- 2 tablespoons lemon juice
- 1/4 teaspoon grated lemon peel

MERINGUE:

- 1 egg white
- 1/4 teaspoon lemon juice
- 1 tablespoon sugar

1) In a small bowl, combine flour and salt; cut in shortening until mixture is crumbly. Gradually add water, tossing with a fork until a ball forms. Cover and refrigerate for 15 minutes or until easy to handle.

2) On a lightly floured surface, roll out pastry to fit a 5-in. pie plate. Transfer pastry to pie plate; trim to 1/2 in. beyond edge of plate. Flute edges. Line unpricked pastry shell with a double thickness of heavy-duty foil. Bake at 450° for 5 minutes. Remove foil; bake 5 minutes longer. Cool on a wire rack.

3) For filling, in a small saucepan, combine sugar, cornstarch and salt. Gradually stir in water until smooth. Cook and stir over medium heat until thickened and bubbly. Reduce heat; cook and stir 2 minutes longer. Remove from the heat. Gradually stir 2 tablespoons hot filling into egg yolks; return all to the pan, stirring constantly. Bring to a gentle boil; cook and stir 2 minutes longer. Remove from the heat. Gently stir in butter, lemon juice and peel. Pour into crust.

4) For meringue, in a small mixing bowl, beat egg white and lemon juice on medium speed until soft peaks form. Gradually beat in sugar on high until stiff, glossy peaks form and sugar is dissolved. Spread evenly over hot filling, sealing edges to crust.

5) Bake at 350° for 10-12 minutes or until meringue is golden. Cool on a wire rack for 30 minutes. Refrigerate for at least 3 hours before serving.

Yield: 2 servings.

NUTRITION FACTS: 1 piece equals 577 calories, 21 g fat (7 g saturated fat), 223 mg cholesterol, 370 mg sodium, 89 g carbohydrate, 1 g fiber, 8 g protein.

PICNIC PECAN PIE

Picnic Pecan Pie

PREP: 10 min. **BAKE:** 40 min. + cooling

Jill Steiner, Hancock, Minnesota

Among the selection of homemade desserts at our family reunion, slices of this timeless treat disappeared fast. It's delectable topped with ice cream or whipped cream. For a milder flavor, you can use light corn syrup in place of the dark.

> 3 eggs
> 1 cup dark corn syrup
> 1/2 cup sugar
> 2 tablespoons butter, melted
> 1 teaspoon vanilla extract
> 1/8 teaspoon salt
> 1 cup chopped pecans
> 1 unbaked pastry shell (9 inches)

1) In a small bowl, lightly beat the eggs. Stir in the corn syrup, sugar, butter, vanilla and salt. Add pecans and mix well.

2) Pour into pie shell. Cover edges loosely with foil. Bake at 350° for 20 minutes. Remove foil; bake 20 minutes longer or until a knife inserted near the center comes out clean. Cool on a wire rack. Store in the refrigerator.

Yield: 8 servings.

NUTRITION FACTS: 1 piece equals 441 calories, 22 g fat (6 g saturated fat), 92 mg cholesterol, 253 mg sodium, 59 g carbohydrate, 1 g fiber, 5 g protein.

PERFECT PECAN PIE ■■■

My pecan pie has just the right amount of sweetness. I add three drops or so of lemon juice and 1/2 teaspoon vanilla to my pecan pie filling. It's yummy!

—*Fern Stewart-Raisch, Mesa, Arizona*

Fudgy Pecan Tartlets

PREP: 30 min. **BAKE:** 20 min. + cooling

Maggie Evans, Northville, Michigan

I usually bake these tiny tarts for the holidays, but they are a hit any time of year. They are easy to make, fudgy and moist. Everyone loves them!

> 1/4 cup butter, softened
> 3 tablespoons cream cheese, softened
> 1/2 cup all-purpose flour

FILLING:

> 1 egg yolk
> 3 tablespoons sugar
> 1-1/2 teaspoons butter, melted
> 1-1/2 teaspoons 2% milk
> 1/2 teaspoon vanilla extract
> 1/2 cup semisweet chocolate chips, melted and cooled
> 12 pecan halves

1) In a small mixing bowl, cream butter and cream cheese until light. Gradually add flour, beating until blended.

2) Roll into 1-in. balls. Press onto the bottom and up the sides of miniature muffin cups coated with cooking spray.

3) For filling, in a bowl, combine the egg yolk, sugar, butter, milk and vanilla; gradually stir in melted chocolate. Fill tart shells three-fourths full. Top each with a pecan half.

4) Bake at 375° for 18-22 minutes or until lightly browned and filling is set. Cool for 10 minutes before removing to a wire rack.

Yield: 1 dozen.

NUTRITION FACTS: 1 tartlet equals 134 calories, 10 g fat (5 g saturated fat), 33 mg cholesterol, 63 mg sodium, 12 g carbohydrate, 1 g fiber, 2 g protein.

FUDGY PECAN TARTLETS

MOM'S CUSTARD PIE

Mocha Chip Pie

PREP: 35 min. + chilling

Sheila Watson, Stettler, Alberta

This mocha pie is chocolaty from top to bottom. The only thing hard about making it is waiting for it to set. Your friends and family will want to dig right in.

- 1-1/2 cups chocolate wafer crumbs
- 1/4 cup butter, softened
- 1 envelope unflavored gelatin
- 1/2 cup milk
- 1/2 cup plus 1 tablespoon sugar, *divided*
- 1/2 cup strong brewed coffee
- 1/4 cup water
- 1/4 teaspoon salt
- 2 squares (1 ounce *each*) unsweetened chocolate, melted and cooled
- 1 teaspoon vanilla extract
- 2 cups heavy whipping cream, *divided*

Toasted sliced almonds, optional

1) In a small bowl, combine wafer crumbs and butter. Press onto the bottom and up the sides of a greased 9-in. pie plate. Bake at 375° for 5-7 minutes or until lightly browned. Cool on a wire rack.

2) In a small saucepan, sprinkle gelatin over milk; let stand for 1 minute. Cook and stir over low heat until gelatin is completely dissolved. Add 1/2 cup sugar, coffee, water and salt; cook and stir for 5 minutes or until sugar is dissolved. Remove from the heat; stir in melted chocolate and vanilla. Transfer to a large bowl; cover and refrigerate until slightly thickened, stirring occasionally.

3) In a small mixing bowl, beat 1 cup cream until stiff peaks form; fold into chocolate mixture. Spread evenly into crust. Refrigerate for 4 hours or until set.

4) Just before serving, in a small mixing bowl, beat remaining cream until it begins to thicken. Add remaining sugar; beat until stiff peaks form. Pipe over pie. Garnish with almonds if desired. Refrigerate leftovers.

Yield: 8 servings.

NUTRITION FACTS: 1 piece equals 433 calories, 33 g fat (20 g saturated fat), 99 mg cholesterol, 286 mg sodium, 33 g carbohydrate, 1 g fiber, 4 g protein.

Mom's Custard Pie

PREP: 25 min. **BAKE:** 40 min. + cooling

Barbara Hyatt, Folsom, California

Just a single bite of this traditional treat takes me back to the days when Mom would fix this pie for Dad and me.

- 1 unbaked pastry shell (9 inches)
- 4 eggs
- 1/2 cup sugar
- 1/4 teaspoon salt
- 1 teaspoon vanilla extract
- 2-1/2 cups milk
- 1/4 teaspoon ground nutmeg

1) Line unpricked pastry shell with a double thickness of heavy-duty foil. Bake at 450° for 8 minutes. Remove foil; bake 5 minutes longer. Remove from the oven and set aside.

2) Separate one egg; set the white aside. In a mixing bowl, beat the yolk and remaining eggs just until combined. Blend in the sugar, salt and vanilla. Stir in milk. Beat reserved egg white until stiff peaks form; fold into egg mixture.

3) Carefully pour into crust. Cover edges of pie with foil. Bake at 350° for 25 minutes. Remove foil; bake 15-20 minutes longer or until a knife inserted near the center comes out clean.

4) Cool on a wire rack. Sprinkle with nutmeg. Store in the refrigerator.

Yield: 8 servings.

NUTRITION FACTS: 1 piece equals 254 calories, 12 g fat (5 g saturated fat), 122 mg cholesterol, 243 mg sodium, 29 g carbohydrate, trace fiber, 7 g protein.

Testing Custard-Type Pies for Doneness

The most common doneness test for custard pies is to insert a table knife about an inch from the center of the pie. If it comes out clean, the pie is done. Or try the jiggle test. Gently shake the pie plate. If the center of the pie slightly jiggles, it's done. As it cools, the residual heat in the filling will finish baking the center.

FALL-FAVORITE PUMPKIN PIE

 CLASSIC: Enjoy old-fashioned goodness with a twist when you serve Walnut-Crunch Pumpkin Pie. A broiled walnut and brown sugar layer tops a traditional filling made with canned pumpkin, evaporated milk, brown sugar and spices for fabulous results.

 TIME-SAVER: It may seem difficult to believe, but Impossible Pumpkin Pie is ready in just one hour. Biscuit/baking mix is the key to this crustless pumpkin pie, which is pleasantly flavored with vanilla and allspice.

 LIGHT: A gingersnap crust is the perfect base for the fluffy filling in Pumpkin Chiffon Dessert. Since it doesn't call for eggs or a pastry crust, it has about a fourth of the calories and fat and a third of the carbohydrates of Walnut-Crunch Pumpkin Pie.

 SERVES 2: Brown sugar and maple flavoring complement the rich filling in Maple Pumpkin Pie. The from-scratch pastry crust is placed in a 5-inch pie plate and bakes into an adorable pie that's perfect for a pair to share.

Walnut-Crunch Pumpkin Pie

PREP: 20 min. **BAKE:** 50 min. + cooling

Edna Hoffman, Hebron, Indiana

- 2 eggs
- 1 can (15 ounces) solid-pack pumpkin
- 1 can (12 ounces) evaporated milk
- 3/4 cup packed brown sugar
- 2 teaspoons vanilla extract
- 1-1/2 teaspoons ground cinnamon
- 1/2 teaspoon salt
- 1/2 teaspoon ground ginger
- 1/2 teaspoon ground nutmeg
- 1 unbaked pastry shell (9 inches)

TOPPING:
- 1 cup chopped walnuts
- 3/4 cup packed brown sugar
- 1/4 cup butter, melted

1) In a large mixing bowl, beat eggs. Beat in the pumpkin, milk, brown sugar, vanilla, cinnamon, salt, ginger and nutmeg. Pour into pastry shell.

2) Cover edges loosely with foil. Bake at 425° for 15 minutes. Reduce heat to 350°. Remove foil; bake 35-40 minutes longer or until set and a knife inserted near the center comes out clean. Cool on a wire rack for 2 hours.

3) In a small bowl, combine the topping ingredients; sprinkle over pie. Cover edges loosely with foil. Broil 3-4 in. from the heat for 2 minutes or until golden brown. Remove foil. Store in the refrigerator.

Yield: 6-8 servings.

NUTRITION FACTS: 1 piece equals 515 calories, 26 g fat (10 g saturated fat), 87 mg cholesterol, 380 mg sodium, 64 g carbohydrate, 3 g fiber, 10 g protein.

Impossible Pumpkin Pie

PREP: 10 min. **BAKE:** 50 min. + cooling

Linda Cummings, Atoka, Tennessee

- 2 eggs
- 1 can (12 ounces) evaporated milk
- 1 can (15 ounces) solid-pack pumpkin
- 3/4 cup sugar
- 1/2 cup biscuit/baking mix
- 2 tablespoons butter, melted
- 2-1/2 teaspoons ground allspice
- 2 teaspoons vanilla extract

Whipped topping, optional

1) In a blender, combine the eggs, milk, pumpkin, sugar, biscuit mix, butter, allspice and vanilla. Cover and process until smooth. Pour into a greased 9-in. pie plate (dish will be full).

2) Bake at 350° for 50-55 minutes or until a knife inserted near the center comes out clean. Cool on a wire rack. Serve with whipped topping if desired. Store in the refrigerator.

Yield: 8 servings.

NUTRITION FACTS: 1 piece (calculated without whipped topping) equals 224 calories, 8 g fat (4 g saturated fat), 74 mg cholesterol, 182 mg sodium, 32 g carbohydrate, 3 g fiber, 6 g protein.

Pumpkin Chiffon Dessert

PREP: 20 min. + chilling

Lynn Baker, Osmond, Nebraska

- 1 cup finely crushed gingersnaps (about 24 cookies)
- 3 tablespoons butter, melted
- 2 envelopes unflavored gelatin
- 1/2 cup fat-free milk
- 1/2 cup sugar
- 1 can (15 ounces) solid-pack pumpkin

1/2 teaspoon salt
1/2 teaspoon ground cinnamon
1/4 teaspoon ground ginger
1/4 teaspoon ground cloves
1 carton (8 ounces) frozen fat-free whipped topping, thawed
Additional whipped topping, optional

PUMPKIN CHIFFON DESSERT

1) In a small bowl, combine cookie crumbs and butter. Press onto the bottom of a greased 9-in. springform pan; set aside.

2) In a large saucepan, combine gelatin and milk; let stand for 5 minutes. Heat to just below boiling; remove from the heat. Stir in sugar until dissolved. Add the pumpkin, salt, cinnamon, ginger and cloves; mix well. Fold in whipped topping. Pour over crust. Refrigerate until set, about 3 hours.

3) Remove sides of pan just before serving. Garnish with additional whipped topping if desired.

Yield: 16 servings.

NUTRITION FACTS: 1 piece equals 125 calories, 3 g fat (2 g saturated fat), 6 mg cholesterol, 172 mg sodium, 22 g carbohydrate, 1 g fiber, 2 g protein.

Maple Pumpkin Pie

PREP: 15 min. + chilling
BAKE: 40 min. + cooling

Vivian Colwell, Goshen, Ohio

1/2 cup all-purpose flour
1/8 teaspoon salt
2 tablespoons shortening
2 tablespoons cold water

FILLING:
1/2 cup canned pumpkin
1/3 cup fat-free evaporated milk
1/4 cup packed brown sugar
1/4 cup egg substitute
2 teaspoons sugar
1/2 teaspoon pumpkin pie spice
1/2 teaspoon maple flavoring
Dash salt

1) In a small bowl, combine flour and salt; cut in shortening until crumbly. Gradually add water, tossing with a fork until dough forms a ball. Cover and refrigerate for 15 minutes or until easy to handle. Meanwhile, in a small mixing bowl, combine the filling ingredients.

2) On a lightly floured surface, roll out dough to fit a 5-in. pie plate. Transfer pastry to pie plate. Trim to 1/2 in. beyond edge of plate; flute edges. Pour filling into crust.

3) Bake at 375° for 40-45 minutes or until a knife inserted near the center comes out clean. Cool on a wire rack. Store in the refrigerator.

Yield: 2 servings.

NUTRITION FACTS: 1 piece equals 419 calories, 13 g fat (3 g saturated fat), 2 mg cholesterol, 346 mg sodium, 65 g carbohydrate, 3 g fiber, 10 g protein.

MAPLE PUMPKIN PIE

DELICIOUS PIE CRUSTS ■■■

For enhanced flavor in your pie crust, add a bit of sugar and a few drops of vanilla to your basic recipe. If you're making an apple or pumpkin pie, also add cinnamon to the crust. Delicious!

—*Bonnie G., Brunswick, Ohio*

CHOCOLATE TRUFFLE PIE

Chocolate Truffle Pie

PREP: 30 min. + freezing

Mercelle Jackson, Rochester, New York

Warm days warrant a cool dessert like this frosty and refreshing pie. The raspberry sauce combined with rich chocolate and ice cream make each slice irresistible. Try out different ice cream flavors and enjoy the results!

> 1 cup chocolate wafer crumbs
> 1/4 cup butter, melted
> 1 pint chocolate ice cream, softened
> 1 cup (6 ounces) semisweet chocolate chips
> 1/3 cup heavy whipping cream
> 1 pint vanilla ice cream, softened
> 2 tablespoons slivered almonds, toasted
> 1 package (10 ounces) frozen sweetened raspberries, thawed
> 1 tablespoon cornstarch

1) In a small bowl, combine wafer crumbs and butter. Press onto the bottom and up the sides of a 9-in. pie plate coated with cooking spray. Freeze for 30 minutes. Spread chocolate ice cream over crust; freeze for 1 hour or until firm.

2) Melt chocolate chips with whipping cream; stir until smooth. Cool slightly. Quickly and carefully spread over chocolate ice cream. Freeze for 30 minutes. Top with vanilla ice cream; sprinkle with almonds. Cover; freeze until firm.

3) For sauce, puree the raspberries in a blender or food processor until smooth. Strain and discard seeds. In a saucepan, combine cornstarch and raspberry juice until smooth. Bring to a boil; cook and stir for 1-2 minutes or until thickened. Cool completely.

4) Remove pie from the freezer 10 minutes before cutting. Serve over raspberry sauce.

Yield: 8 servings.

NUTRITION FACTS: 1 piece equals 435 calories, 26 g fat (15 g saturated fat), 55 mg cholesterol, 197 mg sodium, 51 g carbohydrate, 4 g fiber, 5 g protein.

■ **Favorite Ice Cream Pie:** Substitute your family's favorite flavor of ice cream for either the chocolate or vanilla. Here are some additional combinations: chocolate and coffee, cherry and vanilla or caramel and coffee.

Lime Cheesecake Pie

PREP: 5 min. + chilling

Vivian Eagleson, Lawrenceville, Georgia

This light citrus pie is the perfect treat on a hot day because you don't have to heat up the kitchen to prepare it.

> 1 package (8 ounces) cream cheese, softened
> 1 can (14 ounces) sweetened condensed milk
> 1/3 cup lime juice
> 1-1/2 teaspoons vanilla extract
> 1 graham cracker crust (9 inches)
> 1 carton (8 ounces) frozen whipped topping, thawed

Lime slices and fresh mint, optional

1) In a large mixing bowl, beat cream cheese until smooth. Add the milk, lime juice and vanilla; beat until smooth. Pour into the crust. Refrigerate for 2 hours.

2) Spread with whipped topping; refrigerate 1 hour longer. Garnish with lime and mint if desired.

Yield: 8 servings.

NUTRITION FACTS: 1 piece equals 446 calories, 24 g fat (15 g saturated fat), 48 mg cholesterol, 268 mg sodium, 49 g carbohydrate, trace fiber, 7 g protein.

LIME CHEESECAKE PIE

CHERRY CHEESECAKE PIE

◈ Cherry Cheesecake Pie

PREP: 15 min. **BAKE:** 25 min. + chilling

Sandra Lee Herr, Stevens, Pennsylvania

Cottage cheese is the secret to this creamy slimmed-down dessert. It's festively topped with cherry pie filling.

- 2 eggs, lightly beaten
- 4 ounces reduced-fat cream cheese, cubed
- 1/2 cup fat-free cottage cheese
- 1/4 cup nonfat dry milk powder

Sugar substitute equivalent to 1/4 cup sugar

- 1 tablespoon lemon juice
- 2 teaspoons vanilla extract
- 1 reduced-fat graham cracker crust (8 inches)
- 1 can (20 ounces) reduced-sugar cherry pie filling

1) In a food processor, combine the first seven ingredients; cover and process until smooth. Pour into the crust. Bake at 350° for 25-30 minutes or until the center is almost set. Cool on a wire rack for 1 hour.

2) Cover and refrigerate overnight. Cut into slices; top with cherry pie filling.

Yield: 8 servings.

Editor's Note: This recipe was tested with Splenda No Calorie Sweetener.

NUTRITION FACTS: 1 piece equals 225 calories, 6 g fat (2 g saturated fat), 59 mg cholesterol, 241 mg sodium, 35 g carbohydrate, trace fiber, 7 g protein.

Perfect Cut for Chiffon or Refrigerator Pies

Here's a tip for a smooth, clean cut on a chiffon or other refrigerator-type pie. Warm the blade of a sharp knife in hot water, then dry and make a cut. Clean and rewarm knife before each cut. You'll have a picture-perfect slice of pie.

◈ Strawberry Chiffon Pie

PREP: 25 min. + chilling

Taste of Home Test Kitchen

This scrumptious strawberry chiffon filling is so refreshing. Either a graham cracker crust or chocolate crumb crust will showcase it nicely.

- 2-1/2 cups sliced fresh strawberries
- 1 envelope unflavored gelatin
- 2 tablespoons lemonade concentrate
- 1/4 cup sugar
- 3 egg whites, lightly beaten
- 1 tablespoon orange juice
- 1-1/2 cups reduced-fat whipped topping
- 1 reduced-fat graham cracker crust (8 inches) *or* chocolate crumb crust
- 4 large fresh strawberries, halved

1) Place sliced strawberries in a food processor; cover and process until smooth. Set aside 1-1/2 cups for filling (discard remaining puree or save for another use).

2) In a saucepan, sprinkle gelatin over lemonade concentrate; let stand for 5 minutes. Stir in sugar and reserved strawberry puree. Cook and stir over medium heat until mixture comes to a boil and gelatin is dissolved. Remove from the heat.

3) Stir a small amount of filling into egg whites; return all to the pan, stirring constantly. Cook and stir over low heat for 3 minutes or until mixture is slightly thickened and a thermometer reaches 160° (do not boil). Remove from the heat; stir in orange juice. Cover and refrigerate for 2 hours, stirring occasionally. Fold in whipped topping; spoon into crust. Cover and refrigerate for 2 hours or until set. Just before serving, garnish with halved strawberries.

Yield: 8 servings.

NUTRITION FACTS: 1 piece equals 226 calories, 7 g fat (5 g saturated fat), 12 mg cholesterol, 145 mg sodium, 35 g carbohydrate, 2 g fiber, 4 g protein

STRAWBERRY CHIFFON PIE

RASPBERRY RIBBON PIE

Raspberry Ribbon Pie

PREP: 15 min. **BAKE:** 10 min. + chilling

Anita Ohlson, Cheyenne, Wyoming

We always freeze fresh raspberries when they're in season so we can make this pie year-round.

- 1 cup vanilla wafer crumbs (about 29 wafers)
- 1/4 cup butter, melted
- 1 package (3 ounces) raspberry gelatin
- 1 cup boiling water
- 1/4 cup sugar
- 1 cup fresh raspberries
- 1 tablespoon lemon juice
- 1 package (3 ounces) cream cheese, softened
- 1/3 cup confectioners' sugar
- 1 teaspoon vanilla extract

Dash salt

- 1 cup heavy whipping cream

1) In a small bowl, combine the wafer crumbs and butter; press onto the bottom and up the sides of an ungreased 9-in. pie plate. Bake at 350° for 10 minutes or until golden brown.

2) In a bowl, dissolve gelatin in boiling water. Add the sugar, raspberries and lemon juice. Refrigerate until partially set, about 1-1/2 hours. In a mixing bowl, beat cream cheese and confectioners' sugar until smooth. Add vanilla and salt. In another mixing bowl, beat whipping cream until stiff peaks form. Fold into cream cheese mixture. Spread 3/4 cup over bottom of crust.

3) Spread 3/4 cup raspberry mixture over the top; repeat layers. Refrigerate for 8 hours or overnight before serving. Refrigerate leftovers.

Yield: 8 servings.

NUTRITION FACTS: 1 piece equals 345 calories, 23 g fat (13 g saturated fat), 69 mg cholesterol, 189 mg sodium, 34 g carbohydrate, 1 g fiber, 3 g protein.

■ **Strawberry Ribbon Pie:** Use strawberry gelatin for the raspberry gelatin and use 1 cup sliced strawberries for the raspberries.

Strawberry Tartlets

PREP: 25 min. **BAKE:** 10 min. + cooling

Joy Van Meter, Thornton, Colorado

This elegant-looking dessert is easy to make, and the cute wonton "cups" can be made in advance. They're a different way to present fresh strawberries when entertaining. The recipe is easy to double, too.

- 12 wonton wrappers
- 3 tablespoons butter, melted
- 1/3 cup packed brown sugar
- 3/4 cup Mascarpone cheese
- 2 tablespoons honey
- 2 teaspoons orange juice
- 3 cups fresh strawberries, sliced

Whipped cream and fresh mint, optional

1) Brush one side of each wonton wrapper with butter. Place brown sugar in a shallow bowl; press buttered side of wontons into sugar to coat. Press wontons sugared side up into greased muffin cups. Bake at 325° for 7-9 minutes or until edges are lightly browned. Remove to a wire rack to cool completely.

2) In a bowl, combine the cheese, honey and orange juice. Spoon about 1 tablespoon into each wonton cup. Top with strawberries. Garnish with whipped cream and mint if desired.

Yield: 1 dozen.

NUTRITION FACTS: 1 tartlet equals 214 calories, 16 g fat (9 g saturated fat), 43 mg cholesterol, 84 mg sodium, 16 g carbohydrate, 1 g fiber, 3 g protein.

STRAWBERRY TARTLETS

cupcakes go to high school

Students start a club about baking & giving

No matter how young or how old, everyone can make an impact in their little corner of the world. So says Lily Bussel, 17, of Eugene, Oregon.

Knowing she wanted to help others, she combined her love of cupcakes with fund-raising, and VOILA!

Henry D. Sheldon High School now has its own Cupcake Club.

The idea of giving to others was instilled in Lily at an early age.

"When I was younger, I volunteered at a local soup kitchen," she recalls. "I remember seeing the men's and women's faces light up when I handed them a dinner tray. I received a great sense of satisfaction from that."

Like many other foodies, Lily noticed the increasing popularity of cupcakes and wondered how she could combine her love of baking with the cupcake craze and her desire to help people in her community. The idea for the Cupcake Club was born.

"I met with a vice principal at my high school and felt discouraged after learning about the numerous obstacles I would face in order to have the club approved, but I was determined," she says.

"The majority of students at my school are middle to upper class, and some are unaware of the situation of those less fortunate. Through the Cupcake Club, I hoped to raise awareness among teens about social problems. I also wanted to illustrate the importance of benefiting local charities."

Today, the year-old Cupcake Club has about 35 members who meet, bake and sell their sweet treats after school once a week. In its first six months, the club had raised $900 for local charities.

Lily Bussel

> *Through the Cupcake Club, I hoped to raise awareness among teens about social problems.*
>
> ~Lily Bussel

Recipes

Tips

Cakes

Cakes add a festive air to any meal and usually make an appearance at special-occasion dinners. They are divided into two categories—butter cakes and foam cakes.

Butter cakes get their name because the batter is made from creaming fat—such as butter or shortening—with sugar. The creaming traps air in the batter; this trapped air expands during baking and gives the cake its height. Butter cakes have a fine moist texture and a tender crumb.

Foam cakes contain a high proportion of eggs or egg whites to flour. Beaten eggs give foam cakes their light, fluffy texture. There are three kinds of foam cakes: angel food, sponge and chiffon.

Flour Facts

All-purpose flour is the most commonly used flour and creates a good cake. Cake flour gives a more tender and delicate crumb. Self-rising flour contains the leavening agent and salt, so you only need to measure one ingredient. While you can substitute one type of flour for another, you will need to make some adjustments to the recipe.

- For 1 cup of cake flour, use 3/4 cup plus 2 tablespoons all-purpose flour.

- For 1 cup all-purpose flour, use 1 cup plus 2 tablespoons cake flour.

- For 1 cup self-rising flour, place 1-1/2 teaspoons baking powder and 1/2 teaspoon salt in a measuring cup. Add all-purpose flour to measure 1 cup.

Baking at High Altitudes

High altitude (over 3,000 feet) has less air pressure and drier air. These conditions affect baked goods. The lower air pressure makes the gases created by the leavening agents expand more quickly and causes liquids to evaporate and boil at lower temperatures. The drier air also dries out the flour.

For cakes, this means that there might be excessive rising from the leavening-produced gases. This would cause the texture to be coarse or may even cause the cake to fall before the structure of the cake can be set by baking. Faster evaporation of the liquid, due to a lower boiling point, reduces the amount of liquid and increases the concentration of sugar. This higher sugar concentration may also weaken the structure of the cake.

Some measures to take for butter cakes are to increase the oven temperature 15° to 25°, which will allow cakes to set faster and prevent falling. Fill baking pans half full not two-thirds full, since cakes rise higher. Reduce the leavener, reduce the sugar and increase the liquid.

Here are some general guidelines for adjusting ingredients for butter cakes at different altitudes:

ADJUSTMENT	3,000 FT.	5,000 FT.	7,000 FT.
For *each* teaspoon of baking powder, reduce by:	1/8 teaspoon	1/8 to 1/4 teaspoon	1/4 teaspoon
For *each* cup of sugar, reduce by:	0 to 1 tablespoon	0 to 2 tablespoons	1 to 3 tablespoons
For *each* cup of liquid, increase by:	1 to 2 tablespoons	2 to 4 tablespoons	3 to 4 tablespoons

For foam cakes, beat the egg whites only until soft peaks form. To strengthen the structure of the cake, decrease the amount of sugar by a tablespoon or two and increase the amount of flour or egg component of the cake a little. Increasing the oven temperature by 15° to 25° will also help set the cake structure sooner.

Butter Cakes

Use butter, stick margarine (with at least 80% oil) or shortening. The fat should be softened (at room temperature), meaning it is pliable when touched. Whipped, tub, soft, liquid or reduced-fat products should not be used. Measure all ingredients accurately.

Arrange the oven racks so that the cake will bake in the center of the oven. Preheat oven for 10 to 15 minutes before baking.

Most butter cake recipes call for creaming the butter and sugar. Beat the softened butter or shortening and sugar with an electric mixer or wooden spoon to a light and fluffy consistency, about 5 minutes.

For better volume, allow eggs to stand at room temperature for 30 minutes before using. Or place eggs in their shell in a bowl of warm water while assembling the remaining ingredients.

Mix dry ingredients together to evenly distribute the leavener throughout the flour. This will ensure that it's evenly incorporated into the batter. Stop the mixer occasionally—or between additions of ingredients—and scrape the batter down the sides of the bowl with a rubber or plastic spatula.

It's best to use the pan size recommended in the recipe. For substitutions, check the Bakeware Substitution chart on page 14. Baking times may need to be adjusted. For a tender, golden crust, use aluminum pans with a dull rather than shiny or dark finish. If using glass baking dishes, reduce the oven temperature 25°.

For butter cakes that will be removed from the pans, grease and flour the baking pans. Cakes served from the pans should be greased but not floured. Some cake recipes call for the pan to be lined with waxed paper for easier removal of the cake from the pan. (See Lining a Baking Pan with Waxed Paper on page 607.)

Fill pans half to three-fourths full. A thin batter will rise more than a heavy batter, so only fill the pans half full to allow more room for the batter to rise. Pour thin batters into pans, then tap pans on the countertop to remove air bubbles. Spoon firm batters into pans, then spread gently to even out the batter.

Leave at least 1 in. of space between pans and also between pans and sides of oven for good heat circulation. If using two oven racks, stagger pans in the oven so that they are not directly over one another. Switch pan positions and rotate pans from front to back halfway through the baking time.

Use a kitchen timer. Check for doneness at the minimum recommended baking time, then check every 2 minutes after that. Butter cakes are done when a toothpick inserted near the center of the cake comes out clean. (See Testing Butter Cakes for Doneness on page 607.)

Cool cake for 10 minutes in the pan, unless recipe directs otherwise. Loosen the cake by running a knife around the edge of the pan. Turn out onto a wire rack, place another rack over the cake and flip right side up. Cool completely before filling or frosting unless directed otherwise by the recipe.

If a cake sticks to the pan and will not come out when inverted, return to a heated oven for 1 minute, then try again to turn it out.

Use a serrated knife or use a sawing motion when cutting. Warm the blade of the knife in hot water, then dry and make a cut. Clean and rewarm the knife before each cut.

White Layer Cake

PREP: 15 min. **BAKE:** 30 min. + cooling

Taste of Home Test Kitchen

Every recipe file should contain a standard delicious cake like this. Topped with your favorite flavor of frosting, it's great for any occasion.

- 1/2 cup butter, softened
- 1-1/2 cups sugar
- 4 egg whites
- 2 teaspoons vanilla extract
- 2 cups all-purpose flour
- 1 teaspoon baking powder
- 1/2 teaspoon baking soda
- 1/4 teaspoon salt
- 1-1/3 cups buttermilk
- 2-1/2 cups frosting of your choice

1) In a large mixing bowl, cream butter and sugar until light and fluffy. Add egg whites, one at a time, beating well after each. Beat in vanilla.

2) Combine the flour, baking powder, baking soda and salt; add to creamed mixture alternately with buttermilk, beating well after each addition.

3) Spread evenly into two greased and floured 9-in. round baking pans. Bake at 350° for 30-35 minutes or until a toothpick inserted near the center comes out clean. Cool for 10 minutes before removing from pans to wire racks to cool completely.

4) Spread frosting between layers and over top and sides of cake.

Yield: 12 servings.

NUTRITION FACTS: 1 slice equals 508 calories, 18 g fat (7 g saturated fat), 22 mg cholesterol, 376 mg sodium, 81 g carbohydrate, 1 g fiber, 4 g protein.

Yellow Layer Cake

PREP: 15 min. **BAKE:** 25 min. + cooling

Taste of Home Test Kitchen

Instead of a boxed cake mix, why not try your hand at this easy recipe for a basic yellow cake? You just can't beat the homemade goodness!

- 2/3 cup butter, softened
- 1-3/4 cups sugar
- 2 eggs
- 1-1/2 teaspoons vanilla extract
- 2-1/2 cups all-purpose flour
- 2-1/2 teaspoons baking powder
- 1/2 teaspoon salt
- 1-1/4 cups milk
- 2-1/2 cups frosting of your choice

1) In a large mixing bowl, cream butter and sugar until light and fluffy. Add eggs, one at a time, beating well after each addition. Beat in vanilla.

2) Combine the flour, baking powder and salt; add to the creamed mixture alternately with milk, beating well after each addition.

3) Spread evenly into two greased and floured 9-in. round baking pans. Bake at 350° for 25-30 minutes or until a toothpick inserted near the center comes out clean. Cool for 10 minutes before removing from pans to wire racks to cool completely.

4) Spread frosting between layers and over the top and sides of cake.

Yield: 12 servings.

NUTRITION FACTS: 1 slice equals 576 calories, 22 g fat (10 g saturated fat), 66 mg cholesterol, 425 mg sodium, 89 g carbohydrate, 1 g fiber, 5 g protein.

YELLOW LAYER CAKE

Leveling Layer Cakes

Stacking layers for a layered cake is easier when the layers are level. When the cake is cool, use a long serrated knife to slice the high spot from the bottom layer of a two-layer cake or the bottom and middle layers of a three-layer cake. You can trim off the crown of the top layer or leave it for a domed effect.

Holiday Fruitcake

PREP: 20 min. **BAKE:** 2 hours + cooling

Allene Spence, Delbarton, West Virginia

I came up with this recipe myself and think it has just the right mix of nuts and fruit.

- 3 cups whole red and green candied cherries
- 3 cups diced candied pineapple
- 1 package (1 pound) shelled walnuts
- 1 package (10 ounces) golden raisins
- 1 cup shortening
- 1 cup sugar
- 5 eggs
- 1/4 cup vanilla extract
- 3 cups all-purpose flour
- 3 teaspoons baking powder
- 1 teaspoon salt

1) In a large bowl, combine the cherries, pineapple, walnuts and raisins; set aside. In a large mixing bowl, cream shortening and sugar until light and fluffy. Beat in eggs and vanilla.

2) Combine the flour, baking powder and salt; add to the creamed mixture and mix well. Pour over fruit mixture and stir to coat.

3) Pour into a greased and floured 10-in. tube pan. Bake at 300° for 2 hours or until a toothpick inserted near the center comes out clean. Cool for 10 minutes before removing from pan to a wire rack to cool completely.

4) Wrap tightly and store in a cool place. Slice with a serrated knife; bring to room temperature before serving.

Yield: 16 servings.

NUTRITION FACTS: 1 slice equals 684 calories, 32 g fat (5 g saturated fat), 66 mg cholesterol, 281 mg sodium, 92 g carbohydrate, 4 g fiber, 9 g protein.

OLD-FASHIONED, BUTTERY POUND CAKE

 CLASSIC: If you're craving a luscious, moist cake with a velvety texture, you can't go wrong with Million-Dollar Pound Cake. Vanilla and almond extracts give the batter its homey taste.

 TIME-SAVER: Lemony Pound Cake is ready in about an hour, thanks to a handy package of lemon cake mix and three additional ingredients. It gets richness from cream cheese and eggs and a pretty look from baking in a fluted tube pan.

 LIGHT: Unsweetened applesauce helps slim down this Pound Cake Loaf, which calls for fewer eggs and less butter and sugar. One slice has 300 fewer calories, almost half the cholesterol and about a third of the fat and carbohydrates of a serving of Million-Dollar Pound Cake.

 SERVES 2: Ground almonds, lemon juice and grated lemon peel put a flavorful spin on Almond-Lemon Pound Cake, which is served with a colorful berry sauce. It bakes in a 9-inch pan, yielding just six slices compared to the dozen or more servings that most recipes make.

MILLION-DOLLAR POUND CAKE

Million-Dollar Pound Cake

PREP: 20 min. **BAKE:** 1 hour 40 min. + cooling

George Dunn, Jasper, Texas

 2 cups butter, softened
 3 cups sugar
 6 eggs
 4 cups all-purpose flour
3/4 cup milk
 1 teaspoon almond extract
 1 teaspoon vanilla extract

1) In a large mixing bowl, cream butter until fluffy. Gradually add sugar, beating until light and fluffy, about 5 minutes. Add eggs, one at a time, beating well after each addition.

2) Add flour to creamed mixture alternately with milk, beginning and ending with flour, just until blended. Stir in extracts. Pour into a greased and floured 10-in. tube pan.

3) Bake at 325° for 1 hour and 40 minutes or until a toothpick inserted near the center comes out clean. Cool for 15 minutes before removing from pan to a wire rack to cool completely.

Yield: 16 servings.

NUTRITION FACTS: 1 slice equals 497 calories, 25 g fat (15 g saturated fat), 143 mg cholesterol, 262 mg sodium, 62 g carbohydrate, 1 g fiber, 6 g protein.

Lemony Pound Cake

PREP: 10 min. **BAKE:** 40 min. + cooling

Flora Valdez, San Bernardino, California

 1 package (8 ounces) cream cheese, softened
3/4 cup milk
 1 package (18-1/4 ounces) lemon cake mix
 4 eggs

1) In a large mixing bowl, beat cream cheese until smooth; gradually beat in milk. Add cake mix and eggs; beat until combined. Beat on medium speed for 2 minutes. Pour into a greased and floured 10-in. fluted tube pan.

2) Bake at 350° for 40-45 minutes or until a toothpick inserted near the center comes out clean. Cool for 10 minutes before removing from pan to a wire rack to cool completely.

Yield: 12 servings.

NUTRITION FACTS: 1 slice equals 231 calories, 7 g fat (3 g saturated fat), 78 mg cholesterol, 373 mg sodium, 37 g carbohydrate, 1 g fiber, 6 g protein.

Pound Cake Loaf

PREP: 15 min. **BAKE:** 45 min. + cooling

F. Joyce Grasby, Rochester, New York

1/2 cup butter, softened
3/4 cup sugar
 3 eggs
1/4 cup unsweetened applesauce

POUND CAKE LOAF

1-1/4 teaspoons vanilla extract
1/2 teaspoon grated lemon peel
1-1/4 cups all-purpose flour
1/2 teaspoon baking powder
1/4 teaspoon salt

1) In a small mixing bowl, cream butter and sugar until light and fluffy, about 5 minutes. Add eggs, one at a time, beating well after each addition. Stir in the applesauce, vanilla and lemon peel. Combine the flour, baking powder and salt; add to creamed mixture just until blended.

2) Transfer to an 8-in. x 4-in. x 2-in. loaf pan coated with cooking spray. Bake at 350° for 45-55 minutes or until golden brown and a toothpick inserted near the center comes out clean. Cool for 10 minutes before removing from pan to a wire rack to cool completely.

Yield: 12 servings.

NUTRITION FACTS: 1 slice equals 185 calories, 9 g fat (5 g saturated fat), 74 mg cholesterol, 159 mg sodium, 23 g carbohydrate, trace fiber, 3 g protein.

Almond-Lemon Pound Cake
PREP: 20 min. **BAKE:** 40 min. + cooling

Michaela Rosenthal, Woodland Hills, California

1 teaspoon plus 3/4 cup butter, softened, *divided*
2 teaspoons confectioners' sugar
1 cup slivered almonds
1 cup sugar
2 eggs
1/3 cup sour cream
1 tablespoon grated lemon peel

1 cup cake flour
1 teaspoon baking powder
1/4 cup lemon juice

SAUCE:

1 cup *each* frozen unsweetened raspberries, strawberries and blueberries
1/4 cup sugar
2 tablespoons lemon juice
2 tablespoons confectioners' sugar

1) Grease the bottom and sides of a 9-in. round baking pan with 1 teaspoon butter. Sprinkle with confectioners' sugar; set aside. Place the almonds and sugar in a food processor; cover and process until finely ground.

2) In a small mixing bowl, cream the remaining butter; beat in almond mixture until combined. Add eggs, one at a time, beating well after each addition. Beat in sour cream and lemon peel. Combine the flour and baking powder; add to creamed mixture alternately with lemon juice. Pour into prepared pan.

3) Bake at 350° for 40-45 minutes or until a toothpick inserted near the center comes out clean. Cool for 10 minutes before removing from the pan to a wire rack to cool completely.

4) For sauce, in a heavy saucepan, combine the berries, sugar and lemon juice. Cook and stir over medium-low heat for 10 minutes or until mixture begins to thicken. Sprinkle cake with confectioners' sugar. Serve with berry sauce.

Yield: 6 servings.

NUTRITION FACTS: 1 slice with 3 tablespoons berry sauce equals 654 calories, 37 g fat (17 g saturated fat), 143 mg cholesterol, 334 mg sodium, 76 g carbohydrate, 4 g fiber, 9 g protein.

ALMOND-LEMON POUND CAKE

Lemon Orange Cake

PREP: 20 min. **BAKE:** 25 min. + cooling

Norma Poole, Auburndale, Florida

I love to bake this lovely three-layer cake for Thanksgiving. It has that tangy Florida citrus flavor and isn't any more difficult to make than a two-layer cake.

- 1 cup butter, softened
- 1/4 cup shortening
- 2 cups sugar
- 5 eggs
- 3 cups all-purpose flour
- 1 teaspoon baking powder
- 1/2 teaspoon baking soda
- 1/2 teaspoon salt
- 1 cup buttermilk
- 1 teaspoon vanilla extract
- 1/2 teaspoon lemon extract

FROSTING:

- 1/2 cup butter, softened
- 3 tablespoons orange juice
- 3 tablespoons lemon juice
- 1 to 2 tablespoons grated orange peel
- 1 to 2 tablespoons grated lemon peel
- 1 teaspoon lemon extract
- 5-1/2 to 6 cups confectioners' sugar

1) In a large mixing bowl, cream butter, shortening and sugar until light and fluffy. Add eggs, one at a time, beating well after each addition. Combine the flour, baking powder, baking soda and salt; add to the creamed mixture alternately with buttermilk, beginning and ending with dry ingredients. Beat well after each addition. Stir in extracts.

Preparing a Cake Pan

1) Grease the sides and bottom of the pan by spreading shortening with a paper towel over the interior of the pan.

2) Sprinkle 1 to 2 tablespoons of flour into the greased pan; tilt the pan to coat bottom and sides. Turn pan over and tap to remove excess flour.

GEORGIA PECAN CAKE

Georgia Pecan Cake

PREP: 15 min. **BAKE:** 1 hour + cooling

Carolyn Griffin, Macon, Georgia

This recipe came from my mother and has always been a hit with our family. One taste and you'll see why!

- 1 cup butter, softened
- 2 cups sugar
- 4 eggs
- 1 teaspoon vanilla extract
- 1/2 teaspoon lemon extract
- 3 cups all-purpose flour
- 3/4 teaspoon salt
- 1/2 teaspoon baking powder
- 1/2 teaspoon baking soda
- 1 cup buttermilk
- 1 cup chopped pecans

1) In a large mixing bowl, cream butter and sugar until light and fluffy. Add the eggs, one at a time, beating well after each addition. Beat in extracts.

2) Combine the flour, salt, baking powder and baking soda; set 1/4 cup aside. Add the remaining flour mixture to the creamed mixture alternately with buttermilk. Toss pecans with the reserved flour mixture; fold into batter.

3) Pour into a greased and floured 10-in. tube pan. Bake at 325° for 60-70 minutes or until a toothpick inserted near the center comes out clean. Cool for 10 minutes before removing from pan to a wire rack to cool completely.

Yield: 12-16 servings.

NUTRITION FACTS: 1 slice equals 360 calories, 18 g fat (8 g saturated fat), 84 mg cholesterol, 311 mg sodium, 45 g carbohydrate, 1 g fiber, 5 g protein.

LEMON ORANGE CAKE

2) Pour into three greased and floured 9-in. round baking pans. Bake at 350° for 25-30 minutes or until a toothpick inserted near the center comes out clean. Cool for 10 minutes before removing from pans to wire racks to cool completely.

3) For frosting, in a small mixing bowl, cream butter until light and fluffy. Add the juices, peels and extract; beat until well blended. Gradually add confectioners' sugar, beating until frosting reaches desired consistency. Spread between layers and over top and sides of cake.

Yield: 10-12 servings.

NUTRITION FACTS: 1 slice equals 740 calories, 29 g fat (16 g saturated fat), 151 mg cholesterol, 465 mg sodium, 114 g carbohydrate, 1 g fiber, 7 g protein.

Testing Tube Cakes for Doneness

A standard-size toothpick is too short to accurately test the doneness of a butter cake baked in a tube pan. If you don't have a long wooden pick or metal cake tester to test for doneness, use an uncooked strand of dry spaghetti. Insert it as you would a toothpick; if the spaghetti comes out clean, the cake is done. Discard spaghetti after use.

Poppy Seed Bundt Cake
PREP: 20 min. **BAKE:** 1 hour + cooling

Lois Schlickau, Haven, Kansas

Since this moist cake keeps so well, you can make it the day before serving. It freezes beautifully, too. Flavored with almond extract and poppy seeds, it's great for taking to a picnic or potluck or to present as a hostess gift.

- 3 cups all-purpose flour
- 2-1/2 cups sugar
- 1-1/2 teaspoons baking powder
- 1/2 teaspoon salt
- 3 eggs
- 1-1/2 cups milk
- 1 cup vegetable oil
- 1 tablespoon poppy seeds
- 1-1/2 teaspoons almond extract
- 1-1/2 teaspoons vanilla extract
- 1 teaspoon butter flavoring

GLAZE:
- 3/4 cup confectioners' sugar
- 1/4 cup orange juice
- 1/2 teaspoon almond extract
- 1/2 teaspoon vanilla extract
- 1/2 teaspoon butter flavoring

1) In a large mixing bowl, combine the flour, sugar, baking powder and salt. Whisk the eggs, milk, oil, poppy seeds, extracts and flavoring; add to dry ingredients. Beat on low speed for 30 seconds or just until moistened. Beat on medium for 2 minutes.

2) Pour into a greased and floured 10-in. fluted tube pan. Bake at 350° for 60-70 minutes or until a toothpick inserted near the center comes out clean. Cool for 10 minutes before removing from pan to a wire rack to cool completely.

3) In a small bowl, combine glaze ingredients until smooth. Pour over cake.

Yield: 12-14 servings.

NUTRITION FACTS: 1 slice equals 442 calories, 18 g fat (3 g saturated fat), 49 mg cholesterol, 155 mg sodium, 65 g carbohydrate, 1 g fiber, 5 g protein.

POPPY SEED BUNDT CAKE

DELECTABLE CHOCOLATE CAKE

 CLASSIC: Impress chocolate lovers when you bring out Elegant Chocolate Torte. With moist homemade cake layers, cooked chocolate-pudding-like filling and fluffy chocolate frosting, it's chocolaty through and through. Yum!

 TIME-SAVER: Butterscotch Chocolate Cake lets you dig into a decadent chocolate cake without all the work. This dreamy dessert dresses up chocolate cake from a boxed mix with butterscotch ice cream topping, whipped topping and crushed Butterfinger candy bars.

 LIGHT: Try one bite of Chocolate-Glazed Raspberry Torte (recipe on page 606) and you'll never guess it's light. Egg whites and applesauce in the cake, reduced-fat whipped topping and fresh berries as the filling and a simple glaze make this treat sweet but not sinful. Each slice has less than half the calories and a third of the fat of Elegant Chocolate Torte and just a trace of cholesterol.

 SERVES 2: When you taste Dark Chocolate Pecan Cake (recipe on page 606), you may wish there were leftovers so you could have seconds. This loaf-shaped torte has moist cake, sweetened whipped cream and a praline layer, but makes just enough for two people.

Elegant Chocolate Torte

PREP: 50 min. **BAKE:** 30 min. + cooling

Lois Gallup Edwards, Woodland, California

- 1/3 cup all-purpose flour
- 3 tablespoons sugar
- 1 teaspoon salt
- 1-3/4 cups milk
- 1 cup chocolate syrup
- 1 egg, lightly beaten
- 1 tablespoon butter
- 1 teaspoon vanilla extract

BATTER:
- 1/2 cup butter, softened
- 1-1/4 cups sugar
- 4 eggs
- 1 teaspoon vanilla extract
- 1-1/4 cups all-purpose flour
- 1/3 cup baking cocoa
- 3/4 teaspoon baking soda
- 1/4 teaspoon salt
- 1-1/2 cups chocolate syrup
- 1/2 cup water

FROSTING:
- 2 cups heavy whipping cream
- 1/4 cup chocolate syrup
- 1/4 teaspoon vanilla extract

1) For filling, in a small saucepan, combine flour, sugar and salt. Stir in milk and chocolate syrup until smooth. Bring to a boil over medium heat, stirring constantly; cook and stir for 1-2 minutes or until thickened.

2) Remove from heat. Stir a small amount of hot mixture into egg; return all to the pan, stirring

ELEGANT CHOCOLATE TORTE

constantly. Bring to a gentle boil; cook and stir for 2 minutes. Remove from heat; stir in butter and vanilla. Cool to room temperature, stirring often.

3) In a large mixing bowl, cream butter and sugar until light and fluffy. Add eggs, one at a time, beating well after each addition. Beat in vanilla. Combine the flour, cocoa, baking soda and salt; add to creamed mixture alternately with chocolate syrup and water. Beat just until combined.

4) Pour into two greased and floured 9-in. round baking pans. Bake at 350° for 30-35 minutes or until a toothpick inserted near the center comes out clean. Cool for 10 minutes before removing from pans to wire racks to cool completely.

5) Cut each cake in half horizontally. Place one bottom layer on a serving plate; spread with a third of the filling. Repeat layers twice. Top with remaining cake. In a small mixing bowl, beat frosting ingredients until stiff peaks form; spread or pipe over top and sides of cake.

Yield: 16 servings.

NUTRITION FACTS: 1 slice equals 456 calories, 20 g fat (12 g saturated fat), 126 mg cholesterol, 367 mg sodium, 64 g carbohydrate, 1 g fiber, 6 g protein.

■ **Mocha Chocolate Torte:** Add 1 to 1-1/2 teaspoons instant coffee granules to flour mixture in filling. Proceed as directed.

Butterscotch Chocolate Cake

PREP: 10 min. **BAKE:** 30 min. + chilling

Shelley McKinney, New Castle, Indiana

- 1 package (18-1/4 ounces) chocolate cake mix
- 1 jar (17 ounces) butterscotch ice cream topping
- 1 carton (8 ounces) frozen whipped topping, thawed
- 3 Butterfinger candy bars (2.1 ounces *each*), coarsely crushed

1) Prepare and bake cake according to package directions, using a greased 13-in. x 9-in. x 2-in. baking pan. Cool on a wire rack for 30 minutes.

2) Using the end of a wooden spoon handle, poke 12 holes in warm cake. Pour butterscotch topping over cake; cool completely.

Splitting a Cake into Layers

Using a ruler, mark the center of the side of the cake with a toothpick. Continue inserting toothpicks around the cake. Using the toothpicks as a guide, cut the cake horizontally in half with a long serrated knife. Carefully remove the top half. Frost or fill the bottom half as recipe instructs and replace the top cut side down.

3) Spread with whipped topping; sprinkle with crushed candy bars. Refrigerate for at least 2 hours before serving. Refrigerate leftovers.

Yield: 12-16 servings.

NUTRITION FACTS: 1 piece equals 323 calories, 12 g fat (5 g saturated fat), 40 mg cholesterol, 327 mg sodium, 52 g carbohydrate, 1 g fiber, 4 g protein.

BUTTERSCOTCH CHOCOLATE CAKE

(recipes continued on page 606)

Chocolate-Glazed Raspberry Torte

PREP: 25 min. **BAKE:** 20 min. + cooling

Taste of Home Test Kitchen

- 1 package (18-1/4 ounces) white cake mix
- 1 cup water
- 4 egg whites
- 1/3 cup unsweetened applesauce
- 1 carton (8 ounces) frozen reduced-fat whipped topping, thawed
- 1-1/2 cups fresh raspberries, *divided*
- 1/2 cup sugar
- 1/4 cup baking cocoa
- 1/3 cup fat-free milk
- 4 squares (1 ounce *each*) semisweet chocolate, chopped

1) Coat a 15-in. x 10-in. x 1-in. baking pan with cooking spray. Line with waxed paper and coat the paper with cooking spray; set aside. In a large mixing bowl, combine the cake mix, water, egg whites and applesauce. Beat on medium speed for 2 minutes.

2) Pour into prepared pan. Bake at 350° for 18-20 minutes or until a toothpick inserted near the center comes out clean. Cool for 5 minutes before removing from the pan to a wire rack to cool completely.

3) In a large bowl, combine the whipped topping and 1-1/4 cups raspberries. Cut cake into three 10-in. x 5-in. rectangles. Place one layer on a serving plate; top with half of the berry mixture. Repeat layers. Top with remaining cake.

4) For glaze, in a small saucepan, combine the sugar, cocoa and milk until smooth. Bring to a boil. Remove from the heat. Stir in chocolate until melted; cool slightly. Pour over cake. Refrigerate until serving. Garnish with remaining raspberries.

Yield: 20 servings.

NUTRITION FACTS: 1 piece equals 196 calories, 6 g fat (3 g saturated fat), trace cholesterol, 177 mg sodium, 34 g carbohydrate, 2 g fiber, 3 g protein.

Dark Chocolate Pecan Cake

PREP: 30 min. **BAKE:** 25 min. + cooling

Laura Draper, Garfield, Washington

- 1 tablespoon butter
- 3 tablespoons brown sugar
- 1-1/2 teaspoons heavy whipping cream
- 3 tablespoons chopped pecans

BATTER:

- 2 tablespoons shortening
- 1/4 cup sugar
- 2 tablespoons beaten egg
- 1/8 teaspoon vanilla extract
- 6 tablespoons cake flour
- 2 tablespoons baking cocoa
- 1/4 teaspoon baking soda
- 1/8 teaspoon baking powder
- 1/8 teaspoon salt
- 3 tablespoons water

TOPPING:

- 1/4 cup heavy whipping cream
- 2 teaspoons confectioners' sugar
- 1/8 teaspoon vanilla extract

1) Line a 5-3/4-in. x 3-in. x 2-in. loaf pan with parchment paper; coat with cooking spray. In a small saucepan, melt butter; stir in brown sugar and cream. Cook and stir over low heat until sugar dissolves. Pour into prepared pan. Top with pecans. Cover and refrigerate.

2) In a small mixing bowl, cream shortening and sugar until light and fluffy. Beat in egg and vanilla. Combine the flour, cocoa, baking soda, baking powder and salt; add to creamed mixture alternately with water. Beat just until combined.

3) Pour over pecans. Bake at 325° for 25-30 minutes or until a toothpick comes out clean. Cool completely in pan on a wire rack.

4) For topping, in a small mixing bowl, beat cream until it begins to thicken. Add confectioners' sugar and vanilla; beat until stiff peaks form. Remove cake from pan; split into two horizontal layers. Place bottom cake layer, nut side up, on a serving plate. Spread with half of the topping. Top with remaining cake layer and topping.

Yield: 2 servings.

NUTRITION FACTS: 1/2 cake equals 669 calories, 40 g fat (15 g saturated fat), 126 mg cholesterol, 428 mg sodium, 73 g carbohydrate, 3 g fiber, 7 g protein.

DARK CHOCOLATE PECAN CAKE

Testing Butter Cakes for Doneness

Insert a toothpick in several spots near the center of the cake. If the toothpick comes out clean, the cake is done. If the toothpick comes out with crumbs, the cake needs to bake longer.

GERMAN CHOCOLATE CAKE

German Chocolate Cake

PREP: 30 min. **BAKE:** 30 min. + cooling

Joyce Platfood, Botkins, Ohio

Each layer in this spectacular cake is spread with a coconut-pecan frosting and drizzled with chocolate icing.

  1 package (4 ounces) German sweet chocolate
1/2 cup water
  1 cup butter, softened
  2 cups sugar
  4 eggs, *separated*
  1 teaspoon vanilla extract
2-1/2 cups cake flour
  1 teaspoon baking soda
1/2 teaspoon salt
  1 cup buttermilk

FROSTING:

  1 cup sugar
  1 cup evaporated milk
1/2 cup butter, cubed
  3 egg yolks, beaten

1-1/3 cups flaked coconut
  1 cup chopped pecans
  1 teaspoon vanilla extract
  1 square (1 ounce) semisweet chocolate
1/2 teaspoon shortening

1) Line three greased 9-in. round baking pans with waxed paper. Grease the waxed paper; set aside. In a small saucepan, melt the chocolate with water over low heat; cool.

2) In a large mixing bowl, cream butter and sugar until light and fluffy. Add egg yolks, one at a time, beating well after each. Blend in melted chocolate and vanilla. Combine the flour, baking soda and salt; add to creamed mixture alternately with buttermilk, beating well after each addition.

3) In a small mixing bowl and with clean beaters, beat the 4 egg whites until stiff peaks form. Fold a fourth of the egg whites into the creamed mixture; fold in remaining whites.

4) Pour batter into prepared pans. Bake at 350° for 30 minutes or until a toothpick inserted near the center comes out clean. Cool for 10 minutes. Remove from pans to wire racks. Carefully peel off waxed paper. Cool completely.

5) For frosting, in a small saucepan, heat the sugar, milk, butter and egg yolks over medium-low heat until mixture is thickened and golden brown, stirring constantly. Remove from the heat.

6) Stir in the coconut, pecans and vanilla. Cool until thick enough to spread. Place one cake layer on a serving plate; spread with a third of the frosting. Repeat layers twice. Melt the chocolate with shortening; stir until smooth. Drizzle down sides of cake.

Yield: 12 servings.

NUTRITION FACTS: 1 slice equals 751 calories, 42 g fat (22 g saturated fat), 193 mg cholesterol, 527 mg sodium, 89 g carbohydrate, 2 g fiber, 9 g protein.

Lining a Baking Pan with Waxed Paper

To easily remove cakes from the pan, consider lining the pan with waxed paper. Place pan on a piece of waxed paper. Trace the shape of the pan onto the waxed paper, then cut out. Grease the pan; place the waxed paper in the pan and grease it. Remove the paper as soon as the baked cake is inverted onto a wire rack to cool.

SWEET SHEET CAKE

 CLASSIC: Satisfy a crowd with Favorite Chocolate Sheet Cake. A from-scratch cake prepared with buttermilk and bittersweet chocolate is iced with a cooked chocolate frosting that's sure to please.

 TIME-SAVER: Cut your prep time in half with Coconut Chocolate Cake, which starts with a chocolate cake mix. It's spread with a frosting made with marshmallows and coconut, then covered with a chocolate glaze and sprinkled with slivered almonds.

 LIGHT: Sugar-free pudding mix in both the cake and frosting make Yummy Chocolate Cake light and delicious. Egg whites, fat-free milk and reduced-fat whipped topping are also used to trim it down. A slice has fewer than half the calories, a quarter of the fat and half the carbohydrates of Favorite Chocolate Sheet Cake and only a trace of cholesterol.

 SERVES 2: Indulge in the wonderful flavor of a chocolate sheet cake without all the leftovers, thanks to Tiny Texas Sheet Cakes. Baked in two small loaf pans, this delicious treat—topped with chocolate frosting and pecans—makes enough cake for today and tomorrow.

FAVORITE CHOCOLATE SHEET CAKE

Favorite Chocolate Sheet Cake
PREP: 20 min. **BAKE:** 25 min. + cooling
Mary Lewis, Escondido, California
- 1 cup butter, softened
- 2 cups sugar
- 4 eggs
- 2 teaspoons vanilla extract
- 2-1/4 cups cake flour
- 1 teaspoon baking soda
- 1 teaspoon salt
- 1 cup buttermilk
- 3 squares (1 ounce *each*) bittersweet chocolate, melted

FROSTING:
- 1/4 cup baking cocoa
- 1/3 cup milk
- 1/2 cup butter, cubed
- 1 teaspoon vanilla extract
- 3-1/2 cups confectioners' sugar

1) In a large mixing bowl, cream butter and sugar until light and fluffy. Add eggs, one at a time, beating well after each addition. Beat in vanilla. Combine the flour, baking soda and salt; add to creamed mixture alternately with buttermilk. Beat in chocolate until combined.

2) Pour into a greased 15-in. x 10-in. x 1-in. baking pan. Bake at 350° for 23-27 minutes or until a toothpick inserted near the center comes out clean. Cool on a wire rack.

3) For frosting, in a small saucepan, bring cocoa and milk to a boil over medium heat, stirring constantly. Remove from the heat; stir in butter and vanilla until butter is melted. Whisk in confectioners' sugar until smooth. Drizzle over cake and spread quickly. Let stand until set.

Yield: 16 servings.

NUTRITION FACTS: 1 piece equals 478 calories, 21 g fat (13 g saturated fat), 99 mg cholesterol, 383 mg sodium, 71 g carbohydrate, 1 g fiber, 5 g protein.

Coconut Chocolate Cake
PREP: 10 min. **BAKE:** 20 min. + cooling
Elsie Shell, Topeka, Indiana
- 1 package (18-1/4 ounces) chocolate cake mix
- 1-1/2 cups evaporated milk, *divided*
- 1-1/2 cups sugar, *divided*
- 24 large marshmallows
- 1 package (14 ounces) flaked coconut
- 1/2 cup butter, cubed
- 2 cups (12 ounces) semisweet chocolate chips
- 1/2 cup slivered almonds, toasted

1) Prepare the cake batter according to package directions, using a greased 15-in. x 10-in. x 1-in. baking pan. Bake at 350° for 20 minutes or until a toothpick inserted near the center comes out clean.

2) Meanwhile, in a large saucepan, combine 1 cup milk and 1 cup sugar; bring to a boil, stirring occasionally. Remove from the heat. Add marshmallows and stir until melted. Stir in the coconut. Spread over cake immediately after baking. Cool on a wire rack for 30 minutes.

3) In a small saucepan, combine the butter, and remaining milk and sugar; bring to a boil. Remove from the heat; stir in the chocolate chips until melted. Spread over coconut layer; sprinkle with almonds.

Yield: 16-20 servings.

NUTRITION FACTS: 1 piece equals 454 calories, 22 g fat (14 g saturated fat), 18 mg cholesterol, 285 mg sodium, 66 g carbohydrate, 3 g fiber, 4 g protein.

Yummy Chocolate Cake

PREP: 20 min. **BAKE:** 15 min. + cooling

LaDonna Reed, Ponca City, Oklahoma

 1 package (18-1/4 ounces) chocolate cake mix
 1 package (2.1 ounces) sugar-free instant chocolate pudding mix
1-3/4 cups water
 3 egg whites

FROSTING:

1-1/4 cups cold fat-free milk
 1/4 teaspoon almond extract
 1 package (1.4 ounces) sugar-free instant chocolate pudding mix
 1 carton (8 ounces) frozen reduced-fat whipped topping, thawed

Chocolate curls, optional

1) In a large mixing bowl, combine the cake mix, pudding mix, water and egg whites. Beat on low speed for 1 minute; beat on medium for 2 minutes.

YUMMY CHOCOLATE CAKE

2) Pour into a 15-in. x 10-in. x 1-in. baking pan coated with cooking spray. Bake at 350° for 12-18 minutes or until a toothpick inserted near the center comes out clean. Cool on a wire rack.

3) For frosting, place milk and extract in a large bowl. Sprinkle with a third of the pudding mix; let stand for 1 minute. Whisk pudding into milk. Repeat twice with remaining pudding mix. Whisk pudding 2 minutes longer. Let stand for 15 minutes. Fold in whipped topping. Spread over cake. Garnish with chocolate curls if desired. **Yield:** 16 servings.

NUTRITION FACTS: 1 piece equals 197 calories, 5 g fat (3 g saturated fat), trace cholesterol, 409 mg sodium, 35 g carbohydrate, 1 g fiber, 3 g protein.

Tiny Texas Sheet Cakes

PREP: 25 min. **BAKE:** 20 min. + cooling

Hope Meece, Ambia, Indiana

1/4 cup butter, cubed
1/4 cup water
 1 tablespoon baking cocoa
1/2 cup all-purpose flour
1/2 cup sugar
1/2 teaspoon baking powder
1/4 teaspoon ground cinnamon
Dash salt
 2 tablespoons beaten egg
 2 tablespoons 2% milk

FROSTING:

 2 tablespoons butter
4-1/2 teaspoons 2% milk
 1 tablespoon baking cocoa
3/4 cup confectioners' sugar
1/4 teaspoon vanilla extract
 2 tablespoons chopped pecans, toasted, optional

1) In a large saucepan, bring the butter, water and cocoa just to a boil. Immediately remove from the heat. Combine the flour, sugar, baking powder, cinnamon and salt; stir into butter mixture. Add egg and milk; mix well.

2) Pour into two 5-3/4-in. x 3-in. x 2-in. loaf pans coated with cooking spray. Bake at 350° for 20-25 minutes or until a toothpick inserted near the center comes out clean. Cool for 10 minutes. Remove from pans to a wire rack to cool completely.

3) For frosting, in a microwave-safe bowl, melt butter; add milk and cocoa. Microwave on high for 30 seconds. Whisk in confectioners' sugar and vanilla. Spread over cakes. Sprinkle with pecans if desired.

Yield: 2 cakes (2 servings each).

NUTRITION FACTS: 1/2 cake equals 445 calories, 21 g fat (11 g saturated fat), 80 mg cholesterol, 277 mg sodium, 62 g carbohydrate, 1 g fiber, 4 g protein.

TRIPLE-LAYER BANANA CAKE

Triple-Layer Banana Cake
PREP: 20 min. **BAKE:** 25 min. + cooling

Patty Roberts, Athens, Ohio

My grandchildren can't keep their fingers out of the frosting of this cake. It tastes just like peanut butter fudge!

- 3/4 cup butter, softened
- 2 cups sugar
- 3 eggs
- 1-1/2 cups mashed ripe bananas (about 3 medium)
- 1-1/2 teaspoons vanilla extract
- 3 cups all-purpose flour
- 1-1/2 teaspoons baking powder
- 1-1/2 teaspoons baking soda
- 3/4 teaspoon salt
- 1 cup buttermilk

FROSTING:
- 6 tablespoons creamy peanut butter
- 3 tablespoons butter, softened
- 5-1/4 cups confectioners' sugar
- 8 to 10 tablespoons milk

Peanut halves, optional

1) In a large mixing bowl, cream butter and sugar until light and fluffy. Add eggs, one at a time, beating well after each addition. Beat in bananas and vanilla. Combine the flour, baking powder, baking soda and salt; add to creamed mixture alternately with buttermilk.

2) Pour into three greased and floured 9-in. round baking pans. Bake at 350° for 25-30 minutes or until a toothpick inserted near the center comes out clean. Cool for 10 minutes before removing from pans to wire racks to cool completely.

3) For frosting, in a large mixing bowl, beat the peanut butter and butter until smooth. Beat in confectioners' sugar and enough milk to achieve spreading consistency. Frost between layers and over top and sides of cake. Garnish with peanuts if desired.

Yield: 14 servings.

NUTRITION FACTS: 1 slice equals 583 calories, 18 g fat (9 g saturated fat), 80 mg cholesterol, 498 mg sodium, 102 g carbohydrate, 2 g fiber, 7 g protein.

Frosted Spice Cake
PREP: 15 min. **BAKE:** 25 min. + cooling

Lorraine Darocha, Mountain City, Tennessee

This moist and flavorful spice cake is easy, and you just add cinnamon to prepared vanilla frosting for the fast finishing touch.

- 3 cups all-purpose flour
- 2 cups sugar
- 2 teaspoons baking soda
- 1 teaspoon salt
- 1-1/8 teaspoons ground cinnamon, *divided*
- 1/2 teaspoon ground cloves
- 1/2 teaspoon ground nutmeg
- 2 cups water
- 2/3 cup canola oil
- 2 tablespoons white vinegar
- 2 teaspoons vanilla extract
- 1 can (12 ounces) whipped vanilla frosting

1) In a large mixing bowl, combine the flour, sugar, baking soda, salt, 1 teaspoon cinnamon, cloves and nutmeg. Combine the water, oil, vinegar and vanilla; add to dry ingredients and beat until smooth (batter will be thin).

2) Pour into a 13-in. x 9-in. x 2-in. baking pan coated with cooking spray. Bake at 350° for 25-30 minutes or until a toothpick inserted near the center comes out clean. Cool on a wire rack. Stir remaining cinnamon into frosting; spread over cake.

Yield: 20 servings.

Editor's Note: This recipe does not use eggs.

NUTRITION FACTS: 1 piece equals 283 calories, 11 g fat (2 g saturated fat), 0 cholesterol, 261 mg sodium, 45 g carbohydrate, 1 g fiber, 2 g protein.

Toasting Nuts and Coconut

To toast nuts or coconut, spread in a 15-in. x 10-in. x 1-in. baking pan. Bake at 350° for 5-10 minutes or until lightly browned, stirring occasionally. Or, spread in a dry nonstick skillet and heat over low heat until lightly browned, stirring occasionally.

Raspberry Orange Torte

PREP: 25 min. **BAKE:** 30 min. + cooling

Taste of Home Test Kitchen

Guests are sure to be dazzled by this dessert that's ideal for special occasions. An orange cream filling is spread between the cake layers for a luscious look and taste.

- 1 package (18-1/4 ounces) white cake mix
- 1 package (10 ounces) frozen sweetened raspberries, thawed
- 2 cups heavy whipping cream
- 1 carton (8 ounces) Mascarpone cheese
- 3/4 cup sugar
- 2 tablespoons orange juice
- 1/2 teaspoon grated orange peel
- 2 cups fresh raspberries

1) Prepare and bake cake according to package directions, using two greased 9-in. round baking pans. Cool on a wire rack for 1 hour.

2) Press sweetened raspberries through a sieve; discard seeds. Set raspberry puree aside. In a chilled small mixing bowl and with chilled beaters, beat cream until stiff peaks form. In a large mixing bowl, beat the Mascarpone cheese, sugar, orange juice and orange peel. Fold in whipped cream.

3) Split each cake into two horizontal layers. Place bottom layer on a serving plate. Brush with about 1/4 cup raspberry puree. Spread with about 1 cup cream mixture; top with 1/2 cup fresh raspberries. Repeat layers three times. Refrigerate until serving.

Yield: 10-12 servings.

NUTRITION FACTS: 1 slice equals 541 calories, 34 g fat (16 g saturated fat), 78 mg cholesterol, 335 mg sodium, 57 g carbohydrate, 2 g fiber, 6 g protein.

RASPBERRY ORANGE TORTE

Walnut Torte

PREP: 25 min. **BAKE:** 20 min. + cooling

Kathryn Anderson, Wallkill, New York

A hint of citrus complements the rich walnut flavor of this lovely three-layer flourless cake. Toasted chopped walnuts make a great garnish atop the smooth buttercream frosting.

- 9 eggs, *separated*
- 1 cup sugar
- 1/2 cup water
- 1 tablespoon grated orange peel
- 2 teaspoons grated lemon peel
- 1 teaspoon vanilla extract
- 3 cups finely ground walnuts
- 1/2 cup dry bread crumbs
- 2 teaspoons baking powder
- 1 teaspoon ground cinnamon
- 1 teaspoon ground cloves
- 1/2 teaspoon salt
- 1/4 teaspoon cream of tartar

BUTTERCREAM FROSTING:

- 1/2 cup shortening
- 1/2 cup butter, softened
- 1 teaspoon vanilla extract
- 4 cups confectioners' sugar
- 3 tablespoons milk

Additional walnuts, chopped and toasted

1) Place egg whites in a large mixing bowl; let stand at room temperature for 30 minutes. Line three greased 9-in. round baking pans with waxed paper. Grease the waxed paper; set aside.

2) In another large mixing bowl, beat egg yolks until slightly thickened. Gradually add sugar, beating until thick and pale yellow. Beat in the water, peels and vanilla. Combine the nuts, bread crumbs, baking powder, cinnamon, cloves and salt; add to batter. Beat until smooth.

3) Add cream of tartar to egg whites; beat on medium speed until stiff peaks form. Fold a fourth of egg whites into the batter, then fold in remaining whites.

4) Pour into prepared pans. Bake at 350° for 20-25 minutes or until a toothpick inserted near the center comes out clean. Cool for 10 minutes before removing from pans to wire racks. Carefully peel off waxed paper. Cool completely.

5) For frosting, in a large mixing bowl, cream shortening and butter. Beat in vanilla. Gradually beat in confectioners' sugar. Add milk; beat until light and fluffy. Spread between layers and over top and sides of cake. Garnish with walnuts.

Yield: 15 servings.

Editor's Note: This recipe does not use flour.

NUTRITION FACTS: 1 slice (calculated without additional walnuts) equals 456 calories, 26 g fat (7 g saturated fat), 144 mg cholesterol, 265 mg sodium, 51 g carbohydrate, 1 g fiber, 7 g protein.

TEMPTING CARROT CAKE

 CLASSIC: It's hard to resist a slice of Old-Fashioned Carrot Cake. Two moist layers of spiced cake are spread with a rich, homemade cream cheese frosting dotted with walnuts. The finishing touch of cute frosting carrots only adds to this dessert's timeless appeal.

 TIME-SAVER: You can have Walnut Carrot Cake baking in the oven in just 10 minutes with this recipe, which starts with a yellow cake mix. It's a snap to finish, too, because it relies on prepared cream cheese frosting. To trim even more time, buy a package of shredded carrots from the produce section.

 LIGHT: Treat yourself to Light Carrot Cake without the guilt. It's made with egg whites, calls for only a small amount of oil and is topped with powdered sugar rather than cream cheese frosting. So one piece has 500 fewer calories and 65 fewer grams of carbohydrates than a slice of Old-Fashioned Carrot Cake and no cholesterol.

 SERVES 2: When a large two-layer cake is more than you need, turn to this recipe for Mother's Carrot Cake. It's baked in an 8-inch square pan and yields half the number of servings as Old-Fashioned Carrot Cake.

OLD-FASHIONED CARROT CAKE

Old-Fashioned Carrot Cake

PREP: 30 min. **BAKE:** 35 min. + cooling

Kim Orr, West Grove, Pennsylvania

- 4 eggs
- 2 cups sugar
- 1 cup vegetable oil
- 2 cups all-purpose flour
- 2 to 3 teaspoons ground cinnamon
- 3/4 teaspoon baking soda
- 1/2 teaspoon baking powder
- 1/4 teaspoon salt
- 1/4 teaspoon ground nutmeg
- 2 cups grated carrots

FROSTING:

- 1/2 cup butter, softened
- 1 package (3 ounces) cream cheese, softened
- 1 teaspoon vanilla extract
- 3-3/4 cups confectioners' sugar
- 2 to 3 tablespoons milk
- 1 cup chopped walnuts

Orange and green food coloring, optional

1) In a large mixing bowl, combine the eggs, sugar and oil. Combine the flour, cinnamon, baking soda, baking powder, salt and nutmeg; beat into egg mixture. Stir in carrots.

2) Pour into two greased and floured 9-in. round baking pans. Bake at 350° for 35-40 minutes or until a toothpick inserted near the center comes out clean. Cool for 10 minutes before removing from pans to wire racks to cool completely.

3) For frosting, in a large mixing bowl, cream butter and cream cheese. Beat in vanilla. Gradually beat in confectioners' sugar. Add enough milk to achieve desired spreading consistency. Reserve 1/2 cup of frosting for decorating if desired. Stir walnuts into remaining frosting.

4) Spread frosting between layers and over top and sides of cake. If decorating the cake, tint 1/4 cup reserved frosting orange and 1/4 cup green. Cut a small hole in the corner of pastry or plastic bag; insert #7 round pastry tip.

5) Fill the bag with orange frosting. Pipe 12 carrots on top of the cake, so that each slice will have a carrot. Using #67 leaf pastry tip and the green frosting, pipe a leaf at the top of each carrot. Store cake in the refrigerator.

Yield: 12 servings.

NUTRITION FACTS: 1 slice equals 702 calories, 36 g fat (10 g saturated fat), 99 mg cholesterol, 273 mg sodium, 90 g carbohydrate, 2 g fiber, 8 g protein.

Walnut Carrot Cake

PREP: 10 min. **BAKE:** 40 min. + cooling

Ardyce Piehl, Poynette, Wisconsin

- 1 package (18-1/4 ounces) yellow cake mix
- 1-1/4 cups mayonnaise
- 4 eggs
- 1/4 cup water
- 2 teaspoons ground cinnamon
- 2 cups shredded carrots
- 1/2 cup chopped walnuts
- 1 can (12 ounces) cream cheese frosting

1) In a large bowl, combine cake mix, mayonnaise, eggs, water and cinnamon. Stir in carrots and walnuts. Pour into a greased 13-in. x 9-in. x 2-in. baking pan.

2) Bake at 350° for 40-45 minutes or until a toothpick comes out clean. Cool completely on a wire rack. Spread with frosting. Store in the refrigerator.

Yield: 12-15 servings.

Editor's Note: Reduced-fat or fat-free mayonnaise is not recommended for this recipe.

NUTRITION FACTS: 1 piece equals 424 calories, 26 g fat (6 g saturated fat), 63 mg cholesterol, 408 mg sodium, 44 g carbohydrate, 1 g fiber, 4 g protein.

Light Carrot Cake

PREP: 15 min. **BAKE:** 30 min. + cooling

Ruth Hastings, Louisville, Illinois

- 1/2 cup sugar
- 1/3 cup vegetable oil
- 1/3 cup orange juice concentrate
- 3 egg whites
- 1 cup all-purpose flour
- 1 teaspoon baking powder
- 1 teaspoon ground cinnamon
- 1/2 teaspoon ground allspice
- 1/4 teaspoon baking soda
- 1/8 teaspoon salt
- 1 cup grated carrots
- 2 teaspoons confectioners' sugar

1) In a large mixing bowl, combine the sugar, oil, orange juice concentrate and egg whites; beat for 30 seconds. Combine the flour, baking powder, cinnamon, allspice, baking soda and salt; add to the sugar mixture and mix well. Stir in carrots.

2) Pour into an 8-in. square baking dish coated with cooking spray. Bake at 350° for 30 minutes or until a toothpick inserted near the center comes out clean. Cool on a wire rack. Dust with confectioners' sugar.

Yield: 9 servings.

NUTRITION FACTS: 1 piece equals 183 calories, 8 g fat (1 g saturated fat), 0 cholesterol, 139 mg sodium, 25 g carbohydrate, 1 g fiber, 3 g protein.

MOTHER'S CARROT CAKE

Mother's Carrot Cake

PREP: 25 min. **BAKE:** 35 min. + cooling

Muriel Jones, Hythe, Alberta

- 1 cup all-purpose flour
- 1/2 cup sugar
- 1/2 cup packed brown sugar
- 1 teaspoon baking soda
- 1 teaspoon ground allspice
- 1/4 teaspoon salt
- 1/2 cup vegetable oil
- 2 eggs
- 1-1/2 cups grated carrots

FROSTING:

- 2 tablespoons butter, softened
- 2 ounces cream cheese, softened
- 1 cup confectioners' sugar
- 1/2 teaspoon vanilla extract
- 2 to 4 teaspoons milk
- 2 tablespoons chopped walnuts, optional

1) In a large mixing bowl, combine the flour, sugars, baking soda, allspice and salt. Beat in oil (batter will be stiff). Add eggs, one at a time, beating well after each addition. Stir in carrots.

2) Pour into a greased 8-in. square baking dish. Bake at 350° for 35-40 minutes or until a toothpick inserted near the center comes out clean. Cool on a wire rack.

3) For frosting, in a small mixing bowl, cream butter and cream cheese until smooth. Gradually beat in confectioners' sugar and vanilla. Add enough milk to achieve spreading consistency. Spread over cake. Sprinkle with walnuts if desired. Store in the refrigerator.

Yield: 6-8 servings.

NUTRITION FACTS: 1 piece equals 427 calories, 22 g fat (6 g saturated fat), 69 mg cholesterol, 311 mg sodium, 56 g carbohydrate, 1 g fiber, 4 g protein.

FRUIT-CROWNED UPSIDE-DOWN CAKE

 CLASSIC: Brown sugar, canned sliced pineapple, pecans and maraschino cherries give the distinctive look and taste to Skillet Pineapple Upside-Down Cake.

 TIME-SAVER: Yellow cake mix and apricot preserves hurry along this Simple Pineapple Upside-Down Cake. In fact, this time-trimming version is ready for the oven in just 10 minutes!

 LIGHT: Fresh rosemary is the unusual addition to this better-for-you take on tradition. Rosemary Pineapple Upside-Down Cake calls for less butter and sugar and fewer eggs, so a serving has about two-thirds the calories and half the fat and cholesterol of Skillet Pineapple Upside-Down Cake.

 SERVES 2: A small can of sliced pineapple is just the right size to prepare Mini Pineapple Upside-Down Cake. This sweet little dessert is baked in a 6-inch round baking pan, so it attractively serves four.

SKILLET PINEAPPLE UPSIDE-DOWN CAKE

Skillet Pineapple Upside-Down Cake

PREP: 20 min. **BAKE:** 30 min. + cooling

Bernardine Melton, Paola, Kansas

- 1/2 cup butter, cubed
- 1 cup packed brown sugar
- 1 can (20 ounces) sliced pineapple
- 1/2 cup chopped pecans
- 3 eggs, *separated*
- 1 cup sugar
- 1 teaspoon vanilla extract
- 1 cup all-purpose flour
- 1 teaspoon baking powder
- 1/4 teaspoon salt

Maraschino cherries

1) Melt butter in a 9- or 10-in. ovenproof skillet. Add brown sugar; mix well until sugar is melted. Drain pineapple, reserving 1/3 cup juice. Arrange 7 or 8 pineapple slices in a single layer over sugar (refrigerate remaining slices for another use). Sprinkle nuts over pineapple; set aside.

2) In a large mixing bowl, beat egg yolks until thick and lemon-colored. Gradually add sugar, beating well. Beat in vanilla and reserved pineapple juice.

3) Combine the flour, baking powder and salt; add to batter, beating well. In a small mixing bowl, beat egg whites on high speed until stiff peaks form; fold into batter. Spoon into skillet.

4) Bake at 375° for 30-35 minutes or until a toothpick comes out clean. Let stand for 10 minutes before inverting onto serving plate. Place cherries in center of pineapple slices.

Yield: 10 servings.

NUTRITION FACTS: 1 slice (calculated without cherries) equals 380 calories, 15 g fat (7 g saturated fat), 88 mg cholesterol, 224 mg sodium, 59 g carbohydrate, 1 g fiber, 4 g protein.

Simple Pineapple Upside-Down Cake

PREP: 10 min. **BAKE:** 45 min.

Karen Ann Bland, Gove, Kansas

- 1/4 cup butter, melted
- 1 can (20 ounces) sliced pineapple
- 10 pecan halves
- 1 jar (12 ounces) apricot preserves
- 1 package (18-1/4 ounces) yellow cake mix

1) Pour butter into a well-greased 13-in. x 9-in. x 2-in. baking dish. Drain pineapple, reserving 1/4 cup juice. Arrange pineapple slices over butter; place a pecan half in the center of each slice. Combine the apricot preserves and reserved pineapple juice; spoon over pineapple slices.

2) Prepare the cake batter according to package directions; carefully pour over pineapple.

3) Bake at 350° for 45-50 minutes or until a toothpick inserted near the center comes out clean. Cool for 5 minutes before inverting onto a serving plate. Serve warm.

Yield: 12-15 servings.

NUTRITION FACTS: 1 piece equals 252 calories, 7 g fat (3 g saturated fat), 8 mg cholesterol, 260 mg sodium, 47 g carbohydrate, 1 g fiber, 2 g protein.

SIMPLE PINEAPPLE UPSIDE-DOWN CAKE

Rosemary Pineapple Upside-Down Cake

PREP: 15 min. **BAKE:** 35 min.

Paula Marchesi, Lenhartsville, Pennsylvania

- 1 tablespoon plus 1/4 cup butter, softened, *divided*
- 1/3 cup packed brown sugar
- 1 teaspoon minced fresh rosemary
- 6 canned unsweetened pineapple slices, drained
- 2/3 cup sugar
- 1 egg
- 1 teaspoon vanilla extract
- 1-1/4 cups all-purpose flour
- 1-1/4 teaspoons baking powder
- 1/8 teaspoon salt
- 1/2 cup fat-free milk

Fresh rosemary sprigs, optional

1) Melt 1 tablespoon butter; pour into a 9-in. round baking pan. Sprinkle with brown sugar and rosemary. Top with pineapple slices; set aside.

2) In a small mixing bowl, cream the sugar and remaining butter. Beat in the egg and vanilla. Combine the flour, baking powder and salt; add to creamed mixture alternately with milk. Spoon over pineapple.

3) Bake at 350° for 35-40 minutes or until a toothpick inserted near the center comes out clean. Cool for 5 minutes; run a knife around edge of pan and invert onto a serving plate. Serve warm. Garnish with rosemary sprigs if desired.

Yield: 8 servings.

NUTRITION FACTS: 1 piece equals 264 calories, 8 g fat (5 g saturated fat), 46 mg cholesterol, 207 mg sodium, 45 g carbohydrate, 1 g fiber, 3 g protein.

Mini Pineapple Upside-Down Cake

PREP: 15 min. **BAKE:** 30 min.

Edna Hoffman, Hebron, Indiana

- 1 can (8 ounces) sliced pineapple
- 1/4 cup packed brown sugar
- 3 tablespoons butter, melted, *divided*
- 4 maraschino cherries
- 4 pecan halves
- 3/4 cup all-purpose flour
- 1/3 cup sugar
- 1 teaspoon baking powder
- 1/4 teaspoon salt
- 1/8 teaspoon ground allspice
- 1 egg, lightly beaten
- 1/4 cup 2% milk

1) Drain pineapple, reserving 1 tablespoon juice; set aside. In a small bowl, combine the brown sugar and 2 tablespoons butter; stir until the sugar is dissolved.

2) Pour into an ungreased 6-in. round baking pan. Arrange pineapple slices in a single layer in pan; place cherries and pecans in center of pineapple slices.

3) In a small mixing bowl, combine the flour, sugar, baking powder, salt and allspice. Beat in the egg, milk, reserved pineapple juice and remaining butter just until combined. Spoon over pineapple.

4) Bake at 350° for 30-35 minutes or until cake springs back when lightly touched. Cool for 5 minutes before inverting onto a serving plate. Serve warm.

Yield: 4 servings.

NUTRITION FACTS: 1 slice equals 353 calories, 11 g fat (6 g saturated fat), 77 mg cholesterol, 369 mg sodium, 59 g carbohydrate, 1 g fiber, 3 g protein.

MINI PINEAPPLE UPSIDE-DOWN CAKE

Chocolate Zucchini Cake

PREP: 20 min. **BAKE:** 55 min. + cooling

Peggy Linton, Cobourg, Ontario

The minute I can get my hands on zucchini, I start making this luscious cake. For years, it was an often-ordered dessert at my sister's deli. Tender and chocolaty, it's irresistible with the smooth custard sauce on top.

1-3/4   cups sugar
1/2   cup vegetable oil
1/4   cup butter, softened
2   eggs
1/2   cup buttermilk
1   teaspoon vanilla extract
2-1/2   cups all-purpose flour
1/4   cup baking cocoa
1   teaspoon baking soda
1/2   teaspoon baking powder
1/2   teaspoon ground cinnamon
1/4   teaspoon ground cloves
2   cups finely shredded zucchini
1/2   cup semisweet chocolate chips
1/2   cup sliced almonds

CUSTARD SAUCE:
1/2   cup sugar
2   tablespoons all-purpose flour
2   tablespoons cornstarch
3   cups milk
3   egg yolks, lightly beaten
3   tablespoons butter, cubed
1/4   teaspoon almond extract

1) In a large mixing bowl, beat sugar, oil and butter. Add eggs, buttermilk and vanilla; mix well. Combine the flour, cocoa, baking soda, baking powder, cinnamon and cloves; gradually add to oil mixture. Stir in the zucchini, chocolate chips and almonds.

2) Pour into a greased and floured 10-in. tube or fluted tube pan. Bake at 325° for 55-60 minutes or until a toothpick inserted near the center comes out clean. Cool for 10 minutes before removing from pan to a wire rack to cool completely.

3) For sauce, in a large saucepan, combine the sugar, flour and cornstarch. Stir in milk until smooth. Cook and stir over medium-high heat until thickened and bubbly. Reduce heat; cook and stir 2 minutes longer.

4) Remove from the heat. Stir a small amount of hot filling into egg yolks; return all to pan, stirring constantly. Bring to a gentle boil; cook and stir 2 minutes longer. Remove from the heat. Gently stir in butter and extract. Serve warm sauce with cake; store leftover sauce in the refrigerator.

Yield: 12-16 servings.

NUTRITION FACTS: 1 serving equals 392 calories, 18 g fat (7 g saturated fat), 86 mg cholesterol, 117 mg sodium, 52 g carbohydrate, 2 g fiber, 7 g protein.

Praline Pumpkin Torte

PREP: 25 min. **BAKE:** 30 min. + cooling

Esther Sinn, Princeton, Illinois

This harvest cake stays moist to the last bite. It's perfect for Thanksgiving or holiday gatherings.

3/4   cup packed brown sugar
1/3   cup butter
3   tablespoons heavy whipping cream
3/4   cup chopped pecans

BATTER:
4   eggs
1-2/3   cups sugar
1   cup vegetable oil
2   cups canned pumpkin
1/4   teaspoon vanilla extract
2   cups all-purpose flour
2   teaspoons baking powder
2   teaspoons pumpkin pie spice
1   teaspoon baking soda
1   teaspoon salt

TOPPING:
1-3/4   cups heavy whipping cream
1/4   cup confectioners' sugar
1/4   teaspoon vanilla extract
Additional chopped pecans

1) In a heavy saucepan, combine the brown sugar, butter and cream. Cook and stir over low heat until sugar is dissolved. Pour into two well-greased 9-in. round baking pans. Sprinkle with nuts; cool.

2) For batter, in a large mixing bowl, beat eggs, sugar and oil. Beat in pumpkin and vanilla. Combine

the flour, baking powder, pumpkin pie spice, baking soda and salt; add to pumpkin mixture and beat just until blended. Carefully spoon over praline layer.

3) Bake at 350° for 30-35 minutes or until a toothpick inserted near the center comes out clean. Cool for 10 minutes before removing from pans to wire racks to cool completely.

4) For topping, in a small mixing bowl, beat cream until it begins to thicken. Add confectioners' sugar and vanilla; beat until stiff peaks form.

5) Place one cake layer praline side up on a serving plate. Spread with two-thirds of the topping. Top with second cake layer and remaining topping. Sprinkle with additional pecans if desired. Store in the refrigerator.

Yield: 14 servings.

NUTRITION FACTS: 1 slice (calculated without additional pecans) equals 577 calories, 38 g fat (13 g saturated fat), 118 mg cholesterol, 397 mg sodium, 56 g carbohydrate, 3 g fiber, 6 g protein.

Lemon Curd Cupcakes

PREP: 40 min. + chilling **BAKE:** 20 min. + cooling

Kerry Barnett-Amundson, Ocean Park, Washington

Homemade lemon curd flavors these cupcakes that were made for my brother-in-law's 66th birthday. He loves lemon and gave these a big thumbs-up.

> 3 tablespoons plus 1-1/2 teaspoons sugar
> 3 tablespoons lemon juice
> 4-1/2 teaspoons butter
> 1 egg, lightly beaten
> 1 teaspoon grated lemon peel

LEMON CURD CUPCAKES

BATTER:
> 3/4 cup butter, softened
> 1 cup sugar
> 2 eggs
> 1 teaspoon vanilla extract
> 1 teaspoon grated lemon peel
> 1-1/2 cups cake flour
> 1/2 teaspoon baking powder
> 1/4 teaspoon baking soda
> 1/4 teaspoon salt
> 2/3 cup buttermilk

FROSTING:
> 2 tablespoons butter, softened
> 1/2 teaspoon vanilla extract

Pinch salt
> 2 cups confectioners' sugar
> 2 to 4 tablespoons milk

Edible flowers, confectionery roses *or* additional grated lemon peel, optional

1) For lemon curd, in a heavy saucepan, cook and stir the sugar, lemon juice and butter until smooth. Stir a small amount of hot mixture into egg; return all to the pan. Bring to a gentle boil, stirring constantly; cook 2 minutes longer or until thickened. Stir in lemon peel. Cool for 10 minutes. Transfer to a bowl; cover and chill for 1-1/2 hours or until thickened.

2) In a large mixing bowl, cream butter and sugar until light and fluffy. Add eggs, one at a time, beating well after each addition. Beat in vanilla and lemon peel. Combine the flour, baking powder, baking soda and salt; add to creamed mixture alternately with buttermilk.

3) Fill paper-lined muffin cups three-fourths full. Bake at 350° for 20-25 minutes or until a toothpick comes out clean. Cool 10 minutes before removing from pan to a wire rack to cool completely.

4) Cut a small hole in the corner of a pastry or resealable plastic bag; insert a small round pastry tip. Fill bag with lemon curd. Insert tip 1 in. into center of each cupcake; fill with curd just until top of cupcake begins to crack.

5) For frosting, in a small mixing bowl, combine the butter, vanilla, salt, confectioners' sugar and enough milk to achieve spreading consistency. Frost cupcakes. Store in the refrigerator. Garnish if desired.

Yield: 1 dozen.

Editor's Note: Make sure to properly identify flowers before picking. Double-check that they're edible and have not been treated with chemicals. Look for confectionery roses in the cake decorating aisle of your grocery store.

NUTRITION FACTS: 1 cupcake equals 376 calories, 16 g fat (10 g saturated fat), 94 mg cholesterol, 286 mg sodium, 55 g carbohydrate, trace fiber, 4 g protein.

Coconut Pecan Cupcakes

PREP: 50 min. **BAKE:** 20 min. + cooling

Tina Harrison, Prairieville, Louisiana

I created these fabulous cupcakes for my friend Ann, who said she loved Italian cream cake but didn't want a whole cake.

>   5 eggs, *separated*
>   1/2 cup shortening
>   1/2 cup butter, softened
>   2 cups sugar
>   3/4 teaspoon vanilla extract
>   1/4 teaspoon almond extract
> 1-1/2 cups all-purpose flour
>   1/4 cup cornstarch
>   1/2 teaspoon baking soda
>   1/2 teaspoon salt
>   1 cup buttermilk
>   2 cups flaked coconut
>   1 cup finely chopped pecans

FROSTING:

>   1 package (8 ounces) cream cheese, softened
>   1/4 cup butter, softened
>   1/2 teaspoon vanilla extract
>   1/4 teaspoon almond extract
> 3-3/4 cups confectioners' sugar
>   3/4 cup chopped pecans

1) Place egg whites in a small mixing bowl; let stand at room temperature for 30 minutes. Meanwhile, in a large mixing bowl, cream the shortening, butter and sugar until light and fluffy. Add egg yolks, one at a time, beating well after each addition. Stir in extracts. Combine the flour, cornstarch, baking soda and salt; add to creamed mixture alternately with buttermilk, beating well after each addition.

COCONUT PECAN CUPCAKES

2) Beat egg whites on high speed until stiff peaks form. Fold into batter. Stir in coconut and pecans. Fill paper-lined muffin cups three-fourths full.

3) Bake at 350° for 20-25 minutes or until a toothpick comes out clean. Cool for 10 minutes before removing from pans to wire racks to cool.

4) In a mixing bowl, beat frosting ingredients until smooth; frost cupcakes. Store in the refrigerator.

Yield: 2 dozen.

NUTRITION FACTS: 1 cupcake equals 410 calories, 23 g fat (10 g saturated fat), 70 mg cholesterol, 206 mg sodium, 48 g carbohydrate, 1 g fiber, 4 g protein.

Peanut Butter Chocolate Cupcakes

PREP: 30 min. **BAKE:** 25 min. + cooling

Julie Small, Claremont, New Hampshire

I couldn't find peanut butter-filled chocolate cupcakes (my two favorite flavors), so I experimented and came up with this recipe.

>   1 package (3 ounces) cream cheese, softened
>   1/4 cup creamy peanut butter
>   2 tablespoons sugar
>   1 tablespoon milk

BATTER:

>   2 cups sugar
> 1-3/4 cups all-purpose flour
>   1/2 cup baking cocoa
> 1-1/2 teaspoons baking powder
>   1 teaspoon salt
>   1/4 teaspoon baking soda
>   2 eggs
>   1 cup water
>   1 cup milk
>   1/2 cup vegetable oil
>   2 teaspoons vanilla extract

FROSTING:

>   1/3 cup butter, softened
>   2 cups confectioners' sugar
>   6 tablespoons baking cocoa
>   3 to 4 tablespoons milk

1) In a small mixing bowl, beat cream cheese, peanut butter, sugar and milk until smooth; set aside.

2) In a large bowl, combine the sugar, flour, cocoa, baking powder, salt and baking soda. In another bowl, whisk the eggs, water, milk, oil and vanilla. Stir into dry ingredients just until moistened (batter will be thin).

3) Fill paper-lined jumbo muffin cups half full with batter. Drop scant tablespoonfuls of peanut butter mixture into centers; cover with remaining batter.

4) Bake at 350° for 25-30 minutes or until a toothpick comes out clean. Cool for 10 minutes; remove from pans to wire racks to cool completely.

PEANUT BUTTER CHOCOLATE CUPCAKES

5) In a large bowl, combine frosting ingredients until smooth. Frost cupcakes. Store in the refrigerator.

Yield: 1 dozen jumbo cupcakes.

NUTRITION FACTS: 1 cupcake equals 509 calories, 22 g fat (7 g saturated fat), 60 mg cholesterol, 394 mg sodium, 75 g carbohydrate, 2 g fiber, 7 g protein.

Heavenly Surprise Cupcakes

PREP: 20 min. **BAKE:** 20 min. + cooling

Judie Heiderscheit, Holy Cross, Iowa

The recipe for these filled and frosted cupcakes was handed down by my mother-in-law, who taught this fledgling cook what to do in the kitchen.

> 2 eggs
> 1-1/4 cups sugar
> 1 cup buttermilk
> 2/3 cup vegetable oil
> 1 teaspoon vanilla extract
> 1-1/2 cups all-purpose flour
> 1/2 cup baking cocoa
> 1-1/4 teaspoons baking soda
> 1 teaspoon salt

FROSTING:

> 2/3 cup butter-flavored shortening
> 2/3 cup butter, softened
> 1 cup sugar
> 1 can (5 ounces) evaporated milk
> 1 tablespoon water
> 1/2 teaspoon vanilla extract
> 2 cups confectioners' sugar

1) In a mixing bowl, beat the eggs, sugar, buttermilk, oil and vanilla until blended. Combine the flour, cocoa, baking soda and salt; gradually add to egg mixture. Fill paper-lined muffin cups two-thirds full.

2) Bake at 350° for 20-22 minutes or until a toothpick comes out clean. Cool for 10 minutes before removing from pans to wire racks to cool completely.

3) For frosting, in a large mixing bowl, cream the shortening, butter and sugar. Stir in milk, water and vanilla. Gradually beat in confectioners' sugar.

4) Cut a small hole in the corner of a pastry or resealable plastic bag; insert a small star tip. Fill bag with frosting.

5) Push tip 1 in. into center of each cupcake; fill with frosting just until top of cupcake begins to crack. Pipe frosting in a spiral pattern over the top, beginning near the edge of the cupcake.

Yield: 1-1/2 dozen.

Editor's Note: The texture of this frosting is typical of one made with granulated sugar, even though it's made with confectioners' sugar.

NUTRITION FACTS: 1 cupcake equals 414 calories, 23 g fat (8 g saturated fat), 45 mg cholesterol, 316 mg sodium, 49 g carbohydrate, 1 g fiber, 3 g protein.

Classic Yellow Cupcakes

PREP: 15 min. **BAKE:** 20 min. + cooling

Taste of Home Test Kitchen

Sugar substitute makes these golden cupcakes a wonderfully sweet treat, whether used for dessert or as a fast snack.

> 2/3 cup butter, softened
> 3/4 cup sugar blend for baking
> 3 eggs
> 1-1/2 teaspoons vanilla extract
> 2-1/4 cups cake flour
> 2 teaspoons baking powder
> 1/4 teaspoon salt
> 3/4 cup fat-free milk

Fat-free whipped topping, optional

> 1 teaspoon confectioners' sugar

1) In a large mixing bowl, cream butter and sugar substitute. Add eggs, one at a time, beating well after each addition. Beat in vanilla. Combine the flour, baking powder and salt; add to creamed mixture alternately with milk.

2) Fill paper-lined muffin cups three-fourths full. Bake at 350° for 20-25 minutes or until lightly browned and a toothpick comes out clean. Cool for 10 minutes before removing from pans to wire racks to cool completely.

3) Top with a dollop of whipped topping if desired, then dust with confectioners' sugar.

Yield: 1-1/2 dozen.

Editor's Note: This recipe was tested with Splenda Sugar Blend for Baking.

NUTRITION FACTS: 1 cupcake equals 171 calories, 8 g fat (4 g saturated fat), 54 mg cholesterol, 171 mg sodium, 22 g carbohydrate, trace fiber, 3 g protein.

SPICY HOLIDAY GINGERBREAD

 CLASSIC: A combination of cinnamon, nutmeg and ginger provides the spice in Gingerbread with Chantilly Cream. Squares of this seasonal favorite are wonderful served warm with a dollop of vanilla-flavored whipped cream.

 TIME-SAVER: Skip measuring a dozen or more ingredients with this easy recipe for Pear Gingerbread Cake. A convenient cake mix and canned fruit create the lovely look to this delicious cake that takes just minutes to assemble before baking.

 LIGHT: Unsweetened applesauce, reduced-fat yogurt, whole wheat flour and chopped apples are the healthful additions to Apple Gingerbread. A piece of this spicy cake served with reduced-fat whipped topping has 224 fewer calories, less than half the cholesterol and a mere fraction of the fat of Gingerbread with Chantilly Cream.

 SERVES 2: Pumpkin Gingerbread with Caramel Sauce is a great way for a smaller household to enjoy a holiday favorite. It's baked in a loaf pan, cut into six pieces, then topped with a tasty, from-scratch caramel sauce.

Gingerbread with Chantilly Cream

PREP: 15 min. **BAKE:** 35 min.

Pam Holloway, Marion, Louisiana

- 1/2 cup shortening
- 2 tablespoons sugar
- 1 tablespoon brown sugar
- 1 egg
- 1 cup hot water
- 1 cup molasses
- 2-1/4 cups all-purpose flour
- 1 teaspoon baking soda
- 1 teaspoon ground ginger
- 1 teaspoon ground cinnamon
- 3/4 teaspoon salt
- 1/8 teaspoon ground nutmeg

CHANTILLY CREAM:

- 1 cup heavy whipping cream
- 1 teaspoon confectioners' sugar
- 1/4 teaspoon vanilla extract

1) In a large mixing bowl, cream shortening and sugars until light and fluffy. Beat in egg. Beat in water and molasses. Combine flour, baking soda, ginger, cinnamon, salt and nutmeg; gradually add to creamed mixture.

2) Pour into a greased 9-in. square baking pan. Bake at 350° for 33-37 minutes or until a toothpick inserted near the center comes out clean.

3) In a small mixing bowl, beat cream until it begins to thicken. Add sugar and vanilla; beat until stiff peaks form. Serve with warm gingerbread.

Yield: 9 servings.

NUTRITION FACTS: 1 piece with 3 tablespoons cream equals 427 calories, 21 g fat (9 g saturated fat), 60 mg cholesterol, 368 mg sodium, 55 g carbohydrate, 1 g fiber, 4 g protein.

Pear Gingerbread Cake

PREP: 10 min. **BAKE:** 30 min. + cooling

Cindy Reams, Philipsburg, Pennsylvania

- 1/4 cup butter, melted
- 2 cans (15-1/4 ounces *each*) sliced pears, drained and patted dry
- 1/3 cup sugar
- 1 package (14-1/2 ounces) gingerbread cake mix

1) Pour the butter into a 9-in. square baking dish. Arrange pear slices in rows over butter. Sprinkle with sugar. Prepare cake batter according to package direction; carefully pour over pears.

PEAR GINGERBREAD CAKE

2) Bake at 350° for 30-35 minutes or until a toothpick inserted near the center comes out clean. Cool on a wire rack.

Yield: 9 servings.

NUTRITION FACTS: 1 piece equals 301 calories, 10 g fat (4 g saturated fat), 14 mg cholesterol, 360 mg sodium, 51 g carbohydrate, 1 g fiber, 3 g protein.

Apple Gingerbread

PREP: 15 min. **BAKE:** 30 min.

Pam Blockey, Bozeman, Montana

2/3 cup sugar

1/3 cup unsweetened applesauce

  1 egg

  3 tablespoons molasses

  1 cup all-purpose flour

1/2 cup whole wheat flour

  2 teaspoons ground ginger

  1 teaspoon baking powder

  1 teaspoon baking soda

  1 teaspoon ground cinnamon

1/4 teaspoon ground nutmeg

1/8 teaspoon ground allspice

1/2 cup reduced-fat plain yogurt

1-1/2 cups chopped peeled Granny Smith *or* other tart apples

  1 cup plus 2 tablespoons reduced-fat whipped topping

APPLE GINGERBREAD

1) In a large mixing bowl, combine the sugar, applesauce, egg and molasses; mix well. Combine the flours, ginger, baking powder, baking soda and spices; add to molasses mixture alternately with yogurt, beating just until combined. Fold in the apples.

2) Pour into an 8-in. square baking dish coated with cooking spray. Bake at 350° for 30-35 minutes or until a toothpick inserted near the center comes out clean. Serve warm or cool on a wire rack. Cut into squares; dollop with whipped topping.

Yield: 9 servings.

NUTRITION FACTS: 1 piece with 2 tablespoons whipped topping equals 203 calories, 2 g fat (1 g saturated fat), 24 mg cholesterol, 186 mg sodium, 42 g carbohydrate, 2 g fiber, 4 g protein.

Pumpkin Gingerbread with Caramel Sauce

PREP: 20 min. **BAKE:** 30 min.

Mitzi Sentiff, Annapolis, Maryland

  1 cup plus 2 tablespoons all-purpose flour

1/4 cup sugar

3/4 teaspoon ground ginger

1/2 teaspoon baking soda

1/4 teaspoon ground cinnamon

1/8 teaspoon salt

1/8 teaspoon ground cloves

1/3 cup cold butter

  1 egg

1/3 cup buttermilk

1/4 cup canned pumpkin

1/4 cup molasses

1/3 cup chopped pecans

CARAMEL SAUCE:

1/4 cup butter, cubed

2/3 cup packed brown sugar

  1 tablespoon light corn syrup

1/4 cup heavy whipping cream

1) In a large bowl, combine the flour, sugar, ginger, baking soda, cinnamon, salt and cloves. Cut in butter until mixture resembles fine crumbs. Combine the egg, buttermilk, pumpkin and molasses; stir into crumb mixture just until moistened. Stir in pecans.

2) Pour into a greased 8-in. x 4-in. x 2-in. loaf pan. Bake at 350° for 30-35 minutes or until a toothpick inserted near the center comes out clean.

3) For sauce, melt butter in a saucepan. Stir in the brown sugar and corn syrup; bring to a boil. Reduce heat to medium; cook until sugar is dissolved, about 1 minute. Stir in cream. Return to a boil; remove from the heat. Serve with warm gingerbread.

Yield: 6 servings (3/4 cup sauce).

NUTRITION FACTS: 1 piece with 2 tablespoons sauce equals 516 calories, 27 g fat (14 g saturated fat), 96 mg cholesterol, 327 mg sodium, 66 g carbohydrate, 2 g fiber, 5 g protein.

Foam Cakes

When baking foam cakes in tube pans, set the oven rack in the lowest position. Preheat oven for 10 to 15 minutes before baking.

Separate eggs when they are cold. To ensure egg whites reach their maximum volume, they should stand at room temperature no more than 30 minutes before beating. Also, make sure there are no specks of egg yolk in the white.

Before beating egg whites, make sure your mixing bowl and beaters are clean by washing them thoroughly in hot, soapy water and drying with a clean kitchen towel. Use metal or glass mixing bowls. Plastic bowls, even freshly washed and dried ones, may have an oily film on them. Beat whole eggs or egg yolks until they are thick and lemon-colored.

Gently fold in the ingredients. Using a rubber spatula, gently cut down through the batter, move across the bottom of the bowl and bring up part of the mixture.

Use only the pan size recommended in the recipe. For a tender golden crust, use aluminum pans with a dull rather than a shiny or dark finish.

Do not grease or flour tube pans when baking foam cakes. To rise properly, the batter needs to cling to the sides of the pan. To avoid large air pockets in a baked cake, cut through the batter with a knife to break air bubbles.

It's important to cool foam cakes baked in a tube pan upside down in the pan, otherwise they will collapse and flatten. If using a tube pan with legs, invert the pan onto its legs. If using a tube pan without legs, invert the pan and place the neck over a funnel or narrow bottle.

Foam Cake Tips

1) Foam cakes are done when the top springs back when touched and the cracks at the top of the cake look and feel dry.

2) If your tube pan has legs, invert the pan onto its legs until the cake is completely cool. If your tube pan does not have legs, place the pan over a funnel or the neck of a narrow bottle until cake is completely cool.

Cool cakes completely in the pan before removing. To loosen from the pan, run a thin metal spatula around the edge of the pan and around the center tube using a sawing motion. Gently press the metal spatula between the pan and the cake to loosen more.

If the cake pan has a removable bottom, lift out the cake and run a knife along the bottom of the cake. If the pan is one piece, invert the pan onto a plate; tap the side of the pan with the flat side of a knife and lift the pan away from the cake. Cool the cake completely before filling or frosting.

Cut foam cakes with a serrated knife or electric knife using a sawing motion.

Lemon Angel Food Supreme

PREP: 40 min. **BAKE:** 30 min. + cooling

Linda Blaska, Atlanta, Georgia

Hints of lemon abound in this homemade angel food cake. For variety, eliminate the lemon or add raspberries.

> 1-1/2 cups egg whites (about 12 eggs)
> 1 cup cake flour
> 1-1/2 cups plus 2 tablespoons sugar, *divided*
> 1-1/2 teaspoons cream of tartar
> 1-1/2 teaspoons vanilla extract
> 1/2 teaspoon lemon extract
> 1/4 teaspoon salt

LEMON SAUCE:

> 3 eggs
> 1 cup sugar
> 1/2 cup lemon juice
> 1/4 cup butter, melted
> 1 tablespoon grated lemon peel
> 1/2 cup heavy whipping cream, whipped

Yellow food coloring, optional

1) Place egg whites in a large mixing bowl and let stand at room temperature for 30 minutes. Meanwhile, sift flour and 3/4 cup plus 2 tablespoons sugar together twice; set aside.

2) Add cream of tartar, extracts and salt to egg whites; beat on medium speed until soft peaks form. Gradually add remaining sugar, 2 tablespoons at a time, beating on high until stiff peaks form and sugar is dissolved. Gradually fold in flour mixture, a fourth at a time.

3) Gently spoon into an ungreased 10-in. tube pan. Cut through the batter with a knife to remove air pockets. Bake on the lowest oven rack at 375° for 30-35 minutes or until top springs back when lightly touched and cracks feel dry. Immediately invert pan; cool completely, about 1 hour.

4) Meanwhile, for sauce, whisk eggs and sugar in a heavy saucepan over low heat. Stir in the lemon juice, butter and lemon peel. Cook until mixture

thickens and reaches 160°, about 15 minutes. Transfer to a bowl; refrigerate until chilled.

5) Run a knife around sides and center tube of cake pan. Remove cake to a serving plate. Fold whipped cream and food coloring if desired into sauce. Serve with cake. Refrigerate any leftover sauce.

Yield: 12 servings.

NUTRITION FACTS: 1 slice with about 2 tablespoons sauce equals 318 calories, 9 g fat (5 g saturated fat), 77 mg cholesterol, 158 mg sodium, 55 g carbohydrate, trace fiber, 6 g protein.

■ **Angel Food Cake:** Omit the lemon extract in the cake batter and omit lemon sauce.

■ **Raspberry Angel Food Cake:** Use 1/2 teaspoon almond extract for the lemon extract in the cake batter. After flour has been folded in, fold in 2 cups fresh raspberries. Bake as directed. Omit lemon sauce.

CHOCOLATE ANGEL CAKE

Chocolate Angel Cake
PREP: 25 min. **BAKE:** 35 min. + cooling

Joyce Shiffler, Colorado Springs, Colorado

When I first got married, I could barely boil water. My dear mother-in-law taught me her specialty of making the lightest angel food cakes ever. This chocolate version is an easy, impressive treat.

- 1-1/2 cups egg whites (about 12 eggs)
- 1-1/2 cups confectioners' sugar
- 1 cup cake flour
- 1/4 cup baking cocoa
- 1-1/2 teaspoons cream of tartar
- 1/2 teaspoon salt
- 1 cup sugar

FROSTING:
- 1-1/2 cups heavy whipping cream
- 1/2 cup sugar
- 1/4 cup baking cocoa

- 1/2 teaspoon salt
- 1/2 teaspoon vanilla extract
- Chocolate leaves, optional

1) Place egg whites in a large mixing bowl; let stand at room temperature for 30 minutes. Meanwhile, sift the confectioners' sugar, flour and cocoa together three times; set aside.

2) Add cream of tartar and salt to egg whites; beat on medium speed until soft peaks form. Gradually add the sugar, about 2 tablespoons at a time, beating on high until stiff glossy peaks form. Gradually fold in cocoa mixture, about a fourth at a time.

3) Gently spoon into an ungreased 10-in. tube pan. Cut through the batter with a knife to remove air pockets. Bake on the lowest oven rack at 375° for 35-40 minutes or until the top springs back when lightly touched and cracks feel dry. Immediately invert pan; cool completely, about 1 hour.

4) Meanwhile, for frosting, combine the cream, sugar, cocoa, salt and vanilla in a small mixing bowl; cover and chill for 1 hour.

5) Run a knife around sides and center tube of cake pan. Remove cake to a serving plate. Beat frosting until stiff peaks form; spread over top and sides of cake. Store in the refrigerator. Garnish with chocolate leaves if desired.

Yield: 12-16 servings.

NUTRITION FACTS: 1 slice equals 244 calories, 9 g fat (5 g saturated fat), 31 mg cholesterol, 194 mg sodium, 39 g carbohydrate, 1 g fiber, 4 g protein.

Making Chocolate Leaves

1) Wash several lemon, rose or mint leaves and set aside until completely dry. Melt 1/2 cup chips—semisweet, milk, vanilla or white—and 1/4 teaspoon shortening. With a new small paintbrush, brush melted chocolate in a thin layer on the underside of each leaf. Refrigerate until set, about 10 minutes. Apply a second layer of melted chocolate; chill for at least 15 minutes or overnight.

2) Gently peel leaf from chocolate. If leaves are not to be used immediately, store in a cool dry place in a covered container until needed.

Sunny Sponge Cake

PREP: 40 min. **BAKE:** 20 min. + cooling

Candy Snyder, Salem, Oregon

This golden cake has a light texture and mild orange flavor that makes it a pleasant ending to most any meal.

- 6 egg whites
- 1-1/2 cups all-purpose flour
- 1-1/4 teaspoons baking powder
- 1/4 teaspoon salt
- 3 egg yolks
- 1 cup sugar, *divided*
- 2 teaspoons hot water
- 1/2 cup orange juice, warmed
- 1-1/4 teaspoons vanilla extract
- 3/4 teaspoon grated orange peel
- 1/4 teaspoon grated lemon peel
- 3/4 cup reduced-fat whipped topping

1) Place egg whites in a large mixing bowl, let stand at room temperature for 30 minutes. Meanwhile, sift the flour, baking powder and salt; set aside.

2) In a large mixing bowl, beat egg yolks until slightly thickened. Gradually add 3/4 cup sugar and hot water, beating until thick and pale yellow. Beat in orange juice, vanilla and peels. Gradually fold in reserved flour mixture.

3) Beat the egg whites on medium speed until soft peaks form. Gradually beat in remaining sugar, about 1 tablespoon at a time, on high until stiff glossy peaks form and sugar is dissolved. Fold a fourth of the egg whites into batter, then fold in remaining whites.

4) Spoon batter into an ungreased 10-in. tube pan. Bake on the lowest oven rack at 350° for 20-25 minutes or until cake springs back when lightly touched. Immediately invert pan; cool completely, about 1 hour. Run a knife around sides and center tube of pan. Remove cake to a serving plate. Serve with whipped topping.

Yield: 12 servings.

NUTRITION FACTS: 1 slice with 1 tablespoon whipped topping equals 160 calories, 2 g fat (1 g saturated fat), 53 mg cholesterol, 103 mg sodium, 31 g carbohydrate, trace fiber, 4 g protein.

Ice Cream Cake Roll

PREP: 40 min. **BAKE:** 15 min. + freezing

Kathy Scott, Lingle, Wyoming

This cake roll can be made and filled ahead of time, then once company comes just remove from the freezer 10 to 15 minutes before serving. You can use whatever ice cream flavor you have on hand.

- 4 eggs, *separated*
- 3/4 cup sugar
- 1 teaspoon vanilla extract
- 3/4 cup cake flour
- 1/4 cup baking cocoa
- 3/4 teaspoon baking powder
- 1/4 teaspoon salt
- 3 cups ice cream, softened

CHOCOLATE SAUCE:

- 2 squares (1 ounce *each*) unsweetened baking chocolate
- 1/4 cup butter, cubed
- 2/3 cup evaporated milk, heated to 160° to 170°
- 1 cup sugar

1) Place egg whites in a mixing bowl; let stand at room temperature for 30 minutes. Line a greased 15-in. x 10-in. x 1-in. baking pan with waxed paper; grease and flour the paper. Set aside.

2) In a mixing bowl, beat egg yolks on high for 3 minutes or until lemon-colored. Gradually add sugar and vanilla, beating until thick and pale yellow. Combine the flour, cocoa and baking powder; gradually add to egg yolk mixture. Beat on low until well mixed (batter will be thick).

3) Beat egg whites and salt on high speed until soft peaks form. Fold a fourth of egg whites into the batter, then fold in remaining whites.

4) Spread batter evenly into prepared pan. Bake at 350° for 15 minutes or until cake springs back when lightly touched. Turn cake onto a kitchen towel dusted with confectioners' sugar. Gently peel off waxed paper. Roll up cake in the towel jelly-roll style, starting with a short side. Cool completely on a wire rack.

5) Unroll cake; spread with ice cream to within 1 in. of edges. Roll up again. Cover with plastic wrap and freeze until serving.

6) In a small heavy saucepan, melt chocolate and butter over low heat, stirring until smooth. Gradually add the warm milk and the sugar; stir constantly for 5 minutes or until the sugar is completely dissolved. Serve with cake.

Yield: 10 servings (1-1/2 cups sauce).

NUTRITION FACTS: 1 slice with about 2 tablespoons sauce equals 380 calories, 15 g fat (9 g saturated fat), 120 mg cholesterol, 210 mg sodium, 57 g carbohydrate, 1 g fiber, 7 g protein.

ICE CREAM CAKE ROLL

BANANA CHIFFON CAKE

Banana Chiffon Cake

PREP: 20 min. **BAKE:** 1 hour + cooling

Nancy Horsburgh, Everett, Ontario

Simple yet delicious desserts were my Aunt Allie's specialty. This cake was one of her best.

     5   eggs, *separated*
2-1/4   cups cake flour
1-1/2   cups sugar
     3   teaspoons baking powder
     1   teaspoon salt
  1/3   cup vegetable oil
  1/3   cup water
     1   teaspoon vanilla extract
     1   cup mashed ripe bananas
         (about 2 medium)
Chocolate frosting *or* frosting of
   your choice

1) Place egg whites in a large mixing bowl; let stand at room temperature for 30 minutes. Meanwhile, in another mixing bowl, combine the flour, sugar, baking powder and salt. Whisk the egg yolks, oil, water and vanilla; add to dry ingredients along with bananas. Beat until well blended.

2) Beat egg whites on high speed until stiff peaks form. Fold into batter. Gently spoon into an ungreased 10-in. tube pan. Cut through batter with a knife to remove air pockets.

3) Bake on the lowest oven rack at 325° for 60-65 minutes or until top springs back when lightly touched. Immediately invert baking pan; cool completely, about 1 hour. Run a knife around sides and center tube of pan. Remove cake to a serving plate; frost top and sides.

Yield: 12 servings.

NUTRITION FACTS: 1 slice equals 292 calories, 8 g fat (1 g saturated fat), 89 mg cholesterol, 324 mg sodium, 50 g carbohydrate, 1 g fiber, 5 g protein.

Chocolate Chiffon Cake

PREP: 15 min. **BAKE:** 1 hour + cooling

Dorothy Haag, Mt. Horeb, Wisconsin

There were 11 of us to cook for when I was young. This was a recipe that my mother had. If there were cracked eggs from the laying hens she kept, it was always a good way of using them up!

     7   eggs, *separated*
1-3/4   cups sugar
1-1/2   cups cake flour
  2/3   cup baking cocoa
     1   teaspoon baking soda
     1   teaspoon salt
  3/4   cup water
  1/2   cup vegetable oil
     1   teaspoon vanilla extract
  1/2   teaspoon cream of tartar
Confectioners' sugar

1) Place egg whites in a large mixing bowl; let stand at room temperature for 30 minutes. Meanwhile, in another mixing bowl, combine the sugar, flour, cocoa, baking soda and salt. Whisk the egg yolks, water, oil and vanilla; add to dry ingredients and beat until well blended.

2) Add cream of tartar to egg whites; beat until stiff peaks form. Fold into batter. Gently spoon into an ungreased 10-in. tube pan. Cut through batter with a knife to remove air pockets.

3) Bake on the lowest oven rack at 325° for 60-65 minutes or until cake springs back when lightly touched. Immediately invert pan; cool completely, about 1 hour. Run a knife around sides and center tube of pan. Remove cake to a serving plate. Dust with confectioners' sugar.

Yield: 12-16 servings.

NUTRITION FACTS: 1 slice equals 235 calories, 9 g fat (2 g saturated fat), 93 mg cholesterol, 254 mg sodium, 34 g carbohydrate, 1 g fiber, 4 g protein

CHOCOLATE CHIFFON CAKE

ORANGE TEA CAKE

Orange Tea Cake

PREP: 20 min. **BAKE:** 30 min. + cooling

Beth Duerr, North Tonawanda, New York

This from-scratch sponge cake has a hint of orange in every bite and is wonderful served with a cup of hot tea. It doesn't need frosting—just a dusting of confectioners' sugar.

- 7 eggs, *separated*
- 1-1/2 cups sugar, *divided*
- 6 tablespoons orange juice
- 4-1/2 teaspoons grated orange peel
- 1-3/4 cups all-purpose flour
- 1/2 teaspoon salt
- 3/4 teaspoon confectioners' sugar

1) Place egg whites in a large mixing bowl; let stand at room temperature for 30 minutes. Meanwhile, in another mixing bowl, beat egg yolks until slightly thickened. Gradually add 1/2 cup sugar, beating until thick and lemon-colored. Beat in orange juice and peel. Sift together flour and salt; add to egg yolk mixture. Beat until smooth.

2) Beat egg whites until soft peaks form. Add the remaining sugar, 1 tablespoon at a time, beating until stiff peaks form. Fold a fourth of the egg whites into the batter; fold in remaining whites. Gently spoon into an ungreased 10-in. tube pan. Cut through batter with a knife to remove air pockets.

3) Bake on the lowest oven rack at 350° for 30-35 minutes or until cake springs back when lightly touched. Immediately invert pan onto a wire rack; cool completely, about 1 hour. Run a knife around sides and center tube of pan. Remove cake to a serving plate. Dust with confectioners' sugar.

Yield: 12 servings.

NUTRITION FACTS: 1 slice equals 211 calories, 3 g fat (1 g saturated fat), 124 mg cholesterol, 135 mg sodium, 40 g carbohydrate, 1 g fiber, 6 g protein.

Frosting

Always sift confectioners' sugar before using it for frosting. If there are lumps in the sugar, there will be lumps in the frosting that may clog decorating tips. Frosting needs to be just the right consistency for spreading and decorating. If it's too thin, add a little confectioners' sugar. If it's too thick, add a little milk.

Tint white frosting with liquid, gel or paste food coloring. Liquid gives a pastel color; gel and paste give a deeper color. Add a little at a time, stir in and check the color. You can always add more, but it's hard to lighten the color. The color generally darkens as the frosting dries.

Vanilla Buttercream Frosting

PREP/TOTAL TIME: 10 min.

Diana Wilson, Denver, Colorado

This basic buttery frosting has unmatchable homemade taste. With a few simple variations, you can come up with different colors and flavors.

- 1/2 cup butter, softened
- 4-1/2 cups confectioners' sugar
- 1-1/2 teaspoons vanilla extract
- 5 to 6 tablespoons milk

1) In a large mixing bowl, cream butter until light and fluffy. Beat in sugar and vanilla. Add enough milk to achieve desired consistency.

Yield: about 3 cups.

NUTRITION FACTS: 2 tablespoons equals 124 calories, 4 g fat (2 g saturated fat), 11 mg cholesterol, 40 mg sodium, 23 g carbohydrate, 0 fiber, trace protein.

■ **Almond Buttercream Frosting:** Prepare as directed, except use 1/2 to 3/4 teaspoon almond extract instead of the vanilla.

■ **Chocolate Buttercream Frosting:** Prepare as directed, except use 4 cups confectioners' sugar, 1/2 cup baking cocoa and 6-7 tablespoons milk.

■ **Lemon Buttercream Frosting:** Prepare as directed, except use 5-6 tablespoons lemon juice instead of the milk and add 1 teaspoon grated lemon peel.

■ **Orange Buttercream Frosting:** Prepare as directed, except use 5-6 tablespoons orange juice instead of the milk and add 1 teaspoon grated orange peel.

■ **Peanut Butter Frosting:** Prepare as directed, except use 1/2 cup peanut butter instead of the butter and use 6-8 tablespoons milk.

■ **Peppermint Buttercream Frosting:** Prepare as directed, except use 1/2 to 3/4 teaspoon peppermint extract instead of the vanilla.

Chocolate Ganache

PREP: 15 min. + chilling

Taste of Home Test Kitchen

This satiny frosting will bring a touch of elegance to even the most basic cake. A simple garnish such as fresh fruit, mint or edible flowers adds the finishing touch.

> 1 cup (6 ounces) semisweet chocolate chips
> 2/3 cup heavy whipping cream

1) In a heavy saucepan, melt chocolate chips with cream over low heat. Remove from the heat. Refrigerate, stirring occasionally.

2) For a pourable ganache, cool until mixture reaches 85°-90° and is slightly thickened, about 40 minutes.

3) Pour over cake, allowing some to flow down the edges to completely coat. Spread ganache with a spatula if necessary to evenly coat, working quickly before it thickens. Chill until set.

4) For spreadable ganache, chill until mixture reaches a spreadable consistency. Spread over cake. Chill until set.

Yield: 1-1/4 cups.

NUTRITION FACTS: 2 tablespoons equals 135 calories, 11 g fat (7 g saturated fat), 22 mg cholesterol, 8 mg sodium, 11 g carbohydrate, 1 g fiber, 1 g protein.

Bakery Frosting

PREP/TOTAL TIME: 10 min.

Barbara Jones, Pana, Illinois

This recipe captures the fabulous flavor of cakes from the best bakeries. A big batch of this sweet frosting keeps for 3 months in the refrigerator.

> 2 cups shortening
> 1/2 cup powdered nondairy creamer
> 1 teaspoon almond extract
> 1 package (32 ounces) confectioners' sugar
> 1/2 to 3/4 cup water

Food coloring, optional

1) In a large mixing bowl, beat the shortening, creamer and extract until smooth. Gradually beat in the confectioners' sugar. Add enough water until frosting reaches desired consistency. Tint with food coloring if desired.

2) Store in the refrigerator for up to 3 months. Bring to room temperature before spreading.

Yield: 8 cups.

NUTRITION FACTS: 1/3 cup equals 305 calories, 17 g fat (5 g saturated fat), 0 cholesterol, trace sodium, 39 g carbohydrate, 0 fiber, 0 protein.

TASTY TOPPING FOR CAKES ■■■

Need a tasty topping for cakes and other desserts? I add a little extra flavor to reduced-fat frozen whipped topping with different extracts, such as coconut, cherry, lemon, etc. My family thinks they're getting a real treat!

—Dorothy F., Renton, Washington

Sweetened Whipped Cream

PREP/TOTAL TIME: 10 min.

Taste of Home Test Kitchen

Sometimes a dollop of sweetened whipped cream is all you need to top your favorite cake or other dessert. To make ahead, slightly underwhip the cream, then cover and refrigerate for several hours. Beat briefly just before using.

> 1 cup heavy whipping cream
> 3 tablespoons confectioners' sugar
> 1/2 teaspoon vanilla extract

1) In a chilled small mixing bowl and with chilled beaters, beat cream until it begins to thicken. Add confectioners' sugar and vanilla; beat until soft peaks form. Store in the refrigerator.

Yield: 2 cups.

NUTRITION FACTS: 2 tablespoons equals 57 calories, 6 g fat (3 g saturated fat), 20 mg cholesterol, 6 mg sodium, 2 g carbohydrate, 0 fiber, trace protein.

Simple Frosting Finishes

Peaks

Smooth frosting over top and sides of cake. With an icing spatula or small flat metal spatula, press a flat side of the spatula tip in frosting and pull straight up, forming a peak. Repeat over top and sides of cake.

Swirls

Smooth frosting over top and sides of cake. Use the back of a tablespoon or teaspoon to make a small twisting motion in one direction. Then move the spoon over a little and make another twist in the opposite directions. Repeat until entire cake is covered.

FLUFFY WHITE FROSTING

Fluffy White Frosting
PREP/TOTAL TIME: 20 min.

Georgia Bohmann, West Allis, Wisconsin

For a heavenly light and fluffy frosting, you can't top this variation of the classic 7-minute frosting.

- 1-1/2 cups sugar
- 2 egg whites
- 1/3 cup water
- 1/4 teaspoon cream of tartar
- 1 teaspoon vanilla extract

1) In a heavy saucepan over low heat or double boiler over simmering water, combine the sugar, egg whites, water and cream of tartar.

2) With a portable mixer, beat mixture on low speed for 1 minute. Continue beating on low speed over low heat until frosting reaches 160°, about 8-10 minutes.

3) Pour into a large mixing bowl; add vanilla. Beat on high speed until frosting forms stiff peaks, about 7 minutes.

Yield: about 5 cups.

Editor's Note: A stand mixer is recommended for beating the frosting after it reaches 160°.

NUTRITION FACTS: about 1/3 cup equals 100 calories, 0 fat (0 saturated fat), 0 cholesterol, 9 mg sodium, 25 g carbohydrate, 0 fiber, 1 g protein.

Creamy Chocolate Frosting
PREP/TOTAL TIME: 15 min.

Jeannette Mack, Rushville, New York

Whisking up a batch of smooth-as-silk fudgy chocolate icing is a snap using this short recipe.

- 2 cups heavy whipping cream
- 2 cups semisweet chocolate chips
  or milk chocolate chips
- 3 to 3-1/2 cups confectioners' sugar

1) In a heavy saucepan, bring cream to a simmer, about 180°; remove from the heat. Stir in chips until melted.

2) Place pan in a bowl of ice water; stir constantly until cooled. Gradually whisk in confectioners' sugar until smooth and thick. Store in the refrigerator.

Yield: 2-1/2 cups.

NUTRITION FACTS: about 3 tablespoons equals 388 calories, 23 g fat (14 g saturated fat), 54 mg cholesterol, 18 mg sodium, 49 g carbohydrate, 2 g fiber, 2 g protein.

■ **Creamy White Chocolate Frosting:** Use vanilla *or* white chips instead of chocolate.

Cream Cheese Frosting
PREP/TOTAL TIME: 10 min.

Sharon Lugdon, Greenbush, Maine

This rich, versatile frosting has a delicate vanilla flavor. Most folks agree carrot cake and pumpkin bars wouldn't be complete without it!

- 2 packages (3 ounces *each*) cream cheese, softened
- 1/2 cup butter, softened
- 2 teaspoons vanilla extract
- 1/4 teaspoon salt
- 5 to 6 cups confectioners' sugar

1) In a large mixing bowl, beat the cream cheese, butter, vanilla and salt until smooth. Gradually beat in enough confectioners' sugar until frosting reaches desired consistency. Store in the refrigerator.

Yield: about 3 cups.

NUTRITION FACTS: 1/4 cup equals 234 calories, 9 g fat (6 g saturated fat), 27 mg cholesterol, 127 mg sodium, 38 g carbohydrate, 0 fiber, 1 g protein.

Soft Lemon Frosting
PREP/TOTAL TIME: 5 min.

Madge Robertson, Murfreesboro, Arkansas

This fresh-tasting citrus icing makes a pretty topping for white cake or cupcakes, especially when garnished with grated lemon peel. Plus, it's easy to stir up in a jiffy.

- 1 can (14 ounces) sweetened condensed milk
- 3/4 cup lemonade concentrate
- 1 carton (8 ounces) frozen whipped topping, thawed

1) In a large bowl, combine milk and lemonade concentrate. Fold in whipped topping. Store in the refrigerator.

Yield: about 4 cups.

NUTRITION FACTS: 3 tablespoons equals 96 calories, 3 g fat (2 g saturated fat), 6 mg cholesterol, 21 mg sodium, 15 g carbohydrate, trace fiber, 1 g protein.

comfort food for families

Parents of hospitalized children get help

Amy, Rebecca and Abigail Geiser

"

I love knowing that I'm helping out a parent during a bad time.

~Amy Geiser

Parents dealing with a sick child have one thing on their minds: their child's well-being.

Amy Geiser, mom to twin girls, knows this firsthand. Six years ago, her then 2-year-old daughter, Rebecca, had heart surgery at Akron Children's Hospital in Akron, Ohio. Rebecca made a full recovery and is now a healthy 8-year-old.

Shortly after Rebecca's surgery, Amy heard that the local Ronald McDonald House needed food donations to feed the parents of sick children.

Amy remembered, when her twins were born, receiving homemade casseroles, biscuits, pies and other treats each week from a church friend.

Grateful for the help, Amy told herself that someday she'd pay that kindness forward. Hearing about the need at the Ronald McDonald House, she knew that's how she'd do it.

"I was talking to my mom about the amount of food I'd have to prepare...not to mention hav-

ing two small children at home," Amy says. "I said to her, 'How can I do this?' At that moment, Rebecca walked by and kissed me on the cheek, and I said, 'How can I not do this?'"

For almost 5 years, Amy has prepared meals for 40 people every other month. She buys the ingredients, cooks the dishes in her kitchen and packages them in disposable pans. Volunteers heat and serve her contributions to the families of hospitalized children.

Some of Amy's favorite things to make are beef stew, meat loaf and Pumpkin Gingerbread Trifle.

"At first, I didn't know if I could do this financially," she says. "But I figured it costs less than $1 per person."

"I love knowing that I'm helping out a parent during a bad time," says Amy, a stay-at-home mom. "When I see parents, they're so thankful. They shouldn't have to worry about where they can get something to eat; they're just thinking of getting back to their child."

You can find one of Amy's recipes in the Web exclusive online at tasteofhome.com/ CookbookBonus **Type in access code ICare**

taste**of**home

cooks
who care

DO YOU KNOW A COOK WHO CARES?
If you or someone you know cooks for a charitable, spiritual or other cause, tell us about it at **tasteofhome.com/CookbookBonus**

Recipes

Tips

Desserts

This chapter is filled with ideas for tempting cheesecakes, puddings, ice cream and other tasty classics your family and friends are sure to enjoy.

Cheesecakes

Baking Cheesecake

Before preheating the oven, arrange the oven racks so that the cheesecake will bake in the center of the oven. Preheat the oven for 10 to 15 minutes before baking.

The cheesecake will naturally pull away from the sides of the springform pan as it cools. To help prevent the filling from cracking, grease the bottom and sides of a springform pan.

Measure all ingredients accurately. For best results, use regular cream cheese and sour cream, unless a recipe specifically calls for reduced-fat or fat-free products.

If cream cheese is not softened before mixing, it cannot be smoothed after blending. To avoid lumps, always soften cream cheese at room temperature for about 30 minutes before mixing. To soften in the microwave, place an unwrapped 8-ounce package of cream cheese on a microwave-safe plate; microwave on 50% power for about 30 to 60 seconds or until softened.

Make sure the batter is completely smooth and free of lumps before adding eggs. Add the eggs all at once and beat on low speed just until blended. Avoid overbeating at this step. If too much air is beaten into the mixture, the cheesecake will puff during baking, then collapse and split when cooled.

Stop the mixer occasionally and scrape the batter down from the sides of the bowl with a rubber spatula.

Open the oven door as little as possible while baking the cheesecake, especially during the first 30 minutes. Drafts can cause a cheesecake to crack.

For best results, the springform pan should not be warped and should seal tightly. If in doubt about the tightness of the seal, tightly wrap heavy-duty foil around the outside of the pan to prevent butter in the crust from leaking out. Place pan on a baking sheet.

Use a kitchen timer. Check for doneness at the minimum recommended baking time. A cheesecake is done when the edges are slightly puffed and when the center (about 1 in. diameter) jiggles slightly when the side of the pan is tapped with a spoon. The retained heat will continue to cook the center while the cheesecake is cooling. A cheesecake cooked in a water bath will be just set across the top. The top will look dull, not shiny. Don't use a knife to test for doneness because it will cause the top to crack.

Cool the cheesecake in the pan for 10 minutes on a wire rack, then run a knife around the inside edge to loosen the cheesecake from the springform pan. Don't remove the sides of the pan yet. Cool the cheesecake on a wire rack in a draft-free location for 1 hour. Refrigerate, uncovered, for at least 3 to 4 hours. When the cheesecake is cold, cover it with a piece of foil or plastic wrap across the top of the pan and refrigerate for at least 6 hours or overnight. This allows the cheesecake to set and will make it easier to cut.

Serving Cheesecake

When ready to serve, loosen the latch of the springform and carefully lift the rim of the pan straight up. Slice the cheesecake chilled. But for maximum flavor, allow slices to stand at room temperature for 15 to 30 minutes before serving.

Storing Cheesecake

Cover and refrigerate a cheesecake for up to 3 days. To freeze, place entire cheesecake or individual slices on a baking sheet and freeze until firm. Wrap in heavy-duty plastic wrap and place in a freezer bag. Freeze for up to 2 months. Thaw in the refrigerator.

Cheesecake with Raspberry Sauce

PREP: 1 hour **BAKE:** 50 min. + chilling

Jeanette Volker, Walton, Nebraska

It is a family tradition to make this for our Christmas dinner. And when my daughter was away from home, I made this for her birthday—I shipped it with candles on dry ice.

- 1-3/4 cups graham cracker crumbs
- 1/4 cup sugar
- 1/3 cup butter, melted

FILLING:

- 5 packages (8 ounces *each*) cream cheese, softened
- 1 cup sugar
- 1 cup (8 ounces) sour cream
- 1/2 cup heavy whipping cream
- 2 teaspoons vanilla extract
- 7 eggs, lightly beaten

SAUCE/TOPPING:

- 1 package (12 ounces) frozen unsweetened raspberries, thawed
- 1/2 cup sugar
- 2 cups heavy whipping cream
- 1/2 cup confectioners' sugar
- 1 teaspoon vanilla extract

1) Grease a 10-in. springform pan. In a small bowl, combine cracker crumbs and sugar; stir in butter. Press onto the bottom and 1 in. up the sides of prepared pan. Place on a double thickness of heavy-duty foil (about 17 in. square); securely wrap foil around pan. Bake at 350° for 5-8 minutes. Cool on a wire rack.

2) In a large mixing bowl, beat cream cheese and sugar until smooth. Beat in the sour cream, heavy cream and vanilla. Add eggs; beat on low speed just until combined. Pour into crust.

3) Place springform pan in a large baking pan; add 1 in. of hot water to larger pan. Bake at 350° for 50-60 minutes or until center is almost set. Remove pan from water bath. Cool on a wire rack for 10 minutes. Carefully run a knife around edge of pan to loosen. Remove foil. Cool 1 hour longer. Refrigerate overnight.

4) For sauce, place raspberries and sugar in a food processor; cover and process until smooth. For topping, in a chilled small mixing bowl and with chilled beaters, beat heavy cream until it begins to thicken. Add confectioners' sugar and vanilla; beat until soft peaks form.

5) Remove sides of pan from cheesecake. Serve with raspberry sauce and topping. Refrigerate leftovers.

Yield: 16 servings.

NUTRITION FACTS: 1 slice equals 423 calories, 28 g fat (17 g saturated fat), 180 mg cholesterol, 186 mg sodium, 37 g carbohydrate, 1 g fiber, 6 g protein.

Disguise a Cracked Cheesecake

If the top of your cheesecake has a crack in it, just cover it up! Topping the cheesecake with fruit, a sour cream topping or your favorite jam will offer a delectable disguise.

NO-BAKE LIME CHEESECAKE

No-Bake Lime Cheesecake

PREP: 30 min. + chilling

Robin Spires, Tampa, Florida

Being from the Sunshine State, I love any recipe containing citrus. This one, featuring lime, is quick to mix up and disappears almost as fast.

- 3 cups graham cracker crumbs
- 2/3 cup sugar
- 2/3 cup butter, melted

FILLING:

- 2 envelopes unflavored gelatin
- 1 cup lime juice
- 1/4 cup cold water
- 1-1/2 cups sugar
- 5 eggs, lightly beaten
- 2 teaspoons grated lime peel
- 2 packages (8 ounces *each*) cream cheese, softened
- 1/2 cup butter, softened
- 1/2 cup heavy whipping cream

1) In a large bowl, combine the graham cracker crumbs, sugar and butter. Press onto the bottom and 2 in. up the sides of a greased 9-in. springform pan. Cover and refrigerate for at least 30 minutes.

2) In a small saucepan, sprinkle gelatin over lime juice and cold water; let stand for 1 minute. Stir in the sugar, eggs and lime peel. Cook and stir over medium heat until mixture reaches 160°. Remove from the heat.

3) In a large mixing bowl, beat cream cheese and butter until fluffy. Gradually beat in gelatin mixture. Cover and refrigerate for 45 minutes or until partially set, stirring occasionally.

4) In a chilled small mixing bowl and with chilled beaters, beat cream until stiff peaks form; fold into lime mixture. Spoon into crust. Cover and refrigerate for 3-4 hours or until set. Remove sides of pan. Refrigerate leftovers.

Yield: 12 servings.

NUTRITION FACTS: 1 slice equals 590 calories, 39 g fat (23 g saturated fat), 190 mg cholesterol, 400 mg sodium, 56 g carbohydrate, 1 g fiber, 8 g protein.

■ **No-Bake Orange Cheesecake:** Substitute orange juice and grated orange peel for the lime juice and peel.

Layered Mocha Cheesecake
PREP: 30 min. **BAKE:** 45 min. + chilling

Sue Gronholz, Beaver Dam, Wisconsin

In my search for the perfect mocha cheesecake, I ended up combining a few of my favorite recipes to create this delicious version.

> 1-1/2 cups cream-filled chocolate sandwich cookie crumbs
> 1/4 cup butter, melted

FILLING:
> 2 tablespoons plus 1-1/2 teaspoons instant coffee granules
> 1 tablespoon boiling water
> 1/4 teaspoon ground cinnamon
> 4 packages (8 ounces *each*) cream cheese, softened
> 1-1/2 cups sugar
> 1/4 cup all-purpose flour
> 4 eggs, lightly beaten
> 2 teaspoons vanilla extract
> 2 cups (12 ounces) semisweet chocolate chips, melted and cooled

GLAZE:
> 1/2 cup semisweet chocolate chips
> 3 tablespoons butter

Chocolate-covered coffee beans, optional

1) Grease a 9-in. springform pan. Combine cookie crumbs and butter; press onto the bottom of prepared pan. Place on a double thickness of heavy-duty foil (about 16 in. square); securely wrap foil around pan. Set aside. In a small bowl, combine the coffee granules, water and cinnamon; set aside.

LAYERED MOCHA CHEESECAKE

2) In a large mixing bowl, beat the cream cheese, sugar and flour until smooth. Add eggs; beat on low speed just until combined. Stir in vanilla. Divide batter in half. Stir melted chocolate into one portion; pour over crust. Stir coffee mixture into the remaining batter; spoon over chocolate layer.

3) Place pan in a large baking pan; add 1 in. of hot water to larger pan. Bake at 325° for 45-50 minutes or until center is just set and top appears dull. Remove pan from water bath. Cool on a wire rack for 10 minutes. Carefully run a knife around edge of pan to loosen. Remove foil. Cool 1 hour longer. Refrigerate overnight.

4) In a microwave-safe bowl, melt chocolate chips and butter; stir until smooth. Spread over cheesecake. Remove sides of pan. Garnish with coffee beans if desired. Refrigerate leftovers.

Yield: 16 servings.

NUTRITION FACTS: 1 slice equals 535 calories, 37 g fat (21 g saturated fat), 128 mg cholesterol, 295 mg sodium, 48 g carbohydrate, 2 g fiber, 8 g protein.

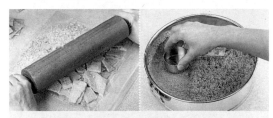

Making a Cheesecake Crumb Crust

1) Place cookies or crackers in a heavy-duty resealable plastic bag. Seal bag, pushing out as much air as possible. Press a rolling pin over the bag, crushing the cookies or crackers into fine crumbs. Or, process cookies and crackers in a food processor.

2) Use a flat-bottomed measuring cup or glass to firmly press the prepared crumb mixture onto the bottom (and up the sides if recipe directs) of a springform pan.

RICH, CREAMY CHEESECAKE

 CLASSIC: Drizzles of caramel and chocolate add an elegant look and extra richness to Caramel Stripe Cheesecake. For the fruit lovers in your house, be sure to try the creamy cherry variation that follows the recipe.

 TIME-SAVER: Chocolate and cherry combine deliciously in no-bake Black Forest Cheesecake. It's a snap to make with a store-bought chocolate crumb crust, whipped topping, cherry pie filling and a handful of other ingredients. It's assembled in just 20 minutes and chilled in the fridge until served, so there's little last-minute prep.

 LIGHT: Reduced-fat cream cheese and 2% cottage cheese help trim down Chocolate Swirl Cheesecake (recipe on page 636), so you can indulge without any guilt. It has less than half the calories and cholesterol and about a quarter of the fat of Caramel Stripe Cheesecake.

 SERVES 2: A 4-inch springform pan makes two perfectly rich servings of Classic Cheesecake (recipe on page 636). Lemon juice and grated lemon peel in the batter give this cheesecake a traditional flavor that's wonderful alone or topped with fresh fruit.

Caramel Stripe Cheesecake

PREP: 35 min. **BAKE:** 40 min. + chilling

Brenda LaBrie, Clark, South Dakota

- 2 cups crushed vanilla wafers
- 1/3 cup butter, melted
- 3 packages (8 ounces *each*) cream cheese, softened
- 1 cup sugar
- 2 tablespoons all-purpose flour
- 3 eggs
- 2 tablespoons heavy whipping cream
- 1 teaspoon vanilla extract

CARAMEL TOPPING:
- 12 caramels
- 2 tablespoons heavy whipping cream

CHOCOLATE TOPPING:
- 1/2 cup semisweet chocolate chips
- 2 teaspoons butter
- 4 teaspoons heavy whipping cream

Whipped cream and coarsely chopped pecans, optional

1) In a small bowl, combine wafer crumbs and butter. Press onto the bottom and 1-1/2 in. up the sides of an ungreased 9-in. springform pan. Place on a

CARAMEL STRIPE CHEESECAKE

baking sheet. Bake at 400° for 10 minutes. Place pan on a wire rack to cool. Reduce the heat to 350°.

2) In a large mixing bowl, beat cream cheese until smooth. Combine the sugar and flour; add to cream cheese and mix well. Add eggs; beat on low speed just until combined. Stir in cream and vanilla. Pour into crust.

3) Return pan to a baking sheet. Bake for 40-45 minutes or until center is almost set. Cool pan on a wire rack for 10 minutes. Carefully run a knife around edge of pan to loosen; cool 1 hour longer. Refrigerate until completely cooled.

4) In a small saucepan, melt caramels with cream over medium heat, stirring constantly. In another saucepan, melt the chocolate chips and butter with cream over low heat, stirring until smooth. Drizzle caramel and chocolate toppings over cheesecake. Refrigerate overnight.

5) Remove sides of pan. Garnish with whipped cream and pecans if desired. Refrigerate leftovers.

Yield: 14 servings.

NUTRITION FACTS: 1 slice equals 442 calories, 30 g fat (17 g saturated fat), 122 mg cholesterol, 283 mg sodium, 40 g carbohydrate, 1 g fiber, 6 g protein.

■ **Creamy Cherry Cheesecake:** For crust, use 1-1/2 cups graham cracker crumbs and 1/4 cup sugar and 6 tablespoons melted butter for the vanilla wafer crumbs and butter if desired. Press into springform pan. Bake cheesecake as directed and let stand for 15 minutes, leaving oven on.

Combine 1 cup sour cream, 1/4 cup sugar and 1 teaspoon vanilla. Spoon topping around edge of cheesecake. Carefully spread over filling. Bake 5 minutes longer. Cool as directed. Refrigerate for about 8 hours.

For cherry topping, in a small saucepan, combine 1/2 cup sugar and 2 tablespoons cornstarch. Drain 1 can (16 ounces) of pitted tart red cherries, reserving juice. Stir juice into saucepan until smooth. Bring to a boil; cook and stir for 2 minutes or until thickened.

Remove from the heat; stir in 1 teaspoon lemon juice, a few drops of red food coloring if desired and reserved cherries. Cool for 5 minutes. Spread over top of cheesecake; refrigerate overnight.

◔ Black Forest Cheesecake
PREP: 20 min. + chilling

Christine Ooyen, Winnebago, Illinois

- 1 package (8 ounces) cream cheese, softened
- 1/3 cup sugar
- 1 cup (8 ounces) sour cream
- 2 teaspoons vanilla extract
- 1 carton (8 ounces) frozen whipped topping, thawed

BLACK FOREST CHEESECAKE

- 1 chocolate crumb crust (8 inches)
- 1/4 cup baking cocoa
- 1 tablespoon confectioners' sugar
- 1 can (21 ounces) cherry pie filling

1) In a large mixing bowl, beat cream cheese and sugar until smooth. Beat in the sour cream and vanilla. Fold in whipped topping. Spread half of the mixture evenly into crust.

2) Fold the cocoa and confectioners' sugar into remaining whipped topping mixture; carefully spread over cream cheese layer. Refrigerate for at least 4 hours.

3) Cut into slices; top each slice with cherry pie filling. Refrigerate leftovers.

Yield: 6-8 servings.

NUTRITION FACTS: 1 slice equals 469 calories, 24 g fat (15 g saturated fat), 50 mg cholesterol, 213 mg sodium, 54 g carbohydrate, 2 g fiber, 5 g protein.

Loosening the Cheesecake

To prevent cracks during cooling, it's important to loosen the cheesecake from the sides of the pan after baking. First cool the cheesecake on a wire rack for 10 minutes. Then carefully run a table knife or small metal spatula between the cheesecake and the inside of the pan. Cool 1 hour longer. Refrigerate overnight before removing the sides of the pan.

(recipes continued on page 636)

Chocolate Swirl Cheesecake

PREP: 25 min. **BAKE:** 40 min. + chilling

Kathy Shan, Toledo, Ohio

- 2 cups (16 ounces) 2% cottage cheese
- 1 cup crushed chocolate wafers (20 cookies)
- 1 package (8 ounces) reduced-fat cream cheese, cubed
- 1/2 cup sugar

Dash salt

- 3 teaspoons vanilla extract
- 2 eggs, lightly beaten
- 1 egg white
- 2 squares (1 ounce *each*) bittersweet chocolate, melted and cooled

1) Line a strainer with four layers of cheesecloth or one coffee filter; place over a bowl. Place cottage cheese in strainer; cover and refrigerate for 1 hour.

2) Coat the bottom and sides of a 9-in. springform pan with cooking spray. Press cookie crumbs onto the bottom and 1 in. up the sides of prepared pan. Place on a double thickness of heavy-duty foil (about 16 in. square); securely wrap foil around pan. Set aside.

3) Transfer cottage cheese to a food processor (discard liquid from bowl); cover and process for 2-3 minutes or until smooth. Add the cream cheese, sugar and salt; cover and process until smooth.

4) Transfer to a large bowl; stir in the vanilla, eggs and egg white just until smooth. Reserve 1 cup of batter; pour remaining batter into prepared pan. Combine the reserved batter with melted chocolate; stir until smooth. Drop by spoonfuls over plain batter; cut through with a knife to swirl.

5) Place springform pan in a large baking pan; add 1 in. of boiling water to larger pan. Bake at 350° for 40 minutes or until center is just set. Turn oven off and open door slightly. Cool cheesecake in oven for 30 minutes.

6) Remove pan from water bath. Remove foil from pan. Carefully run a knife around edge of pan to loosen; cool on a wire rack for 30 minutes. Chill 3-4 hours or overnight. Remove sides of pan. Refrigerate leftovers.

Yield: 12 servings.

NUTRITION FACTS: 1 slice equals 186 calories, 8 g fat (4 g saturated fat), 51 mg cholesterol, 262 mg sodium, 21 g carbohydrate, 1 g fiber, 8 g protein.

Classic Cheesecake

PREP: 35 min. **BAKE:** 30 min. + chilling

Therese Fortier, Grand Rapids, Michigan

- 1/4 cup graham cracker crumbs
- 1 teaspoon sugar
- 4-1/2 teaspoons butter, melted

FILLING:

- 1 package (3 ounces) cream cheese, softened
- 1/4 cup sugar
- 1 egg, lightly beaten
- 1 teaspoon lemon juice
- 1/2 teaspoon grated lemon peel

TOPPING:

- 1/4 cup sour cream
- 2 teaspoons sugar
- 1/4 teaspoon vanilla extract

1) In a bowl, combine cracker crumbs and sugar; stir in butter. Press onto the bottom of a greased 4-in. springform pan. Place on a baking sheet. Bake at 350° for 5 minutes. Cool on a wire rack.

2) In a small mixing bowl, beat cream cheese and sugar until smooth. Add egg; beat on low speed just until combined. Stir in lemon juice and peel.

3) Pour over crust. Return pan to baking sheet. Bake at 350° for 25-30 minutes or until center is almost set. Remove from the oven; let stand for 5 minutes (leave oven on).

4) Combine topping ingredients; carefully spread over filling. Bake 5 minutes longer. Cool on a wire rack for 10 minutes. Carefully run a knife around edge of pan to loosen; cool 1 hour longer. Refrigerate overnight. Remove sides of pan before slicing. Refrigerate leftovers.

Yield: 2 servings.

NUTRITION FACTS: 1 serving equals 488 calories, 32 g fat (19 g saturated fat), 196 mg cholesterol, 323 mg sodium, 42 g carbohydrate, trace fiber, 8 g protein.

CLASSIC CHEESECAKE

CHOCOLATE-COVERED CHEESECAKE SQUARES

Chocolate-Covered Cheesecake Squares

PREP: 1 hour **BAKE:** 35 min. + freezing

Esther Neustaeter, La Crete, Alberta

Satisfy your cheesecake craving with these bite-size treats. Dipped in chocolate, the sweet, creamy delights are party favorites. But be warned—you won't be able to eat just one!

   1 cup graham cracker crumbs
  1/4 cup finely chopped pecans
  1/4 cup butter, melted

FILLING:
   2 packages (8 ounces *each*) cream cheese, softened
  1/2 cup sugar
  1/4 cup sour cream
   2 eggs, lightly beaten
  1/2 teaspoon vanilla extract

COATING:
  24 squares (1 ounce *each*) semisweet chocolate
   3 tablespoons shortening

1) Line a 9-in. square baking pan with foil and grease the foil. In a small bowl, combine the graham cracker crumbs, pecans and butter. Press into prepared pan; set aside.

2) In a large mixing bowl, beat the cream cheese, sugar and sour cream until smooth. Add eggs; beat on low speed just until combined. Stir in vanilla. Pour over crust.

3) Bake at 325° for 35-40 minutes or until center is almost set. Cool on a wire rack. Refrigerate until chilled. Freeze overnight.

4) In a microwave-safe bowl, melt chocolate and shortening; stir until smooth. Cool slightly. Using foil, lift cheesecake out of pan. Gently peel off foil; cut into 49 squares. Remove a few pieces at a time for dipping; keep remaining squares refrigerated until ready to dip.

5) Using a toothpick, completely dip squares, one at a time, in melted chocolate. Place on waxed paper; spoon about 1 teaspoon chocolate over each. (Reheat chocolate if needed to finish dipping.) Let stand for 20 minutes or until set. Store in an airtight container in the refrigerator or freezer.

Yield: 49 servings.

NUTRITION FACTS: 1 cheesecake square equals 141 calories, 10 g fat (6 g saturated fat), 22 mg cholesterol, 48 mg sodium, 12 g carbohydrate, 1 g fiber, 2 g protein.

Pumpkin Cheesecake Dessert

PREP: 20 min. **BAKE:** 35 min. + cooling

Melissa Davies, Clermont, Florida

My family requests this dessert each Thanksgiving. For a change of pace, I sometimes use cinnamon graham crackers instead of plain ones.

  3/4 cup finely chopped walnuts
  3/4 cup graham cracker crumbs (about 12 squares)
  1/4 cup sugar
  1/4 teaspoon ground cinnamon
  1/4 teaspoon ground ginger
  1/8 teaspoon ground cloves
  1/4 cup butter, melted

FILLING:
   2 packages (8 ounces *each*) cream cheese, softened
  3/4 cup sugar
   2 eggs, lightly beaten
   1 cup canned pumpkin
  1/2 teaspoon ground cinnamon, *divided*
   2 tablespoons chopped walnuts

1) In a small bowl, combine the walnuts, cracker crumbs, sugar and spices; stir in butter. Press onto the bottom of an ungreased 10-in. tart pan with a removable bottom.

2) For filling, in a large mixing bowl, beat cream cheese and sugar until smooth. Add eggs; beat on low speed just until combined. Add pumpkin and 1/4 teaspoon cinnamon; beat on low speed just until combined.

3) Pour into crust; sprinkle with walnuts and remaining cinnamon. Place pan on a baking sheet. Bake at 350° for 35-40 minutes or until center is almost set. Cool on a wire rack for 1-1/2 hours. Store in the refrigerator.

Yield: 9-12 servings.

NUTRITION FACTS: 1 serving equals 327 calories, 24 g fat (11 g saturated fat), 87 mg cholesterol, 194 mg sodium, 25 g carbohydrate, 2 g fiber, 7 g protein.

Meringues

Meringue is a sweetened egg white foam that can be shaped into cups to hold fruit or mousse or made into a golden crown on Baked Alaska.

Depending on the amount of sugar beaten into the egg whites, meringue is classified as a soft meringue (as used for Baked Alaska or meringue-topped pies) or hard meringue (as used for meringue shells or cookies).

Since humidity is a critical factor in making a successful meringue, make it on a dry day. Meringues absorb moisture on humid days and become limp or sticky.

Separate the eggs while they are still cold from the refrigerator, then allow the egg whites to stand at room temperature for 30 minutes before beating.

For the greatest volume, place whites in a clean metal or glass mixing bowl. Even a drop of fat from the egg yolk or a film sometimes found on plastic bowls will prevent egg whites from foaming. For this reason, be sure to use clean beaters.

After stiff peaks form, check that the sugar is dissolved. It should feel silky smooth when rubbed between your thumb and index finger.

Swiss Meringue Shells

PREP: 15 min. + standing
BAKE: 1 hour + cooking

Linda Braun, Park Ridge, Illinois

Folks will know you fussed when you bring out these sweet, cloud-like cups topped with fresh berries.

- 3 egg whites
- 1/2 teaspoon vanilla extract
- 1/4 teaspoon cream of tartar
- 3/4 cup sugar

Berries of your choice

Whipped cream *or* vanilla ice cream, optional

1) Place egg whites in a small mixing bowl; let stand at room temperature for 30 minutes. Add vanilla and cream of tartar; beat on medium speed until soft peaks form. Gradually beat in sugar, 1 tablespoon at a time, on high until stiff glossy peaks form and sugar is dissolved.

2) Drop eight mounds onto a parchment paper-lined baking sheet. Shape into 3-in. cups with the back of a spoon. Bake at 225° for 1 to 1-1/2 hours or until set and dry. Turn oven off; leave in oven for 1 hour.

3) Cool on wire racks. Store in an airtight container. Fill shells with berries and whipped cream or ice cream if desired.

Yield: 8 servings.

NUTRITION FACTS: 1 meringue cup (calculated without berries, whipped cream or ice cream) equals 80 calories, 0 fat (0 saturated fat), 0 cholesterol, 21 mg sodium, 19 g carbohydrate, 0 fiber, 1 g protein.

- **Strawberry Meringue Cups:** In a chilled large mixing bowl and with chilled beaters, beat 2 cups heavy whipping cream until it begins to thicken. Add 3/4 cup confectioners' sugar; beat until stiff peaks form. Just before serving, spoon into meringue shells. Top with 1 pint sliced fresh strawberries.

- **Mocha Meringue Cups:** In a heavy saucepan, melt 2 cups milk chocolate chips with 1 cup heavy whipping cream and 1 teaspoon instant coffee granules; stir until smooth. Remove from the heat; stir in 1 teaspoon vanilla. Transfer to a small mixing bowl; refrigerate until chilled. Beat with chilled beaters on high speed until stiff peaks form. Pipe or spoon into meringue cups.

STRAWBERRY SCHAUM TORTE

Strawberry Schaum Torte

PREP: 15 min. + standing **BAKE:** 50 min. + cooling

Diane Krisman, Hales Corners, Wisconsin

This low-fat recipe was handed down from my German grandma. She took great pride in serving this delicate dessert. Whenever I make it, I'm filled with warm memories of childhood.

- 8 egg whites (about 1 cup)
- 1 tablespoon white vinegar
- 1 teaspoon vanilla extract
- 1/4 teaspoon salt
- 2 cups sugar
- 3 cups sliced fresh strawberries
- 1-1/2 cups whipped cream

1) Place egg whites in a large mixing bowl; let stand at room temperature for 30 minutes. Add vinegar, vanilla and salt; beat on medium speed until soft peaks form. Gradually beat in sugar, about 2 tablespoons at a time, on high until stiff glossy peaks form and sugar is dissolved.

2) Spread into a greased 10-in. springform pan. Bake at 300° for 50-60 minutes or until lightly browned. Remove to a wire rack to cool

(meringue will fall). Serve with strawberries and whipped cream. Refrigerate leftovers.

Yield: 12 servings.

NUTRITION FACTS: 1 serving equals 173 calories, 2 g fat (1 g saturated fat), 6 mg cholesterol, 96 mg sodium, 37 g carbohydrate, 1 g fiber, 3 g protein.

Baked Alaska

PREP: 35 min. + freezing **BAKE:** 15 min.

Linda Sanner, Portage, Wisconsin

This is an impressive dessert for any occasion. For Thanksgiving, I make the pumpkin version of this Baked Alaska instead of pumpkin pie.

- 1 quart vanilla *or* chocolate ice cream, softened
- 2 eggs
- 3 tablespoons plus 5 teaspoons water, *divided*
- 1/2 teaspoon vanilla extract
- 1-1/4 cups sugar, *divided*
- 2/3 cup cake flour
- 1/2 teaspoon baking powder
- 1/8 teaspoon salt
- 5 egg whites
- 1/2 teaspoon cream of tartar
- 1 teaspoon rum extract
- 2 tablespoons sliced almonds, toasted

1) Spoon ice cream into a 1-1/2-qt. bowl lined with plastic wrap; freeze until set. Line a greased 9-in. round baking pan with waxed paper; grease the paper and set aside. Place a clean kitchen towel over a wire rack; dust towel with confectioner's sugar. Set aside.

2) In a mixing bowl, beat eggs, 3 tablespoons water and vanilla. Gradually add 1/2 cup sugar, beating until thick and lemon-colored. Combine the flour, baking powder and salt; fold into egg mixture. Pour into prepared pan.

3) Bake at 375° for 12-14 minutes or until cake springs back when lightly touched. Immediately run a knife around edge of pan; invert onto prepared wire rack. Gently peel off waxed paper; cool completely.

4) Place cake on an ungreased foil-lined baking sheet. Unmold ice cream and center on cake. Return to freezer.

5) In a large heavy saucepan, combine the egg whites, cream of tartar and remaining water and sugar; beat on low speed with a portable mixer for 1 minute. Continue beating over low heat until egg mixture reaches 160°, about 12 minutes. Remove from the heat. Add rum extract; beat until stiff peaks form and sugar is dissolved, about 4 minutes.

6) Immediately spread meringue over ice cream and cake, sealing it to foil on sheet. Sprinkle with almonds. Freeze until ready to serve, up to 24 hours.

7) Just before serving, broil on lowest oven rack position for 3-5 minutes or until lightly browned. Serve immediately.

Yield: 12 servings.

NUTRITION FACTS: 1 piece equals 225 calories, 6 g fat (3 g saturated fat), 55 mg cholesterol, 112 mg sodium, 38 g carbohydrate, trace fiber, 5 g protein.

■ **Pumpkin Baked Alaska:** Combine softened vanilla ice cream with 2 teaspoons pumpkin pie spice, then transfer to plastic wrap-lined bowl. Proceed as directed.

Making Meringue and Meringue Cups

1) In a large mixing bowl, beat the egg whites, cream of tartar, vanilla and salt on medium speed until the egg whites begin to increase in volume and soft peaks form. To test for soft peaks, lift the beaters from the white. The peaks of the egg whites should curl down.

2) Add sugar, 1 tablespoon at a time, beating on high speed until stiff peaks form and sugar is dissolved. To test for stiff peaks, lift the beaters from the whites. The peaks of the egg whites should stand straight up; if you tilt the bowl, the whites should not slide around. Sugar is dissolved when the mixture feels silky-smooth between your fingers.

3) For meringue cups, line a baking sheet with parchment paper. Drop meringue into mounds on the paper. Using the back of a spoon, make an indentation in the center of each mound to form a 3-in. cup.

4) Bake as recipe directs. After drying in the oven for 1 hour, remove meringues to cool completely on baking sheet. Carefully remove meringues from paper and store in an airtight container at room temperature for up to 2 days.

Phyllo Dough

Phyllo (pronounced FEE-lo) is a tissue-thin dough, generally sold in the freezer section of grocery stores. It's used for desserts, appetizers and main dishes.

Thaw phyllo according to package directions. Always have all the other ingredients assembled and ready to go before unwrapping the dough. Because phyllo is thin, fragile and tears easily, work on a smooth, dry surface. Phyllo also dries out quickly. So once the dough is unwrapped and unrolled, cover it with plastic wrap and then a damp kitchen towel. Work with one sheet at a time and keep the other sheets covered.

Refrigerate unopened phyllo dough for up to 3 weeks or freeze for up to 3 months. Opened dough can be refrigerated for up to 3 days. Baked phyllo should be stored in airtight containers for up to 3 days or frozen for up to 3 months.

Apple Strudel

PREP: 35 min. **BAKE:** 35 min.

Joanie Fuson, Indianapolis, Indiana

Old-fashioned strudel was too fattening and time-consuming, but this revised classic is just as good. It's best served warm from the oven.

- 1/3 cup raisins
- 2 tablespoons water
- 1/4 teaspoon almond extract
- 3 cups coarsely chopped peeled apples
- 1/3 cup plus 2 teaspoons sugar, *divided*
- 3 tablespoons all-purpose flour
- 1/4 teaspoon ground cinnamon
- 8 sheets phyllo dough (18 inches x 14 inches)
- 2 tablespoons butter, melted
- 2 tablespoons canola oil

1) In a microwave-safe bowl, combine the raisins, water and almond extract. Microwave, uncovered, on high for 1-1/2 minutes; let stand for 5 minutes. Drain. Add the apples, 1/3 cup sugar, flour and cinnamon; toss to coat. Set aside.

2) Place 1 sheet of phyllo dough on a work surface. Combine butter and oil; set aside 2 teaspoons. Lightly brush some of the remaining butter mixture over phyllo dough. Keep remaining phyllo dough covered with plastic wrap and a damp towel to prevent drying.

3) Layer with 7 more sheets of phyllo, brushing each layer with some of the butter mixture. Spread apple mixture over phyllo to within 2 in. of one long side. Fold the short edges over filling. Roll up jelly-roll style, starting from the long side where the apple filling is 2 in. from edge.

4) Place seam side down on a baking sheet coated with cooking spray. With a sharp knife, cut diagonal slits into top of strudel. Brush with reserved butter mixture. Sprinkle with remaining sugar. Bake at 350° for 35-40 minutes or until golden.

Yield: 8 servings.

NUTRITION FACTS: 1 piece equals 205 calories, 7 g fat (2 g saturated fat), 8 mg cholesterol, 121 mg sodium, 35 g carbohydrate, 2 g fiber, 3 g protein.

CRANBERRY PHYLLO TRIANGLES

Cranberry Phyllo Triangles

PREP: 30 min. **BAKE:** 15 min.

Taste of Home Test Kitchen

It's hard to eat just one of these crispy cranberry-filled triangles. If you prefer, make the chocolate version instead.

- 1/2 cup chopped fresh *or* frozen cranberries
- 3 tablespoons sugar
- 2 tablespoons raisins
- 2 tablespoons chopped pecans
- 1 tablespoon honey
- 1/4 teaspoon shredded orange peel
- 20 sheets phyllo dough (14 inches x 9 inches)
- 1/2 cup butter, melted

Confectioners' sugar

1) In a saucepan, combine the cranberries, sugar, raisins, pecans, honey and orange peel; bring to a boil. Reduce heat; simmer, uncovered, for 5 minutes, stirring occasionally. Drain and discard any juice. Cool to room temperature.

2) Lightly brush one sheet of phyllo with butter; place another sheet of phyllo on top and brush with butter. Keep remaining phyllo covered with plastic wrap and a damp towel to prevent drying.

3) Cut the two layered sheets into three 14-in. x 3-in. strips. Place a teaspoon of cranberry filling in lower corner on each strip. Fold dough over filling, forming a triangle. Fold triangle up, then fold triangle over, forming another triangle. Continue folding, like a flag, until you come to the end of the strip.

Making Phyllo Triangles

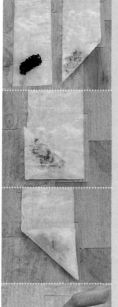

1) Place 1 teaspoon of filling in lower corner on each strip. Fold dough over filling, forming a triangle.

2) Fold triangle up.

3) Fold triangle over, forming another triangle.

4) Continue folding like a flag, until you come to the end of the strip. Brush end of dough with melted butter and press onto triangle to seal. Turn triangle and brush top with melted butter.

4) Brush end of dough with butter and press onto triangle to seal. Turn triangle and brush top with melted butter. Repeat with remaining strips of dough and remaining sheets of phyllo.

5) Place triangles on a greased baking sheet. Bake at 375° for 15-17 minutes or until golden brown. Cool on a wire rack. Sprinkle with confectioners' sugar.

Yield: 30 triangles.

NUTRITION FACTS: 1 triangle (calculated without confectioners' sugar) equals 78 calories, 4 g fat (2 g saturated fat), 8 mg cholesterol, 91 mg sodium, 10 g carbohydrate, trace fiber, 1 g protein.

■ **Chocolate Phyllo Triangles:** Omit the first step of recipe. In a microwave or heavy saucepan, melt 8 oz. chopped semisweet chocolate. Stir in 3/4 cup toasted chopped pecans. Place a heaping teaspoonful of chocolate mixture on phyllo strip in place of the cranberry filling. Fold up and bake as directed.

Working with Phyllo Dough

To avoid cracks and tears, use a soft bristle brush and spread melted butter from the edge of the dough to the center. If you tear a piece, place it in the middle of the layers or just cover with another sheet of phyllo.

Baklava

PREP: 30 min. BAKE: 40 min.

Judy Losecco, Buffalo, New York

Baklava is a very rich Middle Eastern pastry made with phyllo dough, nuts and honey. One pan goes a long way.

   1-1/2 pounds finely chopped walnuts
   1/2 cup sugar
   1/2 teaspoon ground cinnamon
   1/8 teaspoon ground cloves
   2 packages (16 ounces *each*, 18-inch x 14-inch sheet size) frozen phyllo dough, thawed
   1 pound butter, melted

SYRUP:
   2 cups sugar
   2 cups water
   1 cup honey
   1 tablespoon grated lemon *or* orange peel

1) In a small bowl, combine the walnuts, sugar, cinnamon and cloves; set aside. Brush a 15-in. x 10-in. x 1-in. baking pan with some of the butter.

2) Unroll each package of phyllo sheets; trim each stack to fit into pan. Cover dough with plastic wrap and a damp cloth to prevent drying.

3) Place one sheet of phyllo into pan; brush with butter. Repeat 14 times. Spread with 2 cups walnut mixture. Layer with five sheets of phyllo; brush with butter between each sheet. Spread with remaining walnut mixture. Top with one sheet of phyllo; brush with butter. Repeat 14 times.

4) Cut into 2-1/2-in. squares; cut each square in half diagonally. Brush remaining butter over top. Bake at 350° for 40-45 minutes or until golden brown.

5) Meanwhile, in a saucepan, bring the syrup ingredients to a boil. Reduce the heat; simmer for 10 minutes. Strain and discard peel; cool to lukewarm. Pour syrup over warm baklava. Cool.

Yield: 4 dozen.

NUTRITION FACTS: 1 piece equals 271 calories, 16 g fat (5 g saturated fat), 21 mg cholesterol, 162 mg sodium, 30 g carbohydrate, 1 g fiber, 5 g protein.

■ **Pistachio Almond Baklava:** Omit walnuts. In a food processor, process 4 cups unsalted pistachios and 3 cups unsalted, unblanched almonds; until finely chopped. Proceed as directed in step 1.

■ **Chocolate Baklava:** For nut mixture, combine 1 pound finely chopped walnuts, 1 package (12 ounces) miniature semisweet chocolate chips, 3/4 cup sugar, 1-1/2 teaspoons ground cinnamon and 1 teaspoon grated lemon peel. Layer and bake as directed.

For syrup, use 1 cup plus 2 tablespoons orange juice, 3/4 cup *each* sugar, water and honey and 3 tablespoons lemon juice. Bring to a boil. Reduce heat; simmer, uncovered, for 20 minutes. Pour over warm baklava. Cool on a wire rack.

Cream Puffs and Eclairs

Cream puffs and eclairs are airy pastries made from a French dough called "pate a choux" or "choux pastry." The pastry can be formed into a variety of sizes by being dropped from a spoon or by being piped from a pastry bag. The baked puffs are used for desserts as well as appetizers. Cream puffs and eclairs get their puff from the steam that is produced from the water, eggs and fat in the batter. Follow these guidelines for foolproof cream puffs and eclairs.

When baking the dough, it's important not to crowd the baking pan. Leave about 3 in. of space around each puff or eclair. The dough needs room to expand during baking and needs air to circulate so the steam it gives off can evaporate. Cream puffs and eclairs are done when they are golden brown and have a dry, crisp exterior.

For the best flavor, serve cream puffs and eclairs the same day they're made. If necessary, they can be prepared a day in advance. Store unfilled pastries in a plastic bag in the refrigerator. Fill just before serving.

For longer storage, arrange unfilled pastries in a single layer on a baking sheet and freeze. Once they're frozen, transfer to heavy-duty resealable plastic bags and freeze for up to 2 months. Thaw at room temperature for 15-20 minutes before using. If the thawed pastries are a little soggy, reheat them in the oven for a few minutes.

VANILLA CREAM PUFF AND STRAWBERRY CREAM PUFF

Cherry-Chocolate Cream Puffs

PREP: 30 min. + cooling **BAKE:** 30 min. + cooling

Christopher Fuson, Marysville, Ohio

I enjoy cooking and playing with ideas for new recipes. Cherry lovers will enjoy this fun chocolate-filled cream puff that I created.

- 1 cup water
- 1/3 cup butter, cubed
- 1 tablespoon sugar
- 1/8 teaspoon salt
- 1 cup all-purpose flour
- 4 eggs

CHERRY-CHOCOLATE FILLING:

- 1 carton (8 ounces) frozen whipped topping, thawed
- 1/2 cup sugar
- 1/4 cup milk
- 6 squares (1 ounce *each*) semisweet chocolate, chopped
- 3/4 pound fresh *or* frozen sweet cherries, pitted and chopped

Confectioners' sugar

1) In a small saucepan, bring the water, butter, sugar and salt to a boil over medium heat. Add flour all at once; stir until a smooth ball forms. Remove from the heat; let stand for 5 minutes. Add eggs, one at a time, beating well after each addition. Continue beating until mixture is smooth and shiny.

2) Drop by 2 rounded tablespoonfuls 3 in. apart onto greased baking sheets. Bake at 400° for 30-35 minutes or until golden brown. Remove to wire racks. Immediately split puffs open; remove tops and set aside. Discard soft dough from inside. Cool puffs.

3) Let whipped topping stand at room temperature for 30 minutes. In a saucepan, bring sugar and milk to a boil over medium heat; cook and stir until sugar is dissolved. Reduce heat to low; stir in chocolate until melted. Transfer to a large bowl. Cool to room temperature, about 25 minutes, stirring occasionally. Fold in whipped topping.

4) Fill each cream puff with a heaping tablespoonful of cherries; top with chocolate filling. Replace tops. Dust with confectioners' sugar; serve immediately. Refrigerate leftovers.

Yield: 10 servings.

NUTRITION FACTS: 1 cream puff equals 347 calories, 18 g fat (11 g saturated fat), 101 mg cholesterol, 103 mg sodium, 42 g carbohydrate, 2 g fiber, 6 g protein.

■ **Mocha Cream Filling:** Omit cherry-chocolate filling. In a large saucepan, combine 1 cup coffee and 48 large marshmallows. Cook and stir over low heat until marshmallows are melted. Transfer to a large bowl; cool to room temperature, about 20 minutes. Cover and refrigerate just until thickened, about 20 minutes. In a chilled small mixing bowl and with chilled beaters, beat 1-1/2 cups heavy whipping cream until soft peaks form. Whisk coffee mixture for 1-2 minutes. Gradually fold in whipped cream; refrigerate. Just before serving, stir filling. Fill each puff with about 1/3 cup filling. Replace tops; drizzle cream puffs with 1/4 cup warmed hot fudge ice cream topping.

■ **Strawberry Cream Puffs:** Omit cherry-chocolate filling. In a small mixing bowl, beat 2 packages (8 ounces *each*) softened cream cheese and 1 cup sugar until fluffy. Fold in 4 cups whipped cream and 3 cups coarsely chopped strawberries. Fill as directed.

■ **Vanilla Cream Puffs:** Omit cherry-chocolate filling. In a bowl, whisk 1-1/2 cups milk, 1 package

(5.1 ounces) instant vanilla pudding mix and 1/2 teaspoon almond extract for 2 minutes. Let stand for 2 minutes or until soft-set. Fold in 4 cups whipped cream. Fill as directed.

■ **Chocolate Glaze for Cream Puffs:** In a saucepan, melt 6 tablespoons semisweet chocolate chips, 1-1/2 teaspoons shortening and 3/4 teaspoon corn syrup over low heat; stir until smooth. Drizzle over cream puffs.

Banana Cream Eclairs

PREP: 40 min. **BAKE:** 25 min. + cooling

Ruby Williams, Bogalusa, Louisiana

To surprise my banana-loving family, I made this dessert for a reunion, where it stood out among the usual fare. These special treats look and taste delicious.

    1   cup water
    1/2 cup butter, cubed
    1/4 cup sugar
    1/2 teaspoon salt
    1   cup all-purpose flour
    4   eggs

FILLING:

    2-1/2 cups heavy whipping cream
    3   tablespoons sugar
    1   teaspoon vanilla extract
    3 to 4 medium firm bananas

GLAZE:

    1/2 cup confectioners' sugar
    2   tablespoons baking cocoa
    2   tablespoons butter, melted
    1   teaspoon vanilla extract
    1 to 2 tablespoons boiling water
    1/2 cup finely chopped pecans

BANANA CREAM ECLAIRS

Making Cream Puffs

1) Bring water, butter and salt to a boil in a saucepan. Add the flour all at once; stir briskly until the mixture leave the sides of the pan and forms a ball.

2) Remove from heat; let stand for 5 minutes to allow mixture to cool before adding the eggs. Beat well after adding each egg. Continue beating until mixture is smooth and shiny.

3) Drop dough 3 in. apart onto a greased baking sheet. Bake as directed.

4) Remove puffs from pan to a wire rack. Immediately cut a slit in each puff to allow steam to escape; cool. Split puffs and set tops aside; remove soft dough from inside with a fork and discard. Fill as directed.

1) In a large saucepan, bring water, butter, sugar and salt to a boil over medium heat. Add flour all at once and stir until a smooth ball forms. Remove from the heat; let stand for 5 minutes. Add eggs, one at a time, beating well after each addition. Continue beating until dough is smooth and shiny.

2) Insert a 3/4-in. round tip into a pastry bag; add dough. Pipe 3-in. strips about 3 in. apart on a greased baking sheet. Bake at 400° for 25-30 minutes or until golden brown. Remove to wire racks. Immediately split puffs open; remove tops and set aside. Discard soft dough from inside. Cool puffs.

3) In a chilled large mixing bowl and with chilled beaters, beat cream until it begins to thicken. Add sugar and vanilla; beat until stiff peaks form. In another bowl, mash bananas; gently fold in whipped cream. Spoon into eclairs; replace tops.

4) In a small bowl, combine the confectioners' sugar, cocoa, butter and vanilla. Add enough water to make a thin glaze. Spread over eclairs. Sprinkle with pecans. Serve immediately. Refrigerate leftovers.

Yield: 16 servings.

NUTRITION FACTS: 1 eclair equals 323 calories, 25 g fat (14 g saturated fat), 123 mg cholesterol, 176 mg sodium, 22 g carbohydrate, 1 g fiber, 4 g protein.

SUMMERY FRUIT SHORTCAKE

 CLASSIC: Homemade drop biscuits are the key to sweet Strawberry Biscuit Shortcake. Sliced, fresh strawberries are tossed with orange juice and sugar, then tucked inside the golden biscuits along with whipped topping.

 TIME-SAVER: Prepared sponge cakes make Citrus Shortcake oh-so-easy to fix—it's ready in only 10 minutes! Lemon yogurt stirred into the whipped topping and orange juice drizzled on the cakes give this easy strawberry treat its citrusy taste.

 LIGHT: In Strawberry Shortcakes, whole wheat flour and buttermilk put a healthier spin on the shortcakes, while fat-free yogurt and reduced-fat sour cream lighten up the filling. The result is a delicious dessert with about 20% fewer calories and 40% less fat than classic Strawberry Biscuit Shortcake.

 SERVES 2: Fresh berries and peaches are sandwiched inside a pair of home-baked biscuits to create Mixed Fruit Shortcakes. Or fill them with whatever fruit you have on hand, then top with whipped cream.

STRAWBERRY BISCUIT SHORTCAKE

Strawberry Biscuit Shortcake
PREP/TOTAL TIME: 30 min.

Stephanie Moon, Green Bay, Wisconsin

    2 cups all-purpose flour
    3 tablespoons sugar, *divided*
    1 tablespoon baking powder
 1/2 teaspoon salt
 1/4 cup cold butter
    1 cup milk
    2 pints strawberries, sliced
    1 tablespoon orange juice
 1-1/2 cups whipped topping

1) In a large bowl, combine flour, 2 tablespoons sugar, baking powder and salt. Cut in butter until mixture resembles coarse crumbs. Gradually stir in milk until a soft dough forms.

2) Drop dough by heaping tablespoonfuls into eight mounds on a lightly greased baking sheet. Bake at 425° for 12-15 minutes or until lightly browned. Cool on a wire rack.

3) Meanwhile, in a bowl, gently toss the strawberries, orange juice and remaining sugar. Split shortcakes into two horizontal layers. Place bottom halves on serving plates; top with whipped topping and strawberries. Replace shortcake tops.

Yield: 8 servings.

NUTRITION FACTS: 1 strawberry shortcake equals 261 calories, 10 g fat (6 g saturated fat), 19 mg cholesterol, 372 mg sodium, 38 g carbohydrate, 2 g fiber, 5 g protein.

■ **Berry Shortcake:** Use 1 pint *each* fresh blueberries and fresh strawberries.

Citrus Shortcake
PREP/TOTAL TIME: 10 min.

Eileen Warren, Windsor, Ontario

    1 cup (8 ounces) lemon yogurt
    1 cup whipped topping
    4 individual round sponge cakes
 1/4 cup orange juice
 2-2/3 cups sliced fresh strawberries

1) In a small bowl, combine the yogurt and whipped topping. Place sponge cakes on dessert plates; drizzle with orange juice. Spread with half of the yogurt mixture. Top with strawberries and remaining yogurt mixture.

Yield: 4 servings.

NUTRITION FACTS: 1 shortcake with 1/2 cup yogurt mixture and 2/3 cup strawberries equals 238 calories, 6 g fat (4 g saturated fat), 31 mg cholesterol, 214 mg sodium, 40 g carbohydrate, 2 g fiber, 5 g protein.

SUPER STRAWBERRY SHORTCAKE ■■■

Instead of sugar, I add frozen juice concentrate to the berries when I make strawberry shortcake. It adds an unexpected but fun flavor.

—*Beth Walker, Tyler, Texas*

STRAWBERRY SHORTCAKES

Strawberry Shortcakes

PREP: 30 min. **BAKE:** 15 min.

Taste of Home Test Kitchen

- 1/4 cup fat-free plain yogurt
- 2 tablespoons reduced-fat sour cream
- 1 tablespoon confectioners' sugar
- 1/4 teaspoon rum extract *or* vanilla extract
- 1 pint fresh strawberries, sliced, *divided*

DOUGH:

- 2/3 cup all-purpose flour
- 2 tablespoons whole wheat flour
- 2 tablespoons plus 1/2 teaspoon sugar, *divided*
- 3/4 teaspoon baking powder
- 1/4 teaspoon baking soda
- 1/8 teaspoon salt
- 5 teaspoons cold butter
- 1/3 cup buttermilk

1) In a small bowl, combine the yogurt, sour cream, confectioners' sugar and extract. In another bowl, mash 1/2 cup strawberries; stir into yogurt mixture. Cover and refrigerate until serving.

2) Combine the flours, 2 tablespoons sugar, baking powder, baking soda and salt. Cut in butter until mixture resembles coarse crumbs. Stir in buttermilk until a soft dough forms (dough will be sticky). Turn onto a floured surface; gently knead 8-10 times. Pat or roll out to 1/2-in. thickness; cut with a floured 2-1/2-in. round or heart-shaped biscuit cutter.

3) Place on a baking sheet coated with cooking spray; sprinkle with remaining sugar. Bake at 400° for 12-14 minutes or until golden brown.

Cool on a wire rack. Split the shortcakes into two horizontal layers. Spread the yogurt mixture over cake bottoms; top with the remaining strawberries. Replace cake tops.

Yield: 4 servings.

NUTRITION FACTS: 1 shortcake equals 213 calories, 6 g fat (4 g saturated fat), 16 mg cholesterol, 297 mg sodium, 35 g carbohydrate, 2 g fiber, 5 g protein.

Mixed Fruit Shortcakes

PREP/TOTAL TIME: 30 min.

Sue Ross, Casa Grande, Arizona

- 1 cup mixed fresh berries
- 1/2 cup sliced fresh peaches *or* nectarines
- 4 teaspoons sugar, *divided*
- 1/2 cup all-purpose flour
- 3/4 teaspoon baking powder
- 1/8 teaspoon salt
- 2 tablespoons shortening
- 3 tablespoons milk

Whipped cream

1) In a small bowl, combine the berries, peaches and 2 teaspoons sugar; set aside. In another bowl, combine the flour, baking powder and salt; cut in shortening until mixture is crumbly. Stir in milk just until moistened.

2) Drop by 1/3 cupfuls 2 in. apart onto an ungreased baking sheet. Flatten into 2-1/2-in. circles. Sprinkle with remaining sugar.

3) Bake at 425° for 10-12 minutes or until golden brown. Remove to a wire rack to cool. Split shortcakes into two horizontal layers. Spoon fruit onto bottoms; replace tops. Garnish with whipped cream.

Yield: 2 servings.

NUTRITION FACTS: 1 shortcake (calculated without whipped cream) equals 336 calories, 14 g fat (4 g saturated fat), 3 mg cholesterol, 311 mg sodium, 49 g carbohydrate, 5 g fiber, 5 g protein.

MIXED FRUIT SHORTCAKES

Puff Pastry

Frozen puff pastry dough is available in sheets or individual shells. It has dozens of paper-thin layers of dough separated by butter. As the pastry bakes, steam created from water in the dough makes the layers rise up and pull apart, resulting in a crisp, flaky pastry.

Thaw the pastry at room temperature for about 20 minutes before using. Handle as little as possible to avoid stretching and tearing.

Preheat the oven as directed. Cut pastry with a sharp knife or cutter to get a clean edge.

Only brush an egg wash on the top of the dough, not the edges. If the edges are brushed, they will stick together and the pastry won't rise during baking.

Unbaked puff pastry dough may be wrapped tightly in plastic and stored in the refrigerator for 2 to 3 days or frozen for up to 1 month. Baked pastries are best enjoyed the day they are made and don't refrigerate well. Baked, unfilled pastry may be frozen in airtight containers for up to 6 weeks.

RASPBERRY CHOCOLATE PUFFS

Raspberry Chocolate Puffs

PREP: 25 min. **BAKE:** 20 min. + cooling

Anneliese Deising, Plymouth, Michigan

This is my "show-off" dessert because it makes a spectacular presentation that my friends rave about. Although it looks like you fussed, the recipe is actually quick and easy.

- 1 cup vanilla *or* white chips
- 1 cup raspberry *or* milk chocolate chips
- 1 cup chopped pecans
- 1 package (17.3 ounces) frozen puff pastry, thawed
- 1 package (12 ounces) frozen unsweetened raspberries, thawed
- 1 cup confectioners' sugar

Fresh raspberries, additional vanilla, chocolate and raspberry chips and confectioners' sugar, optional

1) In a bowl, combine the chips and pecans. On a lightly floured surface, roll each pastry sheet into a 12-in. square. Cut in half lengthwise and widthwise, making eight 6-in. squares.

2) Spoon the chip mixture in the center of each square. Pull all corners together below the tips of the corners, forming a pouch. Fold the corner tips down.

3) Place on an ungreased baking sheet. Bake at 425° for 18-20 minutes or until golden brown. Remove to a wire rack to cool.

4) In a food processor or blender, puree raspberries and confectioners' sugar. Strain and discard seeds. Spoon raspberry sauce onto dessert plates; top with pastry pouches. If desired, garnish with raspberries and chips; dust with confectioners' sugar.

Yield: 8 servings.

NUTRITION FACTS: 1 puff equals 752 calories, 42 g fat (13 g saturated fat), 6 mg cholesterol, 283 mg sodium, 88 g carbohydrate, 7 g fiber, 9 g protein.

Chocolate Napoleons

PREP: 30 min. **BAKE:** 10 min.

Roberta Strohmaier, Lebanon, New Jersey

Convenience items are the key to these impressive desserts. I use frozen puff pastry for the flaky shells and dress up pudding mix for the yummy chocolate filling.

- 1 sheet frozen puff pastry, thawed
- 2 cups cold milk
- 2 cups (16 ounces) sour cream
- 2 packages (3.9 ounces *each*) instant chocolate pudding mix

TOPPING:

- 1 cup confectioners' sugar
- 2 tablespoons milk
- 2 squares (1 ounce *each*) semisweet chocolate, melted and cooled

1) On a lightly floured surface, roll pastry into a 12-in. square. Cut into twelve 4-in. x 3-in. rectangles. Place on ungreased baking sheets. Bake at 400° for 9-12 minutes or until puffed and golden brown. Remove to wire racks to cool.

2) In a small bowl, whisk milk and sour cream until smooth. Add pudding mix; whisk for 2 minutes or until blended. Refrigerate for 5 minutes.

3) To assemble, split each pastry in half. Spoon pudding mixture over bottom halves and replace tops. Combine confectioners' sugar and milk until smooth; drizzle over top. Drizzle with melted chocolate. Serve immediately.

Yield: 12 servings.

NUTRITION FACTS: 1 Napoleon equals 366 calories, 21 g fat (12 g saturated fat), 58 mg cholesterol, 264 mg sodium, 36 g carbohydrate, 2 g fiber, 6 g protein.

CHOCOLATE TRUFFLE DESSERT

Chocolate Truffle Dessert

PREP: 30 min. **BAKE:** 25 min. + chilling

Taste of Home Test Kitchen

The original version of this unbelievably over-the-top truffle dessert tastes like it took all day to make! But after our makeover, it can be made with just 30 minutes of hands-on work, so you can focus on other things during the busy holiday season.

- 1 package fudge brownie mix (8-inch square pan size)
- 3 cups (18 ounces) semisweet chocolate chips
- 2 cups heavy whipping cream, *divided*
- 6 tablespoons butter, cubed
- 1 tablespoon instant coffee granules
- 3 tablespoons vanilla extract
- 14 to 16 Pirouette cookies, cut into 1-1/2-inch pieces

1) Prepare brownie batter according to package directions. Spread into a greased 9-in. springform pan. Place on a baking sheet. Bake at 350° for 25-30 minutes or until a toothpick inserted near the center comes out clean. Cool completely on a wire rack.

2) Place chocolate chips in a food processor; cover and process until finely chopped. In a small microwave-safe bowl, combine 1 cup cream, the butter and coffee granules. Microwave, uncovered, on high for 1 to 1-1/2 minutes or until butter is melted; stir until smooth. With food processor running, add cream mixture in a slow, steady stream. Add vanilla; cover and process until smooth.

3) Cut a small hole in the corner of a pastry or plastic bag. Fill with 1/4 cup chocolate mixture; set aside for garnish. Transfer remaining chocolate mixture to a large bowl.

4) Remove sides of springform pan. Spread half of the chocolate mixture over brownie layer, spreading evenly over top and sides. In a small mixing bowl, beat remaining cream until soft peaks form; fold into remaining chocolate mixture. Spread over chocolate layer. Gently press cookies into sides of dessert.

5) Pipe reserved chocolate mixture on top. Cover and refrigerate for at least 4 hours or overnight. Remove from the refrigerator 5 minutes before cutting.

Yield: 12-16 servings.

Editor's Note: This recipe was tested with Pepperidge Farm cookies. The amount of vanilla is correct.

NUTRITION FACTS: 1 piece equals 489 calories, 34 g fat (17 g saturated fat), 67 mg cholesterol, 174 mg sodium, 46 g carbohydrate, 3 g fiber, 4 g protein.

Red Raspberry Mousse Dessert

PREP: 10 min. + chilling

Edna Hoffman, Hebron, Indiana

When I need a light and refreshing finish to a special meal, I make this fluffy, fruity mousse. Ladyfingers add an elegant look to this pretty dessert.

- 2 packages (3 ounces *each*) raspberry gelatin
- 1-3/4 cups boiling water
- 2 packages (10 ounces *each*) frozen sweetened raspberries, thawed
- 2 cups heavy whipping cream, whipped
- 23 ladyfingers

Fresh mint, and raspberries and additional whipped cream, optional

1) In a large bowl, dissolve gelatin in boiling water. Stir in raspberries. Refrigerate until partially thickened. Fold in whipped cream.

2) Arrange the ladyfingers with rounded side out around the sides of an ungreased 9-in. springform pan. Carefully spoon raspberry mixture into pan.

3) Cover and refrigerate until firm. Garnish with mint, raspberries and whipped cream if desired.

Yield: 12 servings.

NUTRITION FACTS: 1 piece equals 314 calories, 17 g fat (10 g saturated fat), 131 mg cholesterol, 79 mg sodium, 38 g carbohydrate, 2 g fiber, 5 g protein.

RED RASPBERRY MOUSSE DESSERT

SHOW-STOPPING TRIFLE

 CLASSIC: Introduce fresh strawberries to a traditional Italian dessert and you have delectable Strawberry Tiramisu Trifle. The make-ahead dessert has layers of sliced berries, ladyfingers, grated bittersweet chocolate and a coffee-kissed combination of vanilla pudding, cream cheese and whipped topping.

 TIME-SAVER: Convenience items like hazelnut coffee creamer, instant pudding, canned pie filling, canned cranberry sauce and frozen pound cake make it a cinch to assemble Fruity Hazelnut Trifle. In just 15 minutes, it's dressed to impress.

 LIGHT: Raspberry Strawberry Trifle has lighter nutritional numbers, thanks to fat-free milk, sugar-free instant pudding, angel food cake and reduced-fat whipped topping. One scrumptious serving has two-thirds of the calories and only a fraction of the fat and cholesterol of classic Strawberry Tiramisu Trifle.

 SERVES 2: Two individual dessert dishes hold Mini Mocha Trifles, so they're easy to make and fun to eat. Pound cake cubes are topped with a blend of cream cheese, whipped topping and instant coffee, then sprinkled with semisweet chocolate chips.

Strawberry Tiramisu Trifle
PREP: 30 min. + chilling

Tammy Irvine, Whitby, Ontario

- 1 quart fresh strawberries
- 1-1/4 cups cold milk
- 1 package (3.4 ounces) instant vanilla pudding mix
- 1 package (8 ounces) cream cheese, softened
- 4 tablespoons strong brewed coffee, room temperature, *divided*
- 2 cups whipped topping
- 1 package (3 ounces) ladyfingers, split
- 6 squares (1 ounce *each*) bittersweet chocolate, grated

FRUITY HAZELNUT TRIFLE

1) Set aside three strawberries for garnish; slice the remaining strawberries. In a bowl, whisk milk and pudding mix for 2 minutes. Let stand for 2 minutes or until soft-set.

2) In a large mixing bowl, beat cream cheese until smooth; gradually beat in 2 tablespoons coffee. Beat in pudding. Fold in whipped topping.

3) Brush remaining coffee over ladyfingers. Line the bottom of a 3-qt. trifle or glass serving bowl with half of the ladyfingers. Top with half of the sliced berries, grated chocolate and pudding mixture; repeat layers.

4) Cut reserved berries in half; place on trifle. Cover and refrigerate for 4 hours or overnight.

Yield: 12 servings.

NUTRITION FACTS: 1/2 cup equals 256 calories, 16 g fat (10 g saturated fat), 50 mg cholesterol, 193 mg sodium, 27 g carbohydrate, 2 g fiber, 4 g protein.

Fruity Hazelnut Trifle
PREP/TOTAL TIME: 15 min.

Margaret Wilson, Hemet, California

- 1-1/2 cups cold milk
- 2 tablespoons refrigerated hazelnut nondairy creamer
- 1 package (3.4 ounces) instant vanilla pudding mix
- 1 can (21 ounces) apple pie filling
- 1 can (16 ounces) whole-berry cranberry sauce
- 1 loaf (10-3/4 ounces) frozen pound cake, thawed and cubed
- 2 cups whipped topping

1) In a large bowl, whisk milk, creamer and pudding mix for 2 minutes. Let stand for 2 minutes or until soft-set. In another bowl, combine pie filling and cranberry sauce.

2) Place a third of the cake cubes in a 3-qt. trifle bowl; layer with a fourth of the cranberry mixture and a third of the pudding mixture. Repeat layers twice.

3) Top with remaining cranberry mixture. Garnish with whipped topping. Cover and refrigerate until serving.

Yield: 12-14 servings.

NUTRITION FACTS: 1 cup equals 247 calories, 7 g fat (4 g saturated fat), 35 mg cholesterol, 215 mg sodium, 45 g carbohydrate, 1 g fiber, 2 g protein.

Raspberry Strawberry Trifle

PREP/TOTAL TIME: 20 min.

Patricia Schroedl, Jefferson, Wisconsin

- 3 cups cold fat-free milk
- 2 packages (1 ounce *each*) sugar-free instant white chocolate pudding mix
- 1 prepared angel food cake (14 ounces), cut into 1-inch cubes
- 3 cups sliced fresh strawberries
- 3 cups fresh raspberries
- 1 carton (8 ounces) frozen reduced-fat whipped topping, thawed
- 3 whole strawberries, quartered

1) In a large bowl, whisk milk and pudding mixes for 2 minutes or until slightly thickened.

2) Place a third of the cake cubes in a trifle bowl or 3-1/2-qt. glass serving bowl. Top with a third of the pudding, 1 cup sliced strawberries, 1-1/2 cups raspberries and a third of the whipped topping. Layer with a third of the cake and pudding, 1 cup strawberries and a third of the whipped topping.

RASPBERRY STRAWBERRY TRIFLE

3) Top with remaining cake, pudding, strawberries, raspberries and whipped topping. Garnish with quartered strawberries. Serve immediately or cover and chill until serving.

Yield: 14 servings.

NUTRITION FACTS: 1 cup equals 170 calories, 3 g fat (2 g saturated fat), 1 mg cholesterol, 289 mg sodium, 32 g carbohydrate, 3 g fiber, 4 g protein.

MINI MOCHA TRIFLES

Mini Mocha Trifles

PREP/TOTAL TIME: 15 min.

Taste of Home Test Kitchen

- 1 package (3 ounces) cream cheese, softened
- 4 teaspoons instant cappuccino powder *or* other flavored sweetened instant coffee granules
- 2 teaspoons sugar
- 1 cup whipped topping
- 2 slices pound cake *or* cake of your choice, cut into cubes
- 1/4 cup semisweet chocolate chips

Additional whipped topping and chocolate chips, optional

1) In a small mixing bowl, beat the cream cheese, coffee granules and sugar until blended. Beat in whipped topping.

2) Divide cake cubes between two dessert dishes; top with cream cheese mixture and chocolate chips. Garnish with additional whipped topping and chocolate chips if desired.

Yield: 2 servings.

NUTRITION FACTS: 1 serving (prepared with pound cake) equals 504 calories, 33 g fat (22 g saturated fat), 87 mg cholesterol, 254 mg sodium, 46 g carbohydrate, 2 g fiber, 7 g protein.

Chocolate Fondue

PREP: 15 min. **COOK:** 30 min.

Jane Shapton, Tustin, California

This creamy, delectable dip is a chocolate-lover's dream. You'll want to sample it with a variety of dippers.

- 1-1/2 cups sugar
- 1-1/4 cups water
- 1/4 cup light corn syrup
- 1 cup baking cocoa
- 1/2 cup heavy whipping cream
- 5 squares (1 ounce *each*) semisweet chocolate, chopped

Strawberries, banana chunks, apple slices *or* angel food cake cubes

1) In a small saucepan, bring the sugar, water and corn syrup to a boil. Reduce the heat; simmer, uncovered, for 20 minutes, stirring frequently.

2) In a bowl, combine the cocoa, cream and half of the syrup mixture until smooth; return to the pan. Bring to a boil, stirring constantly. Reduce heat; simmer, uncovered, for 5 minutes. Stir in the chopped chocolate until melted.

3) Serve fondue warm with fruit or cake for dipping. Refrigerate leftovers.

Yield: 2-1/2 cups.

NUTRITION FACTS: 2 tablespoons fondue (calculated without fruit or cake cubes) equals 138 calories, 5 g fat (3 g saturated fat), 8 mg cholesterol, 7 mg sodium, 25 g carbohydrate, 1 g fiber, 1 g protein.

Caramel Pudding Cake

PREP: 10 min. **BAKE:** 40 min.

Lois Litalien, Bonners Ferry, Idaho

This recipe dates back to the 1800s. Place it into the oven before you sit down to dinner for a comforting dessert.

- 1/2 cup butter, softened
- 1/2 cup sugar
- 1-1/2 cups all-purpose flour
- 1 teaspoon baking powder
- 1/2 teaspoon salt
- 1/2 cup milk
- 1/2 cup raisins
- 1 cup packed brown sugar
- 2 cups cold water

1) In a small mixing bowl, cream butter and sugar until light and fluffy. Combine the flour, baking powder and salt; add to creamed mixture with milk. Stir until smooth. Stir in raisins.

2) Spread in a greased 8-in. square baking pan. Combine brown sugar and cold water; pour over batter. Bake at 350° for 40 minutes or until golden brown. Serve warm.

Yield: 9 servings.

NUTRITION FACTS: 1 cup equals 332 calories, 11 g fat (7 g saturated fat), 29 mg cholesterol, 296 mg sodium, 58 g carbohydrate, 1 g fiber, 3 g protein.

Puddings and Custards

Baked custards are a sweetened mixture of milk, eggs and flavoring. They can be baked individually in custard cups or in one large baking dish. They are usually baked in a water bath to help ensure gentle and even baking. (See Making a Water Bath below.) Custards are done when a knife inserted near the center comes out clean and the top looks set.

To unmold a cooled custard, carefully run a knife around the edge of dish to loosen. If possible, lift the bottom edge of the custard with the tip of the knife blade to loosen. Place a serving dish over the top of the baking dish. Invert and remove custard dish.

Bread puddings are made with cubes or slices of bread baked in a custard mixture. They can be enriched with fruits, nuts, chocolate and spices. Bread puddings are served warm or cold and may be accompanied by a sauce. They're done when a knife inserted near the center comes out clean.

Rice puddings are made with cooked rice, a custard mixture, flavoring and spices. They can be served warm or cold. Rice puddings are done when a knife inserted near the center comes out clean.

Store baked custards and puddings in the refrigerator for 1 to 2 days.

Making a Water Bath

Place baking dish in a larger baking pan or dish, then place on rack in oven. Using a kettle or large measuring cup, carefully pour hot or boiling water into larger pan. Fill according to recipe directions.

Coconut Custard Pudding

PREP: 10 min. **BAKE:** 45 min. + cooling

Wilma Lincoln, Grinnell, Iowa

For a change of pace from the coconut, you can modify this recipe to make a yummy vanilla custard pudding.

- 3 eggs
- 1/3 cup sugar

Dash salt

- 2-1/4 cups milk
- 1/4 teaspoon coconut extract
- 1/4 teaspoon vanilla extract

Dash ground nutmeg

1) In a small bowl, whisk the eggs, sugar and salt until the eggs are just blended. In a saucepan, heat milk just to simmering. Gradually whisk into egg mixture. Stir in extracts.

2) Pour into five 8-oz. custard cups. Sprinkle with nutmeg. Place cups in a 13-in. x 9-in. x 2-in. baking pan. Add 1 in. of hot water to the pan. Bake, uncovered, at 350° for 45-50 minutes or until a knife inserted near center comes out clean.

3) Remove cups to a wire rack; cool for 1 hour. Store in the refrigerator.

Yield: 5 servings.

NUTRITION FACTS: 1 serving equals 165 calories, 7 g fat (3 g saturated fat), 142 mg cholesterol, 121 mg sodium, 19 g carbohydrate, trace fiber, 7 g protein.

■ **Vanilla Custard Pudding:** Omit coconut extract. Increase vanilla extract to 3/4 teaspoon. If desired, use 1/3 cup brown sugar in place of the sugar.

Orange Chocolate Mousse

PREP: 25 min. + chilling

Shirley Glaab, Hattiesburg, Mississippi

Easy-to-make, this dessert looks so elegant. Its velvety texture with a hint of orange is a perfect ending to any meal.

    2 eggs, beaten
    2 egg yolks, beaten
    1 cup heavy whipping cream
  1/4 cup packed brown sugar
    3 tablespoons orange juice
    1 to 1-1/2 teaspoons grated
       orange peel
    6 squares (1 ounce *each*) semisweet
       chocolate, melted and cooled
Whipped cream and orange peel
  strips, optional

1) In a saucepan, combine eggs, egg yolks, cream, brown sugar, juice and peel until blended. Cook and stir over medium-low heat for 15 minutes or until the mixture is thickened and reached 160°.

2) Remove from the heat; stir in melted chocolate until smooth. Pour into dessert dishes. Refrigerate

ORANGE CHOCOLATE MOUSSE

for at least 2 hours or until serving. Garnish with whipped cream and orange peel if desired.

Yield: 4 servings.

NUTRITION FACTS: 1 serving equals 542 calories, 41 g fat (23 g saturated fat), 294 mg cholesterol, 63 mg sodium, 41 g carbohydrate, 3 g fiber, 9 g protein.

Old-Fashioned Rice Pudding

PREP/TOTAL TIME: 25 min.

Laura German, North Brookfield, Massachusetts

Try a classic that's a nice way to use up leftover rice. We also like to dress it up with English toffee bits.

    2 cups cooked long grain rice
    2 cups milk
    3 tablespoons plus 1 teaspoon sugar
  1/8 teaspoon salt
    1 teaspoon vanilla extract
Whipped cream, optional

1) In a saucepan, combine rice, milk, sugar and salt. Cook, uncovered, over medium heat for 20 minutes or until thickened; stir often. Remove from the heat; stir in vanilla. Spoon into serving dishes. Serve warm; top with whipped cream if desired.

Yield: 4 servings.

NUTRITION FACTS: 1 serving equals 220 calories, 4 g fat (3 g saturated fat), 17 mg cholesterol, 134 mg sodium, 38 g carbohydrate, trace fiber, 6 g protein.

■ **Toffee Rice Pudding:** Combine 3 tablespoons *each* English toffee bits, miniature semisweet chocolate chips and toasted flaked coconut. Place half of rice pudding in 4 individual dessert dishes and top with half the toffee mixture. Repeat layers.

Chai Rice Pudding

PREP: 10 min. **COOK:** 40 min.

Taste of Home Test Kitchen

Chai refers to tea cooked in warm milk and with spices, such as cardamom, ginger and cinnamon. These same flavors are a wonderful addition to rice pudding.

    8 cups 1% milk
    1 cup uncooked basmati rice
  1/2 cup sugar
  1/4 teaspoon salt
  1/2 teaspoon ground cinnamon
  1/4 teaspoon ground cardamom
  1/4 teaspoon ground ginger
  1/8 teaspoon ground allspice

1) In a saucepan, combine milk, rice, sugar and salt. Bring to a boil. Reduce heat; simmer, uncovered, for 35-40 minutes or until slightly thickened, stirring frequently. Remove from heat; stir in spices. Serve warm or chilled. Refrigerate leftovers.

Yield: 10 servings.

NUTRITION FACTS: 1/2 cup equals 189 calories, 2 g fat (1 g saturated fat), 8 mg cholesterol, 159 mg sodium, 34 g carbohydrate, trace fiber, 8 g protein.

OLD-FASHIONED BREAD PUDDING

 CLASSIC: Buttery croissants, orange peel and a homemade caramel sauce add a sophisticated touch to Elegant Bread Pudding. This recipe makes a large pan of the rich dessert, so you can satisfy a crowd.

 TIME-SAVER: Have a need for speed? Microwave Bread Pudding lets you enjoy a satisfying treat in minutes. With cream cheese, chocolate chips and mini peanut butter cups, it's appealing to all ages.

 LIGHT: Skipping the caramel sauce and using fat-free milk and sugar substitute help slim down this better-for-you Spiced Bread Pudding. One sweet serving has half the calories and cholesterol and less than a third of the fat of classic Elegant Bread Pudding.

 SERVES 2: Only two slices of bread and a small handful of raisins are needed to fix Bread Pudding with Butter Sauce. Custard cups hold the individual servings of this warming dessert, which is served with a flavorful sauce.

Elegant Bread Pudding

PREP: 15 min. **BAKE:** 45 min.

Sharon Runyan, Fort Wayne, Indiana

- 10 cups cubed croissants *or* French bread
- 1/2 cup raisins
- 8 eggs
- 2 cups half-and-half cream
- 1 cup packed brown sugar
- 1 teaspoon ground cinnamon
- 1 teaspoon ground nutmeg
- 1 teaspoon grated orange peel

CARAMEL SAUCE:

- 1 cup packed brown sugar
- 1/2 cup butter
- 1/2 cup heavy whipping cream
- 1 teaspoon vanilla extract

Whipped cream, optional

1) Arrange bread cubes evenly in a greased 13-in. x 9-in. x 2-in. baking dish; sprinkle with raisins. In a large bowl, beat the eggs, half-and-half cream, sugar, cinnamon, nutmeg and orange peel; pour over bread.

2) Bake, uncovered, at 350° for 30 minutes. Cover with foil and bake 15 minutes longer or until a knife inserted near the center comes out clean.

3) For sauce, in a saucepan, combine the brown sugar, butter and whipping cream; cook and stir over low heat until smooth. Remove from the heat; stir in vanilla.

4) Serve bread pudding in bowls with caramel sauce and whipped cream if desired.

Yield: 14 servings.

NUTRITION FACTS: 1 serving equals 377 calories, 17 g fat (9 g saturated fat), 168 mg cholesterol, 270 mg sodium, 49 g carbohydrate, 1 g fiber, 7 g protein.

Microwave Bread Pudding

PREP/TOTAL TIME: 20 min.

Victoria Kvassay, Covina, California

- 3/4 cup heavy whipping cream
- 1/2 cup semisweet chocolate chips
- 1/4 cup whipped cream cheese
- 1/4 cup sugar
- 1 tablespoon butter
- 10 slices white bread, cut into 1-inch cubes
- 15 miniature peanut butter cups, quartered

1) In a large microwave-safe bowl, combine the cream, chocolate chips, cream cheese, sugar and butter. Cover and microwave on high for 2-3 minutes or until chips are melted; stir until smooth. Add the bread cubes; toss to coat.

2) Place half of the bread mixture in a greased 8-in. square microwave-safe dish. Sprinkle with peanut butter cups; top with the remaining bread mixture. Microwave, uncovered, on high for 1-1/2 minutes or until peanut butter cups are melted. Serve warm.

Yield: 6-8 servings.

NUTRITION FACTS: 1 piece equals 332 calories, 20 g fat (11 g saturated fat), 41 mg cholesterol, 295 mg sodium, 37 g carbohydrate, 2 g fiber, 5 g protein.

Spiced Bread Pudding

PREP: 10 min. **BAKE:** 25 min.

Taste of Home Test Kitchen

- 2 eggs
- 2 cups fat-free milk

Sugar substitute equivalent to 1/4 cup sugar

- 1/4 cup sugar
- 1 tablespoon butter, melted

BREAD PUDDING WITH BUTTER SAUCE

1 teaspoon ground cinnamon
1/2 teaspoon vanilla extract
1/4 teaspoon salt
1/4 teaspoon ground nutmeg
1/8 teaspoon ground cloves
5 cups cubed day-old French bread

1) In a large bowl, combine the eggs, milk, sugar substitute, sugar, butter, cinnamon, vanilla, salt, nutmeg and cloves. Add bread cubes; stir gently to coat. Pour into an 8-in. square baking dish coated with cooking spray.

2) Bake, uncovered, at 350° for 25-30 minutes or until a knife inserted near the center comes out clean. Serve warm.

Yield: 6 servings.

Editor's Note: This recipe was tested with Splenda No Calorie Sweetener.

NUTRITION FACTS: 2/3 cup equals 187 calories, 5 g fat (2 g saturated fat), 78 mg cholesterol, 338 mg sodium, 28 g carbohydrate, 1 g fiber, 7 g protein.

Bread Pudding with Butter Sauce

PREP: 15 min. **BAKE:** 35 min. + cooling

Norma Burggraf, Marshfield, Ohio

2 slices white bread, cubed
2 tablespoons raisins
1 egg

1/2 cup evaporated milk
3 tablespoons water
2 tablespoons sugar
1/4 teaspoon ground cinnamon
1/4 teaspoon ground nutmeg

BUTTER SAUCE:
2 tablespoons butter
2 tablespoons sugar
1 egg yolk, beaten
1 tablespoon water
1 tablespoon bourbon, optional

1) Divide bread cubes and raisins between two greased 8-oz. ramekins or custard cups. In a small bowl, whisk the egg, milk, water, sugar, cinnamon and nutmeg. Pour over bread mixture.

2) Bake, uncovered, at 350° for 35-40 minutes or until a knife inserted near the center comes out clean. Cool for 15 minutes.

3) Meanwhile, in a small saucepan, melt butter. Stir in the sugar, egg yolk and water. Cook and stir over medium-low heat for 4 minutes or until sugar is dissolved and mixture comes to a boil. Remove from the heat; stir in bourbon if desired. Serve warm with bread pudding.

Yield: 2 servings.

NUTRITION FACTS: 1 serving equals 451 calories, 21 g fat (12 g saturated fat), 258 mg cholesterol, 351 mg sodium, 52 g carbohydrate, 1 g fiber, 11 g protein.

🍴 White Chocolate Creme Brulee

PREP: 15 min. BAKE: 50 min. + chilling

Carole Resnick, Cleveland, Ohio

When you want a dessert for a special occasion, try this one. Serving two, it's perfect for Valentine's Day or an anniversary dinner. But if need be, you can double the recipe, as I often do for my family.

> 3   egg yolks
> 6   tablespoons sugar, *divided*
> 1   cup heavy whipping cream
> 2   squares (1 ounce *each*) white baking chocolate, finely chopped
> 1/4 teaspoon vanilla extract

1) In a small bowl, whisk the egg yolks and 2 tablespoons sugar; set aside. In a small saucepan, combine the cream, chocolate and 2 tablespoons sugar. Heat over medium-low heat until chocolate is melted and the mixture is smooth, stirring constantly.

2) Remove from the heat. Stir in vanilla. Stir a small amount of hot filling into egg yolk mixture; return all to the pan, stirring constantly.

3) Pour into two 10-oz. ramekins. Place in a baking pan. Add 1 in. of boiling water to pan. Bake, uncovered, at 325° for 50-55 minutes or until center is set. Remove from water bath. Cool for 10 minutes. Refrigerate for 3-4 hours.

4) Remove from the refrigerator 30 minutes before serving. Just before serving, sprinkle remaining sugar over tops. Broil 4-6 in. from the heat for 2 to 2-1/2 minutes or until sugar is caramelized.

Yield: 2 servings.

NUTRITION FACTS: 1 serving equals 854 calories, 62 g fat (36 g saturated fat), 488 mg cholesterol, 86 mg sodium, 70 g carbohydrate, 0 fiber, 9 g protein.

Souffles

Souffles are made from an egg yolk-based custard that is lightened with beaten egg whites. This mixture bakes up into a light, airy creation.

Before working with egg whites, remove all fat residue from your mixing bowl and beaters by washing them thoroughly in hot, soapy water and drying with a clean kitchen towel. Use metal or glass mixing bowls. Plastic bowls, even freshly washed and dried ones, may have an oily film on them.

Separate eggs when they are cold. Make sure there are no specks of egg yolk in the white. Let the separated eggs or egg whites stand at room temperature for 30 minutes before beating. To lighten the batter, fold about a third of the beaten egg whites into the custard base. Then fold in the remaining egg whites.

Spoon or pour custard into baking dish. Souffles rise two to three times the volume of the batter. Bake a four-egg souffle in a 1-1/2- to 2-qt. dish. Bake on middle rack of a preheated oven according to recipe directions.

A souffle is done when the top feels firm and a knife inserted near the center comes out clean. A souffle will fall slightly once it's removed from the oven. For best results, serve the souffle immediately.

An unbaked souffle may be refrigerated up to 2 hours before baking or may be frozen for 3 weeks. If frozen, thaw in the refrigerator before baking. A frozen souffle will not bake up as high as a freshly prepared souffle.

Dark Chocolate Souffle

PREP: 30 min. BAKE: 50 min.

Taste of Home Test Kitchen

Chocolate lovers won't be able to resist this rich souffle. Flavored whipped cream is the crowning touch.

> 1   teaspoon plus 3 tablespoons butter, *divided*
> 1   tablespoon plus 1/2 cup sugar, *divided*
> 1/4 cup all-purpose flour
> 1/4 teaspoon salt
> 1   cup milk
> 4   ounces dark chocolate, chopped
> 4   eggs, *separated*
> 1/2 teaspoon orange extract, optional
> 1/2 teaspoon vanilla extract
> 1/4 teaspoon cream of tartar

TOPPING:

> 1/4 cup confectioners' sugar
> 2   tablespoons baking cocoa
> 1/2 teaspoon vanilla *or* orange extract
> 1   cup heavy whipping cream

DARK CHOCOLATE SOUFFLE

1) Use 1 teaspoon butter to grease bottom and sides of a 1-1/2-qt. souffle dish. Thoroughly coat inside of dish with 1 tablespoon sugar; tap out excess sugar and discard.

2) In a saucepan, combine 1/4 cup sugar, flour and salt. Stir in milk until smooth. Bring to a boil over medium heat; cook and stir for 2 minutes or until thickened. Reduce heat to low; add chocolate and remaining butter. Cook and stir until chocolate is melted; remove from the heat.

3) In a small bowl, beat egg yolks. Stir a small amount of hot filling into yolks; return all to the pan, stirring constantly. Stir in orange extract if desired and vanilla; transfer to a large bowl.

4) In a mixing bowl with clean beaters, beat egg whites and cream of tartar on medium speed until foamy. Gradually beat in remaining sugar on high until stiff peaks form. With a spatula, stir a fourth of the egg white mixture into chocolate batter until blended. Fold in remaining egg white mixture until no white streaks remain.

5) Pour into prepared dish. Bake, uncovered, at 350° for 50-55 minutes or until a knife inserted near the center comes out clean.

6) For topping, in a small chilled mixing bowl and with chilled beaters, combine the confectioners' sugar, cocoa and vanilla. Gradually add cream. Beat on high until stiff peaks form. Serve the souffle immediately with a dollop of topping.

Yield: 6 servings.

NUTRITION FACTS: 1 serving equals 491 calories, 32 g fat (19 g saturated fat), 220 mg cholesterol, 240 mg sodium, 43 g carbohydrate, 2 g fiber, 8 g protein.

Baked Orange Souffle

PREP: 50 min. **BAKE:** 25 min.

Taste of Home Test Kitchen

This souffle with a distinctive orange taste makes a light ending to any meal.

- 1 teaspoon plus 2 tablespoons butter, *divided*
- 2 tablespoons plus 1/2 cup sugar, *divided*
- 5 tablespoons all-purpose flour
- 1/4 teaspoon salt
- 1 cup milk
- 4 eggs, *separated*
- 2 tablespoons grated orange peel
- 1 to 1-1/4 teaspoons orange extract
- 1/8 teaspoon cream of tartar

1) Use 1 teaspoon butter to grease bottom and sides of a 6-cup souffle dish. Thoroughly coat inside of dish with 2 tablespoons sugar; tap out excess sugar and discard.

2) In a saucepan, combine flour, salt and 1/4 cup sugar; gradually whisk in milk. Bring to a boil over medium heat; cook and stir for 2 minutes or until thickened. Transfer to a bowl; whisk in egg yolks, orange peel, extract and remaining butter.

3) In a mixing bowl, beat egg whites and cream of tartar on medium speed until foamy. Gradually add remaining sugar, 1 tablespoon at a time, beating on high until soft peaks form.

4) With a spatula, stir 1 cup of the whites into the orange batter until no white streaks remain. Fold in remaining egg whites until combined. Gently pour into prepared dish.

5) Bake at 400° for 25-30 minutes or until a knife inserted near the center comes out clean. Serve immediately.

Yield: 6-8 servings.

NUTRITION FACTS: 1 serving equals 168 calories, 7 g fat (3 g saturated fat), 119 mg cholesterol, 154 mg sodium, 21 g carbohydrate, trace fiber, 5 g protein.

LOW-CALORIE DESSERTS ■■■

Here are some of my favorite lower-calorie desserts:

I like to top frozen banana and strawberry slices with fat-free whipped topping or fat-free vanilla yogurt. Then drizzle with chocolate syrup for a sweet treat with lower fat and calories.

Prepare a cup of sugar-free hot cocoa, top with fat-free whipped topping, then sprinkle with cinnamon.

Fix your favorite flavor of sugar-free instant pudding with fat-free milk. After it chills, top a serving with a small amount of crumbled graham crackers, chocolate jimmies or candy sprinkles.

—Suzanne R., Grand Rapids, Michigan

Vanilla Custard Ice Cream

PREP: 30 min. + freezing

Margaret Gage, Roseboom, New York

This is the best vanilla custard I've ever had. I like to top it with colorful sprinkles, but you can try different toppings to find your favorite!

>   2 cups milk
>   3/4 cup sugar
>   1/8 teaspoon salt
>   2 eggs, beaten
>   2 cups heavy whipping cream
>   2 tablespoons vanilla extract

Colored sprinkles, optional

1) In a large saucepan, heat the milk to 175°; stir in the sugar and salt until dissolved. Whisk a small amount of the hot mixture into the eggs. Return all to the pan, whisking constantly.

2) Cook and stir over low heat until mixture reaches at least 160° and coats the back of a metal spoon. Remove from the heat.

3) Cool quickly by placing pan in a bowl of ice water; stir for 2 minutes. Stir in whipping cream and vanilla. Press plastic wrap onto surface of custard. Refrigerate for several hours or overnight.

4) Fill cylinder of ice cream freezer two-thirds full; freeze according to manufacturer's directions. Chill remaining mixture until ready to freeze.

5) Allow to ripen in ice cream freezer or firm up in refrigerator freezer for 2-4 hours before serving. Garnish with colored sprinkles if desired.

Yield: 1-1/2 quarts.

NUTRITION FACTS: 1/2 cup equals 227 calories, 17 g fat (10 g saturated fat), 95 mg cholesterol, 70 mg sodium, 16 g carbohydrate, 0 fiber, 3 g protein.

VANILLA CUSTARD ICE CREAM

Tart Lemon Sorbet

PREP: 10 min. + freezing

Susan Garoutte, Georgetown, Texas

On hot summer days, nothing seems to satisfy like the tartness of lemons, especially this light, refreshing sorbet.

>   3 cups water
>   1-1/2 cups sugar
>   1-1/2 cups lemon juice
>   1 tablespoon grated lemon peel

1) In a saucepan, bring water and sugar to a boil. Cook and stir until sugar is dissolved, about 5 minutes. Cool. Add the lemon juice and peel.

2) Pour into the cylinder of an ice cream freezer; freeze according to manufacturer's directions. Allow to ripen in ice cream freezer or firm up in the refrigerator freezer for 2-4 hours. Remove from the freezer 10 minutes before serving.

Yield: about 1 quart.

NUTRITION FACTS: 1/2 cup equals 157 calories, trace fat (0 saturated fat), 0 cholesterol, 1 mg sodium, 42 g carbohydrate, trace fiber, trace protein.

Blueberry Cheesecake Ice Cream

PREP: 25 min. + freezing **BAKE:** 10 min. + cooling

Melissa Symington, Neche, North Dakota

After sampling this flavor at an ice cream stand, I kept trying to duplicate it until it was just right.

>   1/2 cup sugar
>   1 tablespoon cornstarch
>   1/2 cup water
>   1-1/4 cups fresh *or* frozen blueberries
>   1 tablespoon lemon juice

GRAHAM CRACKER MIXTURE:

>   2-1/4 cups graham cracker crumbs
>   (about 36 squares)
>   2 tablespoons sugar
>   1/2 teaspoon ground cinnamon
>   1/2 cup butter, melted

ICE CREAM:

>   1-1/2 cups sugar
>   1 package (3.4 ounces) instant
>   cheesecake *or* vanilla pudding mix
>   1 quart heavy whipping cream
>   2 cups milk
>   2 teaspoons vanilla extract

1) In a saucepan, combine sugar and cornstarch. Stir in water until smooth. Stir in blueberries and lemon juice. Bring to a boil. Reduce heat; simmer, uncovered, for 5 minutes or until slightly thickened, stirring occasionally. Cover and chill.

2) In a bowl, combine cracker crumbs, sugar and cinnamon. Stir in butter. Pat into an ungreased 15-in. x 10-in. x 1-in. baking pan. Bake at 350° for 10-15 minutes or until lightly browned. Cool completely on a wire rack.

BLUEBERRY CHEESECAKE ICE CREAM

3) In a large bowl, whisk the ice cream ingredients. Fill ice cream freezer cylinder two-thirds full; freeze according to manufacturer's directions. Refrigerate remaining mixture until ready to freeze. Whisk before adding to ice cream freezer (mixture will have some lumps).

4) Crumble graham cracker mixture. In a container, layer the ice cream, graham cracker mixture and blueberry sauce three times; swirl. Freeze.

Yield: 2 quarts.

NUTRITION FACTS: 1/2 cup equals 459 calories, 30 g fat (18 g saturated fat), 101 mg cholesterol, 252 mg sodium, 47 g carbohydrate, 1 g fiber, 3 g protein.

Mint Chip Ice Cream
PREP: 15 min. + freezing

Farrah McGuire, Springdale, Washington

We have a milk cow, so homemade ice cream is a regular dessert. This creamy version has a mild mint taste.

- 1-3/4 cups milk
- 3/4 cup sugar

Dash salt

- 3 eggs, lightly beaten
- 1-3/4 cups heavy whipping cream
- 1 teaspoon vanilla extract
- 1/4 teaspoon peppermint extract
- 4 drops green food coloring, optional
- 1/2 cup miniature semisweet chocolate chips

1) In a small saucepan, heat the milk to 175°; stir in the sugar and salt until dissolved. Whisk a small amount of the hot mixture into the eggs. Return all to the pan, whisking constantly.

2) Cook and stir over low heat until mixture reaches at least 160° and coats the back of a metal spoon. Remove from the heat.

3) Cool quickly by placing pan in a bowl of ice water; stir for 2 minutes. Stir in whipping cream, extracts and food coloring if desired. Press plastic wrap onto surface of custard. Refrigerate for several hours or overnight.

4) Stir in the chocolate chips. Fill ice cream freezer cylinder two-thirds full; freeze according to the

manufacturer's directions. Refrigerate remaining mixture until ready to freeze. Transfer to ice cream container; freeze for 2-4 hours before serving.

Yield: 1-1/2 quarts.

NUTRITION FACTS: 1/2 cup equals 244 calories, 17 g fat (10 g saturated fat), 106 mg cholesterol, 59 mg sodium, 20 g carbohydrate, trace fiber, 4 g protein.

Frosty Tiramisu
PREP/TOTAL TIME: 10 min.

Margee Berry, Trout Lake, Washington

Tiramisu is a family favorite but time-consuming to make. So I created an easy, weeknight version.

- 3 tablespoons brewed coffee
- 6 ladyfingers
- 1 quart vanilla ice cream, softened
- 1 container (8 ounces) Mascarpone cheese
- 1 cup chocolate milk
- 2 tablespoons baking cocoa

Whipped cream and chocolate curls

1) Brush coffee over ladyfingers; set aside. In a large mixing bowl, beat ice cream, cheese and milk until smooth.

2) Divide among six parfait glasses. Sprinkle with cocoa. Place a ladyfinger in each glass. Top with whipped cream and chocolate curls.

Yield: 6 servings.

NUTRITION FACTS: 1 serving (calculated without whipped cream and chocolate curls) equals 424 calories, 30 g fat (17 g saturated fat), 132 mg cholesterol, 133 mg sodium, 34 g carbohydrate, 1 g fiber, 9 g protein.

Strawberry Ice
PREP: 15 min. + freezing

Kim Hammond, Watsonville, California

After picking strawberries, we use up many of them in this treat. It's a slushy mixture that kids love.

- 5 cups fresh or frozen unsweetened strawberries, thawed
- 2/3 cup sugar
- 2/3 cup water
- 1/4 cup lemon juice

1) Place berries in a food processor; cover and process until smooth. In a saucepan, bring sugar and water to a boil. Cook and stir until sugar is dissolved, about 5 minutes; cool slightly. Add to food processor. Add lemon juice; cover and process until combined.

2) Pour into a shallow freezer container; cover and freeze for 4-6 hours or until almost frozen. Just before serving, whip mixture in a food processor.

Yield: 6 servings.

NUTRITION FACTS: 1 serving equals 125 calories, trace fat (trace saturated fat), 0 cholesterol, 2 mg sodium, 32 g carbohydrate, 3 g fiber, 1 g protein.

FAMILY-FAVORITE ICE CREAM CAKE

 CLASSIC: The eye-catching colors of Cranberry Pistachio Ice Cream Cake will impress guests, but the fabulous combination of flavors will really wow them. It's handy to fix a day or two before a special occasion and freeze until it's time for dessert.

 TIME-SAVER: Since there's no waiting for layers to set up, Ice Cream Sandwich Dessert is a breeze to make. You can assemble the four store-bought ingredients in only 15 minutes, then pop the pan in the freezer until a few minutes before serving.

 LIGHT: Frozen yogurt and reduced-fat varieties of sandwich cookies, chocolate ice cream and whipped topping lighten up Black Forest Frozen Dessert. A slice of this frosty, layered treat has 150 fewer calories and less than half the fat of a serving of Cranberry Pistachio Ice Cream Cake.

 SERVES 2: It's fun to share dessert when it's a 4-inch round Frozen Raspberry Cheesecake. A shortbread cookie crust is layered with a no-bake cheesecake mixture and raspberry sherbet, then topped with fresh berries. Slice the little dessert in half or simply grab two forks and dig in!

Cranberry Pistachio Ice Cream Cake

PREP: 30 min. + freezing

Quadelle Rose, Springbrook, Alberta

- 1-1/2 cups crushed chocolate cream-filled sandwich cookies
- 1/4 cup butter, melted
- 1-1/2 cups fresh *or* frozen cranberries
- 1/2 cup light corn syrup
- 1/3 cup sugar
- 1/3 cup water
- 6 cups vanilla ice cream, softened, *divided*
- 1/2 cup chopped pistachios, *divided*

1) In a small bowl, combine cookie crumbs and butter; press onto the bottom of a greased 9-in. springform pan. Freeze for 1 hour or until firm.

2) In a small saucepan, combine the cranberries, corn syrup, sugar and water. Bring to a boil; cook over medium heat until the berries pop, about 10 minutes. Cool slightly. Transfer to a blender; cover and process until smooth. Pour into a large bowl. Refrigerate for 30 minutes or until cooled, stirring occasionally.

3) Remove crust from freezer. Spread with half of the ice cream. Set aside 1/4 cup cranberry puree. Pour remaining puree over ice cream. Set aside 1 tablespoon nuts; sprinkle remaining nuts over puree. Freeze for 30 minutes or until firm.

4) Layer with remaining ice cream, puree and nuts. Cover with plastic wrap; freeze for 6 hours or until firm. Remove from the freezer 15 minutes before serving. Remove sides of pan; cut into slices.

Yield: 10-12 servings.

NUTRITION FACTS: 1 piece equals 352 calories, 18 g fat (8 g saturated fat), 39 mg cholesterol, 225 mg sodium, 48 g carbohydrate, 2 g fiber, 5 g protein.

CRANBERRY PISTACHIO ICE CREAM CAKE

Ice Cream Sandwich Dessert

PREP: 15 min. + freezing

Jody Koerber, Caledonia, Wisconsin

- 19 ice cream sandwiches
- 1 carton (12 ounces) frozen whipped topping, thawed
- 1 jar (11-3/4 ounces) hot fudge ice cream topping
- 1 cup salted peanuts, *divided*

1) Cut one ice cream sandwich in half. Place one whole and one half sandwich along a short side of an ungreased 13-in. x 9-in. x 2-in. pan. Arrange eight sandwiches in opposite direction in the pan.

2) Spread with half of the whipped topping. Spoon fudge topping by teaspoonfuls onto whipped topping. Sprinkle with 1/2 cup peanuts. Repeat layers with remaining ice cream sandwiches, whipped topping and peanuts (pan will be full).

3) Cover and freeze for up to 2 months. Remove from the freezer 20 minutes before serving. Cut into squares.

Yield: 15 servings.

NUTRITION FACTS: 1 piece equals 375 calories, 17 g fat (9 g saturated fat), 25 mg cholesterol, 116 mg sodium, 48 g carbohydrate, 2 g fiber, 7 g protein.

BLACK FOREST FROZEN DESSERT

Black Forest Frozen Dessert

PREP: 40 min. + freezing

Ruth Lee, Troy, Ontario

- 1 cup crushed reduced-fat cream-filled chocolate sandwich cookies (about 10 cookies)
- 2 tablespoons butter, melted
- 1 can (15 ounces) pitted dark sweet cherries
- 2 cups black cherry-vanilla swirl frozen yogurt blend
- 3 cups reduced-fat chocolate ice cream, softened
- 1 tablespoon cornstarch
- 2 tablespoons lemon juice
- 3/4 cup reduced-fat whipped topping
- 12 mint sprigs

1) In a small bowl, combine the cookie crumbs and butter. Press onto the bottom of a 9-in. springform pan coated with cooking spray. Place pan on a baking sheet. Bake at 350° for 8-10 minutes or until set. Cool on a wire rack.

2) Drain cherries, reserving syrup. Cover and refrigerate syrup. Chop half of the cherries; refrigerate whole cherries. Spread frozen yogurt evenly over crust; sprinkle with chopped cherries. Cover and freeze for 30 minutes. Spread ice cream over cherries; cover and freeze for 2 hours or until firm.

3) For sauce, in a small saucepan, combine cornstarch and reserved cherry syrup until smooth. Bring to a boil; cook and stir for 2 minutes or until thickened. Remove from the heat; stir in lemon juice and whole cherries.

4) Remove sides of springform pan; cut dessert into slices. Serve with sauce. Garnish with whipped topping and mint.

Yield: 12 servings.

NUTRITION FACTS: 1 slice with 1 tablespoon sauce and 1 tablespoon whipped topping equals 193 calories, 7 g fat (4 g saturated fat), 23 mg cholesterol, 112 mg sodium, 31 g carbohydrate, 1 g fiber, 3 g protein.

Frozen Raspberry Cheesecake

PREP: 15 min. + freezing

Vicki Melies, Elkhorn, Nebraska

- 1/4 cup crushed shortbread cookies
- 1 tablespoon butter, melted
- 1-1/2 ounces cream cheese, softened
- 3 tablespoons sweetened condensed milk
- 1 tablespoon lemon juice
- 1/3 cup raspberry sherbet, softened
- 1/4 cup fresh raspberries

1) In a small bowl, combine the cookie crumbs and butter. Press onto the bottom of a 4-in. springform pan coated with cooking spray. Freeze for 10 minutes. In a small bowl, combine the cream cheese, milk and lemon juice until blended. Spread over crust. Freeze for 2 hours or until firm.

2) Spread sherbet over cream cheese layer; freeze 2 hours longer. Remove sides of pan. Top with raspberries.

Yield: 2 servings.

NUTRITION FACTS: 1 serving equals 391 calories, 22 g fat (12 g saturated fat), 55 mg cholesterol, 288 mg sodium, 43 g carbohydrate, 2 g fiber, 6 g protein.

FROZEN RASPBERRY CHEESECAKE

Fudge Sundae Sauce

PREP/TOTAL TIME: 10 min.

Tammy Mackie, Seward, Nebraska

Mocha flavors are highlighted in this fudgy topping. You can make the sauce without the coffee, too.

- 2 cups (12 ounces) semisweet chocolate chips
- 2 squares (1 ounce *each*) unsweetened chocolate
- 1 cup heavy whipping cream
- 1/4 cup cold strong brewed coffee

Dash salt

- 1 teaspoon vanilla extract

1) In a heavy saucepan, melt the chocolate with the cream, coffee and salt over low heat, stirring constantly. Remove from the heat; stir in the vanilla. Serve warm over ice cream. Store in the refrigerator.

Yield: 2-1/2 cups.

Editor's Note: If you prefer your fudge sauce without the coffee flavor, just omit the coffee and increase the heavy whipping cream to 1-1/4 cups.

NUTRITION FACTS: 2 tablespoons equals 137 calories, 11 g fat (7 g saturated fat), 16 mg cholesterol, 14 mg sodium, 12 g carbohydrate, 1 g fiber, 1 g protein.

Praline Sauce

PREP/TOTAL TIME: 10 min.

Pat Sturze, Campbell River, British Columbia

This is a can't-miss treat over ice cream. You can also serve it over waffles, pancakes or French toast.

- 1-1/2 cups dark corn syrup
- 1-1/2 cups light corn syrup
- 1 teaspoon vanilla extract
- 1/8 teaspoon ground cinnamon
- 1/8 teaspoon ground nutmeg
- 1-1/2 cups coarsely chopped pecans, toasted

1) In a large bowl, combine corn syrups, vanilla, cinnamon and nutmeg until well blended. Stir in pecans. Serve warm or at room temperature. Store in an airtight container at room temperature.

Yield: 4 cups.

NUTRITION FACTS: 2 tablespoons equals 126 calories, 4 g fat (trace saturated fat), 0 cholesterol, 42 mg sodium, 24 g carbohydrate, 1 g fiber, 1 g protein.

Caramel Ice Cream Sauce

PREP/TOTAL TIME: 10 min.

Julee Wallberg, Salt Lake City, Utah

This delightful dessert sauce has a smooth texture and yummy taste. It's terrific drizzled over ice cream.

- 1/2 cup packed brown sugar
- 1 tablespoon cornstarch
- 1/3 cup half-and-half cream

- 2 tablespoons water
- 2 tablespoons light corn syrup
- 1 tablespoon butter, cubed
- 1/2 teaspoon vanilla extract

1) In a saucepan, combine the brown sugar and cornstarch. Stir in the cream, water and corn syrup until smooth. Bring to a boil; cook and stir for 2 minutes or until thickened.

2) Remove from the heat. Stir in the butter and vanilla until butter is melted. Serve warm or cold over ice cream. Store in the refrigerator.

Yield: about 1 cup.

NUTRITION FACTS: 2 tablespoons (calculated without ice cream) equals 96 calories, 2 g fat (2 g saturated fat), 9 mg cholesterol, 31 mg sodium, 19 g carbohydrate, trace fiber, trace protein.

Peppermint Stick Sauce

PREP/TOTAL TIME: 15 min.

Linda Gronewaller, Hutchinson, Kansas

This pepperminty sauce is one of my favorite holiday gifts to give. It's great over ice cream, unfrosted brownies or chocolate cake.

- 1-1/2 cups finely crushed peppermint candies *or* candy canes
- 3/4 cup heavy whipping cream
- 1 jar (7 ounces) marshmallow creme

1) Combine all ingredients in a medium saucepan. Cook over medium-low heat until mixture is smooth and candy is melted, stirring occasionally. Serve warm over ice cream or cake. Store in the refrigerator.

Yield: 3 cups.

NUTRITION FACTS: 2 tablespoons equals 76 calories, 3 g fat (2 g saturated fat), 10 mg cholesterol, 12 mg sodium, 13 g carbohydrate, 0 fiber, trace protein.

PEPPERMINT STICK SAUCE

a very special delivery

Group brings cookies & Christmas spirit to workers

Harlan and Joan Truax

> " I just enjoy
> sharing and
> giving people
> something they
> may not get
> very often.
>
> ~Joan Truax

Today's world is open for business 24/7, so there are always those who have to work on holidays.

Christmas is no exception. From firehouses to gas stations, many people sacrifice time with family and friends to fill the posts on Christmas Eve.

The fact hasn't gone unnoticed by the men's and women's groups at Pittsboro Christian Church in Pittsboro, Indiana. For the past 4 years, dozens of cookies have been delivered to those hardworking men and women who keep things running smoothly the night before Christmas.

The women bake at least six dozen cookies each and bring them to church on Christmas Eve day.

After services, the men's group distributes the cookies to fire-houses, police stations, gas stations, convenience stores and an urgent care medical clinic.

They don't have to wait long for the response: lots of appreciation for the treats.

"The workers are so grateful for the homemade cookies," says Joan Truax, one of the bakers. She makes at least 10 dozen cookies to give away every year.

Joan likes to bake up batches of Gingerbread People cookies. They're tasty and cute; their smiles even get those who work on the holiday to smile back.

Her reward?

That in itself is a priceless Christmas present.

"I just enjoy sharing and giving people something they may not get very often," she says.

Recipes

Tips

Cookies & Bars

Cookies make great snacks, bake sale bundles, homemade gifts and special holiday buffet treats. They are commonly grouped into five categories: drop, shaped, refrigerator, cutout and bars.

The consistency of drop cookie dough allows it to simply be dropped from a spoon onto a baking sheet, making it the easiest kind of cookie to bake.

Shaped cookies are formed by hand into various shapes, such as balls, logs and crescents. Or they're pressed through a cookie press, such as spritz.

For refrigerator (icebox or slice-and-bake) cookies, the dough is shaped into logs, wrapped in plastic wrap and then refrigerated until firm enough to slice and bake.

Cutout cookies have a firmer dough. To make it easier to handle, the dough may need to be chilled before being rolled out and cut into shapes with a cookie cutter.

Bar cookies may be made with a pourable batter, spreadable dough or a crumbly crust that needs to be patted into the pan. The one thing all bar cookies have in common is that they are baked in a pan rather than on a baking sheet. After cooling, they are cut into bars, squares, fingers, triangles or diamonds.

Cookie Baking Tips

Use butter, stick margarine (with at least 80% oil) or shortening. Whipped, tub, soft, liquid or reduced-fat products contain air and water and will produce flat, tough and underbrowned cookies. Measure all ingredients accurately.

Avoid overmixing the dough. If it's handled too much, the cookies will be tough.

Use heavy-gauge dull aluminum baking sheets with one or two low sides. When a recipe calls for greased baking sheets, use shortening or cooking spray. Dark finishes may cause cookies to become overly browned.

Preheat the oven for 10 to 15 minutes. For even baking, make cookies the same size and thickness. Unless the recipe states otherwise, place cookie dough 2 to 3 in. apart on a cool baking sheet.

Leave at least 2 in. around the baking sheet and the oven walls for good heat circulation. For best results, bake only one sheet of cookies at a time. If you need to bake two sheets at once, switch the position of the baking sheets halfway through the baking time.

Check the cookies when the minimum baking time has been reached, baking longer if needed. Follow doneness tests given in individual recipes.

Unless otherwise directed, let cookies cool for 1 minute on the baking sheet before removing to a wire rack. Cool completely before storing.

Let baking sheets cool before placing the next batch of cookie dough on it. Otherwise, the heat from the baking sheet will soften the dough and cause it to spread.

Removing Cookies from a Baking Sheet

If cookies crumble when you remove them from the baking sheet, let them cool for 1 to 2 minutes first. But if cookies cool too long, they become hard and can break when removed. If this happens, return the baking sheet to the oven to warm the cookies slightly so they'll release more easily.

Storing Cookies

Allow cookies to cool completely before storing. Store soft cookies and crisp cookies in separate airtight containers. If stored together, the moisture from the soft cookies will soften the crisp cookies, making them lose their crunch. Flavors can also blend during storage, so don't store strong-flavored cookies with delicate-flavored ones.

Layer cookies in a container, separating each layer with waxed paper. Allow the icing on cookies to completely dry before storing.

Unfrosted cookies can be stored in a cool, dry place in airtight containers for about 3 days. Cookies with a cream cheese frosting should be stored in the refrigerator.

For longer storage, wrap unfrosted cookies in plastic wrap, stack in an airtight container, seal and freeze for up to 3 months. Thaw wrapped cookies at room temperature before frosting and serving. If your crisp cookies became soft during storage, crisp them up by heating in a 300° oven for 5 minutes.

TOFFEE MALTED COOKIES

Drop Cookies

If your mixer begins to strain because the cookie dough is too thick, use a wooden spoon to stir in the last of the flour or ingredients such as nuts, chips or dried fruit.

For even baking, it's important that you make cookies the same size. Use a teaspoon or tablespoon from your flatware set.

Drop cookies generally melt and spread during baking. But sometimes a recipe may instruct you to flatten the cookies with the bottom of a glass dipped in sugar or with a fork, making a crisscross pattern.

Toffee Malted Cookies

PREP: 15 min. **BAKE:** 15 min./batch + cooling

Sharon Timpe, Mequon, Wisconsin

As much as I delight in sharing these goodies, my family considers them "keepers." It's a wonder I ever get them out the door to take to meetings! With their buttery melt-in-your-mouth texture, they're always popular.

> 1 cup butter, softened
> 1/2 cup sugar
> 1/2 cup packed brown sugar
> 2 eggs
> 1 package (3.4 ounces) instant vanilla pudding mix
> 1 teaspoon vanilla extract
> 2-1/4 cups all-purpose flour
> 1 cup quick-cooking oats
> 1 teaspoon baking soda
> 1/2 teaspoon salt
> 1 cup malted milk balls, chopped
> 3/4 cup English toffee bits *or* almond brickle chips

1) In a large mixing bowl, cream the butter and sugars until light and fluffy. Add eggs, one at a time, beating well after each addition. Add pudding mix and vanilla.

2) Combine the flour, oats, baking soda and salt; add to creamed mixture. Fold in the malted milk balls and the toffee bits (dough will be stiff). Drop by rounded teaspoonfuls 2 in. apart onto ungreased baking sheets.

3) Bake at 350° for 12-15 minutes or until golden brown. Cool for 2 minutes before removing to wire racks.

Yield: about 6 dozen.

NUTRITION FACTS: 2 cookies equals 159 calories, 8 g fat (4 g saturated fat), 28 mg cholesterol, 194 mg sodium, 20 g carbohydrate, trace fiber, 2 g protein.

Chocolate Mint Sandwich Cookies

PREP: 20 min. **BAKE:** 10 min./batch + cooling

Bertha Bratt, Lynden, Washington

The minty filling that's sandwiched between two chocolaty cookies is a real treat.

> 6 tablespoons butter
> 1-1/2 cups packed brown sugar
> 2 tablespoons water
> 2 cups (12 ounces) semisweet chocolate chips
> 2 eggs
> 1 teaspoon vanilla extract
> 2-1/2 cups all-purpose flour
> 1-1/2 teaspoons baking soda
> 1 teaspoon salt

FILLING:
   2-1/2 cups confectioners' sugar
    1/4 cup butter
      3 tablespoons milk
    1/2 teaspoon peppermint extract
      3 drops green food coloring, optional

Dash salt

1) In a saucepan, combine the butter, brown sugar, water and chocolate chips. Cook and stir over low heat until chips are melted. Cool.

2) Beat in eggs and vanilla. Combine the flour, baking soda and salt; gradually add to the chocolate mixture. Drop by rounded teaspoonfuls 2 in. apart onto ungreased baking sheets.

3) Bake at 350° for 10-12 minutes or until firm. Remove to wire racks to cool.

4) In a large mixing bowl, combine filling ingredients until smooth. Spread on the bottom of half of the cookies; top with remaining cookies.

Yield: about 15 sandwich cookies.

NUTRITION FACTS: 1 sandwich equals 424 calories, 15 g fat (9 g saturated fat), 49 mg cholesterol, 392 mg sodium, 72 g carbohydrate, 2 g fiber, 4 g protein.

Molasses Raisin Chews

PREP: 10 min. BAKE: 10 min./batch + cooling
Barbara Parker, Middlefield, Connecticut

My aunt always offered a plate of these when we visited her farm. We called them "cry baby cookies" because we thought the three raisins on each one resembled two eyes and a mouth.

  1/2 cup shortening
    1 cup sugar
    1 cup molasses
    4 cups all-purpose flour
    2 teaspoons baking soda
    2 teaspoons ground cinnamon
    1 teaspoon ground cloves
  1/4 teaspoon salt
    1 cup milk
    1 cup raisins

1) In a large mixing bowl, cream shortening and sugar until light and fluffy. Beat in molasses.

2) Combine the flour, baking soda, cinnamon, cloves and salt; add to the creamed mixture alternately with milk, beating well after each addition. Drop by heaping tablespoonfuls 2 in. apart onto greased baking sheets.

3) Arrange three raisins on each cookie. Bake at 350° for 10-12 minutes or until set. Remove to wire racks to cool.

Yield: about 5-1/2 dozen.

NUTRITION FACTS: 2 cookies equals 150 calories, 3 g fat (1 g saturated fat), 1 mg cholesterol, 103 mg sodium, 28 g carbohydrate, 1 g fiber, 2 g protein.

Cranberry Crisps

PREP: 10 min. BAKE: 15 min./batch + cooling
Sandy Furches, Lake City, Florida

I created this recipe after sampling a similar cookie while traveling in North Carolina. These cookies keep well in the freezer, so I always have some on hand for midday munching.

    1 cup butter-flavored shortening
    1 cup sugar
    1 cup packed brown sugar
    2 eggs
    2 teaspoons vanilla extract
  2-1/2 cups old-fashioned oats
    2 cups all-purpose flour
    1 teaspoon baking soda
    1 teaspoon ground cinnamon
  1/2 teaspoon salt
  1/2 teaspoon baking powder
  1-1/3 cups dried cranberries
    1 cup coarsely chopped walnuts

1) In a mixing bowl, cream shortening and sugars until light and fluffy. Add eggs, one at a time, beating well after each addition. Beat in vanilla. Combine oats, flour, baking soda, cinnamon, salt and baking powder; gradually add to the creamed mixture. Stir in the cranberries and walnuts.

2) Drop by tablespoonfuls 2 in. apart onto lightly greased baking sheets. Bake at 350° for 12-14 minutes or until lightly browned. Remove to wire racks to cool.

Yield: 5 dozen.

NUTRITION FACTS: 2 cookies equals 214 calories, 10 g fat (2 g saturated fat), 14 mg cholesterol, 96 mg sodium, 30 g carbohydrate, 1 g fiber, 3 g protein.

Making Drop Cookies

1) Fill a teaspoon or tablespoon with dough. Use another spoon or small rubber spatula to push the mound of dough off the spoon onto a cool baking sheet. Place dough 2 to 3 in. apart or as recipe directs.

2) An ice cream scoop is a perfect utensil for making uniformly sized drop cookies. (A 1 tablespoon-sized ice cream scoop will result in a standard-size 2-in. cookie.) Just scoop the dough, even off the top with a metal spatula and release onto a baking sheet.

MERINGUE FUDGE DROPS

Meringue Fudge Drops

PREP: 30 min. **BAKE:** 30 min. + cooling

Charlotte Elliott, Neenah, Wisconsin

Almond-flavored meringue, a fudgy filling and a sprinkling of pistachio nuts make these bite-size morsels a special addition to any dessert tray.

- 2 egg whites
- 1/4 teaspoon almond extract
- 1/8 teaspoon cream of tartar
- 1/8 teaspoon salt
- 1/2 cup sugar

FUDGE TOPPING:

- 1/2 cup semisweet chocolate chips
- 3 tablespoons butter
- 2 egg yolks, lightly beaten
- 2 tablespoons confectioners' sugar
- 2 tablespoons chopped pistachio nuts

1) Place egg whites in a small mixing bowl; let stand at room temperature for 30 minutes. Line baking sheets with parchment paper; set aside.

2) Beat egg whites with almond extract, cream of tartar and salt on medium speed until soft peaks form. Gradually add sugar, 1 tablespoon at a time, beating on high until stiff peaks form and sugar is dissolved.

3) Drop meringue mixture by teaspoonfuls onto prepared sheets. With a small spoon, make a small indentation in the center of each. Bake at 250° for 30-35 minutes or until dry to the touch. Remove to wire racks to cool completely.

4) For topping, combine chocolate chips and butter in a small saucepan. Cook and stir over medium-low heat until chips are melted and mixture is smooth. Combine egg yolks and confectioners' sugar. Reduce heat to low.

5) Gradually whisk into chocolate mixture. Cook and stir for 1 minute longer or until mixture reaches 160°. Cool to room temperature, whisking several times. Spoon into center of meringue. Sprinkle with pistachio.

Yield: 4-1/2 dozen.

NUTRITION FACTS: 2 cookies equals 56 calories, 3 g fat (2 g saturated fat), 35 mg cholesterol, 32 mg sodium, 6 g carbohydrate, trace fiber, 1 g protein.

Surprise Meringues

PREP: 15 min. **BAKE:** 40 min. + cooling

Gloria Grant, Sterling, Illinois

These crisp, delicate cookies are light as a feather. Mini chocolate chips and chopped nuts are a delightful and yummy surprise in every bite.

- 3 egg whites
- 1 teaspoon vanilla extract
- 1/8 teaspoon cream of tartar
- 1/8 teaspoon salt
- 3/4 cup sugar
- 1 cup (6 ounces) miniature semisweet chocolate chips
- 1/4 cup chopped pecans *or* walnuts

1) Place egg whites in a large mixing bowl; let stand for 30 minutes. Beat egg whites with vanilla, cream of tartar and salt on medium speed until soft peaks form. Gradually add sugar, 1 tablespoon at a time, beating on high until stiff glossy peaks form and sugar is dissolved, about 6 minutes.

2) Fold in the chocolate chips and nuts. Drop by rounded teaspoonfuls 2 in. apart onto parchment paper-lined baking sheets.

3) Bake at 250° for 40-45 minutes or until firm to the touch. Turn oven off; leave meringues in oven for 1-1/2 hours. Remove to wire racks to cool. Store in an airtight container.

Yield: 4 dozen.

NUTRITION FACTS: 2 cookies equals 70 calories, 3 g fat (1 g saturated fat), 0 cholesterol, 20 mg sodium, 11 g carbohydrate, 1 g fiber, 1 g protein.

SURPRISE MERINGUES

- **Peppermint Meringues:** Omit the vanilla extract, chocolate chips and nuts. Finely crush 2 peppermint candy canes. Drop meringue by teaspoonfuls onto parchment paper-lined baking sheets. Sprinkle with crushed candy canes. Bake as directed.

- **Meringue Kisses:** Omit the chocolate chips and nuts. Drop meringue by tablespoonfuls onto parchment paper-lined baking sheets. Press a chocolate kiss into the center of each cookie and cover it with meringue using a knife. Bake at 275° for 30-35 minutes or until firm to the touch. Immediately remove to a wire rack to cool.

SOFT SUGAR COOKIES

Double Orange Cookies

PREP: 20 min. **BAKE:** 10 min./batch + cooling

Pamela Kinney, Traverse City, Michigan

Orange juice concentrate and orange peel make these citrusy treats truly delightful.

- 1 cup butter, softened
- 1-1/2 cups sugar
- 1 cup (8 ounces) sour cream
- 2 eggs
- 1 can (6 ounces) orange juice concentrate, thawed, *divided*
- 4 cups all-purpose flour
- 1 teaspoon baking powder
- 1 teaspoon baking soda
- 1/2 teaspoon salt
- 2 tablespoons grated orange peel

FROSTING:
- 1 package (3 ounces) cream cheese, softened
- 1 tablespoon butter, softened
- 2 cups confectioners' sugar
- 1 tablespoon grated orange peel
- 1 tablespoon reserved orange juice concentrate
- 2 tablespoons milk

1) In a large mixing bowl, cream butter and sugar until light and fluffy. Add sour cream and eggs. Beat until well blended. Reserve 1 tablespoon orange juice concentrate for frosting.

2) Add the remaining concentrate with combined dry ingredients to the creamed mixture; mix well. Stir in the orange peel. Drop by rounded tablespoonfuls onto lightly greased baking sheets.

3) Bake at 350° for about 10 minutes or until edges just begin to brown. Remove to wire racks to cool.

4) In a bowl, combine frosting ingredients. Spread over cooled cookies. Store in the refrigerator.

Yield: about 7 dozen.

NUTRITION FACTS: 2 cookies equals 163 calories, 7 g fat (4 g saturated fat), 29 mg cholesterol, 127 mg sodium, 24 g carbohydrate, trace fiber, 2 g protein.

Soft Sugar Cookies

PREP: 30 min. **BAKE:** 10 min./batch + cooling

Coleen Walter, Bancroft, Michigan

These soft cookies have been a hit in my family for four generations. I often stir up a big batch, and I sometimes add food coloring to the frosting to coordinate with the current holiday.

- 1 cup butter, softened
- 3/4 cup sugar
- 2 eggs
- 1 teaspoon vanilla extract
- 1/2 teaspoon almond extract
- 2 cups all-purpose flour
- 1 teaspoon cream of tartar
- 1/2 teaspoon baking soda
- 1/4 teaspoon salt
- 1/4 teaspoon ground nutmeg

FROSTING:
- 1/4 cup butter, softened
- 3 cups confectioners' sugar
- 1 teaspoon almond extract
- 2 to 4 tablespoons hot water

Food coloring, optional

1) In a large mixing bowl, cream butter and sugar until light and fluffy. Beat in the eggs, vanilla and almond extract.

2) Combine the flour, cream of tartar, baking soda, salt and nutmeg; gradually add to creamed mixture. Drop by rounded teaspoonfuls 2 in. apart onto ungreased baking sheets.

3) Bake at 350° for 8-10 minutes or until light brown. Remove to wire racks to cool.

4) For frosting, in a large mixing bowl, combine the butter, confectioners' sugar, almond extract and enough water to achieve desired consistency. Tint with food coloring if desired. Frost the cookies.

Yield: about 6 dozen.

NUTRITION FACTS: 2 cookies equals 142 calories, 7 g fat (4 g saturated fat), 29 mg cholesterol, 102 mg sodium, 20 g carbohydrate, trace fiber, 1 g protein.

FAMILY-FAVORITE CHOCOLATE CHIP COOKIES

 CLASSIC: Eaten while the chips are warm and melty, Dad's Chocolate Chip Cookies are sure to become a tradition at your house. Don't miss the cranberry chip and white chocolate chip variations that follow the recipe.

 TIME-SAVER: Chocolate Chip Blondies let you enjoy the ooey-gooey goodness of chocolate chip cookies without the work. There's no scooping dough—simply spread into a pan and bake. All that's left to do is cut them into bars and enjoy!

 LIGHT: Reduced-fat margarine and fat-free yogurt help trim calories and fat from lightened-up Chocolate Chip Cookies. They get plenty of flavor from mini chocolate chips and toasted walnuts, so they don't taste lighter.

 SERVES 2: When you're not interested in baking or eating several pans of cookies, turn to this recipe for Jumbo Chocolate Chip Cookies. It makes only one dozen of these larger cookies that feature three kinds of chocolate.

Dad's Chocolate Chip Cookies

PREP: 15 min. BAKE: 10 min./batch + cooling

Art Winter, Trumbull, Connecticut

- 1/3 cup butter, softened
- 2/3 cup shortening
- 1 cup sugar
- 1 cup packed brown sugar
- 2 eggs
- 2 teaspoons vanilla extract
- 3-1/2 cups all-purpose flour
- 1 teaspoon salt
- 1 teaspoon baking soda
- 2 cups (12 ounces) semisweet chocolate chips
- 1 cup chopped walnuts

1) In a large mixing bowl, cream butter, shortening and sugars until light and fluffy. Add eggs, one at a time, beating well after each addition. Beat in the vanilla.

2) Combine the flour, salt and baking soda; add to creamed mixture. Stir in chocolate chips and walnuts. Drop by rounded tablespoonfuls onto ungreased baking sheets.

3) Bake at 350° for 10-11 minutes or until golden brown. Remove to wire racks to cool.

Yield: about 6-1/2 dozen.

NUTRITION FACTS: 1 cookie equals 204 calories, 11 g fat (4 g saturated fat), 19 mg cholesterol, 131 mg sodium, 25 g carbohydrate, 1 g fiber, 3 g protein.

■ **Cranberry Chip Cookies:** Reduce semisweet chocolate chips to 1 cup. Along with the chips and walnuts, stir in 1 cup vanilla *or* white chips and 1/2 cup dried cranberries. Bake as directed.

■ **White Chocolate Chip Cookies:** Omit the semisweet chocolate chips and walnuts. Stir 2 cups vanilla *or* white chips and 1 cup toasted chopped hazelnuts into dough. Bake as directed.

Chocolate Chip Blondies

PREP: 10 min. BAKE: 20 min. + cooling

Rhonda Knight, Laguena Niguel, California

- 1-1/2 cups packed brown sugar
- 1/2 cup butter, melted
- 2 eggs, lightly beaten
- 1 teaspoon vanilla extract
- 1-1/2 cups all-purpose flour
- 1/2 teaspoon baking powder

CHOCOLATE CHIP BLONDIES

1/2 teaspoon salt
1 cup (6 ounces) semisweet
  chocolate chips

1) In a large bowl, combine the brown sugar, butter, eggs and vanilla just until blended. Combine the flour, baking powder and salt; add to brown sugar mixture. Stir in chocolate chips.

2) Spread into a greased 13-in. x 9-in. x 2-in. baking pan. Bake at 350° for 18-20 minutes or until a toothpick inserted near the center comes out clean. Cool on a wire rack. Cut into bars.

Yield: 3 dozen.

NUTRITION FACTS: 1 bar equals 102 calories, 4 g fat (2 g saturated fat), 19 mg cholesterol, 72 mg sodium, 16 g carbohydrate, trace fiber, 1 g protein.

Chocolate Chip Cookies
PREP: 15 min. **BAKE:** 10 min./batch + cooling

Bethany Thayer, Troutville, Virginia

1/2 cup reduced-fat margarine
3/4 cup sugar
3/4 cup packed brown sugar
2 eggs
1/4 cup fat-free plain yogurt
2 teaspoons vanilla extract
2-1/2 cups all-purpose flour
1 teaspoon baking soda
1 teaspoon salt
1-1/2 cups miniature semisweet
  chocolate chips
1/2 cup chopped walnuts, toasted

1) In a large mixing bowl, lightly cream the margarine and sugars. Add eggs, one at a time, beating well after each addition. Beat in yogurt and vanilla.

2) Combine the flour, baking soda and salt; gradually add to creamed mixture. Stir in chocolate chips and walnuts. Drop by heaping tablespoonfuls 2 in. apart onto baking sheets coated with cooking spray.

3) Bake at 375° for 8-10 minutes or until golden brown. Remove to wire racks to cool.

Yield: 4 dozen.

NUTRITION FACTS: 1 cookie equals 95 calories, 4 g fat (1 g saturated fat), 9 mg cholesterol, 94 mg sodium, 15 g carbohydrate, 1 g fiber, 2 g protein.

FREEZING COOKIE DOUGH ■■■

If you make several kinds of cookies during the holidays for a cookie tray at a party or to give as gifts, here's a tip that is sure to simplify your baking. I spend a couple weekends before the holiday rush (sometimes as early as October) mixing up all the cookie dough. Then I freeze it in large freezer bags. When I'm ready to bake, I just put the dough in the refrigerator the night before to defrost.

—Cindi P., Anchorage, Alaska

JUMBO CHOCOLATE CHIP COOKIES

Jumbo Chocolate Chip Cookies
PREP: 20 min. **BAKE:** 15 min. + cooling

Jackie Ruckwardt, Cottage Grove, Oregon

1/2 cup butter, softened
1/2 cup sugar
1/2 cup packed brown sugar
1 egg
1 teaspoon vanilla extract
1-1/4 cups all-purpose flour
1/2 teaspoon baking soda
1/2 teaspoon baking powder
1/2 teaspoon salt
1-1/3 cups flaked coconut
1/2 cup semisweet chocolate chips
1/4 cup milk chocolate chips
2-1/2 ounces white candy coating,
  melted, optional

1) In a large mixing bowl, cream butter and sugars. Beat in egg and vanilla. Combine the flour, baking soda, baking powder and salt; gradually add to creamed mixture. Stir in the coconut and chips.

2) Shape dough by 3 tablespoonfuls into balls. Place 3 in. apart on ungreased baking sheets.

3) Bake at 350° for 12-18 minutes or until lightly browned. Remove to wire racks to cool.

4) If desired, dip one end of cooled cookies in melted candy coating. Allow excess to drip off. Place on waxed paper; let stand until set.

Yield: 1 dozen.

NUTRITION FACTS: 1 cookie equals 292 calories, 15 g fat (10 g saturated fat), 38 mg cholesterol, 261 mg sodium, 39 g carbohydrate, 1 g fiber, 3 g protein.

Chewy Apple Oatmeal Cookies

PREP: 20 min. **BAKE:** 10 min./batch + cooling

Jan Marshall, Fenton, Missouri

My family loves oatmeal raisin cookies, but I wanted to try something new with the classic recipe. We enjoy apples, and I thought the dried fruit would make a good cookie.

    1 cup butter, softened
    1 cup packed brown sugar
  1/2 cup sugar
    2 eggs
    1 teaspoon vanilla extract
1-1/2 cups all-purpose flour
    2 teaspoons ground cinnamon
    1 teaspoon baking soda
  1/4 teaspoon salt
    3 cups old-fashioned oats
  1/2 cup chopped dried apples

1) In a large mixing bowl, cream butter and sugars. Beat in eggs and vanilla.

2) Combine the flour, cinnamon, baking soda and salt; gradually add to creamed mixture and mix well. Stir in oats and apples. Drop by rounded tablespoonfuls 2 in. apart onto ungreased baking sheets.

3) Bake at 350° for 10-12 minutes or until golden brown. Let stand for 1 minute before removing to wire racks to cool.

Yield: 4 dozen.

NUTRITION FACTS: 1 cookie equals 97 calories, 4 g fat (3 g saturated fat), 19 mg cholesterol, 71 mg sodium, 14 g carbohydrate, 1 g fiber, 1 g protein.

CHEWY APPLE OATMEAL COOKIES

- **Maple 'n' Raisin Oat Cookies:** Omit vanilla and apples. Add 1-1/2 teaspoons maple flavoring to the creamed mixture; stir in 1-1/2 cups raisins with the oats. Proceed as directed.
  Yield: 4-1/2 dozen.

- **Chunky Oatmeal Cookies:** Omit the apples. Stir in 1 cup chocolate-covered raisins and 1 cup Reese's pieces or M&M's (plain or peanut butter) with the oats. Bake at 350° for 9-11 minutes.
  Yield: 5 dozen.

Honey Crunch Cookies

PREP: 20 min. **BAKE:** 10 min./batch + cooling

Germaine Stank, Pound, Wisconsin

Honey, coconut and crisp rice cereal add texture and flavor to these crunchy treats. It makes about 5 dozen, so it's a good recipe for a bake sale.

    2 cups all-purpose flour
    2 teaspoons baking powder
  1/2 teaspoon salt
    1 cup butter, softened
    1 cup honey
    2 eggs
    1 cup flaked coconut
    1 cup butterscotch chips
    4 cups crisp rice cereal

1) Sift together the flour, baking powder and salt; set aside. In a large mixing bowl, cream butter until light and fluffy. Add honey, a little at a time, beating well after each addition.

2) Add eggs, one at a time, beating well after each addition. (Mixture will appear to separate.) Gradually add dry ingredients; mix until moistened. Fold in the coconut, chips and cereal. Drop by teaspoonfuls 2 in. apart onto greased baking sheets.

3) Bake at 350° for 12-14 minutes or until golden brown. Remove to wire racks to cool.

Yield: about 5 dozen.

NUTRITION FACTS: 2 cookies equals 196 calories, 10 g fat (7 g saturated fat), 31 mg cholesterol, 181 mg sodium, 25 g carbohydrate, trace fiber, 2 g protein.

Coconut Macaroons

PREP: 10 min. **BAKE:** 20 min. + cooling

Penny Ann Gilliman, Shawano, Wisconsin

These cookies are my husband's favorites. I like that it makes a small enough batch for the two of us to nibble on.

1-1/3 cups flaked coconut
  1/3 cup sugar
    2 tablespoons all-purpose flour
  1/8 teaspoon salt
    2 egg whites
  1/2 teaspoon vanilla extract

COCONUT MACAROONS

1) In a small bowl, combine the coconut, sugar, flour and salt. Stir in egg whites and vanilla; mix well. Drop by rounded teaspoonfuls onto greased baking sheets.

2) Bake at 325° for 18-20 minutes or until golden brown. Remove to wire racks to cool.

Yield: about 1-1/2 dozen.

NUTRITION FACTS: 2 cookies equals 108 calories, 5 g fat (4 g saturated fat), 0 cholesterol, 81 mg sodium, 15 g carbohydrate, 1 g fiber, 1 g protein.

Toffee Cashew Treasures
PREP: 10 min. **BAKE:** 15 min./batch + cooling
Denise Sokolowski, Milwaukee, Wisconsin
After searching for a recipe that combined all my favorites, I decided to create my own cookie. The result is a lacy, crisp cookie that's sure to earn you rave reviews.

 1 cup butter, softened
 1 cup sugar
 1 cup packed brown sugar
 2 eggs
 1 teaspoon vanilla extract
 2 cups all-purpose flour
 2 cups old-fashioned oats
 1 teaspoon baking soda
1/2 teaspoon baking powder
1/2 teaspoon salt
 1 cup flaked coconut
 1 cup English toffee bits *or* almond brickle chips
 1 cup chopped cashews, toasted

1) In a large mixing bowl, cream butter and sugars until light and fluffy. Add the eggs, one at a time, beating well after each addition. Beat in vanilla.

2) Combine the flour, oats, baking soda, baking powder and salt; gradually add to the creamed mixture. Stir in the remaining ingredients. Drop by rounded tablespoonfuls 3 in. apart onto ungreased baking sheets.

3) Bake at 350° for 12-14 minutes or until lightly browned. Cool for 2 minutes before removing to wire racks.

Yield: about 5 dozen.

NUTRITION FACTS: 2 cookies equals 247 calories, 13 g fat (6 g saturated fat), 33 mg cholesterol, 240 mg sodium, 32 g carbohydrate, 1 g fiber, 3 g protein.

Shaped Cookies

Refrigerate the dough until it is chilled for easier handling. If the dough has a high butter content, the heat from your hands can soften the butter in the dough, making it harder to shape. Dust hands lightly with flour to prevent dough from sticking while shaping it.

Pecan Fingers
PREP: 15 min. **BAKE:** 15 min./batch + cooling
Irene Risbry, Colorado Springs, Colorado
You can't go wrong with the combination of butter and pecans in these cookies. I never serve them without receiving requests for the recipe.

 1 cup butter, softened
1/2 cup confectioners' sugar
 2 cups all-purpose flour
1/2 teaspoon salt
 1 cup finely chopped pecans
Additional confectioners' sugar

1) In a large mixing bowl, cream butter and confectioners' sugar until light and fluffy. Combine flour and salt; gradually add to creamed mixture. Stir in pecans.

2) Shape tablespoonfuls of dough into 2-in. fingers. Place 2 in. apart on ungreased baking sheets.

3) Bake at 350° for 15-18 minutes or until lightly browned. Roll warm cookies in confectioners' sugar; cool on wire racks.

Yield: about 4 dozen.

NUTRITION FACTS: 2 cookies equals 149 calories, 11 g fat (5 g saturated fat), 20 mg cholesterol, 126 mg sodium, 11 g carbohydrate, 1 g fiber, 2 g protein.

■ **Cinnamon-Sugar Pecan Fingers:** Reduce pecans to 1/2 cup. Omit additional confectioners' sugar. Combine 3 tablespoons sugar and 1-1/2 teaspoons ground cinnamon. Roll warm cookies in cinnamon-sugar mixture.

■ **Mexican Wedding Cakes:** Omit salt. Add 1/2 teaspoon vanilla extract to creamed mixture. Shape tablespoons of dough into balls. Place 2 in. apart on greased baking sheets. Bake at 350° for 12-15 minutes until lightly browned. Let stand for 2 minutes. Gently roll warm cookies in confectioners' sugar; cool on wire racks.

Lemony Bonbon Cookies

PREP: 15 min. + chilling
BAKE: 15 min./batch + cooling

Linda Nicholson, Palatka, Florida

This recipe is from my great grandmother's collection. When people try one, they ask for the recipe. I always make it for the holidays and any other special event. The pecan on the bottom is a crunchy twist.

- 1/2 cup butter, softened
- 1/3 cup confectioners' sugar
- 1 tablespoon lemon juice
- 3/4 cup all-purpose flour
- 1/3 cup cornstarch
- 24 pecan halves

ICING:

- 1-1/4 cups confectioners' sugar
- 1-1/2 teaspoons butter, softened
- 3 to 4 teaspoons lemon juice

1) In a small mixing bowl, cream butter and confectioners' sugar until light and fluffy. Beat in lemon juice. Combine flour and cornstarch; gradually add to creamed mixture and mix well. Cover and refrigerate for 2 hours.

2) Shape dough into 1-in. balls. Place pecan halves on two ungreased baking sheets. Top each pecan half with a ball of dough; flatten with the bottom of a small glass. Bake at 350° for 14-16 minutes or until cookies are set. Remove to wire racks to cool completely.

3) For icing, combine the confectioners' sugar, butter and enough lemon juice to achieve a spreading consistency. Spread over cooled cookies. Let stand until set.

Yield: 2 dozen.

NUTRITION FACTS: 1 cookie equals 97 calories, 5 g fat (3 g saturated fat), 11 mg cholesterol, 29 mg sodium, 13 g carbohydrate, trace fiber, 1 g protein.

Chocolate Hazelnut Thumbprints

PREP: 20 min. **BAKE:** 10 min./batch + cooling

Ethel Garrison, Puyallup, Washington

Since we live in hazelnut country, I love making these special cookies for festive occasions.

- 2/3 cup butter, softened
- 1/2 cup sugar
- 1 egg
- 1 egg yolk
- 1/2 teaspoon vanilla extract
- 1-1/2 cups all-purpose flour
- 1/4 cup baking cocoa
- 1/2 teaspoon salt
- 2/3 cup ground hazelnuts
- 1/2 cup raspberry preserves

Confectioners' sugar

1) In a large mixing bowl, cream butter and sugar until light and fluffy. Add the egg, yolk and vanilla; mix well. Combine the flour, cocoa and salt; add a third at a time to creamed mixture, beating well after each addition. Stir in nuts.

2) Roll dough into 1-in. balls; place 2 in. apart on ungreased baking sheets. Using the end of a wooden spoon handle, make a 1/2-in.-deep indentation in the center of each ball; fill with 1/4 teaspoon of preserves.

3) Bake at 350° for 10-12 minutes or until set. Remove to wire racks to cool completely. Just before serving, lightly dust with confectioners' sugar.

Yield: about 6 dozen.

NUTRITION FACTS: 2 cookies (calculated without confectioners' sugar) equals 84 calories, 5 g fat (2 g saturated fat), 21 mg cholesterol, 68 mg sodium, 10 g carbohydrate, trace fiber, 1 g protein.

Removing Skins from Hazelnuts

To easily remove skins from shelled hazelnuts, spread the nuts in a single layer in a baking pan. Bake at 350° for 10 to 15 minutes or until the skins begin to flake. Transfer nuts to a clean kitchen towel; rub against the towel to remove the skins. Toasting the nuts also enriches their flavor.

Split-Second Cookies

PREP: 20 min. **BAKE:** 15 min. + cooling

Mrs. Richard Foust, Stoneboro, Pennsylvania

These easy-to-bake cookies feature raspberry jam and are a nice addition to a cookie tray.

- 3/4 cup butter, softened
- 2/3 cup sugar
- 1 egg

SPLIT-SECOND COOKIES

1 teaspoon vanilla extract
2 cups all-purpose flour
1/2 teaspoon baking powder
1/2 teaspoon salt
1/3 cup raspberry jam

1) In a large mixing bowl, cream butter and sugar until light and fluffy. Beat in egg and vanilla. Combine the flour, baking powder and salt; gradually add to creamed mixture and mix well.

2) Divide dough into four equal portions; shape each into a 12-in. x 3/4-in. log. Place 4 in. apart on two greased baking sheets. Make a 1/2-in. depression down center of logs; fill with jam.

3) Bake at 350° for 15-20 minutes or until lightly browned. Cool 2 minutes; cut diagonally into 3/4-in. slices. Remove to wire racks to cool completely.

Yield: about 5 dozen.

NUTRITION FACTS: 2 cookies equals 99 calories, 5 g fat (3 g saturated fat), 19 mg cholesterol, 95 mg sodium, 13 g carbohydrate, trace fiber, 1 g protein.

Cherry Bonbon Cookies

PREP: 15 min. **BAKE:** 20 min. + cooling

Pat Habiger, Spearville, Kansas

This is a very old recipe from my grandma. The sweet cherry filling makes a delightful surprise.

1/2 cup butter, softened
3/4 cup confectioners' sugar
2 tablespoons milk
1 teaspoon vanilla extract
1-1/2 cups all-purpose flour
1/8 teaspoon salt
24 maraschino cherries

GLAZE:
1 cup confectioners' sugar
1 tablespoon butter, melted
2 tablespoons maraschino cherry juice

Additional confectioners' sugar

1) In a mixing bowl cream butter and sugar until light and fluffy. Add milk and vanilla. Combine flour and salt; gradually add to creamed mixture. Divide dough into 24 portions; shape each portion around a cherry, forming a ball. Place on ungreased baking sheets. Bake at 350° for 18-20 minutes or until lightly browned. Remove to wire racks to cool completely.

2) For glaze, combine sugar, butter and cherry juice. Drizzle over cookies. Dust with additional sugar.

Yield: 2 dozen.

NUTRITION FACTS: 2 cookies (calculated without additional sugar) equals 225 calories, 9 g fat (5 g saturated fat), 23 mg cholesterol, 113 mg sodium, 36 g carbohydrate, trace fiber, 2 g protein.

CRACKLE COOKIES

Crackle Cookies

PREP: 15 min. + chilling
BAKE: 10 min./batch + cooling

Ruth Cain, Hartselle, Alabama

My family loves these old-fashioned favorites. Kids can roll them in sugar and place on baking sheets.

1 cup sugar
2 eggs
1/4 cup vegetable oil
2 squares (1 ounce *each*) unsweetened chocolate, melted and cooled
1 teaspoon vanilla extract
1 cup all-purpose flour
1 teaspoon baking powder
1/4 teaspoon salt

Confectioners' sugar

1) In a large mixing bowl, combine the sugar, eggs, oil, chocolate and vanilla. Combine the flour, baking powder and salt; gradually add to sugar mixture and mix well. Cover and refrigerate dough for at least 2 hours.

2) With sugared hands, shape dough into 1-in. balls. Roll in confectioners' sugar. Place 2 in. apart on greased baking sheets. Bake at 350° for 10-12 minutes or until set. Remove to wire racks to cool.

Yield: about 3 dozen.

NUTRITION FACTS: 2 cookies (calculated without confectioners' sugar) equals 127 calories, 5 g fat (2 g saturated fat), 24 mg cholesterol, 63 mg sodium, 19 g carbohydrate, 1 g fiber, 2 g protein.

SHAPING COOKIES ■■■

When making cookies, I use a fork to flatten the dough. I spray it with cooking spray to keep if from sticking to the dough. This works nicely and creates a pretty crisscross pattern.

—Alta R., Pottstown, Pennsylvania

DIPPED GINGERSNAPS

Cardamom Almond Biscotti

PREP: 20 min. **BAKE:** 40 min. + cooling

Verna Eberhart, Watertown, South Dakota

These crunchy slices are requested often during the holidays, particularly by my husband. He likes to dunk them in his coffee.

    1 cup butter, softened
1-3/4 cups sugar
    2 eggs
    2 teaspoons almond extract
5-1/4 cups all-purpose flour
    1 teaspoon baking soda
    1 teaspoon salt
    1 teaspoon ground cardamom
    1 cup (8 ounces) sour cream
    1 cup chopped almonds

1) In a large mixing bowl, cream butter and sugar until light and fluffy. Add eggs, one at a time, beating well after each addition. Beat in extract.

2) Combine flour, baking soda, salt and cardamom; add to the creamed mixture alternately with sour cream. Fold in almonds. Divide dough into fourths; shape each portion into a ball. On two greased baking sheets, roll each ball into a 15-in. log (two logs per pan).

3) Bake at 350° for 30 minutes or until lightly browned and firm to the touch. Transfer to a cutting board; cut at a 45° angle with a sharp knife into 1/2-in. slices. Place cut side down on greased baking sheets.

4) Bake for 5-6 minutes on each side or until lightly browned. Remove to wire racks to cool. Store in airtight containers.

Yield: about 7 dozen.

NUTRITION FACTS: 2 cookies equals 161 calories, 7 g fat (4 g saturated fat), 26 mg cholesterol, 137 mg sodium, 21 g carbohydrate, 1 g fiber, 3 g protein.

Dipped Gingersnaps

PREP: 20 min.
BAKE: 10 min./batch + cooling

Laura Kimball, West Jordan, Utah

Traditional gingersnaps are one of my favorites. These chewy cookies are not only festive looking, but they taste great, too.

    2 cups sugar
1-1/2 cups vegetable oil
    2 eggs
  1/2 cup molasses
    4 cups all-purpose flour
    4 teaspoons baking soda
    1 tablespoon ground ginger
    2 teaspoons ground cinnamon
    1 teaspoon salt
Additional sugar
    2 packages (10 to 12 ounces *each*)
      vanilla *or* white chips
  1/4 cup shortening

1) In a large mixing bowl, combine sugar and oil. Beat in eggs. Stir in molasses. Combine the flour, baking soda, ginger, cinnamon and salt; gradually add to creamed mixture and mix well.

2) Shape into 3/4-in. balls and roll in sugar. Place 2 in. apart on ungreased baking sheets. Bake at 350° for 10-12 minutes or until cookie springs back when lightly touched. Remove to wire racks to cool.

3) In a small saucepan, melt chips with shortening over low heat, stirring until smooth. Dip the cookies halfway into the melted chips; shake off excess. Place on waxed paper-lined baking sheets until set.

Yield: about 14-1/2 dozen.

NUTRITION FACTS: 2 cookies equals 128 calories, 7 g fat (2 g saturated fat), 6 mg cholesterol, 93 mg sodium, 17 g carbohydrate, trace fiber, 1 g protein.

Dipping Cookies in Chocolate

Melt the chocolate chips, baking chocolate or candy coating according to recipe directions. If necessary, transfer the chocolate to a narrow container.

Dip cookie partway into chocolate and scrape bottom of the cookie across the edge of the container to remove excess chocolate. Place on a baking sheet lined with waxed paper and allow to set at room temperature.

Toward the end of the process, when the chocolate is running low, it might be necessary to spoon the chocolate over the cookies. If chocolate cools too much to coat the cookies properly, rewarm before finishing dipping.

CRANBERRY ALMOND BISCOTTI

Cranberry Almond Biscotti

PREP: 20 min. + cooling
BAKE: 40 min. + cooling

Evelyn Bethards Wohlers, Columbia, Maryland

A fellow stay-at-home mom gave me this recipe so we could enjoy our latte breaks more affordably with homemade biscotti. I modified the original version by using a sugar substitute and reducing the fat. Tangy dried cranberries and spices are great additions.

> 2 eggs
> 3 egg whites
> 2 tablespoons molasses
> 3/4 teaspoon almond extract
Sugar substitute equivalent to 1 cup sugar
> 2-1/4 cups all-purpose flour
> 1 teaspoon baking powder
> 1 teaspoon ground cinnamon
> 1/2 teaspoon baking soda
> 1/2 teaspoon ground nutmeg
> 3/4 cup slivered almonds
> 1/2 cup dried cranberries
> 1/2 cup chopped white candy coating

1) In a large mixing bowl, beat the eggs, egg whites, molasses and extract. Beat in sugar substitute. Combine the flour, baking powder, cinnamon, baking soda and nutmeg; gradually add to egg mixture (dough will be sticky).

2) Turn onto a floured surface. Knead in almonds and cranberries. Divide dough in half; shape each portion into a 12-in. x 3-in. rectangle. Transfer to a baking sheet coated with cooking spray.

3) Bake at 325° for 15-20 minutes or until lightly browned. Cool for 5 minutes. Transfer to a cutting board; with a serrated knife, cut each loaf into 16 slices. Place slices cut side down on baking sheets coated with cooking spray. Bake for 12-17 minutes on each side or until firm. Remove to wire racks to cool.

4) In a microwave or heavy saucepan, melt candy coating; stir until smooth. Drizzle over biscotti. Store in an airtight container.

Yield: 32 cookies.

Editor's Note: This recipe was tested with Splenda No Calorie Sweetener.

NUTRITION FACTS: 1 cookie equals 84 calories, 3 g fat (1 g saturated fat), 14 mg cholesterol, 39 mg sodium, 13 g carbohydrate, 1 g fiber, 2 g protein.

Swedish Spritz Cookies

PREP: 15 min. **BAKE:** 10 min./batch + cooling

Susan Bittner, Alberta, British Columbia

A touch of almond extract gives these spritz wonderful flavor. For Christmas, you could tint the dough with red or green food coloring.

> 1 cup butter, softened
> 2/3 cup sugar
> 1 egg
> 1/2 teaspoon almond extract
> 1/2 teaspoon vanilla extract
> 2-1/4 cups all-purpose flour
> 1 teaspoon baking powder

1) In a large mixing bowl, cream butter and sugar until light and fluffy. Beat in egg and extracts. Combine the flour and baking powder; gradually add to the creamed mixture.

2) Using a cookie press fitted with a disk of your choice, press dough into desired shapes 1 in. apart onto ungreased baking sheets. Bake at 375° for 10-11 minutes or until edges are firm and lightly browned. Remove to wire racks to cool.

Yield: 5 dozen.

NUTRITION FACTS: 2 cookies equals 108 calories, 6 g fat (4 g saturated fat), 23 mg cholesterol, 77 mg sodium, 12 g carbohydrate, trace fiber, 1 g protein.

Spiced Spritz Cookies: Omit almond extract and increase vanilla extract to 1 teaspoon. To the flour and baking powder mixture, add 1 teaspoon pumpkin pie spice. Proceed as recipe directs.

Shortcut Christmas Treats

Even if you don't have time to bake, you and your family can still enjoy special Christmas cookies. It just takes a trip to the grocery store and a little creativity! Here are tricks for making purchased cookies your own works of art.

Melt some vanilla or white baking chips. Dip gingersnaps halfway into melted chips…or drizzle the melted chips over the cookies.

Tint your favorite vanilla frosting with food coloring. Use it to pipe holiday designs on sugar cookies.

Purchase chocolate-covered mint cookies, drizzle with contrasting melted white chocolate. Decorate with colored sugar or sprinkles.

KID-PLEASING PEANUT BUTTER COOKIES

 CLASSIC: No matter what your age, you'll have a hard time resisting Peanut Butter Sandwich Cookies. A sweet and creamy filling is tucked between homemade cookies for a doubly delicious peanut taste.

 TIME-SAVER: It's easy to stir up Peanut Butter Kiss Cookies because the recipe calls for only a handful of items. To hurry along baking, put both cookie sheets in the oven at the same time and switch their positions halfway through baking. In minutes, you'll have two dozen chocolate-kissed treats.

 LIGHT: You wouldn't expect chocolate chips and toffee bits in lighter cookies. But Oaty Peanut Butter Cookies have about a third less cholesterol and less than half the calories, carbohydrates and fat of classic Peanut Butter Sandwich Cookies. That's because the recipe calls for reduced-fat margarine, reduced-fat peanut butter, egg whites and old-fashioned oats.

 SERVES 2: Biscuit/baking mix, chocolate chips and three other ingredients make it a snap to whip up a small batch of Chocolate Peanut Butter Bites. It yields 14 cookies, so the two of you can snack on a few today and look forward to a few tomorrow.

PEANUT BUTTER SANDWICH COOKIES

Peanut Butter Sandwich Cookies

PREP: 20 min. BAKE: 10 min./batch + cooling

Debbie Kokes, Tabor, South Dakota

- 1 cup butter-flavored shortening
- 1 cup creamy peanut butter
- 1 cup sugar
- 1 cup packed brown sugar
- 3 eggs
- 1 teaspoon vanilla extract
- 3 cups all-purpose flour
- 2 teaspoons baking soda
- 1/4 teaspoon salt

FILLING:
- 1/2 cup creamy peanut butter
- 3 cups confectioners' sugar
- 1 teaspoon vanilla extract
- 5 to 6 tablespoons milk

1) In a large mixing bowl, cream the shortening, peanut butter and sugars. Add eggs, one at a time, beating well after each addition. Add vanilla. Combine the flour, baking soda and salt; add to creamed mixture and mix well.

2) Shape into 1-in. balls and place 2 in. apart on ungreased baking sheets. Flatten to 3/8-in. thickness with a fork. Bake at 375° for 7-8 minutes or until golden. Remove to wire racks to cool completely.

3) For filling, in a large mixing bowl, beat the peanut butter, confectioners' sugar, vanilla and enough milk to achieve spreading consistency. Spread on half of the cookies and top each with another cookie.

Yield: 44 sandwich cookies.

NUTRITION FACTS: 1 sandwich cookie equals 197 calories, 9 g fat (2 g saturated fat), 15 mg cholesterol, 119 mg sodium, 26 g carbohydrate, 1 g fiber, 4 g protein.

Shaping a Peanut Butter Cookie

Peanut butter cookie dough is generally a stiff dough and needs to be flattened before baking. Using a floured fork, press the balls of dough until 3/8 in. thick. Press again across the lines to make a crisscross pattern.

PEANUT BUTTER KISS COOKIES

Peanut Butter Kiss Cookies

PREP: 20 min. **BAKE:** 10 min. + cooling

Dee Davis, Sun City, Arizona

- 1 cup peanut butter
- 1 cup sugar
- 1 egg
- 1 teaspoon vanilla extract
- 24 milk chocolate kisses

1) In a small mixing bowl, cream peanut butter and sugar. Add the egg and vanilla; beat until blended. Roll into 1-1/4-in. balls. Place 2 in. apart on ungreased baking sheets.

2) Bake at 350° for 10-12 minutes or until tops are slightly cracked. Immediately press one chocolate kiss into the center of each cookie. Cool for 5 minutes before removing from pans to wire racks.

Yield: 2 dozen.

NUTRITION FACTS: 1 cookie equals 123 calories, 7 g fat (2 g saturated fat), 10 mg cholesterol, 57 mg sodium, 13 g carbohydrate, 1 g fiber, 3 g protein.

Oaty Peanut Butter Cookies

PREP: 15 min. **BAKE:** 10 min./batch + cooling

Sherry Craw, Mattoon, Illinois

- 1-1/2 cups reduced-fat margarine, softened
- 1/2 cup reduced-fat peanut butter
- 1/3 cup sugar
- 1/3 cup packed brown sugar
- 1 egg
- 2 egg whites
- 2 cups old-fashioned oats
- 1-1/2 cups all-purpose flour
- 1-1/2 teaspoons ground cinnamon
- 3/4 teaspoon baking soda

- 1 cup (6 ounces) semisweet chocolate chips
- 3/4 cup English toffee bits *or* almond brickle chips

1) In a large mixing bowl, cream margarine, peanut butter and sugars until light and fluffy. Beat in egg and egg whites.

2) Combine the oats, flour, cinnamon and baking soda; gradually add to creamed mixture. Stir in chocolate chips and toffee bits.

3) Drop by tablespoonfuls 2 in. apart onto baking sheets coated with cooking spray; flatten slightly. Bake at 350° for 9-11 minutes or until golden brown. Cool for 2 minutes before removing from pans to wire racks.

Yield: 5 dozen.

Editor's Note: This recipe was tested with Parkay Light stick margarine.

NUTRITION FACTS: 1 cookie equals 82 calories, 4 g fat (1 g saturated fat), 9 mg cholesterol, 59 mg sodium, 11 g carbohydrate, 1 g fiber, 2 g protein.

Chocolate Peanut Butter Bites

PREP/TOTAL TIME: 20 min. + cooling

Terri Keeney, Greeley, Colorado

- 2/3 cup sweetened condensed milk
- 1/3 cup creamy peanut butter
- 1/2 teaspoon vanilla extract
- 1 cup biscuit/baking mix
- 1/3 cup semisweet chocolate chips

1) In a small mixing bowl, beat the milk, peanut butter and vanilla until smooth. Add biscuit mix just until blended. Fold in chocolate chips.

2) Drop by rounded tablespoonfuls 2 in. apart onto ungreased baking sheets. Bake at 375° for 10-12 minutes or until edges are lightly browned. Cool for 2 minutes before removing to wire racks.

Yield: 14 cookies.

NUTRITION FACTS: 1 cookie equals 137 calories, 7 g fat (2 g saturated fat), 5 mg cholesterol, 155 mg sodium, 17 g carbohydrate, 1 g fiber, 3 g protein.

CHOCOLATE PEANUT BUTTER BITES

APRICOT TARTS

Apricot Tarts

PREP: 30 min. + chilling **BAKE:** 25 min. + cooling

Phyllis Hickey, Bedford, New Hampshire

These tiny tarts are an extra-special dessert for any occasion. We love the fruity, nutty flavor.

- 1/2 **cup butter, softened**
- 1 **package (3 ounces) cream cheese, softened**
- 1 **cup all-purpose flour**

APRICOT FILLING:

- 3/4 **cup finely chopped dried apricots**
- 3/4 **cup water**
- 1/3 **cup chopped pecans**
- 1/4 **cup sugar**
- 2 **tablespoons orange marmalade**
- 1/2 **teaspoon ground cinnamon**
- 1/8 **teaspoon ground cloves**

TOPPING:

- 2 **tablespoons cream cheese, softened**
- 1 **tablespoon butter, softened**
- 1/2 **teaspoon vanilla extract**
- 1/2 **cup confectioners' sugar**

1) In a large mixing bowl, beat butter, cream cheese and flour until well blended. Cover and refrigerate for 1 hour.

2) For filling, in a saucepan, bring the apricots and water to a boil. Reduce heat; simmer, uncovered, for 5 minutes. Drain and transfer to a bowl. Add the pecans, sugar, marmalade, cinnamon and cloves; set aside.

3) Shape dough into 24 balls. Press onto the bottom and up the sides of greased miniature muffin cups. Spoon apricot mixture into cups. Bake at 350° for 25-30 minutes or until browned. Cool for 10 minutes; remove from pans to a wire rack to cool completely.

4) For topping, in a small mixing bowl, combine cream cheese and butter. Stir in vanilla. Beat in confectioners' sugar. Place a dollop onto each tart just before serving.

Yield: 2 dozen.

NUTRITION FACTS: 1 tart equals 117 calories, 7 g fat (4 g saturated fat), 17 mg cholesterol, 61 mg sodium, 13 g carbohydrate, 1 g fiber, 1 g protein.

■ **Cashew Tassie Cups:** Prepare cream cheese crust as directed, except omit apricot filling and topping. In a mixing bowl, beat 1/2 cup packed brown sugar, 1 egg and 1 teaspoon vanilla extract until combined. Divide 2/3 cup coarsely chopped cashews among the cups, then spoon brown sugar mixture over tops. Bake at 350° for 20-25 minutes or until filling is set and pastry is golden brown. Cool for 1 minute before removing from pans to wire racks.

Refrigerator Cookies

To make refrigerator cookie dough easier to slice, use nuts and fruits that are finely chopped. Wrap dough tightly to prevent it from drying out in the refrigerator. Refrigerate dough until firm. Generally, the dough can be refrigerated up to 1 week or frozen up to 6 months.

To keep a nice round shape for refrigerated cookie dough, place each roll inside a tall glass and place the glass on its side in the refrigerator. The rounded glass will prevent the bottom of the roll from flattening out.

Use a thin sharp knife to slice through the dough. Cut one roll at a time, keeping additional rolls refrigerated until ready to use. After each slice, rotate the roll to avoid having one side that's flat.

Double Butterscotch Cookies

PREP: 20 min. + chilling
BAKE: 10 min./batch + cooling

Beverly Duncan, Lakeville, Ohio

I also like to make these with miniature chocolate chips or coconut in place of the toffee bits.

- 1/2 **cup butter, softened**
- 1/2 **cup shortening**
- 4 **cups packed brown sugar**
- 4 **eggs**
- 1 **tablespoon vanilla extract**
- 6 **cups all-purpose flour**
- 3 **teaspoons baking soda**
- 3 **teaspoons cream of tartar**
- 1 **teaspoon salt**
- 1 **package English toffee bits (10 ounces) *or* almond brickle chips (7-1/2 ounces)**
- 1 **cup finely chopped pecans**

DOUBLE BUTTERSCOTCH COOKIES

3) Unwrap dough; cut into 1/4-in. slices. Place 3 in. apart on ungreased baking sheets. Place a pecan half in the center of each. Bake at 325° for 20-25 minutes or until lightly browned. Cool for 2-3 minutes before removing to wire racks to cool completely.

Yield: 4-1/2 dozen.

NUTRITION FACTS: 1 cookie equals 100 calories, 6 g fat (4 g saturated fat), 13 mg cholesterol, 83 mg sodium, 10 g carbohydrate, 1 g fiber, 1 g protein.

Chocolate Mint Surprises

PREP: 30 min. + chilling
BAKE: 5 min./batch + freezing

Sheila Kerr, Revelstoke, British Columbia

I came up with this recipe a few years ago and have shared it with many people.

- 3/4 cup butter, softened
- 1 cup sugar
- 1 egg
- 1 teaspoon vanilla extract
- 3 squares (1 ounce *each*) unsweetened chocolate, melted and cooled
- 2-1/2 cups all-purpose flour
- 1-1/2 teaspoons baking powder
- 1/2 teaspoon salt

FILLING:

- 4 cups confectioners' sugar
- 3 tablespoons butter, softened
- 1/4 cup evaporated milk
- 2 to 3 teaspoons peppermint extract
- 1/2 teaspoon vanilla extract
- 2 pounds dark chocolate candy coating, melted

1) In a large mixing bowl, cream butter and sugar until light and fluffy. Beat in egg and vanilla. Add melted chocolate. Combine the flour, baking powder and salt; gradually add to chocolate mixture and mix well.

2) Shape in two 10-in. rolls; wrap each in plastic wrap. Refrigerate for 4 hours or until firm.

3) Unwrap dough and cut into 1/4-in. slices. Place 2 in. apart on ungreased baking sheets. Bake at 375° for 5-7 minutes or until edges are firm. Remove to wire racks to cool completely.

4) For filling, in a bowl, combine the confectioners' sugar, butter, milk and extracts until smooth. Shape into 1/2-in. balls. Place a ball in the center of each cookie; flatten.

5) Freeze for 30 minutes. Dip cookies in melted candy coating to completely cover. Place on waxed paper until set.

Yield: about 6 dozen.

NUTRITION FACTS: 1 cookie equals 148 calories, 7 g fat (5 g saturated fat), 10 mg cholesterol, 51 mg sodium, 22 g carbohydrate, 1 g fiber, 1 g protein.

1) In a large mixing bowl, beat the butter, shortening and brown sugar for 2 minutes or until mixture resembles wet sand. Add eggs, one at a time, beating well after each addition. Beat in vanilla. Combine the flour, baking soda, cream of tartar and salt; gradually add to the creamed mixture and mix well. Stir in toffee bits and pecans.

2) Shape into three 14-in. rolls (mixture will be slightly crumbly); wrap each in plastic wrap. Refrigerate for 4 hours or until firm.

3) Unwrap and cut into 1/2-in. slices. Place 2 in. apart on greased baking sheets. Bake at 375° for 9-11 minutes or until lightly browned. Cool for 1-2 minutes before removing from pans to wire racks to cool completely.

Yield: about 7 dozen.

NUTRITION FACTS: 2 cookies equals 248 calories, 9 g fat (3 g saturated fat), 28 mg cholesterol, 221 mg sodium, 39 g carbohydrate, 1 g fiber, 3 g protein.

Coconut Pecan Cookies

PREP: 30 min. + freezing
BAKE: 20 min./batch + cooling

Betty Matthews, South Haven, Michigan

With this recipe, making sweets has never been easier. Freeze the dough in logs, then slice and bake the cookies when you need them.

- 1 cup butter, softened
- 1 cup sugar
- 1 egg
- 2-1/4 cups all-purpose flour
- 1/2 teaspoon baking soda
- 1/2 teaspoon salt
- 3 cups flaked coconut, *divided*

Pecan halves

1) In a large mixing bowl, cream butter and sugar until light and fluffy. Beat in egg. Combine the flour, baking soda and salt; add to creamed mixture and mix well. Stir in 2 cups coconut.

2) Shape into six 2-in.-diameter logs. Roll in remaining coconut. Wrap in plastic wrap. Freeze for up to 3 months.

Caramel Creams

PREP: 20 min. + chilling
BAKE: 15 min./batch + cooling

Barbara Yongers, Kingman, Kansas

These cookies are delicious plain, but I like to make them into sandwich cookies with the brown butter filling.

- 1 cup butter, softened
- 2/3 cup packed brown sugar
- 2 egg yolks
- 1/2 teaspoon vanilla extract
- 2-1/2 cups all-purpose flour
- 1/3 cup finely chopped pecans
- 1/4 teaspoon salt

FILLING:

- 2 tablespoons plus 1-1/2 teaspoons butter, cubed
- 1-1/2 cups confectioners' sugar
- 1/2 teaspoon vanilla extract
- 2 to 3 tablespoons heavy whipping cream

1) In a mixing bowl, cream butter and brown sugar until light and fluffy. Beat in egg yolks and vanilla. Combine flour, pecans and salt; gradually add to the creamed mixture. Shape into two 10-in. rolls; wrap each in plastic wrap. Refrigerate for 1-2 hours.

2) Unwrap and cut into 1/4-in. slices. Place 2 in. apart on ungreased baking sheets. Bake at 350° for 11-13 minutes or until golden brown. Remove to wire racks to cool completely.

3) For filling, heat butter in a saucepan over medium heat until golden brown. Remove from the heat; add confectioners' sugar, vanilla and enough cream to achieve spreading consistency. Spread on the bottom of half of the cookies; top with remaining cookies.

Yield: about 3 dozen sandwich cookies.

NUTRITION FACTS: 2 each equals 264 calories, 15 g fat (8 g saturated fat), 57 mg cholesterol, 157 mg sodium, 32 g carbohydrate, 1 g fiber, 2 g protein.

CARAMEL CREAMS

Raspberry Nut Pinwheels

PREP: 20 min. + chilling
BAKE: 10 min./batch + cooling

Pat Habiger, Spearville, Kansas

I won first prize in a recipe contest with these yummy swirl cookies a number of years ago. The taste of raspberries and walnuts really comes through in each bite, and they're so much fun to make!

- 1/2 cup butter, softened
- 1 cup sugar
- 1 egg
- 1 teaspoon vanilla extract
- 2 cups all-purpose flour
- 1 teaspoon baking powder
- 1/4 cup seedless raspberry jam
- 3/4 cup finely chopped walnuts

1) In a large mixing bowl, cream butter and sugar until light and fluffy. Beat in egg and vanilla. Combine the flour and baking powder; gradually add to creamed mixture and mix well.

2) Roll out dough between waxed paper into a 12-in. square. Remove top pieces of waxed paper. Spread dough with jam and sprinkle with nuts. Roll up tightly jelly-roll style, starting with a long side; wrap in plastic wrap. Refrigerate for 2 hours or until firm.

3) Unwrap dough and cut into 1/4-in. slices. Place 2 in. apart on ungreased baking sheets. Bake at 375° for 9-12 minutes or until edges are lightly browned. Remove to wire racks to cool.

Yield: about 3-1/2 dozen.

NUTRITION FACTS: 2 cookies equals 159 calories, 7 g fat (3 g saturated fat), 22 mg cholesterol, 66 mg sodium, 22 g carbohydrate, 1 g fiber, 3 g protein.

Cutout Cookies

For tender cookies, use a light touch when handling the dough; overhandling will cause the cookies to be tough.

For easier handling, refrigerate the dough before rolling. This is especially true if the dough was made with butter rather than shortening.

Lightly dust the rolling pin and work surface with flour to prevent sticking. Working too much extra flour into the dough will result in tough cookies.

Roll out a portion of the dough at a time and keep the remaining dough in the refrigerator. Roll out from the center to the edge, keeping a uniform thickness and checking the thickness with a ruler. If the thickness of the dough is uneven, the cookies will bake unevenly. Thinner cookies will be crisp and may burn, while thicker cookies will be chewy.

To prevent the dough from sticking to the cookie cutter, dip the cutter in flour or spray it with cooking spray.

After the dough is rolled out, position the shapes from the cookie cutters close together to avoid having too many scraps. Save all the scraps and reroll them just once to prevent tough cookies.

To keep the cutouts intact before and after baking, transfer them to and from the baking sheet with a large metal spatula or pancake turner that supports the entire cutout.

AUSTRIAN NUT COOKIES

Austrian Nut Cookies
PREP: 30 min. + chilling
BAKE: 10 min./batch + cooling

Marianne Weber, South Beach, Oregon

These are my family's favorite Christmas cookie. If you arrange the slivered almonds in a pinwheel fashion, the cookie resembles a poinsettia.

  1 cup all-purpose flour
2/3 cup finely chopped almonds
1/3 cup sugar
1/2 cup cold butter
1/2 cup raspberry jam

FROSTING:
  1 square (1 ounce) unsweetened chocolate, melted and cooled
1/3 cup confectioners' sugar
  2 tablespoons butter, softened

Slivered almonds

1) In a bowl, combine flour, chopped almonds and sugar. Cut in butter until mixture resembles coarse crumbs. Form into a ball; cover and refrigerate for 1 hour.

2) On a floured surface, roll the dough to 1/8-in thickness. Cut with a 2-in. round cutter and place 1 in. apart on greased baking sheets. Bake at 375° for 7-10 minutes or until the edges are lightly browned. Remove to wire racks to cool completely. Spread 1/2 teaspoon jam on half of the cookies; top with another cookie.

3) For frosting, combine chocolate, confectioners' sugar and butter. Spread on tops of cookies. Decorate with slivered almonds.

Yield: 20 sandwich cookies.

NUTRITION FACTS: 1 cookie equals 146 calories, 9 g fat (4 g saturated fat), 15 mg cholesterol, 58 mg sodium, 17 g carbohydrate, 1 g fiber, 2 g protein.

Sugar Cookie Cutouts
PREP: 30 min. + chilling
BAKE: 10 min./batch + cooling

Elizabeth Walters, Waterloo, Iowa

I must have over 100 different cookie cutters and have had fun putting them to use with this recipe over the years.

  1 cup butter, softened
  1 cup sugar
  2 eggs
1/4 cup half-and-half cream
  3 cups all-purpose flour
  2 teaspoons baking powder
  1 teaspoon baking soda
1/2 teaspoon salt

FROSTING:
1/2 cup butter, softened
  4 cups confectioners' sugar
  1 teaspoon vanilla extract
  2 to 4 tablespoons half-and-half cream

Food coloring and colored sugar, optional

1) In a large mixing bowl, cream butter and sugar until light and fluffy. Add eggs, one at a time, beating well after each addition. Beat in cream.

2) Combine the flour, baking powder, baking soda and salt; gradually add to creamed mixture and mix well. Cover and refrigerate for 3 hours or until easy to handle.

3) On a lightly floured surface, roll out dough to 1/8-in. thickness. Cut with floured 2-1/2-in. cookie cutters. Place 1 in. apart on ungreased baking sheets.

4) Bake at 325° for 6-8 minutes or until edges are lightly browned. Remove to wire racks to cool completely.

5) In another large mixing bowl, cream butter, sugar, vanilla and enough cream to achieve spreading consistency. Add food coloring if desired. Frost cookies. Sprinkle with colored sugar if desired.

Yield: 8 dozen.

NUTRITION FACTS: 2 cookies equals 139 calories, 6 g fat (4 g saturated fat), 25 mg cholesterol, 129 mg sodium, 20 g carbohydrate, trace fiber, 1 g protein.

GINGERBREAD COOKIES

Frosting Gingerbread Cookies

The Gingerbread Cookies at left are a lighter cookie when they are not frosted. If you want to dress up the cookies with some frosting, try piping it on as an outline. For a country look, sponge some thinned frosting on with a piece of sponge from a new, clean sponge. If you're not concerned about the calories, spread the frosting over the cookie and decorate as desired.

Gingerbread Cookies

PREP: 30 min. + chilling
BAKE: 10 min./batch + cooling

Christy Thelan, Kellogg, Iowa

Our two boys linger around the kitchen when these aromatic cookies are baking. I make them throughout the year using a variety of cutters.

- 3/4 cup butter, softened
- 1 cup packed brown sugar
- 1 egg
- 3/4 cup molasses
- 4 cups all-purpose flour
- 2 teaspoons ground ginger
- 1-1/2 teaspoons baking soda
- 1-1/2 teaspoons ground cinnamon
- 3/4 teaspoon ground cloves
- 1/4 teaspoon salt

Vanilla frosting of your choice, optional

1) In a large mixing bowl, cream butter and brown sugar until light and fluffy. Add egg and molasses. Combine the flour, ginger, baking soda, cinnamon, cloves and salt; gradually add to creamed mixture and mix well. Cover and refrigerate for 4 hours, overnight or until easy to handle.

2) On a lightly floured surface, roll dough to 1/8-in. thickness. Cut with floured 2-1/2-in. cookie cutters. Place 1 in. apart on ungreased baking sheets.

3) Bake at 350° for 8-10 minutes or until edges are firm. Remove to wire racks to cool. Decorate with frosting if desired.

Yield: 5 dozen.

NUTRITION FACTS: 1 cookie equals 77 calories, 2 g fat (1 g saturated fat), 10 mg cholesterol, 69 mg sodium, 13 g carbohydrate, trace fiber, 1 g protein.

Hazelnut-Espresso Sandwich Cookies

PREP: 45 min. + chilling
BAKE: 10 min./batch + cooling

Cindy Beberman, Orland Park, Illinois

The inspiration for this cute cookie came from my sister's description of a hazelnut cookie she tried in Italy. She declared my version to be a wonderful approximation. My family likes to help fill them.

- 1 cup butter, softened
- 1-1/4 cups sugar
- 1 egg
- 1 egg yolk
- 4 teaspoons instant espresso granules
- 2 teaspoons vanilla extract
- 2-1/2 cups all-purpose flour
- 1/2 teaspoon salt
- 1/2 teaspoon baking powder
- 1 cup finely ground hazelnuts

FILLING:

- 1 cup heavy whipping cream
- 1-1/4 cups milk chocolate chips
- 1-3/4 cups semisweet chocolate chips, *divided*

HAZELNUT-ESPRESSO SANDWICH COOKIES

1) In a large mixing bowl, cream butter and sugar until light and fluffy. Beat in the egg, egg yolk, espresso granules and vanilla. Combine the flour, salt and baking powder; gradually add to creamed mixture and mix well. Stir in hazelnuts.

2) Divide dough into thirds; flatten each portion into a circle. Wrap each in plastic wrap; refrigerate for 1 hour or until easy to handle.

3) On a lightly floured surface, roll out one portion of dough to 1/8-in. thickness. Cut with a floured 1-1/2-in. cookie cutter; place 1/2 in. apart on ungreased baking sheets. Repeat with the remaining dough.

4) Bake at 375° for 6-8 minutes or until edges begin to brown. Remove to wire racks to cool completely.

5) For filling, in a small saucepan, bring cream to a boil. Remove from the heat; stir in milk chocolate chips and 3/4 cup semisweet chocolate chips until melted. Transfer to a bowl; refrigerate for 1-1/2 hours or until the filling reaches a spreading consistency, stirring occasionally.

6) Spread filling over the bottom of half of the cookies; top with remaining cookies. Melt remaining semisweet chips; drizzle over cookies. Let stand until set. Store in an airtight container in the refrigerator.

Yield: 3 dozen sandwich cookies.

NUTRITION FACTS: 1 cookie equals 214 calories, 13 g fat (7 g saturated fat), 35 mg cholesterol, 85 mg sodium, 23 g carbohydrate, 1 g fiber, 2 g protein.

Making Cutout Cookies

1) For easier handling, chill dough for 1 to 2 hours before rolling out. Lightly flour the surface and rolling pin. Roll out dough as evenly as possible to the recommended thickness.

2) Dip the cutter in flour, then press the cutter into the dough. Lift each cookie with a small metal spatula or pancake turner to support the cookie as it is moved to baking sheet.

3) Bake according to recipe directions. With a metal spatula or pancake turner, remove cookies from the baking sheet to a wire rack, being careful to support the entire cookie. Cool completely before frosting or storing.

Shortbread

PREP: 20 min. **BAKE:** 15 min./batch + cooling

Wendy Masters, Grand Valley, Ontario

Four ingredients is all it takes to mix together this classic shortbread. You can also make them with brown sugar.

> 2 cups butter, softened
> 1 cup sugar
> 1 teaspoon vanilla extract
> 4 cups all-purpose flour

Colored sugar, optional

1) In a large mixing bowl, cream butter and sugar. Add vanilla and mix well. Gradually add flour; mix until dough forms a ball.

2) On a lightly floured surface, roll out dough to 1/2-in. thickness. Cut into 1-1/2-in. squares, diamonds and/or triangles. Place on ungreased baking sheets; sprinkle with colored sugar if desired.

3) Bake at 325° for 14-18 minutes or until edges are lightly browned. Remove to wire racks.

Yield: about 3-1/2 dozen.

NUTRITION FACTS: 1 cookie equals 138 calories, 9 g fat (5 g saturated fat), 23 mg cholesterol, 62 mg sodium, 14 g carbohydrate, trace fiber, 1 g protein.

■ **Spiced Shortbread:** Stir 3/4 teaspoon ground cinnamon, 1/2 teaspoon *each* ground allspice, and ground nutmeg and 1/4 teaspoon ground cloves into the flour. Proceed as directed. **Yield:** 3-1/2 dozen.

■ **Brown Sugar Shortbread:** Omit sugar and colored sugar. Decrease vanilla to 1/2 teaspoon. Cream butter with 1 cup packed brown sugar. Stir in flour. On a lightly floured surface, knead dough for 3 minutes or until smooth. Roll into an 11-in. x 8-in. rectangle. Cut into 2-in. x 1-in. strips. Place 1 in. apart on baking sheets. Prick tops with a fork. Bake at 300° for 22-28 minutes or until bottoms begin to brown. Cool for 5 minutes before removing to wire racks. **Yield:** about 3-1/2 dozen.

■ **Cranberry Nut Shortbread:** Stir in 1 cup dried cranberries and 1/2 cup finely chopped pecans into dough. Roll dough to 1/2-in. thickness; cut into 1-1/2-in. x 1-in. rectangles. Bake as directed. **Yield:** 6 dozen.

SWEET SUBSTITUTE FOR CUTOUTS ■■■

When rolling out dough for cutout cookies, I sprinkle my work surface with confectioners' sugar instead of flour. It keeps the dough from getting too stiff and gives the cookies a sweeter flavor. I also dip the cookie cutters into the confectioners' sugar.

—Karen Ann Bland, Gove, Kansas

Brownies and Bars

Generally, brownies and bars should cool completely on a wire rack before being cut. However, crisp bars should be cut while still slightly warm.

Cover a pan of uncut brownies and bars with foil—or put the pan in a large resealable plastic bag. If made with perishable ingredients, like cream cheese, they should be covered and refrigerated. Once the bars are cut, store them in an airtight container.

Chocolate Cream Cheese Brownies

PREP: 15 min. **BAKE:** 35 min. + cooling

Lisa Godfrey, Temple, Georgia

"Yummy!" That's what I hear every time I make these ooey-gooey treats!

> 1 package (4 ounces) German sweet chocolate
> 3 tablespoons butter
> 2 eggs
> 3/4 cup sugar
> 1/2 cup all-purpose flour
> 1/2 teaspoon baking powder
> 1/4 teaspoon salt
> 1 teaspoon vanilla extract
> 1/4 teaspoon almond extract
> 1/2 cup chopped nuts

FILLING:
> 2 tablespoons butter, softened
> 1 package (3 ounces) cream cheese, softened
> 1/4 cup sugar
> 1 egg
> 1 tablespoon all-purpose flour
> 1/2 teaspoon vanilla extract

1) In a saucepan, melt chocolate and butter over low heat; stir until smooth. Remove from the heat; set aside. In a small mixing bowl, beat eggs. Gradually add sugar, beating until thick and pale yellow.

CHOCOLATE CREAM CHEESE BROWNIES

2) Combine flour, baking powder and salt; add to egg mixture and mix well. Stir in extracts and reserved melted chocolate. Add nuts. Pour half of batter into a greased 8-in. square baking dish; set aside.

3) For filling, in a mixing bowl, beat butter, cream cheese and sugar until light and fluffy. Add egg, flour and vanilla; mix well. Pour over batter in pan. Spoon remaining batter over filling. With a knife, cut through batter to create a marbled effect.

4) Bake at 325° for 35-40 minutes or a toothpick inserted near the center comes out clean. Cool on a wire rack. Cut into bars. Store in the refrigerator.

Yield: about 2 dozen.

NUTRITION FACTS: 1 brownie equals 248 calories, 14 g fat (7 g saturated fat), 74 mg cholesterol, 151 mg sodium, 28 g carbohydrate, trace fiber, 5 g protein.

Marbling Batters

To marble batters, spoon one batter in a random pattern over the other batter. Cut through the batter with a knife. Be careful not to overdo it, or the two batters will blend together and you'll lose the effect.

Caramel Brownies

PREP: 20 min. **BAKE:** 35 min. + cooling

Clara Bakke, Coon Rapids, Minnesota

These rich brownies are full of caramel, chocolate chips and crunchy walnuts. My family and friends just love them.

> 2 cups sugar
> 3/4 cup baking cocoa
> 1 cup vegetable oil
> 4 eggs
> 1/4 cup milk
> 1-1/2 cups all-purpose flour
> 1 teaspoon salt
> 1 teaspoon baking powder
> 1 cup (6 ounces) semisweet chocolate chips
> 1 cup chopped walnuts, *divided*
> 1 package (14 ounces) caramels
> 1 can (14 ounces) sweetened condensed milk

1) In a large mixing bowl, combine the sugar, cocoa, oil, eggs and milk. Combine the flour, salt and baking powder; add to egg mixture and mix until combined. Fold in chocolate chips and 1/2 cup walnuts.

2) Spoon two-thirds of the batter into a greased 13-in. x 9-in. x 2-in. baking pan. Bake at 350° for 12 minutes.

APRICOT PASTRY BARS

3) Meanwhile, in a large saucepan, heat the caramels and condensed milk over low heat until caramels are melted. Pour over baked brownie layer. Sprinkle with remaining walnuts.

4) Drop remaining batter by teaspoonfuls over caramel layer; carefully swirl brownie batter with a knife. Bake for 35-40 minutes or until a toothpick inserted near the center comes out with moist crumbs. Cool on a wire rack.

Yield: 2 dozen.

NUTRITION FACTS: 1 brownie equals 376 calories, 18 g fat (5 g saturated fat), 43 mg cholesterol, 189 mg sodium, 51 g carbohydrate, 2 g fiber, 6 g protein.

Apricot Pastry Bars

PREP: 45 min. **BAKE:** 35 min. + cooling

Nancy Foust, Stoneboro, Pennsylvania

Perfect for a casual gathering or fancier event, these special bars are a crowd-pleaser.

>   4 cups all-purpose flour
>   1 cup plus 2 tablespoons sugar, *divided*
>   3 teaspoons baking powder
>   1/2 teaspoon salt
>   1/4 teaspoon baking soda
>   1 cup shortening
>   3 eggs, *separated*
>   1/4 cup milk
> 1-1/2 teaspoons vanilla extract
>   4 cans (12 ounces *each*) apricot filling
>   1 cup chopped walnuts

1) In a large bowl, combine the flour, 1 cup sugar, baking powder, salt and baking soda. Cut in shortening until mixture resembles coarse crumbs.

2) In a small bowl, whisk the egg yolks, 2 egg whites, milk and vanilla; gradually add to crumb mixture, tossing with a fork until dough forms a ball. Divide in half, making one portion slightly larger.

3) Roll out larger portion of dough between two large sheets of waxed paper into a 17-in. x 12-in.

rectangle. Transfer to an ungreased 15-in. x 10-in. x 1-in. baking pan. Press pastry onto the bottom and up the sides of pan; trim pastry even with top edges. Spread apricot filling over dough; sprinkle with walnuts.

4) Roll out remaining pastry to fit top of pan; place over filling. Trim, seal and flute edges. Cut slits in top. Whisk remaining egg white; brush over pastry. Sprinkle with remaining sugar.

5) Bake at 350° for 35-40 minutes or until golden brown. Cool on a wire rack.

Yield: about 4 dozen.

NUTRITION FACTS: 1 bar equals 125 calories, 6 g fat (1 g saturated fat), 13 mg cholesterol, 63 mg sodium, 16 g carbohydrate, 1 g fiber, 2 g protein.

Mixed Nut Bars

PREP: 15 min. **BAKE:** 20 min. + cooling

Bobbi Brown, Waupaca, Wisconsin

One pan of these bars goes a long way. They get a nice flavor from butterscotch chips.

> 1-1/2 cups all-purpose flour
>   3/4 cup packed brown sugar
>   1/4 teaspoon salt
>   1/2 cup plus 2 tablespoons cold butter, *divided*
>   1 can (11-1/2 ounces) mixed nuts
>   1 cup butterscotch chips
>   1/2 cup light corn syrup

1) In a small bowl, combine flour, sugar and salt. Cut in 1/2 cup butter until mixture resembles coarse crumbs. Press into a greased 13-in. x 9-in. x 2-in. baking pan.

2) Bake at 350° for 10 minutes. Sprinkle with nuts. In a microwave, melt butterscotch chips; stir until smooth. Add corn syrup and remaining butter; mix well. Pour over nuts.

3) Bake for 10 minutes or until set. Cool in pan on a wire rack. Cut into bars.

Yield: about 3-1/2 dozen.

NUTRITION FACTS: 1 bar equals 143 calories, 8 g fat (4 g saturated fat), 8 mg cholesterol, 104 mg sodium, 16 g carbohydrate, 1 g fiber, 2 g protein.

MIXED NUT BARS

FUDGY CAN'T RESIST BROWNIES

 CLASSIC: Chocolate chips and macadamia nuts in the batter and sprinkled on top make Super Brownies one sweet pan of treats. They're so rich and delicious, you can cut them into smaller squares and serve a crowd.

 TIME-SAVER: When time is tight, turn to this handy, make-ahead recipe for Brownie Mallow Bars. It spruces up a pan of fudgy brownies from a mix with mini marshmallows and a luscious layer of peanut butter, chocolate chips and crisp rice cereal.

 LIGHT: Feel free to indulge in Fudgy Brownies and stick to your healthy eating goals, too. Fat-free yogurt and egg whites slim down these fantastic from-scratch treats that are dusted with powdered sugar. Each brownie has less than half the calories, a fraction of the fat and only a trace of cholesterol compared to classic Super Brownies.

 SERVES 2: When a large pan of brownies is too much for your smaller household, turn to this simple recipe for Walnut Brownies. It bakes in a loaf pan and yields eight servings, so lots of leftovers aren't a problem.

Super Brownies

PREP: 20 min. BAKE: 55 min. + cooling

Bernice Muilenburg, Molalla, Oregon

- 1/2 cup butter, cubed
- 1-1/2 cups sugar
- 4-2/3 cups (28 ounces) semisweet chocolate chips, *divided*
- 3 tablespoons water
- 4 eggs
- 5 teaspoons vanilla extract
- 1-1/2 cups all-purpose flour
- 1/2 teaspoon baking soda
- 1/2 teaspoon salt
- 2 cups coarsely chopped macadamia nuts *or* pecans, *divided*

1) In a saucepan, melt butter and sugar over medium heat. Remove from the heat; stir in 2 cups chocolate chips until melted. Transfer to a mixing bowl; beat in water. Add eggs, one at a time, beating well after each addition. Add vanilla.

2) Combine the flour, baking soda and salt; beat into the chocolate mixture until smooth. Stir in 2 cups of chocolate chips and 1 cup of nuts. Pour into a greased 13-in. x 9-in. x 2-in. baking pan. Sprinkle with remaining chips and nuts.

3) Bake at 325° for 55 minutes or until the center is set (do not overbake). Cool on a wire rack. Cut into bars.

Yield: about 3-1/2 dozen.

NUTRITION FACTS: 1 brownie equals 206 calories, 13 g fat (6 g saturated fat), 26 mg cholesterol, 90 mg sodium, 23 g carbohydrate, 2 g fiber, 2 g protein.

BROWNIE MALLOW BARS

Brownie Mallow Bars

PREP: 15 min. BAKE: 35 min. + chilling

Stacy Butler, Lees Summit, Missouri

- 1 package fudge brownie mix (13-inch x 9-inch pan size)
- 1 package (10-1/2 ounces) miniature marshmallows
- 2 cups (12 ounces) semisweet chocolate chips
- 1 cup peanut butter
- 1 tablespoon butter
- 1-1/2 cups crisp rice cereal

1) Prepare brownie batter according to package directions for fudge-like brownies. Pour into a greased 13-in. x 9-in. x 2-in. baking pan.

2) Bake at 350° for 28-30 minutes. Top with the marshmallows; bake for 3 minutes (marshmallows will not be completely melted). Cool on a wire rack.

3) In a saucepan, combine the chocolate chips, peanut butter and butter. Cook and stir over low heat until smooth. Remove from the heat; stir in cereal. Spread over brownies. Refrigerate for 1-2 hours or until firm before cutting.

Yield: 2-1/2 dozen.

Editor's Note: This recipe was tested with Betty Crocker fudge brownie mix.

NUTRITION FACTS: 1 bar equals 259 calories, 14 g fat (4 g saturated fat), 16 mg cholesterol, 138 mg sodium, 32 g carbohydrate, 2 g fiber, 4 g protein.

EASY RASPBERRY BROWNIES ■■■

Growing tired of the ordinary taste packaged brownie mix provided, I decided to use half of the water called for on the box and make up the difference with raspberry syrup. Not only did the syrup add a fun hint of raspberry, but it made the brownies very moist.

—Sheila Bliss, Sacramento, California

⧫ Fudgy Brownies

PREP: 10 min. **BAKE:** 25 min. + cooling

Denise Baumert, Dalhart, Texas

- 1 cup sugar
- 1/2 cup baking cocoa
- 6 tablespoons fat-free plain *or* vanilla yogurt
- 2 egg whites
- 1 teaspoon vanilla extract
- 1/2 cup all-purpose flour
- 1/4 cup chopped walnuts

Confectioners' sugar

1) In a large bowl, combine the sugar, cocoa and yogurt. Stir in egg whites and vanilla. Gradually stir in flour and walnuts just until combined.

2) Pour into an 8-in. square baking dish coated with cooking spray.

FUDGY BROWNIES

WALNUT BROWNIES

3) Bake at 350° for 25-28 minutes or until a toothpick inserted near center comes out clean. Cool on a wire rack. Dust with confectioners' sugar.

Yield: 16 servings.

NUTRITION FACTS: 1 brownie equals 87 calories, 2 g fat (0 saturated fat), trace cholesterol, 12 mg sodium, 18 g carbohydrate, 0 fiber, 2 g protein.

⧫ Walnut Brownies

PREP: 10 min. **BAKE:** 15 min. + cooling

Lorraine Silver, Chicopee, Massachusetts

- 1/4 cup shortening
- 1/2 cup sugar
- 3 tablespoons baking cocoa
- 1 egg
- 1/1 teaspoon vanilla extract
- 1/2 cup all-purpose flour
- 1/4 teaspoon baking powder
- 1/8 teaspoon salt
- 1/4 cup chopped walnuts

1) In a small mixing bowl, cream shortening, sugar and cocoa until light and fluffy; beat in egg and vanilla. Combine the flour, baking powder and salt; gradually add to creamed mixture. Beat on low speed until thoroughly combined. Stir in walnuts.

2) Pour into a greased 8-in. x 4-in. x 2-in. loaf pan. Bake at 350° for 15-20 minutes or until a toothpick inserted near the center comes out clean. Cool on a wire rack.

Yield: 8 brownies.

Editor's Note: This recipe may be doubled and baked in an 8-in. square dish for 20-25 minutes.

NUTRITION FACTS: 1 brownie equals 171 calories, 9 g fat (2 g saturated fat), 27 mg cholesterol, 58 mg sodium, 20 g carbohydrate, 1 g fiber, 3 g protein.

■ **For Double Chocolate Brownies:** Sprinkle 1/4 cup semisweet chocolate chips over batter before baking. Proceed as directed.

BEST-EVER BARS

 CLASSIC: Chocolate chips, walnuts, coconut and toffee bits—Fudgy Toffee Bars have it all. With cocoa in the crust, melted chocolate chips in the filling and even more chips sprinkled on top before baking, these loaded treats are a chocolate-lover's dream come true.

 TIME-SAVER: A jar of caramel ice cream topping is the key to quickly assembling Caramel Butter-Pecan Bars. A three-ingredient crust is topped with pecans and drizzled with caramel. Melting a package of chocolate chips over the warm bars is the fast finishing touch.

 LIGHT: Cranberry Cheesecake Bars get their healthier spin from oats, reduced-fat cream cheese, fat-free sweetened condensed milk and egg whites. Sweet and tangy from cranberry sauce, each rich bar has about 100 fewer calories and 10 grams less fat than classic Fudgy Toffee Bars.

 SERVES 2: Milk chocolate chips and dry roasted peanuts are paired deliciously in Triple-Layer Peanut Bars. Prepared in a loaf pan, the recipe makes six servings—just enough for two of you to enjoy for a few days.

FUDGY TOFFEE BARS

🥄 Fudgy Toffee Bars

PREP: 20 min. **BAKE:** 20 min. + cooling

Diane Bradley, Comstock Park, Michigan

- 1-3/4 cups all-purpose flour
- 3/4 cup confectioners' sugar
- 1/4 cup baking cocoa
- 3/4 cup cold butter
- 1 can (14 ounces) sweetened condensed milk
- 2 cups (12 ounces) semisweet chocolate chips, *divided*
- 1 teaspoon vanilla extract
- 1 cup coarsely chopped walnuts
- 1/2 cup flaked coconut
- 1/2 cup English toffee bits *or* almond brickle chips

1) In a bowl, combine the flour, sugar and cocoa. Cut in butter until mixture resembles coarse crumbs. Press firmly into a greased 13-in. x 9-in. x 2-in. baking pan. Bake at 350° for 10 minutes.

2) Meanwhile, in a saucepan, heat milk and 1 cup chocolate chips over medium heat until chocolate is melted, stirring until smooth. Remove from the heat. Stir in vanilla.

3) Pour filling over crust. Sprinkle with the walnuts, coconut, toffee bits and remaining chocolate chips; press down firmly. Bake for 18-20 minutes or until set. Cool on a wire rack. Cut into bars.

Yield: 3 dozen.

NUTRITION FACTS: 1 bar equals 238 calories, 14 g fat (7 g saturated fat), 15 mg cholesterol, 77 mg sodium, 28 g carbohydrate, 2 g fiber, 3 g protein.

🕐 Caramel Butter-Pecan Bars

PREP: 10 min. **BAKE:** 15 min. + cooling

Mary Jean Hlavac, McFarland, Wisconsin

- 2 cups all-purpose flour
- 1 cup packed brown sugar
- 3/4 cup cold butter
- 1-1/2 cups chopped pecans
- 1 jar (12 ounces) caramel ice cream topping, warmed
- 1 package (11-1/2 ounces) milk chocolate chips

1) In a bowl, combine flour and brown sugar; cut in butter until crumbly. Press into an ungreased

13-in. x 9-in. x 2-in. baking dish. Top with pecans. Drizzle caramel topping evenly over pecans.

2) Bake at 350° for 15-20 minutes or until caramel is bubbly. Place on a wire rack. Sprinkle with chocolate chips. Let stand for 5 minutes. Carefully spread chips over caramel layer. Cool at room temperature for at least 6 hours or until chocolate is set. Cut into bars.

Yield: 4 dozen.

NUTRITION FACTS: 1 bar equals 140 calories, 8 g fat (3 g saturated fat), 9 mg cholesterol, 61 mg sodium, 18 g carbohydrate, 1 g fiber, 1 g protein.

Cranberry Cheesecake Bars

PREP: 15 min. **BAKE:** 30 min. + cooling

Rhonda Lund, Laramie, Wyoming

- 2 cups plus 2 tablespoons all-purpose flour, *divided*
- 1 cup quick-cooking oats
- 3/4 cup packed brown sugar
- 1/2 cup butter, melted
- 1 package (8 ounces) reduced-fat cream cheese
- 1 can (14 ounces) fat-free sweetened condensed milk
- 4 egg whites
- 1 teaspoon vanilla extract
- 1 can (16 ounces) whole-berry cranberry sauce
- 2 tablespoons cornstarch

1) In a large bowl, combine 2 cups flour, oats, brown sugar and butter; mix until crumbly. Press 2-1/2 cups of the crumb mixture into a greased 13-in. x 9-in. x 2-in. baking dish. Bake at 350° for 10 minutes.

2) In a large mixing bowl, beat cream cheese until smooth. Beat in the milk, egg whites, vanilla and remaining flour. Spoon over crust. In a small bowl, combine cranberry sauce and cornstarch. Spoon over cream cheese layer. Sprinkle with the remaining crumb mixture.

3) Bake for 30-35 minutes or until the center is almost set. Cool on a wire rack before cutting.

Yield: 3 dozen.

NUTRITION FACTS: 1 bar equals 142 calories, 4 g fat (2 g saturated fat), 11 mg cholesterol, 67 mg sodium, 24 g carbohydrate, 1 g fiber, 3 g protein.

Triple-Layer Peanut Bars

PREP: 30 min. **BAKE:** 15 min. + cooling

Orlena Berry, Mustang, Oklahoma

- 2 tablespoons butter, softened
- 3 tablespoons brown sugar
- 1 tablespoon peanut butter
- 1/4 teaspoon vanilla extract
- 1/2 cup all-purpose flour

TRIPLE-LAYER PEANUT BARS

FILLING:

- 2/3 cup sweetened condensed milk
- 1 tablespoon butter
- 1/4 cup salted dry roasted peanuts, chopped
- 1 teaspoon vanilla extract

TOPPING:

- 2 tablespoons milk chocolate chips
- 1/4 cup salted dry roasted peanuts, chopped

1) In a small mixing bowl, cream the butter, brown sugar, peanut butter and vanilla until light and fluffy. Gradually add flour until well combined (mixture will be crumbly).

2) Press onto the bottom and 1/2 in. up the sides of an 8-in. x 4-in. x 2-in. loaf pan coated with cooking spray. Bake at 350° for 12-15 minutes or until set and lightly browned. Cool.

3) For filling, in a small saucepan, cook and stir the milk and butter over low heat until mixture comes to a boil and thickens. Remove from the heat; stir in peanuts and vanilla. Spread evenly over crust.

4) Bake at 350° for 15-17 minutes or until set. Immediately sprinkle with chocolate chips; let stand for a few minutes to soften, then spread over filling. Sprinkle with peanuts. Cool on a wire rack. Cut into bars.

Yield: 6 bars.

NUTRITION FACTS: 1 bar equals 326 calories, 17 g fat (7 g saturated fat), 27 mg cholesterol, 216 mg sodium, 38 g carbohydrate, 2 g fiber, 8 g protein.

MAKING LAYERED BARS ■■■

When making bar cookies such as oatmeal layer bars or marshmallow treats, I use waxed paper to press the mixture into the pan. It produces an even layer and keeps your hands clean.

—*Laura J., Largo, Florida*

Apricot Oat Bars

PREP: 15 min. **BAKE:** 30 min. + cooling

Dorothy Myrick, Kent, Washington

With an oat-filled crust and golden crumb topping, these apricot-filled bars are sweet and chewy.

- 1 cup quick-cooking oats
- 1 cup all-purpose flour
- 2/3 cup packed brown sugar
- 1/4 teaspoon baking soda
- 1/4 teaspoon salt
- 1/4 cup canola oil
- 3 tablespoons unsweetened apple juice
- 1 jar (10 ounces) apricot spreadable fruit

1) In a large bowl, combine the oats, flour, brown sugar, baking soda and salt. Add oil and apple juice; stir until moistened. Set aside 1/2 cup for topping.

2) Press remaining oat mixture into an 11-in. x 7-in. x 2-in. baking pan coated with cooking spray. Spread the apricot fruit spread to within 1/4 in. of edges. Sprinkle with reserved oat mixture.

3) Bake at 325° for 30-35 minutes or until golden brown. Cool on a wire rack.

Yield: 16 bars.

NUTRITION FACTS: 1 bar equals 151 calories, 4 g fat (1 g saturated fat), 0 cholesterol, 24 mg sodium, 28 g carbohydrate, 1 g fiber, 2 g protein.

Raspberry Bars

PREP: 20 min. + cooling **BAKE:** 25 min. + cooling

Abby Kuhn, Ellsworth, Maine

A meringue topping tastefully covers a nutty jam filling over a tender pastry crust in these bars.

- 1/3 cup plus 1/2 cup sugar, *divided*
- 1-1/2 cups all-purpose flour
- 3/4 cup butter
- 2 eggs, *separated*
- 1 cup raspberry jam
- 1 cup broken walnuts

1) In a small bowl, combine 1/3 cup sugar, flour, butter and egg yolks. Press into a greased 13-in. x 9-in. x 2-in. baking pan. Bake at 350° for 15 minutes or until golden. Cool. Spread jam over crust; sprinkle with nuts.

2) In a small mixing bowl, beat egg whites on medium speed until soft peaks form. Gradually beat in remaining sugar, 1 tablespoon at a time, on high until stiff glossy peaks form and sugar is dissolved. Spread meringue over nuts.

3) Bake at 350° for 25 minutes or until set and lightly browned. Cool on a wire rack. To cut, use a knife dipped in hot water. Store in the refrigerator.

Yield: 3 dozen.

NUTRITION FACTS: 1 bar equals 118 calories, 6 g fat (3 g saturated fat), 22 mg cholesterol, 42 mg sodium, 15 g carbohydrate, trace fiber, 2 g protein.

LEMON BARS

Lemon Bars

PREP: 25 min. **BAKE:** 10 min. + cooling

Melissa Mosness, Loveland, Colorado

These bars are simple enough for no-fuss dinners, yet elegant enough for special celebrations.

- 1/2 cup butter, softened
- 1/4 cup sugar
- 1 cup all-purpose flour

FILLING:

- 3/4 cup sugar
- 2 eggs
- 3 tablespoons lemon juice
- 2 tablespoons all-purpose flour
- 1/4 teaspoon baking powder

Confectioners' sugar

1) In a small mixing bowl, cream butter and sugar until light and fluffy; gradually beat in flour until blended.

2) Press into an ungreased 8-in. square baking dish. Bake at 350° for 15-20 minutes or until edges are lightly browned.

3) Meanwhile, for filling, in a small mixing bowl, beat the sugar, eggs, lemon juice, flour and baking powder until frothy. Pour over crust.

4) Bake for 10-15 minutes or until set and lightly browned. Cool on a wire rack. Sprinkle with confectioners' sugar. Cut into squares.

Yield: 9 servings.

NUTRITION FACTS: 1 bar equals 250 calories, 11 g fat (7 g saturated fat), 74 mg cholesterol, 99 mg sodium, 35 g carbohydrate, trace fiber, 3 g protein.

Cutting Bars

A large pizza cutter will make quick work of cutting a pan of bars. A bench knife can also be used to cut bar cookies. Press the bench knife down into the cookies to cut; don't drag it through. You'll be rewarded with straight, clean edges on your bars.

this pet project is golden

Rescue mission has truly gone to the dogs

Mary Schmittinger

> ❝ Being able to place a scared, unwanted dog into a loving home is worth the effort it takes to make it happen ❞
>
> ~Mary Schmittinger

Few people get to combine their two loves into something that makes a difference.

Mary Schmittinger of Colgate, Wisconsin, is one of the lucky ones. Her love of baking and dogs has helped further a cause that's close to her heart.

After adopting a beloved family pet from a local dog rescue group, Mary and several members of the group started their own rescue, Wisconsin Adopt a Golden Retriever. The nonprofit group, run by volunteers, provides new beginnings to unwanted dogs that have been surrendered or abandoned.

Last year, 167 of the furry, family-friendly canines were rescued and placed into foster or long-term homes. The group estimates the cost of placing a rescued dog at more than $500 per pooch.

According to the American Kennel Club, the golden retriever is one of the most popular breeds in the United States. Why? These cuddly, cute puppies grow up to be intelligent, handsome dogs

with an eager-to-please attitude. Goldens typically make good hunting companions, guide dogs and search dogs.

"Being able to place a scared, unwanted dog into a loving home is worth the effort it takes to make it happen," says Mary.

Since the rescue group relies solely on donations, numerous fund-raisers are needed to cover veterinarian bills for the dogs, as well as other costs of running the rescue. That's where Mary's knack for baking comes in.

In addition to serving as director and home visit coordinator for the group, Mary has been baking to raise money for the rescuers since 2004. For many of the fund-raisers, Mary starts baking months in advance, freezing her treats until just before the event.

Mary has learned what sweet, tasty specialties will sell the best. She says homemade cookies and bars, quick breads, Amish Friendship Breads and candies, such as Peanutty Candy Bars, are gone in a flash.

taste of home
cooks who care

DO YOU KNOW A COOK WHO CARES?
If you or someone you know cooks for a charitable, spiritual or other cause, tell us about it at **tasteofhome.com/CookbookBonus**

You can find some of Mary's recipes in the Web exclusive online at tasteofhome.com/ CookbookBonus **Type in access code ICare**

Recipes

Tips

CANDIES

Candies

Homemade candies are fun to make, serve and give to friends and family. With these tips and recipes, you should have delicious, sweet treats every time.

Candy Making Tips

Always measure and assemble all ingredients for a candy recipe before beginning. Do not substitute or alter the basic ingredients. Use real butter for best results or stick margarine (with at least 80% oil).

Use heavy-gauge saucepans that are deep enough to allow candy mixtures to boil freely without boiling over. Use wooden spoons with long handles for safe stirring when preparing recipes with hot boiling sugar.

Humid weather affects results when preparing candies that are cooked to specific temperatures or that contain egg whites. For best results, make candy on days when the humidity is less than 60%.

Store homemade candies in tightly covered containers unless otherwise directed. Don't store more than one kind of candy in a single container. Individually wrap chewy candies like caramels, popcorn balls and taffy.

Using a Candy Thermometer

The best and most reliable way to check the temperature of candy is to use a candy thermometer. If none is available, use the Cold-Water Test for Candy on page 695.

Always use a thermometer designed for candy making. It must have a movable clip to secure it to the side of the pan and to keep the end of the thermometer off the bottom of the pan.

Check your candy thermometer for accuracy each time you make candy. Place the thermometer in a saucepan of boiling water for several minutes before reading. If the thermometer reads 212° in boiling water, it is accurate. If it rises above or does not reach 212°, add or subtract the difference to the temperature called for in the recipe.

A candy mixture will cook very slowly when boiling until it reaches 220°, then it will cook quickly. It's important to closely watch the thermometer at this point. Some digital thermometers will beep when they reach the preset temperature. When finished using the thermometer, allow it to cool before washing to avoid breakage.

Chocolate Basics

Recipes may call for chocolate chips, baking chocolate or candy coating. Chocolate chips are available in standard, miniature and larger "chunk" sizes as well as a variety of flavors (semisweet, milk and vanilla or white). Specialty flavors such as raspberry or mint are sometimes available.

Baking chocolate is available in unsweetened, semisweet, milk and German sweet chocolate as well as white. It is commonly sold in 8-ounce packages that are divided into 1- or 2-ounce squares or bars.

Baking chocolate is designed for melting. For faster melting, chop baking bars into smaller pieces. Chips can be melted in place of semisweet, milk or white baking chocolate. Simply substitute 6 ounces of the appropriate flavored chips for 6 ounces of baking chocolate.

Candy coating or almond bark is available in dark, milk or white chocolate varieties. It is commonly sold in large individual blocks, in bags of flat discs and in packages of individual 1-ounce squares. Candy coating is used as a coating for candies, cookies, fruits or nuts.

HARD MAPLE CANDY

☙ Hard Maple Candy

PREP: 5 min. **COOK:** 30 min. + cooling

Dorothea Bohrer, Silver Spring, Maryland

During the war, the women at my grandmother's church would donate sugar rations throughout the year to make candy as a fund-raiser at Christmas. I'm lucky enough to have inherited this tried-and-true recipe.

- 1-1/2 teaspoons butter, softened
- 3-1/2 cups sugar
- 1 cup light corn syrup
- 1 cup water
- 3 tablespoons maple flavoring

1) Grease a 15-in. x 10-in. x 1-in. pan with butter; set aside. In a large heavy saucepan, combine the sugar, corn syrup and water. Cook over medium-high heat until a candy thermometer reads 300° (hard-crack stage), stirring occasionally.

2) Remove from the heat; stir in maple flavoring. Immediately pour into prepared pan; cool. Break into pieces. Store in airtight containers.

Yield: 1-3/4 pounds.

NUTRITION FACTS: 1/3 ounce equals 46 calories, trace fat (trace saturated fat), trace cholesterol, 5 mg sodium, 11 g carbohydrate, 0 fiber, 0 protein.

■ **Anise Hard Candy:** Use 2 teaspoons anise extract for the maple flavoring. Add 6-9 drops red food coloring with the extract if desired.

Butterscotch Hard Candy

PREP: 10 min. **COOK:** 30 min. + cooling

Darlene Smithers, Elkhart, Indiana

I love making this classic butterscotch recipe. We think these irresistible bites are better than the store-bought variety. They never last long!

- 1 teaspoon plus 1 cup butter, softened, *divided*
- 2-1/2 cups sugar

- 3/4 cup water
- 1/2 cup light corn syrup
- 1/4 cup honey
- 1/2 teaspoon salt
- 1/2 teaspoon rum extract

1) Butter a 15-in. x 10-in. x 1-in. pan with 1 teaspoon butter; set aside. Cube remaining butter and set aside.

2) In a large heavy saucepan, combine the sugar, water and corn syrup. Cover and bring to a boil over medium heat without stirring. Cook, uncovered, until a candy thermometer reads 270° (soft-crack stage).

3) Add the honey, salt and remaining butter; stir constantly until the mixture reaches 300° (hard-crack stage). Remove from the heat. Stir in the rum extract.

4) Pour into prepared pan without scraping; do not spread. Cool for 1-2 minutes or until the candy is almost set. Score into 1-in. squares; cool completely. Break squares apart. Store in an airtight container.

Yield: 1-1/2 pounds.

NUTRITION FACTS: 1 piece equals 144 calories, 6 g fat (4 g saturated fat), 17 mg cholesterol, 109 mg sodium, 23 g carbohydrate, trace fiber, trace protein.

TERRIFIC TOFFEE

Terrific Toffee

PREP: 10 min. **COOK:** 25 min. + standing

Carol Gillespie, Chambersburg, Pennsylvania

This buttery toffee is one of those must-make treats my family requests for the holidays.

- 1-1/2 teaspoons plus 1 cup butter, softened, *divided*
- 1 cup semisweet chocolate chips
- 1 cup milk chocolate chips

1 cup sugar
3 tablespoons water
2 cups coarsely chopped almonds, toasted, *divided*

1) Butter a large baking sheet with 1-1/2 teaspoons butter; set aside. In a small bowl, combine semisweet and milk chocolate chips; set aside.

2) In a large heavy saucepan, combine sugar, water and remaining butter. Cook and stir over medium heat until a candy thermometer reaches 290° (soft-crack stage). Remove from the heat; stir in 1 cup almonds. Immediately pour onto prepared baking sheet.

3) Sprinkle with chocolate chips; spread with a knife when melted. Sprinkle with remaining almonds. Let stand until set, about 1 hour. Break into 2-in. pieces.

Yield: about 2 pounds.

NUTRITION FACTS: 1 ounce equals 187 calories, 14 g fat (6 g saturated fat), 18 mg cholesterol, 69 mg sodium, 15 g carbohydrate, 2 g fiber, 3 g protein.

■ **English Toffee:** Omit semisweet chocolate chips and almonds. Prepare toffee as directed. Spread in pan. Sprinkle 1 cup milk chocolate chips over hot toffee; spread with a knife when melted. Sprinkle with 1 cup chopped pecans. Let stand until set, about 1 hour.

■ **Hazelnut Toffee:** Omit milk chocolate chips and almonds. Prepare toffee as directed, stirring in 1/3 cup chopped hazelnuts. Spread in pan. Sprinkle 2 cups semisweet chocolate chips over hot toffee; spread with a knife when melted. Sprinkle with 1/2 cup finely chopped hazelnuts. Let stand until set, about 1 hour.

Saving Toffee

Sometimes when you make toffee, the ingredients separate during cooking and there is a buttery layer on top and a thicker layer underneath. To save the batch of toffee, add about 1/2 cup hot water and stir until well blended. Continue cooking as recipe directs.

Cold-Water Test for Candy

Thread Stage (230°-233°). Dip a metal spoon into the hot candy mixture. Hold the spoon over the cold water. The mixture should fall off the spoon in a fine thread.

Soft-Ball Stage (234°-240°). Drop a small amount of the hot candy mixture into the cold water. When cooled and removed from the water, the ball will flatten immediately and run over your finger.

Firm-Ball Stage (244°-248°). Drop a small amount of the hot candy mixture into the cold water. When cooled and removed from the water, the ball will hold its shape and not flatten.

Hard-Ball Stage (250°-266°). Drop a small amount of the hot candy mixture into the cold water. When cooled and removed from the water, the candy will form a hard yet pliable ball.

Soft-Crack Stage (270°-290°). Drop a small amount of the hot candy mixture into the cold water. When cooled and removed from the water, the candy will separate into threads that are hard but not brittle.

Hard-Crack Stage (300°-310°). Drop a small amount of the hot candy mixture into the cold water. When cooled and removed from the water, the candy will separate into hard brittle threads.

Mixed Nut Brittle

PREP: 5 min. **COOK:** 30 min. + cooling

Norma Francel, Edwardsburg, Michigan

Nut fanciers have a lot to love about this irresistible brittle. The variety of nuts is what makes it so different. It's one of the first sweet treats to appear on my Christmas candy tray...and also the first to disappear!

- 1-1/2 teaspoons plus 3 tablespoons butter, softened, *divided*
- 1-1/2 cups sugar
- 1 cup water
- 1 cup light corn syrup
- 1 can (10 ounces) mixed nuts (without peanuts)
- 1 teaspoon vanilla extract
- 1-1/2 teaspoons baking soda

1) Butter a baking sheet with 1-1/2 teaspoons of butter; set aside. In a large heavy saucepan, combine the sugar, water and corn syrup. Cook over medium heat until a candy thermometer reads 270° (soft-crack stage), stirring occasionally.

2) Add nuts; cook and stir until the mixture reaches 300° (hard-crack stage). Remove from the heat; stir in vanilla and remaining butter. Add baking soda and stir vigorously.

3) Quickly pour onto prepared baking sheet. Spread with a buttered metal spatula to 1/4-in. thickness. Cool before breaking into pieces.

Yield: about 1-3/4 pounds.

NUTRITION FACTS: 1 ounce equals 148 calories, 7 g fat (2 g saturated fat), 4 mg cholesterol, 164 mg sodium, 22 g carbohydrate, 1 g fiber, 2 g protein.

■ **Peanut Brittle:** Use 2 cups peanuts for the mixed nuts.

■ **Macadamia Almond Brittle:** Use 1 cup each coarsely chopped macadamia nuts and coarsely chopped almonds for the mixed nuts.

Angel Food Candy

PREP: 40 min. + standing **COOK:** 45 min. + standing

Carrol Holloway, Hindsville, Arkansas

Dipped in white and dark candy coating, this two-tone treat stands out on any goody tray.

- 1 teaspoon butter, softened
- 1 cup sugar
- 1 cup dark corn syrup
- 1 tablespoon white vinegar
- 1 tablespoon baking soda
- 1/2 pound white candy coating
- 1/2 pound dark chocolate candy coating

1) Butter a 13-in. x 9-in. x 2-in. pan with the butter; set aside. In a large heavy saucepan, combine the sugar, corn syrup and vinegar.

2) Cook and stir over medium heat until sugar is dissolved. Cook, without stirring, until a candy

ANGEL FOOD CANDY

thermometer reads 290° (soft-crack stage). Remove from the heat; stir in baking soda. Pour into the prepared pan. Do not spread candy. Cool, then break into pieces.

3) In a microwave or small heavy saucepan, melt white candy coating; stir until smooth. Dip the candies halfway into melted coating, shaking off excess. Place on waxed paper-lined baking sheets until set.

4) Melt dark chocolate coating; dip uncoated portion of candies in coating. Return to waxed paper until set. Store in an airtight container.

Yield: 1-1/2 pounds.

NUTRITION FACTS: 2 ounces equals 343 calories, 11 g fat (10 g saturated fat), 1 mg cholesterol, 360 mg sodium, 64 g carbohydrate, trace fiber, trace protein.

Sugared Peanut Clusters

PREP: 15 min. + cooling

Gail McClantoc, Sweet Water, Alabama

Coffee and cinnamon provide the flavor in these nutty treats. Remember to work quickly to form the small clusters!

- 2 teaspoons butter, softened
- 1-1/2 cups sugar
- 1/2 cup brewed coffee
- 1 tablespoon light corn syrup
- 1 teaspoon ground cinnamon
- 1 teaspoon vanilla extract
- 1 jar (16 ounces) dry roasted peanuts

1) Butter two baking sheets with the 2 teaspoons butter; set aside. In a large heavy saucepan, combine the sugar, coffee, corn syrup and cinnamon.

2) Bring to a boil over medium heat, stirring occasionally. Cook until a candy thermometer reads 234°-240° (soft-ball stage). Remove from the heat; stir in vanilla. Add peanuts; stir quickly.

3) Pour onto prepared baking sheets. Quickly separate into small clumps with two forks. Cool completely. Store in an airtight container.

Yield: 6 cups.

NUTRITION FACTS: 1/4 cup equals 165 calories, 10 g fat (1 g saturated fat), 1 mg cholesterol, 158 mg sodium, 17 g carbohydrate, 2 g fiber, 4 g protein.

Toasted Almond Caramels
PREP/TOTAL TIME: 30 min. + cooling

Mae Ondracek, Pahrump, Nevada

Preparing these caramels never fails to put me in the holiday spirit. Later, when I'm passing them around, that cheerful feeling becomes contagious.

>   1 teaspoon plus 1/4 cup butter, softened, *divided*
>   2 cups sugar
>   1 cup light corn syrup
> 1/4 teaspoon salt
>   1 cup heavy whipping cream
>   1 teaspoon vanilla extract
>   1 cup chopped almonds, toasted

1) Line an 8-in. square dish with foil; butter the foil with 1 teaspoon butter. Set aside. In a large heavy saucepan, combine the sugar, corn syrup, salt and remaining butter. Bring to a boil over medium heat, stirring constantly. Reduce heat to medium low; boil gently without stirring for 4 minutes.

2) Remove from the heat; slowly stir in the cream. Return to the heat; cook, without stirring, over medium-low heat until a candy thermometer reads 245° (firm-ball stage). Remove from the heat; stir in vanilla and almonds.

3) Pour into prepared pan (do not scrape sides of saucepan). Cool completely. Using foil, lift the caramel out of pan. Discard foil; cut caramel into squares. Wrap individually in waxed paper or foil; twist ends.

Yield: about 4 dozen.

NUTRITION FACTS: 1 caramel equals 94 calories, 4 g fat (2 g saturated fat), 10 mg cholesterol, 33 mg sodium, 14 g carbohydrate, trace fiber, 1 g protein.

■ **Nutty Chocolate Caramels:** Omit chopped almonds. Add 4 squares (1 ounce each) chopped semisweet chocolate to the saucepan along with the sugar. Proceed as directed until mixture reaches 245°. Remove from heat; stir in 2 teaspoons vanilla and 1 cup chopped walnuts. Proceed as recipe directs.

Southern Pralines
PREP: 30 min. + cooling

Bernice Eberhart, Fort Payne, Alabama

These are a real Southern treat that I've used to fill many holiday gift tins!

>   3 cups packed brown sugar
>   1 cup heavy whipping cream
>   2 tablespoons light corn syrup
> 1/4 teaspoon salt
> 1/4 cup butter, cubed
>   2 cups chopped pecans
> 1-1/4 teaspoons vanilla extract

1) In a large heavy saucepan, combine the brown sugar, cream, corn syrup and salt. Bring to a boil over medium heat, stirring constantly. Cook until a candy thermometer reads 234° (soft-ball stage), stirring occasionally.

2) Remove from the heat; add butter (do not stir). Cool until candy thermometer reads 150°, about 35 minutes.

3) Stir in the pecans and vanilla. Stir with a wooden spoon until candy just begins to thicken but is still glossy, about 5-7 minutes. Quickly drop by heaping teaspoonfuls onto waxed paper; spread to form 2-in. patties. Let stand until set. Store in an airtight container.

Yield: about 3-1/2 dozen.

NUTRITION FACTS: 1 praline equals 130 calories, 7 g fat (2 g saturated fat), 11 mg cholesterol, 35 mg sodium, 17 g carbohydrate, 1 g fiber, 1 g protein.

SOUTHERN PRALINES

Using a Candy Thermometer

For accurate temperature readings, the candy thermometer should be attached to the side of the saucepan but not touching the bottom of the pan.

SWEET, CREAMY FUDGE

 CLASSIC: This big batch of Two-Tiered Fudge is made the traditional way for a wonderful creamy texture that's worth the wait. Both the chocolate nut layer and the cherry vanilla layer are brimming with old-fashioned goodness.

 TIME-SAVER: You can get your fudge fix in minutes with this easy recipe for Candy Bar Fudge. It's prepared in the microwave using convenience items such as canned frosting, two kinds of chips and candy bars.

 LIGHT: Fat-free sweetened condensed milk helps slim down chocolaty Marshmallow Fudge, which has broken graham crackers and mini marshmallows throughout. Although slightly larger than a piece of Two-Tiered Fudge, one square of this lighter fudge has half the fat, almost 30 fewer calories and about half the carbohydrates.

 SERVES 2: When you're craving fudge, but don't want all the work or a big pan of sweet treats, turn to Peanut Butter Fudge Cups. Mini muffins cups are the perfect containers for six single servings of sweet peanut butter fudge.

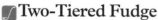

Two-Tiered Fudge

PREP: 40 min.   **COOK:** 40 min. + cooling

Christine Richburg, Brewton, Alabama

CHOCOLATE NUT LAYER:

- 2 teaspoons plus 2 tablespoons butter, softened, *divided*
- 2-1/4 cups sugar
- 1 cup milk
- 3 squares (1 ounce *each*) unsweetened chocolate
- 1 tablespoon light corn syrup
- 1 teaspoon vanilla extract
- 1/2 cup chopped nuts

CHERRY VANILLA LAYER:

- 1 teaspoon plus 2 tablespoons butter, softened, *divided*
- 2-1/2 cups sugar
- 1/2 cup half-and-half cream
- 1/2 cup milk
- 1 tablespoon light corn syrup
- 1/4 teaspoon salt
- 1 teaspoon vanilla extract
- 1/3 cup chopped candied cherries

1) Line a 9-in. square pan with foil; butter the foil with 1 teaspoon butter. Set aside. For chocolate nut layer, butter the sides of a large heavy saucepan with 1 teaspoon butter; add the sugar, milk, chocolate and corn syrup.

2) Cook and stir over medium heat until sugar is dissolved. Bring mixture to a boil. Boil until mixture reaches 236° (soft-ball stage), stirring occasionally. Remove from the heat.

3) Add vanilla and remaining butter (do not stir). Cool to 110° without stirring. Stir with a clean dry wooden spoon until fudge begins to thicken; add nuts. Continue stirring until fudge becomes thick and begins to lose its gloss, about 10 minutes. Immediately spread into prepared pan; set aside.

4) For cherry vanilla layer, butter the sides of a clean large heavy saucepan with 1 teaspoon butter; add the sugar, cream, milk, corn syrup and salt. Cook and stir over medium heat until sugar is dissolved. Bring to a boil. Boil until mixture reaches 236° (soft-ball stage), stirring occasionally. Remove from the heat.

5) Add vanilla and remaining butter (do not stir). Cool to 110° without stirring. Stir with a clean dry wooden spoon until fudge begins to thicken; add cherries. Continue stirring until fudge becomes thick and begins to lose its gloss, about 8 minutes. Immediately spread over first layer.

6) Score into squares while still warm. Using foil, lift fudge out of pan. Discard foil; cut fudge into 1-in. squares. Store in an airtight container at room temperature.

Yield: about 2-1/2 pounds.

NUTRITION FACTS: 1 piece equals 70 calories, 2 g fat (1 g saturated fat), 3 mg cholesterol, 19 mg sodium, 13 g carbohydrate, trace fiber, 1 g protein.

■ **Chocolate Nut Fudge:** Line a 9-in. x 5-in. x 3-in. loaf pan with foil and butter the foil. Prepare chocolate layer as directed and pour into prepared pan. Score into squares while still warm.

■ **Chocolate Fudge:** Line a 9-in. x 5-in. x 3-in. loaf pan with foil and butter the foil. Prepare chocolate layer as directed, except omit nuts. Pour into prepared pan. Score into squares while still warm.

■ **Cherry Vanilla Fudge:** Line a 9-in. x 5-in. x 3-in. loaf pan with foil and butter the foil. Prepare Cherry Vanilla Layer as directed and pour into prepared pan. Score into squares while still warm.

Candy Bar Fudge

PREP: 20 min. + chilling

Bonnie Ayars, Mechanicsburg, Ohio

 1 teaspoon butter, softened
 1 cup semisweet chocolate chips
 1 cup butterscotch chips
 1 can (16 ounces) chocolate fudge frosting
 2 Snickers candy bars (2.07 ounces *each*), cut into 1/4-inch chunks, *divided*

1) Line a 9-in. square pan with foil and grease the foil with the butter; set aside. In a large microwave-safe bowl, melt the chocolate and butterscotch chips; stir until smooth. Stir in frosting and half of the candy bar pieces.

2) Spread into prepared pan. Sprinkle with remaining candy bar pieces. Refrigerate for 1 hour or until set. Using foil, lift fudge out of pan. Discard foil; cut fudge into 1-in. squares or cut out with small cookie cutters. Store in an airtight container in the refrigerator.

Yield: about 1-1/2 pounds.

NUTRITION FACTS: 1 piece equals 93 calories, 5 g fat (3 g saturated fat), 1 mg cholesterol, 30 mg sodium, 13 g carbohydrate, trace fiber, trace protein.

MARSHMALLOW FUDGE

Marshmallow Fudge

PREP: 15 min. + chilling

Holly Mann, Temple, New Hampshire

1-1/3 cups semisweet chocolate chips
 2/3 cup fat-free sweetened condensed milk
 1 teaspoon vanilla extract
1-1/3 cups miniature marshmallows
 2 whole reduced-fat graham crackers, broken into bite-size pieces

1) Line an 8-in. square pan with foil and coat with cooking spray; set aside. In a large heavy saucepan, melt chocolate chips with milk over low heat; stir until smooth. Remove from the heat; cool for 2 minutes. Stir in vanilla. Fold in the marshmallows and graham crackers.

2) Pour into prepared pan. Refrigerate for 1 hour or until firm. Using foil, lift fudge out of pan. Discard foil; cut fudge into 48 pieces. Store in an airtight container.

Yield: 4 dozen.

NUTRITION FACTS: 1 piece equals 41 calories, 1 g fat (1 g saturated fat), 1 mg cholesterol, 10 mg sodium, 7 g carbohydrate, 1 g fiber, 1 g protein.

Peanut Butter Fudge Cups

PREP: 15 min. + chilling

Lori Brown, Manhattan, Illinois

 1 cup confectioners' sugar
 2 tablespoons 2% milk
 1 tablespoon creamy peanut butter
2-1/2 teaspoons baking cocoa
 1 teaspoon butter, softened
 1/2 teaspoon vanilla extract

1) In a small microwave-safe bowl, combine all the ingredients. Microwave, uncovered, on high for 30 seconds. Stir until smooth. Pour or press into six paper-lined miniature muffin cups. Refrigerate until set. Store in an airtight container.

Yield: 6 servings.

NUTRITION FACTS: 1 piece equals 105 calories, 2 g fat (1 g saturated fat), 2 mg cholesterol, 22 mg sodium, 21 g carbohydrate, trace fiber, 1 g protein.

Stirring Fudge

Allow fudge to cool to 110° undisturbed. Agitating the fudge at this stage may cause it to become grainy. Once it reaches 110°, beat with a clean, dry wooden spoon.

As you continue to stir, the temperature will continue to drop and the mixture will start to become thick and harder to stir. It may also have lighter colored streaks in it. Once the fudge starts to loose its sheen (which could take up to ten minutes), immediately pour into the prepared pan.

Determining the point when the fudge is ready to pour is important to its success. If it is poured too soon, it will be soft; if stirred too much, it will be grainy or will set up right in the bowl.

Macadamia Nut Fudge

PREP: 15 min. + chilling

Vicki Fioranelli, Cleveland, Mississippi

My aunt lives in Hawaii and keeps us supplied with macadamia nuts. But when I run out, I make this fudge with pecans.

- 2 teaspoons plus 1/2 cup butter, softened, *divided*
- 4-1/2 cups sugar
- 1 can (12 ounces) evaporated milk
- 3 cups chopped macadamia nuts, *divided*
- 3 packages (4 ounces *each*) German sweet chocolate, chopped
- 1 package (12 ounces) semisweet chocolate chips
- 1 jar (7 ounces) marshmallow creme
- 2 teaspoons vanilla extract
- 1/2 teaspoon salt, optional

1) Line two 9-in. square pans with foil; butter the foil with the 2 teaspoons butter. Set aside. In a large heavy saucepan, combine the sugar, milk and remaining butter. Bring to a gentle boil. Cook for 5 minutes, stirring constantly.

2) Remove from the heat; Stir in 2 cups nuts, chopped chocolate, chocolate chips, marshmallow creme, vanilla and salt if desired.

3) Pour the fudge into prepared pans; sprinkle remaining nuts over top and press in lightly. Refrigerate until firm. Using foil, lift fudge out of pans. Discard foil; cut fudge into 1-in. squares.

Yield: about 5 pounds.

NUTRITION FACTS: 1 piece equals 72 calories, 4 g fat (1 g saturated fat), 2 mg cholesterol, 16 mg sodium, 10 g carbohydrate, trace fiber, 1 g protein.

■ **Pecan Nut Fudge:** Use 3 cups chopped toasted pecans in place of the macadamia nuts.

Double Chocolate Truffles

PREP: 20 min. + chilling

Ruth Gordon, Lakewood, New York

Chocolate lovers of all kinds will appreciate these yummy truffles. Another nice combination is the flavor of orange extract in place of the vanilla.

- 1-1/3 cups semisweet chocolate chips
- 1/3 cup heavy whipping cream

DOUBLE CHOCOLATE TRUFFLES

- 3 tablespoons butter, cubed
- 1 teaspoon vanilla extract
- 1 cup vanilla *or* white chips
- 2 tablespoons shortening, *divided*
- 1 cup milk chocolate chips

1) In a microwave-safe bowl, melt the semisweet chocolate chips with whipping cream and butter at 50% power for 2-3 minutes; stir until blended. Add vanilla; cool. Refrigerate until almost solid but still workable, about 1 hour.

2) Shape into 1/2-in. balls. Microwave white chips and 1 tablespoon shortening at 30% power until melted; stir until smooth. Dip balls in white chocolate mixture to coat. Place on waxed paper; let stand until set.

3) Microwave milk chocolate chips and remaining shortening at 30% power until melted; stir until smooth. Dip balls into milk chocolate mixture to coat. Place on waxed paper; let stand until set.

Yield: 2-1/2 dozen.

NUTRITION FACTS: 1 truffle equals 122 calories, 9 g fat (5 g saturated fat), 9 mg cholesterol, 23 mg sodium, 11 g carbohydrate, 1 g fiber, 1 g protein.

■ **Orange Truffles:** Use 3/4 teaspoon orange extract in place of the vanilla extract.

Dipping Candy into Chocolate

Place candy on a table fork or a special two-tined candy fork; dip into the melted chocolate to cover entirely. Remove from the chocolate; scrape off any excess chocolate on the side of the bowl. Place on waxed paper to cool and harden.

Coconut Bonbons

PREP: 25 min. + chilling

Beverly Cray, Epping, New Hampshire

Family and friends always request these bonbons. Luckily, this recipe makes a huge batch to meet the demand.

- 1/2 cup butter, softened
- 2 pounds confectioners' sugar
- 1 can (14 ounces) sweetened condensed milk
- 4 cups chopped pecans
- 1 package (10 ounces) flaked coconut
- 1 teaspoon vanilla extract
- 2 cups (12 ounces) semisweet chocolate chips
- 1 tablespoon shortening

1) In a large mixing bowl, cream butter and sugar until light and fluffy. Add the milk, pecans, coconut and vanilla; mix well. Shape into 1-in. balls. Refrigerate for 30-45 minutes or until firm.

2) In a microwave, melt the chips and shortening; stir until smooth. Dip balls and place on waxed paper to set. Store in an airtight container.

Yield: about 21 dozen.

Editor's Note: Candies can be frozen for up to 3 months before dipping in chocolate. Thaw in refrigerator before dipping.

NUTRITION FACTS: 1 bonbon equals 48 calories, 3 g fat (1 g saturated fat), 2 mg cholesterol, 9 mg sodium, 6 g carbohydrate, trace fiber, trace protein.

Melting Chocolate

Break or chop large pieces of chocolate so they melt more evenly. Melt chocolate in a dry, heavy saucepan over low heat; stir until smooth. Even small amounts of water will cause the chocolate to seize (become thick and lumpy) and to be unusable. If the chocolate needs to set up after melting (such as when it's used for dipping or garnishes), add 1/4 to 1/2 teaspoon of shortening for every 6 ounces of chocolate.

To melt chocolate in the microwave, place it in a microwave-safe bowl. Melt semisweet chocolate at 50% power, and milk chocolate and vanilla or white chocolate at 30% power. Stir frequently until the chocolate is melted; do not overheat.

Lemon Cream Bonbons

PREP: 30 min. + freezing

Ann Barber, Creola, Ohio

I used to save these special treats just for Christmastime. But they're in such demand with my family that I now keep them on hand all year-round.

- 2 packages (8 ounces *each*) cream cheese, softened
- 3 tablespoons lemon juice
- 2 tablespoons grated lemon peel
- 1 teaspoon lemon extract
- 1 cup confectioners' sugar
- 1 pound dark chocolate candy coating, melted
- 1/4 pound white candy coating, melted

1) In a large mixing bowl, beat the cream cheese, lemon juice, peel and extract. Gradually beat in confectioners' sugar. Cover and freeze for 2 hours.

2) Using a small ice cream scoop, drop mixture by 1-in. balls onto waxed paper-lined baking sheets. Cover and freeze for 1 hour.

3) Dip frozen balls, a few at a time, into dark chocolate; place on waxed paper. Let stand until set. Spoon melted white coating into a heavy-duty resealable plastic bag; cut a small hole in a corner of bag. Drizzle over candies. Store in the refrigerator. Remove just before serving.

Yield: about 4 dozen.

NUTRITION FACTS: 2 pieces equals 177 calories, 10 g fat (8 g saturated fat), 10 mg cholesterol, 28 mg sodium, 22 g carbohydrate, trace fiber, 1 g protein.

Vanilla Popcorn

PREP/TOTAL TIME: 10 min.

Carolyn Roney, Scipio Center, New York

We enjoy traveling, and this recipe makes the perfect driving snack. It can be ready to go in about 10 minutes.

- 3 quarts popped popcorn
- 1 cup sugar
- 1/2 cup butter, cubed
- 1/4 cup light corn syrup
- 1/4 teaspoon baking soda
- 1/2 teaspoon vanilla extract

1) Place popcorn in a large bowl; set aside. In a saucepan, combine the sugar, butter and corn syrup. Bring to a boil over medium heat; boil and stir until mixture is golden, about 2 minutes.

2) Remove from the heat; stir in baking soda and vanilla. Pour over popcorn and toss to coat. Cool slightly; break apart while warm.

Yield: 3 quarts.

NUTRITION FACTS: 1 cup equals 206 calories, 11 g fat (5 g saturated fat), 20 mg cholesterol, 209 mg sodium, 28 g carbohydrate, 1 g fiber, 1 g protein.

VANILLA POPCORN

Peanut Candy Popcorn Balls

PREP: 20 min. + standing

Alida Jaeger, Ixonia, Wisconsin

Kids love these colorful novelties, which feature popcorn, nuts, M&M's and marshmallows.

> 4 quarts popped popcorn
> 1-1/2 cups salted peanuts
> 1-1/2 cups chopped pecans
> 1 package (16 ounces) green and red milk chocolate M&M's
> 1/2 cup butter, cubed
> 1/2 cup vegetable oil
> 1 package (16 ounces) miniature marshmallows

1) In a large bowl, combine the popcorn, peanuts, pecans and M&M's; set aside. In a large heavy saucepan, combine butter, oil and marshmallows; cook and stir until smooth. Pour over popcorn mixture; mix well.

2) When cool enough to handle, shape into popcorn balls. Let stand at room temperature until firm before wrapping in plastic wrap or stacking.

> **Yield:** about 20 popcorn balls.

NUTRITION FACTS: 1 popcorn ball equals 440 calories, 29 g fat (8 g saturated fat), 15 mg cholesterol, 195 mg sodium, 43 g carbohydrate, 3 g fiber, 6 g protein.

Caramel Pecan Candy

PREP: 35 min. + chilling

Dick Deacon, Lawrenceville, Georgia

These yummy, layered squares are sweet and chewy. I have also made this recipe in a 9-inch pie pan and cut it into very small pieces. You can't eat very much at one time.

> 1/3 cup plus 1/2 cup butter, *divided*
> 20 cream-filled chocolate sandwich cookies, crushed
> 1 package (14 ounces) caramels
> 3 cups chopped pecans, toasted

TOPPING:

> 3/4 cup semisweet chocolate chips
> 3 tablespoons butter, cubed
> 3 tablespoons heavy whipping cream
> 3 tablespoons light corn syrup
> 3/4 teaspoon vanilla extract

1) In a large saucepan, melt 1/3 cup butter over medium heat; stir in the cookie crumbs. Press into an ungreased 9-in. square baking dish. Bake at 325° for 10-12 minutes or until set. Cool on a wire rack. Meanwhile, in a small saucepan, melt caramels and remaining butter over low heat. Stir in the pecans. Pour over crust. Cool.

2) For topping, in a small saucepan, combine the chocolate chips, butter, cream and corn syrup. Cook and stir over low heat until smooth. Remove from the heat; stir in vanilla. Pour over caramel

layer. Cool on a wire rack. Refrigerate until chocolate sets. Let candy stand at room temperature for 5-10 minutes before cutting into 1-in. squares. Store in an airtight container in the refrigerator.

> **Yield:** about 6-1/2 dozen.

NUTRITION FACTS: 1 piece equals 94 calories, 7 g fat (3 g saturated fat), 7 mg cholesterol, 55 mg sodium, 8 g carbohydrate, 1 g fiber, 1 g protein.

ORANGE JELLY CANDIES

Orange Jelly Candies

PREP: 15 min. **COOK:** 10 min. + standing

Leah Jackson, Washington, Utah

Making candy is my favorite thing to do. I've been collecting candy recipes for more than 40 years.

> 2 teaspoons butter
> 1 package (1-3/4 ounces) powdered fruit pectin
> 1/2 teaspoon baking soda
> 3/4 cup water
> 1 cup sugar
> 1 cup light corn syrup
> 1/8 teaspoon orange oil
> 5 drops *each* red and yellow food coloring

Additional sugar

1) Butter a 9-in. square pan with 2 teaspoons butter; set aside. In a heavy saucepan, combine pectin, baking soda and water (mixture will be foamy).

2) In another large heavy saucepan, combine sugar and corn syrup. Bring both mixtures to a boil. Cook until foam on pectin mixture thins slightly and sugar mixture comes to a full rolling boil, about 4 minutes. Gradually add pectin mixture to boiling sugar mixture, stirring constantly. Boil for 1 minute, stirring constantly.

3) Remove from the heat. Stir in orange oil and food coloring. Immediately pour into prepared pan. Let stand at room temperature for 3 hours or until set.

4) Sprinkle waxed paper with additional sugar; invert pan onto sugar. With a knife dipped in warm water, cut candy into 1-in. squares; roll in

additional sugar. Place on a wire rack. Let stand, uncovered, at room temperature overnight. Store in an airtight container.

Yield: 81 pieces.

NUTRITION FACTS: 3 pieces (calculated without additional sugar) equals 76 calories, trace fat (trace saturated fat), 1 mg cholesterol, 41 mg sodium, 19 g carbohydrate, 0 fiber, trace protein.

Caramel Marshmallow Treats

PREP/TOTAL TIME: 30 min.

Tamara Holschen, Anchor Point, Alaska

I created this candy by combining my husband's favorite cookie recipe and my mom's caramel dip. These sweets really appeal to kids. Plus, they can help make them.

    5   cups crisp rice cereal, coarsely
        crushed
    1   can (14 ounces) sweetened
        condensed milk
    1   package (14 ounces) caramels
    1   cup butter, cubed
    1   teaspoon ground cinnamon
  1/2   teaspoon vanilla extract
    1   package (16 ounces) large
        marshmallows

1) Line two baking sheets with waxed paper; set aside. Place cereal in a shallow bowl. In a large heavy saucepan, combine milk, caramels and butter. Cook and stir over low heat until melted and smooth. Remove from heat; stir in the cinnamon and vanilla.

2) With a toothpick, dip each marshmallow into warm caramel mixture; turn to coat. Press marshmallow bottoms in cereal; place on prepared pans. Let stand until set.

Yield: 5 dozen.

NUTRITION FACTS: 2 pieces equals 106 calories, 4 g fat (3 g saturated fat), 11 mg cholesterol, 80 mg sodium, 17 g carbohydrate, trace fiber, 1 g protein.

Creamy Pastel Mints

PREP: 40 min.

Janice Brady, Seattle, Washington

Easy and versatile, these mints can be cut into any shape you want. Vary the colors for each season.

    1   package (3 ounces) cream cheese,
        softened
  3/8   teaspoon peppermint extract
    1   drop red food coloring
    1   drop blue food coloring
    1   drop yellow food coloring
    3   cups confectioners' sugar

1) Divide cream cheese equally among three small bowls. Stir in 1/8 teaspoon mint flavoring into each bowl. Using the food coloring, tint one portion red, one blue and the remaining portion yellow. Gradually stir 1/2 cup sugar into each portion.

2) Knead 1/2 cup of the remaining sugar into each color until smooth. Roll out to 1/4-in. thickness. (No sugar or flour is necessary on the rolling surface.) Use 1-in. cookie cutters to cut out various shapes. Store tightly covered in the refrigerator.

Yield: about 5 dozen.

NUTRITION FACTS: 1 piece equals 28 calories, 1 g fat (trace saturated fat), 2 mg cholesterol, 4 mg sodium, 6 g carbohydrate, 0 fiber, trace protein.

Chocolate Peppermint Bark

PREP: 15 min. + chilling

Keslie Houser, Pasco, Washington

These candies are such a snap to prepare, I almost feel guilty serving them. But the chocolate and mint flavors always bring guests back for more!

    6   squares (1 ounce *each*) white
        baking chocolate
    1   cup (6 ounces) semisweet
        chocolate chips
    1   cup crushed peppermint candies,
        divided

1) Line a baking sheet with waxed paper; set aside. In a microwave-safe bowl, melt white chocolate at 30% power; stir until smooth. Microwave chocolate chips at 50% power; stir until smooth. Stir 6 tablespoons of crushed peppermint candies into each bowl. Drop white chocolate and semisweet chocolate in alternating spoonfuls onto prepared pan.

2) With a metal spatula, cut through chocolate to swirl, spreading to 1/4-in. thickness. Sprinkle with remaining crushed candies. Chill until firm. Break into pieces. Store in an airtight container in the refrigerator.

Yield: about 1 pound.

NUTRITION FACTS: 2 ounces equals 167 calories, 8 g fat (5 g saturated fat), 1 mg cholesterol, 11 mg sodium, 27 g carbohydrate, 1 g fiber, 1 g protein.

■ **Pistachio Cranberry Bark:** Omit peppermint candies. Stir 3 tablespoons toasted chopped pistachios and 2 tablespoons dried cranberries into each bowl of melted chocolate. Proceed as directed. Sprinkle top with 2 tablespoons toasted chopped pistachios and 2 tablespoons dried cranberries.

CHOCOLATE PEPPERMINT BARK

CARAMEL PRETZEL STICKS

Caramel Pretzel Sticks

PREP: 2 hours **COOK:** 35 min.

Mary Bown, Evanston, Wyoming

Homemade caramel, smooth almond bark and chopped nuts make these pretzel rods sinfully delicious. This treat is always a huge hit at holiday parties. People think you spent all day in the kitchen!

    2 teaspoons butter, softened
    2 cups sugar
    1 cup light corn syrup
    1 cup butter, cubed
    1 can (14 ounces) sweetened
       condensed milk
    1 package (10 ounces) pretzel rods
    6 to 12 ounces white candy coating
    6 to 12 ounces milk chocolate
       candy coating
  3/4 cup finely chopped walnuts,
       optional

1) Grease a large baking sheet with the butter; set aside. In a large heavy saucepan, combine the sugar, corn syrup and butter. Bring just to a boil over medium heat, stirring constantly. Continue boiling, without stirring, at a moderate-steady rate for 4 minutes. Remove from the heat; stir in milk. Return to the heat. Reduce to medium-low; cook and stir until a candy thermometer reads 245° (firm-ball stage).

2) Pour 2 cups caramel mixture into a 2-cup glass measuring cup. Quickly dip each pretzel halfway into caramel. Allow excess to drip off. Place on well-buttered prepared pan; let stand until set.

3) In a microwave-safe bowl or measuring cup, melt white candy coating; stir until smooth. Dip half of the caramel-coated pretzels into coating. Melt milk chocolate coating; dip remaining pretzels. Drizzle white-coated pretzels with milk chocolate coating; drizzle milk chocolate-coated pretzels with white coating. Sprinkle with walnuts if desired. Store in an airtight container.

Yield: about 2-1/2 dozen.

Editor's Note: Any remaining caramel mixture may be poured into a well-buttered 8-in. x 4-in. x 2-in. loaf pan. Cool to room temperature before cutting into squares and wrapping in waxed paper.

NUTRITION FACTS: 1 pretzel stick equals 284 calories, 11 g fat (8 g saturated fat), 22 mg cholesterol, 223 mg sodium, 46 g carbohydrate, trace fiber, 2 g protein.

Peanut Butter Balls

PREP: 1 hour + chilling

Rhonda Williams, Mayville, Michigan

It's a tradition for my sister and me to bring these chocolaty confections to functions and family gatherings.

    2 cups creamy peanut butter
  1/2 cup butter, cubed
    4 cups confectioners' sugar
    3 cups crisp rice cereal
    4 cups (24 ounces) semisweet
       chocolate chips
  1/4 cup shortening

1) Line a baking sheet with waxed paper; set aside. In a small saucepan, combine peanut butter and butter. Cook and stir over medium-low heat until smooth. Remove from the heat.

2) In a large bowl, combine confectioners' sugar and cereal. Pour peanut butter mixture over cereal; toss to coat. Roll into 1-in. balls; place on the prepared pan. Refrigerate until chilled.

3) In a large microwave-safe bowl, melt chocolate chips and shortening; stir until smooth. Dip balls in chocolate mixture; allow excess to drip off. Return to baking sheets; refrigerate until set.

Yield: about 5-1/2 dozen.

Editor's Note: Reduced-fat or generic brands of peanut butter are not recommended for this recipe.

NUTRITION FACTS: 1 piece equals 138 calories, 9 g fat (3 g saturated fat), 4 mg cholesterol, 59 mg sodium, 15 g carbohydrate, 1 g fiber, 2 g protein.

Easy Chocolate Treats

Making candy doesn't need to be a time-consuming task. Here's a simple recipe for making chocolate-covered treats. Chop eight 1-ounce squares of semisweet chocolate. Melt chocolate and 1 teaspoon shortening in a microwave or heavy saucepan; stir until smooth. Dip fresh or dried fruit, nuts, pretzels or cookies in chocolate; let excess chocolate drip off. Place on waxed paper until set. Or stir chopped nuts, flaked coconut, raisins or chow mein noodles into the melted chocolate. Drop by spoonfuls onto waxed paper and let stand until set. Store the chocolate candies in an airtight container.

'the goodie lady' soothes others

TLC comes with delivery of homemade treats

Rita Cotten

"

She's a wonderful person. She came through even when we had so much snow that the Post Office was closed.

~Rita Gower

Wednesdays are special days at Guardian Family Services, a shelter for victims of domestic violence and homeless women and children in Metropolis, Illinois.

That's the day residents can enjoy the homemade goodness of fresh muffins, brownies or other baked items from Rita Cotten, affectionately known as "The Goodie Lady."

Rita has been baking goodies for the residents every Wednesday for more than five years—in fact, she has never missed a week, says Rita Gower, the shelter's program director.

"She's a wonderful person. She came through even when we had so much snow that the Post Office closed and even on the weeks that her husband was in the hospital. This proves to me she is a loyal and dependable friend of the shelter."

Rita Cotten started her weekly deliveries when her employer introduced a program that encouraged staff members to volunteer in the community by cleaning up the riverfront, rebuilding homes

and various other projects.

"I have arthritis and carpal tunnel in my hands, so I couldn't participate in those efforts," Rita explains. But she wanted to do something, and she knew about the shelter's mission.

"I've never been in that situation but I knew these people needed some tender loving care," Rita says. So she turned her love of baking into a sweet delivery for the women and children who might be staying there.

"If my little contribution makes them happy, even for a moment, then it's worth it," she says.

Rita's contribution might be two or three dozen muffins, four dozen cookies or a pan of super-rich brownies, all of which get rave reviews from the residents. Many of the recipes she uses were handed down from her mom, while others she found in magazines or were shared by friends.

"I have gotten some of the most wonderful thank-you letters and cards from these ladies," Rita says. "It makes you want to do more."

taste of home
cooks who care

DO YOU KNOW A COOK WHO CARES?
If you or someone you know cooks for a charitable, spiritual or other cause, tell us about it at **tasteofhome.com/CookbookBonus**

You can find one of Rita's recipes in the Web exclusive online at tasteofhome.com/CookbookBonus
Type in access code ICare